East Siberian

Sea

CHUKCHI

Sea

Sea

Plain

erian

Chersky Range

Verkhoyansk Range

Bering

Sea

Sea
of
Okhotsk

Irkutsk

Blagoveshchensk

Vladivostock

metres
2000+
1000-2000
200-1000
0-200

0   100   200 km
0   50   100   150 miles

The Russian Empire (1913)

ARMENIA

AZERBAIJAN

BELARUS

ESTONIA

GEORGIA

KAZAKHSTAN

KYRGYZSTAN

LATVIA

LITHUANIA

MOLDOVA

TAJIKISTAN

TURKMENISTAN

UKRAINE

UZBEKISTAN

RUSSIA

The Cambridge Encyclopedia of
Russia

*and the former
Soviet Union*

Edited by **ARCHIE BROWN**
PROFESSOR OF POLITICS
UNIVERSITY OF OXFORD

MICHAEL KASER
READER IN ECONOMICS
UNIVERSITY OF OXFORD

and **GERALD S. SMITH**
PROFESSOR OF RUSSIAN
UNIVERSITY OF OXFORD

Associate Editor **PATRICIA BROWN**

The Cambridge
Encyclopedia of
Russia
*and the former
Soviet Union*

CAMBRIDGE
UNIVERSITY PRESS

Published by the Press Syndicate of the University of Cambridge
The Pitt Building, Trumpington Street, Cambridge CB2 1RP
40 West 20th Street, New York, NY 10011-4211, USA
10 Stamford Road, Oakleigh, Melbourne 3166, Australia

First published as *The Cambridge Encyclopedia of Russia
and the Soviet Union* 1982
Reprinted 1984
Second edition published as *The Cambridge Encyclopedia of Russia
and the former Soviet Union* 1994

Printed in Great Britain at the University Press, Cambridge
Colour origination by Typongraph, Verona, Italy
Typeset by Rowland Phototypesetting, Bury St Edmunds

A catalogue record for this book is available from the British Library

Library of Congress cataloging in publication data applied for

ISBN 0 521 35593 1 hardback

A CAMBRIDGE REFERENCE BOOK

Consultant editor, Art and Architecture Professor John E. Bowlt,
Department of Slavic Languages, University of Southern California,
Los Angeles
Editorial assistant Alex Hollingsworth
Design Dale Tomlinson (Peter Ducker and Andrew Shoolbred)
Maps and diagrams European Map Graphics
Picture research Callie Kendall
Index Barbara Hird

*The title page shows
an early-morning
view of St Petersburg
across the river Neva*

Contents

Cyrillic alphabet	Latin alphabet
А а	a
Б б	b
В в	v
Г г	g
Д д	d
Е е	} e
Ё ё	
Ж ж	zh
З з	z
И и	i
Й й	y
К к	k
Л л	l
М м	m
Н н	n
О о	o
П п	p
Р р	r
С с	s
Т т	t
У у	u
Ф ф	f
Х х	kh
Ц ц	ts
Ч ч	ch
Ш ш	sh
Щ щ	shch
ъ	
ы	y
ь	'
Э э	e
Ю ю	yu
Я я	ya

In proper names initial E- (with occasional exceptions for familiar names) is rendered Ye- and terminal -ый and -ий are simplified to -y (Dostoevsky); well-known Russian names are given in the form in which they have become familiar to English-speaking readers (Nicholas II, Peter the Great, Alexander Solzhenitsyn).

Some other exceptions to consistency are also made for the sake of familiarity. Thus, for example, *perestroyka* and *glasnost'* are rendered as perestroika and glasnost. Certain place-names appear with more than one spelling. This is partly a result of changes over time (and of the dominant power in the region) and partly reflects the linguistic conventions of the different nationalities inhabiting the territory. For instance, even in Soviet times Moldova was what the Romanian-speaking Moldovans called their republic, although to Russians and – following Russian and Soviet usage – to the English-speaking world it was Moldavia.

Contributors

TA **Thomas Adshead**
European Bank for Reconstruction and Development, London

SA **Dr Shirin Akiner**
*Director, Central Asia Research Forum, School of
Oriental and African Studies, University of London*

RA **Dr Roy Allison**
*Senior Lecturer in International Security,
University of Birmingham; Head of Russian and CIS Programme,
Royal Institute of International Affairs*

GDA **Dr Gregory D. Andrusz**
Kazakhstan-UK Centre, Middlesex University, Enfield

TEA **Dr Terence E. Armstrong**
*Formerly Reader in Arctic Studies, Scott Polar Research Institute,
University of Cambridge; Emeritus Fellow, Clare Hall*

AÅ **Professor Anders Åslund**
Director, Stockholm Institute of East European Economics

DTB **Professor Derek Bailey**
Professor of Accounting, Thames Valley University, Ealing

JB **Dr Jennifer Baines**
Lecturer in Russian, Magdalen College, Oxford

RPB **Dr Roger P. Bartlett**
*Reader in Russian History, School of Slavonic and
East European Studies, University of London*

JHB **Professor James H. Bater**
*Dean, Faculty of Environmental Studies,
University of Waterloo, Ontario*

AVB **Dr Andrey Berezkin**
Head, Political Geography Laboratory, Moscow University

MJB **Dr Michael J. Berry**
Lecturer in Russian for Social Scientists, University of Birmingham

MTB **Professor Milka T. Bliznakov**
*Department of Architecture and Urban Design, Virginia
Polytechnic Institute and State University, Blacksburg*

TB **Dr Terence Boddington**
Department of Physical Chemistry, University of Leeds

MB **Professor Morris Bornstein**
Department of Economics, University of Michigan, Ann Arbor

MAB **Canon Michael Bourdeaux**
Director, Keston Institute, Oxford

JEB **Professor John E. Bowlt**
*Department of Slavic Languages,
University of Southern California, Los Angeles*

JMB **Dr Jozef M. van Brabant**
*Principal Economic Affairs Officer, Department of Economic and
Social Development, United Nations, New York*

AHB **Professor Archie Brown FBA**
*Professor of Politics, University of Oxford;
Director, Russian and East European Centre, St Antony's College*

WCB **Professor William C. Brumfield**
Professor of Slavic Languages, Tulane University, New Orleans

WB **Professor Włodzimierz Brus**
*Formerly Professor of Economics, University of Oxford;
Emeritus Fellow, Wolfson College*

MB **Dr Mary Buckley**
Senior Lecturer in Politics, University of Edinburgh

AMC **Aldyth M. Cadoux**
Tutor in Russian, Fettes College, Edinburgh

RWC **Professor Robert W. Campbell**
*Distinguished Professor of Economics,
Indiana University, Bloomington*

CC **Dr Catherine Cooke**
*Lecturer in Design, Faculty of Technology,
The Open University, Milton Keynes*

BC **Dr Brian Cooper**
Cambridge

JMC **Professor Julian Cooper**
*Professor of Russian Economic Studies; Director, Centre for
Russian and East European Studies, University of Birmingham*

OC **Professor Olga Crisp**
*Emeritus Professor of Economic History, School of Slavonic and
East European Studies, University of London*

RWD **Professor R.W. Davies**
*Emeritus Professor of Soviet Economic Studies,
University of Birmingham*

CMD **Dr Christopher M. Davis**
*Lecturer in Russian and East European Political Economy,
University of Oxford; Fellow of Wolfson College*

KD **Professor Karen Dawisha**
Professor of Government, University of Maryland, College Park

MD **Martin Dewhirst**
*Lecturer in Russian, Department of Slavonic Languages
and Literatures, University of Glasgow*

HBFD **Dr H.B.F. Dixon**
Lecturer in Biochemistry, University of Cambridge

CD **Professor Charlotte Douglas**
*Chair, Department of Slavic Languages and Literatures,
New York University*

ASD **Andrew Duncan**
*Assistant Director for Information,
International Institute for Strategic Studies, London*

NJD **Dr John Dunstan**
Senior Lecturer in Russian Studies, University of Birmingham

DAD **Dr David A. Dyker**
*Reader in Economics, School of European Studies,
University of Sussex, Brighton*

RGE **Richard G. Eales**
Lecturer in History, University of Kent, Canterbury

JE **Dr Jonathan Eyal**
*Director of Studies, Royal United Services Institute
for Defence Studies, London*

AERF **PROFESSOR ANN FARKAS**
Brooklyn College, City University of New York

MFe **PROFESSOR MURRAY FESHBACH**
Department of Demography, Georgetown University, Washington DC

IPF **PAUL FOOTE**
Lecturer in Russian, University of Oxford; Fellow of The Queen's College

MMF **DR MARIAMNA M. FORTOUNATTO**
Icon painter and restorer, London

MF **THE REVEREND MICHAEL FORTOUNATTO**
Archpriest at the Russian Orthodox Cathedral, London

SF **DR SIMON FRANKLIN**
Lecturer in Russian, University of Cambridge; Fellow of Clare College

RAF **DR R. A. FRENCH**
Senior Lecturer in Geography, University College, London

KWG **KENNETH W. GATLAND FRAS**
Editor, Spaceflight

VJG **DR VLADIMIR GELMAN**
Institute of Sociology, Russian Academy of Sciences, St Petersburg

MVG **THE LATE MICHAEL GLENNY**
Writer and translator

IG **DR IGOR GOLOMSTOCK**
BBC Russian Service, London

NG **NOEL GOODWIN**
Associate Editor, Dance and Dancers

JG **JULIAN GRAFFY**
Senior Lecturer in Russian Language and Literature, School of Slavonic and East European Studies, University of London

PG **PROFESSOR P. GRAY**
Master, Gonville and Caius College, Cambridge

PRG **PROFESSOR PAUL R. GREGORY**
Department of Economics, University of Houston, Texas

SH **DR SERGEI HACKEL**
Formerly Reader in Russian Studies, University of Sussex, Brighton

BH **DR BASIL HAIGH**
Formerly Physician, British Embassy, Moscow

HH **HARRY HANAK**
Reader in International Relations, School of Slavonic and East European Studies, University of London

PH **PROFESSOR PHILIP HANSON**
Professor of the Political Economy of Russia and Eastern Europe, University of Birmingham

MH **DR MURIEL HEPPELL**
Emeritus Reader in the Medieval History of Orthodox Eastern Europe, University of London

RJH **PROFESSOR RONALD J. HILL**
Professor of Comparative Government, Trinity College, Dublin

LH **THE LATE DR LUKASZ HIRSZOWICZ**
Formerly Editor, East European Jewish Affairs, London

DH **PROFESSOR DAVID HOOSON**
Department of Geography, University of California, Berkeley

GAH **PROFESSOR GEOFFREY A. HOSKING FBA**
Professor of Russian History, School of Slavonic and East European Studies, University of London

GMH **PROFESSOR G. MELVYN HOWE FRSE FRGS FRSGS**
Emeritus Professor of Geography, University of Strathclyde

JH **DR JANA HOWLETT**
Lecturer in Russian, University of Cambridge; Fellow of Jesus College

CH **DR CAROLINE HUMPHREY**
Lecturer in Social Anthropology, University of Cambridge; Fellow of King's College

RH **DR RAYMOND HUTCHINGS**
Editor, Abstracts Russian and East European Series

AJ **DR ANTHONY JONES**
Associate Professor of Sociology, Northeastern University, Boston

SFJ **DR STEPHEN JONES**
Associate Professor, Program of Russian and Soviet Studies, Mount Holyoke College, South Hadley, Massachusetts

DJ **PROFESSOR DAVID JORAVSKY**
History Department, Northwestern University, Evanston, Illinois

PRJ **PROFESSOR PAUL R. JOSEPHSON**
Professor of Science, Technology and Society, Sarah Lawrence College, New York

MCK **DR MICHAEL KASER**
Reader in Economics, University of Oxford; Fellow of St Antony's College

AK-W **DR A. KEMP-WELCH**
Senior Lecturer, School of Economic and Social Studies, University of East Anglia, Norwich

AK **ANNA KISSELGOFF**
Chief Dance Critic, New York Times

RIK **DR RONALD I. KOWALSKI**
Senior Lecturer in History, Worcester College of Higher Education

HL **DR H. LEEMING**
Emeritus Reader in Slavonic Languages, School of Slavonic and East European Studies, University of London

RAL **DR R. A. LEWIS**
Director, Centre for European Studies, University of Exeter

HML **DR HARALD M. LIPMAN**
Medical Adviser to the Foreign and Commonwealth Office, London

LWL **DR L. W. LONGDON**
Formerly Professor of Mathematics and Ballistics, Royal Military College of Science, Shrivenham

CHM **PROFESSOR CARL H. McMILLAN**
Professor of Economics, Carleton University, Ottawa

AM **ALASTAIR McAULEY**
Reader in Economics, University of Essex, Colchester

EM **PROFESSOR ELLEN MICKIEWICZ**
James R. Shepley Professor of Public Policy Studies, Duke University, Durham, North Carolina

PPM **PROFESSOR PHILIP P. MICKLIN**
Department of Geography, Western Michigan University, Kalamazoo

JHM **JOHN MILLER**
Reader in Politics, La Trobe University, Melbourne

SM **DR SIMON MITTON FRAS**
Group Director, STM Publishing, Cambridge University Press

PM **DR PATRICK MOORE CBE, FRAS**
Editor, Year Book of Astronomy

JN **DR JOAN NEUBERGER**
Assistant Professor of History, University of Texas, Austin

WWN **DR WALTER W. NEWEY**
Formerly Senior Lecturer in Biogeography,
University of Edinburgh

MAN **DR MICHAEL A. NICHOLSON**
Lecturer in Russian, University of Oxford;
Fellow and Senior Tutor, University College

AN **THE LATE PROFESSOR ALEC NOVE FBA**
Formerly Professor of Economics, University of Glasgow

JN **PROFESSOR J. NUTTING F.Eng**
Emeritus Professor of Metallurgy, University of Leeds

FO'D **DR FELICITY O'DELL**
Learning Centre Co-ordinator, Eurocentre, Cambridge

JP **DR JUDITH PALLOT**
University Lecturer in the Geography of Russia,
University of Oxford; Official Student of Christ Church

RP **PROFESSOR ROGER PARSONS**
Professor Emeritus of Chemistry, University of Southampton

RHP **DR RIITTA PITTMAN**
Research Fellow, St Antony's College, Oxford

ABP **PROFESSOR ANTONY B. POLONSKY**
Professor of East European Jewish History,
Brandeis University, Waltham, Massachusetts

HMP **THE LATE PROFESSOR H. M. POWELL FRS**
Formerly Professor of Chemical Crystallography,
University of Oxford

AP **DR ALEX PRAVDA**
Lecturer in Russian and East European Politics,
University of Oxford; Fellow of St Antony's College

PBR **PROFESSOR PETER REDDAWAY**
Professor of Political Science and International Affairs, George
Washington University, Washington DC

TTR **THE LATE DR TAMARA TALBOT RICE**
Writer and art historian

JR **PROFESSOR JAMES RIORDAN**
Professor of Russian Studies, University of Surrey, Guildford

BAR **PROFESSOR BERNARD RUDDEN**
Professor of Comparative Law, University of Oxford;
Fellow of Brasenose College

RR **PROFESSOR ROBERT RUSSELL**
Professor of Russian, University of Sheffield

TR **DR TIM RYBACK**
Deputy Director, Salzburg Seminar, Salzburg

LBS **THE LATE PROFESSOR LEONARD SCHAPIRO CBE, FBA**
Formerly Professor of Political Science,
London School of Economics

GS **DR GERALD SEAMAN**
Associate Professor of Musicology, University of Auckland

DJBS **DR DENIS J. B. SHAW**
Lecturer in Geography, University of Birmingham

JGS **JAMES SHERR**
Lecturer in International Relations, Lincoln College, Oxford;
Research Fellow, Royal Military Academy, Sandhurst

AS **DR ANDREW SHERRATT**
Senior Assistant Keeper, Ashmolean Museum, Oxford

MHS **MICHAEL SHOTTON**
Formerly Lecturer in Russian, University of Oxford;
Emeritus Fellow of St Catherine's College

HS **DR HAROLD SHUKMAN**
Lecturer in History, University of Oxford;
Fellow of St Antony's College

LVS **DR LEONID SMIRNYAGIN**
Associate Professor of Geography, Moscow University;
Member of the Presidential Council, Russian Federation

GES **DR GRAHAM SMITH**
Lecturer in Geography, University of Cambridge;
Fellow of Sidney Sussex College

GSS **PROFESSOR GERALD S. SMITH**
Professor of Russian, University of Oxford; Fellow of New College

RS **PROFESSOR RICHARD STITES**
Department of History, Georgetown University, Washington DC

NS **PROFESSOR NORMAN STONE**
Professor of Modern History, University of Oxford;
Fellow of Worcester College

RGS **PROFESSOR RONALD GRIGOR SUNY**
Alex Manoogan Professor of Modern Armenian History,
University of Michigan, Ann Arbor

LJS **PROFESSOR LESLIE J. SYMONS**
Emeritus Professor of Geography, University College, Swansea

RT **DR RICHARD TAYLOR**
Reader in Politics and Russian Studies, University College, Swansea

VGT **PROFESSOR VLADIMIR G. TREML**
Department of Economics, Duke University,
Durham, North Carolina

EKV **DR ELIZABETH VALKENIER**
Resident Scholar, The Harriman Institute,
Columbia University, New York

K-EW **DR KARL-EUGEN WÄDEKIN**
Formerly Professor of East European and International
Agrarian Policy, Justus Liebig University, Giessen

GW **DR GREGORY WALKER FLA**
Head of Acquisitions, Bodleian Library, Oxford

MW **DR MAX WALTERS**
Formerly Director, University of Cambridge Botanic Gardens

SLW **PROFESSOR STEPHEN WHITE**
Department of Politics, University of Glasgow

SDW **DR STEPHEN WHITEFIELD**
Tutor in Politics and Fellow of Pembroke College, Oxford

FCMW **DR FAITH WIGZELL**
Senior Lecturer in Russian Language and Literature, School of
Slavonic and East European Studies, University of London

HTW **H. T. WILLETTS**
Formerly Lecturer in Russian History, University of Oxford

DSMW **DR D. S. M. WILLIAMS**
Formerly Lecturer in the History of Asiatic Russia, School of
Slavonic and East European Studies, University of London

NJRW **N. J. R. WRIGHT**
Director (Regional Studies), Phillips Petroleum, Woking, Surrey

WHZ **DR W. H. ZAWADZKI**
Abingdon

IZ **DR ILIANA ZLOCH**
Faculty Associate, Department of Economics, Harvard University

This book is a successor volume to the *Cambridge Encyclopedia of Russia and the Soviet Union*, published in 1982. The twelve years since then have been amongst the most momentous in the history of Russia. The country has undergone dramatic change, both domestically and in its relations with the outside world, while the Soviet Union, a feared 'superpower' a mere decade ago, has ceased to exist. Yet Russia is still the largest country on the planet and it remains at least as important in the 1990s as it was in the early 1980s, if for different reasons.

Russia retains its power both to inspire and destroy. The whole world, and not just the hundred and fifty million citizens of Russia, will be affected by this vast country's success or failure in establishing political democracy and a market economy and in preserving and building upon the intellectual and cultural freedom attained during the late 1980s.

Russia's cultural heritage – including one of the greatest literatures in the history of civilization – is a source of enduring strength, whereas the Socialist Realist approach to culture and Marxist-Leninist doctrine more generally (notwithstanding its huge impact on Russian and world history) are already recognized as having offered 'a road to nowhere'. But without a stable and democratic political order, the darker side of post-Soviet Russia's inheritance will present a threat extending well beyond Russian borders. For not only is Russia the world's second military power after the United States, with the capacity to destroy life on earth, but large parts of the country constitute an ecological disaster area crying out for responsible and responsive government.

The principal focus of this volume is on Russia, in all its major facets, from the earliest times to the present day. Discussion is, however, by no means confined to the Russians, but embraces the other nationalities which made up the Russian Empire and the Soviet Union. While there are a number of entries – for example, on earlier Russian history and literature – which are carried over from the previous book, the greater part of the text is published for the first time. This volume is much more a new work than a second edition. Compared with the 112 authors of the 1982 book, the new Encyclopedia has 132. Contributors are drawn from nine countries, with British scholars making up the largest single category. Apart from the book's extended timescale, its thematic coverage is also more extensive. Moreover, some entries have not only been newly written but *re*written over the past two years as Russia changed its political and economic system and its role in world affairs.

If the speed of change made life more difficult for the editors and authors, the completion of the book only after the Soviet Union ceased to exist is a great advantage. Although the chronological sweep of the work is far wider than the 74 years of the USSR, this becomes, among other things, the first volume to examine the Soviet period as a whole from so many different angles – not only in the history section, where there is particular emphasis on political history, but in the sections on art and architecture, peoples, religion, language and literature, cultural life, the sciences, politics, the economy, society, the military, international relations, and even the physical environment where pollution is so severe a legacy of the Soviet era.

Within the Soviet period, particular attention is devoted to the last ten years of Communist rule since they were a time when transformation of a great many aspects of Soviet and Russian life occurred or got seriously underway. The Gorbachev era (1985–1991), and the advent of perestroika and glasnost, bulks especially large, for seldom have so many far-reaching changes been packed into so few years. Much fresh information became available during that time of radical reform and still more new material came to light with the collapse of the Soviet system. Western scholars had better accesss to Russian decision-makers than hitherto, some archives were opened, and Russian-language published sources became far more revealing from the late 1980s than ever before in the Soviet era. This book is able, therefore, to offer not only as comprehensive a survey of Russia past and present as is consistent with a single-volume publication, but in many respects a fresh interpretation of the last years of Soviet rule, based on the up-to-date research of its specialist contributors.

Attention is devoted also to post-Soviet Russia, for enough time has elapsed since the demise of the USSR in December 1991 for a number of important new tendencies in political, economic and cultural life to be identified, even though this has also been a period of political struggle and constitutional confusion. In addition to the Russian Federation, the divergent experiences of the other successor states of the former Soviet Union receive attention in several sections of the Encyclopedia.

Among the many features distinguishing the present volume from its predecessor (which, after reprinting, has been out-of-print for some years) are its illustrations. The new book contains more pictures as well as more text. Most of the photographs are different from those in the 1982 edition, some having been specially commissioned for this volume. A number of the maps are new; the others have been updated and entirely redrawn.

The 1982 *Cambridge Encyclopedia of Russia and the Soviet Union* had four editors, of whom two – Archie Brown and Michael Kaser – remain. The others, John Fennell and Harry Willetts, had retired from their posts at Oxford University before we embarked on the new venture and Professor Fennell, we record with great sadness, died on 9 August 1992. To re-establish a breadth of scholarly experience in the humanities as well as the social sciences, Gerald Smith – John Fennell's successor as Professor of Russian at Oxford – became the third member of the editorial team for the present volume.

We are deeply grateful to our numerous authors, not least those writing on the areas changing fastest, for their friendly co-operation. We should like to record also our warm thanks to Sir Isaiah Berlin for several most helpful and constructive suggestions. With such a large number of contributors, and so many changes taking place in the object of their study, this has been a complicated book to produce. A great part of the organizational burden has been borne by the Associate Editor, Patricia Brown; we wish to express our deep appreciation of her work. Thanks are due also to our editorial assistant, Alex Hollingsworth, especially for his help with the maps and panels. We are most grateful, finally, to Cambridge University Press for their excellent work on the technical side and for having enough confidence in the volume to price it modestly in relation to its substantial size and lavish illustration.

Readers should note that the year of birth and, where relevant, the year of death of a person named in the text of the book are normally given only on the first substantive reference. When dates do not accompany a particular reference, it is usually possible to find them by looking up the first page reference to that person in the index.

ARCHIE BROWN
MICHAEL KASER
GERALD S. SMITH

The physical environment

The natural landscape

The varied landforms within the territorial vastness of the former Soviet Union assume the shape of a colossal amphitheatre. The towering Caucasus, Pamir, Tyan'-Shan', Altay, Sayan and Far East mountain ranges along the southern and eastern borders slope down to the vast East European (Russian) Plain, the West Siberian Plain and the Turan-Caspian Lowland. However, such a simple pattern of peripheral mountains and plains belies a complex geological structure and evolutionary history.

TECTONIC STRUCTURE

The land area comprises two large, very ancient and deep-seated stable blocks or continental platforms: the East European (Russian) platform in the west and the Siberian platform in the east. Both are composed of extremely tough igneous and metamorphic rocks of Pre-Cambrian (Archaean) age lying at varying depths below geologically more recent strata. These basal complexes have proved, in general, to have been resistant to later fold or mountain-building movements and overlying deposits are almost horizontal and only slightly disturbed. Occasionally the ancient foundations outcrop at the surface as 'shield' areas. In European Russia they are exposed in Karelia and Azov-Podolia; in Siberia, in the Aldan and Anabar shields.

The broad belt of Palaeozoic (Primary) strata between the two great platforms was folded in Hercynian times. These structures are exposed at the surface in the low ranges of the Ural Mountains and in the Kazakh Uplands (which also contain some Caledonian elements) but are buried beneath younger sediments in the West Siberian Lowland. Structural elements of Mesozoic (Secondary) age occur in eastern Siberia and the Far East. They include the great geosyncline or depression (marking an ancient fold in the strata) through which the Lena River flows.

Along the southern and eastern margins of the Pre-Cambrian, Palaeozoic (Caledonian and Hercynian) and Mesozoic structural zones lies part of the great belt of Cainozoic (Tertiary, Alpine) folding – originally the northern border of the great Tethys geosyncline. It includes a small section of the eastern Carpathians, the Crimean Mountains, Caucasus, Kopet-Dag and Pamirs. Volcanic activity here belongs to the recent geological past and earth movements and extinct volcanoes (such as Mt Elbrus) are common. A second belt of more recent Cainozoic formations borders the earlier tectonic zones along the Pacific seaboard. Within Russian territory the belt includes the Koryak ranges, Kamchatka, Sakhalin, the Kuril Islands and the coastal ranges of Sikhote-Alin'; it is composed of fold mountains with which are associated much seismic and volcanic activity.

The Pre-Cambrian platforms lie deep below the lowlands of the European part of Russia and beneath low but well-dissected plateau blocks in Siberia. Where exposed at the surface these and other areas of ancient folding (such as the Ural Mountains) represent but vestigial remains of former greatness. They are usually low in altitude with exposed roots and inverted relief. In contrast, in areas of Cainozoic folding, denudation has had only a relatively short time in which to work, tectonic structures are conformable and landscapes youthful in character. Slopes are steep and mountain peaks high and jagged; upfolds continue to form the mountain summits, and downfolds the intervening valleys.

Past periods of mountain-building are of undoubted importance in the evolution of the landscapes, but possibly of greater significance were the frequent advances and withdrawals of the sea, which occurred particularly west of the Urals. During these movements sedimentary strata were alternately laid down, largely giving rise to the variety in age and character of the surface deposits over much of the country.

GLACIATION

The ice ages of Pleistocene (Quaternary) times were the last major event in the evolution of the landscape. The four major advances and retreats of the ice-sheet from centres in Scandinavia, northern Karelia, Novaya Zemlya, the northern Urals and the Altay, Sayan, Pamir and Caucasus mountains, have

Previous spread.
'Mountains': an Armenian landscape by Martiros Sar'yan, 1923

Tectonic zones

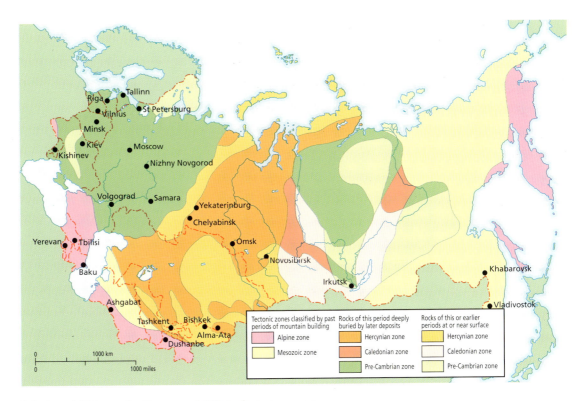

Tectonic zones classified by past periods of mountain building

- Alpine zone
- Mesozoic zone

Rocks of this period deeply buried by later deposits

- Hercynian zone
- Caledonian zone
- Pre-Cambrian zone

Rocks of this or earlier periods at or near surface

- Hercynian zone
- Caledonian zone
- Pre-Cambrian zone

left an indelible mark. The second (Oka) glaciation was the most extensive: it penetrated southwards to the edge of the Central Russian Upland with a great lobe down the basin of the Don River and thence along the foot of the Volga Upland to the middle Ural Mountains. The contemporary (Dem'yanka) glaciation in western Siberia did not extend so far south as over the plains to the west. A lobe of ice associated with a third glaciation (Dnieper), from a mainly Scandinavian source, penetrated well south along the Dnieper Lowland. The fourth glaciation (Valday) did not extend as far south as the Dnieper-Don stage, neither did it affect Siberia, but because it was the last it has left most evident traces and accounts for many features of the landscape.

Near the ice centres, particularly in more northerly latitudes, the effects of the ice were mainly erosive: as it crept over the land surface soils were removed and hollows gouged out of the bedrock which are now occupied by myriads of lakes, as in Karelia. Beyond, in northern European Russia and southwards to the limit of the ice-sheets, is a region of glacial deposition with extensive dumps and spreads of morainic deposits such as boulder clay, glacial sands and gravels and terminal moraines. These deposits have impeded drainage and left behind a diffuse drainage pattern, innumerable ponds and lakes and extensive swamps and marshes. Beyond the southernmost limit of the ice front is a broad region of water-eroded relief and finely graded and sorted deposits laid down by melt-water streams and wind action; these now form spreads of deep, fertile loess.

PERMAFROST

Many landforms and processes owe their origin to permafrost or perennially frozen ground, which underlies about 47 per cent (9 million sq km) of the territory of the former USSR in a relatively narrow coastal strip north of the Arctic Circle in European Russia, a broader zone in western Siberia and almost the whole of the country east of the Yenisey River, to the Pacific. The upper, so-called 'active layer' thaws in summer and is up to 2m thick; the perennially frozen layer beneath may be more than 1000m thick. Patterned ground, pingos or frost boils and thermokarst topography marked by sinks and other irregularities are examples of the surface effects of permafrost. The impervious perennially frozen layer retains moisture near the surface and encourages solifluction – mudflows and landslides on slopes.

RELIEF

The surprising variety of landforms and scenery is the result of a long and complex geological history, of unremitting surface erosion and of deposition and erosion by sea, river and ice. Even so, such is the territorial immensity of the country that the relief units which comprise it appear vast, monotonous and unchanging and extend for thousands of kilometres. The overall pattern is one of extensive lowlands and tablelands girdled by great ranges of mountains.

Limits of glaciation and permafrost

The East European (Russian) Lowland extends from the western frontiers of the country to the Urals and from the Arctic Ocean to the Black Sea and the Caspian Sea, covering almost the whole of European Russia. Its average elevation is 100–200m above sea-level, although there are parts where altitudes of 300–400m are attained. Hilly terrain such as the Valday Hills, Central Russian Uplands and Volga Upland alternates with practically flat lowlands such as the Dnieper, Oka-Don and Black Sea lowlands.

The Valday Hills, north-west of Moscow, are a jumbled mass of hills where a dissected carboniferous limestone escarpment is crossed by a terminal moraine and other glacial debris. The highest summits are more than 300m and form the drainage divide between the headwaters of the four main river systems of the area – Volga, Dnieper, Western Dvina (Daugava) and Msta, which are connected at their sources in a vast bog. The Central Russian Upland is a heavily dissected loess-covered plateau with many recent and developing ravines. Its average height is 230–250m and the highest points in the Tula district reach 290m. The Volga Heights, which reach 350m and stretch almost meridionally along the west bank of the Volga from Nizhny Novgorod to Volgograd (Stalingrad), like the Central Russian Upland, form an asymmetrical plateau which descends comparatively steeply in the east to the valley of the Volga.

The broad depression of the Dnieper Lowland (50–150m), principally occupying the plain on the left bank of the Dnieper, separates the Volyno-Podol'sk shield from the Central Russian Upland. During the Dnieper glaciation the lowlands were occupied by a lobe of the ice-sheet which left them extensively covered with sands and clays, with swamps and a poorly developed drainage system. These conditions prevail in the Pripyat Marshes of the Polesye Lowland, but on the lower Dnieper the lowland, which extends east of the Dnieper for more than 150km, has long dried out. The alluvial Oka-Don Lowland (160–180m) fills the broad depression between the eastern slopes of the Central Russian Upland in the west and the Volga Heights in the east. Broad river terraces covered with loess-like sandy soils are the principal landscape form. The Black Sea Lowland is a relatively thin belt (100–200km) stretching along the northern shores of the Black Sea and the Sea of Azov, and including the Crimean Plain. The surface, which only occasionally exceeds 100m, is flat and loess-covered, and in places reaches the coast in cliffs up to 30m high.

The Kola-Karelian region in the extreme north-west of European Russia lies wholly within the shield area of Pre-Cambrian crystalline rocks. It is an area of ice-scoured plateaux, mostly below 300m, although the massif of the Khibiny Mountains in the Kola Peninsula reaches more than 900m at one point. The numerous lakes are a legacy of the Quaternary glaciations.

The Ural Mountains, which separate the European and Asian parts of the former USSR, comprise a composite and much denuded north–south mountain system, broken by transverse valleys. These mountains, generally 300–800m high (highest peak Mt

The Tunka valley in Buryat-Mongolia

Narodnaya, 1894m), appear as no more than a gentle swelling within the vast Russian–West Siberian Plain. The West Siberian Plain extends from the Arctic Ocean to the steppes of Kazakhstan and eastwards 200km to the Yenisey. It is only insignificantly above sea-level, its highest points are mostly below 200m and in parts even below 100m. This, the largest area of level land on the earth, is drained by the mighty rivers Ob', Irtysh and Yenisey which cause extensive flooding in the spring.

Central Asia is almost essentially the Turan-Caspian Lowland which lies to the south of the West Siberian Plain and beyond the low Turgay Plateau. It is an area of inland drainage extending from the shores of the Caspian Sea to the mountains of Central Asia, which tower to heights of 5000–7000m. The region consists of flat plains around the northern shores of the Caspian Sea and clayey and dune-covered deserts – the Kara Kum and Kyzyl Kum – separated by the Ust-Urt Plateau. An abrupt change in the landscape takes place east of the Yenisey River. Here the greater part of the countryside is taken up by the heavily dissected and thickly forested Central Siberian Plateau, 400–1000m, bordered to the south by the mountains of southern Siberia and to the east by the trough-like valleys of the Lena and Vilyuy. In north-eastern Siberia the character of the landscape changes yet again. This extensive and imperfectly explored territory, bounded to the east by the mountains of the Pacific margins, is mainly highland country, including high ranges (1800–3000m) around the Verkhoyansk and Kolyma tablelands.

The Russian Far East is a comparatively narrow strip of land extending from north-east to south-west for practically 4500 km. In the north the rugged

Dzhugdzhur range along the Sea of Okhotsk separates the region from Siberia proper; in the south the low (600–1000m) ranges of the Sikhote-Alin' system face the Sea of Japan. Structurally associated with the outer ranges of the Sikhote-Alin' and separated by the Gulf of Tartary is Sakhalin, a mountainous island formed of two parallel chains with a central depression. The Koryak range, Kamchatka (with 30 active volcanoes) and the Kuril Islands are part of the arc-shaped system which runs the length of the east coast of Asia to form a section of the 'fiery girdle of the Pacific'.

Not only eastern Siberia and the Russian Far East are characterized by mountains; a highland belt of Alpine-type fold mountains and associated plateaux also encircles the Russian Lowland, Central Asia and the West Siberian Plain in the south and east. In the south-west are the Ukrainian Carpathians, 1000–1800m high; the relatively low Crimean range (reaching 1500m) on the southern margins of the peninsula is a further link in the southern mountain belt. The Caucasus, extending between the Black and Caspian seas, is a system of ranges of which the highest is Mt Elbrus (5642m). East of the Caspian the Kopet-Dag attains 800m in Turkmenistan but lies mainly in Iran, where the greatest elevations are reached. The cloud-shrouded and permanently snow-covered Pamir-Altay and the Tyan'-Shan' mountains have summits rising to over 6000m (Mt Communism, 7495m). These ranges are interspersed with deep valleys and rounded highlands. Between the Tyan'-Shan' and the Altay mountains lies the relatively low Djungarian Gate, the historic gateway from China across Mongolia to the Kazakh steppes and thence to the Volga. The Altay mountains in southern Siberia are followed eastwards by the high ranges, tablelands and depressions of the Western and Eastern Sayan Highlands in the west and the Yablonovy and Stanovoy ranges in the east, the whole area forming a complex of rounded ranges and basins. GMH

Mountains in Turkmenistan: a virtual 'lunar' landscape

Rivers and drainage

Right. *A mountain lake in Dagestan (Caucasus)*

The territory of the former USSR has an average annual river flow estimated at 4720 cu km, 93 per cent arising within its boundaries and 7 per cent entering from adjacent countries. The area accounts for 10.7 per cent of the 41,000 cu km flow of the world's rivers – second after Brazil. However, in terms of flow per unit of land area, the former Soviet Union at 211,000 cu m/sq km per year was below the world average of 273,452 cu m/sq km per year. Average annual per capita river flow in 1989 was over 16,000 cu m per person – double the world figure of near 8,000 cu m per person.

River flow is unevenly distributed. Moist regions (north-west and northern European Russia, Siberia, and the Far East) account for 87 per cent of average annual flow but cover only 71 per cent of the area. The remaining 13 per cent of river flow crosses the mainly dry southern regions which make up 29 per cent of the territory. The largest rivers flow northward to the Arctic Ocean or eastward to the Pacific. Only the Volga among major rivers discharges southward.

DRAINAGE BASINS

There are five major drainage basins. The largest by far in area and runoff is the Arctic Ocean Basin stretching from the Kola Peninsula in the north-west to the Far East. It covers 54 per cent of the former USSR and accounts for 63 per cent of river discharge. The largest and longest rivers are found in the Siberian part of this basin. The Yenisey has a mouth discharge of 603 cu km per year (first in the former USSR and sixth in the world). Its length is 4090 km and basin area 2,580,000 sq km. The Lena is the second heaviest flowing river at 515 cu km with a

length of 4400 km and drainage area of 2,490,000 sq km. Third is the Ob' at 397 cu km, with a length of 5410 km (including its tributary the Irtysh) and basin of 2,975,000 sq km. The European part of the Arctic Basin holds two major rivers: the Pechora (130 cu km; 1809 km; 322,000 sq km) and the Northern Dvina (110 cu km; 1302 km; 360,000 sq km). Rivers of the Arctic basin are characterized by a lengthy ice cover (from five months for the European Arctic to eight months for eastern Siberia) and heavy spring flows from the melting of accumulated snow in their basins.

Second in runoff is the Pacific Ocean Basin which accounts for 21 per cent of average annual surface discharge and covers 15 per cent of the territory. The major artery is the Amur at 392 cu km (fourth in the former USSR), with a length of 4510 km and basin area of 1,855,000 sq km. This river and its right-bank tributary, the Ussuri, form a long border with China. The Amur is frozen for five months. It is chiefly rain fed by the summer monsoon with repetitive floods throughout the warm season, which reach their peak in August and September.

The Caspian–Aral Sea Basin is third in runoff with 9 per cent of the total for the former USSR, though it covers 23 per cent of the territory. The distinguishing feature of this basin is that rivers flow into three large terminal lakes, saline and with no outlets. These are the Caspian Sea, the Aral Sea, and Lake Balkhash. The Volga is the heaviest flowing river (254 cu km; 3700 km; 1,380,000 sq km) and discharges into the Caspian. Fifth in flow in the territory as a whole and first in European Russia, it is the area's most famous river and one that has played a key role in the historical, cultural, and economic development of the Russian state.

Two rivers are tributary to the Aral Sea, the Amu Dar'ya and Syr Dar'ya. Since they flow through deserts, average discharge in their upper courses where they exit the Tyan'-Shan' and Pamir mountains (Amu 73 and Syr 37 cu km) is considerably larger than where they enter the Aral Sea (Amu 40

The Lena – Russia's second biggest river

and Syr 15 cu km). The Amu stretches 2620 and the Syr 3078 km; respective basin areas are 465,000 and 462,000 sq km.

The Baltic Sea Basin is fourth in runoff with 4 per cent of the discharge of the former USSR, covering 2 per cent of its area. The Neva is the chief river with an average annual flow of 82 cu km and drainage area of 282,300 sq km. The Neva stretches only 74 km since it flows out of Lake Ladoga which acts as a regulating reservoir and creates an unusually even annual flow regime.

The Black Sea Basin is last in runoff volume accounting for only 3 per cent of the former USSR's river flow but its basin covers 6 per cent of the territory. Two large rivers enter this southern sea: the Dnieper (52 cu km; 2280 km; 504,000 sq km) and the Don (29 cu km; 1870 km; 422,000 sq km).

ECONOMIC DEVELOPMENT

The region has an abundance of surface flow resources. But economic use of many of the heaviest flowing and longest rivers is severely hindered by their location in sparsely inhabited, climatically unfavourable northern or eastern regions as well as their northward flow to the frozen Arctic. Only 16 per cent of surface discharge crosses the central and southern regions where 75 per cent of the population, 80 per cent of economic activity, and 80 per cent of the crop land, including the most fertile, are found. In these regions, rivers have been intensively mastered for transportation, industrial and municipal water supply, irrigation, hydro-electricity, and for fishing.

The Soviet government concentrated development on the major rivers of central and southern European Russia. Cascades of dams with hydro-electric capacity, navigation locks, and large reservoirs were built along the two major rivers of these regions, the Volga and Dnieper, between the 1930s and 1980s, transforming them into chains of huge lakes. The Volga system (including its right bank tributary, the Kama) has 11 large reservoirs and hydrocomplexes with an installed generating capacity of 11 million kilowatts. The river is navigable for 3550 km and large vessels travel from the Caspian in the south to the Rybinsk reservoir in the north and for a considerable distance up the Kama. It is connected by navigation canals to the Don river (thereby to the Azov, Black and Mediterranean seas) as well as to the White and Baltic seas.

The Volga–Baltic water route can handle ships to 5000 metric tonnes. The Volga system carries more tonnage than any other river in the former USSR (over half of the river-generated tonnes per km) with oil and refined products, forest products, con-

struction materials, industrial raw materials, coal, machinery and grain the dominant cargoes. Passenger traffic is also very heavy along the Volga. The Dnieper Cascade consists of six dams, reservoirs, and hydrocomplexes with an installed capacity of 3.6 million kilowatts. This river has also been made navigable for over 2000 km; large vessels can navigate its lower and middle courses but upstream reaches are limited to shallow-draught craft.

Large amounts of water are withdrawn for irrigation from the Dnieper, Volga, Don and other rivers flowing across southern European Russia and the Caucasus, where about half the former Soviet Union's irrigated area of 20 million hectares is located. However, irrigation has been most intensively developed in Central Asia and southern Kazakhstan. Located amidst the Kyzyl Kum and Kara Kum deserts, this region's economy is based on irrigated agriculture. Consequently, the flow of the two largest rivers here (Amu and Syr Dar'ya) has been almost entirely consumed before it reaches the Aral Sea to irrigate over 7 million hectares of land. Large hydrocomplexes have also been built along the upper courses of these rivers to regulate flow and produce electricity.

Rivers in northern European Russia, in Siberia, and the Far East have so far received less economic development. The major Arctic flowing rivers such as the Pechora, Northern Dvina, Ob', Yenisey, and Lena have considerable transportation importance, particularly in summer when freight movement along the Northern Sea Route is in full swing. For many communities not served by hard-surfaced

Right. Irrigation in Kyrgyzstan

The Pechora river in the Urals – typical landscape of much of northern Russia

The Angara river, an important source of hydropower, near Lake Baykal

roads or railways, they are the main supply routes (even in winter when their frozen surfaces are used as roads). Since the 1950s the Siberian rivers Ob' and Yenisey have also been the sites for the construction of large hydropower stations. Several of the world's largest hydrostations have been built along the Yenisey and its principal tributary, the Angara. Installed capacity of the five stations completed and one under construction is 26 million kilowatts. Two major hydroelectric stations have been built on tributaries of the Amur, but the river's main economic importance is transportation, including a growing trade with Japan.

The geographical disparity between the concentration of population, industry, and agricultural potential on the one hand and abundant river flow on the other has stimulated a long-term interest in large-scale transfers of water between northern drainage basins of perceived water surplus and southern drainage basins of perceived water shortage. The Soviet government pursued serious water transfer planning from the 1930s. In the early 1960s a scheme to transfer 40 cu km per year from the Vychegda and Kama rivers of northern European Russia into the Volga River Basin was nearly implemented but abandoned on environmental and economic grounds.

In the 1970s and early 1980s water management design agencies formulated projects to divert 20 cu km and 27 cu km annually, respectively, from the north of European Russia into the Volga Basin and from the Ob' River Basin into the Aral Sea Basin. These plans were subsequently approved by the government. Preparatory construction work for the European scheme began in 1984 while final construction designs for the Siberian plan were being prepared. When Gorbachev became leader in 1985, the plans came under widespread and bitter public criticism as ill-founded and inordinately expensive vehicles of environmental and cultural destruction. An August 1986 decree of the Council of Ministers and Central Committee of the CPSU ordered all construction and design work for north–south transfers to be halted but allowed for continued research into their environmental and economic aspects.

POLLUTION

As in other industrialized countries, rivers in the Soviet Union have suffered at the hands of man. Pollution has most seriously affected rivers in the more economically developed and populated central and southern portions of European Russia. The Volga, Dnieper, Neva, Don, and other smaller streams receive large volumes of industrial and municipal waste. In the southern, drier portion of the region, irrigation runoff containing salts, pesticides and herbicides, and fertilizers is also a problem. Major clean-up efforts have been under-way since the early 1970s, particularly on the Volga, but the situation remains severe.

In other regions pollution is also a concern. In northern European Russia, Siberia, and the Far East timber-rafting litters rivers with bark and sunken logs; in Western Siberia, oil development has tainted the Ob'; and in Central Asia irrigation runoff has made what is left of the waters of the Amu and Syr Dar'ya unfit for drinking.

The chains of dams and reservoirs placed along the major rivers have radically altered their natural ecosystems. Annual flow variation has been reduced, nutrients and sediments have accumulated in reservoirs, migratory fish have been cut off from spawning grounds, and conditions for fish have dramatically changed in the lake-like environments of reservoirs compared to those of free-flowing rivers. Forests and agricultural lands have also been flooded for reservoirs.

The most severe problems are associated with the Volga Cascade where Caspian sturgeon and salmon have been cut off from most of their spawning areas, spring discharges below the lowest dam (Volgograd) have been cut to levels harmful to fish, and huge, shallow reservoirs have flooded 22,400 sq km, of which 51 per cent was formerly agricultural land.

Human activities have also depleted river flow. The primary causes are reservoirs and irrigation. The former permanently trap water in 'dead storage' and increase evaporative losses, and irrigation only returns part of the water withdrawn, the remainder being lost to evaporation, transpiration, and filtration. For 1976–80, depletion of the Volga, Dnieper and Don was estimated at 8 per cent, 41 per cent and 24 per cent, respectively.

By far the most dramatic case of flow diminution is in Central Asia where the discharge of the Amu and Syr Dar'ya into the Aral Sea, formerly the world's fourth largest lake, was reduced to near zero by the 1980s as the result of excessive irrigation. Consequently, the level of the Aral between 1960 and 1993 dropped more than 16m, its area shrank by 45 per cent and water volume decreased by 25 per cent.   PPM

The Aral Sea disaster

One of the world's worst environmental disasters, taking place in the Central Asian region of the former USSR, is the drying up of the fourth largest lake in the world, the Aral Sea. As a result of extensive and hugely wasteful irrigation along the lengths of the two main rivers that feed it, the Aral Sea is almost at the point of no return. Without prompt action, the lake will die.

During the 1980s, the shrinking Aral split into two smaller seas, which are already developing their own water balances. The deltas of the two rivers that feed the Aral, the Amu Dar'ya and the Syr Dar'ya, once lush havens for a diverse flora and fauna, have been all but destroyed. In the sea itself a formerly thriving fishing industry is now extinct, fishing ports finding themselves miles inland as the water recedes, the fish killed by the increasing salinity of the water.

The effects of the tragedy stretch well beyond the Aral; salts and dust blown up from the exposed seabed are damaging plants over a wide area, and are probably the cause of a dramatic increase in levels of respiratory disease and certain types of cancer among the local population. The reduced flow of the rivers has meant that pollution levels in their lower reaches are now extremely dangerous. In Karakalpakia, the region that borders the southern half of the Aral Sea, infant mortality rates can exceed 100 per 1,000 live births, four times the average for the former USSR. Medical surveys in the region in the late 1980s showed that 66 per cent of adults and 83 per cent of children were suffering from illnesses directly attributable to water and air pollution.

The effort necessary to avert total disaster is huge. In order to maintain the sea at its present level, 33 cubic kilometres of water is needed per year. To restore it to its 1961 levels, a minimum of 56 cu km per year is required. The present average annual flow is a mere 7 cu km.

Fishing vessels stranded far from the retreating Aral Sea

Climate

Right. *Dolbai-Ulgen Gorge in Stavropol' Territory*

The extent of latitude in the European part of the former Soviet Union provides a temperature gradation from the Arctic north to the sub-tropical south. But the vast longitudinal dimension across northern Eurasia, mainly in high and middle latitudes, and the consequent remoteness of Siberian regions from the moderating influences of the Atlantic, result in the predominance of extreme features of climatic continentality. These are manifested by great contrasts between mean summer and winter temperatures and by brief transitional spring and autumn seasons, together with generally moderate or low levels of precipitation. The heat received from direct solar radiation increases from north to south in accordance with the increase in the noon elevation of the sun, but this is modified by the greater cloudiness of the European region, resulting from the effect of the greater frequency of depressions in that area as compared with Siberia, an area remote from the Atlantic Ocean, which is the chief source of moisture.

Winter is the dominant season during which an anticyclonic ridge of very high pressure forms over much of Russia, associated with a continental air mass which creates very low temperatures and generates cold, dry winds. The Siberian region becomes increasingly cold eastwards; thus Oymyakon, at latitude 63°N in eastern Siberia, has the lowest absolute temperature anywhere in the northern hemisphere: −67.7°C. The proximity of the frozen Arctic and the mountainous relief all contribute to the severity of winter in this region. The great mountain barrier in the south excludes warm tropical air, but there is no such relief barrier in the north, so that cold polar air has almost complete access to the great lowland areas. Only in the far south, along the Black Sea coast of the Crimea and in parts of Transcaucasia are winter temperatures above freezing.

Winter snowfall produced by the passage of depressions – which also bring brief thaws – is particularly heavy west of the Urals. The duration of snow cover is still long, varying from a mean of about 160 days in St Petersburg to 80 days in Kiev. In the very high mountains of the south, the snow and ice last all the year, and in the Moscow region the Moskva, Oka and Volga Rivers freeze before December and remain frozen until mid-April.

In spring the anticyclone weakens as the great land mass warms rapidly; the snow melts, the rivers thaw and by midsummer a broad belt of warmth with temperatures between 20°C and 16°C extends across the country from the west to mid-Siberia. The highest summer temperatures occur in subtropical

Below. *Siberian mountains – the East Sayan*

Below right. *Moscow in winter*

Right. *The climate of the former Soviet Union. From top to bottom: winter temperatures, summer temperatures, and precipitation*

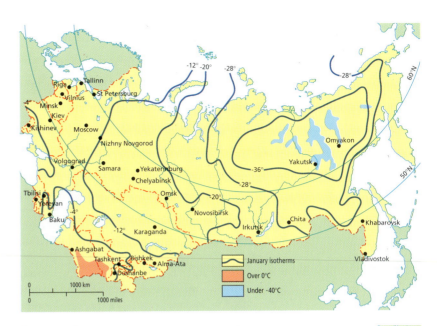

Below. *Waterlilies in a woodland lake near St Petersburg*

southern areas such as Georgia and in the hot, arid areas of Central Asia where, for example, Tashkent records a July mean of 25°C.

Summer is the season of highest precipitation, except in the Black Sea region where moist air from the Mediterranean produces mainly autumn and winter rains. The Atlantic is again the principal source of precipitation, producing a central belt of moderate amount (400–800 mm) from which there is a decrease eastwards, southwards and northwards, except in mountainous areas. Summer rainfall in eastern Siberia is low and irregular, but the driest region is the desert zone east of the Caspian Sea where less than 100 mm are recorded. Summer monsoon rains occur in the Far East from the Pacific source region, but the highland relief of that area restricts the heaviest falls to maritime areas, minimizing their effect in eastern Siberia. WWN

11

Flora and fauna

ECOLOGICAL ZONES

Natural vegetation and soil constitute two of the region's principal renewable organic resources, as they form the basis of agriculture and source of many types of raw materials. After the Pleistocene glaciations, the process of natural selection produced plant communities dominated by species closely adapted to the local environment. Both the flora and the soil broadly corresponded to a broad latitudinal gradation in temperature, rainfall, potential evaporation and irradiation. In the far north were the treeless cold deserts or tundras; farther south, higher temperatures and longer growing seasons allowed the formation of great forested zones. Southwards again, the forests were succeeded by steppes or treeless prairie grasslands, more suited to sub-humid climates. These in turn gradually

Vegetation and soil

yielded to semi-desert and desert where plant life was adapted to prolonged drought.

Each major plant type provided food and shelter for many kinds of mammals, birds and insects, forming a set of complex ecosystems represented today within a growing number of nature reserves. In each zone human influence over time gave rise to varying degrees of transformation of the ecosystem by, for example, replacing natural vegetation by agricultural systems – though even then the basic relationships between organisms and the environment could remain functionally unaltered.

Today each vegetation zone can be seen to be closely related to a particular kind of soil. It is formed by the interaction of five factors, namely the parent rock, the climate, living organisms (particularly vegetation and fauna), the geology of the land, and the time over which the soil has developed. The combination of these environmental influences gives rise to distinctive soil layers, commonly characterized as surface soil, subsoil, and the substratum of rock material. Much of the former USSR

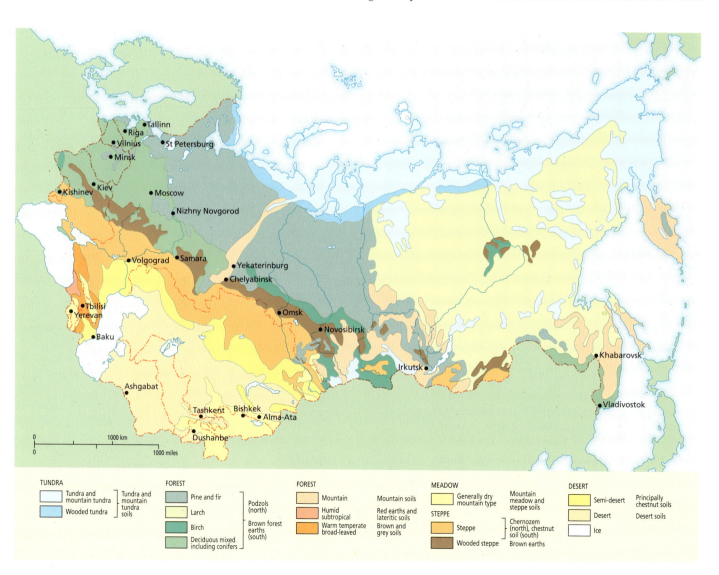

TUNDRA		
☐ Tundra and mountain tundra	Tundra and mountain tundra soils	
☐ Wooded tundra		

FOREST		
☐ Pine and fir		Podzols (north)
☐ Larch		
☐ Birch		Brown forest earths (south)
☐ Deciduous mixed including conifers		

FOREST		
☐ Mountain		Mountain soils
☐ Humid subtropical		Red earths and lateritic soils
☐ Warm temperate broad-leaved		Brown and grey soils

MEADOW		
☐ Generally dry mountain type		Mountain meadow and steppe soils
STEPPE		
☐ Steppe		Chernozem (north), chestnut soil (south)
☐ Wooded steppe		Brown earths

DESERT		
☐ Semi-desert		Principally chestnut soils
☐ Desert		Desert soils
☐ Ice		

Scale: 0 — 1000 km; 0 — 1000 miles

Cities labelled: Tallinn, Riga, Vilnius, St Petersburg, Minsk, Kishinev, Kiev, Moscow, Nizhny Novgorod, Volgograd, Samara, Yekaterinburg, Chelyabinsk, Tbilisi, Yerevan, Baku, Omsk, Novosibirsk, Irkutsk, Khabarovsk, Vladivostok, Ashgabat, Tashkent, Bishkek, Alma-Ata, Dushanbe

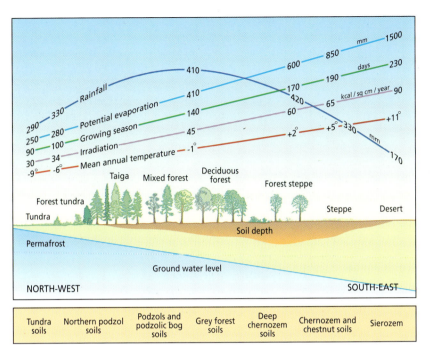

Climate, vegetation and soil profiles of European Russia

is lowland terrain, substantially uniform topographically and geologically. The influence of climate and vegetation upon soil formation is thus apparent over wide areas as potential variables such as geology and relief are in practice largely constant. Soil types accordingly correspond closely to the zones of vegetation established by interacting climatic elements and form broad belts trending west to east, except in mountain areas. There, the more rapid variations in physical factors of climate and relief due to altitude produce a near-vertical zonation of soil and vegetation.

Tundra

Climate: arctic; soil type: arctic desert and tundra soils

The tundra or treeless cold desert covers almost all the extreme north of European and Siberian Russia from the Arctic coast to the northern margin of the coniferous forest. It also extends southwards into mountainous areas above the tree-line. Winters are prolonged and very cold, with up to nine months of sub-zero temperatures, so that the subsoil remains permanently frozen (permafrost). All biological activity is thus confined to a shallow upper soil layer, the 'active layer' which thaws only during the short summer. It is usually waterlogged, as moisture cannot drain through the solidly frozen permafrost beneath. The soil therefore lacks air, restricting the decomposition of organic matter and the release of nutrients by bacteria and fungi. An acid, peaty layer tends to form on the surface above a lower horizon of blue clay or loam, but soil layers are usually disturbed by frost action, which thrusts stones upwards to the surface where they form circular or polygonal patterns.

Almost all tundra plants are dwarfed, no taller than a few centimetres, and commonly with a prostrate, creeping form of growth close to the soil surface, giving them protection from wind-chill or desiccation. In the coastal 'high Arctic desert', the low fertility, scanty precipitation and brief growing season exclude all plant life but mosses, lichens and algae; farther south, a longer frost-free period allows growth of a 'typical tundra' consisting of flowering herbs, grasses, sedges and shrubs. Such vegetation grows rapidly during summer when daylight continues after midnight and temperatures rise above freezing. At this time plants store up food reserves in their enlarged root systems for the renewal of growth in the following spring, a phase contrasting with mid-winter conditions of total darkness and consequent plant dormancy.

The plant life forms the primary food component of an ecosystem which supports uniquely important bird and mammal populations. Reindeer and lemming are prey for wolves and foxes, and most birds are migrants visiting the tundra for breeding in summer and returning southwards in autumn. But all Arctic plants and animals exist in delicate balance with their harsh environment, now increasingly threatened by the immense soil disruption created by the exploitation of northern mineral deposits. Atmospheric quality is damaged by toxic emissions of gases from smelting industries which are injurious to all plant growth; freshwater resources are polluted by sewage and other effluent from urban and industrial developments in northern Siberia and the Kola peninsula.

Boreal forest

Climate: sub-arctic; soil type: podzols; gleyed podzols; peats

The tundra passes gradually southwards into a zone of transition, the wooded tundra or forest-tundra where stunted boreal tree species are intermingled with tundra plant communities. This margin between the forest proper and the true tundra coincides approximately with the July isotherm of 10°C and extends southwards east of the Urals where the Siberian climate increases in severity.

The boreal forest, or taiga, covers almost all the sub-Arctic north of Russia extending from Europe eastwards to the Pacific Ocean. It is the largest coniferous forest in the world, containing about half the earth's reserve of softwood timber. In addition to its economic importance, it is of great global significance in its favourable influence on atmospheric conditions and in its regulation of stream flow and of soil moisture reserves. Among the dominant coniferous species, pine and spruce are the most valuable for industry and cover large areas in the west, though larch is the commonest beyond western Siberia. However, the forest contains also numerous stands of deciduous species such as birch and aspen which replace the conifers after fires or logging operations. The trees and their undergrowth sustain a rich and varied bird and mammal fauna, the latter including bears, wolves and smaller mammals, which may, like the mink, yield valuable fur resources.

Although cleared areas of the taiga produce limited riverside pastures or crops, neither its climate nor its soil favour high-yielding agriculture. The low temperature and high humidity create a podzol soil with a black, acid surface layer of coniferous leaf litter; below it is a grey infertile layer formed by downward percolation of water through the soil, causing leaching of its nutrients. Some nutrients are retained in the compact red-brown subsoil together with iron and aluminium compounds, but most are lost in drainage. 'Gleyed' soils, in contrast, are poorly drained and accumulate in depressions; they lack oxygen, as do the organic peats, which form treeless bogs and marshes like the immense Vasyugansk morass of Western Siberia. Drained peat-bog terrain is converted to agriculture and peat is used as a power-station fuel, or as a source of chemicals.

The widespread extraction of fossil fuels and metal ores which lie under the taiga, the accompanying industrial developments, and vast areas of forest destroyed by flooding for reservoir construction, have all had a catastrophic impact on the forest ecosystem. Such development takes precedence over the urgent need for conservation of the forest environment, including the huge freshwater resource of its river systems.

Mixed forest

Climate: temperate continental; soil type: brown podzolic

South and west of the taiga the European Russian lowland used to consist of mixed forests comprising a mosaic of coniferous pines or spruce trees and broad-leaf deciduous oak, beech and maple, but as the latter occupied the more fertile soils they have largely been cleared for agriculture. This region has a longer growing season than that of the taiga, with a warm summer (Moscow's July mean is 19°C) but a long winter with heavy snowfall.

The soils of the deciduous woodlands are brown podzolic forest soils. Although moderately acid, they are richer than podzols, as their weathered parent rocks, plus the abundant humus produced by the annual leaf fall, generate more nutrients, losses of which are reduced because leaching by rainwater is lessened. Such soils and the warm, humid summer give rise to a greater diversity of plant and animal life than that of the taiga: vegetation is multi-layered, with separate strata of shrubs, herbs and mosses below the canopy of the dominant trees. Each stratum contains characteristic fauna, birds

The taiga near Lake Baykal

and invertebrates occupying different layers. Below ground, there is abundant earthworm and insect activity which breaks down the fallen leafy organic matter and releases nutrients. The conifer stands occupy poorer soils or replace the deciduous trees above the deciduous tree limit.

The forests and soils of the lower Amur basin of the Far East are similar to those of the European region, although the forests are richer in flora and fauna, being a mixture of both temperate and tropical elements.

Steppe

Climate: temperate semi-arid; soil type: chernozem and chestnut

Southwards of the mixed forest, as the climate becomes warmer and drier, the vegetation changes to a transitional zone of forest-steppe where groves of oak are interspersed with grassland, both now transformed by agriculture. Beyond it to the south is the true steppe or prairie grassland. At one time the habitat of herds of migratory deer, wild horses and other grazing animals, the steppe now provides the Commonwealth of Independent States (CIS) with its best arable land, extending from Ukraine for 4000 km into Siberia.

With decreasing precipitation, increasing summer heat and evaporation southwards, trees disappear except in the moist valleys, and the landscape becomes open steppe. The soils here are black earths or chernozems famous for their thick upper layer

The East Siberian steppe

The central Caucasus,
Svanetia (Georgia)

of black organic matter or humus, the residual product of decayed roots and feather grass foliage, sedges and other flowering herbs. It contains abundant earthworms and other soil fauna, whose activity releases nitrogen, calcium and other plant nutrients, providing great reserves of fertility. These nutrients are not leached out as rainfall is light and counteracted by evaporation produced by hot dry winds (*sukhovei*). Fertility is also enhanced by the parent material of the soil; this is generally loess, a fine-textured wind-blown deposit rich in lime.

The natural fertility of all the grassland soils is reduced by the frequent droughts, and wide areas have been degraded or lost through agricultural misuse; soft and friable, they are easily eroded by running water and by wind during dust storms. Hence protective wind-shelter belts have been important in soil conservation.

Semi-desert and desert

Climate: semi-arid/arid; soil type: chestnut-brown; saline and desert

A further increase in aridity southwards is accompanied by less abundant vegetation and consequently a shallower humus layer in the topsoil. These features characterize the southern chernozems, which grade to the south into the chestnut soils found in a broad belt extending mainly east of the lower Volga into western Siberia and Kazakhstan. The chestnut soils have dark-brown upper layers formed by a plant cover of grasses, short-stemmed

herbs and small shrubs, the latter often drought-resistant and salt-tolerant, qualities required by the presence of saline deposits drawn up to the surface by strong evaporation of soil moisture. Cultivation of such soils, even with irrigation, is hazardous and is followed by destructive dust storms.

The extreme south, occupied by the Central Asian states, is an intensely dry region, very hot in summer and cold in winter, with irregular rainfall. The plant cover consists of ephemeral herbaceous species appearing only after rain, and drought-resistant perennial shrubs, grasses, and small trees, which provide livestock grazing.

The soils vary widely and are often highly saline, such as the solonchaks which are loams with a surface crust of sodium chloride, like those of the chestnut soil zones. Sandy soils are widespread and form mobile dunes in the Kara Kum and Kyzl Kum. The most productive soils are the grey sierozems of the foothill oasis areas which may yield good crops with irrigation.

The subtropics

Climate: humid subtropical; soils: red podzolic

South of the main ranges of the Caucasus, largely in Georgia, the natural vegetation is broad-leaved warm-temperate forests, very rich in species and luxuriant in character. Most of the plant cover is sustained by deep, acid, leached, well-drained soils, reddish in colour due to the abundance of iron-oxides. These areas, when cleared of forest, yield crops of tea and citrus fruit. Eastwards in Azerbaijan, in the lower Kura valley, the climate is drier and colder and sustains steppe or semi-desert vegetation and soil, crop production requiring irrigation. In contrast, the Crimean peninsula in the extreme south has a Mediterranean climate with winter rainfall and warm dry summers, to which the mainly evergreen, drought-resistant plant life is adapted.

The Caucasus

These ranges are Alpine-type mountains rising higher than 5000m and well above the treeline. They form a climatic divide, separating continental steppe or semi-desert in the north from the more humid sub-tropical conditions in the south. Increasing elevation from lower to higher slopes creates zonal differences in climate, reflected in vegetation, soil, animal life and land utilization. The warm-temperate mountain forests of deciduous species on lower slopes are supported by brown or grey forest soils; above them, with increasing precipitation, are dark coniferous forests growing to the treeline, above which, extending up to the snow-line, are rich sub-alpine and alpine tundra meadows. Extended forest clearance to provide land for agriculture has made anti-erosion measures essential.　　WWN

Kara Kum desert in the
Repetek reserve

15

FAUNA

Owing to the variety of environmental conditions encountered and a great latitudinal extent, the fauna of the region is extremely varied. In the high Arctic are the polar bear (*Thalarctos maritimus*), Arctic fox (*Alopex lagopus*), musk-ox (*Ovibos moschatus*), lemming (*Lemmus* and *Dicrostonyx* sp.), snowy owl (*Nyctea scandiaca*), raven (*Corvus corax*) and ptarmigan (*Lagopus lagopus*). The wild reindeer (*Rangifer tarandus*) of much of the tundra has been crowded out of its grazing grounds by the domesticated reindeer and its numbers are decreasing. Elk (*Alces alces*), bear (*Ursus* sp.) and many small fur-bearing animals such as the sable (*Martes zibellina*), squirrel (*Sciurus vulgaris* and *S. Fuscombens*), fox (*Vulpes* sp.), marten (*Martes martes*) and ermine (*Mustela erminea*) frequent the taiga in European Russia, Siberia and the Far East. The musk-rat, introduced from Canada in 1930, has adapted well to the swampy environment. The mixed forest zone of European Russia has been much depleted of wild life by man. The roebuck (*Capreolus capreolus pygargus*), wolf, fox and squirrel are still common, but the brown bear and badger (*Meles meles*) less so. The beaver (*Castor fiber*) is found in the marshes of the west.

The varied fauna of the former Soviet Union: brown bear, hazel grouse, a saiga antelope, and spotted deer

Wild life in the extensively cultivated steppelands has been sadly depleted and many species such as wild horses, cattle and the marmot have been exterminated while others, such as the saiga antelope (*Saiga tatarica*), have migrated into the semi-desert regions. The dormouse, hamster, mole-rat, and ground-squirrel remain, however, as do several species of birds including the great bustard or strepet (*Otis tarda*). The ground-squirrel (*Citellus fulvus, C. dauricus*), jumping mice and other rodents together with the gazelle (*Procapra gutturosa*) frequent the semi-deserts and deserts. The Volga delta is no longer rich in wild-fowl but cormorants (*Phalacrocorax carbo*), geese and egrets are numerous. Mountain fauna is made up of a great variety of species. In the Caucasus, for example, the wild life includes mountain goats (*Capra aegagrus, C. ibex caucasica, C. ibex severtzovi*), the chamois, red deer, roe-deer and mountain sheep. Northern taiga and southern species are found in the Far East of the country. These include the Manchurian and Caspian tigers (*Panthera tigris altaica* and *P. tigris virgata*), leopard (*Panthera pardus orientalis*), raccoon dog (*Nyctereutes procyonoides ussuriensis*), an endemic Manchurian hare (*Lepus mandschuricus*), elk, musk-deer, sable and brown bear.

Significant ecological protection legislation has been passed to cover the conservation of a wide range of species, including insects and soil fauna.   GMH

Resources and conservation

NATURAL RESOURCES

With approximately 22.4 million sq km of territory, or about 16 per cent of the world's total land area, the former USSR is richly endowed with natural resources. Not all, however, are well located with respect to the distribution of population and economic activity, nor have they been wisely utilized. Only about 10.7 per cent of the territory, for example, can be used for arable farming, though the natural hayland (2.6 per cent), pasture (14.2 per cent) and the reindeer pastures of the north (14.8 per cent) are also agriculturally significant. Expansion of the arable areas at the expense of swamp and marsh (8.5 per cent of the territory) and of forest and scrubland (37.2 per cent) has met limited success. The remaining 12.0 per cent of the territory is classified as unsuitable or unoccupied land.

Despite the size of the country, the authorities have shown continuing concern about losses of agricultural land to construction and other uses. In the twenty-five years to 1989, for example, approximately 22 million hectares of arable land were lost, of which 12 million were taken for construction purposes and 10 million for hydro-electric power projects.

Right. Sparse forest and bog in the Tyumen oil and gas basin

Below. Log-rafting on the Kama river

Forests

The former USSR has over one fifth of the world's forested land and over one half of its coniferous standing timber. The reserve amounts to over one quarter of the world's growing stock. The actual forested area is some 811 million ha, representing 86,000 million cu m of timber; 75 per cent of the forested area is coniferous. Approximately three quarters of the forested area lies in the often remote Asiatic part of the country, a region containing only a quarter of the population, but the harsh climate produces a thinner stand and a slower annual growth rate than in the European territory. The timber industry is oriented towards the more accessible forests, and 60 per cent of the total national growing stock is classified as mature or over-mature.

Game

Rich resources of fauna exist: of the 125–130 thousand known species found, special importance attaches to commercial land game, over 40 species of which live mainly in the forest zone. The tundra (polar fox and northern reindeer) and taiga together provide about 80 per cent of all the furs and 90 per cent of the forest game.

Water

One of the most important of the territory's resource problems is water. Although receiving about 10 per cent of the world's precipitation, and possessing about one-eighth of the world's surface runoff, water resources are extremely unevenly distributed. Considerable areas suffer from an over-abundance of water, especially in the forest zone. Peat bog, however, makes a small but important contribution to the energy supply from an estimated 60 per cent of the world's peat resources. A much greater problem is aridity: 30 per cent of the territory, especially in Central Asia and the southern European area, has only 2 per cent of the total surface water resources. Of the annual surface runoff, 62 per cent is lost to the Arctic Ocean and 20 per cent to the Pacific, leaving only 18 per cent, corresponding with the internal and Atlantic drainage basins, available for 80 per cent of the population. Although only about 7 per cent of the annual surface runoff is currently utilized, this amounts to more than 20 per cent of the reliable flow. Inefficient use of water helps to promote water shortages not only in the southern regions but also in industrialized and urbanized areas further north.

Minerals

The Soviet Union was able to provide for most of its own needs in minerals – possessing, for example, the world's greatest reserves of iron ore. Many of the metallic deposits are in convenient locations.

The European territory is well endowed with iron ore, though considerable reserves are also believed to lie in remoter parts of the east. Manganese (of which the deposits are very large, probably exceeded only by South Africa's) and other ferro-alloys are scattered in various locations across the European region, the central and southern Urals, southern Siberia and parts of Central Asia. Some, such as nickel and cobalt, are mined in remote areas of the north. The territory is well endowed in copper, lead, zinc, gold, silver, diamonds, asbestos, mercury and antimony; supplies of bauxite appear to be less abundant and those of tin are mainly in inaccessible regions.

Energy

Most of the energy resources are found in the eastern zones which also supply more than half of the fuel needs despite the fact that 75 per cent of the population and 80 per cent of the industry (both in terms of fixed assets and value of production) are located in the west. Ninety per cent of the potential coal reserves, for example, lie in Siberia and the Far East; estimates suggest that the country possesses half of the world's potential reserves. Siberia and the Far East contain 63 per cent of the total explored reserves which equal 281 thousand million tons (the world's second largest explored reserve). Sixty per cent of this consists of hard coal. The USSR ranked second after China in hydroelectric power potential, only 20 per cent of which was used. Two thirds of the potential lies in Siberia and the Far East, 16 per cent in Kazakhstan and Central Asia, and 18 per cent in Europe which has half the installed capacity. Reserves of hydrocarbons are also believed to be very extensive, although once again distribution is very much oriented towards the east. Western estimates suggest that the former USSR contained 10–12 per cent of the proved oil reserves of the world; unexploited deposits in East Siberia, the Far East, the northern continental shelf, Kazakhstan and Turkmenistan have since substantially raised this total. The territory also boasts some 40 per cent of the world's natural gas reserves, most of which are in Siberia, though increasing deposits are now being revealed in Central Asia. There is a large gas condensate reserve, and considerable potential for developing alternative energy sources.   DJBS

The distribution of natural resources in the former Soviet Union. Below: iron ore reserves. *Above right:* non-ferrous mineral reserves. *Below right:* coal reserves and exploitation

Asbestos · **Fluorspar** · **Antimony**
Gold · **Mercury** · **Tin**
Copper · **Mica** · **Uranium**
Diamonds · **Lead** · **Zinc**

Tallinn
Riga
Vilnius
St Petersburg
Minsk
Kiev
Kishinev
Moscow
Nizhny Novgorod
Volgograd
Samara
Yekaterinburg
Chelyabinsk
Tbilisi
Yerevan
Baku
Omsk
Novosibirsk
Irkutsk
Khabarovsk
Vladivostok
Ashgabat
Tashkent
Bishkek
Alma-Ata
Dushanbe

0   1000 km
0   1000 miles

Riga
Tallinn
Vilnius
St Petersburg
VOLYNIAN BASIN
Minsk
DNIEPER BASIN
Kishinev
Kiev
MOSCOW BASIN
Moscow
Nizhny Novgorod
PECHORA BASIN
DONBAS BASIN
Samara
Volgograd
Chelyabinsk
Yekaterinburg
Tbilisi
Yerevan
Baku
TUNGUS BASIN
LENA BASIN
Omsk
KANSK-ACHINSK BASIN
KUZBAS BASIN
Novosibirsk
SOUTH YAKUTIAN BASIN
BUREYA BASIN
Ashgabat
KARAGANDA BASIN
Irkutsk
Khabarovsk
SUCHAN BASIN
Tashkent
Bishkek
Alma-Ata
Vladivostok
Dushanbe

Hard coal deposit
Hard coal mining centre
Brown coal deposit
Brown coal mining centre

0   1000 km
0   1000 miles

19

Right. The Baku oilfields are heavily polluted by leakage

ENVIRONMENTAL PROTECTION

Central planning and ownership of the means of production did not enable the Soviet Union to escape the problems of environmental deterioration. The principal reasons appear to have been a commitment to rapid economic growth, the failure to put a price on many natural resources, lack of co-ordination and foresight, and an unwillingness to enforce conservation measures. Also important has been belief, especially under Stalin, in an inexhaustible supply of many resources and in society's ability to modify nature to suit its own purposes. Continued dependence on inefficient industrial processes utilizing outdated technologies has, however, not only wasted valuable resources but had serious consequences for the environment.

Decrees on the conservation of the environment date back to the earliest years of Soviet power, but it was not until the late 1950s and early 1960s that concern at the environmental consequences of industrialization became widespread. Between 1957 and 1964 all fifteen Union Republics adopted comprehensive laws on the management and conservation of natural resources. Various sections of republican criminal codes were adapted to provide penalties for infringements of conservation laws.

Legislative bases were adopted for the management of land (1968), water (1970), minerals (1975) and forest (1977). Natural landscapes were protected in a system of nature preserves and reserves, and other measures were taken to conserve endangered plant and animal species.

Responsibility for conservation was exercised at many levels, including the national and republican governments, and an important role was played by the sectoral ministries and agencies. Local soviets

Hydrocarbon basins and exploitation

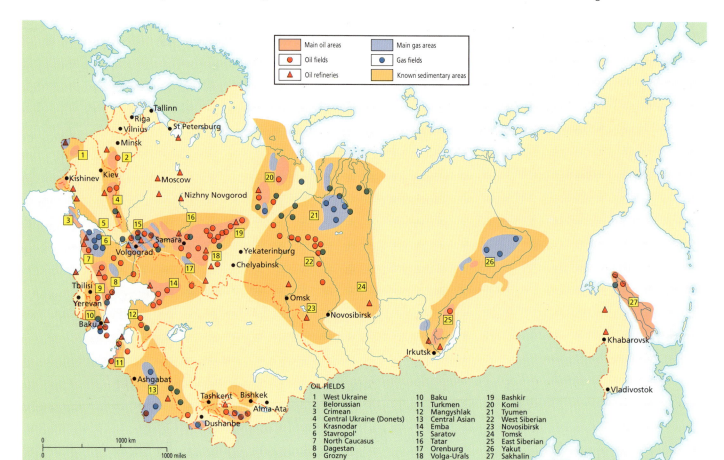

Legend:
- Main oil areas
- Oil fields
- Oil refineries
- Main gas areas
- Gas fields
- Known sedimentary areas

OIL FIELDS

1	West Ukraine	10	Baku	19	Bashkir
2	Belorussian	11	Turkmen	20	Komi
3	Crimean	12	Mangyshlak	21	Tyumen
4	Central Ukraine (Donets)	13	Central Asian	22	West Siberian
5	Krasnodar	14	Emba	23	Novosibirsk
6	Stavropol'	15	Saratov	24	Tomsk
7	North Caucasus	16	Tatar	25	East Siberian
8	Dagestan	17	Orenburg	26	Yakut
9	Grozny	18	Volga-Urals	27	Sakhalin

0   1000 km
0   1000 miles

had a conservation mandate within their administrative districts. The USSR State Committee for Environmental Protection, established in January 1988, was supposed to supervise the work of the many conservation agencies which were often poorly co-ordinated in the past. Such failures to implement conservation laws derived not only from the traditional political weakness of key environmental agencies but also from the fact that important conservation responsibilities were vested in agencies primarily concerned with the exploitation of environmental resources.

During the Gorbachev era (1985–91) much more information was made available on environmental issues from which it became clear that, in spite of the legislation and conservation activity of the post-Stalin period, many regions were suffering from severe environmental disruption. Serious air pollution, for example, afflicts numerous industrial cities; 50 million people (18 per cent of the population) are said to live in cities where air pollution levels periodically exceed permitted levels by a factor of ten or more. The consequences for health are predictably damaging.

No less widespread is the pollution of water. The waste water discharged into inland lakes and seas

Right: Magnitorgorsk, where annually two tons of harmful substances are released per inhabitant, more than in any other Russian city

increased by over four times in twenty years; more than 25 per cent of this effluent is discharged without treatment. The Volga–Caspian basin, the Black, Azov and Baltic seas, and such inland lakes as Baykal, Issyk-Kul and Ladoga are gravely polluted, with dire economic and social consequences. In spite of special measures supposedly taken to conserve the ecologically unique Lake Baykal, the water is still contaminated by cellulose production taking place on the shores of the lake, and by millions of tons of waste water discharged by industrial and agricultural enterprises. In Central Asia diversions of water from the rivers Syr Darya and Amu Darya for irrigation of cotton have caused the rapid shrinking of the Aral Sea, a major ecological catastrophe.

Losses and deterioration of land through opencast mining, flooding for hydrological schemes, drilling for oil and gas, soil erosion, salinization and desertification afflict different regions. Of major international concern was the accident at the Chernobyl' nuclear power plant in the Ukraine in April 1986, the direct effects of which in the short term were 31 deaths, many hospitalizations, and the long-term evacuation of 135,000 people from a 30 km zone around the plant, and a pall of radioactive pollution over a large area of northern and western Europe. There will be thousands of premature deaths and the Soviet authorities stand accused of failing to take adequate counter-measures. The vociferous anti-nuclear lobby which the catastrophe generated halted an ambitious nuclear power programme.

The successor states, being more responsive to public opinion, may make significant improvements in environmental conservation, through increased government expenditure, enhanced environmental consciousness, green movements and tougher laws. Economic reform in itself moves conservation away from planning measures and towards the greater use of economic incentives and sanctions.   DJBS

Above. Children swimming at Krasnoyarsk

Extent of gully erosion in European Russia

ДА ЗДРАВСТВУЕТ
ЕДИНСТВО И БРАТСТВО ТРУДЯЩИХСЯ
ВСЕХ НАЦИОНАЛЬНОСТЕЙ СССР!

The peoples

Settlement

The settlement of northern Eurasia began with the 'Neolithic revolution', which ushered in agriculture and permanent habitation. About the start of the fifth millennium BC agriculture first appeared in the extreme south of Turkmenistan. From here agriculture, based on irrigation and settled societies with urban characteristics, spread to the river valleys of Central Asia. A second introduction of agriculture and settled life came into European Russia from the Danubian lands in the shape of the Tripol'e culture of the third millennium BC. Thereafter successive agricultural societies, living in permanent villages, occupied the forest-steppe zone and gradually penetrated northwards into the zone of mixed forest. Last in this succession were the East Slav tribes, who had spread through the mixed forest of European Russia by the sixth century AD. The open steppes north of the Black Sea remained the home of successive nomadic peoples, although some, notably the Khazars, farmed and founded towns.

Among the Slavs slash-and-burn cultivation supported small village kinship communities, linked into tribal groupings. Near the southern forest frontier with the steppe, most villages were fortified with ditches and earthen banks, topped by wooden palisades. Some fortified places, the seats of chieftains, grew into towns as tribute from adjacent regions provided surpluses for craft manufacture and trade. The formation of the Kievan state in the ninth century stimulated the processes of forest clearance for agriculture, the establishment of new villages and urban foundations. By 1238 there were nearly 300 Russian towns. Russian village settlement extended north to the Gulf of Finland and east to the middle Volga.

The Tatar invasion long retarded Russian settlement, but as Tatar power declined colonization was resumed, at first northwards into the largely unpopulated basins of the White and Kara seas. Monasteries, such as that at Arkhangel'sk, often formed the nuclei of towns, but severities of climate and soil conditions greatly limited rural settlement. In the mid-sixteenth century Ivan the Terrible's defeat of the Tatars at Kazan' and Astrakhan' opened the way southwards and eastwards to Russian expansion. The southern frontier of Russian colonization

into the steppe was protected by successive, lengthy defensive lines from Tatar raids; many towns began existence as fortresses guarding Muscovy's southern flank. The rich 'black earth' soil encouraged intensive agricultural settlement in villages strung out along the steppe rivers; much larger than the hamlets of the forests to the north, these villages spawned daughter villages in side valleys, as settlement intensified after the Russians reached the Black Sea coast in the eighteenth century. Often Germans and other foreigners were settled by the government in large 'plantation' villages of regular layout, while private landowners transferred serfs to their new, extensive steppe estates.

Eastwards, Yermak's Cossacks in the later sixteenth century had opened the way for colonizing Siberia. In explorations motivated initially by the wealth of furs, Russian settlers had reached the Pacific by the mid-seventeenth century. Wooden forts guarding the long river routes eastward rapidly acquired town status as centres of the fur trade, but it was only in the eighteenth and, even more, the nineteenth centuries that there was large-scale agricultural settlement of more favourable areas in southern Siberia by official colonists, runaway serfs and persecuted religious groups.

The nineteenth century saw the tardy start to industrialization in Russia and, with it, numerous urban foundations based on manufacturing. In the central region earlier serf craft settlements became textile towns; on the Donbas coal-field a group of mining and metallurgical towns emerged. The ancient Baltic ports, important since Hanseatic times, were now rivalled by new Black Sea ports. Serf emancipation was decreed in 1861 but it was only with the 1906 Stolypin agrarian reforms that rural settlement began to undergo a major change. Peasants could opt out of common-field cultivation, enclose their own holdings and build their house on the enclosure. The traditional, tightly nucleated Russian village began to be replaced in some areas (notably the Baltic lands) by widely dispersed individual farmsteads.

However, before this process had much effect, the 1917 Revolution and the collectivization of agriculture after 1928 halted and even reversed it. The Soviet government (in its General Scheme of Settlement) pursued a policy of consolidating small, rural settlements into larger places with modern services to achieve the Marxist aim of abolishing differences

Previous spread. A poster of 1934 idealizing the 'Unity and Brotherhood' of Soviet nationalities

between urban and rural living standards, but with limited success and often hardship in villages being phased out. Ultimately it was hoped to reduce the 470,000 rural settlements of 1970 to only 175,000. Meanwhile rapid industrialization has in 70 years created more new towns than the whole pre-revolutionary period and developed new industrial areas, especially in Asiatic parts of the country. The post-Second World War period has seen increased concentration of the urban population in cities and agglomerations of over one million people.   RAF

Population

Until modern industrialization began in the second half of the nineteenth century the characteristics of Russian demography were those of medieval Europe. The rapid increase implicit in a high birth rate was checked by famine and disease. Around 1200 the population of Russia is estimated at 7.5 million, and it had only doubled (to some 15.5 million) by the death of Peter the Great. Natural growth accelerated in the eighteenth century and with the addition of nearly 9 million by the acquisition of new territory the population stood at 42.75 million at the Imperial Revision of 1811–12; of these just on 1.5 million were in Siberia. It was in the last six decades of the Tsarist Empire that population magnitudes were transformed, as the breakdown below indicates.

POPULATION OF RUSSIA, 1857–1910

	1857 estimate	1897 Census	1910 estimate
Russia-in-Europe	59.3	94.2	118.7
Poland	4.8	9.4	12.1
Siberia	4.3	5.7	8.2
Caucasus	4.3	9.2	11.7
Central Asia	—	5.7	10.0
TOTAL	72.7	124.2	160.8

Source: W. H. Parker, *An Historical Geography of Russia*, London, 1968, p. 308

Mortality was still high – at 31 per thousand the rate was double that of contemporary Britain – but the birth rate was still higher – at 47 per thousand. The annexation of Central Asia and of some of the Chinese borderlands was only partly offset by westward emigration – between the 1897 Census and the First World War 2.5 million emigrated to the United States alone.

By the mid-1920s emigration was no longer a factor in the demography of what was by then the

USSR. Many left during and just after the Civil War, but transatlantic migration had been severely checked by the imposition of quotas by the United States in 1921. Until emigration was allowed to resume in the closing years of Soviet power the only periods when fertility and mortality did not alone determine population growth were the exodus in the wake of hostilities – in the 1930s from Central Asia during the forcible suppression of nomadism and of the Basmachi resistance, and in the 1940s from the German-occupied territories in the west. But the oscillations of Soviet times in both births and deaths were far more extensive than those experienced by other industrial nations. Extreme peaks in mortality occurred during the Civil War and the famine of 1921–22, during collectivization and the ensuing famine in the Volga zone and Ukraine, and during the Second World War and the 1946 famine. The mass separation of men from women in conditions of war, the spread of disease and poor nutrition among mothers and children steeply lowered birth rates. Without the impact of these events the population of the USSR would have been well over 300 million in 1980 instead of an actual 265 million.

When the Union disintegrated at the end of 1991, the population stood at just under 292 million. All the successor states but Georgia fell into one of two categories: measured by divergence from the all-union average on 1989 data, the three Slav republics and the three Baltic states exhibited low birth rates and high death rates while the five Central Asian states, Armenia, Azerbaijan and Moldova, showed high birth rates with low death rates; Georgia had low rates for both births and deaths.
                                                                    MCK

RECENT BIRTH RATES

At the end of the Second World War demobilization, the return of evacuees, the relative normality of food supply (rationing was lifted in December 1947), and improved health care brought the baby boom familiar in other combatant states. However, fertility soon resumed the downward trend of the 1930s. The birth rate decreased from 26.7 per thousand population in 1950 to 17.0 in 1969. This largely, but not entirely, reflected the growing urbanization of the population, the increase in educational attainment among women and their increased participation in gainful employment, and the continued housing shortage. Simultaneously, regional differentials remained very significant. Thus, within the then Soviet Union, the crude birth rate in Estonia declined from a high of 16.6 births per thousand population in 1960 to a low of 14.2 in 1967; it subsequently increased to 16.0 by 1988 but declined again to 15.4 in 1989. In Uzbekistan, the largest

NATIONAL COMPOSITION OF THE SUCCESSOR STATES, 1989

Ethnic groups	Population (thousands)	Ethnic groups	Population (thousands)	Ethnic groups	Population (thousands)	Ethnic groups	Population (thousands)
Russia		Tatars	468	**Georgia**		**Lithuania**	
Russians	119,866	Karakalpaks	412	Georgians	3,787	Lithuanians	2,924
Tatars	5,522	Crimean Tatars	189	Armenians	437	Russians	344
Ukrainians	4,363	Koreans	183	Russians	341	Poles	258
Chuvash	1,774	Kyrgyz	175	Azeris	308	Belorussians	63
Bashkir	1,345	Others	846	Ossetes	164	Others	86
Belorussians	1,206			Greeks	100		
Mordva	1,073		19,810	Abkhaz	96		3,675
Chechen	899			Others	168		
Germans	842					**Turkmenistan**	
Udmurt	715	**Kazakhstan**			5,401	Turkmen	2,523
Mari	644	Kazakhs	6,535			Russians	339
Kazakhs	636	Russians	6,228			Uzbeks	317
Avars	544	Germans	958	**Tajikistan**		Kazakhs	88
Jews	537	Ukrainians	896	Tajiks	3,172	Others	256
Armenians	532	Uzbeks	332	Uzbeks	1,198		
Buryats	417	Tatars	328	Russians	388		3,523
Ossetes	402	Uygurs	185	Tatars	72		
Kabarda	386	Belorussians	183	Others	263	**Armenia**	
Yakuts	380	Koreans	103			Armenians	3,084
Others	4,939	Others	716		5,093	Azeris	85
						Kurds	56
	147,022		16,464			Russians	52
				Moldova		Others	28
				Moldovans	2,795		
Ukraine				Ukrainians	600		3,305
Ukrainians	37,419	**Belarus**		Russians	562		
Russians	11,356	Belorussians	7,905	Gagauz	153	**Latvia**	
Jews	486	Russians	1,342	Bulgarians	88	Latvians	1,388
Belorussians	440	Poles	418	Others	137	Russians	906
Moldovans	325	Ukrainians	291			Belorussians	120
Bulgarians	234	Jews	112		4,335	Ukrainians	92
Poles	219	Others	84			Others	161
Hungarians	163						
Romanians	135		10,152				2,667
Others	675			**Kyrgyzstan**			
				Kyrgyz	2,230	**Estonia**	
	51,452			Russians	917	Estonians	963
		Azerbaijan		Uzbeks	550	Russians	475
		Azeris	5,805	Ukrainians	108	Ukrainians	48
Uzbekistan		Russians	392	Germans	101	Belorussians	28
Uzbeks	14,142	Armenians	391	Tatars	70	Finns	17
Russians	1,653	Lezghins	171	Others	282	Others	34
Tajiks	934	Others	262				
Kazakhs	808				4,258		1,565
			7,021				

Source: Soviet census of 1989: *Vestnik statistiki* 10-12/90, 1, 4, 6/91. Permanent residents only.

republic with a Muslim population, the rate of births was recorded as 39.8 in 1960, was at a low of 32.8 in 1969, increased again to 37.8 in 1986, and slightly declined to 33.3 in 1989. The prospect now is that the crude birth rate will increase because of an emigration of large numbers of non-Muslims, with their lower fertility patterns, back to their eponymous successor states (chiefly Russia and Ukraine) and of Jews to Israel and elsewhere.

The Union average declined in every year of perestroika. Among the factors were greater uncertainty about the future, acute shortages of contraceptives which led to frequent resort to abortion and low reproductive health among potential mothers. This decline was particularly marked among Russians: the birth rate in the Russian Federation dropping from slightly over 17 per thousand population in 1986 to 12 in 1991. Because 17 per cent of the Federation's population were non-Russian, many of the others being of Muslim origin with

BIRTH, DEATH, AND NATURAL INCREASE RATES, JANUARY 1979 AND 1989
(per thousand population)

	Crude birth rate		Crude death rate		Natural increase rate	
	1979	1989	1979	1989	1979	1989
Russia	15.8	14.6	10.8	10.7	5.0	3.9
of which, Russians	15.0	13.4	10.9	10.9	4.1	2.5
Ukraine	14.7	13.3	11.1	11.6	3.6	1.7
of which, Ukrainians	14.7	13.6	11.4	11.9	3.3	1.7
Belarus	15.8	15.0	9.5	10.1	6.3	4.9
of which, Belorussians	15.7	14.9	9.8	10.5	5.9	4.4
Moldova	20.2	18.9	10.5	9.2	9.7	9.7
of which, Moldovans	22.1	21.0	10.9	9.0	11.2	12.0
Estonia	14.9	15.4	12.3	11.7	2.6	3.7
of which, Estonians	14.2	16.3	14.4	13.6	−0.2	2.7
Latvia	13.7	14.5	12.7	12.1	1.0	2.4
of which, Latvians	13.0	15.1	14.9	13.5	−1.9	1.6
Lithuania	15.3	15.1	10.3	10.3	5.0	4.8
of which, Lithuanians	15.2	15.4	10.3	10.3	4.9	5.1
Armenia	23.0	21.6	5.6	6.0	17.4	15.6
of which, Armenians	22.5	23.3	5.6	6.4	16.9	16.9
Azerbaijan	25.2	26.4	7.1	6.4	18.1	20.0
of which, Azerbaijani	27.5	28.8	6.3	5.8	21.2	23.1
Georgia	17.8	16.7	8.3	8.6	9.5	8.1
of which, Georgians	17.6	16.1	8.2	8.5	9.4	7.6
Kazakhstan	24.0	23.0	7.7	7.6	16.3	15.4
of which, Kazakhs	30.3	31.1	6.6	6.3	23.7	24.8
Kyrgyzstan	30.1	30.4	8.3	7.2	21.8	23.2
of which, Kyrgyz	38.4	38.3	7.7	6.3	30.7	32.0
Tajikistan	37.8	38.7	7.7	6.5	30.1	32.2
of which, Tajiks	42.1	42.9	7.7	6.1	34.4	36.8
Turkmenistan	34.9	35.0	7.7	7.7	27.2	27.3
of which, Turkmen	38.1	38.6	7.2	7.6	30.9	31.0
Uzbekistan	34.4	33.3	7.0	6.3	27.4	27.0
of which, Uzbeks	38.6	37.4	6.6	5.9	32.0	31.5

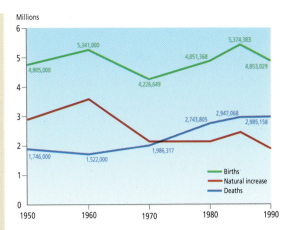

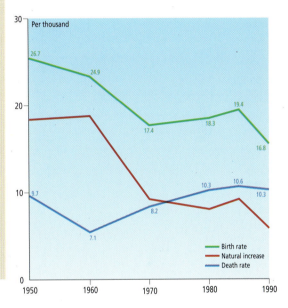

Above right. Population trends in the former USSR, 1950–1990. The top diagram charts total births and deaths per annum, and the net natural increase in population annually; the lower shows birth, death, and natural increase rates per thousand population

higher fertility patterns, the rate for Russians alone would be even lower – perhaps lower than simple reproduction. This will lead to a net decline in their number after a period of time when current patterns are affected even more by the decline in age-specific fertility rates (ASFR).

The ASFR is a more precise measure of fertility patterns than the crude birth rates because the latter divides births not only by all females – especially those of very young ages and older ages when fertility has not begun or has been completed – but also by all males. The divisor in an ASFR is restricted to females of reproductive age. Thus, it measures those under age 20, conventionally the 16 to 19 year-old females, then by five-year age group up to and including 45 to 49 years of age (a grouping in which very few births are recorded outside the Muslim-related southern tier). Of the 485,085 births recorded in 1988 for those under 20 years of age, 2,404, or less than half a per cent, were born to young females under 16. Separate data for births to women age 50 and over are not available; their

birth numbers are included with the 45 to 49 year-old age group.

The Union ASFR for 16 to 19 year-old females showed a steady increase after 1965, and particularly in 1989. These increases are undoubtedly related to changes in conscription. Thus the draft of 18 year-old males for two years instead of 19 year-old males for three years of military service, made males available for marriage at age 20 upon discharge from the armed forces, not at 22 as before 1967. The 1989 increment was affected by the return of troops from the war in Afghanistan. In all other age groups a general decline in ASFRs was witnessed after 1986/87 following an increase in all groups after 1980/81. This factor will become less significant in the successor states as the armed forces are reduced, or as individuals fail to appear for conscription.

Among the successor states, all of which are affected by adverse social, economic and nationality-conflict conditions as well as by health and environmental problems, the Slav republics exhibit a simple reproduction rate (number of children born

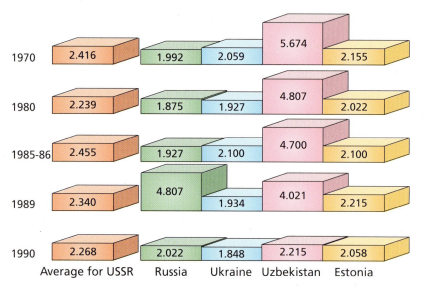

1970	2.416	1.992	2.059	5.674	2.155
1980	2.239	1.875	1.927	4.807	2.022
1985-86	2.455	1.927	2.100	4.700	2.100
1989	2.340	4.807	1.934	4.021	2.215
1990	2.268	2.022	1.848	2.215	2.058
	Average for USSR	Russia	Ukraine	Uzbekistan	Estonia

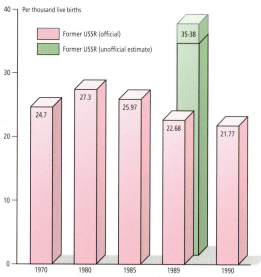

Per thousand live births

Former USSR (official)
Former USSR (unofficial estimate)

1970	1980	1985	1989	1990
24.7	27.3	25.97	22.68 / 35-38	21.77

The 51 living descendents of Gulam and Sadaf Agayev, Turkmenistan, 1984

Top. Fertility rates for the former USSR and four of its constituent republics, 1970–1990. Top right. Infant mortality, 1970–1990

to women 16–49) at or below the level of 2.1, with urban rates below this. The six Muslim majority republics exhibit high ASFRs, albeit at a lower level than previously. For example, in Uzbekistan, the ASFR for 1988 was 5.410 children per woman 16 to 49 years of age, whereas in 1975/76 it had peaked at 7.543; this compares with the much lower level in Ukraine (2.436) and the much higher level in Tajikistan (6.417) recorded in 1988.

In the final years of Soviet power, the combination of a sharp decrease in the birth rate in Russia with increased death rates spread throughout the Federation. Thus, in 1988 three oblasts out of 73 manifested higher crude death rates than crude birth rates, in 1989 in ten, in 1990 in 21, in 1991 in 30, and it was estimated this occurred in about 70 of the 73 oblasts in 1992. Continued disruption of living conditions in most of the successor states further disturbed normal demographic patterns.　MFe

RECENT DEATH RATES

The pattern of mortality can never have been considered normal in the former Soviet Union; the conditions affecting it were always complex, highly differentiated by location, and unpredictable.

If normal demographic growth demonstrates a general tendency to decline other than when fertility decreases so far that the ageing of the population becomes the driving force toward increases, in the former Soviet Union changes due to factors other than aging are of much greater significance. For example, infant mortality (the number of infant deaths between birth and age one year per 1,000 live births), was increasing in the later years of the Soviet era and was probably some 50 per cent higher than the official figures. Infant mortality was officially recorded at a high of 31.4 in 1976, after a low of 22.9 in 1971; publication then stopped for about a decade until retroactive estimates became available. It declined to an official low of 21.7 in 1990. Errors of omission and of commission (whereby a child who dies in the tenth month, for example, may be retained on the hospital register until the thirteenth or fourteenth month when it 'dies', and is hence no longer classed as an 'infant' death) may bring the true infant mortality to 38 deaths per 1,000 live births in 1989. The official figures for infant mortality rates range from about 12 for Lithuania to a high of 50 or so for Turkmenistan, but the actual rates are closer to 20 and 100 respectively. The rate for Turkmenistan could even be 120 deaths per 1000 live births, which is on a par with the least developed countries.

Adjusting for the estimated under-reporting of infant deaths, the official life expectancy at birth of 69.3 in 1990 for both sexes should be lowered by about 0.5 years. Moreover, because of current trends

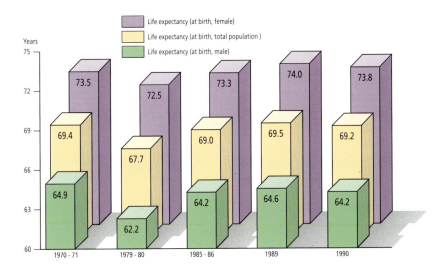

Life expectancy in the former USSR, 1970–1990

in mortality, even this figure – distinctly lower than that of all industrially developed countries – is likely to decrease. In historical context that estimate of just under 69 years should be compared with the mere 32 years estimated for 1896–97 and 44 years for 1926–27. However, the trend of the last quarter-century of the Soviet era was downward. For males, the 1990 expectancy of 64.3 (an official calculation for 1990) was some three years lower than the high of 66.1 in 1966–67. Although slightly exceeded in 1989 (at 74.0 years life expectancy at birth) for women, the high of 73.8 years in 1966–67 was virtually identical to the 1990 level of 73.9 years. The range in the republics was from an official 69.7 in Turkmenistan to 76.3 in Georgia and 76.4 in Lithuania. As nationality conflicts continue in the successor states, excess deaths will also occur.

Although the suicide rate was falling in the last years of the Soviet Union's existence (27 per 100,000 population in 1980, 30 in 1984, but 21 in 1989 and 1990), economic conditions may lead to increases in suicide among the elderly, and to increases in stress, smoking, accidents, and other causes which already put the share of deaths among the male working-age population (officially defined as 16 to 59 years of age) at 40 per cent of all male deaths in 1991. Average male life expectancy at birth among the Peoples of the North (Nentsy, Evenki, Chukchi, etc.) was 46 years of life and was about as bad as that in Pskov and Kursk oblast and still lower in Zhitomirskaya oblast (due to the Chernobyl' meltdown of 1986, which the Ukrainian government in 1992 estimated cost 8,000 lives). These were levels akin to those found at the beginning of the century in developed countries.

Conditions affecting mortality include shortages of medicines and of basic diagnostic equipment; high air, land and water pollution levels, compounded by a pervasive radioactivity. This is not merely the cloud-trail of the Chernobyl' disaster (of caesium-137, strontium-90 and plutonium-239 and 240) but the dumps of radioactive waste which litter the country – more than 600 are scattered around Moscow and at least as many in St Petersburg.

A serious outcome of all these conditions is the increase in birth defects (*defekty*) and birth deformities (*urodstva*) in many regions of the country, especially noticeable in the 1980s. Maternal mortality rates are (officially) some six to seven times higher than those of the United States, the United Kingdom, Germany and Japan (and after adjustments recommended by a former Soviet Deputy Minister of Health, some 20 per cent higher than the reported figure of 46–49 deaths per 10,000 women). Lack of proper nutrition, given the disruption in the economy, food distribution problems and inflation may also contribute to a further growth in this health measurement.

Mortality among the younger population (under 20 years of age) may rise in the successor states due to epidemics. If in the United States fewer than ten cases of diphtheria were recorded each year (no deaths), for a population of 250 million, the experience of Moscow is more than extraordinary: with a population of nine million, the number of recorded cases of diphtheria increased from fewer than 100 each year in 1988 and 1989, to 688 in 1990 and about 1,100 in 1991 (out of about 1,800 nationwide in that year). Diphtheria deaths were some 50 to 60 persons in 1989 alone, and rose to hundreds annually in Moscow and St Petersburg in 1992 and 1993. Many life-saving medications are not available and some estimates put at over one million the excess deaths throughout the former USSR in 1992 due to lack of medicines. Cases of polio quadrupled to 312 cases in 1991.   MFe

Migration and emigration

'Russia's history is the history of a country colonizing itself,' wrote the historian O.V. Klyuchevsky (1841–1911). For Russians migration and the opening up of new territory, especially to the south and east, were for centuries familiar concepts, as was the idea of a turbulent frontier beyond which the tsar's writ might not run. The history of the United States offers parallels.

The state took great interest in colonization also, and not only as an adjunct to penal policy. It was after his defeat of the Tatar khanates of Kazan'

(1552) and Astrakhan' (1556) that Ivan the Terrible gave the Stroganov family their commission to embark on what became the colonization of Siberia. By 1645 (before the British and French had left the Atlantic seaboard of America) the chain of Russian forts and trading posts had reached Okhotsk on the Pacific coast. Russia held Alaska from 1741 to 1867 and as Napoleon was entering Moscow a small settlement was being set up in northern California. Territories like the Semirech'e and the Altai *krai* were still being opened up for agriculture at the beginning of the twentieth century.

Given the origins, traditions and policies of the Soviet regime, it is not surprising that it sought to bring labour and resources together by means of state-sponsored migration, nor that it used coercion as well as incentives to promote this policy. Millions of people flocked into the towns during the early Five-year Plans, and millions were displaced by the collectivization of agriculture, the Great Terror and the deportation of nationalities, mainly to the Far North, Siberia and Kazakhstan. In 1929 81 per cent of the Soviet population had lived on the land; the figures for 1939 and 1959 are 68 and 52 per cent respectively.

By the time of Stalin's death most of the Soviet Union's precious and strategic metals and a great deal of its lumber was worked by forced labour, and such settlements were the origin of several of Siberia's industrial cities. We should not forget either the settlement for political reasons of immigrants in Kaliningrad (the former Königsberg) and in the south of Sakhalin; much of the Russian immigration into the Baltic union republics will have had a similar motive.

Khrushchev preferred to encourage migration to the Far North, Siberia and Kazakhstan by less drastic means: substantial wage bonuses; organized recruitment of workers (*Orgnabor*) and compulsory placement of graduates in their first jobs; and campaigns of orchestrated enthusiasm for pioneering projects such as that in the 'Virgin Lands'. It was at this time that the largely European settlement of northern, central and eastern Kazakhstan was consolidated.

Also under Khrushchev workers regained the right to change jobs at will, a move which left only the internal passport and *propiska* systems as obstacles to spontaneous migration. Little firm information has been published about spontaneous migration, but it is clear that it greatly exceeded state-sponsored migration in volume, and obscured and cut across the objectives of state migration policy. Spontaneous migration had three basic trends. The first was to continue the massive flight from country to town: between 1959 and 1989 there was a net rural-to-urban redistribution of up to 50 million people, so that by 1989 no more than 34

per cent of the Soviet population (and 26 per cent of that of the RSFSR) was counted rural. This migration was fuelled more by dissatisfaction with rural life than by urban demand for labour. The migrants were disproportionately young adults: conscripted males, for instance, who learned a trade in the armed forces and used this to negotiate urban residence and then invite women from their home villages to join them.

By the 1970s and 1980s the consequences were, for the countryside, an ageing workforce and an excess of deaths over births throughout most of the European part of the Soviet Union; and for urban life severe pressure on housing and services. Despite controls, many cities faced problems of illegal immigration, or of semi-legal, casually employed *limitchiki* (so called because they were obliged to reside outside city limits). Bad as they were, these problems would have been considerably worse if it had not been for the antipathy to migration among Central Asian Muslims.

In addition the population of the European Soviet Union shifted southwards, apparently attracted by the more hospitable southern climate. Between 1959 and 1989 the population of the Lower Volga and North Caucasus regions with the Ukrainian Black Sea coast and Moldavia increased by about 40 per cent, that of the rest of the European Soviet Union by less than 20 per cent and that of Siberia by 30 per cent.

Little of this variation can have been due to fertility differences and it suggests that the southern belt made a net gain of some 4 million immigrants. The economy of the southern regions emerged more prosperous and balanced than that of the north and centre, whilst in the Non-Black Earth Zone of northern Russia agriculture declined and thousands of villages became depopulated. Both rural-to-urban and north-to-south migration slackened in the 1970s and 1980s, helped in part by special programmes (from 1974) to revive the Non-Black Earth Zone.

The third migratory trend was one making for ethnic consolidation: the movement of members of ethnic minorities to areas of homogeneous settlement of their own people, typically to their titular national territorial formations. Though never as massive as rural–urban or north–south migration, this movement became marked after ethnic unrest broke out in several parts of Transcaucasia and Central Asia in 1988–90, and its antecedents can be traced back to the 1970s and earlier. In 1959 some 44 per cent of Soviet Armenians lived outside the Armenian SSR, but in 1989 only 33 per cent; between 1970 and 1989 the Russian population of Transcaucasia and the Autonomous Republics of the North Caucasus declined from 1.97 million to 1.67 million. Nevertheless the collapse of the Soviet Union left numerous minorities outside their titular states, most importantly a diaspora of some 25 million Russians living outside the Russian Federation.

In the early 1920s some two million opponents of the Soviet regime emigrated from the USSR, and upwards of 300,000 displaced persons did not return after the Great Fatherland War. But in the 1930s and after 1945 the Soviet government did its best to prevent emigration to other countries. Effective pressure for Jewish emigration emerged at the beginning of the 1970s and was an important strand in the dissident movement; about a quarter of a million Jews left the Soviet Union in the late Brezhnev period.

Emigration resumed in 1987 with Jews and Germans (pioneers because they could command foreign support) prominent among émigrés. In May 1991 a *Law on Exit from and Entry into the USSR* was passed by the Supreme Soviet, designed to come into effect in January 1993; it defined and liberalized citizens' rights to travel abroad and to emigrate, leaving acquisition of convertible foreign currency the principal obstacle to such movement.   JHM

Ethnic groups

SLAVONIC PEOPLES

Below. *The facial characteristics of these Muscovites strikingly reflect the varied ethnicity of the Russian republic. Below right. Demonstrators marching in support of Ukrainian independence*

The Slavonic peoples fall into three groups: Western Slavs (Poles, Czechs and Slovaks); South Slavs (Serbs, Croats, Slovenes, Bulgarians and Macedonians); and Eastern Slavs (Russians, Ukrainians and Belorussians). Apart from some three million descendants of settlers in the Americas, Western

Europe and Australasia, the Eastern Slavs live almost entirely in what was formerly the Soviet Union – 145.2 million Russians, 44.2 million Ukrainians and 10.0 million Belorussians according to the 1989 census. Russians and Ukrainians were the largest and second largest of the Union's many nationalities.

Russians plainly derive their name from the Varangian foundation of Rus' with its centre at Kiev, but (like so much else) the ethnic make-up of Kievan Rus' is obscure. It is likely that 'Russian-ness' was defined initially in religious terms – simply by adherence to the Russian Orthodox Church – and that the Russian state always included people (Varangians, Khazars, Finns, Tatars) whose native language was not Slavonic, but who worshipped in Church Slavonic, used Russian as a *lingua franca* and were readily absorbed into the Russian identity. By the nineteenth century, however, Russians and the other Eastern Slavs were coming increasingly to be defined by religious and language criteria, if not by the latter only.

Still more obscure and controversial is the process whereby the Ukrainians (before the twentieth century 'Little Russians') and the Belorussians (or 'White Russians') came to see themselves, and to be seen, as nationalities distinct from the Russians (who may still be called 'Great Russians' in literary or ceremonial language).

Suffice it to sketch the geopolitical background to this divergent evolution. Kievan Rus' was destroyed by the Mongols in 1240, and by the 1360s Belorussia and the west and centre of what later became Ukraine had been absorbed into Lithuania, which in turn was soon to be united with Poland (1386). Meanwhile at the beginning of the fourteenth century successive Primates of the Russian Orthodox Church moved their seat from Kiev to Moscow and took the name Rus' with them. It was from this northern centre that the conquest of the Tatars, the 'unification of

The principal ethnic groups in the former USSR

Legend:

- Slav
- Turkic
- Latvian, Lithuanian
- Finno-Ugric
- Caucasian
- Mongol
- Iranian
- Moldavian
- Peoples of the north
- Sparsely inhabited territories

the Russian lands' (*sic*) and the colonization of Siberia were embarked upon: an expansion principally towards the east and south-east. Kiev was not again part of a Russian state until 1654; Belorussia and the west bank of the Dnieper not until the Partitions of Poland (1772–95); whilst Galicia – where Austria had cultivated an Eastern Slavonic consciousness as distinct as possible from that of Imperial Russia – had never been ruled from Moscow before it was taken into the Soviet Union in 1945. By the late nineteenth century the tsarist authorities were giving tacit acknowledgement to the existence of a Little Russian identity, but they continued to hamper vernacular publication and schooling in Ukrainian and Belorussian, and neither they nor their Soviet successors tolerated national church organizations other than the Russian Orthodox Church.

In 1989 there were 119.9 million ethnic Russians in Russia proper (the RSFSR), forming 81.5 per cent of its population. More than three-quarters now live in urban areas. Despite 500 years of colonial expansion, only some 27 million of them live in Siberia, mostly in a belt along its southern boundary, tapering ever more thinly towards the east, so that inland from the Pacific the densely settled zone is sometimes no more than 100–150 kilometres on either side of the Trans-Siberian Railway.

There are three regions of Russia where Russians are not the overwhelming majority. In the Ural Mountains and along the rivers flowing west from the Urals live significant minorities of Turkic and Finnic peoples (the residue of the khanate of Kazan'); in eleven oblasts or ASSRs of this region Russians amount to about 64 per cent of the population. Notice on the map how narrow is the neck of Russian settlement in the Orenburg and Chelyabinsk *oblasti* that separates Tatars and Bashkirs to the north from their fellow Turkic-speaking Muslims in Kazakhstan. Second, Russia conquered but never assimilated the northern slopes of the Caucasus; in six national territorial formations here Russians are no more than 23 per cent of the population, and a dwindling community too. In these two regions the Tatars and the Chechen saw the collapse of the Soviet Union as an opportunity to try to break with Russia. Third, across vast tracts of East Siberia (the Yakut, Buryat and Tuvinian Autonomous Republics) Russians are slightly more than half the population.

A further 25.3 million Russians (17.4 per cent) live outside the Russian Federation, a diaspora that cannot help but influence Russia's relations with the other successor states. Three of these Russian communities are of particular significance as possible foci of pressure for political change. Almost a quarter of the population of Ukraine (11.4 million) are Russians living predominantly in the east (Donbas and Khar'kov) and south (the Crimea, Odessa), where they abut the further half million Russians in Moldova. They are contiguous with the Russians of the Rostov and Voronezh oblasts and their loyalties are likely to be watched closely by Ukrainian and Russian governments alike.

The 7.1 million Russians of north and east Kazakhstan and north Kyrgyzstan form another Russian community of long standing that is contiguous with Russia (the boundary between Siberia and Kazakhstan is an arbitrary product of the 1920s). If this community seeks common cause with the Russian Federation it will be difficult for the states of Kazakhstan and Kyrgyzstan to survive. A further 2.7 million Russians live in Belarus, Latvia and Estonia, predominantly in urban areas and in industrial employment; in Latvia they are a third of the population and the largest ethnic group among urban residents.

Ukrainians within the Soviet Union numbered 44.2 million in 1989, 37.4 million of them in Ukraine itself, which had a population of 51.5 million. By far its largest national minority is its 11.4 million Russians. Outside Ukraine there are 6.8 million Ukrainians living scattered throughout European Russia (3 million), in Siberia (1.3 million), Kazakhstan (0.9 million) and Moldova (0.6 million). Almost half the population of the Kuban' considered itself Ukrainian in the 1926 census, but this community has been registered as Russian ever since – initially, it seems, as a consequence of official instructions.

Of the 10.0 million Belorussians, 7.9 million live in Belarus and 2.1 elsewhere, largely in Russia, Ukraine, Kazakhstan and Latvia. Under the Empire Belorussians were largely rural dwellers, and this may account for the fact that the development of a

Below. Belorussians in national costume. Below right. A vigorous assertion of Estonian independence

conscious Belorussian identity has been largely a twentieth century phenomenon.

All three Eastern Slavonic nations experienced an ethnic revival during the 1980s. Among Russians this took the form of increasing rejection of one of the Soviet regime's cardinal myths – that the interests of Russia were intrinsically identical with communist and (all-union) Soviet interests. In Ukraine the nationalist movement, Rukh, based largely in the west, succeeded in persuading increasing numbers in the centre, south and east, Russians included, that Ukraine would be better off severing its ties with Moscow.   JHM

BALTIC PEOPLES

The Lithuanian, Latvian, Estonian and Karelian peoples are located on the eastern shores of the Baltic Sea. Following the 1939 Molotov–Ribbentrop Secret Protocol, the national homelands of the three most southern of these peoples were incorporated into the Soviet Union and were made Soviet Socialist Republics. As part of the former Soviet Union, over 90 per cent of the 2.9 million Lithuanians, 1.5 million Latvians and 1.0 million Estonians resided within the boundaries of their respective republics at the 1989 census while nearly all the remainder were to be found in the towns of Russia, Belarus and Ukraine. In contrast, the Karelians, whose national territory was down-graded from a Soviet Socialist Republic to an Autonomous Soviet Socialist Republic in 1956, have only half their 131,000 total within Karelia. Sizeable Karelian communities are also located in Kalinin and Murmansk oblasts, the St Petersburg area and in neighbouring Finland.

The national languages of the Latvians and Lithuanians belong to the Baltic group, an Indo-European sub-group. Although Latvian and Lithuanian are

Poles in the USSR

The Poles made up one of the largest minorities in the Soviet Union, but did not attain the level of autonomy granted to other much smaller nationalities. Other than the Germans and the Crimean Tatars, both of whose political institutions were abolished by Stalin in the 1940s, the Poles were the largest ethnic group in the Soviet Union without a territory bearing their name.

Before 1939 the Polish population of the USSR was very small, but the territory annexed in 1939 and 1940 was inhabited by about 2 million Poles. Over 500,000 of these were deported, mainly to Siberia and Central Asia, between 1939 and 1941. According to the 1989 census there were approximately 1.13 million Poles living in the USSR (although other estimates put the figure at nearer 2 million), with the highest concentration living in the area around the border of Belorussia and Lithuania. The largest Polish community in the successor states to the Soviet Union is in Lithuania, centred on the Vilnius region (which was in Poland until 1939); the Lithuanian Poles have been agitating for more autonomy, but as of 1993 this had not been granted by the Lithuanian government.

During the Soviet period the Poles had no official region, although there were a few Polish language schools, and this led to a loss of cultural identity and to the assimilation of Poles into local populations. They were, however, often treated as foreigners in the USSR because the great majority of their ethnic group lived outside its borders.

The Poles are hoping that this will change in the successor states.

mutually unintelligible, both languages are characterized by a similar lexical development and structure. The more northerly Estonians and Karelians belong to the Finno-Ugric language group, a branch of the Uralic language family.

In terms of cultural development, the Estonians have more in common with their southern neighbours than with the Karelians. The character of the Estonian, Latvian and Lithuanian languages and cultures owes much to the rise of nationalist movements in the last quarter of the nineteenth century and to their parallel literary revivals, continuing through the period of independent statehood between 1918 and 1940. The Lutheran religion in nineteenth-century Estonia and Latvia also influenced the high level of literacy found among the indigenous peasantry. Lutheranism in Estonia and Latvia, and Catholicism in Lithuania set these peoples apart from their eastern Slav neighbours. The only exception to this congruity between ethnicity, language and religion was a large Catholic community in Eastern Latvia (Latgalia), an area occupied by Poland in the sixteenth century. Cut off from coastal Latvia, Latgalia developed a regionalism manifest in dialect, religion and rural institutions – the latter characterized by the *mir* (village community) whereas the individual farmstead was usual in the rest of Latvia, in Estonia and in Lithuania. Within the overwhelmingly Lutheran-based Estonian ethno-linguistic community there is also another small ethnographic group, the Setu, who inhabit south-east Estonia and areas adjacent to Pskov oblasts and who are Orthodox Christians.

The Karelians, with close linguistic and cultural ties to neighbouring Finland, have a less distinctive social and cultural identity than the other three Baltic peoples. This is partly explained by the drift of Karelians to other regions of the USSR, and the predominance of Russians who outnumber the eponymous nationality by six to one in Karelia itself. Outnumbered as they are, most Karelians are necessarily bilingual.

Throughout their period as part of the USSR, the Lithuanians, Latvians and Estonians saw their predominance within their respective republics challenged. This was primarily as a result of the immigration of Russians and to a lesser extent Ukrainians and Belorussians, mainly into the region's cities. As in Karelia, one of the main reasons behind such an influx was industrialization. In contrast to the Karelians, Lithuanians, Latvians and Estonians remain the predominant nationality groups within their national homelands. Higher rates of immigration combined with lower birth rates in highly urbanized societies has however meant that in contrast to Lithuanians, both Latvians and Estonians have declined in numerical importance within their republics. By 1989 Latvians constituted 50.7 per cent of their republic's population, Estonians registered 61.5 per cent, while Lithuanians made up 80 per cent.

The Estonians, Latvians and Lithuanians were also the first peoples of the Soviet Union to take advantage of Gorbachev's policy of glasnost and put forward demands for the re-establishment of their former independent states. During mid-1988 in all three republics, nationalist-based Popular Fronts emerged and quickly moved from calling for greater political autonomy to promoting outright sovereign statehood. Within the following eighteenth months

Right. A Latvian vigil for independence, 18 January 1991

these broad-based Popular Fronts replaced the local Communist Parties as the *de facto* governments of all three republics. On 11 March 1990 Lithuania's Popular Front-based government, Sajudis, declared Lithuania to be an independent state, and within the following three months both Estonia and Latvia had declared their intention to follow Lithuania's example.

The abortive Moscow coup of August 1991 finally paved the way for all three Baltic peoples to rejoin the world community of sovereign states with Estonia and Latvia following Lithuania in declaring themselves to be independent states on 20 and 21 August respectively. In September 1991 all three Baltic states were admitted to full membership of the United Nations.   GES

ARMENIANS

The Armenians are an ancient people who speak an Indo-European language and have traditionally inhabited the border regions between Turkey, Iran, and the former USSR. Living in a mountainous land of more than 260,000 sq km continuously from the sixth century BC until driven out of the Turkish-held areas in 1915, the Armenians were peasant farmers who withstood invasions and nomadic migrations for centuries, creating a unique culture blended of Iranian social and political structures and Hellenic, later Christian, literary traditions. Today more than three million Armenians live in Armenia, which

The 560 km chain of two million Balts from Vilnius to Tallinn for Baltic States' independence on the 50th anniversary of the Nazi–Soviet Pact, 2 August 1989

occupies 29,000 sq km of the north-eastern corner of historic Armenia; another million live in other parts of the successor states to the USSR, and perhaps as many as two million live in the Armenian diaspora in other countries of the world. The capital of Armenia, Yerevan, is a city of more than a million people.

Armenia was first settled about six thousand years BC, and the first major state was the kingdom of Urartu, with its centre around Lake Van. Shortly after the fall of Urartu, the Indo-European-speaking proto-Armenians migrated, probably from the West, onto the Armenian plateau and mingled with the local Hurrian peoples. The first mention of the Armenians dates from the mid-sixth century BC. Ruled for many centuries by the Persians, Armenia became a buffer state between the Greeks and Romans to the west and the Persians or Arabs of the Middle East. It reached its greatest size under King Tigran II the Great (95–55 BC), but was soon conquered by Rome.

Christians since the early fourth century AD, Armenians claim theirs was the first state to have adopted Christianity as its official religion. Early in the fifth century, Saint Mesrop, known as Mash-tots, invented an alphabet for Armenian, and religious and historical works began to appear as part of the effort to consolidate the hold of Christianity. Yet unity eluded the Armenians as the various noble houses of Armenia fought with one another and with their kings. The country was seldom unified under a single monarch. After the invasions of of the Seljuk Turks in the eleventh century, the independent kingdoms within Armenia proper collapsed, and a new Armenian state, the Kingdom of Lesser Armenia, formed along the Mediterranean in Cilicia. As an ally of the Crusader kingdoms, Cilician Armenia fought against the rising Muslim threat to Christendom until it was overrun by Mamelukes in 1375.

From the fifteenth century until the early twentieth century most Armenians were under the rule of the Ottoman Turks, governed through the *millet* system that allowed the Armenian church to administer the Armenians. Eastern Armenia, ruled by the Persians until 1828 when it was annexed by the Russian Empire, developed more rapidly and along more western lines than Turkish Armenia. Young nationalists formed the most active revolutionary parties determined to liberate the Armenians of Turkey. The plight of Turkish Armenians, suffering from discrimination, arbitrary taxation, and the periodic attacks of armed Kurds, aroused the Great Powers to propose a series of reforms to the Porte. Though much talk revolved around the so-called 'Armenian Question', few lasting reforms were carried out, though European public opinion was

briefly aroused in 1894–96 when hundreds of thousands of Armenians were massacred by the Kurds and Turks with the sanction of the 'Bloody Sultan' Abdul Hamid II.

Hopeful that the Young Turk Revolution of 1908 would bring them a period of peace and development within the Ottoman Empire, Armenians instead found themselves torn between Russia and Turkey when the First World War broke out. The Young Turks decided to deport Armenians from their historic homeland into the deserts of Mesopotamia. In the process a million or more Armenians died or were massacred in what has been called 'the first genocide' of the twentieth century. Many survivors fled to Russian Armenia, where in 1918 an independent republic was established. Ruled by the nationalistic Dashnak party, independent Armenia lasted only until the end of 1920. Threatened by the Kemalist movement in Turkey, the Dashnak government turned the new state over to Communists as the lesser danger to Armenian existence.

A land of refugees and disease, Soviet Armenia recovered slowly through the 1920s and benefited from the forced modernization directed from Moscow. While a large number of Armenians migrated to the Armenian republic and established a modern nation in part of their historic homeland, the Armenian republic exported a large number of intellectuals and professionals to other parts of the USSR. A process of 'nativization' made Armenia ever more ethnically and culturally Armenian, but thousands suffered from the cruel repressions of Stalin's rule.

Faced by ecological problems induced by industrialization, a corrupt and entrenched political élite,

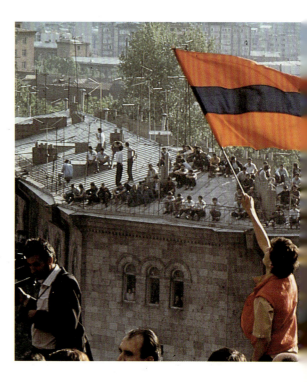

per cent of whom are Georgians. The remaining 29.9 per cent, is ethnically heterogenous with nine national groups of over 30,000. The largest minorities are the Armenians (8.1%), Russians (6.3%), Azeris (5.7%), South Ossetians (3.00%), Greeks (1.9%) and Abkhazians (1.8%). The non-Georgian Abkhazians and the Muslim Georgians of south-west Georgia (known as the Adzharians) have their own Autonomous Republics. Abkhazians and Adzharians make up 17.1 and 80.1 per cent respectively of their Autonomous Republics. From 1922 to 1990, the linguistically Iranian South Ossetians occupied their own Autonomous Region (constituting 66.4 per cent of that region's 1989 population). The Region's abolition by the Georgian Supreme Soviet in December 1990 and the renaming as Samachablo, the Georgians' own name for it, brought violent reaction for integration with the majority of Ossetians in North Ossetia, part of the Russian Federation.

The urban population of Georgia in 1989 was 56 per cent, an increase of 4 per cent since 1979. Yet it was still the least urbanized republic in Caucasia. The population of the capital, Tbilisi, increased 18 per cent over the same period to one and a quarter million. Ninety-five per cent of Georgians live in their own republic, the second highest residential concentration of all ex-Soviet republics after Lithuania. It is estimated that there are at least 120,000 Georgians in north-eastern Turkey and 12–14,000 in Iran. There is a small Georgian community in France, émigrés of the 1920s and the Second World War.

Georgia contains considerable natural resources including sizeable deposits of manganese, coal and oil. It has significant hydroelectric and forestry potential and its metallurgical production in 1989 was third among the ex-Soviet republics. Although only 20 per cent of Georgian land is cultivated, it produced 90–95 per cent of the USSR's tea and citrus fruits, 15 per cent of its grapes and 10 per cent of the silk and tobacco. However, Georgia imported a quarter of its electricity, 96 per cent of its oil, 100 per cent of its gas, 94 per cent of its grain and 98 per cent of its sugar, most of which came from the rest of the then Soviet Union. This dependence, combined with a collapsing infrastructure, chronic pollution problems, recurring natural disasters and a declining national income adds up to a bleak economic picture for independence.

The pre-Soviet period

Georgians have a long history of independent statehood, but their strategic position in Caucasia and their conversion to Christianity in the fourth century led to continuous wars with larger empires, particularly from the Muslim south. From the sixteenth century onwards, Georgian kings sought Russian

and frustration over the failure of the Soviet government to resolve their national claims to lost territory in Turkey and the neighbouring Soviet republic of Azerbaijan, Armenians began a series of demonstrations in February 1988 for the return of Nagorno-Karabakh to Armenia. On 7 December 1988 an earthquake devastated north-western Armenia, focusing world attention on the Armenians. The Armenian national movement came to power in 1990 and declared Armenia independent in 1991. War with Azerbaijan prevented economic recovery in the early years of the new republic.

RGS

GEORGIANS

The Georgian Republic (the description 'Soviet Socialist' was dropped by the Georgian Supreme Soviet in October 1990), occupies 69,300 sq km in the western part of the Caucasian isthmus. The republican population in 1989 was 5.4 million, 70.1

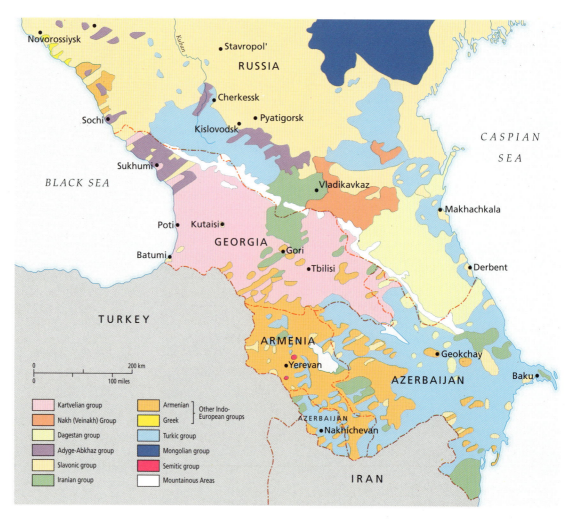

Peoples of the Caucasus

An opposition group in Tbilisi, Georgia

(Christian) protection. In the first decades of the nineteenth century, a weakened and divided Georgia was incorporated piecemeal into the Russian empire. The modernizing Russian state created an active Georgian intelligentsia and native working class. By the 1890s a nobility-led Georgian nationalism was replaced by a homegrown Marxism. Georgian social democrats (almost entirely Menshevik) effectively took power in February 1917 and after a brief experiment with Armenia and Azerbaijan as part of a Transcaucasian Federation (April–May 1918), the Georgian social democrats declared an independent Georgian Democratic Republic. Socialist in orientation, the republic was invaded by the Red Army in February 1921 and incorporated into the new Soviet state.

The Soviet period and after

From 1922 to 1936 Georgia was part of a Transcaucasian Federal Soviet Socialist Republic along with Armenia and Azerbaijan. A national communist movement among Georgian Bolsheviks was crushed in the 1920s and Lavrenty Beria, as Georgian First Party Secretary (1931–38), supervised the implementation of mass terror in the republic. In 1944 approximately 100,000 Meskhetians who lived in southern Georgia, were expelled to Central Asia. Under Khrushchev, Georgians regained significant local control in the republic, but a quasi-official Georgian nationalism and economic corruption under V.P. Mzhavanadze (b. 1902), the Georgian Party First Secretary (1953–72), led to his replacement by (1972–85) E.A. Shevardnadze (b. 1928), and to an attempt by Moscow to reassert its power. Shevardnadze's anti-corruption campaign was unsuccessful and Georgians continued to express antagonism towards Russian linguistic and cultural inroads. In the 1970s a Georgian dissident movement emerged, which, though ineffective, produced its martyrs for Georgian religious and national rights.

Gorbachev's innovative policies rapidly undermined the Georgian Communist Party. It lost all credibility after a demonstration for Georgian independence was brutally suppressed by Soviet and MVD troops on 9 April 1989. The Georgian nationalist opposition, characterized by bloody infighting, finally captured power in the Georgian Supreme Soviet elections of October 1990 when the 'Round Table' bloc under former human rights activist, Zviad Gamsakhurdia, won an overwhelming majority. The new government's Georgianization programme led to continued inter-ethnic conflict with the Abkhazians and Ossetians. In a referendum in March 1991, Georgians voted overwhelmingly for independence and the following month (on 9 April) the Georgian Supreme Soviet formally declared its independence.

Kalmyks

Dispossessed of their territory between 1943 and 1957, the Kalmyks returned from exile to their pastoral livelihoods: the adjoining illustrations are of racehorses at the Ut-Sala stud. Four-fifths of the agricultural area is pasture and much of the ploughland is sown to fodder. Livestock produce and Caspian fish supply important food-processing plants, and with oil and gas extraction industrialization had by 1992 brought the urban share to nearly half the population of the newly-named Republic of Kalmykia-Khal'mg Tangch.

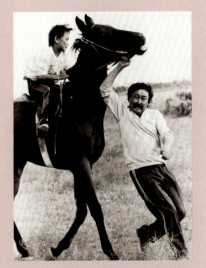

North Caucasians

The Confederation of Mountain Peoples of the Caucasus is one of Russia's youngest political bodies, but it has quickly proved itself to be one of the most potentially troublesome.

The Confederation grew out of an Assembly of the Mountain Peoples of the Caucasus which first met in Sukhumi, the capital of Abkhazia, in 1989. While the Assembly was largely symbolic, the Confederation that was created in the same city in 1991 has proved to be more formidable.

The purpose of the Confederation, theoretically at least, is to protect the Mountain Peoples from the two major ethnic groups living to the north and south of the Caucasus mountains: the Russians and the Georgians. Troops under the banner of the Confederation fought in Abkhazia against the Georgians in 1992, and the Confederation clashed with Russia in a dispute between Ingushetia and North Ossetia in the same year.

Apart from the Russians and the Georgians, the Christian, pro-Russian and linguistically Iranian Ossetians are regarded as enemies. The reasons for the antipathy between the Ossetians and the remainder of the Caucasian peoples seem to be almost exclusively linked to their pro-Russian stance, and the related fact that Ossetia gained territory as the result of Stalin's mass deportations of Caucasian peoples during the Second World War.

In January 1992 Zviad Gamsakhurdia was overthrown by a military coup, and the following March Eduard Shevardnadze returned as chair of a newly-formed State Council.   SFJ

TURKIC PEOPLES

Over 90 per cent of the Turkic peoples of the USSR are historically of the Muslim faith, and over 90 per cent of these inhabit Central Asia and Kazakhstan. The remainder of the Turkic Muslims live in the Caucasus, Siberia, and the Volga region. The Gagauz and Chuvash living in Europe and the Yakuts and Tuvinians living in East Asia have never been affected by Islam. Physical features common to all the Turkic peoples are hard to discern, and the only common cultural feature is language. With the exception of those spoken by such non-Muslim peoples as the Gagauz and Yakuts, the Turkic languages strongly resemble one another, most of them being to some extent mutually intelligible. Under the Soviet regime all the Turkic languages were greatly developed and provided with literary forms. By the late 1930s they were using varieties of the

Cyrillic alphabet but there are now strong preferences for the latin script in the form adopted by Turkey.

Smaller groups of Turkic peoples are: the Muslim Kumyks, Karachays, Balkars and Nogays living in the North Caucasus, and the partly pagan and partly Christian Khakass and the Altay of southern Siberia.

Uzbeks

The Uzbeks are the largest Turkic people in the former USSR and the largest in the world after the Turks of Turkey. They were the third most numerous nationality in the USSR and, of the total of 16.7 million, 85 per cent lived in the Uzbek SSR (the precursor of present day Uzbekistan), which was formed in 1924 and in which Uzbeks constituted 69 per cent of the population. The remainder are more or less equally divided between the adjoining

Below. Uzbeks in local dress in the streets of Samarkand. Bottom. Tatar activists in Moscow

successor states. Their name was probably derived from Uzbek, one of the khans of the Golden Horde.

In the fifteenth century the Uzbeks occupied the land between the lower Volga and the Aral Sea. Moving south early in the sixteenth century, they conquered the settled regions of Bukhara and Samarkand and, later, Urgench and Tashkent, and eventually became mixed with the earlier settlers in these regions, including the ancient Iranian population of Khorezm and Soghdia. They constituted more than half of the former khanate of Khiva, and a third of that of Bukhara. Originally nomads, the Uzbeks have been sedentary for the last three centuries. There are also over one million Uzbeks in Afghanistan and about 800,000 in the Sinkiang-Uygur Autonomous Region of China.

Tatars

Of the total of 6.6 million Tatars about 26 per cent live in Tatarstan and about 15 per cent in Bashkiria; 10 per cent live in Uzbekistan, 5 per cent in Kazakhstan and smaller numbers in Kyrgyzstan, Tajikistan and Turkmenistan and in the Mordva, Udmurtia, Chuvashia and Yakut-Sakha regions. Other Tatar elements are widely scattered throughout Russia. A distinct Tatar community numbering about 500,000 and known as the Krym (Crimean) Tatars inhabited the former Crimean Tatar ASSR (after 1956 part of Ukraine) until they were expelled in 1945 for alleged collaboration with the German invaders. Several Krym Tatar families have been allowed to return to their homeland; the remainder are still living in Uzbekistan and other parts of Central Asia.

Kazakhs

Of the 8.1 million Kazakhs, 80 per cent inhabit Kazakhstan, of which they comprise only 40 per cent of the population. The Kazakh territory was originally constituted an ASSR in 1920, but was raised to the status of SSR in 1936. Under the tsarist administration the Kazakhs were known as Kirgiz, the true Kirgiz being called Kara Kirgiz.

The origin of the Kazakhs is obscure, their name not appearing in Turkic language records until the eleventh century. The historian V.V. Bartol'd describes them as 'Uzbeks who in the fifteenth century detached themselves from the bulk of their nation and consequently had not taken part in the conquest of the Timurid kingdom'. The three 'hordes' into which the Kazakhs formed themselves after the break-up of the Golden Horde in the fifteenth century were distributed over a vast steppe area including Lake Balkhash, the north and central part of what is now Kazakhstan, and the western part of the latter near the Caspian Sea and the Ural River. Although now largely stabilized, the Kazakhs were originally nomadic and since the coming of the Russians there

Above. *Kazakhs. A woman and a shepherd in traditional headdresses, and Kazakh women brewing tea*

have been large migrations between Russian and Chinese territory. About one million now live in the Sinkiang-Uygur Autonomous Region of China.

Azeris

Of the 6.8 million Azeris in the former USSR, 86 per cent live in Azerbaijan, of which they constitute 83 per cent of the population; the remainder live in Georgia, Armenia and Dagestan. Under the tsarist regime the Azeris were known as Tatars, with whom they have no direct ethnic connection, despite being of Turkic origin. They came under Muslim influence in the seventh century and were conquered by the Seljuks in the eleventh century. They were incorporated in the Safavid Iranian empire in the sixteenth century and their territory began to attract the attention of Russia in the eighteenth century, being finally annexed at the beginning of the nineteenth century.

After the Revolution, the Azeris achieved a brief independence in 1918, but were overrun by the Red Army in 1920 and formed into the Azerbaijan Soviet Republic. This was at first included in the Transcaucasian Federal Republic but in 1936 was constituted an SSR. During the Iranian occupation many Azeris adopted the Shi'a rite to which they still adhere whereas virtually all the other Turkic groups in the former USSR are Sunni Muslims. The republic

adjoins the Iranian province of Azerbaijan in which live about another 4.5 million Azeris.

Turkmens

Of the total of 2.7 million Turkmens, 93 per cent live in Turkmenistan, of which they constitute 68 per cent of the population. The remainder inhabit Uzbekistan. The Turkmens were the most distinctive among the Turkic peoples of the USSR; their origin is obscure but their long-shaped heads suggest intermingling with some ancient non-Turkic stock. Tradition connects them with the Oguz tribes, to which the Seljuk and Osmanli Turks also belonged. Until the 1880s the Turkmens were under varying degrees of domination by the khanates of Khiva and Bukhara, and by Iran where some 500,000 of them still live. After the final Russian conquest in the 1880s, a large part of their territory was constituted the oblast of Transcaspia. Originally semi-nomadic, the Turkmens are now mainly stabilized. Approximately 400,000 inhabit northern Afghanistan.

Kyrgyz

Of the total of 2.5 million Kyrgyz (formerly known as Kirgiz) in the former USSR, 88 per cent live in Kyrgyzstan where they constitute 52 per cent of the population. The origin of the present-day Kyrgyz is

Right. *Funeral for victims of Soviet/Azeri conflict, 20 January 1990.* Far right. *Turkmens with traditional astrakhan headwear*

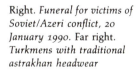

uncertain but they are probably of mixed descent from the Kirgiz who inhabited the upper reaches of the Yenisey River between the sixth and ninth centuries, and various invading Mongol and Turkic tribes. The Kirgiz came finally under Russian domination in 1876. Under the Soviet regime they were first constituted an autonomous oblast in 1924, an ASSR in 1926 and an SSR in 1936, finally becoming the independent republic of Kyrgyzstan in 1991. There are also some 80,000 Kirgiz in the Sinkiang-Uygur Autonomous Region of China.

Karakalpaks

The vast majority of the 423,500 Karakalpaks are concentrated in the Karakalpak Autonomous Republic within Uzbekistan, originally formed in 1925 as an autonomous oblast within the Russian Republic. They are closely allied to the Kazakhs, both ethnically and linguistically. Their main occupation is now agriculture; since the dessication of the Aral Sea there is no longer a fishing industry.

Uygurs

A national minority numbering 262,643, the Uygurs live mainly in the Alma-Ata oblast of Kazakhstan and in the Fergana valley. They originate from what is now the Sinkiang-Uygur Autonomous Region of China, where there are about 6 million Uygurs.

Bashkirs

Numbering 1,449,000 in 1989, the Bashkirs live mainly in Bashkiria, where they constitute about one-quarter of the population. Muslims since the fourteenth century, they came under Russian domination in the sixteenth century. In 1917 a Bashkir nationalist government was formed but in 1919 it joined the Bolsheviks and was constituted an ASSR.

Gagauz

The majority of the total of 197,768 Gagauz live in Moldova. After Moldovan independence they demonstrated forcibly against the republic's government on the grounds that their autonomy was inadequately protected. There are also small groups living in the Zaporozhe oblast of Ukraine, in the North Caucasus and in Kazakhstan. Their origin is not clear. Those living in the territories of the former USSR are Orthodox Christians who migrated from Turkish territory during the eighteenth and nineteenth centuries. Their language is Turkic, but they have no other affinities with the Turkic peoples.

Chuvash

The majority of the 1,842,000 Chuvash live in Chuvashia and constitute about three-quarters of

Below. Kyrgyz falconers, and Kyrgyz boys at the Manas (epic hero) festival

its population. They are thought to be descended from the medieval Volga Bulgarians. Their territory was annexed to Russia with the conquest of Kazan' in 1552. They became Orthodox Christians and all traces of Islamic civilization have disappeared. Although their language is Turkic, it is strongly aberrant. Since 1940 it has been written in a modified Cyrillic script.

Yakuts

The largest people of the Altaic family, the 381,922 Yakuts live in Yakut-Sakha (founded as the Yakut ASSR in 1922) and the remainder in neighbouring areas of East Siberia. They have been subject to Russia since the seventeenth century. Their language is Turkic but strongly aberrant: it is now written in a modified form of Cyrillic.

Tuvinians

The majority of the 206,629 Tuvinians live in what was the independent People's Republic of Tannu Tuva between 1921 and 1924; incorporated in the USSR in October 1944, it was designated the Tuvinian Autonomous Region (AR) until 1961, when it became an ASSR. Their Turkic language has been written in Cyrillic since 1940. They are Lamaist Buddhists.   GWH/SA

IRANIAN PEOPLES

Small Iranian communities are the Kurds (152,717, though unofficial estimates are much higher), Tats and Talysh living in Transcaucasia, and Baluchis in Tajikistan.

Tajiks

Of the total 4,215,000, some 75 per cent of Tajiks live in Tajikistan, of which they constitute 62 per cent of the population. Of the remainder, 20 per cent live in Uzbekistan and 0.8 per cent in Kyrgyzstan. The Tajiks are without doubt the oldest ethnic element in Central Asia, being the descendants of the ancient Soghdian and Bactrian population. But traces of the ancient Iranian civilization are no more marked in them than in the Uzbeks, except among the so-called mountain Tajiks of Gorno-Badakhshan. Before 1921 the Tajiks were mainly concentrated in the khanate of Bukhara, but they also made up a large part of the so-called Sarts (a term no longer in use) living in the Fergana, Zeravshan and Gissar valleys. Their language closely resembles the Dari spoken in Afghanistan. Many Tajiks are bilingual in Tajik and Uzbek. The Islamic Tajiks mainly follow the Sunni rite but some of the mountain elements follow the Ismaili Shi'a rite. There are over two million Tajiks in northern Afghanistan and a few thousand also in the Sinkiang-Uygur Autonomous Region of China.

Ossetes

An Iranian people numbering 598,000, the Ossetes mostly live in their eponymous territory, the division of which between Russia (North Ossetia) and Georgia (South Ossetia) generated hostilities with Georgia on the break-up of the USSR. Ossetes are descended from the medieval Alans. In the eighteenth century they came under strong Russian influence and were annexed to Russia early in the nineteenth century. They are mostly Orthodox Christians with a small Sunni Muslim element.   GWH/SA

Mongol peoples

Mongol peoples within Russia fall into two large groups: the Buryats and the Kalmyks. Although other Asian peoples such as the Tuvinians, Altays

Below. Bashkirs at the Sabantui (ploughman's) festival. The Bashkir poet Mustai Karim, in city dress, is here being greeted by young people in traditional costume

Below right. A Tajik family assembled for a celebratory meal

Above. *A fully bearded Buryat, and a Buryat woman in traditional, richly embroidered, headgear*

and some of the Evenki have been strongly influenced by Mongol culture, their languages are not from the Mongol group and hence they must be considered separately. Only a very small percentage of the Mongol peoples count Russian as their native language; although there has been a strong Russian influence in dress and living habits, the end of Soviet power allowed both Buryats and Kalmyks to revive their national and religious culture.

Buryats

The Buryats numbered 421,000 in 1989, most living in Buryatia, to the south and east of Lake Baykal. Other groups live to the west of the lake in the Ust'-Ordynsk autonomous area, and in the east, in the Aginsk Buryat autonomous area. Some tens of thousands of Buryats also live in Mongolia and in the north-west of China.

In the seventeenth century, the Buryats were a series of loosely-connected nomadic pastoralist tribes. Many of them had been subject to the Mongol khans, but after a border was established between Mongolia and Russia the majority decided to stay on the Russian side. They were under the indirect rule of the tsarist government, and kept many of their own traditions. Their early religion, shamanism, was superseded by lamaism during the nineteenth century in the eastern parts of Buryatia – despite the border, the Mongolian influence was still strong.

The basis of the Buryat economy was livestock herding, and the eastern Buryats continued to be nomadic until after the Revolution. The western Buryats were strongly influenced by Russian culture, developed an agricultural tradition and a more settled life, and were even converted in a rather superficial way to Orthodox Christianity. Ousted by Russian peasant settlers from their lands west of Lake Baykal, they began to migrate to the eastern side; the eastern Buryats in their turn moved even further, towards Mongolia and Manchuria. A fairly large migration of this kind took place after the Civil War in the 1920s.

Today, both western and eastern Buryats have a diversified economy and are settled in villages and towns. They conduct mixed farming in the rural areas, and some are employed in engineering and other industries in the towns along the Trans-Siberian Railway.

Kalmyks

The Kalmyks, like the Buryats, speak a dialect of Mongolian. They numbered 174,000 in 1989. Most now live in Kalmykia, near the mouth of the Volga where it enters the Caspian Sea, in an area of grassland steppe suitable for the nomadic pastoralism which used to form the basis of their economy.

The Kalmyks previously lived in Western Mon-golia (Dzhungaria) and fled from there to the Volga region in the early seventeenth century under pressure from feudal wars. By the eighteenth century they had been converted from shamanism to lamaism, their cultural links still being primarily with Mongolia. Later, under pressure from the tsarist government, some fled back over the steppes as far as China, an immense trek in which many lost their lives. Nearly all the remaining Kalmyks were registered in the Astrakhan' province of the Russian Empire. Like the Buryats, the Kalmyks were ruled indirectly and had their own tribal princes. After the Revolution nomadism gradually became less important as agriculture was taken up, and after collectivization in the 1930s it ceased altogether. In Kalmykia and Buryatia lamaism was essentially destroyed in the 1930s, leaving only a few token monasteries.

During the Second World War part of Kalmykia was occupied by the Germans, and as a punishment for alleged disloyalty on the part of the Kalmyks, Stalin's government abolished the Kalmyk ASSR in 1943 and expelled its population to various parts of Siberia. The republic was re-established in 1957, and most of them were allowed to return to it. The Kalmyks now have a diversified economy: mixed farming, with some industry around the capital town of Elista.   CH

PEOPLES OF THE NORTH

The indigenous peoples of the Russian north are both more diverse and more numerous than those of Arctic and sub-Arctic America. Soviet ethnographers used the phrase 'the small peoples of the north', which connoted 26 peoples but excluded the two largest northern groups, the Komi and Yakuts. These are listed here with three others (Mordva, Udmurt, Mari) who, although not normally considered northern, round out the Finno-Ugrian peoples. The Estonians and Karelians are also Finno-Ugrians, but are grouped here under Baltic peoples.

At the beginning of the Soviet period the numerically larger peoples were the dominant groups in their homelands, but since a massive immigration of Russian settlers, all except the Komi-Permyaki are minority groups. The historical characterization of these people as reindeer-breeders is only a general indication of their current occupations; increasing numbers in all national groups have moved into industrial and professional jobs having no special relationship to national background.

The official Soviet contention that many of the smaller peoples were dying out under tsarism may be justified in some cases, but reversal of that trend has not been spectacular, for the increase in numbers between 1926 and 1970 was under 10 per cent. It

A Siberian Komi reindeer-breeder

is likely that there was much assimilation into Russian or other immigrant groups. About half the peoples numbering under 30,000 received instruction in written languages in Soviet times, and the looseness of the Federation Treaty of 1992 now offers a brighter outlook for their cultural survival. Even before the USSR broke up, an association of the small peoples of the north was set up in April 1990 to guard their interests.

The Uralian family live in northern Russia, in Europe or in north-west Siberia. The Finno-Ugrian peoples are predominantly pastoralists. The most southerly members – Mordva, Udmurt, and Mari – are the most numerous, and their importance was recognized in the Soviet period by the establishment in each case of an Autonomous Soviet Socialist Republic (ASSR) on the group's homeland, the Volga and Kama basin. Uralians have played a role in the history of the Russian plain since earliest historical times, making contact with Russian principalities and city states.

Further north, in the boreal forest, live the Komi and their less numerous cousins, the Komi-Permyaki. All are relatively sophisticated peoples, a significant proportion of their members having higher education. The remaining members of the

Khanty reindeer-breeders of the Western Siberian plain

Finno-Ugrian group are the Khanty and Mansi, collectively known as Ob' Ugrians, two related peoples who were until recently mainly hunters and fishers, with some interest in reindeer-herding. Finally, the Saami tend reindeer in the vicinity of Murmansk; they are related ethnically and linguistically to the Lapps (Sami) of Scandinavia.

The remaining group in the Uralian family is composed of Samoyedic peoples. The name Samoyed was dropped for the peoples (it implies 'cannibal' in Russian), but is retained for the group. They live on or near the coast on the Barents and Kara seas, and are still primarily hunters, fishers, and reindeer-herders.

In the Altaic family, the most important component are the Yakuts, who call themselves Sakha and live as pastoralists in the middle Lena basin. They have had close contact with the Russians for three centuries and are well educated; many have entered the professions. Yakut language and culture thrive, and the people, formerly an ASSR, promoted themselves to the State of Sakha in 1991. The language is Turkic, the Yakuts being the most north-easterly of the Turkic-speaking peoples. Others in the north are the Dolgany, reindeer-herders of Taymyr who speak Yakut but are of

Chukot nomads

mainly Tungus origin, and a very small group, the Tofa, who are now mostly fur-farmers and live near Irkutsk.

The other Altaic group are the Tungus-Manchurians, reindeer-herders, hunters and fishers of the Far East forests. The largest are the Evenki (formerly called Tungus, the name now used for the group as a whole), who range across a huge belt of territory from the Yenisey to the Pacific and into Manchuria. Their cousins, the Eveny, live to the north-east, on the shores of the Sea of Okhotsk and the Arctic Ocean, while the remaining members inhabit the lower Amur valley and, in the case of the Oroki, the island of Sakhalin.

The Palaeoasiatic peoples live chiefly in the far north-east and also are hunters, fishers and reindeer-herders. The term was coined to embrace peoples whose languages belonged to none of the major groups. In fact the Chukchi, Koryak, and Itel'men languages are related, thus giving some unity to the peoples of the Chukotka and Kamchatka peninsulas. The Eskimo (Inuit) and Aleut are the Asiatic representatives of those two related peoples whose main populations lie in North America. The Yukagiry, on the Kolyma River, have largely been assimilated into neighbouring groups. The Nivkhi are separated physically as well as linguistically and live on Sakhalin. The Kety, living on the Yenisey, are even more widely separated and their provenance (or language affiliation) has always been something of a mystery.   TEA

JEWS

There were 5 million Jews in Russia in 1897, 2.7 million within the reduced area of the USSR in 1926,

and about 4.8 million in the enlarged USSR in 1941; they were recognized as a nationality under Soviet law.

According to censuses conducted in the post-war era, they numbered 2.3 million in 1959, 2.15 million in 1970, 1.81 million in 1979 and 1.45 million – 0.5 per cent of the population – in 1989. The reasons for this decline in number are the losses of over 2.5 million in the Second World War and the holocaust and the emigration of over 300,000 in 1948–88; approximately 300,000 more left in 1989 and 1990. About 60 per cent of the emigrants went to Israel. These losses should be seen against the background of the 'natural' decline due to the small size of families, mixed marriages and assimilation.

The Jews are dispersed throughout the country. In 1989 most of them lived in Russia (537,000), Ukraine (486,600), Belorussia (now Belarus) (112,000), Uzbekistan (84,100) and Moldavia (now Moldova) (65,800). In 1979 there were 10,200 Jews in the Jewish Autonomous Region in the Far East (capital city Birobidzhan), 5.4 per cent of the population there. About 98 per cent of Jews inhabit urban areas; a quarter live in the largest cities of Moscow, St Petersburg and Kiev.

Ninety-five per cent are Ashkenazi Jews whose language has been Yiddish. The Central Asian Jews, Mountain Jews, Georgian Jews and the tiny Krymchak community constitute the remainder. In 1989 11.1 per cent of the Ashkenazi Jews declared Yiddish as their mother tongue and another 4.0 per cent regarded it as their second language; 86.6 per cent stated that Russian was their mother tongue. The percentage of linguistic Russification is much lower (24.9 per cent) among the non-Ashkenazi Jews.

The Jews are a highly educated population. According to 1975 figures, Jews, who formed less

The Jews became part of the Russian Empire after the Polish partitions under Catherine II. It was in the former Polish territory that the important movements of Hassidism, Zionism and Jewish socialism emerged. Under the tsars they were subject to many disadvantages, and they suffered great losses in the Civil War. The Sovietization of the Jewish minority included economic upheaval, the suppression of their religious life, the liquidation of their public and political life, and also from the 1930s the progressive elimination of Soviet Jewish culture. In a reversal of earlier policies, the Jews were increasingly excluded from politically sensitive occupations and discrimination was introduced in many fields. This policy became manifest in Stalin's last years (1948–53): campaigns against Jewish nationalism and 'cosmopolitanism' were followed by the closing down of all Jewish Soviet institutions and publications, the mock trial of fifteen prominent Jewish leaders and writers and their execution on 12 August 1952, and the notorious 'Doctors' Plot'. Many Jews lost their jobs and a great number were jailed.

Some improvement occurred under Stalin's successors. This included a very modest resumption of Yiddish publications (a literary monthly and a few books) as well as theatrical activities. But basic discriminatory policies were not reversed.

As a result of the 1967 Six-Day War in the Middle East and the emergence of Soviet dissent, a Jewish movement for emigration to Israel developed and an unofficial Jewish culture appeared in the form of samizdat publications in Russian, the teaching of Hebrew and the holding of seminars. At the same time, the official propaganda against Zionism and Israel intensified and in many cases acquired antisemitic features. The prevailing virtual prohibition on emigration was partially lifted in the 1970s, but restrictions were tightened in the early 1980s.

Considerable changes in the situation of the Jews took place under Gorbachev (1985–91). Emigration was resumed and became massive. Altogether over 750,000 Jews emigrated between 1971 and 1991, mainly to Israel and the USA. Jewish cultural bodies emerged all over the country, publications appeared in many towns and in 1989 an umbrella organization, the Vaad, was created. Activities which were hitherto prohibited or virtually non-existent, such as the teaching of Hebrew and Yiddish, Jewish history and religion, could be openly conducted; many of the discriminatory measures were dismantled and the official anti-Zionist propaganda was toned down. Links between the Jews and the State of Israel are expanding and the post-Soviet states have established relations with Israel which had been severed by Moscow in 1967. But at the same time active grass-roots anti-semitic and xenophobic movements

Top. Jewish emigrants from the USSR arriving in Tel Aviv, Israel. Above. Inside a Moscow synagogue

than 0.8 per cent of the total population, constituted 4.1 per cent of all employees with higher education and 1.4 per cent of those with specialist secondary education. In 1987, when the Jews represented about 0.5 per cent of the population, they formed 1.4 per cent of the workforce with higher and specialist secondary education, 3.85 per cent of all scientific personnel and 10.3 per cent of the doctors of science. They are also strongly represented among lawyers, doctors, cultural and artistic workers, writers and journalists. There were few in the direct service of the Party or state apparatus (military, security and diplomatic services) although they had been prominent there during the first decades of Soviet power. The rapid decline of the number of Jewish students (112,000 in 1968–69, 41,000 in 1984–85) and postgraduates indicated a process of decline in the Jews' role in the economy and intellectual life.

emerged in many parts of the former USSR. An extremist expression of it are the Pamyat societies and similar bodies which operate in many Russian towns. Anti-semitic attitudes also find support in conservative Russian nationalist and neo-Stalinist circles.   LH

MOLDOVANS

Until 1991 Moldova was known by its Russified name of Moldavia. Despite strenuous Soviet efforts, nationhood distinct from Romanian remained little more than a political concept. According to the usual definitional criteria, the titular nationality is Romanian, Moldovans sharing the same religion, language, culture and historical experience. The present state occupies Romanian lands seized by the tsars in 1812.

Imperial Russia made little effort to regard the inhabitants of the region as a distinct nation (preferring instead to classify them as 'Bessarabians'). Their ethnic allegiance became crucial only after the province seized the opportunity presented by the collapse of central authority in 1917 and opted for union with Romania. The recovery of Bessarabia remained a major plank in Soviet foreign policy between the World Wars but, while Lenin always formulated his country's claims to the area in ideological or historical terms, Stalin considered that such claims should be strengthened by regarding the inhabitants as a separate nation.

The Moldavian Autonomous Soviet Socialist Republic was established on Ukrainian territory in 1924 precisely in order to represent a nucleus for this nation; it was, however, often ruled by members of other Soviet ethnic groups. As part of the Molotov–Ribbentrop Pact of 23 August 1939, the Soviet Union annexed the province in June 1940 and established the Moldavian Soviet Socialist Republic (MSSR) two months later. However, Stalin also demanded another part of Romania which had not previously been subjected to Russian rule, the northern part of Bukovina. In order to emphasize that the inhabitants of the MSSR were indeed a separate nation, the Bukovinians remained classified as Romanians and were annexed to the Ukraine. In Soviet terms 'Moldavian' applied to the Romanian speakers only in the MSSR who, according to the results of the 1989 Soviet census, numbered 2,795,000 people. They remained indistinguishable from the 20,353,000 of their kin in Romania and a further 557,000 Moldovans in other parts of the USSR.

Soviet policies were ineffectively aimed at gaining the population's acceptance for the continuance of Moldova within the USSR. Much effort was directed towards two parallel but inherently contradictory efforts. On the one hand, the Soviet authorities aimed to strengthen their claims that a Moldovan nation really existed, through a careful separation of the region's historical and cultural connections with Romania and through the encouragement of distinctive local characteristics. Stalin believed that a nation required a separate language and sought to manufacture one for Moldova. However, the effort was clumsy and ultimately doomed to failure, for it concentrated mainly on the the replacement of the Romanian Latin alphabet by Cyrillic.

Precisely because other means to create a separate nation were lacking, the Soviet Union also attempted to dilute the preponderance of Moldovans in their own republic. The local intelligentsia and the majority of land-owning peasants were eliminated in two deportations (the first in 1941, the second in 1945–46) and the forced collectivization of agriculture resulted in a famine which had claimed the lives of 100,000 Moldovans by the end of 1947. At the same time the authorities encouraged an influx of Russians and Ukrainians.

Thus, while the overall number of Moldovans increased by 45.5 per cent in the 1941–79 period, that of the ethnic Russians grew by 168.9 per cent. The capital of Chişinău (Kishinev) and the cities of Tiraspol, Tighina (Bendery) and Bălţi (Beltsy) became essentially Russian settlements while Moldovans remained confined to the countryside and excluded from most administrative positions: their share among local 'white-collar' workers was only half of their numerical preponderance in the republic.

Moldovans were also purposely excluded from the Communist Party, finding their promotion prospects limited because most senior party members were Russians: no fewer than two Soviet leaders – Leonid Brezhnev and Konstantin Chernenko – started their political careers in Moldova (the first as party leader in the early 1950s and the second as ideology chief).

Despite subsequent attempts to co-opt Moldovans onto governing bodies, the local party has continued to be dominated by other ethnic groups since Russians and Ukrainians (together 27 per cent of the population) accounted for almost half of the party's membership in 1989.

The endemic ethnic and political gulf between leaders and population, coupled with a particularly repressive regime, not only failed to contain the Moldovans but actually increased their attachment to other Romanians for two reasons. First, Romania itself embarked on a carefully executed strategy of differentiation from its other Warsaw Pact allies in the 1960s, a policy which required the manipulation of nationalism. While the Romanian government

Gagauz protest meeting, September 1990

never made explicit demands for the recovery of Soviet territory, its officially sponsored nationalism struck a chord with Soviet Moldovans.

More importantly, by pursuing a double-edged policy which on the one hand proclaimed the existence of a separate Moldovan nation, and on the other devalued the importance of that nation, the Soviet authorities left the Moldovans in a state of cultural and political limbo which only heightened their conviction that the reassertion of their Romanian identity was a question of survival, rather than of mere preference.

In any case, efforts to dilute the ethnic character of the republic ultimately failed because Moldovans still registered the highest birth-rate in the European USSR (20.1 per 1,000 at the end of the 1970s) and thus retained their share of the population (currently 64 per cent). Moldovans also started migrating to the cities: Chişinău's population grew by 30 per cent between the 1979 and 1989 censuses. And, despite the fact that they suffered from the lowest educational standards among the ethnic groups in their own republic (and one of the lowest in the USSR), a new Moldovan intelligentsia emerged in the capital and some rural areas. From 1987 educated Moldovans (particularly writers and journalists) spearheaded a campaign of cultural revival which culminated in the formation of a Popular Front in the spring of 1989. Simeon Grossu, the Moldavian party First Secretary (and the last Brezhnevite republican leader to survive in the USSR), was ultimately overwhelmed by the Front's very simple tactic: realising that to advocate closer relations with Romania was then still out of the question, opposition groups simply challenged their leader to accord them the real attributes of the nation to which he claimed they belonged.

Unlike his counterparts in the Baltic Republics, Grossu not only could not afford to encourage local nationalism, he could not contemplate even symbolic concessions granted in most other Soviet republics, for the MSSR did not have its own language or historical existence as an established state. Indeed, the leadership quickly discovered that every symbol of nationhood could only be Soviet or Romanian, not Moldovan. As a result, it resolved to oppose all popular demands. However, after a prolonged period of demonstrations (some drawing as many as 500,000 people), the authorities abandoned their previous linguistic and cultural policies. The Latin alphabet was restored, and Romanian was decreed a state language in 1989.

This political crisis was exacerbated by a steadily worsening economic situation. Moldova's economy remained essentially geared to the supply of agricultural products for export. The republic's national income was 15 per cent lower than the Soviet average, and while Moldova produced meat and vegetables in great quantities, local supplies were scarcer than in any other European republic in the former USSR. Under perestroika the adoption of enterprise autonomy and the beginnings of a market economy fuelled demands to cut their export of food products and to transform Moldova into a truly independent entity.

When independence was achieved as the state of Moldova in 1991, the event was marred by hostilities with two national minorities, Russian and Gagauz. The Russians established their 'Republic of Transdnestria' on the left bank of the Dniester in open conflict with the Moldovan government and the Gagauz declared an autonomous republic in the southern region they inhabit.   JE

GERMANS

The oldest settled German communities within the Russian Empire were the Baltic Germans, social élites of the Baltic provinces which Russia acquired in the eighteenth century. Baltic German status, deriving from medieval hierarchies, was finally lost after the 1917 Revolution, when the Baltic peoples formed independent states. Following Soviet annexation in 1940, most Baltic Germans were transferred to Germany. A second small group of Russian Germans included descendants of immigrant entrepreneurs, merchants, and military, technical or cultural specialists.

Most present-day Germans in Russia and Ukraine, however, are descended from immigrant peasant farmers, who settled principally on the lower Volga near Saratov and around the Black Sea in the later eighteenth and the nineteenth centuries. In the 1870s land shortage and the cancellation of special privileges produced some re-emigration, then chiefly to the Americas, which has continued intermittently ever since. After 1917 the Volga Germans were the first Soviet ethnic minority to receive local autonomy, in the Workers' Commune of the Volga Germans (1918), from 1924 until 1941 the Volga German Autonomous Soviet Socialist Republic. Many German communities suffered severely in the Civil War, and in the great southern famine of 1921–22. Thereafter until 1941 they shared the common life and experiences of the USSR.

With the invasion by Hitler's Germany, however, the German communities were deported eastwards *en masse* as traitors: the total involved was probably 650–700 thousand. The Volga German ASSR was liquidated. The German advance cut short the deportation of Ukrainian Germans; the invaders removed the remainder westwards, into Poland and Germany. After 1944–45 many were returned to the USSR and sent to join their exiled fellows. Rehabilitation came in decrees of 1955 and 1964. But prohibition of return to former homelands was lifted only secretly, without publication, in 1972; Soviet German history and status remained taboo subjects. In their exile – in the Komi ASSR and Urals region, but especially the Central Asian republics and south-western Siberia – they lived largely scattered among other nationalities. After 1955 German-language schools were established in areas with significant German population and very limited religious facilities were allowed. An all-union German-language newspaper, *Neues Leben*, founded in 1956, was followed by some local German-language newspapers and radio broadcasts. While employment was chiefly in agriculture (including lumbering), a technical and intellectual stratum also emerged, and a significant minority became assimilated.

The 1989 Soviet census showed 2,039,000 Germans, of whom 57 per cent (67 per cent in 1970) gave German as their first language. Perestroika belatedly promised radical change in their status. In 1988 they became a discussion topic in the Soviet media, and restoration of an autonomous area came under active official consideration in late 1989. Cultural and religious facilities, and public representation, improved: 1988 saw a new Soviet Evangelical-Lutheran Bishop, and the first German full Central Committee member since 1941. Informal groupings emerged, and in 1989 the 'initiative group' *Wiedergeburt* (Rebirth) was founded. Emigration to Germany was already increasing from previous low levels before the collapse of Soviet power and has been large from all the successor states in which Germans had been exiled. Although prospects for a restoration of the Autonomous Republic on the Volga faded, a German national district in Altay Kray was revived in 1992, to which the German government made an initial grant of ten million Deutschmarks for housebuilding in the German style.   RPB

GYPSIES

According to the 1989 census there were 262,000 Gypsies living in the Soviet Union but the real figure may be closer to 500,000. The discrepancy arises partly because the nomadic life of many Gypsies makes it difficult to record their numbers accurately, and partly because parents sometimes do not register their children as Gypsies at birth. Their population has in fact trebled over fifty years, despite the killing of many thousands in the German-occupied areas during the Second World War (nomadic Gypsies being classified with the Jews).

Most Gypsies live in European Russia, Belarus, Ukraine and the Baltic states. They arrived in two waves: the first from the south, via the Balkans in the fifteenth and sixteenth centuries and the second via Germany and Poland in the sixteenth and seventeenth centuries; by the early eighteenth century a small number had established themselves in Siberia. They speak Romani, which derives from the Indo-Aryan branch of the Indo-European family of languages and is common to all Gypsies (who call themselves 'Rom'), but each group has been influenced by the language of the surrounding people. Because the majority passed through the Byzantine Empire in the Middle Ages, their language has a strong Balkan influence. Despite living in widely scattered communities, the Gypsies seem to have

At the airport: a woman emigrant of the German minority

Gypsy family in the Volga region

resisted linguistic assimilation. Before the Revolution, the Gypsies lived mainly by horse-trading (men) and fortune-telling (women), but also undertook smithing, woodwork and basket-making. Most were wandering people, but they regularly visited peasant markets and festivals, and some settled in St Petersburg and Moscow, where they gained a living as singers, fiddlers and dancers.

A separate group of about 8,000 Gypsies lives in Central Asia; they call themselves 'Mugat', but are known as 'Lyuly' by the Uzbeks and 'Dzhugy' by the Tajiks. Most speak two languages: either Uzbek or Tajik, and their own argot, which is a mixture of Tajik and the secret language of the wandering people of Central Asia, a language which goes back to the Middle Ages. These Gypsies have no legends about their origin, which scholars suppose to have been Indian, since their dark physical features and custom of tattooing the forehead suggest a southern origin. They formerly lived in patrilineal groups descended from a common ancestor, in winter gathering in particular neighbourhoods at the edges of towns, and in summer moving off through the countryside. In addition to the usual Gypsy occupations, they specialize in folk medicine.

Because of the Gypsies' lack of a regular work tradition, it was difficult for the Soviet authorities to include them in the socialist economy. An all-Gypsy collective farm called 'Kommunism' soon disintegrated, and even in farms where Gypsies were mixed with other people the Gypsy section often gave up and moved away. On the several collective farms with Gypsy brigades members had settled houses, sent their children to school and made use of Soviet medical help and bank loans.

Many, nevertheless, resisted attempts to settle them in permanent jobs. In 1956 a decree of the Supreme Soviet made it an offence punishable by 'corrective labour' for a Gypsy to live a nomadic life. Such measures had little effect, and were not in fact rigorously enforced. Only partial success was achieved in persuading Gypsies to educate their children and large numbers maintained their wandering traditions and lived in tents.

The Gypsies' most noted influence on Russian culture is perhaps in music. The vogue for Gypsy revelry began in the late eighteenth century when Count A.G. Orlov brought a Gypsy choir from Moldavia to perform for Catherine II, and throughout the nineteenth century Gypsy singers, dancers and musicians were among the most popular entertainers, whether in noble houses (many of whose owners maintained their own Gypsy troupes) or in the taverns and restaurants of Moscow and St Petersburg. Yet the 'Gypsy romance' – the most widely known and performed genre of 'Gypsy' song from the mid-nineteenth century to the present – is in fact a Russian invention, with no roots in native Gypsy tradition.

After the Revolution Gypsy troupes were at first criticized as artificial creations of the old aristocratic regime, but from the late 1920s they were encouraged to develop their own culture. Two Romani journals were established (*Rómany Zórya* in 1927, and the monthly *Nevo Drom* in 1929), and Romani school textbooks appeared. Publishing in Romani lapsed after the Second World War until the early 1970s. In 1931 the 'Romen' Gypsy theatre was founded, and after a shaky start – the initial problem was to find Gypsies with the education and experience to run it – it became one of the most popular theatres in Moscow.   SF/CH

Religion

Christianity

THE RUSSIAN ORTHODOX CHURCH

The beginnings of Russian Christianity may be traced back to the ninth century, but the evidence is fragmentary. A 'Russian' diocese seems to have been established by the Byzantines in 867, though its location is not certain. In 944 there were Russian Christians among the signatories of a Byzantine–Russian treaty; by the middle of the tenth century (*c*.955) Princess Ol'ga (regent of Kiev, 945–64) was herself baptized. However, her own baptism was not the prelude to an immediate conversion of her people. On the contrary, the Kievan realm was to experience something of a pagan revival under her son Svyatoslav (962–72) and, even more markedly, under the young Vladimir (980–1015), her grandson. Under Vladimir, indeed, there was an attempt to create a new Nordic pantheon, with Perun (the god of thunder) at its head. It was the same Vladimir who was to demolish its monuments and desecrate its shrines in the last decade of the century, for the new pantheon proved to be an anachronism.

Conversion

The principality of Kiev was surrounded by powerful neighbours, each of whom had accepted one of the great monotheistic religions in the course of the preceding century. Vladimir must have perceived that his country's political and economic – not to mention spiritual – welfare depended on conversion to one or another of these faiths, whether Judaism, Islam or Christianity. His investigations persuaded him that Byzantine Christianity had most to offer.

Negotiations with Constantinople led to Vladimir's marriage to the emperor's sister (989) and to its necessary precondition, his baptism (988). It was a baptism which was to determine the religion of the Russian people for centuries to come.

At the outset 'conversion' was the policy of an élite, which showed no hesitation in promoting it by force. Although the new religion spread with remarkable speed and Rus' was soon able to display all the marks of a flourishing Christian civilization, paganism was to linger for many centuries, however covertly, especially in the rural areas.

Rus' inherited a fully-developed Christian tradition from the Byzantine world. The converts were not expected to engage in any major theological controversies (the age of the great Ecumenical Councils had come to an end with the Council of 787). Nor were they required to devise new liturgical forms. For their worship and instruction the Byzantines provided them even with a corpus of Slavonic translations. The new faith was communicated in a language which was accessible to the local population, an important factor in its diffusion and acceptance.

Organization

It remains unclear which diocese of the new Church had precedence until 1037. The matter is complicated by the existence of several missionary centres prior to the conversion of the Kievan realm. But although there were briefly to be metropolitans in Chernigov and Pereyaslavl' even in the second half of the

Previous spread. *Members of the Holy Synod receiving saintly relics formerly in the Kremlin Museum, 1988*

Below. *The archangel Gabriel. Eleventh century mosaic, St Sofia Cathedral, Kiev*

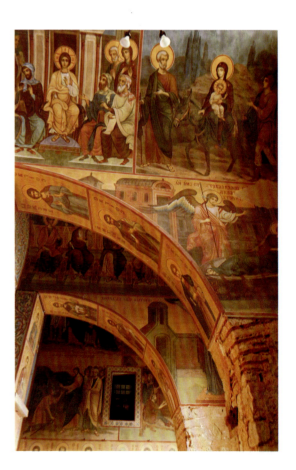

Right. The church of
St Theodore Stratilates,
Novgorod, completed in
1361

eleventh century, the appointment of a metropolitan of Kiev (Feopempt) in 1037 determined the location of the primatial see throughout the pre-Mongol period and its designation for some time after. Under Kiev at least seven other dioceses were soon established; their number was to rise to 15 by the time of the Mongol conquest. The first metropolitan was a Greek, as were most of his successors for some time to come. An exception, such as the Russian Metropolitan Ilarion, was not likely to gain the approval of Constantinople: Ilarion remained in office for barely a year (1051–52). Not until the fifteenth century did the Russian Church begin to take decisions in such matters entirely for itself: formally, it remained a province of the patriarchate of Constantinople until at least 1448.

As members of that patriarchate the Russians were party to Constantinople's ever-increasing estrangement from Rome, of which the Schism of 1054 was but one expression. The 'missionary' inroads of the Swedes (1240) and the Baltic Teutonic Knights (1242), successfully resisted by Alexander Nevsky (c.1220–63), were to confirm their worst suspicions of the heretical West.

Early monasteries and first saints

The Kievan Monastery of the Caves (1051) grew up around two saintly figures, Antony (d.1072/73) and Feodosy (d.1074). If not the first, it was certainly the most important of the early monastic foundations. These were to number 68 by the time of the Mongol invasion. Almost all had an urban location and a commitment to their secular environment. They were valued for their educational, artistic and philanthropic work, as well as for their spiritual life.

The growing maturity of the Church was demonstrated by the canonization of several saints. First among these were the princes Boris and Gleb (d.1015); their feast was celebrated three times a year. Feodosy, who attended the translation of their relics in 1072, was soon to follow them into the ranks of saints (1108). Vladimir himself was not to be canonized until 1240, the very year in which his old capital was sacked by the Mongols. Thus began a new and sombre period.

Mongol toleration

The devastation which accompanied the Mongol invasion affected the Church no less than any other institution. But the toleration of the Mongol rulers for all religions (which was to outlive their subsequent conversion to Islam) led them to safeguard, even to enhance, the position of the Church. Its beliefs and practices were to be respected; moreover it was to be exempt from all taxation. The tolerance of one khan even led to the establishment of a new see at the Mongol capital of Saray (1261).

Left. Twelfth-century fresco
in St Sofia with scenes from
the life of Christ painted
under Byzantine influence

Kiev–Vladimir–Moscow

The sack and consequent decline of Kiev persuaded Metropolitan Maksim (d.1305) to transfer his residence to the city of Vladimir. For less obvious reasons, his successor Petr (d.1326) moved to the as yet unimportant township of Moscow (1325). In due course the alienation of Kiev (it fell under Polish-Lithuanian dominion) provided yet one more reason for the metropolitan to change his title to that of 'Moscow and all Rus'' (1458). A separate metropolitanate of Kiev was established, first under Roman auspices (1458), then under Constantinople (1470).

Monastic revival

The most significant church figure of the fourteenth century was not a metropolitan but a humble monk, Sergy of Radonezh (1314–92). Around his hermitage in the wilds 70 km north-east of Moscow at the place subsequently named after him, Sergiev Posad (in Soviet times Zagorsk), was to develop one of the greatest of Russian monasteries, dedicated to the Holy Trinity (and eventually also to its saintly founder). Sergy's work provided the stimulus for a revival of monastic life. New foundations proliferated, by contrast with the pre-Mongol period, in areas which were hardly populated, even unexplored. In Sergy's lifetime there were perhaps 50 new monastic houses; the number was to be trebled within a century of his death.

The monastic colonizers often acted as missionaries. None made such an impact as the great missionary of the Zyrian (Komi) people, Stefan of Perm' (1340–96), who translated the Scriptures and the liturgy into the local language and created a Zyrian alphabet for the purpose. He followed in the footsteps of SS. Cyril and Methodius (the ninth-century apostles of the Slavs, creators of a Slavonic alphabet) and paved the way for the missionary translators of later centuries, particularly the nineteenth. Unlike many a later Russian missionary, however, St Stefan resolutely refused to have his work exploited in the interests of the Russian state.

Rome–Constantinople–Moscow

The independence of the Muscovite Church was hastened, though it was not determined, by the formal (and short-lived) reunion of Rome and Constantinople – the Catholic and Orthodox Churches – brought about at the Council of Ferrara–Florence (1438–39). Metropolitan Isidor of Moscow had been a member of the Council and party to its decisions. But Moscow would have none of them. On his return to Moscow Isidor was at first imprisoned by the grand prince (1441), then allowed to flee the country. Isidor, while residing as cardinal in Rome, remained nominally metropolitan of Moscow until his death in 1463. But his replacement had been chosen long before, and by the Russian Church alone – without even a token preliminary reference to Constantinople. Metropolitan Iona (d. 1461), the new metropolitan in Moscow, became head of an effectively independent (autocephalous) Orthodox Church in 1448.

Constantinople was soon to fall to the Turks (1453). In Muscovy it was said that this was a punishment for acceptance of the Union with Rome. The termination of Byzantium's political independence, together with the growth of Muscovy's power and self-esteem, encouraged the Russians to seek unequivocal validation of their Church's independence. The century which began with the monk Filofey's attempt to popularize the concept of Moscow as the Third Rome (successor to the Second Rome, Constantinople) ended with the Second Rome's acceptance of Moscow's patriarchal status (1589). The first patriarch of Moscow and all Rus' (1589–1605) was to be Metropolitan Iov of Moscow, formerly archbishop of Rostov. His patriarchate was allotted fifth place in order of precedence by the ancient Eastern patriarchates in 1593; it retains this position to the present day.

Church and state

The negotiations which led to the patriarchate's establishment had been conducted by the tsar. In the course of the sixteenth century the Church had become ever more closely identified with the state, despite the proclamation by the Moscow *Stoglav* ('hundred chapters') Council of 1551 to the effect that the Byzantine principle of 'symphony' between Church and state was to be followed. An attempt to secularize monastic landholdings in the early years of the century had come to nothing – though there had been some support for such a policy from among 'non-possessor' monks, such as Nil Sorsky (1433–1508), as well as from the would-be beneficiaries of the secular world. However, the victor in the dispute between 'possessors' and 'non-possessors', Abbot Iosif of Volokolamsk (1439–1515), nevertheless sought to further the ever-increasing authority of the state. Ivan IV was to demonstrate its power most brazenly: at one stage he not only dismissed the metropolitan of Moscow, Filipp (1568), but had him strangled. Moves to canonize Metropolitan Filipp began within 21 years of his death. His name was soon to be added to the calendar of Russian saints which had been so greatly augmented under the auspices of his persecutor-to-be and at the initiative of the enterprising Metropolitan Makary (1481–1563). At the Councils of 1547 and 1549 the Church had approved the canonization of no fewer than 39 new Russian saints.

The Time of Troubles

The Time of Troubles (*Smuta*) at the beginning of the seventeenth century involved the heroic 16-month long défence of St Sergy's Trinity monastery against a besieging army of 30,000 Polish invaders (1608–09) and, at a different level, the repulse by the Russian Church of Catholic overtures and machinations. The aged Patriarch Germogen (1606–12) died witnessing to the integrity of Orthodoxy. His successor Patriarch Filaret (1612–34) was to pursue a markedly anti-Catholic policy. The

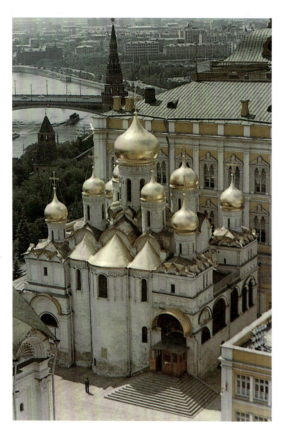

Cathedral of the Annunciation, Moscow Kremlin. Fifteenth century

Patriarch Filaret, Father of Mikhail, the first Romanov Tsar

West-Russian Orthodox hierarchs under Polish rule had earlier accepted Union with Rome at yet another Council (Brest, 1596) at which the Uniat Church was created. Filaret, a prisoner of the Poles for eight years preceding his enthronement (1619), had no intention of tolerating such arrangements. Filaret occupied a curiously privileged place in the state since he was also father (and mentor) of the new tsar, Mikhail Romanov. He therefore took the title of Great Lord (*Velikiy gosudar'*).

Nikon's reforms

In the mid-century a later patriarch, Nikon (1652–81), was also to insist on this title in an attempt to assert not only the equality, but the supremacy of the Church in church–state relations. His policies, and in particular his autocratic manner of pursuing them, led to disarray in Church and state alike. Indeed, their mutual relations were to be affected for centuries to come. Nikon's reign may be seen as a watershed in the history of the Russian Church. His failure to establish (he would have argued, re-establish) the primacy of the Church cleared the way for the ecclesiastical reforms of Peter the Great.

The Ecclesiastical Regulation

At the death of Patriarch Adrian (1691–1700), Peter let the patriarchate lapse. He gave his support successively to two clerics of a Protestant orientation, Metropolitan Stefan Yavorsky (1658–1722) and Archbishop Feofan Prokopovich (1681–1736). The latter was to prove all-important as the effective author of Peter's *Ecclesiastical Regulation* (1720). It was a document drawn up in camera by the emperor's nominee. Although it was subsequently signed by the Russian bishops and other senior clergy, these were no longer free agents (as the document itself made plain). Their successors remained subordinate and largely subservient until the end of the empire.

The Holy Synod

The *Regulation* established an Ecclesiastical College (*Kollegium*) which was almost immediately re-named Holy Synod. This was essentially a government department. Charged with its oversight was a secular administrator, the Chief Procurator or *Ober-Prokuror*. Significantly, this was a German title, with no roots in Orthodox history. For Peter's entire programme for the subjugation and administration of the Church was unashamedly borrowed from the West. In particular, he turned for guidance to the Lutheran G.W. Leibnitz (1646–1716).

Education

Paradoxically, while the administration took on a Protestant appearance, the Church initially provided its future leaders with an education which was based principally on Catholic models. Throughout the seventeenth century Ukraine (strongly influenced by the Catholic West) had provided Muscovy with teachers and scholars, many of them trained under Uniat auspices. The integration of much of Ukraine and Muscovy (1654) and the transfer of the Kievan metropolitanate from Constantinople to Moscow (1685–87) served to confirm this tendency. The syllabus of the Helleno-Greek Academy of Moscow (1685) followed a scholastic pattern. Its first masters were the Greek brothers Ioaniky and Sofrony Likhud, who had gained their doctorates in Padua. Perhaps appropriately, the Academy eventually took the name Slavo-Latin (1700–75) before becoming Slavo-Greco-Latin (1775–1814). This was to make way for the Moscow Ecclesiastical Academy at Sergiev Posad (1814). Three other institutions had also gained the title of Academy by this time: Kiev (1701), St Petersburg and Kazan' (1797). All four were to survive until the Revolution of 1917; two of them (in Leningrad and Zagorsk) were to be re-established after the Second World War.

Secularization of the monasteries

The secularization of monastic properties which had been successfully resisted by Abbot Iosif of Volokolamsk was undertaken by Catherine II in 1763–64, soon after her accession to the throne (1762). The Church was deprived of extensive landholdings and of almost two million serfs, and thus became more dependent on the state. The unfortunate metropolitan of Rostov, Arseny Matseevich (1696–1772), was one of the few to protest against the actions of the government. He was demoted and imprisoned.

Spiritual elders

Yet an inner revival of monastic life was on the horizon. Poverty was exactly what Bishop Tikhon of Zadonsk (1724–83) sought and propagated; his humble way of life was to be remembered with more affection than Metropolitan Arseny's naive triumphalism. But none was to gain more renown than the meek recluse Serafim of Sarov (1759–1833). His radiant ministry served as a reminder that the Church was left inwardly unscathed by the administrative and fiscal reforms which had come its way.

The influence of the Moldovan Elder Paisy Velichkovsky (1722–94) was to transform the life of a number of monasteries in the course of the nineteenth century. He translated the recently compiled *Philokalia* ('Love of Beauty') into Slavonic (1793), propagated the use of the Jesus Prayer and ensured that the institution of spiritual elders (*startsy*) gained widespread approval. The great monastery at Kozel'sk, Optina Pustyn', was to

Church of the Transfiguration, Urals region. Late eighteenth century

Glukharev (1792–1847) of the Altay mission; Metropolitan Innokenty Veniaminov (1797–1879), who worked in Kamchatka, Alaska and the Aleutian Isles; and Archbishop Nikolay Kasatkin (1836–1912), the first saint of the now autonomous Orthodox Church of Japan.

The Established Church

Few voices were raised in protest against the restrictions under which the Church had to operate in the nineteenth century, and even these were muted by censorship. Among those who accepted the status quo the most noteworthy were the statesmanlike metropolitan of Moscow, Filaret Drozdov (1782–1868) and the devout but ultra-conservative Chief Procurator K.P. Pobedonostsev (1827–1907). But the revolutionary events of 1905 gave impetus to reformers; there was new hope for a restoration of the Church's independence from the state. Removal of numerous restrictions from the hitherto underprivileged (and not infrequently persecuted) non-Orthodox religious bodies of the empire (1905) encouraged the Orthodox to work towards a Council of the Russian Orthodox Church. It seemed lamentable that a body of such age, dignity and size should not be permitted to regulate its own affairs. By 1914 it possessed 73 dioceses, 54,174 churches (not to mention a comparable number of chapels) and 1,025 monastic foundations. With its 291 hospitals and its 35,528 parish schools it had a social as well as a liturgical role to perform, though it favoured the latter. But the tsar remained obdurate and convened no Council. The work of the Pre-Conciliar Commission of 1906 and the Pre-Conciliar Consultation of 1911–12 was set aside. Only with the end of the Orthodox monarchy did the Church gain some opportunity to compensate for the preceding centuries of Synodal rule. But the moment came late and it was far too brief.

The office of Chief Procurator was abolished at the request of its last incumbent A.V. Kartashev (1875–1960) in the summer of 1917. That same summer the first Council of the Russian Orthodox Church for two and a half centuries began its sessions. The first session (15 August 1917) took place at the very heart of the old Third Rome, in the Cathedral of the Assumption in the Moscow Kremlin. The Council's sessions continued until the following summer. Not least of its acts was to re-establish the patriarchate. It also elected three candidates for the post of patriarch. The final choice was by lot: this fell on Tikhon, newly elected metropolitan of Moscow (1865–1925).

Separation of Church and state

The Church which he was called upon to lead was faced with unprecedented problems. The new politi-

become a renowned centre for *startsy* until its closure in the 1920s. Among its most revered elders were Leonid (1768–1841), Makary (1788–1860), Amvrosy (1812–91) and Nektary (1856–1928).

Nineteenth-century missions

Although it used the designation *Russian* Orthodox, the Church had come to minister to a considerable variety of ethnic groups both within the borders of the empire and beyond its confines. Not only Zyrians but Tatars, Chuvash, Cheremis, and Votyaks were among the tribes or nationalities which provided converts in their tens of thousands. The missionary enterprise had its disreputable aspect as an arm of Russian imperialism. But there were saintly figures among missionaries and converts alike. Russian missions abroad left their mark in Alaska (from 1794) and Japan (from 1861). Among the great missionaries of the nineteenth century mention should be made of Archimandrite Makary

Patriarch Tikhon

cal situation rendered void or inapplicable the carefully elaborated legislation of the 1917–18 Council. The integrity of a Tikhon was therefore all the more needed in the regulation of Church affairs. With him began a new line of martyrs and confessors, for although the Church was suddenly separated from the state the new establishment was to subject it to every kind of indignity and constraint. With the old certainties swept aside, the Church was now to be proved by fire.

The Bolshevik government's decree of 23 January 1918 on the separation of Church and state and of schooling from the Church affected all religious bodies, but none so obviously or so immediately as the formerly established Church of the Russian Empire. Under the Provisional Government of 1917 there was still talk of the Orthodox Church preserving some kind of privileged position among the other confessions and religions. Now the Church found itself, like any other of these bodies, deprived even of the rights of a person at law.

The confiscation of Church property (legitimized by the same decree) soon led to confrontations. The newly elected patriarch's first encyclicals expressed a severity which bordered on militancy (19 January and 7 November 1918). But his insistence that the new leaders acted 'in a manner contrary to the conscience of the people' could only serve to confirm the Bolsheviks in their resolve to mould that conscience in accordance with their own ideology. For the Bolsheviks sought not only to undermine the Church economically: their intention was to displace it as the mentor of the people, and an intensive (generally crude) anti-religious propaganda campaign was put into operation as soon as the Civil War ended in 1922.

Reform movements in the 1920s

There was a more insidious device intended to diminish the authority of the Church. From 1922 the secular authorities gave support to a reform movement within the Orthodox Church: in effect, they fomented schism. The reform movement (usually termed Renovationist) was led by clergy who professed virtually unqualified loyalty to the new state and to its aspirations. Prominent among its leaders was Archpriest – subsequently Metropolitan – Aleksandr Vvedensky (1889–1946).

The arrest of Patriarch Tikhon (1922) was used as an opportunity to usurp his authority and, eventually, to depose him at the reformers' second Council (1923). However, their movement was not a united one, nor was it well supported. Despite the premises and facilities which were made available to it, the movement was to lose its impetus before the outbreak of war (1941) and it was to be disbanded before its end.

Similar reform movements surfaced briefly in the 1920s among the Lutherans, the Armenian Orthodox, the Jews, the Muslims and the Buddhists of the USSR.

Confiscation of valuables

The Patriarch's arrest was the result of another plan (Trotsky's) to discredit the Church. The intention was to take possession of the Church's movable property under the guise of famine relief. The state would gain financially; the Church would be disgraced by any resistance which might be offered to the confiscation of sacred items. In the event, Tikhon (who was willing to donate unconsecrated objects) legitimized such resistance. There followed clashes, deaths and arrests. Among those to be tried and executed, in 1922, was the meek and popular metropolitan of Petrograd, Veniamin Kazansky.

Patriarch Tikhon's succession

The patriarch emerged from prison in 1923 with a declaration that he was 'no longer an enemy of the Soviet government'. The declaration was to be echoed in his final testament, signed on the day of his death (7 April 1925). However, neither declaration resulted in government recognition of the Orthodox Church or of its administration. On the contrary, fresh confusion resulted from the arrest and exile (1925) of the patriarch's *locum tenens* Metropolitan Petr Polyansky (1863–1936). Most of the remaining bishops who had been designated possible successors were also in prison or in exile.

Nor was the confusion dispelled by the release from prison of Metropolitan Sergy Stragorodsky, or by his successful application for legalization (1927). For many churchmen believed that Sergy's declaration of loyalty to the state, however well-intentioned, was too compliant. They refused to recognize his authority, and further schisms resulted, led by such figures as Metropolitan Iosif Petrovykh (1872–?1937).

New restrictions

Metropolitan Sergy (1861–1944) became the 'deputy *locum tenens*' of the patriarchal throne on the eve of Stalin's First Five-year Plan, and of all the consequent or associated regimentation of life. The new order in respect of religion found its legal expression in the decree of 8 April 1929, a decree which was to remain in force until revised (c. 1962) and published in its revised form in 1975. Like the decree of 1918 it affected all religious bodies.

Among its stipulations was that each religious association should be registered as such by the competent secular authorities – who, in the process, could be expected to gain some control of the association's administration. No religious association was

Right. *The Lutheran church on the Nevsky Prospekt, St Petersburg, was converted by the Soviet local authority to a swimming pool, but is now being returned to religious use*

permitted to give material aid to its members, and this despite the fact that the clergy were already deprived of civil rights (even of ration cards), while yet subjected to punitive taxation. A memorandum (1930) from Metropolitan Sergy to the government official charged with religious questions protested against some of the new requirements, but to no avail.

Meanwhile the state Constitution was amended. Whereas the text of 1918 permitted 'freedom of religion and anti-religion to every citizen', the revised formulation restricted the 'freedom of religion' permitted by the text of 1918 to 'freedom of worship'. Anti-religious propaganda was permitted as before, but the right to issue any sort of religious propaganda was tacitly withdrawn (16 May 1929). The 1936 Constitution was to restore civil rights to the clergy, but religious propaganda was to remain unconstitutional in the revised Constitution of 1977 as in that of 1936.

The 1930s saw a drastic reduction in the number of churches, the apparently final dissolution of the monasteries, and the imprisonment of countless clergy. At the outbreak of war, hardly four bishops were at liberty to exercise their pastoral role within the narrow limits permitted by the authorities. And yet within and despite these limits – and even in the most appalling conditions – there were church members in their tens of millions who adhered heroically to their faith.

The impact of the Second World War

The war created an entirely new situation. On Soviet territory the government was brought to see the patriotic potential of the Orthodox Church. The first to point in this direction was Metropolitan Sergy, who made a dignified, immediate and apparently independent appeal for the defence of the homeland (22 June 1941). Stalin granted him an audience (4 September 1943) and permitted the convocation of a Council (8 September 1943). This Council proceeded to the election of Sergy as patriarch of Moscow and all Rus'. His death early in the next year was followed by another Council (1945) and the election of Metropolitan Aleksy Simansky (1877–1970) as his successor.

All this symbolized the revival of public life for the Church. Throughout the war churches were reopened and clergy restored to diocesan and parochial duties. By 1944 an Orthodox theological college was inaugurated in Moscow (the first since the 1920s): within a few years there were nine others.

The German invaders had permitted to some extent the revival of church life in the occupied regions. This revival outlived the liberation. The many monasteries which had sprung to life in the western regions (as well as those which had survived

the 1930s on non-Soviet territory) thus came to enrich the life of the post-war Church in the USSR. Sixty-nine monastic houses were to remain open until the early 1960s.

The patriotic role played by the Church was noted: new opportunities were to be found for it in the diplomatic field after the war. Its steadfast support for the state's foreign policy was the condition of the concordat achieved under Stalin. Such support was offered in the World Peace Council (from 1949), in the Christian Peace Conference (from 1958) and in the World Council of Churches (from 1961). In this respect the Orthodox Church did not differ from other religious bodies in the USSR, most of which were expected to engage in similar activities. The most prominent Orthodox leaders concerned with foreign affairs were (successively) two brilliant metropolitans, Nikolay Yarushevich (1892–1961) and Nikodim Rotov (1929–78).

The Khrushchev programme

But the state was not always to keep its side of the unwritten (or at least unpublished) concordat. At the end of the 1950s the concessions won by the Church in wartime came into question; the period of Khrushchev's ascendancy saw the launching of a relentless campaign against religion (1958–64). Something like two-thirds of the Orthodox churches, seven out of the ten theological schools and the great majority of the monasteries were abruptly closed under one pretext or another. Anti-religious propaganda was once more intensified. There was a rash of well-publicized apostasies and, in response to them, several (in the circumstances courageous) excommunications (1959). Apart from a dignified speech in protest (1960) the aged Patriarch Aleksy maintained a sorrowful silence on the subject of the persecution. Khrushchev's fall (1964) brought an end to the worst excesses. But there was not to be any significant restoration of the Church's facilities. However, the death of Aleksy after a quarter of a century as patriarch was at least followed

Right. *President Gorbachev with Patriarch Aleksy II, March 1991*

by another Council (1971) at which Metropolitan Pimen Izvekov (1910–90) was elected as his successor.

The persistence of religion

From the Revolution of 1917 until perestroika began in 1985 religious bodies in the USSR were subjected to every conceivable strain, and the proportion of the population which overtly practised a religion significantly declined. By the end of the Khrushchev period, however, there were church members who manifested a new vigour in pressing for an improvement in the situation. At the very least they urged that the Soviet authorities abide by the legal and constitutional standards which they themselves had established. Prominent among those who adopted a 'dissident' position in respect of the establishment were Archbishop Ermogen Golubev (1896–1978) and the priests Nikolay Eshliman, Gleb Yakunin and Dimitry Dudko. In 1977 Yakunin was one of those who established a 'Christian Committee for the Defence of Believers' Rights' in Moscow.

For the next ten years this and all other religious groups which took initiatives for religious liberty or against state interference in church affairs continued to face concerted persecution. Only with the accession to power of Mikhail Gorbachev were some 400 prisoners of all denominations released. Other concessions followed.

In 1988, coinciding with the millennial celebrations of Russian and Ukrainian Christianity, a major reversal of policy became apparent. Gorbachev himself inaugurated this when he met the leaders of the Russian Orthodox Church in April, stating that believers and non-believers shared one destiny and calling for Christian help in the social aspect of

perestroika. In June the state supported the millennial celebrations in a remarkable way, granting the return of some key church buildings and allowing full television coverage of all main events. New legislation was passed, giving the church the right to print literature, to organize religious instruction and to develop its social programme.

All official anti-religious policy ceased with the dissolution of the Soviet state at the end of 1991. The Orthodox alone still numbered many tens of millions, and in all the successor states religion remained a potent force. Under Boris Yel'tsin the Russian government accorded official recognition and due honour on public occasions to the Orthodox Church, but the situation inherited by the Ukrainian government of Leonid Kravchuk was complicated by the opposition of an autocephalous group to the establishment retaining allegiance to the Russian Orthodox Church. In 1992 the refusal of Metropolitan Filaret of Kiev to resign following damaging revelations regarding his personal life and KGB connections further complicated a volatile situation.   SH/MAB

THE GEORGIAN ORTHODOX CHURCH

The Georgian Church traces its history back to the fourth century AD. It was already subjected to various pressures by the imperial Russian government in the nineteenth century; indeed, from 1811 it was incorporated into the Russian Church. It regained its independence at the time of the Revolution (an independence which the Moscow Patriarchate was to recognize only in 1943), but was to suffer depredations under the rule of Stalin, at one time its seminarist (Tbilisi, 1894). At its head is the Catholicos-Patriarch of all Georgia, Archbishop of Mtsekheta and Tbilisi. Under the present incumbent, Ilya II (Shiolashvili), a long-awaited revitalization of church life is in progress much complicated by the current political instability. There is a small seminary at Mtsekheta (opened in 1964), and an academy at Tbilisi (opened in 1988).   SH

Patriarch Aleksy II celebrating a service in Moscow

THE ARMENIAN CHURCH

Armenia also possesses its own Church, which was established no fewer than sixteen centuries ago. Unlike the Georgian Church, it is not of the same communion as the Russian Orthodox Church, belonging as it does to the family of Churches – formerly (and misleadingly) designated 'Monophysite' – which refused to accept the formulations of the Council of Chalcedon (451).

The experience of the Armenian Church in the USSR until 1941 was an unhappy one. By the end of the 1930s most of its churches, if not all, were closed. But Stalin's gesture in giving an audience to the future Catholicos, Kevork Cheorekchian, in April 1945 indicated that improvements were to be expected. Under the cautious Catholicos Kevork (1867–1954) the holy city of Echmiadzin was allowed to recover some of its dignity and facilities (including a seminary). Among other things it was given every opportunity to become a religious centre for the international Armenian community. It has continued to act as such in the reign of Kevork's successor Vazgen I (L.K. Palchian, b.1908).   SH

THE OLD BELIEVERS

Though formerly an integral part of the Russian Orthodox Church, the Old Believers (or Old Ritualists) separated from it in the mid-seventeenth century because of Patriarch Nikon's reforms of the 1650s. However, they have long ceased to form one body or even to adhere to a common set of beliefs. They differ most obviously on the question of church order. No bishops adhered to the Old Believer schism in the early days. Many Old Believers thus felt bound to remain without ordained clergy. Others subsequently restored their orders through a former Orthodox bishop at Belo-Krinitsa in the Austro-Hungarian Empire (1846). But it is not simply a question of belonging to the 'priestly' or the 'priestless' category. There are numerous subdivisions (*tolki*) under each heading, particularly

the latter. Among the most important are the Archepiscopate of Moscow and all Rus' (the Church of the Belo-Krinitsa Concord) which – as its name implies – possesses ordained clergy; and the Transfiguration Community of Old Believers (Staropomorsk Concord), which is priestless. The Old Believers were subjected to persecution by the tsarist authorities; the antagonism of the Soviet state therefore did not find them unprepared. Their profound conservatism, as well as their tendency to settle on the periphery of the realm, have always helped to preserve their way of life. They number several millions.   SH

RUSSIAN SECTS

There are sects whose origins may be traced to the Old Believer movement. Others have their separate history. Some, like the Molokans or the Dukhobors, can look back to the eighteenth century, but several are of recent origin. Among these may be noted the True Orthodox Christians, who see Patriarch Tikhon as the last legitimate head of Russian Orthodoxy and who have taken a critical stance towards the official Church as well as to the government since 1925. They have now emerged from the underground and act as an opposition to the Moscow Patriarchate.   SH

Worship in an Old Believers' church

Right. The 'Hill of Crosses', a Lithuanian demonstration of piety and nationalism in the Soviet period

EVANGELICAL CHRISTIANS AND BAPTISTS

This title has, since 1944, referred to a united Protestant denomination which brought together several pre-revolutionary evangelical groups (commonly called Baptists). Lenin, because of their earlier subjugation, granted them some privileges, such as maintaining a theological school, long after the abolition of these within the Russian Orthodox Church. Stalin oppressed all denominations equally, but then allowed some churches to re-open during the war in return for moral support.

The leading body established at that time, the All-Union Council of Evangelical Christians and Baptists, has maintained political loyalty to the Soviet regime ever since, even during the Khrushchev period, when a new wave of church closures affected all republics. Apparent passivity in the face of persecution which went far beyond the letter of the law led to sharp criticism of this leadership, with the emergence of a would-be independent body of unregistered Baptists which soon went into schism with the recognized leadership. In the 1970s the state began to permit the autonomous registration of some of these churches, but many others either refused or were not permitted to legalize themselves. The three different groupings persisted into the Gorbachev era.

The reform movement encountered systematic persecution until 1987–88, when the last of several hundred prisoners were released. Of the original leaders, Georgy Vins (b.1928) was expelled to the United States in 1979, while Gennady Kryuchkov ran the unregistered church for fifteen years, while remaining in hiding from the KGB. The official church gradually won concessions in return for its loyalty, being permitted some small printings of the Bible and opportunities for the leadership to travel extensively and sometimes even to study abroad. All groups experienced much greater freedom under Gorbachev, and prospects for re-unification improved with the collapse of the USSR. There are some 400,000 adherents, of whom perhaps a quarter belong to the unregistered churches.   MAB

THE CATHOLIC CHURCH

Between the two World Wars Catholicism had, at most, a tenuous existence with no firm base on Russian soil. However, the advance of the Red Army into Lithuania and Western Ukraine in 1944–45 saw the Soviet Union acquire a large indigenous Catholic population by conquest. Stalin's policy was immediately to subjugate these churches by persecution, in some instances worse than that

experienced by the Russian Orthodox Church in the previous decade.

In Lithuania and neighbouring areas of Belorussia not only bishops, but the intellectual leadership of a whole generation of the Roman Catholic Church, were liquidated or sent into exile. This did not prevent the loyalty of 80 per cent of Lithuania's 3.5 million people remaining with the church.

Stalin treated the Eastern-Rite Catholics (Uniats) of Western Ukraine even worse than others: legal existence (registration) was simply denied them after 1946. The alternatives were either enforced absorption into the Orthodox Church or imprisonment for those who resisted. These believers, numbering some 4 million, were the world's largest banned religious body.

One outcome of this persecution was the spread of Catholicism to the exile areas of Siberia and Central Asia, providing the small beginnings of a religious revival which has progressively affected all denominations. The election of a Polish Pope in 1978 provided further stimulus, ensuring all Soviet Catholics were fully prepared to take maximum advantage of the new opportunities afforded by perestroika when they arose.

The years 1988–89 saw the return of key buildings to the faithful, such as Vilnius Cathedral and the 'Queen of Peace' Church in Klaipeda, which had been confiscated immediately after its construction in 1961. A second seminary opened in Lithuania, bishops returned from exile, the Vatican elevated Vincentas Sladkevičius to the rank of Cardinal, and the legalization of the Ukrainian Catholic Church played its part in that republic's drive to independence in 1991.   MAB

THE LUTHERAN CHURCH

The liquidation of the Lutheran Church leadership in its heartland of Estonia and Latvia immediately after the Second World War had a more devastating effect than parallel events within the Catholic Church, because the regime managed to put compliant men in their place. Membership dwindled from the majority of the population to some 600,000, including scattered new congregations in the places of exile.

Just before the inception of perestroika there were new stirrings: pastors preaching a revivalist gospel tinged with nationalism. This led to increased persecution, which furthered the renewal, heralding major gains when conditions improved. In April 1989 the governing body of the Latvian Church, a twelve-member Consistory, voted .out Archbishop Eriks Mesters and replaced him by Karlis Gailitis, a strong supporter of the Popular Front movement. Riga Cathedral is now in use for worship once again and new Christian journals are appearing.   MAB

Judaism

Judaism always was a recognized religion in the USSR, but was in a considerably worse situation than other recognized denominations with regard to national and regional organization, contacts with co-religionists abroad and educational facilities.

The religious community (*kehilla*) which was the main framework of Jewish public life was dissolved by the Soviet authorities in 1919. Except for the years of relative relaxation, such as the war years (1941–45) and the immediate post-Stalin years (1954–57), Judaism came under sustained pressure from the Soviet state. It greatly suffered in Khrushchev's anti-religious drive. In the Brezhnev period, the anti-Zionist campaign included a strong anti-semitic component.

As a result of these policies the number of synagogues – 1,103 in 1926 and about 450 in 1959 – was reduced to as few as 60 in the 1970s and 1980s, of which about half were in Transcaucasia and Central Asia where only a fraction of Soviet Jews lived. The massive flow of the Jews towards the great cities and their occupational and social upward mobility reinforced the process of secularization.

In 1956 a *yeshiva* at the Moscow Choral Synagogue was licensed, but it had a precarious existence. A few Soviet graduates who had been permitted to study at the Budapest Rabbinical Seminary began to officiate as rabbis in the USSR in the 1980s. Since

Right. Jewish worship in a Moscow synagogue

the late 1950s thousands of Jews have gathered at synagogues on holidays, particularly Simhat Torah (Rejoicing in the Law). The Jewish movement of the 1970s was accompanied by a religious revival in certain circles and this continued with greater vigour under Gorbachev. Lively contacts developed with Jewish communities abroad and a Union of Jewish Communities was set up, embracing religious bodies throughout the country. In mid-1992 forty rabbis were functioning instead of the small number only a few years earlier. Religious study circles are spreading and yeshivot have been established in Moscow and St Petersburg. Many Jewish educational establishments at all levels (from kindergarten to university courses in Moscow, Kiev and Vilnius among others) in over 60 cities now have a religious orientation. Many synagogues are being returned to worshippers, notably the Polyakov synagogue in Moscow, and synagogues in L'viv and Kharkiv.   LH

Islam

Below. The Dalai Lama in the Kremlin with Metropolitan Pitirim, 1991
Bottom. *A Buddhist temple in Buryatia*

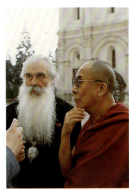

There were some 55 million Muslims in the former USSR, one of the largest Muslim populations in the world. The great majority are Sunni (Hanafi), but there are some 5 million Shi'a in Azerbaijan and a few thousand Isma'ilis in Tajikistan. About 60 per cent of the Muslims inhabit Central Asia, 20 per cent Transcaucasia and Northern Caucasus, 20 per cent the Volga region and Siberia.

In the first decade of Soviet rule Islam was treated with some tolerance, but from the late 1920s up to the Second World War it underwent severe repression. Thereafter the situation improved somewhat; a few mosques were reopened, and two *madrassa* (Muslim religious colleges) were allowed to function. Four Spiritual Boards were created to administer Islamic affairs (in Tashkent, Baku, Ufa and Makhachkala). During this period Islam survived more as a cultural phenomenon than a religion; knowledge of prayers and ritual was almost obliterated.

Perestroika and glasnost wrought dramatic (though belated) changes in official attitudes to Islam. These date from 1989, when a new young Mufti, Muhammad Sadyq Mamayusupov, became Chairman of the Tashkent Spiritual Board. In the following months more mosques were opened than in the preceding several decades; 1,500 pilgrims were allowed to undertake the *hajj* (annual pilgrimage to Mecca), a fifty-fold increase over the previous year.

The independence of the Central Asian states brought Islam fully back into the public arena. Several Muslim functionaries (including Mufti Mamayusupov) hold official positions in local and national government. There are demands for a return to the Arabic script (abolished in 1930) and in the six states with predominantly Islamic populations there have been proposals for the re-introduction of elements of the *sharia* (Muslim law).   SA

Buddhism

Buddhism in Russia follows the Tibetan reformed Gelug-pa tradition. There were at the time of the 1917 Revolution probably several hundred thousand Buddhists, principally in Buryatia and Kalmykia. The power and wealth of the monasteries (*datsan*) and monks (lamas) provoked Soviet counter-measures and Buddhist institutions were effectively annihilated in the late 1930s. Two small monasteries, with some tens of lamas, were re-opened after the Second World War at Ivolga and Aga, regions inhabited by Buryats. The administration of the Buddhists in the USSR was entrusted to the Buddhist Religious Central Board, with the Bandido Khambo Lama of Ivolga at its head. In the late 1980s and early 1990s small monasteries were reestablished in Buryatia, Tuva, and Kalmykia.   CH

History

Origins

THE EARLIEST PEOPLES

Although in earlier prehistory Russia was a frontier region, remote from the main centres of economic and cultural development in the Old World, it came to play a crucial role in history as the birthplace of a new way of life which profoundly affected surrounding areas: steppe nomadism.

Nomadism

It was in the early fourth millennium BC that the tribes living in the lower reaches of the rivers flowing through the Ukrainian steppes – Dnieper, Dniester and Don – began to use the herds of wild horses which roamed the dry areas between as more than a source of meat. Finds from the site of Dereivka, near Kiev, include fragments of horse-bits, indicating that these animals were used for the first time for riding. This innovation produced major changes in this area. People spread on to the steppe areas, using their new mobility to keep herds of sheep and using solid-wheeled wooden carts (drawn by oxen) which were first constructed by groups living on

the fringes of Near Eastern civilization in the Caucasus. The dead were buried in subterranean chambers under round mounds, which can still be seen in enormous numbers on the steppes, giving the name Pit-grave or *Kurgan* culture. Its later phases are distinguished as the Catacomb-grave and Timber-grave cultures. In some of these burials, models or actual remains of carts have been found, as in the famous find in the Tri Brata tumulus on the Kalmyk Steppe. Metal objects show connections with the flourishing metal-working area of the Caucasus. Settlements of this period, such as Usatovo and Mikhaylovka near Odessa, show that wealthy communities lived in defended settlements.

The way of life which crystallized in Ukraine was the key to the occupation of the dry zone which stretched eastwards across to the Altay. Movements of population, probably speaking Indo-European languages, carried communities of millet-farmers and sheep herders who used the horse and the Bactrian camel for transport in a wave of eastward expansion. Archaeologically these are represented by the Andronovo and Karasuk cultures, which are known as far east as the Minusinsk depression (along the upper Yenisey River) in the early second millennium BC. It was the southern wing of this movement, around the eastern side of the Caspian, which brought Indo-European languages into Iran and ultimately as far south as India. The combination of horses and wheeled vehicles led to the first construction of the light chariot by the people of the steppes, whose military advantage allowed them to penetrate deeply into the older urban civilizations to the south. By the middle of the second millennium BC wheeled vehicles of steppe origin were in use in China by the founders of the first Chinese state, the Shang dynasty.

This Indo-European domination of the steppes (whose later representatives were the historically-recorded Scythians, Sarmatians and Sakas) came to an end only in the first millennium AD when groups of oriental origin reversed the eastward flow of population to appear in history as invading Huns, Avars and Khazars.

AS

Scythians and Sarmatians

Russian history proper can be said to begin along the northern shore of the Black Sea and in the steppe beyond. Here it was that the peoples of southern

Previous spread. Peter the Great, founder of the Russian Empire: Falconet's equestrian statue of 1782 erected in St Petersburg by Catherine the Great

The Andronovo culture of the second millennium BC

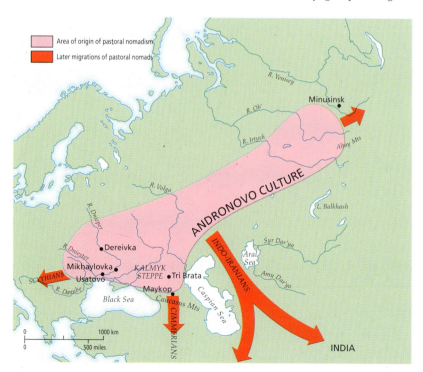

Russia came into contact with the ancient world of Greece and Rome through the Greek colonies which began to appear along the Black Sea coast from about the seventh century BC. The Greek historian Herodotus, who lived in the fifth century BC, spent some time in the Greek colony of Olbia at the mouth of the river Bug and left a valuable description of the surrounding region and its population. The knowledge provided by this account and by other fragmentary writings of the same period has been verified and greatly augmented by archaeological evidence from excavations carried out both in imperial Russia and, on a larger scale, in the Soviet Union. The excavation of burial-mounds in southern Russia has proved a rich source of information. Material from the so-called 'frozen tombs' of Pazyryk in Siberia has proved even more valuable. Although outside the Scythian area of influence, much of this material bears a striking similarity to finds in southern Russia, and provides evidence in support of references in Herodotus.

The earliest in the succession of peoples who appeared in southern Russia from about the year 1000 BC in the course of waves of invasion from Asia are thought to have been the Cimmerians; it appears that they spoke an Indo-European language and ruled southern Russia from about 1000 BC to 700 BC. The Scythians, a new wave of invaders, defeated them and destroyed their state. The new rulers, who spoke an Iranian language, held sway in southern Russia from the seventh to the end of the third century BC; according to Herodotus, their dominions extended from the Danube to the Don and from the shore of the Black Sea a twenty-day journey northwards. At its greatest extent the Scythian state probably stretched south of the Danube and across the Caucasus into Asia Minor.

The Scythians lived a life typical of nomads. They were effective in warfare and established a strong military state, so strong that not even the Persians could defeat them in their own territory. Herodotus describes their state as a tribal confederation ruled by the 'royal Scythians', who always provided the monarch and 'counted all other Scythians their slaves'. He also distinguishes the 'Scythian-farmers' and the 'Scythian-pastoralists', although it seems unlikely that the whole population of the region was Scythian. Some historians think that the successive waves of invaders formed only the ruling group in southern Russia while the bulk of the population was indigenous and continued steadily to develop their own culture.

Some time in the third century BC the Scythians were displaced by the Sarmatians, another wave of Iranian-speaking nomads from Central Asia, who ruled until the beginning of the third century AD. Sarmatian social organization was similar in many

ways to the Scythian, and they seem to have fitted easily into the culture and economy of the region.

It was during the Scythian-Sarmatian period that the interaction between Greek civilization and the nomadic way of life led to the appearance in the steppe and on the shores of the Black Sea of a highly-developed culture known as the Graeco-Iranian. The nomads brought a distinctive art and craftsmanship, especially in metal-work, and an original style in decorative art known as the Scythian animal style. They made no sustained effort to destroy the Greek colonies of southern Russia, but traded with them and developed other close contacts, thus making a distinctive contribution to classical civilization, and leaving their imprint on the land that was to become known as Russia.

Goths

Sarmatian rule in the steppe region north of the Black Sea was brought to an end in about 200 AD by the Goths, Germanic invaders from the north-east, probably from the region of the Baltic. They were divided into several tribes, of which the most important were known as the Ostrogoths and the Visigoths. The Ostrogothic empire in southern Russia reached its zenith under Hermanric (who reigned from about 350 to 370 AD), when it stretched from the Black Sea to the Baltic. Little is known of their system of administration, and their cultural level was probably considerably lower than that already prevailing in southern Russia. About 362 AD the Goths penetrated the Crimea, where they established town-like settlements and buried their princes and other notables in graves which often closely resemble earlier Scythian burial-mounds.

Huns

The empire of Hermanric was shattered by the Huns, who descended upon the Goths about 370 AD. The Huns, who came in a mass migration from Central Asia, are thought to have been originally a Turkish-speaking people with the addition of large groups of Mongols, but by the time they reached central Europe they were a much more mixed group containing large Iranian and Germanic elements they had conquered and absorbed in the course of their irresistible surge along the great steppe road from Asia into Europe. Although one of the most primitive peoples to break into southern Russia, the Huns had sufficient energy and military ability not only to conquer the region, but to go on to play a vital part in the period of the 'Great Migrations' in Europe. They penetrated deep into France and, although defeated at the battle of Châlons in 451, invaded Italy. However, with the sudden death of their leader, Attila, in 453, the primitive and poorly-organized Hunnic empire quickly disintegrated.

A ritual goblet from third century BC Azerbaijan

Avars

The Avars were another Turkic-Mongol group from Asia, whose invasion of southern Russia in 558, like that of the Huns, changed the whole political system of east-central Europe. It caused a new wave of migrations of Germanic and Iranian tribes, although on a more limited scale than the general displacement caused by the Huns. The centre of the Avar empire lay in the basin of the middle Danube, and at the height of their power their sway extended to eastern Russia. Control of Russia was lost after about a hundred years, but the Avar state lasted about two and a half centuries, in the course of which it threatened Byzantium and waged wars in the west against the empire of Charlemagne. In the end the Avar state fell quickly to pieces and disappeared virtually without trace – the common fate of politically weak nomad empires.

Khazars

The next organized power to emerge in Russia dates from the seventh century AD. This was the state of the Khazars, which covered the region of the lower Volga and the south-eastern Russian steppe. They were yet another Turkish-speaking people from Asia, whose arrival split up a powerful tribal confederation known as Great Bulgaria, which had occupied the region of the lower Volga and north Caucasus since the collapse of the Hunnic empire; one group settled in the Balkans, to be absorbed by the Slavs and give its name to present-day Bulgaria, while another went north-east and eventually established a prosperous trading state on the middle Volga.

The Khazar state lay in an even more favourable position across important trade routes, and the Khazars, although originally a nomadic people, built towns, developed commerce and played an important role in the international politics of the period. They fought stubbornly against the Arabs and succeeded in blocking the spread of Islam into Europe. In the eighth and ninth centuries the ruler and the upper class embraced Judaism – another curious development in an unusual history. The Khazar state survived until about the year 1000, although it never really recovered from the shattering series of blows dealt it by the Kievan prince Svyatoslav in 965.

Slavs

The history of the peoples and cultures of southern Russia before the ninth century AD forms an essential background to Kievan Russia, but the inhabitants of the Kievan state who became known as Russians were not Scythians, Huns or Khazars – they were Slavs. The first written references to the Slavs occur in early classical writers such as Pliny the Elder, and it is now assumed by many historians that the Slavs composed a significant part of the population of southern and central Russia from the time of the Scythians. Surviving successive invasions and migrations, they make their appearance in the Russian Primary Chronicle, where at the dawn of Kievan history a number of East Slavonic tribes are recorded paying tribute to the Khazars.   DSMW

THE LAND OF RUS'

The Russian Primary Chronicle (edited in the early twelfth century) opens by announcing its intention to reveal 'the origins of the land of Rus' . . . the source from which the land of Rus' had its beginning'. However, faced with a distant and undocumented past, the chronicler had to content himself with a stylized introduction to Russian history, much of which resembles myth or saga. He was not to know that he would thereby kindle a controversy which has yet to run its course.

According to the chronicle, three Scandinavian (Varangian) brothers, Ryurik, Sineus and Truvor, came with their followers to the land of Rus' (c. 860–62) in answer to an invitation from the local east Slav tribes: 'Our whole land is great and rich, but there is no order in it. Come to rule and reign over us.' Whether the brothers came from Denmark or Sweden remains unclear. Even less clear is the meaning of the term Rus', which is applied to them, as well as to their host land. But perhaps the most crucial question which remains unanswered concerns the extent of their influence and that of their successors on the Slavs who allegedly invited them.

The chronicle suggests that the land was 'great and rich'. Yet another long-standing controversy relates to the source of this apparent wealth. Were the peoples of Rus' principally engaged in agriculture or in trade? Archaeology tends to provide support for the former; the literary sources give preference to the latter. In either case, the new Varangian overlords undoubtedly imposed order by taxation. They also sought to increase prosperity by extending and safeguarding trade routes. Chief among these (and perhaps the lure which brought them to Rus') was the Dnieper–Black Sea route 'from the Varangians to the Greeks' which linked Scandinavia with the fabled wealth of Constantinople.

The lure of Constantinople

Thus Ryurik's associates Askol'd and Dir seized the township of Kiev (860) and used it as their base for an ambitious attack on Constantinople itself. The assault was not brought to a successful conclusion, but the Byzantines were never to forget it. It forced them to take cognizance of their bellicose northern

Kiev, with the statue of Prince Vladimir in the foreground

called the Byzantine capital). His expedition of 907 (if the evidence of the Russian chronicle is to be accepted) was successful enough to result in a favourable Russo-Byzantine treaty (911). Under Ryurik's son Igor' (913–45) two more expeditions were launched against Constantinople (941 and 944), resulting in a second treaty. Though somewhat less advantageous to the Russians than the first, it still provides evidence of the extent to which the two parties valued each other's trade and collaboration.

The baptism of Igor''s widow Ol'ga (regent 945–64) under the sponsorship of the Byzantine emperor paved the way for even closer collaboration. Ol'ga was received by the emperor in Constantinople itself (957). But her example was followed by few, and certainly not by the Kievan state as a whole. Ol'ga was widowed as the result of local Slav (Drevlian) resentment at her husband's main alternative source of income, tribute. The Drevlians had been required to pay an exceptionally heavy tribute after an earlier uprising against Igor'. In 945 they rose once more, captured Igor' and executed him. In the chronicle Ol'ga is remembered almost as much for the terrible revenge which she took on the Drevlians – she killed their envoys, burned their town and put 5,000 of its inhabitants to death – as for her subsequent conversion to the religion of mercy and peace.

Svyatoslav (962–72)

Askol'd and Dir had captured Kiev from the Khazars, whose empire lay to the south-east, centred on the Volga basin. Ol'ga's son Svyatoslav was to go further and to undermine the empire itself. He was a brilliant tactician – in the years 963–66 and again 968–69 he moved tirelessly from one victory to another – but he was deficient in strategy: he failed to exploit his dismemberment of Khazaria and moreover failed to compensate for it. In the process a buffer state vanished and Rus' was subjected to endless inroads from nomads who replaced the Khazars – at first the Pechenegs, subsequently the Polovtsy (Cumans). The Pechenegs demonstrated their new strength by killing Svyatoslav himself (972) as he returned from an abortive attempt to extend his power to the Balkans. Earlier, he intended to make Pereyaslavets on the Danube his capital (967), unabashed by the resulting confrontation with the combined forces of Bulgaria and Byzantium.

Svyatoslav's three sons were left to resolve their differences as to who should rule in Kiev. For Kiev, rather than Novgorod (where Ryurik settled), had by now acquired a pre-eminence which it was to retain, if only in theory, for many years to come. According to the Russian Primary Chronicle, it had been designated 'the mother of Russian cities' by Oleg as long ago as 882; the same chronicle

neighbours and to plan for their containment. It is not clear whether Askol'd and Dir became Christians before their death at the hands of Ryurik's councillor Oleg (882). But the eventual baptism of the Kievan rulers Ol'ga and Vladimir was clearly consonant with Byzantium's desire to reduce the risk of further such incursions.

Meanwhile, however, Oleg (882–912) followed Askol'd and Dir to Mikligard (as the Norsemen

Medieval stone icon found by archaeologists in Novgorod

contained a legend to the effect that its future site had once been blessed by no less a visitor than the Apostle Andrew.

Vladimir I (980–1015)

The would-be successors' struggle for power (unlike many that were to follow) was comparatively brief. Prince Vladimir emerged the sole survivor. In an attempt to unite the Rus' lands he fostered the creation of a pagan pantheon at Kiev. He furthered stabilization by regulating the collection of tribute from the various provincial capitals, in each of which he placed one of his twelve sons as ruler. He also sought to counteract the work of Svyatoslav by building a line of forts to the east as a protection against the Pechenegs. Instead of overextending his frontiers to the west, he attempted to stabilize them by capturing the Cherven cities' from Poland (981).

All this provides evidence of an astute mind, though it hardly prepares for that demonstration of statesmanship which was to ensure Vladimir's lasting fame and bring Rus' firmly within the bounds of the Byzantine commonwealth.

The conversion of Rus'

The creation of an indigenous pantheon could bring few benefits in the field of foreign relations. The Khazars had been converts to Judaism; the eastern Bulgars were Muslim; the homeland of the Varangians had recently turned to western Christianity, as had the Poles and Hungarians; to the south and south-west lay the Orthodox world, in the midst of which Svyatoslav had hoped to settle. The acceptance of any one of the great monotheistic religions would facilitate new alliances and further trade. Vladimir seems to have pondered the options for some time. Ultimately, he chose to follow his grandmother's example in his acceptance of Orthodox

Christianity. This choice was diplomatically the more attractive since support for the Byzantine emperor (Basil II) brought him the coveted reward of the emperor's sister in marriage. Vladimir's baptism (*c.* 988) was the necessary prelude to such a match.

In the event, the emperor was reluctant to proceed with his part of the bargain: Vladimir needed to capture the Crimean city of Kherson from the Byzantines (989) to prompt the despatch of his bride. He returned to Kiev later that year with the necessary zeal and support to initiate the accelerated (and often forcible) conversion of his subjects. It was a turning-point in Russian history.

The Russian Primary Chronicle paints an excessively laudatory portrait of the Christian Vladimir. But there is no reason to doubt the sincerity with which he accepted the new faith, nor the efficiency with which he established and disseminated it. Kiev was soon graced with a stone cathedral (990–96), church statutes were elaborated (996/1007–11) and bishoprics were established. However, the new faith was not enough to ensure amity among Vladimir's offspring. His death (1015) immediately provoked the kind of internecine strife which was to become a depressingly familiar feature of early Russian political life.

Yaroslav the Wise (1036–54)

The Kievan throne was now seized by Svyatopolk (1015–19). According to the subsequently elaborated narratives of the Chronicle, he immediately ordered the assassination of his rivals Boris, Gleb and Svyatoslav. If only on this account, Yaroslav of Novgorod disputed Svyatopolk's succession. The ensuing war (with Yaroslav supported by Varangians, Svyatopolk by Poles and Pechenegs) ended in victory for Yaroslav (1019).

But Yaroslav did not thereby become sole ruler of the Russian territories. Most important among his remaining rivals was Mstislav of Tmutarakan', whose successful struggle with Yaroslav (1024–26) ultimately ended in an agreement to divide the country, using the Dnieper as frontier. Yaroslav retained Novgorod, Kiev and the right (west) bank: Mstislav's territory extended from the left bank to include Chernigov and Pereyaslavl', as well as Tmutarakan'. Only Mstislav's death without issue (1036) reunited these areas.

Yaroslav's unchallenged reign proved to be an exceptional one. Though remarkable as much for consolidation as for innovation, it was to earn him the sobriquet *mudryy*, 'the wise'. Kiev gained notably in grandeur and prestige. Adam of Bremen (d.1074) went so far as to call it 'the rival of Constantinople's realm, the brightest ornament of the Greek [Orthodox] world'. Under Yaroslav began the construction of the great cathedral of St Sofia (1037–

Detail from the Russian Primary Chronicle depicting the marriage of Vladimir to Anna, daughter of the Byzantine emperor, Basil II, in 988

46). This was to be the seat of Kiev's metropolitan (the head of the Church), normally the legate of Constantinople. However, at one stage Yaroslav sponsored the election of a native Russian (Ilarion) to this exalted post (1051–52), as if to demonstrate his independence of the Byzantine world. Possibly by way of redress, he arranged the marriage of his son to a Byzantine princess (1052). It was one of many such marriages by which Yaroslav sought to cement good relations with the outside world. His own immediate family was linked to the royal families of Sweden, Norway, Poland, Hungary, France and Germany.

Yaroslav's work in the legal sphere was to prove more lasting than his diplomacy. Early in his career (about 1016) he had seen to the codification of Russian law (*Pravda russkaya*); this was revised and amplified two decades later. Although it began life as a local Novgorodian codex, it was to serve Russian law-makers as a source and model for centuries to come.

The troubled succession

Regrettably, Yaroslav seems to have developed no legislation or guidelines to regulate the complex succession to his throne. Though some kind of rota system may have been followed by his immediate successors, this would seem to have been the result of their pragmatic decisions rather than of any pre-conceived plan. Thus the death of Yaroslav presented a challenge to centralized government in the Kievan

realm, a challenge which it was ill-prepared to withstand. Only by the mutual agreement of Yaroslav's three most powerful successors – Izyaslav, Svyatoslav and Vsevolod – was fragmentation of the realm delayed. All three ruled successively in Kiev: Izyaslav, the eldest, with two significant interruptions, both caused by the popular discontent he provoked (1054–68, 1069–73 and 1077–78). Like Svyatopolk before him, Izyaslav regained his throne with Polish help in 1069. But neither Poles nor Germans were anxious to offer him support in his second exile, from which he returned briefly only on his supplanter's death.

That only one of Yaroslav's sons (Vsevolod) remained to rule in the years 1078–93 by no means ensured stability. Troubles were compounded by the appearance of a new enemy in the steppe. The defeat of the Pechenegs in Yaroslav's time had simply made way for the Polovtsy who from 1061 were to harass the Russian principalities. Worse, they were later to be employed by one principality against another.

The reign of Svyatopolk II (1093–1113) produced no resolution of Russia's political problems, despite the unprecedented attempt to bring them to the conference table at Lyubech in 1097. At first a reconciliation of the various princes and power groups seemed to have been achieved; but the very participants in the conference soon suspected one another of conspiracy, and the treacherous arrest and blinding of Yaroslav's grandson Vasil'ko (1097) revealed the fragility of that same year's agreements.

Vladimir Monomakh (1113–25)

Ironically, it was one of the staunchest defenders of the Lyubech accord who was to deviate from it and thus offer Kievan Rus' the security and stability which had evaded it for so long.

Vladimir Monomakh's reign in Kiev began democratically with an invitation from the Kievan *veche* (city assembly). The riots which preceded and provoked the invitation (as well as those which followed Monomakh's initial refusal to serve) were ended by his promptly effected social and fiscal reforms. His military prowess had already been displayed in his successful campaigns against the Polovtsy – notably in 1111. Such campaigns were to be continued by his son Yaropolk (1116 and 1126).

The authority of Vladimir rested, however, on more than the ability to wage war or conduct diplomacy. It is clear that his personal integrity was a cohesive force of paramount importance. Some indication of its character is provided by the magnificent *Testimony* (*Pouchenie*), incorporated into the Russian Primary Chronicle, which was edited and revised in his reign.

The fragmentation of Kievan Russia, 1054–1238

The twelve principalities of Russia in 1100

Ustyug
Belozersk
Ladoga
REPUBLIC OF NOVGOROD
VLADIMIR-SUZDAL
Reval
Novgorod
Yaroslavl'
Kostroma
R. Volga
Pskov
Torzhok
Rostov
Riga
Izborsk
Suzdal'
Vladimir
Tver'
VOLGA BULGARS
R. Dvina
Baltic Sea
Moscow
Murom
LITHUANIA
Polotsk
SMOLENSK
Ryazan'
Kovno
Vitebsk
MUROM-RYAZAN'
POLOTSK
Smolensk
Minsk
CHERNIGOV
POLAND
Pinsk
Turov
NOVGOROD-SEVERSK
R. Vistula
TUROV
Chernigov
Cracow
VOLYNIA
KIEV
PEREYASLAVL'
Kiev
GALICIA
Pereyaslavl'
Galich
Carpathian Mts
CUMANS or POLOVTSY
R. Dniester
R. Dnieper
R. Don
R. Volga
HUNGARY

0   500 km
0   250 miles

Black Sea

Constantinople

Muscovite Russia

The decline of Kiev

The days of Kiev's primacy were numbered. Mono-makh's sons Mstislav (1125–32) and Yaropolk (1132–39) were able to follow successfully in their father's footsteps, but the succeeding years saw end-less disputes and power struggles involving a prize of ever-decreasing value. Chernigov had long been an alternative centre of power. In the western regions, Galicia and Volynia (to be united in 1199) tended ever more to go their own way. And in the north-west, Novgorod had always retained a certain independence; it had its own trade connections via the Baltic with the west, and its mercantile concerns, as well as its distinctive form of government, were to further its separate development. Nowhere was the *veche* and its council to gain such status, nowhere was the prince to become so much its servant.

The city of Vladimir

Kiev could no longer hope to influence (let alone control) Novgorod after 1136, and a hitherto com-paratively obscure principality of the north-east began to manifest its pretensions in this respect by the mid-twelfth century. With the accession of the most forceful of Monomakh's grandsons, Andrey, to the throne of Rostov and Suzdal' (1157–74), the centre of gravity was to move to his newly established capital Vladimir on the Klyaz'ma. The succeeding half-century saw Vladimir's embellish-ment as rival and supplanter of Kiev. Its impressive Cathedral of the Assumption (*Uspenskiy sobor*) (1158–60/1185–89) still stands as a memorial to Andrey's ambitions, which were fully shared by his successor, Vsevolod III (1176–1212). The decline of Kiev was calculatedly emphasized by Andrey, who captured and sacked the old capital in 1169 but spurned it as his seat.

Right. The plundering of Kiev by the Tatars, from a mid-sixteenth century miniature in the Illustrated History of Chronicles

The end of Kievan Rus'

In due course Vladimir itself suffered depredations and decline. Six years before the death of Vsevolod III, a 'supreme emperor' had been proclaimed in the Far East: in Mongolian his title read 'Chingis [or Genghis] Khan'. By 1223 his advance battalions entered Polovtsian territory from the south on a victorious reconnaissance for the main Mongol army. A combined force of Russians and Polovtsy was defeated by them on the Kalka River (1223). The Mongols' subsequent withdrawal should have engendered no complacency for they were to return in full force (1237). Ultimately only a few western cities were to escape the widespread destruction which established Mongol suzerainty and ushered in a new age.

THE MONGOL CONQUEST

In the autumn of 1237 a Mongol army led by Batu, grandson of Genghis Khan, swooped down upon the Russian city of Ryazan'. This was the beginning of the Mongol invasion of the 'western lands', the final stage in a programme of conquest planned by an assembly of Mongol chieftains in 1206. Batu's army then proceeded methodically through north-eastern Russia, capturing and sacking many cities, including Vladimir on the Klyaz'ma, which fell in February 1238. By the time the Mongols (or Tatars as they are more commonly known in the Russian sources) arrived there Prince Yury Vsevolodovich, grand prince of Vladimir, had left the town (trusting that its strong walls would protect it) and retreated north-wards with his army. He hoped that a long march of pursuit would weaken the invaders; but he under-estimated the toughness and endurance of the Mongol horsemen, who could spend long hours in the saddle with little need for food or rest. When Batu's army caught up with Yury on the banks of the river Sit' the Russians were defeated and Yury himself was killed. Batu then turned west, towards the wealthy commercial city of Novgorod. However Novgorod was saved by a change in the weather: in 1238 the spring thaw came unusually early, making the ground too swampy for Batu's mounted troops to advance.

Alexander Nevsky

Alexander Nevsky is one of Russia's most revered historic figures. His name has been invoked in times of crisis by leaders as disparate as Peter the Great and Stalin, and he retains a prominent position in the folklore of the country to this day.

Alexander was the son of Yaroslav I, Prince of Vladimir. When only in his early twenties, he was invited by the leaders of Novgorod to become their prince. The city was unique in Russia at that time in that its civilian leaders formed the seat of real power; the prince's responsibilities were strictly limited to military leadership, and on at least one occasion Novgorod's prince was dismissed by the people. Alexander's victories against first the Swedes in 1240 and then the Teutonic (or Livonian) Knights in 1242 consolidated his position as prince, but it was his diplomatic skills in dealing with the Mongol invaders that were to keep him there.

Alexander ruled Novgorod as an ally of the Mongol horde, and by doing so prevented the invasions and destruction that occurred elsewhere in Russia. At the time this policy was the cause of much bitterness, but in later years it came to be

seen as the salvation of much of the culture and, more importantly, the religion, of north-western Russia.

In 1380 Alexander, who had taken monastic vows on his deathbed, was canonized by the Orthodox Church. He was already a hero of the Church, as Muscovite monks writing down his story had infused it with anti-Catholicism; his victories were now seen not just as successes against invading forces from the west, but as triumphs over the Roman enemy.

Peter the Great sought legitimacy for his new city by transferring the remains of the warrior-monk from their resting-place in Vladimir to a new monastery in St Petersburg. Stalin used his name in a call-to-arms at the beginning of the 'Great Patriotic War'. The film *Alexander Nevsky* (1938) by Eisenstein, had music by Prokofiev subsequently reworked as a cantata. These are just two twentieth-century examples of many artistic works about this first great hero of Russia.

Fresco depicting Alexander Nevsky by Simon Ushakov, 1666. Cathedral of the Archangel Michael, the Kremlin, Moscow

During the year 1239 Batu undertook no major campaigns; then in the summer of 1240 he struck again, this time in a south-westerly direction. The cities of Chernigov and Pereyaslavl' were captured and sacked, and finally Kiev itself, in December 1240. This completed the conquest of Russia and inaugurated the period of Mongol overlordship described in Russian chronicles as the 'Tatar yoke', which was to last for nearly two and a half centuries. At the same time as the Russians faced the Mongol onslaught they were also threatened from the west, by the armies of Sweden and the Teutonic Knights, who attacked Novgorod in 1240 and Pskov in 1242. Both attacks were repulsed by the prince of Novgorod, Alexander Nevsky (so called for his victory over the Swedes on the Neva River, 1240), his second victory being the famous Battle of the Ice on Lake Peipus. The scale of this engagement has probably been exaggerated by posterity, but this has not lessened Alexander Nevsky's importance as a warrior hero and cult figure.

The Tatar yoke

After 1240 the whole of what was formerly Kievan Russia became part of the vast Mongol empire, of which it formed the western section. Batu, now its khan, or ruler, established his capital at Saray near the mouth of the Volga. At first this was a large camp, since the Mongols continued to follow their nomadic life-style, but in time it became more like a conventional town, with settled inhabitants.

The khan and his entourage at Saray were known collectively as the Golden Horde (from the word *orda*, meaning camp). The Golden Horde did not administer the conquered territory as a single unit, a fact which was to influence the future course of Russian history. The middle Dnieper area was ruled directly from Saray by Mongol officials, while the rest of Russia remained under the control of its princes, as vassals of the Golden Horde. This meant that each prince had to go to Saray, make a formal act of obeisance to the khan and then receive a *yarlyk* or patent authorizing him to rule his principality, though under the watchful eye of a resident Mongol overseer called a *baskak*. The *yarlyk* had to be renewed every time there was a new prince or khan, so that visits to Saray became part of the normal pattern of life for the Russian princes. Sometimes they would spend many months there, competing for the khan's favour by means of bribes and flattery, since this was the surest way to political success in their quarrels with each other. Only two princes, Daniil of Galicia and Alexander Nevsky's brother Andrey, attempted serious military resistance; both

Mongol archers depicted in a Persian manuscript of the fourteenth century

were forced into submission by Mongol counter-attacks.

To the ordinary people Mongol rule meant two things: financial tribute and compulsory military service. The Mongols, who used the decimal system, at first demanded a tenth of everything. Later the tribute was commuted to money payments, assessed separately for towns and rural areas. The tribute was first collected by tax-farmers, then subsequently, after the reign of Khan Mengu-Temir (1266–79), by specially appointed tax-gatherers. Finally under Khan Uzbeg (1313–41) the duty of collecting taxes became the prerogative of the leading Russian princes. For military service the

Reconstruction of medieval Novgorod, even the roadway formed from a corduroy of logs

Mongols conscripted 10 per cent of the male population; they also forced many skilled craftsmen to work for them. In order to make accurate assessments for the purpose of taxation and conscription the Russian population was 'counted', in four successive stages, during the second half of the thirteenth century.

The heavy burden of taxation and conscription, following after the devastation caused by the invasions, had a depressing effect on the economy of the Russian lands. Outside the city of Novgorod, which reached the height of its prosperity during the fourteenth and fifteenth centuries, commerce declined and the Russian economy became more agrarian in character. As a result landowners became the most important social and economic group in the community; this led Soviet historians to describe this period of Russian history as 'feudal'. (It must be noted, however, that this term does not mean the same as it does when applied to western Europe in earlier centuries.)

The Church under Mongol rule

The period of Mongol rule proved important in the development of the Orthodox Church in Russia. Khan Mengu-Temir issued a *yarlyk* exempting all church lands from taxation, and all people working on them from military service. The Church thus became a specially privileged institution. The reason for this was that it was part of Mongol tradition, preserved in a document known as the Great Yasa, 'to respect the learned and wise men of all peoples', and the monks and priests of the Orthodox Church were so regarded in the lands subject to the Golden Horde. In time these privileges proved to be double-edged: they strengthened the Russian Church as an institution, and thus helped it to keep alive such cultural activities as chronicle-writing and icon-painting; but increasing wealth also led to worldliness and corruption among some of the monks and clergy. Moreover in time princes began to covet church lands, which caused tension between secular rulers and church authorities.

Although the Russian Church continued to be a single unit of ecclesiastical administration controlled by a metropolitan appointed and consecrated by the patriarch of Constantinople, from the beginning of the fourteenth century onwards it became more national in character: a number of Russian metropolitans were appointed, and Russian princes made determined efforts to secure the election of favoured candidates. At times this caused tension with the patriarchs of Constantinople, but the formal tie of dependence continued until 1448, when a synod of Russian bishops elected one of their own number as metropolitan because of their opposition to the act of union with the Western Church signed at the Council of Florence in 1439. From then on the Russian Church had its own head. There were also attempts to establish a separate area of jurisdiction with its own metropolitan in the west Russian lands which had been wrested from the Mongols and conquered by the Lithuanians during the fourteenth century. But these attempts did not prove to be permanent.

Monastic life flourished during the period of Mongol rule: at least 180 monasteries are known to have been founded, including the famous Trinity Monastery of St Sergy, founded by St Sergy of Radonezh, and the Solovetsky Monastery founded in 1429 on an island in the White Sea. Both these houses, and many others, owed their foundation to a revival of the ascetic ideals and practices of early Christian monasticism, of which St Sergy was a notable exponent. As many monasteries were founded in hitherto uninhabited areas, they performed an important economic role by attracting settlers and opening up new lands to agriculture.   MH

The rise of Moscow, 1261–1533

Principality of Moscow by 1462

Further expansion of Moscow by 1533

THE RISE OF MOSCOW

In the years after the Mongol conquest the process of political fragmentation and resultant inter-princely strife continued, a fact which helped the Golden Horde to maintain its supremacy. However, during the fourteenth century, one principality achieved a position of political predominance: Moscow.

At the time of the Mongol invasions Moscow was a relatively minor city of the grand principality of Vladimir, which did not acquire the status of a separate principality with its own prince until 1301, when it was assigned to Daniil, a younger son of Alexander Nevsky. It was then a modest 1,300 sq km in extent, an area which Daniil's descendants were to increase thirtyfold.

However, territorial expansion was not the only factor in Moscow's rise to power. While it was still quite small one of its early rulers, Ivan I (1325–40), usually known as *Kalita* or 'Moneybag', acquired the coveted *yarlyk* for the office of grand prince of Vladimir, though he had to share it with Prince Alexander Vasil'evich of Suzdal' until the latter's death in 1331. This title conferred special prestige on its holder since he was considered the most senior of all the Russian princes. For some years this *yarlyk* had been ferociously contested between the princes of Moscow and those of Tver', who belonged to a more senior branch of the prolific Ryurikovichi (the descendants of Ryurik). It was only after Ivan I had helped the Golden Horde to suppress a popular revolt in Tver' in 1327 that he was finally granted the *yarlyk* as a reward. From then on it was held almost exclusively by the princes of Moscow, though not always without a struggle. The Moscow princes also benefited from their position as the chief financial agents of the Golden Horde, and from the transference of the seat of the metropolitan of the Russian Church to Moscow after 1328.

During the middle decades of the fourteenth century the Golden Horde itself became prey to internal dissensions, a fact which proved advantageous to the Russian principalities, especially Moscow. Palace (or tent) revolutions were frequent, and between 1360 and 1380 there were 25 khans, some of whom reigned only a few weeks. In such circumstances the Golden Horde was in no position to enforce the payment of tribute, much of which went into the coffers of the prince of Moscow. However, later in the century a vigorous grand vizier named Mamay assumed effective power at Saray and demanded the payment of arrears, even organizing a punitive expedition to enforce his request.

The prince of Moscow at this time was Dmitry Ivanovich, a grandson of Ivan I. Although he was somewhat reluctant to risk a military confrontation with the Mongols, when he heard that their army

Ivan I, known as Kalita: 'Moneybag'

was advancing towards Moscow he decided to resist it, with help from some other Russian princes. The armies met at Kulikovo Field near the river Don on 8 September 1380, and after a hard-fought battle the Russians emerged victorious; in honour of this victory Prince Dmitry came to be known as Dmitry Donskoy ('Victor of the Don').

The battle of Kulikovo certainly did not mean the end of the 'Tatar yoke'; indeed two years later a Mongol army raided and burnt Moscow and re-enforced the payment of tribute for some years. But the victory of Kulikovo is rightly considered an important landmark in Russian history because it shattered the legend of the military invincibility of the Mongols.

During the rest of the reign of Dmitry Donskoy and those of his successors Vasily I (1389–1425) and Vasily II (1425–62) Moscow further increased its territory and maintained its political predominance, in spite of a prolonged internal dynastic conflict during the reign of Vasily II. It was his son Ivan III and his grandson Vasily III who were destined to bring all the east Russian lands under their rule, and lay the foundations of a united Russian state. MH

IVAN III (1462–1505)

Ivan III, sometimes known as Ivan the Great, became grand prince of Moscow and Vladimir in 1462. Although he inherited a territory many times larger than that of his ancestor Prince Daniil Alexandrovich, there were even larger areas of the future Russian state which lay outside his control. It was to be his major achievement to bring these under his rule. They comprised two different types of territory: appanages within Muscovy granted to his four younger brothers, and independent principalities ruled by their own princes, descended, like Ivan III himself, from different branches of the Ryurikovich dynasty. The most important of these principalities were Yaroslavl', Rostov, Ryazan' and Tver', Moscow's ancient rival.

Territorial unification

In the task of territorial unification Ivan III displayed both political acumen and diplomatic skill, but he was also helped by good luck. For example two of his brothers, Yury and Andrey the Younger, died without heirs and their appanages reverted to Ivan. Uglich, the appanage of Andrey the Elder, was confiscated because he refused to participate in a campaign against the Kazan' Tatars. The regions outside Muscovy were likewise acquired by varied means; the princes of Yaroslavl' and Rostov renounced their sovereign rights in return for financial compensation

Ivan III

(in 1463 and 1474 respectively); Tver' was annexed in 1485 when its prince tried to make an alliance with Casimir IV of Poland (thus breaking the terms of a previous treaty with Moscow); Ryazan' came under Ivan's control (though not formally annexed) as the result of a dynastic marriage, arranged between its heir, Prince Vasily Ivanovich and Ivan III's sister in 1464.

Perhaps Ivan III's most difficult task was the subjugation of the city-republic of Novgorod, which controlled a vast colonial territory. Although nominally part of the grand principality of Vladimir, Novgorod had long been autonomous, governed by officials appointed by its own *veche*. Relations with the suzerain princes of Moscow had often been tense, but it was Ivan III who finally abolished the political privileges of Novgorod. The circumstances of the final confrontation in 1477 were complicated, and Ivan III was able to take advantage of social and political dissensions within the city which provided him with an opportunity for intervention.

The acquisition of so much new territory raised problems of administration. Ivan III tried to centralize this as much as possible, by appointing provincial governors responsible to himself, known as *namestniki*. In some cases, however, their powers were modified by local charters making specific administrative and judicial arrangements for those areas. A few of these have survived, for example the Beloozero Charter of 1488, which provides for some participation by elected local inhabitants. In 1497 he issued a *Sudebnik* or law-code to establish uniform legal norms throughout his dominions.

Border consolidation

Ivan III pursued a vigorous foreign policy in relation to his immediate neighbours, the Tatar khanates and the grand principality of Lithuania, itself dynastically linked to the kingdom of Poland. In the middle of the fifteenth century the once-powerful Golden Horde split up into three separate units: the Crimean Tatars (under the suzerainty of the Ottoman Empire after 1475), the Kazan' khanate and the so-called Great Horde, or remnants of the Golden Horde.

Although the overlordship of the Golden Horde had become merely nominal even before Ivan III's accession, and was formally renounced in 1480, the Tatars remained dangerous neighbours because of their frequent and destructive raids into Russian territory. Ivan III attempted to neutralize this danger in two ways: he cultivated friendly relations with the Crimean Tatars and made a treaty of alliance with their khan Mengli-Girey in 1480; in the case of Kazan' he intervened in its internal political power struggles with a view to securing subservient and pro-Russian khans. Several military expeditions

Vasily III

against Kazan' were organized for this purpose during Ivan III's reign.

Ivan's policy towards Lithuania was more aggressive, since he regarded the Dnieper area which the Lithuanians had conquered from the Mongols as part of his territorial patrimony. At first activities against Lithuania were limited to border skirmishes, the so-called 'small war' of 1487–94, in which Ivan III was not even officially involved; but from 1500 to 1503 there was a period of open warfare in which Russian troops had considerable success, though they failed to take the important city of Smolensk. The war was concluded by a six-year truce, leaving Russia in possession of all the territory it had occupied.

Ivan III's last years were darkened by quarrels within his family as to who should succeed him, the main protagonists being Yelena, the wife of his deceased eldest son Ivan, and his masterful second wife Sofia Paleologue (niece of the last Byzantine emperor), each of whom desired the succession of her own son. Ivan finally decided in favour of his eldest son by Sofia, who succeeded him as Vasily III in 1505.   MH

VASILY III (1505–33)

Under Vasily III the administration of the Russian state was consolidated and its territory further extended, notably by the annexation of Ryazan' and Pskov (formerly a subsidiary town of Novgorod), and the capture of Smolensk. The circumstances following the annexation of Pskov gave rise to the dictum describing Moscow as the Third Rome, and thus by implication the heir of the Byzantine Empire recently conquered by the Ottoman Turks. The famous words occur in a letter written by the monk Filofey, member of a monastery near Pskov, urging Vasily III to be less harsh in his treatment of the citizens of that town.   MH

IVAN IV, THE TERRIBLE (1533–84)

Ivan the Terrible

When Vasily III died in 1533 he was succeeded by his eldest son, Ivan, then only three years old; hence a regency was necessary. In 1547 Ivan IV announced that he was of age to govern, and his first official act was to have himself crowned tsar in a ceremony closely modelled on that used for the coronation of the Byzantine emperors, his crown being the legendary Cap of Monomakh, said to have been presented to Ivan's ancestor Vladimir Monomakh by his own imperial grandfather, Constantine IX. Ivan IV, generally known as Ivan the Terrible (though this word does not accurately render the Russian word *Groznyy* by which he was known and some historians term him 'The Dread'), possessed qualities which promised well for his task as ruler of Russia, including physical energy, a keen intelligence and an awareness of the needs of his large but backward realm. Unfortunately these were counterbalanced by an over-exalted sense of the importance of his office, a deep suspicion of others that amounted to paranoia, and an uncontrolled aggression.

His reign began with a series of useful administrative, legal and military reforms, including the promulgation of a revised *Sudebnik* in 1550. In this task the tsar was assisted by a group of able advisers known as the Chosen Council. But this 'good phase' did not last: in 1565 Ivan IV's morbid suspicion of all those around him, especially the boyars (representatives of the titled and non-titled senior nobility and aristocracy), caused him to divide his country into two parts, one of which was placed under his complete personal dictatorship. This was known as the *oprichnina*, 'special court territory' or 'realm apart'. Within this area the tsar's will was enforced by the *oprichniki* or members of the 'special court'. Before long their activities spread beyond the boundaries of the *oprichnina* and subjected the entire Russian land to a reign of terror, culminating in a large-scale massacre of the citizens of Novgorod in 1569 (on the pretext of treasonable plotting with the king of Poland), and a similar pogrom in Moscow in 1572. The activities of the *oprichniki* then gradually diminished, but not before they had inflicted immense physical and psychological damage on the country.

Ivan IV's reign opened well in the sphere of foreign policy. His grandfather's attempts to curtail the aggressive activities of the Tatar khanates by means of alliances and pro-Russian puppet rulers had broken down, and it was clear that bolder measures were necessary. Ivan IV therefore undertook three campaigns against the Kazan' khanate with a view to annexing its territory; the third of these, in 1552, was successful. Some of his advisers thought that he should then have turned against the Crimean Tatars; but he preferred to pursue a policy of westward expansion at the expense of Lithuania and the Livonian Order who controlled the Baltic coast. This involved him in a complex series of military operations known as the Livonian War (1558–83). In spite of some setbacks, a considerable amount of territory was occupied by the Russian armies; but all this was lost when the new Polish king Stefan Batory organized a series of determined counter-offensives (1578–81).

Ivan IV's strong desire for more contact with the West, an area in which he anticipated Peter the Great, also caused him to welcome Richard

Procession of Russian boyars, followed by merchants trading in furs, at the Court of the Holy Russian Emperor, Maximillian II. Woodcut by Michael Peterle, 1576

Chancellor and the English sailors who made their way overland from the mouth of the Northern Dvina River to Moscow in 1553. This resulted in the establishment of regular trade with England conducted by the Muscovy Company, founded in 1555.   MH

FEDOR I (1584–98)

Fedor I

Ivan IV was succeeded by his eldest surviving son Fedor. He was intensely interested in religious observances and had little taste or aptitude for the tasks of government. These were consequently left to his advisers, especially his brother-in-law, the boyar Boris Godunov. Under his direction Russia gradually recovered from the stresses of the years preceding Fedor's accession, and further progress was made in the economic development and colonization of Siberia, which had begun under Ivan IV. Fedor's reign also saw the gradual erosion of the freedom of movement of the peasantry, which had been guaranteed, though on a restricted basis, by the *Sudebniki* of 1497 and 1550. This process was closely linked with the increase in the number of *pomest'e* estates (land granted in return for military service) for which it was essential to secure an adequate labour force.   MH

BORIS GODUNOV (1598–1605)

Fedor I's death in 1598 marked the end of the Ryurikovich dynasty. The succession problem was solved by the election of Boris Godunov as tsar, by an assembly known as the *Zemsky sobor* (Assembly of the Land); although this consisted mainly of boyars, ecclesiastical dignitaries and service gentry, it also included some representative elements. Boris Godunov proved an intelligent and efficient ruler, but nevertheless he was not popular; the older nobility resented his authority, and he was suspected of having contrived the murder of Ivan IV's youngest son Dmitry, who had died in mysterious circumstances in 1591. Boris hoped that his son might succeed him; but in fact his sudden death in 1605

Right. Boris Godunov, immortalized in the nineteenth century by Pushkin and by Musorgsky's famous opera of 1874

was followed by a prolonged succession crisis, only finally resolved by the election of Mikhail Romanov as tsar in 1613.   MH

THE TIME OF TROUBLES

The years between the death of Boris Godunov and the accession of Mikhail Romanov are usually known as the *Smutnoe vremya* (Time of Troubles).

Right. *Fedor III, depicted in the manner of an icon by the Russian painter, B. Saltanov*

This was a period of civil war in which the issues were very confused, since the search for a ruler was complicated by smouldering social discontent, political tensions and the dynastic ambitions of the king of Poland. The prominent part played by successive pretenders claiming to be the Tsarevich Dmitry was symptomatic of the deep-seated malaise in Russia at that time.   MH

THE EARLY ROMANOVS

During the period 1613–82 Russia was ruled by three tsars: Mikhail Romanov (1613–45), his son Aleksey (1645–76) and his grandson Fedor III (1676–82). Seen in retrospect, this time appears relatively calm and uneventful compared with the tumultuous and dynamic periods which preceded and followed. However, it was by no means a time of stagnation; old problems continued to exercise the minds of rulers and their advisers, and important new developments in home and foreign policy were initiated.

The first task of Mikhail Romanov after his election was the restoration of internal order; this included the expulsion of the Poles and Swedes who had occupied Moscow and other places during the Time of Troubles. It was also necessary to regulate the government's relations with the Cossacks, who had played an active part in the recent unrest, and to restore the country's shattered economy. This involved increasing the financial burdens of the already oppressed peasantry; there was also further economic development in Siberia, which in 1637 acquired its own *prikaz* or government office. Dur-

Tsar Aleksey Mikhailovich

ing the earlier part of his reign Mikhail Romanov was much influenced by his masterful father, Patriarch Filaret, who had been forced to retire to monastic life by Boris Godunov.

In foreign policy the most important development during this period was the continuation of Russia's westward territorial expansion into the middle and lower Dnieper area, the area later generally known as Ukraine. This was closely linked with the government's relations with the Dnieper and Zaporozhian Cossacks who inhabited the region. Nominally subjects of the king of Poland, the Cossacks were Orthodox in religion and disinclined to submit to any kind of rigid governmental control. In 1653 Bogdan Khmel'nitsky, the elected *hetman* or leader of the Zaporozhian Cossacks offered to place his followers, who then included the Dnieper Cossacks, under the suzerainty of Tsar Aleksey instead of that of the king of Poland. After some hesitation this offer was accepted. Not surprisingly it led to war between Russia and Poland, the progress of which was

The entry into Moscow, 1613, of Tsar Mikhail Romanov

complicated by the intervention of Poland's inveterate enemy Sweden, and dissensions amounting to civil war among the Cossacks themselves. This war was concluded by the Treaty of Andrusovo in 1667, which left Russia in control of the left bank of the Dnieper, including Kiev.

The Assembly of the Land

An interesting aspect of this period of Russian history was the participation of the *Zemsky sobor* (Assembly of the Land). It met ten times in Mikhail's reign and several times during that of Aleksey, who consulted it in 1653 on the issue of accepting suzerainty over the Zaporozhian and Dnieper Cossacks. Though not empowered to initiate legislation, it could present petitions, and much of the content of the enlarged law-code of 1649 known as the *Sobornoe ulozhenie* was based on such petitions.

The Old Believers schism

The reign of Aleksey saw the first and only major conflict between the secular and ecclesiastical power in Russia, which culminated, in 1668, in the formal deposition of Patriarch Nikon. He had tried to introduce changes in ritual designed to bring the Russian Church into conformity with other Orthodox communions, particularly the Greek. Though seemingly trivial on the surface, Nikon's reforms and his manner of introducing them symbolized deeper changes in the Russian Church and roused strong opposition among the more conservative elements. Some of these eventually broke away and formed a schismatic group known as the Old Believers.

Patriarch Nikon

Enserfment

All these developments contain some element or promise of progress in the Russian state; but the position of the peasants remained economically and culturally backward, while their legal status further deteriorated as a result of the removal of any time limit for reclaiming runaway peasants, which was included in the *Sobornoe ulozhenie* of 1649. This completed the process of the enserfment of the Russian peasantry, which lasted until 1861. The discontent of the peasants with their hard conditions led to frequent desperate attempts to seek escape by flight, and occasionally to uprisings. One of these, under the leadership of the Cossack Sten'ka Razin in 1670–71, reached the dimensions of a major rebellion, which was brutally suppressed. Russia at the threshold of the modern age thus carried a burden which undoubtedly hindered progress. MH

Imperial Russia

PETER THE GREAT (1682–1725)

The death of Fedor III in 1682 left no clear heir to the throne, and brought to a head conflict between the factions at court. The election as tsar of ten-year-old Peter (1672–1725), son of Aleksey Romanov's second wife, was overturned in a bloody *coup d'état*. Peter's half-sister Sofia (1657–1704) seized power as regent, creating her sickly brother Ivan (1666–96) co-tsar with Peter.

In the following years Peter lived away from court and was left largely to his own devices. This unorthodox education freed him from the constraints of Muscovite tradition, and gave scope both to his great energy and to the passion for things military which were to become hallmarks of his reign. Discovery of an old boat led to a fascination with ships and the sea, and ultimately to the creation of a powerful navy. The 'toy regiments' recruited for his amusement from among noble companions and serving-boys helped him to overthrow Sofia in 1689, and later became the Guards regiments which formed the élite of his modernized army. Only after his mother's death in 1694 did Peter personally take up the reins of government, and it was characteristic that his first major undertaking was military: an attack upon the Turkish fortress of Azov in 1695.

The technical problems which he encountered before he was able to reduce Azov in 1696, as well as a desire to revitalize the international alliance of the 1680s against the Turks, took Peter on a 'Grand

The Grand Embassy

The purpose of Peter the Great's Grand Embassy, which set off in March 1697, was to develop a military coalition against the Ottoman Empire. This kind of embassy was far from unusual in Muscovite history. However, Peter's presence made the expedition something very much out of the ordinary. He became the first Russian sovereign to cross the borders of his state on a peaceful mission for over 700 years.

Peter decided to travel incognito, using the name Peter Mikhailov. However, he did not go unrecognized by the many officials and rulers and ordinary people that he met (perhaps because he was remarkably tall, even by today's standards). While much of his time was spent in discussions about the putative alliance against the Turks, he concentrated most of his energy in learning from the West.

The extent of this learning process was not limited to practical concerns: Peter studied everything from culture to clothes and manners, with an eye to taking them back to Russia. It was, though, technical expertise and skills that he most sought. He was particularly interested in ships, an

Peter the Great dressed as a ship's carpenter

infant technology in his own country. Peter had had from an early age an obsessive interest in boats and all things nautical; indeed, in 1694 he had established a dockyard at the White Sea port of

Arkhangel'sk, and designed and built his own sea-going ship there.

One of the most famous stories about the Grand Embassy was the period that Peter spent as a carpenter at the Dutch shipyards at Zaandam and Amsterdam; the small hut where he is supposed to have lived in the former still stands. Peter also came to England, met King William III, and, as elsewhere, visited dockyards, factories and other places where he sought new ideas, and skilled workers to develop those ideas in Russia.

Peter returned home in the summer of 1698 to deal with an attempted revolt. He took with him many ideas for improving Russia, and in particular its military. It is doubtful, though, how much he fully absorbed; his progress across Europe was marked by the drunken orgies of which he was so fond, and he left behind a trail of destruction and shocked and outraged dignitaries. The diarist John Evelyn, who had lent Peter the use of his house at Deptford, near London, had good reason to remember the tsar's visit: it was said that everything breakable in both house and garden had been wrecked!

Princess Sofia, as depicted by the nineteenth-century Realist painter Il'ya Repin

Embassy' to Western Europe in 1697–98. The journey proved seminal. It showed Peter that the anti-Turkish alliance was dead, and turned his eyes northwards to the Swedish territories on the Baltic: with Augustus of Poland he planned an attack on Sweden which opened the Great Northern War (1700–21). It showed him, too, the wealth and the power of the world beyond Muscovy's borders.

Reforms

The tasks of fighting Sweden, and of modernizing his country along advanced, Western, lines, became Peter's two major preoccupations of the next twenty-five years. Each fed upon the other. 'War was the mother of the Petrine reforms' in so far as it compelled Peter to change the country's governmental and economic structure, in order to withstand the power of Charles XII of Sweden and to underpin the huge land and sea forces which Muscovy built up. The decisive battle of the war was Peter's crushing victory over Charles at Poltava (1709); although in 1711 he suffered near-disaster on the river Pruth at the hands of the Turks, with whom Charles had taken refuge. The end came in 1721, with the Treaty of Nystad, which showed the balance of power decisively in Muscovy's favour. To mark the peace, Peter assumed the title of emperor:

Peter the Great, painted in London by Sir Godfrey Kneller when he arrived with the Grand Embassy in January 1698

of administration and policy was vested in a new Senate. The Russian Orthodox Church was subordinated to the state: a Holy Synod under a lay Procurator replaced the patriarchate (established in 1589).

Attempts to reorganize provincial and municipal government remained unsuccessful. More effective were Peter's efforts to mobilize the financial and human resources of the nation. The capitation or 'soul' tax, levied on every male subject, nobles and clergy excepted, largely solved the government's constant need for greater tax revenue. The upper classes were also pressed into more effective service. The Inheritance Law of 1714 and the Table of Ranks (1722) provided a closely co-ordinated service structure for the nobility. Under Peter their position as land- and serf-owners was consolidated, but so were their obligations to the state.

Peter's reforms were conducted at first on an *ad hoc* basis, under the pressures of the time; after Poltava he had the leisure, and the experience, to be more systematic. His measures were informed by a rationalistic, pragmatic spirit which reflected the political wisdom of contemporary Europe. They reached down to the minutiae of popular daily life; and they contributed to a strengthening of state power at home which was as great as the influence on the international scene achieved through the defeat of Sweden. However, the range and the speed of change were bound to provoke opposition, even though little that Peter did was totally without precedent. His ruthless subjection of all classes to the vastly expanded demands of the state, his subjugation of the Church, his insistence on Western forms and skills, all produced discontent and resistance. The most important of several popular opposition movements was Kondraty Bulavin's Cossack revolt of 1707–08.

Among the upper classes conservative dissent was kept in check by brutal police methods, but crystallized around the feckless heir apparent, the Tsarevich Aleksey. Confrontation between father and son led finally to the death of Aleksey (1690–1718) under interrogation and torture in 1718, and Peter changed the law of succession to safeguard his reforms. The new law of 1722, repealed only at the end of the century (1797), provided for the monarch to choose his own heir. But Peter's death in 1725 was too sudden to allow him to make the choice.   RPB

Muscovite Russia became the Russian Empire.

But if military imperatives hastened the transformation of Muscovy, Peter's wars were themselves only means to a greater end which that transformation also served, the establishment of Russia as a great European power. His broader aspirations are represented by the elegant Western architecture of his new port and capital, St Petersburg, founded in 1703 on territory captured from Sweden, and by the Academy of Sciences, set up in 1725 after previous consultation with G.W. Leibnitz.

Renewal and expansion of the armed forces were followed by reforms in almost every sphere. The central government administration was reorganized into a system of boards or Colleges; co-ordination

CATHERINE I (1725–27)

The grandees around the throne at once sought to fill the vacuum left by the absence of an official successor. The crown now passed to Peter's widow, his second wife Catherine (1684–1727, Martha

Skavronska, Catherine I), a woman of low birth and little education from Livonia. Captured in Peter's early Baltic campaigns, she was the mistress of Field-Marshal Sheremet'ev (1652–1719), then of Peter's close assistant Prince Aleksandr Menshikov (1673–1729), before moving to Peter's own bed and subsequently becoming his wife and empress. Now she owed her elevation essentially to Menshikov and to the Guards regiments which he brought to the palace to acclaim her. Menshikov was also of common birth; and during Catherine's reign he was all-powerful. The new rulers' low social origin again reflected Peter's assault on Muscovite tradition, although the ruling élite continued to be drawn largely from old families. The intervention of the Guards in the succession set a fashion for the rest of the century.   RPB

PETER II (1727–30), AND ANNA (1730–40)

Under Catherine, who took no interest in matters of state, power had been exercised by a Supreme Privy Council in which Menshikov played an important role. The Council retained power under her successor Peter II (1715–30), the young son of the ill-fated Tsarevich Aleksey, although Menshikov lost his position. On Peter II's sudden death from smallpox in 1730, the Privy Councillors decided to offer the throne to Peter I's niece Anna, Dowager Duchess of Courland (1693–1740), who lived in her Baltic duchy in poverty-stricken obscurity; they took the opportunity to impose on Anna conditions which would ensure her dependence upon them.

Initially Anna accepted the Council's 'Points' or proposals; but finding that they lacked the support of the majority of the nobility, who feared oligarchy more than a single absolute ruler, she tore up the 'Points' in a melodramatic confrontation with the Councillors, and assumed full autocratic powers. In return for their support, the nobility gained improvements in the conditions of their service to the state.

Anna's reign brought German pre-eminence at Court, personified by the favourite Biron (E.J. von Bühren, 1690–1722) whom she made Duke of Courland. The serious state of national finances produced oppressive measures to regularize taxation. In-fighting continued among the élite. Court style lacked refinement (Anna shared her uncle Peter's penchant for dwarves and monsters) and the high German profile offended some Russian sensibilities – hence the later term *Bironovshchina*, 'the bad rule of Biron'. There were, however, more positive sides. This was also a time of cultural development, with the introduction of opera into Russia, from Italy,

under court patronage. Russia made its weight felt in Europe in the crisis over the Polish succession (1733–35); and a successful war with Turkey (1735–39) regained Azov, lost by Peter in 1711.

Anna died childless in 1740, leaving the crown to her infant great-nephew Ivan Antonovich (Ivan VI) (1740–64), under the regency of his mother Anna Leopol'dovna (1718–46) and her husband the Duke of Brunswick. Biron's initial domination of the new regent was broken in months by a coup, which did not, however, end the prominence of Germans at the head of the government. But in November 1741 a further coup, backed by the Guards and financed with French money, brought Peter I's daughter Elizabeth (1709–61) to the throne.   RPB

ELIZABETH (1741–61)

Like her immediate predecessors, Elizabeth took little interest in political affairs. Her particular contribution was to encourage the western luxury and expensive tastes which had already begun to show themselves under Anna, and which accorded well with Elizabeth's extravagant pleasure-seeking and love of social life. In the absence of firm guidance from the sovereign, influence in government lay with favourites.

Until his fall in 1758 A.P. Bestuzhev (1693–1763) dominated foreign affairs, while the Shuvalov family – Aleksandr, Petr, Ivan – became prominent in internal matters. Petr Shuvalov interested himself

Right. Empress Elizabeth, by Pietro Rotari

Empress Anna, after a portrait by Amiconi

85

in things social and economic, to the country's and his own personal advantage. Ivan was a noted patron of the arts and sciences. Together with Russia's 'universal genius' M.V. Lomonosov (1711–65), he was instrumental in the founding of Moscow University in 1755. Lomonosov, son of a White Sea fisherman, made a name in many fields, as poet, historian, scientist, ending his days in 1765 as a prominent cultural administrator and an Academician. The new university was followed by the establishment of the first Russian theatre (1756) and of an Academy of Fine Arts (1757). These and other developments heralded the cultural efflorescence of the last decades of the century.

In international affairs Russia's position continued to grow stronger. The Swedish declaration of war in 1741 rapidly proved futile. Russia's part in the international complications of the Austrian succession was a relatively minor one, but in the Seven Years War (1756–63) Elizabeth's determined hostility to Frederick of Prussia and the campaigns against him of the Russian armies were instrumental in bringing Prussia to its knees. Final victory, however, eluded Elizabeth. To Frederick's great relief she died late in 1761.   RPB

PETER III (1761–62)

Peter III (1728–62), born in Holstein and brought to Russia as grand prince and heir apparent, was Elizabeth's nephew and successor. Maladjusted and boorish, Peter had an unconcealed scorn for things Russian and was a fervent admirer of Prussia. He not only withdrew Russian forces from the anti-Prussian coalition but at once gave up all Russia's conquests and pledged his support for Frederick. Such blatant disregard for Russia's interests, as well as Peter's attitude to the established government and the national church, provoked intense resentment. Some measures of Peter's government were of considerable importance: a manifesto freeing the nobility from compulsory service; decrees on trade; concessions to the Old Believers. But these did not save him. In June 1762, his wife Catherine, whose own position was jeopardized by Peter's infatuation with a mistress whom he threatened to marry, mounted a coup with the help of her lover and his brothers, popular Guards officers. Peter abdicated and was murdered soon after.   RPB

CATHERINE THE GREAT (1762–96)

Catherine II (1729–96) was a German princess, married at the age of fifteen to the Grand Prince Peter (later Tsar Peter III), and consequently had no proper title to the Imperial throne. In the event she became one of eighteenth-century Russia's most successful rulers: her long reign was marked by spectacular success abroad, important internal reforms, and the consolidation of the social order. Her strong personality and vivid private life have attracted many biographers. Traditionally she has been included among the so-called enlightened despots, absolute monarchs who in the age of the Enlightenment applied the ideas of the time to the tasks of government. However, the ideas most influential in the absolute governments of eighteenth-century Europe were those not of the socially radical French Enlightenment, but of the German Enlightenment and the German political economists of the time (the 'cameralist' school), whose concerns were essentially with the wealth and strength of the state.

Social and political reform

Catherine inherited a social and political order in

Catherine the Great

which the country was under-governed and under-developed. The nobility, corporately reconstituted and newly educated by the measures of Peter I, had steadily gained freedom from service constraints and by now monopolized higher public office and private landownership to its own advantage. Peter III's 1762 Manifesto abolishing compulsory service to the state was a significant step in this development. The Russian nobility enjoyed rights unusual even in hierarchical *ancien régime* Europe, in particular virtual life-and-death powers over the servile peasantry.

As an eighteenth-century absolute monarch, Catherine wished to maintain the existing order, took privilege for granted, and relied politically upon the noble élite. She also wished, however, to modernize and develop the country, which involved safeguarding the status and the productive capacity of other social groups. She took pride in creating many new towns, although real urban growth was minimal and society remained overwhelmingly agrarian. Early thoughts of improving the peasants' lot foundered for lack of social support; attempts to expand and to clean up the civil service had similar ill success. Furthermore the great peasant revolt led by the Cossack Ye. I. Pugachev (1726–75) in 1773–75 showed the dangerous weakness of government outside the centre. What I. de Madariaga has called Catherine's 'reforming decade' (1775–85) opened with the 1775 reform of provincial government. This heralded an extensive decentralization of state administration and gave a significant role to the gentry in the provinces. The 1785 Charter to the Nobility finally completed the establishment of the nobility as a separate estate within society, codifying its privileges.

At the same time, nevertheless, Catherine issued a parallel Charter to the Towns of the Empire and worked on the draft of another for the state peasantry: in short, she envisaged the organization of Russian society along the lines of west European estates. The social group ignored here were the landowners' serfs, who had suffered a steady decline in rights and status parallel to the rise of the gentry. Catherine's government did little to lessen the subjugation of the Empire's peasants, and in some respects increased it. It is especially in this area that the gap between her declared intentions and political rhetoric and actual results achieved have provoked charges, often exaggerated, of cynicism or hypocrisy. However, her personal concern with the 'peasant question' was a direct cause of the increasingly public discussion of the peasantry's position within society, which began seriously in the 1760s.

The difficulties of reform were fully demonstrated by the clashes of interest in the famous Legislative Commission of 1767; Pugachev showed the dangers

Pugachev in the cage in which he was brought to Moscow in 1775. Following his execution, his head was exhibited on a pole

of loss of control. In her political theory Catherine was eclectic; but her policies aimed basically to maximize all the resources of the country, and so its wealth and power. To this end she actively encouraged trade and industry; agriculture was much discussed but little improved. Another important object of policy, common to most contemporary European governments, was expansion of the population.

In many respects Catherine's reign completed developments begun or furthered under Peter I. Her secularization of Church estates in 1764 made final the subordination of Church to state. The position of the major social classes remained basically unchanged after 1785 until the peasant emancipation of 1861. Economic developments were the fruits of Peter I's beginnings, while Catherine's successes against the Ottoman Empire and the foundation of Odessa (1794) on the Black Sea finally opened the way to Mediterranean commerce.

In cultural affairs, the century's latter decades saw a great flowering: the educational demands made on the nobility by the Petrine service structure, and Russia's new openness to Europe, now produced an élite interested in cultural pursuits. The development of a modern literature accompanied an increasing engagement with European intellectual currents: Russia too was involved in the Enlightenment. One result was the emergence of political dissent. A.N. Radishchev (1749–1802), in his *Journey from St Petersburg to Moscow* (1790), combined the form of Lawrence Sterne's *Sentimental Journey* with a fierce attack on the institutions of serfdom and autocracy. Following the outbreak of the French Revolution, however, Catherine would not tolerate such heterodoxy: Radishchev, 'the father of Russian radicalism', was condemned to death, a sentence commuted to exile in Siberia.

Foreign affairs

In foreign affairs, Catherine II's reign marks a high point of Russian prestige and influence. On her accession in 1762 she withdrew Russian support from Frederick II, but did not renew hostilities against him. Common Russian and Prussian interests in Poland led eventually to the three partitions (with Austria) of 1772, 1793 and 1795 and the extinction of Polish statehood, and established a long tradition of Russian–Prussian co-operation. Catherine's two Turkish Wars of 1768–74 and 1787–91, and the 1783 annexation of the Crimea, removed the old Tatar threat in the south and gave the Empire final control over the northern Black Sea littoral. Russo-French mediation of the War of the Bavarian Succession (1779) left Russia the co-guarantor of the Holy Roman Empire; while the success of the maritime Armed Neutrality (1780)

Right. *Emperor Paul,
by V. L. Borovikovsky*

showed Catherine's ability to challenge the greatest naval power, Britain, on the seas. A last effort by Sweden in 1787–88 to reassert herself in the Baltic, while Russia was preoccupied with the Turks, failed completely. RPB

PAUL (1796–1801)

Catherine II was succeeded by her son Paul (1754–1801). Well-educated and well-intentioned, but resentful both of his mother and her favourites, he combined an unbalanced temperament with an excessively exalted view of the tsar's position. Significant administrative change was begun in his reign, recentralizing government, and Paul's militarization of society presaged the reigns of his sons Alexander I and Nicholas I. His regime however proved capricious and despotic. The apparent vagaries of his foreign policy, and his humiliating and unpredictable treatment at home of nobility and courtiers, army and government, made his rule intolerable, even to his son and heir the Grand Prince Alexander. With Alexander's consent a coup deposed Paul on 1 March 1801; during a scuffle with the conspirators he was strangled. RPB

ALEXANDER I (1801–25)

Alexander I (1777–1825) came to the throne as a result of the murder of his father, Paul, in 1801. He was obliged to begin his reign with undertakings

to restore for the nobles their status under Catherine the Great. But his own inclinations were romantic, and he tended towards the ideals of the European Enlightenment. In 1802 and 1803 he established a 'Secret Committee' in which four close friends, including the Polish Prince Adam Czartoryski, discussed methods of bringing enlightenment to Russia. But social reform, especially in the question of serfdom, was beyond even the tsar's powers; and the reforms were mainly concerned with matters of government, in which the efficiency of the Senate

Military parade during the reign of Emperor Paul

Right. Alexander I, by George Dawe. Far right. A. A. Arakcheev, after a portrait by W. Wagner, 1818

in its executive and legislative functions was improved and a beginning was made towards harmonious ministerial government.

Alexander's reign was dominated by foreign affairs. Russia had vacillated between French and English connections under Tsar Paul, but Alexander opted in 1805 for an English and Austrian alliance, largely because he feared Napoleon's ambitions in Germany and the eastern Mediterranean. This policy failed, in a series of Allied defeats which ended with the battle of Friedland in summer 1807.

Alexander then opted for alliance with Napoleon, a policy promoted after a meeting on the river Niemen at Tilsit. Relations between France and Russia worsened over Polish and economic matters and Napoleon invaded Russia in June 1812. His army, 600,000 strong, was over twice as large as the Russian armies, badly supplied and prone to disease. It gradually pushed back the Russian forces (which, contrary to legend, did not deliberately retreat), but losses were such that Napoleon had to fight a major battle outside Moscow, at Borodino, with only 100,000 men. He entered Moscow, which – in circumstances that have never been clarified – burnt down. He stayed on, hoping that the tsar would come to terms. But Alexander, buoyed up by a great wave of patriotic emotion, would not do so. Napoleon retreated, in ever-worsening military circumstances, and re-crossed the Niemen with only 30,000 men. In the next three years, Russian forces dominated Europe and played a prominent rôle in the fall of the Napoleonic Empire.

Mikhail Speransky

Alexander wavered between extremely religious conservatism and the Enlightenment of his youth. But the Russian situation was such that serious reform made little headway. Alexander's main reforming statesman, M.M. Speransky (1772–1839), was dismissed in 1812 because he offended powerful conservative, aristocratic interests (he had written: 'There are no truly free persons in Russia except beggars and philosophers'). The dominant voice in the latter part of Alexander's reign was that of the militarist A.A. Arakcheev (1769–1834). Alexander's liberalism was confined to the conquered lands of Finland (taken from Sweden in 1808) and Congress Poland, to which he gave a constitution. He died in 1825, thought by some merely to have hidden away from the burdens of rule.   NS

NICHOLAS I (1825–55)

Alexander I's successor, his brother Nicholas, was of much harsher character. He was a lover of Prussia and wished to keep a large police establishment. He was known as 'the gendarme of Europe', and Russia's role throughout his reign (and especially in 1848) was highly conservative. Russian armies crushed revolt in Poland in 1830–31 and in Hungary in 1849. They did intervene in the Balkans against Turkey and in favour of small Balkan peoples of Orthodox faith, but the intervention was limited. Nicholas was mainly concerned to keep the peace

Nicholas I

ditions for the state serfs, but the effect was limited. Nicholas continued to rule through the police, reorganized (under A.K. Benckendorff, 1783–1844) as Third Section of the Tsar's Chancery, and the army. Little was done for education; his aim was a static society: 'glitter at the top, rot at the bottom' was one comment on it.

But change came just the same. The economy was gradually shifting, with the towns expanding (in 1864 there were three times as many towns with a population of over 50,000 as in 1830) and the population doubling between 1800 and 1860 (when it reached 60 million). Many nobles were unable to keep pace, and three-quarters of their serfs were mortgaged to the state by 1855. Moreover, Europe no longer tolerated the Russian claim to dominate the Near East. In 1854 Great Britain and France came to the support of Turkey, and landed troops in the Crimea. Sevastopol', a Russian naval base in the Black Sea, was captured. Nicholas I, dismayed that his Austrian ally had abandoned him, died, and his son Alexander II made peace in 1856.   NS

in Europe, a freedom that enabled him to expand Russia's frontiers in the southern Caucasus at Persian expense, and to a lesser extent in Central Asia.

The 'Decembrists'

At home Nicholas imposed a rigid, bureaucratic rule. He was challenged at the outset of his reign by a conspiracy of army officers (known as the 'Decembrists' from the date of their uprising, 14 December 1825) who had picked up doctrines of European liberalism and were full of ideas for a free, constitutional, federative Russia. But these officers were not well-organized, nor did they have any serious support. Their uprising, centred on Senate Square outside the Winter Palace, soon fizzled out, and the leaders were either hanged or exiled for lengthy terms in Siberia. Thereafter, Nicholas imposed strict censorship, to which many literary figures, including Pushkin, fell victim.

Serfdom and emancipation

Nicholas maintained serfdom, which embraced almost four-fifths of the population, whether as serfs of the nobles or of the state. He, and many other Russians, appreciated that serfdom was corrupting both the serfs and their owners by preventing the establishment of a free class of prosperous farmers, and driving much of the peasant population towards shiftlessness and alcohol. But if he abolished serfdom, the nobles would no longer maintain administration, discipline, and taxation, and the country might then fly apart. The Tsar's assistant P.D. Kiselev (1788–1872) ameliorated con-

Right. *Alexander II with his wife*

ALEXANDER II (1855–81)

Russia had reached a considerable crisis. Its foreign policies were a failure, and the 'Black Sea Clauses' of the peace treaty prevented it from moving warships into or out of the Black Sea. The peasantry were becoming restive, and agrarian protests against serfdom grew in scale. Finance was in disarray, for

Alexander II with his manifesto on the emancipation of the serfs

the state could not sustain for ever the burden of a noble class whose mortgages accounted, in 1859, for 450 million rubles of the 750 million in circulation. In the circumstances, Alexander II, though himself a man of conservative inclinations, saw no alternative but radical reform.

In 1861 emancipation of the serfs was proclaimed. No longer would the peasants formally belong to a nobleman. But personal freedom was only a start, for there remained many complicated questions. Now that the nobles no longer directly administered serfs, who would do this job? How much land should the former serfs be given? Should the nobles have compensation? These questions were not satisfactorily solved, though a better effort was made than some idealists imagined. The peasants acquired (with very great regional variations) roughly two-thirds of the land they had previously worked, and they undertook to pay 'redemption dues' of annual cash payments to the state, which advanced compensatory lump sums to the nobles. Not surprisingly, the peasants protested, and efforts to recover redemption payments were not successful. Even forty years later (when they were written off) the payments were in arrears.

The state also limited peasants' freedom: they were included in village communes which owned the land and assigned parts of it to individual peasants, generally according to their families' size. This was administratively convenient, and suited the peasants' own ways in much of the country, but it acted as a block on rural economic progress, for a man

could not count on having the same land for even half of his working life. Russian agriculture, though capable of producing great quantities of grain for export, was never as efficient as western agriculture, and there were some devastating famines.

Alexander II had to create a new bureaucracy, for which he also created schools and colleges; the State Bank came into existence in 1859; elected county councils (*zemstva*) were set up in 1864 to deal with local administration, and the system of taxation was overhauled. Many Russians hoped that Alexander would go further, and grant a constitution, but in the tsar's view Russia was simply too large and too varied to allow any other system of rule but autocracy – certainly not rule by a small noble class. He grew irritable when constitutional changes were suggested by *zemstvo* leaders, two of whom he exiled. His reforms therefore stopped short, and this encouraged radical opposition to tsarism.

There was no coherent popular protest for most of the nineteenth century, and the opposition movements of intellectuals and some of the nobility were necessarily confined in scope. Opposition was also divided in aim. German liberalism and Hegelianism acted as a spur for the 'Westerners', at their head Petr Chaadaev (1793–1856), in the 1840s; the Decembrists had anticipated this inspiration from the West. In the 1850s and 1860s the opposition was particularly shaped by Alexander Herzen, whose journal-in-exile, *The Bell*, was even read by the tsar, and who aimed at a synthesis of Russian tradition and the western ways which, in pure form, he despised.

Counter to these traditions ran the ideas of the 'Slavophiles' (especially A. S. Khomyakov, 1804–60) who despised legal forms and advocated Slav institutions: a free Russia based on the village commune and the old Russian form of parliament. Such opposition necessarily remained academic, and literary: the exiles, with their confused finances, opinions and (still more) private lives, were typical.

In the 1860s there arose a more popular opposition, based on the 'intelligentsia' – a phrase that now began to be used to describe educated, rebellious young people usually of lower middle-class extraction. Expansion of the educational system, though not generous (and considerably less than in other European countries), had been forced on the tsarist state by the needs of modernity. It created a number of aspiring and educated young people who did not have secure employment, and who lived from hand-to-mouth. They had no stake in society, and yet had lost their roots. The result was a plethora of dissident doctrines. With N.G. Chernyshevsky (1828–89) there arrived an opposition movement, populism, that had lost touch even with the Herzen-inspired opposition movements of the earlier period. Chernyshevsky and his like rejected religion, order, the family. They were, in Turgenev's word, 'nihilists'.

The limitation of Alexander II's reforms was such that more and more of these young people were driven into a radical opposition. In the 1870s they attempted to carry their doctrines 'to the people', and they went out to the villages in an effort to convince the peasantry. They failed. The peasants were suspicious of all townsmen and did not take kindly to the women students. The populists succeeded in arousing the peasantry only when they happened on traditional grievances, expressed in traditional ways (a pretender-tsar, for instance). Elsewhere the peasantry handed them over to the police.

In despair, a section of the populists established a terrorist organization, 'Land and Liberty', which plotted assassinations. The most successful of these was the shooting by Vera Zasulich, of General Trepov, police chief of St Petersburg, in 1878. She was pronounced not guilty by a sympathetic jury, which caused the tsar to whittle down the entire jury system. Attempts were made on the tsar himself, culminating in his assassination in March 1881.   NS

ALEXANDER III (1881–94)

Alexander III absorbed the lesson of his father's murder, and resolved that there should be no further liberalizing measures. Thereafter, a vicious circle developed: the government became harsher and regarded liberal reforms as merely an incitement to greater opposition; while the opposition was pushed further and further towards extremism.

The constitutional experiment with which Alexander II had been toying on the eve of his death was shelved. Alexander listened to his adviser K.P. Pobedonostsev (1827–1907), an uncompromising highly religious reactionary, whose beliefs were of a type unfamiliar in Europe since the mid-seventeenth century. Efforts were made to resuscitate the declining nobility by, for example, the provision of mortgages through a Land Bank (1883), and to provide greater police-coverage in the towns and the countryside. The activities of the zemstva (county councils) were cut back. In the short run, this policy succeeded, and active opposition inside the country collapsed.

The 1880s brought considerable economic change. As Russia developed railways, it was able to export grain and to stimulate metallurgical extraction and working. The state lacked capital, but by the 1890s it was able to acquire considerable capital from abroad, especially France, and its resources began to be seriously exploited – with some 260 foreign companies well to the fore. Native Russian capitalists did exist, notably in the Moscow area, where the textile industry became quite advanced, but on the whole they were clumsy and parasitical.

This again developed into a vicious circle. The government retained a somewhat cumbersome measure of state control, mainly because it did not trust the capitalists on their own; and the capitalists responded by developing a bureaucratic, rather than an entrepreneurial, mentality. Where they were menaced (as in the depression of 1900–03) they responded, not by technological inventiveness, but by cartellization and price-fixing, often at the expense of employment and wages. Russian industry and banking therefore became highly monopolistic, and corruption seems to have played a considerable part. Moreover, foreign skills and capital were important to the progress that Russian industry unquestionably made in the 1890s. In 1897 Russia conformed to world practice and adopted the gold standard, under the finance minister S. Yu. Witte. This procured foreign investment, but did so, it has been suggested, at the expense of native credit-institutions.

The Russian worker was badly-paid, was forbidden to form unions, and then had to pay high prices for the goods he needed. Any threat from workers could easily be checked by an influx of fresh labour from the countryside, where agriculture underwent a similarly patchy development.

The peasant commune (mir) was far from being an ideal base for agrarian capitalism, and yet it

Alexander III as a young man, by Alexander Doborovin

Right. Nicholas II

continued to flourish in the latter part of the century. To some extent, government policy was responsible: the government needed the administrative services of the village elders, and therefore left them in charge of the community. But it was mainly the interests of the bulk of the peasantry that kept communes together in most of European Russia. The commune gave a man land when he had mouths to feed from it, and, by the same token, hands to work it.

At a time when population was rising fast (from 60 million in 1860 it rose to 130 million in 1905) and land was under pressure, the commune carried out an obvious service in the short run. The difficulty was of course that no peasant without hereditary tenure had much interest in developing his land, and agriculture remained very backward. A few noble estates did well, and in some areas where communal tenure was weak there were adequately efficient independent farmers. Grain made up two-fifths of Russia's exports in the late nineteenth century, but the agricultural problem was quite as serious for the tsars as it was for their successors.

Alexander III responded with timid efforts to promote peasant property (a Peasants' Land Bank being established in 1885), but he tended to head off peasant discontent in the direction of the Jews or the non-Russian peoples; an aggressive, Panslav foreign policy was another part of the system. The tsars had tried to confine Jews to the Pale of Settlement in eastern Poland and White Russia, but the Jewish and non-Jewish populations did clash, and from 1881 onwards there was a series of pogroms against Jews. Jewish emigration, fostered by railways, went ahead, but even as late as 1891 measures of almost eighteenth-century style were being used against Jews (for instance, their expulsion from Moscow and Kiev). The Jewish population responded by producing its own nationalism and social-democratic opposition (the *Bund*).

Government agents acted similarly against the non-Russian peoples of the empire – Poles, Ukrainians, even Baltic Germans whose university at Dorpat near Riga was Russified. This reaction stimulated native nationalist movements. It should be said, however, that in most cases these nationalistic movements were not separatist.   NS

NICHOLAS II: AUTOCRACY UNDER ASSAULT (1894–1904)

Nicholas II came to the throne amid hopes that he might relax the authoritarian rule of his father, Alexander III. Nicholas quickly dashed those hopes in his contemptuous response to a delegation of moderate noble leaders who, using the occasion of

their address to the new tsar, had expressed their desire for constitutional reform. The tsar's reply, word of which spread quickly through educated society, was to denounce such talk as 'senseless dreams' and to promise to rule in the manner of his 'unforgettable father'. Disillusion extended to Russian workers and peasants after thousands of them were accidentally crushed to death at the tsar's coronation in 1896. Nicholas's decision to continue the celebrations that evening in disregard of the tragedy was typical of his poor political judgment and lack of human sensitivity. His distaste for the business of politics and his pledge to rule as a traditional autocrat did not, however, prevent him from presiding over the industrial transformation of the empire.

Industrialization and urbanization

The government's industrialization programme picked up steam in the 1890s under the direction of Minister of Finance, Sergey Witte. Following the extension of Russia's railway lines, there was dramatic expansion in textile production and almost every area of heavy industry – iron and steel production, oil drilling, coal mining – although the country still lagged behind many of its European competitors. Internally, rapid economic growth was deeply disruptive of Russian society and traditional culture, and, coming as it did on the heels of the social transformation unleashed by the Great Reforms, industrialization accelerated the evolution

of a more open and active society whose aims were often in direct conflict with those of the autocracy. In the countryside the early stages of rapid industrialization had produced massive peasant famine in the previous reign in 1891. Whether the agrarian sector was beset by acute economic crisis is disputed, but all agree that peasants were still bitterly resentful of the Emancipation land settlement, which left the bulk of the land in noble hands, and that peasant discontent was potentially explosive.

From the late 1890s until the outbreak of the First World War in 1914, millions of peasants left their ancestral villages for industrial wage labour in cities. Their arrival shifted the arena for political and social conflict from the countryside to the new urban centres. When migrants began flooding the cities and gathering in settlements on their outskirts, the autocracy was unprepared and unwilling to expend scarce resources on their basic necessities. The unusually prominent role the government played as industrial sponsor tied politics directly to the fortunes of industry, made the autocracy a natural target of working-class discontent and led the government to repress harshly the efforts of the growing strike movement to improve conditions and mobilize workers.

As Moscow and St Petersburg and other large cities were inundated with peasants in search of work, the burgeoning middle classes of small traders and shopkeepers felt increasingly besieged. Crime rates soared, as did tensions between privileged and non-privileged sectors of society. Cultural conflict heightened class tensions in ethnically mixed cities such as Tiflis, Riga, and Baku on the borderlands and Warsaw, Odessa and other industrial cities located in the Pale of Settlement. Political unrest sharpened hostility between Slavs and Jews, resulting in mass pogroms against Jews and Jewish property. An official policy of Russification, also intensified in the 1890s, increased ethnic strife and damaged tsarist authority in the non-Russian periphery. Social and cultural fragmentation was reflected in the remarkable artistic efflorescence at the turn of the century. Rejecting the realism and political didacticism of the nineteenth-century intelligentsia, Silver Age artists explored the breakdown of social and individual unity, often in apocalyptic terms which questioned Russia's hold on 'civilization', and contributed to society's sense of disorientation and disintegration.

Opposition movements

The urban educated élite produced the new radical and liberal opposition movements that would battle for power during the revolutionary era. In the 1890s urban professionals were joined by noble *zemstvo* (county council) activists to form a liberal opposition, which clamoured for a voice in the political system, limitations on the tsar's powers, and some guarantee of civil rights. The movement represented a broad spectrum ranging from the most moderate constitutionalists, led by D.N. Shipov, who favoured a weak consultative parliament, to radicals who called for a freely elected legislative body and later adopted socialist programmes for a major redistribution of the land. By 1904 moderate *zemstvo* liberalism had been largely supplanted by its more outspoken branch of urban intellectuals, led by Paul Milyukov and a former Marxist, Peter Struve, publisher of *Osvobozhdenie* (*Liberation*), the liberal organ. The founding of the Union of Liberation in 1903 maintained a fragile unity among liberals, provided an umbrella for moderate discontent in educated society at large, and served as the critical political weapon against the autocracy in the 1905–07 Revolution.

Two radical movements vied for popular support after the famine of 1891 brought a new generation face to face with rural poverty. Populists who later formed the Socialist-Revolutionary Party (SRs), believed that ancient collective peasant institutions

Below left. Flogging a prisoner on Sakhalin island, late nineteenth century

Below right. Prisoners in a Siberian forced labour camp around 1900

Rasputin

Grigory Rasputin (1869–1916) was one of the most extraordinary figures in the history of Russia. The story of how an unkempt and uncouth holy man from Siberia became influential in the running of a Great Power in the twentieth century is one that has fascinated people ever since.

Rasputin, a semi-literate peasant, was one of a loose fraternity of pilgrims, or unordained religious teachers (*starets*), who travelled through Russia living off the gifts of those to whom they preached. Their doctrines were often far from orthodox: Rasputin taught that great sins made possible great repentances, a view of life sometimes interpreted to mean that the path to eternal salvation lay in sexual excess.

Rasputin was already established as a guru among the upper classes of St Petersburg when he was introduced to the tsarina in 1905. His apparent successes in healing the haemophiliac Tsarevich Alexis quickly made him Alexandra's trusted confidant. The tsarina, although reluctant at first, had become a highly enthusiastic convert to the Orthodox faith, particularly its more spiritual aspects, and to her Rasputin seemed to be the embodiment of Russia and Orthodoxy. She began to seek his advice on political as well as personal matters.

Rasputin, once he had become aware of his potential power, made use of it, but not in an overtly political way; he had his friends promoted to important posts in the government, where they all too often proved to be utterly incompetent.

His influence had been attacked by members of the Duma for many years, and by 1916 he and the German-born tsarina were being openly accused of treachery against Russia. Eventually on 17 December 1916 he was murdered by a group of arch-conservatives led by the Grand Duke Dmitry Pavlovich and Prince Yusupov.

Rasputin's death was as dramatic and unconventional as much of his life. It is said that he consumed a vast quantity of poison, was shot, beaten and finally dumped under the ice of a frozen river before he died.

would allow Russia to avoid capitalism and, through violent revolution, progress directly to socialism. They obtained broad and enduring peasant support for their advocacy of land redistribution. An extreme Socialist-Revolutionary wing embarked on an assassination campaign against tsarist officials, which achieved spectacular results in exposing government vulnerability. Dozens of officials were killed by SR bomb-throwers, including the obdurate Minister of Interior, V.K. Plehve, whose murder in 1904 was greeted by indifference and even celebration on the streets of St Petersburg.

Bolsheviks and Mensheviks

Some young radicals believed that the populist reliance on a uniquely Russian path to socialism was blind to the inroads capitalism had already made both in the countryside and the city. Marx's view that capitalism was both inevitable and a necessary step towards socialism offered them a more practical strategy of organizing among urban workers in the growing cities. 'Scientific' Marxist theories did not always reflect the actual needs of the working class

but Social Democratic leaders provided education, guidance, and organizing skills for the working-class activists. In 1903 Russian Social Democrats (SDs) split over their proper relationship with the proletariat and with liberalism. Lenin – the alias of Vladimir I'lich Ul'yanov (1870–1924) – who provoked the split, believed that workers could never develop revolutionary consciousness except under the tutelage of the intelligentsia, and that only a centralized, disciplined party of professional revolutionaries would be safe from the tsarist secret police. His Bolshevik faction rejected alliances with any other parties, even for the purpose of overthrowing the autocracy.

The Mensheviks, led by Yuly Martov and the venerable former populist Georgy Plekhanov, favoured a broadly based, open party and sought to train a worker-intelligentsia to lead the labour movement. They also favoured temporary alliance with liberals for the overthrow of autocracy. While membership in the revolutionary parties was minuscule before 1905, radical educational and agitational efforts began bearing fruit as rising mass protest

Nicholas II with his family

Father Georgy Gapon

The path to revolution

THE PSEUDO-PARLIAMENTARY PERIOD, 1905–14

By 1904, when war with Japan broke out, Russia was in ferment. The professional classes, identified with the *zemstvo* movement, were demanding representative government, and organizing themselves to become the Constitutional Democratic Party (Kadet). The land hunger and poverty of the peasants was exploding in violence and arson. The students, influenced by all shades of revolutionary thought – Marxist, populist, anarchist – were demonstrating against the government's educational policies, and its refusal to grant autonomy to the universities. Among the working class, economic and political demands, formulated since the 1880s under Marxist guidance, had created a strike movement which by 1904 achieved mass proportions.

'Bloody Sunday'

In August 1904 the Minister of the Interior was assassinated. With the army in the Far East, the government seemed weak and the police disoriented. The turbulence increased. On Sunday 9 January 1905 (OS), a huge procession of workers with their families, led by the priest/police-agent Fr Gapon (1870–1906), marched to the Winter Palace in St Petersburg to present a pious petition to an absent tsar. After giving warnings to disperse, the troops fired into the crowds, killing at least 200. Throughout Russia and in the West, 'Bloody Sunday' provoked outrage.

Appeasement and repression

Nicholas II offered consultative representation, provoking further demands by this show of weakness, worsened by disasters in Manchuria and the total loss in May of the Russian Baltic Fleet at Tsushima. In August peace was concluded at Portsmouth, USA, and the government offered the opposition movement a legislative assembly – the Duma. It was to be elected on a restricted suffrage and satisfied nobody. The unrest continued, culminating in a general strike which paralysed the empire from 7 to 17 October (OS). Under extreme pressure from his closest advisers, Nicholas II now issued his October Manifesto, granting personal inviolability, freedom of conscience, speech, assembly, and association, and promising a State Duma, elected on a popular franchise, to approve all future laws. Count Sergey Yulevich Witte (1849–1915), author of the Mani-

manifested itself in hundreds of organized strikes which in 1905 would provide the power behind the masses' opposition to autocracy.

On the eve of 1905, a decade after Nicholas came to the throne, nearly every group in Russian society had reason to be discontented. Even the conservative gentry grumbled openly about the urban-oriented government policies that had been undercutting noble prestige and economic well-being since the emancipation of the serfs. New restrictions on student activities sent university students to the streets in 1899. Workers' fortunes weathered a sharp setback in the economic downturn of 1900, but the hardships of recession produced an upsurge in labour unrest from 1903 when the economy began to improve. In 1902–03 massive peasant uprisings engulfed two southern provinces and, on the borderlands, anti-Russian sentiment was smouldering.

The outbreak of the Russo-Japanese War in 1904 and Russia's humiliating defeat at the hands of what many people thought to be an obscure and culturally inferior nation ravaged much of what was left of the tsar's authority. Russia was ripe for revolution.

JN

festo, was appointed prime minister and Russia appeared to have embarked on constitutional reform. Nicholas's concessions, however, had merely whetted the opposition's appetite and the unrest mounted. The police were unable to cope, and the strikers escalated their demands: constituent assembly, civil rights, an eight-hour day; then, as professional revolutionaries came to the fore, democratic republic, amnesty, arming of the workers.

The movement in St Petersburg was led by a soviet, or council, which began as a central co-ordinating strike committee and developed into the mouthpiece for the entire revolutionary labour movement. Nevertheless, when the government arrested all 562 deputies in December, the workers did not react. In Moscow, meanwhile, the local Bolsheviks had been campaigning ardently for armed uprising, and when by December sufficient arms had been collected, an insurrection was staged, only to be crushed by government troops after a week's bloody fighting. The revolution had reached its zenith with the general strike in October and thereafter the government was regaining lost ground. Having granted civil liberties and promised a democratically elected assembly, Nicholas II brought his army back from the war and set about 'pacifying' the country.

The October Manifesto had split the opposition movement. Moderates advocated the peaceful reconstruction of the country on the basis of the Manifesto and formed themselves into the Octobrist Party.

Liberals were now prepared to cut their ties with the revolutionaries and adopt parliamentary methods, but were not satisfied with the scope of the concessions and formed themselves into the Kadet Party, with the aim of working legally towards full constitutional government. The Prime Minister, Witte, was unable to attract liberals or moderates into his cabinet, because they could not countenance the traditional tsarist methods being employed to crush the revolution. Under Witte's successor, P. A. Stolypin (1862–1911), the gallows, nicknamed 'Stolypin's necktie', were in constant use, and field courts martial were the normal means used by him for the summary trial and execution of thousands of insurrectionaries in 1906–07.

The repressions were accompanied by a powerful upsurge of Russian chauvinism and violent anti-semitism. Aided, even prompted by the police, pogromists wreaked vengeance on the Jews for the humiliations recently heaped upon the tsar and the Russian people, in war and revolution. The post-1905 period saw the greatest waves of Jewish emigration.

The Duma

The Duma was to be elected by all classes, through indirect franchise. Laws would be passed only with Duma approval, though legislation also required the approval of the State Council and the tsar.

The first two Dumas (1906 and 1907) were unworkable. The first reflected the temper of recent

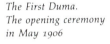

The First Duma. The opening ceremony in May 1906

P.A. Stolypin

events and was hence powerfully liberal, with a token number of the extreme left, since the Socialist Revolutionaries, the Bolsheviks and the Mensheviks had at first boycotted the elections, thus losing much support to the Kadets. Stolypin knew co-operation from such an assembly was impossible and dissolved it after two months. The second Duma came with stronger left-wing and conservative elements, a token extreme right and a weakened Kadet centre. Again, the government was unable to find support in the assembly and it was dissolved after three months.

Stolypin's reforms

Stolypin had a vast programme of legislation, including land reform, freedom of religion, inviolability of the person, civic equality, workers' national insurance, income-tax reform, *zemstvo* reform, introduction of *zemstva* into the western provinces, compulsory primary education, secondary- and high-school reform, and police reform, none of which he felt able to risk in the Duma. By the simple act of temporarily suspending the Duma and invoking Article 87 of the Fundamental Laws, which permitted the government to legislate when the Duma was not in session, Stolypin was able to pass most of his legislation, though he would have preferred to grace it with the air of constitutionality the Duma could have provided.

To this end, in June 1907 he altered the electoral law and achieved a third Duma that provided him with support from the Octobrists and the Right, greatly reduced the Kadets and all but eliminated the socialists and national groups. The third Duma ratified Stolypin's land reform, which permitted peasants to leave the commune freely, and which encouraged those willing to try independent farming, so furthering his aim of building Russia's rural stability on a class of free, prosperous farmers.

Before 1914 Russian nationalism grew rabid,

Troops supporting the February revolution, Petrograd, 1917

reaching a climax in the Beilis Affair (1913), when the accusation of ritual murder against a Jew aroused widespread indignation at home and abroad. The Right saw Russia's traditional institutions declining, and in Stolypin's increasing power a threat to the tsar's personal standing. In 1911 Stolypin was assassinated, probably by a police agent.

Elections in the following year produced a fourth Duma much like the third. Though the government had majority support, the opposition parties maintained continual criticism of state policy, and even of court life – criticism that established the strained relations that would deteriorate to the point of collapse between the government and its critics during the First World War.   HS

WAR AND REVOLUTION

The patriotic upsurge accompanying Russia's entry into the First World War gave way to anxiety when it was seen that the country was poorly prepared and no match for Germany. The absolutist psychology of the tsar, barely touched by the pseudo-parliamentary experience, dictated that war was the business of government. Only after persistent efforts on the part of liberal politicians and industrialists, and after serious military defeats, did Nicholas II agree to allow some degree of public organization of the war effort.

Relations between the tsar, who from mid-1915 was supreme military commander, and his critics, sharpened as defeat followed defeat, and the country's economic position grew worse, with galloping inflation, transport chaos and food shortage. The tsar at GHQ, the empress's mismanagement of the ministers, and her close relationship (for her son's sake) with the notorious Rasputin made the imperial family a clear target for the opposition, who by the end of 1916 were openly proclaiming that Russia's misfortunes were the result of either treason or stupidity in high places. Duma spokesmen were saying the tsar must go. Even bureaucrats and military leaders saw this as the only way to save the war effort and the monarchy.

Revolution

On 23 February 1917 (OS) bread riots occurred in Petrograd (St Petersburg until 1914), spreading quickly to working-class quarters where the violence increased. Two days later some regiments of the vast garrison, consisting of peasant raw recruits and convalescent troops from the front, joined the rioters. The next day the Duma elected a Provisional Committee of moderate, liberal and radical leaders. Later that day, strikers and revolutionaries formed the Petrograd Soviet of Workers' Deputies in the

Tauride Palace, where the new Provisional Committee also sat. One of its deputy chairmen was A.F. Kerensky (1881–1971), also a member of the Provisional Committee.

The government lost its head. The ministers were arrested, and the tsar, totally isolated from his supporters, did not oppose the revolutionary government, and on 2 March (OS) abdicated. His brother and chosen heir, Michael, refused the crown unless it were given to him by a democratically elected constituent assembly and thus the Romanov dynasty was at an end. The Provisional Government, which now emerged, immediately enacted liberal laws, abolishing the police and replacing them by a people's militia. Also on 2 March, the Soviet issued its Order No. 1, calling for the creation of soviets (revolutionary councils) in army units to monitor officers. This, combined with the shock of the tsar's abdication and (despite war conditions) the total freedom of speech, generated an atmosphere of political anarchy so rampant that Lenin could call the Russia of 1917 the freest country in the world.

Lenin had spent the war in Swiss exile, returning to Russia only in April, with the aid of the German government. Lenin's wartime propaganda had tried to persuade the belligerent armies to turn the imperialist war into civil war, and this policy, in the context of 1917, meant attacking the new regime in Russia for its determination to prosecute the war. The Provisional Government was committed to improving Russia's military fortunes, despite the reluctance of the soviets, swollen by deserters and troops unwilling to go to the front. At first, the Petrograd Soviet, and the local Bolshevik leaders, took the line that they would support the new government 'in so far as its actions were not counter-revolutionary'. In spirit, the Soviet and the crowds which thronged it were for immediate peace.

Lenin was to exploit this gap, which divided the interests of the two organs of power that coexisted since March, by advocating defeatism in the rear and fraternization at the front. He brought the Petrograd Bolsheviks into line, and with large funds channelled to him by the Germans via his agents in Scandinavia he mounted a virulent campaign against the government, against the war, and in favour of the transfer of all power to the soviets. Although the Bolsheviks were a minority in the soviets, Lenin's purpose was to use this potential weapon to knock the government off balance.

Erosion of the provisional government

In May a new coalition came into being, when the foreign and war ministers, P.N. Milyukov (1859–1943) and A.I. Guchkov (1862–1936), the most committed to war, resigned. The government now promised to make peace without annexations or indemnities – the Petrograd Soviet's socialist formula – but was still compelled by patriotic inertia to defend the country and the revolution, a policy which appeared contradictory. Also in May, a new wave of returning professional revolutionary internationalists, Bolshevik and Menshevik, flooded the Petrograd Soviet, stiffening its militancy.

In July the liberals resigned from the government, the Galician offensive collapsed, with the troops deserting wholesale, and thousands of armed soldiers, sailors and workers poured on to the streets of the capital shouting 'all power to the soviets'. The Soviet declined to seize power and, unsure of the government's military support, Lenin, too, hesitated to lead the armed mobs.

To press the government's fragile political advantage at this moment, Kerensky, now prime minister as well as war and navy minister, caused documents to be published, albeit prematurely, alleging that Lenin's party had been receiving money from the Germans to conduct defeatist fraternization and agitation. Tipped off in advance, Lenin had gone into hiding in Finland, but the revolutionary masses, who now saw in the July demonstrations a German-backed manipulation of their revolution, turned against the Bolsheviks, and the Bolshevik Red Guards were disarmed.

Kerensky and the army commander L.G. Kornilov (1870–1918) agreed now to demonstrate the government's strength and resolve by a show of force against the mobs in the capital, aimed at restoring discipline in the army and submission in the Soviet. But while Kornilov's troops were moving towards Petrograd, Kerensky, fearing that he might be overthrown by Kornilov, reversed his orders. The troops and Kornilov were confused and demoralized, but not before the Soviet, panicked by Kerensky, had rearmed the Bolshevik Red Guards. From this moment the Provisional Government had no credible forces at its disposal.

The Bolshevik coup

By September the Bolsheviks had majorities in the Petrograd and Moscow Soviets, and Lenin was frantically urging them to seize power, but it was Trotsky (Lev Davidovich Bronstein, 1879–1940), President of the Petrograd Soviet, who planned and executed the coup. On 24 October (OS) the garrison troops acknowledged the Soviet as sole power, and next day the Peter and Paul Fortress with its arsenal went over to the Soviet. The seizure of the Winter Palace took place that night. The Provisional Government, intimidated by a blank shot from the cruiser *Aurora*, refused to use force in its own defence. Five soldiers, one sailor, and no defenders were killed, and the October Revolution was an accomplished fact. HS

The Soviet era

LENIN AS LEADER (1917–24)

When the II All-Russian Congress of Soviets opened at 11 p.m. on 25 October 1917 (os) the total strength of the Bolsheviks and their supporters was 370 or 380 out of 650, but their position was much fortified when the socialist delegates walked out in protest against the Bolshevik coup. The Congress voted at 5.30 a.m. the following morning to vest power in an all-Bolshevik Council of People's Commissars, headed by Lenin. The Bolsheviks had already by 10 October won majorities in the Petrograd and Moscow Soviets and in other urban centres, and for some time earlier Lenin, from his Finnish hiding-place, had been bombarding his colleagues with calls to seize power.

In the end the uprising was fixed to coincide with the Congress meeting, largely owing to the insistence of Trotsky that the coup must be clothed with the legitimacy of a transfer of power to the soviets – as against Lenin's view that power should be seized as soon as possible. The evidence suggests that the decision to launch the operation was taken only at the last minute.

Although Lenin always had in mind a seizure of power by his party, Trotsky's plan to make it appear as a soviet take-over was fully justified, since both the workers in the capital and Bolshevik delegates to the Congress itself supported a coalition of socialists and Bolsheviks as represented in the Congress of Soviets. Under threat of a strike from the Union of Railway Workers the Bolsheviks agreed to a coalition with the breakaway Left Socialist Revolutionaries (LSRs), which proved to be short-lived. The 'neutrality' of the Petrograd garrison ensured that there was virtually no resistance in the capital; in Moscow the conflict lasted a little longer.

Bolshevik propaganda had fully supported the convening of a Constituent Assembly to decide the future of Russia, and had blamed the Provisional Government for delaying the elections. These were duly held on the days it had appointed, 12 and 13 November, and all the evidence suggests that the vast majority of the electorate voted freely. The Bolsheviks secured about one-quarter of the total votes cast; half the country voted for socialism and against bolshevism. When the Constituent Assembly opened on 5 January 1918, it rejected by 237 votes to 136 a Bolshevik declaration endorsing the first decrees adopted by the All-Bolshevik Council of People's Commissars. The Bolsheviks and their LSR allies then walked out, and on the following day the Red Guards refused to admit the remaining delegates to the adjourned meeting of the Assembly. About a week later the III All-Russian Congress of Soviets, the elections to which had been carefully rigged, approved by an overwhelming majority the forcible dispersal of the first and – until more than 70 years later – the last freely elected representative body in Soviet history.

Below. Distributing revolutionary newspapers, Moscow, February 1917.
Below right. Revolutionary leaflet distributed on the eve of the Bolshevik coup, October 1917

Russian soldiers with revolutionary flags and banners on the Galician front, 29 October 1917

Civil War and the Red Terror

One of the first acts of the II Congress of Soviets was to adopt a decree on peace, which the Central Powers at first ignored. But on 2 December 1917 an armistice was signed, and after protracted negotiations in which the Powers increased the severity of their terms, violent dissensions appeared among the Bolshevik leaders, many of whom demanded a 'revolutionary war'. Peace was eventually signed on crippling economic terms at Brest-Litovsk on 3 March 1918 (NS). One result of the peace was the end of the coalition with the LSR who were incensed both by the capitulation to Germany and by Bolshevik policy towards the peasants. On 6 July the German ambassador was assassinated by a member of the LSR, and small-scale revolts by that party took place in Moscow and Petrograd. Thereafter it was forced out of existence, though many of its adherents joined the Bolsheviks (Communist Party as they became after March 1918).

The second result was civil war. During July there were several anti-communist insurrections, and anti-communist forces began their advance into the heart of Russia. On 30 August an attempt was made on Lenin's life, and the Bolsheviks inaugurated the mass arrests and executions, accompanied by the suppression of virtually all surviving non-Bolshevik newspapers, known as the Red Terror.

The Civil War lasted in effect from the summer of 1918 until November 1920, when the last of the anti-Bolshevik (or White) forces were evacuated from the south of Russia. They were commanded first by General A.I. Denikin (1872–1947) and later by General P.N. Wrangel (1878–1928). Apart from the attack in the south, Admiral A.V. Kolchak (1870–1920), allied with the Czech Legion, attacked from Siberia, while in the north-west General Yudenich's thrust got very near to Petrograd by October 1919. The approach of the White forces to Yekaterinburg (Sverdlovsk during the Soviet period) where the former emperor Nicholas II and his family were held in captivity, motivated the communists' decision to kill the emperor, his wife and children, his doctor and three servants on 16 July 1918.

Communist fortunes varied in the course of the war, but the ultimate victory meant a great lift to their self-confidence. Victory was mainly due to three factors. The first was the energy and organizing ability of Trotsky who, as People's Commissar for War, rebuilt the demoralized Imperial Army into the Red Army, making use in the process of tens of thousands of former officers. The second was the fact that the peasant population, though it did not support the communists, disliked them less than the White forces, whose policy was to restore the land acquired by peasants under the Bolsheviks to its former landlords. The third factor was the presence of enthusiastic communists at key points to maintain drastic discipline and morale. The much-publicized Allied intervention was originally motivated by the desire to restore the eastern front which had collapsed owing to Bolshevik policy, thus enabling the Germans to move troops to the west. Although ill-planned, ill-supported, and militarily of virtually no importance, this intervention played a big part in communist propaganda as a rallying call against a hostile capitalist West.

War Communism

The period of extreme communization which lasted from mid-1918 until spring 1921 was called 'War Communism'. It is uncertain whether this was a deliberate ideological plan or a series of improvisations in response to events. The Bolsheviks had inherited enough chaos from the Provisional Government: their own measures considerably added to it. In October nationalization of land, with the right of cultivation assured to the peasants, unleashed anarchy in the villages; in the following month industry was disorganized by a decree on workers' control. Before long stringent economic centralization was introduced, and workers' control was abandoned in favour of disciplinary management. The problem of food shortage was the most acute: compulsory requisitioning of food from the peasants was soon decreed, and class war broke out in the villages on the setting up of 'committees of the poor'. The immediate response of the peasants was to reduce production, and to try to unload their products on the extensive black market. But in time their resistance took on military form and by the end of 1920 a virtual guerrilla war was in operation

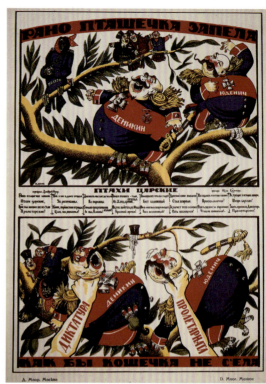

Above. 'Death to World
Imperialism', Civil War
poster, Moscow, 1919.
Above right. 'Early birds
sang as the cat ate them'.
Bolshevik poster from 1919
showing the White Generals
Denikin, Kolchak and
Yudenich being devoured by
the 'dictatorship of the
proletariat'

in parts of the country. About half the work-force
left the towns for the villages. An attempt to
nationalize almost the entire industry of the country
did not prevent economic collapse: by 1921 gross
output had fallen to less than a third, and foreign
trade had disappeared – in part owing to the Allies'
blockade. The sufferings of the population through
death, famine, disease, civil war and communist
terror were enormous.

Internal dissension

It is not surprising that with this background the
new regime should have been faced with serious
opposition. The forces opposed to the Revolution
mostly rallied to the various White armies. The
liberal parties were quite early on destroyed by
murder, arrest and exile. The two main socialist
parties, the Mensheviks and the Socialist Revolu-

tionaries (SRS), were never (except for a few months)
outlawed, and indeed throughout the Civil War
continued to return fair-sized contingents in elections to the soviets. But, as their criticism of the
communists became more vocal, they were increasingly harassed and impeded in their political aims
by arbitrary violence and deprived of their press.
The accusation of counter-revolutionary violence
levelled against them was untrue. The SRS did for
some months attempt to collaborate with one of the
governments set up by the White forces, but soon
abandoned both that attempt and general political
activity. The Mensheviks relied expressly on strictly
constitutional means, and expelled individuals who
took part in violence. The conclusive proof that
the socialist parties were not counter-revolutionary
(though certainly anti-communist) is provided by
the fact that many thousands of their adherents
were left at their official posts throughout the Civil
War and only afterwards removed from public service. The reasons for their destruction by arrest,
exile, and – in the case of the SRS – by a show
trial in 1922, were their increasingly effective and
popular criticism of Communist Party policy and
its arbitrary violence.

Within the Party also critical factions developed
in 1920 – such as the Democratic Centralists who
demanded more autonomy for the communists in
the soviets, and the Workers' Opposition who
claimed more independence for trade-union communists. In March 1921 the crews and garrison at the
naval base of Kronstadt revolted, demanding an end

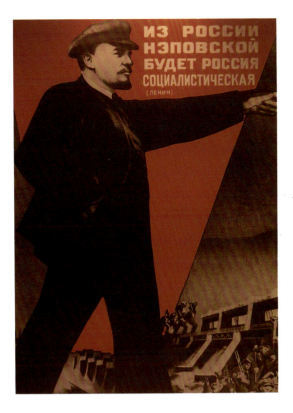

Poster of V. I. Lenin from the early Soviet period

to communist monopoly of power and more freedom for workers and peasants. Faced with crisis, Lenin presented the X Congress of the Communist Party with a series of measures which reflected the Party's panic in face of the threat to its sway. At the same time the Kronstadt rebels were mown down with heavy casualties, with the full support of the Congress including the members of the opposition factions. Lenin's measures, apart from the New Economic Policy (NEP), included the prohibition of factions on pain of expulsion, severe limitations on freedom of discussion within the Party, and a call for the suppression of the socialist parties (the Men-

Taking the salute on Lenin's Mausoleum, Moscow, 1924. Left to right: Voroshilov, Trotsky, Kalinin, Frunze, Budenny (behind), Klara Zetkin and Yenukidze

sheviks had, indeed, for some time been advocating a policy very similar to NEP).

Reorganization of the state

After the Bolshevik seizure of power, legislative authority was technically vested in a Central Executive Committee, in session between the intermittent All-Russian Congresses of Soviets. In practice, legislative power was exercised more often by the Council of People's Commissars, and by the Council of Workers' and Peasants' Defence, of which Lenin was also the Chairman; its main tasks were the supply of the Red Army and the militarization of the population and industry for Civil War needs. As for the legal system, the entire body of law left intact by the Provisional Government, as well as the bar and the judiciary, were abolished by decree, and on 24 November 1917 Revolutionary Tribunals were set up. These were directed to decide cases by their 'revolutionary conscience' but even after 1922, when codes of civil and criminal laws were promulgated, a great deal of discretion was left in the hands of the courts and of the, often, lay judges who presided over them.

Also, on 6 December 1918 the All-Russian Extraordinary Commission of the Council of People's Commissars for Combating Counter-Revolution, Sabotage and Speculation, known as Vecheka, was set up. Although its authority was, by the decree, limited to investigation and confiscation of property and ration cards, the Vecheka soon assumed the powers of imprisonment and execution without trial. Administrative arrests were followed by deportation and consignment to prison camps for forced labour, where conditions were appalling.

The first Constitution of the RSFSR was adopted on 10 July 1918. Its characteristic features were: indirect elections to the soviets, inequality of franchise, disfranchisement of certain classes and omission of any reference to the real force in government – the Communist Party. It included clauses guaranteeing civil rights, but provided no method for their enforcement. A new but similar Constitution was adopted on 6 July 1923, embodying the 'voluntary' union of the Ukrainian, Belorussian and Transcaucasian SSRs into the Union of Soviet Socialist Republics (USSR). Since the will that decided for union was that of the local Communist Parties only, its voluntary nature is open to doubt. The mortally ill Lenin warned his party in 1922 against excessive Great Russian chauvinism in the treatment of national minorities. Yet in 1921 Lenin had apparently authorized the invasion by the Red Army of Menshevik-controlled Georgia in support of a rebellion staged by local communists – in flagrant breach of the treaty of 7 May 1920 between Georgia and the RSFSR.

Lenin

Lenin was born Vladimir Il'ich Ul'yanov in Simbirsk in 1870, the son of a provincial school inspector who had risen to gentry rank through promotion. His father died in 1886, but it was the arrest and execution of Lenin's older brother Alexander for his part in a plot to assassinate Tsar Alexander III the following year that was to leave a more lasting impression.

Lenin studied law at Kazan' University, and graduated as an external student from St Petersburg University in 1891, by which time he was a leading figure in both legal and illegal Marxist circles. He was arrested and imprisoned in 1895, and subsequently exiled to Siberia in 1897. During his three years there he wrote a large number of revolutionary and theoretical works and married Nadezhda Krupskaya, a friend and

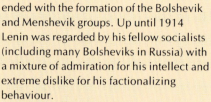

Above. *V. I. Lenin, 1922.*

ended with the formation of the Bolshevik and Menshevik groups. Up until 1914 Lenin was regarded by his fellow socialists (including many Bolsheviks in Russia) with a mixture of admiration for his intellect and extreme dislike for his factionalizing behaviour.

The outbreak of war brought about a change in many of Lenin's basic ideas; by 1917 he was associated with the extreme left of the European socialist movement. He returned to Russia with the help of the German government, after the February Revolution. However, within a few years of taking power after the October Revolution, Lenin's health, already weakened by an assassination attempt in 1918, had collapsed, and following a long illness he died in January 1924.

fellow Marxist revolutionary from St Petersburg, who was also in exile.

After his release, Lenin moved abroad, devoting great energy to imposing his will on the fledgling Russian Social Democratic Labour Party (RSDLP). During this period, Lenin brought about several splits in the party, the most famous of which in 1903

Left. *Lenin with his wife, Krupskaya.*
Right. *Lenin and Stalin.* Below. *Lenin addressing a rally in Red Square, 1919*

Trotsky

If Lenin was the uncontested leader of the Bolsheviks, it was Leon Trotsky who became their organizational genius. Trotsky was born Lev Davidovich Bronstein in Ukraine in 1879. Already anti-regime as a teenager, he became a Marxist, was arrested, and was sentenced to Siberian exile in 1900.

He escaped and fled to London, where he met Lenin in 1902. After the split in the RSDLP in 1903 Trotsky avoided either faction and took an independent line, arguing that the Russian bourgeoisie was too weak to carry out its revolution, and that the proletariat should directly usurp power from the Romanovs. This radical theory of permanent revolution was very similar to that espoused by Lenin in 1917, but at the time it won Trotsky little support.

During the 1905 revolution Trotsky became the leader of the St Petersburg Soviet. Following its collapse he was arrested and exiled to Siberia once more, but again he escaped abroad. After 1905 he worked to create a united Marxist party; this put him into direct, often bitterly personal, opposition to Lenin.

Leon Trotsky, 1920

Trotsky inspecting the newly-formed Red Cavalry during the Civil War, 1918

By 1917 Trotsky believed that the Bolsheviks, whom he then joined, shared his views. He played a decisive role in planning and executing the October coup, and he created and led the victorious Red Army to victory in the Civil War. However, after 1921 Trotsky found himself gradually outmanoeuvred by rivals in the leadership, particularly Stalin. Trotsky was deported in 1928 and murdered at Stalin's behest in Mexico in 1940.

Lenin suffered his first stroke in May 1922, and thereafter could work only intermittently until March 1923. In April 1922 Stalin, with Lenin's full approval, had become General Secretary of the Central Committee of the CPSU. By the end of 1922 Lenin had expressed doubts about Stalin's fitness for the post (in a letter to the forthcoming Party Congress, which Stalin succeeded in suppressing) but when he died on 21 January 1924 Lenin had not suggested his own successor.   LBS

STALIN GAINS ASCENDANCY

At Lenin's death, the immediate succession fell to G. Ye. Zinov'ev (real name Radomysl'sky, 1883–1936), L. B. Kamenev (real name Rozenfel'd, 1883–1936) and J. V. Stalin (real name Dzhugashvili, 1879–1953). The son of a Georgian shoemaker, Stalin was expelled in 1899 from the Tiflis Orthodox seminary as a Marxist agitator and became a full-time professional revolutionary in 1901. He first attracted Lenin's attention in 1905, became a member of the Bolshevik Central Committee in 1912, and was from then on one of the most prominent Bolshevik leaders inside Russia.

Trotsky, with whom Stalin clashed during the Civil War, had made many enemies in the Party, and had already been defeated in debate in the party organs which Stalin largely controlled. Stalin also enjoyed the full support of the right wing of the Party, headed by N. I. Bukharin (1888–1938), since until 1928 he fully supported NEP of which Bukharin was then the main advocate. The opposition of Zinov'ev and Kamenev was easily routed by the XIV Congress of the CPSU at the end of 1925, the composition of which was manipulated by Stalin as General Secretary. Trotsky was already defeated and discredited on theoretical issues such as 'Socialism in One Country' versus 'World Revolution'. Early in 1926 he joined with Zinov'ev and Kamenev in a United Opposition against Stalin's growing dictatorship. Events soon showed that the struggle was hopeless, owing to Stalin's control over the organs of the Party through his Secretariat. In such conditions, the Left Opposition to NEP, which probably commanded much support in the Party, was irrelevant. On 14 November 1927 Trotsky and his supporters were expelled from the Party and exiled, and the following year Trotsky was ejected from the USSR.

Trotsky's dictatorial practices, together with the fact that he was a Jew, made it unlikely that he could ever rally wider support in the Party – quite apart from the obstacle of Stalin's control of the apparatus. Bukharin, described by Lenin as 'the favourite of the Party', was in quite a different position. The policy which he advocated, and which Stalin for a time seemed to support, was squarely based on Lenin's thoughts, as expressed in his last writings.

NEP, according to Lenin, was in no sense a temporary device in order to secure a breathing-space: it was part of a plan designed to last 'not centuries, but generations'. The Bolsheviks had in 1917 been 'forced' to take power in circumstances in which the population was not ripe for socialism. The period of reconciliation between town and country which NEP offered would provide an opportunity for the peasants to acquire political maturity, and to learn by experience the virtues of co-operation: in no circumstances, according to Lenin, should this be forced. NEP was popular with many sections of the population: it repaired the ravages of the Civil War – the level of previous production in agriculture was reached by 1925, while the real wages of workers in terms of purchasing power rose to 108.4 per cent of the 1913 level in 1926/27. Intellectual life enjoyed a freedom that it was not to know for another sixty years. There was therefore every incentive for a man as jealous of political rivals as Stalin to eliminate Bukharin and his supporters once their alliance against the Left Opposition was no longer necessary to him.

Stalin's primary motive in ending NEP may have been not so much the desire to remove Bukharin as economic and political considerations. The economic argument was the alarming drop in grain supplies to the towns. The peasants were eating better and were, as usual, reluctant to sell grain unless compelled while industry was providing few products for them in exchange; attempts at the beginning of 1928 to stimulate deliveries were unsuccessful. Again, all were agreed that both collectivization of agriculture and the industrialization of the country were desirable: the debatable question was one of pace.

Bukharin, who accepted Lenin's time-scale of 'generations', believed that capital should be extracted from the peasants by first developing light industries which would produce the kind of goods that the peasants would buy in exchange for their produce. Supporters of the Left Opposition believed in some kind of compulsion against the peasants, although no one advocated the all-out war against 100 million people that Stalin unleashed, at the cost of millions of their lives and of long-term damage to agriculture.

Apologists for Stalin have sometimes justified his policy on the grounds that it was necessary in order to ensure rapid industrialization in face of the rising menace of attack by Germany – but this looks like being wise after the event.

It is not known exactly when Stalin decided on the 'Third Revolution' – enforced collectivization of agriculture and industrialization at breakneck speed. Clear signs of the impending change appeared by the spring of 1928. But rumours of the ending of NEP were indignantly denied, and Stalin proceeded with great caution in the face of known opposition inside the Party. He also showed great skill in out-manoeuvring Bukharin and the right wing of the party leadership. This operation occupied the whole of 1928. By the 16th Party Conference in April 1929 Bukharin and his supporters had been condemned: they were later expelled from the Politburo. At this Conference the ambitious First Five-year Plan and a policy of rapid collectivization of agriculture were adopted unanimously. For nearly five years thereafter the Party was to be engaged in open war against a terrorized, hostile and desperate people. By 10 March 1930 over half of all farms had been collectivized in a campaign which had lasted only five months, and engaged 25,000 party workers.

On 2 March 1930 Stalin, in a *Pravda* article which referred to 'dizziness from success', attempted to divert odium from his policy on to the subordinates who carried out his orders. But the respite which followed was only temporary, and the XVI Party Congress, in June and July 1930, urged a further determined struggle. To make it more effective for the control of industry, this Congress also reorganized the apparatus of the Communist Party, which by then numbered over one million, having quadrupled since October 1917. LBS

Right. *The Red Army looting and decommissioning an Orthodox Church in Moscow, 1925*

STALIN'S AUTOCRACY (THE 1930S)

Immediately after Stalin gained political ascendancy, he set about the social and economic transformation of the country. A hectic process of state-building took place, in which much that became familiar in the Soviet scene was born. Large-scale ministries and collective farms were formed, vast construction sites started to cover the countryside with towns and industry, and the repressive organs extended outwards, including their major manifestation: the growing GULag empire of concentration camps, forced labour camps and transit prisons. All levels of society changed places: peasants became workers, millions of whom migrated annually to the towns (until stopped by the restoration of the internal passport), workers poured into offices and the swelling ranks of lower administration, and the top echelons coalesced into an amorphous and privileged élite, misleadingly entitled the 'Soviet intelligentsia'.

But this was not the work of Stalin alone. His 'great break' of 1929 quite consciously harnessed the energies of younger party cadres, of Komsomols and even schoolchildren, in a gigantic effort to reshape the culture and economy of the countryside. They formed 'raiding parties' of 'light cavalry' which transformed every area of social life, from grain requisitioning to philosophy, into the struggle with 'alien tendencies' and 'class enemies' on each particular 'front'. However carefully they were oriented by the party leadership, such forces had an identity of their own, and formed part of the social basis for Stalinism. In addressing them, Stalin and other oligarchs were appealing to a quite authentic, if often suppressed, stream of the original bolshevism. Since 1921 the whole pattern of policy had been retreat: a mixed economy, peasant agriculture, compromise with 'bourgeois specialists' and a prospect of socialism that would take (in Lenin's words) 'years and years'. Stalin's policies promised advance at last, enacted with much of the rhetoric and militancy of the Civil War period, but literally too: for younger cadres this was their own civil war, the one against the peasantry.

Stalin and the Party

Stalin's leadership transformed the CPSU into a mass organization, whose size had swelled from 1.3 million (1928) to 3.5 million (when recruitment was halted) in January 1933. Of these, the first intake was primarily of workers. Over a million production and transport workers were admitted in 1930/31, with mass applications often received from workshops and even factories in the first stage of the Five-year Plan. By April 1930, 48.6 per cent of party members were manual workers. But the target of one worker for every two communists was not achieved; thereafter 'proletarian' enrolment fell away, simultaneously with the reduced status of the 'working class' in the official definitions of society. Peasant intake also rose in the early months to reach a high point of one new recruit in five during 1930. Most came from the newly-constituted collective

Below. *Church used as a grain store during collectivization in the early 1930s*
Below right. *Workers at the 'Trekhgornaya' textile mills applying to join the Communist Party, 1930*

Stalin in the company of collective farmers, 1933

farms whose party cells and 'political departments' formed the new focus of party influence in the countryside. All was not well in these first stages, and Stalin attempted to blame 'excesses' of collectivization on the fervour of local party workers. Further indication of resistance may be seen in the fact that some 40,000 individual peasants (uncollectivized) still held party membership in January 1931. This was not the last of the political difficulties with the countryside.

But out of the recruitment policies which Stalin pursued there soon emerged a third and most decisive element. As the dust settled, it became clear that the beneficiaries of the incipient Stalin order were neither the working class nor least of all the peasantry. At the heart of this new policy, which found expression in party membership quite early on, was the appeal to a new stabilizing factor: a new 'middle' in Soviet society, and one through which it could properly be said that the country was being ruled. This third estate, which lumped together such disparate strata as the local administrators, factory managers, technical intelligentsia and 'specialists', both old and new, rose steadily as a proportion of party membership through the 1930s. Among industrial managers, party members increased from 15 per cent (1930) to 70 per cent (1933), and among top officials in agriculture, the jump was from 15 per cent (1930) to 83 per cent (1933). In the central apparatus of state, the Party soon came to achieve predominance – even saturation – while at some crucial levels of local government, such as the *rayon* (district), it reached an average of 97 per cent. Thus party members of this rank became a vital link between the political leadership and the society they were administering.

Stalin and society

At the first stage of Stalin's ascendancy, in which 'proletarian' forces were unleashed originally against the Party's right and thereafter upon the whole society, positive discrimination was exercised in their favour. Access to higher education was thought vital to a working class which would treble in size (from 6 to 20 million) during the 1930s. The special faculties which prepared workers for universities were vastly expanded from an annual intake of 160,000 to some 511,000 students by 1933. A new technical intelligentsia was similarly recruited after 1928 according to a stringent *numerus clausus* on class lines, and a series of show trials of 'wreckers' between 1928 and 1931 served as a reminder that 'bourgeois' technical specialists were capable of sabotage and every ingenious trick to destroy the country's industrial effort.

In June 1931 Stalin suddenly reversed this line, and denounced the 'specialist-baiting' and anti-intellectual discrimination which he had earlier fostered. In parallel pronouncements he laid down theoretical bases for inegalitarianism: the 'new stage' he had inaugurated needed specialist skills and was willing, he clearly hinted, to pay for them. Quality of work, not social origin, would be the new basis of reward and discrimination. A similar line was followed, in April 1932, towards the cultural intelligentsia, when militant and proletarian associations in literature and the arts were suddenly disbanded and replaced (on orders of the Central Committee) by more broadly-based bodies: the cultural unions.

Such a shift in policy was well-grounded in economic necessity, and reflected the determination to produce greater balance, proportion, internal consistency and realism in the targets for the Second Five-year Plan (1933–37). It also reveals the relationship between Stalinism and society. Whereas, at the previous stage, Stalin had sought to mobilize the pre-existing elements who most opposed – and now destroyed – the remnants of the NEP society, at the second stage (from 1931/32 on) he showed himself a conscious social manipulator, breaking with his previous supporters, and looking ahead towards the stabilizing policies which would enable him to rule a now-transformed country with some greater degree of assurance and regularity. This shift in attitude, however, may also have been determined by a change in Stalin's personal political position.

Opposition to Stalin

While no outright opposition to Stalin emerged before the XVII Party Congress, there had previously been significant rumblings of discontent behind the scenes. During 1929 all leaders were 'Stalinist' in that they upheld basic tenets: collective farming imposed at whatever cost (at least 6 million peasant deaths during the resulting famines); industrial development by force where necessary; and forced labour by the growing camp and prison populations. Yet despite these original assumptions, opposition started to appear. Already during 1930 serious divisions on policy could be discerned within the Stalinist leadership. Two top officials of the party and governmental apparatus, S.I. Syrtsov (1893–1937) and V.V. Lominadze (1897–1935), appear to have drawn up a secret manifesto, which condemned the violent repression of the peasantry, the megalomania of such large industrial projects as the Stalingrad (now Volgograd) tractor factory, and Stalin's autocratic conduct. Little had come of this before they were expelled from the Party as a 'left-right bloc' in December 1930.

In the summer of 1932 a new opposition document appeared, the (M.N.) Ryutin (1890–1937) manifesto, some 200 pages of analysis which was disseminated quite widely in upper party circles. It argued that N.I. Bukharin's warnings against adventurist economic policies had been vindicated, proposed an economic retreat, including scaled-down investments and dismantling of the collective farm system, a general amnesty, and reinstatement of expelled party members. Much of the text which remained unpublished until 1990–91 was devoted to criticism of Stalin, whose personal vindictiveness and power-seeking were held to be the ruin of the Revolution. Stalin responded with extreme vehemence and is known to have demanded the death penalty for the ringleaders, a request refused by the Politburo, among whom the Leningrad party secretary, S.M. Kirov (1886–1934), is now known to have been particularly firm. No doubt other leaders were united in the expectation that, if the request had been granted, they would be potential victims, and Stalin himself may have meant this in the famous telegram of September 1936, which told the security organs that they were 'four years behind' in the work of exposing enemies within the Party.

The XVII Party Congress (the 'Congress of Victors') assembled in January 1934 ostensibly to celebrate the defeat of 'enemies of socialism' in the Soviet Union. Collective agriculture had been established, industrial production put on a firm footing and above all, as Stalin's speech insisted, the hopes expressed abroad that the 'Soviet experiment' would founder had themselves been confounded. But there were other murmurings behind the scenes, of which the most important concerned Stalin's personal position.

During 1933 a new set of tendencies had emerged within Soviet society, that may be summarized as the call for order. Much earlier than anyone could have anticipated, the new social structure – with its growing hierarchies and inequalities – had begun to settle down, exerting pressures, even perhaps demands of its own. In the cultural sphere, as championed by Gor'ky, these took the form of a campaign for 'quality' and a rejection of the shoddy literary standards of the First Five-year Plan. In education this involved an end to the *numerus clausus*, renewal of academic standards and a largely conservative school reform.

From the Soviet establishment, with its swelling organs of administration, came the call for routine, predictability, the laying-down of directives and even of legal regulations. Of the latter, Kirov seems to have been champion. He warned that the agricultural administration was ineffective, calling for the abolition of its much-hated political departments (a measure enacted later in 1934). Further, he condemned 'extremism' in dealing with the countryside, particularly the punitive expulsion from collective farms, which amounted often to sentence to death by starvation. Kirov probably intended to restrict the sweeping powers of the secret police in their usurped judicial role (widened in a circular of July 1929) to the functions simply of arrest and preliminary investigation. Finally, though not publicly expressed at the Congress, came criticism of Stalin's leadership, implying that any restoration of legality would have to begin at the top. Secret ballot figures show about 300 votes against Stalin, who then ceased using the title 'General Secretary'. Kirov was promoted from Leningrad to a position alongside him in the Moscow Secretariat – a transfer prevented by his assassination in December 1934.

The Great Terror

The Kirov murder was the signal for a new stage in Soviet history, one of mass repression which began in earnest in 1936 and did not subside until 1939. Paradoxically, the descent into lawlessness

Right. Red Square, May Day 1934. Left to right: Kalinin, Stalin, Voroshilov and Kuybyshev

Stalin and the Soviet
leadership on the Lenin
Mausoleum, May Day,
1938

was accompanied by public gestures of legality. Promulgation of the Stalin Constitution ('the most democratic in the world') took place simultaneously with the great purges and trials of 1936. Bukharin, its main author, appears genuinely to have believed that legal limits could be put on Stalin's power; he contemplated a project (articulated on a foreign journey of 1936) of setting up a 'second party' of loyal socialist intellectuals who would criticize the status quo from an independent viewpoint. Stalin had other ideas. Rather than sanction a second party he resolved to rule without one.

Until the end of 1934 Soviet policies came, nominally at least, from the Party and were confirmed by periodic, though less and less frequent, meetings of its oligarchs and upper echelons. These upper ranks were a prime target of subsequent repression – 70 per cent of the Central Committee elected at the XVII Congress was executed during the following five years. Of ordinary delegates, some 1,108 were arrested or executed in the same period, and only 59 of the original 1,966 reappeared as delegates to the next Congress in 1939.

Analysis of those purged within the Party shows that terror moved steadily closer to the centres of power. This was signalled by the first 'show trial' of top leaders (G. Ye. Zinov'ev, L.B. Kamenev and 14 others) in the summer of 1936. Those of other leaders (G.L. Pyatakov (1891–1937), K.B. Radek (1885–1939) and 'accomplices') followed in January 1937, while Bukharin and others (including A.I. Rykov (1881–1938), Kh. G. Rakovsky (1873–1938) and G.G. Yagoda (1891–1938)) were retained for the grand finale in 1938. With the exception of Yagoda's, all these guilty verdicts were posthumously annulled in 1988/89.

Terror against the Party was renewed at the plenum of February 1937. Stalin and his supporters forced through – against various doubters – a resol-

ution which demanded further 'intensification of the struggle' against 'enemies of the people'. That opened the door to mass arrests in all sections of society, though particular severity was given to leading groups: senior administrators, managers, the intelligentsia, military officers and so on.

For total arrests, above 8 million (about 5 per cent of the population) is a likely figure. Of those arrested, some 800,000 (one in ten) were probably executed, while the remainder faced incarceration or transportation to the camp system. As to the death-rate in camps, a figure of 10 per cent in 1933, rising to 20 per cent in 1938, is probably conservative, but even so would mean a death rate annually of well over one million persons for the purge years. Given that 10 years was a standard sentence, it can easily be seen that only a small fraction of those convicted can have survived.

Stalin's use of power

Four instruments were essential to Stalin's rule. First was his mastery of the Party through its apparatus – a tendency which worried Lenin, who had promoted him – and his consequent ability to select delegates to the Party Congresses which would choose him. As the party institutions atrophied during the 1930s, he relied ever more closely on his private secretariat. Second was a compliant Procuracy – a quite familiar feature of old Russia – and the willingness of jurists to subordinate themselves to his orders. Of these, the most infamous was A. Ya. Vyshinsky (1883–1955), Chief Prosecutor in the 'show trials'. Stalin's third instrument was the secret police, who came to constitute a state within the state, omnipresent, and significantly entrusted (after the apparent suicide of Stalin's second wife, Nadezhda Alliluyeva, in November 1932) with the management of his households. Last, at the apex of the terror system, was the GULag:

Photographs as propaganda

Like their counterparts in Hollywood, photographic retouchers in Soviet Russia spent long hours smoothing out the blemishes of imperfect complexions, helping the camera to falsify reality. Stalin's pock-marked face demanded exceptional skills with the airbrush. But it was during the Purges that a new form of falsification emerged. The eradication of Stalin's political opponents at the hands of the NKVD was swiftly followed by their obliteration from all forms of pictorial existence.

Photographs for publication were retouched and restructured with airbrush and scalpel to make once famous personalities vanish. This reworking was often clumsily executed, perhaps intentionally, so that the disappearances would serve as a warning to others. Paintings too were often withdrawn from galleries so that compromising faces could be blocked out of group portraits.

At the same time a parallel industry was in full swing, glorifying Stalin as the 'great leader and teacher' through Socialist Realist paintings, monumental sculpture and, in many cases falsified, photographs representing him as the only true friend, comrade and successor to Lenin.

Entire editions of works by denounced politicians and writers were banished to the closed sections of the state libraries. Trotsky's writings were removed by state decree in 1935. Ordinary citizens were forced to take part in this charade, afraid of the consequences of being caught in possession of material considered 'anti-soviet' or 'counter-revolutionary'.

The murderous leaders of the NKVD did not escape obliteration themselves when they fell from favour. N.I. Yezhov's bloody rule ended suddenly in 1939 and in one photograph he was transformed, almost surrealistically, into wooden panelling.

Perhaps the strangest example of all came years later with Beria's downfall, following Stalin's death in 1953. To replace his fawning biography, subscribers to the *Great Soviet Encyclopedia* were sent a four-page insert carrying a full-page picture and new information on the Bering Sea. The substitute photograph showed whalers harpooning their catch – perhaps an ironic reference to the fate of Stalin's blubbery henchman.

David King

The St Petersburg League of Struggle for the Emancipation of the Working Class, 1897. The League was founded by Lenin (seated, centre) and Yuly Osipovich, known as Martov (seated, right), who on his death was publicly mourned by Bolsheviks as 'their most sincere and selfless opponent'. This explains why he survived in the version of the picture published in 1939 (below), from which A.L. Malchenko (standing, left) was touched out.

Stalinist disappearances. The upper photograph, taken in April 1925, shows, left to right, Lashevich, Frunze, Smirnov, Rykov, Voroshilov, Stalin, Skrypnik, Bubnov, and Ordzhonikidze. When published in 1949 (below), rearrangement and retouching had reduced the group to four: Frunze, Voroshilov, Stalin and Ordzhonikidze. More than half the meeting had been erased from history.

D.A. Nalbandyan's famous picture celebrating the opening of the White Sea–Baltic Canal. Stalin is flanked by Kirov (left) and Voroshilov. On the left, the figure of Yagoda, chief of the NKVD secret police, shot in 1936 on Stalin's orders, has been obliterated by overpainting.

Blacked out faces from Ten Years of Uzbekistan, 1934. There is hardly a publication from the Stalinist period that does not bear the scars of political vandalism: photographs defaced with Indian ink or savagely attacked with scissors. Sometimes entire pages were torn out.

this quite quickly grew to be a basic element of his rule and, not surprisingly, the word with which Stalinism became synonymous.

Yet terrifying and destructive though it was, this period still produced achievements. The 1930s saw the USSR industrialize, largely through its own resources, and such show pieces as the Moscow Metro railway system, the gigantic power-stations in the Urals and the machine-building combines were concrete evidence of what could be done. Other of the 'prestige projects' – such as the White Sea-Baltic Canal – were economically worthless, and amounted to pyramids in honour of Stalin, after whom the largest were named. Throughout the decade, therefore, colossal waste accompanied construction. Not until Gorbachev's speech in November 1987 was the official balance sheet of achievements versus costs finally tilted to the latter.   AK-W

The USSR at war (1941–45)

On the eve of war the ordinary Soviet citizen could, it seemed, look forward to a period of relative stability. Real wages were still lower than in 1926 and would remain so until 1952. Many items of food were in short supply: the massacre of livestock during collectivization had left the country with fewer cattle than in 1913. The prison camps of Central Asia, Siberia and the Far North were choked with slave labourers. But the population at large, especially the office-holders and the educated, had been, as a Soviet writer would later put it, 'frightened once and for all' by the Great Terror, and were reliably subservient. Police activity had therefore been reduced. Stalin himself said that there would in future be no need for mass purges. (He should have added that the population would none the less be systematically culled both to refresh their memories of 1936–38 and to provide cheap labour for industries and areas which held little attraction for free workers.) Collectivization and the Five-year Plans, for all the waste and confusion of the early 1930s, had laid the foundations of a modern economy. Stalin had silenced those of independent standing who might challenge his authority; exile did not save his sternest critic, Trotsky, who was murdered on Stalin's orders in Mexico in June 1940. The central organs of government were staffed with his creatures, the middle levels of authority in all sectors with people who had made themselves accomplices in the bloodletting and who joined loudly in the rites of the Stalin cult. Science, culture and education were by now as tightly controlled, and as rigidly subordinated to central planning, as were industry and agriculture.

It might appear that the country could concentrate on the two huge tasks which Stalin had set it – overtaking the leading capitalist countries in economic performance and producing by education and indoctrination 'Soviet man', a new type of human being fit to live in the communist society of the future. Many in the USSR were ready to believe that the 'Stalin Constitution', though scarcely relevant to the present, was a genuine blueprint for a happier future. Many were prepared to overlook, as temporary tactical necessities, glaringly unsocialist or inhumane features of the system: the draconian labour legislation, the fees charged in the higher classes of schools, the special shops selling to the privileged goods inaccessible to other citizens, and even the corrective labour camps, the full horror of which seems to have been concealed with remarkable success from the population at large.

In June 1941 the 'sudden and perfidious' attack by his recent partner in the Molotov–Ribbentrop Pact ruined Stalin's hopes of a period of intensive economic development and social engineering.

The course of the war

In the early stages of the war the Soviet regime was preserved by the mistakes of the enemy and by luck rather than by its own efforts. Though it is scarcely credible that Hitler took the ever-suspicious Stalin by surprise, he certainly found him ill-prepared. The Great Purge had weakened the Soviet armed forces. The first Soviet commanders in the three main sectors were incompetent old Civil War hacks. In the western regions – and particularly in Ukraine and Belorussia – the inhabitants at first often welcomed the German invaders as liberators. By

Right. Poster with anti-Hitler caricature

The Siege of Leningrad

The siege that the city of Leningrad endured for two and a half years during the Second World War was the worst suffered by any city in modern times. The destruction, in human lives and in the fabric of the city itself, was immense.

Leningrad (St Petersburg) lies on a narrow strip of land bounded on one side by the Baltic Sea and on the other by Lake Ladoga. By August 1941 the Finns attacking from the north had sealed off the city from that direction. On 30 August the Germans captured the small town of Mga and cut the last rail link to the rest of the Soviet Union. The siege began.

Leningrad's food supplies were limited, and several factors made the situation worse: few people had been evacuated; food was still being sent out of the city as the Germans surrounded it; and bombing destroyed the main food warehouse. During the winter of 1941–42 the daily ration was as low as two slices of bread per person. Thousands died every day of hunger and illness, often caused by the inedible ingredients such as wood shavings put in the bread to increase its bulk. Very soon there were no domestic animals to be seen in Leningrad: dogs, cats and the city's pigeons and sparrows went to feed the starving people. Leather was boiled to make jelly.

In mid-November 1941 the famous 'Road of Life' across the frozen Lake Ladoga was opened, but it was not until mid-January 1942 that more food was entering the city than was being eaten. On 1 January there was less than two days' supply of food left.

Hundreds of thousands starved to death during that winter, the coldest for decades.

The bodies were kept in piles on the snow, or in one room of an apartment, while the survivors lived in another. There were few places to dig graves, and fewer people with the strength to dig them. Many bodies were not buried until the spring thaw.

By mid-1942 the population of the city was down to one-third of its size just eight months earlier; by the end of 1943 it was

Above left. *Transporting the dead, Nevsky Prospect, 1941*
Above right. *Winter, 1942*
Left. *Anti-aircraft battery installed near St Isaac's Cathedral, Leningrad, 1942*

less than a quarter of the 1941 level. While many of these people were evacuated in 1942 and 1943, it is estimated that between 1.3 and 1.5 million people, or approximately half of those trapped by the siege, were either killed in the fighting or died of starvation.

The first break in the German lines was achieved in January 1943 and the siege was finally lifted on 27 January 1944, 880 days after it had begun. The diary of a seventeen-year-old schoolgirl sums up the feelings of the people of the city:

All of us Leningraders are one family, baptized by the monstrous blockade – one family, one in our grief, one in our experience, one in our hopes and expectations.

Second World War poster showing the Allies strangling Hitler

Soviet filmed images of the Second World War.
Below. *Children sheltering during a German bombing raid*
Below right. *Resistance from young and old*

November 1941 one of the three main invading armies was outside Leningrad (which the Germans never succeeded in taking, though over a million died in the beleaguered city), the second was 20 miles from Moscow, and the third deep in Ukraine.

Moscow, however, was saved by Hitler's own miscalculation in diverting armour from the central sector to the other two, and by the early onset of a very severe winter. The Soviet regime retained its main centre of command and communications, and succeeded in evacuating to the rear some 1,500 industrial enterprises, the output from which, together with the material aid supplied by the Allies, ensured that in the last two years of the war the Soviet forces were better armed and equipped than the enemy. In 1942 the German drive towards Baku, intended to cut off Soviet oil supplies, was checked, and Hitler made his second great mistake in concentrating too much of his strength on Stalingrad (Volgograd) – an objective of more symbolic than strategic importance. The defeat of Field-Marshal

von Paulus at Stalingrad (January 1943), and the capture of his huge army, was the turning-point in the war.

In the next 18 months the Soviet armies recovered all the territory taken by the Germans, and thereafter swept westward and southward into Romania, Bulgaria, the Baltic states, Poland, Hungary, Austria and Czechoslovakia. On 22 April 1945 Soviet forces surrounded Berlin, and linked up with American troops on the Elbe. The unconditional surrender of Germany to the Allies followed on 7 May. On 8 August (two days after the USA had dropped an atomic bomb on Hiroshima) the USSR joined in the last phase of the war against Japan and rapidly captured the Japanese forces in Manchuria, to justify the territorial gains promised at the Yalta Conference.

The war had inflicted enormous losses, human and material, on the USSR: 27 million killed according to the latest estimates (half of them civilians or prisoners), 1,710 urban centres destroyed, 25 million people left homeless, thousands of enterprises and thousands of kilometres of railway put out of action.

Territories under German occupation

Still grosser than Hitler's military blunders were the political errors committed by the German authorities in the occupied territories. Those Ukrainians, Belorussians and – a smaller proportion of their national group – Russians who met the invader with the symbolic 'bread and salt' hoped in vain for deliverance from the most objectionable features of the Soviet system. Though the German commanders often recommended more tactful and realistic treatment of the local population, the SS (the Nazi Party troops) and the political authorities on the whole favoured ruthless exploitation and the ultimate extermination of Slav 'submen' (*Untermenschen*). The Law for Restoration of Private Land

Soviet Second World War poster

A.V. Suvorov (1729–1800), M.I. Kutuzov (1745–1813) – than of Marx and Engels. Guards regiments and divisions were set up again, specifically military decorations (the Orders of Suvorov and Kutuzov) introduced, epaulettes and saluting (both previously regarded as symbols of the old caste system) were brought back. Stalin promoted his most successful commanders marshals, and himself took this title, as well as the unique style of 'Generalissimus'. The abolition (in March 1943) of the Comintern convinced many at home and abroad that Russian nationalism had finally triumphed over communist internationalism.   HTW

THE REVERSION TO STALINIST NORMALITY

The great victories of 1943–45 might seem to have demonstrated conclusively the loyalty of the bulk of the Soviet population and of the army in particular, and to have shown that the regime was firmly and efficiently in control of the country and its resources. It had certainly raised Soviet power and Stalin's personal authority (indeed, his personal popularity) to an unprecedented level. But if the Soviet peoples expected that after the war the leadership would reward their tremendous efforts by relaxing its heavy political and economic pressures upon them, they were to be disappointed.

After the Second World War Stalin was, if anything, still more morbidly obsessed with problems of security, internal and external, than he had been before. Those sections of the population which had passed out of Soviet control during the war – and this included prisoners of war and those deported to forced labour in the Third Reich, as well as civilians who had lived under German occupation – were automatically suspect, as were the inhabitants of newly annexed regions. Tribunals with powers of summary punishment followed in the wake of the liberating Soviet armies, condemning to execution or imprisonment not only actual traitors but others who had done no more than continue to teach Soviet schoolchildren, or live in their own homes with German soldiers billeted upon them. Perhaps the most tragic of Stalin's victims were the displaced persons forcibly repatriated to the USSR by its Western allies.

Population transfers for reasons of security modified the ethnic map of the USSR. In 1941, in the path of the German advance, the Volga Germans had been moved from what had been their home for nearly two centuries. After the German retreat, the Soviet authorities uprooted whole peoples – the Crimean Tatars, the Caucasian Chechen Ingush and the Kalmyks – alleged to have collaborated with

(February 1942) did not in fact result in the general dismantling of collective farms. The execution of civilian hostages, the massive levies for forced labour in Germany and elsewhere, and the ruthless ill-treatment of prisoners of war held in the occupied areas helped to convince the local population that they had exchanged a bad master for a worse.

The powerful Ukrainian nationalist movement from mid-1943 onwards considered itself at war with both Nazis and communists. By the autumn of 1943, 10 per cent of German fighting troops in the USSR were engaged against partisan units – many of which were also viewed with suspicion and anxiety from Moscow. Though the Germans had in their hands a sufficient number of Soviet volunteers to launch an anti-communist crusade in the USSR itself, and a general of proven talent willing to command it (General A.A. Vlasov (1900–46), captured outside Leningrad in July 1942), they decided that the enterprise might rebound upon them.

The patriotic revival

Stalin, for his part, showed great psychological acumen in his handling of the Soviet population. Although the regime since its inception had propagated 'militant atheism' and at times actively persecuted believers, he recognized the importance of the Orthodox Church as a focus of patriotic feeling by receiving Metropolitan Sergy in September 1943, and permitting the re-establishment of the Holy Synod. Writers and artists were allowed a measure of creative freedom unknown since the late 1920s. Foreign cultural imports – particularly films – were accepted for their entertainment value, with little regard to ideological content. Propaganda for the home front centred around 'patriotic' rather than narrowly communist themes: more was heard of old Russia's military heroes – Alexander Nevsky,

The Soviet Union in World War II

Above. *Home to ruins: the Western Front, 1942*

Below. *The battle of Stalingrad (storming a house), November, 1942*

Above. *The battle of Kursk, July 1943*

Below left. *Soviet troops advance towards the centre of Berlin, 1945*

Below right. *Berlin, 1945*

The progress of the war in Russia, 1941–44. The Soviet border is shown as it stood on the eve of the German invasion in 1941

The Soviet Union	Frontline December 1941
Axis and occupied territories 22 June 1941	Frontline November 1942
Neutral countries	Frontline December 1943
Soviet border 1938	Frontline December 1944
Soviet border 22 June 1941 (Day of Nazi invasion)	Post-War borders

the occupier. Mass deportations from the Baltic republics helped to clear the way for Russian immigration. The persecution of 'homeless cosmopolitan' writers and critics, during the campaign to restore ideological discipline in the arts, opened up a new era of official anti-semitism.

Post-war reconstruction of the country's battered and distorted economy was in itself a task which might have taken a decade. Stalin, however, proclaimed a much more ambitious and exacting programme: a series of Five-year Plans to treble pre-war industrial output and 'guarantee our motherland against all eventualities'. Relations between the USSR and its wartime allies had deteriorated quickly as communist regimes were installed by force or fraud in Eastern and Central Europe. Soviet propagandists proclaimed once again the division of the world into two camps, and the alleged threat of an 'imperialist' onslaught on the USSR was used to justify the narrow concentration of Soviet economic resources on heavy industry and military production.

Progress in these sectors was impressive. By 1948 the country had basically reconstructed its war-damaged industries, and expansion thereafter was rapid. By 1949 the USSR had acquired a nuclear weapon. Light industry, and more particularly agriculture, were starved of capital to make all this possible. Meat, fats, sugar, flour, clothing and footwear were always in short supply. The war-devastated cities of Ukraine, the mid-Volga region and South Russia were rebuilt with remarkable speed, but in the congested older cities the housing shortage grew increasingly acute.

Nowhere were increased investment and generous incentives more necessary than in agriculture, and nowhere were they so heartlessly denied. The means by which Stalin hoped to increase agricultural output – higher norms for compulsory deliveries, tighter labour discipline, administrative reorganization, grandiose schemes to 'transform nature' by for instance raising great shelter belts in the path of the drying east winds, and generalizing 'ley rotation' farming – were utterly ineffectual, and the country was in sight of a grave crisis of supply on the eve of his death.

In the ageing dictator's last years the stultifying effect of what his successors would call 'the cult of

Territory annexed by the USSR, 1939-40 and
re-incorporated in 1945

Former German and Czechoslovak territory
annexed by the USSR in 1945

States liberated by the Soviet army, and/or in which communist
regimes came to power between 1945 and 1948

Soviet occupation zones in Austria
(evacuated 1954) and Germany

British, French and United States occupation zones

USSR IN 1938

The iron curtain in 1948

Eastern and southern frontiers of areas of pre-war
Germany incorporated into Poland in 1945

The Soviet Union in Eastern Europe, 1945–48

its centre pages to polemical articles on linguistic science, in preparation for a pronouncement of stunning banality on this subject by J. V. Stalin. His only significant contribution to the proceedings of the XIX Congress of the CPSU in 1952 (the first since 1939) was a comically crude pamphlet on 'The Economic Problems of Socialism'.

Stalin's jealous and vainglorious insistence on his own intellectual and political supremacy had more sinister results than these. In 1949 he authorized the execution of N.A. Voznesensky (1903–50), a member of the Politburo and chairman of the State Planning Commission, and a number of other senior officials. The 'Leningrad Affair' (as it is called, since several of those concerned had connections with Leningrad and with A.A. Zhdanov (1896–1948), who had been in charge of the city during the war) was a warning that even the highest office-holders could be summarily destroyed if they aroused Stalin's suspicions. In 1952 it appeared that others might shortly follow Voznesensky into oblivion. At the XIX Party Congress in October the Politburo was enlarged and renamed 'Presidium'. According to Khrushchev, in his 'secret speech' of 1956, this was in preparation for the elimination of older leaders in favour of 'less experienced' persons. It became obvious that Stalin was contemplating bloodshed when in January 1953 *Pravda* reported that nine doctors had confessed to the murder of Zhdanov and to plotting against other prominent persons on the orders of the US intelligence services. When Stalin died two months later, these charges were dropped and the police officials and false witnesses responsible for them were punished. HTW

THE KHRUSHCHEV YEARS, 1953–64

After the death of Stalin no single individual attained the dictatorial power which he had wielded during the last twenty years or more of his life. The collective leadership which was established in the first two years following Stalin's death on 5 March 1953 was a product not so much of agreement among his heirs as of disagreement on policy issues and of personal rivalry among the leaders. The struggle for power which took place behind the cloak of collective leadership was, moreover, one between powerful bureaucratic machines as well as between leaders. Those who immediately emerged as potential supreme leaders were G.M. Malenkov (1902–88) who, as Chairman of the Council of Ministers, headed the government; L.P. Beria (1899–1953), Minister of Internal Affairs and head of the security police (later the KGB); and N.S. Khrushchev (1894–1971), a party secretary who quickly became *de facto* head of the party organization and who in

the personality' became more and more obvious in all sectors of public life. To judge from its coverage in the Soviet press, by far the most important event in the immediate post-war period was the seventieth birthday of J. V. Stalin in 1949. His prejudices and whims governed the activities not only of administrators but of scholars, writers, artists and scientists: incalculable damage to Soviet agriculture, as well as to science, was caused by his unqualified support of the pseudo-genetics of Lysenko, and the development of automation in the USSR was impeded by his conviction that 'cybernetics is a bourgeois delirium'. In 1949 *Pravda* for several days devoted

September 1953 was officially accorded the title of First Secretary of the Central Committee of the Communist Party (CPSU). It was not difficult for a majority of central party leaders and government ministers to agree on the need to keep the security police in a much more subordinate role than it had played under Stalin. Beria's ambitions threatened this policy and though the secret-police chief tried to add political support to the coercive force he could command by attempting to appeal to the non-Russian nationalities, both Malenkov and Khrushchev had much stronger followings at the centre where power in the Soviet Union was at that time concentrated. In July 1953 it was announced that Beria had been arrested and in December it was officially confirmed that he had been executed.

Malenkov initially had the upper hand over Khrushchev and until mid-1954, when alphabetical order was adopted, the former's name headed the list of members of the Central Committee's Presidium (Politburo until 1952, and again from 1966 to 1991). But already before the end of 1953 Khrushchev had apparently taken over from Malenkov primary responsibility for agricultural policy and he championed the claims of heavy industry against Malenkov's attempt to place a new emphasis on the consumer goods sector. By so doing, Khrushchev no doubt won additional support from the powerful bureaucratic agencies whose interests he thus served. In February 1955 Malenkov was forced to resign his chairmanship of the Council of Ministers and engage in self-criticism, whereby he took the blame for the failures of past agricultural policy and accepted that the foundation of the economy on heavy industry was correct.

N.A. Bulganin (1895–1975) took Malenkov's place as Chairman of the Council of Ministers and he, in turn, was replaced as Minister of Defence by the war hero, Marshal G.K. Zhukov (1896–1974). Khrushchev's standing within the leadership was becoming greater, but was by no means unchallengeable. Partly no doubt to strengthen his own position in relation to such senior rivals as Malenkov and V.M. Molotov (1890–1986) and partly because of his genuine revulsion against Stalin's style and methods of rule, Khrushchev took the initiative – and the risk – of denouncing the man to whom, in his years as supreme leader of the country, god-like qualities had been attributed. Malenkov and Molotov (as well as Khrushchev's mentor, L.M. Kaganovich, 1893–1991) were more intimately involved in some of Stalin's worst excesses than Khrushchev had been and so stood to lose more from an exposure of Stalin's misdeeds. Khrushchev was far from having been without sin in Stalin's time, but with characteristic boldness he was prepared to cast the first stone.

The XX Party Congress and de-Stalinization

The scene of Khrushchev's attack on Stalin was the XX Congress of the CPSU held in February 1956. In a four-hour speech in closed session at the end of the Congress (which was issued in only a limited Soviet edition for party workers, but which none the less soon became widely known throughout the USSR and Eastern Europe and was shortly published in full in the West) Khrushchev attacked the cult of Stalin's personality and drew attention to many of the injustices and crimes he had perpetrated. In discussing the Terror, Khrushchev deplored the execution and imprisonment on trumped-up charges only of party members and did not concern himself with the fate of non-members of the CPSU. This breakthrough into relative frankness had momentous consequences. It contributed to a freer intellectual atmosphere within the Soviet Union itself, though it was a great shock to many communists and helped to stimulate unrest in Eastern Europe (especially Hungary and Poland) and dissension within the international communist movement.

Though these consequences of the XX Congress undoubtedly caused great concern within the party leadership, they did not deter Khrushchev from returning to the de-Stalinization theme at the XXII Party Congress in 1961. There in open session he made points which he had included only in his 'secret speech' of 1956, and other speakers provided further details of Stalin's crimes. Symbolically, Stalin's body was removed from the mausoleum in Red Square where it had lain, since his death in 1953, alongside Lenin's. Places named after Stalin ceased to bear the name of the discredited leader; even the famous Stalingrad became Volgograd. These changes had been preceded in the mid-1950s by the much more important release and rehabilitation of hundreds of thousands of political prisoners and the posthumous rehabilitation of others, though the process was far from complete.

The anti-party group crisis

The struggle for power between Khrushchev and his rivals came to a head in June 1957 when his leading opponents combined to outvote him in the Presidium (Politburo) and made a determined attempt to remove him. The seven-to-four majority against Khrushchev included such important leaders as Malenkov, Molotov, Kaganovich and Bulganin. Malenkov and Molotov had taken somewhat different policy lines in the recent past and the coalition was united in little but their desire to be rid of Khrushchev. His opponents were, however, labelled 'the anti-party group' by Khrushchev and it is true that Khrushchev's support lay, above all, in the party apparatus, since a majority of the secretaries

Khrushchev on a visit to the Stalingrad Hydro-Electric Station, 1958

Right. Khrushchev meeting the stars of the American show, 'Holiday on Ice', Moscow, 1959

The traditional greeting of bread and salt for Krushchev at the railway station of the Moldavian capital, Kishinev, May 1959

at the Central Committee of the CPSU, union republican and regional levels had been appointed during his incumbency as First Secretary of the Central Committee and looked to him as their patron. Khrushchev, backed by A.I. Mikoyan (1896–1978) among the most senior of Politburo members and by Marshal Zhukov, insisted on taking the dispute to a plenary session of the Central Committee which supported him against the majority of the Presidium. This victory enabled Khrushchev to strengthen his position by ousting from the party leadership (in 1957–58) Malenkov, Molotov, Kaganovich and Bulganin, among others, and when Bulganin was relieved also of his chairmanship of the Council of Ministers in 1958, Khrushchev himself took over the post and headed both Party and government from then until his removal from the political scene in October 1964.

Khrushchev's record

Though Khrushchev will probably be remembered above all for his contribution to the cause of de-Stalinization, he was not averse to imposing his own views on his colleagues, and his policies were marked by inconsistency and over-optimism. The inconsistency was especially notable in cultural policy and was symbolized by Khrushchev's refusal, on the one hand, to allow publication of Boris Pasternak's novel, *Doctor Zhivago* (and his forbidding Pasternak to

accept the Nobel Prize for Literature in 1958) and, on the other, by his personal approval for publication of Alexander Solzhenitsyn's *One Day in the Life of Ivan Denisovich* in 1962.

In foreign policy Khrushchev took the important step of recognizing that war between states with 'different social systems' was not inevitable; he was very conscious of the destructive power of nuclear weapons. At the same time his heavy emphasis on nuclear rather than conventional forces helped to lose him the support of the Soviet military. Similarly, his tolerance of attacks on Stalin and the Stalin period alarmed the KGB and conservative party officials and helped to undermine his support in those quarters.

In other areas Khrushchev combined reformist initiatives with a tendency to push particular policies too far. He upgraded the status of agriculture within the Soviet economy, but his division in 1962 of regional party organs into industrial and agricultural sections alienated many in the party apparatus. Nevertheless, the living standards of the mass of the people received far more attention under

Khrushchev than they had under Stalin. Having earlier supported the claims of heavy industry in the course of his struggle against Malenkov, Khrushchev, in the years of his ascendancy, put his own weight behind the effort to make life easier for the Soviet citizen. One reflection of this was the massive house-building programme, notwithstanding the fact that the quality of the hastily-built apartment blocks left much to be desired.

A new Party Programme adopted in 1961 set hopelessly over-ambitious targets to be met by 1980 and failure to come anywhere near achieving them became an embarrassment to Khrushchev's successors. In addition to approving the Programme, the XXII Congress of the CPSU in 1961 approved new Party Rules. These, in the main, remained in force until the Gorbachev era, but one disturbing innovation was rescinded at the first post-Khrushchev Party Congress (the XXIII in 1966). This was Article 35 which stated that at each regular election not less than a quarter of the membership of the Central Committee and its Presidium, not less than one-third of the Union Republican Central Committees and of the regional party committees, and not less than one half of the membership of town and district party committees and of primary party organization committees or bureaux must be renewed. It was widely held that Khrushchev had introduced the compulsory percentage turnover in order to be able to move people from party office at will, while maintaining himself and his supporters in positions of authority by invoking the escape clause which safeguarded the position of those of especially great prestige and ability. (A much less specific sentence on systematic renewal was added to Article 24 when the Rules were revised at the XXIII Congress, a change which strengthened the security of tenure of party office-holders.)

The fall of Khrushchev

Khrushchev's style of rule helped to lose him the support he had earlier built up. It is evident from his own memoirs as well as from the writings of his Soviet critics that he took many important decisions alone and that latterly he frequently put more reliance upon his personal advisers than upon officials within the appropriate party and government agencies. Some of his personal initiatives – notably the decision to put missiles in Cuba in 1962 – were also fraught with danger and when they turned out to be less than wholly successful, it was clear where responsibility lay.

A coalition of Khrushchev's disgruntled party colleagues, with the tacit support of the military and the much more active support of the KGB, finally brought his remarkable political career to an end. There was no repetition of the 1957 events when Khrushchev attended the Central Committee session on 14 October 1964. This time the top leadership (Politburo and Secretariat) were almost completely united against him and the Central Committee had no longer any collective desire to come to his support. Ostensibly, Khrushchev 'retired' on grounds of old age – he was seventy – and failing health, but the subsequent exclusion of his name from the Soviet press, as well as attacks in which he was clearly the unnamed target, made plain to Soviet citizens that he had been toppled against his will.

Khrushchev's career and personality were not lacking in contradictions. He was a hard and ruthless politician who yet possessed a warm humanity; a Stalinist from his youth who did more than anyone to shake the foundations of Stalinism; a poorly educated worker of peasant origin who had a sharp intelligence and a remarkable capacity for learning (not least from his trips to the West); and a true believer in the illusory goal of a humane world communism who did not hesitate to send tanks into Budapest to crush with armed force the Hungarian uprising of 1956.   AHB

THE BREZHNEV ERA, 1964–82

Of the two highest political positions in the country held by Khrushchev, the more powerful post – First Secretary (in 1966 renamed General Secretary, a return to the nomenclature of Stalin's time) of the Central Committee of the CPSU – went to L.I. Brezhnev (1906–82) and the chairmanship of the Council of Ministers to A.N. Kosygin (1904–80). It is one measure of the re-establishment of collective leadership that until 1980 both men, by this time in their mid-seventies, held the same posts, and that there were then two other survivors of Khrushchev's Presidium still holding Politburo membership (as well as

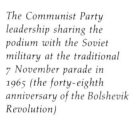

The Communist Party leadership sharing the podium with the Soviet military at the traditional 7 November parade in 1965 (the forty-eighth anniversary of the Bolshevik Revolution)

One of the most influential Soviet leaders over many years, M.A. Suslov, pictured above on 26 February 1981 (just under a year before his death)

Right. Painting of Brezhnev as he liked to be portrayed, bedecked with medals

secretaryships of the Central Committee): M.A. Suslov (1902–82) and A.P. Kirilenko (1906–90). Under this oligarchical leadership the division of labour among the various party and governmental bodies became more clear-cut, and though party controls, in a broad sense, remained as strong as ever, there was less arbitrary interference by the leadership in the work of specialist institutions. Brezhnev, unlike Khrushchev, accepted that he could not take personal decisions in every policy area from foreign policy to family law and from agriculture to literary culture.

Brezhnev's enhanced status

While Brezhnev did not come to wield the individual power of a Khrushchev, still less that of a Stalin, he gradually strengthened his position in relation to his colleagues and acquired a greater prominence in the 1970s than he had had in the 1960s, becoming the leading Soviet spokesman on foreign affairs and overshadowing Kosygin who had earlier often engaged in 'summit talks' on behalf of the Soviet Union. Brezhnev was also able to strengthen his position within the Politburo by securing the promotion to full membership of such protégés and supporters as F.D. Kulakov (1918–78), D.A. Kunaev (b.1912) and V.V. Shcherbitsky (1918–90) in 1971, and K.U. Chernenko (1911–85) in 1978, and by removing from the leadership such potential opponents as P.Ye. Shelest (b.1908) in 1973, A.N. Shelepin (b.1918) in 1975 and N.V. Podgorny (1903–83) in 1977.

The removal of Podgorny facilitated a further enhancement of Brezhnev's position – his elevation to the chairmanship of the Presidium of the Supreme Soviet (a post which Podgorny had held since 1965 when he succeeded Mikoyan). This was the first time in Soviet history that a party General Secretary had combined that post with the formal headship of state and though it was a less powerful combination of offices than Khrushchev's combining the party leadership with the chairmanship of the Council of Ministers, in terms of status it increased the distance between Brezhnev and his colleagues. Brezhnev, indeed, became the recipient of a whole series of official honours each more absurd than the last – for example, the Lenin Peace Prize, 1973; Marshal of the Soviet Union, 1976; the Order of Victory (the highest military honour), 1978; and the Lenin Prize for Literature (for his ghosted memoirs), 1979. While the leadership changes of the 1970s were to Brezhnev's advantage, and his public honours surpassed those accorded to Khrushchev, it was noteworthy that turnover in the Politburo, Secretariat and Central Committee (and among party officials generally) was much slower than under either of Brezhnev's predecessors. This reflected both his cautious, consensus-seeking style

and the desire of his colleagues to maintain some counterweights to him within the leadership.

Under Brezhnev's leadership many of Khrushchev's policies were modified or even reversed. A number of his administrative reforms were speedily annulled. Military expenditure was increased. The de-Stalinization process begun by Khrushchev was not only stopped, but attacks upon Stalin and the Stalin period were virtually forbidden. The great purges were not so much exonerated as ignored. While fewer rash and grandiose promises were made by Brezhnev than by Khrushchev, reality continued to be gilded by propaganda; bad news – if it arose within the Soviet Union – was, as before, suppressed.

Foreign policy

In foreign affairs the Soviet leadership under Brezhnev exercised greater caution than Khrushchev had displayed, but they devoted substantial resources and attention to expanding their influence in post-colonial Africa and showed a firm intention to maintain the Communist status quo in Eastern Europe. The latter policy was ruthlessly underlined when the Soviet Union intervened militarily in August 1968 to put an end to the 'Prague Spring', even though the reform process in Czechoslovakia over the previous eight months had been embarked upon by the Communist Party of that country under the leadership of Alexander Dubček. The invasion of Czechoslovakia was a blow to reformers within the Soviet Union itself. For many of them it was

The aged oligarchy was fond of presenting one another with awards, the party leader, Leonid Brezhnev, being the most frequent recipient. Here Brezhnev is presented with an Order of Lenin and 'Hero of the Soviet Union' gold star on his seventy-fifth birthday, 19 December 1981. Mikhail Suslov is reading the citation. Others, left to right, in the foreground, are Kirilenko, Tikhonov, Chernenko, Gromyko and Ustinov. Gorbachev is at the back between Chernenko and Gromyko

confirmation that the Brezhnev years were to be ones of conservative Communism and that their hopes for change, first kindled by the XX Party Congress in 1956, would be long deferred.

The riskiest foreign adventure undertaken by the Soviet Union in the Brezhnev era was the military intervention in Afghanistan in 1979. This provoked a more hostile American response than the ending of the Czechoslovak reforms, since Czechoslovakia – unlike Afghanistan – was a Warsaw Pact country. It also turned out to be a more obvious failure for the Soviet Union. Whereas the intervention in Czechoslovakia produced the short-term results which the Brezhnev leadership sought, Soviet troops in Afghanistan found themselves bogged down in a guerrilla war which they could not win outright and which was costly politically as well as in human lives. It was not, however, until the Gorbachev era that the full folly of the enterprise was admitted and Soviet troops were withdrawn.

During much of the 1970s Soviet–Western relations improved and there was significantly more East–West contact than hitherto. This was a period of more frequent 'summit talks' between Brezhnev and his successive American counterparts, Presidents Nixon, Ford and Carter. The signing of the Helsinki Agreement (the Final Act of the Conference on Security and Co-operation in Europe) on 1 August 1975 was an event of special, albeit ambiguous, importance. While the Agreement could be presented to the Soviet public as a victory for the USSR inasmuch as it appeared to have secured a long-standing Soviet goal – official acceptance by the Western powers of the borders which had existed *de facto* since the end of the Second World War – it had unintended consequences for the Soviet Union. Provisions in the Agreement, which Western negotiators had insisted upon – on human rights, cultural co-operation and dissemination of information – which the USSR did not, in fact, begin to implement seriously until the late 1980s, were a source of embarrassment to the Brezhnev leadership. They

gave added force to Western criticisms of Soviet practices – especially following the election of President Carter in the United States in 1976 and the stress he laid on human rights – and encouragement to the small but courageous band of Soviet dissidents.

The last years of the Brezhnev era were ones of deteriorating East–West relations. A combination of the Soviet invasion of Afghanistan in December 1979 and the election of Ronald Reagan as American President in 1980 produced a new chill in Soviet–American relations in particular. Soviet foreign policy was being made by an aged group of senior Politburo members – Brezhnev himself, within the limits of his rapidly failing physical powers; Andrey Gromyko (1909–89) who had been Foreign Minister since 1957 and a full member of the Politburo since 1973; Dmitry Ustinov (1908–84), the Minister of Defence (who had also been in the Politburo since 1973); and Yury Andropov (1914–84), the KGB chief since 1967 who had been elevated to the Politburo simultaneously with Gromyko and Ustinov in 1973. Just outside this inner circle stood the even older and no less conservative figure of Boris Ponomarev (b.1905) who had been head of the International Department of the Central Committee of the CPSU since 1955, an office he continued to hold until 1985.

A network of institutes, capable of offering the Soviet leadership advice on foreign policy, was established in Moscow during the Brezhnev era and it did have the effect of making the leaders and, to a certain extent, a broader public, somewhat better-informed about the outside world. Several of these bodies – for example, the Institute of the United States and Canada, headed by Georgy Arbatov (b.1923) – included well-informed and sophisticated analysts (as well as hacks and KGB agents), but even the best of them had to operate within the limits of an agenda set by the aged political oligarchs.

Domestic developments

For most Soviet citizens the Brezhnev era was one of rising living standards and it was politically the most tranquil of all periods of Soviet history. But a heavy price was paid for these achievements, such as they were. The apparent economic advance and incessant talk about the 'scientific and technological revolution' supposedly taking place on Soviet soil obscured the facts that the technological gap between the Soviet Union and most Western countries was widening in favour of the West and that several of the newly-industrializing countries of Asia were also better exemplars of the latest technological developments. The Brezhnev years as a whole saw a decline in the rate of Soviet economic growth and by the end of the 1970s and beginning of the 1980s this had reached the point of stagnation. Such econ-

Aleksey Kosygin, Chairman of the Council of Ministers from 1964 to 1980, was an influential economic administrator in the Soviet Union over many years. His first ministerial appointment – in January 1939 as People's Commissar for the Textile Industry of the USSR – occurred when he was only thirty-four

omic development as took place was at a heavy ecological price – as indeed had been the case in earlier Soviet periods. In the Brezhnev era, however, there was an added dimension of danger as atomic power was increasingly used as a source of energy. The badly-constructed nuclear power-stations which proliferated, and the nuclear waste unsafely disposed of, represented a major threat to future generations – and not only within the territory of the Soviet Union and its successor states.

The superficial political tranquillity was also attained at a price which had to be paid later. Real problems – including inter-ethnic tensions and the variety of deeply-felt grievances of many of the nations within the multi-national Soviet state – were swept under the carpet. After a brief period between 1965 and 1968 when modest economic reform was being promoted by Kosygin, *reform* (of any sphere of Soviet activity) became a taboo concept. Thus, problems accumulated as only tinkering attempts could be made to resolve them. While ultimately reform in the Soviet Union – in the Gorbachev era – brought into the open the internal contradictions of the Communist system, the postponement of reforms did nothing to ease the pain of transition.

In a few respects – in addition to a general rise in the material standard of living – there was under Brezhnev modest change for the better as compared with Khrushchev's time. Churches were less persecuted than they had been by Khrushchev, although they continued to be objects of surveillance and of anti-religious propaganda. Natural scientists (including geneticists) achieved greater intellectual freedom than they had enjoyed under Khrushchev (not to speak of Stalin), but social scientists were still kept within an ideological straitjacket. Some of the latter, however, managed to bend Marxism-Leninism to their own purposes to a limited extent even in their published works while in private they freed themselves still further from official dogma.

Public political dissent, as distinct from private criticism, was, however, an activity confined to a small minority of the population. It had first surfaced in the mid-1960s when Khrushchev's successors looked as if they might not only stop criticism of the Stalin period but even formally rehabilitate Stalin himself. The opposition to such a rehabilitation of a vocal group of prominent intellectuals helped to impose limits on the extent to which the clock was turned back. But the authorities took pains to ensure that the dissident movement did not became a mass one. The dissidents' motives could easily be misrepresented by the tightly-controlled official mass media and a wide variety of repressive measures could be brought into play against those who contined to engage in independent political activity. Thus, for example, of the two

leading figures in the dissident movement, Alexander Solzhenitsyn (b.1918) was arrested and deported from the Soviet Union in February 1974 and Academician Andrey Sakharov (1921–89) was exiled to the city of Gor'ky (Nizhny Novgorod) in January 1980. By the end of the Brezhnev era manifestations of overt dissent had been reduced to a trickle.

Basic foodstuffs in Soviet shops were still heavily subsidized by the state as one of the ways of keeping the population quiescent, but this led to shortages of meat and of dairy products – especially in provincial towns, for the authorities took care to give a higher priority for distribution to Moscow, Leningrad and the republican capitals where a growth of social discontent might have had the most serious political consequences. Social malaise was, however, indicated by an increase in alcoholism and drunkenness, an associated decline in the life expectancy of adult males and higher infant mortality rates.

For the party-state élite the Brezhnev era was one of unprecedented calm. They did not have to fear for their lives, as in Stalin's time, or even for their jobs, as in Khrushchev's. Security of tenure in high office led to the entire party and governmental leadership growing old together. At the beginning of 1982, the last year of Brezhnev's life, the average age of the Politburo was over seventy. Patron–client relationships, which had always been a feature of Soviet political life, flourished as never before, while corruption grew in response to the lessening of the fear of retribution and to the loss of belief in the ultimate goals of the system. If the Brezhnev era was both politically and socially the most stable of all periods of Soviet history, it was also the most cynical.   AHB

ANDROPOV AND CHERNENKO, 1982–85

Compared with the sweeping changes which affected the Soviet Union in the late 1980s the periods of 15 months (from November 1982 until February 1984) when Yury Andropov (1914–84) led the Soviet Union and of 13 months (February 1984 to March 1985) during which Konstantin Chernenko (1911–85) was at the helm might be regarded as indistinguishable. That would, however, be to ignore differences of atmosphere and in priorities which were observable at the time.

Andropov had an ambiguous past. Between 1957 and 1967 he was regarded as a relatively enlightened department head in the apparatus of the Central Committee of the CPSU. He brought in as consultants a number of young and intelligent people who were to become prominent reformers in the

Yury Andropov addressing a meeting of East European leaders, June 1983. Front row (left to right): Dmitry Ustinov, Nikolay Tikhonov, Andropov and Andrey Gromyko

perestroika years. Andropov, although more open-minded than Brezhnev, was, however, no liberal, as he demonstrated fully when he was head of the KGB from 1967 until early 1982, following which – after the death of Mikhail Suslov (1902–82) – he returned to party work.

On Brezhnev's death Andropov became General Secretary of the Communist Party with the support both of those who hoped to see some economic reform and of others whose demand was for greater discipline within society. Although Andropov's health began to fail as early as February 1983, he made some cautious nods in the direction of reform and more vigorous moves towards counteracting the drunkenness and general sloth which had characterized the later Brezhnev years. With the people as a whole (as opinion surveys from the era of glasnost were later to confirm) he was much more popular than was either his predecessor or successor. Andropov appealed to a substantial body of opinion within Soviet society at that time which held that the greatest need was for more order and firm government. The shortness of his term as party General Secretary meant that the reality whereby he had no fundamental solutions to offer to the problems of the Soviet system was obscured by the myth that what the country needed most was a strong leader and that Andropov embodied that ideal.

Under Andropov a sterner line was adopted to combat alcoholism, absenteeism and corruption while at the same time a few tentative steps towards economic reform were taken. A number of industrial enterprises were given greater decision-making autonomy by way of 'experiment' and Mikhail Gorbachev (b.1931) was allowed to advocate the 'collective contract' in agriculture whereby groups of farmers were to be given greater autonomy, responsibilities and incentives by contractual agreement with their parent state or collective farm.

By the standards of the Brezhnev years, personnel change in the upper echelons of the party apparatus and the government was brisk. In retrospect, the most important single action taken by Andropov was to extend the responsibilities of Gorbachev within the top leadership team, making him overseer of the economy as a whole and not only of agriculture. Other people brought into relatively senior positions by Andropov included Yegor Ligachev (b.1920) and Nikolay Ryzhkov (b.1929), both of whom were to be important figures in the perestroika era. Some of the most corrupt of Brezhnev's cronies were dismissed from office. A degree of change did not, however, constitute a break with Leninist orthodoxy. Overt dissidents were persecuted with at least as much vigour as Andropov had displayed when he still headed the KGB, although there was a broadening of the limits of permissible 'within-system' criticism.

The modest domestic change was not matched by any improvement in the Soviet Union's relations with the outside world. Although Andropov signalled an interest in ending the Sino-Soviet dispute, no fundamental change took place in Soviet relations with any other country. East–West relations remained extremely strained and were further exacerbated at the beginning of September 1983 when a civilian Korean airliner which had flown over Soviet territory was shot down with the loss of 269 lives. This action did fresh damage to the Soviet Union's international reputation and, taken in conjunction with Andropov's failing health, postponed any hopes of breaking the East–West deadlock.

When Andropov succumbed to his long illness in February 1984 at the age of 69 he was succeeded by the 72 year old Chernenko rather than by Gorbachev, who was 20 years younger. Andropov had attempted towards the end of his life to pave the way for

Yury Andropov lying-in-state in the Hall of Columns, Moscow, 11 February 1984. Members and candidate members of the Politburo and Secretaries of the Central Committee of the CPSU are seen paying their last respects to him. Andropov's successor, Konstantin Chernenko, is third from the left in the front row and Gorbachev is in the centre of the picture

Chernenko (looking every one of his seventy-three years) taking the salute at the Bolshevik Revolution anniversary celebrations on 7 November 1984

Gorbachev to succeed him, but his wishes were ignored by the Brezhnevite old guard who turned with relief to one of their own, Chernenko, who had been close to Brezhnev since the early 1950s. Already in indifferent health when he became General Secretary, Chernenko was able to leave no mark on Soviet history, but made a temporary difference in the sense that the modest policy changes – whether of a disciplinarian or reformist character – introduced by Andropov were now pursued with less vigour. The only change that took place in the top leadership team (the Politburo and Secretariat of the Central Committee of the CPSU) was that occasioned by the death of Defence Minister Ustinov in December 1984. There was a strong sense of interregnum and Chernenko, like his predecessor, did not have a single 'summit meeting' with the American President. In view of Chernenko's declining health and the fact that he was not particularly well versed in international affairs, A.A. Gromyko (1909–89) was never more dominant in Soviet foreign policy-making than during these 13 months. It was only with Chernenko's demise on 10 March 1985 – the third death of a Soviet General Secretary in less than three years – that the leadership passed to a new generation.   AHB

THE GORBACHEV ERA, 1985–91

When Mikhail Gorbachev succeeded Konstantin Chernenko as General Secretary of the Central Committee of the CPSU on 11 March 1985 he had more radical reform in view than was realized by the party apparatus and the population as a whole, but hardly so far-reaching as the changes he was actually to espouse between 1989 and 1991. Moreover, neither Gorbachev nor his political opponents within Russia imagined or intended that this era of reforms would end with the dissolution of the Soviet Union itself – an outcome inconceivable in 1985, even to committed nationalists in the non-Russian republics. Yet in retrospect it is far from clear that a politically and economically transformed Soviet Union could have been kept intact by anyone, given the scale of the pent-up national grievances which the new openness and freedoms of the Gorbachev era allowed to be aired and to become the subject of conflicting political demands.

By lifting the lid on independent political and intellectual activity which had first been placed on it by Lenin – and kept there for almost seven decades – Gorbachev and his reformist allies within a far-from-united Soviet leadership saw a mass of complex issues spill on to the political agenda. Some of them were put there by Gorbachev himself who, with great political skill, was to grasp and hold the political initiative during his first four years as Soviet leader.

From the Spring of 1989 until his resignation on 25 December 1991 Gorbachev was, however, increasingly responding to events beyond his control. Even then, he had crucial choices to make and it was of the utmost importance that he refused to allow Soviet troops to stand in the way of the independence movements in Eastern Europe and that, while making concessions to conservative forces at home, he would not authorize the state of emergency and comprehensive crackdown on democratic forces he was being pressed to introduce by hard-line opponents and by senior colleagues alike. In the end the Prime Minister, the Chairman of the KGB, the Minister of Defence, the Minister of Internal Affairs, the head of military industry, and a number of communist party officials took the law into their own hands and staged their attempted coup. By so doing, they achieved the opposite of what they intended and made certain the destruction of the very Soviet state they had been bent on preserving at all costs.

Beginnings, 1985–86

All Soviet leaders inherited a top leadership team which they could not instantly change and Gorbachev was no exception. He was surrounded by members of the Politburo and Secretaries of the Central Committee who had been promoted to those posts either under Brezhnev or by Andropov. Some were thinly-disguised opponents of Gorbachev (as well as of any reform worthy of the name), others were conditional supporters; none – until the promotion of Eduard Shevardnadze (b.1928) from candidate to full membership of the Politburo in July 1985 – was a like-minded and wholehearted supporter. Already, however, in April 1985, Nikolay Ryzhkov and Yegor Ligachev had been elevated to full membership of the Politburo, while retaining the Secretaryships of the Central Committee to which they had been promoted by Andropov. Ryzhkov and Ligachev both fell into the category of conditional allies of Gorbachev, but the alliance at that time was more important than the conditionality as the new General Secretary set about building a coalition which would replace the Brezhnevite old guard.

Ligachev became in this period the *de facto* number two to Gorbachev within the party leadership. One of the earliest policies to be endorsed by the Politburo and actually implemented was an anti-alcohol campaign in which the prime mover was Ligachev but which became identified with the name of Gorbachev who defended it publicly. Although alcoholism and alcohol-related disease and crime in the Soviet Union were on a scale sufficient to justify extreme concern, the actual measures adopted – the closing-down of production units

(including the destruction of some valuable vineyards) and the drastic reduction of retail outlets – had unintended consequences. They were a stimulus to illicit distilling and led to a serious loss of budgetary revenue as a result of the sharp drop in the legal sales of alcoholic drinks. In the later years of the Gorbachev era the restrictions on the sale of alcohol were relaxed but by then much damage had been done, both in terms of the revenue and of the developing use of unlicensed and especially dangerous intoxicants.

A number of important personnel changes conducive to policy innovation were made in Gorbachev's first year. These included the removal from the Politburo in early July 1985 of the ambitious and backward-looking Grigory Romanov who had been the Secretary of the Central Committee supervising the army and defence industry; the replacement at the same time of Andrey Gromyko as Foreign Minister by Shevardnadze (although Gromyko was given a prestigious – but less powerful – post in compensation, being elevated to the Chairmanship of the Presidium of the Supreme Soviet as titular head of state); the replacement of the veteran Brezhnevite Nikolay Tikhonov (b.1905) by Ryzhkov as Chairman of the Council of Ministers in September; and the appointment in December 1985 of Boris Yel'tsin (b.1931) as First Secretary of the Moscow City Committee of the Communist Party in succession to Viktor Grishin (1914–92) who had harboured hopes of succeeding Chernenko as Soviet leader. Yel'tsin – who was later to be a more serious rival to Gorbachev than Grishin had been – became a candidate (non-voting) member of the Politburo in February 1986.

The promotion of Aleksandr Yakovlev (b.1923), although less publicly visible, was of comparable importance to those mentioned above. Yakovlev was appointed head of the Propaganda Department of the Central Committee in July 1985 and became a Secretary of the Central Committee in March 1986. Of those who sat round the Politburo table, the most radical were now Shevardnadze, Yakovlev and Yel'tsin, with Gorbachev himself who, while he found it necessary to take account of different viewpoints, was especially close to Shevardnadze and Yakovlev both politically and personally. It was, moreover, to Gorbachev that they owed their promotion. (By the summer of 1987 – thanks to Gorbachev's decisive backing – Yakovlev was a full member of the Politburo as well as of the Central Committee Secretariat, even though at the beginning of the previous year he was not even a member of its much larger outer body, the Central Committee.)

The XXVII Congress of the CPSU in February 1986 came too early in Gorbachev's General Secretaryship

Aleksandr Nikolaevich Yakovlev, an important Gorbachev ally of the 1980s

Mikhail Gorbachev

Mikhail Gorbachev was born into a peasant family in the village of Privol'noe in the southern Russian territory of Stavropol' on 2 March 1931. Within the next few years Stalin's forcible collectivization of agriculture, and the associated famine, had killed a third of the inhabitants of the village. In the course of the 1930s both Gorbachev's grandfathers were arrested.

Having survived this harsh decade and the war years, the young Gorbachev was able in 1950 to enter the Law Faculty of Moscow University, a success he owed not only to excellent school grades but also to receiving the Order of the Red Banner of Labour as an exemplary worker. In 1951 he met Raisa Titorenko – a bright student in the Philosophy Faculty – and they were married in 1953. Upon graduation in 1955, Gorbachev returned to his native Stavropol' area and rose through the Komsomol and Communist Party regional hierarchy (he was party First Secretary for the Stavropol' area from 1970 until 1978) before being summoned to Moscow as the Secretary of the Central Committee responsible for Agriculture.

By the end of 1980 Gorbachev was also a full member of the Politburo, but it was when Yury Andropov succeeded Leonid Brezhnev as Soviet leader in November 1982 that Gorbachev's powers and responsibilities were significantly extended. Although Andropov wished Gorbachev to be his successor, the aged Soviet oligarchy preferred the 72-year-old Konstantin Chernenko when Andropov died in February 1984. Only after Chernenko's death in March 1985 did Gorbachev, then aged 54, become party leader and the most powerful person in the Soviet Union.

As General Secretary Gorbachev embarked upon an ambitious programme of reforms which changed the character of the Soviet political system and left Russia a freer country than it had ever been. His perestroika also had, however, unintended consequences. Reform left the economic system in limbo and inter-ethnic problems, long suppressed, came to the surface as a result of glasnost and the new liberties. Gorbachev strove to maintain a union, either by turning the USSR into a genuine federation or by going even further and accepting that the USSR – to be renamed the USS or Union of Sovereign States – become a loose confederation. In this he was unsuccessful. He left, however, a huge imprint on twentieth-century history not only through the changes he brought about, both wittingly and unwittingly, in the Soviet Union, but also by his contribution to the ending of the Cold War and his abandonment of Soviet domination of Eastern Europe.

Gorbachev visiting the Kuybyshev region of Russia, April 1986

Mikhail and Raisa Gorbachev during Gorbachev's years in power

for him to have marshalled support for as radical a political agenda as he was to succeed in setting in 1987 and 1988. Nevertheless, a number of ideas which were fresh in the Soviet context were aired and significant personnel changes were made. Gorbachev used the word, 'reform'; for the first time and, indeed, went further, arguing that 'radical reform' of the economy was necessary. It was also at the XXVII Congress that Yel'tsin first achieved country-wide prominence by delivering a speech notable for its forthrightness. In a foretaste of things to come, he attacked the duplication of state organs by the Communist Party Central Committee apparatus and criticized the work of the department of the Central Committee responsible for party organizational work, a department which, as the cognoscenti were aware, was supervised by Ligachev.

The term, 'New Political Thinking', entered Soviet vocabulary early in the Gorbachev era and, increasingly, *perestroika* (reconstruction) became the favoured all-purpose word for the reform of the system which got under way. In the first two years of the perestroika period, *uskorenie* (acceleration) and *glasnost'* (openness) were also much-used terms. But there was no economic breakthrough of the kind that the concept of uskorenie was intended to encapsulate, and glasnost during the new leadership's first year represented only a modest advance in frankness compared with what was to come later.

The disaster at the Chernobyl' nuclear power station in Ukraine on 26 April 1986 was catastrophic not only ecologically, socially and economically (with widespread nuclear contamination of parts of Ukraine and Belorussia in particular), but a serious setback for glasnost. The first reports of the disaster emanated from the West; Soviet acknowledgment of it came only with a minimally informative announcement on Soviet television on the evening of 28 April. The attempts both at local and national level to play down the scale of what had in fact been the world's worst nuclear accident to date provoked serious criticism abroad and, increasingly, inside the Soviet Union. Within a few months of Chernobyl', the degree of openness in the Soviet mass media began to expand significantly, and with each successive year in the second half of the 1980s the boundaries of the permissible were pushed ever wider.

Important early stimuli to glasnost from above were the appointments of Vitaly Korotich (b.1936) as editor of the weekly magazine, *Ogonek*, and of Yegor Yakovlev (b.1930) as editor of the weekly newspaper, *Moscow News*, in the summer of 1986. Another landmark was the general release of the Georgian film, *Repentance* – an artistically impressive and politically effective indictment of Stalinism – in November of the same year. It was typical of the times that the issue of the film's release had to be considered at the highest political levels where it was supported by Gorbachev, Shevardnadze and Yakovlev and opposed (unsuccessfully) by Ligachev.

Even at this early stage of the Gorbachev era, signs of new thinking on the Soviet Union's relations with the outside world began to emerge and Gorbachev and Shevardnadze brought a very different style to the conduct of foreign policy from that of their aged predecessors. The replacement as head of the International Department of the Central Committee in early 1986 of the veteran ideologist Boris Ponomarev (b.1905) by the long-serving Soviet Ambassador to Washington, Anatoly Dobrynin (b.1919), was another indicator of a growing pragmatism. The first Soviet-American summit meeting since 1979 took place in November 1985 when Gorbachev met with President Ronald Reagan in Geneva. The meeting inaugurated a more co-operative phase of Soviet-American relations, although the Reykjavik summit a year later – at which more far-reaching proposals on the reduction of strategic and medium-range missiles were discussed – ended without agreement.

Two important events in December 1986 offered different portents of the future. One was the nationalist tinge to the rioting which occurred in Alma-Ata on 16 December when the veteran Brezhnevite and Kazakh national, Dinmukhamed Kunaev, was replaced as First Secretary of the Communist Party in Kazakhstan by a Russian, Gennady Kolbin (b.1927). The other was Gorbachev's telephone call to Academician Andrey Sakharov on 19 December in his place of exile in the city of Gor'ky (now Nizhny Novgorod), informing him that he was free to return to Moscow. This was important symbolically, as it signified both to Russian intellectuals and to the outside world a new toleration of dissent. It was also of direct political consequence, for Sakharov was to go on to play an important part in the new Soviet institutions which emerged in 1989, the last year of his life.

Radical political reform, 1987–88

It was characteristic of the first four years of perestroika that the most important political initiatives came from the top of the Communist Party hierarchy and that the most consequential political struggles took place within the higher party echelons. Thus, it was two plenary sessions of the Central Committee of the CPSU – in January and June 1987 – which put, first, serious political reform and, second, significant economic reform firmly on the political agenda. Gorbachev had wished to put forward proposals for political reform to a plenary session of the Central Committee in 1986 but met with opposition. The plenum which was eventually held in January 1987 had been postponed three times. It was at this meeting that Gorbachev gave his first explicit support to competitive elections and stressed the need, more generally, for 'profound democratization'. In June of the same year it was the turn of economic reform to be launched. The major report endorsed by the plenum observed that radical economic reform was a key component of perestroika and condemned the over-centralization of the Soviet economy.

Although the June plenum was a step forward in terms of recognition of the deficiencies of the unreformed Soviet economic system, the half-measures it adopted – support for greater enterprise autonomy within what remained, basically, a non-market economic environment – did more harm than good. The plenum did pave the way, however, for the introduction of co-operatives and later of private enterprise by extending to the economy the principle enunciated by Gorbachev, 'Everything is permitted which is not prohibited by law'. Previously, the only safe assumption in Soviet conditions had been that nothing new by way of economic (or political) organization was allowed unless explicit permission had been given for it. (In September 1987 the entitlement of individuals and co-operatives to open small shops was, in fact, made explicit.)

In May 1987 a bizarre episode provided Gorbachev with the opportunity to make several changes in the military high command. On Border Guards' Day (28 May) a young West German, Mathias Rust, flew a light plane into the Soviet Union and eventually landed just off Red Square in Moscow. While many Russians found this more entertaining

Andrey Sakharov

Andrey Sakharov (1921–89) became the best-known of the Soviet dissidents during the Brezhnev period and in the Gorbachev era one of the Soviet Union's first true parliamentarians. After studying physics at Moscow State University, and working in an arms factory during the Second World War, Sakharov became involved in the USSR's fledgling nuclear weapons programme. He played a crucial role in the development of the Soviet Union's first hydrogen bomb, and was elected a full member of the Academy of Sciences in 1953.

Sakharov received many state honours during the 1950s, but despite this he came increasingly into conflict with the regime. In 1968 he wrote an essay that explicitly called for Soviet-American co-operation and convergence. As a result of its publication in the West, Sakharov lost many of the privileges he had previously enjoyed.

During the 1970s Sakharov campaigned tirelessly for the protection of human rights in the USSR, publicizing abroad cases of abuse. For this work he was awarded the Nobel Peace Prize in 1975. Eventually, in 1980, the Brezhnev regime banished him to the closed city of Gor'ky. Here he undertook a series of hunger strikes in an effort to secure permission for his wife, Yelena Bonner, to receive medical treatment overseas. He remained in Gor'ky until he received the now famous telephone call from Mikhail Gorbachev in December 1986, inviting him to return to Moscow.

Sakharov spent the last years of his life working for a thorough democratization of the USSR, more comprehensive than that initially proposed by Gorbachev. Elected to the Congress of People's Deputies in 1989, he immediately became one of the leading figures in the new legislature. His sudden death in late 1989 deprived the Soviet Union of a democrat of huge moral authority and deeply-felt humanitarian beliefs.

than annoying, the military leadership was not amused. Gorbachev took advantage of their embarrassment in order to remove several senior military officials, including the Minister of Defence, Marshal Sergey Sokolov (b.1911). Sokolov was replaced by General Dmitry Yazov (b.1923) who, however, as an active participant in the August 1991 attempted coup, was later to let Gorbachev down in a much more fundamental way.

A Central Committee plenary session which was called in October 1987 for the express purpose of approving Gorbachev's draft speech for the celebration of the seventieth anniversary of the Bolshevik Revolution became more important as the occasion when Yel'tsin burned his bridges so far as the party hierarchy was concerned – an event which set back his career in the short run but before long was to stand him in very good stead with the broader public. The influence of the latter was still indirect and very limited in 1987 but Yel'tsin's popularity with Muscovites may well have been a factor in his not being sent as ambassador to a small and distant country. He was, however – at a meeting in November 1987 at which he was harangued in a manner reminiscent of the unreconstructed Communist past – removed from his Moscow party organization First Secretaryship; at the next plenum of the Central Committee of the CPSU (in February 1988) he was dropped from candidate membership of the Politburo. Nevertheless, he remained a member of the Central Committee and he was granted a governmental post as First Deputy Chairman of the State Construction Committee. Yel'tsin's offence had been to say that perestroika was proceeding too slowly, to criticize the way Ligachev ran the Secretariat of the Central Committee and to claim that there was excessive adulation of Gorbachev within the Politburo. The transcript of the October plenum of the Central Committee, including Yel'tsin's speech, was not published until February 1989, but rumours about it soon spread in 1987. By the standards of two years later Yel'tsin's critical remarks were mild, but their impact was great partly because of the discordant note they struck at a meeting convened for other purposes and also because they confirmed the popular view of the future Russian leader as someone not afraid to challenge the party establishment.

Gorbachev's speech on the seventieth anniversary of the Bolshevik Revolution in November 1987 was a compromise account of Soviet history which did not entirely please either conservatives or radicals. It partially promoted the rehabilitation of Bukharin and of Khrushchev and declared that Stalin's guilt was 'immense and unpardonable'. Gorbachev also noted that the process of rehabilitation of the victims of Stalin had effectively stopped in the mid-1960s

Boris Yel'tsin

Boris Nikolaevich Yel'tsin secured his place in Russian history in June 1991 when he became the first leader of Russia to be directly and democratically elected by the people. With the breakup of the Soviet Union in December of that year, he became the first President of the independent Russian state.

In some respects Yel'tsin's path to the leadership of a democratic movement in Russia was an unlikely one. Born into a poor peasant family in the Sverdlovsk region of central Russia in 1931, he graduated from the Ural Polytechnical Institute and worked as an engineer in the construction industry. A Communist Party member from 1961, he was a full-time party functionary from 1968 until the perestroika era.

As First Secretary of the Sverdlovsk regional party committee in Brezhnev's time, he had been responsible for bulldozing, at the behest of his Central Committee superiors, the building in Sverdlovsk (Yekaterinburg) in which the last Tsar of Russia, along with the Tsarina and their children, had been murdered – to prevent it becoming a possible place of pilgrimage.

After his move to Moscow, however, and especially as First Secretary of the Moscow city committee of the Communist Party from December 1985 until late 1987,

Yel'tsin rapidly gained popularity as he clashed with the established party bureaucracy. Matters came to a head in late 1987 and Yel'tsin was removed from his Moscow party post, although he remained a member of the Central Committee of the CPSU until he resigned from the Communist Party in 1990.

As the Communist Party became increasingly unpopular, Yel'tsin's willingness to challenge its leadership enhanced his standing with the wider public. In elections in 1989 (for the Congress of People's Deputies of the USSR), in 1990 (for the Congress of People's

Deputies of the Russian Federation) and in 1991 (for the Presidency of Russia) he received massive support.

In post-Soviet Russia Yel'tsin put his weight behind price liberalization, privatization and movement to a market economy, but found the political problems of power more difficult to overcome than those he faced in opposition. He lost the support of a number of former allies, among them Ruslan Khasbulatov (b. 1942) and Aleksandr Rutskoy. In 1993 he forcibly dissolved the legislature which Khasbulatov chaired and held a referendum on a new Constitution together with elections for a new parliament. On a low turnout of voters the Constitution was approved but the new parliament was almost as critical of Yel'tsin's policies hitherto as its predecessor had been.

and announced the setting-up of a new commission to review unresolved cases of victims of repression.

The following month Gorbachev became the first Soviet leader since Nikita Khrushchev in 1959 to visit the United States when he held his third summit meeting with President Reagan, this time in Washington. The two leaders signed a treaty on the elimination of Soviet and US medium-range nuclear missiles. At this stage of the perestroika era improved East–West relations and the reduction of international tension bolstered Gorbachev's popularity at home, compensating in some measure for the lack of economic improvement. Soviet citizens had for many years feared war, and official propaganda up until the Gorbachev era had exploited to the full the notion of an external threat. As the threat of war visibly receded, the new Soviet foreign policy was welcomed at home as well as abroad and perceived to be one of the successes of perestroika. That mood was reinforced when the fourth summit meeting between Gorbachev and Reagan took place in Moscow at the end of May and beginning of

June 1988. It came shortly after another generally welcomed reversal of Brezhnevite foreign policy; in April an agreement on the withdrawal of all Soviet troops from Afghanistan, and on the ending of the war there, had been signed in Geneva.

Domestically, 1988 saw an intensification of the struggle between reformers and those who feared (not without reason) that the pillars of the Soviet system were being destroyed. A letter from a neo-Stalinist Leningrad chemistry lecturer, Nina Andreeva, was turned into a major article in the newspaper, *Sovetskaya Rossiya*, and published on 13 March 1988. It defended Stalin from his contemporary critics in the Soviet Union, attacked Westernizing liberals in Soviet society and, by implication, blamed Jews for most of Russia's troubles. The article was praised by Ligachev at a meeting with editors of other newspapers and reprinted in many local papers. It had been published, with the connivance of conservative Communists in the Central Committee apparatus, on the eve of Gorbachev's departure for Yugoslavia and of Yakovlev to Mongolia. The lack of a prompt critical response led many people to interpret the article as a change of official line and there was an almost universal public silence on the article and the issues it raised until an authoritative response to the Andreeva line was published in *Pravda* on 5 April. Gorbachev and Yakovlev had persuaded the Politburo that the Andreeva article was, in effect, an anti-perestroika manifesto which required a comprehensive rebuttal.

Gorbachev and his supporters in the leadership placed many of their hopes for further radical reform in the 19th Party Conference held in mid-summer. Although the election of delegates – which had been supervised by the party apparatus – produced a majority by no means well disposed to radical reform, Gorbachev cajoled and outwitted them into accepting proposals which, upon implementation, were to make the Soviet political system different in kind from what it had been before. Extensive television coverage made the conference participants more conscious of public opinion and may have helped to inhibit party officials from giving full vent to their negative thoughts on the proposals for democratization. Soviet citizens could also see and hear for the first time criticism (on television and radio) of members of the Politburo and they witnessed an open clash between Yel'tsin and Ligachev, with Gorbachev also responding critically to Yel'tsin's plea for 'party rehabilitation'. The main importance of the 19th Conference was that it approved a range of far-reaching political reforms, the most significant of which was the decision to create a new legislature, the Congress of People's Deputies of the USSR (which would, in turn, elect an inner body, the Supreme Soviet) and, in a vital break with the past, to do this in competitive elections. It was also agreed that a new post of Chairman

Mikhail Gorbachev playing host to President Ronald Reagan in the Kremlin, May 1988

of the Supreme Soviet of the USSR (*Predsedatel' Verkhovnogo Soveta SSSR*) be created and that office-holders from top to bottom within the Communist Party and in the soviets be restricted to two terms of five years each.

Gorbachev followed up his political success at the 19th Party Conference with a radical restructuring of the Communist Party apparatus in September of the same year. Along with a number of personnel changes, he succeeded in abolishing more than half of the departments of the Central Committee and in greatly restricting the role of the Secretariat, partly through the creation of six somewhat more broadly-based commissions (which possessed less *de facto* power than the organs they largely replaced). One of the senior officials who thereby lost ground was Ligachev who had previously supervised a number of departments and policy areas in the Central Committee, including ideology and agriculture. Now he found himself restricted to agriculture as head of the new Agricultural Commission. While this was a definite demotion for Ligachev, it did no favours to agriculture.

Gorbachev was elected Chairman of the Presidium of the (still unreformed) Supreme Soviet in October 1988, in succession to Gromyko, and that Supreme Soviet session approved the constitutional amendments which would bring into being the successor legislature the following year. Now head of state as well as party leader, Gorbachev had a fifth and final summit meeting with Reagan in New York in December. On that same visit he made a major speech to the General Assembly of the United Nations in which he set out the Soviet new thinking on global issues and also pledged a unilateral cut of 500,000 troops.

Although 1988 was a year of important political reform and of foreign policy achievements, it was also the time when the issue which, above all others, was to be the downfall of the Soviet Union – the national question – became increasingly salient. Early in the year Armenians both in their enclave of Nagorno-Karabakh within Azerbaijan and in the Armenian capital of Yerevan demonstrated in large numbers in favour of the incorporation of Karabakh into Armenia. They thus brought back on to the political agenda an issue which had long been a cause of latent or active conflict between Armenians and Azeris. Once there, it continued to defy solution and before long degenerated into violent confrontation. (As of 1993 fierce armed clashes between Armenians and Azeris on and around the territory of Nagorno-Karabakh were persisting.) And this was not the only tragedy to overtake Armenia. On 7 December 1988 an earthquake struck the republic, killing some 25,000 people and rendering tens of thousands homeless.

If 1988 saw the resurgence of the Karabakh issue, it was also the year in which Estonians, Latvians and Lithuanians asserted their rights to national self-determination and brought into the open their well-founded grievances about being forcibly incorporated in the Soviet Union in 1940. Popular Fronts were formed in all three republics and in November Estonia declared its sovereignty. That did not yet mean full independence and Gorbachev and the reformist wing of the Soviet leadership – who had underestimated the depth of nationalist feeling – hoped that any separatist tendencies could be held in check by turning the Soviet Union from a unitary state which only purported to be a federation into a genuine federal union. Opinion among the Balts in particular was not, however, to be assuaged by such means.

Transformation at home and abroad, 1989–90

The all-union elections for the Congress of People's Deputies of the USSR, held in March 1989, constituted a decisive turning-point in Soviet political life. Inasmuch as in a number of republics, most notably the Baltic ones, they provided an opportunity to organize on behalf of, and elect, nationally-minded deputies, they might be regarded as one of the important steps along the road to the breakup of the Soviet Union. But, more immediately, they introduced significant elements of pluralism and of democratization into the political system, even though it still fell far short of being a fully-fledged democracy. Of the 2,250 members of the Congress, 1,500 were drawn from territorial constituencies, with 750 seats distributed among the various parts of the country on the basis of population density and 750 divided among the national-territorial units ranging from union republics down to the so-called autonomous regions. One of the limitations on the democratic character of the elections was the selection of a further 750 deputies from officially-recognized 'public organizations', among them the Communist Party itself (it sent 100 deputies, including Gorbachev and most of the top leadership who, thereby, did not need to fight a competitive election in a territorial constituency), the Komsomol, the trade unions and the Academy of Sciences. While the third of the deputies from public organizations included many people chosen for their assumed reliability and conformism, some of these organizations – not least, the Academy of Sciences and the Film-Makers' and Theatre Workers' Unions – elected a number of the most radical and outstanding deputies. Thus, rank-and-file scholars defeated the attempts of the leadership of the Academy of Sciences to foist upon them a list of candidates which excluded Andrey Sakharov and other politically active scientists and scholars of distinction. The

deputies eventually elected from the Academy included not only Sakharov but others committed to radical change, including the head of Soviet space research, Roal'd Sagdeev (b.1932), and the economist and creative writer, Nikolay Shmelev (b.1936), who topped the poll.

In the territorial elections to the new legislature, there was more than one candidate in approximately three-quarters of the electoral districts. Although these were competitive elections, they were not multi-party ones, for parties other than the CPSU did not yet exist. But that did not mean that there were no serious clashes of opinion and of interest. Of the candidates whose names appeared on the ballot papers, 85.3 per cent were Communist Party members and 87.6 per cent of those actually elected belonged to the CPSU. But the fact that Yel'tsin was a party member, as was his factory manager opponent, in a constituency embracing the whole of Moscow did not make the contest any the less real. Yel'tsin's achievement in gaining around 90 per cent of the votes of Muscovites in spite – or partly because – of the efforts of the party apparatus to favour his opponent made him the first Soviet politician to have a power base which rested on overwhelming electoral support.

Although there were many districts where as a result of apathy or the machinations of local party officials more radical prospective deputies were kept off the ballot paper and others in which the party boss succeeded in having only one name – his own – on the ballot, the latter stratagem did not ensure electoral success. A candidate had to obtain more than 50 per cent of the votes in order to be elected and in a number of major cities, including Leningrad, a majority of electors crossed out the name of the single nominee – usually a local party leader – and forced a second election in that district.

The First Congress of People's Deputies which met on 25 May and continued in session until 9 June made a colossal impact on Soviet society. A mere two years later this all-union legislature was held in fairly low esteem, but enormous enthusiasm greeted its earliest debates. Two decisions were especially important in that regard. The first was that Gorbachev made it clear, at a pre-session meeting with the majority of deputies who were party members, that they would not be subject to the old-style party discipline and would be free to speak and vote according to their judgement. The second was the decision to broadcast the proceedings of the First Congress live on both radio and television. The speeches – many of them highly critical of party leaders – were thus heard by an audience estimated to be almost a hundred million. One speech, which left listeners hardly able to believe their ears, was entirely devoted to an attack on the KGB; the speaker,

Yury Vlasov (b.1935) – a weightlifter turned writer – said it should be moved out of its central Moscow headquarters to 'a modest building in the suburbs' and be held accountable for its activities to the new Supreme Soviet.

The Congress was chaired by Gorbachev who was elected to the new post of Chairman of the Supreme Soviet which made him, in effect, Speaker of that assembly, while continuing to be *de facto* head of the executive as party General Secretary. One of the most contentious issues to come up at the First Congress of People's Deputies was the ruthless dispersal of a peaceful demonstration by Soviet troops in the Georgian capital of Tbilisi on 9 April 1989. At least 18 young people were killed and many more injured. A parliamentary commission to investigate the circumstances was set up under the chairmanship of the academic lawyer and reformist deputy (later Mayor of St Petersburg) Anatoly Sobchak (b.1937). The deaths of the demonstrators, far from halting the growth of nationalist feelings, enraged Georgian public opinion and provided a tremendous boost to separatist sentiments.

Even though there was a relatively conservative majority within both the Congress of People's Deputies of the USSR and the new Supreme Soviet, there were enough authoritative nonconformist figures to ensure that, at the very least, the new legislature became a forum for criticizing the executive, embracing such previously taboo targets as the party leadership (including Gorbachev), the KGB and the military establishment. Although the 542-person Supreme Soviet, elected by the First Congress of People's Deputies to be the permanently working part of the legislature, was criticized as being 'Stalinist-Brezhnevite' by the radical deputy, Yury Afanas'ev (b.1934), it was by no means entirely docile. This, the Chairman of the Council of Ministers Nikolay Ryzhkov discovered to his cost when the new legislature made full use of its power to approve ministerial appointments; as many as 11 of Ryzhkov's nominees failed to get through the confirmatory process.

The new legislative assemblies – both Congress and Supreme Soviet – contributed also to an extension of glasnost, for the mass media could report the critical remarks of deputies and then follow them up with fresh criticism of their own. In a parallel extension of freedom of publication, one formerly banned book after another was published in journal or book form, among them George Orwell's *Nineteen Eighty-Four* and Alexander Solzhenitsyn's *The Gulag Archipelago*. In what might have been a setback to the new freedom of publication, Gorbachev put pressure on the editor of the weekly newspaper *Argumenty i fakty*, Vladislav Starkov (b.1940), to resign, but Starkov, backed by his staff, refused to go and he was still occupying his editorial

chair when Gorbachev himself resigned as President of the USSR more than two years later. Gorbachev showed more determination, and had more success, in removing an editor from the other end of the Soviet political spectrum – the conservative Communist editor of *Pravda*, Viktor Afanas'ev (b.1922) who was replaced by a Gorbachev aide, Ivan Frolov (b.1929), in October 1989.

The year was one of growing national assertiveness and of inter-ethnic discord. Lithuania and Latvia followed the lead of Estonia (the previous year) in declaring their sovereignty, as did Azerbaijan. In June violent clashes took place in the Fergana region of Uzbekistan between Uzbeks and Meskhetians. September saw the imposition by Azerbaijan of a rail blockade of Armenia. Significant developments of a more orderly kind in large republics included the return of the First Secretaryship of the Communist Party of Kazakhstan to Kazakh hands with the election of Nursultan Nazarbaev (b.1940) – later President of Kazakhstan – in June 1989 and the founding congress of the Ukrainian popular front, Rukh, in September. At the beginning of the following year there was an escalation of violence in the Caucasus. The Azerbaijan capital, Baku, was the scene of atrocities in January 1990 when pogroms against Armenian residents were followed several days later by ruthless action by Soviet troops against Azeris in which at least 83 people died.

The bicentenary of the French revolution, 1989, was a year of decisive breakthrough to independence of the countries of Eastern Europe. Until the Gorbachev era it had been taken for granted that the Soviet Union would intervene militarily to prevent the establishment of non-Communist regimes in any Warsaw Pact country. While Gorbachev hoped that leaders of a similar disposition to his own would be chosen in Eastern and Central Europe, he and his allies with responsibilities in that area (notably Shevardnadze and Yakovlev) accepted the logic of the doctrine of non-interference in the affairs of their neighbours which they had proclaimed and did not prevent the collapse of the Communist order in what used to be called 'the Soviet bloc'. In October 1989 it was officially accepted by the Soviet leadership that member states were free to leave the Warsaw Pact alliance.

While the developments in Eastern Europe in 1989–90 enhanced Gorbachev's already high standing in the West (and led to his being awarded the Nobel Peace Prize in October 1990), they were of little help to him at home. While many Soviet citizens were indifferent to these foreign developments, some powerful groups and institutional interests – including the army, the KGB, military industry and the Communist Party apparatus – were increasingly alarmed by the disappearance of

Soviet soldiers leaving Czechoslovakia

Eduard Shevardnadze, the Soviet Foreign Minister, here seen with US Secretary of State James Baker, December 1990

been for the removal of Article 6 of the Soviet Constitution which asserted the dominant role of the Communist Party within the political system. Gorbachev could not accede to this demand until he had persuaded the Central Committee of the party he led to give up their monopoly of power; he did this at a Central Committee plenum in February 1990. A few days before – in the biggest political demonstration seen in Moscow since it became the capital in 1918 – more than 100,000 people marched to the Kremlin in support of democratic reforms. By then popular opinion had become a factor to be reckoned with in Soviet politics.

At the Third Congress of People's Deputies of the USSR, convened in March 1990, Article 6 was duly repealed and so the substantial elements of political pluralism which had been becoming an increasing reality at the end of the 1980s now had a legal basis. The system remained, however, a mixed one, retaining important authoritarian features, such as the power of the party apparatus in many localities and a KGB which, if it could no longer suppress dissidents as it once did, continued its activities of surveillance. At the all-union level and in several republics the party leadership, was, however, losing ground to the new state institutions. Gorbachev got the approval of the March meeting of the Congress for the creation of an executive presidency and of two new collective bodies attached to it which the President (*Prezident*) would chair. The first of these, the Presidential Council, was intended to take over many of the functions of the Politburo. To some extent it did so, but it was an institution without structural supports. When the old Politburo took a decision the entire Communist Party apparatus was at its disposal to implement it. Many decisions taken by the new presidential organs were left hanging in the air. The creation of a second collective body, the Council of the Federation, was intended to offer a voice to all republics at the centre, give meaning to the federal principle and thereby hold the union together. Unlike the Presidential Council, which was appointed by the President, the Council of the Federation was to consist of the Presidents of the Supreme Soviets of the union republics – chosen by their own republican Congresses of People's Deputies or Supreme Soviets following elections which were to take place in every republic during 1990. In several cases, however, these elections produced majorities of deputies in favour of separatism and thus leaders who had no interest in participating in the Council of the Federation.

Gorbachev was elected unopposed in a secret ballot of deputies for the post of President of the USSR. Many radical deputies held that such an election should have been by the whole people and it was

Communist systems in the 'fraternal countries' and concerned that their own patrimony was similarly endangered. Thus, if foreign policy had earlier brought Gorbachev more credit than blame at home, the opposite became the case in 1989–90, even though reformers within the Communist Party ranks and non-party democrats welcomed the renunciation of the policy which had brought Soviet tanks into Hungary in 1956 and into Czechoslovakia in 1968.

The first summit meeting between Gorbachev and President George Bush was held aboard ship off Malta in early December 1989. In the same month the Second Congress of People's Deputies was convened and during it – on 14 December – the most authoritative and morally consistent critic of the Soviet executive among the deputies, Andrey Sakharov, died.

One of the demands made by Sakharov and others at the Second Congress of People's Deputies had

Above. *Mikhail Gorbachev and Anatoly Luk'yanov at the opening of the third session of the USSR Supreme Soviet, 1990*

Above right. *Boris Yel'tsin with his wife, Naina, a poster of Lenin in the background*

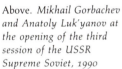

agreed that in future that would be the case. In the event, however, the Soviet Union had ceased to exist well before Gorbachev's first five-year term of office had ended and he thereby became both the first and last Soviet President. The Chairmanship of the Supreme Soviet was separated from the state Presidency in March 1990 and Anatoly Luk'yanov (b.1930), who had previously been Vice-Chairman, succeeded Gorbachev as Chairman and before long was exercising considerable authority within the Soviet legislature.

The republican elections produced nationalist majorities in all three Baltic republics, and the 'nationalities question' reached crisis proportions for the all-union leadership in Moscow in the first half of 1990. Declarations of independence by Lithuania and Estonia (in March) and Latvia (in May) went beyond previous declarations of sovereignty. But since the centre still insisted that such decisions could not be taken unilaterally by any republic, and the Baltic states argued that they did not need to abide by any agreed procedure since they had not consented to incorporation in the Soviet Union in the first place, there was a stalemate between the Balts and the all-union authorities. In many respects the Baltic peoples did proceed to govern themselves, but they did not yet have fully independent statehood. There were, for example, large numbers of Soviet troops on their soil, whose senior officers co-operated with political groups opposed to Baltic separatism, and Moscow had not accepted that its writ no longer ran in Lithuania, Latvia and Estonia.

Elections for the Congress of People's Deputies of the Russian republic (RSFSR) produced a divided assembly, but one with a somewhat higher proportion of reformers than was to be found in the all-union legislature. After a lengthy political

struggle, Boris Yel'tsin – who had again enjoyed overwhelming electoral support, this time from his native Sverdlovsk – was elected Chairman of the Supreme Soviet of the RSFSR in May. The following month the Russian republic declared its sovereignty. While this was not yet the full independence claimed by the Baltic states, it was a more damaging blow to the USSR, for a collision between the political leadership of the RSFSR (which occupied some three-quarters of the territory of the union and had more than half of its population) and the union 'centre' – each located in Moscow – threatened to make the country ungovernable. It was in many ways the greatest challenge yet posed to the future of the union.

Other republics followed the Russian lead. Before the end of 1990 every one of them had declared sovereignty. Gorbachev argued that such sovereignty – as distinct from outright independence – was consistent with the creation of a renewed union, but he was subjected to cross-pressures from those, such as Yel'tsin, on the one hand, who were moving towards support for a looser confederation, and, on the other, hard-liners who were mounting a backlash against the pluralization of Soviet politics, the loss of power of the centre and the threat of further disintegration. One manifestation of this was pressure for the creation of a separate Communist Party organization for the Russian republic – a development Gorbachev sought to avoid, for he saw it as an attempt to create a second centre within the CPSU which would attempt to restore traditional Communist norms. Nevertheless, disgruntled party officials in Russia insisted upon its creation and at its founding conference in June 1990 many of the policies Gorbachev, Yakovlev and Shevardnadze had been pursuing came under severe attack. It was fully in keeping with the tone of the proceedings that the hardline Ivan Poloz'kov (b.1935) was elected First Secretary of the Communist Party of the RSFSR.

Gorbachev appeared, however, to turn the tables on his conservative Communist opponents at the XXVIII Congress of the CPSU, held in July 1990. Conceding the strength of national consciousness within the union republics, he called for 'a real union of sovereign states' and for a new union treaty to replace that of 1922. His radical critics in Russia viewed this move as coming too late, but – from the other side – there was great resistance on the part of the central organs of power to giving up any of their prerogatives, even though in practice some of these were already slipping from their grasp. The Congress also adopted a programmatic document called 'Towards a humane and democratic socialism' which not only adopted the terminology of 'democratic socialism' long anathema to Communists but, in a number of respects, brought the doctrine of the CPSU closer to the ideas of West European democratic socialist parties. Gorbachev's ability to use such levers of party power as he possessed did not, however, mean that a majority of the delegates who voted for change were in fact committed to implementing it.

The time was, in any case, past when party congresses could determine the political agenda of the country. Radical democrats since at least the beginning of 1990 had increasingly looked to Yel'tsin (who announced his resignation from the CPSU during the Congress), rather than Gorbachev, as their standard-bearer. Having seen off, as he thought, the threat from 'the right' (as the conservative Communists were known to democrats in the Soviet Union), Gorbachev attempted to re-establish a coalition with the liberal and democratic 'left'. In August, in a move which completely bypassed the

Communist Party, he co-operated with Yel'tsin on the setting-up of a working group to make recommendations on how the Soviet Union could move speedily to the establishment of a market economy. A team of economists, all committed to the need for marketization and evenly divided between people close to Gorbachev and Yel'tsin associates, formed a group under the leadership of Academician Stanislav Shatalin (b.1934). Subsequently known as the 'Shatalin Plan' or the '500 Days Programme', the document they produced represented a total break with Soviet-style socialism. Indeed, it did not even attempt to reconcile its advocacy of economic transformation – involving rapid marketization, privatization and a huge devolution of economic power to the republics in what would be a new voluntary union – with socialist principles of any kind. Although the timetable for drastic change was almost certainly over-optimistic, the Shatalin group proposals appeared to offer a new impetus to reform and the opportunity of reconciliation between Gorbachev and Yel'tsin, both of whom expressed their approval of the team's work.

Winter of discontent, 1990–91

The tentative attempt of Gorbachev and Yel'tsin to work together in 1990 was short lived. Gorbachev, under great pressure from the Council of Ministers (not least, its Chairman, Ryzhkov), and from the military-industrial complex, the KGB and the party apparatus, searched for middle ground between the Shatalin plan and a plan drawn up by the Ryzhkov government. The economist Abel Aganbegyan (b.1932) was prevailed upon to draw up a compromise document. Its ideas were much closer to the views of Shatalin than to those of Ryzhkov, but it was seen as a retreat by Gorbachev from more radical measures and was approved as the President's

Below. Barbara Bush (left) and Raisa Gorbachev at Wellesley College, Massachusetts, June 1990. Below right. President George Bush with Mikhail Gorbachev in Helsinki, September 1990

Above. *Muscovites protest against price rises, and in support of Yel'tsin, 1991*
Above right. *An anti-Gorbachev demonstration on Sovetskaya Square, Moscow, 23 December 1990*

programme by the USSR Supreme Soviet in October. The urgent deadlines of the Shatalin Plan were lost, as was the political momentum, and the fragile coalition embracing reformers in the union structures and those with republican (especially Russian) affiliations was broken. Shatalin himself, who had been Gorbachev's nominee, was critical of the Soviet President.

As more and more of his former liberal supporters deserted him, Gorbachev made a tactical shift to 'the right'. Under threat from both the conservative forces (who appeared, in the most literal sense, to include the big battalions) and the radicals and democrats, Gorbachev apparently believed that the danger from the former was greater. Although that was by no means an implausible view, events the following year showed its limitations. Gorbachev himself was later to accept that this had been a time for decisive choice and that he had been mistaken in trying to pursue a centrist course. As politics became more polarized centrists were increasingly isolated. In retrospect Gorbachev's success in persuading the XXVIII Congress to accept ideas in which a majority of the delegates did not believe had been a pyrrhic victory. It would have been better to split the party rather than paper over the cracks.

The winter of 1990–91 was a time of conservative backlash to which Gorbachev made major concessions. While it is possible that without this tactical shift a coup might have been brought forward by 18 months – with greater chance of short-term success – the appointments Gorbachev made did nothing to discourage those who wished to turn the clock back. Not surprisingly, though, they lost him further support among the democrats. These appointments included that of Boris Pugo (1937–91) as Minister of Internal Affairs and of General Boris

Gromov (b.1943) as his First Deputy; the promotion of Gennady Yanaev (b.1937) to a new post of Vice-President; the appointment of Valentin Pavlov (b.1937) as Prime Minister (formerly called the Chairmanship of the Council of Ministers); and of Leonid Kravchenko (b.1938) as head of radio and television.

There was also a highly significant departure from Gorbachev's team; Eduard Shevardnadze, who had been subjected to increasing attacks for his conduct of foreign policy and for the 'loss' of Eastern Europe, resigned as Foreign Minister on 20 December 1990 and, in an impassioned speech, warned of a coming dictatorship. In November 1990 Gorbachev had abolished the Presidential Council on the grounds that it had been ineffective as an executive organ; he intended to work instead through a new government and through the Council of the Federation.

The Orthodox Christmas on 7 January 1991 was celebrated as an official public holiday for the first time in Soviet Russia and the midnight liturgy from the Cathedral of the Epiphany in Moscow was televised live. January, however, brought no other relief from the impending gloom. Within a few days Soviet special troops occupied the television tower in the Lithuanian capital, Vilnius, and their attack left 14 people dead and 110 wounded. A demonstration in Moscow on 20 January of almost 100,000 protesters demanded the resignation of Gorbachev, along with that of the Minister of Defence, the Chairman of the KGB and the Minister of Interior.

In February relations between Yel'tsin, who had added his political weight to those who opposed the repression in the Baltic states (of which the Vilnius television tower attack was intended by hardliners in the Gorbachev administration to be but a first step towards a more comprehensive crackdown), and Gorbachev reached a new low. In a live television interview on 19 February Yel'tsin called for Gorbachev's resignation as Soviet President. Large numbers of people responded to the call of the Democratic Russia movement to join demonstrations in Moscow in defence of Yel'tsin (whom the Supreme Soviet of the USSR had accused of violating the Soviet Constitution) and of the independence of the mass media.

Gorbachev, determined to preserve a union (albeit one which was unlikely to include the three Baltic states), held a referendum in March on the question, 'Do you consider it necessary to preserve the USSR as a renewed federation of equal sovereign republics, in which rights and freedoms of all nationalities will be fully guaranteed?' Apart from the three Baltic states, Armenia, Georgia and Moldova also refused to participate. In the nine republics in which the question was put, the overall turnout was 80 per cent and 76 per cent voted for the union.

A miners' strike added to the social turmoil, but a huge demonstration in Moscow on 28 March in support of Yel'tsin passed off peacefully, in spite of the fact that 50,000 militia had been drafted in to maintain order. The senior office-holders in the Gorbachev administration who were later in the year to stage a coup were constantly trying to create the conditions for a state of emergency which they had long been pressing Gorbachev to declare. Although Gorbachev had warned of such a possibility with reference to Lithuania in particular – as a way of attempting to persuade the Lithuanians to moderate their immediate demands – he did not at any time resort to presidential rule by taking up the emergency powers available to him.

In addition to the Baltic states, there was national ferment in the Caucasus. On 9 April 1991 Georgia declared its independence and just under a week later its popularly elected President, Zviad Gamsakhurdia (1939–93), encouraged civil disobedience against Soviet institutions.

The Novo-Ogarevo process

Gorbachev's zig-zag tactics of 1990–91 took another turn in April 1991 when he built new bridges to those favouring radical change. Stressing the need to get agreement on the terms of a new union treaty, he launched a fresh dialogue with all the republican leaders prepared to enter into it, including Boris Yel'tsin. This came as a blow to the conservative Communists in the union leadership; the extent to which Gorbachev was prepared to meet republican demands more than half way was the most important single reason for the August putsch. Only nine of the fifteen republics participated in the talks on a union treaty. Lithuania, Latvia, Estonia and Georgia already regarded themselves as independent states, and Armenia and Moldova also boycotted the

meetings. The discussions came to be known as the '9 + 1 talks' or the 'Novo-Ogarevo process'. The former name referred to the nine republics whose leaders participated, the 'one' being the all-union leadership and Gorbachev in particular. Novo-Ogarevo was the name of the dacha outside Moscow in which the discussions were held.

In an attempt to keep the initials USSR as the name of the country, the participants reached provisional agreement by early June on 'Union of Soviet Sovereign Republics', 'Sovereign' replacing 'Socialist' in the old name. However, by 17 June, this had been changed to 'Union of Sovereign States' (USS). On 29 July Gorbachev and Yel'tsin agreed on one of the most contentious issues – the collection and distribution of taxation – and on 2 August Gorbachev announced that the USS, a new 'genuinely voluntary union' of sovereign states would be the successor in law to the USSR. The draft Union Treaty was published in Moscow on 14 August. It had critics both in the all-union political structures and in the republics; but Russia, Belorussia, Kazakhstan, Uzbekistan and Tajikistan declared their willingness to sign it, and four other participants in the Novo-Ogarevo process – Ukraine, Azerbaijan, Turkmenistan and Kyrgyzstan – were expected to append their signatures later. The initial signing ceremony was fixed for 20 August.

Apart from the issue of what kind of union, if any, was to survive or be recreated, the most important single happening in this period was the June election for the Russian Presidency. The candidates represented very different political standpoints, and the outcome was a triumph for Boris Yel'tsin and the 'Democratic Russia' movement. By convincingly defeating his five opponents – securing 57.30 per cent of the votes cast in a ballot in which 74.66 per cent of the adult population voted – Yel'tsin became the first leader in Russian history to be popularly elected. This not only increased his standing at the time but, crucially, gave him the legitimacy and authority to speak for Russia at the time of the attempted putsch a little over two months later. On the same day as the presidential election Gavriil Popov (b.1936) was elected Mayor of Moscow and Anatoly Sobchak Mayor of Leningrad (the city voting at the same time to change its name back to St Petersburg).

The following month Gorbachev, who was clearly losing ground at home to Yel'tsin, attended the G7 economic summit – a 7 +1 meeting of the leading industrial nations – in London. Seeking Western financial backing for the Soviet economic reforms, he had to return to Moscow empty-handed, in spite of a show of goodwill by Western leaders. The reform package he brought to the talks lacked coherence, being a composite document which took account of the relatively conservative 'anti-crisis programme' put forward by Pavlov's government, the more radical measures of the economist, Grigory Yavlinsky (b.1952), and the recommendations of the International Monetary Fund and the European Bank of Reconstruction and Development.

In spite of the spirit of compromise (in comparison with the winter of 1990–91) which animated the Novo-Ogarevo talks, there were also in the summer of 1991 further signs of political polarization. Soviet troops under the jurisdiction of the Minister of Interior, Pugo, took over the Vilnius telecommunications centre for several hours on 26 June and cut Lithuania off from the outside world during that time. In contrast, at the beginning of July a group of prominent politicians, including Eduard Shevardnadze and Aleksandr Rutskoy (b.1947), launched a Movement for Democratic Reform.

From a different part of the political spectrum there appeared on 23 July an open letter of sinister intent, 'A Word to the People', published in the newspaper, *Sovetskaya Rossiya*. Signed not only by prominent Russian nationalist writers but also by two members of the government – General Boris Gromov, the First Deputy Minister of the Interior, and General Valentin Varennikov (b.1923), a Deputy Minister of Defence – it attacked those who had renounced the power of the Communist Party and handed it over to 'frivolous and clumsy parliamentarians'. In a thinly-veiled attack on Gorbachev, the letter asked how the country had allowed into power those 'who seek advice and blessings across the seas'. Later, this document – which expressed confidence that the army would step forward as the bulwark of all the healthy forces in society – was rightly seen as an ideological forerunner of the August coup.

One day earlier Yel'tsin had issued an important decree banning the organizational structures of political parties in the workplace in Russia. This applied equally to new parties (of which by this time 300 were registered in the Soviet Union as a whole) and to the Communist Party. It was to the CPSU, however, that it came as a body-blow, for the primary party organization at the place of employment had been one of its major means of influence and control.

When a plenary session of the Central Committee of the CPSU took place a few days later, members vented their wrath equally on the Yel'tsin decree and on a draft programme – for a special Party Congress due to take place later in the year – presented to them by Gorbachev. The programme appeared to bring party doctrine and goals closer to those of a social democratic party than ever before. A reluctant plenum accepted the programme provisionally, having been assured that there would be

an opportunity later for further changes. Some of those present were doubtless aware that before long they would not have to rely on persuasion alone; they awaited the measures foreshadowed in 'A Word to the People'.

The August 1991 coup and its aftermath

The short-lived coup began on 18 August. Gorbachev, on holiday in the Crimea but preparing to return to Moscow for the signing of the union treaty, was put under house arrest. An eight-man State Committee for the State of Emergency in the USSR (SCSE) was set up and a delegation from it demanded that Gorbachev declare a state of emergency or resign. He refused to go along with either demand, and so the would-be leaders of the country announced on the morning of 19 August that Gorbachev was unable to carry out his presidential duties 'for health reasons' and that these functions would be performed by the Vice-President, Gennady Yanaev. The putschists were unsuccessful in isolating Yel'tsin, who was able to make his way to the Moscow 'White House' – the Russian parliament building – which became the focal point of resistance to the coup (although there were massive demonstrations against it also in St Petersburg where Sobchak took the lead in opposing the SCSE).

The White House was surrounded by tanks, but thousands of Moscow citizens stood between them and the building. Yel'tsin denounced the SCSE and, addressing the crowd from the top of a tank on 19 August, proclaimed that he was taking control of army and KGB units on Russian territory. By 20 August the number of people around the White House had grown to about 50,000 at any one time; while scarcely a military obstacle, this greatly raised the potential political cost of storming the building.

On 21 August the coup collapsed. There were five main reasons for its failure. First, crucially important was Gorbachev's refusal to give the delegation from the SCSE any kind of endorsement in response to their ultimatum. If the orders for a state of emergency had come from the head of state and commander-in-chief of the armed forces and CPSU General Secretary (Gorbachev was all three), the responsiveness of army and KGB units to the commands would almost certainly have been greater than to those of a self-appointed committee.

Second, Yel'tsin's popularity among Russians, the legitimacy conferred upon him by his recent election as President, and his determination and courage played a decisive role in rallying the democratic forces opposed to the putsch. Third, the fact that over the three days several hundred thousand people were prepared to come out on to the streets in Moscow and St Petersburg in defence of their recently-won freedoms made it harder for the scse to arrest Russia's elected leaders and uncertain whether conscript soldiers would obey orders to fire on their fellow-countrymen. Fourth, the coup leaders – KGB Chairman Kryuchkov, Minister of Defence Yazov, Prime Minister Pavlov, Vice-President Yanaev, military industry chief Baklanov and Minister of Interior Pugo (who committed suicide on 22 August), among them – displayed incompetence and indecisiveness. In the longer term, they could not possibly have succeeded, but the fact that they failed so quickly owed something to their own inhibitions, including a desire (reflecting some impact even on them of the perestroika years) to give their take-over a semblance of legality. It is noteworthy that only three citizens were killed in Moscow and none in St Petersburg. Fifth, international (especially western) support for Gorbachev and Yel'tsin was immense; foreign radio stations (most notably, the BBC, Radio Liberty and Voice of America) played an important part in keeping the peoples of the USSR informed at a time when the Soviet mass media had once again been subjected to strict censorship.

The most obvious coup leaders were arrested immediately after its collapse and at the end of the month they were joined in prison by the Chair-

Anti-coup demonstration in Red Square, August 1991

man of the Supreme Soviet of the USSR, Anatoly Luk'yanov, who was said to have conspired with them. The coup leaders were initially accused of high treason, but in 1992, after the Soviet state had ceased to exist, the charges were amended. (They were released from custody in 1993 and, though brought to trial, the court proceedings were almost immediately suspended. Whether they would ever be sentenced for their activities in August 1991 was, in early 1994, still unclear.)

The involvement of the most senior figures in the all-union leadership in the attempted putsch helped, following their failure, to shift the balance of power still further towards the republics and away from the centre. In particular, it ensured that Yel'tsin now had more *de facto* power and greater authority than Gorbachev. The Soviet President, isolated during the coup, did not help his cause by vowing on his return to Moscow to continue to fight to reform the Communist Party. Yel'tsin's view that the CPSU was beyond salvation was more in tune with the popular mood. On 23 August, in the presence of Gorbachev (whom he went out of his way to humiliate) in the Russian parliament, Yel'tsin issued a decree banning the functioning of the Communist Party in the Russian republic. Gorbachev protested unavailingly against this, but a day later he resigned as General Secretary and endorsed the suspension.

The independence of the Baltic states was recognized by the Soviet Union on 6 September 1991; Belorussia formally changed its name to Belarus on 19 September; and four days later Armenia declared its full independence. In Russia Ruslan Khasbulatov was elected Chairman of the RSFSR Supreme Soviet on 29 September and two days later the RSFSR Congress of People's Deputies voted to restore the old red, white and blue Russian flag. In early November Yel'tsin became acting prime minister of Russia in addition to being President.

Gorbachev had formed a new administration – bringing, for example, Anatoly Sobchak and Gavriil Popov into consultative positions as well as restoring to senior posts the most reform-minded members of his old team, notably Eduard Shevardnadze (who returned to his former job as Soviet Foreign Minister in November), Aleksandr Yakovlev and Vadim Bakatin (b.1937). The last-named, appointed Chairman of the Committee of State Security in late August, was given the important task of cutting the KGB down to size and bringing it under democratic political control. None of these appointments were, however, to be of any avail, for the bandwagon of republican independence was rolling fast and in Moscow itself the new Russian leadership did not want to share power with anyone else – even a Gorbachev team shorn of its reactionaries and strengthened by the return of its best members who had been marginalized in the winter of 1990–91.

A referendum on independence and presidential elections in Ukraine on 1 December turned out to be an especially important step towards the breakup of the Soviet Union. Whereas a majority of the Ukrainian electorate had voted for a 'renewed union' earlier in the year, some 90 per cent now opted for independence. The experience of the coup – and the possibility it raised of the Soviet clock being turned back – as well as the sometimes tense relations with the Russian leadership which had prevailed in the several months since then had clearly affected public opinion. Russia recognized Ukrainian independence on 3 December.

Virtually the final nail in the coffin of the union was hammered in five days later when at a meeting in Brest the Presidents of Russia, Ukraine and Belarus agreed to form a Commonwealth of Independent States (CIS) with its headquarters, never in fact established, in Minsk. Conscious that they were about to bury the union, they stated that the USSR was 'ceasing its existence as a subject of international law and geopolitical reality'. The new Commonwealth – which developed very little by way of institutional structures in the year that followed – did not become, as some hoped and others feared, simply an association of the Slav states; at a meeting in Alma-Ata on 21 December those attending increased to eleven – all of the former Soviet union republics except the three Baltic ones and Georgia.

In the early part of December Gorbachev was still struggling against the odds to maintain some kind of union, but by 18 December he had recognized that this was a forlorn hope. He announced that he would resign as Soviet President when the transition from union to Commonwealth had been completed. His actual departure from office came on 25 December when he signed a decree divesting himself of his authority as President of the USSR and transferring his powers as Commander-in-Chief of the armed forces, with the control over nuclear weapons which that entailed, to Yel'tsin. Gorbachev made a televised resignation speech and on the same day the Red Flag was lowered over the Kremlin. The following day (26 December 1991) the USSR Supreme Soviet abolished itself and declared that 'the Soviet Union no longer exists'.   AHB

AFTER THE SOVIET UNION

With the collapse of the Soviet Union, the fifteen former union republics, now separate states, were faced by economic difficulties worsened by the breakdown of long-standing economic ties and by heightened inter-ethnic tensions. The Commonwealth of Independent States (CIS) was an attempt, in principle, to maintain co-operation and put it on a new basis. Eleven of the newly-independent countries were more or less closely associated with it. The three Baltic states shunned the CIS from the outset, and Georgia also did not join, although – unlike Estonia, Latvia and Lithuania – it sent observers to CIS meetings. The other eleven former Soviet republics were represented at the various meetings of the CIS, but two of them – Azerbaijan and Moldova – did not ratify the CIS treaty in 1992, although Azerbaijan eventually did so in September 1993 after its former Communist leader, Gaydar Aliev, returned to power. Georgia followed its example in December 1993 and Moldova, too, drew closer to CIS membership.

To a certain extent the CIS provided a mechanism for crisis management, but its extremely slender institutional base did little to promote economic co-operation. Some of the Soviet Union's successor states were much more interested in co-operation than others. Belarus, under the leadership (until 1994) of Stanislav Shushkevich, and Kazakhstan, whose President was the astute former Communist First Secretary of the Kazakh republic, Nursultan Nazarbaev, along with a majority of the Central Asian states, tended to favour the maintenance of economic links with Russia and some measure of political co-operation. In the case of Kazakhstan – territorially the second largest (after Russia) of the successor states – this was no doubt connected with the fact that almost as many Russians as Kazakhs lived there and with the Kazakh leadership's laudable desire to maintain good inter-ethnic relations. Armenia also favoured closer security and economic links with Russia.

The major successor state least inclined to develop institutional ties with Russia and the other former Soviet republics was Ukraine, although the Ukrainian President, Leonid Kravchuk, like Nazarbaev, took pains to reassure the large Russian minority living within Ukraine. In his relations with the Russian state, however, Kravchuk – like a number of leaders in the other CIS states, a former senior official in the Communist Party – was careful not to leave himself open to the charge of continuing to look to Moscow for guidance. By asserting Ukrainian national interests, he was able to shrug off the attacks of those with longer-standing Ukrainian national (or nationalist) credentials. When, however, in January 1994 Kravchuk finally agreed, under American and Russian pressure, to give up Ukraine's nuclear weapons, he was subjected to strong criticism at home. One damaging dispute between Russia and Ukraine in 1992 was over control of the Black Sea fleet which led some Russian politicians to call for a return of the Crimea to Russian jurisdic-

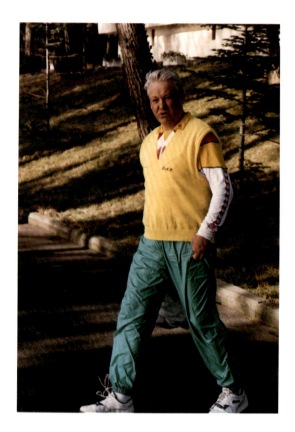

tion. President Yel'tsin did not back any such revision of borders and a compromise on the fleet was reached in 1994. Russian-Ukrainian relations, however, remained delicate.

Moscow, for its part, had to contend with centrifugal forces within Russia itself; its control over outlying regions during the first two years of independent statehood was even less than it had been in the last two years of Soviet rule. Yet Russia, compared with many other former Soviet republics, was able to preserve relatively peaceful inter-ethnic relations. The hostilities that presented it with the biggest problems were in other republics, especially since Russian troops were still stationed there. At home the violence which was a major source of concern was that arising out of ordinary crime. Popular perceptions of greatly increased criminal activity were confirmed in August 1992 when it was officially announced that the crime rate so far that year had been one-third higher than in the corresponding period of 1991.

Worse problems afflicted several of the other successor states to the Soviet Union. In Georgia, civil war led to the overthrow of Zviad Gamsakhurdia and the return of Eduard Shevardnadze – the former Soviet Foreign Minister and, before that, First Secretary of the Georgian Communist Party – as Chairman of the Georgian State Council. Following elections in October 1992 Shevardnadze became Chairman of the Georgian parliament. This change, although welcomed by most Georgians, did not, however, end the conflict between the authorities in Tbilisi and the followers of Gamsakhurdia, until Gamsakhurdia's death, apparently by suicide, at the end of December 1993. Nor did it stop increasingly bitter hostilities between Georgian armed forces and the Abkhaz minority, although Russian mediation helped to reduce the level of conflict which had arisen also between Georgians and Ossetians.

Elsewhere in the Caucasus, the armed struggle between Armenians and Azeris over the predominantly Armenian enclave of Nagorno-Karabakh in Azerbaijan continued into 1994, in spite of CIS and Russian efforts to bring about a ceasefire. In Moldova there was conflict between the mainly Russian population of the Dniester region and forces loyal to the independent Moldovan state. Civil war in Tajikistan led to the overthrow in September 1992 of the President, Rakhmon Nabiev, a former First Secretary of the Tajik Communist Party who had been sacked by Mikhail Gorbachev in 1985. Nabiev had earlier replaced as President his successor as Communist Party leader, Kakhar Makhamov; the latter was forced to resign in the wake of the August 1991 putsch which he was accused of supporting. In many of the new states old scores, which had their origins under Communist rule (or even earlier), were still being settled, although there was no longer an authority capable of imposing ultimate control.

Post-communism also presented the new, or not-so-new, leaderships in the former Soviet republics with difficult economic choices. There was a fairly widespread recognition that there was no alternative to movement towards a market economy, but disagreement from one state to another on how fast the movement should be and concerning the degree of regulation of the market economy which was required. The size of the Russian economy, and the willingness of Yel'tsin and the young economic reformers in his government to embark on serious reform, meant, however, that other successor states had to respond to Russian initiatives. This was notably the case with price decontrol in Russia on 2 January 1992; within the month all the former Soviet republics were forced to liberalize prices. The high degree of integration of the former Soviet economy meant that a tight money policy in Moscow in the first half of 1992 (it was thereafter slackened) had an immediate impact on the other ex-Soviet republics; some of them, but by no means all, broke away from the 'ruble zone'. High trade dependence established under central planning meant that even in 1993–94 production failures in one of the new states meant loss of supplies and production slowdowns in another.

Within Russia itself there was growing resistance to implementing shock therapy. Yel'tsin had ceded the post of acting prime minister to the radical young economist, Yegor Gaydar early in 1992. However, when he proposed him for the actual Prime Ministership, this was rejected by the Seventh Congress of Peoples' Deputies in December 1992. The older and more cautious Viktor Chernomyrdin (b.1938) was elected instead. Gaydar returned as First Deputy Prime Minister in autumn 1993, but resigned in January 1994, dissatisfied with Chernomyrdin's economic policy and in the wake of the December 1993 parliamentary elections which produced a legislature majority opposed to Gaydar's approach.

One of the major psychological and political problems was that people who, whatever their nationality, had previously lived within a common state, suddenly at the end of 1991 found themselves living 'abroad'. Given the dominating position of Russians within the former union, the demise of the USSR made the difficulties of the 25 million Russians living outside Russia an especially delicate problem – one to which the Russian government and parliament became increasingly sensitive. With the titular nationalities of virtually all of the successor states asserting themselves more than hitherto, the social and political status of the Russians declined. A high proportion of Russians in the population, as in Kazakhstan, did not of itself necessarily lead to a *modus vivendi* between them and the eponymous nationality of the state. Of the three Baltic states, for example, it was in Lithuania – where the Russian population was proportionately much smaller than in Latvia and Estonia – that the Russians had fewest complaints of being turned into second-class citizens or even non-citizens.

Economically, it was virtually unavoidable that standards of living would get worse before they got better. Certainly, 1992 saw a drop in average real incomes in all of the successor states, together with high inflation and greater job insecurity. This, in turn, made the management of inter-ethnic relations more difficult than it would have been under conditions of growing prosperity. For many citizens of the former Soviet Union, especially outside Russia, the new national independence made the hardships a price worth paying, but the standpoint varied from one nationality to another. Minority nationalities within particular Soviet republics had often looked to Moscow as a counterweight to the majority nationality in their own republic. In the absence of institutional structures within the CIS which could take up, and improve upon, the functions of mediation (or simply imposition of order) performed by the former union, disputes between the titular nationality and minorities within state borders increasingly resulted in violence. It was clear that skilful and far-sighted political leadership would be required if this tendency were to be reversed and if

The breakdown of politics. The Moscow White House set alight by bombardment from troops loyal to President Yel'tsin, 4 October 1993. This was the finale of a standoff between executive and legislature which came to a head when Yel'tsin dissolved the Supreme Soviet and the Congress of People's Deputies of the Russian Federation on 21 September

SOVIET AND POST-SOVIET HISTORIOGRAPHY

Lenin, Trotsky and other Marxist revolutionary leaders wrote extensively about Russian and world history before the 1917 revolutions. But there were few Marxists among the professional historians. The most prominent was Mikhail Nikolaevich Pokrovsky (1868–1932). On the eve of the First World War Pokrovsky published his *Russian History from Earliest Times*, which advanced the view that history had followed the same broad pattern in Russia as in the rest of Europe: feudalism had been succeeded by capitalism in the sixteenth century. But he also argued that the distinctive feature of Russian history was the long predominance of commercial rather than industrial capitalism; this economic basis of society was defended and maintained by the autocratic bureaucracy.

the former Soviet Union were to avoid the extremes of inter-ethnic tension which had afflicted the former Yugoslavia. As the territory of what used to be the USSR was saturated with far more extensive – as well as much more destructive – weaponry than ex-Yugoslavia, the development there of political toleration and of institutional means of resolving conflict assumed an importance of the first magnitude.

Relations between the executive and the legislature, in fact, broke down in Russia in September–October 1993. President Yel'tsin dissolved the Congress of People's Deputies and Supreme Soviet on 21 September and the resistance of many of the deputies to these measures was only broken on 3–4 October when a group of deputies urged on by Vice-President Rutskoy tried but failed to capture the Ostankino television centre. Troops loyal to President Yel'tsin stormed the 'White House', at that time the home of the legislature.

Elections for a new bicameral parliament were held in December 1993 and resulted in a strong showing by relatively conservative and even extreme nationalist forces with radical reformers again in a minority.   AHB

Some professional historians emigrated in the aftermath of the 1917 Revolution, but the majority remained within the Soviet Union. Until the end of the 1920s many 'bourgeois' historians were able to continue their research and teaching without great interference, side by side with the growing Pokrovsky school of young Marxist historians.

The years of relative tolerance ended in 1928–29, and in the next few years militant Marxists, with the support of the party leadership, waged a bitter campaign against the bourgeois historians, who were treated as class enemies. Many were arrested and accused of counter-revolutionary crimes; the most prominent non-Marxist historian, S. F. Platonov (1860–1933), a monarchist by political conviction, died in internal exile. The different Marxist groups and trends also debated bitterly among themselves; by the time of his death in April 1932 Pokrovsky's influence was waning.

In the second half of the 1930s previously-condemned non-Marxist historians of the pre-revolutionary period such as Tarlé and Bakhrushin returned to positions of influence. The Pokrovsky conception was replaced by an amalgam of socio-economic analysis and a more traditional and more patriotic political and diplomatic history, all within a prescribed framework.

In twentieth-century Russian history, and particularly the history of the Communist Party, the prescribed viewpoint was very firmly imposed. In October 1931, in his letter 'Some Questions Concerning the History of Bolshevism', Stalin attacked 'archive rats' who sought to re-examine Lenin's role. He also condemned the 'rotten liberalism' of those who treated Trotskyism as a mistaken group within Communism, and insisted that it was counter-revolutionary. Henceforth historical debate about the Soviet period was almost extinguished.

Aleksandr Rutskoy in militant pose during the standoff between President Yel'tsin and the Russian Supreme Soviet, October 1993

Then the textbook *History of the Communist Party of the Soviet Union (Bolsheviks): Short Course*, written with the active participation of Stalin, was published in 1938; after that all publications, syllabuses, films and broadcasts had to conform precisely to its judgments and periodization.

After Stalin's death frankness about the past greatly increased, encouraged by Khrushchev's de-Stalinization campaigns of 1956 and 1961. The most important single event was the publication by V.P. Danilov (b.1925) and others of critical articles, based on party archives, on the collectivization of agriculture and 'dekulakization'.

The historian, M.N. Pokrovsky

But within a couple of years of Khrushchev's fall in October 1964 the boundaries of discussion again greatly narrowed, though they did not return to the crippling limits of the Stalin years. The publication of an important book on collectivization, edited by Danilov, was cancelled; and from 1967 to 1985 many creative historians were demoted and silenced. After 1985 a mental revolution took place in the Soviet view of the past. Articles in newspapers and journals, and films and TV programmes, thoroughly re-examined the Soviet past, condemning Stalin's policies and seeking to explain why they triumphed. The revelations and the discussions were eagerly followed by tens of millions of Soviet citizens, in an intense public interest in the past which was without any historical precedent. In the Politburo this critical frankness about the past was strongly but unsuccessfully resisted by Ligachev and Chebrikov, but supported by Gorbachev and Yakovlev.

In the public discussions many different assessments of the past were hotly defended. In 1988 there was a consensus among radical reformers that the New Economic Policy (NEP) of the 1920s should have continued and that the forcible collectivization of agriculture was a disaster; for the reformers, the whole Stalinist period was a substantial departure from socialism. All the reformers agreed in their condemnation of the bureaucratic system (some say, bureaucratic ruling class) which developed after Lenin's death.

From the autumn of 1988 onwards, articles began to appear which rejected both Leninism and the whole course of Soviet development since the Bolshevik Revolution of October 1917. According to these critics, the Bolsheviks had driven Russia down a false road, leading away from her pre-revolutionary evolution towards democratic capitalism. NEP failed because the role of the state was excessive. Stalin's policies essentially continued those of Lenin. What was now needed, those radical critics claimed, was a return to the traditions of the

Provisional Government or even of late tsarism. During 1989 and 1990 the media were flooded with information previously unpublished in the Soviet Union about the repressions under Lenin, the famine of 1933 in which many millions died, and the labour camps. By the summer of 1990, in a public atmosphere increasingly critical of Gorbachev's reforms, an anti-Communist interpretation of the past was accepted by the majority of the Moscow and Leningrad intelligentsia. Following the defeat of the August 1991 coup, this viewpoint dominated most of the media.

Rival views, however, continued to be expressed both before and after the coup. Many writers, politicians and ordinary Russian citizens are convinced that the radicals reject too much of the Soviet past. Some claim that in spite of repressions the Stalin period was a major stride towards socialism; more defend Lenin and the October Revolution. The Russian nationalists take a strong line of their own. They stress the continuity between the pre- and post-revolutionary eras, which they present as the triumphant story of the emergence of Russia as a great world power. They differ among themselves in their attitude to Stalin and Stalinism: some regard Stalin as a great leader of Russia, most condemn Stalin's collectivization for destroying Russian peasant traditions. One extreme nationalist wing attributes the disasters of the Soviet period to the machinations of Jews and freemasons, and regards the radical intelligentsia of the perestroika era as their agents.

Among professional historians major changes did not take place until 1988, when the editors of two important historical journals were replaced and the staff of the Institute of the History of the USSR (now the Institute of Russian History) of the Academy of Sciences elected an open-minded director. From 1989 onwards both Soviet and foreign historians were permitted far wider access to the state archives, and after August 1991 the former Central Party Archives became more accessible. Important new publications of archival material are under way, but now they are hindered not by political but by commercial considerations.

Frankness does not imply complete objectivity. Even professional historians sometimes display obvious bias in their zeal to expose past falsifications of their history and accept unreliable information provided it sheds an unfavourable light on the Soviet past. But this is a new world, in which as a rule arguments are much more closely related to evidence than in the past, and rival views are openly presented.   RWD

Art and architecture

Early arts and architecture

SCYTHIAN ART

The Scythians, warlike nomads who dominated the steppes north of the Black Sea during the seventh to the fourth centuries BC, are famous for their art, mostly practical or decorative objects such as jewellery, weapons, cups and bowls, often made from or adorned with gold. Like most nomads, they carried their wealth with them, so their trappings and equipment had to be valuable as well as useful and easily portable. Since these warriors were buried with their earthly possessions, Scythian art is found in graves. The richest examples have been discovered in princely kurgans or burial-mounds such as Kelermes in the north-west Caucasus (sixth century BC), Chertomlyk near the river Dnieper (fourth century BC) and Kul' Oba in the eastern Crimea (fourth century BC). Here chieftains were buried in elaborately furnished underground tombs, sometimes accompanied by slain horses and human attendants.

The origins of Scythian art are still not fully understood, but it is possible that some elements can be traced back to tribes who lived in Siberia and Central Asia during the third millennium BC. An early version of Scythian or steppe art has been discovered in the Golden Kurgans, in the Chiliktin Valley of Kazakhstan. These finds, dating from the seventh century BC, include small gold-foil felines in coiled form, stags, boars and vultures (to be seen in the Hermitage Museum, St Petersburg). Perhaps a little later in the seventh century BC, gold objects said to come from the site of Ziwiyeh in north-west Iran may reflect a westward migration of the Scythians (Archaeological Museum, Tehran, and Metropolitan Museum of Art, New York).

The stylistic affinities in this early art reveal the wide-ranging connections of these nomads through trade, migration and warfare. At Chiliktin, contact with China is suggested by the coiled feline decorations, a motif which persists throughout the history of Scythian art. The Ziwiyeh gold work has links with Near Eastern art, an influence which continues

in the objects from early steppe kurgans like Kelermes. During the sixth to the fourth centuries BC, when the Scythians ruled the steppes and traded with the Greek cities on the Black Sea, Scythian art took on a noticeably Greek tinge. The Kul' Oba tomb includes some pieces made for a nomadic chief by Greek craftsmen, as well as purely Greek objects which apparently pleased the taste of the wealthy barbarian.

Scythian art is commonly described as 'animal' art, because the subject matter is often animals, typically single figures in curled-up poses or with legs dangling. Certain motifs (stags, birds of prey, felines) were used throughout the history of Scythian art, and may well have had totemic or magical significance. However, with the passage of time, Greek influence increased and the original simplicity was often lost; this transformation is particularly obvious in representations of stags. In early examples, like the early sixth-century BC gold plaque shaped like a stag from Kostroma Kurgan in the north-west Caucasus (in the Hermitage), the animals are clearly reindeer, native to the regions of eastern Asia where the Scythians probably originated. By the fourth century BC, the memory of reindeer seems to have become faint. The famous Kul' Oba gold stag in the Hermitage was obviously made by a Greek craftsman who slavishly followed a model which he scarcely understood. Nevertheless, although the richness and splendour of late nomadic art testify to the exotic tastes cultivated by these once-primitive steppe dwellers, the persistence of animals such as the stag suggests the power and importance that traditional imagery retained for the Scythians.   AERF

Above. Scythian gold plaques for sewing onto garments. Right. Scythian pectoral of gold found at Tolstoe, southern Ukraine

WESTERN TURKESTAN (UZBEKISTAN)

Although there were periods in antiquity when high artistic standards were attained in various parts of Central Asia, it was not until the Christian era that a distinct school of fine arts came into being in Western Turkestan. Its development there took place in two phases. The first, as revealed by recent excavations, extended from roughly the first century AD to c.720, when the Arabs conquered the region and put an end to its figurative arts. The second period was launched in the ninth century by Ismail the Samanid, who abandoned Zoroastrianism in favour of Islam and established his capital in Bukhara. The style reached its peak under Timur (1336–1405) and his grandson, the astronomer-poet Ulug Beg (1394–1449), lingering on well into the seventeenth century.

Even in Bactrian times (sixth to fifth centuries BC) urbanism, and thus architecture, had flourished in Soghdia unimpeded by the nomads. By the fourth to fifth centuries AD cities such as Afraosiab (ancient Marakanda/Samarkand), princely domains such as Varaksha, and citadels such as Mug or Balalyk Tepe contained a variety of weapons, tools, domestic utensils and decorative and precious objects. The artistic styles and town plans are well represented at Panjikent, a walled fifth- to sixth-century town containing a chieftain's citadel, residential area, suburbs and cemetery. Its buildings of unbaked brick were often two-storied, with porticos or eiwans (three-walled vaulted chambers with tall, inverted-V-shaped, entries) and vaulted or domed roofs, occasionally supported by wooden columns, even by caryatides. Some buildings contained as many as 150 rooms. Rectangular reception halls had a continuous bench inserted into the three walls with paintings extending above it to the ceiling or to a frieze formed of stucco statues, many of them portraits of individuals.

The vast mural compositions are outstanding. Their subjects range over ceremonial scenes, battle, genre and religious themes, hunting subjects and illustrations of epics inspiring those immortalized by the poet Firdausi (c.935–1020). The men are wasp-waisted, the women elegant. The style is monumental, accomplished, and colourful; Sassanian influences prevail but the impact of Hellenism, as transmitted by Parthia, is evident, alongside that of Buddhism. The costumes are made of expensive contemporary materials, some obviously imports from Persia, others indubitably of local make; recent research has revealed the existence in Soghdia, following the establishment of the silk-route and the end of China's monopoly in making silk, of a silk production and weaving industry there. The cut of the caftans is similar to that found in contemporary paintings in Eastern Turkestan.

Throughout this period figurines, decorated ossuaries and painted vessels were made in unglazed pottery. In Samanid times Samarkand's potters discovered a slip which prevented their painted designs from running. They were able to decorate their glazed wares with superb script and abstract, geometric or floral designs executed in black (often on a white ground), brown and green. By the tenth century their creations were widely admired and their influence was felt in Persia. In the fourteenth and fifteenth centuries they provided the glazed tesserae and tiles which testify to the excellence of this period's buildings.

From Samanid times onwards, figural representations were replaced by decorations which, stimulated by advances in mathematics and astronomy, were chiefly geometric in character, although often accompanied by plant arabesques. In architecture the introduction of baked bricks enabled many designs to be produced by varying the disposition of the bricks, as in the ninth- to tenth-century domed and cube-shaped Samanid mausoleum at Bukhara, the earliest example of a style which spread to Persia. In the 47m high Kalyan minaret (1127–29) at Bukhara the designs are disposed in thirteen bands with, at its summit, the oldest recorded glazed blue tiles with relief designs that were to become so important in Timurid times. In the twelfth to thirteenth centuries decorations were incised on terracotta and alabaster

Western Turkestan

slabs, as, for example, on the twelfth-century Magok Attari Mosque at Bukhara and, at Usgen, on the eleventh-century mausolea of Nasr ben' Ali, of Jalal-al-din al-Husein (1152) and that dated to 1186. Later, script became a superb form of decoration.

In towns the walled citadel – the Ark – was surrounded by a defended residential area – the shahristan – its main roads, lined with open water-channels, connecting the *registan* (main square) to the gates. The garden suburbs lay outside the walls. Sections of some walls survive, as at Bukhara.

Architecture is represented by mosques, madrasahs (Muslim establishments of higher education), round and slightly tapered minarets, and mausolea. Timur's ruined palace in his birthplace, Shahr-i-Sabz (ancient Kesh), provides the only extant example of domestic architecture, Ulug Beg's sextant at Samarkand the only scientific relic. Domes, eiwans and porticoes are the style's main features, the mosques being roofed. Only the twelfth-century Kalyan Mosque at Bukhara and the Bibi Hanum (1399–1404), built by Timur in Samarkand in honour of his Chinese wife, recall in their ground plans the open-court layout of Arab mosques. Stalactite vaulting is customary while glazed-tile panels and majolica mosaics adorn the porticoes, eiwans and drums, sometimes over-flowing on to the walls. Bukhara's chief monuments include the fourteenth-century mud-brick Chashma Ayub mausoleum and the Madrassa of Miri-Arab (1535–36), Kukeltash (1568–69), Abdulla Khan (1588–90), and Char Bakr (sixteenth-century). Turcoman Tekke rugs are often miscalled 'Bukharas', probably because many were sold there.

Above. The cube-shaped mausoleum of the Samanid dynasty at Bukhara, Uzbekistan, late ninth to early tenth century, the earliest baked-brick building in Central Asian architecture. As the Balo-Uhaz mosque (right) shows, a similar style was still influential in Bukhara in the early twentieth century

Samarkand contains two of Islam's finest architectural creations. The earlier, the fourteenth- to fifteenth-century Shah-i-Zinda, is a street of mausolea; entrance to its steep flight of stairs – made, as in India, of marble – is through Ulug Beg's portico. The earliest tomb, situated at its summit, belongs to Kasim; those bordering the street include two belonging to Timur's ladies and are distinguished by the ridged, melon-shaped domes associated with Timur. All the mausolea are sumptuously decorated with glazed ceramics, but the isolated Gur Emir (1403–04) is the most glorious. Built by Timur to serve as the mausoleum of a favourite son, it became his own burial-place. Samarkand's *registan* is bordered on three sides by the fine Madrasahs of Ulug Beg (1417), Shir-Dor (1619–36) and Tillya Kari (1646–59), but many of the smaller mosques are scarcely less beautiful. TTR

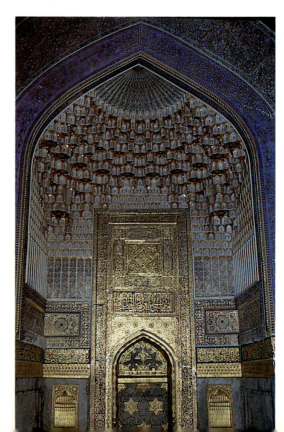

Right. The Kalyan minaret (1127–29) at Bukhara, Uzbekistan. Far right. *The Shah-i-Zinda, Samarkand: the Ulug Beg portico, 1372*

Monuments of Samarkand. Above. The dome and minarets of the Shir-Dor Madrasah (1619–36). Right. The Gur Emir (1403–04). Below. The registan, *with its three Madrasahs*

TRANSCAUCASIA

During much of their history the buffer kingdoms of Armenia and Georgia were coveted by Persia, which competed for them first with Rome, then with Byzantium and, finally, with Russia. In addition Arabs and Ottoman Turks attempted to annex them and convert them to Islam. However, their trials were to some extent offset in the artistic field, where their talents and skills enabled them to benefit from their enemies' cultural achievements.

On adopting Christianity (Armenia in 303, Georgia by 330) the attention of both countries veered towards Byzantium, yet they met their need for churches by adopting the basilical type in use at the time in Palestine and Asia Minor. Stone — sandstone, tufa, basalt and granite — became their customary building material. They cut it into blocks dressed inside and out, and set in fine mortar.

In both countries architecture developed along parallel though quite distinct lines so that, at much the same time as the Georgians were building the stylish, three-aisled basilica at Bolnisi, dated by their earliest stone-cut inscription to AD 478–91, the Armenians were doing so at Yereruk (c.600). Both kingdoms must have realized simultaneously that their rituals required churches with an internal cruciform plan rather than a basilical, preferably roofed with a dome at the intersection of the aisles. Although by the third century AD the Romans were attempting to place a dome above a square by experimenting with the pendentive (or coved corner), the Sassanians, possibly even the Assyrians, had already succeeded in effecting this transition by evolving the squinch arch. The Transcaucasians must surely have acquired the technique from these eastern neighbours since, between 586 and 604, the Georgians used the squinch at Jvari, near Mtskheta, and, around 600, the Armenians did so at Avan. The church at Jvari is shaped on the inside as a tetraconch (a building with four semicircular apses), each bow linked to the central area by niches aligned to frame a square roofed by a dome resting on squinches. After that, all that was needed to increase the size of the central area in buildings of this type was the introduction of four free-standing piers or columns to serve as supplementary supports for the dome, an experiment tried out in Georgia, at Tzromi between 626 and 634. Where buttresses were required, barrel-vaults were used to bind them to round or octagonal drums surmounted by domes, which in both kingdoms were pyramid-shaped.

The Golden Age

In the seventh century the Arab conquest of Transcaucasia checked all activity, even in Armenia where domestic architecture had become established in

The late sixth-century Church of the Cross at Jvari, Georgia

Urartian times (ninth to sixth centuries BC) and had flourished under the Arsacid dynasty (53–128 AD) – as, for example, at Garni. However, the Muslims who settled in the region (particularly Azerbaijan) erected some striking mosques, mausolea, baths, and other purely Islamic monuments during the succeeding centuries. Conditions improved in the ninth century for the region's Christian inhabitants, towns became more prosperous, and architecture revived. Palaces were built for notables and bishops, castles were enlarged and modernized, bridges were steeply arched to bear flood water more effectively, monasteries were expanded and, in Georgia's Upper Svanetia, from 1096 at any rate, stone look-out towers replaced the wooden ones incorporated in larger houses.

Church-building became more ambitious. In 964, at Kumurdo in Georgia, the architect Sacotsari built a domed cathedral with a cruciform exterior into

which he inserted a sixth aisle, setting it at right angles to the five-aisled nave. When Ashot III of Armenia (952–77) chose Ani as his capital he embellished it with splendid palaces, cathedrals and fortifications, and when Georgia was unified under King David IV (1089–1129) both kingdoms entered upon a golden age.

In architecture the style of these regions is distinguished by the sophistication of the façades and by the height and spaciousness of the churches. By blending features belonging to the basilical and domed-cruciform types, church interiors came to resemble double basilicas. Their roofs acquired several levels, porches were added, transepts were emphasized, choirs were included and pillars, often grouped in clusters as later in western Gothic, marked the divisions of the aisles. At Ani some pillars were already joined by slightly pointed arches but at Mtskheta those in Sveti-Tskhoveli (1010–29) were still rounded. The building's architect, Arsukidze, broke the exterior of the cathedral's east wall into five tall sections, adding two niches for the preacher's use, and split the north and south fronts into three divisions. Often churches were paved with marble slabs, inlay or glazed tiles; in Georgia alone a low marble or stone screen formed of carved panels set between pilasters, never an iconostasis, separated the nave from the sanctuary. Gradually, thicker mortar was used and brick courses were inserted in the masonry. In the thirteenth century further development was halted by the Mongol invasion. Yet much solid building continued to be erected between the sixteenth and eighteenth centuries, although bricks were increasingly used and decoration often became excessive.

Sculpture and murals

Transcaucasian stone is an excellent sculptor's material. In Armenia single slabs, sometimes enormous in size, were carved with elaborate, often foliated crosses (*khachkars*). Set up in the open, they symbolized the Christian faith and date from all periods. In Georgia (for example at sixth-century Khandisi) carved slabs surmounted by crosses, recalling Saxon counterparts, gradually fell out of use while tall, slender wooden crosses encased in embossed sheet-gold, often accompanied by a small, pyramid-shaped gold cap, were placed inside some cathedrals and were probably also carried in processions.

Already at Jvari, sculptures of a distinctive character embellished the church's exterior. With the years they became more numerous, appearing on the tympana, architraves, vaults, cornices, arches and capitals, framing windows and entrances, and decorating the wooden shutters and doors. Some scholars discern Romanesque features in them, others perceive

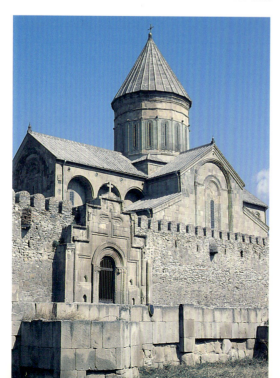

Sveti-Tskhoveli Cathedral (1010-29), Mtskheta, Georgia

eastern elements in the animal forms and interlaced and geometric designs. However, it is the Byzantine style which prevails. Subjects range from the religious, animal and vegetal, with the vine given prominence, to symbolic crosses, rosettes, bosses and, as already at Jvari, royal donor and related portraits (for example, in Armenia, King Gagik at Aghtamar and a master mason at Zvartnotz). Portraits were also included among the interior mural paintings (in Georgia, George III and Queen Tamara in the twelfth-century church in the rock-cut townlet of Vardzia).

In both kingdoms the mural paintings adhered to the Byzantine tradition but Constantinople's influence is stronger in the rare wall mosaics (such as the twelfth-century Virgin and Child at Gelati, Georgia) while the Syrian tends to prevail in the paintings. In Armenia, where mural painting was done in Urartian times, the finest Christian examples are perhaps to be found at Ani and Aghtamar, the most elegant Georgian murals at Ateni and Urbnisi. Few artists signed their paintings, though a notable exception occurs in Upper Svanetia, where an artist called Tevdore (Theodore) worked c.1096–1112.

Applied arts

In architecture the Georgians and Armenians must be ranked equally; but whereas the Armenians may have produced the finer artists, the Georgians were perhaps the better jewellers. Manuscripts were illuminated in both kingdoms, but the Armenians appear as the more individualistic and wider-ranging in their choice of subjects, showing a more marked bent for elaborate interlaced designs. Artists in both countries worked in the Byzantine style, although Syrian influences are often to the fore in the religious scenes, while the Persian tend to dominate in the secular, especially in battle pieces (such as the fifteenth-century Georgian Jruichi Psalter). The earliest Armenian miniatures to survive adorn the Lazarev Gospel of 887 and some that are bound up with the Echmiadzin Gospel of 989; the oldest Georgian miniatures illustrate the Ardishi Gospel of 897 and the Jruichi Gospel of 936–40, where the draperies are rendered with particular skill.

Georgia's love of the sumptuous and elegant is especially evident in metalwork, a craft which flourished there in the second millennium BC. In Christian times Georgia alone, with the exception of Kiev, was able to produce cloisonné enamels of the Byzantine type. Mastering that most difficult technique, the Georgians achieved brighter, clearer and more varied colours than the Kievans. In the twelfth century the enameller Asan of Tchkondidi may have had a workshop at Martvili. The earliest enamels (those adorning the Virgin of Kobi associated with Leo III of Abkhazia (957–67) and the

Right. St John the Baptist. Detail from embossed and chased silver cover of the Bertsk Gospel (c. 1184–93), by Beshken of Opiza

earlier enamels on the Khakhuli triptych) have a green background.

The delicacy of Georgian filigree, wire and granular decoration has seldom been equalled. These techniques are seen at their best on the exquisitely wrought gold triptych known as the Khakhuli, once the property of Gelati Monastery. Here they provide a setting for delicate chased and repoussé designs, cabochon jewels and over 100 cloisonné enamels, 32 of them Georgian. The latter include a Virgin's head which cedes little in humanism to the near-contemporary Byzantine panel painting known as the icon of the Virgin of Vladimir (Vladimirskaya, now in the Tret'yakov Gallery, Moscow).

The Georgians' talent for embossing and chasing very thin sheets of metal – gold, silver, silver-gilt, copper and copper-gilt – led them to substitute such plaques for painted icons, as well as using them as book-covers. The earliest plaques to survive are a fifth-century silver-gilt representation of St Gregory the Illuminator and a sixth- or seventh-century silver-gilt disk of St Mamas. The monasteries of Opiza, Tbeti and Gelati became important centres of production. Only two jewellers are known by name: the more individualistic Beka who, in 1193, worked the cover of the Tselkendili Gospel; and his near contemporary, Beshken of Opiza, who signed one of his gospel covers.

That the Armenians were almost equally skilled is evident from the silver Skevra reliquary which the Catholicos Constantine presented to King Hetun in 1293. There was a large demand for jewellery in both countries, but more fine pieces of medieval date survive in Georgia. Later, excellent silver niello work was produced, once again chiefly in Georgia.   TTR

Folk art

RUSSIA

Russian folk art is, of course, as old as the people themselves, but the material available for its study before the middle of the nineteenth century is scanty. With advancing prosperity, its products increased greatly, becoming more widely known, and although now influenced by competing mass-produced goods, they retain enough of their previous character to enable us to fill in the gaps in the earlier material and to form a picture of the whole tradition.

The main characteristics of Russian folk art – imaginative use of the available raw materials and rich decoration – are attributable to the conditions of peasant life. The geographical isolation of the villages, caused by the lack of roads, made it necessary for people to be almost entirely self-sufficient, and the long winters, when no work might be done in the fields, gave them ample time to perfect elaborate ornamentation. The decorative motifs they used naturally often illustrate ancient folk beliefs.

The State Historical Museum in Moscow and the State Russian Museum in St Petersburg contain rich collections of domestic and craft products, such as embroidery, wooden distaffs, gingerbread moulds and printing blocks. Not surprisingly embroidery, which requires only a background of woven material and a needle and thread, provides a fair proportion of the exhibits; much is no older than the eighteenth century, but two fifteenth- or sixteenth-century pieces have recently been discovered. The embroidered figures include fantastic buildings, animals (deer, unicorns), birds (peacocks, two-headed eagles), birds with human faces (the legendary *sirin* and *alkonost*) and a woman flanked either by two horses, which she holds by their bridles, or by two birds standing on her hands, thought to represent a pagan mother-goddess with fertility connotations. Some of these designs survive, and are also found painted and carved on distaffs and carved on wooden door-lintels. The carved horse or cock often adorning the end of the main roof-beam in northern houses is also a pre-Christian symbol, bringing good and warding off evil. The birds on wedding-towels signify love, and the flowering bush frequently seen on gingerbread moulds is a symbol of rebirth.

It was customary for gingerbread to be given at the village festivals held on church holidays, and at weddings and funerals. The earliest moulds found date from the twelfth and thirteenth centuries. The designs vary with the occasion: on St George's day the gingerbread was in the shape of birds, cows and sheep. The carvers knew all the traditional shapes by heart, and adhered to them until the beginning of the nineteenth century, when they began to look for new patterns in *lubki* (chapbooks or single printed sheets – 'broadsides' – with text and pictures prepared from wooden blocks).

In every household the women were engaged for much of the time in spinning, and distaffs were often given by men as presents to their wives, daughters and sweethearts. Datable specimens in the Russian collections go back to 1783, although of course the instrument is as old as spinning itself. Russian distaffs are larger than those of any other country, and are held upright in a base provided with a hole for that purpose and serving also as a seat for the spinner. Both the blade at the upper end which holds the wool and the base often display carved or painted designs, geometric and representational.

The production of wooden blocks for the printing of designs on dress-materials, table-cloths, church banners, and book-covers is supposed to have originated with the icon painters, who worked in towns; but by the end of the eighteenth century this had become village work. In the 1830s mechanization was introduced, but shawls and kerchiefs continued to be hand-printed from wooden blocks; by the end of the nineteenth century whole districts were supported by this industry. The earliest designs were geometric, but in the nineteenth century representational designs appear, for example gallants and ladies in traditional costumes. These, like the designs on nineteenth-century gingerbread moulds, were copied from *lubki*. The earliest surviving *lubok* (1619–24) represents the Dormition of the Mother of God; the early subject-matter was always religious. *Lubki* were hawked outside monasteries, but later they also conveyed political opinions expressed in religious symbols: at the time of Peter the Great broadsides appeared for and against the tsar.

Porcelain 'Whale-dish' from Gzhel', near Moscow; the plastic style and painted cobalt decoration are typical. Porcelain manufacture, taking advantage of the local clays, began at Gzhel' in the early eighteenth century

Folk art

Above left. *Caucasian shepherd, lamb and henwife in Ukrainian dress*

Above right. *Ukrainian vodka flask in the shape of a bear*

Left. *Modern wall-hanging based on the traditional 'Cat of Kazan'' design*

Right. *Kargopolski whistle from central Russia with a whistle from the New Jerusalem Monastery*

Below. *Troika made by Yegorov (b. 1918)*

The emancipation of the serfs in 1861, along with growing industrialization and economic expansion, influenced folk art through the style of factory-produced goods and the contact of peasants with urban life. For instance, one home-made distaff bears a picture of a fashionable tea-party with a lady standing by a samovar, welcoming guests. Rich townsfolk began to take notice of peasant art and concerned themselves to investigate, conserve and reproduce it. The beginning of this tendency is marked by the appearance in 1872 of the book by V.V. Stasov (1824–1906) called *Russian Folk Decoration*. An important patron was S.I. Mamontov (1841–1918), a leading figure in the Moscow-centred movement known as the Wanderers. On his estate at Abramtsevo near Moscow he assembled in the 1870s gifted enthusiasts who not only conducted research into popular art but also set up craft schools where traditional designs were embodied in articles for contemporary use. With their own hands they built the church, traditional in form, which is still there. V.D. Polenov (1844–1927), a painter and archaeologist, added a museum of national peasant art which also survives; its first exhibit was a carved lintel which he found in a nearby house.

Other estate colonies of craftsmen basing their designs on peasant work were organized, notably that founded by Princess Tenisheva at Talashkino near Smolensk. She not only helped to design the products, but also made a major collection of village articles in everyday use. Other important collections were those of P.I. Shchukin (now in the State Historical Museum in Moscow) and of Princess Aleksandra Sidamon-Eristov and N. de Chabelskoy. By the 1880s interest in Russian folk art, especially embroidery, had spread to other European countries: the Broderie Russe Company opened shops in London, Paris and other capitals, as outlets for work made or collected in Russia. Later (1911–20), the continuing interest in Britain was catered for by Madame Pogorsky's Russian Peasant Industries shop in London, stocking books of translated Russian folk-tales illustrated by I.Ya. Bilibin (1876–1942) in a style based on designs collected in Siberia, and still in print.

Traditional embroidery all but disappeared after 1920 through lack of materials. There was, however, a brief renaissance in the early 1980s when lessons in crochet, knitting and embroidery were advertised on cards pinned to trees in Moscow streets. Beadwork too has enjoyed a revival, using modern and adapted traditional designs. Yet while beads are available, there is the greatest difficulty in obtaining suitable needles and thread.

Since the Gorbachev era the most obvious change in folk art is its greater availability. To supplement falling incomes, people are remembering half-forgotten skills, like a young engineer encountered on the Arbat, who learned from his grandfather the art of making baskets out of bast (the inside layer of lime-tree bark).   AMC

CAUCASIA

Caucasian folk art differs widely from Russian, its products reflecting the strong local and ancient traditions of fiercely independent non-Slav peoples. Their artefacts include the well-known knotted carpets and rugs, of which one unusual feature is quilting: a thin layer of wool is inserted between the rug and the lining. Knitted work, especially socks of wool or silk, sometimes incorporating gold threads, shows decoration in a contrasting colour, using figures of birds, the tree of life, the *buta* (a curved motif familiar from Paisley shawls), and other geometric shapes. The earliest example of beadwork is a hookah stem of the fourteenth century; tambour work may be seen on the Azerbaijan national costume and resembles some kinds of Bukharan and Indian embroidery, the *buta* motif also being employed. Georgian embroidery is characterized by the free use of metal threads, and is based on traditions established in the seventeenth and eighteenth centuries in workshops supplying church vestments and icons. The pottery of Dagestan includes glazed ware with impressed designs and unglazed ware with painted designs, in either case geometric. Jewellery, daggers, drinking horns and other domestic articles are decorated with damascening or niello work.

Right. Caucasian daggers, chased silver inlaid with niello, nineteenth century

CENTRAL ASIA

This region is the home of peoples mainly of Turkic origin and tongue and traditionally of nomadic habits; important cities such as Bukhara and Samarkand established themselves on the great trade-route between East and West and encouraged the production of goods of high quality. The nomadic Kazakhs, like other peoples of this area, made woven and knotted rugs, but are specially remarkable for the felt matting (made from sheep's wool) with which they covered the floors and walls of the *yurts* (movable pavilions) in which they lived. Bold simple shapes were cut out of two superimposed squares of felt of different colours, often the black and white of the undyed wool. The cut-outs were then interchanged and the resulting patterned squares were joined in chequer-board fashion, the joins being covered with braid, and the whole mat sometimes surrounded with a fringe of dyed horsehair. Such mats were expected to last some fifty years. Bukhara has given its name not only to carpets and rugs but also to embroidered wall-hangings and bed-covers of the nineteenth century, though these were often in fact made in Nurata, Fergana, Tashkent or Samarkand. The floral designs are usually embroidered in silk on cotton, sometimes with the tambour stitch used by Uzbeks, Tajiks, Kyrgyz and Turkmens. Embossed leather was used to make flagons for koumiss (fermented mares' milk), milking pails, cases for drinking vessels and other domestic articles.   AMC

Sacred art

ICONS

The word 'icon' (Greek: 'image' or 'likeness') is applied to mosaics, frescoes, wooden panels, embroidery, sculpture and metalwork depicting subjects relevant to worship in the Orthodox Church. When Russia officially accepted Christianity from Byzantium in 988 it was a conscious choice resting on an experience of liturgical beauty and meaning, combining word, song, architecture and image: an interrelated theological and artistic reality. From Byzantium and Bulgaria the Russians inherited a mature tradition, with a coherent and theocentric world view.

Almost without exception, icons are unsigned: the name inscribed on the icon is that of the saint depicted. The universal creative principle underlying this culture is the fact of the Gospel message and the doctrine of the Incarnation of Christ: God has become visible and therefore depictable, and remains adored. His image – and that of each of the saints – is scrupulously and authentically personal, historical, offering an insight into the invisible and divine reality of the holy in the context of eternity. Because the nature of any image is to make present the person depicted, iconic reality derives from the indwelling of the holy one in his image, which both the painter and the beholder approach with awe. They venerate the image, but worship God.

As elsewhere in traditional Orthodox iconography, Russian icons of Christ are essentially of two kinds: the 'Pantocrator' (Almighty), with all its derivations, and the 'Holy Face' or 'Icon of Christ not made by hand'. All bust and whole figure portraits of Christ depict the 'Pantocrator': whether in the dome or gallery of a cathedral; whether depicted alone on a wooden panel, or with others in one of the Gospel scenes; or whether severe as the Judge of the Last Days, as in Feofan (Theophanes) the Greek's (1335–c. 1410) Pantocrator in the dome of the Church of the Transfiguration of the Saviour, Novgorod (1378), or gentle as the God of Mercy, as in Andrey Rublev's (?–1430) panel icon from a Deesis row in Zvenigorod, now in the Tret'yakov Gallery in Moscow.

Traditionally, Christ, when on His own, faces the beholder, His right hand raised in blessing, His left holding the Gospel Book, either open displaying a chosen text or closed to show the jewelled cover. His garments are traditional and in royal colours: a purple or brown tunic covered in part by a blue *himation*. These are also the traditional garments of the Apostles, each identifiable by his own colours and physiognomy. Christ in Glory is seated on a throne, surrounded by a mandorla. Here, the royal colours are outshone by the Light of His Divinity represented in white and gold (Luke 9:29).

With icons of the Mother of God and Child, Russian icon painters again faithfully followed their Byzantine masters by adopting four basic traditional types: the 'Hodigitria' (Pointer of the Way), 'Of the Sign', 'Of Tenderness' and 'Enthroned'. The Hodigitria icon had two well-known variants – the *Tikhvinskaya* and the *Kazanskaya* – both late Russian developments showing the Child in slightly different poses, and named after the towns where they made their first miraculous appearances, in 1383 and 1579 respectively. Russia's most famous Mother of God icon, the *Vladimirskaya*, is of the 'Tenderness' type. It was a twelfth-century gift from Byzantium to the court of the Kievan Rus' at Vladimir, the town is where it remained for four centuries until brought to Moscow to be venerated by court and people in the Kremlin Cathedral of the

Dormition of the Mother of God. Since the Revolution it has hung in the Tret'yakov Gallery.

Other icons depict the Mother of God in various forms of intercession and veneration by the faithful. With Mother of God icons, as with Christ icons, expressions vary from severe to tender. Although the Child often looks at his Mother and clasps her, she always looks firmly out at the beholder; never do Mother and Child exchange tender looks which would exclude the beholder. Nor is the Mother depicted alone: she is always in some way related to her Son. In her integrity, her position among men was unique for, pure in heart, she was 'able to see God'. The iconography of the Mother of God and Child is based on sound theology, and it celebrates the doctrine of the Incarnation. The Mother remains the Theotokos, the one who 'bore God'.   MMF

ICONOSTASIS

The God-centred attitude is further exemplified in the interior of a Russian church: the iconographic programme inherited from Byzantium includes the iconostasis, as well as four specific areas of wall-painting within the architecture of the building. The iconostasis is an 'icon of the Church' in its growth, depicting in its various tiers the history of salvation from Adam to the Last Judgment. It delineates the borderline and manifests the unity between two worlds, the eternal and the temporal; the sanctuary representing the Kingdom of God, and the nave where the people stand in active vigilance and wor-

ship. The doors through which the celebrants proceed during the liturgy make this visually apparent.

In its complete form the iconostasis incorporates five tiers, a counterpart of what is proclaimed in word and song in the Orthodox liturgy. The upper tier, of the Forefathers, represents the Old Testament from Adam to Moses; the centre holds the icon of the Holy Trinity (the Three Angels appearing to Abraham). Below this is the row of the Prophets, from Moses to Christ; they hold scrolls prophesying the Incarnation. In the centre is the icon of the Mother of God of the Sign, a depiction of Isaiah's prophecy about the virgin and the child Emmanuel. Below is the tier of Festivals, representing the New Testament. These icons depict the life of the Mother of God and Christ, as they are celebrated in the Church year. They include, among others, the Presentation of the Mother of God in the Temple, the Nativity of Christ, the Transfiguration. The next tier is called Deesis, 'prayer'. Here, angels and saints are set in relation to the central triptych where Christ is approached by His Mother and St John the Baptist in an attitude of intercession. This triptych was the kernel of the original templon iconography. The templon in Middle Byzantine churches consisted of a number of columns carrying an architrave which, in turn, carried from one to three rows of icons. The Deesis triptych remained the most important iconography on the screen. Below is the 'local' tier: icons of locally-venerated saints or events, and two large icons of Christ and the Mother of God on either side of the Holy Doors which show the Annunciation and the Four Evangelists, symbolizing the advent of the Kingdom.

It was in fifteenth-century Russia that, under the brushes of Feofan the Greek and Andrey Rublev the iconostasis rose to unprecedented heights, carrying five and later even six rows of icons, so that what had in more ancient times been a more or less open screen and a curtain, in Russia became a solid wall, pierced by three doors.

The outlining iconographic arrangement on the walls, in the dome, in the apse and on the west wall is given as a graphic narrative of Christ's ministry and of the lives of the saints. The early use of mosaics was soon replaced by fresco painting. As a symbol of Heaven, the central dome contains Christ Pantocrator surrounded by angels and prophets, and in the drum the Twelve Apostles, while the Four Evangelists are in the four pendentives (coved corners). The apse contains a row of hierarchs of the early Church. Above this is represented the Communion of the Apostles, echoing the eucharistic action by the clergy in the sanctuary. Higher still is a large icon of the Mother of God interceding for the world. The rest of the vaults, arches and walls are covered with scenes from the Life of Christ and the Sunday Gospels in the high places; pillars, pilasters and the lower parts of the walls depict the martyrs and other saints. The narrative iconography thus reproduces for the eyes of the faithful what their ears hear in lessons and hymns.

The comprehensive mural programme and the structure of the iconostasis was a logical, conscious development within a theocentric Church, the result of a living process in which tradition was understood as a dynamic and creative presence in the world, a culture nurtured on worship and the Gospels.

Below. A sixteenth-century freestanding iconostasis, showing the five tiers of pictures. Below right. A page from the Podlinnik, *showing (left to right) St John of Damascus, St Savas, St Nicholas the Miracle Worker, and St Ambrose*

THE PAINTING OF ICONS

The icon painter is, first of all, a theologian: not in the academic sense, but as a man or woman who worships God and venerates the saints. He is the first to venerate what he has made on behalf of the Church, and hence does not consider the icons as his exclusive achievement.

The only iconographic canon is the *Podlinnik*, the painter's handbook, an anthology of outlines for every saint and sacred event, with indications of symbols and conventions aimed at preserving the identity and likeness of the saint. The style of the icon derives from the same iconographic and theological tradition of the Church, in a language of lines and colour which the Russians have unhesitatingly adopted. Significantly, the Greek and Slavonic words for icon painting are 'icon writing'. The lines and contours follow a logical structure. They are never arbitrary, neither do they ignore the shape of the body; the order is cosmic, not chaotic. The drapery follows the movement of the body it envelops without being merely naturalistic. The structure is architectural, the contours are emphatic, and the principal lines uninterrupted, directing the lesser lines and supporting the overall structure.

Paint is applied in superimposed transparent layers, shading from an all-enveloping dark to smaller areas of lighter shades, and ending in the minute concentrations of light which provide the characteristic luminosity of the icon. The only source of light is from within the saint. There is no limit to this light, which by its very nature casts no shadows: the Uncreated Light of God. Indicating

St George with scenes from his life, fourteenth century, with peasant or folk stylistic elements

divinity, the mandorla, an all-embracing halo, and 'assist', a fine network of gold lines, are reserved for Christ alone – and only in icons recording events where he had revealed his Godhead, depicting him outside his mission on Earth – with the exception of his Childhood and the icon of the Transfiguration. We see him in the Ascension, the Dormition, the Last Judgment and in icons of individual saints blessing them from Heaven, arrayed in white and gold, or gold ochre. The 'assist' sometimes spills over from Christ onto the very people or objects he touches: his Mother, the Book, the Throne.

In respect of perspective the arrangement of space and the geometry of volumes are, in principle, distorted when depicted on the flat surface of an icon panel. The medieval painter reduced depth of field by using undistorted parallel lines (furniture, buildings, books). He simultaneously endeavoured to enhance the visual amplitude of forms through linear or inverted perspective, instinctively alternating them to bring important features of the painting to the fore. The complexities of perspective are thus subordinated to the overriding artistic composition of the icon.

Overall stylistic diversity is mild. One cannot speak of independent 'schools' in the sense of Renaissance schools, but must rather envisage different strands within the same tradition. Painters travelled, and the icons travelled; this often makes it difficult to date and place an icon. However, there are local characteristics reflecting the distinctive quality of the earths and minerals used for paints in a particular

region, or the influence of certain masters in a given area. Added to this, there is an over-all 'Russian' character in the forms and shapes of bodies and faces; in some bizarreness of architectural features, and in the use and application of colours and specific painterly techniques. This is the case whether an icon dates from the early eleventh century beginnings or half a millennium later. Broadly speaking, the tradition is faithfully observed until the sixteenth century.

From the time of Russia's official conversion in 988 under Prince Vladimir I of Kiev local artists collaborated with their Byzantine masters. But soon the Russians worked on their own, from time to time inspired by Byzantine work or by visiting masters. In the decoration of churches such as St Sofia Cathedral enough mosaic and fresco work remains as examples of iconic work of that period. No panel icons can be attributed to Kiev with any certainty. The earliest panel icons are from Novgorod, strongly influenced in the eleventh and twelfth centuries by Byzantine icons. The Annunciation Cathedral in the Moscow Kremlin has a magnificent St George with the large dominating eyes typical of the twelfth century, the face finely modelled by the fusion technique and the features brought to life by direct, firm, expressive lines. The Saviour 'made without hands' in the Tret'yakov Gallery, Moscow (based on the traditional King Abgar Mandylion) is another Byzantine-based icon executed with the most economical, direct means to make the highest impact. Other icons in this early category characterized by very large expressive eyes, strong lines and painterly modelling by fusion are the head of the Archangel with golden hair in the Russian Museum, the so-called Yaroslavl' Mother of God of the Sign and the Ustyug Annunciation, both in the Tret'yakov Gallery.

Right. The Saviour 'made without hands', Novgorod, twelfth to thirteenth centuries

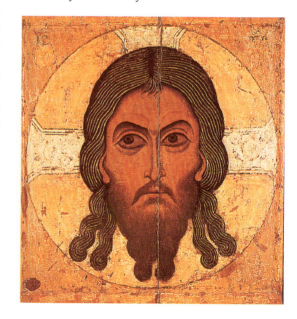

Above. *Christ Pantocrator, from a Deesis from Chernokulovo village, Vladimir, fifteenth century*

Far right. *Fourteenth century icon of SS Paraskeva, Gregory the Theologian, John Chrysostom and Basil the Great, from Pskov*

The Ustyug Annunciation, Yur'ev Monastery, Novgorod, twelfth century

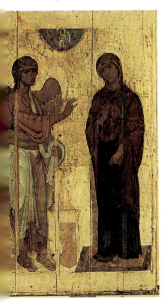

Areas such as Rostov-Suzdal' with Vladimir as its capital, Yaroslavl' and Pskov are all famous for their early icons. The famous *Vladimirskaya* Mother of God, in Vladimir after 1155 (originally a gift by Constantinople to Kiev), must have made a great impact there, on the faithful and artists alike, as indeed must other such documented gifts of Byzantine masterpieces. Two Deesis panels also in the Tret'yakov Gallery, one of Christ Emmanuel between two Angels, the other the adult Christ between the Mother of God and St John the Baptist, both from Vladimir-Suzdal', are reminiscent of this, as is the St Dmitry icon, also in the Tret'yakov Gallery, dated twelfth or thirteenth century.

The Tatar (or Mongol) inroads in the thirteenth and fourteenth centuries destroyed much of Russian works of art; they put a brake on further work and impeded contacts with Byzantium and the Balkans. Novgorod and Pskov remained free to continue creating, local characteristics coming more and more to the fore as Byzantine influence receded. The fourteenth and fifteenth centuries are considered the greatest in Novgorod. The themes were to the point, the means remained economic, direct, the colours were pure, bright, with flaming red predominating; white was used lavishly. Often the figures were short with biggish heads, the attitudes frontal in icons of Novgorod's favourite saints such as Paraskeva, Anastasia, George, Elijah, Nicholas and Blaise as well as Florus and Laurus. A small Mother of God of the Sign is often inserted as a semi-spherical icon below the upper frame of such groups of saints, as the documented Protectress of the town of Novgorod. Often red, the nearest colour to gold in the solar spectrum, was used for the background colour. Such icons as the Prophet Elijah in the Tret'yakov Gallery, St George in the Russian Museum and SS Varlaam Khutynsky, John the Almsgiver, Paraskeva and Anastasia, also in the Russian Museum, are good examples of this period in Novgorod.

In the fifteenth century the figures became elongated and the heads small; the impact of the colours remained strong and unmixed but superimposed. Painterly means became more sophisticated: examples include, in the Tret'yakov Gallery: Holy Women at the Sepulchre (*c.*1475), SS Florus and Laurus; in the Russian Museum, St Petersburg: the Quadripartite Icon; and in the Museum of History in Novgorod: the icons on canvas, such as Christ among the Doctors.

Pskov icons are characterized by a strong dark green and bright orange, often dotted and decorated with white. The modelling of the faces, with their important luminosity, is often achieved by short thick white strokes or patches and parallel lines. A typical example is the Mother of God's Assembly in the Tret'yakov Gallery (*c.*1351–1400). The four-teenth-century icon of SS Paraskeva, Gregory the Theologian, John Chrysostom and Basil the Great in the Tret'yakov Gallery is a superb example of the scrupulous care which the painter took to be true to the saints' personal, authentic features. A famous icon from Tver', the Blue Dormition, fifteenth century, can also be found in the Tret'yakov Gallery.

When Moscow became the centralizing power in the fourteenth and fifteenth centuries much that had been created in Vladimir-Suzdal' was absorbed in the new rising culture and continued there. Moscow iconography also came under Paleologue influence. Feofan the Greek, after working in Novgorod, painted in the Kremlin in Moscow together with the young Andrey Rublev in the Annunciation Cathedral in 1405. They developed the iconostasis to unprecedented heights. Rublev's most famous icon, painted for the Trinity Monastery of St Sergy, is the Holy Trinity icon in the Tret'yakov Gallery – perfect in expressing consent and assent by the Three Persons to the Sacrifice symbolized in the Chalice on the Table. He achieved the ultimate in luminosity and transparency in paint, his lines are delicate and direct; compassion, gentleness, dignity in humility are what he expresses. Among others the St Michael from Zvenigorod in the Tret'yakov Gallery is a good example of his work. His influence was enormous in Russian icon painting.

Dionisy (*c.*1441–1508) is the last name of known great icon painters coming within this same tradition. His figures are elegant, refined, with light colours superbly blended and harmonious. Detail becomes important and that whole era of icon painting, with the refinement, aesthetic values, preciousness and ornamental detail characterizing the sixteenth and seventeenth centuries is already hinted at here.

Andrey Rublev

A contemporary of Van Eyck, Masaccio and Piero della Francesca, Andrey Rublev was widely acknowledged during his lifetime, but after his death he became famous as the greatest Russian icon painter when the Council of a Hundred Chapters in 1551 recommended his works as models for the painting of icons.

Little is known about his life. He took monastic vows as a young man at the Monastery of the Trinity, which had been founded in 1345 by St Sergy of Radonezh. Rublev later moved to Moscow as a monk of the Andronikov monastery. The ancient chronicles mention works by him that were commissioned by Russian princes and Church notables, including the decoration of the Cathedral of the Assumption at Zvenigorod (c. 1400), the Cathedral of the Assumption at Vladimir (1408, the most substantial and significant of his surviving cycles of frescoes), and the Cathedral of the Nativity at Zvenigorod (c. 1415–20).

In about 1405, with Feofan

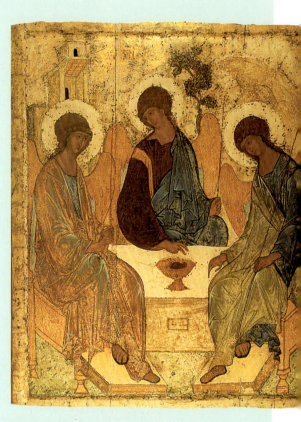

(Theophanes) the Greek and the elder Prokhor of Gorodok, he helped to create the iconostasis of the Cathedral of the Annunciation in Moscow with its enormous figure of the deity (over two metres tall) and its extensive ranks of celebrants from which the classic Russian iconostasis originates. Many other icons are attributed to Rublev, the most famous of them being the Old Testament Trinity of 1410–20 (right), now in the Tret'yakov Gallery, Moscow.

While adhering strictly to the iconography and painterly canons of medieval painting (the symbolism of details, flatness, reverse perspective and so on) Rublev introduces elements of a new renaissance perception of the world. He is often called the 'Russian Fra Angelico'; both were monks who overcame medieval asceticism and brought a human note into art. In the history of Russian art, Rublev was the first master (along with Feofan) with an individual style and the most important artist of the pre-Petrine period.

Above. *Icon of the Protecting Veil* [Pokrov], *seventeenth century, Stroganov school*

Right. *Mother of God icon, eighteenth-nineteenth century*

The elongated figures of the so-called Stroganov school, perfect in technique to the point of virtuosity, and the 'verbosity' and fussiness in the narrative icons tell of a time in Russian icon painting when to simple statements of faith was added philosophical speculation. The Court and the mighty of the more regulated secular world have also left their impact here. From being an art founded in a spiritual reality developing out of an unfragmented world view and faith, iconic painting absorbed more and more secular matter while retaining the exterior shell. Introduction to Western naturalistic painting based on the Renaissance (which was partly pagan in inspiration) proved an irresistible temptation to the Russians. Simon Ushakov (1626–86) attempted a fusion of both worlds – the naturalistic and the transfigured – but instead of a 'spiritual body' (St Paul) he painted glistening flesh. The vision had become distorted and psychological states were mistaken for spiritual ones. However, side by side with this decadent phase in the Church and its art went another current which continued in the tradition of asceticism and spiritual life, producing sacred art. This is why, in this century, icons are still being created from within the Church, true to its tradition and experience, alive in the spirit which perpetuated it.   MMF

Architecture

MEDIEVAL ARCHITECTURE

With the acceptance of Christianity by Prince Vladimir in 988, the construction of masonry churches spread throughout Kievan Rus'. The largest and most complex of these early churches was Kiev's Cathedral of Divine Wisdom (St Sofia, 1037–50s), commissioned by Yaroslav the Wise and built under the direction of Greek masters and artisans. The interior contained extensive mosaics as well as frescoes. Other major churches of this period include the St Sofia Cathedral in Novgorod (1045–52), the Cathedral of the Transfiguration of the Saviour in Chernigov (1031–50s), and the Cathedral of the Dormition in the Kiev Cave Monastery (1073–78).

Regardless of size, the churches rapidly evolved toward a simplified plan known as the 'inscribed cross', with a cuboid core structure and two main aisles whose intersection was marked by the central dome, elevated on a drum and supported by four piers. The interior bays were delineated on the exterior by pilasters culminating in curved gables known as *zakomary*, whose shape reflected the barrel vaulting of the interior. The application of stucco to church walls, typically built of thin brick, rough stone, and heavy mortar, began towards the end of the twelfth century. Although modest in size, the Church of the Transfiguration at Mirozhsky Monastery, Pskov (1156) and the Church of the Transfiguration on the Nereditsa, near Novgorod (1198, rebuilt after the Second World War) were notable for their twelfth-century frescoes.

In addition to Kiev, Novgorod, and neighbouring cities, the third centre of masonry construction in pre-Mongol Rus' was the Vladimir-Suzdal' principality, whose limestone churches were distinguished by carved decoration and precision of design. The first of these were commissioned by Yury Dolgoruky, including the Church of the Transfiguration in Pereslavl'-Zalessky (1152–57). His son Andrey Bogolyubsky initiated the great era of limestone building in the Vladimir area with the Cathedral of the Dormition, Vladimir (1158–60); his palace church at Bogolyubovo (1158–65, only fragments extant); and the Church of the Intercession (*Pokrov*) on the Nerl' (1165). His successor, Vsevolod III, enlarged the Dormition Cathedral (1185–89), and built the Cathedral of St Dmitry, Vladimir (1194–97), whose upper tier is covered with elaborate carving representing biblical and secular motifs. Other churches of this period include the Cathedral of the Nativity of the Virgin in Suzdal' (1222–25) and St George in Yur'ev-Pol'sky (1234), both of which

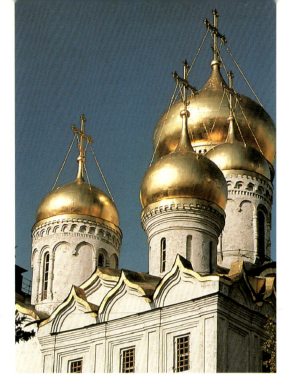

collapsed in the fifteenth century and were substantially modified when rebuilt.

Following the Mongol invasion of 1237–41, church construction declined precipitously; but by the middle of the fourteenth century masonry construction reappeared on a large scale, particularly in Novgorod, whose Church of St Theodore Stratilates (1360–61) and the Transfiguration Church on Elijah Street (1374, frescoes by Feofan the Greek) exemplified a distinct local style characterized by steeply-pitched trefoil roofs.

Moscow also witnessed the beginnings of an architectural revival, but not until the last quarter of the fifteenth century did the major monuments of the Kremlin take shape under the direction of Italian masters imported by Ivan III. In building the Cathedral of the Dormition (1475–79), Aristotele Fioravanti used the Vladimir Dormition Cathedral as a model but introduced technical improvements such as deep foundation trenches with oak pilings, strong brick used in vaulting, and iron tie-rods. As a result the interior, with its round columns, seemed unusually spacious and well-lit.

Brick soon replaced limestone for most masonry construction: Alevisio Novi used it in his Cathedral of the Archangel Michael (1505–09), which had a number of Italianate elements. Italian influence was also pronounced in Marco Fryazin and Pietro Antonio Solari's design of the Faceted Palace (1487–91), and in the Kremlin walls and towers built by Antonio Fryazin, Marco Fryazin, Solari, and others (1485–1516, with major additions in the seventeenth century). The dominant element of the Kremlin, the Bell Tower of Ivan the Great, was constructed in two stages: the lower two tiers in 1505–08 by Bon Fryazin, and the upper tier with cupola in 1599–1600.

Above. *Interior, Cathedral of the Annunciation, in the Kremlin, Moscow.* Right. *St Basil's Cathedral, at the south end of Red Square, Moscow (1555–61)*

Below. *A window on the tiled façade of the Krutitskoe podvor'e, Moscow (1694), built following the example of Jonah Sysoevich's residence chambers in Rostov*

During the sixteenth century, Moscow's brick votive churches displayed remarkable forms (also with Italian influence). The Church of the Ascension at Kolomenskoe (1530–32) established the 'tent' tower form, while the Decapitation of John the Baptist at Dyakovo (c.1550) exemplified another interpretation of the tower church. These prototypes were combined in the most spectacular of Russian churches, the Cathedral of the Intercession on the Moat, popularly known as St Basil's (1555–61). Built to commemorate Ivan IV's conquest of Kazan' and Astrakhan', the structure consists of a central tent tower (dedicated to the Intercession) surrounded by eight tower churches. Colourful onion domes were added around 1600, while attached structures and much of the decoration appeared throughout the seventeenth century. The logic of the central plan resembles concepts of ideal architecture developed during the quattrocento, but applied in a radically idiosyncratic manner by builders from Pskov.

After the devastations of the Time of Troubles, masonry churches were built on an unprecedented scale during the long reign of Aleksey Mikhailovich. Of special note are two large complexes: Patriarch Nikon's New Jerusalem (or Resurrection) monastery near Moscow, with its cathedral (1658–85) based on the plan of Jerusalem's Holy Sepulchre church; and in Rostov, Metropolitan Jonah Sysoevich's walled ensemble of churches and residence chambers (1670–83). In a related development, many of Moscow's monasteries underwent a major rebuilding in the late seventeenth century (Novodevichy, Novospassky, Simonov, Donskoy, Andronikov) as did the great Trinity-Sergius Lavra at Sergiev Posad. The proliferation of lavishly ornamented churches occurred throughout Muscovy, with particularly fine examples in Yaroslavl'.

As Russia experienced increased contact with the West through Ukraine and trade with northern Europe, elements of the baroque appeared in numerous churches commissioned primarily by the Naryshkin and Sheremetev families. Examples of the 'Naryshkin Baroque' show a revival of the tower church form, often on a quatrefoil base as in the Churches of the Intercession at Fili (1690–99), the Trinity at Troitskoe-Lykovo (1698–1703), and the Transfiguration at Ubory (1694–97). The latter two churches are attributed to Yakov Bukhvostov, who also built the great Dormition Cathedral in Ryazan' (1693–99). During the seventeenth century the use of brick in secular construction increased, mainly in Moscow, with its brick *palaty* and the tiered Sukharev Tower (1692–1701). None the less, the history of masonry architecture in pre-Petrine Russia is largely a matter of church, monastery, and fortress construction.   WCB

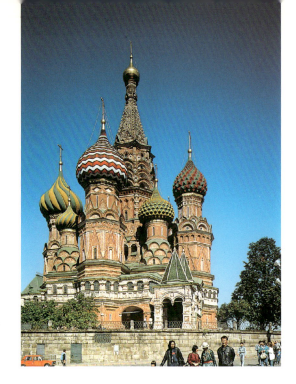

WOODEN ARCHITECTURE

Throughout Russian history wood has been used for virtually every type of construction, from large churches and fortress walls to peasant dwellings. Medieval chronicles refer to early wooden churches of complex design, such as the first church of St Sofia in Novgorod, with thirteen 'tops'. There is no firm evidence as to the appearance of wooden structures before the late sixteenth century, although the small church of St Lazarus from the shores of Lake Onega (now at the Kizhi Museum of Wooden Architecture) is tentatively dated c.1390. However, the basic forms are presumably rooted in the traditions of many centuries, as are the construction techniques.

The most distinctive examples of wooden architecture are churches, which include the simple 'cell' (*klet*) church resembling the peasant's house; the 'tent' tower (*shatyor*) placed on an octagon over the cube of the main structure; and the 'tiered' church, a pyramidal structure composed of ascending octagonal levels. The logs – usually heartwood of pine, either squared or rounded – were notched and joined horizontally. The domes, as well as the 'barrel' gables, are typically of aspen shingles, which age to a bright silver hue. Despite the decorative carving, only the simplest of tools were used until the nineteenth century, when many of the churches were covered with milled plank siding. Remarkable for their construction logic, wooden churches also display elaborate configurations, exemplified by the Church of the Transfiguration at Kizhi (1714), whose pyramid of recessed levels supports twenty-two cupolas. Although such structures achieved great height, the church interior was defined by a much lower ceiling.

Right. *Preobrozhenskaya Church (1714) on the island of Kizhy in Karelia. The church has 22 cupolas, many of them visible here*

Below. *Detail of wooden house, Suzdal'. Bottom. Wooden house, Tbilisi, Georgia*

Log houses likewise ranged from simple huts to large three-storey dwellings – peculiar to the far north – containing space for the family and shelter for livestock during the winter. Wooden housing is still extensively used not only in the Russian countryside but in provincial cities (particularly in Siberia and the Far East), where the houses often have plank siding and intricately carved decorative elements. Because of the significant role of wooden architecture in Russian history, open air museums have been established throughout Russia (Novgorod, Kizhi, Kostroma, Suzdal', and Vologda) for the purpose of reassembling and preserving some of the best examples of log structures.

ST PETERSBURG (LENINGRAD)

Founded by Peter I in 1703, the city became the Russian capital in 1711 and plans for its development were submitted by the architects Jean Baptiste Le Blond (1679–1719) and Domenico Trezzini (1671–1734). Le Blond's influence was pervasive in defining the early Baroque style in St Petersburg, but his untimely death precluded a more extensive architectural legacy. Trezzini enjoyed a prolific career that included monuments such as the Cathedral of SS Peter and Paul (1712–32), the Building of the Twelve Colleges (1722–41), Peter I's Summer Palace (1711–14), and the first design of the Alexander Nevsky Lavra with the Church of the Annunciation (1717–22). Other notable buildings include the Kunstkammer (1718–34), by Georg Mattarnovi, with a central tower after a design by Andreas Schlüter. In its early stages St Petersburg's architecture was much indebted to the northern European Baroque, particularly of Sweden and Holland.

Bartolomeo Francesco Rastrelli (1700–71) defined the lavish high Baroque style during the reigns of Anne and Elizabeth. Among his major projects were Elizabeth's Summer Palace (1741–43, not extant), the Stroganov Palace (1752–54), the final version of the Winter Palace (1754–64), and the Smol'ny Convent with its Resurrection Cathedral (1748–64). In addition Rastrelli greatly enlarged the existing Imperial palaces at Peterhof (1746–52) and Tsarskoe Selo (1748–56). During this period Russian architects such as Mikhail Zemtsov (1688–1743) and Savva Chevakinsky (1713–80) made significant contributions to the city's development. Chevakinsky's masterpiece, the Cathedral of St Nicholas (1753–62), rivals the best work of Rastrelli.

In the transition from the Baroque to the Neoclassicism favoured by Catherine II, Jean-Baptiste Vallin de la Mothe (1729–1800) played a pivotal role with the design of the Academy of Arts (1764–88), the Small Hermitage (1764–75), the New Holland Arch (1765–80s), and the arcaded trading centre Gostiny Dvor (1757–85). A pleiade of architects endowed the city during the second half of the eighteenth century with a grandeur inspired by classical Rome and Palladianism: Antonio Rinaldi (c.1710–94) built the Marble Palace (1768–85, one of the city's few buildings surfaced in natural stone); Giacomo Quarenghi (1744–1817) designed the Hermitage Theatre (1783–87), the Academy of Sciences (1783–89), the Smol'ny Institute for Noblewomen (1806–08) as well as the Alexander Palace at Tsarskoe Selo (1792–96); and Georg Friedrich Veldten (1730–1801), builder of the Chesme palace and church (1777–80) in the pseudo-Gothic style, enhanced the beauty of the city with his quays along the left bank of the Neva.

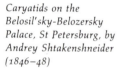

Caryatids on the Belosil'sky-Belozersky Palace, St Petersburg, by Andrey Shtakenshneider (1846–48)

Charles Cameron (c.1740–1812), the leading proponent of Palladian architecture in Russia, designed the palace at the imperial estate of Pavlovsk (1780–96) as well as the pavilions in the estate park. At Tsarskoe Selo he redecorated in the manner of Robert Adam and Clérisseau a number of rooms in Rastrelli's Catherine Palace, and attached the superb Cameron Gallery (1783–86), with connecting pavilions, to the south wing of the palace. Construction in the city continued with Emperor Paul's Mikhaylovsky Palace (1797–1800), an Italianate design by Vincenza Brenna and Vasily Bazhenov. Ivan Starov (1744–1808), whose understated classicism

The Cathedral of the Resurrection in the Smol'ny Convent (1748–64), St Petersburg, by Rastrelli

in the design of the Tauride Palace (1783–89) was widely admired as a model for estate architecture, completed the ensemble of the Alexander Nevsky Lavra with his Roman-style Trinity Cathedral (1776–90). A still more striking example of Roman influence in church architecture occurred in Andrey Voronikhin's Cathedral of the Kazan' Mother of God (1801–11), with its imposing colonnade attached to the north (Nevsky Prospekt) façade. Voronikhin (1759–1814) also designed the Mining Institute (1806–11), whose Doric portico exemplifies the revival of interest in archaic Greek architecture. Similarly Jean Thomas de Thomon (1760–1813) used the Greek temples at Paestum as a model for the Bourse, or Stock Exchange (1805–10), on the tip of Vasilevsky Island.

The construction and site plan of the Bourse provided a focus to one of the city's major strategic points, and thus initiated Alexander I's campaign to provide an interconnecting system of architectural ensembles and public space throughout the centre of St Petersburg. The rebuilding of the Admiralty (1806–23) by Andreyan Zakharov (1761–1811) reaffirmed that structure, and its spire, as a dominant element in the city plan; but the culmination of the imperial design was left to Carlo Rossi (1775–1849) who created four great ensembles: the Mikhaylovsky Palace and Park (1819–25); the General Staff Building and Arch (1819–29), facing Palace Square; the Alexandrine Theatre and surrounding buildings (1828–32); and the Senate and Holy Synod (1829–34) facing Senate Square, the site of Etienne Fal-

Above left. St Petersburg: view through the arch of the General Staff building (Rossi, 1819–29) into Palace Square, with Montferrand's monolithic Aleksandr column (1829–34) and the Winter Palace (Rastrelli, 1754–64). Left. Portico of the Smol'ny Institute, by Quarenghi (1806–8); the Institute served as Lenin's HQ after the October Revolution. Above right. Inside the dome of St Isaac's Cathedral, St Petersburg, by Auguste Montferrand

conet's monument to Peter I ('The Bronze Horseman', 1768–82). Vasily Stasov complemented Rossi's work with a number of late Neoclassical churches, including the Church of the Icon of the Saviour (1817–23), with the attached building of the Court Stables extending on either side along the Moika. During the reign of Nicholas I, classical unity yielded to eclecticism and new developments in construction engineering, both of which are evident in the final version of St Isaac's Cathedral (1818–58) by Auguste Montferrand (1786–1858) and in mid-nineteenth century palaces by Andrey Shtakenshneider (1802–65).   WCB

NEO-CLASSICAL MOSCOW

Moscow's most extensive use of the neo-classical style occurred in mansions for the nobility and wealthy merchants in the central city, as well as on suburban estates such as Kuskovo, Ostankino, and Arkhangel'skoe. Many of the estate houses were designed by skilled serf architects, but the most prominent classicists in Moscow were Matvey Kazakov (1738–1812) and Vasily Bazhenov (1737–99). It is assumed that Bazhenov designed the Pashkov House (1784–86, later the Rumyantsev Museum); and he also drew up, at the request of Catherine II, a grandiose plan for rebuilding the Kremlin in the neo-classical style. Among the major neo-classical institutional buildings are the Sheremetev Pilgrims' Refuge by Quarenghi (1792–1803); the Old Gostiny Dvor (1791–1805) by Quarenghi and Kazakov; the main building of Moscow University (1782–93), the Senate (1776–87, in the Kremlin), and the Noblemen's Assembly (1793–1801), all by Kazakov. A number of imposing neo-classical churches were built, including Matvey Kazakov's Church of the Metropolitan Philip (1777–88), and the Church of Martin the Confessor (1782–93) by Rodion Kazakov (1755–1803). After the fire of 1812, damaged structures such as the Pashkov House and Moscow University were rebuilt, while new houses appeared in the Empire style as interpreted by Domenico Gilardi (1788–1845), Osip Bove (1784–1834), and Afanasy Grigor'ev (1782–1868).   WCB

HISTORICISM

Even before the waning of neo-classicism, period styles such as the pseudo-Gothic had appeared in the work of Georg Velten, Vasily Bazhenov, and Matvey Kazakov. In the 1770s and 1780s Bazhenov and Kazakov were involved in the building of a Gothic imperial estate at Tsaritsyno, near Moscow, but the project was abandoned by Catherine II. In the nineteenth century the Gothic revival reappeared, as in Mikhail Bykovsky's (1801–85) design for the estate of Marfino (1831–45). More significant, however, was the Russo-Byzantine style, supported by Nicholas I and implemented by Konstantin Ton (1794–1881), builder of the Great Kremlin Palace (1838–49). The major work in this style, which prevailed in church architecture throughout the century, was Ton's Church of Christ the Redeemer (1837–83, not extant), built in Moscow as a memorial to Russian valour in the 1812 war.

Secular architecture in St Petersburg and Moscow during the mid-nineteenth century was largely an eclectic combination of various periods in the history of Western architecture, but by the 1870s there arose arose a new national style based on decorative elements from sixteenth- and seventeenth-century Muscovy as well as on motifs from folk art and wooden architecture. Among the early proponents of the Russian Revival style were Ivan Ropet (Petrov; 1844–1908) and Viktor Hartman (1834–73). Examples in Moscow include the Historical Museum (1874–83) by Vladimir Shervud (1833–97); the Moscow City Duma (1890–92) by Mikhail Chichagov (1837–89); and the Upper Trading Rows

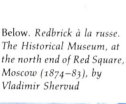

Right. *Interior, the Upper Trading Rows, Red Square, Moscow, by Aleksandr Pomerantsev, 1889–93; after the Revolution this became the State Universal Store (GUM), and is now leased to Western firms such as Benetton and Dior*

Below. *Redbrick à la russe. The Historical Museum, at the north end of Red Square, Moscow (1874–83), by Vladimir Shervud*

(1889–93) by Aleksandr Pomerantsev (1848–1918). In Petersburg the Russian style was used by Alfred Parland (1845–92) for the Church of the Resurrection of the Saviour 'on the Blood' (1883–1907). In Moscow a number of mansions were built in the style, and its influence continued through the turn of the century as the 'romantic', or neo-Russian, component of the *style moderne*. Painters such as Viktor Vasnetsov (designer of the entrance to the Tret'yakov Gallery, *c*.1905) and Sergey Malyutin were particularly active in using the traditional Russian decorative arts as part of a new architectural aesthetic.   WCB

THE CLASSICAL HERITAGE

Patronized by Catherine II and Alexander I during the eighteenth and nineteenth centuries, Russian classicism had spread widely, and its revival at the beginning of the twentieth century could be seen as a revival of Russia's own heritage rather than as a new wave of Westernization. This neo-classical style was applied not only to private residences and apartment buildings but with even greater enthusiasm to public buildings.

The stronghold of the style was in St Petersburg. Among the leading architects there were Ivan Fomin (1872–1936) and Vladimir Shchuko (1878–1939), both of whom continued to play an important role in the post-revolutionary years. Ivan Fomin's Polovtsev mansion of 1911–13 (later a trade union sanitorium) demonstrates his commitment to neo-classicism. In the same style he designed the Workers' Palace for the Peterhof district in 1919, unexecuted but used later in a simplified version for

Gateway to the south: the Kiev Station, Moscow (1912–17) by Rerberg

the Mossovet (Moscow Soviet of Workers', Peasants' and Soldiers' Deputies) building (1928–30). He reverted to a more ornate neo-classicism in his competition project for the Academy of Sciences of the USSR (1934, unexecuted). Before the Revolution Shchuko built several apartment buildings in St Petersburg in the neo-classical style. He also used classic colonnades for the propylaea (or entrance) of the Smol'ny Institute (1923), a classic version for the Lenin Library in Moscow (1928–39) with Vladimir Gel'freykh (1885–1967), and gained fame with his winning project for the Palace of the Soviets in Moscow in collaboration with Boris Iofan (1891–1976) and Gel'freykh.

Although neo-classicism was less popular in Moscow than in St Petersburg, it was applied to such diverse edifices as the Bryansk (today's Kiev) railway station of 1912–17 by Ivan Rerberg (1869–1932) and V.K. Oltarzhevsky (1880–1966); the Alexander

Below. The propylaea of the Lenin Library, Moscow, by Shchuko and Gel'freykh (1928–39). Below right. The Ryabushinsky house (1900–02), Moscow, by Shekhtel', inhabited by Maksim Gor'ky after his final return to Stalin's Russia in 1931, now housing his museum

III (today's Pushkin) Museum of 1912 by Roman Kleyn (1858–1924); and to the commercial building of the Treugol'nik Association of 1916 by M.S. Lyalevich (1876–1944), as well as to apartment buildings and private houses. The most ardent and influential promoter of neo-classicism was Ivan Zholtovsky (1867–1959), who after the Revolution was appointed head of the architectural section of the Department of Visual Arts (IZO) of the Commissariat of Enlightenment (NKP) as well as of the architectural office of the Mossovet. He was the planner of the Russian Agricultural Exhibition in Moscow of 1923, designing many of the pavilions, though the most innovative and best-known pavilion of the exhibition was the Makhorka pavilion by Konstantin Mel'nikov (1890–1974).   MB

ART NOUVEAU AND THE NEO-RUSSIAN STYLE

Two other styles were more important to Moscow's architectural scene at the beginning of the twentieth century than neo-classicism. One was imported from France and accepted in Russia by its French name, the *style moderne* (or Art Nouveau, as it is known in English-speaking countries). The other was the outcome of a renewed interest in the Russian national tradition and medieval heritage, known as the neo-Russian style. While churches often followed historical precedents with utmost fidelity, as, for example, the Church of the Intercession of the Virgin for the Convent of Martha and Mary (1908–12) by Aleksey Shchusev (1873–1949), the neo-Russian forms were also adapted in the twentieth century to contemporary uses with unusual freedom. The most outstanding examples are Shchusev's Kazan' railway station (1913–26) and the Yaroslavl' railway station (1902–04) by Fedor Shekhtel' (1859–1926). Shchusev, in fact, is best known for his Lenin Mausoleum (1924–30), the Ministry of

Novoslobodskaya metro station

Agriculture (Narkomzem) building (1928–33), where he reverted to contemporary architectural forms, and the hotels Moskva (1930–35) and Borodino (1947) in the official Socialist Realism style. Shekhtel' was one of Moscow's leading exponents of a clearly international Art Nouveau, as demonstrated by his Ryabushinsky house (1900–02, now the Maksim Gor'ky Memorial Museum) and the Derozhinsky house (1901). Art Nouveau was also applied in a more austere form for commercial buildings, as, for example, in the Utro Rossii printing-house (1907) and the Moscow Merchants' Society building (1909), both by Shekhtel'.   MB

THE AVANT-GARDE

The years of the First World War, the Revolution and the Civil War brought architectural activities to a virtual standstill and gave architects the time for conscious re-examination of their professional roles, ideological commitments, social obligations and environmental contributions. Immediately after the Revolution, avant-garde circles consisting of architects, painters and sculptors began to search for ways to achieve the eternal ideal of fusing art with life. They envisaged a world where all man-made objects contributed to continuous harmony of experiences and where life was nothing less than a total work of art. The first step toward the creation of such a world was the eradication of the differences between architecture, the arts, the crafts and the design of utilitarian objects.

This attitude was promptly adopted by artists such as Kazimir Malevich (1878–1935) with his *arkhitektony*; Vladimir Tatlin (1885–1953) with his constructions and the Monument to the Third International (Comintern); the brothers Naum Gabo (1890–1978) and Anton Pevsner (1886–1962)

with their constructions; and by architects such as the Vesnin brothers (A.A. Vesnin, 1883–1959 and V.A. Vesnin, 1882–1950) with their stage designs. Other exponents were L.M. Lisitsky (pseud. El' Lissitzky, 1890–1941) with his *Prouns* ('projects for the assertion of the new') and Ladovsky and Krinsky with their experimental projects for a communal house.

In May 1919 Nikolay Ladovsky (1881–1941), Vladimir Krinsky (1890–1971) and the sculptor Boris Korolev (1884–1963) initiated the so-called Commission for Sculpture-Architecture Synthesis (*Sinskul'ptarkh*). While at the beginning the group was dominated by architects, by the end of 1919 this circle was joined by painters such as Aleksandr Rodchenko (1891–1956) and Aleksandr Shevchenko (1882–1968), and renamed *Zhivskul'ptarkh* (Painting-Sculpture-Architecture Synthesis). The group provided the initial membership of the Institute of Artistic Culture (INKHUK) when it was founded in May 1920 as well as the leading faculty of the Higher State Art-Technical Studios (Vkhutemas), organized that summer. INKHUK and Vkhutemas became the common forum for both artists' and architects' research and exchange of ideas.   MB

CONSTRUCTIVISM

Although architecture was hailed as the leader of the arts and the culmination of the Constructivists' search, theoretical differences quickly divided architects into factions. One group, led by Ladovsky, with El' Lissitzky, Vladimir Krinsky and Nikolay Dokuchaev (1891–1944), formed Asnova (the Association of New Architects) in 1923. The second group, with Moisey Ginzburg (1892–1946), the Vesnin brothers and Andrey Burov (1900–57) among its leaders, formed OSA (the Society of Contemporary Architects) in 1925. Asnova's members devoted most of their energy to developing a rational, scientific method for the education and development of artistic creativity that was pertinent to all art forms and to any artistic endeavour (hence their name – the 'rationalists'). Since there were few possibilities of actual construction owing to the economic crisis, most of the new architectural ideas were expressed only in drawings and competition projects.

However, Lenin's New Economic Policy (NEP) began to present some opportunities for building. Ladovsky, deeply interested in the spatial perception of the pedestrian, had a few executed projects (the pavilion of the Lermontov underground railway station in Moscow of 1935 is one example). He expanded his research in 1928 to include urban design and new town planning and in the same year

founded ARU (the Union of Architects-Urbanists). Konstantin Mel'nikov is the best-known member of Asnova probably because he was least involved in the theoretical and educational activities of the group, devoting his time during the 1920s and 1930s to competitions and to design for a wide variety of buildings. He gained international recognition with his Soviet Pavilion at the Paris International Exhibition of Decorative Arts (1924–25) and fame at home with five workers' clubs (Rusakov, Kauchuk and Frunze in 1927, all in Moscow; Pravda in 1928 in Duleva; Burevestnik in 1929 in Moscow), all of which are still functioning. Mel'nikov's own house on Krivoarbatsky Pereulok in Moscow (1927–29) is one of the most unusual and exciting examples of contemporary architecture in Moscow.

For the most part, OSA united practising architects, although Ginzburg was as much a theoretician and educator as practitioner. His theoretical works were published in the Society's own magazine *Modern Architecture (Sovremennaya arkhitektura)*, as well as in several books, such as *Ritm v arkhitekture (Rhythm in Architecture)*, 1923. His deep concern with multi-family housing is demonstrated by his Sovnarkom (Council of People's Commissars) housing complex on Novinsky Boulevard in Moscow (1928–30); his contributions to public buildings could be seen as far as Kazakhstan (namely, in the Alma-Ata party headquarters of 1927–31); and his ability to design and co-ordinate large complexes was demonstrated in a sanatorium complex for the Ministry of Heavy Industry in Kislovodsk (1933–37).

The Vesnin brothers have been called leaders of Russian Constructivist architecture. They established a joint practice in Moscow in 1911 and, apart from private residences, designed three chemical factories and two industrial plants with workers' settlements before 1917. The best example of their work before the Revolution is the post office on Myasnitsky Street of the 1910s. Their project for the Palace of Labour competition, the first national architectural competition after the Revolution,

received only third prize but was widely publicized as marking the beginning of modern architecture in the Soviet Union. During the 1920s the Vesnin brothers won many competitions and built numerous structures, all demonstrating the translation of Constructivist theory into actual forms and materials. Still standing in Moscow, for example, are their Palace of Culture at the Likhachev Automobile Works (1930–37) in the former grounds of the Simonov Monastery, and the House of Cinema Actors (1931–34), originally built for the Society of Political Prisoners.

The architectural scene of the 1920s would be incomplete, however, without mention of the Golosov brothers (Panteleymon, 1882–1945; and Il'ya, 1883–1945) both active members of OSA and accomplished architects – as demonstrated by Panteleymon's *Pravda* newspaper building (1929–34) and Il'ya's Zuev Club (1925–29). Grigory Barkhin's (1880–1969) *Izvestiya* newspaper building (1925–27), likewise in Moscow, is also an important Constructivist achievement. MB

Above. Konstantin Mel'nikov's Soviet Pavilion at the Paris International Exhibition (1924–25).
Above right. The Zuev club, Moscow (1925–29) by Il'ya Golosov

Below. The Rusakov workers' club, Moscow, by Mel'nikov, 1927. Below right. The Pravda *building, Moscow (1929–34), by Panteleymon Golosov*

STATE INTERVENTION

All experiments ceased by the end of 1932 due to three crucial governmental actions. First, in that year all architectural organizations were abolished and architects were forced into a single Union of Soviet Architects. Private practice was banned and architects could work only in governmental planning and design studios that were organized in 1933. Secondly, the state demonstrated its desired direction for architectural development through its choice of the winning project in the competition for the Palace of the Soviets (1931–33). Finally, a controlling organization – Arplan – was established in 1933 to review and approve every project before construction began. The aesthetic canon of the state was thus easily enforced and the results were clearly reflected in Soviet buildings of the subsequent decades.   MB

ARCHITECTURE SINCE THE 1930S

Architecture and town-planning after 1930 involved the interaction of two areas of concern, which were themselves shifting and evolving over the period in relation to wider political and economic circumstances. One concern was quantitative, one qualitative.

The First Five-year Plan was the only one until the Khrushchev period to promise a housing construction programme commensurate with the acute housing need. But its fate was to typify the constant vulner-

ability of the whole Soviet building effort, and of civic (as opposed to industrial or military) construction, to national and international pressures.

The main qualitative, or stylistic, concern over the period was the achievement of an ideologically correct balance between 'national' and 'international'. From the inauguration of 'Socialism in One Country' in the mid-1920s, architecture and town-planning felt varying degrees of 'anti-cosmopolitan' pressure. This was greatest in the late 1920s and early 1930s, and in the Cold War years after the Second World War. Within the constant overall determination to create an architecture and a settlement structure reflecting the 'national' characteristics of the Soviet Union, there likewise waxed and waned a concern to reflect republican nationhood in both its aesthetic and social dimensions. There was also an attempt to reflect those regional differences conditional upon climate and geology which more mechanically determine both spatial organization and constructional methods in the built environment.

These remained live themes in Soviet professional debate. Their convergence with many concerns of the post-Modernism now prevalent in the West perhaps increased Western sympathy towards stylistic shifts in Soviet architecture and town-planning which had been regarded hitherto as incomprehensible abnegations of 'modernity'.

The turning-point in the formulation of a Soviet socialist approach, the architectural equivalent of the Urbanist-Disurbanist planning debate, was the Palace of Soviets competition of 1931–33. This enormous symbolic building for central Moscow represented a testbed for the adequacy of 'modernist' modes of composition and the stylistic treatment of the propagandist role of public building, in the conditions of mass aesthetic taste at that time. Official competition commentaries spoke of the need for achieving 'a critical assimilation of the architectural heritage'; for 'utilizing the best of both modern and historical architecture, combining them with the highest technical achievements of today to create a distinctive architecture of the socialist age'. This general formulation was canonized as 'Socialist Realism' by the First Congress of Soviet Architects in 1937. Some of its most mature achievements were to be erected in the post-war period, when the prevailing 'anti-cosmopolitanism' produced greater incorporation of republican and regional decorative themes than had been usual in the 1930s. The Hotel Leningrad in Moscow was an example. Having attracted a Stalin Prize for Architecture in 1948, this building was criticized by Khrushchev in his 1954 speech to the All-Union Conference of Builders, Architects and Workers, which took an anti-decorative stance as part of a redirection of

Below. *A Stalinist 'wedding cake': The Ministry of Foreign Affairs, Smolenskaya Square, Moscow. Tall buildings of this kind were designed to overwhelm a skyline previously dominated by churches*

Soviet architecture on to a line recognized in the West as 'modern'. His emphasis on techniques for quantity production gave rise to a broader anti-aestheticism which was later blamed by architects for a lowering of their status in relation to other professions. This had a serious impact on recruitment.

Among factors which helped to revive concern for regional and local expression in architecture was the increasing attention to community buildings. Such buildings were natural vehicles for experimentation in the richer handling of local micro-climatic problems; for reviving regionally characteristic decorative and spatial languages and palettes of colour and light; in short, for continuing the synthesis of the new with the 'popular' (narod-nyy), which was seen as the basis of socialist 'assimilation' in these fields of public creative work. A highly regarded republican example of this trend was the Karl Marx Public Library in Ashkhabad by Abdulla Akhmedov, built in the mid 1970s.   CC

TOWN-PLANNING SINCE THE 1930S

The massive new-towns building programme of the First Five-year Plan provoked a far-reaching discussion of principles: the so-called Urbanist-Disurbanist debate. This concerned the proper nature of that 'new settlement of mankind' which Marx, Engels and Lenin had predicted would emerge when socialist economic relationships were combined with transmissible energy and mass-production technologies. It brought together two well-known economists (Yu. Larin, real name M.Z. Luré, 1882–1932; and L.M. Sabsovich) on one side, and Constructivist architects (led by Moisey Ginzburg and sociologist M.A. Okhitovich) on the other, all united against the uncontrolled growth of urban development threatening the USSR in the later 1920s, which they saw as inherently capitalist. Intimately involved with issues of collectivization in agriculture and urban daily life, this debate was a major turning-point in identifying the range of factors determining form in this field, and in deciding the proper shape of Soviet settlement patterns during the era of 'transition to socialism'.

Various Communist Party decisions (1930–32) canonized gradualism in collectivization of the urban way of life (byt). Preference was given to cluster patterns of limited-sized industrial and agricultural settlements and to heavy masonry (kapital'nye) construction systems rather than to the rapid erection of temporary stock. Principles governing the internal planning of Soviet towns derived from these decisions. The smallest planning unit, the kvartal, was seen as that unit within which the socialist state (or local government) would provide those daily-use services (public catering, laundry and infant care) which the individual bourgeois housewife hitherto performed within her private 'domestic economy'. The exact sizes of kvartaly varied with conditions. They were grouped into housing districts (rayony), offering the next level of educational, recreational and retail facilities. Groups of these comprised urban rayony, certain of whose more specialized facilities might serve the town as a whole.

This simple hierarchical structure was based upon such pervading features of the Soviet Union as the non-existence of a normal market in goods, services or land. It could also be accommodated within the Party's hierarchical agitational and supervisory structure. The very uniformity of rayon structure and building type over the whole urban area was itself seen as a direct reflection of politics. It was the 'elimination of the difference between centre and periphery' – a division very marked in Russia's pre-revolutionary cities. Residential and productive zones would ideally be located to minimize both journeys to work and industrial pollution. With climatic and productive conditions varying greatly across the continent there were many 'model' new towns.

Perhaps the most complicated problem facing town-planners in this period, however, was the 'socialist reconstruction' of existing towns and cities on to a similar pattern. Surgery was also applied to the dense inherited urban fabric to provide for public transport arteries, green space, sunlight and fresher air; for basic public utilities such as running water, sewerage, gas, electricity (generally for the first

Post-war rebuilding in the Stalinist style: on the Kreshchatik, the main street of Kiev, Ukraine

A corner of Akademgorodok, a bleakly geometric new city of the 1960s

*Which one is mine?
A suburban Moscow
apartment block of the
1970s*

*Which city is this?
Large-panel construction in
a Leningrad apartment
block*

time), and for rationalized locations for certain important factories in relation to industrial needs. The 1935 Moscow Plan was the model for this process. Prepared under the direction of the pioneer of pre-revolutionary garden cities, Vladimir Semenov (1874–1960), it was among the world's first fully integrated city plans.

Regional planning was regarded as particularly demonstrating the benefits of socialism over capitalism. Here too the 1930s saw the need for theory and practice to develop virtually from first principles, both in overall resource planning and in tailoring the agreed cluster and satellite forms of settlement to local conditions. For practical reasons as much as ideological ones, the various planning and architectural design networks were by then rather more centralized than during the 1920s. With expertise extremely short, any competent professional – save those regarded as irredeemably determined to pursue 'abstract scheming' (*prozhekterstvo*) – was usefully employed within them.

Stringent pressures during the 1930s naturally distorted intended allocations and planning patterns. The most acute setback, however, was that caused by German destruction in the Second World War, summarised in Soviet figures as 1700 towns and cities and 70,000 urban settlements and villages 'completely or almost completely destroyed' (many of these, of course, were newly built in the 1930s). The total loss of six million buildings left 25 million people homeless. One dimension of the post-war 'anti-cosmopolitanism' in architecture and planning was thus a passionate nationalism that, understandably, existed within the profession even before it was reinforced by wider campaigns. Meticulous reconstruction of architectural monuments was one expression of this; another was greatly increased emphasis upon that preservation of historic urban plan-forms which had been a central, and at the time controversial, tenet of the 1935 Moscow Plan.

The need to re-establish complete urban infra-

structures sucked resources from residential construction once more, and in the early 1950s the living space per head in the urban housing stock was again down around 4 sq m, below half the agreed 'sanitary minimum' of 9 sq m. First steps towards commensurate action were launched by Khrushchev's speech to the All-Union Conference of Builders, Architects and Workers of 7 December 1954: 'On the widespread introduction of industrial methods, improvement of quality and lowering of costs in construction'. By 1959 new building techniques had been sufficiently developed for the Seven-year Plan to promise a doubling of the total Soviet urban housing stock. About 85 per cent of the promised 15 million new apartments were constructed, and they form much of the inner area of Russian cities even today.

The mixing of two-storied facilities with higher residential buildings and, generally open, green site-planning was typical of Soviet housing. Construction in the 1930s was lower, limited to four or five storeys by lack of lifts, and generally of parallel-block form. Districts built in the post-war Stalin years were commonly of more enclosed design, grouped around extensive park-like courtyards. In the first large-panel construction systems of the later 1960s and early 1970s, craning constraints produced rather open layouts and simple building geometry, but technical developments subsequently permitted more varied composition and the use of more interesting sites. Greater diversity of elevational treatment and apartment type was also becoming possible through dimensional and technical integration of the former multiplicity of 'closed' constructional systems into a 'unified catalogue' for each region. In the virgin outskirts of cities such as Moscow, St Petersburg, Tbilisi and the Siberian centres, the late-1970s house-building programme averaged one finished apartment per minute, and much of this housing is around fifteen storeys, often of linear curving 'wall' form rather than in isolated tower blocks. When transport and services are adequate, these areas are generally much appreciated for their quietness, their immediate access to the countryside, and the modern living standards which their apartments provide.

Urban developments in the extreme north have long been the subject of special studies and employ climatically suitable building types. The appropriateness of the temperate-zone housing models to southern, Central Asian climates (and lifestyles) became a subject of debate, as did issues of improving the distribution services and facilities. The future model town structure embodied in the Moscow Plan of 1971 focuses upon relief of centre–periphery travel by creation of secondary retail and civic centres between these outer housing areas.   CC

Art

The eighteenth century was a period of dramatic change in all walks of Russian life. The policy of rapid Westernization initiated by Peter the Great had an immediate and destructive effect on the patriarchal traditions of Russian culture. One of its direct results, however, was the formation of an important school of secular Russian painting that gained in momentum from the middle of the century – a school that differed radically from the long tradition of icon-painting. The centre of this new movement came to be the Imperial Academy of Arts founded in 1757. Its influence on Russian art was considerable. Russia's first professional easel painters, such as Vladimir Borovikovsky (1757–1825), Dmitry Levitsky (1735–1822) and Fedor Rokotov (c.1736–1808), were all closely associated with the Academy.

Right. Vladimir Borovikovsky, M. I. Lopukhina, 1797

THE ACADEMY OF ARTS

The principal style favoured by the Academy during the last decades of the eighteenth century and during the nineteenth was a Western, classical one supported and propagated by its teaching-staff who were mainly French, German and Italian. Levitsky's *Portrait of E.I. Nelidova* (1773) embodies the aesthetic principles of the early Academy: the very genre of the portrait, the virtuoso technique, the idealization of subject, the emphasis on pose and dress, the neglect of background and landscape – such elements are also identifiable with the Western European mainstream of the eighteenth century and bring to mind the portraits of Gainsborough and Reynolds.

During the 1800s and 1810s the influence of the classical canon of beauty was maintained at the Academy, affecting the important Russian painters of the time such as Orest Kiprensky (1782–1836), Karl Bryullov (1799–1852) and Aleksandr Ivanov (1806–58). Moreover, these artists were among the many Russian intellectuals who lived in Italy for short or long periods between 1810 and 1840 and who moved in the same circles as Gros, Ingres and the Nazarenes (a group of German artists living in Rome in the early nineteenth century). Although it would be misleading to call Kiprensky, firmly rooted in the classical tradition, a Romantic, he was acquainted with the philosophies of Novalis, Schelling and Schlegel as well as with German and French Romantic painters. For example, in his portraits Kiprensky concentrated on the individual psychology, on the spontaneous and natural gesture of the sitter, as is demonstrated by his famous *Portrait*

Below. Dmitry Levitsky, Portrait of E. I. Nelidova, 1773. Below right. The romanticized classicist: Orest Kiprensky, Portrait of the Poet Aleksandr Pushkin, 1827

of the Poet Aleksandr Pushkin of 1827. Kiprensky's vigorous portraits reflect his endeavour to overcome the limitations of the strict academic system by choosing a freer, more energetic style.

Kiprensky always complained that material circumstances forced him to paint portraits and that his patrons denied him the opportunity to use historical subjects. No doubt, he envied the fate of Russia's most successful son of the Academy – Bryullov. Bryullov's painting also relied on the classical ideals of the Academy, and the artist attained prestige at home and abroad as an excellent portrait painter,

Karl Bryullov, Last Day of Pompeii, *1830–33*

Aleksandr Ivanov, The Appearance of Christ to the People, *1837–57*

to which works such as the *Portrait of Princess Samoylova Leaving the Ball* (1838–42) testify. But unlike Kiprensky, Bryullov worked in various genres and media, including historical and mythological painting, and his celebrated *Last Day of Pompeii* (1830–33) is one of the grand flourishes of the nineteenth century. Together with other rhapsodical compositions of that time, the *Last Day of Pompeii* owes much to Raphael (*The Fire in the Borgo*) and Poussin (*The Plague of Ashdod*). Bryull-

ov's masterpiece interprets a popular theme, repeating Giovanni Pacini's opera of the same name and foreshadowing Bulwer Lytton's novel *The Last Days of Pompeii* of 1834. Some observers, such as Alexander Herzen (1812–70), saw a prophetic meaning in the painting, identifying the eruption and imminent destruction of the noble Pompeians with the contemporary predicament of aristocratic Russia, threatened also, so it was maintained, by an inevitable cataclysm. In this respect, it is relevant to recall that Bryullov's picture was painted in the same decade that Gogol' began his epic novel *Dead Souls*, the description of a Russia tired and sick at heart.

The pathos and melodrama of *Last Day of Pompeii* link it with the concurrent achievements of Western European artists such as Delacroix, Delaroche and Géricault. The work is very different from the painting of Bryullov's fellow-countryman and contemporary, Ivanov. This fanatical and fervent artist considered art to be the expression of a profound religious and moral experience, and he attempted to communicate this idea in his major work *The Appearance of Christ to the People* (1837–57). As in the case of Bryullov's canvas, the prototypes of *The Appearance of Christ to the People*, a huge painting measuring 540 by 750 cm, were entirely Western, ranging from Raphael's *Transfiguration* to the paintings of the Nazarenes. Still, the intent of Ivanov's picture was of particular relevance to Russia, for the artist regarded Moscow as the Third

Rome and the Russian people as the future witness of the Second Coming. It is not surprising, therefore, that Ivanov should have included the deeply religious and patriotic Gogol' as well as a self-portrait among the observers of Christ's appearance. Of course, this interpretation does not alter the fact that *The Appearance of Christ to the People* depends on academic or at least Western artistic principles. On the other hand, Ivanov's water-colours of scenes from the Bible from the 1840s and 1850s depart radically from traditional concepts. The musical, prismatic quality of these renditions distinguishes them from the heavy narrative style of most nineteenth-century historical painting, and these curiously refractive images have been compared to the work of William Blake and to the Symbolist visions of Mikhail Vrubel' (1856–1910). JEB

THE RUSSIAN SCHOOL

Ivanov marked the culmination of the Western academic style in Russian art. From the 1850s Russian art became increasingly 'Russian', favouring scenes from everyday Russian life instead of aristocratic portraits and mythological episodes. Pavel Fedotov (1815–52) and the Realists of the 1860s to 1880s developed this trend, producing their visual commentaries on the 'accursed questions' of Russian contemporaneity. Fedotov, for example, used Hogarth-like satires of Russian mores in order to focus critical attention on topical issues such as the inequality of women (*The Major's Betrothal*, 1848) and the impoverishment of the aristocracy (*The Unexpected Guest*, 1849–50). However, it is impor-

Pavel Fedotov, The Major's Betrothal, *1848*

tant to remember that even before Fedotov and parallel to the achievements of Kiprensky, Bryullov and Ivanov, a number of artists were supporting an indigenous, more primitive style of painting based on commonplace themes from Russian life. In particular, there were Vasily Tropinin (1776–1857), a liberated serf who brought a homeliness and simplicity to his portraits and genre scenes, and, above all, Aleksey Venetsyanov (1780–1847).

In their establishment of an artistic code alternative to the Western academic tradition, Tropinin, Venetsyanov and their pupils maintained the patriotic mood of the 1812 epoch, when caricaturists such as Ivan Terebenev (1780–1815) ridiculed Gallic civilization and glorified the qualities of the ordinary Russian people. While appreciating some elements of the academic system, Venetsyanov also turned to the theme of Mother Russia, finding artistic inspiration in the ingenuous activities of the Russian peasant. His paintings such as *Spring Ploughing* (1830s) influenced a whole generation of provincial painters in Russia, not least Grigory Soroka (1823–64). In turn, Soroka's distinctive luminist style, exemplified by the painting *The Fishermen* (1840s), bears a curious resemblance to American rural painting of the same period (cf. George Bingham's *Boatmen on the Missouri*, 1846). In America and Russia this kind of painting heralded the emergence of a new and powerful movement: Realism. JEB

REALISM

Realism, the dominant trend in the second half of the nineteenth century, gave Russian art its modern, national idiom. What Pavel Fedotov had been searching for – new subject matter, an appropriate pictorial language, and ethnic identity – found full expression in the works of the Realist painters. Hardly known and not highly valued in the West, they have played as important and continuing a role in Russian culture as the great writers Turgenev, Tolstoy and Dostoevsky. Although Realism passed through different phases during the more than three decades of its pre-eminence, it had one distinct, overall characteristic: an intense commitment to Russian subjects and scenes, which was grounded in the conviction that art should serve a social function – conveying civic, moral or national values – rather than concentrate on aesthetic expression and stylistic refinement. Realism was born in the 1860s, a decade of reforms that began with the emancipation of the serfs. Although such long-overdue changes were instituted from above, intellectuals were swept up with national renovation. Yet in the absence of a free press, painters, like writers, had to comment covertly on current political and social issues in their works. The foremost critic of the day, Nikolay Chernyshevsky (1828–89), aptly expressed the prevailing spirit of civic motivation at the outset of the movement when he wrote: 'The goals of art are to understand reality, and then to apply its findings for the use of humanity.' Because of these historical circumstances, both dedication and 'literariness' characterized Russia's first modern art style.

The Wanderers

Vasily Perov (1833–82) best exemplified the initial political motivation. His *Village Procession* (1861) is not merely a meticulous depiction of drunken priests and peasants setting out to celebrate Easter. It is more than an indictment of clerical laxity, for in the eyes of the articulate public the Orthodox Church was a principal mainstay of autocracy. The censor's removal of the canvas from an exhibition confirmed for the politically alert intellectual that art was actively enlisted in agitation against the regime. Other first-generation Realists tended to be less outspokenly political. Their small-size narrative pictures were critical exposés of such social problems as rural poverty, drunkenness, child labour, or women's rights.

During the 1870s Realism attained maturity. The episodic and critical commentary of the opening phase gave way to more general statements on Russian themes; the range of subjects was enlarged; and the painters' technique improved. This art – produced outside the patronage of the Imperial Academy of Arts and in defiance of the neo-classical standards of 'high art' it upheld – was popularized by the first professional society of independent painters. Founded in 1870, it was named the Association of Travelling Art Exhibitions and was headed by Ivan Kramskoy (1837–87), who had organized a secession of graduating students from the Imperial Academy in 1863. For the next twenty years the Association counted the most talented and innovative painters among its members, and in annual exhibitions introduced their work in the two capitals,

Two versions of the pastoral dream. Below left. Arkhip Kuindzhi, The Birch Grove, *1897. Right. Aleksey Savrasov,* The Rooks Return, *1871*

St Petersburg and Moscow, as well as in the major provincial towns. So successful was this educational and cultural mission that Realism and *peredvizhnichestvo* ('the art of the travelling exhibitions') became synonymous.

The fortunes of contemporary art were also buoyed by the appearance of middle-class patrons. Foremost among them was the textile manufacturer, P.M. Tret'yakov (1832–98), who bought the best works at each Travelling Exhibition and in 1892 bequeathed to the city of Moscow an art gallery with his collection of some 800 works of the new national school.

Landscape was among the most popular themes introduced by the *Peredvizhniki*, or 'Wanderers', as members of the Association were called. The unassuming beauty of the Russian countryside had been celebrated in literature since Pushkin, but it was the Realists who undertook to picture their native land with lyrical insight. Among the prominent landscape painters were Aleksey Savrasov (1832–97), Ivan Shishkin (1832–98), Fedor Vasil'ev (1850–73), Arkhip Kuindzhi (1842–1910), and Vasily Polenov (1844–1927). Their manner varied greatly, from Shishkin excelling in an almost photographic rendition of forest and trees to Kuindzhi experimenting with the bold use of unusual colour schemes in depicting the Ukrainian countryside.

The Wanderers also created a national portrait gallery. These likenesses are so forceful that to this day they are *the* mental images Russians have of their great writers, composers and scholars. The explanation, in part, is that the portraitist sought to create an inspiring image, to convey his subject's commitment and resolve. Thus, Perov represented Dostoevsky as a writer racked by the problems of the times, and Kramskoy showed the civic-minded poet N.A. Nekrasov (1821–77) composing even on his death-bed.

Historical paintings were, at first, oblique commentaries on current issues. Nikolay Ge's (1831–94) canvas of Peter the Great confronting his sullenly resistant son (1871) spoke to viewers of the diminishing tempo of the reform movement; the picture (1885) of Ivan the Terrible cradling the blood-stained body of the son he had just struck with mortal blows (Il'ya Repin, 1844–1930) was a reminder that all too often in Russia brute force alone decided matters of state or an individual fate. Similarly, the pictures of Vasily Vereshchagin (1842–1904) denounced war at a time when Russia was conquering Turkestan. But a change occurred in the 1880s with the surge of nationalism, and Russian history found a panegyric chronicler in Vasily Surikov (1848–1916). He started by extolling in rich and colourful detail the defenders of old Russian traditions who opposed Peter the Great's Westernization programme (*The Morning of the Strel'tsy Execution*, 1881; *Boyarinya Morozova*, 1887), and went on to glorify Russian military exploits (*Yermak's Conquest of Siberia*, 1895; *Suvorov Crossing the Alps*, 1899).

Repin was the most talented and versatile painter of the Russian Realist school. One of his themes was the peasantry, and the large-scale *Volga Barge Haulers* (1873) won him immediate acclaim with its sympathetic commentary on the lot of the people and its bold diagonal composition and striking colour. The individual portraiture in that multi-figure canvas typified one treatment of the peasant theme: giving the lowly the same respectful attention hitherto reserved for those much higher in the social scale; and Perov, Repin and Kramskoy produced a varied gallery of peasant types. Others, like Vasily Maksimov (1844–1911), objectively documented peasant customs or, like Sergey Ivanov (1864–1910), concentrated on the peasants' squalor and misery.

The revolutionary movement figured prominently in the work of the Realists. Not that the painters openly supported the radicals, but they reflect the dilemma which the selflessness and persistence of the movement posed to men of principle. Repin painted the most memorable and artistically valuable canvases on the subject: *Under Conveyance* (1876); *The Propagandist's Arrest* (1878–92); *Refusal of Confession* (1879–85); and *They Did Not Expect Him* (1883–88), in which a returning prisoner facing his family suggests the theme of sacrifice and suffering in the symbolic references to Golgotha. Portraits of idealized revolutionary types were produced by Nikolay Yaroshenko (1846–98).

In these several themes the Realists were relating much of the story of Russia during the decades of their ascendancy. Other social genres documented the changes brought on by industrialization: Konstantin Savitsky (1844–1905) depicted peasants working on the railway; Nikolay Kasatkin (1859–1930) and Abram Arkhipov (1862–1930) chronicled the emergence of the proletariat; while Vladimir Makovsky (1846–1920) concentrated on the tribulations of the urban poor and the mores of the upper classes.   EKV

Vasily Surikov, Boyarinya Morozova, 1887; she defiantly makes the anathematized two-fingered Old Believer sign of the cross as she is taken into exile

An intelligentsia exile returns from Siberia. Il'ya Repin, They Did Not Expect Him, 1884–88

DECORATIVISM

The vigour of the Realist movement declined towards the end of the 1880s as artists achieved popular and personal success. The former positivist and utilitarian ethos began to lose its claim on younger artists, and reaction set in. The new generation was frankly interested in art *per se*, and more and more sought their training in the West. The Vasnetsov brothers, Viktor (1848–1926) and Apollinary (1856–1938), introduced fancy and the purely decorative into their paintings of mythical knights and medieval Moscow; Mikhail Nesterov (1862–1942) tried to capture the unique spirituality of the Russian Orthodox religion; Isaak Levitan (1861–1900) turned to painting landscape outdoors; Valentin Serov (1865–1911) and Konstantin Korovin (1861–1939) made use of the colour discoveries of the Impressionists; while Vrubel' experimented with Symbolist decorative forms.

By the 1890s Russian Realism, having dominated the scene much longer than was the case elsewhere in Europe, was on the wane and the stage was ready for a new revolution in painting.   EKV

Valentin Serov,
Ol'ga Orlova, 1911

MODERNISM

Between the last decade of the nineteenth century and the October Revolution the arts in Russia manifested one of the foremost expositions of Modernism in the Western world. In addition to a generation of brilliant modern writers, such artists as Vrubel', Vasily Kandinsky (1866–1944), Kazimir Malevich and Vladimir Tatlin achieved artistic maturity during this time. In addition, these were crucial years of growth and learning for a 'second generation' of the avant-garde, El'Lissitzky, Aleksandr Rodchenko and the many Constructivists of the 1920s. The multiplicity of centres available in Russia for artistic training, renewed and vigorous contact with Western European centres of art and the growth of a wide audience among the middle class, all contributed to the vitality of modern art. A time of change, germination and blossoming, this period of thirty years became known as the Silver Age of Russian culture.   CD

THE WORLD OF ART ASSOCIATION

In the late 1880s and early 1890s a group of students – the future World of Art association – including Konstantin Somov (1869–1939), Leon Bakst (1866–1924), Alexandre Benois (1870–1960) and Sergey Diaghilev (1872–1929) set themselves to study a wide range of topics, particularly eighteenth- and early nineteenth-century Russian art and eighteenth century and contemporary French culture. Under the organizational leadership of Diaghilev, the World of Art in the late 1890s brought to the Russian public exhibitions of Scandinavian and European art and, through the lavish *World of Art* journal, published from 1898 to 1904, gave wide distribution to the art and ideas of such Western painters as Degas, Monet and Whistler, as well as to the group's own artistic endeavours.

The World of Art turned attention away from the large historical and social canvases of the Academy and the Wanderers to a smaller, more intimate genre, for the most part works done on paper in water-colour, gouache, ink and similar secondary media. The artists of the World of Art emphasized aesthetic quality and images of the 'beautiful' in its many connotations. Instead of the commonplace everyday subjects of their predecessors, they painted retrospective landscapes – Benois' *Feeding the Fish* (1897) and *The Pyramid at Versailles* (1906) – and morbid and erotic scenes such as Somov's *Harlequin and Death* (1907). Bakst and Somov drew portraits of themselves and their friends in a sensitive, precise late-academic style – Bakst's *Portrait of Andrey Bely* (1906) – and Benois and Bakst produced many stage and costume designs.   CD

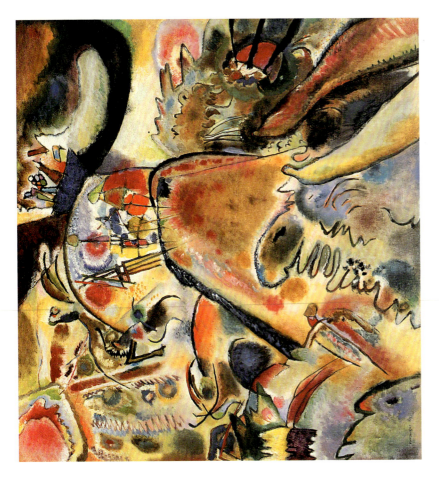

Vasily Kandinsky,
Small Pleasures, *1913*

THE SYMBOLISTS

The most significant theoretical and philosophical ideas for the development of modern styles in art derived from the Symbolist movement. The belief in a higher realm of existence, of which this world is only a reflection, and in the importance of art to the creation of a higher psychological and aesthetic consciousness in society, was shared by many artists at the turn of the century. In trying to express simultaneously both this world and another, they developed a variety of innovations in painting style. Favourite Symbolist motifs included women idealized as incarnations of grace and eternity, divine

Mikhail Vrubel',
Demon Seated, *1890*

and demonic subjects, and archetypal events. Above all, Symbolist artists made it difficult for the viewer clearly to see and understand what was depicted. By making his work 'difficult' the artist hoped to induce in the viewer a subjective or intuitive perception of both worlds.

Although not officially associated with any Symbolist group, Mikhail Vrubel' painted in a uniquely expressive style which appealed to artists of Symbolist and other artistic persuasions. His famous *Demon Seated* (1890) and *Demon Cast Down* (1902), two of more than a dozen of Vrubel''s depictions of the protagonist of Lermontov's poem *Demon* (1839), were admired by World of Art artists for their precise, although complex, linearity and the romantic literary subject matter; by the Blue Rose Symbolists for their dominant blue and lavender colours – especially 'mystical' and 'ethereal' according to Symbolist tenets – and for the portrayal of an unearthly being; and, later, by avant-garde groups, who considered his work a direct stylistic predecessor of Cubism. The talent of Vrubel', a major artist of the modern era who worked in many media, went unrewarded in his lifetime.

Viktor Borisov-Musatov (1870–1905), a Symbolist painter of women in landscapes of indeterminate time and place – *At the Pool* (1902), *Phantoms* (1903), *Slumber Divine* (1904–05) – was towards the end of his life associated with the outstanding group of Moscow literary Symbolists. He was also, for a time, the teacher of Pavel Kuznetsov (1878–1968) who from 1904 to 1907 followed an expressly Symbolist programme. During this time Kuznetsov produced beautiful but melancholy blue and grey paintings of scarcely discernible fountains and mysterious foetal creatures – *Blue Fountain* (1905), and *Birth* (1906–07). In 1907 Kuznetsov organized the major Blue Rose exhibition, devoted almost entirely to Symbolist work.

Kuznetsov and other Symbolist painters were allied with the progressive *Golden Fleece* (*Zolotoe runo*) journal (1906–10) which sponsored Symbolist, post-Impressionist and Fauvist ideas and artists, both Russian and Western European. In its 'Salon' exhibitions of 1908 and 1909 the *Golden Fleece* presented the most advanced art of the time, including Gauguin, Matisse and Van Gogh, to the Russian public.

Vasily Kandinsky, who earlier had shared the contemporary Russian interest in folk art and Symbolist painting, from about 1909 displayed in his work the dominant Symbolist concern for the depiction of higher, archetypal events. Kandinsky, like other Russian Symbolists, made his pictures 'difficult', relying on colour and barely discernible Biblical subjects to affect the viewer subliminally, as in *Small Pleasures* (1913).   C.D.

THE AVANT-GARDE

In 1910 Mikhail Larionov (1881–1964) and others organized an exhibition society called the 'Knave of Diamonds'. The name was chosen for its lack of Symbolist associations and in opposition to the 'pretty' names – Blue Rose, World of Art – of earlier societies. The work of the Knave of Diamonds artists also contrasted sharply with that of its predecessors. Like the Symbolists, the fledgling avant-garde used colour for its own sake rather than naturalistically, however, they preferred the clear, bright colours of the French Fauves and the German Expressionists to the misty and formless blues of the Blue Rose Symbolists.

Among the artists exhibited at the first Knave of Diamonds exhibition (December 1910) were Aristarkh Lentulov (1878–1943), Aleksandra A. Ekster (1884–1949), Robert Fal'k (1886–1958), Petr Konchalovsky (1876–1956), Il'ya Mashkov (1884–1944), David Burlyuk (1882–1967), Malevich, Kandinsky, Natal'ya Goncharova (1881–1962) and Larionov. Current French and German work was also shown. Typical of the Knave of Diamonds' interests at this time were bright colours, strong patterning and simplified forms, such as may be seen in Goncharova's *Washing Linen* (1910).

Larionov, Goncharova, Malevich and others soon left the Knave of Diamonds to organize their own exhibition in 1912, 'The Donkey's Tail'. The group advocated more primitive forms, even brighter colour and peasant subjects to make their work strong and vital. Malevich, for example, exhibited at The Donkey's Tail his *On the Boulevard* (1911) and *Man With a Sack* (1911), which show large bright figures with oversized, childishly drawn hands and feet. Their 'Target' exhibition (March 1913) was the first to show Larionov's and Goncharova's Rayist style.

Slightly earlier than the Knave of Diamonds in Moscow, the Union of Youth was organized in St Petersburg. Initiated by Mikhail Matyushin (1861–1934) and Yelena Guro (1877–1913), the organization exhibited many of the painters associated with Moscow groups as well as their own members. Early in 1913 a group of poets and painters which adopted the name 'Cubo-Futurists' became formally allied with the Union of Youth. Headed by David Burlyuk, it had earlier been allied with the Knave of Diamonds. The decision to change affiliations coincided with the departure of Malevich and Tatlin from Larionov's organization, and they, too, associated themselves with the Union of Youth. During 1913 Malevich worked closely with Burlyuk's group, especially the poet Aleksey Kruchenykh (1886–1968), and with some members of the Union of Youth, most notably the painter and composer Matyushin and Ol'ga Rozanova (1886–1918).

The Cubo-Futurists had a strong theoretical and analytical orientation derived from both French Cubism and Italian Futurism as well as native literary and philosophical sources. They fractured their subjects into abstracted planes and volumes and sometimes reduced the illusionistic sense of space, as can be seen in Rozanova's *Man in the Street* (1913). The Cubo-Futurists also were attracted to the irrational, the accidental and the absurd. Malevich's *Englishman in Moscow* (1914) shows objects apparently unrelated to each other in size and narrative meaning combined on the canvas with words and parts of words without obvious significance.

Malevich, Matyushin and Kruchenykh also produced an opera, *Victory Over the Sun*, which was performed in St Petersburg early in December 1913. A landmark in the history of theatrical performances, the opera features songs in Kruchenykh's language of the future set to Matyushin's music. Malevich's geometricized costumes and scenery, depicting partial objects and individual letters and musical notes, produced an impression of ambiguity and absurdity.

Tatlin in the spring of 1914 began to construct his assemblages of various materials, including glass, wood and metal, to form Cubist and abstract three-dimensional works. These 'reliefs' were first shown publicly at 'The V Trolley' exhibition (March 1915).

The '0.10' exhibition (December 1915) was one of the most advanced of its time. There Malevich and a group of followers showed abstract Suprematist paintings for the first time. The new canvases, which depicted bright rectangles of colour against a white background – *Eight Red Rectangles* (1915) – did not suggest objects or forms abstracted from nature. Some conveyed a sense of weightlessness or flight;

Kazimir Malevich, Dynamical Suprematism, 1914

one consisted of a single large black square. At the same exhibition Tatlin displayed his 'corner reliefs', three-dimensional constructions suspended across the corners of a room – *Corner Relief* (1915).

The Cubo-Futurists and Suprematists felt their art to be more faithful in its rendering of things physically real than the art of previous times. They were especially aware of history and of scientific advances in physics, psychology and physiology, and sought radically innovative styles in their art in order to express these new interpretations of the world. Thus, from the beginning of the Symbolist movement at the end of the nineteenth century until the Revolution in 1917, the primary motivation of many Russian artists was the depiction of some non-visible reality. After the Revolution the world was to seem much more visible and concrete.   CD

POST-REVOLUTIONARY ART

The Revolution of October 1917 exerted an immediate and transformative effect on Russian art. Artists such as Malevich and Tatlin who, before 1917, had occupied an uncertain position in bourgeois society, now assumed administrative and pedagogical duties. Within the Department of Visual Arts (IZO) of the Commissariat of Enlightenment headed by A. V. Lunacharsky (1875–1933), many radical artists played influential roles in Soviet artistic life, propagating their innovative ideas on an unprecedented scale thanks to the new state exhibitions, publications, art schools and research institutions.

The ranks of the avant-garde were filled by the return of artists from abroad such as Marc Chagall (1887–1985), Naum Gabo (1890–1977), Kandinsky and David Shterenberg (1881–1948), and IZO NKP acquired many works for metropolitan and provincial museums.

Under the auspices of IZO NKP artists prepared an ambitious programme of reconstruction. New art schools known as *Svomas* (Free State Art Studios) were opened in Moscow, Petrograd (St Petersburg) and other centres, enabling artists such as Ivan Klyun (1870–1942), Malevich, Aleksandr Rodchenko (1891–1956) and Tatlin to disseminate their ideas. Similarly, 1920 saw the foundation of an Institute of Artistic Culture (INKhUK) in Moscow, which sought to conduct researches into the psychological and physical properties of art. Kandinsky compiled an intricate programme for INKhUK, although it was rejected by his colleagues, who favoured a more straightforward, rational approach. Indeed, some artists and critics associated with INKhUK such as Boris Arvatov (1896–1940), Lyubov' Popova (1889–1924) and Rodchenko felt that studio art was incapable of further development and advocated a move to industrial design, contributing to the emergence of Constructivism in 1921. The Petrograd affiliation of INKhUK, organized in 1922, retained a more intimate, aesthetic stance, experimenting in form and colour theory under Malevich and Matyushin and their students – Il'ya Chashnik (1902–29) and Boris Ender (1893–1960).   JEB

CONSTRUCTIVISM

Indicative of the sudden transference of allegiance from the studio to the street was the exhibition called '5 x 5 = 25' held in Moscow in 1921 at which five artists – Aleksandra Ekster, Lyubov' Popova, Rodchenko, Varvara Stepanova (1894–1958) and Aleksandr Vesnin – each with five works, presented their latest and last investigations into abstract art. For example, Rodchenko's contribution included three canvases painted in red, yellow and blue, a

Aleksandr Rodchenko, Non-Objective Composition, 1918

Varvara Stepanova, camera portrait by Rodchenko

gesture that demonstrated the apparent impasse into which modern art had fallen. In 1922, therefore, the theoretician and apologist of Constructivism Aleksey Gan (1893–1942) felt justified in calling for 'Labour, technology, organization!' instead of the traditional media.

The Constructivists of the early 1920s attempted to remove the individualistic, 'bourgeois' impetus from art and to concentrate on a mechanical or scientific approach, resorting to the use of industrial materials such as aluminium and glass. The constructions of Rodchenko, especially his remarkable *Suspended Constructions* of 1921, reflect this tendency, although, in fact, these works were no less idiosyncratic and subjective than pre-revolutionary works.

Even Tatlin moved from the pure art of his reliefs to utilitarian design, as demonstrated by his model for the 1919–20 Monument to the Third International (Comintern). Commissioned by the Soviet government, Tatlin designed a fantastic project incorporating four levels rotating at different speeds and encased within a single metal and glass thermos. Tatlin's Monument was to have been taller than the Eiffel Tower and, while never built, signalled the advance of Soviet Constructivist architecture and interior design.

Poster art

For Mayakovsky they were the 'flowers of the revolution'; and posters on political and other themes were certainly among the most striking features of the early Soviet system. The population was still largely illiterate, so there was little point in appealing for their support through the printed word. During the Civil War both the Bolsheviks and their opponents resorted to other means to make their point: above all the political poster, nearly four thousand of which were issued in tens of millions of copies during these years.

Poster art was relatively late to develop in pre-revolutionary Russia. Poster artists, however, could draw on other traditions. Icons, with their use of colour and simple composition, were an important source. So, too, were newspaper cartoons and the satirical journals that arose after the 1905 revolution. The new regime, after 1917, was quick to develop this potential, and a stream of bold images began to carry their appeals to a nationwide audience. Dmitry Moor's 'Have you volunteered?' (1920) was particularly influential; so too was his 'Help!', inspired by the Volga famine of 1921.

Later, in the 1920s, poster artists turned to public health and education. In the 1930s,

often using photo-montage, they embraced industrialization; during the Second World War they took up defence and foreign policy. Toidze's 'Motherland-mother calls' (1941) was inspired by his own wife as she told him of the outbreak of hostilities.

The poster enjoyed a brief revival during the years of perestroika, as it exposed bureaucracy and Stalinist iniquities. It adapted less successfully to market conditions, and the end of communist rule marked the end of the poster as a form of political communication, although it remains important – as in other countries – for advertising purposes.

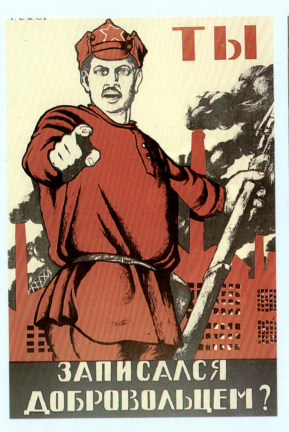

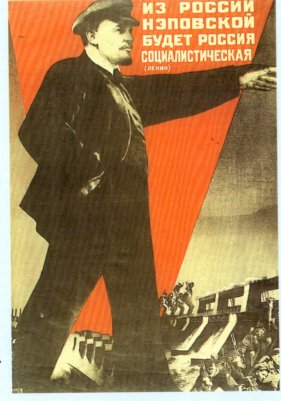

The riches of Soviet poster art. Left. 'The Proletarian's Ten Commandments'. This page, clockwise from top left: 'Have you volunteered?', 'Capital', 'Motherland-mother calls', and 'From NEP Russia will come Socialist Russia' (Lenin)'.

RETURN TO REALISM

Many young Soviet artists worked on functional projects during the 1920s, experimenting in many fields such as stage design (Aleksandra Ekster, Popova), porcelain and book design (Natan Al'tman, 1889–1970; El' Lissitzky), and posters and textiles (Dmitry Moor, 1883–1946; Varvara Stepanova). However, many artists also continued to paint and to sculpt, not necessarily in an experimental manner but rather in a more realist, 'readable' vein. Symptomatic of this counter-movement was the establishment in 1922 of the Association of Artists of Revolutionary Russia (AKhRR) with its wish to 'depict the present day: the life of the Red Army, the workers, the peasants, the revolutionaries and the heroes of labour'. The theoretical premise of AKhRR and the reportorial style of its key members such as Isaak Brodsky (1884–1939) and Yevgeny Katzman (1890–1976) came to serve as a departure-point for the Socialist Realist programme from 1934 onwards. While AKhRR quickly emerged as a powerful artistic force, it did not completely overshadow the cultural arena, and alternative styles were followed at least until the early 1930s.

With the inauguration of Lenin's New Economic Policy (NEP) in 1921, the private art market was re-established and a new bourgeois patron appeared, encouraging the development of an artistic style that was neither abstract, nor documentary, but reminiscent of Symbolism, Expressionism and even Surrealism. This representational but still subjective movement was closely identifiable with the group

known as the Society of Easel Artists (OST) led by Shterenberg, Aleksandr Deyneka (1899–1969), Yury Pimenov (1903–78) and Aleksandr Tyshler (1898–1980). These artists painted scenes from contemporary Soviet life – factory workers, athletes, and construction sites – emphasizing the expressive qualities of line and using anatomical distortion to bring the image of man closer to his mechanical, technological environment. Pictures such as Pimenov's *Give to Heavy Industry* (1927) exemplify this trend.
JEB

GOVERNMENT CONTROL OF THE ARTS

The coexistence of Constructivism, the Association of Artists of Revolutionary Russia (AKhRR) and the Society of Easel Artists (OST) was indicative of the artistic diversity of the Soviet 1920s. Of course, thanks to the consolidation of the party apparatus after 1922, the government came increasingly to dictate its will in cultural matters, and it was clear ever since Lenin's 'plan for monument propaganda' of 1918 (when Lenin had commissioned monuments to socialist and revolutionary heroes) that art and politics were to be linked indissolubly under the Soviet regime. But even in the late 1920s artists were still free to experiment with industrial design and abstraction, although they were no longer encouraged to do so and the leftists were removed from positions of power. In 1929 Malevich was granted his last Soviet one-man show, but in 1930 the long-awaited one-man show of Pavel Filonov (1883–1941) was cancelled after pressure from AKhRR members. In the same year the group known as 'October' opened its single exhibition, presenting examples of industrial design, photography and architectural projects by Gustav Klucis (1895–1938), El' Lissitzky, Rodchenko and others, but by 1932 the artistic and political climate had so changed that October was criticized for committing 'vulgar mistakes' and 'abolishing art'.

Such accusations were made by those artists, critics and administrators who sought to impose Realism as the correct and exclusive style on all Soviet artists. In practical terms, they achieved their goal by means of two important procedures. The first of these was the party decree *On the Reconstruction of Literary and Artistic Organizations* of 1932 whereby existing cultural groups were suppressed, and writers, artists, musicians and architects were urged to join the appropriate, exclusive unions (the Union of Artists of the USSR was formally set up only in 1939). This prepared the way for the establishment of Socialist Realism as the single, legitimate artistic and literary style in 1934 at the

The revolution can still have elements of abstraction: Aleksandr Deyneka, The Defence of Petrograd, 1927

Feast in the time of plague: Aleksandr Gerasimov, Collective Farm Festivities, 1937

First All-Union Congress of Soviet Writers. Dicta such as 'we must depict reality in its revolutionary development' and 'create works with a high level of craftsmanship, with high ideological and artistic content' endorsed by the delegates to the Congress, constituted the basis of Soviet cultural policy for many years. Artists such as Aleksandr Gerasimov (1881–1963) and Boris Ioganson (1893–1973), proponents of Socialist Realism, attained national renown and political favour as 'court painters' to the Stalin regime. JEB

SOCIALIST REALISM

Monolithic Socialist Realism replaced the search for new forms of artistic expression during the two decades which followed the dissolution of art organizations in 1932. The term Socialist Realism evolved out of a literary debate as a description of the basic creative method of socialist society. In the visual arts it became synonymous with a style which earned itself the following anonymous definition:

Isaak Brodsky, Lenin at the Smol'ny, *1930*

'Socialist Realism is a method of praising our leaders in a way even they will understand.' The imposition of this style upon Soviet art was largely due to the influence of a group of artists who subscribed to the aesthetic principles first enunciated by the Wanderers (Association of Travelling Art Exhibitions) in the 1860s. They considered that art could be evaluated only in terms of its effectiveness as a social weapon, and that the aim of art should be the depiction of 'the plain truth'. In a socialist Russia, these neo-Wanderers argued, the truth lay in 'the heroic and optimistic reality of Soviet life'. It was the duty of the artist to capture this truth by means of an art which was 'national in form and socialist in content'.

In 1932 a new All-Russian Academy of Arts was established, and in 1934 the government appointed Brodsky its director. A pupil and disciple of Repin, Brodsky had already established a reputation as an accomplished painter before the October Revolution with such works as *The Demonstration of the Tsar's Faithful Servants in Gratitude for the Saving of their Fatherland* (1914), and portraits of Kerensky and other members of the Provisional Government. After the Revolution Brodsky devoted his talents as a portraitist primarily to the depiction of Lenin: *Lenin against the Background of the Kremlin* (1924); *Lenin against the Background of Smol'ny* (1925); *Lenin against the Background of a Demonstration* (1927); and so on. His portrait of *Lenin at the Smol'ny* (1930), became particularly well known, especially as over five million reproductions of the work were printed between 1934 and 1937.

In 1928 artists of the 'left' had accused Brodsky of attitudes characteristic of a member of the 'reactionary bourgeoisie'. But after becoming director of the Academy of Arts in 1934, he ensured that artists of the 'left' (Constructivists, Suprematists, Analytical Expressionists) were replaced in art education by those committed to representational art. Artists of the 'left' also ceased for the most part to exhibit officially, except as theatre, book, or textile designers. Thereafter they were to have little room for manoeuvre – they could turn to design as did Al'tman, they could renounce their 'formalist mistakes' and try to adapt to Socialist Realism, like Vladimir Lebedev (1891–1967), or face hardship, obscurity and even active persecution, as did Filonov and Malevich. Nevertheless, at first it seemed as if the work of representational artists with varying stylistic approaches could comply with the vague definition of Socialist Realism. Former members of the World of Art, Blue Rose, Knave of Diamonds, OST and other groupings exhibited and taught alongside the neo-Wanderers. Indeed the 'positive', 'life-assertive' portraits and still-lifes by former Knave of Diamonds artists such as Aleksandr Kuprin (1880–

1960), Mashkov, Fal'k and Konchalovsky were at first singled out for praise, as was the 'social consciousness' of Kuz'ma Petrov-Vodkin (1878–1939).

But by 1939 the increasing isolation of the Soviet Union and growing xenophobia gave rise to the demand that true Soviet art dissociate itself from any form of expression developed during the years of free exchange of artistic ideas between Russia and Western Europe. As a result, all artists departing from the static, idealized canon of style introduced by the neo-Wanderers were accused of 'formalism' and 'decadence'. Even the OST painters Deyneka, Pimenov, and Petr Vil'yams (1902–47) and Yevgeniya Zernova (b.1900) came under attack: '[they] have not yet shaken the dust of formalism from their feet. They like machines and know them. Indeed too well. In Zernova's *Transfer of the Tank* the latter takes up half the canvas. Meanwhile the tank crew remain without facial expression. There is no new man here' (attributed to a contemporary Soviet critic by the historian G. Loukomski).

Brodsky died in 1939 and the leadership of Socialist Realism in art was taken over by Aleksandr Gerasimov, who started his career with a portrait of K. Ye. Voroshilov (Chairman of the Presidium of the Supreme Soviet, 1953–60) and devoted his life's work to the faithful portrayal of the great leader: *Stalin at the XVI Congress of the Communist Party* (1933), *Stalin and Voroshilov at the Kremlin* (1938), and so on. His portraits and other works earned him four Stalin Prizes, the Chairmanship of the Organizing Committee of the Union of Soviet Artists (founded in 1939), and in 1947, presidency of the USSR Academy of Arts.

'Stalin and the Soviet Peoples', an exhibition held in 1939 in the Tret'yakov Gallery, Moscow, further defined the official attitude towards art as a 'literary' form. The works exhibited were divided according to subject: Revolutionary and Historical Themes; Portraits of Distinguished Soviet Citizens; Man Transformed by Labour – the Image of our Motherland; and Soviet Industry. The neo-Wanderers were predominant. The painters exhibiting included Aleksandr Gerasimov, Sergey Gerasimov (1885–1964), Yevgeny Katzman, Brodsky, Georgy Ryazhsky (1895–1952), Vasily Yefanov (1900–78), Ioganson, Moisey Toidze (1871–1953). Sculpture was represented by the works of Nikolay Tomsky (1900–84), Matvey Manizer (1891–1966), Ivan Shadr (1887–1941) and Vera Mukhina (1889–1953), whose *Worker and Collective Farm Woman*, designed for the 1937 Paris International Exhibition, now stands outside the Exhibition of Economic Achievements in Moscow.

The official art of the Second World War and of the early post-war years was primarily devoted to Russia's heroic past – as in *Morning on Kulikovo*

Femina sovietica in corpore sano: Aleksandr Deyneka, Broad Vistas, 1944

Field (1943–46), by Aleksandr Bubnov (1908–64), depicting Dmitry Donskoy's victory over the Tatars in 1380 – and to its tragic but 'heroic' present, for example, works by the Kukryniksy collective, the painters Mikhail Kupriyanov (b.1903), Porfiry Krylov (b.1902) and Nikolay Sokolov (b.1903). The latter were as well known for their political cartoons as for their easel paintings, such as *The Fascist Retreat from Novgorod* (1944–46).

Until the late 1950s the neo-Wanderers' naturalistic representation of an idealized reality was the sole form of official artistic expression permitted. Art other than Soviet art, except for the Social Realism of artists such as Courbet and Millet, was criticized as bourgeois and was not on view.

The three decades following 1939 were barren and joyless; even the gentle sensuality which characterized the portraits of women workers in the 1930s

The commanding heights: Aleksandr Gerasimov, Stalin and Voroshilov at the Kremlin, 1938

Above. *Vasily Yefanov,* An Unforgettable Encounter, *1936. Stalin's entourage includes (left to right) Ordzhonikidze, Molotov, Kalinin (seated), Khrushchev, Kaganovich, Voroshilov, and Budenny, all of whom survived the Purges; Ordzhonikidze committed suicide in 1939, and Molotov's wife was arrested.* Right. *Male hammer and female sickle: Vera Mnukhina's* Worker and Collective Farm Woman, *1937, at the entrance to the Soviet state's showground, the Exhibition of Economic Achievements (VDNKh), Moscow*

The Avenue of the Cosmonauts, Moscow. In the forground is the first woman in space (1963), Valentina Tereshkova (b. 1937). Cynical Muscovites refer to the rocket-topped monument as 'the impotent's dream'

was replaced by the ungainly massiveness of the female ideal of the wartime years. Nevertheless a few official artists were able to maintain a distinctive identity. Since Socialist Realism was 'national in form', artists of the non-Russian republics such as the Armenian Martiros Sar'yan (1880–1972) and the Georgian Lado Gudiashvili (1896–1980) could produce and exhibit paintings which, had they been the work of Russians, would have been dismissed as 'formalist'.

Graphic artists, many of them 'exiles' from easel art, also continued to produce varied and original work. The illustrations and engravings of such artists as Vladimir Favorsky (1886–1964), Aleksey Pakhomov (1900–73), Tyshler, Lebedev, Andrey Goncharov (1903–79), Petr Miturich (1887–1956) and Dmitry Mitrokhin (1883–1973) are of enduring quality. JH

ART AFTER THE THAW

In 1957 the republican Artists' Unions were finally united into the Union of Soviet Artists. The election of Konstantin Yuon (1875–1958) as the first chairman of the Union demonstrated that the 'thaw' had reached the visual arts. Yuon had never been closely associated with the Wanderers. A member, before 1932, of World of Art, the Union of Russian Artists and the Association of Artists of Revolutionary Russia, he had renounced the symbolism of his early work (for example, *The New Planet*, 1921) for the 'realism' of the 1930s, but retained his inventive use of colour. After Yuon's death in 1958 and for the next decade the Union of Soviet Artists was headed by Sergey Gerasimov and Ioganson. In 1968 for the first time, the chairman was an artist whose career had begun after the Revolution, Yekaterina Belashova-Alekseeva (1906–71), a sculptor who first exhibited in 1934.

Right. *Il'ya Glazunov, The Return of the Prodigal Son, 1977*

From 1957 Soviet art began to show a real diversity. As the neo-Wanderers' version of Socialist Realism showed signs of losing its pre-eminence, artists of the first three decades of this century were being reappraised. The early works of former members of World of Art, Blue Rose, Knave of Diamonds, the Union of Russian Artists and the Society of Easel Artists (OST) were again to be seen in the galleries, a number of books on art movements of the pre-1932 period appeared, and Western art, both figurative and non-figurative, became more accessible. This, together with the direct influence through art-school teaching of artists of the 1920s and early 1930s, played a great part in shaping late Soviet art. In style, if not in spirit, the early 1980s art scene resembled that of the 1930s, and although official art remained exclusively representational, membership of the Union of Artists did not necessarily preclude experimentation with unofficial styles and tendencies.

The influence of the neo-Wanderers is, however, still apparent. There is little to distinguish *Motherhood* (1964) by Eduard Bragovsky (b.1923) or *The Parting* (1967) by Gely Korzhev-Chuvelev (b.1925) from the work of Ioganson. The works of Igor' Simonov (b.1927) and Boris Okorokov (b. 1933) are faithful to the traditions of Socialist Realism in their 'heroic' portrayal of reality and their assumption that 'great ideas' require large canvases. The influence of OST can be seen in the spacious, almost monochromatic compositions of Tair Salakhov (b.1928). Mikhail Savitsky's (b.1922) *Partisan Madonna* (1967), owes an obvious debt to Kuz'ma Petrov-Vodkin. The post-Impressionism of the Knave of Diamonds survives in the works of Vyacheslav Stekol'shchikov (b.1938) and is to be discerned in the semi-abstract experiments with colour by Nikolay Gritsyuk (b.1922).

Tair Salakhov, The Composer Kara Karaev

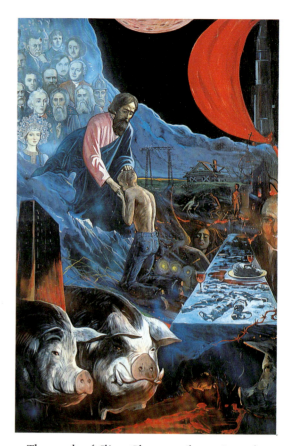

The work of Il'ya Glazunov (b.1930), perhaps the only Soviet artist whose work received official recognition at home and commercial success abroad, used Russia's realist tradition in an interesting manner, exemplified by *The Return of the Prodigal Son* (1977). This is full of references to Russia's past and present. Depictions of rulers, churchmen and writers, closely modelled on well-known works by other artists, flank the central figure from *The Appearance of Christ to the People* by Ivanov, an artist from the Wanderers group. On the table lies a head from an icon of St John the Baptist and corpses in the snow from the Kukryniksy's *The Fascist Retreat from Novgorod*. The whole scene is observed from the right by one of Brodsky's portraits of Lenin.

An impressionistic simplicity distinguishes the work of artists from the Baltic republics, such as the Latvian Jemma Skulme (b.1925) and the Lithuanian Jonas Švažas (b.1925).

Soviet art overall was adversely affected by the isolation which characterized the period 1934 to 1957. Sculpture, most dependent upon state patronage, remained almost static: size rather than concept seemed to be the criterion. Graphic and easel art, however, show signs of recovery. Recent evaluations of Russia's artistic heritage, the influence of unofficial art and the increased exchange of ideas with other countries should now enable art in the former Soviet Union to follow new paths. JH

ART IN THE NON-RUSSIAN REPUBLICS

Many of the artists associated in the West with modern Russian art – Mikalojus Čiurlionis (1875–1911), Klucis, Dmitry Nalbandyan (b.1906), Sar'yan, Salakhov, Niko Pirosmanashvili (1860/3–1918), Aleksandr Volkov (1886–1957), and Vrubel' – were not born in Russia. This impressive list of names indicates the substantial debt of Russian and Soviet art to the ethnic minorities comprising the non-Russian republics, especially of Georgia, Armenia, Azerbaijan, Uzbekistan and the Baltic states.

The art and architecture of twentieth-century Georgia warrants particular attention. Before the Revolution Tiflis (now Tbilisi) enjoyed a vigorous cultural life and, for example, was exposed to the avant-garde through artists and writers such as Kirill Zdanevich (1892–1969), his brother Il'ya (Iliazd) (1894–1975) and the primitive Niko Pirosmanashvili. In the years 1918–19 Tiflis became a Futurist centre, witnessing the activities of the Dada group known as '41°' and the appearance of a whole series of unorthodox books and journals. After the incorporation of Georgia into the Soviet Union in 1921, its independent artistic life continued to flourish and to maintain international connections, especially with Paris, where Lado Gudiashvili and David Kakabadze (1889–1952), perhaps Georgia's most talented twentieth-century artists, studied. While retaining the decorative quality of traditional Georgian art, Gudiashvili brought an Expressionist, sometimes apocalyptic force to his painting, as in *Fish* (1920) and *The Underprivileged* (1930). In contrast, Kakabadze created skilful abstract works during the 1920s, organized and restrained.

Inevitably, the move towards Socialist Realism, ratified in Moscow in the early 1930s, affected the development of Georgian art, producing its own 'protocolists' such as Ketevan Magolashvili (1894–1973) and Iraklii Toidze (b.1902), whose portraits of Stalin earned him a high position in Soviet cultural life. But because of Georgia's strong national traditions and comparative remoteness from the Kremlin, the doctrine of Socialist Realism did not gain the exclusive control of art it achieved in Russia. A number of Russian artists – Yevgeny Lancéray (E.E. Lansere, 1875–1946), Aleksandr Shevchenko, Vasily Shukhaev (1887–1973) – made their home in Georgia during the 1930s. This was symptomatic of a general drift from the main Russian cities to Central Asia of many artists and writers, including Aleksandr Drevin (1889–1938), Fal'k, Kuz'ma Petrov-Vodkin, Kuznetsov and Nadezhda Udal'tsova (1885–1961).

Naturally, Georgian painting, architecture and design enjoyed substantial goverment patronage during the hegemony of Stalin and the powerful G.K. Ordzhonikidze (1886–1937), often providing exotic combinations of Western European and indigenous motifs. Many buildings of the 1930s and 1940s in Tbilisi, multi-storey and constructed of ferro-concrete, have the appearance of ornamental rugs. Further, this oriental influence from Georgia (and from Armenia, Kazakhstan and Uzbekistan) manifested itself in the façades, mosaics and reliefs of the Stalin 'wedding-cakes' such as the Hotel Moskva in Moscow. After experiencing an Impressionist phase in the late 1950s and early 1960s, Georgian painting entered the so-called 'severe style' represented by Konstantin Makharadze (b.1929) and Radish Tordiia (b.1936). In turn, this movement contributed to the remarkable recent efflorescence of Georgian monumental art.

Armenia, annexed to the Soviet Union in 1920, strove to retain its cultural identity, although its most famous painter, Sar'yan, perhaps took his inspiration more from Gauguin and Matisse than from the traditions of the Armenian decorative arts

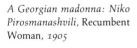

A Georgian madonna: Niko Pirosmanashvili, Recumbent Woman, *1905*

Martiros Sar'yan, Old Yerevan, *1928*

Right. Jemma Skulme, Women of Nice

and miniature. During the 1920s and 1930s a number of experimental artists came to the fore, including Georgy Grigoryan (b.1897) and Akop Kodzhorian (1883–1959), whose dramatic *Shooting of the Communists* (1930) is a compelling example of Armenian Expressionism. From the mid-1930s onwards the exuberance and decorativeness of traditional Armenian art yielded to the anonymous narrative style of Socialist Realism, of which Dmitry Nalbandyan, a last survivor from Stalin's 'court painters', is the most typical representative. The same process was evident in Azerbaijan and Uzbekistan, whose few avant-garde painters of the late 1920s and early 1930s – such as Gazanfar Khalykov (b.1898), Shmavon Mangasarov (b.1907), Ural Tansykbaev (1904–74) and Usto-Mumin (pseudonym of Aleksandr Nikolaev, 1897–1957) – were replaced by orthodox defenders of the Socialist Realist faith. Tair Salakhov, First Secretary of the Union of Artists of the USSR, added some interest to this trend when he contributed to the 'severe style' of the 1960s, supported by Sarkis Muradyan (b.1927). Their colleague, Torgul Narimanbekov (b.1930) has succeeded in retaining the ornamental, colourful bias of his national culture.

While the Baltic states (Lithuania, Latvia and Estonia) were incorporated into the Soviet bloc only in 1940, they had long-maintained cultural ties with Russia. The Symbolist Čiurlionis lived in Lithuania before moving to St Petersburg in 1908; the etcher Vasily Masyutin (1884–1955), the critic and painter Waldemars Matvejs (Vladimir Markov, 1877–1914), the abstract painter and designer Klucis and the sculptor Teodor Zalkaln (1876–1972) were all Latvian. Jemma Skulme, the daughter of the celebrated painter and sculptor Otto Skulme (1889–1967), upheld the family's artistic tradition by heading the Latvian affiliation of the Union of Artists of the USSR. The painter Indulis Zarin (b.1929) is

also worthy of mention. Tallinn in Estonia is the centre of a veritable renaissance of the graphic arts represented by Leonhard Lapin (b.1947), Malle Leis (b.1940), Raul Meel (b.1941), Mare and Tonis Vint (both b.1942), artists who are the worthy successors to Eduard Wiiralt (1898–1954), one of the great visionaries of twentieth-century European art. Among the non-Russian cultures of the Soviet Union in the 1970s, Baltic art showed the greatest vigour, independence and potential.   JEB

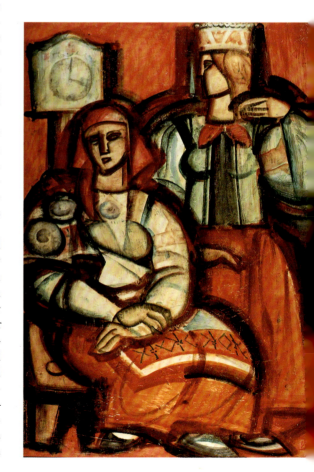

THE ALTERNATIVE TRADITION

The early 1930s saw the stifling of Russia's revolutionary atmosphere, and the revolutionary avant-garde suffocated in the cultural vacuum of Socialist Realism. Yet some major figures of that avant-garde did remain inside Russia (among others, Malevich, Tatlin, El' Lissitzky, Rodchenko, Al'tman) and continued to work. Outcasts from official life, they applied themselves either to book and graphic design – mainly in propaganda journals published for foreign consumption (El' Lissitzky, Rodchenko) – or to design for the theatre (Natan Al'tman, Tyshler, and others). Malevich and Tatlin painted figurative portraits and still life, not because they had any desire to adapt to new demands, but because the collective structure of their creative activity had collapsed, and without it there was no point in avant-garde experimentation. The traditions of the avant-garde went underground, to be continued in private. Rodchenko, in 1943–44, painted a vast canvas entitled *Expressive Rhythm* which anticipated the spontaneous methods of what was to become *tachisme*. V. V. Sterligov (1904–73) continued to develop the theories of his master, Malevich. El' Lissitzky was, to the end of his life, producing projects for towns of the future. In such conditions, however, these activities were merely isolated episodes, with no direct consequences. Anything outside the realm of Socialist Realism remained in the studios, confined to a close circle of the artists' friends, and thus played no part in the public aesthetic life of society. This alternative tradition became a broad movement only after the death of Stalin.

Open opposition

From 1956 to 1963 cultural links with the West were more intense than at any other period of Soviet history. For the first time in a quarter of a century major exhibitions of French, English, Belgian and American art were held in Moscow and Leningrad. Articles on the subject began to be published; they may have been critical, but they did at least contain scraps of objective information. This first encounter with contemporary foreign art was decisive for Soviet art.

The opposition movement in art arose in the mid-1950s from two sources. First, a 'left wing' appeared within the official Union of Soviet Artists. Without directly confronting the principles of Socialist Realism, young artists (many of whom entered art school straight from the front, wounded and decorated) sought to extend the notion of 'truth to life', and in order to express that truth, to master the entire range of modern methods. They painted portraits and landscapes, scenes of war and of work, and they made memorials to the dead; but all this was done not in the pompous style of official Socialist Realism but in an attempt to reflect life's dramatic, and sometimes tragic, confrontations. This line of Soviet art of the late 1950s and early 1960s has come to be termed the 'severe style'. Boris Birger (b.1923), Vadim Sidur (1924–86), Ernst Neizvestny (b.1926), Vladimir Veysberg (b.1924), Nikolay Andronov (b.1929), Pavel Nikonov (b.1930) and others gained widespread popularity and were featured in the Soviet press as the most talented representatives of the younger generation of artists.

The other and main source of this movement flowed from those who from the very beginning had not accepted the dogmas of official ideology. The older among them were of various backgrounds and followed various paths to non-conformism: some arrived at it via the prison camps (Boris Sveshnikov, b.1927; Lev Kropivnitsky, b.1922), and others thanks to their teachers, or as a result of particular circumstances (for example, Oskar Rabin, b.1928; Vladimir Nemukhin, b.1925). The majority, however, were students (Dmitry Plavinsky, b.1937; Anatoly Zverev, 1931–88; Oleg Tselkov, b.1934; Vladimir Yankilevsky, b.1938; and others). Like the artists of the 'severe style', they viewed their art, at that time, as 'forms of reflection of reality', but they filtered this reality through the prism of Surrealism, Expressionism, the grotesque, fantastic realism, as they tried to penetrate the social, spiritual and existential bases of life.

A far smaller proportion of them embraced abstractionism (Lidiya Masterkova, b.1929; Mikhail Kulakov, b.1933; and others) or pure form-creation. At the start of the 1960s, however, the 'Movement' group (Lev Nusberg, b.1937; and others) was formed – the only body proclaiming direct descent from the traditions of the revolutionary avant-garde. At present, this line is continued in the 'Author Working Group', led by Francisco Infante (b.1943).

Political reaction

The existence of an artistic opposition successfully competing with Socialist Realism posed a serious threat to official Soviet ideology. In December 1962 the main guardians of this ideology – the members of the USSR Academy of Arts – were able to convince the party leader, Khrushchev, that this was indeed the case. At a major exhibition of the Union of Soviet Artists at the Manège (Moscow's most important exhibition hall), they pointed out to him the new trends, and branded them as ideological deviations threatening the very foundations of the Soviet state. That was the start of a nationwide campaign against 'liberal tendencies' in culture, which were seen as stemming from the influence of 'hostile Western ideology'. Harsh criticism was aimed not only at the outsiders, but also at the members of the Union of Soviet Artists who had created the 'severe style'. Some of them were forced to compromise, but the most talented were gradually shunted out of official life and were, in effect, transformed into 'unofficial' artists (Birger, Veysberg, Sidur, Neizvestny and others).

Nevertheless, throughout the 1960s the opposition movement expanded; fresh followers joined it in their hundreds; it spread to Leningrad and to the towns of the union republics. Its stylistic range became broader, and it developed with a more intense dynamism. In an amazingly brief period, individual artists and groups of artists made the transition from Surrealism and Russian Constructivism to Western pop-art, photo-realism, happenings and conceptualism, expressed in the work of artists such as Erik Bulatov (b.1933) and Il'ya Kabakov (b.1933). The opposition movement had, in fact, joined the mainstream of European art. It had mastered the basic rules, and had created its own national variations on fundamental European themes, such as the 'sots-art' of Vitaly Komar (b.1943) and Aleksandr Melamid (b.1945) which openly parodied the values of the official ideology, or the grob-art ('grave-art') of Sidur.

From the inception of the opposition movement, the only channels of communication between the artists and the public were exhibitions arranged semi-legally in workers' clubs, research institutes and private apartments. Although such exhibitions were few, and although their duration was brief – for they were usually closed by the authorities as soon as discovered – they did create the impression of a living unofficial art, and inspired hope for the future. Through them information about the opposition movement in the USSR leaked abroad. From the mid-1960s the exhibitions were strictly prohibited; all mention (even critical) of the unofficial artists disappeared from the Soviet press; it was as if their art had been silently declared non-existent. It was death for the artists' work.

On 15 September 1974 a group of artists went out to a patch of waste ground in Moscow to display their work. This first free open-air exhibition was smashed by the authorities with the aid of bulldozers, fire-hoses and plainclothes militia. A number of pictures were burned on the spot. Some of the foreign correspondents present were subjected to physical harassment, with the result that the artistic opposition movement in the USSR received the full attention of the Western media. At the same time, members of the movement continued doggedly to press for their right to show their works. These were the factors which largely determined the situation in Soviet art until the 1980s.

Relationship to Socialist Realism

The authorities were now forced into making certain concessions. They permitted a number of brief exhibitions of unofficial art (passed over in total silence by the press); and in 1976 an organization which admitted nonconformist artists (the Graphic Artists Section of the city committee of soviets) was set up in Moscow as a buffer between the Union of Soviet Artists and the flood of unregulated unofficial art. However, pressure on the most active participants in the movement was increased and many were compelled by threats to leave the country. The early 1970s therefore saw the start of a second stream of emigration from the country, the first having taken place in the 1920s. Mikhail Shemyakin (b.1943), Neizvestny, Nusberg, Rabin, Tselkov, Masterkova, Eduard Zelenin (b.1938) and many others left.

These events gradually undermined the monolith of Stalin's Socialist Realism. Soviet artists – who at one time were united and tightly integrated – became divided by personal interests, creative platforms, and different groups. From the early 1960s onwards we can identify three main movements or tendencies which were mutually hostile. Firstly, the upholders of Socialist Realism who occupied the key positions in Soviet artistic life throughout this period. Secondly, many members of the Union of Soviet Artists who were aspiring to expand the frontiers of Realism, to introduce certain stylistic elements from artists of the 1920s (such as Kuznetsov, Petrov-Vodkin and Sar'yan) and to borrow from Western trends. Their artworks, which characterized so many of the Soviet exhibitions of the 1960s, constituted a rich mixture of the most diverse influences, even though their common denominator was still Socialist Realism with its social orientation and affirmative optimism. Thirdly, those artists who opposed both camps – and not just those who supported the unofficial movement with its orientation towards contemporary Western art and the Russian avant-garde, but also those who (both inside and outside the Union) wished to revive the 'elevated subject' in the form of the majesty of Russia, her history, and the national character of her people in the traditional forms of Russian Realism. Such artists – Il'ya Glazunov and others – regarded the liberal tendencies in contemporary Soviet art as a product of Western Modernism and as something alien to the Russian spirit. However, their opposition expressed itself merely in a certain displacement of the ideological axis away from official patriotism towards a popular Orthodoxy.

Perestroika and glasnost

On 11 September 1986 the Central Committee of the Communist Party of the Soviet Union and the Council of Ministers of the USSR issued the resolution

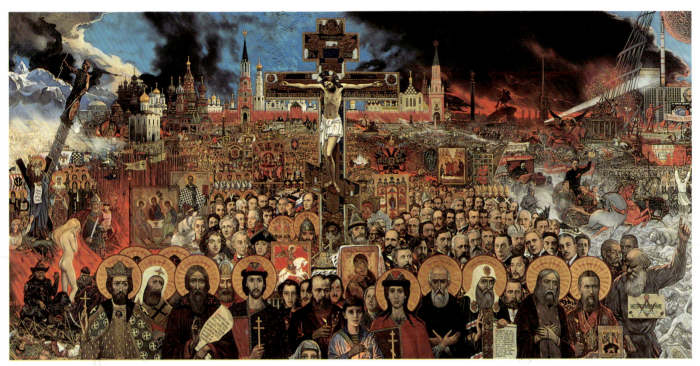

Il'ya Glazunov, Eternal
Russia

'Concerning Measures for the Further Development of the Visual Arts and the Promotion of their Role in the Communist Education of the Workers'. This decree relied upon a Stalinist vocabulary in its endeavour to reinforce the sacred principles of Socialist Realism, to intensify the struggle against Western influences, and so on. However, few people mentioned this decree at the Seventh Artists' Convention at the beginning of 1987. In fact, Socialist Realism itself came under attack: participants suggested that it be the subject of critical re-evaluation and some even concluded that Socialist Realism had brought no less damage to Soviet art than Lysenko had to biology and agriculture.

During the next three years the opposition, now unleashed, swept away all the official barriers, emerged in the public arena, and began to occupy most of the exhibition halls and the press. Gradually, semi-legal groups of young artists assumed official status and articles began to appear about names once forbidden, praising them as vital contributors to the development of Soviet art in the 1960s and 1970s (Birger, Kabakov, Sidur, Zverev).

Today, the distinctive characteristic of artistic life is pluralism – a pluralism that has replaced the single party line that used to control all artistic matters. One can now see works by the former unofficial artists and the practitioners of Socialist Realism at the same exhibitions, while the radical innovations of the young neo-avant-gardists can be seen right next to the canvases of the populist, patriotic champions of the 'Russian idea'. Each of these tendencies attracts its supporters, defenders and apologists – and from all walks of life and in the most diverse publications. Each group now has the opportunity to advance its cause and does so. In effect thanks to perestroika and glasnost, each of these movements is an alternative one.   IG (trans. SF and JEB)

*Dissident artists Sergey
Shukhov (left) and Vladimir
Koval*

Language

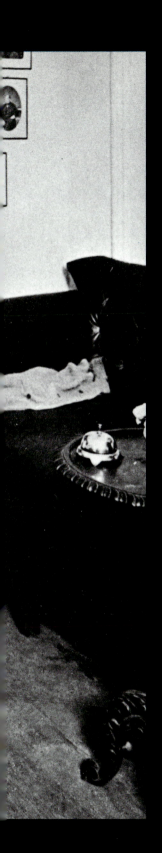

and literature

Language

RUSSIAN, UKRAINIAN AND BELORUSSIAN

Russian, Ukrainian and Belorussian together form the East Slavonic group of the Slavonic branch of the Indo-European family of languages, the other groups being West Slavonic (Czech, Slovak, Polish and Lusatian) and South Slavonic (Slovene, Serbo-Croat, Bulgarian, Macedonian and Old Church Slavonic). The accompanying tabulation of dates summarizes linguistic development.

Long before their earliest recorded history, the East Slavonic dialects had developed some of the main characteristics which distinguish them from West and South Slavonic. The acquisition of literacy came with the conversion to Christianity in 988; early literature confined to religious themes was written in Old Church Slavonic, with an admixture of East Slavonic dialectal features. Secular documents made use of the local vernaculars, which, up to the fourteenth century, were close enough to be dubbed either simply East Slavonic or Old Russian, in the wide sense of ancestors of the three modern languages, containing in embryo their divergent characteristics, with the exception of accretions, chiefly lexical, from outside sources. Among the

most important dialects were those of the Ilmen' Slovenes and Krivichi (North Great Russian), the Radimichi, Vyatichi and Severyane (South Great Russian), the Polyanians and Volynians (Ukrainian) and the Dregovichi (Belorussian). From the tenth century until its sack by the Tatars in 1240 Kiev was the chief East Slavonic cultural centre; after that date there was a westward shift of power and influence to Galicia and Volynia which heralded the emergence of Old Ukrainian (fourteenth to sixteenth centuries). From the thirteenth century divergent tendencies may be observed in Great Russian (for example, confusion of hiss and hush sibilants – ts/ch in Novgorod; ts/ch, s/sh, z/zh in Pskov) but disintegration was forestalled by the growth of Moscow, through the annexation of minor principalities and the suppression of the independent republics of Novgorod and Pskov, to become the undisputed political and cultural centre of Great Russia. The language which took shape in Moscow admitted elements from both North and South Great Russian, a happy blend which is reflected in the modern standard pronunciation with plosive *g* from the former and reduction of unstressed vowels (*akan'e*) from the latter.

Polish and Lithuanian domination of western areas encouraged the development of Old Belorussian and Old Ukrainian, at this stage (fourteenth to sixteenth centuries) so close to each other as to be given the common name of Ruthenian by some

The relationship of Russian, Belorussian and Ukrainian to other Indo-European languages

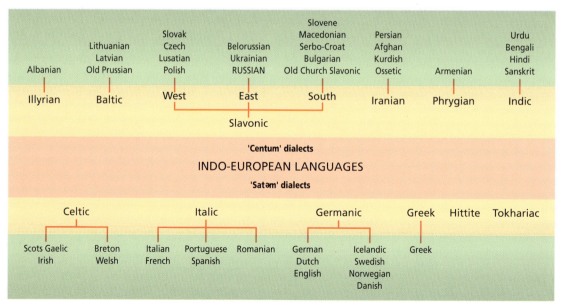

Previous spread. Lev Tolstoy in his study at Yasnaya Polyana, 1908

scholars. First confined to legal documents, by the sixteenth century these dialects had become an adequate medium for contemporary literary genres such as Orthodox religious polemical tracts, vivid personal reminiscence, and syllabic verse on the Polish and Latin pattern. The most striking feature of the Ruthenian literary language was its use of Polish and not Old Church Slavonic as a source of neologisms.

The growth of Russian power under Peter the Great and Catherine II and the transfer of Ukrainian and Belorussian territories to the Russian state interrupted the further development of Ukrainian and Belorussian. The publication of I.P. Kotlyarevs'ky's (1769–1838) parody of the *Aeneid* (1798) and the first collection of poems *The Minstrel* (1840) by T.G. Shevchenko (1814–61), national poet of the Ukraine, mark the re-emergence and consolidation of modern Ukrainian as a literary language. During the second half of the nineteenth century, when publication in Ukrainian was severely restricted by the tsarist authorities, the Austrian government encouraged the development of Ukrainian in Galicia. Since Galicia admitted a much stronger Polish element than the language of the other cultural centres, Kiev and Kharkiv, the upshot was a legacy of strains and contradictions which are still being resolved.

The renaissance of Belorussian (or White Russian) as a literary medium and official language of the Belorussian SSR began rather later and was eventually confirmed by the writings of the poets Yanka Kupala (1882–1942) and Yakub Kolas (1882–1956). Ukrainian and Belorussian are now firmly established as the official languages of independent Ukraine and Belarus. Some of their distinguishing characteristics from Russian are shown in the chart overleaf, but it is in the vocabulary, above all, that they differ, because of the relative infrequency of Church Slavonic and the richness of Polish elements in Ukrainian and Belorussian. For example, Russian has *obeshchat'* = 'to promise' and *sokrovishche* = 'treasure' from Church Slavonic, whereas the equivalent words in the two other languages – Belorussian *abyatsats'*, *skarb* and Ukrainian *obitsyaty*, *skarb* – are from Polish.

HL

Right. The Ukrainian national poet Taras Shevchenko. Statue in Kiev by Matvei Manizer

IMPORTANT DATES IN LINGUISTIC HISTORY	
2nd millennium BC	Split of Indo-European into 'satem' and 'centum' dialects (so designated on the basis of the term used for 'one hundred')
1st millennium BC	Formation of Common Slavonic; in the second half, close association of Baltic and Slavonic
c. 500–800 AD	Distintegration of Common Slavonic into East, West and South dialect groups
863	Mission of SS Cyril and Methodius to Slavs of Moravia and Pannonia; Slavs acquire an alphabet and a written language (Old Church Slavonic)
988	Conversion of Eastern Slavs to Christianity; introduction of alphabet and written language
1056–57	The oldest dated manuscript book written by a Russian scribe: Prince Ostromir's Gospel-book
1130	The earliest dated secular document; the deed of Prince Mstislav Volodomirovich and his son Vsevolod
1491	Earliest Church Slavonic books for Eastern Slavs printed by Fiol in Cracow
1517	Dr Francis Skaryna commences publication of the Belorussian translation of the Bible: 1517–19 in Prague; 1522–25 in Wilno (Vilnius)
c. 1553	First printing in Moscow
1596	The first Church Slavonic grammar and dictionary by the Belorussian monk Lavrenty Zizany, printed in Wilno (Vilnius)
1627	The first Church Slavonic-Ukrainian dictionary by the Ukrainian Pamvo Berynda, Kiev; 2nd edition, Kuteina, 1657
1755	Publication of Lomonosov's Russian grammar; founding of Moscow University
1798	I. P. Kotlyarevs'ky's parody of the *Aeneid* marks the rebirth of the Ukrainian literary language
1820–37	Pushkin's mature work: the perfecting of the Russian literary language
1840	T. G. Shevchenko's collection of poems in Ukrainian, *Kobzar* (The Minstrel)

RUSSIAN LITERARY LANGUAGE

The Russian literary language is the direct heir of Old Church Slavonic, the first written language of the Slavs, which came into being to answer the needs of a people newly converted to Christianity. Its roots are firmly set in the confident Graeco-Slavonic bilingualism of SS Cyril and Methodius (the ninth-century missionaries of the Slavs) and their followers, who transplanted a whole vocabulary of spiritual and moral concepts from Christian Hellenic ground into a new idiom in which it still lives and serves the purposes not only of the Slavonic branches of the Orthodox Church but also, in its Russian context, the secular state.

In spite of an attempt by Lomonosov to codify the functions within Russian of the Church Slavonic elements it was not until the nineteenth century that a complete integration was achieved in the work of Pushkin. Russian continues to draw neologisms and derivatives not only from its dialectal base but also from the Church Slavonic thesaurus, as great a treasure-house for Russian as Latin is for the languages of western Europe. Some evidence of its use as an inexhaustible source for neologisms and derivatives, especially those of a moral, didactic or scientific character, may be noted in the following examples (Church Slavonic words capitalized): *vsya VLAST' SOVETAM* = 'all power to the soviets' (a revolutionary slogan); LeninGRAD, VolgoGRAD,' as against the native Novgorod; *MLECHnyy put'* = 'Milky Way' as against the native *molochnye produkty* = 'dairy products'; *GLAVA* = 'chief, chapter' as against the native *golova* = 'head' (part of the body).

The West European languages began to make a significant contribution to the Russian vocabulary first via Polish mediation between the fifteenth and seventeenth centuries and later directly: German and Dutch in Peter the Great's time, French later in the eighteenth century, German, and increasingly English, in the nineteenth and twentieth centuries. Russian has also acquired many loan-words from the Turkic and Finno-Ugrian peoples on the eastern borders. All these diverse elements have played their part in making Russian a language of immense power and beauty, rich in synonyms, capable of expressing the subtlest nuances of meaning, the worthy instrument of the great novelists of the nineteenth century.   HL

DISTINGUISHING FEATURES OF RUSSIAN, BELORUSSIAN AND UKRAINIAN

Belorussian	Russian	Meaning
• Soft consonants *ts'*, *dz'*	*t'*, *d'*	
Example: *khadzits'*	*khodit'*	'to go'
• Reduction of unstressed *o* and *e* to *a* and *ya*		
Example: *malako*	*moloko*	'milk'
vyaliki	*velikiy*	'great'
• No soft '*r*'		
Example: *berah*	*bereg*	'bank, shore'
• Absence of *n* between preposition and personal pronoun		
Example: *da yaho*	*k nemu*	'to him'

Ukrainian	Russian	
• Pronunciation of certain vowels *i* as ee in 'sweet'	*e* or *o*	
Example: *sino*	*seno*	'hay'
nis	*nes*	'he was carrying'
nis	*nos*	'nose'
• Pronunciation of *y* as i in 'bit'	*i* or *y*	
Example: *bytv*	*bit'*	'to beat'
• Consonants are pronounced hard before the vowels *y* and *e*		
Example: *dyvo* (hard *d*)	*divo* (soft *d*)	'wonder'
den' (hard *d*)	*den'* (soft *d*)	'day'

Belorussian and Ukrainian	Russian	
• Fricative *h*	*g*	
Example: BR *holas*,		
UKR *holos*	*golos*	'voice'
• Initial *vo*, *vu* in some words	*o* or *u*	
Example: BR *voka*	*oko*	'eye'
UKR *vohon'*	*ogon'*	'fire'
BR *vulitsa*, UKR	*ulitsa*	'street'
vulytsya		

Distribution of speakers of the Slavonic languages

WEST SLAVONIC (Pomeranian) Polish 38.1 — EAST SLAVONIC
(Polabian) Lusatian 0.1
Czech 10.2
Slovak 4.7
Belorussian 10.0
Russian 145.2
Ukrainian 44.2
(Old Church Slavonic)
Slovene 1.9
Serbo-Croat 15.7   Macedonian 1.2
Bulgarian 7.6
SOUTH SLAVONIC

ES distinct from WS and SS: R *gorod, bereg, molod, moloko*
Sn *grad, brěg, mlad, mleko*
Cz *hrad, břeh, mladý, mléko*
Pol *gród, brzeg, młody, mleko*
(Note that Czech and Slovak here diverge from the other WS languages and follow the SS line.)

WS distinct from SS and ES: (1) Pol *kwiat*; R *tsvet*
(2) Pol *szary, wsze*; R *seryy, vse*
(3) Pol *mydło*; R *mylo*

SS distinct from WS and ES: (1) SCt *lakat*; Pol *łokieć*; R *lokot'*
(2) OCS *rabota*; Pol *robota*; OR *robota*

Early literature

RUSSIAN FOLKLORE

Folklore is the traditional culture of the Russians, passed down from generation to generation. Originally much of it was connected with East Slavonic paganism, but after the introduction of Christianity in the tenth century, it increasingly became the sole form of secular popular entertainment. Ritual folklore, often given Christian overtones, accompanied every event of significance in daily life, while non-ritual folklore, particularly the more artistic form, was brought to the people by travelling minstrels or mummers, called *skomorokhi*. The Church fulminated against them, but they were not suppressed until the mid-seventeenth century. Then they disappeared into the countryside to pass on their skills to talented peasants. Thanks to Russia's economic and social backwardness, folk literature was a rich and vital tradition right up to the Revolution, and even now is not defunct.

One of the most ancient and prolific folk genres is the tale. The Russians possess variants of well-known fairy tales such as Snow White or Cinderella, as well as many original subjects, each in countless different versions. Folk tales are of three kinds: fairy tales, animal tales and tales of everyday life.

Best known are the fairy tales, perhaps originally connected with the shamanistic beliefs of the Ural-Altaic peoples, attributing power over good and evil to the tribal priest-doctor. Their hero is either a prince or a low-born fool, Ivanushka Durak, who ultimately marries the princess. Fairy tales centre on a dangerous quest, during which the hero encounters the famous figures of peasant folklore, such as the witch Baba Yaga, who lives in a house on chicken legs, and the dragon Koshchey the Immortal who can only be killed if the egg that contains his death can be discovered. To enable him to combat evil, the hero receives help usually either from magical animals or from objects like the comb that can turn into a forest or the purse that never empties.

Animal tales, probably connected once to animistic beliefs, describe comic encounters between animals, who, as in the Brer Rabbit stories, are given a distinguishing human characteristic. Thus the most popular character, the Fox Lizaveta or Lisa Patrikeevna (*lisa* means fox), specializes in sweet words and flattery. Fearsome animals are turned into figures of fun: Mishka or Mikhail Ivanych, the Bear, though known for his strength as 'the uprooter of trees', is slow and clumsy. Even more stupid is the 'grey fool', the Wolf, who is constantly outwitted. Full of lively dialogue, rhymes and snatches of song, animal tales are still popular with Russian children.

The tales of everyday life are generally of more recent origin. They are based on the motif of the triumph of the underdog: the fool over the clever man. Their comic and satiric touches (the priest and the landlord are figures of fun) and their lively colloquial style ensure their popularity.

Rich and varied though folk tales are, they are less striking than the epic songs of Russia, the *byliny*. Preserved in the far north of Russia until relatively recent years, *byliny* were sung – or rather intoned – by peasant *skaziteli* (singers), who were famed for their narrative skill, poetic sensibility and, not least, their memory. Most *byliny* were composed before the sixteenth century. A few with superhuman heroes such as Svyatogor the giant, or Volkh Vseslavich who can turn himself into an animal, probably go back to pre-Christian times. Most others were composed either during the period of Kievan greatness (eleventh and twelfth centuries), or after the Tatar invasion. It is hard to tell, for the heroes – the *bogatyri* Il'ya of Murom, Alesha Popovich, Dobrynya Nikitich – are the same, and precise historical details are few. Whatever the period of composition, events are related back to an idealized heroic Kievan age. Other *byliny* are set in Novgorod. Unlike the Kievan *bylina* cycle, which is usually concerned with heroic battles or love, the Novgorod *byliny* are altogether more prosaic: Vasily Buslaevich, the 'hero' of some, is little more than a drunken braggart. *Byliny* depend for their effect upon the skill of the singer, who must compose his text from memory with the aid of stock poetic formulas and situations; thus the description of saddling a horse is always the same, hands are

Right. Mishka the Bear, as illustrated in a 1963 Soviet book of folk tales for children

always white, a maiden always fair. Epic features include threefold epic retardation and hyperbole – a *bogatyr'* wielding a weapon with such force that he clears a roadway through the ranks of the enemy.

With time, *byliny* gave way to historical songs and ballads. Sung in the same tonic (accentual) metre as *byliny*, but shorter and lacking the heroic tone and stock situations, historical songs present popular, sometimes spurious accounts of historical episodes or personages. Ballads, on the other hand, have little or no connection with history though they may once have had one. Mainly composed between the thirteenth and early eighteenth centuries in a slightly freer tonic verse than *byliny*, ballads are dramatic tales of the fates of individuals such as the wife who murders her husband, or the wife slandered by her mother-in-law and killed by her husband.

Folk-songs are not all narrative. Large numbers of lyric songs exist which were, and are, sung not by special singers but by ordinary people, very often women. The majority of songs describe peasant life, mainly its sadder sides: perhaps the most persistent theme is that of unhappy love and marriage. Other groups of songs centre round soldiers, bandits or barge-haulers. The poetics of lyric songs depend to a great extent on a range of beautiful traditional nature symbols. Apart from these songs expressing personal feeling, Russian folklore possesses a wide range of ritual songs connected with festivals and ceremonies such as weddings. Even now in the north the age-old tradition of funeral laments is not entirely defunct. Using folk poetic expressions, the singer expresses her own and the family's profound grief by improvising a lament, which reflects the character and occupation of the deceased. Christian themes are also found in the *dukhovnye pesni*, spiritual songs, which present popular versions of biblical and hagiographical stories.

Some forms of folklore such as drama were less well-developed than in Western Europe. Modern times have produced their own forms, notably the *chastushka*, a four-line verse, often comic, satiric or bawdy in character. But though most of the traditional forms are in decline, not all have yet disappeared. They and the pithy sayings and proverbs that are part of colloquial speech are reminders that the average Russian today is still in touch with the traditional oral culture of the people.

FCMW

LITERARY GENRES

Russian literature developed as a consequence of the conversion of the people to Christianity by the prince of Kiev, Vladimir I, in 988. In adopting the Eastern Orthodox form of Christianity from Byzantium rather than from Rome, the Russians received a liturgy in a Slavonic language, Old Church Slavonic, which in spite of its Greek syntax and specialized vocabulary was readily comprehensible. This facilitated the appearance of a literature in a language close to the vernacular within a mere half-century of the introduction of writing. In western Europe where the lingua franca was Latin, vernacular literatures evolved more slowly. Ultimately, the Russians were the losers, for they were isolated from intellectual movements in western Europe. The Renaissance and Reformation scarcely affected them, and Russian literature continued along medieval lines until the seventeenth century – far later than in western Europe.

Since literature followed upon conversion, much of it was naturally of an ecclesiastical nature – sermons, lives of saints and edifying works of various kinds. Even where it was secular it was still didactic; chronicles recorded events of significance, satirical and polemical works attacked abuses or proposed change, military tales told of great victories or defeats. The early Russian writer, who until the sixteenth century was usually a monk, saw himself as a medium for the conveying of information. He therefore was not interested in making up fictitious plots or inventing new literary forms. Indeed, the more a work conformed to the conventions of a given genre, the more it would be worthy of respect. But though didactic and traditional, Russian literature did not lack entertainment value: vivid stories, dramatic scenes, even wit and humour are present, but are always subordinated to tendentious aims. Similar attitudes are evident in the use of source materials: anything that served the purpose of a work could be included, and information that conflicted might be omitted with impunity.

Because of the fairly low literacy rate, early Russian literature was generally intended for reading aloud, in church, monastery or court, and, later, in the houses of the wealthy. Ecclesiastical literature which had to convey ethical concepts and abstract arguments took account of this fact by employing rhetoric; repetition and euphony of the most varied kinds helped to make the work more pleasing to the ear. By contrast, secular literature, which tended to be more narrative, at least until the sixteenth century, inclined towards simple syntax which made it easy to follow.

FCMW

KIEVAN LITERATURE

The literature of this period is usually termed 'Kievan' though works may actually have been written in one of the lesser principalities. At this stage regional differences are minimal.

The chronicles

Perhaps the most impressive of the literary works of the period is the Russian Primary Chronicle, or the *Tale of Bygone Years*, which covers the period up to 1118. As in Byzantine annals, material is placed under the heading of a given year. Since no annalist of the early twelfth century could be expected to remember precise dates for more than a few years, it is obvious that the Chronicle is a compilation. It was mainly written by monks of the Kievan Monastery of the Caves, among them Nestor, its first redactor or editor. Aptly termed a literary mosaic, the Chronicle includes folk legends, accounts of battles, lives of saints and a will, each written in the style appropriate to the subject matter. Subsequently it was imitated all over Russia. Local chronicles reflect regional tastes and preoccupations, and those from rival towns often provide fascinatingly varied views of the same events. They also often incorporate complete literary works such as the *Instruction of Vladimir Monomakh*, found in the *Tale of Bygone Years*. This unusual document, composed by one of Russia's most energetic and talented princes, consists of series of precepts for his sons followed by an amazingly long list of his campaigns. The advice contained in the first section, which is largely culled from Byzantine sources, is particularly valuable for its picture of the ideal Kievan prince.

Sermons

Through translation the Russians received many of the best examples of the Byzantine art of homily. That they were appreciated is evident from native Russian sermons, which, though not original in their theology, reveal remarkable skill with argument and its expression. The most impressive is Metropolitan Ilarion's *Sermon on Law and Grace* (1037–51) probably intended as a stimulus to the canonization of Vladimir I. Ilarion opens with a succession of beautifully balanced antitheses between Grace, the gift of Christ, and the Law of the Old Testament. Grace, he argues, is superior to Law not least in its availability to all peoples, the Russians included. And so he turns to the specific theme of the conversion of Russia, and as he does, he skilfully raises the emotional tone of the work until it culminates in a superb lyrical eulogy of Vladimir and his son, the ruling prince of Kiev, Yaroslav. By contrast, the sermons written by the twelfth-century bishop from Turov, Kirill, lack both Ilarion's patriotic tone and his skill with logical argument. Instead Kirill employs an ornate style to paint charming symbolic pictures of nature in which each detail reflects an aspect of the Church festival on which the sermon was to be pronounced.

Hagiography

Lives of saints were very popular in Kievan times, perhaps partly because the Byzantine model for rhetorical biography had been imperfectly absorbed, thus permitting realistic character portrayal and episodes inconsistent with traditional concepts of sanctity. Thus, of the versions of the deaths of the young princes Boris and Gleb, cruelly butchered by their elder brother Svyatopolk in 1015, only *The Lection on the Blessed Martyrs Boris and Gleb*, written c.1078 by Nestor, conforms to Byzantine canons. Logically structured and carefully written, it presents an idealized portrait of the young princes, but is much less enjoyable than the more popular *Tale of the Holy Martyrs Boris and Gleb*. Though the *Tale* is an awkward fusion of conflicting legends, it contains dramatic episodes and vivid portraits of the two brothers, especially of Gleb as he begs for mercy from his murderers. Even Nestor's *Life of St Feodosy of the Monastery of the Caves* ignores convention with its superb portrayal of Feodosy's possessive bullying mother, who goes to all ends to thwart her son's monastic calling. Kievan literature also boasts its own patericon, a collection of edifying stories about monks. The *Patericon of the Kievan Monastery of the Caves*, begun in the early thirteenth century, recounted episodes from the lives of former monks of the monastery. Simply told, and often fantastic in character, some, such as the tale of Moisey Ugrin who virtuously resisted the blandishments of a Polish beauty, are well-developed narratives.

The Tale of Igor''s Campaign

One of the most famous works in all Russian literature, *The Tale of Igor''s Campaign*, was apparently composed about 1187 by a court bard. It tells of the disastrous expedition led by Igor', Prince of Novgorod-Seversk, against the nomadic Polovtsians. The work is such a unique combination of folk poetry and literary traditions that doubts have frequently been cast on its authenticity, especially as the sole manuscript was destroyed in the great fire of Moscow in 1812. Written in a highly poetic prose full of nature imagery and symbol, the *Tale* gives an impressionistic description of the battle and defeat. Then follows the grand prince of Kiev's ominous dream and an exhortation to the powerful princes of Rus' to unite against the common foe. In the last section of the work, Igor''s wife Yaroslavna laments the loss of her husband, but Nature responds to her grief by facilitating Igor''s escape and return home. The work ends on a note of muted happiness. Although the *Tale's* authenticity may never be established completely, it none the less remains a work of undisputed genius.   FCMW

THE TATAR PERIOD

The main theme of *The Tale of Igor''s Campaign*, the need for unity in the face of danger, appears frequently from the twelfth century on. It evidently was the subject of the tantalizing fragment, the *Tale of the Destruction of the Russian Land*, a poetic lament for past glory. After the crushing Tatar invasion of 1237–40, princely strife no longer seemed an adequate explanation of the current state of affairs. As Serapion of Vladimir (d.1275) declared in his *Sermon on the Merciless Heathen*, the defeat of the Russians was divine punishment for their sins. In a period of isolation and national decline, it is not surprising that literature draws little from Byzantium, concentrating rather on those familiar literary genres that reflected current preoccupations – the recording of events in the chronicles and particularly of battles, some in independent military tales. The *Tale of the Capture of Ryazan' by Batu* describes the first encounter between the main Tatar army and the Russians in 1237. It provides a good example of a compilatory work: a basic story to which dramatic episodes and emotional colouring have been added over a period of time, in this case up to the second half of the fifteenth century. The defeat of the Ryazan' army and the sack of Ryazan' by Batu are part of the original story, but into this framework touching or dramatic scenes, often of dubious veracity, have been placed. Thus Prince Oleg the Fair, who refuses to be converted to Batu's 'false faith' and is chopped into pieces with knives, actually did not die until 1258. This and other epic stories – such as the tale of Yevpaty Kolovrat, who dies a glorious death after valiantly attempting to avenge the Ryazan' army against hopeless odds – were drawn from epic folk-songs. The author's aim is to increase the sense of patriotic grief for Ryazan'.

A period which valued military prowess was not likely to appreciate saintly virtues so well. It is not surprising that hagiography languishes at the expense of a hybrid genre, the secular biography of princes, which combined hagiographical and annalistic motifs and techniques. The *Life of Alexander Nevsky*, for example, which was written in the early 1280s, paints an idealized portrait of Alexander as warrior, statesman and Defender of the Orthodox Faith. To do so, the author was obliged to alter or ignore his less noble exploits. Thus both his battles, against the Swedes at the mouth of the Neva and against the Teutonic Knights on the ice of Lake Peipus, are falsely depicted as epic conflicts. To assist the author's intention of promoting Alexander as a hero saint, he is even shown performing miracles.

Not all the extant works of this period are concerned with battles and the Tatar invasion: the *Supplication of Daniil the Exile* is a curious twelfth-century work, which was greatly added to by later copyists. The author seems to have been one of the retinue of the prince of Pereyaslavl'. Feeling badly treated by his prince, he complains bitterly in a series of pungent aphorisms drawn from the Scriptures, translated Byzantine works and folklore. FCMW

MUSCOVITE LITERATURE

Ecclesiastical literature

About 1330 a religious revival started in Russia. Scores of people seeking a life of contemplation left the towns for the inhospitable countryside. As disciples joined them, monasteries grew up, which were to spearhead a renaissance of religious art and literature. The most important, the Trinity Monastery founded by St Sergy at Sergiev Posad (Zagorsk) sheltered icon painters such as Andrey Rublev and the brilliant hagiographer Epifany the Most Wise (d.1420). Given this name on account of his elaborate prose style called 'word-weaving', Epifany is the author of two highly ornate biographies, the *Life of St Sergy* (1417–18) and, about 1396, the *Life of Stefan of Perm'*, his friend who had converted a Finnic tribe to Christianity. Epifany was so overcome with veneration towards his subjects that he was forced into ever more elaborate word patterns to express himself. Such efforts were essential if Stefan were to be considered a worthy candidate for canonization, for he had performed no miracles, the normal prerequisite for a saint.

With the fall of Bulgaria and Serbia to the Turks at the end of the fourteenth century, numbers of South Slav writers fled to Russia. They brought with them a more controlled form of 'word-weaving' and a similar interest in the exploits of the saintly individual. The many lives and eulogies of saints composed by the fifteenth-century Serbian hagiographer Pakhomy Logofet display a good grasp of rhetoric but lack the deep feeling of Epifany. And yet because Pakhomy's writings were controlled in style, they became the model for later Muscovite hagiography, and 'word-weaving', losing its spiritual intensity, descends into a florid rhetoric which is increasingly found in secular literature of an official character.

Secular literature

The cultural revival of the late fourteenth century coincided with the first signs that the Tatars were not invincible. The battle of Kulikovo Field (1380), though little more than a psychological victory, was celebrated in a variety of literary works, from the ornate biography of Dmitry Donskoy, prince of Moscow, to epic military tales. The most interesting of the latter is the *Zadonshchina*, composed in an epic style very similar to that of the *Tale of Igor''s Campaign*.

Secular literature in the second half of the fifteenth century is of two kinds: either ideological, attempting to bolster the political or religious claims of a principality or ruler, or non-didactic. The move to free literature from the shackles of tendentiousness was unfortunately suppressed in the sixteenth century, which was dominated by an oppressive intellectual atmosphere.

Sixteenth-century literature

Moscow was by now head of a centralized Russian state and bitter debate ensued over the question of autocratic power. For the first time, writers are drawn from varied social groups, and literature depicts their respective viewpoints and the burning issues of the day. Of particular interest is the correspondence (1564–79) between Tsar Ivan the Terrible and a former close associate, Prince Kurbsky. In elegant prose, Kurbsky argues the case for the old aristocracy, the boyars, whom he feels Ivan has slighted, and asserts their ancient right to change their allegiance, as he himself has done by leaving Russia for Lithuania. Ivan's response, couched in a language alternately lofty and crude, is to name Kurbsky's action as that of a traitor, insisting that he, Ivan, is the sovereign chosen by God and that the boyars must submit to him. The views of another social group, the 'service gentry', are presented by Ivan Peresvetov. Ostensibly describing the last days of the Byzantine Empire and the first of Turkish rule in Istanbul, Peresvetov's works are thinly disguised allegories about the Russia of his day, permitting him to make bold criticisms and advocate a programme of reform. It is interesting that many of his less radical proposals were actually taken up by the tsar.

Probably more bitterness surrounded the religious controversies of the sixteenth century. The so-called Trans-Volga Elders, advocates of monastic poverty and a life of contemplation, clashed with the Josephians (followers of Iosif of Volokolamsk), who were in favour of monastic property, which enabled the Church to fulfil an active charitable role. Both sides, Nil Sorsky (1433–1508) and Vassyan Patrikeev for the Trans-Volga Elders, Iosif of Volokolamsk (c.1439–1515) for the Josephians, defended their views, and elaborated their teachings. The eventual defeat of the Trans-Volgans destroyed a vital spiritual spark in the life and literature of Muscovy. Free-thinking in the form of heresy was ruthlessly suppressed – a number of polemical anti-heretical tracts testify to their vigour. Even secular life was regulated; the *Domostroy*, a prosaic guide to everyday behaviour, was drawn up under the auspices of Metropolitan Makary (1481–1563), who also reorganized hagiographical literature, ensuring where necessary the writing and rewriting of saints' lives in florid rhetorical style. The heavy weight of officialdom, secular and ecclesiastical, hung over literature.

Seventeenth-century literature

The great social upheavals of the Time of Troubles (1598–1613) did much to dissipate the oppressive social atmosphere, but it had little effect on literature. Works of the period still employ heavy Muscovite rhetoric, though a new interest in rhyme is evident. But as time went on, it was clear that the conventions that had held Russian literature together for so long were breaking down. The reading public had expanded, creating a market for entertaining stories. Most were still heavily didactic, like the *Tale of Savva Grudtsyn* in which a young man is seduced by a married woman, falls into the clutches of the Devil, but eventually seeks salvation in a monastery. The exception is the *Tale of Frol Skobeev*, where lively narrative is not burdened by any kind of moral: Frol is a rogue, who seduces a rich man's daughter and by cunning succeeds eventually in gaining his father-in-law's blessing. A further innovation is the deliberate use of folklore as a literary source, as in the *Tale of Woe-Misfortune* about a Prodigal Son who comes to grief through drink. The tonic (accentual) verse and many of the motifs and expressions are drawn from folk poetry.

The masterpiece of the seventeenth century came not from the secularization of culture but from the religious reaction to it, the Schism in the Russian Church of the 1650s and 1660s. The leader of the Old Believers (as the Schismatics came to be called), the Archpriest Avvakum (c.1620–82), composed his autobiography between 1672 and 1675 while in a subterranean prison in the cold far north of Russia. Though termed a Life, this differs from others of the genre, being a detailed autobiography which presents a vivid picture of the indomitable Avvakum and his forbearing wife and children as they endure years of appalling privation in Siberia. Writing in a pithy crude style close to the vernacular, Avvakum heaps abuse on his enemies, portrays his friends and family with tender affection and himself emerges as the first rounded portrait in Russian literature.

Avvakum's desire for a return to old Russian piety was partly a reaction to the growth of Western influence in Russia. Those scholars who, after the annexation of Ukraine in 1654, moved from Kiev to Moscow brought with them new literary forms, the poetry and drama of the Baroque. Though there had been various attempts at verse in the first half of the century, it was Simeon Polotsky (1629–80), a product of the Kievan Academy, who really established literary verse. Written in rhyming couplets with a regular number of syllables, Simeon's verse is notable for its verbal effects and serious content. Western influence also accounted for the emergence of secular court drama in the 1660s. Though the plays of this period, including those by Simeon Polotsky, lack dramatic qualities, they helped set Russian literature upon a Western path of development. After 1700, the old forms of literature either died away or disappeared from the forefront of literary development to form a sub-culture among the broad mass of the people. FCMW

Eighteenth-century literature

KANTEMIR, TREDIAKOVSKY, LOMONOSOV, SUMAROKOV

The gulf separating Russian literature from the literatures of Western Europe at the beginning of the eighteenth century was wide. Verse-writing and drama had made only a scant first appearance in the last third of the seventeenth century, and in 1700 there were effectively no authors, no reading public, no secular press, no theatre. The reign of Peter the Great produced no significant literature, but the Western cultural orientation provided by his reforms led to the emergence of a sophisticated, europeanized literature from the 1730s. The period 1730–1800 saw a rapid development of literary culture from the crude beginnings in the works of Kantemir and Trediakovsky to the compositions of N.M. Karamzin and V.A. Zhukovsky, who could stand comparison with their Western contemporaries.

This rapid progress owed much to the fact that Russia began its literary apprenticeship in the age of classicism, which provided a comprehensive genre system and a wealth of models to follow. Two other important factors in the development of a modern literature were the creation of a balanced literary language, which exploited the resources of Russian and Church Slavonic, and the adoption of the syllabo-tonic (or syllabic-accentual) system of versification in place of the purely syllabic system inherited from the seventeenth century.

The first 'modern' Russian writer was A.D. Kantemir (1708–44), a product of the Petrine age and a man of broad European culture. He is known principally for his nine verse satires (1729–39),

The polymath Mikhailo Vasil'evich Lomonosov

unpublished in his lifetime, which were written in defence of enlightenment and contain many lively portraits of its enemies. He was the last author of note to use syllabic verse, on which he wrote a treatise.

Three authors dominated Russian literature until 1760: Trediakovsky, Lomonosov, and Sumarokov. All occupied positions in institutions of the state, which reflected the restricted, 'official' scope of literary activity at the time. In the theory and practice of literature, however, they achieved much and laid solid foundations for its further development.

V.K. Trediakovsky (1703–69), after studying in Holland and France, was employed in the Academy of Sciences. More a scholar than an artist, he wrote on literary history and theory, on prosody (notably, his pioneering treatise on the syllabo-tonic system, 1735) and on language. His original compositions were lifeless and cumbrously written, and his principal achievements were in the field of translation (Tallemant's *Voyage à l'île d'amour*, 1730; Fénelon's *Télémaque*, 1766).

M.V. Lomonosov (1711–65) has been called the 'Peter the Great of Russian literature'. Of humble family, he had a phenomenal career, achieving distinction as scientist, philologist and man of letters. A professor at the Academy of Sciences, he was the author of scientific works, a Russian grammar and a manual of rhetoric; in his *Letter on the Rules for Russian Verse* (1737) he extended the prosodic reforms of Trediakovsky; and in his essay 'On the usefulness of church books' (1757–58), he prescribed the 'three styles' of language appropriate to the main divisions of literary genres. He embodied the civic tradition of classical literature and is, above all, famed for his twenty 'solemn' odes (1737–64) celebrating events of state, victories, royal anniversaries and so on. The constant theme of the odes is the need to continue the policies of Peter the Great for enlightenment and the scientific and economic advance of Russia. These celebratory odes, which are heavily ornate in style, show great skill in form and language. Lomonosov also wrote religious and philosophical odes, sparser and more natural in style, of which the two 'Reflections (Morning and Evening) on the greatness of God' are outstanding.

A.P. Sumarokov (1717–77) was of gentry stock. He served in the army and, until 1761, occupied positions at court. He was the first Director of the Russian Theatre (1756–61) and the most wide-ranging writer of his day. Following Boileau's *L'Art poétique*, he set out the canons of classicism in two verse epistles (on language and on poetry, 1747) and exemplified all the main genres in his own prolific writings. He is best known for his introduction of the classical tragedy into Russia (*Khorev* (1747) and eight others) and his cultivation of the lighter genres of verse (songs, fables), in which he moved towards more natural forms of expression, both in language and verse structure. Though less talented than Lomonosov, he was more immediately influential in broadening the scope of literature and stimulating the growth of personal, as distinct from civic, themes. He favoured clarity in style and was critical of the embellished odes of Lomonosov. IPF

DRAMA

From the 1760s literary development accelerated. There were more writers and more readers, and literature became more closely concerned with the problems of contemporary life. Western literature also became increasingly accessible through translations.

The drama flourished. The classical tragedy was continued in the works of M.M. Kheraskov (1733–1807), Ya. B. Knyazhnin (1740–91), N.P. Nikolev (1758–1815), V.A. Ozerov (1769–1816) and others. Comedy became a popular genre, especially satire, which, with its attack on social follies and vices, provided both entertainment and moral instruction. In comedy, Sumarokov played a pioneering role in the 1750s. The comic repertoire expanded rapidly in the following decades, with translations and adaptations of French plays, for example, those of V.I. Lukin (1739–94), as well as many original comedies by Knyazhnin, Nikolev, A.O. Ablesimov (1742–83), P.A. Plavil'shchikov (1761–1812) and others. The best verse comedy of the period is *Chicanery* by V.V. Kapnist (1758–1823), which, as well as being skilfully written, went beyond the satire of 'general' social vices and had political overtones.

The outstanding comedy writer of the century was D.I. Fonvizin (1744–92). He wrote two celebrated plays in prose: *The Brigadier* (1766–69) and *The Minor* (1782). The first is a salon comedy, close to life in its humorous attack on corrupt morals, ignorance, and the current gallomania. *The Minor* is an indictment of domestic tyranny and false education, and it touches also on larger social questions, such as serfdom. While written in accordance with the classical 'unities' and, in the case of *The Minor*, slowed down by *raisonneur* moralizings, both these plays by Fonvizin are lively and entertaining, and merit their lasting place in the Russian theatrical repertoire. IPF

The dramatist Denis Ivanovich Fonvizin

THE NOVEL AND THE LITERARY JOURNAL

The novel and the literary journal, which were unknown in the classical canon and reflected the broadening scope and function of literature, appeared in Russia in the 1760s. The first Russian novels were those of F.A. Emin (1735–70), a Hungarian or Pole by origin, who between 1761 and 1770 produced over twenty-five books, some original, some translations. The best known of these is *The Letters of Ernest and Doravra* (1766), an epistolary novel influenced by Rousseau's *La nouvelle Héloïse*. M.D. Chulkov (c.1743–92) was the author of entertaining novels written in popular style – *The Mocker* (1766–68), and *The Comely Cook* (1770). Both these authors also engaged in journalism. Sumarokov had published the first Russian journal, *The Industrious Bee*, in 1759, and from the late 1760s journals had a regular place in Russian literary activity, partly through the stimulus of Catherine the Great, who had literary interests and herself published a journal – *All Sorts* – in 1769. The English *Spectator* was the prime model for the early Russian journals. The outstanding figure in the journalistic movement in the 1770s and 1780s was N.I. Novikov (1744–1818), who published a succession of satirical journals – *The Drone* (1769–70), *The Tatler* (1770), *The Painter* (1772), and others. IPF

DERZHAVIN

Novels and journals appealed to a wide public by their entertainment value and interest in mundane affairs, but they made little immediate impact on the established literary tradition. There, the revolution came from within, from a poet who began writing in the tradition of Lomonosov, but then abandoned its restrictions: G.R. Derzhavin (1743–1816), the most original Russian writer of the eighteenth century.

Derzhavin had a career as soldier (ten years in the ranks) and official (his last post was Minister of Justice). His major literary achievement was to move away from the rigid genre system and to bring life into Russian poetry. He abandoned the impersonality of classical authorship and gave the imprint of his own character to most of what he wrote. His best works are experience-based and noted for the accuracy and realism of their descriptions, particularly of nature. Derzhavin adopted a new approach to odic themes in his epoch-making *Felitsa* (1782), a poem about Catherine the Great, which, unlike the traditional panegyric ode, is light in tone, human in scale, and breaks the genre code by combining panegyric with satiric themes. Derzhavin maintained the solemn odic tradition in poems on national themes, but these too are more down-to-earth and more natural in expression than the odes of his predecessors.

Borovikovsky's portrait of the poet Derzhavin, 1795

His many outstanding works include robust civic poems (*To Rulers and Judges, The Grandee*), philosophical poems (*God, The Waterfall*), and domestic poems containing memorable, colourful descriptions of everyday life (*Invitation to Dinner, Life at Zvanka*). His style, sometimes rough, was rich and original and broke with many of the clichés of classical verse.   IPF

FABLES

By the 1770s the balance was shifting from the more solemn genres to lighter forms of literature. The decade which saw the completion of Russia's first epic poem – M.M. Kheraskov's *Rossiada* – saw also the appearance of the mock-epic *Elisey* of V.I. Maykov (1728–78) and of *Dushen'ka*, the light-hearted narrative poem of I.F. Bogdanovich (1744–1803).

Lighter genres, however, could still be serious in purpose – a characteristic exemplified by the fable, which enjoyed great popularity. Sumarokov had led the way with over 350 fables, written in vigorous, earthy free iambs. Later, more formal writers in the genre included I.I. Khemnitser (1745–84) and I.I. Dmitriev (1761–1837).

The greatest Russian fabulist, who ranks with the best of any country or age, was I.A. Krylov (1769–1844). He began his literary career as dramatist and journalist in the 1780s; later he turned to fable-writing (200 fables, 1807–34). The distinction of Krylov's fables lies in the originality of their themes, the harmony of their content and form, and the richness of their language.   IPF

Nikolay Mikhaylovich Karamzin

SENTIMENTALISM

In the last quarter of the century classicism was ceasing to be the dominant literary mode. The European movement of Sentimentalism exerted its influence in Russia from the 1760s (in the novels of F.A. Emin, and the poems of M.N. Murav'ev (1757–1807)). The central figure in Russian Sentimentalism was N.M. Karamzin (1766–1826), who had a lasting influence on the development of Russian literature and the literary language. Prose was his chief medium, and he was the first author to write readable, elegant Russian, which he based on the ordinary language of educated society. After travelling in Europe, he published *Letters of a Russian Traveller* (1791–92), which followed the tradition of sentimental travel literature with its casually intimate observations of life. The emphasis on the emotional and psychological aspects of human experience is reflected in Karamzin's stories of 1792–1803, the most famous of which is *Poor Liza* (1792), a tale of a peasant girl abandoned by her noble lover. Certain of his stories, such as *The Island of Bornholm* (1794) and *Sierra Morena* (1795), are more romantic in theme and mood. Karamzin was also a journalist, and his *European Herald* (1802) established the pattern for the 'thick' monthly literary-political journal which has flourished in Russia ever since. From 1803 Karamzin abandoned literature to write his major work, *The History of the Russian State*.

Throughout the eighteenth century, directly or indirectly, the state exercised control over literature by censorship, and Russia's first literary martyrs date from this time. The best known is A.N. Radishchev (1749–1802), author of *Journey from St Petersburg to Moscow* (1790). Radishchev's book, which contained radical criticism of Russian institutions (in particular, serfdom), was banned as seditious and the author was exiled to Siberia.   IPF

EARLY ROMANTICISM

The century ended with the appearance of the first poems of V.A. Zhukovsky (1783–1852), the major Russian representative of early Romanticism. Zhukovsky's verse was reflective, elegiac, the direct expression of experience and feeling. He wrote original verse, but most of his works were translations, chiefly from German and English poets, whose works harmonized with his own mood. He introduced the narrative ballad into Russia with translations from G.A. Bürger, Sir Walter Scott, Robert Southey and others and with original compositions, such as *Svetlana*. The outstanding feature of Zhukovsky's verse is his command of form and language,

The poet Vasily Andreevich Zhukovsky, 1817

which provided a norm of poetic expression for the following generation of poets. Zhukovsky became the friend and adviser of both Pushkin and Gogol' and thus provided a direct link between the traditions of two centuries.

A comparison of the work of Zhukovsky with that of Kantemir indicates how much Russian literature had progressed in a mere seventy years. In this time Russia had assimilated the experience of European literature, mastered existing techniques, created the formal and linguistic base on which the great writers of the nineteenth century were to build, and, in Lomonosov, Derzhavin, Karamzin and Zhukovsky, had shown signs of its own original genius.   IPF

Nineteenth-century literature

GRIBOEDOV

The term nineteenth-century Russian literature refers to the period 1820 to 1917, which has a recognizable wholeness, a discreteness, surpassing that of most conventional eras in any national literature. It is marked at the beginning by the first major published work of Pushkin, and at the end by the Bolshevik Revolution.

The early years of Pushkin's fame coincide with the tragically brief career of A.S. Griboedov (1795–1829). Both writers were steeped in the Russian and European literature which preceded them: but both

Aleksandr Sergeevich Griboedov, dramatist and diplomat

subjected existing literary tradition to critical review, thus establishing styles and intellectual preoccupations which set the pattern for their successors. Griboedov was a man of precocious and diverse talents. Born into the Moscow gentry, he took degrees in science and law, privately studied history and literature, and was known as a musician, an amateur of philosophy and a wit. Though intimately associated with Masonic and revolutionary circles, he enjoyed a brilliant career in the diplomatic service. Cleared of all suspicion that he had been indirectly involved in the Decembrist revolt, he was promoted and, after Russia's victory in the war with Persia (1828), led a mission to Tehran to enforce the peace treaty. An enraged mob stormed the Russian legation, and Griboedov was killed.

Griboedov wrote only one genuinely original work, the play *Woe from Wit* (no translation does justice to the multiple implications of the Russian *Gore ot uma*). Superficially a satire after the manner of Molière and D.I. Fonvizin (1744–92), it is at core a work of portentous philosophical purpose. The focus of the drama is its central figure, Chatsky, the size of whose role relative to the whole text is rivalled only by that of Hamlet. Chatsky is a Russian type, yet also a model of modern European man, as that man will be seen through nineteenth-century Russian eyes. A natural product of cultural evolution through the Renaissance, the Enlightenment and the incipient scientific-industrial age, Chatsky is characterized above all by *um* – intellectual idealism, a conviction that man can and will achieve, through the exercise of intellect, a perfect individual and social life. Griboedov charts the tragic destiny of this human type, from the initial sacrifice of his emotional world (expressed in Chatsky by his futile adoration of the heroine Sofia) to alienation from human society, madness and oblivion. The tragic consequences of a Promethean arrogance based on the power of human intellect were to be more fully explored by Lermontov, Tolstoy and Dostoevsky. A second important theme is touched upon, if lightly. Though the plight of Chatsky is not seen to be of specifically Western origin, much satirical play is made upon the pernicious mimicry of Western manners in Muscovite society; and Sofia falls victim to a sentimental idealism born of European literary fashion.

Woe from Wit is richly innovatory in other ways. Cutting a swathe through the rigid neo-classical concept of genre, it blends its central tragedy with high satirical comedy, though Griboedov's 'gallery of types' are always more absurd than vicious. In addition, the playwright moulds the disorderly rhythms of contemporary speech into a strict iambic metre. Thus, in its partial rejection of the rigid canons of neo-classicism, its absorption into literature of the currency of everyday speech, its exploration of the theme of intellectual man, and its study of a question of *bytie* (human destiny) within a context of *byt* (ordinary human life), it did much to trigger off the sustained literary explosion of the next century. None the less, Griboedov's achievements are overshadowed by those of his contemporary, Pushkin.   MHS

PUSHKIN

Kiprensky's portrait of Pushkin

Born into the landowning gentry, Aleksandr Pushkin (1799–1837) was educated at the Lyceum at Tsarskoe Selo and by the age of 20 had already acquired a considerable reputation as poet, rebel and rake. He was exiled in 1820 for his revolutionary and often blasphemous verse and epigrams, and thus preserved from direct involvement in the Decembrist revolt. In 1826 Tsar Nicholas I appointed himself Pushkin's 'patron', thus effectively putting the writer's movements, finances and the publication of his literature under official control. In 1834 Pushkin was appointed a 'gentleman of the chamber', a calculated slight devised by the tsar also as a means of ensuring the presence at court of Pushkin's beautiful but vacuous wife, Natal'ya. In 1837 Pushkin was lured into a duel in defence of his wife's honour and killed.

After a frivolous but witty exercise in mock-heroic (*Ruslan and Lyudmila*, 1820), Pushkin captured the attention of the Russian literary world with a series of narrative-descriptive poems on ostensibly Byronic themes. In *The Robber Brothers* (1821), *The Captive in the Caucasus* (1821) and *The Fountain of Bakhchisaray* (1822) he emulated perfectly the rich

A signed self-portrait by Pushkin

exoticism of Byron's Eastern poems: in mood and theme, however, Pushkin's poems constitute a deliberate rebuttal of Byronic Romanticism. Pushkin's quasi-Byronic figures embody not human freedom and unfettered individuality but their antithesis; they illustrate the internal and external factors (habit, passion, environment, history, nature) which limit the individual pursuit of freedom. *The Gypsies* (1824) summarizes Pushkin's scepticism: no man in any setting, wild or urban, is less un-free than the next, except he recognize that this is so, and thus find tranquillity. It also marks a final break with the Byronic manner. Its structure is a complex of narrative, description, song, dramatic dialogue and authorial observation. Its style is taut, stripped of ornamentation and packed with subtle parallels and ironies – clear indications of Pushkin's own mature voice.

Pushkin's novel in verse, *Yevgeny Onegin* (1823–30), is his most famous and influential work. Written over the whole central period of his literary career, it records and reflects in style, content and theme the process of maturation in Pushkin's art and outlook during those years. The heady effervescence of the first of its eight cantos (or chapters) gradually gives way to a more sombre and reflective manner. Its plot is slender; the novel is a complex experimental web of narrative, description and digression – a sustained discussion of the art of literature and a brilliant display of various poetic modes. While on one level *Yevgeny Onegin* can be seen as a metaphor of Pushkin's life as man and artist, of the tensions and processes at work within him, it treats also of vital Russian themes, notably the tension between East and West in Russian culture and the Russian psyche. The hero Yevgeny's essential Russian character is obscured by the assumed masks of an alien Western culture, absorbed in a second-hand form from the fashionable life of Petersburg. He is reduced ultimately to a pathetic wraith, knowing neither who he is nor what he feels. In counterpoint the heroine Tat'yana survives the transitory influence of European Sentimentalism, from which springs a youthful infatuation with Yevgeny; nourished by the good earth of rural Russia, she emerges as dignity and morality incarnate, the integrated personality at peace with itself and with the world.

Pushkin's only full-length play, *Boris Godunov* (1825), was modelled in broad approach, and also extensively in detail, upon Shakespeare. Combining elements of tragedy and history play, it has proved too concentrated and experimental an amalgam to function effectively on the stage. It is a study primarily of the ironies inherent in the movement of history, and of the illusoriness of freedom through power.

The so-called 'Little Tragedies' of 1830 (*Mozart and Salieri, The Feast at the Time of the Plague, The Covetous Knight, The Stone Guest*) and the unfinished *The Water Nymph* (1824–32) and *Scenes from the Days of Chivalry* (1831) are Pushkin's only other ventures into drama. The 'Little Tragedies' are concentrated experiments in the exposure of character and psychology through dialogue and soliloquy. They are replete with irony, and typical of Pushkin's art of saturating the text with meaning.

The narrative poem *The Bronze Horseman* (1833) is Pushkin's most perfect and mature display of poetic artistry; it also summarizes his complex view of the destiny of Russia and of individual man. The poem opens with a triumphant eulogy on the godlike figure of Peter the Great, who in his divine wisdom and in defiance of nature, built St Petersburg – a 'window into Europe', a fortress, and a city of beauty and delight. Petersburg is destiny: the triumphal prologue concludes with an exhortation to nature to reconcile itself with Peter's visionary creation. In the narrative section of the poem both nature – in the form of the river Neva – and man – in the form of a petty clerk – rebel. The river retreats: the petty clerk is driven to hallucination, madness and extinction. The poetry of *The Bronze Horseman* is rich in euphony, image, delicate epithet and hidden symmetry, and displays Pushkin's total mastery of a range of poetic styles.

In the late 1820s Pushkin recorded, in *Yevgeny Onegin* and elsewhere, his intention to shift from poetry to prose. Poetry was 'the language of feeling', associated with youth and romanticism: prose he called 'the language of thought' – of maturity and realism. Between 1830 and his death he wrote mostly in prose, and developed a uniquely laconic

Hermann threatens the Countess; a still from Yakov Protazanov's film The Queen of Spades, *1916*

A poem by Pushkin

The time has come, my friend! For rest my heart
                                    is asking.
The days fly fast away, each single hour takes
                                    off
A particle of being, but meanwhile you and I
Propose to live together . . . then all at once,
                                    we'll die.
There is no happiness here, but there is rest and
                                    freedom.
I've long been dreaming of an enviable fate —
Long since, a weary slave, I plotted my escape
To some far sanctuary of work and pure delight.

Aleksandr Pushkin, untitled fragment, 1834
Translated by G. S. Smith

and expressive prose style. His *Tales of Belkin* (1830) mocked the ornate cliché-ridden language and stereotyped characters of Romanticism and Sentimentalism, suggesting their total inappropriateness to Russian life, manners and literature. *The Queen of Spades* (1834) is a complex and intricate work whose central figure, Germann, in his obsessive pursuit of power through wealth and demonic egocentricity, foreshadows characters in Dostoevsky. *The Captain's Daughter* (1836), an historical romance after the manner of Walter Scott, is a masterpiece of stylistic economy.

Of all Pushkin's works his lyrics lend themselves least to translation. The dominant themes are love, friendship, poetry, the poetic vocation, reminiscence and the pursuit of tranquillity. His lyrics are noted above all for their precise laconic delineation of complex feeling, their absolute mastery of poetic euphony, their delicately interlocking imagery and their ability to elevate Pushkin's personal experience to one of general relevance and appeal.

Pushkin's writing also includes reworkings of traditional Russian folk literature, notably *The Tale of the Priest and his Workman Balda* (1830) and *Tsar Saltan* (1824–31); other genres of narrative verse – the heroic *Poltava* (1828), the anecdotal *Count Nulin* (1825) and the comic-realistic *The Little House in Kolomna* (1830); reviews, critiques and travel notes such as *A Journey to Arzrum* (1836) and historical studies. Pushkin is recognized, in Russia at least, as the outstanding genius of Russian letters. His genius expressed itself in the range of styles and genres in which he experimented, and his remarkable achievements in all of them; in his moulding of a rich expressive language for both verse and prose; in his establishment of motifs and themes which his successors would develop; and above all in his endowing Russian literature with a genuine and unique national identity. **MHS**

THE PUSHKIN PLEIAD

So dominant was the figure of Pushkin that a group of not inconsiderable poets of the same period have become known collectively as the 'Pushkin Pleiad' – a term which does less than justice to their individual talents. Baron A.A. Del'vig (1798–1831) is noted for the paucity of his output and the cold, formal brilliance of his verse. D.V. Davydov (1784–1839) wrote spirited verse predominantly on themes of warfare and debauch. Prince P.A. Vyazemsky (1792–1878), endowed with a superb gift for word-play, penned elegant rhymes on universal themes. K.F. Ryleev (1795–1826), executed as a ringleader in the Decembrist revolt, is known for his rousing and rebellious civic verse. Undoubtedly the brightest star in the Pleiad was Ye.A. Baratynsky (or Boratynsky: 1800–44). Much influenced by Pushkin, Baratynsky none the less developed a uniquely sonorous and compact poetic style, and achieved the difficult feat, rarely essayed by Pushkin, of converting the contemplation of abstract intellectual questions into pure poetry.   MHS

LERMONTOV

The tragedy of Pushkin's death sparked into life another remarkable literary talent – that of M. Yu. Lermontov (1814–41). The descendant of a seventeenth-century Scottish migrant, George Learmont, he was intellectual, vain and introspective by nature. He entered Moscow University at the age of sixteen but quickly abandoned formal study and joined the Guards, dissipating his energy in debauch-

Mikhail Yur'evich Lermontov in military uniform

ery, and his intellect largely in the compiling of obscene verse for the amusement of his comrades. Enraged by the death of Pushkin, he wrote a poem (*Death of a Poet*, 1837) inveighing against those corrupt forces in and around the court who had conspired in Pushkin's destruction. For this rhetoric Lermontov paid with a year's exile to the Caucasus. The episode was his salvation as a writer.

Before 1837 Lermontov's poetry (excluding the unprintable) was immature, imitatively Byronic and packed with the jumbled imagery and sentiments of conventional melancholic Romanticism. Only a few isolated pieces hinted at his potential as a major lyricist. Among them are *The Cup of Life* (1831), *Desire* (1831), *The Sail* (1832), *The Angel* (1832) and *As the Flame of a Falling Star at Night* (1832). His romantic melodrama *Masquerade* (1835) is important only in that its central figure foreshadowed Pechorin, the protagonist of his greatest work, *A Hero of our Time* (1840).

In the remaining four years of his life, Lermontov developed and displayed a startlingly original literary talent. Two narrative poems, dating back in early draft to 1829–30, were revised and completed (*The Demon*, 1839; *Mtsyri*, 1839). Purely Romantic in spirit, they are remarkable for the sustained richness of their style and for a strain of genuine feeling which contrasts brightly with the simplistic poses of the early lyrics. Lermontov's lyric poetry of the period 1837–41 is distinct from the earliest immature work in two fundamental ways: first, in its rapprochement with the real world – if the lyric hero is still persecuted and oppressed, it is now by identified forces in reality; secondly, in its rapprochement in style with the Pushkinian virtues of terseness, expressiveness and shape. Some outstanding examples are: *When the Yellow Cornfield Ripples* (1837), *I Do Not Wish the World to Know* (1837), *Meditation* (1838), *The Poet* (1838), *Trust Not Yourself* (1839), *The Cliff* (1841). He also experimented in other poetic genres, notably the martial ballad (*Borodino*, 1837) and the epic folk poem, such as *The Story of the Merchant Kalashnikov* (1837).

Lermontov's novel *A Hero of our Time*, generally regarded as his greatest work, continues the Pushkinian tradition of experimentation in the novel form, though the nature of Lermontov's experiment is unique. It is composed of five parts, all ostensibly modelled on such conventional prose genres as the Caucasian travel memoir and the diary: the chronology of events is shuffled and rearranged and the hub of the work, its hero Pechorin, is observed from various angles of view. This sophisticated structure is perfectly geared and subordinated to the book's main dynamic – a gradually sharpening focus on the character and psychology of the hero. The prose has all the clarity and delicacy of the mature lyrics, and Lermontov catches perfectly the respective 'voices' of his various narrators, from a simple army captain to his own introspective hero. The psychological make-up – and plight – of Pechorin marks a natural progression from Griboedov's Chatsky and Pushkin's Germann. Pechorin is a further model of modern man, whose inner life is so dominated by the power of analytical intellect that emotion is stifled, and human relationships are reduced to a deadly, one-sided game, conceived of and controlled by the mind. In Pechorin the tragic consequences of the tyranny of intellect over emotion and instinct are fully mapped. Acceptance of no external authority, moral, social, or divine, leads to ennui and the yearning for death. Pechorin admirably illustrates modern man's loss of wholeness, of oneness with the world. The proud Byronic hero is reduced, under realistic scrutiny, to a psychological cripple.   MHS

GOGOL'

Lermontov's death brought the Golden Age of Russian poetry to its end. For sixty years Russian literature was to be dominated by prose, especially the novel, while poetry and drama became secondary genres. The first great prose-writer to follow Lermontov was N.V. Gogol' (1809–52), who was born in Ukraine and moved to St Petersburg at the age of nineteen. Meditative, but profoundly ambitious, he was initially stunned by his failure to achieve instant success in either literature or the public service. Early collections of short stories, however, soon established him among the literary élite and, apart from a short-lived and generally disastrous spell as Professor of History at St Petersburg University in 1834–35, Gogol' thereafter devoted himself to literature. Encouraged by Pushkin, and lauded by, amongst others, the critic Belinsky and the emerging Slavophiles, he became obsessed not only by his art, but also by the sense of a divine vocation to purge Russia of its 'sins' and, through his works, lead it to salvation and the realization of its messianic destiny. Between 1836 and 1848 he resided in Rome, returning only periodically to Russia. Lapsing gradually into religious mysticism, he died a melancholic semi-recluse.

Gogol''s fiction falls into three categories: short stories, the novel Dead Souls and drama. His short stories comprise three cycles. Evenings on a Farm near Dikan'ka (1829–32), Mirgorod (1833–35) and the cycle conventionally titled 'Petersburg Tales' (1831–41). The Dikan'ka stories, based on Ukrainian folklore, are romantic in spirit and conjure up a world of rustic harmony, shared by men, nature and the forces of the supernatural. Outrageous fun

and Gothic horror merge in this version of a Slavonic Arcady. In Mirgorod to Arcady is added – in the story Taras Bul'ba – Gogol''s rose-tinted notion of an heroic Slavic past, when Cossack heroes of Homeric stature rode out in defence of Orthodoxy against the infidel Pole. But this idyll of rural and historic Russia is already tainted by the destructive forces which characterize modernity. In The Old-World Landowners the harmonious existence in nature of two old people is based on mere gluttony. Later, their rustic paradise is swiftly reduced to ruin by the incursion of alien urban forces, in the form of a wastrel heir and lackadaisical trustees. Even the spiritual and familial unity of the Cossacks in Taras Bul'ba is undermined by the forces of materialistic greed and sexuality. The magnificently mock-heroic The Tale of How Ivan Ivanovich Quarrelled with Ivan Nikiforovich (The Two Ivans) is in perfect counterpoint to Taras Bul'ba, revealing in already finished form Gogol''s nightmare vision of the degeneracy of modern man. Where the Cossacks rode shoulder to shoulder against the common foe, the two Ivans quarrel even unto death over some knick-knack or trifling insult and pursue their feud through petty litigation. It is a drab, disheartening world – but for Gogol' a rich source of comic invention. The grotesquely comic mock-epic manner of The Two Ivans clearly foreshadows his prose masterpiece Dead Souls.

The 'Petersburg Tales' expose the full nightmare of modern urban life which so terrified the mystic and prophet in Gogol' yet, paradoxically, so richly nourished his fertile artistic imagination. Wit, fantasy, absurdity and the grotesque flourish in such tales as The Nose and The Notes of a Madman, while in Nevsky Prospekt and The Portrait art and the artist are shown as specific and vulnerable targets of the demonic forces of corruption. The Overcoat describes an hilariously squalid petty clerk, who is lured to destruction by the dream of a new coat – this dream being rich in Freudian undertones. The wretched hero returns in phantom shape after death to take his vengeance on the city. The 'Petersburg Tales' are replete with a surrealistic fantasy which not only expresses Gogol''s view of a demon-ridden urban world but simultaneously allows him to take his vengeance upon it.

A recurrent theme in Gogol''s stories is the conflict between noble dream (of man or artist) and base reality. The motif of dream is modified and redeployed in his theatrical masterpiece The Government Inspector (1836). Khlestakov, a rascally non-entity, while passing through a symbolically anonymous provincial town, is taken by the town officials to be a government inspector incognito. Both Khlestakov and the mayor are dreamers, but their dreams are of power, rank and wealth – the

Gogol' in 1841

ignoble dreams of vulgar men. The mayor's dream is compounded by nightmare visions of retribution for the sins of corruption. Gogol' creates a situation where the dreams of the various parties collide to complement and foster each other. The bubble finally bursts: Khlestakov melts away to perform his mischief elsewhere. To the discomfiture of the mayor is added that of the audience, whose sense of well-being, induced by their privileged knowledge, is shattered in the last act by a series of devices which turn the stage into a mirror. Gogol''s play has no equal in Russian for the sustained brilliance of its comic inventiveness.

In *The Two Ivans* and *The Government Inspector* the didactic and artistic impulses in Gogol' are perfectly in tune; the inevitable rift between them occurred in his greatest literary project – the novel *Dead Souls*. His intention was to write a three-part novel akin to Dante's *Divine Comedy*. Part I ('Inferno') is complete. Only fragments of Part II remain, Gogol' having burned the original completed draft in 1846. Part III was never written.

If the original project was based on Dante, it is the influence of Homer which pervades Part I – the novel as we now have it. As in *The Two Ivans* the essential manner is mock-epic: indeed, in broad structure Gogol''s *poema* is a splendidly ironic replica of *The Odyssey*. His anti-hero Chichikov roams the world of provincial Russia, driven by the single force of greed. He encounters all manner of half-monsters and half-men – Russian landowners, from whom he would buy dead serfs. His notion is to pawn them before the next census officially registers their death. The style is a travesty of the epic manner. The trivial, the base, the vulgar become objects for detailed and fantastical description; the utterly banal is treated as though it were the infinitely noble. Meanwhile, in a series of lyrical digressions, in which the figure of Gogol' himself, prophet and teacher, looms large, a vision of the 'real' Russia is evoked, a land bright with colour, enriched by a tongue superior to all others and endowed with a messianic destiny among the nations of the world. Gogol''s voice is rarely absent from the work. Like Sterne and Pushkin, Gogol' for ever intrudes upon the text, manipulating, commenting, even merging here and there, in a sort of masochistic glee, with the wretched Chichikov himself. The all-pervasive theme of sin, purgation, salvation and the realization of a divinely ordained destiny pertain always as much to the writer as to his native land. There is no cause to lament the absence of the second and third parts of the novel. Part I of *Dead Souls* is a perfect expression of the whole, integrated Gogol'. His mischievous artistic imagination is wonderfully excited by the 'Inferno' of reality, which the teacher in him abhors. Part II, one senses, was

The critic Vissarion Belinsky

written predominantly by the teacher and committed to the fire by the artist.

As though to replace Part III, Gogol' wrote *Selections from a Correspondence with Friends* (1847), a publicistic work in epistolary form. Seemingly in a last effort to discover within contemporary Russia the seeds of his imagined Slavonic Utopia, Gogol' here heaps praise on (among other things) Russian Orthodoxy, literature, women and the paternalistic autocratic-feudal society. The tone of the piece is at once coyly self-castigatory and unrelentingly didactic. This melancholy victory of teacher over artist offers interesting parallels with the later part of Tolstoy's career.   MHS

BELINSKY

The 1840s can be seen as a transitional period in the evolution of Russian literature. It is marked, first, by the emergence of four writers – Goncharov, Turgenev, Dostoevsky and Tolstoy – whose mature work would compose the great age of the Russian realistic novel; second, by the full flowering of the dispute between Slavophiles and Westernists on the future cultural and historical evolution of Russia; and third, by the career of the critic V.G. Belinsky (1811–48). A *raznochinets* (an educated man of the 'middle', non-gentry, class), he had a vital and enduring effect upon Russian literary attitudes, largely through his critical reviews published in the journals *Notes of the Fatherland* and *The Contemporary* during the 1840s. Acknowledged as the leader of progressive Westernist thought, he asserted that literature must be realistic in manner, relevant to the problems of real life and inspired by progressive socio-political ideas. Having mistakenly assumed that Gogol''s work was motivated above all by an abhorrence of Russia's social and political institutions, he reacted to *Selections from a Correspondence with Friends* with the famous *Letter to Gogol'* (1847) in which he scathingly rebuked his former idol for ostensibly betraying their shared ideals. Belinsky's conception of literature as primarily a vehicle for the expression of 'civic' ideas became deeply embedded in intellectual attitudes towards literature for the remainder of the nineteenth century and found further, more radical, expression in the works of N.G. Chernyshevsky (1828–89) and N.A. Dobrolyubov (1836–61). It was Belinsky too who through his critical columns welcomed into literature the great prose writers of the future – Turgenev, Goncharov and Dostoevsky.   MHS

TURGENEV

I.S. Turgenev (1818–83) was born of gentry stock. Educated in Moscow, St Petersburg and Berlin, he

Repin's portrait of Ivan Turgenev

travelled extensively in Europe and was a lifelong admirer of European art and culture. His first literary success came with the publication of *A Hunter's Notes* (1847–52). This collection of sketches of peasant life, manners and character, superficially dispassionate, yet profoundly compassionate, was impressive not just for its lyricism of style, elegance of composition and delicate characterization, but also for its treatment of the peasantry as human beings in their own right. Turgenev was lionized by the progressive Westernist faction, who quite overlooked the work's underlying mood of Romantic pessimism. This fatalistic philosophy, which saw man as the hapless and impotent plaything of nature, was the dominant force shaping the lives of men throughout Turgenev's writings: it is explicitly expounded in such diverse pieces as *A Journey to Poles'e* (1857) and the *Senilia* (or *Poems in Prose*, 1879–83).

Turgenev subsequently worked almost exclusively in the genres of *povest'* (novella) and novel. In both, his central preoccupation is always the delineation of human character. The love story, upon which the Turgenev plot is most commonly built, is never an end in itself, but only an instrument by means of which the characters of the individuals concerned may be more penetratingly explored.

Turgenev's prose is carefully wrought, yet remarkably at ease, striking a mean between the stark economy of Pushkin and the uninhibited effusiveness of Gogol'. It has measure, clarity and balance; it is the most natural of all Russian styles.

Outstanding among the *povesti* are *A Quiet Spot* (1854), *Asya* (1858), *First Love* (1860), *The Torrents of Spring* (1872) and *A King Lear of the Steppe* (1870).

In his novels, Turgenev sets his study of human fate and human types within the context of contemporary Russian affairs. Having suggested, in the essay *Hamlet and Don Quixote* (1860), a polarity in human type between 'Hamlets' – introspective, inactive egoists – and 'Don Quixotes' – extrovert altruists – he set out in the novels to measure figures from the contemporary Russian landscape against these two archetypes. The result is curious. The essentially Quixotic type, whom Turgenev lauded in his essay as a force for progress, is revealed in *On the Eve* (1860) as humourless, wooden and damned; the arrogant assumption of the hero, Insarov, that he can change the world is punished by nature through death from disease. The predominantly Hamlet types (Rudin in the novel of the same name, 1856; Lavretsky in *A Nest of Gentlefolk*, 1859) talk and dream, but risk no active challenge to the fates. Rudin's 'heroic' death upon the 1848 Paris barricades is in fact no more than a final act of submission. If the Hamlets, by and large, survive, it is because they instinctively know what Turgenev knows – that any human challenge to that order and equilibrium established by nature, be it in the form of political commitment or the pursuit of a great love, will bring certain retribution.

Turgenev's greatest novel, *Fathers and Sons* (1862), is notable above all for its superbly tragic hero, Bazarov. Modelled upon the scientifically-minded and materialistic 'nihilists' of the 1860s, Bazarov utters a Promethean challenge to nature, but discovering within himself natural forces of instinct and emotion which defy intellectual analysis and control, he is reduced to woeful contemplation of his own triviality and to an acceptance of death as an act of reconciliation. *Fathers and Sons* surpasses Turgenev's other novels not only in its hero, but also in its finely worked narrative structure and its freedom from a 'Turgenevan heroine' – that insipidly Victorian epitome of integrity and morality which, introduced to throw his male figures into darker relief, mars the earlier works.

Harassed by critics of all political persuasions who could not, or would not, see that his novels were studies in human character, not political doctrine, the novelist himself finally succumbed. His last novels *Smoke* (1867) and *Virgin Soil* (1877) sank beneath a burden of talk on contemporary issues, and blatant authorial prejudice.

Apart from such pieces as *The Torrents of Spring* and *A King Lear of the Steppe* the last twenty years of his life were a period of decline. Turgenev died in France in 1883. MHS

GONCHAROV

I.A. Goncharov (1812–91) was the son of a provincial merchant, and followed a career in government service, much of it as an official censor. Apart from the travel memoir *The Frigate Pallada*, written after an uncomfortable trip to Japan in 1854, and a few minor prose pieces, his work was limited to three novels, upon which he worked in desultory fashion for a total of nearly thirty years.

The first, *An Ordinary Story* (1847), returns to the Griboedovan theme of the conflict between ideals and reality, and traces in its hero the inevitable transition from youthful idealism to the sober and practical attitudes of later life. The third novel, *The Precipice* (1869), is marred by the intrusion of crotchety authorial attitudes, a schematic story line and wooden treatment of character. Like Turgenev's late novels, it is the work of a writer in decline.

Goncharov's fame rests almost exclusively on his second novel, *Oblomov* (1849–59), the eponymous hero of which has achieved almost mythic status. Oblomov is the eternal dreamer, adrift in a real world which does not answer to his dream. Ensconced in his flat within the dizzy modern world of St Petersburg, Oblomov nurtures his half-remembered, half-imagined dream of a provincial Russian Arcady.

Totally transcending its immediate context, Oblomov's dream represents the eternal yearning of man for the Golden Age, and of the adult for the innocent and secure world of childhood – both refuges from a threatening world. Resisting the efforts of Shtol'ts (Stolz), a symbolically half-German man of affairs, who attempts fruitlessly to stir Oblomov from his contemplative torpor, and the attentions of Ol'ga, a girl who loves in him not what he is, but what she can make of him, Oblomov finally discovers a surrogate for his dream in the undemanding love and care offered him by the plump widow Pshenitsyna. His tranquil death is likened to the running-down of a clock, which someone has forgotten to wind.

The central theme of *Oblomov* has a long literary pedigree. What distinguishes Goncharov's treatment of it is above all the delicate and sustained irony with which the author treats his hero, and his hero's dream. If Goncharov recognizes the undying appeal of the dream, he also recognizes its hopelessness. Yet the overall rhythm of the novel reinforces that concept of time which lies at the basis of Oblomov's vision of existence: time is the rhythm of the seasons and of the geological evolution of the planet, not the dash of modern man to change the world before he dies. The emblematic quality of Oblomov is unrivalled even by the great characters of Dostoevsky.   MHS

Ivan Goncharov

DOSTOEVSKY

The son of a Moscow doctor, F.M. Dostoevsky (1821–81) achieved instant fame in 1845 with his first novel *Poor Folk*. In the next four years he completed *The Double* (1846), *The Landlady* (1847), *White Nights* (1848) and a considerable volume of shorter pieces. Throughout the 1840s Dostoevsky dabbled in radical politics. In 1849 he was arrested for his association with the socialist group known as the Petrashevsky circle (from its founder, the political dissident M.V. Butashevich-Petrashevsky), and sentenced to eight years' imprisonment and exile – though not before having been subjected to a traumatic mock execution, staged by the tsarist authorities. He returned to St Petersburg only in 1859.

Of his early pieces, *Poor Folk* is notable primarily for its sentimentally sympathetic treatment of the downtrodden and its grotesquely naturalistic manner; *The Double*, for its introduction of the theme of the divided personality; and the unfinished *Netochka Nezvanova* (1849), for the first appearance of another notable Dostoevskyan type – the demonically wilful 'infernal' woman.

After Siberia Dostoevsky quickly re-established his literary reputation with *The Humiliated and the Insulted* (1861), a novel highly reminiscent of his 'philanthropic' works of the 1840s, and *Notes from the House of the Dead* (1861–62), an account of his period of penal servitude, which, apart from its vivid descriptions of criminal types, gave first expression to two ideas which were to find an important place in his later thought: first, that sin can be punished and expiated only by conscience; secondly, that the intelligentsia must re-establish their bond with the people and with the 'soil' of Russia.

Dostoevsky's outlook had, indeed, undergone a fundamental change. Abandoning his previous Westernist and progressive sympathies, he now propounded a mystic and conservative Slavophilism. A visit to Europe in 1862–63 strengthened his conviction that Russia must resist the insidious influence of European culture and civilization, based on atheism and materialism. The years from 1860 to 1864 were a period of personal crises. His first marriage, contracted in Siberia, had broken down. A passionate affair with Apollinaria Suslova in 1862–63 and heavy losses in her company at the roulette tables of Europe were followed in 1864 by the deaths of his wife and his beloved brother Mikhail (with whom he had co-edited the ill-fated journals *Time* and *The Epoch*), and finally by bankruptcy.

During the remaining seventeen years of his life Dostoevsky proceeded to write a series of works which have made a unique contribution to the world's literature of ideas. Their starting point was the extraordinary *Notes from Underground* (1864).

Written in first-person 'confessional' form, *Notes from Underground* is ostensibly an attack, in the name of individual liberty and freedom of the will, upon all scientific, rational and materialistic theories of man. The result is paradox. The anonymous 'Underground Man' argues his case against reason *by* reason. Perversely he asserts that man's best interest lies in demonstrating his inalienable freedom by going against his best interests. The result is total unfreedom – symbolized by the wretched bolt-hole from which he speaks – inertia, alienation, and the certainty that all he can believe is that he does not know what he believes. The key to his plight, never overtly stated, is hinted at in the figure of a prostitute, Liza, who responds to his malicious taunting with a display of selfless, unthinking humility.

Dostoevsky's first classic novel *Crime and Punishment* (1865–66) expands the themes of *Notes from Underground*. Its hero, Raskol'nikov, commits a murder apparently in the name of rational altruism. Subsequently, a deeper motive is revealed – demonic self-will, based not upon love, but upon absolute contempt for his fellow men. These apparently contradictory impulses within a single man are explained by Dostoevsky in terms of a sinister interconnection. Socialistic theory, based on 'enlightened self-interest' or 'rational utilitarianism' is no more than a mask for tyranny. As for the Underground Man, so for Raskol'nikov, redemption is promised through the agency of a prostitute, Sonya, representing the force of faith, humility and self-abnegation.

In 1867 Dostoevsky married his secretary, Anna Snitkina; under her stabilizing influence he gradually rid himself of gambling fever and debt. Driven abroad by dunning creditors in 1867, he was able to return to Russia in 1871. Meanwhile, under intense financial pressure, he had produced two more great novels, *The Idiot* (1868) and *The Devils* (1871).

In Prince Myshkin, the hero of *The Idiot*, Dostoevsky attempted to incarnate those Christian virtues of humility, selflessness and altruistic love previously outlined in the figures of Liza and Sonya. Myshkin, introduced into a corrupt Petersburg world dominated by the evil forces of materialism and lust, proves neither sufficiently human nor sufficiently divine to affect the hearts and minds of those whom he would save. As Myshkin finally lapses into insanity, Dostoevsky, playing the devil's advocate as always with disturbing ease, traces unerringly the inevitable victory of darkness over light.

In *The Idiot* Dostoevsky more clearly than ever before defined the opposing forces battling for the soul of Russia. At the devil's elbow stood the forces of West European culture and civilization – atheism, urbanism, materialism, rationalism, rampant individualism, and the twin systems of political tyranny – socialism and Roman Catholicism. On the side of Holy Russia were faith ('the Russian Christ'), *narodnost'* (a spirit of oneness with the simple masses) and *sobornost'* (the innate, instinctive and religiously-based communistic spirit of the Russian people). Russia, he believed, must pass through suffering to salvation and thence to the fulfilment of its messianic destiny among the nations of the world.

In *The Devils* Dostoevsky considers the battle primarily on its political front. The devils of the title are nihilists who threaten to infect Russia with the virus of materialistic socialism. The novel is rich in exotic and terrifying characters, embodying various aspects of Dostoevsky's nightmare vision of the fate of modern man, who, rejecting faith, would arrogantly elevate himself to Man-God status.

Dostoevsky's last great novel, *The Brothers Karamazov* (1880), concludes and summarizes the cycle. In the various members of the Karamazov family the writer presents a composite picture of the body, mind and soul of contemporary Russia and of the forces at work within it. Their common heritage – 'Karamazovism' – represents a phenomenal energy, which can find its expression equally in insatiable lust, demonic amoralism, intellectual scepticism, or in faith, humility and love.

The four great novels are all intensely dramatic in form. The narrative itself is rich in the stuff of melodrama – passion, murder, suicide – but the essential drama lies elsewhere, either in the conflict between different characters embodying opposing

Right. Dostoevsky in 1880

Right. *Tolstoy as a volunteer officer in the Caucasus, 1854*

ideas, or in the internal conflict raging within the divided individual. This drama of ideas is enacted primarily through talk: dialogue between characters or within a single character, or the direct exposition of idea or theory. Melodramatic incident and dramatic dialogue, combined with elements of outrageous humour, move the novels along at a frenetic pace against a background of seamy contemporary life. There are no easy resolutions; the Dostoevskian novel concludes in uncertainty.

Other important works of the later period are *The Eternal Husband* (1870), *The Adolescent* (1875) and *A Writer's Diary* which, published in serial form from 1876, was a primarily publicistic work devoted to the promulgation of the writer's increasingly conservative views.

A career begun in debt and despair ended in domestic happiness, financial stability and fame. Having achieved a new pinnacle of public acclaim with his famous address on the occasion of the unveiling of a statue to Pushkin in Moscow in 1880, Dostoevsky died in 1881. His funeral procession was followed by thousands.   MHS

TOLSTOY

The 'wholeness' of nineteenth-century Russian literature is in no way better illustrated than by the remarkable similarities in basic outlook between Dostoevsky and his great contemporary Tolstoy – two men who, astonishingly, never met, and who in social origin, temperament, life-style and attitudes towards literature could barely have had less in common.

L.N. Tolstoy (1828–1910) was an aristocrat by nature as he was by origin. Orphaned by the age of seven, he none the less enjoyed a secure and contented childhood. He entered university at the age of sixteen; at nineteen he dropped out, and returned to the family estate of Yasnaya Polyana to conduct an abortive experiment in rural reform. Four years in Moscow and St Petersburg pursuing the pleasures of the flesh were followed by military service as a volunteer in the Caucasus.

His first work of fiction was experimental and ambitious. In *The Diary of Yesterday* (1851), which survives as an unfinished fragment, Tolstoy set out to record every single thought, feeling, word and action in one day of its narrator-hero's life. The personal diary which Tolstoy kept intermittently from 1847 also offers many clues to his subsequent personal and literary development. In terms of its sustained and penetrative analysis of (his own) character, interspersed with passages of philosophical rumination, it is a characteristic piece.

In 1852 Tolstoy dispatched from the Caucasus to N.A. Nekrasov, editor of the journal *The Contem-*

porary, a semi-fictional memoir of childhood. Its success was instantaneous. *Childhood*, together with its two sequels *Adolescence* (1854) and *Youth* (1857), is a seminal work for the understanding of Tolstoy's literature; here in embryonic form is the essence of his thought and literary art. It is first a fiction based upon, and tied to, personal experience; but above all it is a work dominated by the image of the child and the child's view. In *Childhood* Tolstoy sings the innocence of childhood, its instinctive moral virtue, emotional spontaneity, blissful security from intellectual introspection (and thus from the 'accursed questions' of existence) and the sexual instinct. All later theories of 'simplification' stem from this. At the same time the child's view, translated into literary art, becomes the very basis of Tolstoy's method in his fictional and non-fictional works alike. It is the simple, direct and innocent view, untouched by prejudice or conventional attitude, uninhibited by delicacy or deference, untainted by manners: its moral basis is that of instinct and conscience alone. It is experimental in that it recognizes no constraints of convention on form: it simply says what it wants to say in the way it feels it can best be said.

Adolescence and *Youth* mark the fall from innocence. Contact with the world of men, the awakening of intellect and sexuality, the competitive urge, all conspire to erode and destroy that perfect image of man embodied in the child. Tolstoy's subsequent career would be largely devoted to a pursuit of the means by which the grown man may rediscover the perfect goodness and innocence of the child, and so be liberated from the spectres of evil and death.

The many short prose works which Tolstoy wrote in the following ten years are consistently experimental and informed by an irreverent and iconoclastic attitude towards the form and topics of conventional literature. At the same time they amply illustrate a central Tolstoyan paradox. Tolstoy attempts to reduce man and human experience to a series of intellectually conceived and perceived rules, principles and categories, doing so through the profoundly intellectual medium of art. Simultaneously, however, he identifies intellect – man's consciousness of himself and the world – as the very bane of existence, debarring man from assimilation into life, moral virtue, and the acceptance of death. Not for nothing did Tolstoy wear a medallion of Rousseau round his neck.

In *The Raid* (1853), *The Wood Felling* (1855) and *Sevastopol' Sketches* (1855–56) Tolstoy subjects to scathing scrutiny conventional attitudes towards war, courage and the Caucasus, glorifying the unconscious and unsung bravery of the peasant soldier at the expense of the sham heroics of the educated officer class. In such blatantly 'moral' tales as *Notes of a Billiard Marker* (1853–55), *Two Hussars* (1856), *Lucerne* (1857), *Albert* (1858), *Three Deaths* (1858), *Polikushka* (1862) and *Kholstomer* (1863, published 1885) he consistently contrasts the vanity and immorality of civilized, intellectual – and frequently Western – man with the instinctive nobility and morality of 'simple' man, or (in a typically Tolstoyan *reductio ad absurdum*) of a horse or a tree. Simultaneously, the eighteenth-century technique of discovering truth by exposing reality to the unprejudiced and innocent eye is developed by Tolstoy to sometimes extraordinary lengths. Thus *Sevastopol' in December* is conducted in the second-person mode (Tolstoy tells you not what *he* sees, but what *you* see), while in *Kholstomer* human behaviour is observed by a horse.

Family Happiness (1859), written partly as an apology for Tolstoy's sterile flirtation with one Valeria Arsen'eva, is an analysis of the slow but ineluctable transformation of a marriage relationship between a young girl and an older man. Seen entirely from the point of view of the girl, it is a fine example of Tolstoy's ability to 'transfer' himself into a fictional character.

The Cossacks (1862), ostensibly another critical examination of the back-to-nature theme, sets its introspective hero Olenin amidst a Cossack tribe who live by purest instinct. The central embodiment of 'simple' virtue, the old hunter Yeroshka embraces a view of man and nature which transcends conventional morality. Lust and murder, in so far as they are part of a natural 'instinctive' existence, are not to be condemned. Olenin expresses a fundamental

Tolstoyan dilemma. Striving consciously to emulate the natural virtue of the Cossacks, he is forced ultimately to recognize that no man can think himself into a state of virtue.

Having twice travelled to Western Europe, in 1857 and 1860–61, and seen nothing to please him, Tolstoy determined never to go again. In 1862 he married, and, blissfully ensconced at Yasnaya Polyana, set to writing *War and Peace*.

This work traces the interlocking fates of individuals and Russia itself during the turbulent years of the Napoleonic wars. Its central heroes, Andrey Bolkonsky and Pierre Bezukhov, are largely projections of Tolstoy himself and of his struggle to understand the meaning and purpose of his existence, while the heroine Natasha Rostova is Tolstoy's most perfect incarnation of his ideal of innocent simplicity. *War and Peace* brought to full fruition all the promise of Tolstoy's early works, and pushed forward the frontiers of the novel form to a degree matched only perhaps by Sterne's *Tristram Shandy*. Combining elements of the family chronicle, the historical epic, the novel of ideas and the fictionalized autobiography, it is a superb expression of the whole Tolstoy, both man and artist, and of the paradoxes within him. Describing life and historical event with the apparently beguiling objectivity of an innocent, it does so constantly in order to persuade. Proclaiming the primacy of the simple and uncultured over the civilized and the intellectual, it draws its characters almost exclusively from the upper echelons of Russian society. It denounces art, while superbly displaying Tolstoy's total command of literary artifice. Debunking conventional interpretations of history, it finds no better explanation for history than blind determinism, and tampers with historical fact

Right. Ivan Kramskoy's portrait of Tolstoy in middle age

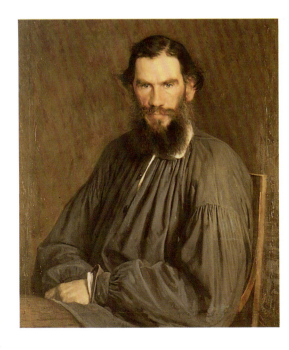

Right. *Tolstoy sets out on his last journey, 1910*

From *Anna Karenina*

Her thirst for life, increased by her physical recovery, was so strong and her circumstances were so new and pleasant that Anna felt unforgivably happy. The more she got to know Vronsky, the more she loved him. She loved him for himself and for his love for her. Possessing him completely was a constant joy for her . . . In everything he said, thought, and did, she saw something specially noble and elevated. Her rapture often made her afraid; she looked for, but could not find, anything that was not beautiful. She dared not reveal to him her sense of her mediocrity compared to him. She thought that he, seeing this, might well stop loving her; and there was nothing she feared so much now, although she had no reason at all to do so . . . He was such a masculine person, but towards her not only did he not go against his own will, but he had no will, and seemed to be occupied only with anticipating her desires . . .

Vronsky, meanwhile, notwithstanding the complete fulfilment of everything he had desired for so long, was not completely happy. He soon came to feel that the fulfilment of his desires had given him only one particle of the mountain of happiness he had anticipated. This fulfilment seemed to him to be the eternal mistake that people make when they think that happiness is getting what you want . . . In his heart he soon felt the desire for desires, ennui. Despite his intuition, he began grasping at every passing caprice, taking it for desire and aim . . . just as a hungry animal grabs at everything that comes its way, so Vronsky completely unconsciously grabbed at politics, new books, pictures.

Lev Tolstoy, *Anna Karenina* (Part 2, ch. VIII) 1877
Translated by G.S. Smith

as suits its purpose. It is the crystalline accuracy with which Tolstoy creates his illusion of human experience which makes the book so persuasive. Absorbed by its detail, we are induced to overlook the fallibility of its broad assertions. And when it is overtly polemical, it is brilliantly so: Tolstoy tears down with arrogant ease the idols of received ideas.

In *War and Peace* Tolstoy came as close as he ever did to persuading himself that the key to life's mystery was within his, and our, grasp. It lay in the absorption of the individual, and of human consciousness, into the stuff of 'simple' life – birth, marriage, procreation, the domestic round, tilling the earth. But like all of his 'solutions', it represented not so much an answer to the 'accursed questions', as a means of attaining that blissful state (akin to early childhood) when the questions never arise.

Anna Karenina (1873–77) demonstrates clearly the fragility of the solutions suggested in *War and*

Peace. Tolstoy's second great novel is his most honest work and his least conclusive. The optimism of *War and Peace* gives way to despondency. Death – an event of mystic grandeur in *War and Peace* – is now seen as ugly and bewildering.

Conceived originally as a tale of sin and expiation, the novel expanded to take a broader, balanced view of its adulterous heroine, Anna, and to incorporate a contrapuntal story – that of Levin, a Russian landowner, whose search for happiness and the meaning of life has (like that of Andrey and Pierre) its base in Tolstoy's own experience. Like *War and Peace*, *Anna Karenina* is a superbly organized novel, built upon the interlocking stories of Anna and Levin, two fundamentally different, yet in some ways curiously similar, characters, each dedicated to the pursuit of individual fulfilment. The novel is rich too in its treatment of a host of contemporary social and political issues, the discussion of which is more closely integrated into the text than were the philosophical digressions in *War and Peace*.

In certain ways *Anna Karenina* foreshadows two of the major works of Tolstoy's later years – *A Confession* (1882) and *What is Art?* (1897). The years during which he was working on the novel were a period of personal crisis too. The steady deterioration of his relationship with his wife made family life a less reliable refuge from the 'accursed questions'. Several deaths in his family reminded him forcibly of his own mortality. More convinced than ever of the futility of a rational approach to life's mystery, Tolstoy took the leap into faith:

characteristically, however, the faith he now proclaimed was rebellious, intensely personal and, for all its intuitive base, developed and pursued with a dogged rationalism. *A Confession* is the dramatic account of Tolstoy's 'conversion' to a Christianity stripped of ritual and dogma, founded upon, and perceived through, the dictates of conscience.

What is Art?, worked on by Tolstoy over a long period before publication, represents the writer's final view of the nature and function of art. It is a typically Tolstoyan treatise – perverse, mischievous, iconoclastic, brilliantly destructive, numbering Shakespeare, Pushkin and Homer among its many victims. Its central thesis is that art must be simple, accessible to all men, and must infect those who experience it with good and moral feelings.

The major part of Tolstoy's work during the last thirty years of his life consists of efforts to fulfil, through fiction and treatise, the dictates of *A Confession* and *What is Art?*. Outstanding among the fiction of the period are *The Death of Ivan Il'ich* (1886), *Master and Man* (1895), *Hadzhi Murat* (1896–1904), and two treatments of the theme of sexuality, *The Kreutzer Sonata* (1889) and *The Devil* (1889). Tolstoy also experimented in drama, notably in *The Power of Darkness* (1887) and *The Fruits of Enlightenment* (1889).

As Tolstoy's fame and following spread throughout the world, his home became a place of pilgrimage. Although he was excommunicated by the Orthodox Church for his 'heresies' in 1901, Tolstoy's reputation saved him from governmental persecution. His domestic life, however, was reduced to endless series of quarrels and recriminations. In autumn of 1910 he fled his home, and shortly afterwards died at the wayside railway station of Astapovo.   MHS

POETRY AND DRAMA

For half a century or so the thunder of the great novelists almost completely obliterated the gentler sounds of poetry. Yet two fine lyric poets, Tyutchev and Fet, were at work throughout this period; and it is not surprising that they owe their present high reputation not to their contemporaries, but to their 're-discovery' by the poets and critics of the early twentieth century.

F.I. Tyutchev (1803–73) came of noble stock and spent most of his adult life as a diplomat abroad. His early poetry is predominantly of a philosophical nature, grandiloquent, elegant, replete with archaisms and expressing a metaphysical system based largely on ideas of the German Romantics. In later life he wrote political verse expressing his increasingly reactionary Slavophile views. His finest achievement is his love poetry, and in particular the darkly passionate verses inspired by his liaison with E.A. Denis'eva, his children's governess.

A.A. Fet (real name Shenshin: 1820–92) is very much a 'poet's poet'. The range and depth of feeling, the sensitivity to nature and human emotion achieved in his poetry totally belied the staid, strait-laced exterior which he presented to the world. Richly metaphorical, saturated in feeling, exquisitely euphonic, his verse is sometimes philosophical, more commonly a pure celebration of love, nature or the poetic muse.

Neither Tyutchev nor Fet found much favour among the critics of their day, who saw literature's function as no more than the propagation of progressive ideas. The only civic themes in Tyutchev's poetry were mystic and reactionary. Fet, himself a political conservative, totally eschewed such unpoetic themes. The third major poet of the period,

Left to right: *Tyutchev, Repin's portrait of Fet, and Nekrasov*

Left to right: Ostrovsky, Kramskoy's portrait of Saltykov-Shchedrin, Leskov in the early 1880s

N.A. Nekrasov (1821–77), combined an ambitious, self-indulgent and snobbish character with a radical political credo, which found consistent expression in his verse. Though frequently lapsing into sentimentality or rhetoric, his verses on the Russian people, the poverty of their lives and the richness of their spirit, are sincerely felt and expressed with often formidable power. His finest works, *Red-Nosed Frost* (1863) and the unfinished *Who Can Live Happily in Russia?* (1863–77) draw widely on the motifs and the manner of folk poetry, and are among the finest celebrations of the 'simple people' in Russian literature.

Drama in the mid-century succumbed almost entirely to the dominance of the novel. Only two native dramatists made any significant contribution to the repertory of the Russian stage – A.V. Sukhovo-Kobylin (1817–1903) and A.N. Ostrovsky (1823–86). Both were primarily satirists, and interest in their work has diminished with time. Of Sukhovo-Kobylin's three plays, *Krechinsky's Wedding* (1855) has survived on the strength of a superbly contrived comic plot. Ostrovsky wrote some fifty plays: a handful are still staged, notably *The Thunderstorm* (1859) and *The Forest* (1871). These two plays owe their survival to the playwright's success in grafting the conflict between moral and sexual instinct on to a satirical treatment of purely contemporary types.   MHS

LESSER PROSE WRITERS

M.Ye. Saltykov (pseudonym Shchedrin: 1826–89) wrote mainly in a genre falling midway between fiction and pamphlet. His *History of a Certain Town* (1869–70) is a microcosmic parody of Russian history, disguised as the chronicle of a small town. *Provincial Sketches* (1856–57), *Gentlemen of Tashkent* (1869–72) and similar pieces suffer from an excess of topical allusions and an 'Aesopic' language,

devised to foil the censorship, which reduce their accessibility to the modern reader. Saltykov's outstanding work is *The Golovlev Family* (1872–76), which traces the decay of a family of provincial landowners, ultimately destroyed by their own greed, bestiality and hypocrisy. It is a powerful but unrelievedly depressing study in human decadence.

N.S. Leskov (1831–95) is an original talent who has found little honour in his own land. A *raznochinets* (educated man of the 'middle', non-gentry, class) by birth, he acquired a profound first-hand knowledge of the manners, culture and language of the provincial masses. His career in literature began badly with two long novels, *No Way Forward* (1864) and *At Daggers Drawn* (1870–71), which alienated the critics by their overtly hostile treatment of the young radicals.

Cathedral Folk (1872) is one of his finest works. A 'chronicle' centred upon a study of the provincial clergy, it is a marvellous compendium of the poignant and the hilarious, and establishes a fundamental theme in Leskov – that of the 'righteous man'. This *pravednik* is a uniquely Russian type, simple, selfless and submissive, yet endowed with many qualities of the *bogatyr'*, the epic folk-hero, nonconformist and antagonistic to authority. Leskov's 'righteous men' are moved by conscience, instinct and a zest for life which takes no heed of conventional morality.

Outstanding among Leskov's other longer works are *The Enchanted Wanderer* (1874), *The Sealed Angel* (1874) and *The Hare Park* (1894, pub. 1917), while the most famous of his shorter pieces are *The Lady Macbeth of the Mtsensk District* (1865), *On the Edge of the World* (1876), *The Left-Handed Craftsman* (1882) and *The Sentry* (1887).

Though working within a prose tradition which at the best of times took little heed of formal convention, Leskov is by far the most daring and innovatory stylist of his age. Favouring the first-person narrative mode, particularly that vernacular variety known in Russian as *skaz*, Leskov's narratives are characterized by a defiant disorder – a formal expression of his belief in the primacy of the natural and the instinctive. Nor has any other writer made such effective use of the rich expressive resources of Russian provincial dialects.   MHS

CHEKHOV

With the death of Dostoevsky and the decline in Tolstoy's imaginative art after *Anna Karenina*, the 1880s were a relatively barren interlude; by the early 1890s, however, two new talents had emerged – A.P. Chekhov (1860–1904) and Gor'ky.

Anton Chekhov's literary career was born of necessity. His father, a provincial shopkeeper, was reduced to bankruptcy in 1876. Chekhov was thus obliged in the early 1880s to combine his medical studies with the production of sketches and anecdotes for a variety of comic papers in order to support himself and the family. Itself of little intrinsic literary merit, this work afforded Chekhov valuable experience in the observation of human foibles and in the art of artistic compression. The writer's superficially comic but essentially gloomy view of a world of scoundrels, hypocrites and fools is occasionally enlivened by a sympathetic glance at children or some of society's hapless victims.

Gradually the focus of Chekhov's stories shifted from anecdotal incident to the inner world of his characters: at the same time he developed an impressionistic technique for psychological description which became fundamental to his mature manner. In such pieces as *The Kiss* (1887), *Happiness* (1887) and *The Steppe* (1888) narrative, description and

image are transmitted largely via the perception of the central characters: herein lay the key to that particular Chekhovian phenomenon known as 'mood'.

Chekhov's first works for the stage were a series of superb short farces – *The Bear* (1888), *The Proposal* (1888), *The Wedding* (1889) and *The Anniversary* (1891) – together with two longer pieces – *Ivanov* (1887) and *The Wood Demon* (1889) – which gave some indication of his subsequent evolution as a major dramatist. By 1890 – in which year he made an arduous journey to the penal colony on Sakhalin Island to conduct a single-handed census – Chekhov had come to see himself as a 'serious' writer and to give precedence to his literary, over his medical, vocation.

The body of short stories written during the remainder of his short life offers a comprehensive picture of Russian life and manners of the period; yet it is the individual psychological experience with which Chekhov is always chiefly preoccupied. Such tales as *A Dreary Story* (1889), *Ward No. 6* (1892), *My Life* (1896) and *The Peasants* (1896) take a largely critical view of Tolstoyism and its psychological implications. In *A Woman's Kingdom* (1894), *A Doctor's Visit* (1898) and *In the Ravine* (1900) he examines the impact of industrial capitalism. In others the baneful influence upon the human psyche of religion (*Three Years*, 1895) or the contemporary cult of pessimism (*The Wife*, 1892) is delicately observed. Stories on a love theme – *About Love* (1898), *Lady with a Little Dog* (1899) – take a sceptical view of conventional morality; while a host of others trace the pernicious afflictions of greed, complacency, ambition and self-indulgence. Chekhov observes the world with detachment and irony, content to let his readers be the judges. Though his characters are seen predominantly in spiritual or moral decline, pessimism is often averted by the implication that man can and will live better than he does.

Chekhov's fame in the West rests largely upon the four plays *The Seagull* (1895–96), *Uncle Vanya* (1897), *Three Sisters* (1900) and *The Cherry Orchard* (1903). All four are studies of the moribund provincial gentry class of Chekhov's day, but have transcended their age to become classic studies of human hope, frustration and despair. As in his stories, Chekhov concentrates upon the internal world of his characters: drama consists in the emotional interplay between characters or in the struggle of the individual to preserve hope and integrity in a hostile world. Meanwhile, within dialogue and action he develops a system of symbols, clues and allusions which illuminate the inner world of thought and emotion. Not that Chekhov rid his plays entirely of the artifices of conventional theatre.

Chekhov reads The Seagull *to the cast of the Moscow Arts Theatre in 1898; Stanislavsky is on his right*

Anton Chekhov near the end of his life

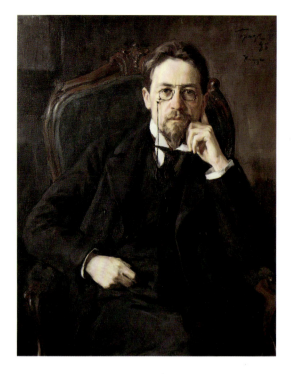

Though such climactic events as suicides in *The Seagull* and *Three Sisters* or the crucial auction in *The Cherry Orchard* are shifted off stage, they, together with the framing device of arrival and departure, remain as vestigial traces of the traditional 'plot'. Moreover, the superficially naturalistic Chekhovian dialogue is so replete with implied meanings as to seem ultimately at least as contrived as the more overtly dramatic dialogue of conventional theatre.

Perhaps Chekhov's greatest contribution to literature as a means by which man may understand himself lies in his pervasive irony, suggesting, as it does, that what we do or say is at best a very indirect way of expressing what we actually mean or feel; and that the narrow pursuit of individual happiness is perhaps a betrayal of man's true calling. It is to be concluded from Chekhov's writing that whereas in success the human spirit dies, through misfortune it is tempered and regenerated. The unique blend of ironic scepticism and dogged idealism above all gives Chekhov's work its distinctive flavour.   MHS

Right. Boris Grigor'ev's portrait of Gor'ky, 1926

GOR'KY

Maksim Gor'ky (1868–1936), whose real name was Aleksey Maksimovich Peshkov, was the son of a Nizhny Novgorod carpenter. His finest work, the trilogy *Childhood* (1913), *Amongst People* (1916) and *My Universities* (1923) is a vivid record of the forging of Gor'ky's extraordinary personality in a world of poverty and brutality, alleviated only by such rare examples of human warmth as his

maternal grandmother, and by books and the pursuit of knowledge. His first published writing, and the adoption of the pseudonym Gor'ky (meaning 'bitter'), date from 1892. In romantic rebellion against the prevailing atmosphere of political oppression and intellectual stagnation, his early stories evinced a burning faith in human freedom. In *Makar Chudra* (1892) and *The Old Woman Izergil'* (1894) figures drawn from gypsy myth and folklore are set in a richly romantic landscape of forest and steppe. In *Emel'yan Pilyay* (1893) and *Chelkash* (1894) there emerged a new hero, the *bosyak*, loosely modelled on the itinerant labourers he had encountered on his travels about Russia, and embodying – in Gor'ky's romanticized version – the very essence of freedom, independence and will. As reality, in the form of wharves, slums and dosshouses, began to impinge upon the earlier mythical settings, so too the psychology of the characters was treated with greater verisimilitude. In *Chelkash* Gor'ky's awareness of the psychological fragility of the self-isolated individual is already discernible. By *Konovalov* (1896) and *Boles* (1897) he had come to acknowledge the destructive potential of his earlier proclaimed ideal – the escape from an ugly world into a beautiful lie. His novel *Foma Gordeev* (1889) convincingly describes the inevitable crushing of the individual and inarticulate rebel by superior hostile forces in society.

By the turn of the century Gor'ky's fame as a writer was matched in Russia only by Tolstoy's: with fame came some measure of protection from police persecution. Drawn increasingly into political affairs, Gor'ky became associated with the Bolsheviks, for whom he was a valuable source of funds; thus began a long and tortuous relationship both

with the Bolshevik Party and, more particularly, with Lenin. Forced to flee after the 1905 revolution, Gor'ky eventually settled on Capri, to return after the general amnesty of 1913.

His literary output, meanwhile, was prodigious. To the novels *Three of Them* (1901), *Mother* (1907), *A Confession* (1908), *Okurov Town* (1909) and *Matvey Kozhemyakin* (1910) were added his first attempts at the drama, notably *The Petty Bourgeois* (1901), *The Lower Depths* (1902), *Summer Folk* (1904) and *Enemies* (1906). Of the novels, *Mother* was lauded by Soviet criticism as a forerunner of 'Socialist Realism'. It is crude, tendentious and unconvincing – yet enlivened for all that by the curious religious-political philosophy of 'God-building' which underpins it. This contemporary crackpot synthesis of Marxism-Leninism and Christianity, to which Gor'ky (to Lenin's dismay) strongly adhered at the time, found even more eloquent and overt expression in *A Confession*. Gor'ky's plays are marred by a crude aping of modernist techniques and an immoderate tendentiousness – with the exception of *The Lower Depths*, whose dosshouse setting, vivid dialogue, colourful characters and delicately ambiguous treatment of the theme of 'ugly truth and beautiful lie' ensured it an initial *succès de scandale* and subsequent survival on the world's stage.

Of Gor'ky's writing after 1910 only such non-fictional pieces as the autobiographical trilogy, his *Recollections* (notably of Tolstoy, Chekhov and Leonid Andreev) and *Notes from a Diary* (1924) are truly memorable. The novels *The Artamonov Business* (1925) and the unfinished *The Life of Klim Samgin* (1927–36) are monumental accounts of the evolution of the merchant class and the intelligentsia respectively. One late play, *Yegor Bulichev and Others* (1932), still enjoys some popularity.

After publishing a series of virulently anti-Bolshevik articles in 1917–18 and making heroic efforts in the aftermath of revolution to save starving members of the old intelligentsia, Gor'ky left the USSR again in 1921. Lured back in 1928, he became the figurehead of emerging literary Stalinism; he died, in mysterious circumstances, in 1936.   MHS

LITERARY REVOLUTION

The years 1890 to 1910 were marked in Russia by a profound cultural and aesthetic upheaval on several interconnected fronts – art and art criticism, religion, philosophy and literature. It involved not only a rediscovery and reinterpretation of the ideas of the past, but also the promotion of new approaches. At its heart lay a rejection of those principles of social

and moral utilitarianism which had so preoccupied the Russian mind for a half-century or more. The old gods of progress, reform and moral improvement were replaced by those of beauty, mysticism and unfettered individualism. In the field of art the leading spirits of the movement were Sergey Diaghilev (1872–1929), founder of the influential journal *World of Art* and Alexandre Benois (Benua, 1871–1960), the painter and art critic. The outstanding religious-philosophical thinkers of the period were N.A. Berdyaev (1874–1948), V.V. Rozanov (1856–1919) and L.I. Shestov (real name Shvartsman, 1866–1938). A fundamental reappraisal of the work of Tolstoy, Dostoevsky and Gogol' was effected by the critical studies of D.S. Merezhkovsky (1865–1941).

The crowning expression of this 'revolution' in literature itself is the Symbolist school of poetry. The major poets associated with this school are Blok, Bely, V. Ya. Bryusov (1873–1924), Bal'mont and Fedor Sologub (real name F.K. Teternikov, 1863–1927).

K.D. Bal'mont (1867–1942) is known mainly for six books of original verse written between 1894 and 1904, in which he experimented in rhythm, euphony and pure sound. Bryusov, an early admirer of the French Symbolists, and an expert in the history and techniques of poetry, is now better remembered for his promotion of poetry through translation and commentary than for his own – often fine – original verse.

Sologub's poetry is overshadowed by his extraordinary novel *The Petty Demon* (1892–1902), in which a provincial Russian town and its inhabitants are elevated to symbols illustrating the author's curious metaphysical system and morbid sensuality. Yet his poetry is often exquisite, matching in its delicate structures and meanings the finest poetry of Tyutchev.

Andrey Bely (real name B.N. Bugaev, 1880–1934), a prolific writer of both verse and prose, was certainly in terms of personality – and, at the time, notoriety – the most influential member of the movement. Falling at various times under the influence of such religious-political mystics as V.S. Solov'ev (1853–1900), Rudolf Steiner and R.V. Ivanov-Razumnik (1878–1946), his poetry was marked always by metaphysical mysticism and formal experimentation. His finest prose work, the novel *Petersburg* (1910–16), is packed with vivid incident and character and written in an elaborately ornamental style. Yet its central theme, the mystic conflict in Russia between forces of East and West, now seems trite. For all its brilliant craftsmanship, Bely's work always lacked the spontaneity and intensity of feeling which was the hallmark of the poetry of Blok.   MHS

BLOK

Blok in 1907

A.A. Blok (1880–1921) is the outstanding genius of the Russian Symbolist movement. Two early cycles of verse, *Ante Lucem* (1898–1900) and *Verses about the Beautiful Lady* (1904), are the finest examples in Russian of pure Symbolist poetry, trapping elusive visions from beyond reality in a gossamer net of symbol, image and poetic music. The dimly perceived object, here as in much of Blok's verse, takes female form: it is associated with V.S. Solov'ev's mystic concept 'Sofia, Goddess of Wisdom' – and to some degree with the poet's wife. Reality subsequently encroached increasingly upon Blok's poetic vision. In *The Stranger* and *The Puppet Show* (1906) the early mood of reverent anticipation is replaced by ironic disillusion. From an ethereal world, Blok's verse descends into a landscape of brothels, pot-houses and dimly-lit streets. *The Snow Mask* (1907), a cycle of verse inspired by a stormy love affair, is dominated by the image of swirling blizzards, while *The City* (1904–08) and *The Terrible World* (1909–16) record Blok's visionary response to such contemporary phenomena as factories, aviation and modern warfare.

In the cycle *Homeland* Blok first gave clear voice to a mystic Slavophilism latent in much of his verse, and expounded also in articles such as *The People and the Intelligentsia* (1908) and *The Intelligentsia and the Revolution* (1918). These works hark back clearly to mainstream literary ideas of the nineteenth century, particularly those of Dostoevsky. The Russian intelligentsia, Blok suggests, had, by fostering the alien rational-scientific culture of the West, lost touch with Russia, its people, its mystic spirit and its messianic destiny. Further boosted by Blok's association in 1916–17 with R.V. Ivanov-Razumnik, this mystic-religious nationalism found its finest expression in two major poems of the revolutionary period – *The Twelve* and *The Scythians* (1917–18).

The Scythians is an impassioned plea to the West to reconcile itself to the Revolution and its mystic import, or suffer the consequences. The nature of this mystic import is eloquently suggested by *The Twelve*. This culminating masterpiece of Blok's literary career shocked and enthralled the reading public. Incorporating the imagery of storm, movement and colour of his early work with popular song, revolutionary slogan and the rough language of the streets, Blok created in *The Twelve* a rich texture of harmony and dissonance, of sacred and profane. Twelve Red Guards who patrol revolutionary Petrograd, brutally sweeping away all remnants of the past, are led – though they do not know it – by Christ: thus is the Revolution revealed as an apocalyptic cataclysm, heralding the Second Coming, and the fulfilment of Russia's messianic destiny. As revolutionary rapture gave way to the harsh realities of Civil War, famine and reconstruction, Blok was rapidly overtaken by a sense of disillusion, which contributed to his early death in 1921.

Blok was not alone in viewing the Revolution through a rose-tinted lens of mystical idealism. Other writers – notably Bely, Yesenin, Mayakovsky and Pil'nyak, and even Gor'ky in his time – had awaited or welcomed the Revolution as a prelude to the establishment of a new 'Christian' era in Russia. All of them, with the possible exception of Gor'ky, were to suffer in their individual ways the same disillusionment.

MHS

Post-revolutionary Russian literature

THE NEW REGIME

The impact of the October Revolution on the established literary world was inescapable, although its reception varied considerably according to the political attitude and artistic inclinations of individual writers. Unlike their nineteenth-century predecessors, they were forced to declare their allegiance in an atmosphere where even the composition of lyric poetry, with its disregard for the surrounding turmoil, seemed to betoken a political stance. Immediately after the Revolution and during the early years of NEP (the New Economic Policy, 1921–28) state interference was minimal and subordination to party dictates was voluntary. More tangible attempts at external control followed quickly and the history of this period is that of greater or lesser pressure by the Party, through organized literary channels, to influence both the subject and its presentation in literature. The freedom and independence of the individual in their artistic as well as their personal life became the central preoccupation of those who resisted this regimentation; the assimilation of the individual into the collective was that of those who submitted, willingly or after a struggle.

Many groups, by virtue of their dubious claims to be the spokesmen of the masses, unsuccessfully sought the literary 'hegemony' only to discover A.V. Lunacharsky's determination to resist any attempt to monopolize the direction of art. These included Mayakovsky and the Futurists, Yesenin and the Imaginists, and Proletkul't, the association of proletarian writers founded in 1918.

JB

Above. *Mayakovsky*

Right. *A photomontage by Aleksandr Rodchenko illustrating Mayakovsky's* About This, *1923*

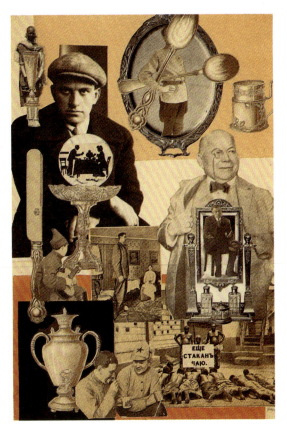

MAYAKOVSKY AND THE FUTURISTS

An instinctive revolutionary, V.V. Mayakovsky (1893–1930) joined the Bolshevik Party at the age of fifteen, was arrested three times in consequence and spent eleven months in prison for underground propaganda activity. A founder of the Russian Futurists, who denounced writers of the past while praising technological innovation and revolutionary ideas in their poetry, Mayakovsky never went as far as V.V. Khlebnikov (1885–1922), whose 'trans-sense' language was intended to liberate the word totally from its conventional meaning. But he did use a deliberately coarse and unpoetic diction, set in a declamatory, highly rhythmical form, to stifle the lyricism he had displayed in pre-revolutionary works (*Vladimir Mayakovsky*, 1913; *A Cloud in Trousers*, 1915), and tried to curb his egocentricity by hyperbolic eulogies of the Revolution and the people – *Mystery Bouffe* (1918), a dramatic poem for the theatre; *150,000,000* (1920), a heavy-handed satire against the capitalist West, personified by Woodrow Wilson, to whom he opposes the heroic Russian peasant Ivan with his 150 million heads. However, in spite of his enthusiastic writing of agit-poetry (propaganda verse) and jingles for state advertising and his longer political works (*Vladimir Il'ich Lenin*, 1924; *It's Good*, 1927), the suppressed lyricism breaks through in *I Love* (1922) and *About*

Yesenin in the year of his suicide

This (1923), a tragic poem with personal motifs, culminating in the beautifully written *At the Top of my Voice* (1930), where despair in his unhappy private life and disillusion in his commitment to a revolution which had allowed bourgeois values to reassert themselves are painfully revealed. This despair and petty harassment by the bureaucratic Russian Association of Proletarian Writers contributed to his unexpected suicide, a severe blow to the prestige of officially-approved literature.   JB

YESENIN AND THE IMAGINISTS

Born in a village in provincial Ryazan', S.A. Yesenin (1895–1925) was a genuine peasant in origin. The emotional, lyrical poetry he brought to Petrograd in 1915, with its colourful rustic imagery and religious symbolism, made him immediately famous as the voice of peasant 'wooden' Russia. Like Blok, he welcomed the Revolution as a force for spiritual renewal and foresaw in his anti-urban, anti-Western poem *Inoniya* (1918) the imminent arrival of a peasant paradise. In 1919 he moved to Moscow and joined the Imaginists, who were claiming the succession to the then 'defunct' Futurism as the leaders of poetic taste. They took to extremes the coarse language, the crude imagery and the public rowdyism of their predecessors, but replaced Futurist optimism with a morbid pessimism. Yesenin's *Confession of a Hooligan* (1920) and *Tavern Moscow* (1923–24), however, show true unhappiness: disillusionment with the anti-peasant, proletarian course of the Revolution and a despair exacerbated by his brief and disastrous marriage to Isadora Duncan and the drunken scandals which characterized the public image he had adopted. He attempted without success to adjust to the changes in village life under the soviets (*Soviet Rus'*, 1924), but the source of his sweet, melodious lyrics had altered beyond recognition; nor could he reconcile himself with Russia's rapid industrialization. His dramatic suicide – he wrote a farewell poem in his own blood – symbolized for many the fate of rural Russia.   JB

PROLETARIAN GROUPS

The Proletkul't, led by A.A. Bogdanov (real name Malinovsky, 1873–1928), aimed to produce a specifically proletarian literature and to this end organized studios where an incongruous selection of pre-revolutionary writers, such as V. Ya. Bryusov, Andrey Bely, N.S. Gumilev (1886–1921) and Ye. I. Zamyatin (1884–1937) taught. Emphatically anti-individualist and anti-Modernist groups claiming

Mikhail Sholokhov

proletarian origin, such as the Smithy and Cosmos organizations, wrote hymns to the proletarian collective, with no individual heroic figures; these productions often degenerated into the catchy propaganda jingles masquerading as poetry churned out by such as Dem'yan Bedny (real name E.A. Pridvorov, 1883–1945). In prose Serafimovich (real name A.S. Popov, 1863–1949), in his realistic novel *The Iron Flood* (1924), described the mass movement of an army while D.A. Furmanov (1891–1926), in *Chapaev* (1923), recorded peasant guerrilla operations under a leader whose job was merely to direct the heroic peasant mass. Others do feature individual communists, as did Yu. N. Libedinsky in *A Week* (1922) – its subject a peasant revolt against communist rule – with an emphasis on individual psychology which lesser talents such as A.A. Fadeev (1901–56) or S.A. Semenov were to continue. By far the best known is M.A. Sholokhov (1905–84), with his epic *The Quiet Don* (1928–40), a complex and realistic panorama of the revolutionary period, with its clash of ideologies and parties. His hero, Grigory Melekhov, is an individualist who belongs to no party, and a fierce Cossack chauvinism imbues the whole narrative. Since publication Sholokhov has been suspected of plagiarism from an author killed during the Civil War, whose diary manuscript he adapted. JB

THE FELLOW-TRAVELLERS

Between 1921 and 1932 the prevailing liberalism, made official in a decree of 1925, resulted in a wide variety of sophisticated and high-quality literature, mostly from the pens of the 'fellow-travellers' (Trotsky's term) who, while not with the regime, were either generally sympathetic to its aims or at least not its active opponents.

The Serapion Brothers

One such group, the Serapion Brothers (after a character in E.T.A. Hoffman's *Tales*), exemplify the extreme individualism persisting into the 1920s, their one common principle being freedom of thought and action, in literature as in politics. Inevitably the Revolution, the Civil War and its aftermath became their main subjects, frequently treated with a certain romanticism by those, such as V.V. Ivanov (1895–1963) (*Armoured Train No. 14-69*, 1922), more favourably inclined to the Bolsheviks; but all these authors concentrated on realistic description with often gruesome details of the fighting, and, most importantly, on the intellectual's task of defining his position in the new, generally alien world. K.A. Fedin's (1892–1977) *Cities and Years* (1924) was the first novel attempting to analyse rather than

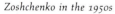
Zoshchenko in the 1950s

describe or eulogize the Revolution, through its weak, sentimental hero – a modern version of the nineteenth-century superfluous man, who is willing but unable to subordinate the values of an intellectual and his own self-interest to those of the new society. The novel's construction, with the closing scene transposed to the opening pages and other time-shifts, was hailed as unusual and inventive. V.A. Kaverin (real name V.A. Zil'berg, 1902–89) was one of many to develop the theme of freedom as a prerequisite for the work of the artist (*Artist Unknown*, 1931). M.M. Zoshchenko's (1895–1958) short sketches paint with the humour of cynical despair the sometimes cruel, sometimes absurd behaviour of Soviet citizens in mundane life.

Zamyatin

The most prominent and influential Serapion was Ye. I. Zamyatin (1884–1937). His reputation, which grew from his satirical tales of English life, written from personal experience (*The Islanders*, 1918; *The Fisher of Men*, 1922), was firmly established by stories of more immediate topicality, such as his moving account of the cold, hunger and human misery of War Communism in Petrograd in *The Cave*, where the city is in the grip of a new ice age, mammoths stalk abroad and humans retreat to their cave-flats and god-stoves, their morality becoming ever closer to that of their primeval ancestors. The use of a central metaphor and the careful interweaving of related imagery transform the factual material of this logically narrated tale into something distinctly surrealistic. Zamyatin's independent viewpoint and aggressive individualism brought him continuous trouble with the Party, culminating in the publication abroad (1927) of his futuristic fantasy *We* (written 1920–21). Loss of human dignity as a result of ideological fanaticism put into practice concerns him deeply in this consciously Dostoevskian polemic against the utopian socialist dogma, adopted by the Bolsheviks, that material well-being should have primacy over the individual's free will. In *We* its logical extreme, happiness without freedom for the many under the benevolent tyranny of a few, is realized in the One State, ruled by its Benefactor (with a sinister *ante diem* resemblance to Stalin) and the Guardians who save its citizens, identified only as numbers, from the consequences of their irrational instincts in a regimented society based on purely rational principles, where unity is all and rebellion is easily suppressed. Only when Zamyatin was permitted to leave for France in 1931 did the persecution provoked by *We* cease.

Other fellow-travellers

Those outside the Serapion group, but holding similar views, included Yu. K. Olesha (1899–1960) and V.P. Kataev (1897–1986). Olesha's *Envy* (1927) presents the conflict between a fanciful poet doomed to failure and a solid, successful bureaucrat of the new order. Kataev in *The Embezzlers* (1927) relates the somewhat unsavoury scenes glimpsed through a drunken haze by two absconding officials travelling through Russia. He also provided the idea for his younger brother and a co-author which became the hugely popular satirical novel *The Twelve Chairs* (1928) by Il'f and Petrov (real names I.A. Fainzil'-berg, 1897–1937 and Ye. P. Kataev, 1903–42), with its memorable crook Ostap Bender pursuing diamonds hidden in a set of chairs dispersed round Russia during the NEP period. L.M. Leonov's (1899–1990) works treat the outcasts of the new society with a sympathy reminiscent of Dostoevsky: *The Badgers* (1925) revolves around a group of peasant rebels who reject the Revolution as the old conflict between town and village takes on a new slant: *The Thief* (1927), set in the NEP period, has as its hero the leader of a gang of thieves disillusioned with life under Soviet rule. Leonov's concern for the variety and multiplicity of life, threatened by the sinister myth of equality – in practice conformity with a colourless norm – and his (then uncommon) interest in ethical questions – the sanctity of human life, the hypothetical right to kill – are similarly Dostoevskian in feeling. Among those loosely connected with the fellow-travellers it was the greatest talents, Pil'nyak, Babel' and Bulgakov, who later attracted the fiercest denunciations.

Pil'nyak

The novel *The Naked Year* (1922) by Boris Pil'nyak (real name B.A. Vogau, 1894–1937) was the first to treat the Revolution and its effects on Russian life. Like others of his so-called novels (such as *Machines and Wolves*, 1925), it is a collection of episodes without a unifying plot, depending for its unity on devices such as repetition or verbal refrains. The influence of Andrey Bely's *Petersburg* and *The Silver Dove* can be seen in the many lyrical or historico-philosophical digressions, rhetorical questions and exclamations, the highly involved syntax and the time-shifts, which set a style for many aspiring writers. Russia's historical destiny as part-East, part-West fascinated both Pil'nyak and Bely. Pil'nyak interpreted the Revolution as a cleansing blizzard which preceded a renewal of social morality and justice for the downtrodden. He became disillusioned and began to incur displeasure, notably with his *Tale of the Unextinguished Moon* (1926), which was taken as an allusion to the suspicious death on the operating table of the Civil War general M.V. Frunze. It was *Mahogany* (1929), published in Berlin before the Soviet censor had time to reject it, which caused the furore leading to his expulsion

from the Russian Association of Proletarian Writers (RAPP). It treats with sympathy the romantic revolutionaries who mourn the passing of genuine communism, and its attitude to Soviet administrative personnel is distinctly critical. The same themes recur in *The Volga Flows into the Caspian Sea* (1930), Pil'nyak's hopelessly unsuccessful attempt at reparation for the crimes of *Mahogany*, which was his contribution to Five-year Plan literature and dealt ostensibly with plans to reverse the flow of the Volga. Humiliating public recantations could not ensure his survival: he was shot in 1937.

Babel'

An orthodox Jewish upbringing and an early love of French literature produced in I.E. Babel' (1894–1939) a distinctive writer at his finest in short, impressionistic sketches, usually founded on one incident and remarkable for their extraordinary style, highly concentrated, yet exotic in its ornamentalism. His masterpiece is the collection *Red Cavalry* (1926), tales from his own experiences in Marshal S.M. Budenny's First Cavalry Army in the Soviet-

> ## Platonov
>
> The novels, short stories, and essays of Andrey Platonovich Platonov (1899–1951) were increasingly suppressed during his lifetime; republished from the late 1950s, they have only been fully available in Russia since the late 1980s, leading to a widely-held recognition that Platonov is the most important Soviet prose writer of the inter-war period. Born in Voronezh, Platonov worked at a variety of technological jobs and as a journalist before moving to Moscow as a professional writer. His work refers to the shattering events of his lifetime – civil war, famine, collectivization, cultural revolution, industrialization, terror, world war, – but not in order to document them. Instead, they are the surreally depicted circumstances in which his heroes search for meaning; his characters tend to be ideologically and politically naive, grotesquely credulous, linguistically clumsy and ungifted, and often physically damaged. *The Foundation Pit* (written 1929–30, published abroad 1973, in Russia 1987) lays waste the idea of social, moral, and technological progress; Platonov's masterpiece *Chevengur* (one fragment published 1929, published abroad 1972, in full in Russia 1988), set in the provincial steppes in 1921 and dealing with the brutal imposition of Communism, is one of the great Russian dystopias.   GSS

Polish war. Contrast and paradox abound – the weak Jewish intellectual leading a band of crude and brutish Cossack troops (traditionally viciously anti-Semitic), the blind cruelty of the Revolution and the humanity of its ideals, the almost sadistic details of the bloodshed and the poetic nature descriptions. Babel''s *Odessa Tales* (1931) are a unique literary record of the misery of a persecuted minority: childhood recollections of pogroms and the heavy seriousness of Judaism are, however, alleviated by the panache and exuberance of Jewish gangsterism in the archetypal figure of Benya Krik, the 'king' of Odessa's criminal life. Odessa Jews also feature in his play *Sunset* (1928); the poor reception of his detached ironic style made him decide to cultivate the 'genre of silence', only to be harassed for some years before disappearing to his death in prison.

Bulgakov

The short stories of M.A. Bulgakov (1891–1940) in his collection *Devilry* (1925), and in particular the science fantasies *Heart of a Dog* and *The Fatal Eggs* (1924), use humour and satire in their trenchant criticism of Soviet society, especially of the ignorant and uncultured ex-peasants and workers who reached positions of influence. His major novel, *The White Guard* (1924), later adapted into a successful play under the title *Days of the Turbins*, describes Kiev in the worst years of the Civil War. The close family life and cultural heritage of the upper classes are defended to the death from a fundamentally hostile Revolution. That the play was staged at all is surprising: in *A Theatrical Novel* (1937) Bulgakov describes the difficulties of staging any of his works and his love–hate relationship with the Moscow Arts Theatre (мкhат). His masterpiece, *The Master and Margarita* (1930–40; published 1966), is probably the outstanding novel of post-revolution Russia. Its main concern, which permeates all Bulgakov's work, is the conflict of the spiritual with the mundane, materialist world, here at its most acute in the confrontation of Christ, a figure of impressive dignity and simplicity, with Pontius Pilate in ancient Jerusalem, paralleled by that of the Devil (under his traditional name of Woland) and his motley attendants with the inhabitants of Moscow in the 1930s. Hilarious slapstick comedy in the antics of Woland's hangers-on, as they relentlessly expose the human weaknesses of the Muscovites, does not mask the conclusions he reaches during his visitation – namely that cowardice and avarice (inevitably accentuated by the conditions under Stalin) are as much the ruling passions as during the time of Pilate, but are here frequently mitigated by a saving compassion and faith in the power of art and the spiritual world.

Bulgakov in 1928

Journals

The principal organ for fellow-travellers, the journal *Krasnaya nov'* edited by A.K. Voronsky (who supported their right to a platform in spite of their ideological instability) was the victim of a prolonged campaign by the proletarian writers' organizations, particularly from their magazine *Na postu* which demanded a unified party line in literature. In 1927 Voronsky and 'The Pass' group which shared his ideas and included writers of some talent such as V.P. Kataev (1897–1986) or A.P. Platonov (real name Klimentov, 1899–1951) and well-known critics such as D.A. Gorbov (b.1894) and I. Lezhnev (real name I.G. Al'tshuler, 1891–1955), were attacked, and Voronskyism became a term of abuse as a synonym for nonconformity.

The Formalists

The same fate awaited the Formalist critical group Opoyaz (Society for the Study of Poetic Language), led by V.B. Shklovsky (1893–1984) and featuring critics of stature such as R.O. Jakobson (1896–1982), Yu. N. Tynyanov (1894–1943), V.M. Zhirmunsky (1891–1971) and O.M. Brik (1888–1945). The extreme Formalists reduced the study of a work of art to the 'sum of its stylistic devices'. Words, not images or emotions, are the real material of poetry, and the normal perception of the subject is distorted and deliberately 'made strange' by undue emphasis on one specific factor, such as metre or syntax; any connection between the work and the author's individuality is strenuously denied. Although the group's views moderated in the late 1920s, study of form as opposed to socially useful content became anathema. Even Marxist critics such as Trotsky, A.V. Lunacharsky (1875–1933) and N.I. Bukharin (1888–1938), who advocated tolerance of variety, were losing their influence.

M.M. Bakhtin (1895–1975), one of the most independent and original thinkers of this period, produced new theories on topics in metaphysics and (among others) Freudianism, Marxism, Formalism, linguistics and the evolution of the novel. Like the Formalists, he fell foul of the authorities; he was exiled in Kazakhstan (1930–36) and later in provincial towns, but continued to develop his ideas and to expand and revise his early works until the end of his life. JB

THE POETS

The four major poets of the early Soviet period were all well known before the Revolution: none, however, preserved the freedom to write as they chose and the consequence in their personal lives was as tragic as for their nineteenth-century precursors.

Pasternak

Before he became famous with *My Sister Life*, a collection of poems written in 1917 in direct response to the excitement and upheavals of that year, B.L. Pasternak (1890–1960) had studied philosophy and music, belonged briefly to a Futurist sub-group, and produced two well-received volumes of verse. The startling freshness and originality of his poems result equally from his astonishing metaphors, the novelty of his perception, his musical, yet taut, forms and his juxtaposition of the poetic with the highly prosaic. His theme is almost exclusively man and nature and their interaction. Attempts at longer poems more in tune with the predominant novel form in the 1920s (*The Year 1905*, 1927; *Spektorsky*, 1931) were unsatisfactory, and a new volume of lyric verse (*Second Birth*, 1932) signalled a return to his natural idiom. In 1936 he was censured for the personal and aesthetic aspects of his work and thereafter published nothing but translations, especially from Shakespeare, until *On Early Trains* (1943), half of whose poems reflected wartime experiences, as did the collection *The Terrestrial Expanse* (1945), in a more direct, less sophisticated style. The publication in Italy of his idiosyncratic and highly poetic novel *Dr Zhivago* (1958), and the subsequent scandal in the Soviet Union which forced him to refuse the Nobel Prize, shattered his life; persecution over it continued until his death.

Mandel'shtam

The early work of O.E. Mandel'shtam (1891–1938) is filled with a sober gratitude for this world, with man as its centre, which he shared with his fellow-Acmeists Akhmatova and Gumilev, and which remained his major poetic theme throughout his life. His collection *Tristia* is resonant with the majestic tones of the classical world in its elegy for the culture symbolized in the city of St Petersburg, which he saw rapidly being transmuted into Hades. His reassessment in his work collected under the title *Poems 1921–25* of the changed and apparently hostile world around him brought about a loss of self-belief in his right to be a lyric poet. He filled the poetic silence with prose, the incisive semi-autobiographical *Noise of Time* (written 1923) and *The Egyptian Stamp* (1928), a longish surrealistic novella of some brilliance, set in the Kerensky summer of 1917. Poetry returned in 1930, after a systematic campaign to erase him from literature had restored his will to fight, and in 1934 he was arrested for a superbly vicious anti-Stalin epigram and exiled to Voronezh, where he composed the poems of his three *Voronezh Notebooks*, none of which was published in his lifetime. Like Pasternak, Mandel'shtam was highly sophisticated, European in his modes of thought and purely Russian in his

loyalties, with the further dimension of a Jewish background. Mandel'shtam's work is wider-ranging than Pasternak's and relies on intellect rather than on instinct; there is the same command of metaphor, coupled with great vigour and *élan* within the austerely traditional forms from which he rarely departed. Mandel'shtam's arrests, the second leading to his disappearance and death in a transit camp, form the subject of the impressive memoirs of his widow, Nadezhda Mandel'shtam (1899–1980), published first in the West (*Hope against Hope*, 1970, and *Hope Abandoned*, 1972).

Akhmatova

The pre-revolutionary poetry of Anna Akhmatova (real name Gorenko, 1889–1966) is imbued with the despair of unrequited love, repentance for sensual pleasures and a religious sense of being justly punished for them. The restraint of her terse, classical form contrasts sharply with the depth of passion in her stanzas. In the 1920s these qualities in her verse and the fact of her earlier marriage to N. S. Gumilev (shot as a White conspirator in 1921) led to her being called an 'internal émigré' and forced her to stop publishing her intensely private, self-analytical poems. Maturity and later suffering – the fourteen years spent in labour camps by her son and the arrest of close friends such as Mandel'shtam – gave her work a new, broader dimension to the point where, in her magnificent *Requiem* (1935–61), she became the voice of all those Russian women whose menfolk had been shot or imprisoned during the

Pasternak in the mid-1920s

Right. *Akhmatova in old age*

Mandel'shtam in 1929

purges. Thus when A.A. Zhdanov's infamous 'half-nun, half-harlot' accusation of 1946 ushered in a new period of disgrace for her, her personal dignity and poetic reputation remained undiminished. Her *Poem Without a Hero* (1940–56) is a brilliant, impressionistic masquerade based on her Petersburg literary friends, with their often tragic relationships, who make surrealistic, ghostly appearances from the mists of the year 1913, the last before the 'true twentieth century' of war and mass destruction arrived. Finally rehabilitated, she was permitted to travel abroad to receive honorary degrees in 1965.

Tsvetaeva

The early collections of Marina Tsvetaeva (1892–1941) show a romantic and idealistic personality obsessed with the exceptional and the heroic, epitomized in the figure of Napoleon, whereas *Juvenilia* (1916) is more austere and decidedly pacifist in the wake of real warfare. *Versts I* (1916), a lyrical diary of her personal life in her native Moscow in that year, presents a calm historical perspective impossible thereafter: her later comparisons of the Revolution and Civil War with the destruction of culture by the Tatar hordes show her firmly committed to the White cause espoused by her husband. In 1922

Tsvetaeva in 1914

she left Russia to join him, living in near-destitution in Paris from 1925 onwards; her unconventional personality made it impossible for her to conform with the rigid attitudes of the émigré group there and her finest collection, *After Russia* (1928), with its disparate elements of Russian Futurism, folk lament, *byliny* (epic songs) and even the Bible, was poorly received. She returned to the Soviet Union in 1939 and, after a period of increasing misery, she committed suicide. Immense energy and verbal force characterize her work – the reactions of a vivid and impulsive personality expressed in a direct, exclamatory style, often hectoring, rarely contemplative and never matched by its imitators.   JB

SOCIALIST REALISM IN LITERATURE

Various groups from the Proletkul't, the ex-Futurist LEF (Left Front of Art), the Constructivists, with their emphasis on scientific and technical vocabulary, and RAPP (Russian Association of Proletarian Writers) in its various mutations, which claimed to speak for the Party itself, flourished until the adoption of the First Five-year Plan in 1928, when *Pravda* and other official organs attacked their lack of commitment to social tasks, and campaigns against individuals such as Zamyatin and Pil'nyak were launched. The Stalinist period, when writers were used for education and propaganda purposes only, was established with the liquidation of all groups and enforced membership in a Union of Soviet Writers under the control of the Party, at whose First Congress in 1934 Socialist Realism was adopted as the union's literary policy. Stalinists (L.M. Kaganovich, P.F. Yudin and L.Z. Mekhlis) controlled the channelling of production and hence the livelihood of all writers, and during the Terror the union secretary, Stavsky (real name V.P. Kirpichnikov, 1900–43), was responsible for the imprisonment and often the death of numerous authors.

The phrase 'Socialist Realism' was in itself a contradiction; 'realistic' description of actual life had simultaneously to depict the ideal 'socialist' reality, with its communist heroes and their inspiring deeds, while any criticism of substance was strictly forbidden. Since the term had no meaning other than obedience to party directives, the period up to and immediately after the Second World War is one of almost total literary sterility. The majority of novels have but one plot: sentimentally idealized communists struggle, in hackneyed political clichés, against the unscrupulous class enemies or saboteurs whom they invariably defeat. Novels such as N.A. Ostrovsky's (1904–36) *How the Steel was Tempered* (1935), in which a poor boy joins the underground and, in spite of poverty, wounds and lack of education, becomes a militantly communist writer, or *The Story of a Real Man* (1946), by Boris Polevoy (real name B.N. Kampov, b.1908), where a Soviet pilot is shot down by the Germans, losing both feet, but returns to fight in the air, were written to inspire communist ideals in the young. 'Shock workers' feature in *The Second Day* (1935) by I.G. Erenburg (1891–1967) or *Time, Forward!* (1932) by V.P. Kataev (1897–1986); directors of gigantic industrial projects are the protagonists in Leonov's *Road to the Ocean* (1935) and F.V. Gladkov's (1883–1958) *Energy* (1939); P.A. Pavlenko wrote of progress in the Soviet Far East (*In the East*, 1937); Yu.P. German described a woman's regeneration through learning and work (*Our Friends*, 1936). In drama Nikolay Pogodin's (real name N.F. Stukalov, 1900–62) *Tempo, Poem about an Axe* and *Snow* (all 1930) are typical Five-year Plan plays, like his *Aristocrats* (1934), whose heroes are three Cheka-men (political police) against the background of the White Sea Canal. A.N. Afinogenov's play *Fear* (1931) has an old scientist repenting of his anti-Soviet actions. In poetry A.A. Prokof'ev, E.A. Dolmatovsky and A.A. Surkov delivered the requisite socially responsible works.

Although Erenburg and A.N. Tolstoy (1883–1945) became apologists for the regime, Tolstoy's *Road to Calvary* (1920–41) or *Peter the First* (1925–45) and Erenburg's *The Extraordinary Adventures of Julio Jurenito and his Disciples* (1922) or *Out of Chaos* (1933) are not without quality. M.M. Prishvin (1873–1954) and K.G. Paustovsky (1892–1968) with their works on nature and A.S. Grin (real name Grinevsky, 1880–1932), with his fantastic and romantic tales, chose uncontroversial subject-matter and remained relatively unaffected. But most gifted writers fell silent or were silenced.   JB

Right. Stalin's cultural overseer, Zhdanov

WAR LITERATURE

A brief period of relative freedom came with the Second World War. K.M. Simonov's (1915–79) *Days and Nights* (1944) and V.P. Nekrasov's (1911–87) *In the Trenches of Stalingrad* (1945) convey the immediacy of the siege of Stalingrad (now Volgograd) in a natural, unforced manner impossible a few years previously. Most established authors contributed to the war effort as both journalists and writers, thus working from experience. A.A. Fadeev's (1901–56) *The Young Guard* (1945) centres on an underground group of Komsomol members in the German occupation; L.M. Leonov's (1899–1990) play *Invasion* (1942), which won one of the Stalin Prizes instituted in 1939, and Simonov's *Russian People* (1942) are self-explanatory. Simonov, A.A. Surkov, N.S. Tikhonov (1896–1979) and two

women poets, Margarita Aliger (b.1915) and Ol'ga Berggol'ts (1910–75), all wrote lyrical and hortatory verse about the war. The immensely popular *Vasily Terkin* of A.T. Tvardovsky (1910–71) is a 'typical' folksy Russian soldier who, in the course of the eponymous long poem (1941–45), demonstrates – not without humour – his specifically Soviet courage at the front. His creation is perhaps the most memorable official work of the war.   JB

ZHDANOVISM

A sudden but predictable end to the relaxation of the war came with a Central Committee resolution of August 1946 in which the works of M.M. Zoshchenko were denounced as bourgeois, apolitical and vulgar, and those of Anna Akhmatova as aesthetic, pessimistic and amoral, and journals were censured for publishing them. This signalled the tightening of controls and the opening of a virulent campaign, master-minded by A.A. Zhdanov, against the literary world. Enthusiastic optimism, glorification of the system and its successes (real or desired), extreme chauvinism associated with an open encouragement of anti-Semitism, and idolization of Stalin make the literature of the years 1946–53 a wilderness. Although K.A. Fedin, V.A. Kaverin, V.S. Grossman (1905–64) and F.I. Panferov (1896–1960) obliged with novels adhering strictly to requirements and N. Ye. Virta (1906–76), S.V. Mikhalkov and V.M. Kozhevnikov produced suitably anti-Western and anti-'cosmopolitan' plays, many writers had to wait for the death of Stalin to publish their true work.   JB

Emigré and dissident literature

A scholarly bibliography listing works of émigré literature published between 1918 and 1968 includes some 17,000 entries. This rich chapter in the history of Russian literature is largely inaccessible to the English-speaking reader. Any tendency to wither away has been retarded in the literary life of the expatriate Russian communities by new waves of Soviet emigration, bringing widely different experiences and attitudes.

THE FIRST EMIGRATION: 1918 ONWARDS

Right. Vladimir Nabokov

As a result of the Bolshevik assumption of power, the collapse and evacuation of the White armies, the famine of 1921 and the selective expulsion of intellectuals, approximately one million Russians had left their homeland by the early 1920s. They were widely dispersed from the Far East to Western Europe and included an impressive number of established literary figures. Paris became the political, and eventually literary, capital of the Russian Emigration, but in the first half of the 1920s it was Berlin which saw the most feverish literary and publishing activity. The Berlin publishing house of Z.I. Grzhebin, largest of many, catered for both the émigré and Soviet markets. It was in the Berlin newspaper *The Helm (Rul')* that Vladimir Nabokov (real name Sirin, 1899–1977) regularly published his early verse. But of some 600 émigré literary journals, almanacs and anthologies which have appeared since 1918 pride of place must go to the Paris-based *Sovremennye zapiski*. Published from 1920 up to the very fall of France in 1940, it became the literary embodiment of, and monument to, the First Emigration.

A number of writers now regarded as 'Soviet' spent periods abroad in the years after the Revolution. Il'ya Erenburg took an active part in émigré literary life, whereas Maksim Gor'ky held himself aloof. Aleksey Tolstoy was not alone among emigrants in coming to terms with the Revolution in the spirit of the 'Change of Landmarks' movement of 1921 onward and eventually returning to the Soviet Union. Unrivalled, however, was the agility with which Tolstoy effected the transition from ardent propagandist of the White cause to Stalin Prize-winning classic of Socialist Realism. Some writers of the older generation adjusted to the stresses of emigration better than others. Aleksandr Kuprin (1870–1938) failed to repeat his pre-revolutionary successes as a creator of realistic prose fiction and returned, already ill, to the Soviet Union a year before his death. In sharp contrast, Aleksey Remizov (1877–1957) maintained his extraordinary output of fiction, fantasy and documentary throughout a long career in emigration. It was in emigration too that Ivan Bunin (1870–1953) attained the height of his powers as a lyrical and psychological realist with the strongly autobiographical *Life of Arsen'ev* (1927–39) and the collections of stories *Mitya's Love* (1925) and *Dark Alleys* (1943). His Nobel Prize of 1933 lifted the morale of the émigré literary world. Boris Zaytsev (1881–1972), whose best prose is marked by an exquisite lyrical and impressionistic manner (*Pattern of Gold*, 1926; *House in Passy*, 1935) exemplifies a widespread reversion to religious themes and intonations. Other celebrated prose-writers were Ivan Shmelev (1873–1950), Dmitry Merezhkovsky and Aldanov (Mark Landau, 1889–1957). Aldanov's historical novels of the 1920s and 1930s brought him world-wide recognition.

Outstanding among a cohort of poets which included Zinaida Gippius (1869–1945) and Georgy Ivanov (1894–1958) were Vladislav Khodasevich (1886–1939) and Marina Tsvetaeva (1892–1941). Tsvetaeva wrote some of her finest work in emigration (*After Russia*, 1928); she returned to the Soviet Union in 1939, there to die by her own hand. Khodasevich's last lyrics (*European Night*, 1927) are among the supreme achievements of émigré literature. He subsequently devoted himself to criticism. Khodasevich's influence among younger émigré poets was at least equalled by that of Georgy Adamovich (1894–1972), a poet and a brilliant if impressionistic critic whose judgement was highly valued by the younger generation of Paris poets such as Anatoly Shteyger (1908–44).　　MAN

THE SECOND EMIGRATION: 1945 ONWARDS

The war dealt a heavy blow to émigré culture as a whole, putting an end to Russian-language publishing in Paris, Prague, the Baltic states and China. Several writers perished in concentration camps or in the ranks of the French Resistance. Some were affected by a damaging polarization towards 'Soviet patriotism' on the one hand and fascism on the other. With the dispersal of existing cultural centres many émigrés, including Vladimir Nabokov, moved to the United States, and the Russian-language literary journal *Novy zhurnal*, founded in New York in 1942, grew quickly to prominence. The end of the war brought an influx of Soviet citizens via the displaced-persons camps of Europe, and the new literary voices among them were generally well received by the older emigration. Of the prose writers none could match the success of Sergey Maksimov (1917–67) with his widely translated novel *Denis Bushuev* (1949). Notable among the poets were Ivan Yelagin (1918–86) and Nikolay Morshen (b.1918); Igor' Chinnov (b.1914), brought up in emigration, emerged as a major poet. The establishment of the literary and socio-political journal *Grani* in Germany in 1946 was an initiative of the Second Emigration. The literary aspirations of both emigrations were greatly furthered by the founding of the Chekhov Publishing House (New York) in 1951 and the appearance of the almanacs *Bridges* and *Aerial Ways* in the late 1950s and 1960s. There was no significant new emigration in those years.　　MAN

Il'ya Erenburg

THE KHRUSHCHEV THAW

Concern over the stifling cultural legacy of Zhdanov had been publicly voiced before 1953, but with the death of Stalin criticism became more concrete and comprehensive. Symptoms of inauthenticity and insincerity in recent Soviet literature were discussed in 1953–54 by Fedor Abramov (1920–83) and Vladimir Pomerantsev (1907–89), while Ol'ga Berggol'ts appealed for the rehabilitation of genuine lyric poetry. If the mood of the 'Thaw' was captured in the short novel of that name (1954) by Il'ya Erenburg, then opposition to it was epitomized in the dismissal of Aleksandr Tvardovsky from the editorship of the literary journal *Novy mir* in 1954 and certain speeches at the Second Congress of the Soviet Writers' Union the same year. Thematic novelty was the outstanding feature of Erenburg's *The Thaw* and of such characteristic works of 1956 as the novel *Not by Bread Alone* by Vladimir Dudintsev (b.1918), the short story *The Levers* by Aleksandr Yashin (1913–68) and the drama *Petrarch's Sonnet* by Nikolay Pogodin. In these works the Stalinist model of leadership is exposed as dogmatic, corrupting and sterile. The intuition and conscience of individuals emerge as beneficial to the collective, while private life, including marital infidelity, is shown as unamenable to intervention on ideological grounds. This preliminary assertion of the right to treat complex human issues had a declarative, programmatic ring, entirely in the spirit of Khrushchev's condemnation of Stalin at the XX Party Congress in 1956. Its mirror image may be found in the 'anti-thaw' novel *The Yershov Brothers* (1958) by Vsevolod Kochetov (1912–73), part of the back-lash prompted by the Hungarian uprising of December 1956. Such oscillations were a feature of the 1950s. The rehabilitation of liquidated or incarcerated writers and increased access to foreign literature were leavening ingredients, but in 1958 a Writers' Union of the RSFSR, of orthodox complexion, was established to counter free-thinking tendencies in existing literary organizations. Direct political intervention in literary affairs, though sporadic, could be harsh. The rejection for publication in his own country of the novel *Dr Zhivago* by Boris Pasternak (1890–1960) was followed by a foreign edition (1957), the award of a Nobel Prize and a scandal at home culminating in his expulsion from the Writers' Union and threats of deportation.　　MAN

'YOUNG' WRITING

After 1956 the younger generation, grown weary of authority, found new cult figures and filled sports stadia to hear recitals by its heroes. This audience responded not only to the pugnacious, declamatory verses of Yevgeny Yevtushenko (b.1933), but also to the technical virtuosity of Andrey Voznesensky (b.1933) and the robust lyricism of Bella Akhmadulina (b.1937). The enthusiasm of the young poets, which was by no means without support from older colleagues, stimulated the appearance of typewritten verse anthologies in the late 1950s, foreshadowing that upsurge in uncensored literary and publicistic expression known from the mid-1960s as *samizdat* ('self-publishing'). It was with officially published stories of disorientated and disaffected youngsters that Anatoly Gladilin (b.1935, exiled 1978) and

237

GULag punishment cells, Magadan, Siberia

Vasily Aksenov (b.1932, exiled 1980) made their names. Characteristic of their works (Aksenov's *Starry Ticket* (1961) is best known) is a rejection of epic continuity and narrative omniscience in favour of fragmentary structure and shifting point of view reflecting the preoccupations and jargon of the central figures. J.D. Salinger and Ernest Hemingway are often cited as influences.   MAN

THE LEGACY OF THE PAST

A powerful, if short-lived stimulus to literary ferment was the XXII Party Congress of 1961 and the symbolic removal of Stalin's remains from the Lenin Mausoleum. From the mid-1950s onwards returning political prisoners had begun to appear as minor characters in literary works and allusions to the atmosphere of the purges had been permitted. However, the November 1962 issue of *Novy mir* carried a work which remains the most forceful treatment of the labour camp (GULag) theme to be published in the Soviet Union. *One Day in the Life of Ivan Denisovich* by Alexander Solzhenitsyn (b.1918) meticulously recreates the point of view of a non-intellectual prisoner in conditions of average severity. It achieves more through understatement than did Boris D'yakov (b.1902) with his *Experiences Recounted* (1964), an attempt to preserve the image of the Party unsullied amidst the horrors of the camps. Upon Khrushchev's removal from office in 1964 his successors declared the labour camp theme exhaustively ventilated, leaving to *samizdat* and foreign publishers the accomplished and harrow-

From *The GULag Archipelago*

The people who had direct personal experience of twenty-four years of Communist happiness knew by 1941 what nobody else in the world knew: that on this whole planet and in the whole of history there had never been a regime more evil, more bloody, and at the same time more deviously wily than the Bolshevik regime, which had arrogated to itself the title 'Soviet'. They knew that in terms of the number of people tormented, the sense of long-term entrenchedness, the far-reaching concept of its mission, and its thoroughgoing unified totalitarian nature, no other regime on earth could compare with it, not even the juvenile Hitler regime, which at that time was darkening all eyes in the West.

Alexander Solzhenitsyn, *The GULag Archipelago*, Vol. III
Translated by G. S. Smith

ing *Kolyma Stories* of Varlam Shalamov (1907–81), the novel *Faculty of Unneeded Things* (1964–75) by Yury Dombrovsky (1909–78) and Solzhenitsyn's remaining works on the subject. These include two 'polyphonically' constructed novels: *The First Circle* (1968) explores the contrasts and affinities between the closed world of a prison research institute and other circles of Stalin's inferno; in *Cancer Ward* (1968) it is not only the patients who are compelled to reconsider the meaning of their lives, but the diseased body politic and Soviet society as a whole. Solzhenitsyn's *The GULag Archipelago* (1973–75), which spans many volumes and several genres, caused a sensation unmatched by any previously published account of the labour camp world. Although this is the theme with which the Nobel Prize-winning writer is chiefly identified, he himself regards it as a necessary distraction from his main literary task – the creation of a vast epic cycle devoted to the history of the Russian Revolution, *The Red Wheel* (completed 1991). Solzhenitsyn's works began to be published in the USSR in 1989, and by the end of 1991 almost all of them had appeared there.

In contrast, the Second World War remained a living theme in official literature. Its manifestations ranged from routine tales of heroism and pathos to such documentary reconstructions as *Brest Fortress* (1964) by Sergey Smirnov (1915–76) and *Blockade* (1968–73) by Aleksandr Chakovsky (1913–91). One of the first to combine motifs of de-Stalinization with the war theme was Konstantin Simonov. His novel *The Living and the Dead* (1959), with its depiction of the culpably misdirected defence of the Soviet Union in the opening stages of the war, won a Lenin Prize. Other works stand out for their rejection of formulistic jingoism in favour of an unidealized examination of the psychological and moral stresses of life in the trenches: such are the stories of Vasil' Bykov (b.1924), the poems of Boris Slutsky (1919–86), and the novels *The Battalions Request Fire Support* (1957) by Yury Bondarev (b.1924), and *An Inch of Ground* (1959) by Grigory Baklanov (b.1923). De-heroization could not be practised with impunity. In *Good Luck, Schoolboy* (1961) Bulat Okudzhava (b.1924) introduced a lovable but decidedly non-bellicose adolescent hero, only to be accused in some quarters of slandering a whole generation of Soviet youth. An outrageous satirical novel, *The Life and Extraordinary Adventures of Private Ivan Chonkin* (1963–70) by Vladimir Voynovich (b.1932, exiled 1980), could only be published abroad and circulate in *samizdat*. MAN

'VILLAGE' PROSE

This category is sufficiently loose to embrace many of the most vigorous tendencies of post-Stalin Soviet literature – the quest for spiritual values, the reappraisal of the past, the rejection of formal and thematic determinateness. A precursor was Valentin Ovechkin (1904–68), whose cycle of sketches, *Weekdays in the District* (1952–56), cast an unprecedentedly critical eye upon *kolkhoz* life. No less influential have been the sketches and diaries of Yefim Dorosh (1908–72) and Vladimir Soloukhin (b.1924). Soloukhin's *Vladimir Country Roads* (1957) and subsequent works are marked by that lyrical, religiously tinged sense of national identity which, during the 1960s, found frequent expression

in the journal *Molodaya gvardiya*. In his novel trilogy *The Pryaslins* (1958–73) Fedor Abramov chronicles the hard life of a North Russian peasant family since the war. Sergey Zalygin (b.1913) sets his short novel *On the Irtysh* (1964) in a Siberian village during the collectivization of agriculture, a process which he depicts without euphemism. Memorable among the gallery of Russian peasant types are the heroine of Solzhenitsyn's *Matrena's Home* (1963), Ivan Afrikanovich, the patient, perplexed and endearing creation of Vasily Belov (b.1932) in his *Same Old Story* (1966), and the tougher eponymous hero of *From the Life of Fedor Kuz'kin* (1966) by Boris Mozhaev (b.1923). Vasily Shukshin (1929–74) devotes some of the best of his deceptively simple short stories to the social and moral disorientation of uprooted peasants. Salutary for Soviet literature as a whole was the village-writers' rediscovery of the richness of authentic non-literary speech. MAN

OFFICIAL VERSUS UNOFFICIAL LITERATURE

The years between the fall of Khrushchev and the Gorbachev period saw the reimposition of thematic taboos and the stabilization of literary-political relations, with periodic reprisals against recalcitrant writers. These extend from the conviction of Andrey Sinyavsky (pseud. Terts, b.1925, exiled 1974), and Yuly Daniel' (pseud. Arzhak, 1925–89), in 1966 for publishing 'defamatory' works abroad to the deportation of Solzhenitsyn in 1974 and extrajudicial measures taken in 1979 against the organizers of the uncensored anthology *Metropolis*. Throughout the 1960s *Novy mir*, under the renewed editorship of Aleksandr Tvardovsky had served as first refuge of the liberal-minded writer and direct opposite of Vsevolod Kochetov's (1912–73) orthodox journal *Oktyabr*. The dispersal of the *Novy mir* editorial board in 1970 marked a watershed. At the same time, readers of *samizdat* had precarious access to a substantial alternative literature, which included the major novels of Solzhenitsyn, the verses of such officially neglected poets as Iosif Brodsky (b.1940, exiled 1972; Nobel Prize for Literature 1987), and the tape-recorded ballads of Bulat Okudzhava, Vladimir Vysotsky (1938–80) and Aleksandr Galich (1919–77, exiled 1974).

By the 1970s the boundaries between official and unofficial channels of expression became more difficult to draw and the prose of Andrey Bitov (b.1937), Georgy Vladimov (real name Volosevich, b.1931) and Fazil' Iskander (b.1929) became known in the Soviet Union either through the official press or through *samizdat*; but with an increasing number

*Unlicensed dissidents:
Andrey Sinyavsky
(foreground) and Yuly
Daniel' on trial in 1966*

of writers leaving the country, either voluntarily or under constraint, the picture grew more complicated. New works were written in emigration and earlier censored works were restored. Some émigré writings then found their way back into the Soviet Union. Among the better-known expatriate writers of the 1970s were the poets Brodsky, Galich and Naum Korzhavin (b.1925), and the prose-writers Solzhenitsyn, Sinyavsky, Anatoly Gladilin (b.1935), Viktor Nekrasov (1911–87) and Vladimir Maksimov (b.1932). At the same time, the official literature of the Brezhnev period may not be dismissed out of hand. For example, the vitality and integrity of the Siberian village-writer Valentin Ras-

putin (b.1937), as seen in his short novel *Live and Remember* (1975), and the incisive exploration of urban morality undertaken in the stories of Yury Trifonov (1925–81) were not worthless simply because they were officially tolerated. The fine play *The Joker* (1966) by Viktor Rozov (b.1913) and the consistently high achievement of his fellow playwright Aleksandr Vampilov (1937–72) were as much a part of Soviet theatre as were the embattled experiments during the 1960s and 1970s of Yury Lyubimov, director of Moscow's Taganka theatre. The selective republication in the 1970s of such suppressed twentieth-century classics as those by Boris Pil'nyak, Osip Mandel'shtam, Marina Tsvetaeva, Mikhail Bulgakov, and Aleksey Remizov (1877–1957) was welcome even though it was principally intended for export.   MAN/GSS

*Licensed dissidents:
Yevgeny Yevtushenko (left)
and Valentin Rasputin
(right)*

THE 'THIRD WAVE': 1970 ONWARD

During the 1970s there were some 200,000 legal emigrants from the Soviet Union, the majority travelling on Israeli visas. A number of well-known 'dissidents' and unamenable writers, both Jews and non-Jews, chose, or were compelled, to go abroad. Apart from Israel, the main centres of settlement were Paris and New York. The longest-running journals of the Third Emigration are *Vremya i my*, Tel-Aviv, *Continent*, founded by Vladimir Maksimov, and *Syntax*, edited by Andrey Sinyavsky. All three began to be legally published in Moscow

Joseph Brodsky

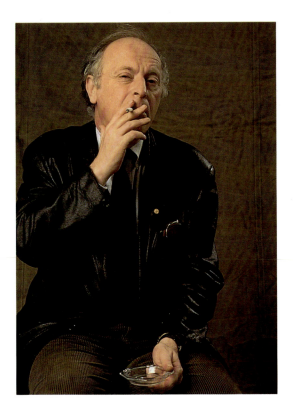

in 1991. The major publishing house is 'Ardis', founded in Ann Arbor, Michigan in 1971 by the American scholars Carl (1938–84) and Ellendea Proffer. The literary life of the 'Third Wave' has been characterized by vigorous internecine polemic. But during the 1970s and early 1980s more important literature was written and published outside Russia than inside: it includes the prose of Vasily Aksenov, Sergey Dovlatov (1938–91), Andrey Sinyavsky (Abram Tertz), Sasha Sokolov (b.1943), Alexander Solzhenitsyn, and Vladimir Voynovich, the poetry of Dmitry Bobyshev (b.1936), Joseph Brodsky, Natal'ya Gorbanevskaya (b. 1936), Yury Kublanovsky (b.1948), Lev Loseff (b.1937), and Aleksey Tsvetkov (b.1948). From late 1987 this work began to be freely published and discussed in the USSR, and writers made return visits. Emigration continued during the Gorbachev period and after; by the end of 1991 there were about 400,000 Russian speakers in Israel, supporting a vigorous literary community.   MAN/GSS

GLASNOST AND
THE LITERARY PRESS

From the early 1930s there were traditionally two centres of power and influence in Soviet literature: the heavily bureaucratized Unions of Writers (for the USSR as a whole, for individual republics and for Moscow); and the large-circulation weekly and monthly literary newspapers and journals. While the Unions as such played no significant role in the opening up of Soviet literature that occurred during the Gorbachev period, a number of liberally inclined journals and newspapers were at its forefront, especially after the Central Committee plenum of January 1987 which took a decision in principle to weaken censorship and to introduce the policy of glasnost. In fact, as early as 1986 changes in the editorship of key publications were already preparing the ground. In October 1986 the veteran writer Sergey Zalygin became editor-in-chief of *Novy mir*, a journal with an intermittent tradition of radicalism, and proceeded to rejuvenate its editorial board. The writer Grigory Baklanov did the same to *Znamya* after he was made editor in August 1986. That same summer Vitaly Korotich took over the illustrated weekly *Ogonek* and Yegor Yakovlev the weekly magazine *Moscow News*. Changes in editorial policy led to massive increases in circulation. That of *Novy mir* trebled to 1,500,000 between 1987 and 1989, while *Ogonek* was by then selling 3,000,000. Other magazines that trod the radical path include the Leningrad *Neva, Yunost'* (the young people's monthly, also selling 3,000,000 in 1989) and *Druzhba narodov*. Mention should also be made of the newspaper *Argumenty i fakty*, which, as its title implies, specialises in supplying its readers with concrete information, and which at the height of its circulation was selling 33,000,000 copies per week. Not all of the press was so audacious, however, and some newspapers and magazines took up an explicitly conservative position, notably *Nash sovremennik*, a journal closely associated with Russian nationalism, and *Molodaya gvardiya*, an official publication of the Komsomol. Thus for the first time in decades the Soviet press broadly reflected the existing range of opinion in Soviet society.

For all the rhetoric of 're-building' associated with the Gorbachev years, Soviet society was paradoxically just as intent on looking backwards, in an endeavour to reclaim the Soviet and pre-Soviet past and tell the truth about it. In the literary press this mission of reclamation was reflected in several ways. The great writers and thinkers of the period of Russian modernism have been re-published on a grand scale, including such figures as Nabokov and Zamyatin, the very fact of whose emigration had hitherto placed them beyond the pale. A large number of works devoted to contentious periods of Soviet history appeared, from Pasternak's *Doctor Zhivago* (finally published by *Novy mir* in 1988) and Akhmatova's *Requiem* to Rybakov's *Children of the Arbat*, Grossman's *Life and Fate* and beyond. After a period of nervousness, late in 1987 the journals plunged into the publication of living émigrés, the writers of the 'third emigration', returning Brodsky, Aksenov, Voynovich, Sinyavsky and many others to their native readers. This process reached its apogee with the massive reclamation of the works of Solzhenitsyn, which began in the summer of 1989. New publication on this scale had the effect of promoting a fundamental reappraisal of literary values, and of rendering school and university literary textbooks obsolete. In their absence the literary press became an evolving literary encyclopaedia. Because the journals continued to include essays on historical, political, philosophical and other subjects, and because in those areas old sources had also become discredited, they became historico-political encyclopaedias as well. Amid all this retrospection there were anguished (and justified) cries that new young writers could scarcely be heard. Nevertheless, a number of hitherto little published writers (not all of them very young) established their reputations with Soviet readers during the Gorbachev period; they include the prose writers Tat'yana Tolstaya (whose stories have appeared in English as *On the Golden Porch*, London, 1989 and *Sleepwalker in a Fog*, London, 1992), Yevgeny Popov (*The Soul of a Patriot*, London, 1992), Sergey Kaledin (*The Humble Cemetery*, London, 1990), Victor Yerofeev (*Russian Beauty*, London, 1992), and the dramatist and short story writer Lyudmila Petrushevskaya.

The heady excitement in the journals gradually led to upheaval in the world of Soviet publishing. Traditionally in the Soviet Union there was a substantial gap between the appearance of a work in a journal and hard cover publication, and the book publishing cycle was notoriously slow. In the Gorbachev period Soviet publishing houses began competing with each other, and with the journals, to bring out rival editions of popular works, introducing a system of 'express publication' and engaging in consumer research to establish the needs of the market. This marketization was also reflected in large increases in the prices of books. This period also saw the appearance of a number of new small and semi-independent publishers and the beginnings of private publishing.

While all these phenomena were clearly evidence of a new vitality in Soviet publishing, there were signs before the end of 1991, as in other spheres of Soviet life, that the boom was coming to an end, and with it the euphoria. The journals encountered problems as diverse as publication ceilings, paper shortages, distribution difficulties, decrease in revenue consequent upon cover price rises, attempts by the newly-confident conservatives to remove radical editors, and threatened and actual returns to censorship. Journals as diverse in profile as *Novy mir* and *Nash sovremennik* told their readers that failure to supply them with enough paper was a surreptitious attempt to silence them; a number of established

journals fell up to a year behind in their publication schedules. Others experienced alarming falls in circulation, while some ceased to appear at all. The potentially thriving unofficial press encountered particular problems by being locked into the remnants of the state printing and distribution networks. The period in which the literary press played (splendidly) its part in the opening up of Soviet society, ended with the collapse of that society.

In the new Russia of 1992 the financial and existential crisis facing long-established journals and newspapers became even more acute. Print runs continued to plunge. Delays in appearance were commonplace. Many journals balanced precariously on the edge of closure. Some did close. Serious book publishing experienced the same cold breeze of market forces, and many long-cherished projects, impossible before 1987 for ideological reasons, were now abandoned on financial grounds. On the other hand, new and lively organs, notably *Nezavisimaya Gazeta* and the weekly magazine *Stolitsa*, flourished. The present situation is one of lively, chaotic flux. In part because of their very success in pluralizing society, the journals (like other ex-Soviet media such as the cinema), no longer speak with a central and universally audible voice.   JG

POST-SOVIET LITERATURE

The August 1991 coup accelerated the fragmentation of the writers' professional organization, which had been set up in the 1930s at Stalin's initiative to supervise and control Soviet literature. The process was initiated by the establishment of *Aprel'* (April, or 'Writers in Support of Perestroika'), in early 1989 as a protest movement within the USSR Writers' Union, and of other independent writers' associations. It culminated, in the immediate aftermath of the coup, in the takeover of the USSR Writers' Union by Yevgeny Yevtushenko and his liberal-minded colleagues, and in the breaking away of the alternative Russian Writers' Union from the reactionary RSFSR Writers' Union, and of the Moscow Writers' Union from the 'stagnant' Moscow Writers' Organization. Timur Pulatov (b.1939), an Uzbek writer, was elected First Secretary of the former USSR Writers' Union; and Vladimir Ognev (b.1923), a literary scholar and critic, as the head of its financial arm, the *Litfond*. In January 1992 the old Union was officially transformed into the *Sodruzhestvo Soyuzov Pisateley* (SSP) (Commonwealth of the Writers' Unions), as outlined in a declaration which was signed by twelve different writers' organizations, including the Belorussian and Central Asian PEN Centres and the international European Forum.

By March of the same year, the dissatisfaction of the pro-democracy writers with their new leadership came to a head in the form of a second revolt. The chief causes for complaint were Timur Pulatov's dictatorial style of leadership at the head of the SSP, his and Yevtushenko's lavish use of the organization's scarce funds for extensive foreign travel and, most important of all, the revelation that Pulatov had conspired with the reactionary Russian writers in order to consolidate the united forces of Islam and Orthodoxy against the influence of 'pragmatic, soulless Western civilization'. The second putsch replaced Pulatov with a triumvirate: the journalist and politician Yury Chernichenko (b.1929); the 'current affairs' writer Andrey Nuykin, and the poet Nikolay Panchenko (b.1924). The liberal writers acknowledged readily that direct influence in the 'corridors of power' was vital for the future of their organization. Thus with Chernichenko – the leader of the Peasant Party and an adviser to Aleksandr Rutskoy – as one of the group heading the SSP its registration, previously delayed, became a straightforward matter.

Inevitably, the changes forged in the old Union were rejected by the reactionary writers, who accused their liberal colleagues of offending against the Union's Constitution. After the August coup, the RSFSR Writers' Union and the literary newspaper *Den'*, whose editorial board includes Aleksandr Prokhanov (b.1938) (editor-in-chief), Stanislav Kunyaev (b.1932), Valentin Rasputin (b.1937), Igor' Shafarevich (b.1923) and the notorious television journalist, Aleksandr Nevzorov, emerged, even more prominently and aggressively than before, as the chief bastions of the forces hostile to change.

The long-awaited Ninth Writers' Congress finally took place in Moscow in June 1992. The participants, the majority of whom represented conservative writers' factions, resolved to found yet another writers' association, the International Association of Writers' Unions (IAWU). Timur Pulatov was chosen as leader and it was declared the only legitimate successor to the former USSR Writers' Union. Inevitably, the SSP disagreed strongly with this claim. The question of 'succession' was temporarily resolved in July 1992 by a statement from the Justice Department of the Russian Federation, which noted that neither the rules of the newly established IAWU, nor the rules of the SSP, included any mention of either of these organizations being a legitimate successor to the USSR Writers' Union. A mere act of official registration with the appropriate ministry did not automatically make one organization successor to another; it simply endowed it with a legal status. In this instance the question of 'succession' would have to be resolved in court.

Any correspondence between the writers' professional organizations and genuine literature has historically been tenuous. The (mainly) political ferment at and the post-coup changes within the Writers' Unions have not altered this basic fact. With regard to literature, in the course of 1991 the mood among writers and critics became increasingly characterized by frustration and growing despair: before 1985 their works were not published for political reasons; now they could not be published for commercial reasons or because the publishing industry had more or less collapsed. Paper and other raw materials of publishing were scarce and prohibitively expensive. Literary journals gained a better chance of acquiring materials if they invited the Russian Ministry of Mass Media to become one of their founders; this meant, however, that the Ministry could wield influence on the editorial policy of the given publication if it chose to do so.

On the aesthetic level, the struggle between 'young' writers and the writers of the 1960s generation continued to intensify. In general, 'young' writers rebelled against the literary conventions (both stylistic and thematic) prevalent in the 1960s and 1970s. They were intent on destroying the paradigms inherited from the literary culture of the 'Khrushchev thaw' and the 'stagnation' period, through delving into the art of satire, the grotesque, the surreal and the *very* real and ordinary. Viktor Yerofeev, Sergey Kaledin (b.1949), Vladimir Sorokin (b.1955), Zufar Gareev and Valeriya Narbikova (b.1958), among other prose writers, partook in the process of stripping, layer by layer, literary heroes and heroines of the positive characteristics with which official literature had persistently endowed them in the past. While, in the early 1990s, the censor no longer shaped or curtailed literary creativity in the former Soviet Union, it became evident that the potential of post-Soviet Russian literature would be realized only if sufficient material means could be found to make the newly-acquired freedom manifest.   RHP

Cultural life

Music

RUSSIAN MUSIC

Russian music is notable for its directness, colour, melodic richness, rhythmic vitality and strong emotional appeal. Symphonic works sound well, since Russian composers are invariably excellent orchestrators. Orchestral music tends to cover a wide range of timbres and dynamics. Instrumental music is often characterized by brilliant idiomatic writing, though this is less evident in vocal music, where long-flowing cantabile lines are often preferred. The distinctive plaintive quality frequently discernible in Russian music may partly be explained by the presence of the folk idiom (for much Russian music contains certain intervals and melodic shapes characteristic of Russian folk music) and by employment of certain chords, especially those of the augmented fifth and the augmented sixth.

The development of Russian music can best be understood if it is viewed in the historical perspective of the development of Russia itself. During the first millennium of the Christian era the various Slav tribes were in a state of continual movement, although by the end of the ninth century the Eastern Slavs had established themselves in towns such as Kiev, and subsequently Novgorod and Moscow. The adoption of Christianity in 988 linked Kiev with the Byzantine Empire and culture; the arts (including sacred chant) flourished. When the Mongols overran Russia in the early thirteenth century, Kiev was captured and devastated, but Novgorod escaped, and the maintenance of its trading links with Western Europe brought economic and artistic benefit. Folk music particularly developed: both Kiev and Novgorod are notable for their cycles of *byliny* (heroic ballads). Tatar domination until the mid-fifteenth century left lasting traces on folk culture. During this time Moscow gradually established itself as the capital of the Russian state. First steps at conscious emulation of West European music were taken in the mid-seventeenth century, when linear (five-line) notation was introduced and attempts were made at polyphonic composition and the writing of secular music. Still closer ties with Western Europe were fostered by Peter the Great, whose policy was continued through the eighteenth century by the

Empresses Anna, Elizabeth and Catherine the Great; Catherine's magnificent palace, the Hermitage, became a centre of musical and theatrical activity. Prominent foreign composers (Cimarosa, Paisiello, Traetta, Galuppi) were invited to Russia, where they did much to stimulate musical education, and young performers of talent were sent to study in Italy.

Russia's first acquaintance with foreign opera took place in 1731 with the visit of two foreign opera companies, after which there followed a steady stream of Italian, French and German opera enterprises. By 1780 operas were being written and performed by Russian musicians, vocal and instrumental music (mainly taking the form of keyboard sonatas and variations on Russian songs) were being composed, instruments were being manufactured, and musical scores printed. The violin compositions of Ivan Khandoshkin (1747–1804) show good understanding of violin technique. The nobility established their own theatres on their estates, with performers drawn from their own serfs, but it was only after the turmoil of the Napoleonic wars that professional theatres (as opposed to the popular street theatres) became accessible to a broader section of the community. Orchestral music in Russia dates back to this period, when orchestras in the Italian fashion were established at Court and in the houses of the nobility. A curiosity of the second half of the eighteenth century was the Russian horn band, in which each serf musician played only a single note on instruments varying from 95 mm to 2.25m in length. Such bands, some having up to forty players, had an extensive repertoire, including symphonies and overtures, and were extremely disciplined. The horn band persisted until the 1830s and the guitar and the harp remained popular domestic instruments for many decades, both as solo instruments and for accompanying sentimental songs.

Nineteenth-century Russia fell under the influence of Western Romanticism, manifested particularly in the operas of Spontini, Cherubini, Weber and Meyerbeer – talents against which no Russian composer could at first compete. With the coming of M.I. Glinka (1804–57), however, a strong creative personality emerged to change completely the face of Russian music; his distinctive treatment of folk materials, both in orchestral music and in his operas, provided models for succeeding generations.

Previous spread. Aleksandr Benois' decor for Stravinsky's opera The Nightingale, 1914

Right. *Glinka.* Far right. *Repin's portrait of Modest Musorgsky*

Whereas *A Life for the Tsar* (1836) is concerned with the theme of patriotism in the person of the sturdy peasant, Ivan Susanin (an alternative title to the opera), *Ruslan and Lyudmila* (1842), based on the poem by Pushkin, is more innovative from the harmonic and orchestral points of view, and employs Georgian, Turkish, Arabian and Finnish elements and the whole-tone scale. Though foreign influences may be discerned in his work, Glinka's achievement was a remarkable one and may be compared with the role of Pushkin in formulating a Russian literary language.

Though national elements may be found in the music of A.S. Dargomyzhsky (1831–69) and A.N. Serov (1820–71), Glinka's real successor was M.A. Balakirev (1836–1910), who further developed orchestral music on national lines, both in his symphonies and his symphonic poems and orchestral overtures utilizing Russian themes. His chief piano work, the oriental fantasy *Islamey*, inspired by Liszt, is important in its imaginative treatment of exotic material and may be said to have had some effect on subsequent piano composers both in Russia and in Western Europe. It was Balakirev who gathered round him the group of five known as the *Moguchaya kuchka* (literally the 'Mighty Handful' – the name given to the group in 1867 by the critic V.V. Stasov (1824–1906)), comprising Balakirev himself, A.P. Borodin (1833–87), C.A. Cui (1835–1918), M.P. Musorgsky (1839–81) and N.A. Rimsky-Korsakov (1844–1908). All were amateur musicians. Stasov was their literary spokesman and ideologist. Despite the disparity of their styles and personalities, each composer (influenced to some

extent by the theories of the Slavophile and Populist movements) shared the common credo expressed by the composer Serov: 'Music, like any other human language, must be inseparable from the people, from the soil of the people, from its historical development. . . . In repeating the ancient Hellenic myth of Antaeus, who remained invincible so long as he rested firmly on the earth, Russian art can draw inexhaustible forces from the folk element.' Nowhere is the desire for identification with the Russian people better seen than in the songs of Musorgsky (many of which use natural speech inflections and peasant expressions) and in his masterpiece, the opera *Boris Godunov* (1869, revised 1872, première 1874). Drawing inspiration from Dargomyzhsky's experiments in musical realism, as well as from innovative elements in the music of A.G. Rubinstein (1829–94) and Serov, Musorgsky succeeded in creating a nationally coloured melodic and harmonic language of striking originality; indeed, one so original that it was largely misunderstood by his contemporaries.

The compositions of Borodin, though not large in number, are notable for their emotional warmth and lyricism (in which effective use is made of chromaticism), rhythm, clear formal structure and skilful treatment of the thematic material. This is seen particularly in his heroic opera *Prince Igor* (1869–87, left unfinished on his death and completed by Rimsky-Korsakov and Glazunov), with its colourful orchestration and vivid characterization, and in his songs, chamber and orchestral work.

Rimsky-Korsakov's music, while lacking the dramatic intensity of that of Musorgsky and the heroic

Aleksandr Glazunov, by Repin

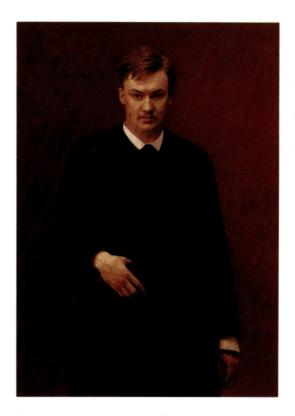

lyricism of that of Borodin, is nevertheless outstanding in its coruscating orchestration and striking and sonorous harmonies. Though his operas are uneven in quality, at their best, as in *The Snow-Maiden* (1881, première 1882) and *The Golden Cockerel* (1907, première 1908), they make most effective theatre. Especially successful are the folk scenes and picturesque orchestral episodes reflecting Rimsky-Korsakov's interest in Russia's pantheistic and historical past. His orchestral suite *Sheherazade* (1888) shows his creative talents at their best. He was also of importance as a teacher, among his pupils being A.K. Glazunov (1865–1936), A.K. Lyadov (1855–1914), N.Y. Myaskovsky (1881–1950), I.F. Stravinsky (1882–1971) and many others.

Apart from their work as composers, Musorgsky, Borodin, Rimsky-Korsakov and Cui (whose music lacks the strength and originality of the others) were all active at various times as letter-writers and critics. Examination of Cui's letters and writings alone, however (he contributed regularly to the *St Petersburg Gazette* from 1864 to 1917), is sufficient to demonstrate that the Five were far from united in their outlook and that their work was not received by their contemporaries in their native land with anything like the enthusiasm which it is accorded today.

A unique place in Russian nineteenth-century music is occupied by Anton Rubinstein, one of the few musicians of that era whose work was at all known outside the frontiers of his native country. A brilliant pianist, a talented and prolific composer,

Petr Tchaikovsky

it was Rubinstein who succeeded in establishing the first Russian Conservatory (that of St Petersburg in 1862), thus placing music on a more professional footing. The Moscow Conservatory was founded by his brother Nicholas (1835–81) in 1866. Despite Rubinstein's immense contribution to Russian music (for he did much to popularize music by Russian composers in his concerts throughout Europe and to promote Russian-born performers), at present Rubinstein's efforts are largely ignored – a strange quirk of fate, since in nineteenth-century Europe Rubinstein was regarded as the outstanding representative of Russian music, Tchaikovsky's music becoming popular only at the end of the century.

If the musical activities of the 'Mighty Handful' were centred primarily in St Petersburg, those of P.I. Tchaikovsky (1841–93) were based largely in Moscow. Tchaikovsky enjoys the distinction of being the first professionally trained Russian musician, a graduate of the St Petersburg Conservatory. While a patriot in outlook (for folk elements feature prominently in his work), he was an admirer of West European music, particularly that of Mozart and French opera (Gounod, Thomas and Bizet). His vast output of vocal, orchestral, chamber, ballet and operatic music, however, is notable for its excellent craftsmanship and his chief compositions have subsequently achieved international acclaim.

The nineteenth century saw the real flourishing of orchestral music, the St Petersburg Philharmonic Society being founded in 1802 and the Russian Musical Society in 1859. Branches of that Society were subsequently established in all main centres. Concerts were also given at the Free Music School (an organization set up in opposition to the St Petersburg Conservatory in 1862), the Moscow Philharmonic Society in 1883, and Belyaev's Russian Symphony Concerts in 1885, which he founded expressly for the performance of Russian music. Outlets for the work of Russian composers were provided by the publishing houses of M.P. Belyaev (1836–1904), P.I. Jürgenson (1836–1904) and V.V. Bessel' (c.1843–1907).

Russian orchestral music from the start found itself in a unique position, having come into being almost entirely in the nineteenth century. With no symphonic tradition to fall back upon, Russian composers modelled their first orchestral compositions on West European Romantic prototypes. It was not from classical composers that they drew their inspiration but rather from certain works of Beethoven, Berlioz, Schumann and (at a slightly later date) Liszt. In all this music may be detected an unconventional attitude towards musical form, a particular penchant towards cyclic structure – that is, unification of a work by means of a recurring

Right. *Sergey Rakhmaninov by Somov, 1925*

theme, often melodically and rhythmically metamorphosed – and (following the formal structures of Berlioz and Liszt) less concern with counterpoint and development but with greater emphasis on harmony, colour and rhythm.

Characteristic of the Russian nationalist composers (the music of Anton Rubinstein is more classical in structure, although it still contains Romantic features) is a tendency towards programme composition and the employment of folk elements, which have been consistently utilized from the time of Glinka onwards. One of the difficulties in using a folk-tune lies in its development, since it is already a highly developed entity. Glinka's solution was to repeat a folk-tune almost verbatim, but to introduce changes in orchestration and harmonization – a 'changing background' technique employed in his orchestral fantasy *Kamarinskaya* (1848) and frequently used by his successors. Rimsky-Korsakov in his suite *Sheherazade* (1888) utilizes a mosaic-like structure, in which basic musical motifs, incessantly varied, succeed one another in a dazzling display of orchestral and harmonic colour, though the work is also unified by a number of orchestral motto-themes.

Apart from the existence of a small number of pieces for organ (mostly written by Glazunov), by far the greatest proportion of Russian keyboard music is for the piano. Since the piano was a much favoured instrument in Russia during the nineteenth century, nearly all composers wrote extensively for it, in consequence of which there exists a large repertoire for piano solo, piano duet, or two pianos, ranging from the simplest children's pieces, mazurkas, impromptus, berceuses, preludes, bagatelles, polonaises, to studies, sonatas and operatic paraphrases, in many of which the influence of Chopin and Liszt is apparent. Among outstanding Russian piano works are Balakirev's oriental fantasy *Islamey*, Musorgsky's *Pictures from an Exhibition*, and works by Rubinstein, Tchaikovsky, A.N. Scriabin (1872–1915) and S.V. Rakhmaninov (1873–1943).

Russian chamber music mostly takes the form of string quartets, occasional larger ensembles, and works for piano and strings. Though some pieces for piano and wind do exist (for example Rimsky-Korsakov's Piano Quintet), compositions for wind alone are a rare phenomenon. Apart from its colour and vitality and emphasis on melody, Russian chamber music is characterized by brilliant writing for the individual instruments. Among the outstanding Russian chamber works are Glinka's *Trio Pathétique* for piano, clarinet and bassoon, the string quartets of Borodin, Tchaikovsky and Glazunov, Tchaikovsky's String Sextet (*Souvenir de Florence*), Arensky's Piano Trio and the collective com-

position *Les Vendredis*. Rakhmaninov's Cello Sonata in G Minor is highly esteemed. During the nineteenth century the Russian Musical Society organized in its branches chamber music concerts, in which foreign virtuosi participated. The Petersburg Chamber Music Society was established in 1872 and the Belyaev Quartet Evenings in 1891.

In the years preceding the Revolution diverse tendencies were apparent. While some composers such as Glazunov, Lyadov and Rakhmaninov continued to compose along traditional lines, others sought new means of expression: Scriabin explored the world of symbolism and mysticism; S.S. Prokofiev (1891–1953) developed a highly personal language, full of astringent dissonances; commissioned by the impresario Diaghilev, Igor' Stravinsky (1882–1971) startled the Western world with his ballets *The Firebird* (1910) and *The Rite of Spring* (1913); the composer N.A. Roslavets (1881–1944) experimented with serial (atonal) music. Of these composers Stravinsky may be regarded as one of the most influential and innovative figures of the twentieth century. Despite the heterogeneous nature of his style, however, Russian elements are to be found in the majority of his works. While revealing to West European audiences a vigour and colour perhaps hitherto unknown, his ballets mark the culmination of the music of the Russian Nationalist school.

GS

SOVIET MUSIC

After the Revolution of 1917 the majority of Russian composers continued either to follow their former style of composition or to write music in accordance with the new communist ideals. Some left Russia permanently; Prokofiev departed in 1918 to return again in 1932. Lenin himself saw music as fulfilling a valuable ideological role, a means of mass propaganda, and shortly after the Revolution created the Commissariat of Enlightenment (NARKOMPROS), of which A.V. Lunacharsky was appointed Commissar. An important division of NARKOMPROS was the section devoted to music and a conscious effort was made to bring music to the masses. At the same time, however, Lunacharsky resisted pressure from such extremist groups as the *Proletkul't*, which favoured a new radical 'proletarian culture', having little or no connection with Russia's traditional musical past. A temporary lessening of state control occurred in 1921 with the New Economic Period (NEP), an era which also saw improved relations with the West. While the first few years after the Revolution were essentially a time of consolidation, a number of organizations came into being that were to play an important part in the country's musical development. Such were the Association of Proletarian Musicians (founded in 1923 and renamed the Russian Association of Proletarian Musicians in 1929) and the Association of Contemporary Music (1925). As with the literary and pictorial arts, a notable factor in the musical life of this period was the element of experiment, manifest in the work of such composers as D.D. Shostakovich (1906–75), A.V. Mosolov (1900–73), and others. To the innovators, modernism was the order of the day; close attention was paid to developments in avant-garde West European music. Concert programmes included music by advanced contemporary Western composers such as Paul

Dmitry Shostakovich

Dmitry Shostakovich was born in 1906 into a family of Polish origin; the composer's grandfather had been exiled to Siberia for his part in Polish revolutionary activities during the reign of Tsar Alexander II. Shostakovich showed musical talent from an early age, and entered the St Petersburg Conservatory in 1919. He graduated twice, first as a pianist in 1923, and then as a composer in 1925. The First Symphony, which was his graduation composition, was widely acclaimed both in the USSR and abroad.

During the 1920s Shostakovich developed his style along constructivist lines, a process which culminated in his surrealist opera *The Nose*, based on Gogol''s story, which utilized Meyerhold's experimental theories of theatre. At the beginning of the 1930s, however, he began to move away from the extremes of the avant-garde, and his 1934 opera *The Lady Macbeth of the*

Mtsensk District made use of many aspects of traditional Russian culture.

The opera was highly popular with the public, but not with the person whose opinion mattered most: Stalin. Two editorials in *Pravda* in 1936 attacking Shostakovich seemed to signal the composer's imminent arrest in the purges, but, almost miraculously, he remained free, in body if not in spirit. He cancelled the première of his Fourth Symphony (it was not performed until 1961), and under severe pressure produced in 1937 a Fifth designed to conform to the requirements of the regime. His most popular work with contemporary audiences, and perhaps his most famous, is the Seventh 'Leningrad' Symphony, written in the city as the German armies approached in 1941. Shostakovich was ordered to leave the city for his own safety – much against his will – as the siege began.

In 1948 Shostakovich again became the target of attacks by the regime. Most of his works were banned, and he was forced to rely on writing cinema music for a living. These restrictions were lifted after Stalin's death, although Shostakovich again came into conflict with the regime over the use of Yevtushenko's poems in his works in the 1960s. His last symphony, the Fifteenth, was written in 1971.

Shostakovich died in Moscow in 1975, hurt but not bowed by the attempts to control his art. He was criticized by left and right for being both 'conservative' and 'decadent'. However, his resilience when faced with huge pressure to conform was demonstrated by the use in his music – right up until his death – of literary compositions that were officially frowned upon.

Hindemith, Ernst Krenek and Franz Schreker, while Alban Berg attended in person the Leningrad première of his expressionistic opera *Wozzeck* in 1927. Experiments in electronic musical instruments were carried out by L.S. Termen (b.1897), whose Théréminvox was subsequently demonstrated in Europe and America. Having made a striking début with his First Symphony in 1925, Shostakovich was officially commissioned in 1927 to write a symphony to celebrate the tenth anniversary of the October Revolution, and incorporated the sound of a factory whistle in the score, while into his Third Symphony, sub-titled 'First of May', he introduced a chorus singing a contemporary text.

In 1932, however, the Russian Association of Proletarian Musicians, together with other writers' associations, was dissolved by the Communist Party and replaced by the Union of Soviet Composers, branches of which were established in the principal cities. Its journal *Sovetskaya muzyka*, which superseded existing music periodicals, was founded in 1933. To this period belongs the commencement of the official doctrine of Socialist Realism, which was defined as 'the truthful, historically concrete presentation of reality in its revolutionary development'. This marks the true beginning of Soviet music, of which the opera *Quiet Flows the Don*, written by the composer I.I. Dzerzhinsky (1909–78) in 1934, is regarded as a classic example.

The establishment of new artistic criteria had far-reaching consequences. Shostakovich's opera

The Lady Macbeth of the Mtsensk District, which had played to packed houses in Leningrad since 1934, was, two years later, severely criticized in the press and subsequently withdrawn; the première of his Fourth Symphony was cancelled. It was not until the end of 1937 that Shostakovich reappeared with his Fifth Symphony, sub-titled 'A Soviet Artist's Reply to Just Criticism', a work which won general acclaim. To this period belong Prokofiev's ballet *Romeo and Juliet*, the First Symphony by the Armenian-born composer A.I. Khachaturyan (1903–78) and the mass songs of I.O. Dunaevsky (1900–55); immediately before the outbreak of the Second World War Prokofiev wrote the cantata *Alexander Nevsky* – originally incidental music to a film by S.M. Eisenstein (1898–1948) – and Yu.A. Shaporin (1887–1966) his *On the Field of Kulikovo* (1939). Shostakovich's Seventh Symphony was completed during the siege of Leningrad and its score was microfilmed and flown to the West, where its frequent performance helped to foster support for the Soviet war effort. Other orchestral works of this period were Shostakovich's Eighth Symphony (1943), Prokofiev's Fifth Symphony (1944) and Khachaturyan's Violin Concerto (1940). Shostakovich's Piano Quintet (1940) and Piano Trio (1944), together with Prokofiev's Piano Sonatas Nos 7–9 and his Sonata for Flute and Piano (1943–44), are outstanding chamber works. Khachaturyan's ballet *Gayane*, from which comes the well-known *Sabre Dance*, was written in 1942.

The party decree of 10 February 1948 accused a number of Soviet composers of 'formalism', singling out Muradeli's opera *The Great Friendship* for particular admonition (though this was mitigated by another decree ten years later). Prokofiev died on the same day as Stalin in 1953. Shostakovich continued to dominate the scene as a composer of orchestral music, but his Thirteenth Symphony,

Sergey Prokofiev. Drawing by Henri Matisse

Alfred Shnittke

written in 1962 to verses by Yevgeny Yevtushenko on the subject of Baby Yar (the scene of a massacre of Jews) ran into ideological difficulties over the text and was revised. His secular oratorios *Song of the Forests* (1949) and *The Execution of Stepan Razin* (1964) achieved success abroad. V.P. Solov'ev-Sedoy (1907–79) gained wide acclaim with his song *Evenings in the Moscow Woodlands*. The *Oratorio Pathétique* by G.V. Sviridov (b.1915), first performed in 1959 with words by V.V. Mayakovsky (1893–1930), was much praised in the Soviet musical press and was awarded a Lenin Prize; other notable works of this period were Prokofiev's last opera *War and Peace* (première 1955), Shaporin's opera *The Decembrists* (1953) and Khachaturyan's ballet *Spartacus* (première 1956). The music of the composers G.I. Ustvol'skaya (b.1919) and A.N. Pakhmutova (b.1929) also attracted attention.

The period following 1965 saw profound changes in Soviet musical life, including the loss of two leading composers – Shostakovich and Khachaturyan. By the time of his death in 1975 Shostakovich had completed 15 symphonies and 15 string quartets, which virtually constitute a history of Soviet music. His conversations with Solomon Volkov, published under the title *Testimony* in 1979, were dismissed as spurious in the Soviet Union and evoked mixed responses in the West; they suggest, however, the presence of programmatic elements in a number of his symphonies, a fuller understanding of which may become apparent in the course of time. An edition of his works, begun in 1978, has now appeared. Soviet composition over the last twenty-five years, however, has revealed an increasing familiarity on the part of the new generation of Soviet composers with West European contemporary techniques. Aleatoric and serial elements (though used with tonal implications) are found, for instance, in the *Concerto Buffo*, written in 1966 for a combination of flute, trumpet, piano, percussion and strings by S.M. Slonimsky (b.1932), a work which was both published and recorded, while the score of *Poetoriya* (published 1975) by R.K. Shchedrin (b.1932) has a decidedly 'new look'. In his scores Shchedrin employs a host of technical devices – note rows, aleatoric elements, collage techniques, as well as unconventional approaches to form, while his opera *Dead Souls* (première 1977) abounds in novel sound effects often recalling electro-acoustic music – a medium at that time officially discouraged. During the 1970s Slonimsky frequently included jazz elements with beat accompaniment in his compositions, though in most of his works may be found fragments of folk-song, which were incorporated, no doubt, to meet the ideological requirements of the time.

Of the many (literally) thousands of composers in the former Soviet Union (the Moscow Branch of the Union of Soviet Composers had 600 members alone), one of the most gifted is A.G. Shnittke (b.1934), whose polystylistic compositions have been acclaimed both in the USSR and abroad. Drawing his inspiration from diverse sources (his *Fourth Symphony* of 1984, for instance, utilizes sacred elements from Russian Orthodox, Roman Catholic and Protestant chant, Lutheran chorale and Jewish cantillation), such works as his Third Violin Concerto (1978) and Cello Concerto (1986) have achieved international success. In 1988 he was composer in residence at Aldeburgh; in 1989 a Schnittke Festival was held in Stockholm; and in 1990 he was guest-of-honour at the Huddersfield Contemporary Music Festival together with the gifted composer S. Gubaydulina (b.1931). Shnittke is now living in the West. The music of composers such as E. Denisov (b.1919), the Estonian Arvo Pärt (b.1935), V. Artemov (b.1940), A. Knaifel (b.1943), V. Lobanov (b.1947), D. Smirnov (b.1948), E. Firsova (b.1950), V. Genin (b.1958) and others, is universally highly regarded.

The impact of glasnost on music has been considerable. After 1935 Soviet composers had to ensure that their music was ideologically sound (the symphony had to be programmatic; song, opera, secular oratorio and cantata to employ appropriate texts; chamber and keyboard compositions to contain folk intonations). A much more liberal attitude towards musical composition was eventually displayed by the state with the result that the doctrine of Socialist Realism finally became meaningless. By 1992 sacred music was not only being published and records produced, but also publicly performed. Music before 1750 (once *terra incognita*) is now being explored, the organ studied, history texts rewritten, rock music encouraged and a far franker discussion of musical life is evident in the musical press. The ever-increasing cultural exchanges with the Western

Right. Street musicians on the Arbat, Moscow

world (particularly with the United States) are indubitably leading to a cross-fertilization of ideas in a manner which only a decade ago would have been inconceivable. While the general standard of musical performance remains at a consistently high level, electronic technology is far less developed and the extent to which composers will avail themselves of electronic media in the future, raises an interesting question. GS

MUSIC IN THE FORMER SOVIET REPUBLICS

While some republics, such as Ukraine, Armenia and Georgia, possessed well-developed musical cultures before the Revolution, elsewhere acquaintance with the forms and practices of West European music has been a comparatively recent phenomenon. By 1992 virtually all fifteen former republics of the USSR possessed opera and ballet theatres, a state conservatory, music and choreographic schools, a Union of Composers, performing groups attached to radio and television, and a philharmonic organization embracing symphony orchestras, orchestras of folk instruments, and choral and instrumental groups. While much was done to encourage local musical life and to maintain interest in national customs (ensuring at the same time development along correct ideological lines), composers and musicians were reminded that they formed an integral part of the Soviet Union and shared a common policy. However, as a result of glasnost and the creation of the Commonwealth of Independent States, this policy is being reassessed. This is especially true of those republics with a strong ethnic or non-Christian culture.

Ukraine has a long musical tradition and it was from Ukraine and Belorussia that polyphony, based on that of the Catholic Church, was introduced into

Russian sacred music in the seventeenth century. Ukrainian singers and composers, notably D.S. Bortnyansky (1751–1825), were prominent at the Russian Court in the eighteenth century. The operas of N.V. Lisenko (1842–1912) were of national importance in the nineteenth century. Of the modern Ukrainian composers (some of whom are Jewish), R.M. Glière (1874–1956) was probably the best known outside the USSR, other figures being the violinist D. F. Oistrakh (1908–74), the pianist Emil Gilel's (1916–85), the conductor N.G. Rakhlin (1906–79) and the bass singer B.R. Gmyra (b.1903). Odessa has long been renowned for its musical life and has been the home of many outstanding musicians.

Armenia is particularly rich in musical traditions. The Armenian Church, with its wealth of sacred chant, was established in the fourth century, and there is a strong idiosyncratic folk music. Of the Armenian composers of the nineteenth century S.G. Komitas (1869–1935) and A.A. Spendiarov (Spendiaryan) (1871–1928) are notable, while among more recent composers are numbered A.G. Arutyunyan (b.1920), A.A. Babadzhanyan (b.1921) and E.M. Mirzoyan (b.1921). The single most outstanding composer is A.I. Khachaturyan (1903–78). Prominent Armenian musicians include the conductor A.S. Melik-Pashaev (1905–64), the coloratura soprano G.M. Gasparyan (b.1922) and the mezzo-soprano Zara Dolukhanova (b.1918).

There is evidence that music has existed in Georgia since pre-Christian times, notable being the folk music with its highly individual choral polyphony, and the sacred music (the Christian Church in Georgia was established in the fourth century). Georgia was annexed by Russia in 1801. During the nineteenth century an important part in the country's musical development was played by M.M. Ippolitov-Ivanov (1859–1935), other more recent composers being A.M. Balanchivadze (b.1906), V.I. Muradeli (1908–70), O.V. Taktakishvili (b.1924), whose piano concerto is often performed in the West, S.F. Tsintsadze (b.1925) and G. Kancheli (b.1935). Tbilisi, the capital, has a fine opera house, in which a prominent performer was the veteran dancer and ballet-master V.M. Chabukiani (b.1910). The Georgian State Dance Company is well known.

The musical development of Azerbaijan has been influenced by the Muslim religion; recently several local composers have come to the fore, among whom K.A. Kara-Karaev (b.1918) and A.D. Melikov (b.1933) are outstanding.

In the Baltic area, Lithuania, Latvia and Estonia are all musically active, and each has a distinctive profile. But whereas a national music did not develop in Estonia and Latvia until the mid-nineteenth cen-

Jazz quartet playing beneath the flag of an independent Ukraine

tury because of foreign cultural domination, music in Lithuania has a much longer and more developed history, extending back to at least the fourteenth century. In Estonia L. Auster (b.1912), A.I. Kapp (1878–1952), V.K. Kapp (1913–64), J.P. Rääts (b.1932) and, especially, A. Pärt (b.1935), who lives abroad, have all produced interesting compositions. An outstanding singer was the baritone G. Ots (1920–75). In Latvia J. Vītols (1863–1948), J.A. Ivanovs (b. 1906) a prolific composer of symphonies, R.S. Grinblat (b.1930), V. Barkauskas (b.1931), P. Dikcius (b.1933), and O. Balakauskas (b.1937) have all made contributions, while in Lithuania notable are the artist-composer M. Čiurlionis (1875–1911) and the symphonist J.A. Juzeliunas (b.1916).

There is also much musical activity in Belarus, Moldova and in Asian states such as Kyrgyzstan, Uzbekistan, Tajikistan, Kazakhstan and Turkmenistan, with some of their composers now known in the West.

Opportunities to assess developments in music of the Soviet republics were provided by the various annual gatherings and plenums held in Moscow or in regional capitals, where new works from the republics were performed and discussed. With the break-up of the Soviet Union in December 1991 no doubt radical changes will take place in musical life, linked both to nationalism and religion. In those countries where familiarity with European music is less than a hundred years old, especially those where strong Islamic fundamentalist movements arise, these changes could well be dramatic.   GS

SACRED MUSIC

It is fairly certain that sacred chant was introduced into Russia from Byzantium after the adoption of Christianity by Vladimir, Grand Duke of Kiev, in 988. In the course of the following two centuries it underwent a gradual process of transformation. Like the Byzantine rite the Russian was unaccompanied, no instruments being permitted in its performance apart from the human voice. It also shared with Byzantium similar melodies, hymn texts (probably translated into Russian), and the system of eight 'modes', though these were not modes in the West European sense of the word but rather melodic formulae. Though at first no specific Russian notation existed, various systems gradually evolved, of which the *znamenny* notation (from the word *zna-mya*, meaning 'sign') is the most important. The *znamenny* chant, which dates from about the eleventh century, is the foundation of Russian sacred music. Like Gregorian chant in Western Europe, Russian chant had no fixed metre and followed the inflection of the words.

During the sixteenth century an attempt was made to rid the chant of corruptions which had crept into it over the preceding centuries and which had arisen through developments in the Russian language. Through the insertion of extra syllables in the chant, and the addition of excessive ornamentation by singers, the services had increased greatly in length. The ecclesiastical assembly (the *Stoglav* Council) convened by Ivan IV in 1551 introduced reforms, among which was the creation of special schools for the preparation of singers and precentors. Attempts were made to improve and simplify the *znamenny* notation and two important choirs were formed, belonging to the Tsar and the Patriarch respectively. Some rudimentary attempts were made at sacred polyphonic writing, at that time highly developed in Western Europe.

It was in the seventeenth century, however, that great changes occurred which affected sacred music. In order to offset the increasing influence of the Catholic Church (whose sacred polyphonic music had a strong emotional appeal) and to strengthen the power of the Russian Orthodox Church, from 1654 onwards Moscow was visited by Greek, Ukrainian and other scholars, who introduced a kind of sacred polyphonic part-song, utilizing a five-line notation, a type never previously employed in Russia. The enforcing of polyphony and the new notation, with other radical changes in religious usage, were among the causes of the Great Schism, resulting in the flight of many Old Believers to remote parts of the country. The *Musical Grammar* by N. Diletsky (c.1631–90), written about 1680, is of importance, in that it was the first work to introduce West European musical terminology to Russia and to explain some of the principles of polyphonic composition. Further attempts at correcting errors in the books of sacred chant were made by A. Mezenets in 1655 and 1668. The last part of the seventeenth and the first part of the eighteenth centuries saw the rise of a number of composers of sacred music in Russia, among them V. Titov, though technically this music, comprising concertos, psalms and polyphonic chants, was inferior to West European counterparts.

During the second half of the eighteenth century, as with most other arts, Russian music fell under Italian influence, an important part being played by the Italian masters Galuppi and Sarti. Galuppi's most outstanding pupil during his time in Russia (1765–68) was the Ukrainian Bortnyansky, who, having studied in Italy, was appointed to the Court Chapel, of which he later became director. Under his aegis the singing of the Imperial Chapel reached a high degree of technical perfection, while his own sacred music, though influenced by the Italian idiom, served as a model for future generations.

Notable during the nineteenth century was the work of A.F. L'vov (1787–1870), director of the Imperial Chapel, who not only raised the standard of singing to unprecedented heights, but, having assembled a huge body of chants, undertook the immense task of publishing the complete cycle of liturgical chants for the church year – the *Obikhod*. Glinka also composed sacred music, in which he was influenced by the writings of Prince V. Odoevsky (1804–69), a particularly well-informed man for his time and a connoisseur of sacred chant. Odoevsky appears to have been the first Russian scholar to draw attention to the existence of theoretical writings on Russian chant, and, by discussing the manuscripts of Mezenets and others, did much to provoke interest in the subject. Before the Revolution sacred music was written in St Petersburg by composers such as Rimsky-Korsakov, Lyadov, G. L'vovsky (1830–94), and especially A.A. Arkhangel'sky (1846–1924), who was one of the first to use women's voices in sacred Russian chant.

The chief centre of sacred composition in Moscow was the Moscow Synodal School, where much valuable work was undertaken by its director, S. Smolensky (1848–1909) and the assistant choirmaster A.D. Kastal'sky (1856–1926). In his arrangements Kastal'sky strove to devise a homogeneous musical language, in which the harmony and counterpoint arose spontaneously from the chant, particular attention being paid to the words. Fine choral works were also written by other members of the Moscow School – P.G. Chesnokov (1877–1944), A.T. Grechaninov (1864–1956), V.S. Kalinnikov (1866–1901), S.I. Taneev (1856–1916), Rakhmaninov and others. Rakhmaninov is remembered for his *Liturgy* in free style (1910) and for his *All-Night Vigil* (1915). Tchaikovsky composed a *Liturgy of St John Chrysostom* (1878) for unaccompanied choir, which is one of the few attempts at setting a complete service, and an *All-Night Vigil* (1881). Mention should also be made of Anton Rubinstein's sacred operas and oratorios, such as *Paradise Lost, The Tower of Babel, Moses, Sulamith* and *Christus*, which were performed outside Russia.

The mid-nineteenth century onwards saw an increasing interest in the study of Russian chant, important works being written by D.V. Razumovsky (1818–1889), Yu. Arnol'd (1811–1898), and later I. Voznesensky (1838–1910), S. Smolensky, V. Metallov (1862–1926) and A. Preobrazhensky (1870–1929). After the Revolution research into sacred music in Russia virtually ceased until the 1960s, when there was a revival of interest. Indeed, investigations into Russian sacred chant were conducted almost entirely by scholars in the West.

In recent times, however, there has been a remarkable change of attitude by the state towards Russian sacred music. The return of the Danilov Monastery to the Church in 1984, the granting of permission for the Church to resume its headquarters in Moscow, the allowing of a new cathedral to be built in the Soviet Union for the first time since the Revolution, were recognitions by the state that the Church and its music could play an important and cohesive social role. Nor is it without significance that the year 1988 commemorated the thousandth anniversary of the establishment of the Russian Church and the founding of the Russian State. Whereas a few years ago performances of sacred music (either Russian or Western) were a comparative rarity, today churches are being restored, choirs re-formed, and records of liturgical music publicly sold, the important musical roles often sung by leading operatic performers. Sacred works, previously omitted from the so-called 'complete editions' of the music of Glinka, Rimsky-Korsakov and Tchaikovsky, are to be included in forthcoming publications, and the whole attitude towards sacred music and its performance and investigation is currently being re-appraised.   GS

LITURGICAL BACKGROUND

Mainly known in its choral form, Russian sacred music embraces a range of participants: being a function of the total worship of the Orthodox Church, this liturgical singing concerns as much the worshippers, who participate through their attention and singing, and the officiating clergy, as it does the more specialized choir and individual singers and readers. Inherited from Byzantium, Christian worship in Russia has its particular vocal expression in the chanting and singing of the human voice, the most sensitive of all musical instruments. Psalmody, melody and harmony combine to make the music of the liturgy. Ordinary speech is never used: only when he delivers a sermon does the priest 'speak'. Bells to summon the people to attend the various services through their elaborate harmonies and sparkling rhythms hang outside each church building; being incapable of verbal expression, all other instruments have been barred from use in the liturgy.

The language used in the liturgy is Church Slavonic, a linguistic relative of Russian, dating back to the ninth century and having its own history of development. Beloved by the believer for its beauty and depth of meaning, this near-vernacular, through its employment in the liturgical re-enactment of sacred events and festivals considerably influences the making and interpretation of church melodies; in turn, these have a powerful didactic role. The essential experience of the collective liturgy is that

Nikolay Rimsky-Korsakov

of the personal divine presence in the Church, in which God – not only the people – is the prime 'listener'. Any noticeable departure from this basic liturgical attitude (such as theatrical or concert performances) must be deemed untypical and worldly.

The character of the singing varies according to the role of the participants: the deacon chants the litanies and the Holy Scripture and conducts the congregation in prayer; there are no pews and everybody stands in worship. The priest, both a living image of Christ the High Priest and a representative of the people, voices the words of the sacraments, sings the Gospel and addresses God on behalf of all. Through the skill of their voices the choir-leaders with their choirs, the individual singers and the readers are able to express in the liturgy the mind and feeling of the Church (repentance, joy, praise) and to convey the continuity of its teaching in the festal, lenten and ordinary hymnographies. In monasteries the antiphonal form is in use: the alternative singing of two choirs and their coming together in prominent liturgical sequences such as the Evensong Hymn at vespers or the Great Doxology at matins; the movements of the clergy (when they cense the icons and the people, or carry the Gospel book in solemn procession to the ambo); and the iconographic layout in the church – all reveal the spatial, architectural purpose and shape of the sacred building. Similarly, in cathedrals and major parishes two choirs often share the choral programme of the liturgy: a senior choir on the right-hand side of the sanctuary is more skilled and technically ambitious; that on the left is simpler. In many ordinary parishes a single choir suffices. The risk now, as the post-Soviet economic crisis worsens, is that lack of funds may reduce the activity of many senior choirs or even squeeze them out of existence entirely.

The liturgical forms of worship may be classified as follows:

- The life-cycle of a person: in sacraments such as baptism, the Eucharist, marriage and unction, and services of prayer held on occasion of trials and joys (journeys, illness, new undertakings) and of death (funeral and memorial services) the Church sanctifies the entire existence of a Christian, emphasizing the many manifestations of joy, grief, hope, endurance, love, entreaty, trust and faith.

- The yearly lenten and festal cycles: in the movable Easter cycle the seven weeks' lenten preparation gives rise to the liturgical climax of Good Friday, without which neither the peace of Saturday in Holy Week nor the festivities of Easter can be understood. The fixed festal cycle centres on Christmas and embraces nine feasts of the Lord and His Mother, as well as numerous saints' days throughout the year.

- The weekly cycle: this focuses on Sunday and culminates in the Divine Liturgy, the Eucharist, for which (due to its largely unchanging shape) many composers have written a variety of original settings reminiscent of the Western motet or anthem, as well as complete liturgies sung by the right-hand choir. A popular service of praise is the *akathist*, which is sung by the priest and the congregation.

- The daily cycle: this is best represented by its music in the Saturday night vigil where, apart from occasional anthems, considerable use is made of the eight-tone musical system, the *Oktoikh*, which gives the liturgy a definite stylistic consistency.   MF

FOLK MUSIC

Russian folk-song is remarkable for its wealth and diversity. In its oldest form it reaches back into the period before Russia's conversion to Christianity in the tenth century; texts of the most ancient folk-songs contain references to the worship of pagan deities and reverence for primeval forces. The early songs, such as the *khorovod* (round dance) and calendar song (relating to the seasonal year), are of limited compass and of simple structure, often consisting of variations on a basic theme. A unique place in both literature and music is occupied by the *byliny* (heroic ballads), which were composed primarily in the towns of Kiev and Novgorod and describe events occurring from the eleventh to sixteenth centuries, in which typical subjects are heroes, such as Il'ya of Murom, Dobrynya Nikitich, Sadko and others. Some of the *byliny* were taken over by the 'historical' songs, of which the subjects were more concerned with specific historical events. Their full flowering occurred between the sixteenth and eighteenth centuries. The *dukhovnye stikhi* (spiritual verses) are melodically similar to the *byliny* and historical songs, but employ subject matter taken from the Bible and the lives of the saints; this genre was until recently largely neglected by Soviet scholars.

A special and substantial place in Russian folk music is occupied by wedding songs. Collated over a long historical period (and thus showing great diversity of structure) they formed an essential part of the traditional peasant wedding, a long and elaborate ritual accompanied by songs and laments. Comic or humorous songs were performed by the *skomorokhi* (the Russian clowns or buffoons, equivalent of the West European merrymen, *Spielmänner* or *jongleurs*). Unique in Russian folk-song is the so-called 'lyrical' song, which came to full fruition

Right. Village musicians in the Volga region with guitar and concertina

during the sixteenth and seventeenth centuries. Notable for its rich melodic content, rhythmic freedom and wide vocal range, the lyrical song may be said to express the poetic feelings of the performer; in its language often symbolic and metaphorical, the singer draws extravagant parallels between personal emotions and natural phenomena (the sun, the dew, rivers, birds and trees). The lyrical song is often performed in a special kind of folk polyphony, which is improvised in accordance with certain traditions; it may be regarded as the culmination of Russian folk-song composition, for in the eighteenth century, new song forms influenced by West European music began to appear particularly in the towns, among them the 'town song', the recruit song, and (at a later date) the *chastushka* (witty jingle). Other types of song include Christmas carols, soldiers' and sailors' songs, prison songs, revolutionary songs, and children's songs.

The first attempts at collecting the words and music of Russian folk-songs were made in the eighteenth century; V. Trutovsky, a Ukrainian, issued four volumes (1776–95), followed by that (1790) of J. Práč (d.1818) and a collection, made in the 1780s and attributed to Kirsha Danilov, that was first published in full in 1818.

Important nineteenth-century collections, inspired by the Slavophile or Russian Nationalist movement, were those of Balakirev (1866), Tchaikovsky (1868–69) and Rimsky-Korsakov (1876), all of whom included folk songs in their own compositions. It was not until the last part of the century, however, that musicians began to realise that many of the Russian folk-tunes were modal in nature (not

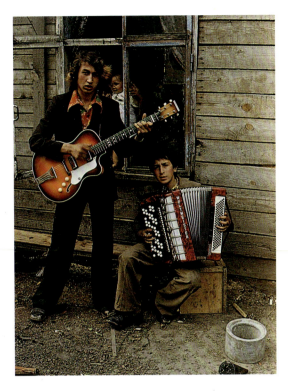

written in the conventional major-minor system), that folk-songs were not sung each time in exactly the same manner but were melodically and rhythmically varied, and that certain types of folk-song and folk music could be sung and performed polyphonically – factors which may be seen in the collections (1879, 1885) of Yu. N. Mel'gunov (1846–93), and (1904, 1909) of Ye. E. Lineva (1853–1919) and others. Lineva was one of the first Russian folk-song collectors to record folk-songs on a phonograph.

During the Soviet period there was intensive research into virtually all aspects of folk music. Following the pattern set by the Imperial Russian Geographical Society in the years preceding the Revolution, numerous expeditions were sent to collect folk-songs in remote districts. The results were analysed and in part published. Collections of folk instruments were established, substantial numbers of folk-songs were recorded, though only a fraction of these has been issued commercially on disc, and volumes of folk-songs were published from time to time. Poor funding and lack of facilities and trained personnel have been a recurring problem. There is by no means total agreement among scholars as to the precise structure of Russian folk-song and scholarship is constantly being reassessed.   GS

Title page of the first edition of Práč's collection of folk songs, St Petersburg, 1790

СОБРАНIЕ
НАРОДНЫХЪ РУСКИХЪ
ПѢСЕНЪ
съ ихъ ГОЛОСАМИ
на
МУЗЫКУ положилЪ
ИВАНЪ ПРАЧЪ.

Печатано
въ
Типографiи
Горнаго училища
1790.

VOCAL AND CHORAL MUSIC

Of the many songs written by Russian composers during the nineteenth century, those of Musorgsky are outstanding in their melodic and harmonic originality, the melodies themselves often revealing folk influence. Not only is there a close link between words and music but many of the songs show psychological insight into the life and condition of the Russian peasant. Musorgsky's song cycle, *The Nursery* vividly portrays events seen through the eyes of a child. The songs of Tchaikovsky and Rakhmaninov are also well known outside Russia. Among Soviet composers the songs of Prokofiev, Shostakovich, Kabalevsky (1904–87), G. V. Sviridov, Slonimsky and Shnittke all deserve attention.

If secular choral music in pre-revolutionary Russia tended to be overshadowed by sacred (one of the few outstanding secular choral works is Rakhmaninov's *The Bells*, written in 1913), the Soviet era saw the appearance of a number of secular oratorios and cantatas, among them Prokofiev's *Alexander Nevsky* (1938), Shaporin's *On the Field of Kulikovo* (1939), Koval's *Yemel'yan Pugachev* (1942), Shostakovich's *Song of the Forests* (1949), Salmanov's *The Twelve* (1957), Sviridov's *Poem in Memory of Sergey Yesenin* (1955) and *Oratorio Pathétique* (1959). Petrov's *Peter the First* (subtitled 'vocal-symphonic frescoes, utilizing original texts and historical documents and ancient folksongs', 1974) and Shchedrin's *Poetoriya* to words by A.A. Voznesensky (b.1933) (a concerto for poet, accompanied by a woman's voice, mixed chorus and symphony orchestra, including a beam of light, 1975) both excited favourable comment and were widely performed in the USSR.

Among recent choral works to attract attention are the secular oratorios *From 'The Russian Primary Chronicle'* for soloists, chorus and chamber orchestra, using a text from the eleventh-century Chronicle, written in 1983 by G. Dmitriev (b.1942) and *Lament for Andrey Bogolubsky, Grand Duke of Vladimir* (1987), likewise based on ancient Russian chronicles, folklore and historiographic sources by the young composer V. Genin (b.1958).   GS

The baritone Dmitry Hvorostovsky in a production of Eugene Onegin, *London 1993*

OPERA

Russian opera differs from West European opera in its more extensive employment of folk material, its use of national subjects, its wide use of choral elements, its emphasis on male vocal roles and the relative absence of female coloratura. Though the first Russian operas were composed in the eighteenth century, it was in the hands of Glinka that the real foundations of national opera were established. In his two operas *A Life for the Tsar* (*Ivan Susanin*) (1836) and *Ruslan and Lyudmila* (1842) he ingeniously combined Italian arioso, Germanic counterpoint and heterogeneous folk materials to form a distinctive musical language. In style, however, his operas are markedly different. Whereas *A Life for the Tsar* is in the epic tradition with considerable emphasis on the peasant folk element, *Ruslan and Lyudmila* is harmonically and orchestrally more adventurous, with oriental dances, richly ornamented arias, powerful choruses and brilliant orchestral numbers.

Throughout the nineteenth century Russian composers were influenced by Glinka's operas; Musorgsky's *Boris Godunov* and Rimsky-Korsakov's *The Tsar's Bride* continued the epic vein, while *Khovanshchina* (by Musorgsky, completed by Rimsky-Korsakov) and Rimsky's *The Golden Cockerel* both exemplify the exotic tradition. Of Rimsky-Korsakov's other operas *May Night* utilizes a plot by Gogol', while his *Sadko* employs *bylina* (heroic ballad) material from the Novgorod cycle. *The Golden Cockerel*, based on Pushkin's poem, completed in 1907, encountered difficulties with censorship and its performance was never permitted in the Imperial Theatres. Though Tchaikovsky was also a prolific opera composer, only his *Eugene Onegin* and *The Queen of Spades* (in which he exploited and sentimentalized Pushkin's plots) have achieved lasting success outside Russia. A unique place is occupied by Borodin's *Prince Igor* – perhaps the finest manifestation of the heroic element in Russian opera. While support for opera came primarily from the Imperial Theatres, a private opera company was founded by S.I. Mamontov (1841–1918) in Moscow in 1885, and was succeeded by S.I. Zimin's (1875–1942) opera theatre in 1904. The season of Russian opera given by the impresario Diaghilev in Paris in 1908, which included Musorgsky's *Boris Godunov* with Chaliapine (Shalyapin) in the title role, made an unforgettable impression on Western Europe. Stravinsky's *The Nightingale* was written in 1914 and his *Mavra* in 1922.

Of the many operas composed since 1917, those of Prokofiev and Shostakovich are of special importance. Whereas Prokofiev's *The Love for Three Oranges* (1919) and *The Fiery Angel* (1927) were

Right. *The pianist Svyatoslav Rikhter*

written during his absence from Russia, *Semyon Kotko* (1939), *The Duenna* (1940), *The Story of a Real Man* (1948) and *War and Peace* (1952) all show the influence of Socialist Realism. Shostakovich's best-known operas are *The Nose* (1928) and *The Lady Macbeth of the Mtsensk District* (1932) – the latter subsequently performed in a modified version under the title *Katerina Izmaylova*. The music and text of Glinka's *A Life for the Tsar* were likewise altered, and the opera retitled *Ivan Susanin*. While many operas by Soviet composers were highly rated in the USSR – for example, Shchedrin's *Not Love Alone* (1961), Slonimsky's *Virineya* (1967), and Shchedrin's *Dead Souls* (1977) – only a few became known outside the former Soviet Union; Shaporin's opera *The Decembrists* (performed in 1953) was a rare example. Operetta also enjoyed great popularity in the USSR and attracted the attention of composers such as Shostakovich, Dunaevsky, Kabalevsky and Khrennikov.

Operatic productions are generally created on a lavish scale, with large casts and realistic scenery. Stage effects are frequently employed and many operas include choreographic elements. Singing has always varied in quality and according to region. Orchestral accompaniments are of a consistently high standard. Until recently only few selected Western works were in the current repertoire, these being selected primarily for their ideological rather than musical significance. Russian opera is now discussed on a regular basis in the Western press in such journals as *Opera*.   GS

PERFORMERS

Among the many outstanding performers, mention may be made of the pianists Anton Rubinstein, Vladimir de Pachmann, Sergey Rakhmaninov, Sergey Prokofiev, Lev Oborin, Yakov Zak, Svyatoslav Rikhter, Emil' Gilel's, Vladimir Ashkenazy, Yury Yegorov, and Yevgeny Kissin; the violinists David and Igor Oistrakh, Leonid Kogan, Valery Klimov, Gidon Kremer and Viktor Tret'yakov; the cellists Daniil Shafran and Mstislav Rostropovich; the sopranos Valeriya Barsova, Goar Gasparayan and Galina Vishnevskaya; the mezzo-sopranos Nadezhda Obukhova, Irina Arkhipova, Zara Dolukhanova and Yelena Obraztsova; the tenors Leonid Sobinov, Sergey Lemeshev, Vladimir Atlantov and Vladislav P'yavko; the basses Fedor Chaliapine (Shalyapin), Mark Reyzen, Ivan Petrov, Aleksandr Vedernikov and Yevgeny Nesterenko.

The annual International Tchaikovsky Competition, held in Moscow since 1958, attracts widespread interest and has served as a launching-point for many distinguished performers.   GS

ORCHESTRAS

A novel experiment in the early days of the Soviet period was the 'Persimfans' – an orchestra without a conductor, which existed in Moscow 1922–23. The most famous Soviet orchestra, however, was the Leningrad (now St Petersburg) Philharmonic (1917), which developed from the former Court Orchestra, while in Moscow of chief importance were the State Symphony Orchestra of the USSR (1936), the Bol'shoy Symphony Orchestra of Radio and Television, the Symphony Orchestra of the Moscow Philharmonic (1953), the Moscow State Symphony Orchestra (1955), and the Moscow Chamber Orchestra, directed until his emigration in 1976 by Rudol'f Barshay. The conductors Yevgeny Mravinsky, Kirill Kondrashin, Yevgeny Svetlanov and Gennady Rozhdestvensky have all achieved international renown.   GS

MUSIC EDUCATION

Until the middle of the nineteenth century music education in Russia was not organized on a systematic basis, though there is evidence of tuition being provided by sacred bodies, orphanages, theatre schools, universities and visiting foreign musicians. The Moscow Synodal School for the study of sacred chant was opened in 1857, and was also the first educational establishment in Russia to introduce a scheme for the study of folk music. With the inception of the Russian Musical Society in St Petersburg (1859), thanks to the efforts of Anton Rubinstein, music classes were opened; the Conservatory there was founded in 1862, and that of Moscow in 1866; other branches of the Society set up music classes during the course of the century. For lack of skilled teachers in Russia, Rubinstein drew many of his staff from Western Europe, especially Germany, and the imprint of Germanic thought and method had far-reaching effects. Music education in Russia then relied largely on textbooks translated from foreign writers; however, Tchaikovsky's manual on harmony, Taneev's book on counterpoint and Rimsky-Korsakov's volumes on harmony and orchestration are all internationally known. Despite the fact that the Russian Musical Society and the Conservatories were founded for the benefit of Russian music, strong opposition was encountered from Slavophiles such as Balakirev, who (with Lomakin) opened his own Free School of Music in 1862 as a rival establishment. In 1883 the Moscow Philharmonic Society started a School of Music and Drama. Around the turn of the nineteenth century there were several initiatives towards education for the masses, among which may be mentioned the People's Conservatory opened in Moscow in 1906. The Gnesin Music Institute, founded in Moscow in 1895, is still in existence.

During the Soviet period music education was standardized. Detection of musical talent began at kindergarten level; at about the age of six, students of outstanding ability entered a 'ten-year school' where children's normal academic studies were augmented by special musical instruction, often conducted by leading musicians. Children less musically gifted were sent to a 'seven-year school', then entered a secondary specialized school after which successful pupils from both this and the 'ten-year school' could enter a state conservatory, the most prestigious being those at Moscow and Leningrad. Tuition at the conservatory lasted for five years, after which a further period of postgraduate study was possible. Employment was usually arranged by the Union of Soviet Composers, an organization which was not concerned with composition alone. Political training played an important part in the life of the Soviet musician and much emphasis was placed on correct ideological attitudes; to write music for children in particular was a task expected of all Soviet composers. Music education today, however, is in a state of flux.   GS

A bandura class at the Leontovich music school in Vinnitsa, Ukraine

POPULAR TOURING ENSEMBLES

During the nineteenth century a number of Russian ensembles toured abroad, among them the peasant choirs conducted by Prince Yu. Golitsyn (1823–72) and D. Agrenev-Slavyansky (1834–1908); the latter group, formed in 1869, specialized in folk-song. An unusual ensemble for the period was the Vladimir Hornplayers, formed by N. Kondrat'ev in the 1870s, whose music was played polyphonically on shepherds' horns (in no way connected with the single-note metal horns of the earlier Russian horn band). The first orchestra of folk instruments was that of V.V. Andreev (1861–1918): his Great-Russian Folk Orchestra (founded 1886) toured extensively and included 'families' of balalaikas and domras, constructed to his own specifications. M. Pyatnitsky (1864–1927) founded his folk chorus in 1910.

After the Revolution great attention was paid to popular ensembles. The Andreev Ensemble, enlarged in size, instruments and repertoire, became known as the Osipov Russian Folk Orchestra. The Pyatnitsky Russian Folk Chorus retained its name, but since 1938 has been augmented by a dance group and folk orchestra. The Radio and Television Orchestra of Russian Folk Instruments, formed in Moscow in 1945, is well known in Russia, while the Ensemble of Song and Dance of the Soviet Army (1928), the Moiseev Ensemble (1937), and Berezka Ensemble (1948) have achieved world renown. Also outstanding have been the Voronezh Ensemble (1943), the Georgian State Dance Company (1945), and the Siberian Omsk Folk Chorus (1950).

Choral ensembles too are extremely popular. The oldest surviving choir in Russia today is that of the Academic Kapella in St Petersburg, which traces its origins back to the Grand Ducal Singing Clerks established by Ivan III in 1489 to participate in services in the Cathedral of the Assumption in the Kremlin. After the foundation of St Petersburg, the Singing Clerks were transferred to the new capital, and were named in 1763 the Imperial Court Chapel Choir – a title that was retained until 1917. The Choir of Patriarchal Singing Clerks came into being in 1589, being renamed the Moscow Synodal Choir in 1721; its tour of Europe in 1911 was a memorable event. The St Petersburg Philharmonic Society was founded in 1802, Beethoven's *Missa Solemnis* being given its first performance there in 1824. Also noteworthy are the Russian Choral Society founded in Moscow in 1878, and Aleksandr Arkhangel'sky's mixed choir, established in 1880, which performed sacred and secular Russian works both in Russia and abroad.

Outstanding among present-day choral ensembles are the Academic Russian Choir (1936), the

Republican Choir (1942), the Moscow State Chorus (1956) (all based in Moscow), and the Academic Kapella and the Kapella Boys' Choir in St Petersburg. Well-trained choral ensembles are also maintained by radio and television, the best being the Moscow State Radio and Television Chorus. GS

JAZZ

Soviet jazz had a peculiar history. It faced three main problems: periodic persecution by the state, competition from other genres of popular music, and the need to establish its own authentic voice. The earliest forms of jazz (ragtime and related dance music) appeared in the last decade of tsarist rule and began to pick up a following among the urban upper classes. After the hiatus of war and revolution, jazz returned to Russia along with other forms of popular culture. The political, social, and cultural climate of NEP made this possible although many Bolsheviks opposed jazz as decadent and foreign. As in the previous epoch, jazz was initially an élitist trend. The first jazz concert (1922) shared billing with a poetry reading; avant-garde figures such as Vsevolod Meyerhold on the stage and Dziga Vertov on the screen used jazz to symbolize capitalist decay. By the late twenties new Soviet bands had replaced the visiting Negro ensembles and formed the basis of the jazz era of the 1930s.

Photomontage by Rodchenko for Mayakovsky's About This, *1923, using jazz motifs*

The original Soviet jazzmen came mostly from the educated class and the ethnic minorities – A.K. L'vov-Velyaminov, Sigizmund Kort, Georgy Landsberg, and the better known Leonid Utesov and Aleksandr Tsfasman. Their music, highly derivative, had by 1928 conquered large segments of the urban middle classes, NEP businessmen, some workers, and a few powerful official sponsors. Some government officials even considered jazz suitable music at congresses. Both foreign and domestic bands ranged from hot and swingy to smoother salon styles. With jazz came the dance craze. On stage and in the higher-toned dining rooms, the salon dance reigned – imported and erotically suggestive acrobatic steps such as 'Tango of Death' were sometimes performed by celebrity dance couples. The new and revived dance styles won over young and old. But party and Komsomol moralizers saw *fokstrotizm* and *tangoizm* as harmful maladies. Opposition to jazz and the dances it spawned sprang, as elsewhere, from a fear of the body and of mass corruption. Dance-and-music battles were sporadic in the first decade of the Revolution; they would escalate into a long war beginning in 1928.

The bitter campaign against jazz during the cultural revolution codified a decade of invective. In 1928 the recently returned Gor'ky identified jazz with homosexuality, drugs, and bourgeois eroticism – charges that were later recycled to fit the rock culture of the day. Komsomol activists patrolled public dance places and anti-jazz lecturers marched into schoolrooms. But in the early thirties, a reversal took place and the war on popular music, including jazz, was scaled down. Foreign hits were heard all over Moscow, and European jazz bands played in the major Moscow hotels and in dozens of cities. The kings were Aleksandr Tsfasman and Leonid Utesov. Tsfasman, the son of a Jewish barber in Ukraine, rose to become one of the richest men in the USSR, leader of half a dozen bands, and star of radio, concert hall, and film. Tsfasman saturated the Soviet musical scene in the 1930s and 1940s with songs like 'The Man I Love', 'Shanty Town', and the Glenn Miller classic, 'Chattanooga Choo-choo'. Utesov – musically far less gifted – was actually more popular partly because of the spectacular success of his comedy film *Happy Fellows*, but mostly because his Odessa background and his circus and carnival road experience on the southern 'borshch belt' gave him a clowning manner like that of his idol, Ted Lewis. In fact Utesov was the typical *estrada* entertainer – quick-witted, versatile, and funny. He was not only one of the stars of the 1930s but also a personal favourite of Stalin.

At the moment of its peak, jazz fell victim to a new assault by envious musicians from other genres and by nationalists and conservatives resentful of imported culture. Ambivalence reigned for a while, but when the purge came, it hit hard: one band leader was arrested on the podium. Others were sent to camps. Tsfasman, Utesov, and a few others remained untouched, but only at the price of converting their jazz into a Soviet product, cleansed of 'decadence'. State Jazz (later Estrada) Orchestras were formed, large well-dressed ensembles that played an assortment of ballroom music, classics, and smoothed out 'jazz' in carefully written arrangements with an emphasis on orchestral colour and texture rather than on swinging spontaneity. As a whole, Stalin's dilution of jazz resembled that in Hitler's Germany, where dance music had to be slow and smooth, with strings and some 'folk' instruments added to the 'jazz' complement.

During the Second World War official shackles on jazz were somewhat loosened and frontline jazz band concerts were very popular. Bands popped up among railwaymen, aviators, cooks, and the NKVD and publishing houses produced 'anti-fascist' songs and marches for them. The ensembles of Boris Rensky, Skomorovsky, Tsfasman, Utesov, and others were warmly received at the front and in the fleet. There was never enough jazz music for the troops. When *Sun Valley Serenade* appeared on Soviet screens in 1944, the popularity of Glen Miller's style rose even further. The wartime jazz star was 'Eddie' (Edi or Adi in Russian) Rosner. The son of a Polish-Jewish shoemaker in Berlin, he fled into Soviet territory at the beginning of the war. Rosner headed the Belorussian jazz ensemble and then moved to Moscow and toured the front. An admirer of the American trumpeter and band leader, Harry James, Rosner banished the balalaika and concertina from his orchestra and played straight American jazz. During the Zhdanov cultural purge that followed the war, jazz was again assaulted as a Western disease. Musicians were arrested and their music banned – at one point the authorities actually 'arrested' all the saxophones in the country.

From the beginning of the Khrushchev period, the severe bans were lifted, although jazz was still seen by many as an alien art, and it continued to fight for a place in the galaxy of popular music and public performance – not to mention recording and radio programming. The smooth estrada jazz was ever present on bandstands and in restaurants. It was the music of the jitterbugs and *stilyagi* and of hundreds of thousands of youngsters who tuned in to the jazz programmes of Willis Conover on The Voice of America which started in 1955. Dixieland groups, combos, and jazz clubs proliferated in Soviet towns where couples danced at parties to the strains of Peggie Lee and Duke Ellington.

Jazz reached its peak of development in the Brezhnev era and became fully accepted. Cool, hot, pro-

gressive, and dixie were heard on radio and recordings and at numerous festivals, and jazz became the subject of books, lectures, and discussions. Jazzmen could even offer upbeat arrangements of Russian folk-songs and Soviet hits from the forties. Ironically, the triumph of jazz coincided with its decline in popularity among the young. Some of its brightest stars – many of them Jews – emigrated. But more important, jazz had ceased being raucous dance music and had become a concert art that required reverence and even study. Young people who wanted to shake no longer found sufficient energy in jazz. In the 1960s and 1970s rock succeeded in edging it out among the young.

Jazz still has a following among the intelligentsia, not only those who grew up on it in the forties, but among young people as well. There may be as many devotees of American jazz in the former Soviet Union as in the land of its birth, although it has been clearly overshadowed by rock. The Leningrad Jazz Club, directed by the multi-talented David Goloshchekin, has full houses. In Moscow the Igor Brill Quartet continues to play with brilliant technical virtuosity the classic idiom of the 1950s. Apostles of New Jazz or Free Jazz, like Vyacheslav Ganelin, Vladimir Chekasin, Vladimir Tarasov, Sergey Kurekhin, and other avant-gardists have abandoned the decorum of the 'cool' era for an explosive emotionalism, experimental individualism, and political iconoclasm. A promoter of Free Jazz has called it 'the most democratic music on this planet'; but it has not captured a mass audience.   RS

ROCK AND POP MUSIC

Rock music first entered Soviet cultural life in the late 1950s as official constraints on jazz began to lift. Despite Soviet criticism of rock as a form of 'alien primitivism' (Dmitry Shostakovich) and 'an explosion of the basest instincts and sexual urges' (Dmitry Shepilov) jazz bands were quick to include rock numbers in their repertoires. Nevertheless, a music ensemble was as likely to play a boogie-woogie or calypso tune as it was a rock or jazz number. Rock and roll remained of marginal cultural significance.

In the mid-1960s the Beatles transformed rock into a mass cultural phenomenon. While the Soviet press dismissed the Beatles as a short-lived musical fad, hundreds of amateur rock groups appeared in schools, factories and institutions of higher learning. A rock band was even formed by cadets at Suvorov, the prestigious Soviet military academy. By the late 1960s Moscow alone had over 250 amateur groups.

After failed attempts to suppress young people's enthusiasm for rock through intimidation, including the arrest of band members and concert organizers on charges of tax evasion, the Ministry of Culture took steps to co-opt the rock movement. In 1966 the first Vocal Instrumental Ensembles (VIAs) were formed under official auspices. These state-sponsored rock bands – the Happy Fellows, the Singing Guitars and the Blue Guitars – had their appearance, their texts and their decibel levels carefully monitored by the state. In return they were supplied with Western equipment, given the opportunity to release records on Melodiya and sent on domestic and foreign concert tours.

Despite resistance from conservative quarters rock music made significant inroads into Soviet culture throughout the 1970s. In 1973, Stas Namin became the first rock musician to join the composers' union. In that same year David Tukhmanov released on Melodiya what is regarded as the first real Soviet rock album, 'How Beautiful Is This World'. Alla Pugacheva emerged as the Soviet Union's most popular performer and, with nearly two hundred million records sold, ranks as one of the top soloists in the history of recorded sound.

The restrictions placed on state-sanctioned VIAs inspired a thriving underground rock culture. An official estimate from the mid-1970s placed the number of professional VIAs at 150, compared with over 100,000 unofficial bands. The most popular underground group was the legendary Moscow band Time Machine, many of whose songs became anthems for the disenchanted youth of the Brezhnev era. Following the Soviet invasion of Afghanistan in December 1979 and the subsequent deterioration of East-West relations in the early 1980s, the Soviets launched a campaign to purge the Soviet music scene of Western influences. Tours by Western rock bands were cancelled; domestic rock ensembles were accused of ideological subversion; hundreds of discotheques were closed for promoting decadent Western values. By the mid-1980s the official rock scene had been devastated.

The popular music scene became one of the first areas of Soviet life to feel the effects of the Gorbachev reforms. Three months after Gorbachev came to power, a Soviet rock band, Avtograf, participated in the international benefit concert for Africa, Live Aid. A year later Moscow rock bands organized their own benefit for the victims of the Chernobyl' disaster. By 1987 formerly underground bands, most notably Aquarium, were receiving domestic and international acclaim. Films like *Assa* (1987) and *The Burglar* (1987) explored Soviet rock culture.

The official acceptance of rock music caused a crisis on the Soviet rock scene. Not only did Soviet bands now have to compete with Western rock – increasingly available from tours and recordings – even more importantly, formerly underground bands, whose existence and following had been built on the idea of resistance to the state, found they had lost their *raison d'être*. As a result, commercial success has generally replaced moral and spiritual commitment as the driving force behind the current rock scene.   TR

The First Moscow Rock Festival, 1989

MUSIC THEATRES

The principal Russian music theatres are centred in Moscow and St Petersburg. The best known in Russia is the Moscow Bol'shoy, which originated in 1776. A theatre was erected on its present site in 1821–24, but it was badly damaged by fire in 1853, being rebuilt with substantial alterations by Alberto Kavos (Cavos) in 1856. Opera and ballet by Russian composers have been performed there since 1825 and since the 1930s the Bol'shoy has attracted the finest performers. Since 1961 the Bol'-shoy Company has also appeared at the Palace of Congresses, a huge hall seating 6,000 people, located in the Kremlin. Operas and ballets are likewise staged at the Stanislavsky and Nemirovich-Danchenko Theatre, founded in 1941, whose repertoire tends to include lesser-known works, and at the Opera Studio of the Moscow Conservatory. Music plays an important part in the programme of the Moscow Gypsy Theatre and the Moscow Music Hall, and there is also an Operetta Theatre. Concerts are given in the many palaces of culture and halls, in particular the Palace of Congresses, the Concert Hall of the Moscow Conservatory, the Tchaikovsky Hall (both of which contain an organ), the Rakhmaninov Hall and the Gnesin Music Institute.

In St Petersburg pride of place is occupied by the Mariinsky Theatre (known as the Kirov during the Soviet era), which occupies the site of the former Imperial Mariinsky Theatre. After the founding of a Russian dramatic theatre by Catherine II in 1756, the Directorate of the Imperial Theatres was established in 1766. From 1783 performances were given in St Petersburg at the Kamenny ('Stone') Theatre (also known as the Bol'shoy). In 1855 the opera

company moved to a new building, the Theatre-Circus, which was renamed the Mariinsky Theatre in 1860, to which the ballet company returned in 1886. The former Kamenny Theatre was rebuilt in 1889 by the Russian Musical Society and is now the home of the St Petersburg Conservatory. Many notable first performances of works by Russian composers were given at the Kamenny and Mariinsky Theatres which were also visited by celebrated foreign opera singers, such as Patti, Tamburini and Rubini. To this day operas and ballets are presented in a sumptuous, grandiose manner, abstract décor being eschewed in favour of realistic staging. Operas are also given at the Maly Theatre, founded in 1918, and at the Studio of the St Petersburg Conservatory. Operettas are performed at the Musical Comedy Theatre (founded 1929).

Of the many concert halls in St Petersburg, those belonging to the Philharmonic (of which the larger was formerly the 'Hall of the Nobility') and the Concert Hall of the St Petersburg Conservatory are notable. Concerts are also given in the Hermitage and in the Hall of the Academic Kapella. Opera and ballet companies, operetta and music hall, are well established throughout the former Soviet republics and each large city has its own theatres, symphony orchestras and concert halls. Seats are relatively inexpensive and subscription concerts are popular. At the present time lack of financial support has, however, created problems for all aspects of musical life, especially for the major theatres.   GS

Scene from Yury Olesha's Three Fat Men *at the Moscow State Children's Musical Theatre, 1968*

MUSIC MUSEUMS AND LIBRARIES

Materials relating to the eighteenth-century serf theatre are to be found in the Sheremet'ev Palace at Ostankino. The Bol'shoy Theatre in Moscow and the Mariinsky Theatre in St Petersburg both possess extensive libraries and archives of programmes, letters, model sets, costumes, décors and musical sketches. The Maly Opera and Ballet Theatre, St Petersburg, also contains musical and theatrical materials such as posters, photographs, letters, concert programmes, while music holdings and recordings are also found in the St Petersburg Theatrical Institute. The Music Library of the Mariinsky is one of the richest of its kind and contains many sets of orchestral parts and a host of other materials relating largely (but by no means exclusively) to the history of Russian opera.

The largest music museum is the Glinka Museum, situated in the building of the Moscow Conservatory, which contains more than 20,000 original manuscripts of Russian and West European composers, including Glinka, Borodin, Rimsky-Korsakov, Tchaikovsky, Prokofiev, Shostakovich, as

The theatre at Count Sheremet'ev's palace, Ostankino, near Moscow

well as Wagner, Liszt, Grieg, Ravel, Saint-Saëns and others. It also contains a large library of recordings as well as materials on folk music and the music of the former Soviet republics. The Russian State (formerly Lenin) Library in Moscow possesses the largest collection of music bibliographical materials in Russia; important also is the Central State Archive of Literature and Arts. Music library holdings in general, and those of the St Petersburg Public Library and the St Petersburg Conservatory in particular, are substantial and contain many bibliographical rarities. Much can also be found in the Library of the Institute of Theatre Music and Cinematography (though this is currently being redistributed), in the library of the St Petersburg Conservatory, the St Petersburg Philharmonic, the Academic Kapella, the St Petersburg Radio, the University Library, the Central Historical Archive and the Academy of Sciences. The St Petersburg Conservatory possesses a large collection of recordings, some of them unique, while the Phonogram Archive of Pushkin House contains a considerable collection of recorded folk music, both Russian and from the republics.

The Hermitage contains many iconographic materials relating to Russian and non-Russian music, taking the form of paintings, drawings, sketches and sculptures. There are also House Museums devoted to specific composers such as the Tchaikovsky House in Klin (established 1894), the Tchaikovsky Museum in Votkinsk (established 1940), the Scriabin Museum in Moscow (established 1922), and the Rimsky-Korsakov Museum in Tikhvin (established 1944).

In St Petersburg's Alexander Nevsky cemetery lie the graves of many Russian composers, including Glinka, Balakirev, Musorgsky, Borodin, Rimsky-Korsakov, Tchaikovsky, Serov and Rubinstein. GS

Tchaikovsky's grave at the Alexander Nevsky cemetery, St Petersburg

MUSIC PERIODICALS

The first music periodicals appeared in Russia in the late eighteenth century, although these were all short-lived. It was not until 1840 that a music journal was firmly established; this was the *Nouvelliste*, which survived in various forms until 1916. The major music periodicals were *Russkaya muzykal'naya gazeta* (1894–1918), *Muzyka* (1910–16) and *Muzykal'ny sovremennik* (1915–17), but substantial articles on music and related subjects are found in a host of other publications such as the *Yearbooks of the Imperial Theatres* (1892–1917). A number of periodicals, mostly of only a few years' duration, appeared in the 1920s and the early 1930s. They included *Sovremennaya muzyka* (1924–29), *Muzyka i revolyutsiya* (1926–29) and *Proletarsky muzykant* (1929–32), but all these were superseded by the journal *Sovetskaya muzyka*, which, with the exception of a few years during the Second World War, has appeared regularly since 1933. The journal *Muzykal'naya zhizn'* founded in 1957, is more lightweight in content. GS

MUSIC CRITICISM

The first Russian writer to have a regular music column in a newspaper appears to have been Nikolay Kashkin (1839–1920) in the 1860s in Moscow. Among notable Russian music critics are Prince V. Odoevsky, A. Serov, V. Stasov, César Cui, A. Famintsyn (1841–96), M.M. Ivanov (1849–1927), G. Larosh (1854–1904), N.F. Findeyzen (1868–1928) and B.V. Asaf'ev (1884–1949). Discussion of international contemporary music and reportage of musical events was a feature of Russian journals during the 1920s, but, after the early 1930s, apart from occasional articles in leading newpapers and periodicals, musical criticism (primarily of musical life within the Soviet Union) was found mostly in the official journal *Sovetskaya muzyka*. There is available in the English language a large body of memoir literature relating to Russian composers, including writings by Glinka, Rimsky-Korsakov, Musorgsky, Tchaikovsky, Chaliapine and Prokofiev.

Among the notable nineteenth-century music publishers were the firms of Bessel, Jürgenson, Gutheil (Gutkheyl) and Belyaev. Kusevitsky's firm, the Russian Music Publishing House, was founded in 1909 in Berlin. From 1918 music was published by Muzgiz (State Publishing Company) and since 1964 by Muzyka.

Contrary to Western custom, reviews of concerts rarely appear on the day following the event, but usually many days, even weeks, later. Until recently, criticism in general was determined by ideological factors, but a more liberal attitude became evident in the Gorbachev era together with a more sympathetic approach to Western music and mass musical culture, especially rock. For the first time since the 1930s new music periodicals began to appear.   GS

INSTRUMENT MANUFACTURE

Russian folk instrumental music is closely connected with vocal music. Of the stringed instruments important are the *gusli*, the *domra*, the balalaika and the *gudok*. The *gusli*, counterpart of the West European psaltery, is one of the oldest Slav instruments and is plucked with both hands, the instrument being placed on the player's lap. The *gudok* (equivalent of the West European rebec) was a three-stringed instrument, played with bow, dating back to about the eleventh century. The *domra* was a three-stringed plucked instrument often employed by the *skomorokhi* in the sixteenth and seventeenth centuries, while the triangular-shaped balalaika, which gradually replaced the *domra*, consists of two or three strings plucked with a plectrum. The balalaika became popular at the end of the nineteenth century, when other similar instruments were constructed and popularized by folk orchestras. Among the wind instruments are the *rog* (primitive horn), the *truba* (wooden trumpet), the *rozhok* (wooden horn with finger holes); there are the *dudka* or *sopel'* (types of flute), and the double end-blown flute – the *svirel'*; reed instruments include the *zhaleyka* and the *surna*, while the *volynka* is the equivalent of the Scottish bagpipe. The *garmon'* (concertina) came into popular use from the nineteenth century onwards. Of especial interest is the

kuvikly or *kuvichki*, consisting of a cluster of cane pipes held loosely in the hand. Percussion instruments include *bubny* (tambourines), *lozhki* (a type of castanets), as well as rattles, jew's harp and different species of drum. A large collection of folk instruments of the world's peoples and other musical instruments is found in the Institute of Theatre, Music and Cinematography, St Petersburg.

Of the musical instruments manufactured in Russia before 1917, the work of the violin-, cello-, and guitar-maker I.A. Batov (1767–1841) and of the guitar-maker J.F. Arkhuzen (1795–1870) is noteworthy. During the nineteenth century a piano-making industry was established in St Petersburg which accounted for 80 per cent of all keyboard instruments produced in Russia. This relied almost entirely on imported parts, which were then locally assembled. After the Revolution it was on the basis of the existing companies of Bekker (Becker) and Shreder (Schröder) that Krasny Oktyabr' was established, which became the largest piano-manufacturing enterprise in the USSR. The Zimmermann wind-instrument factory, opened in St Petersburg in 1876, was nationalized in 1917. Plucked instruments (balalaikas, harps, mandolins, guitars) were produced at the Leningrad Lunacharsky factory from 1926, while accordions (using either keys or buttons) are produced in large numbers. The experimental work of L.S. Termen in the early 1920s, resulting in the invention of the *Théréminvox*, followed in the 1930s by further work

The tuva, a modern folk instrument

on electrical musical instruments by A.V. Rimsky-Korsakov (b.1910) and A.A. Ivanov (b.1907) in St Petersburg, led to the invention of the *Emeriton*, various models of which have subsequently appeared. Instrument-making classes are held in the St Petersburg and Moscow Conservatories.

Rare musical instruments, including music-boxes, violins and harps, are to be found at the Hermitage. The State Collection of Unique Musical Instruments, founded in Moscow in 1919, contains about fifty instruments by Italian, French, German and Russian craftsmen, including violins, cellos and violas by Stradivarius, Amati, Montagnana and Guarneri. These may be borrowed by musicians for occasions such as international competitions. GS

THE RECORDING INDUSTRY

The first factory to produce records within the Russian Empire was established by the English Gramophone Company in Riga at the beginning of the twentieth century. The first factory in Russia itself was opened by Pathé in 1907. In 1913 Moscow alone had ten stores devoted to the sale of records. By 1915 there were six factories in Russia producing 20 million discs per year. After the Revolution, following the nationalization of all industry, record factories were set up on an extensive scale. In 1964 the national record firm Melodiya was established under the direction of the Ministry of Culture and

in 1975 produced nearly 200 million records, of which 13 million were purchased in Moscow, nearly two million of them at the Melodiya Store in Kalinin Prospekt (opened 1969). Of the records produced, 31 per cent are said to be of 'serious' music (consisting primarily of works by Russian and Soviet composers and some Western composers); the remainder include light music, folk music, mass songs, children's records, verse and speech records. Though jazz records are produced, these are often in short supply and the lack of liaison between producers and sellers is frequently criticized in the press. A new improved stereo record-player is now available, though cassette recorders and tapes are far less common than in the Western world. In 1975 all Shostakovich's symphonies were issued by Melodiya in conjunction with HMV. A notable event was the issuing of 'Band on the Run' by Paul McCartney's group 'Wings' in 1976.

The whole attitude towards rock music in the Soviet Union has recently undergone change. Records by Led Zeppelin, the Commodores and other Western groups were put on sale in 1988, though demand far exceeds supply. Compact disc players are now produced commercially and the quality of disc recording has much improved. Video recorders are also a scarce commodity and there is a basic shortage of all electronic materials. GS

Dancer at a Moscow rave, 1992

Popular culture

In current parlance, 'popular culture' pertains to urban culture produced for a mass audience, thus differentiating it from 'high culture' – fine art, classical music, legitimate theatre, ballet, opera, *belles-lettres* and so on; and from 'folk culture', which is produced in the countryside by peasants. There has been a constant interchange among these since the swelling of popular culture in the last century, fuelled largely by urbanization and technological change. In the Russian empire, the rise of popular culture was marked by a quickening of commercial activity at the turn of the century, a mass press, the importation of photographic, cinematic and phonographic techniques, the arrival of European and American entertainment (music hall, revue, ragtime, tango, the motion picture), the spread of restaurants and cafes, and a general shift in reading and listening habits of the lower and lower-middle classes of the towns. In the last decades of the Old Regime, popular culture – songs, sheet music, *estrada* shows, pulp and boulevard fiction, and cinema – were characterized by commercialism, sim-

Right. *Acrobat of the Moscow State Circus*

plified narrative, performance, and musical structures, exotica, a touch of eroticism, and audiences of mixed gender, age, and class. The movie melodrama produced by native studios from about 1908 to 1917 combined these features and was the most popular single genre of mass entertainment. Although a broad spectrum of educated public opinion criticized popular entertainments on aesthetic and moral grounds, it had no power to restrict them in a serious way. Nor did the tsarist censorship, operating at a low key after 1905, exert much real pressure upon them.

All this changed in the Soviet period. After a few years of confusion and absence of a coherent policy, the regime nationalized almost the entire popular entertainment industry – film studios, the stage, circus, the press, and public performance. Government control diminished during the NEP period; and the resultant partial resurgence of 'vulgar' commercial entertainment revealed that the urban masses, when given a choice, chose it over the often politicized heroics of Bolshevik artistic and cultural offerings. In cinema for example, they preferred comedy, adventure, intrigue, and crime stories with clear plots, strong characters, and plenty of action to the revolutionary spectacles of Eisenstein and Pudovkin or the experimental documentaries of Dziga Vertov.

After several complicated reversals during the Five-year Plans, a Stalinist system of 'mass' culture based on Socialist Realism was established and lasted in its most rigid form (except for a slight relaxation during the war of 1941–45) until the death of Stalin in 1953; and in many of its essential forms until the advent of glasnost and perestroika in 1985. This system of mass culture – rooted in the values of the élitist intelligentsia but modified and expanded by a need to reach the masses – excluded erotic, introverted, and mystical-religious themes as well as experimental or avant-garde artistic forms. Instead it offered realistic representation, hagiography of state leaders, and the values of construction, revolutionary adventure, and optimism. Mass culture fea-

Below. *Lyubov' Orlova.*
Below right. *Alla Pugacheva*

tured hundreds of songs for youth, workers, and soldiers; an elaborate system of folkloric ensembles; a politicized comedy stage and circus arena; tales of aviation, exploration, socialist construction, and defence; and musical comedy films which combined entertainment, lavish production values, and social messages. The film star, Lyubov' Orlova, became one of the cultural icons of the age remembered by millions down to the present, though she remains virtually unknown outside the USSR.

Soviet popular culture reached a level of maturity and accommodation in the Khrushchev and Brezhnev decades. A continued prohibition of the forbidden themes together with continued promotion and even financing of official motifs and forms was combined with a loosening up, a selective allowance of Western imports, and a revival of once proscribed genres such as jazz. In this era, the great stars of mass Soviet culture emerged and held sway: Alla Pugacheva the queen of popular song, Arkady Raykin the king of stage satire, Oleg Popov the circus clown, Eldar Ryazanov the film comedy director, and Yulian Semenov the master of the spy thriller. Such artists enjoyed immense popularity not only in live performance (or on the printed page) but also on television (an adaptation of Semenov's *Seventeen Moments of Spring* was a blockbuster TV-movie hit of the late 1970s). The works of these media figures were consumed on a mass scale and they themselves became national celebrities and household words.

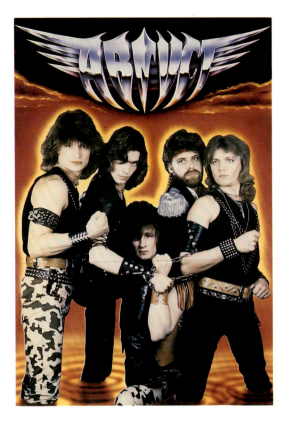

The Russian heavy metal group 'Avgust'

Elitist bias, cultural diplomacy and ignorance of Soviet tastes and preferences have led Western observers to ignore the vast realm of popular culture and to believe that the artists, musicians and writers known to the outside world were automatically the favourites of Soviet citizens as well.

Since 1985 the old structures of state-sponsored culture have been shaken and new organisms are feeding the tastes of the younger generation. Rock music, films featuring scenes of sex and violence, foreign imports and music video are on the cutting edge of popular culture. The censorship, firmly in place for more than fifty years, is virtually gone. Old-style big bands and crooners, folk groups, political or ideological films, and tendentious plays are being nudged off stage and screen – the silver, the 'blue' (television), and the 'third screen' (video) – in favour of entertainment that contains the novelty and shock effect that citizens of the former Soviet Union – at least of the younger generation – thirst for. Since older persons continue to cherish the cultural forms of their youth (war songs and movies for example), the generational tension that has always existed has taken on sharp forms, sometimes expressed in ideological and political language. Conservative nationalist Russians or Russophiles have taken particular offence at the provocative gestures, clothing, music and lyrics of certain rock singers and bands. Thus popular culture, virtually ignored in Soviet scholarship of the past, has now surfaced as a visible social and political phenomenon.   RS

Theatre

Russian theatre

The theatre came late to Russia; apart from crude fairground shows and performances at court by foreign actors, there was virtually no theatre in Russia until the Empress Elizabeth established the first public theatre at St Petersburg in 1756, with an annual subsidy of 5,000 rubles, under the direction of the poet and playwright A.P. Sumarokov. Originally somewhat artificial, socially exclusive entertainments confined to the capitals and a few provincial cities, the first plays were translations or clumsy Russian imitations of foreign works. The theatre was, however, much fostered and popularized by Catherine the Great, herself a playwright; she inaugurated the Imperial Theatre Administration (which for nearly a century monopolized control of all Russian theatres), founded the Imperial Theatre School in 1779 and authorized in 1780 the building in Moscow of the Petrovsky (now Bol'shoy) Theatre. The first truly original Russian playwright was D.I. Fonvizin (1744–92); his comedy *The Minor* (1782), a vigorous satire on contemporary manners, is still played today. Uniquely Russian was the serf theatre; rich landowners built theatres and trained companies of actors from among their more talented serfs, many of whom achieved such fame that their owners were obliged to emancipate them.

Under Alexander I and Nicholas I the number of theatres increased, notable foundations of the period being the Maly Theatre in Moscow (1808) – where the great actor M.S. Shchepkin (1788–1863) established a distinctively Russian school of acting – and the Alexandrinsky (now Pushkin) Theatre (1832) in St Petersburg. A Theatre-Circus was built there (1847–49) for pantomime and circus shows and the first permanent circus was established in 1877. In 1839 Nicholas I gave the Imperial Theatres comprehensive statutes which remained in force, virtually unchanged, until 1917. Poets and novelists of genius

Right. Façade of the Bol'shoy Theatre, Moscow

(Pushkin, Gogol', Lermontov, Turgenev) began writing for the stage, although many of the best plays of that era were banned by censorship for many years – as happened with the wittiest, most mordant social satire of them all, *Woe from Wit* by A.S. Griboedov. Written in 1823, its full version was not staged until 1869. Even Aleksandr Pushkin, Russia's greatest poet, suffered under the theatre censorship: his great chronicle play *Boris Godunov* (1825) was not performed until 1870. Also unstaged until 1862 was M.Yu. Lermontov's *Masquerade* (1835), a romantic drama of character.

The best known of all Russian plays dates from this period: *The Government Inspector* (1836) by N.V. Gogol', a classic comedy of mistaken identity. To the comedy of social criticism inaugurated by Griboedov and Gogol', I.S. Turgenev added a new element: a subtle but keen awareness of the psychological tensions that underlie conventional human relationships. Turgenev's masterpiece in this genre is the ever-popular *A Month in the Country* (1850; first performed 1872). The following decades saw the rise of authors who were first and foremost playwrights; prominent among them was A.V. Sukhovo-Kobylin (1817–1903), whose own bizarre life-story (falsely accused of murder, he spent decades in the toils of the archaic Russian legal system) provided much material for his grotesque satirical comedies, *Krechinsky's Wedding* (1855), *The Case* (1861; first performed in 1882) and *The Death of Tarelkin* (1869; first performed 1900), which prefigure Kafka in their nightmarish indictment of a vast, oppressive bureaucracy.

Alexander II's more liberal reign relaxed theatrical censorship; it also nourished the career of Russia's most protean man of the theatre, A.N. Ostrovsky (1823–86), who in his 57 plays (seven written in collaboration) created many quintessentially Russian characters. His influence as director and teacher equalled his popularity as a playwright; best known is his tragedy *The Thunderstorm* (1859). A.K. Tolstoy (1817–75) and L.N. Tolstoy (1828–1910) added enduring plays to the repertoire: of A.K. Tolstoy's historical trilogy, *Tsar Fedor Ioannovich* is a moving verse drama; contemporary themes were treated naturalistically in L.N. Tolstoy's *The Power of Darkness* (1887; first performed 1895) and *The Living Corpse* (written 1900; published and first performed 1911), and humorously in his comedy *The Fruits of Enlightenment* (first performed 1891).

At the turn of the century the Russian theatre experienced a creative renaissance, beginning in 1898, when K.S. Stanislavsky (real name Alekseev, 1863–1938) and V.I. Nemirovich-Danchenko (1858–1943) founded the Moscow Arts Theatre (МКХАТ). Three principal elements underlay its worldwide influence: respect for the author's inten-

Vsevolod Meyerhold

Vsevolod Meyerhold (1874–1940) began his theatrical career as an actor in the Moscow Art Theatre's original productions of Chekhov's *The Seagull* and *The Three Sisters*, playing opposite the playwright's future wife, Ol'ga Knipper.

Meyerhold's growing interest in Symbolist drama led Stanislavsky in 1905 to put him in charge of an experimental theatre studio where he was able to realize his belief in the primacy of movement in stage drama. Influenced by stylized Japanese *kabuki* theatre and the ideas of the English stage designer Gordon Craig, Meyerhold developed the theory of biomechanics, which reduced the actor to a highly trained marionette and acting, lighting, décor and the other elements of theatre to mere tools for the realization of the director's grand design.

Meyerhold's total vision of theatre was too radical for its time, and he was sacked. From 1908 to 1918 he directed the Imperial Theatres in St Petersburg but was simultaneously engaged in experimental studio work under the pseudonym 'Dr Dapertutto'. He was the first director to welcome the Revolution and in 1920 Lunacharsky put him in charge of the state-run Theatre Division, where he attempted to develop his idea of a 'Theatrical October'.

Meyerhold pioneered the production of Mayakovsky's plays, including *The Bed-bug* (1929) and *The Bath House* (1930). With actors reduced to robots and sets to a minimum, he changed the face of Russian theatre. However, the ideas and practices he unleashed acquired their own momentum and the advent of Socialist Realism in the 1930s exposed him to accusations of 'formalism' and 'cosmopolitanism'.

In 1938 Meyerhold lost his company. Arrested on 20 June 1939 (his wife, the actress Zinaida Raikh, was later found brutally murdered), he was finally shot on 2 February 1940. He was one of the greatest innovators in modern theatre history.

МЕЙЕРХОЛЬД

Scene from A.K. Tolstoy's drama Tsar Fedor Ioannovich *at the Maly Theatre, Moscow*

tion; rigorous training to analyse and express character truthfully; subordination of individual performances to ensemble. The MKhAT also 'discovered' A.P. Chekhov (1860–1904). When *The Seagull* (1895–96) failed in St Petersburg, the MKhAT production (1898) made it triumphantly successful and thereafter it gave premières of *Uncle Vanya* (1899), *Three Sisters* (1901) and *The Cherry Orchard* (1904). Maksim Gor'ky's long career as a playwright (20 plays) also began with the MKhAT 1902 productions of *The Lower Depths* and *The Philistines*. Symbolist influence on the theatre culminated in the experimental, non-realistic productions by V.E. Meyerhold (1874–1940) at the St Petersburg theatre of actress and manager Vera Komissarzhevskaya (1864–1910), notably his 1906 production of Blok's *The Puppet Show*.   MVG

SOVIET THEATRE

In the years immediately following the Revolution a fierce political debate raged over the direction to be taken by the newly nationalized Soviet theatre. Radical theoreticians advocated a complete break with the tradition of realistic professional theatre, and some of the leading companies were only saved from extinction through the intercession of Lunacharsky.

During the 1920s and 1930s the number of theatres in Soviet Russia increased dramatically, attracting a wider audience. The traditional, highly professional realism of MKhAT and the Gor'ky Theatre in Leningrad coexisted with the work of three outstanding innovative directors. Meyerhold's longstanding interest in non-realistic theatre resulted in his adoption of Constructivism, in which the set was generally an abstract machine containing

ladders and scaffolding, and the parallel technique of biomechanics, by means of which he trained actors to use their bodies for maximal expressiveness. Whereas Stanislavsky advocated creating a role 'from the inside', Meyerhold's techniques revealed psychology 'from the outside' through mime and gesture.

Yevgeny Vakhtangov (1883–1922) began as a pupil of Stanislavsky but later moved towards Meyerhold's principles, particularly in the use of fantasy and the grotesque. Aleksandr Tairov (real name Kornblit, 1885–1950) founded the Moscow Kamerny Theatre where, during the 1920s, he pioneered the introduction of stage Constructivism. His approach may be termed 'synthetic', aiming for an effect based on all the elements of theatre: the art of the 'master actor', especially bodily movement; musical rhythm; maximum use of spatial possibilities.

Soviet drama up to 1956 suffered from political constraints to an even greater degree than prose writing, especially in the period of Zhdanovism, which saw the introduction of so-called 'no-conflict drama'. Nevertheless, during the 1920s important plays were written by Mikhail Bulgakov, Nikolay Erdman (1902–70), and Vladimir Mayakovsky. Among the authors of canonical Socialist Realist plays were Nikolay Pogodin and Vsevolod Vishnevsky (1900–51).

The period since 1956 has seen the rise to prominence of a number of talented directors. Under Yury Lyubimov (b.1917) Moscow's Taganka Theatre became one of the most significant companies in the world. Georgy Tovstonogov (1915–89) had a long and distinguished career at the Gor'ky Theatre in Leningrad. Other notable directors include Oleg Yefremov (b.1927), Anatoly Efros (1925–87), and

Right. The director Yury Lyubimov in his office at the Taganka Theatre, Moscow

Yevstigneev as Lunacharsky (left) and Kvasha as Sverdlov in Shatrov's The Bolsheviks *at the Sovremennik Theatre, Moscow*

Dance

FOLK-DANCE

Russian folk-song and folk-dance are closely connected; indeed, from the earliest period of Russian history there is evidence to show that folk-dance played an important part in pagan (and subsequently Christian) ceremonies. The annual festival of *Svyatovit* was celebrated after the harvest with worship, songs and dances, ending with a general feast; the cult of *Rok* ('fate' or 'destiny') persisted up to the sixteenth century, likewise being accompanied by dancing, while the festivities on St John's Night, celebrated with dancing and people leaping across the flames of a crumbling bonfire, persisted until recent times. The various events of the seasonal year were commemorated in song and dance, such being the singing game 'And we were sowing millet'. An important place in all these customs and rituals was played by the *khorovod*, a round dance performed originally only in the spring, accompanied by dramatic action and singing; it is widespread amongst the Slav peoples, being known as the *kolo* (literally 'wheel') in Yugoslavia, and the *vesnyanki* in Ukraine. *Khorovody* are found in the first collections of Russian folk-songs published in the eighteenth century and they have been widely studied.

Examples of dance-songs are also found in the first printed collections. With melodies in some cases clearly of great antiquity, the dance-songs are in rapid tempo and full of rhythmic vitality, the tunes often being constructed on a variation principle. Such dances must have formed part of the repertoire of the *skomorokhi* who appeared not only at secular festivals but also at Court, certainly up to the time of Peter the Great. Dances must also have included the squatting dance and dances with bent knees.

The *trepak*, which comes from the old Russian verb *trepat'*, to stamp with the feet, is a dance in 2/4 time performed at a lively tempo: the *trepak* in Tchaikovsky's *Nutcracker* suite is well known. The *kazachok* and *gopak* are both Ukrainian dances.

All these dances have formed an essential part of the repertoire of companies such as the Ensemble of Song and Dance of the Soviet Army, the Moiseev Ensemble, and the Georgian State Dance Company and many others, for folk-dance music and folk instrumental music are closely interwoven.   GS

Lev Dodin (b.1940), who turned the Leningrad Maly Dramatichesky into one of the Soviet Union's leading theatres.

Since 1956 relatively few major dramatists have emerged, with a high proportion of productions being based on dramatizations of prose works. Among the best playwrights of this period are Viktor Rozov (b.1913) and Aleksey Arbuzov (1908–86), who depicted human relationships with notable honesty. From the 1970s onwards younger dramatists addressed the ethical and social problems faced by Soviet citizens. Aleksandr Vampilov (1937–72) wrote poignant comedies which reveal the influence of Chekhov. The plays of Aleksandr Gelman (b.1933) deal with the interaction between public and personal morality. Lyudmila Petrushevskaya (b.1938) writes about the everyday problems faced by Russian men and – especially – women. Mikhail Shatrov (real name Marshak: b.1932) specializes in revolutionary-historical plays which present in dramatic form key moments in Soviet history and in which Lenin, Trotsky, Stalin and other Soviet leaders feature as characters. His plays of the 1980s, especially *Onward, Onward, Onward!* (1987), represented a major contribution to the literature of glasnost.   RR

Dancers of the Ukrainian State Dance Company

THE RUSSIAN BALLET

Ballet in Russia today is the heir to almost 250 years of continuous tradition, and a rapid expansion of activity since 1945 which established permanent companies in each of the constituent republics of the former Soviet Union. These formed a pyramid of 34 companies in 32 cities, with Moscow and Leningrad (each having two or more companies) at the peak. They ranged in size from about 45 dancers in the smaller companies to over 150 in the largest. Most of their dancers joined as graduates from 20 or so State Choreographic Schools, of which more than half provided a complete nine-year course in vocational and general education. All companies and schools were state-financed and, continuing a practice established since the eighteenth century, the special nature of a dancer's career was recognized by the provision of a full pension after 20 years' professional work.

Origins

The origins of theatrical dance in Russia are found in Court entertainments on the one hand, and folk-dances on the other, together with the groups of privately-owned serf-dancers maintained by rich estate owners at least until 1806, when the last large group of such entertainers was bought by the Imperial Theatres in Moscow. As early as 1624, Tsar Mikhail, first of the Romanov dynasty, engaged a dancing-master, Ivan Lodygin, to teach children of humble origin who became Court entertainers, and on 8 February 1673 the first recorded ballet in Russia, *The Ballet of Orpheus and Eurydice*, was performed for Tsar Aleksey at the then summer palace of Preobrazhenskoe, near Moscow. After the Court was moved to St Petersburg by Peter the Great (who had already set up a *Teatral'naya khoromina*, or 'theatre room' in the Kremlin), with his encouragement of dancing as a social accomplishment, the French ballet-master Jean-Baptiste Landé was invited to St Petersburg in 1734. Four years later he received permission to open there the first Russian ballet school, where children of palace servants and orphans were taught the technique of the *danse de l'école* as it had originated in France. Their training took three years, the school becoming the basis for the ballet element in the state system of imperial theatres initiated by Catherine II in 1756. The Directorate of the Imperial Theatres was formally constituted in 1766, with the ballet division an integral part of the theatre school and state pensions for the artists.

From 1759 the Vienna-born dancer and choreographer, Franz Hilverding, was given charge of the ballets in St Petersburg and Moscow, where he developed the narrative *ballets d'action* on the principles formulated by Jean-Georges Noverre, as did Hilverding's pupil, the Milanese Gasparo Angiolini, and Noverre's pupil, Charles Le Picq. The first Russian ballet-master of renown was Ivan Val'berkh (1766–1819), who studied under Angiolini, danced under Le Picq and was appointed inspector (general manager) of the company at St Petersburg's Bol'shoy Theatre and director of the ballet school there in 1794.

Meanwhile, an Italian dancer in St Petersburg, Filippo Baccari, was engaged in 1773 to give dancing lessons to children at the Moscow Orphanage over a three-year period. At the end of that time he was to receive 250 rubles for each qualified solo dancer and 150 rubles for any other who attained an agreed standard. The results exceeded expectations, and from 1776 ballets began to be staged regularly for public entertainment in Moscow. They were first performed at the Znamensky Theatre until it was destroyed by fire in 1780, and then at the Petrovsky Theatre which opened in that year on the site where Moscow's Bol'shoy Theatre now stands. The Bol'shoy Ballet of today is the direct heir of the dancers who first appeared at the Znamensky, and the company therefore dates its origin from 1776, having celebrated its bicentenary accordingly.

Val'berkh moved to Moscow in 1807, where he reorganized the ballet school and company, while St Petersburg came under the lasting influence of another Noverre disciple, Charles-Louis Didelot (1767–1837), first from 1801 to 1811, when he revised the teaching system and laid the foundation for what became the renowned St Petersburg style of ballet, and again from 1816 until his death. During this time he staged a number of significant ballets, notably *Raoul de Créquis* (1819), *La Fille mal gardée* (1827) and the first Pushkin ballet, *The Prisoner of the Caucasus* (1823). Pushkin declared of Didelot: 'There is more poetry in his ballets than in all the French literature of his times', and it was Pushkin's reference (in *Yevgeny Onegin*) to 'the Russian Terpsichore's soul-inspired flight' that summarized in one sentence the entire spirit and character of the Russian school of ballet.

The nineteenth century

In their elements of human interest, local colour and greater bodily freedom, with even a rudimentary use of *pointe* dancing for the ballerinas at moments of emotional climax, Didelot's ballets were true precursors of the nineteenth-century Romantic ballet first embodied by Marie Taglioni (1804–84). This style, with its emphasis on lightness, grace and modesty, gave a fresh purpose to theatrical dance, enabling it to become more poetic and imaginative, an art of illusion rather than illustration. Taglioni brought the seeds of Romantic ballet to Russia with her début in St Petersburg in 1837 in her father's production of *La Sylphide* (1832), following its original success in Paris. She and her contemporaries from the West also performed other outstanding Romantic ballets such as *Giselle* (1841), which established Yelena Andreyanova (1819–57) as the first Russian Romantic ballerina in St Petersburg; her Moscow counterpart was Yekaterina Sankovskaya (1816–78).

Sankovskaya also choreographed her own version of *Le Diable à quatre* in Moscow four years before Taglioni's former partner, Jules Perrot (1810–92), staged the ballet in St Petersburg during his tenure as ballet-master from 1848 to 1859. Perrot, one of the creators of *Giselle*, who first made London an important centre for ballet during the 1840s, mounted new versions of his London and Paris successes as well as creating other ballets which extended the prestige of the St Petersburg style. He was succeeded by another Frenchman, A. Saint-Léon (1821–70), whose ballets included *The Little Humpbacked Horse* (1864) based on Yershov's fairy-tale, which contained national dances in a stylized form and became a classic of Russian ballet for generations. Saint-Léon moulded Marfa Murav'eva (1838–79) as a ballerina of brilliant technique.

Ballet at this time continued along parallel lines in Moscow and St Petersburg, often sharing the same productions, sometimes pursuing independent ideas. St Petersburg reflected courtly taste and interests, while Moscow, the mercantile centre, drew its audiences from a wider public and tended to be more independent. The native Russian flavour in ballet was consolidated by *The Fern* (1867), with choreography by Sergey Sokolov, a student of Saint-Léon, and music by Yury Gel'ber, first violin and conductor of the Bol'shoy Theatre Orchestra in Moscow. Two years later the St Petersburg company came under the despotic control of Marius Petipa (1818–1910), whose 46 original ballets include some of the greatest glories of the Imperial Russian Ballet.

Right. Tamara Karsavina

The Imperial Ballet

Petipa, born in Marseilles, first went to St Petersburg in 1847, having already toured in France, Spain and the USA, and was a leading dancer of the Imperial Russian Ballet until 1858, when he became second ballet-master under Saint-Léon. In this capacity he staged his first important ballet, *Pharaoh's Daughter* (1862), with music by Cesare Pugni, then staff ballet composer to the Imperial Theatres. Petipa's mixture of Perrot's dramatic principles with exotic *divertissements*, fantastic transformations and multiple apotheoses constituted the new *ballet à grand spectacle*, a type which dominated Russian ballet for the rest of the century. *The Sleeping Beauty* (1890), in which Petipa and Tchaikovsky first collaborated, remains the outstanding example, but scenes and *pas de deux* by Petipa have survived from other ballets such as *Don Quixote* (1869), *Bayaderka* (1877), *Paquita* (1881) and *The Corsair* (1899), as well as from his 1895 production of *Swan Lake*.

Anna Pavlova

This, the best-known of all Russian ballets, had its origins in a domestic entertainment for Tchaikovsky's family, probably about 1871, but it was first staged professionally as a four-act ballet at Moscow's Bol'shoy Theatre in 1877, where the ballet-master Julius Reisinger was responsible for the first, not very successful choreography. It continued in the repertory through a new choreographic version by Joseph Hansen in 1880, but disappeared after 1883. It then remained unperformed until after Tchaikovsky's death, when the most famous version by Petipa and his assistant, Lev Ivanov (1834–1901), was originally mounted in St Petersburg in 1895, in the wake of the greater successes of *The Sleeping Beauty* and *The Nutcracker* (1892), for the second of which Ivanov was largely responsible.

Ivanov worked so much in the shadow of Petipa, mostly revising older ballets, that the transitory nature of unrecorded choreography has denied him much posthumous fame, but the known share of his contribution to *Swan Lake*, preserved in the familiar lakeside scene of Act 2, is evidence of his choreography's exceptional (and musical) distinction. Soviet historians have also pointed to his original choreography for the Polovtsian Dances in the first production (1890) of Borodin's opera, *Prince Igor*, on which the better-known version by M.M. Fokin (1880–1942) 20 years later was to some extent based. At the end of his life, however, Ivanov had to petition the Imperial Theatres for financial assistance after 50 years' service, and he died in poverty.

Vaclav Nijinsky in 1913

During Petipa's ascendancy at St Petersburg, ballet in Moscow went into a relative decline for want of comparable artistic direction, although there was no lack of outstanding individual dancers for both centres. Many were trained by the Swedish-born Christian Johansson (1817–1903), regarded as one of the chief architects of the Russian school of ballet. His most celebrated pupils included: Mathilda Kshesinskaya (1872–1971) – she and the Italian-born Pierina Legnani (1863–1923) were the only dancers ever to be officially awarded the title 'prima ballerina assoluta'; Ol'ga Preobrazhenskaya (1870–1962); Pavel Gerdt (1844–1917) – the most famous Russian male dancer of his time; and the brothers Nikolay and Sergey Legat.

Moscow ballet revived under A. A. Gorsky (1871–1924), who was born and trained in St Petersburg under Petipa, and went to Moscow as ballet-master in 1900. He adapted to ballet the principles of dramatic expression propounded by Konstantin Stanislavsky (1863–1938) at the Moscow Arts Theatre (MKhAT), and achieved a form of realistic drama in choreographic terms that revivified the art of dance. Gorsky began with his own revisions of Petipa's *Don Quixote* and *Raymonda*, made no fewer than five progressive versions of *Swan Lake* which became the basis of the Bol'shoy Ballet's subsequent presentations of that work, and was the first choreographer anywhere to set a classical ballet on a pre-composed symphony, using A.K. Glazunov's

(1865–1936) Fifth Symphony in 1915. He also initiated the recording of ballets in 'Stepanov notation', a system devised by Vladimir Stepanov (1866–96) which was of crucial importance when the classic Russian ballets were first mounted by British companies in the 1930s.

After Petipa's retirement in 1903, new directions were sought at St Petersburg. Following unrest among the dancers, these crystallized around Fokin, whose approach to choreography may also have had some influence from the American free-style dancer Isadora Duncan when she first appeared in Russia in 1905. Fokin, whose distinguished career took wing with such ballets as *Les Sylphides*, *The Firebird* and *Petrushka*, and other dancers from St Petersburg including Anna Pavlova (1881–1931), Tamara Karsavina (1885–1978) and Vaclav Nijinsky (1889–1950), together with Igor' Stravinsky as composer, became more widely known through Sergey Diaghilev. Diaghilev's touch of genius changed the face and fortune of classical ballet within five years through the seasons of ballet he organized and presented in Paris and London, from 1909 to 1914, with dancers from both St Petersburg and Moscow. Some then remained with him in emigration, but Fokin returned to St Petersburg in 1912 and was made ballet-master; he added several more works before the Revolution of 1917, but thereafter he rejoined his fellow-émigrés in the West.   NG

Sergey Diaghilev

Besides winning a new status for the art of dance on an international scale through the Ballet Russe company which he formed in 1911 and presented for nearly twenty years, Sergey Diaghilev influenced European trends in music and theatrical design, and his interests also embraced Russian painting, iconology and literature.

He was born in the Selishchev army barracks in the province of Novgorod in 1872, the son of an army officer who inherited a family estate and distillery at Perm', in the Urals. Diaghilev grew up in a cultured home surrounded by books, pictures and music. Sent to St Petersburg to study law, he devoted more attention to music, but his hopes of becoming a singer or composer foundered for lack of talent.

Instead he helped to found in 1899 an influential journal, *Mir iskusstva* (*World of Art*), and the same year obtained a post at the Imperial Theatres 'for special missions', which included editing the theatres' official yearbooks.

Diaghilev (right) with Jean Cocteau

A less than discreet homosexuality and other factors brought his dismissal in 1901.

Believing that Russian art deserved to be more widely known, Diaghilev from 1906 organized in successive years in Paris an exhibition of fine art, concerts of Russian music, and a season of Russian opera. Financial cutbacks in 1909 meant that more attention was focused on a ballet troupe touring with the opera, the impact of which gradually brought the Ballet Russe into existence as an independent company.

The company was fired by Diaghilev's belief in a composite art-form of dance, music and design with all the elements chosen and commissioned by him to make a balanced whole. These included his gamble on the unknown Igor' Stravinsky whose music for *The Firebird* (1910) launched his career. Diaghilev's entrepreneurial flair and artistic judgement kept the venture going until his sudden death in 1929 in Venice, where he was buried in the cemetery of San Michele.

SOVIET BALLET

Ballet in the Soviet Union after 1917 has usually been identified with the nineteenth-century classics and a vigorous, heroic style of dance-drama that was fostered from the 1930s until the end of the 1950s. Yet this period, which coincided with the imposition of Socialist Realism in all the arts, may now be seen as constituting only one, albeit dominant, stage in the evolution of Soviet ballet.

Actually, this development was marked by four distinct phases. Firstly, the immediate post-Revolutionary period and the 1920s encouraged avant-garde experiments in various styles. A short-lived proliferation of 'free dance' groups such as the Nikolay Foregger (1892–1939) troupe with its 'machine dances' coincided with the state's conscious preservation of classical ballet. It was the view of Anatoly Lunacharsky, the first People's Commissar for Education, that traditional ballets should be preserved as a national heritage for a mass public.

Secondly, the 1930s until the end of the 1950s focused on uplifting themes accessible to wide audiences. 'Formalism' was condemned, which meant that plotless ballets – common in the West – were suppressed, usually in favour of full-evening narrative productions. These included revised versions of nineteenth-century classics such as *Swan Lake*, in which emotional expressiveness was encouraged even in abstract pure-dance passages. There were also new ballets drawn from literary sources such

as Pushkin's *The Fountain of Bakhchisaray* (1934) choreographed by Rostislav Zakharov (1907–84) and *Romeo and Juliet* (1940) by Leonid Lavrovsky (1905–67). Ballets in a realistic style with political themes were presaged in 1927 with *The Red Poppy* by Vasily Tikhomirov (1876–1956) and Lev Lashchilin (1888–1955). This type of ballet ranged from *The Flames of Paris* (1932), a spectacular paean to the French Revolution by Vasily Vaynonen (1901–64) to *The Shore of Happiness* (1948) a dramatic work about the Second World War by Vladimir Bourmeister (1904–71).

An attempt in this era to instill Stanislavsky's acting principles into ballet as 'Choreodrama' was eventually diluted into a genre called *Drambalet*, in which dance steps were subordinate to gesture. Thirdly, the period from the 1960s to the late 1980s saw a reaction to *Drambalet's* tendency to degenerate into silent acting. Choreographers, especially Yury Grigorovich (b.1927), who left the Kirov Ballet in Leningrad in 1964 to become artistic director of the Bol'shoy Ballet in Moscow, sought to restore the ascendancy of ballet's academic idiom by eliminating mime. Other directions were visible by the 1970s through the plotless ballets of Maya Murdmaa (b.1933) in Tallinn, and Georgy Aleksidze (b.1941) in Tbilisi. Fourthly, the beginning of the 1990s, as a result of perestroika and glasnost, witnessed the growth of new ballet troupes throughout the Soviet Union. The Bol'shoy, under Grigorovich, and the Kirov – the Mariinsky Ballet of Tsarist times, directed since 1977 by Oleg Vinogradov (b.1937) – remained the two major state companies. But compared with the Soviet Union's 35 other opera-house troupes, their repertoires were limited; creativity was more marked elsewhere in the various republics as well as among temporary or permanent touring troupes directed by former members of the major companies. Small experimental groups known as studios sprang up with young choreographers seeking to work outside ballet conventions and to find the equivalent of the modern-dance vocabulary common in the West.

Generally, Soviet ballet technique, modernized by the teaching method of Agrippina Vaganova (1879–1951), was considered the most advanced in the world until the 1980s. The technical prowess of Rudolf Nureyev (1938–93) and Mikhail Baryshnikov (b.1948) was not matched in the Western companies they joined after leaving the Kirov. Technique was extended also through the artistic innovations of choreographers like Fedor Lopukhov (1886–1973) and Kasyan Goleyzovsky (1892–1970). Both, bowing to political pressures, produced more conservative works after the 1920s. Later, another major choreographer, Leonid Yakobson (1904–75) was accused, like Goleyzovsky, of

Mikhail Baryshnikov. Born in Latvia, Baryshnikov trained at the Riga Choreography School and then with the Kirov Ballet in Leningrad. He defected to the West in 1974 whilst on tour in Canada, and has since worked principally with the American Theater Ballet

Rudolf Nureyev

Rudolf Nureyev, one of the greatest male dancers of the second half of the twentieth century, was born on a train in Siberia on 17 March 1938. He grew up in the town of Ufa and began his training as a ballet dancer with private teachers there. Joining the Vaganova ballet school in Leningrad at the relatively late age of seventeen, he was immediately accepted upon graduation as one of the leading dancers of the Kirov company. During the Kirov's first major tour to the West in 1961, Nureyev was acclaimed by Parisian audiences, but his independent behaviour led his Soviet overseers to insist that he return to Moscow, ostensibly to dance at a Kremlin gala. Realizing that his nonconformism might make this his last trip to the West, Nureyev evaded his minders and applied for asylum in France.

He was to become much the best-known male dancer of his generation in the West. His soaring leaps and magnetic power were matched by a few dancers of his generation in Russia – for example, Vladimir Vasil'ev (b. 1940) of the Bolshoy Ballet – but Nureyev's performances with the Royal Ballet in London, the Paris Opera Ballet, the American Ballet Theater, the Martha Graham Dance Company and the Boston Ballet made him far better known to Western audiences. Television and film helped to turn him into a superstar, the one male ballet dancer universally recognized.

The Western part of Nureyev's career ended where it began – in Paris. He achieved new success as a director of the Ballet of the Paris Opera, although he continued almost until the end to tour as a dancer (beyond the time when he could fulfil the expectations he aroused). At a late stage in his career Nureyev demonstrated his

Nureyev with the British ballerina Margot Fonteyn, his most famous partner

versatility and musicality by embarking on a new career as an orchestral conductor; moreover, as a director of ballet he did much to restore the fortunes of the company of the Paris Opera. He returned twice to Russia, in 1987 and 1989, but made his final public appearance on the stage of the Paris Opera in October 1992 when his new production of *La Bayadère* was rapturously received and he himself – obviously dying, and physically supported by the principal dancers – took his last curtain call. He died in Paris on 6 January 1993.

injecting eroticism into ballets that used expressive movement outside the classical idiom.

With creativity stifled for many years, Soviet ballet turned inward and concentrated on technique and artistry, producing great dancers. Marina Semenova (b.1908), the first major ballerina schooled in the Soviet aesthetic, and Galina Ulanova (b.1910), Soviet ballet's most celebrated ballerina, both moved from the Kirov to the Bol'shoy. Yelizaveta Gerdt (1891–1975) taught two generations of stars: Maya Plisetskaya (b.1925), Raisa Struchkova (b.1925) and Yekaterina Maksimova (b.1939). The prototype of the new Soviet male bravura dancer was Aleksey Yermolaev (1910–75). He was followed by Vakhtang Chabukiani, Konstantin Sergeev, Aleksandr Lapauri, Nikolay Fadeechev, Maris Liepa and in Nureyev's generation, Yury Solov'ev, Vladimir Vasil'ev and Nikita Dolgushin.

Natal'ya Dudinskaya, Irina Kolpakova, Alla Shelest, Alla Sizova, Natal'ya Bessmertnova and Natal'ya Makarova (who defected in 1970) were among the other excellent dancers. Nina Ananiashvili and Irek Mukhamedov came to the fore in the 1980s. But with the new freedom to travel and to appear as guest artists abroad, leading Soviet dancers performed less frequently at home (Mukhamedov joined the Royal Ballet in London in 1990).

Dancers and critics complained about the dearth of new Soviet choreography and what they perceived as the decline of the dominant opera-scale style with which Grigorovich won acclaim in *Spartacus* (1968) and even in *The Golden Age* (1984). Ballets by Western choreographers like George Balanchine were staged for the first time in Tbilisi and Leningrad. Attention shifted to choreographers like Nikolay Boyarchikov (b.1935), director of the

Right. *Yekaterina Maksimova and Vladimir Vasil'ev in* Spartacus *at the Bol'shoy Theatre, Moscow, 1974.* Far right. *Tat'yana Shemetovets and Vladimir Komkov of the Belorussian Ballet in* Bolero

Musorgsky Ballet (formerly the Maly) in Leningrad, Valentin Yelizarev (b.1947) in Minsk and Boris Eifman (b.1946) in Leningrad.

But it was clear that as companies and individual dancers increasingly toured abroad to earn hard currency, Soviet (and post-Soviet) ballet was in disarray. The old cohesive style, without a major choreographer as inspiration, had splintered – mirroring the society around it.   AK

Film

BEFORE THE REVOLUTION

In Russia, as elsewhere, the cinema began life as a music-hall novelty and a fairground attraction. The first demonstration of the new machine took place in St Petersburg in May 1896 between two acts of an operetta called *Alfred Pasha in Paris*. The novelty spread like wildfire, proving very popular at the Nizhny Novgorod Fair, where Gor'ky first saw it in 1898, describing it as the 'kingdom of the shadows'. To the tsar, Nicholas II, it was and remained 'an empty, totally useless, and even harmful form of entertainment'. (Nevertheless he allowed a filmed record of his family to be kept

which was later shown in cinemas and proved a rich source of material for documentary film makers.) In the early years of the cinema films were very short and simple. They were shown by travelling projectionists who moved town as their audiences and supply of films were exhausted. Initially, the monopoly of production and distribution for these films lay with French firms like Pathé and Gaumont, but in 1908 the first Russian films were produced. By the outbreak of the First World War the audience for the cinema exceeded that for all other forms of public entertainment in Russia's towns put together. Films were becoming longer and more complex but 90 per cent of them, and all film stock and equipment, were still imported. On the outbreak of the war the Russian cinema was thrown back on its own resources: by 1916 imported films were down to 20 per cent of those shown. Many films were made to stir the patriotic feelings of the audience, but even more were made to offer them escape from the realities of war. At this time the two first major Russian directors emerged: Yevgeny Bauer (1865–1917) and Yakov Protazanov (1881–1945). The government was on the point of taking the cinema under its control when the revolutions of 1917 swept it away.   RT

SOVIET CINEMA

The Bolsheviks had always been acutely aware of the need for political agitation and propaganda and in this light Lenin remarked that: 'Of all the arts, for us the cinema is the most important'. The cinema already had an enormous audience in the cities and one of the principal tasks of the 1920s was to spread this audience to the countryside: partly to this end agit-trains were sent all over the country during the Civil War and the early years of Soviet power. They showed short films called *agitki* ('living posters') which through their simplicity and essentially visual impact were ideal vehicles to communicate the basic principles of the new ideology to a backward, illiterate and multilingual population. As most peasants had never before seen a moving picture the impact upon them was all the greater: the Bolsheviks became associated in the popular mind with modern technology and, by implication, with progress.

The October Revolution caused most of the pre-revolutionary entrepreneurs to flee the country, taking their much-needed equipment, films and personnel with them. The disruptions of the Civil War reduced the cinema to chaos. There was no stock with which to make the necessary films but students at the new State Film School perfected new techniques in so-called 'films without film'. These techniques were applied in practice as film stock became available. After several abortive deals, supplies of the necessary materials and equipment were restored through Willi Münzenberg's Workers' International Relief movement, a subsidiary of the Communist International, based in Germany and operating throughout Europe. The Soviet cinema was taken into state ownership in August 1919 and the first centralized state cinema enterprise, Goskino, was established in 1922. It failed to live up to rather exaggerated expectations and was reorganized in 1924 into Sovkino. This organization presided over what is known as the 'golden era of Soviet film' (1925–30), after which it was superseded by Soyuzkino, with the task of bringing the cinema firmly under Communist Party control. After further changes the Soviet cinema was finally placed under a separate Ministry of Cinematography in 1946.

The Soviet cinema was always regarded, by Party and film makers alike, as *the* art form of the Revolution. After the late 1920s little was left to chance and from 1930 cinema was organized to ensure that it reflected the official view. Before then, in its 'golden era', it expressed the spontaneous enthusiasm of those active in the industry. This was the period when all the most famous Soviet silent films were made: S.M. Eisenstein's (1898–1948) *The Strike* (1925), *The Battleship Potemkin* (1926), *October* (1927), *The Old and the New* and also *The General Line* (1929); V.I. Pudovkin's (1893–1953) *The Mother* (1926), *The End of St Petersburg* (1927), *Storm Over Asia* (1929); Dziga Vertov's (1896–1954) *Forward, Soviet!* (1926), *A Sixth Part of the World* (1926), *The Eleventh Year* (1928) and *The Man with the Movie Camera* (1929); and A.P. Dovzhenko's (1894–1956) *The Earth* (1930), criticized officially for its 'defeatism'. Although all these film makers were united in their enthusiastic support for the Revolution, they were divided in their method of expression. The 1920s and early 1930s were marked by increasingly bitter polemics between those who felt that the documentary film was the major revolutionary art form, that the newsreel was the most appropriate vehicle for revolutionary propaganda, or that the fictional feature film fulfilled this role more effectively. Within the latter category there were partisans of editing (montage), as opposed to acting, on the one hand, and of different schools of acting on the other. Some directors (Eisenstein) portrayed the mass as collective hero, while others (Pudovkin) chose individual stereotypes as representative of the mass. The avant-garde techniques developed at this time have exerted a profound influence on subsequent generations of film makers throughout the world.

Despite the immense importance of this period from the standpoint of cultural history, there is ample evidence to suggest that the films from this

Right. *Scene from Pudovkin's* The Mother, *1926. Far right. Close-up from the Odessa Steps sequence in Eisenstein's* Battleship Potemkin, *1926*

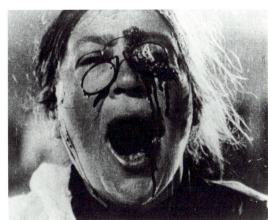

era that are now famous were not at all popular with contemporary audiences, who were looking for entertainment and enjoyment rather than experimentation. *The Battleship Potemkin* was taken off early in 1926 after two weeks because audiences preferred to see Douglas Fairbanks Snr. in *Robin Hood*. In fact it was not until ten years after the Revolution, when imports were deliberately reduced, that box-office receipts from Soviet films exceeded those from imports. Until then Soviet films continued to be more popular abroad than they were at home: *Potemkin* showed in more cinemas in Berlin alone that in the whole of the USSR. Soviet films gained access to the world market through subsidiary organizations of the Communist International such as Prometheus and Weltfilm in Germany. Soviet enterprises also co-produced films with these companies: because such films were made for export they were less polemical, more 'entertaining', and thus also more successful with Soviet audiences too. But the most popular Soviet films were the melodramas produced with the support, and often the active participation, of Lunacharsky, the People's Commissar for Education: these films – among them the serial *Miss Mend*, 1926 (F. Otsep, 1895–1949 and B.V. Barnet, 1902–65), *Salamander*, 1928 (G.L. Roshal 1899–1983), *The Bear's Wedding*, 1926 (K. Eggert 1883–1955) – were modelled on American productions. Many had little or no overt political content and were denounced as 'bourgeois' and 'counter-revolutionary'.

At the end of the 1920s, with the resignation of Lunacharsky, the end of the silent film and the advent of the First Five-year Plan, the 'golden era' of experimentation came to an end. Henceforth the cinema was to be harnessed directly by the Party to confront the enormous tasks of the 'cultural revolution' that was to accompany the social and economic transformation of the country's life. New levels of censorship were introduced, party cells vetted films at all stages of their production, and before distribution all films were submitted to an audience of selected workers to ensure that they were 'intelligible to the millions'. This system survived more or less intact until the advent of perestroika.

The films themselves began to reflect the official view much more closely. The collective or mass hero gave way to the individual leader figure: the Gor'ky trilogy of Mark Donskoy (1901–81); *Chapaev*, 1934 (Vasil'ev brothers: G.N., 1899–1946 and S.D., 1900–59); *Peter the First*, 1939 (V.M. Petrov, 1896–1966, and S.I. Bartenev, b. 1900); and *Alexander Nevsky*, 1938 (Eisenstein) are obvious examples. It is even more instructive, however, to compare *October*, 1927 (Eisenstein) or *The End of St Petersburg*, 1927 (Pudovkin) with *Lenin in October*, 1937 (M.I. Romm, 1901–71) and *The Man with a Gun*, 1938 (S.I., Yutkevich 1904–85). Film makers were no longer able to portray reality as they perceived it, but had instead to portray reality as the Party perceived it. This enhanced reality was baptized 'Socialist Realism'. The cinema became what Trotsky would have described as a 'hammer' for social change, rather than a 'mirror' reflecting society and its problems.

During the Second World War the cinema, like other art forms, was fully mobilized for the war effort. Many leading film makers went to the front, bringing back some of the most remarkable war footage ever shot. Feature films, to boost morale, portrayed the great heroes of the past: *Suvorov*, 1941 (Pudovkin and M. Doller, 1889–1952), *Bogdan Khmel'nitsky*, 1941 (I.A. Savchenko, 1906–50), *Kutuzov*, 1944 (Petrov), and *Ivan the Terrible*, 1941–46 (Eisenstein), were all immortalized on film

The battle on the ice from Eisenstein's Alexander Nevsky, *1938*

Right and centre. *Nikolay Cherkasov in the title role of Eisenstein's* Ivan the Terrible *(1941–46)*

Below. *Bondarchuk's epic,* War and Peace, *1963–67*

as examples for contemporary audiences; in 1946 Stalin himself appeared with a halo in M.E. Chiaureli's (1894–1974) *The Vow*. In the same year the Party's Central Committee signalled a further tightening of ideological controls in its resolution, denouncing *A Great Life*, 1946 (L.D. Lukov, 1909–63) and other films, including the second part of Eisenstein's *Ivan the Terrible*. This was banned, its very existence denied, until after Khrushchev's 1956 secret speech denouncing Stalin's 'personality cult'.

After the death of Stalin the Soviet cinema entered a new and much more fruitful period. Earlier technical problems were overcome: the ravages of war were made good and both stationary and mobile sound cinema installations covered the entire country. The industry was completely self-sufficient in the production of film stock and equipment. Many films were still imported and these were often shown mainly to film workers to keep them abreast of Western developments; much was also exported and an increasing number of films, such as I. Talankin's (b.1927) *Tchaikovsky* (1970) or A. Kurosawa's *Dersu Uzala* (1975), were co-produced with foreign organizations.

For some 20 years after the Second World War the Soviet cinema was known abroad principally for its re-creations of that war in films such as *The Cranes are Flying*, 1957 (M.K. Kalatozov, 1903–84) or *The Ballad of a Soldier*, 1959 (G.N. Chukhray, b.1921) and for its screen versions of classics of Russian literature – *The Lady with the Lapdog*, 1960 (I. Ye. Kheyfits, b.1905), *The Nest of Gentlefolk*, 1969 (A. Mikhalkov-Konchalovsky, b.1937) or the 12-hour version of *War and Peace*, 1963–67 (S.F. Bondarchuk, b.1920). From the 1960s this stereotyped view became less and less applicable as the Soviet cinema turned to grapple with contemporary problems. Sometimes this was done indirectly through the historical epic (*Andrey Rublev*, 1966 (A. Tarkovsky, 1932–86)), or the science-fiction epic *Solaris*, 1972 (Tarkovsky). On other occasions the problems were tackled more openly and directly as in *The Beginning*, 1970 (G. Panfilov, b.1934). In any case the Soviet cinema, although still operating within the overall constraints of the principles of Socialist Realism, became much more flexible in its interpretation and application of those principles. This could also be seen in the rapid increase in the number of films from the Union Republics with a distinctly national flavour, such as Mikhalkov-Konchalovsky's *The First Teacher* (Kirghizia, 1965), S.I. Paradzhanov's (1924–90) *Shadows of Our Forgotten Ancestors* (Ukraine, 1964) and G.N. Shengelaya's (b.1937) *Pirosmani* (Georgia, 1971).

By the 1970s Soviet cinema had the highest per capita audience figures in the world. It seemed to have resisted the encroachments of both radio and television and to have remained, if not (as Lenin had prophesied) the most important, then at least among the 'most important of all the arts'. It seemed entirely appropriate therefore that one of the first signs of the impact of perestroika in cultural affairs should have been the coup that swept the old guard in the Union of Cinematographers from power in May 1986. It was deeply significant that the new First Secretary of the Union, Elem Klimov (b.1933), had had five of his six feature films 'arrested' for varying lengths of time.

One of the first actions of the new Union leadership was the establishment of a 'Conflict Commission' to review the films that had been 'shelved' during the era of stagnation. Its decisions resulted in the release of sixty previously banned pictures, including Aleksandr Askol'dov's *The Commissar*, which had been shelved for two decades because of its sympathetic portrayal of Jewish life. But, in addition to coming to terms with its own past as a censored art form, Soviet cinema took on the responsibility of helping Soviet audiences to con-

front the suppressed realities of their own past and come to terms with the phenomenon of Stalinism. Ironically, the two most important films in this regard had been made in the Brezhnev period and promptly banned. Aleksey German's (b.1938) nostalgic evocation of the innocent idealism of the 1930s before the Terror, *My Friend Ivan Lapshin* (made 1983; released 1985), was first shown on national television in order to avoid the obstructionism then still prevalent in the distribution network. The other film was Tengiz Abuladze's (b.1924) *Repentance*, completed in Georgia in 1984. When it was unshelved in 1986 it attracted a record audience of 17 million within three weeks. Through a fantastic allegory centring on a grotesque stereotype of a dictator, the film dealt openly with the Great Terror for the first time on the Soviet screen. Its success was, at least in part, a *succès de scandale*.

Other films have taken the criticism of aspects of contemporary Soviet life to new extremes. Juris Podnieks' (1950–92) *Is It Easy to Be Young?* (Latvija Film, 1987), a documentary made in Riga, examined

Andrey Tarkovsky

Andrey Tarkovsky is the best known Soviet film director after Sergey Eisenstein, whose work he despised, partly because for Tarkovsky's generation the montage tradition that Eisenstein represented had degenerated into a ritual straitjacket.

Tarkovsky wanted to make cinema anew, defining it as 'sculpted time'. He worked within the framework of official Soviet cinema, while constantly pushing it to its uttermost limits. Many of his artistic techniques could be contained within the changing guidelines of Socialist Realism but the central concern of his works – the struggle of the individual against his environment in the search for inner truth – caused endless friction with the Soviet authorities.

Tarkovsky's first clash with those authorities came with the colour sequence

which concludes his film of the life of the icon painter *Andrey Rublev* (1969), a celebration of the freedom of artistic creativity. The film had only a limited release in the USSR and it was substantially cut for Western distribution. His next film, the science-fiction epic *Solaris* (1973) marked a transition towards the more directly metaphysical concerns of his later Soviet films *The Mirror* (1975) and *Stalker* (1980). *Stalker* explores the search for inner meaning as far as was possible in the Soviet context without overtly resorting to a religious solution.

Top. Andrey Tarkovsky in 1986, shortly before his death. Left. Andrey Rublev. Right. The Mirror, one of Tarkovsky's most enigmatic films, withheld from overseas distribution for six years after completion

Tarkovsky moved to Italy for *Nostalgia* (1983). At the Cannes Film Festival the Soviet authorities managed to prevent it winning the main prize: it won a special jury prize instead. This official hostility impelled Tarkovsky towards the permanent exile which, like other Soviet artists, he dreaded, as it cut him off from his creative roots in Russia. His final film *The Sacrifice* (1986) was made in Sweden: it examines the meaning of life, death and time.

Tarkovsky died in exile in Paris. During the final stages of his cancer there were moves towards reconciliation. After his death, and even before the collapse of the old Soviet power structures, he was fully rehabilitated. Time has secured Tarkovsky's own reputation as one of the leading figures in post-war Soviet – or, more accurately, Russian – cinema.

Above. From Abuladze's
Repentance, *1984. Right.*
Andrey Fomin as Andrey,
Natal'ya Negoda as Vera,
and Aleksandra Tabakova
as Lena in Pichul's Little
Vera, *1988*

bum (1987), which examined the roots of evil through the increasingly criminal actions of a sixteen-year-old vigilante. Vasily Pichul's *Little Vera* (1988), which wrongly became notorious in the West as the 'first Soviet sex film', was in fact a searing indictment of the pressures of Soviet family life.

However, the audience's appetite for new revelations has gradually become blunted and cinema attendance figures have plummeted. Television proved not only more exciting, but also more convenient to watch, and the battlefield of perestroika has left people with less leisure time overall. As in wartime, audiences turn to the media to be entertained rather than confronted with the sordid side of everyday reality, which impinges on them all too readily. Soviet audiences are turning increasingly to video, either in their private homes, or in local 'video-salons', which frequently purvey pirated copies of imported films, or sheer *erotika*. At the same time, the film industry has been reorganized along commercial lines, so that each studio has to make a profit from its own film productions to reinvest in replacing equipment that is several decades behind that in the West.

As in so many sectors of the Soviet economy, the peak that Soviet cinema appeared to have reached in the 1970s proved to be illusory, or at best a temporary bastion against the floodgates of a harsh reality. Soviet cinema in its final years – and, still more, post-Soviet cinema – had to learn to accommodate itself to the rigours of the market economy and to seek a new relationship with its no longer captive audience, one based on the principle of supply and demand in a period of flux, uncertainty and growing chaos. A flood of Western imports now threatens a potentially fatal struggle for the lowest common denominator to attract viewers and finance.   RT

the whole gamut of problems facing Soviet youth, including the shadow of military service in Afghanistan. Vadim Abdrashitov (b.1945) built upon a reputation for courage established with *A Train Has Stopped* (1982), a study of local corruption following a railway accident in a provincial town, with *Plyum-*

The sciences

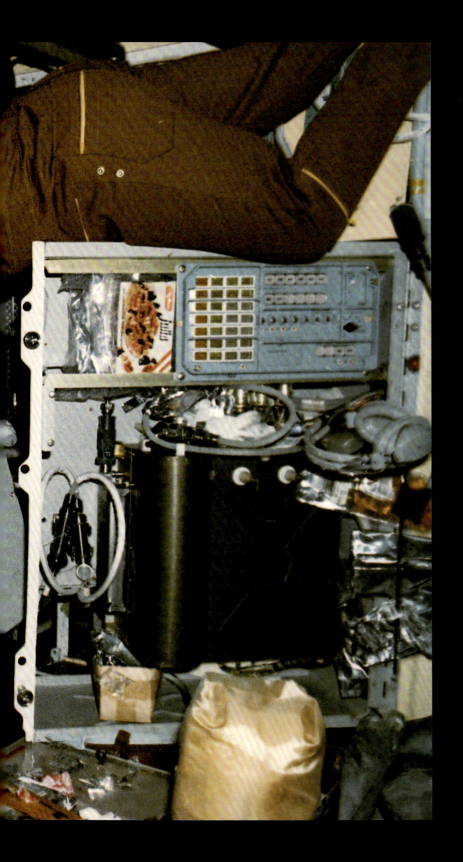

Scientific development

SCIENCE IN THE RUSSIAN EMPIRE

The first stirrings of a scientific attitude in Russia occurred in the seventeenth century at the time of the Scientific Revolution in Western Europe, but there was strong opposition from the Orthodox Church to independent secular thought. The real beginning of scientific enquiry had to await the modernization drive of Peter I. During his foreign travels as a young man, Peter had made himself familiar with the latest developments in science and technology. He was to maintain contact over many years with Leibnitz the German scientist. Foreign scholars were encouraged to visit Russia and young Russians were sent abroad. The culmination of the tsar's policies was to be the creation of the Academy of Sciences as a Russian equivalent of London's Royal Society and Paris's Académie des Sciences; it was opened in 1725 just after his death with an original membership of foreign scholars. The Academy's initial strength lay in mathematics and in 1727 the young Swiss mathematician Leonhard Euler arrived in St Petersburg, where he was to stay for thirteen years. The publication of his *Mechanica* in 1736 was one of the landmarks of eighteenth century science. The Academy was also involved in the organization of expeditions to survey and investigate the natural history of the far-flung regions of the Empire. However, the infant institution suffered from an internal conflict between Russian and German factions. This division was linked to a debate concerning the relative importance of science and technology in its activities. The balance between pure learning and work of direct practical benefit has been an issue which has subsequently sporadically recurred within the Academy.

The most notable of the young Russian scholars who began to appear was M.V. Lomonosov (1711–65). His interests covered a wide range of the sciences. Most notably, Lomonosov was one of the scholars who laid the foundation for the development of physical chemistry. It can be claimed that he revolutionized historical writing in Russia. He was also a poet and a member of a group who sought to standardize literary Russian. Further, he was to play a leading role in the creation of Moscow University which opened in 1755.

Science was slow to establish firm domestic roots as periods marked by a favourable atmosphere for the development of scientific thought and scholarship were interspersed with times of obscurantism and Orthodox Church domination. Thus, the early years of Alexander I's reign saw the creation of a Ministry of National Education (1802) and the foundation of new universities. However, the government was subsequently to order that theology be made a required subject in all universities and to ban certain textbooks. The crushing of the Decembrist uprising against Alexander's successor in 1825 resulted in further censorship and political oppression. Against this background the embryonic Russian scientific community struggled to survive. However, even in these unpropitious times the tradition in mathematics was revived through the work of M.V. Ostrogradsky (1801–61), V.Ya. Bunyakovsky (1804–89) and, in particular, N.I. Lobachevsky (1792–1856), who was the founder of the first non-Euclidean geometry.

Defeat in the Crimean War and the era of reform which followed had an effect on the country's scientific life as great as it did on other areas of Russian society. The development of science in its broadest sense was considered to be a corollary of the drive for social and economic modernization. A new statute for the universities was approved in 1863 which provided for an expansion in higher education and gave the universities and their professors a greatly increased level of autonomy. These more liberal times produced the first real wave of Russian scientists. They included: A.M. Butlerov (1828–86), who played a key role in the development of structural theory in chemistry; P.L. Chebyshev (1821–94), who maintained Russia's mathematical tradition; the comparative embryologists A.O. Kovalevsky (1840–1901) and I.I. Mechnikov (1845–1916, Nobel Prize 1908); the great D.I. Mendeleev (1834–1907), who, in 1869, unveiled his periodic table of chemical elements; I.M. Sechenov (1829–1905), later to be described as the father of Russian physiology; and K.M. Timiryazev (1843–1920), a pioneer in the study of photosynthesis.

Previous spread. Yury Grechko and Yury Romanenko in the Mir space station

Dmitry Mendeleev

Dmitry Mendeleev (1834–1907) was one of the greatest scientists of the nineteenth century. His discovery of the periodicity of chemical elements can be compared to Darwin's work in biology or Newton's in physics in terms of the scale of the achievement. Yet for much of his life Mendeleev was largely unappreciated by his fellow-countrymen.

The event that led to Mendeleev's discoveries was his appointment to the Chair of Chemistry at St Petersburg University in 1867. Finding that there was no suitable textbook for his students, he set out to write his own, synthesizing his 15 years of study of the properties of elements. To help him with his work he wrote down on cards (he was an avid patience player) the properties of the known elements. As he arranged them, he was struck by the patterns that were formed. Indeed, so convinced was Mendeleev of the value of his discovery that he decided there were errors in existing scholarship and predicted the existence of three new elements to fit the gaps in his table. Although when it appeared in 1869 the table was greeted with almost universal scepticism, the discovery of the three missing elements quickly led to its acceptance. Element no. 101 is named mendelevium after him.

Mendeleev was treated with great respect outside Russia, but not so in his own country. His fiery temper and his support for the political demands of the students put him constantly into conflict with the authorities, and his second marriage, to an artist, was bigamous under Russian law although he was never prosecuted. As a result he was never admitted to the Academy of Sciences, which was full of his conservative enemies. Many other institutions all over the world honoured him, however, and he is now regarded as one of the pioneers of modern chemistry.

The expansion of scientific research was concentrated in the universities which thus replaced the Academy as the centre of Russian science. The latter remained a conservative institution and refused to admit to membership some pioneering scientists. There was considerable outcry when it excluded no less a person than Mendeleev.

By the last quarter of the nineteenth century a critical mass had been achieved in science. The domestic scientific community was now strong enough to withstand the next period of reaction. Although some scholars were driven abroad by the unfavourable conditions, most remained to train their successors. Contact and mutual support were maintained through a growing number of learned societies. Outstanding amongst the rising generation was I.P. Pavlov (1849–1936). While he is best remembered for his work on the nervous system, it was for his work on the digestive process that in 1904 he was to be awarded the first Nobel Prize to be received by a Russian scientist. Russia at the time possessed an increasing number of scientists doing high-class work. There were physicists such as P.N. Lebedev (1860–1912) and A.F. Ioffe (1880–1960). V.I. Vernadsky (1863–1945) undertook important studies in radioactivity and in geochemistry. Ye.S. Fedorov (1853–1919) was a pioneer in crystallography and A.A. Markov (1856–1922) was to make a major contribution to probability theory (Markov chains). V.M. Bekhterev (1857–1927) was, like Pavlov, a neurophysiologist.

However, the size of the research community and of Russia's scientific and technical intelligentsia as a whole was still relatively small when compared with the major industrial powers. The institutional structure was also underdeveloped. In particular, Russia lagged seriously in the more applied areas of research. The industrialization of its economy was greatly dependent on the import of capital and technology. There were few resources devoted to the development of domestic technology. Russian scientists and inventors who produced work of possible practical application found it difficult to get support. This failing was sharply exposed by the outbreak of the First World War which cut Russia off from Germany, its major source of modern technology. In response the government made more resources available for scientific work and new research groups and organizations were established. RAL

SCIENCE IN THE SOVIET UNION

While the tsarist government had contained a strand of opinion which saw science as dangerous and subversive, the Bolshevik government which came to power after the Revolution of October 1917 had an ideology which considered modern science and technology as one of the keys to progress. Scientists, who had previously lobbied somewhat fruitlessly for the creation of a system of research laboratories on the model which was being developed

Peter Kapitsa

Astrophysical laboratory developed by the Academy of Sciences of the USSR, Crimea

in the world's major industrial economies, now received positive responses. Many institutes which became leading organizations in the Soviet research and development system had their roots in the immediate post-revolutionary period. At the same time, in response to a combination of pressure from some of its members and from the government, the Academy of Sciences began to change from a scientists' club into a large research organization. The prospects of a career in science opened up for more young people and also for a wider cross-section of the population.

In the nineteenth century most of the leading scientists came from an aristocratic background. For many parts of society, access to higher education was difficult if not impossible. For example, there was a policy which sought to control the number of Jews who were able to enter the universities. The decade after the Revolution was a time of increasing productivity in science as bright young minds were attracted to research. During these years three future Nobel laureates, P.L. Kapitsa (1894–1984), N.N. Semenov (1896–1986) and L.D. Landau (1908–68), began their research careers at the physics institute which had been established by Ioffe in Petrograd after the Revolution.

As in other areas of Soviet life, the First Five-year Plan brought radical change in science. A rapid expansion in the numbers of research and development organizations, funding and staff took place. The increase was particularly large in establishments doing work related to industry and was linked to the goal of ensuring that the Soviet Union achieved

technological independence from the West. The number of research workers and university teaching staff, which had been under 12,000 in 1913, was to be nearly 100,000 in 1940. The universities, however, were overburdened with teaching in the drive to produce large numbers of trained specialists for the growing economy, and they lost much of their research role to independent research institutes controlled by the ministries which were responsible for the various sectors of the economy or which were created within the Academy of Sciences.

While the size of the Soviet Union's scientific effort dramatically increased, the climate in which research was undertaken became less propitious. Central control and planning began to stifle initiative and the purges and oppression of the 1930s were to have a devastating effect. Growing Soviet isolationism resulted in the breaking of the wide international contacts so vital for a thriving scientific community. Many scientists were imprisoned. Virtually all the Soviet Union's top aircraft designers found themselves working as prisoners in establishments run by the NKVD. N.I. Vavilov (1887–1943), a pioneer of scientific plant-breeding and plant genetics was to die in prison, while dictatorial control over biology and agricultural science was exercised by the pseudo-scientist T.D. Lysenko (1898–1976). Research on genetics was to be virtually halted.

In the West, as a result of the perceived contribution of science and scientists to the war effort and the development of science-based branches of industry, the post-war years brought a continuing high commitment to funding scientific research. In the Soviet Union too, further rapid growth in the scientific effort took place. By 1990 there were more than 1.5 million research workers and university teachers.

This expansion was marked by the development of large and, frequently, overly bureaucratic organizations. The Academy of Sciences of the USSR, for example, had a scientific staff of more than 60,000. On the other hand, Soviet contributions to world scientific development did not match the size of its research effort, nor did the rate of technological progress in the economy reflect the resources spent on applied research and development. Soviet scientists received relatively few Nobel Prizes. These were awarded almost totally (six out of seven) in physics, which has been considered an area where Soviet research achieved world standing. Since 1990, the breakup of the Soviet Union, the collapse of the economy and the need to control escalating budget deficits have resulted in a crisis in the support of science. This is reflected in a significant 'brain-drain' abroad of the most talented scientists and a flight from state-funded science to better paid private and co-operative commercial activities.   RAL

MEDICINE AND HEALTH CARE

Before the reign of Peter the Great medical care in Russia was provided by a few, chiefly foreign, doctors recruited by the Apothecaries' Chamber established in 1581 and renamed in 1620 the Apothecaries' Office. A significant event in preventive medicine was the establishment of the first quarantine posts in 1592. Peter's programme of Westernization after his tours of Western Europe required a greatly expanded medical service, primarily for the army and navy but also for the new industrial communities and growing cities. Physicians were recruited abroad, mainly in England, Scotland, Holland, Germany and Sweden. The Medical Chancellery legislated on such matters as burial of the dead and the wholesomeness of food. The whole medical organization was presided over by the Imperial Physician: the first occupant of this post was a Scot, Dr Robert Erskine (d. 1718). To train Russian doctors a 'Gofshpital' with a medical school was founded in Moscow in 1706; others followed in St Petersburg and Kronstadt (1733). Peter's Admiralty Regulations (1722) defined the medical service for the navy and dockyard workers and served as the basis for General Regulations on Hospitals (1735) and for later health legislation in industry. The first factory hospital, staffed by a surgeon, was set up at Sestroretsk naval ordnance factory in 1724 and more ambitious arrangements were made at the new Urals industrial centre of Yekaterinburg in 1734.

In 1739 public health boards were appointed in Moscow and St Petersburg, chaired by a Town Physician, for medico-legal duties and to organize the urban medical services. In 1775 Russia was divided into provinces (*gubernii*) and these into counties (*uezdy*), each with its medical officer. Provincial medical boards were established in 1797 by Paul I to ensure local observance of central governmental regulations and to organize measures against epidemics, which were becoming a major problem. Inoculation against smallpox, introduced by Dr Thomas Dimsdale at Catherine the Great's invitation (1768), was vigorously pursued.

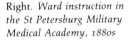

Right. *Ward instruction in the St Petersburg Military Medical Academy, 1880s*

These administrative measures were generally unsuccessful, largely because of the shortage of doctors, and steps were taken to improve the supply. The first university faculty of medicine opened in Moscow in 1775. The 'Gofshpital' schools were replaced by medico-surgical academies, with a more scientific, less practical curriculum, in St Petersburg and Moscow (1799). The St Petersburg Academy, reorganized in 1805 by a Viennese physician, Dr Peter Frank, and later enlarged, became the Imperial Medico-Surgical Academy in 1809, with the Scot Sir James Wylie as its first president. It trained doctors mainly for the army, and in 1881 was renamed the Military Medical Academy.

Private medical practice existed only in the towns, where there were sufficient people wealthy enough to afford it. Charitable hospitals were built, many of them on a magnificent scale, to meet the needs of the poorer citizens. Outside the large towns, however, medical aid was virtually non-existent; the only time a peasant might see a doctor was when being medically examined for military service. Rural hospitals, staffed mainly by German or Polish doctors who rarely spoke Russian, were in a deplorable state and most of the work was done by nominally supervised medical auxiliaries (*feldshers*).

Local medical care

The introduction of the *zemstvo* system of local government under Alexander II was a major milestone in pre-revolutionary Russian health care: the 1864 laws made the *zemstva* responsible, 'within legal and economic limitations', for the health of the community, and aimed at a uniform availability of medical care throughout the country, free to all who paid their contributions. Each county was divided into four or more districts (*uchastki*), each to have a central hospital (on average one per 20,000 population in central Russia and one per 60,000 population in eastern Russia). Various types of staffing were tried, with one or more physicians per county, assisted by *feldshers*. The medical departments of the provincial *zemstva* managed their own hospitals (which served the whole province for psychiatric cases) and funded hospital construction in the counties. They organized *feldsher* training schools, convened congresses of *zemstvo* doctors (the first in 1871) and published some remarkably erudite statistical and medico-topographical surveys. The control of epidemics was, nevertheless, their most important function and some established herds of calves for vaccine preparation, and bacteriological laboratories for making antisera against rabies and diphtheria. *Zemstva* were functioning

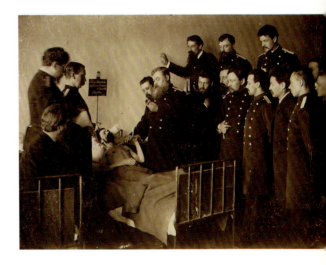

Right. *Infant mortality in the nineteenth and early twentieth centuries*

by 1890 in 34 out of the 50 provinces of European Russia excluding Poland and the Caucasus; in those provinces of European Russia (other than Poland and the Caucasus) without *zemstva* the central government was gradually establishing a medical service, but far inferior in staffing ratio.

Laws of 1870 and 1892 required the urban authorities to provide a public health service and some personal health care, but the general situation left much to be desired, especially outside the main cities. In the period 1884–87, 40 per cent of persons dying in the better-off districts of Odessa and 94 per·cent of those dying in the poorer quarters had not sought medical advice. In 1882 a free universal medical service was established for the poor of St Petersburg through government doctors (nearly half of them women). It was intended originally to deal with epidemics of diphtheria and scarlet fever, but in 1883 it became permanent, and in 1885 provided 215,000 consultations and 49,000 domiciliary visits.

A law of 1866 required factories to have a hospital with beds at the rate of one per 100 workers, but at most factories the medical service existed only on paper (in the 1880s only 67,000 of a total workforce of 150,000 in Moscow province enjoyed an actual medical service). By 1890 there were 9,892 doctors in civilian posts (four times as many as in military practice) and of these the number employed in industry was rising steadily; the first All-Russian Congress of Factory Doctors was held in Moscow in 1909. By that year, of a total of 19,866 civilian doctors (1,328 women), 14,398 lived in towns and 5,468 in rural districts, making one doctor to 7,800 inhabitants. On average in the towns there was one doctor to 1,500 inhabitants and in rural districts, one to 24,600. The situation was aggravated by their irregular distribution: even the better-served area of European Russia compared unfavourably with other countries of Europe both in the absolute level of infant mortality and in the rate of its decline during the three decades before the First World War.

Education and research

From an early date the right to practise medicine in Russia was limited to those who had passed official examinations, and the University Code of 1844 accepted only candidates who had completed ten semesters. In 1896 there were ten medical schools: the Military Medical Academy and the Universities of Moscow, Kiev, Kharkiv, Warsaw, Kazan', Yur'ev, Dorpat (now Tartu), Helsingfors (now Helsinki) and Tomsk; Odessa University opened a medical school in 1900. Russia was the first country to organize postgraduate medical specialization, at the Medico-Surgical Academy in 1841. The Grand

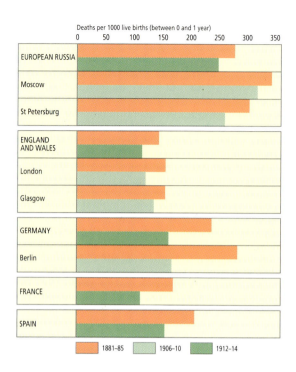

Deaths per 1000 live births (between 0 and 1 year)

EUROPEAN RUSSIA · Moscow · St Petersburg · ENGLAND AND WALES · London · Glasgow · GERMANY · Berlin · FRANCE · SPAIN

1881–85 · 1906–10 · 1912–14

Duchess Yelena Pavlovna Clinical Postgraduate Medical Institute, the first such establishment in the world, was founded in 1885. In the 32 years until 1917 it trained 9,906 doctors. After the Revolution medical education was radically reorganized (1930): a shortening of the course was made possible by early separation into specialities. Research was fostered by the creation of an Academy of Medical Sciences in 1944.

On the territory of what is now Uzbekistan an important medical school had flourished in Samarkand a millennium earlier: the *Canon of Medicine* of the Arab physician Ibn Sina or Avicenna (980–1037) served as a textbook in East and West for some five centuries. It was not, however, until the mid-nineteenth century that Russian medical research began.

The most notable of the pre-revolutionary Russian medical scientists were N.I. Pirogov (1810–81) in military and orthopaedic surgery, anaesthesia and anatomy; I.I. Mechnikov (1845–1916) in the pathology of inflammation and the discovery of phagocytosis; S.S. Korsakov (1853–1900) in psychiatry; V.M. Bekhterev and N.Ye. Vvedensky (1852–1922) in neurology; I.M. Sechenov and I.P. Pavlov in neurophysiology (particularly the discovery of conditioned reflexes); F.F. Erismann (1842–1915) in preventive medicine, and D.I. Ivanovsky (1864–1920), who has a sound claim to be regarded as the founder of virology. Russian doctors and scientists also made important additions to knowledge of the epidemiology and pathology of plague, cholera and typhus fever.   BH

Scientific institutions

SCIENCE POLICY

From the earliest days of the Soviet regime the development of science was considered a matter of the highest priority. In the difficult years immediately after the Revolution measures were taken to retain the services of scientists, many of whom were unsympathetic to the new order, and to expand the network of research organizations, in particular by creating institutes able to assist in the country's industrial development. By the end of the 1930s the country possessed a relatively large and diverse research base. In terms of personnel and finance, expansion occurred at a rapid pace after the war, but from the mid-1970s the rate of growth of personnel slowed and in recent years the share of GNP devoted to research and development has stabilized.

The principal agencies concerned with science policy until 1991 were the State Committee for Science and Technology (GKNT), the USSR Academy of Sciences, and the State Planning Committee (Gosplan). The GKNT was responsible for securing a coherent national science and technology policy in accordance with party and government directives. Its brief included the elaboration, with the Academy of Sciences and Gosplan, of draft plans of research work, co-ordination and oversight of major national research and development programmes, management of the country's scientific and technical information network and the inventions and patents system. It also handled many international matters relating to applied research and technology. Military research and development was co-ordinated by the Military-Industrial Commission.

Policy in the field of fundamental research was the responsibility of the USSR Academy of Sciences, which co-ordinated its plans with the GKNT and Gosplan. The latter also planned the practical application of results. Until perestroika, when active intervention diminished, the Party exerted inordinate influence, frequently harmful, on policy and the appointment of personnel through the Central Committee's science and educational departments. Since 1991 Russia has been attempting to reorganize the former Soviet science policy institutions to make them compatible with the requirements of a market economy. The Ministry for Science and Technology Policy now has overall responsibility, working in association with the Russian Academy of Sciences. The principal policy concerns have been the minim-ization of damage to the country's science base arising from a severe contraction of funding, and the adoption of measures to transform the research and innovation system. In the other successor states it has proved necessary to create completely new science policy institutions and to restructure the research establishments located on their territories in order to form independent national research systems. It remains to be seen to what extent the traditional USSR-wide research network will be maintained, but the scientists of the newly-independent states now have an opportunity to become full participants in the wider international scientific community.

JMC

PERSONNEL AND FINANCE

The growth of scientific potential in the former USSR can be judged from the number of those recorded as 'scientists' (all persons with a higher degree or academic title and others employed as professionals in scientific, academic and industrial-research work regardless of their formal qualifications): 12,000 in 1913, 98,300 in 1940, 927,700 in 1970 and 1,522,200 at the beginning of 1989. Of the latter, those with higher degrees comprised 493,100 candidates of science (equivalent to a western Ph.D.) and 49,700 doctors of science (D.Sc.). By international standards the republics of the former USSR have a high proportion of women scientists: almost 40 per cent of all scientists are women, though their proportion in the most highly qualified categories is much lower: 13 per cent of doctors of science, and 28 per cent of candidates of science. Of the 1989 total, 10 per cent worked in organizations of the Academy of Sciences and other academies, 36 per cent at higher educational establishments, 43 per cent at research institutes subordinate to industrial and defence ministries, and the remaining 11 per cent at industrial enterprises, ministries and government departments. Since 1991 the number of scientists in Russia employed as such has fallen by at least one-third.

Expenditure on research and development expanded at a rapid pace: total expenditure in current prices rose from 11,700 million rubles in 1970, to 22,300 million in 1980 and more than 40,000 million in 1989. Most fundamental research and all military and some high priority civilian projects were funded from the state budget. In 1989 state budget funding amounted to 21,500 million rubles, of which 15,300 million (71 per cent) was for military purposes. Most applied research and development was funded from the retained earnings of enterprises and various ministerial funds. Much research was undertaken for contracts between client organizations and

Above. *The Tokamak 15 experimental nuclear fusion plant, Kurchatov Institute, Moscow, 1989. Above right. The Russian Academy of Sciences, Moscow*

research establishments, and such contract research played a large role in the higher educational sector and, increasingly, the Academy system.

The biggest problem in the later Soviet period was the inadequate provision of modern research equipment, in particular the shortage of computers. Governments of the successor states have now been compelled in the interests of monetary stabilization to slash their expenditure. Redundancy among scientific personnel and the closure of entire research institutes has become widespread, trends reinforced by swingeing cuts in military procurement and the shedding by civilian enterprises of their research establishments. JMC

THE ACADEMY OF SCIENCES

The leading centre of Soviet science was the USSR Academy of Sciences, which was responsible for much of the country's fundamental research and for general scientific leadership of all research in the natural and social sciences. The Academy was founded by a decree of 1724 and officially began its activities in St Petersburg in the following year. By the end of the nineteenth century the Imperial Academy of Sciences, as it was then known, had become the main scientific centre of the country, although its contribution to Russia's economic and technical development was modest. After the February 1917 revolution it was renamed the Russian Academy of Sciences. In the 1920s a new charter was adopted and other steps were taken to increase the relevance of the Academy's work to the country's development and also to enhance the influence within it of the Communist Party. The designation 'of the USSR' was adopted in 1925 and in 1934 the headquarters moved from Leningrad to Moscow. Concern with practical problems increased sharply during the Second World War, but in the early 1960s many of the Academy's technically-oriented institutes were transferred to the industrial research network.

At the beginning of 1989 the Soviet Academy had 909 full members (academicians) and corresponding members and 138 honorary foreign members. Research was undertaken within the Academy at almost 300 institutes, observatories and other scientific establishments, employing 62,000 scientists and a total staff of more than 200,000. The supreme body of the Academy was the General Assembly of all academicians and corresponding members, which met at least twice a year to discuss the development of science in the country as a whole, to resolve important issues of policy and organization, and to elect new members. All elections were by secret ballot. The Academy had enjoyed a large measure of autonomy and internal democracy, and sought to preserve them, not always successfully, in the face of attempted intervention at various times by the Communist Party and other external bodies. The leading executive body was the Presidium, elected every four years by the General Assembly, and headed by the President of the Academy. The successive Presidents were A.P. Karpinsky (May 1917–

36), a geologist; V.L. Komarov (1936–45), a botanist; S.I. Vavilov (1945–51), a physicist; A.N. Nesmeyanov (1951–61), an organic chemist; M.V. Keldysh (1961–75), a mathematician; A.P. Aleksandrov (1975–86), a nuclear physicist; and G.I. Marchuk (1986–91), a mathematician and computer specialist. Prior to becoming President of the Academy, Marchuk (b.1925) served for six years as chairman of the State Committee for Science and Technology. As President he was assisted by the Academy's chief scientific secretary, I.M. Makarov (b. 1927).

The Presidium had four sections which controlled the work of departments and research establishments: physical-technical and mathematical sciences; earth sciences; chemical-technical and biological sciences; and social sciences. Each section consisted of a number of departments (recently eighteen) organized on the basis of disciplines and headed by academician secretaries. In November 1986 the Academy adopted a reform enhancing the managerial role of the departments, with a corresponding reduction of the powers of the central Presidium. This move was part of a more general effort since 1985 to revitalize and democratize the Academy in order to enhance its research capability.

The USSR Academy of Sciences had three regional divisions (Siberian, Urals and Far Eastern), three research centres (Leningrad, Saratov and Kola), and several smaller branches. The Siberian Division, founded in 1957, was the most important. It had dual subordination to the Academy's Presidium and the RSFSR Council of Ministers, and included the Novosibirsk science city, Akademgorodok. The Academy had more than 200 advisory scientific councils which played a role in defining research, an extensive network of libraries, including a Central Library in Leningrad, and responsibility for one of the oldest and largest scientific publishing houses in the world (founded in 1727), 'Nauka', which annually issued over 3,000 books and 185 journals.

Each of the union republics, with the exception of the RSFSR, had its own Academy of Sciences. At the beginning of 1989 the 14 republican Academies employed a total of 56,000 scientists working in 400 establishments. There were also four USSR branch Academies: the All-Union Lenin Academy of Agricultural Sciences, founded in 1929 and employing 21,000 scientists in 1988, the Academy of Medical Sciences (founded in 1944), the Academy of Pedagogical Sciences (1966), and the Academy of Arts (1947).

The formation of a separate Russian Academy had begun, even before the USSR body was dissolved, and it then took over the institutions and personnel on Russian territory. Of the Academies in other successor states, the largest and oldest is that of Ukraine, founded in 1919; the youngest that of Moldavia, founded in 1961. Some of the institutes occupied leading positions in the Soviet period and made a substantial contribution to the economic and cultural lives of their respective republics.   JMC

RESEARCH BASES

Higher education

The higher education system in the former Soviet Union employed over half a million lecturers and full-time research scientists, but their contribution to the country's research effort was not large. The research institutes and laboratories of higher educational establishments (VUZY) accounted for less than 10 per cent of total research and development in terms of expenditure. Research in the VUZY was undertaken in academic departments, in research institutes and in departmental laboratories classed either as 'problem-oriented' (engaged primarily in fundamental research funded through the state budget), or 'branch' (applied work contracted with ministries and enterprises). In the successor states a determined effort is being made to enhance the research facilities of the higher education sector.

Branch organizations

The largest component of research in terms of personnel and expenditure was the network of establishments under the branch ministries and government departments, in particular those of industry, agriculture and other sectors of the economy. In industry alone at the beginning of 1989 there were almost 1600 research establishments, half being concerned with engineering – civil and military. In recent years efforts were made to overcome a long-standing problem, the organizational separation of research from production, partly through the creation of 'science-production associations' – amalgamations of research and development establishments with enterprises. By 1989 there were more than 450

Azimuth telescope at the Russian Academy of Sciences Observatory, Stavropol' Territory

such associations in industry, more than double the number in 1980.

Intersectoral organizations

In an effort to improve the management of large research projects, the 'interbranch scientific and technical complex' (known by the initials MNTK) was inaugurated in 1985. By 1989 there were 23 MNTK for such major national research programmes as the development of personal computers, robotics, lasers and new materials. The MNTK was a grouping of research and development organizations, usually belonging to a number of different ministries, under the guidance of a 'lead institute'. Some were headed by Academy institutes; others by branch organizations.

Research and development

The traditional organizational structures of Soviet science have tended to be excessively large and cumbersome, lacking in flexibility, with limited mobility of personnel. In the late 1980s a new sector began to form, consisting of co-operatives and other small-scale units engaged in research, design, innovation and similar activities for the promotion of technical progress. By the spring of 1989 there were almost 4,000 co-operatives of this type, involving more than 100,000 people. As marketization proceeds in the successor states such bodies outside the public sector could become an important feature of research and development facilities.

Inventions and discoveries

Both in the former USSR and in the successor states responsibility for questions relating to inventions is vested in a Committee for Inventions and Discoveries (an independent State Committee under the USSR Council of Ministers until 1988, but then attached to the State Committee for Science and

Solar power installation in the Kara Kum, Turkmenistan

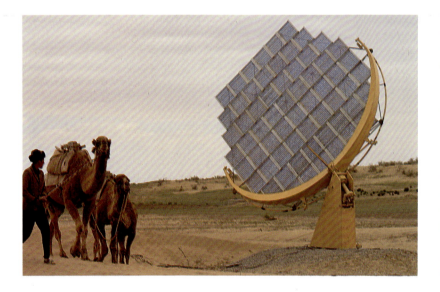

Technology). The Committee provides expertise for the confirmation of inventions, maintains a register of them and promotes their use in the economy. An inventor receives a 'certificate of authorship' for a confirmed invention, which then becomes the property of the state, plus a payment on a scale determined by the estimated economic return gained from the practical application of the invention. A register of major new scientific discoveries is also maintained, those responsible for scientific breakthroughs receiving diplomas and financial rewards. Patents during the Soviet period were usually only granted to foreigners. Transition to market economies has stimulated discussion of a replacement of the inventions system and the successor states are likely to adopt legislation like that of Western countries.

Voluntary scientific activity

There is a long tradition of participation of scientists and engineers in voluntary activity to promote the popularization of science and technology. The system of Scientific and Technical Societies (NTO), which originated in the Russian Technical Society founded in 1866, consisted of 29 independent voluntary societies co-ordinated by a USSR Union of Scientific and Engineering Societies, founded in 1988. They had a total membership of almost 12 million scientists, engineers, technicians and workers, who participated in a wide range of activity concerned with research and innovation. The Union published a popular monthly journal, *Tekhnika i Nauka*. There was also a mass movement for the promotion of inventions, the All-Union Society of Inventors and Rationalizers (VOIR) founded in 1958 and sponsored by the trade unions: in 1989 it claimed a membership of 14 million people. The Society published a monthly, *Izobretatel' i Ratsionalizator*. The popularization of science was the principal activity of yet another organization, the All-Union Knowledge Society (*Znanie*), founded in 1947, organizing lectures and publishing a wide range of literature on scientific and political themes, including the popular monthly journal, *Nauka i Zhizn'*.   JMC

SCIENTIFIC INFORMATION NETWORK

The former USSR had an elaborate network of organizations concerned with the gathering, processing and dissemination of scientific and technical information. This system was developed in part to compensate for the country's relative isolation from world science and technology. The principal organization was the long-established All-Union Institute of Scientific and Technical Information (VINITI) –

Right. Inside the Dubna Nuclear Research Institute, near Moscow

subordinated jointly to the State Committee for Science and Technology and the USSR Academy of Sciences. Other national organizations included the Academy's Institute of Scientific Information in the Social Sciences (INION), the All-Union Scientific and Technical Information Centre, which registered and analysed information on current research being undertaken in the USSR, and the All-Union Institute of Interbranch Information, which served the defence industry and helped to diffuse its technologies to the civilian economy. The entire national information service employed some 200,000 people. It was supplemented by a national network of scientific libraries, headed by the State Public Scientific and Technical Library in Moscow. The majority of these agencies were taken over by the Russian government on the dissolution of the USSR, but it and other successor governments undertook considerable rationalization in the interests of financial retrenchment.

Scientific and technical literature is published not only by Nauka, but also by a number of universities and a range of specialized publishing houses concerned with particular technologies or branches of industry. In 1988 approximately 19,000 scientific books and brochures were published, together with more than 200 journals devoted to the natural sciences and mathematics.   JMC

INTERNATIONAL RELATIONS

Under Stalin Soviet science became increasingly isolated from the rest of the international scientific community. Relations gradually revived during the 1950s and 1960s, and more vigorously during the period of détente during the 1970s. However, the situation under Brezhnev was far from satisfactory with many obstacles to international scientific contacts and exchanges. Under Gorbachev the situation

improved, permitting a substantial increase in visits abroad by Soviet scientists, much greater access to foreign scientific publications, and more active participation in international research projects. Freedom of movement reached the point where there was mounting Soviet concern about a 'brain drain' of scientists to leading western countries. As before, the most extensive collaboration took place within the framework of Comecon, including participation in bilateral and multilateral projects. Examples of the latter included the 'Interkosmos' space research programme and an international programme for the development of computers. In the past relations with western countries were often based on intergovernmental scientific and technical co-operation agreements, but the improved international climate led to the development of more diverse, decentralized, forms of co-operation between Soviet and western organizations. Areas of strong interest for international collaboration, particularly with Russian and Ukrainian organizations, include space research, astronomy, energy (including research into nuclear fusion based on the Tokamak installations), medicine and the environment. Scientists from western as well as eastern countries participate in the work of the Joint Nuclear Research Institute at Dubna near Moscow.

The USSR Academy of Sciences was the organization primarily responsible for international links in fundamental research, but the State Committee for Science and Technology played an active role in applied research and development. From 1965 the USSR adhered to the Paris Convention for the protection of industrial property, since when Soviet participation in international patent matters increased, but it was still at a very low level considering the scale of the country's research potential when the Soviet state collapsed. Sales of licences, handled by the specialized agency, Litsenzintorg, were also on an extremely modest scale in the Soviet period. In 1987 only 390 licences were sold abroad, of which 101 went to developed western countries.   JMC

Helen Sharman, the first Briton in space, with Anatoly Arbatsky and Sergey Krikalev, in Soyuz, May 1991

Scientific research

EXPLORATION

In many people's minds the Russians are less closely associated with exploration than the English, Spanish and Dutch, yet Russia has a long history of expeditions into little known territories of the globe. In 1500 the Russian state was confined to the forests west of the Ural mountains but during the following century expansion took place into Siberia, to which early expeditions were usually financed by merchants, led by Cossack fortune-hunters and motivated by the quest for furs. The economic motive for exploration remained dominant until the reign of Peter the Great when the search for scientific knowledge became a driving force, with the state providing encouragement and backing for many expeditions of discovery, and the leaders of such expeditions being of the 'gentleman explorer' category familiar in the West. The tradition of scientific exploration has remained with the Russians to the present day.

The breakthrough into Siberia was made in 1581 by a band of Cossacks led by the outlaw Yermak (d.1584), and within sixty years the first Russian reached the Pacific coast. The so-called 'conquest of Siberia' opened a new world for exploration. Moving up the Siberian rivers Russians reached the northern coast and, taking to their flat-bottomed boats (*kotchi*), they entered the Arctic seas and explored the northern coast, although little was made of the discoveries there until the eighteenth century, when the Great Northern Expedition was launched. During the course of several shipping seasons exploratory parties, under constant threat from ice and scurvy, mapped the northern coastline, and the charts produced remained in use for two centuries.

Interest in the area was inspired partly by the desire to discover whether a north-east passage to the Orient existed. Discovery of the passage is credited to another Cossack, S.I. Dezhnev (*c.*1605–72/3), who supposedly set sail in 1648 from the Kolyma river in his *kotch*, rounded the easternmost cape of Asia (now Cape Dezhnev) and endured shipwreck to arrive, after a long overland trek, on the river Anadyr which flows into the Pacific. Expeditions in the centuries following confirmed the existence of the passage and made further discoveries in the north-west Pacific. V.I. Bering (1681–1741), a Dane serving in the Imperial Navy, and A.I. Chirikov (1703–48) between 1725 and 1743 sailed

from Okhotsk through the Bering Strait to the eastern cape and later discovered Alaska and the Aleutian Islands. In 1820–24 F.P. Vrangel' (1796–1870), travelling by dog-sledge over the frozen sea, charted the coast west of the cape and discovered the island which now bears his name.

Exploration was not confined to the cold lands of Siberia: from the seventeenth century Russians explored as far afield as Mongolia, China, India, Africa and Brazil; they also carried out detailed investigations of Middle Asia and the Caspian Sea basin. In the first half of the nineteenth century Russian ships for the first time circumnavigated the globe, while 1819–21 saw the voyage of F.F. Bellingshausen (1779–1852) and M.P. Lazarev (1788–1851) to the Antarctic ice barrier and the discovery of Peter I and Alexander Land.

In Siberia and the other places they visited, Russians gave to Europe often the first detailed knowledge of places hitherto poorly represented on maps. For the seventeenth and eighteenth centuries the most celebrated traveller-scientists include F.I. Soymonov (1682–1780), V.V. Atlasov (*c.* 1662–1711) and S.P. Krasheninnikov (1711–55) and for the nineteenth and twentieth centuries, V.A. Obruchev (1863–1956), P.P. Semenov-Tyan-Shansky (1827–1914) and P.K. Kozlov (1863–1935).

Soon after the 1917 Revolution the frontier of exploration shifted to the Arctic Ocean and here the new Soviet government pioneered the use of aircraft in polar research. The first Russian flight in the Arctic was made in 1914 but it was not repeated until the 1920s. Since that time aircraft have increasingly been used in the Arctic and in the early days some spectacular flights were made, such as the transpolar flight to America in 1937 of V.P. Chkalov (1904–38). In 1941 I.I. Cherevichny (1909–71) made a return flight to the northern 'pole of inaccessibility', stopping *en route* at a number of points on the ice for scientific observations. The expedition lasted 68 days and covered 15,000 miles, and firmly established the principle of using aircraft for reconnaissance work and to service surface expeditions.

Drifting ice stations have also been used in polar exploration – the first in 1937 when a team led by I.D. Papanin (1894–1986) was set down on a North Pole ice-floe to observe sea-ice drift. They remained on the ice for nine months before being taken off, having drifted to the Greenland coast. This drift was followed by others in the post-war years and, together with air exploration, they helped to establish Soviet research workers as undisputed experts on the central Arctic region.   JP

GEOGRAPHY

The Middle Volga from an atlas of the Imperial Academy of Sciences (St Petersburg, 1745) 'in conformity with the rules of geography and with the latest observations'

Geography in pre-revolutionary Russia had a long, varied and distinguished history, still inadequately recognized in the rest of the world. Moreover its progress and emphases were unusually responsive to the distinctive developments and needs of the country and its people. Notable geographical work

in Russia dates from the time of Peter the Great, whose interest in map-making, geographical expeditions, and the discovery and appraisal of natural resources resulted in the first national atlas, edited by I.K. Kirilov (d.1737). All in all, the achievements of geography probably outshone those of other sciences during his modernizing reign. A large number of original studies were published in the eighteenth and nineteenth centuries, combining in a distinctively Russian way exploration and scientific analysis with a reforming zeal for the betterment of the life of the peasant and, to this end, searching for the most appropriate regional systems. P.P. Semenov-Tyan-Shansky, for instance, who directed the Russian Geographical Society for several of its most vigorous decades, was a member of the Committee for the Emancipation of the Peasants from the Bonds of Serfdom at the same time as he was organizing his expeditions to the Tyan'-Shan' mountains, and also assembling his comprehensive statistical survey of the Russian Empire.

The Imperial Russian Geographical Society, founded in 1845, was generally recognized as the most successful of the many learned societies before the Revolution, in tune with contemporary national aspirations, crises, needs and ways of thought. Regional branches with their own publications and lectures, were set up in Siberia and Caucasia, as well as in Russia proper, and the Society assumed initial responsibility for geology, meteorology, anthropology and archaeology.

Russian geography, in its Golden Age from about 1880 to the First World War, compares well with that of any other country of the period. Its major figures, notably A.I. Voeykov (1842–1916), V.V. Dokuchaev (1846–1903) and D.N. Anuchin (1843–1923), as well as Semenov-Tyan-Shansky, were both scientists and humanists. Dokuchaev's theory of soil formation and natural zonation and Voeykov's theory of heat and moisture balance clearly derived from their experience with the dominant natural zones, such as the 'black-earth' steppe and the podzol *taiga* (coniferous forest) and eventually had a considerable influence on world science. Voeykov's monumental *Climates of the World* (1884) established his reputation as a world pioneer of climatology. He taught at St Petersburg University, but the major figure in university geography as such was Anuchin, who taught it (with anthropology) at Moscow University from 1884 until his death in 1923. During this period Prince Peter Kropotkin (1842–1921), who had early made his mark as a geographer in Russia, and kept up this scientific interest throughout his life, was in exile in Britain. Other famous Russian scientists, such as the chemist D.I. Mendeleev, the geochemist V.I. Vernadsky and the plant geneticist N.I. Vavilov, were also active contributors to geography and to the Geographical Society.

Thus there was a vigorous body of geographical scholarship and tradition in Russia by the time of the Bolshevik Revolution, combining natural scientific and humanist approaches, and focusing on human environmental and regional studies. While this tradition carried over into the 1920s, it was – as were most aspects of life and thought in Russia – severely disrupted in the Stalinist period (1928–53). Geography's humane and international cast was submerged by the formation and mobilization of large bodies of specialists who were directed towards practical tasks. Since much of the urgent work was of a primary nature and human-oriented studies tended to be politically vulnerable, geography had changed overwhelmingly into a physical science by the mid-1950s; it had also become heavily fragmented, since official doctrine discouraged those integrated studies of man and his environment that had been central to the subject before 1930. However, in spite of the difficulties, elements of the broken heritage were kept alive, notably through the 'landscape school' of L.S. Berg (1876–1950) and the 'regional school' of N.N. Baransky (1881–1963).

The post-Stalin decade under Khrushchev was characterized by a ferment of vigorous disputation about the nature and direction of geographical studies, in which the most prominent and successful advocate of a more integrated and humanized geography was V.A. Anuchin (1913–84), whose catalytic book, *Theoretical Problems of Geography*, appeared in 1960.

As a result of this 'revolution', more human-oriented work was done in geography between the mid-1960s and mid-1980s (later dubbed 'the period of stagnation'), but the discipline remained under the control of the Party as before. Dramatic changes had to wait until 1988, following glasnost, new leadership and the fall-out from Chernobyl'. Two examples of these must suffice here: it was finally admitted that Soviet maps had been deliberately distorted for fifty years and a new series was promised; and political geography, which had been practically forbidden since 1930, suddenly emerged as the most dynamic new branch of the subject, focusing on the real communities of the country, and their relation to ethnic, ecological, economic, and international questions. The tragedy is that the collapse of the Soviet Union, which has freed the brightest minds to work on these vital topics (which are in the spirit of the pre-revolutionary traditions), has also seen the dwindling of resources needed to support them in Russia, and even more in the successor states of the former Soviet Union.   DH

Right. Laying out the drill for a depth of 12 km in the geological exploration of the Kola Peninsula

GEOLOGY

Mineral exploration

There may be as many as 250,000 earth scientists and technicians currently working in the former USSR, where the geologist was lauded as a pioneer in the struggle to develop an enormous Motherland. The role of geology here has been unequivocal – to search for and discover new mineral wealth. Primary geological exploration and mapping, particularly east of the Urals, has also always been a principal preoccupation. Pre-revolutionary Russian geology had a strong mining tradition dominated by the famous Mining Institute in St Petersburg, founded in 1773; coal and metal mining were concentrated largely in European Russia, although the construction of the Trans-Siberian Railway in the 1890s gave considerable impetus to the investigation of Siberia's natural resources. The gigantic prospecting operations conducted in Central Asia, Siberia and the Far East since the Revolution have resulted in a greatly increased level of economic mining activity: for coal, iron and precious metals from southern West Siberia, the Kuznetsk basin and the Altay; for copper and nickel from Noril'sk, inside the Arctic circle; for tin and gold from the Far East.

The Baku oilfields were first developed in the late eighteenth century, and are still productive although reserves are low. The search for new petroleum deposits involves a high degree of geological input,

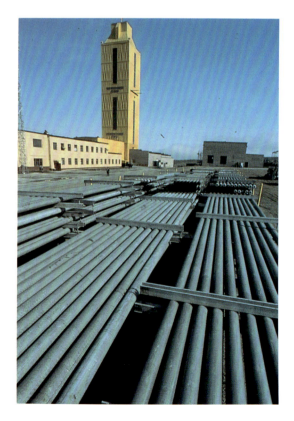

and the discovery by I.M. Gubkin (1871–1939) of major reserves in the Volga-Urals petroleum zone (the 'second Baku') is regarded as a major achievement of Soviet petroleum geology. This was followed by massive discoveries in the West Siberian basin (the 'third Baku') during the 1960s and by the current development of the Peri-Caspian basin; several other major sedimentary basins in Siberia and the Far East are being explored. Appropriate technology still lags behind the West but active steps have been taken to improve the situation, partly through co-operation with western companies. It is widely recognized in the western oil industry that the former Soviet Union not only has gigantic undeveloped or under-developed fields such as Tengiz on the Caspian, but also represents one of the last real exploration frontiers. A wide variety of oil companies and consortia have signed agreements with various governments and administrative bodies in the region, but the rapid changes in political and commercial circumstances have made some of these contracts uncertain at best, and relatively little real investment has so far taken place. What is certain, however, is that given political stability and satisfactory commercial arrangements a major new phase of oil exploration and development will begin in which western companies will be heavily involved.

Mapping

The history of systematic geological mapping in Russia began in 1881 with the establishment of the Geological Committee which undertook to map Russia on a scale of 1:420,000 (the *desyativerstka* maps – ten versts to an inch). This ambitious project was never achieved, although about 10 per cent of maps and a number of more detailed surveys of mining districts had appeared by the end of the century, and a small-scale map (1:2,500,000) of European Russia was produced before the 1897 International Geological Congress in St Petersburg.

A.P. Karpinsky (1847–1936), widely regarded as the father of Soviet geology, headed the Geological Committee from 1885 to 1903, before going on to help establish, and for many years lead, the post-revolutionary Academy of Sciences. The Committee survived the Revolution virtually intact, and was expanded considerably in the 1920s when particular emphasis was placed on mapping east of the Urals. Priority was naturally given to regions of known economic potential (such as the Kuznetsk and Tungus coal basins, the Kolyma gold-fields) but extensive reconnaissance surveys using air, boat, horse or even reindeer transport were made and by the 1937 International Geological Congress in Moscow it was possible to produce the first geological map of the entire Soviet Union, albeit on a small scale (1:5,000,000). Much of the detail of regional

geological surveying, particularly that accomplished since the 1940s, is contained in the series *Geologiya SSSR*. This massive work, published in 48 parts, gives in a fairly standard format the detailed stratigraphy, igneous and metamorphic history, tectonics, geomorphology and a synthesis of geological development of each region. The volumes are accompanied by geological maps, on scales of 1:1,000,000, 1:1,500,000, or 1:2,000,000, along with correlation charts, cross sections and so on. The first volumes appeared in the 1940s, but most have been published since 1963 under the general editorship of A.V. Sidorenko (b.1917); the series occupies about 2m of library shelf. A new set of geological maps covering the USSR in 16 sheets was published in 1983, edited by D.V. Nalivkin (1889–1982).

Stratigraphy and palaeontology

A strength of Soviet geology was its ability to direct large numbers of specialists to specific tasks, such as the palaeontological description and correlation of sequences. The aim was, through exhaustive palaeontological study, to extend standard stage terminology and correlate biostratigraphic horizons throughout the USSR, often at the expense of the original lithostratigraphic terminology. The work of V.V. Menner (1905–89) was influential in this field for fifty years. A number of interdepartmental committees were set up in the 1950s to supervise this 'unification' and the main results published in another major book series, *Stratigrafiya SSSR* (14 volumes, also edited by Nalivkin).

Tectonics

A Russian school of tectonics, which emphasized vertical oscillations during geological time, had developed during the nineteenth and early twentieth centuries, and is particularly associated with the work of Karpinsky. Working primarily on the Russian platform, Karpinsky and his followers recognized a close dependence of palaeogeography on oscillatory vertical movements controlled by fundamental tectonic structures ('Karpinsky lines').

The first tectonic maps covering the whole country were compiled under N.S. Shatsky (1895–1960) during the 1950s. An atlas of 'lithologo-palaeogeographic' and palaeotectonic maps was published during 1967–69, edited by A.P. Vinogradov (1895–1975). This massive work is in four volumes with over 70 stage-by-stage palaeogeographic and 20 palaeotectonic maps at 1:7,500,000 scale as well as 50 larger-scale regional maps. A new series of palaeotectonic compilation maps, with even more detail (1:5,000,000) and accompanying text, began publication in 1977, edited by T.N. Spizharsky. These works were a major achievement in the Karpinsky tradition and represent an enormous task in compilation and cartography; nothing quite like them existed outside the USSR. While following this tradition, Soviet tectonic geologists remained aloof from developments in the West, from Alfred Wegener's first proposal of continental drift in the late 1920s to the 'plate tectonic' scientific revolution of the late 1960s. These global theories emphasizing large-scale horizontal movements were anathema to leading scientists such as V.V. Beloussov (b.1907), but recently some Soviet geologists, such as L.P. Zonenshayn began to examine evidence for, and application of, this 'new global tectonics'. The re-evaluation of the geology of this vast country will accelerate with increased western contact, such as the current co-operation with western oil companies, bringing many new interpretations of geological history.   NJRW

ECOLOGY

Nature reserves in the former Soviet Union

While elements of ecological thinking can be traced back to such eighteenth-century pioneers of Russian science as P.S. Pallas (1741–1811) and I.I. Lepekhin (1740–1802), it was the work of Charles Darwin which provided the major impetus to ecological science in Russia and the Soviet Union. N.A. Severtsov

(1827–85), for example, theorized about the interrelationships between fauna and their natural environment, and applied concepts of natural selection and environmental variability to explain changes through time and space. V.I. Vernadsky pioneered ideas about the development of the biosphere and humanity's actual and potential role in the evolution of the earth. In the first decade of the twentieth century the zoologist G.A. Kozhevnikov (1866–1933) developed the notion of the *etalon*, which involved the idea of creating a series of *zapovedniki*, or areas of virgin nature, which would be dedicated to the study of biocenoses or ecological communities. The period witnessed the beginnings of a Russian conservation movement. Meanwhile, Russian ecology developed in close association with other sciences, such as the soil science of V.V. Dokuchaev and geography as propagated by D.N. Anuchin, A.I. Voeykov and L.S. Berg.

In the wake of the 1917 Revolution, ecology received official encouragement, with government policies to promote conservation and the establishment of a network of nature reserves by Lenin's decree of 16 September 1921. Among important work in this period can be cited that by V.N. Sukachev (1880–1967) on vegetational classification, L.G. Ramensky (1884–1953) on vegetational conti-

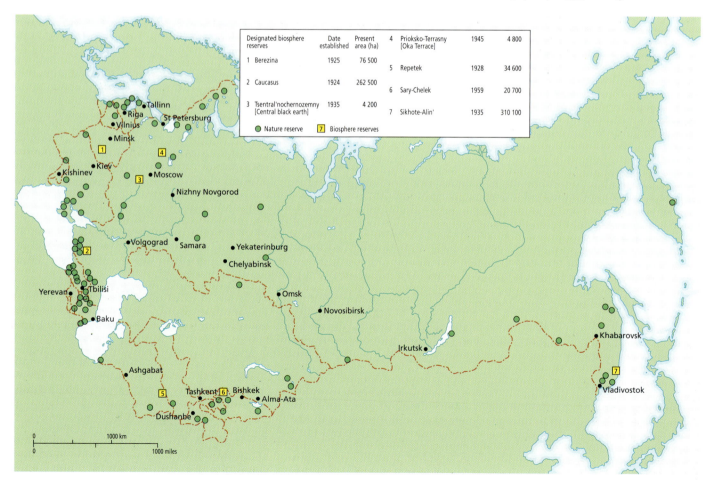

Designated biosphere reserves	Date established	Present area (ha)
1 Berezina	1925	76 500
2 Caucasus	1924	262 500
3 Tsentral'nochernozemny [Central black earth]	1935	4 200

	Date	Present area (ha)
4 Prioksko-Terrasny [Oka Terrace]	1945	4 800
5 Repetek	1928	34 600
6 Sary-Chelek	1959	20 700
7 Sikhote-Alin'	1935	310 100

● Nature reserve   [7] Biosphere reserves

nuity and species individuality, and V.V. Stanchinsky on trophic dynamics. However, these advances were soon to be challenged by the onset of Stalin's industrialization drive. Particularly prominent in this regard was I.I. Prezent (1902–c.70), a collaborator of T.D. Lysenko, who denounced the network of inviolable nature reserves as a device for promoting counter-revolutionary resistance to key economic programmes involving far-reaching environmental change. Certain ecologists were arrested while others were dismissed following the liquidation of many of the reserves in 1951. After the Stalin period, however, ecological and conservationist thinking underwent a gradual revival and the network of nature reserves expanded once more. Yet there were still numerous debates between those ecologists favouring concepts supportive of a highly preservationist attitude towards nature and others with a more pragmatic or even exploitative approach.

No more than in other countries has it proved easy to endow ecology with a universal methodology or set of principles, or to provide it with a secure place in the academic hierarchy. This is probably the central reason why it has tended to fall prey to political pressures and why ecologists have felt the need to engage in debates with political and social connotations. Soviet ecology was influenced by the international debates between proponents of continuum and association in vegetation studies, but this was given a particular slant because of a widespread belief until the 1970s in the notion of the closed, self-regulated ecological system or biocenosis. The latter idea had conservationist implications. Related to this notion has been the tendency to define the term 'ecology' narrowly by comparison

The Repetek Biosphere Reserve, Kara Kum desert, Turkmenistan

with western definitions, and to use the term 'biogeocenology' for the field in general. This results from ecology's close associations with geography and soil science, and constituted the basis for Sukachev's claim that ecology was a separate science from biology and geography. The biogeocenose represents the most basic landscape unit of the biogeosphere, the biotic and abiotic components of which have a high degree of spatial uniformity. The concept thus allowed ecologists to claim a distinct unit of study, but it has now been rejected by many ecologists in favour of the more flexible western term, 'ecosystem'.

In spite of such difficulties and uncertainties, the post-Stalin period witnessed the gradual development of ecology with the founding of new research institutes and many new field and experimental stations undertaking work ranging from vegetation mapping to process studies and systems ecology. Interdisciplinary links have been strengthened because of the growing concern of other sciences with environmental issues and because of the increased realization of the complexity of the human impact on the environment. Ecology and other disciplines have thus fostered subdisciplines such as social and human ecology. Ecology's development has also been influenced by new theoretical concepts, changing public attitudes towards nature, and political events. Just as the science's importance was emphasized in the 1950s and 1960s by ecological catastrophes associated with steppe reafforestation and Virgin Lands schemes, so in the 1980s and 1990s the Chernobyl' accident and the many official revelations about environmental disruption have had a similar effect. While ecology as an organized science will doubtless suffer as a result of the political and economic upheavals of the early 1990s, its medium- and long-term significance for the post-Soviet republics seems assured. DJBS

SYSTEMATIC BOTANY

In mid-1964 250 years' study of scientific botany in Russia culminated in the completion of the 30-volume *Flora SSSR*, describing and systematizing 17,500 species. It was published during the years 1934 to 1964 and prepared by staff of the Komarov Botanical Institute of the Academy of Sciences, founded in 1714 as *Aptekarsky Ogorod* by Peter the Great to supply medicinal herbs to his army.

Still based in St Petersburg, the Institute is probably second only to Kew in number of herbarium specimens (six million in 1967) and has one of the world's major botanical libraries (450,000 volumes in 1966). The landmarks in its history are the landmarks in Russian botany. Three of its members are the heavyweights of Russian plant systematics in this century: B.A. Fedchenko (1872–1947); V.L. Komarov (1869–1945); and B.K. Shishkin (1886–1963). V.L. Komarov, after whom the Institute was named in 1940, was editor-in-chief of *Flora SSSR* and, although most of the work fell on Shishkin (who succeeded him as head of the Institute's Department of the Systematics and Geography of Higher Plants) and on E.G. Bobrov, he imposed his own taxonomic philosophy. He regarded morphologically homogeneous geographical races as distinct species and promoted the series (*ryad*) as a group of genetically related geographically variant species (though many of these series were no more than single polymorphic species). Application of his species concept led to much taxonomic splitting, with morphological variants often elevated to species, while subspecies and botanical varieties were rarely recognized.

To many botanists, Russian and foreign, Komarov was therefore a taxonomic splitter, in contrast to the so-called lumpers, who favour a few large species divided into many infraspecific taxa. As Shishkin put it, 'the complicated nomenclature being used in many publications in the West, according to which the species is divided into subspecies, the subspecies into varieties, . . . was not accepted'. The difference between the splitter and lumper approach may be illustrated by one of the world's major crops, wheat (*Triticum*), a recent classification of which lumps the diploids all under *T. monococcum* (as subspecies *boeoticum*, *thaoudar* and *monococcum*), the tetraploids under *T. timopheevii* (subspp. *araraticum*, *timopheevii* and *militinae*) and *T. turgidum* (subspp. *dicoccoides*, *dicoccum*, *palaeocolchicum*, *carthlicum* and *turgidum*, the last being further subdivided into convars., *turgidum*, *durum*, *turanicum* and *polonicum*) and the hexaploids under *T. aestivum* (subspp. *spelta*, *vavilovii*, *macha*, *vulgare*, *compactum* and *sphaerococcum*) and *T. zhukovskyi*. Splitters, among them many Soviet botanists, regard each of these infraspecific taxa as individual species, so that for example *T. turgidum* subsp. *turgidum* convars. *durum* and *turgidum* are widely treated as *T. durum* (macaroni wheat) and *T. turgidum* (rivet wheat).

Komarov stamped his taxonomic outlook on a generation of Soviet taxonomists. More recent Soviet botanists have admitted the excesses to which Komarov's method was carried and have advocated reassessing the rank of many species described by Soviet taxonomists; for instance A.L. Takhtadzhyan (b. 1910), who succeeded Shishkin as head of the Department of Higher Plants in 1963, favours a biological concept of species, arguing that some species consist of many geographical races and ecotypes. A partial new edition of *Flora SSSR* is contemplated.

Its English translation *Flora of the USSR* (published during the 1960s and 1970s) increases the accessibility of *Flora SSSR*, though linguistic barriers are minimal in systematic botany owing to use of the International Code of Botanical Nomenclature, by which a Latin binomial is the agreed name for every species, and Latin diagnoses are required to validate new taxa. *Flora SSSR* provides not only Latin but also Russian binomials, with a generic and specific epithet often closely reflecting the Latin, e.g *pshenitsa tverdaya* (=*Triticum durum*).

The completion of *Flora SSSR* in 1964 coincided with the first volume of the five-volume *Flora Europaea* (completed in 1979), for which one of the advisory editors was Aleksey A. Fedorov (b. 1908) of the Komarov Institute, who later initiated and edited *Flora evropeyskoy chasti SSSR*, the fifth volume of which appeared in 1981.

Another important contribution of Soviet systematic botany is *Kul'turnaya flora SSSR*, begun with a first volume on wheat in 1935 under the general editorship of one of the greatest contributors to the study of botanical populations, the plant geneticist N.I. Vavilov, and still being published irregularly (volume 11 in 1984, volume 14 in 1983, volume 18 in 1985, volume 21 in 1982) and with revisions, including a new edition of volume one which appeared in 1979. BC

FLORISTIC CONSERVATION

The international movement to stimulate the production of national *Red Data Books* dealing with the rare and threatened species of the country concerned was impressively supported in the USSR. For example, the second edition of Volume 2 of the *Red Data Book* covering all the plants of the Soviet Union, published in Moscow in 1984, is a handsome volume of 475 pages bound in red. Each species has a coloured illustration and a dot distribution map. A similar volume, slightly smaller in format, covering all the rare plants of the Russian Republic (*Krasnaya kniga RSFSR*) was published in Moscow in 1988; its coloured illustrations are even more lavish, with blocks of excellent photographs taken in the wild, 130 in all. Both these works, though in Russian with no Western language summary, can of course be used by all botanists via the Latin names which are indexed.

In addition to the *Red Data Books*, there are many other regional guides to nature reserves and protected areas, which mostly cover both plants and animals. An exceptionally beautiful book in English, with superb colour photographs and authoritative text, is that by the Lithuanian naturalist and conservationist, Algindas Knystautas, entitled *The Natural History of the USSR* and published in London in 1987. SMW

GENETICS

The science of genetics has had a unique history of official support (1917–35), condemnation (1936–64), and renewed support (1965 onwards). The condemnation of genetics has been ascribed to a supposed Marxist fondness for Lamarckism (the doctrine that acquired characteristics are inherited) because of an imagined affinity between Lamarckism and meliorism – the faith in human self-improvement that Marxists share with many other people. This widespread explanation is without basis in logic or in history: Lamarckism can just as readily subvert faith in progress on the assumption that centuries of deprivation and oppression have bred inferiority into the lower classes and the darker races. In any case, Marxists do not have a special record of unusual fondness for Lamarckism, and Soviet support for genetics was originally based on meliorist dreams. N.I. Vavilov, an eminent plant scientist who studied in England with William Bateson before the Revolution, argued that genetics would show breeders how to 'sculpt organic forms at will'. In the 1920s he won support for a great network of research institutions under VASKhNIL (the All-Union Academy of Agricultural Sciences named after Lenin) and fostered pure research in such institutions as the Institute of Genetics of the USSR Academy of Sciences. By the end of the 1920s geneticists of Marxist persuasion, such as A.S. Serebrovsky (1892–1948), won ascendancy for the belief that genetics is the realization of dialectical materialism in biology.

Collectivization precipitated the crisis of Bolshevik faith in genetics. Soviet leaders expected that their new agrarian system would facilitate rapid adoption of the most advanced techniques, such as the replacement of scraggy peasant varieties of plants and animals by high-yielding – and highly demanding – improved varieties. Such expectations were cruelly disappointed: the new agrarian system generated such massive disincentives that even the simplest old techniques declined in efficiency. Central agricultural authorities were drawn to admiration of T.D. Lysenko, an agronomist of peasant extraction who had a flair for public relations and fanatical faith in his intuition for agronomic panaceas. The first and most famous was 'vernalization', originally a word he coined for moistening and chilling seed before planting, and ultimately his catch-all term for almost any kind of seed treatment, and for an imaginary period in plant development. His claim of great practical benefits to agriculture was based on crude, brief tests of his recipes; careful statistical testing was in official disfavour as the 'bourgeois' specialists' way of subverting revolutionary enthusiasm. Scientists who criticized Lysenko's theoretical justifications of his agronomic schemes exposed themselves to accusations of separating theory from practice.

By the mid-1930s the central authorities were persuaded that Lysenko had created a distinctive Soviet science, called agrobiology or Michurinism (after the plant-breeder I.V. Michurin, 1855–1935), in advance of 'bourgeois' plant physiology and genetics. Research and teaching in genetics were sharply curtailed and subjected to waves of harsh criticism, which culminated in utter condemnation of the science at a highly publicized meeting of VASKhNIL in 1948. Within a few years, however, the disappointing practical results of Lysenko's concepts began to disturb the agricultural authorities. Starting in the last year of Stalin's life and accelerating after his death, there was a revival of the contest for official favour between genetics and Lysenkoism. In 1965, after the fall of Khrushchev, the appropriate statistical study of some Lysenkoite proposals, such as training cows to improve their heredity, destroyed his claim to practicality for good. The government gave its complete support to the restoration of research and education in genetics, but repressed efforts to examine the scandalous record of the 35 years preceding 1965.

Historical discussion of the Lysenko affair began within the USSR at the end of the 1980s as part of glasnost. No one has supported agrobiology or Michurinism, which showed once again the total dependence of that pseudo-science on tyrannical power. Indeed, expression of indignation has tended to overwhelm genuine historical discussion of long-term causes and effects.

The most remarkable accomplishment of Soviet geneticists may have been simply keeping their science alive during the bitter era which destroyed the leading position their predecessors were winning in

The Vavilov Gene Bank, St Petersburg

the 1920s and early 1930s. The great names of Soviet genetics are still those of an abortive past: S.S. Chetverikov (1880–1959), who pioneered the mathematical theory of natural selection before he was arrested; N.V. Timofeev-Resovsky (1901–81) and Theodosius Dobzhansky (1900–75), who made their major contributions to the science in Germany and in the USA; and N.K. Kol'tsov (1872–1940), who might have led the race to analyse the molecule of heredity, if his research institute had not been taken from him and ruined. The revival of genetics after 1965 has not restored the brilliance of the immediate post-revolutionary years, but that may be part of the general mediocrity that afflicted most areas of Soviet science, and intellectual life at large, during the post-Stalin decades.   DJ

SOVIET MEDICINE

As the social upheaval after the Revolution was resolved, the authorities developed a centralized health-care system, building upon and expanding pre-revolutionary medical provisions. In particular they offered comprehensive medical care to the widely dispersed war- and famine-devastated population and, most significantly, largely controlled infections such as typhus, smallpox, cholera, malaria, diphtheria, poliomyelitis, pertussis, tularemia, brucellosis and tuberculosis (Ye.N. Pavlovsky, 1884–1965; K.I. Skryabin, 1878–1972). Unfortunately, in recent years there has been a resurgence of some of these illnesses as medical facilities have deteriorated.

After many years of isolation from the West and in some instances because of political policies, there was often duplication of research occurring outside the USSR, and development of original ideas only to a relatively low technological level. However, the development of extra-corporeal circulatory systems by S.S. Brykhonenko (1891–1960) permitted the introduction of cardiac surgery by P.A. Kuprinov (1893–1963) and thoracic and oesophageal surgery by S.S. Yudin (1891–1950).

Developments in anaesthesia (A.V. Vishnevsky, 1874–1948) permitted both neurosurgery (N.N. Burdenko, 1876–1946) and plastic surgery (V.P. Filatov, 1875–1956). The latter was particularly stimulated by treatment of casualties during the Second World War. Under the auspices of the Academies of Sciences and of Medical Sciences much basic and clinical research has been undertaken in many fields including molecular biology and genetics, basic physiology, mechanisms of illness and recovery, reconstructive surgery and microsurgery, diagnosis, treatment and rehabilitation in cardiovascular disease, aetiology and the treatment of neoplasms, methods of reducing infant mortality, prophylaxis

and treatment of viral diseases, diagnosis and prophylaxis of metabolic disturbances, study of memory and treatment of neurological disorders, occupational diseases, diet, synthesis of hormones, enzymes and antibodies, and studies of ageing.

Particular mention should be made of the Institutes of Oncology (N.N. Blokin, b. 1912), Cardiology (Ye.I. Chazov, b. 1929), Neurology (V.M. Bekhterev), Gerontology (D.F. Chebotarev) and the studies in neuropsychology (A.R. Luriya, 1902–1977).

The high priority of space exploration has necessitated development of space medicine, in particular assessment of potential cosmonauts and of the effects of weightlessness (B.B. Yegorov, b. 1937). Unfortunately, the majority of the population has not in general benefited from these developments, as is shown by the rising levels of adult and infant morbidity and mortality in the last two decades.

Traditional remedies have been widely used, particularly 'adaptogens' (I.I. Berkman) to stimulate the body's natural defences. More recently manufactured substances such as Interferon have been introduced. Treatment of cardiac and renal disease with hyperbaric oxygen is widely practised. In recent years shortage of allopathic medicines has increased the usage of traditional remedies, including cupping and also increased application of alternative medical procedures such as acupuncture, hypnotism and faith healing.

Treatment of sporting injuries had high priority in the USSR, although facilities for the chronically disabled are still very limited. The concept of hospices is just being introduced. More recently, new techniques in surgical treatment of myopia (S.N. Fedorov, b.1927) and orthopaedic problems (G.A. Ilizarov) have been developed and although controversial have gained considerable worldwide recognition.

Right. Svyatoslov Fedorov, an innovative eye-surgeon with a worldwide practice

In recent years international contacts expanded and formal agreements for co-operation in research and health-care were made with the UK, USA, France, Finland and Italy in addition to Eastern European countries. The USSR actively participated in the World Health Organization and in 1978 hosted in Alma Ata an international conference on primary health care.

Ye.I. Chazov (Minister of Health, 1987–90) expressed the hope that by the year 2000 health-care in the USSR would have achieved a level comparable with that of other developed countries. However, standards greatly deteriorated with the end of the Soviet state. In all the successor countries budgets had to be severely cut for the current needs of hospitals, the provision of drugs and medical equipment fell sharply with the breakdown of domestic trade and the shortage of foreign currency (the ruble much depreciated) to pay for imports. Low-paid health-care personnel increasingly left the profession.   HML

PSYCHOLOGY AND PSYCHIATRY

In nineteenth-century Russia, as in the West, modern psychology and psychiatry emerged out of the conviction that the human mind is a process of nature and must therefore be explained scientifically, by empirical study rather than philosophical or theological speculation. In Russia the two disciplines were relatively late and weak in developing, by comparison with such centres as France and Germany, and therefore Russian specialists showed a tendency to emphasize preliminary theorizing. Those peculiarities made them especially vulnerable to the intrusion of state ideology, which was strong in the 1850s, then ebbed away, but revived with enormous force after 1917. Communist leaders insisted on a distinctive Soviet approach, which was allegedly Marxist and Pavlovian, and many people accepted that claim at face value. But realistic appraisal of the two disciplines reveals scant evidence of Pavlovian or Marxist influence in concrete psychological inquiry or in psychiatric practice, behind the façade of ideological profession.

In 1850 the tsarist government abolished psychology within universities, fearing that it subverted belief in the immortal soul, and thus was linked to the recent revolutions in the West. In 1863, after defeat in the Crimean War had shown the need to modernize Russia, the government restored a modern curriculum. P.D. Yurkevich (1827–74), who brought psychology to Moscow University, tried to keep it subordinated to Orthodox doctrine, but increasingly the discipline came under the control of those who insisted on separating the science

of the mind from religious views on the soul. They divided into rival schools, as psychologists did in the West, and the disciples of Wilhelm Wundt (1832–1920) proved to be dominant. One of them, G.I. Chelpanov (1862–1936), created a strong research centre at Moscow University and then, in 1912, Russia's first Institute of Psychology, which has remained the major centre for research.

I.M. Sechenov is often credited with starting Russian psychology on the path to Pavlovian doctrine, but his actual achievement was different, and more significant. In the 1860s he founded modern physiology in Russia, and achieved international fame for showing that stimulation of the brain could inhibit the spinal reflexes of a frog. He reasoned that thought is an interruption of reflexes and leaped to the conclusion that he had discovered the way to find the neural bases of all animal behaviour, including human thought. But further neurophysiological experimentation on central inhibition took him into a dead end. He turned to a different field of research, the absorption of gases in the blood, while continuing to speculate on the connections between neural and psychic processes. At the same time he encouraged his students, most notably N.Ye. Vvedensky and A.A. Ukhtomsky (1875–1942), to continue research on neural inhibition, which led them away from psychology, to processes of neural excitation and inhibition that are present at every level of nervous systems. Thus Sechenov established in Russia the line of rigorous neurophysiology for which Charles Sherrington (1857–1952) is celebrated. Sherrington gave him credit, but the veneration of Pavlov has obscured Sechenov's real achievement.

I.P. Pavlov was a physiologist who resisted both lines of Sechenov's work, that is, both the speculation on connections between neural and psychic processes and the rigorous study of neural inhibition. He disdained psychology and restricted himself for a long time to vivisection of dogs in pursuit of the nervous systems that regulate the organs of digestion. For that he won a Nobel Prize in 1904, when he was just beginning the studies of conditioned reflexes that would make his name a byword for a thoroughgoing reduction of mental processes to neural mechanisms. In fact Pavlov's studies of conditioning failed to establish the actual mechanisms by which the ringing of a bell or the flashing of a light causes a dog to salivate. He stubbornly brushed off critical disproof of his intuitive leap from behaviourist experiments to imagined processes in the cortex of the dog's brain, and so drew his school of neurophysiologists into a dead end. The rival school of V.M. Bekhterev, though espousing a more audacious reduction of all mental phenomena to 'reflexology', was more cautious and more rigorous

Ivan Sechenov (1829–1905), outstanding Russian neurophysiologist

Ivan Pavlov (1849–1936), physiologist and Nobel prize winner

in actual brain studies. In the United States behaviourist psychologists revered Pavlov as a founder of their school, ignoring the neural schemes that seemed to him and his Soviet colleagues the essence of his achievement.

Russian psychiatry in the pre-revolutionary decades tended to follow German models, especially the nosological approach that Emil Kraepelin (1856–1926) made famous. In this view mental disorders are diseases of the nervous system; psychiatrists must therefore establish the precise categories of mental disease in their courses of development, while simultaneously seeking neurophysiological explanations. In nosology S.S. Korsakov (1854–1900) was especially noteworthy for establishing the syndrome of neural paralysis and mental disorder that alcoholism can cause. In neurology V.M. Bekhterev became most eminent, as he did in psychiatry at large. An outspoken radical in politics, as the leaders of the pre-revolutionary medical profession tended to be, he was also a wide-ranging experimenter and theorist. His doctrine of 'reflexology' was supposed to unify all the scientific disciplines that study animal behaviour.

The Bolshevik Revolution brought enthusiasm for new departures and tyranny to push them along. In the 1920s a student of Chelpanov's, K.N. Kornilov (1879–1957), demanded a Marxist transformation of the psychoneurological sciences, and won command of the Institute that Chelpanov had founded. He and the Party's ideologists were tolerant of pluralistic division in approaches to that transformation, and took for granted the similarity of such divisions with 'bourgeois' schools of psychology. On that basis L.S. Vygotsky (1896–1934) developed a challenging project for an historico-cultural approach, which was aborted in the early thirties by the Stalinist 'revolution from above'. Psychologists, Kornilov and Vygotsky included, were obliged to condemn their previous ideas in favour of some new school that would be completely different from the 'bourgeois' schools of the West and would serve the practical needs of Soviet society, most notably in education.

Out of those obligations a distinctive Stalinist school emerged. The 'classics of Marxism-Leninism' and the latest decisions of the Central Committee were the frame of reference, even though they contained little that was relevant to the would-be science of psychology. S.L. Rubinshtein (1889–1960) emerged as the most learned discussant of psychology within that Stalinist framework – except for the early 1950s, when the 'anti-cosmopolitan' campaign ruled him out. When Pavlov became pro-Soviet in the mid-1930s, the ideological establishment added his doctrine to the canon that required genuflection and banned critical

thought. In 1950–52 highly publicized conferences chastised neurophysiologists, psychiatrists and psychologists for genuflecting to Pavlov's doctrine without using it in their research and teaching.

Stalin's death in 1953 and the period of Khrushchev's liberalization legitimized such perfunctory orthodoxy as a cover for the revival of 'bourgeois' scholarship. The school claiming Vygotsky as its mentor emerged as the most significant without, however, doing much for his grand historico-cultural project. Such leaders as A.R. Luriya (1902–77) had responded to the constraints of the Stalin era by focusing on neuropsychology, with special attention to the problems of brain damage and the development of children, areas in which they won the respect of specialists around the world. The advent of glasnost in the late 1980s made it possible to open up discussion of such previously forbidden topics as the 'Pavlov Sessions' of the early 1950s. In the ex-Soviet state psychology could at least start afresh.

In psychiatry the Revolution brought major changes gradually. Freudianism was virtually banned in the late 1920s, as an ideology of accommodation rather than revolutionary transformation. The effect of that ban, though great in Soviet culture at large, was rather small in psychiatry, where only a few specialists had shown a sympathetic interest in psychoanalysis. The use of psychiatry for exculpation of criminals was also condemned fairly early; punishment in prisons or camps, not coddling in hospitals, was called for. In the 1930s there was also a drive against loose diagnoses of schizophrenia, the disturbance that confines more patients than any other in mental hospitals, which were terribly overcrowded at the time. In the post-Stalin era the Soviet Union caught up with the West in numbers of mental hospitals and of psychiatrists, and surpassed the West in diagnoses of schizophrenia. A.V. Snezhnevsky (1904–87), who became the power in Soviet psychiatry during the 'anti-cosmopolitan' campaign of the early 1950s, built a school committed to the supremacy of the clinician's intuitive judgment, which expressed itself most notoriously in indiscriminate diagnoses of schizophrenia, sometimes for blatantly political purposes. Under perestroika there was some reform of such abuses. The

Right. Psychiatric consultation at the Serbsky Institute, Moscow, after the termination of its horrific penal functions

ten Special Psychiatric Hospitals, including the infamous Serbsky Institute in Moscow, were transferred from the patently penal Ministry of Internal Affairs to that of Health. Improvements were taking place in the successor states, but not very fast.   DJ

CHEMISTRY

The origins of chemistry in Russia and of Russian chemical and general scientific language are usually traced to the polymath M.V. Lomonosov. He recorded his chemical work in Latin and subsequently translated it into Russian. His device for rendering 'international' (Greek/Latin) scientific terms was stem-by-stem translation (hydrogen = *vodorod*). Although this natural mechanism is still productive (supersonic = *sverkhzvukovoy*), it is now at least matched in importance by the direct adoption of international terms, to which are added Russian terminations (physical chemistry = *fizicheskaya khimiya*). This shift has slightly eased scientific communication with non-Russians and easily survived Stalin's attempt to russify science. The scale of effort in chemistry in the former USSR was comparable with that in the USA. It is tempting to speculate that the readiness of the two languages Russian and English to adopt foreign words, with their extensive mechanisms for word formation, have contributed to their pre-eminence, in weight of publication at least, in a realm which lives by its novel concepts.

Russian contributions to chemistry have assumed large proportions only in this century. However, the nineteenth century saw the publication of that supreme synthesis of chemical knowledge, D.I. Mendeleev's periodic classification of the elements (1869–71) – a codifying of family resemblances and trends in the properties of scores of diverse chemical elements, which has since become a cornerstone of chemical thinking. K.K. Klaus (1796–1864) discovered ruthenium, and F.F. Beilstein (1838–1906), with others, systematized the documentation of organic chemistry. Other distinguished names of this period are G.I.Hess (1802–50), V.N. Ipat'ev (1867–1952), N.A. Menshutkin (1842–1907), P.Walden (1863–1957) and L.A. Chugaev (1873–1922). After the Revolution, Russian chemistry significantly increased its pace; its organization and development paralleled that of physics. Between the wars many research institutes were established which produced notable work in physical chemistry, inorganic chemistry, electrochemistry and radiochemistry; organic chemists such as N.D. Zelinsky (1861–1953), S.V. Lebedev (1874–1934), A.Ye. Arbuzov (1877–1968), A.N. Nesmeyanov (1899–1980) and N.A. Preobrazhensky were particularly recognized for work on hydrocarbon transformations, organo-metallic compounds, and organo-phosphorus chemistry.

Chemistry and science generally had to survive the political-philosophical intrusions of Stalin's era; one example was the proscription of the valence bond method, a valuable theoretical tool in the description of chemical bonding, reputedly because it invoked an abstract concept (that of a resonance 'end-form') deemed incompatible with socialist philosophy. Since Stalin's death a freer climate has prevailed, yet the partial isolation of Russian chemistry before 1953 has led to some interesting examples of independent and simultaneous discovery in both chemistry and physics. Chemistry research facilities both within the Academy of Sciences network and in universities have been expanded since the 1950s and useful industrial applications have been developed; significant achievements have been mainly in electrochemistry and combustion science.

COMBUSTION SCIENCE

Soviet research in the field of combustion, flame and explosion is pursued by a very large number of workers, mainly in research institutes, and particularly in those of the Academies of Sciences. The volume of fundamental work published (nearly all in Soviet journals) is substantial. Much applied work is also done; its volume can only be guessed at.

On the fundamental side, one man's influence has been continuing and is unsurpassed: that of N.N. Semenov. A physicist by training, his own earliest work was done in the A.F. Ioffe Institute in Leningrad. Since 1931 he has headed the Institute of Chemical Physics there (which moved to Moscow in 1941), and attracted and led other scientists of immense distinction and varied background, pre-eminent among them V.N. Krondrat'ev (1902–79), D.A. Frank-Kamenetsky (1910–70) and Ya.B. Zel'dovich (1914–87). With its daughter institutes at Chernogolovka near Moscow and at Novosibirsk, it remains a major focus of activity.

A less personal tradition, probably of equal significance, is the support afforded by Russian and Soviet traditions of excellence in applied mathematics, on which combustion scientists have been able to draw; the relative ease with which distinctly uncommercial books could be published may also have helped here.

Chemical pathways in combustion

The complexity of organic oxidations was recognized by A.N. Bach (1857–1946), who, at the same time (1897) as Engler, advanced the 'peroxide theory' of slow oxidation. The next distinctively Russian

Nikolay Semenov (1896–1986), whose research was fundamental to understanding the combustion process

contribution in this field was the application by Semenov of branched-chain ideas: degenerate branching or secondary initiation was proposed to interpret slow oxidation reactions. Contemporaneously, Kondrat'ev (1930) identified the species emitting light in cool flames, and soon after inaugurated Soviet mass-spectrometric studies of related reactions, a line expanded by V̇.L. Tal'rose (b.1922). General work on cool flames was begun by M.B. Neimann and others from 1932. These themes have continued, and electron-spin-resonance techniques have subsequently been applied by A. Nalbandyan (b.1918) and V.V. Voevodsky (1917–67). Many liquid-phase oxidations in biological as well as in chemical systems are now studied by N.M. Emanuel (b. 1915) and his team.

Thermal explosion and chain-branching theory

Soviet workers from Semenov onwards have made fundamental and continuing contributions in the areas of thermal explosion and branched-chain explosion (which overlap with each other) as well as with related problems of flame propagation and detonation.

The idea of chain reactions is due to Bodenstein and Nernst. The most extreme form is afforded by branching chains, in which one free radical is replaced by more than one. This idea was put forward by Semenov in 1927 to explain features of the oxidation of phosphorus vapour, long known but not understood, and soon applied by him (and by Sir Cyril Hinshelwood in England) to the hydrogen-oxygen reaction, for which work they were awarded a Nobel Prize. The next development was the idea, also due to Semenov, of degenerate branching, or secondary initiation, in hydrocarbon oxidation.

The branching-chain reactions most familiar today are those of nuclear fission, nuclear fusion and astrophysics; after pioneering contributions in chemical fields both Frank-Kamenetsky and Zel'dovich moved to these fields of physics.

Semenov perceived (1928) common ground between the problems of dielectric breakdown and those of thermal explosion; he rediscovered and made famous the geometrical representation of criticality and was the first to give an algebraic analysis. He established the small degree of self-heating necessary to cross the brink of instability and found the relationships between critical conditions and temperature.

In the 1930s O.M. Todes and P.V. Melent'ev opened up the investigation of induction periods and non-steady states and also discussed exothermic, autocatalytic reactions. In 1938–39, the conductive theory of thermal explosion was inaugurated by Frank-Kamenetsky. Forty years of study have not displaced this more general starting point, and the

Institute (especially its section at Chernogolovka) continues to house the largest group of workers in the world on these themes, to which significant contributions have been made by A.G. Merzhanov, F.I.Dubovitsky and S.I. Khudyaev.

Heterogeneous combustion and catalysis

In 1938–39 Frank-Kamenetsky put forward the unifying thermokinetic theory of ignition and extinction in exothermic heterogeneous reactions, first exemplified by the combustion of coal and later (1946) by a catalytic oxidation. In translation (1955) his book became known to western combustion scientists if not chemical engineers.

Reactor stability in open systems

In 1941 Zel'dovich and Yu.A. Zysin published their original and authoritative work on the theory of exothermic, first-order reaction in a well-stirred reactor, predicting multistability and explaining ignition and extinction. In 1948 another contribution of striking originality was made by I.E. Sal'nikov in the systematic application of stability-of-motion studies to chemical reactions. The early stationary-state work was codified by L.A. Vulis and modern experimental and theoretical reactor studies pursued at the Institute of Catalysis and Kinetics under G.K. Boreskov (b.1907).

Flame propagation

Soviet workers have made significant experimental and theoretical advances in all types of flame propagation. Pioneering descriptions in the nineteenth century were inadequate, though V.A. Mikhel'son (1860–1927) gave an early (1890) and correct description of the pre-heating zone. A proper solution of the appropriate eigenvalue problem was reached in the West in the 1930s. Subsequent Soviet work promptly gave an adequate approximate solution (Zel'dovich and Frank-Kamenetsky, 1938). It might be said that much of Soviet theoretical research is characterized by this striving for intelligible and adequate models capable of lending physical insight, whether or not solutions or more complete models are to hand.

Important contributions to combustion studies have been made by K.K. Andreev, A.A. Shidlovsky, Merzhanov and A.F. Belyaev (burning of solid mixtures; propellants, pyrotechnics and explosives), by I.M. Gel'fand (b.1913), L.D. Landau (1908–68), K.P. Stanyukhovich and Zel'dovich (theories of complex heat transfer and fluid flow), by A.Ya. Apin, Belyaev, Ya.B. Khariton, R.I. Soloukhin, K.I. Shchelkin (study of the steps from small stimulus to flame to detonation) and by Zel'dovich, Voevodsky, Kondrat'ev, Semenov, L.N. Khitrin, Nalbandyan and A.S. Sokolik (ignition in the gas phase).

Detonation

The phenomenon of stable detonation (supersonic combustion) was clearly identified in Paris in 1881. The motion was correctly associated with shock waves, and an expression for detonation velocity was derived in 1895 (Chapman, Jouguet). In Russia Mikhel'son made some early studies of detonation and shock, and the simple course of the variation of pressure with density in a steady detonation is known in the former USSR as the Mikhel'son line. In the 1930s and 1940s significant theoretical and experimental progress was reported, much of it from the Institute of Chemical Physics.

Wide-ranging studies of the build-up to, and propagation of, detonation especially in solids and liquids were made by Khariton, Belyaev, Apin, Andreev, S.D. Roginsky and V.K. Bobolev. In the early 1940s came the first solution of the structure of the steady one-dimensional detonation wave in the absence of dissipative processes. It was independently found by J. von Neumann (USA), by W. Döring (Germany) and by Zel'dovich (USSR). Further Russian work shows close correspondence in content and timing with that in the West, usually with American studies in the vanguard. Significant progress has been made in the realms of instabilities in the growth and propagation of detonation (A.N. Dremin, Soloukhin, Shchelkin) and in theoretical descriptions of important but complex configurations and effects (Zel'dovich, Stanyukhovich).

TB/PG

ELECTROCHEMISTRY

Research in electrochemistry in the USSR was probably on a larger scale than anywhere else in the world. This development from a relatively small effort at the beginning of the twentieth century was largely due to the outstanding contribution and influence of A.N. Frumkin (1895–1976). Born in Moldova, he received his early education in Odessa and began research in Strasbourg and Bern. During the First World War he carried out the work for his thesis 'On electrocapillary phenomena and electrode potentials', which was published in Odessa in 1917. This laid the basis for much of his subsequent work, which was concerned with the structure of charged interfaces and the kinetics of electrochemical reactions. He provided a clear explanation of the source of the electromotive force of a galvanic cell which was the subject of a long controversy between nineteenth-century physicists and chemists, as well as developing a clear understanding of the properties of the charged layer at the junction between two phases.

In 1922 Frumkin moved to Moscow, where he founded a department in the Karpov Institute. During the Second World War he was director of the Colloido-Electrochemical Institute (later the Institute of Physical Chemistry) of the Academy of Sciences. In 1958 he formed a new Institute of Electrochemistry and remained its director until 1976.

V.E. Kazarinov succeeded him and in the 1970s the Institute numbered several hundred people working on themes such as theoretical electrochemistry, photoelectrochemistry, bioelectrochemistry and optical techniques.

Of many other institutes working on electrochemical problems, often with senior members trained in Frumkin's laboratory, probably the most important are the Karpov Institute, Moscow, under Ya.M. Kolotyrkin (b.1910) studying fundamental problems of corrosion; the Institute of Power Sources under N.S. Lidorenko (b.1916) studying new batteries and fuel cells; the Institute of Organic Catalysis and Electrochemistry, Alma-Ata, under D.V. Sokol'sky studying the relation between electrochemical and heterogeneous catalysis; the Institute of General and Inorganic Chemistry, Kiev, under A.V. Gorodysky (previously under Yu.K. Delimarsky) studying mainly the electrochemical properties of molten salts; the Institute of Metallurgy (attached to the Sverdlovsk Polytechnic Institute) formerly under O.A. Yesin, studying the electrochemical properties of slags and other industrially-important ionic melts; and groups in Moscow State University, the Georgian Academy of Sciences in Tbilisi and Tartu State University.

The strength of electrochemistry as it developed in the USSR lies in its contributions to the fundamental problems of the subject, although there are undoubtedly many applications in technology. These contributions include the development of the concept of the potential of zero charge as a characteristic property of an electrode; detailed analysis of the structure of the interfacial layer and adsorption properties of a wide variety of electrodes in many solvents; the development of methods for the study and control of electrode reactions, notably the alternating current method and the rotating-disk electrode and the ring-disk electrode; the understanding of semiconductor electrodes; the laws of photoemission from electrodes; the development of the quantum theory of charge transfer between metal and electrolyte; and the effect of the structure of the interface on the kinetics of electrode reactions. The electrochemical nature of corrosion processes was first explained in terms of conjugated charge transfer reactions by Frumkin and many electrochemical problems in physicochemical hydrodynamics were solved by V.G. Levich.

RP

BIOCHEMISTRY

Biochemistry shared in the general development of Soviet science in the 1920s, and V.A. Engel'gardt's (1894–1984) work demonstrating that the oxidation of foodstuffs in various tissues was accompanied by the synthesis of organic phosphates appeared in 1930. In 1939 V.A. Belitser (b.1906) and E.T. Tsybakova more directly established the existence of oxidative phosphorylation – the use of the energy of respiration to synthesize adenosine triphosphate (ATP). Engel'gardt's demonstration (with his wife, M.N. Lyubimova), also in the 1930s, that myosin, a major component of muscle fibrils, was the enzyme that broke down ATP, was the first step towards the understanding of the mechanism by which chemical energy is converted into the mechanical work done by muscle. A further important advance was the discovery by A. Ye. Braunstein (1902–86) of transamination, the process by which nitrogen can be exchanged from one amino acid to another, with the result that several of the amino acids needed for protein synthesis can be made in the body and are thus not essential components of the diet of animals.

The harsher political conditions of 1930–53 and the Second World War hit biochemistry even more than many other sciences. This was because of the imposition of the views of Lysenko in place of the firmly established findings of genetics, with disastrous consequences in biological education. *Biokhimiya* (the biochemistry journal first published in 1936) became filled with much routine work on agricultural products, virtually excluding fundamental science.

The expansion of biochemistry after Stalin's death was marked by the foundation of many institutes in Moscow or its environs (Pushchino), and throughout the country (Akademgorodok near Novosibirsk). The Institute of Molecular Biology in Moscow opened in 1959, although it was called the Institute of Physico-Chemical and Radiation Biology until 1965, Lysenko's views having some official backing until 1964. Many scientists who had earlier avoided the biological label came to the subject from physical and chemical institutes. A journal of molecular biology, *Molekulyarnaya biologiya*, started publication in 1967. In the 1970s Soviet biochemical work diversified greatly, studies spreading to genetic engineering, to the arrangement of DNA (deoxyribonucleic acid) in chromosomes, to the mechanisms of photosynthesis and oxidative phosphorylation, and to the structure of ribosomes, organelles involved in protein synthesis. Enzyme mechanisms had long been studied, and x-ray crystallography joined the methods used. Well-established work on peptides, steroids, antibiotics and other natural products was recognized, after M.M. Shemyakin (1908–70) died, by the renaming of the institute he had directed (until then the Institute of the Chemistry of Natural Products) as the Shemyakin Institute of Bio-organic Chemistry, housed since the mid-1980s in new and lavish buildings.

Many institutes joined in a project (1974–78) on reverse transcriptase, an enzyme produced in animal cells by tumour-causing viruses, which had been discovered in the USA. The project included isolation of the enzyme and its direct scientific study, as well as many applications, especially (as in other parts of the world) the programming of bacteria to make plant or animal products by making DNA for incorporation into the bacterial genome from plant or animal messengers. Approaches ranged from the purely chemical (building on the great Russian tradition of organophosphorus chemistry to synthesize

Trofim Lysenko

The story of how Trofim Lysenko (1898–1976) was able to control the direction of Soviet agriculture and biology for nearly 30 years exemplifies the irrationality of the Soviet system. Lysenko was able to use his influence over party leaders and a fanatical ambition to promote his theories, although the facts would have supported those of his rivals.

He first came to prominence with his theory of 'vernalization', or seed treatment. One of the major reasons for his popularity with the Soviet leadership was the fact that his techniques promised quick results; above all, they were very cheap. Lysenko took advantage of Stalin's distrust of statistics and statisticians to convince the leadership of the potential of his ideas without producing any evidence that they would work.

In the 1930s Lysenko gradually became an important political figure as well, and in 1940 he was able to have his former mentor, the geneticist N. I. Vavilov, arrested and exiled to the GULag, where he died. Lysenko took over his post at the head of the Academy of Sciences' Institute of Genetics. In 1948 he led an attack on genetics that ended with its virtual destruction as an academic discipline in the USSR. Lysenko, an enthusiastic Stalinist, did for science what Zhdanov did for culture.

Under Khrushchev, Lysenko at first lost favour, but then gradually regained some of his former influence. However the combination of Khrushchev's removal from power in 1964, successful work on DNA in the West, and the long-overdue testing of Lysenko's methods in a scientific manner finally proved what had been long suspected – that all his techniques were useless – and he was dismissed from his official posts. His influence was none the less so strong that he was able to keep control of his research station until his death in 1976.

RNA primers needed for the start of transcription), through use of the enzyme for determining RNA sequences, to those of applied biology. Most biochemical work, however, is less centrally coordinated and planned.

G.P. Georgiev (b.1933) discovered hnRNA (heterogeneous nuclear RNA), the precursor of messenger RNA, and thus a link in the expression of genomic DNA in proteins, and he characterized the particles that contain and process it. He and his group have also studied mobile genetic elements from animals, isolating and cloning them. V.P. Skulachev (b.1935) made several advances in the understanding of the pumping of ions across mitochondrial membranes in animals and chloroplast membranes in plants. He observed the 'sodium cycle', a bacterial alternative to the proton cycle of plants and animals. A.S. Spirin (b.1931) gave the first qualitative description of macromolecular RNA, observed structural alterations in ribosomes, and discovered their powers of self-assembly in the 1960s. He discovered 'informasomes' and developed a molecular model of how ribosomes worked. He showed that extracellular protein synthesis could be achieved with structurally modified ribosomes. A.A. Krasnovsky (b.1913) discovered the reverse photochemical reduction of chlorophyll, and proposed chemical models for the evolution of photosynthesis.

The ingenuity of supporting physics and engineering was one the assets in the Soviet development of biochemistry and molecular biology, but the difficulties and delays in obtaining what western scientists regard as generally available apparatus, materials, and reagents were major handicaps. This led the All-Union Biochemical Society to put great effort into negotiating joint projects to enable Soviet scientists to obtain financial support in foreign currency. By the mid-1970s much Soviet work was being published in western journals, and although modest in comparison with that of other developed countries, it was already making a considerable contribution to world science – a great change from a generation earlier.   HBFD

PHYSICS

From modest beginnings at the time of the Revolution, physics became the leading scientific discipline in the Soviet Union and the largest in the world in terms of numbers of physicists, institutions, and publications. Centred initially in Moscow and Leningrad, physics spread to Kiev, Kharkiv and Novosibirsk, and to all union republic capitals. There were 80 physicists in Russia in 1917, perhaps 1,000 on the eve of the Second World War. By 1990

there were tens of thousands. Initially under the jurisdiction of a number of different commissariats, nearly all fundamental research institutes were embraced by the Academy of Sciences. Applied research fell under various ministries, while physics education took place in universities. This separation of training and research was in contrast to practice in the USA and Britain. Soviet physics was characterized by a strong theoretical tradition, in part owing to material backwardness.

While Soviet physicists were among world leaders in high energy, nuclear, condensed matter, and solid state physics, by many standards they failed to perform effectively. Soviet physicists and chemists won only eight Nobel prizes, primarily for work done before the Second World War, and according to scientific citation indices, western scholars do not cite their Soviet colleagues at a level which reflects the quantity of Soviet scientific journals. The system proved capable of pioneering efforts in space (Sputnik), nuclear fusion (Tokamak) and fission, elementary particle and theoretical physics, but it often proved incapable of maintaining a lead or catching up in areas where it was behind. Many of the reasons for these failings lie in the structural, ideological, and administrative impediments to successful scientific performance which were part of the Stalinist legacy.

In the 1920s the physics enterprise grew rapidly under the leadership of the research 'schools' of the experimentalists A.F. Ioffe and D.S. Rozhdestvensky (1876–1940), and the theoreticians Ya.I. Frenkel' (1894–1952), I.Ye. Tamm (1895–1971) and L.I. Mandel'shtam (1879–1944). Mandel'shtam is known for the discovery in 1928 of the combinational scattering of light simultaneously with the Indian physicist Raman (the 'Raman effect'). The absence then of a national science policy enabled physicists to find the wherewithal from several bureaucracies to fund their research. Tens of institutes and physics departments were founded, primary among them being the Leningrad Physico-Technical Institute, the State Optical Institute in Leningrad, and the Institute of Physics and Biophysics in Moscow. In the late 1920s and 1930s a series of new institutes in Sverdlovsk, Kharkiv, Dnepropetrovsk and Leningrad were created under the leadership of the Physico-Technical Institute. The Physics Institute of the Academy of Sciences and the Institute of Physical Problems were also founded in Moscow.

Rapid industrialization and the collectivization of agriculture triggered expansion of physics research; the state saw physics as fitting neatly with plans for 'socialist reconstruction', while physicists took advantage of increased support to expand research in such areas as semi-conductor and nuclear physics. At the same time, Stalinist policies were introduced for science which resulted in centralization of administration, emphasis on applied at the expense of fundamental research, the subjugation of the physicists' professional society to party organs, and the creation of 'autarky' (international isolation and censorship of information) in science. The Stalin period was also characterized by an attack on alleged 'idealism' in relativity theory and quantum mechanics, and arrests and executions of scientists accused of holding such views. During the Great Terror of the late 1930s as many as one hundred physicists were arrested, including V.A. Fok (1898–1974), specialist in quantum mechanics, and L.D. Landau, a Nobel prize-winner; both were later released, but at least ten others were executed. Again, during the post-war Zhdanovshchina, physics as a discipline fell under attack, although work on the atomic bomb project afforded some protection.

In spite of these policies, Soviet physicists were able to make significant advances. In 1934 P.A. Cherenkov (b. 1904) observed that fast electrons moving through matter emit light; Tamm and I.M. Frank (1908–91) soon provided a theory of radiation for an electron moving at a velocity exceeding the phase velocity of light in a given medium. In the physics of condensed matter (the properties of liquids and solids, best studied at low temperatures), Landau explained superfluidity of helium in 1937, a theory which had been discovered by P.L. Kapitsa, also of the Institute of Physical Problems in Moscow. Landau later offered a general theory of Fermi liquids which related to Helium III and the modern theory of electrons in metals. V.L. Ginzburg (b.1916) also made significant contributions to the theory of superconductivity and to astrophysics.

Under Khrushchev and in the de-Stalinization 'thaw', ideological encroachment abated and the physics discipline grew rapidly. Successes in nuclear physics and nuclear power were striking. During the Brezhnev years, nevertheless, an overly-centralized system dominated by several institutes and individuals remained in place, and research was waylaid by censorship, outdated equipment, poor computer facilities and political intolerance, which resulted in the exile of A.D. Sakharov and widespread anti-semitism.

The post-war years are marked none the less by accomplishments in several fields. In plasma physics Sakharov, Tamm, I.V. Kurchatov (1902–60), head of the atomic bomb project, L.A. Artsimovich (1909–73), and M.A. Leontovich (1903–81) advanced the idea of magnetic containment of thermonuclear processes in the Tokamak fusion reactor. In elementary particle and high energy physics, V.I. Veksler (1907–62) suggested the principle of synchronous or phase-stable acceleration. His work was discovered simultaneously by E.M. MacMillan in the USA in 1945. On the basis of that work, a 10 GeV proton accelerator (synchrophasotron) was constructed at Dubna in 1957, followed by a 76 GeV proton synchrotron in 1967, and the nearly complete 3,000 GeV accelerator, 'UNK', at Serpukhov. Under the direction of G.I. Budker (1918–77), physicists at the Institute of Nuclear Physics in Novosibirsk built colliding beam accelerators for electron-electron and electron-positron interactions from 1965 to 1967, about the same time as physicists at Stanford. In relativistic cosmology the work of Ya. B. Zel'dovich, D.A. Kirzhnits (b.1926) and A.D. Linde is noteworthy, as is the work of several scholars in the theory of solar neutrinos. In quantum electronics, the work of N.G. Basov (b.1922) and A.M. Prokhorov (b.1916) of the Physics Institute of the Academy of Sciences in 1954, elaborated independently by the American Charles Townes, led to the development of the maser and laser.

The Synchrophasotron accelerator, and (bottom) the Phobos spectrometer at Dubna

Under Gorbachev, and later Yel'tsin, a series of reforms was advanced to revitalize physics: decentralization of funding and administration through grants, contracts, co-operatives and foundations; the democratization of administration at the institute level of research, and the decline and fall of the Party; the acceleration of retirement of entrenched bureaucrats; efforts to speed the flow of information, travel and study abroad; and an increasing role for the newly founded Physics Society in place of the Russian Association of Physicists, founded in 1919 and disbanded by the Party in 1931.　　　PRJ

CRYSTALLOGRAPHY

Crystallography was much studied in the USSR, as elsewhere, both for the specific scientific interest in crystals and substances that crystallize (including biological macromolecules) and for the application to crystalline mineral resources, in which the country was particularly rich. Research in this field being pursued in many universities and institutes has important applications in industry and in a wide range of uses for the armed forces, from satellites to submarine detection.

Although the name crystallography suggests the mere drawing of crystals, the subject embraces their study in many ways, all based on the recognition of a crystal as a lattice-like repeating structure. An outstanding Russian contribution to theories of three-dimensional repeating patterns involving considerations of symmetry was Ye.S. Fedorov's (1853–1919) derivation (the first, 1890) of the 230 'space groups' that represent all the possible ways in which a basic structural component (atom or complex set of atoms) may repeat to form a crystal (assumed, for this purpose, to be perfect). Several methods, the most widely-practised being diffraction of x-rays by the crystal, are now available for determining the dimensions of the repeating pattern directly and the details of the basic component less directly: Soviet research played a leading role in developing the use of electron diffraction for these purposes. In Moscow the Institute of Crystallography, first director A.V. Shubnikov (1887–1970), grew from a laboratory of the Academy of Sciences; it now numbers its personnel in hundreds and is particularly well equipped. The subjects of theoretical studies there include antisymmetry, colour symmetry and imperfections; the crystal chemistry of silicates and the structures of very large biologically important molecules are among the objects of crystal structure determinations. Also investigated are the mechanical, optical, thermo-optical and electrical properties of crystals. The Institute's fundamental work on the growth of crystals has resulted in a

Boris Paton (b. 1918), Ukrainian metallurgist, an innovator in welding technology

national industry for the production of monocrystals, which are indispensable for the development of radio, quantum and semiconductor electronics and of optical and acoustic apparatus.　　　HMP

METALLURGY

The post-war developments in the field of physical metallurgy took a somewhat different course in the USSR from that in Western Europe and the USA. In the non-communist world, the seeds of the dislocation theory of the plastic properties of metals which had been sown in the immediate pre-war years began to germinate after the war and their growth dominated metallurgical thought for the next decade. The belief that many of the properties of metals and alloys were controlled by 'imperfections' in the metallic lattice may have proved a difficult ideological concept for those who believed that if 'imperfections' were removed a better society would result. Research on physical metallurgy in Russia during the period 1945–55 was hence influenced almost entirely by techniques that depended upon lattice perfection such as x-ray and electron diffraction.

By 1957 the experimental evidence in support of the role of dislocations in the plastic flow of metals had become incontrovertible with the first direct observation in the electron microscope of dislocations and their movement in thin metal foils. These observations led to a general acceptance by Soviet metallurgists of the implications of lattice imperfections and from then on the patterns of research followed closely those in other countries; electron optical methods for the study of metallurgical structures assumed a dominant role in Russia, as elsewhere.

The application of metals and alloys in gas turbines made it necessary to examine their behaviour at high temperature, and a significant Soviet development was in the field of high-temperature metallography, where special optical microscopes, linked with stage straining devices, have become widely available to research laboratories.

The formulation of new alloys is a direct consequence of the general understanding and quantification of structure-property relationships that have been the pervading theme of physical metallurgy in the USSR and the rest of the world for the past thirty years. However, alloy development is also influenced by national needs: the high cost of extracting nickel in the remote North led to much study of manganese in a wide variety of steels in which the nickel is replaced by manganese, an element abundant in the Caucasus; and the ready availability of titanium led to Soviet metallurgists becoming the leading authorities in the extraction of this metal from its ores and its subsequent alloying and fabrication. From this work a titanium alloy hull for a nuclear submarine was developed. As in the West, older heat-treated low-alloy steels are still in use.

It has always seemed that there must have been a hidden metallurgical agenda, the details of which did not appear in the Russian literature. However, with the opening up of the Soviet research institutions, the agenda is now becoming apparent and a number of licensing agreements for hitherto unknown metallurgical processes have been signed with the West. The full impact of these developments has yet to be assessed. JN

MATHEMATICS

Medieval Samarkand and Khorezm were the birthplace of major mathematical advances: the first word of the ninth-century treatise on quadratic equations, *Al-jebr wa'lmuqābala*, gave the term 'algebra', and the author's name, Al-Khorezmi, the term 'algorithm'. Ibn Sina (known in the West as Avicenna) was an original mathematician as well as compiler of all existing knowledge of medical science, while Al-Biruni (known also as Beruni) was a mathematician as well as historian. The territory that was the USSR did not lose mathematicians as the intellectual glory of Samarkand faded in the seventeenth-century, for the first of Peter the Great's scientific institutions in Russia was a School of Mathematics and Navigation founded early in the eighteenth century. The great names of Russian mathematics are of the following century, however – N.I. Lobachevsky in non-Euclidean geometry, P.L. Chebyshev in number theory and polynomial approximation of functions, and later, A.M. Lyapunov (1857–1918) in stability theory, A.A. Markov the elder in probability theory, and V.A. Steklov (1863–1926) in analysis. Many mathematics institutes bear Steklov's name.

Many of the modern centres of research in mathematics in the USSR were set up in the first few years after the October Revolution. Although research was influenced by established mathematicians such as V.V. Stepanov (1889–1950) (trigonometrical series), and N.N. Luzin (1883–1950) and M.Ya. Suslin (1894–1919) (operations on sets), the 1920s saw the inauguration and development of important trends. In topology, P.S. Aleksandrov (1896–1982) and P.S. Uryson (1898–1924) jointly or separately made significant contributions to the theory of compact and locally compact topological spaces, the homology theory of general topological spaces, and dimension theory. A.N. Tikhonov's (b. 1906) now classical result on the topological product of an arbitrary set of compact topological spaces dates from this period. L.A. Lyusternik (1899–1981) and L.G. Shnirel'man (1905–38) developed a topological apparatus that was used to estimate the number of solutions of variational problems. In probability theory, S.N. Bernshtein (1880–1968) investigated limit theorems for Markov series and sums of stochastically independent random variables, and contributed to the theory of heterogeneous Markov chains. Pre-Revolution research on the law of large numbers was completed by A.N. Kolmogorov (1903–87), who with A.Ya. Khinchin (1894–1959) generalized the law of iterated logarithm to sums of independent variables. In analysis, D.Ye. Men'shov (1892–1988) obtained results on the representation of functions by trigonometric series, and the monogeneity of functions of a complex variable. Variational-geometric methods were developed to solve extremal problems arising in hydrodynamics and later in oscillating wing theory. The contributions to the theory of quasi-conformal mappings initiated by M.A. Lavrent'ev (1900–80) and work on approximation of functions and applications to problems of plane elasticity are noteworthy. The Russian group-theoretical school was founded by O.Yu. Shmidt (1891–1956) in the late 1920s.

All these directions continued in the 1930s. Kolmogorov's work on analytical methods in probability theory laid the foundation for the theory of Markov processes; developments in stationary stochastic processes and fields progressed naturally to Kolmogorov's famous work on universal equilibrium theory in turbulent flow (1941). Urgent and complicated problems arising in aircraft construction resulted in the contributions of M.V. Keldysh (1911–80) to the theory of oscillations and self-oscillations of aircraft structures, and unstable flow; studies on the oscillation of systems with a dissipation of mechanical energy later led to work on non-self-adjoint operators in functional analysis. In the 1930s functional analysis was emerging as an independent branch of mathematics, and significant contributions were made by L.V. Kantorovich (1912–86) and M.G. Kreyn (vector lattices), and by

Ibn Sina or Avicenna (980–1037), mathematician and successor to Galen as a comprehensive medical authority

I.M. Gel'fand (Banach algebras). Important contributions to the topology of real algebraic curves and to the theory of systems of partial differential equations were initiated by I.G. Petrovsky (1901–73), and links between Markov processes and solutions to certain problems in the latter field were investigated. Methods and results in partial differential equations had important applications in the theory of elastic shells; the beginnings of a theory of generalized functions appeared in work of S.L. Sobolev (1908–89). In the 1920s and 1930s V.V. Stepanov, N.N. Bogolyubov (b. 1909) and others contributed to the substantial development of the theory of almost periodic functions created by the Danish mathematician H. Bohr. N.N. Bogolyubov stated and developed the now classical method of averages for investigating general non-conservative systems with a small parameter.

The 1930s saw a creative contribution to a new branch of group theory (the theory of soluble and nilpotent groups) by A.G. Kurosh (1907–71) and co-workers, while significant developments on topological groups were made by L.S. Pontryagin (1908–88). By 1950 numerical methods had been developed to handle a wide range of problems involving infinite systems, partial differential and integral equations; fundamental results on the approximation of functions by polynomials are due to Lavrent'ev and Keldysh.

These directions of research were developed and extended in the post-war years and the 1950s. Substantial contributions were made to the qualitative theory of systems of partial differential equations, ergodic theory and the classification of dynamical systems. The results and ideas of Petrovsky in the topology of algebraic varieties and in partial differential equations had and still have a great influence on research in these fields. Men'shov obtained fundamental results on the representation of functions by trigonometric series. In non-linear analysis Yu.A. Mitropol'sky (b.1917) investigated oscillation processes in non-linear systems, while M.A. Krasnosel'sky and others used functional methods to study problems involving non-linear integral equations. The introduction of generalized functions of any class by Gel'fand and G.Ye. Shilov (1917–75) stimulated investigations into the behaviour of solutions of general systems of partial differential equations. The mathematical theory of viscous incompressible flow was developed by O.A. Ladyzhenskaya (b.1922). In computational mathematics algorithms were devised to improve the effectiveness of difference methods for the solution of multidimensional non-stationary problems in gas dynamics and elsewhere. The studies of Gel'fand, M.A. Naimark and others on infinite-dimensional representations of groups were applied to problems in elementary particle physics and the quantum theory of fields. A.Ya. Khinchin's work on probability theory added to the mathematical foundations of information theory begun by Shannon.

In 1957 the Siberian Section of the Academy of Sciences of the USSR was created with M.A. Lavrent'ev as its president. Section scientists contributed to the solution of problems vital to the industrial strength of Siberia, and taught at the University of Novosibirsk (founded 1959). Lavrent'ev initiated a scheme of attracting large numbers of young people to study mathematics and physics at the Institutes of Akademgorodok by carefully searching for and selecting pupils in the senior classes in schools.

The subsequent decades saw significant research in many areas: the factorization of groups and locally finite groups, topology (P.S. Novikov (b.1938) was awarded in 1970 the Fields Medal of the International Mathematical Union), global analysis, non-linear differential equations with variable coefficients, quasi-periodic systems and pseudo-differential operators. Ladyzhenskaya and others investigated general non-linear and non-stationary Navier-Stokes equations. O.A. Oleynik (b.1925) made profound contributions to the study of discontinuous solutions of non-linear partial differential equations, to systems with rapidly oscillating discontinuous coefficients in perforated domains, and in boundary layer theory. Regularization methods were developed to solve a wide class of ill-posed problems, and for operator equations and inverse problems. Advances were made in reliability theory, Markov processes and the solubility of partial differential equations with infinitely many variables, singular integral equations, in computational mathematics, and in the mathematical simulation of biophysical and other processes. Several mathematicians were honoured by the award of the Lenin Prize, and on some were conferred the prestigious Lobachevsky Prize (they include A.N. Kolmogorov in 1987). In 1977 the Academy of Sciences gave M.A. Lavrent'ev the Lomonosov Gold Medal for his distinguished work.　　　　　LL

AUTOMATION

Until the 1930s developments in automatic control theory originated from the classical methods of E.J. Routh in England, A. Hurwitz in Germany, and I.A. Vyshnegradsky (1831–95) and A.M. Lyapunov in Russia for the stability analysis of linear and non-linear (Lyapunov) systems. The importance to science, industry and agriculture of the subject was recognized by the formation in 1939 of the Institute of Automation and Remote Control in

Moscow. The late 1930s and the 1940s saw significant developments in several directions: the introduction of frequency methods; the extension of the Nyquist stability criteria for linear feedback systems to closed loop systems, distributed parameter systems, and those with a lag; the structural stability of control systems; the automation of multivariate systems and its application to the control of power systems. The work of L. V. Kantorovich (1912–86) on mathematical methods for the organization and planning of production (1939) (which merited a Nobel Prize for Economics in 1975) was the starting point for the subsequent construction of a theory of optimal macroeconomic planning. The stimulus provided by A. A. Andronov (1901–52) (with his collaborators) and the leading schools in non-linear oscillation theory led to the development of a theory of non-linear systems with piecewise linear components, and its application to servo-mechanism design. The harmonic balance method of N.M. Krylov (1879–1955) and N.N. Bogolyubov led to the development of methods for analysing self-oscillations in certain non-linear systems; these methods and others resulted in a comprehensive transient analysis of non-linear systems.

The mathematical theory of optimal control began to develop in the early 1950s; a significant contribution to it was due to L.S. Pontryagin and co-workers who developed a maximum principle permitting the solution of a very extensive class of problems with an arbitrary performance index and equality and inequality constraints. The principle has been proved for linear pulse systems, extended to distributed parameter systems, and formulated in an abstract framework to investigate extremum problems in linear topological spaces.

Investigations in stochastic optimal control theory based on the work of A.N. Kolmogorov in the USSR and of N. Wiener in the USA resulted in the creation of broad methods of synthesizing linear and non-linear optimal control systems with any statistical performance index. In 1953 the ideas of Wiener and other western cyberneticists had been denounced in the principal Soviet philosophical journal as a pseudo-science serving capitalist interests. Recognition of the industrial significance of cybernetics, and increasing pressure from Soviet scientists themselves (including Kolmogorov, who withdrew his earlier opposition) soon reversed this view. In 1958 an Academy of Sciences Scientific Council on Cybernetics under A.I. Berg (1893–1979) pioneered development, a periodical was founded, and in 1963 an Institute of Cybernetics was set up in Kiev under V.M. Glushkov (b. 1923). Subsequent research found widespread applications in the economy.

In the early 1970s N.N. Krasovsky (b.1924) and co-workers produced methods of estimating from given observations the state of a controlled system that is subject to random perturbations. Many practical problems in the control of processes in the most diverse branches of science and engineering (chemical technology, diffusion processes, acoustics, thermal physics, geofiltration) led to the emergence and development by A.G. Butkovsky and others (in the late 1970s and the 1980s) of a theory of optimal mobile control of distributed systems, and its application in many areas. Ya.Z. Tsypkin's (b. 1919) work on the foundations of the theory of learning systems is now seen as an important forerunner of new developments in artificial intelligence and the application of artificial neural networks.   LL

TECHNOLOGY

Technology appears to be one of the decisive areas where a socialist system has not succeeded in matching the achievements of a market economy and a political democracy. It was not the case that the Communist Party of the Soviet Union did not recognize its importance. On the contrary, the Party attached great importance to the technology of production processes as a factor in economic growth. The Party fostered research with the aim of accelerating technical progress, but not to the exclusion of a certain continuity of production processes, as exemplified in the emphasis laid on a basic production of iron and steel, and on preservation – unchanged as far as possible – of the specifications of final products. Especially in the first post-revolutionary years the popular presentation of technological policy was in terms of electrification and mechanization, but electrification was a real and continuous influence in the Soviet development strategy as well as being a slogan: Lenin, when defining communism as equalling 'Soviet power plus the electrification of the whole country', envisaged this as a universal force for modernizing and transforming economy and society. In 1931, during Stalin's First Five-year Plan, mechanization was formulated as an objective wherever manual work was laborious (this spirit did not, of course, infuse the widespread construction carried out by forced labour which simultaneously began to be used). In many directions mechanization has since become extensive, although frequently – as in coal-mining, agriculture, or factory handling of materials – markedly uneven; for instance, agricultural field work was mechanized much more than livestock rearing. Automation jumped into official favour even where economically hardly justified, yet nationwide it is not particularly advanced. Until the 1960s (as regards industrial design) refined aspects of person–machine relationships – as affected, for

Right. *Assembly line at the Belarus Tractor Factory, Minsk*

example, by differences in skill or in the organization of the workplace, or other ergonomic influences – received slighter attention.

The bias in favour of scientific progress may have distracted attention away from solving problems in production technology, but has probably favoured military-scientific purposes; in the late 1950s twice as much was spent on pure science as on technology whereas in the USA more was spent on technology than pure science. Both military and institutional considerations have apparently had the result of promoting a special emphasis on welding, research into which is headed by the Paton Institute of the Ukrainian Academy of Sciences. For instance, welding is the key to joining materials intended for extremely stressful conditions, such as are encountered by a deep-diving submarine hull. A second bias was the denial until 1956 of obsolescence as possible under socialism; machinery once installed had to be run until physically worn out. Correspondingly, and because also (up to 1965) equipment was not resold to enterprises, the practice became engrained of ordering only the latest and best equipment, normally that embodying the largest scientific contribution. Far from being always economically justified, this practice left no scope for introducing 'intermediate' (low capital-intensive) technology. Among negative effects of the technological profile of Soviet industrialization may be mentioned substantial environmental problems, polluting water

Irrigation works on the Chu River, Kyrgyzstan

more than air. The ecological results of dam- and canal-building have been far from satisfactory, having resulted in disastrous pollution and ecological interference in, for example, the Aral Sea.

Much heed was paid to standardization, especially as expressed in state standards. Characteristic of the Soviet space programme, and conferring significant advantages in the production and deployment of defence supplies, standardization was also widely diffused in Soviet consumer goods. Unfortunately this militated against variety and choice. Large-scale processes were favoured, which seemed to match both the economy's needs for large-volume output and the abundance of most natural resources. Where the technique had originally been imported, the creation of larger versions ('scaling-up') was common. Miniaturization correspondingly tended to be backward. The problem of discovering appropriate criteria of plan-fulfilment reacted upon design: reckoning machinery by weight not surprisingly led to the production of unduly heavy machines. While the main emphasis in Soviet development was on quantity, much more attention was paid in the 1970s to bettering quality; for instance, to improving operational reliability (where absolutely necessary there may be recourse to duplication of equipment), or to achieving production without defects. However, this brought no breakthrough and the average quality of Soviet-made goods remained low.

Imported technology

Russian pre-revolutionary economic development was founded overwhelmingly on imported technologies and this remained almost equally true of Soviet economic development, despite the creation of a greatly diversified capability for scientific and technical research with a more than hundredfold multiplication over 60 years in the number of people qualified in these spheres. Among the exceptions before the Revolution was oil refining, where the technology applied in Russia (though partly based on foreign inventions) was relatively advanced, having outgrown an earlier hindrance imposed by the Excise. The creation of new techniques in Soviet laboratories, followed by their industrial application, was of comparatively minor importance, exemplified in the manufacture of synthetic rubber. By contrast, imported technology or 'know-how' has been identified in all major sectors. Foreign prototypes also have been imported and reverse-engineered (often, naturally, with their faults as well as their virtues) and then assimilated into production cycles. Where equipment has been imported, the indigenous contribution has sometimes been restricted to providing a building and its appurtenances. Certain adaptations to conform with local conditions or national

standards have little more than modified this overall picture.

Technologies, somewhat more than designs, often seem to have been selected; thus, such items as caterpillar tractors or cameras were in the 1960s produced in quantities surpassing (relative to other needs) domestic requirements. In a number of cases, however – including those just mentioned – choices appear to have been influenced by the feasibility of employing either the manufacturing technique or the final product for military as well as civilian purposes. Whereas in the earliest stages of Soviet industrialization equipment was imported primarily for the extractive and basic materials branches, there was later a shift towards imports embodying very advanced technology with a high scientific content. Soviet reliance upon such imports from western countries increased markedly between 1966 and 1979, but was checked at the beginning of 1980 by the US embargo as a response to the Soviet invasion of Afghanistan. Obversely, the years 1961–65 represented a peak in the number of new types of equipment – machinery, apparatus and instruments – created first in the USSR.

Technological imports had a most important economic effect, although (because of organizational or other circumstances) it may not necessarily be possible to raise the productivity of imported equipment to that achieved in its country of origin. The impact of western technology in the Soviet economy was nevertheless estimated for the 1970s at three to four times that of the same volume of investment in technology of home origin. Soviet exports of machinery also increased, but those to western countries in the late 1970s were below 10 per cent of imports from those countries.

Eastern Europe, especially the GDR and Czechoslovakia, was also an important technological supplier: about three-quarters of total Soviet equipment imports came from other communist countries. The import of technology other than that embodied in equipment was achieved through licensing and industrial co-operation agreements, particularly with Eastern Europe, through intergovernmental arrangements. The All-Union Institute of Scientific and Technical Information (VINITI), perused and translated extracts from some 30,000 publications received from over one hundred countries; industrial espionage too played a part. The 'technological gap' between the USSR and the most advanced countries was nevertheless not being narrowed, even when reliance on importing highly advanced technologies was at its peak in the 1970s.

Technological level

The extremely wide range of technology in the former USSR needs to be borne in mind when its

Right. Workstations in the Commercial Bank for Innovations, Moscow

level is assessed. On the whole, while the level was below that of other advanced countries, the gap tended to be smaller in industry than in other sectors, and also within a given branch was highly variable between factories. Defence industries were probably on average more efficient than the civilian sector, although not to the extent that was suggested by western evaluations in the 1960s. Heavy industry tends to be more efficient than light industry, and production of capital goods than of consumers' goods. Service branches, ancillary branches such as factory handling, and also trade and distribution are especially backward.

The USSR was fairly advanced – and indeed in some subdivisions may have been considered advanced – in applications of materials science, such as metallurgy (notably chemical inhibition of corrosion), ceramics, chemical composites and fibres, and welding (a long tradition, culminating in the application of lasers). Also advanced were many branches of engineering, notably machine tools (although metal-cutting, as distinct from forging and pressing, was over-emphasized, and numerically-controlled technology lags behind by some years); electronics (including microchips), energy transmission systems for electricity at very high voltage and for coal as slurry (although compressors for gas-pipelines had to be bought in the West).

Techniques in building, building materials (glass-making technology has been imported) and the extractive industries are in the main on a somewhat lower level; the USSR adopted prefabrication in construction on a large scale from 1957 onwards (in sharp contrast to the traditional means still used in individual house-building) and produced very large items of machinery for open-cast mining, construction and civil engineering, a group of sectors which as a result had a low priority in imports. The chemi-

cal industry, especially 'small chemistry' (as distinct from large-volume output used in industrial processes, such as the production of sulphuric acid) and synthetic fibres, heavily depended on foreign purchases of high technology. The same may be said of the motor vehicle industry, which was backward in almost all respects (excluding some go-anywhere vehicles). Here the immense FIAT plant at Togliatti has effected a change. Textiles and clothing, timber, pulp and paper, and the food industries (except processing on-board ship) are also behind, having benefited relatively little from imported technology since 1932.

Computers were slow to develop. Hardware evolved faster than software, where systems were adopted and copied from the USA; as a consequence of the 'Ryad' programme in Comecon, software was improved, though problems remain in diffusion, in maintenance and in the range and distribution of peripherals. The lag behind the USA in the development of information technology is estimated to be almost ten years.

Civil engineering has been responsible for immense hydroelectric constructions, such as the damming of the Volga and Angara rivers and canal-building (the present century being the country's great canal age). Railway construction too, facilitated by the generally flat terrain, has continued on a fairly substantial scale. On the other hand, road-building has been backward and has not yet provided an adequate network of highways. The programme of military construction (of missile silos, for example) has been very large, but technical details are not published.

The Soviet fishing fleet is modern; the relatively unspecialized composition of the mercantile marine permits more flexible utilization, including military use. The aircraft industry is advanced in producing large helicopters, and has developed aircraft with variable geometry and vertical take-off; on the other hand the air conditioning system of Aeroflot has a poor reputation. Much Soviet military equipment appears fairly advanced, yet is easy to maintain and service. Tanks are given good nuclear-biological-

Control room, Bratsk Hydroelectric Station

The IL-96-300 Aerobus
(11,000 km range,
300 passengers) under
construction in Voronezh,
1990

chemical (NBC) protection and now in addition reactive armour; the AK-47 assault rifle is the guerrillas' favourite; the latest generation of warships has shown remarkable originality, especially in the development of long-range ship-to-ship missiles. Recently, however, the Gulf War (1991) suggested that the effectiveness of much Soviet military equipment had been overestimated – even if allowance is made in this case for the inferior quality of Iraqi troops and their mistaken tactics. Gradual improvement, rather than dramatic innovation, is characteristic of most Soviet military designs, which as a rule are probably more novel than the technologies employed in arms manufacture.

Finally, the extent to which the USSR seemed latterly to have become accident-prone must be mentioned. Although Chernobyl' was by far the most devastating example, there have been numbers of other serious accidents. The phenomenon has perhaps not grown as much as reporting might suggest – previously accidents were ordinarily not reported – but a rising trend does appear to be present. It provides clear evidence of poor construction, design, maintenance, or avoidable human error.   RH

ASTRONOMY AND ASTROPHYSICS

Astronomers in the USSR have made many notable contributions to the science. Historically the dominant person is Ulug Beg (1394–1449), an eminent Uzbek astronomer, who at the age of fifteen became governor of Samarkand and towards the end of his life ruler of an immense territory in Western Turkestan. Here he gained an international reputation, compiling a catalogue of 1,018 stars, mainly based on observations made at his observatory. Archaeological investigations have shown that the main instrument was a sextant of 40m radius made of polished marble set in a rock-hewn trench on the meridian. This would have been used for measuring the altitude of the Sun; trigonometrical tables correct to the ninth decimal place were computed at the observatory to allow important astronomical constants to be determined to high accuracy. Ulug Beg's results first became available to Europeans in 1643, when John Greaves (1602–53), Professor of Astronomy at Oxford University, compiled astronomical tables based on Beg's observations. When these were first published in Europe, catalogues requiring extended observation and exacting reductions were rare. They had considerable practical value because methods of determining terrestrial longitudes, a pressing problem for navigation, depended on precise star positions.

The nineteenth century saw the establishment by Nicholas I in 1839 of a major observatory at Pulkovo, which remains one of the centres of Russian astronomy, having both optical and radio telescopes. The famous Struve dynasty practised astronomy there for almost a century. V. Ya. Struve (1793–1864), of German birth, was appointed director of the Dorpat observatory; in 1824 he perfected the first clock-driven telescope and commenced classic work on double stars, which he continued after his move to Pulkovo in 1839. His son Otto (1819–1905) followed his father and became director in 1861; in turn, Otto's sons Karl (1854–1920) and Gustav (1858–1920) became directors of the Berlin (1904) and Kharkiv (1894) observatories respectively. Gustav's son Otto (1897–1963), born at Kharkiv, fought with the White Army in the Revolution and eventually reached the USA in 1921, where he was director successively of the Yerkes, McDonald, and National Radio Astronomy Observatories. Four of the Struves (Karl excepted) received the Gold Medal of the Royal Astronomical Society.

Between the mid-twentieth century and 1980 Soviet astronomers steadily built up their observational facilities to include several instruments of world class. The 6m reflector (1976) at Mt Simirodriki in the Caucasus was the world's largest optical telescope for fifteen years. At the same site is a

Ulug Beg's fifteenth century sextant, Samarkand

major radio telescope (1978) some 600m in diameter. The Crimean observatory possesses a 2.64m reflector and in Armenia the Byurakan observatory has a 2.6m instrument. Radio astronomy is vigorously pursued at the Crimea and Pulkovo observatories. The 6m Bolshoy Telescope at the Special Astrophysical Observatory (Crimea) was the first large telescope in the world to employ the altazimuth design, which seemed revolutionary at the time, but is now standard practice for large telescopes worldwide.

The greatest achievements in this century have unquestionably been made by theoretical astronomers, and western scientists have gone to considerable lengths to visit them in Moscow and invite them to international symposia. The Copernicus Astronomical Institute (1978) in Warsaw was the major meeting point throughout the 1980s, and was specifically funded by the USA to improve the exchange of ideas.

I.S. Shklovsky (b.1916) has made numerous contributions to the theory of radiation; he gave the first correct account (1952) of the production of radio waves in objects such as radio galaxies and the remnants of exploded stars. In particular he predicted from his theory that the visible light from such an object would be polarized; this was confirmed in 1953 by V.M. Dombrovsky, working at Byarakan. After a brilliant start the Moscow school has continued a distinguished tradition, V.L. Ginzburg (b.1916) and S.P. Syrovatsky having written the standard works on the subject. Another important area has been cosmology and gravitation, particularly the development of knowledge of the early universe, to which Ya.B. Zel'dovich and the Moscow school have made significant contributions concerning the behaviour of elementary particles in the first

second in the life of the universe. I.I. Novikov made outstanding contributions to our understanding of black holes, and their role in astrophysics and cosmology.

In space astronomy the main achievement apart from selenology is the landing of Venera 9 and 10 on the surface of Venus (October 1975). These craft functioned at high temperature (485°C) and pressure (90 atmospheres) for about one hour, long enough to transmit the first photographs ever obtained on the surface of another planet.   SM

SELENOLOGY AND SELENOGRAPHY

Soviet astronomy covers all branches of the subject, but although lunar research was no exception, it is fair to say that before space-flight became feasible studies of the Moon were confined to a relatively few enthusiasts. Many theoretical papers were, however, published in the immediate post-war period, notably by N.P. Barabashov and A.V. Markov, who put forward theories of the nature of the Moon's surface which proved very close to the truth.

In the USA most authorities consider the major formations on the Moon's surface of impact origin. Opinion in the USSR (and in much of Europe) was more divided, and it was felt that both internal and external processes played major roles in the moulding of the surface. An important contribution was made on 3 November 1958 by N.A. Kozyrev, using the large refractor at the Crimean Astrophysical Observatory: he recorded a red event in the crater Alphonsus, and obtained spectrographic confirmation. Though his interpretations have been questioned, there seems little doubt that an event did occur, proving that the Moon is not completely inert. Other 'transient phenomena' have been recorded both before and since, but Kozyrev's observation is probably the most significant of its kind.

The main Soviet contribution to lunar study has been in the field of space research. The first successful lunar probes were launched in 1959: Luna 1 (January) passed within 5,955 km of the Moon, Luna 2 (September) made an uncontrolled landing, and Luna 3 (October) made a circumlunar trip, sending back the first photographs of the Moon's far side – never visible from Earth because (allowing for some oscillation) 41 per cent of the total surface is permanently averted. From the Luna 3 results the Soviet authorities were able to publish the first maps of the far side, and named some of the features, notably the Mare Moscoviense (a dark plain) and the important, dark-floored crater Tsiolkovsky. These designations have been officially adopted, though some errors were also made; the so-called 'Soviet Mountains' proved to be non-existent.

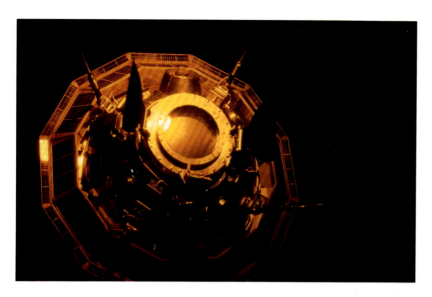

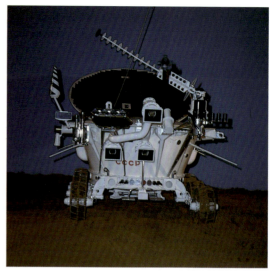

Above. *Lunokhod 3*
Above right. *Lunokhod 1*
Right. *Luna 3's historic photograph of the far side of the Moon*

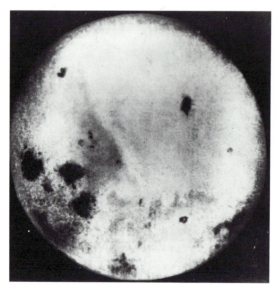

The next few Luna probes were not successful, and meanwhile the US Orbiter programme (succeeding the Ranger series of crash-landing vehicles) enabled American astronomers to compile much improved maps of the lunar surface. However, an important advance was made on 31 January 1966 with the automatic Soviet probe Luna 9, which made a controlled landing in the grey plain named the Oceanus Procellarum, conclusively disproving the theory that the lunar maria were covered with deep layers of soft dust.

Many years later it was revealed that the Soviet authorities had intended to make a manned lunar landing during the 1960s. However, a series of failures with their powerful launchers, together with the premature death of their chief designer, S.P. Korolev (1906–66), caused the project to be abandoned, and subsequent lunar research was carried out with unmanned vehicles. Of these, three (Lunas 16, 20 and 24) have been returned to Earth, carrying samples of Moon material, and two set down mobile vehicles, termed Lunokhods. The first Lunokhod was carried to the Moon in Luna 17 (November 1970), and operated for eleven months; the area photographed exceeded 80,000 sq m involving 200 panoramic pictures and 20,000 photographs; a distance of over 10 km was travelled before its power failed. It also made soil analyses and transmitted back the results.

Lunokhod 2, carried in Luna 21 (January 1973), had a shorter active life of four months, but was able to travel a distance of 37 km: whereas Lunokhod 1 had descended in the Mare Imbrium, well away from the site of any Apollo landing, Lunokhod 2 operated in the Le Monnier area, only 180 km from the landing-point of the US astronauts Eugene Cernan and Harrison Schmitt in the previous December.

Results from the Soviet probes were in good accord with those of the manned and unmanned American vehicles. The samples obtained from the automatic Soviet recovery vehicles were of great value because they involved entirely new areas of the Moon, despite the fact that the amount of material brought back was relatively small. There was a pleasingly free exchange of Soviet and American lunar samples, and so far as lunar research is concerned there continues to be full co-operation between the various national teams.

The Soviet Union also launched lunar satellites; for instance, Luna 19 (28 September 1971) remained in contact for over 4,000 lunar orbits. Among the features studied were the enigmatical mascons (a convenient acronym for *mass concentrations* below some of the maria and large walled plains) which had been discovered in 1968 by the American astronomers, P. Muller and W.L. Sjögren, from studies of the movements of Orbiter 5. Here again the Soviet and American results were in good accord.

Sergey Korolev

Sergey Korolev (right) with Yury Gagarin, the world's first cosmonaut, 1961

The father of the Soviet space programme, and the creator of many of the USSR's most famous rockets, Sergey Korolev was for many years known to the Soviet public as 'The Designer'. This sobriquet was not a mark of his prowess, however; a prison record meant that his name could not be mentioned in the press.

Korolev was born in 1906 in Zhitomir in Ukraine. After graduating in 1930, Korolev began work as an aircraft designer but was soon inspired by a colleague, K. E. Tsiolkovsky (1857–1935),

to switch his attention to rocketry. His research was, however, rudely interrupted in 1938 when he was arrested by the NKVD, accused of selling blueprints of aircraft designs to the Germans. He was imprisoned until 1944, and during this time he both suffered solitary confinement and lived in the design camps with other imprisoned specialists in the field, such as Andrey Tupolev (1888–1972).

After his release, Korolev was allowed to join a team of Soviet scientists visiting the V-2 rocket bases in occupied Germany. His first designs for long-range missiles were based on the V-2, but he soon began to develop his own ideas, and in 1957 the first Soviet intercontinental ballistic missile was successfully flown. In October of the same year Sputnik 1 was launched.

Korolev was also in charge of the development work for Yuri Gagarin's historic manned flight in 1961, as well as for the first lunar and interplanetary flights. Unfortunately, he died in January 1966, just three weeks before the first successful landing of a Soviet space capsule on the Moon.

Korolev was rehabilitated to a certain extent after Stalin's death in 1953, and he even joined the CPSU. However, despite several official prizes and honours, he was never identified to the Soviet public as the leader of the space programme in his lifetime. Notoriously difficult to work with, he was to a large degree responsible for the flying start in the space race enjoyed by the USSR.

The Discoverers of Space monument, Baikonur cosmodrome, Kazakhstan

Up to 1993 there have been no lunar probes since August 1976, when Luna 24 landed in the grey plain of the Mare Crisium, drilled down to a depth of 2m, collected samples, and landed back on Earth on 22 August. Regardless of how many missions may be launched in the future, in the meantime many theoretical papers continue to appear in Russian astronomical journals.   PM

SPACE RESEARCH

Sputnik

On 4 October 1957 the Soviet Union astonished the world by launching the first artificial satellite from a secret base in Central Asia. Called Sputnik 1, it was little more than a radio transmitter encased in an aluminium sphere from which long 'whip' aerials extended, but the regular 'bleep-bleep' of its transmitter picked up all around the world signalled the dawn of a new age. That it was the USSR which had

achieved this breakthrough from a less advanced technological base than the USA was the major shock, and its political and military impact was deeply felt in the western world.

Two men were primarily responsible for this 'golden day' in Soviet history: the brilliant spacecraft designers S.P. Korolev, who headed the rocket teams, and V.P. Glushko (1906–89), who designed the engines. Both had played pioneer roles in Soviet rocketry before the Second World War.

Their crowning achievement would not have been possible, however, without the political support given from the time of Stalin to the development, in the military programme, of an intercontinental ballistic missile (ICBM) bigger than anything conceived in the West. The plan to use this rocket to launch satellites is said to have sprung from a recommendation by Korolev himself. The ICBM was to become the mainstay of the Soviet space programme, which for some time continued to outpace that of the USA.

Right. Cosmonauts Gagarin, Nikolaev and Tereshkova with party leader Khrushchev, 1963

Sputnik 2 carried a dog, Laika, into orbit and Sputnik 3 took the form of a 1,327 kg geophysical observatory. Modifications to the basic launch vehicle, including the addition of another rocket stage, soon produced even·more spectacular results. Selenological research proceeded with unmanned Luna space probes, which in 1959 passed, hit and circumnavigated the Moon; Luna 3 sent back the first pictures of the Moon's far side by television. The Soviet leadership under Khrushchev was quick to realize the political importance of space achievement for enlarging Soviet prestige and influence, and continually pushed the rocket teams to greater effort. Before the USA could launch the first Americans into space, Yu.A. Gagarin (1934–68) was making his single orbit of the earth in a Vostok spacecraft. His epic flight on 12 April 1961 lasted 108 minutes and was the final act that set America on course for the Moon in Project Apollo, soon announced by President J.F. Kennedy to a joint session of Congress (25 May 1961).

The Soviet teams maintained their pace: the cosmonauts who followed Gagarin included the first woman in space, Valentina Tereshkova (b.1937), who circled the earth 48 times in Vostok 6, in a journey lasting 70 hours 50 minutes. On 18 March 1965 A.A. Leonov (b.1934), clad in a pressure suit and wearing life-support equipment on his back, became the first man to walk in space from the orbiting Voskhod 2. To make this possible, Korolev modified a Vostok by fitting an extensible airlock. The first successful landing of an instrument capsule, Luna 9, on the Moon followed on 3 February 1966: pictures were transmitted from the Ocean of Storms, west of the craters Reiner and Marius.

In the meantime, the first Soviet space probes had been sent to Venus and Mars in a determined effort to roll back new frontiers. Instruments landed on Venus in the early 1970s endured atmospheric pressures 90–100 times greater than on earth and temperatures exceeding 470°C; and yet in 1975, despite these hostile conditions, the first television pictures were obtained directly from the surface. However, success with Mars was to be denied in 1971 when an instrument capsule made a heavy landing in a dust storm between the regions of Electris and Phaethontis. The television transmitter stopped after only 20 seconds.

A bold attempt to investigate Phobos, the inner moon of Mars, at close quarters – even to land instruments – failed in 1988–89 when the space probes Phobos 1 and Phobos 2 suffered communications problems. The latter, however, having swung into orbit round Mars, did return data of a more general kind before contact was lost during final approach manoeuvres to the tiny moon.

Kosmos

An ambitious new project, Kosmos, began in 1962 initially at Kapustin Yar (east of Volgograd) but later at the original Sputnik base of Tyuratam-Baykonur (in the Karaganda region of Kazakhstan) and at Plesetsk (south of Arkhangel'sk). The first objective was to extend investigation of the earth's atmosphere and cloud cover, ionosphere, magnetic field, radiation belts and the influence of solar radiation and cosmic rays upon the general environment. Satellites for this purpose were generally of a standardized construction using common components; the scientific investigation was later expanded to include experiments from other countries within the Interkosmos programme. A second range of Kosmos activity included the testing of satellites which later emerged as fully-fledged operational systems, of which early examples were the Meteor weather and Molniya communications satellites. Projected manned space systems were also tested under the Kosmos label. The third category concerned the testing of military space systems. A large family of reconnaissance and surveillance satellites also operated within the Kosmos programme.

The Molniya communications satellite, part of the Kosmos rocket programme, on the launch-pad at Plesetsk

Soyuz, Salyut and Mir

Further success in developing manned spacecraft after Vostok and Voskhod was not achieved without mishap. After experiencing difficulty with the control of Soyuz 1, cosmonaut V.V. Komarov (1927–67) was killed when the parachute lines of his capsule became entangled as he tried to land. The tragedy delayed the Soyuz programme for a year and a half, but eventually cosmonauts were able to fly extended missions in earth orbit drawing electrical power from solar 'wings' which opened out in space. It was also possible to use craft of this type to obtain experience in the art of space docking, a step towards the Salyut space station.

Soyuz was later modified for ferrying cosmonauts to Salyut stations but after the Soyuz 11 incident in June 1971, when three men died in a depressurization accident while returning to earth, the spacecraft was made into a two-seater and was given extra safety equipment. The cumbersome solar wings were removed and the craft made dependent on chemical batteries which could be recharged from the solar panels on the space station after the craft had docked. Later, Soyuz designers restored a three-person crew in a spacecraft with improved solar panels and computer controls.

One of the major achievements of the Soviet space programme had been the ability to dock unmanned Progress cargo ships with Salyut which brought fuel, equipment, food, water and other supplies. If necessary they could act as 'space tugs' using their engines to push the station into a different orbit. These versatile craft, developed from Soyuz, were later filled with waste materials, separated from the station and made to burn up harmlessly over the Pacific Ocean.

Cosmonauts were thus able to use the Salyut workshop for extended periods of research. In 1978 two Russians, V.V. Kovalenok (b.1942) and A.S. Ivanchenkov (b.1940), were aloft for a record 139 days 14 hours 48 minutes, far exceeding the maximum stay of 84 days by Americans aboard the Skylab space station. In 1979 came another record-breaking flight in which two Salyut 6 cosmonauts, V.A. Lyakhov (b.1941) and V.V. Ryumin (b.1939), spent 175 days in earth-orbit – not far short of the flight time for a journey to Mars. In 1978 and 1979 cosmonauts of other communist countries (Czechoslovakia, Poland and the GDR) made week-long visits to Salyut stations in conjunction with Soviet colleagues. More joint flights followed, including cosmonauts from Hungary, Bulgaria, Vietnam, Cuba, Mongolia, Romania, France, India and Britain; and Ryumin, making another flight with a Soviet commander, set a new duration record of 184 days, 20 hours, 12 minutes.

Salyut 7, with more crew comfort, appeared in

1982, giving research opportunities to a growing family of cosmonauts, both Soviet and foreign. Work performed aboard Salyut included astronomical observations, study of the earth's natural resources, pollution monitoring and research in medicine and biology. There were also 'space-factory' experiments in which materials were melted in electric furnaces to discover how they behave under micro-gravity conditions prevailing in space. This research included the testing of new metal alloys free of the distortions caused by gravitational pull; the formation of ultra-pure semiconductor materials such as gallium arsenide, of great potential for the electronics industry; and efforts to produce glasses of high purity which could find wide application in fibre-optics and optical instruments (telescopes, cameras). Then, in 1986, came the space station Mir (Peace) with six docking ports for the attachment, in successive launchings, of lab modules: first Kvant (Quantum) 1 in March 1987, for astronomy and astrophysics; then Kvant 2 in November 1989 with new environmental and research

Right. Buran space shuttle
on the Baykonur launch-pad

equipment, an enlarged airlock and the manned
manoeuvring unit Icarus used by cosmonauts for
extra-vehicular activity. In June 1990 came Kristall,
a pilot 'space-factory' for materials processing. Still
to be added were Spektr and Priroda.

Returning from the Mir-Kvant 1 complex on 29
December 1987, Yuri Romanenko (43) established
a new duration record of 326 days in space. By
March 1990 Soviet cosmonauts had made 12 space-
walks from Mir totalling 45 hours, 16 minutes.

Zond

Soviet ambitions at the time of the United States
manned landing on the Moon were unclear, for
Zond spacecraft were being flown unmanned around
the Moon and back to earth. They resembled the
Soyuz spacecraft except that they omitted the orbital
module used for experiments in earth orbit.

In September 1968 Zond 5, carrying tortoises and
other biological specimens, looped the Moon and
returned to splash down in the Indian Ocean. Similar
spacecraft – Zond 6 (November 1968) and Zond 7
(August 1969) – made an aerodynamic 'skip' when
they encountered the earth's atmosphere which
enabled them to land back on Soviet territory. Zond
8 (October 1970), the last of the series, splashed
down in the Indian Ocean. We now know these were
trial runs for a man-around-the-Moon spectacular
intended to head off the Americans. In the event,
Apollo 8 intervened and no Soviet manned flight
occurred, although ingenious robot devices were
landed which drilled into the Moon's soil and flew
home with small samples, and roving vehicles performed soil tests.

The super-boosters

After a huge N-1 multi-stage booster bigger than
America's Saturn V moon rocket failed disastrously
on test in 1969–72, the USSR developed the heavy-
lift rocket Energiya, first launched unmanned on 15
May 1987. The second test mission on 15 November
1988 launched the Soviet space shuttle Buran (Snow-
storm) unmanned: it was recovered under automatic
control at the Tyuratam-Baykonur cosmodrome

after completing two Earth orbits in 3 hours, 25
minutes.

In 1989 the Soviets confirmed belatedly that the
'old' N-1 booster, with a payload of 95 tonnes, had
been developed to race the Americans to a Moon
landing (though Khrushchev had claimed there was
no Moon Race). Energiya was expected to launch
elements of a larger modular space station, Mir 2,
said to have a total mass of 500–600 tonnes, in the
late 1990s. According to scientists before the Soviet
collapse, it was also the key to sending cosmonauts
to the Moon and Mars.

Space policy

What seemed to be a breakthrough in bilateral collaboration reached its climax in July 1975 when an
Apollo spacecraft carrying a special docking attachment linked with a Soyuz above the earth; while
the craft were together their crews exchanged visits
and conducted simple experiments. Not only did this
symbolic meeting between East and West involve
astronauts and cosmonauts visiting each others'
countries for training but Soviet and United States'

Right. Yury Romanenko
returning from a record
duration in orbit,
December 1987. *Far right.*
The Apollo–Soyuz link-up,
July 1975

The Mir space station in orbit

common docking facilities allowing them to take part in co-operative programmes of space research. Preliminary discussions of a possible link-up between a future space station and an American space shuttle took place.

The Mir space station, with its 'plug-in' laboratory modules and a new generation of satellites for meteorology, Earth observation, communications and navigation, gave the USSR, in the era of glasnost and perestroika, the opportunity to work with a wider international community, in particular through commercial agreements. The breakthrough had begun with the exchange of scientific instruments some years before; discussions were also undertaken between Soviet and American scientists to co-operate in future projects for exploring the Moon and Mars.

The economic problems of the Soviet successor states greatly modified these ambitions; two, Kazakhstan and Russia inherited the major facilities and soon placed emphasis on outlets of more immediate commercial appeal.   KWG

research teams collaborated to render compatible the docking facilities of the two dissimilar ships. The joint mission was a complete success and it was planned that spacecraft of both countries would have

The stranded cosmonaut

One of the strangest stories arising from the collapse of the Soviet Union in 1991 was that of the cosmonaut who watched events unfold for months from the isolation of the Mir space station 500 kilometres above Earth.

Sergey Krikalev returned home to a land that was remarkably different from the one that he had left. Yet, while his story attracted a great deal of interest in the West, the Soviet space programme no longer excited the attention in its own country that it once had, and the plight of the 'last Soviet citizen' went almost unnoticed.

Krikalev was born in Leningrad in 1958, a year after the historic flight of Sputnik 1. He trained as an aviation technician, and fulfilled a lifelong dream by being accepted for the cosmonaut programme in 1985.

Before the flight that put him in the headlines, Krikalev spent five months in space in 1988–89; while there he got to know the Flight Controller, who later became his wife.

Krikalev blasted off for his second period in space in May 1991; one of his fellow-cosmonauts on the mission was the first Briton in space, Helen Sharman. He was scheduled to spend five months in orbit, but three months into the flight he and his companion were informed in a brief message from base that an anti-Gorbachev coup had taken place. They spent several days unaware of what was going on below; once the coup was defeated, their position became even more uncertain.

Because of the shortage of money for the space programme, and because of his expertise as an engineer on Mir, Krikalev was asked to stay in space 'until further notice'. He stayed on for another six months, welcoming the many paying guests from the West that the space programme was forced to accept in order to make ends meet. Eventually funds provided by Germany and the arrival of another engineer meant Krikalev was able to return to Earth after 310 days in space. In this time his country had vanished, and with it much of the space programme.

Politics

Pre-revolutionary institutions and ideas

THE AUTHORITARIAN INHERITANCE

The nature of the tsarist Russian political system was determined by the fact that it had to provide for a huge multi-national empire on the basis of meagre or underdeveloped resources. Russia was economically and institutionally the most backward of the European great powers, which meant that it had to devote a greater proportion of its resources than any other to the sheer business of defending and administering its territories.

The principal sinews of the Russian state were thus concerned with recruiting an army and police force and raising the means to pay for them. Until 1861 the key institution was serfdom, under which peasants were tied to the land and required to provide the means, either in labour, money or kind, to enable the landlord to devote himself to state service and to discharge taxes on their behalf. Until 1874 a small number of serfs were drafted into the army each year, but they served for up to twenty-five years; they were freed from personal bondage and seldom returned to the village after demobilization. In 1861 the serfs were emancipated, and thereafter paid their taxes direct to the treasury, but they remained segregated in 'village societies', where their property rights and freedom of movement were less than those enjoyed by the rest of the population.

At the apex of the system the autocrat ruled by divine right. Subjects obeyed him or her, as the Fundamental Law put it, 'for fear and for conscience'. Until 1825 the autocrat relied heavily on the landed nobles for the practical exercise of his or her rule, and Catherine II awarded them a charter in recognition of their services. No other social estate enjoyed any corporate rights. After 1825, when officers from the landed nobility rebelled against Nicholas I, the tsars relied more on the bureaucracy (where there were many landless nobles), the political police (the Third Department,

reorganized in 1880 as the Department of Police), the ordinary police and the army. The Orthodox Church was organizationally virtually a branch of the state, and, having little land of its own, relied on state subsidies: it therefore exercised very little independent influence on political or intellectual life.

The executive branch of government was headed by the tsar himself. Since there was no united Council of Ministers, or cabinet, except briefly in 1880–81 and after 1905, he had personally to coordinate the policy of the different ministries. This task imposed a great strain on him and made his qualities of leadership a matter of national importance. Access to him was crucial and was the subject of lively intrigue, described in embittered detail in their memoirs by many former officials and courtiers. The tsar was assisted from 1810 by the State Council, a gathering of senior or retired officials appointed by himself to elaborate legislative proposals which he was free to accept, amend or reject. After 1906 the State Council included elected members from the nobility, local government and other established institutions, and became the upper house of the new legislature. Otherwise, to deal with non-routine business, the tsar would set up *ad hoc* inter-departmental committees, like those which drafted the laws emancipating the serfs, or the Committee on the Trans-Siberian Railway, which was founded in 1891 to co-ordinate measures relating to that project.

From 1722 to 1917 officials in the state service all held a position on the Table of Ranks, which established parallel hierarchies for military, civilian and court service. Individuals would be promoted partly on the basis of educational qualifications, partly on merit and partly on seniority. In principle one's rank corresponded to the post which one held: at a certain rung on the ladder one became eligible for noble status. Social position thus depended on authoritative assessment of one's achievements and promise in state service, a basic feature of Russian society right up to 1917.

In the 1860s Alexander II began trying to create the institutions of civil society such as might eventually have moderated the power of autocracy. He established independent law courts and elective local government assemblies, the zemstvos. He eased censorship, opened higher education to all social classes, and expanded the secondary and primary school

A. N. Radishchev: portrait by A. Laktionov

network. He opened the army officer corps to all social estates, and made all male adults liable (at least in theory) for military service.

It was not until 1906, however, and then only under pressure of revolution, that his grandson Nicholas II set up an elected legislative assembly at the centre, the State Duma. Its rights were not negligible, but the tsar retained the right to dissolve it and to appoint the government himself, and in practice sometimes used the emergency provisions of the Fundamental Laws to pass legislation he suspected the Duma would reject. Nevertheless, the Duma performed one of the vital tasks of a parliament: it educated both the public and the government on the facts of political life, and provided a variety of views on how the problems might be tackled.

Because before 1905 the political system offered so few opportunities for participation, the first political parties were radical or revolutionary in nature. Land and Freedom (1876) aimed to propagandize the peasants and workers on the advantages of socialism and to turn Russia into a federation of village communes and workers' co-operatives. It soon spawned a terrorist wing, the People's Freedom (1879), which devoted itself to the assassination of government officials and eventually of the tsar himself. The traditions of both were resumed by the Socialist Revolutionary Party (1901). The Social Democratic Party (1898) drew its inspiration from Marx, and concentrated its efforts on fomenting a workers' revolution, though the Bolshevik wing, led by Lenin, also aimed to involve the peasants. The 1905 revolution prompted the creation of non-socialist parties, of which the most important were the Constitutional Democrats or Kadets (radical liberal) and the Union of 17 October (moderate liberal). Right-wing nationalist and monarchist parties, often anti-Semitic, gained a good deal of public attention, but did not fare well at the ballot box until the electoral law was altered to favour their constituency.   GAH

POLITICAL AND SOCIAL THOUGHT

If pre-revolutionary Russian political institutions offered variations on an authoritarian theme, political thought was by no means so circumscribed, although publication of radical ideas was seldom easy. While the influence of many of the most notable pre-revolutionary Russian political thinkers on the autocracy was negligible (other than the negative impact of provoking the authorities into acts of repression), the corpus of Russian thought embraced notable liberal and constitutionalist thinkers as well as conservative and revolutionary ones.

Russian thought, nevertheless, had a number of dominating themes and characteristics. These included the yearning for absolutes so characteristic of the Russian intelligentsia (which coalesced in the 1840s); a longing for the integrated wholeness of the individual; a sense of alienation from contemporary Russian society, perceived usually as the long-term effect of the Petrine reforms; a sense of guilt concerning the peasantry, even after the reform of 1861; and anxiety about the true nature of Russia – its history and destiny. Since the intelligentsia conducted its debates in a political context in which censorship hampered free discussion and publication, many ideas were mediated through creative literature and literary criticism.

As early as the eighteenth century there was some real diversity of view among Russian political thinkers. Several produced their own versions of enlightened absolutist doctrine, among them I.T. Pososhkov (1652–1726) and N.M. Karamzin (1766–1826). One of the clearest defences of the rights of the nobility, accompanied by the claim that their upbringing made them uniquely qualified to rule, was provided in the writings of Prince M.M. Shcherbatov (1733–90). In contrast, S.Ye. Desnitsky (c. 1740–89), the first Russian professor of law in Moscow University, advocated political reform aimed at reducing the power of the nobility in his *Proposal on the Establishment of Legislative, Judicial and Executive Powers in the Russian Empire*, submitted to Catherine II in 1768. Desnitsky, who studied in Glasgow University from 1761 to 1767, elaborated a number of ideas of his Scottish professors, Adam Smith and John Millar, in his writings between the late 1760s and late 1780s; he also translated into Russian the first volume of Blackstone's *Commentaries on the Laws of England*. A better-known eighteenth-century thinker of radical disposition was A.N. Radishchev (1749–1802), whose *Journey from Petersburg to Moscow* (1790), although published under a pseudonym, led to his imprisonment and exile. Radishchev had absorbed Western ideas of liberty and enlightenment, but although some of his views anticipated those of the nineteenth-century intelligentsia, he differed from the latter inasmuch as he served as a state official for most of his adult life.

One of the most important Russian political thinkers of the first half of the nineteenth century was P.Ya. Chaadaev (1794–1856). In some respects a romantic conservative rather than a liberal, Chaadaev was an admirer of the achievements of Christianity in Western Europe and a critic of the extremes of religious nationalism which he observed in the emerging Slavophile movement within his own country. Not only did Chaadaev find it difficult to publish his heterodox views, but the Russian

Alexander Herzen

translation in 1836 of a work he had written in French in 1829 led the authorities to declare him insane.

Alexander Herzen

The Decembrists – the group of young army officers who attempted to seize power in Russia in December 1825 – can be regarded as Russia's first revolutionaries. But the elaboration and development of revolutionary theory was to come later in the century. More evolutionary than revolutionary was the thought of the founder of Russian populism and one of the country's earliest socialists, A.I. Herzen (1812–70). Unlike many later Russian socialists and populists, Alexander Herzen rejected all deterministic theories of progress and held fast to the absolute value of liberty as an end in itself. He combined advocacy of socialism with arguments for individualism, seeing the former as providing conditions for the free development of human personality while refusing to sacrifice personal freedom on the altar of an abstract concept. In the great nineteenth-century debate between Westerners and Slavophiles, Herzen's position is not open to simple categorization. Although his receptiveness to European ideas is characteristic of the Westerner, it is combined with a distinctively Slavophile contempt for the Western bourgeoisie and admiration for the Russian peasant commune. Along with the numerous contributions to his newspaper, *The Bell*, published abroad over a ten-year period beginning in 1857 (Herzen himself having left Russia a decade earlier), Herzen's important political reflections included *From the Other Shore*, *The Russian People and Socialism* and his remarkable memoirs, *My Past and Thoughts*. Herzen's political ideas contrasted in many ways with the militant anarchism of his fellow exile, Mikhail Bakunin (1814–76).

Slavophiles and Westerners

The heated debate which took place between Slavophiles and Westerners in the 1840s was to be a recurrent theme in Russian history, one which still has a strong resonance in the Russia of the 1990s. The nineteenth-century Slavophiles stood for the supremacy of the Russian cultural tradition, of which the keystone was Orthodox Christianity. They combined belief in Russia's spiritual superiority with an emphasis on the unifying and integrating character of the national idea. Among the most important exponents of Slavophile political views were A. S. Khomyakov (1804–60), I.V. Kireevsky (1806–56), the brothers, K.S. and I.S. Aksakov (1817–60 and 1823–86) and Yu. F. Samarin (1819–76).

The Westerners, whose emphasis on Russian 'backwardness' was anathema to the Slavophiles,

Konstantin Leont'ev

tended to be atheists, materialists, internationalists and advocates of Western political as well as scientific ideas. Their thought decisively shaped the attitudes and actions of the intelligentsia in the half-century before the 1917 Revolution. Their belief in human progress was often of a simplistic character and, within the revolutionary strand of Westernism – as represented, for example, by P.N. Tkachev (1844–86) – it was frequently blinkered and fanatical. Westernism was, however, a movement of great intellectual diversity.

Apart from the notable but ambiguous role played in it by Herzen, its most formidable adherents included the literary critic, V.G. Belinsky (1811–48), the leading 'nililist', D.I. Pisarev (1841–68), the vehemently anti-Establishment N.A. Dobrolyubov (1836–61) and the radically revolutionary writer, N.G. Chernyshevsky, whose novel, *What Is to be Done?* (1863) provided the title for a much more influential political tract, written by Lenin, some forty years later.

A Westerner of utterly different outlook from Chernyshevsky was B.N. Chicherin (1828–1904). A philosopher and jurist, Chicherin was an anti-socialist who supported private property, argued against the peasant commune, advocated freedom of contract and, in contrast with the greater part of the intelligentsia, held that Russia's most imperative need was to develop the rule of law. While in favour of a strong state, Chicherin insisted that the state authorities must themselves be bound by law and that the courts must be completely independent. A gradualist in politics, he insisted that legal order must come before political freedom.

An influential writer who rejected both Westernism and Slavophilism and, for good measure, official conservatism was Konstantin Leont'ev (1831–91). Profoundly anti-liberal and anti-democratic, Leont'ev argued that the peasant needed a firm master and that the Russian people generally responded best to a strong and even ruthless leader. Holding that Russia was already being adversely affected by a decaying Europe, Leont'ev firmly believed in a distinctive 'Russian alternative'. One writer on whom Leont'ev drew for inspiration was N.Ya. Danilevsky (1822–85), the author of *Russia and Europe*, who argued against the idea of universal values and in favour of ideals which he saw as the product of distinctive Russian and Slavic experience. A Pan-Slavist, he believed in the existence of a specific 'Slavic historico-cultural type' and thus rejected the universalism of many of the Slavophiles as well as, more obviously, Westernism.

Attitudes to revolution

In the 1870s and 1880s conflict between left (liberals, populists and socialists) and right (conservative and reactionary monarchists and imperialist nationalists) hardened in the face of governmental intransigence. In the ensuing polarization of attitudes, Lenin (whose ideas are discussed in the next entry) eventually became the most expressive and influential thinker on the obdurate left. The visionary philosopher Vladimir Solov'ev, was the most important figure in a flowering of idealist thought that began in the late nineteenth century and was eventually driven out by the Bolshevik Revolution.

One of the most remarkable manifestations of the intelligentsia's heart-searchings was the symposium, *Landmarks* (*Vekhi*), published in Moscow in 1909. The contributors included the religious philosophers, N.A. Berdyaev (1874–1948) who in emigration after 1922 emerged as one of the most influential modern Russian thinkers, S. N. Bulgakov (1871–1944) and S.L. Frank (1877–1950), and the economist, P.B. Struve (1870–1944). This was an attempt by liberal intellectuals, some of them former Marxists disillusioned with deterministic theories, to make sense of the 1905 war and revolution and, more generally, of Russia's historical destiny; it had seemed to many intellectuals that the Apocalypse was at hand and that they had precipitated it. The paramount concern was to warn the country about the catastrophic prospect of revolution.

The first concerted attempt at a theoretical assessment of the events of 1917 was another collection, *From Out of the Depths* (*Iz glubiny*). The contributors included many from *Landmarks*, among them Berdyaev, Bulgakov, Frank and Struve (the last-named being the driving force). The catastrophe had happened and was interpreted as the fatal result of an uncritical Russia embracing and absolutizing Western ideas and failing to respect native institutions making for stability. The national culture had to be restored through Church and State; only then would real democracy be possible. The book was set up in type in Moscow in 1918, banned, confiscated after another attempt to print it in 1922, brought out of Russia by Berdyaev and published in the West.

The post-revolutionary cultural and political theory of Eurasianism was announced in the symposium, *Exodus to the East* (*Iskhod k Vostoku*), published in Sofia in 1921 by a group of young émigré thinkers. They included the great linguist, N.S. Trubetskoy (1890–1938); the theologian, G.V. Florovsky (1893–1979); and the historian, G.V. Vernadsky (1887–1973). The group continued its activity throughout the 1920s and was the most important manifestation of 'change of landmarks' thinking. Political theory on both left and right was held to be bankrupt and a synthesis was sought that would truly represent Russia's nature and history as a country of both East and West.

After many years of subterranean existence, the collections of 1909, 1918 and 1921, the highest expression of the intelligentsia's quest, have not only been published in Russia but have become also the subjects of intense discussion, although accompanied now by a sense of loss on the part of the intelligentsia of its earlier prestige. Westernism, 'the Russian idea' and Eurasianism – with their long intellectual histories – have re-emerged as important, and competing, ways of looking at the world in post-Soviet Russia.

AHB/GSS

The Soviet political system

MARXISM-LENINISM

As defined in official Soviet theory, Marxism-Leninism was a comprehensive and scientific system of philosophical, social and political views constituting the world outlook of the working class and the Communist Party, and thus the ruling ideology of the USSR and all socialist states. Marxism-Leninism comprised a philosophical method (dialectical materialism), a theory of historical development (historical materialism), a critique of the political economy of capitalism, and a theory of the development of socialism and communism (scientific communism). Departing from the official terminology, Marxism-Leninism could be seen as consisting of three parts: a philosophical method, a set of doctrines laying down laws of social development, and an action programme derived from the above and continually modified in the light of changing political realities.

The materialist interpretation of the world and its historical development formulated by Heinrich Karl Marx (1818–83) – a German national of Jewish extraction – constituted the basis of the philosophical and doctrinal foundations of Marxism-Leninism. According to Marx, just as man's material situation determines his social, spiritual and political life, so the forces of production condition his relationship to his work as well as the class relations within society as a whole. Together these economic and social factors and relations (the base) largely condition the legal, religious, institutional and political superstructure. Historical development is generated by technological change rendering production relations outdated and thereby undermining the whole social and political edifice that perpetuates

Marx and Engels

Karl Marx was born in Trier in the German Rhineland in 1818. His family was part of the middle-class establishment of one of the oldest settlements in Germany, his father a Jew who had converted to Protestantism.

One of the earliest influences on Marx's life was a friend of his father, the liberal nobleman Baron Ludwig von Westphalen, who encouraged the young Marx to pursue an academic career, initially in Bonn (1835–36). A move to Berlin in 1836 introduced Marx to the ideas of Hegel, and after leaving the University he went in 1843 to Paris where he began to develop Hegel's thought along his own lines. He took with him his new wife, Jenny, the daughter of Baron von Westphalen.

In the 1840s Marx began to develop his theories with the help of Friedrich Engels. In 1848 they published the *Communist Manifesto*, a forcefully-argued pamphlet that applied Marx's philosophy to human affairs as a guide to, and predictor of, action. Within weeks of the *Manifesto* appearing, the revolutions of 1848 broke out all over Europe. All were eventually suppressed and Marx became *persona non grata* in Germany because of his journalistic work in support of the revolutionaries. In 1849 he and his family fled to London, where they remained for the rest of their lives.

The first few years in exile were spent in poverty, mostly because Marx was very bad at living within his means. The situation was gradually eased by financial support from Engels, and Marx was able to carry on writing, publishing one volume of *Das Kapital* before his death in 1883.

Marx's time in London was marred by family tragedy. Both his legitimate sons died in the 1850s; his wife and beloved eldest daughter also predeceased him. However, on occasion the mischievous student in Marx was seen. A friend and biographer tells the story of the time he and Marx fled through the streets of Soho being pursued by a group of London policemen; their crime was hardly political – they had been caught smashing streetlights with cobblestones after an evening in the pubs of Oxford Street.

Friedrich Engels (1820–95), although often seen as Marx's junior partner, is of interest in his own right. While he did not have the theoretical rigour of his friend, he was regarded by contemporaries as one of the most knowledgeable writers of the time.

Engels was born in Barmen (now part of Wuppertal) in the Rhineland, an industrial town with a strong Pietist tradition. He did not attend University after leaving school, working instead in an office in Bremen, and was largely self-taught. However, in 1842 Engels visited Berlin, and quickly became known as one of the ablest members of the Young Hegelians' circle. In the same year he went to Manchester to work in his father's cotton factory, and here witnessed the full horrors of working-class poverty in northern England. His *Condition of the Working Classes in England* appeared in 1845.

Engels spent the late 1840s in Europe with Marx, organizing the fledgling Communist movement and writing articles for Marx's newspaper, the *Neue Rheinische Zeitung*. After fighting on the side of the revolutionaries in Bremen, he too went into exile in Britain.

For many years Engels helped to run the family factory in Manchester; he was well paid, and eventually was able to support Marx as well as his own household. This household was somewhat unconventional. His common-law wife for many years was Mary Burns, who had formerly been a domestic servant. When she died in 1864 (an event which caused the only recorded argument between Engels and Marx over the latter's unsympathetic reaction), her sister Lizzie took her place. Engels ultimately married Lizzie Burns a few hours before her death in 1878.

While in Manchester, Engels wrote prodigious numbers of perceptive articles on the military and the art of war. He moved to London in 1870 in order to work more closely with Marx. After the latter's death, Engels edited and published Marx's works, including the two remaining volumes of *Das Kapital* (1885, 1894), as well as many of his own works. When he died in 1895, his ashes were scattered in the sea off Beachy Head.

Below. The title page of the Russian edition of Marx's Das Kapital. *Left.* Marx, *photographed in London, 1872. Right.* Friedrich Engels, c 1872

КАПИТАЛЪ.

КРИТИКА ПОЛИТИЧЕСКОЙ ЭКОНОМІИ.

СОЧИНЕНІЕ
КАРЛА МАРКСА.

ПЕРЕВОДЪ СЪ НѢМЕЦКАГО.

ТОМЪ ПЕРВЫЙ.

КНИГА I. ПРОЦЕССЪ ПРОИЗВОДСТВА КАПИТАЛА.

С.-ПЕТЕРБУРГЪ.
ИЗДАНІЕ Н. П. ПОЛЯКОВА.
1872.

Soviet propaganda poster portraying (left to right) Lenin, Engels and Marx

distinction between the bourgeois democratic and proletarian revolutions, Lenin greatly telescoped development between these two stages, insisting that the proletariat, allied with the peasantry, could hasten the end of the bourgeois phase and ensure an uninterrupted transition to the socialist revolution.

The key to this whole process was the revolutionary party. Experience of the revolutionary movement in Russia and analysis of its lack of progress in western Europe made Lenin highly sceptical about the proletariat's inherent revolutionary consciousness – in which Marx had so much confidence. Left to themselves, workers under capitalism would develop a 'trade-union consciousness' that would restrict their demands to narrow economic bounds. Such 'spontaneous' development had to be avoided by means of a consciousness-building exercise mounted by a party of revolutionaries who alone could lead the workers to proletarian revolution. Lenin accordingly called for a small, highly-disciplined party of professional revolutionaries organized along democratic centralist lines. All this had important repercussions for Lenin's elaboration of post-revolutionary development. Whereas Marx had only once distinguished between an initial and a higher stage of communism, Lenin drew a clear line between what he called socialism and communism. Communism broadly corresponded to Marx's definition: a classless, harmonious and self-governing society. The concept of socialism transformed what Marx had envisaged as a short transitional phase, in which social, economic and political inequalities and a state machine would continue to exist, into a fully-fledged stage of post-revolutionary development. Having to contend with the prospect of considerable opposition after the Revolution, Lenin made the proletarian state – the dictatorship of the proletariat – a central feature of the post-revolutionary order. His dictatorship of the proletariat emerged as a powerful, one-party-dominated state using all available means of coercion for a considerable time and persisting *qua* state for decades rather than the years or even months envisaged by Marx. The one factor that could shorten this long-drawn-out post-revolutionary development was world revolution, the prospects for which, Lenin argued, were altered by the expansion of imperialism. Colonialism prolonged the life of capitalism in imperialist countries but it harnessed the struggle for national liberation to the revolutionary cause.

The diminishing prospects of international revolution by the mid-1920s prompted Lenin's successor Stalin to formulate the doctrine of 'socialism in one country' which declared that the Soviet Union could build socialism without external help. To justify his centralized and bureaucratic system of rule, Stalin

the power of the ruling exploitative class. The focus of Marxian analysis is on the process of change from capitalism to communism in which the conflict between the old and the emerging order is embodied in the class conflict between the bourgeoisie and the proletariat. As mounting endemic crises plague the capitalist economy and de-stabilize its political superstructure, so the proletariat grows in numbers, misery and revolutionary consciousness to become the prime force in the social revolution that ushers in the transition to communism. As the post-revolutionary system develops towards full communism, exploitation and all class antagonisms cease and their political counterpart, the state, rapidly gives way to self-administration. Marx stressed throughout his writings that no new system comes into existence without first ripening within the fully developed, and therefore conflict-ridden, framework of the preceding mode of production. Thus the proletarian revolution would not occur until capitalism had reached its highest stage of development.

As a Russian revolutionary, Lenin was concerned primarily with the prospects for revolution not in developed capitalism but in a largely agrarian economy with a small capitalist sector and proletariat and with embryonic rather than fully mature bourgeois democratic institutions. Essentially, Lenin's contribution to the ideology consists of modifications in Marxian doctrine and the addition of an action programme designed to facilitate a Marxist revolution in conditions of backwardness. Lenin invested social and economic backwardness with a new revolutionary potential by contending that the uneven development of capitalism meant that conflicts were often most exacerbated where advanced capitalism penetrated largely pre-capitalist social and political orders. Thus the 'weak links' in the capitalist chain could be the first to break. While retaining Marx's

Charlatan Soviet scientist Trofim Lysenko expounding his ideas to Nikita Khrushchev. Immediately to the right of Khrushchev is Mikhail Suslov, second from the left Anastas Mikoyan

Right. *Leonid Brezhnev at the opening of the XXV congress of the CPSU, February 1976. Immediately behind are Politburo members Fedor Kulakov (left) and Viktor Grishin (right). Behind Grishin is Cuban leader Fidel Castro*

extracted from Lenin's writings an official Leninism which emphasized their most authoritarian features and transformed many revolutionary expedients into dogmatic law. In so doing, Stalin changed Marx's and Lenin's varied revolutionary doctrine and strategy into the monolithic ruling ideology of Marxism-Leninism. This ideology centred on a militarized Communist Party which held a monopoly of political power reducing all other organizations to transmission belts for its policies and using bureaucratic and coercive methods to engineer rapid social and economic transformation. Egalitarianism was denounced and communism reduced to the attainment of high levels of economic growth and material prosperity. In 1936 Stalin declared that the Soviet Union had achieved socialism 'in the main'; the paradoxical growth of coercive state power was justified by two purportedly dialectical insights. Stalin contended that the elimination of classes involved the intensification of class struggle and that the state would die away only by becoming stronger. Furthermore, it was declared that the state would continue to exist even under communism if the Soviet Union were still confronted with hostile capitalist governments.

While the main body of Marxism-Leninism as codified under Stalin was left unchanged, these two additions were rescinded as part of the de-Stalinization process. The replacement of 'capitalist encirclement' by 'peaceful coexistence' not only shifted relations with the West from out-and-out confrontation to ideological and economic competition, but also removed the major doctrinal justification for the persistence under socialism of coercive state power. According to the 1961 Party Programme, social unity had become sufficient for the dictatorship of the proletariat to be superseded by an 'all-people's state'. The Programme was itself the high spot of a general shift under Khrushchev to a more dynamic and forward-looking ideology which emphasized the role of mass consciousness and participation in building a communist society based on material abundance, equality and self-government. A timetable was even established for this task which stipulated that the material and technical basis of communism would be created by 1970 and a communist society built 'in the main' by 1980.

Khrushchev's timetable was quietly forgotten by his more pragmatic and cautious successors. Soviet discussions in the Gorbachev era dubbed Khrushchev the last of the 'romantics', for he was perhaps the last leader to believe in the basic assumptions and historical optimism of the original revolutionary ideology. Those who followed treated ideology simply as a means of legitimating their rule and justifying their policies. Brezhnev tried to give institutional continuity and policy incrementalism the semblance of historical progress by making the concept of 'developed socialism' the centrepiece of ideological innovation. Academic departments of scientific communism justified their existence by producing sterile elaborations of the various stages of 'developed socialism' in an attempt to camouflage the conservatism of the Brezhnev era which deteriorated from the early 1970s into what Gorbachev subsequently termed 'stagnation' (*zastoy*).   AP

NEW THINKING: THE DOMESTIC CONTEXT

While the term, 'New Thinking' (or 'New Political Thinking') quickly gained currency after Mikhail Gorbachev succeeded Konstantin Chernenko as General Secretary of the Soviet Communist Party, it was soon clear that this was something much more than the latest catch-phrase. Extremely important changes of doctrine were embodied in the new corpus of ideas, some of which turned previous Soviet ideology on its head. While few, if any, of the ideas were new in a global sense, they were novel indeed in the Soviet context.

One of the first concepts to be discarded was the Brezhnevian idea that the Soviet Union had reached the stage of 'developed socialism'. Addressing the XXVII Party Congress in early 1986, Gorbachev noted that this concept had become a cloak for conservatism. The terms the new Soviet leader brought into the forefront of political discourse were *perestroika* (reconstruction), *glasnost'* (openness), *uskorenie* (acceleration) and *demokratizatsiya* (democratization).

The importance of the term, perestroika, was that it opened up wider opportunities for advocacy of change. Its very ambiguity was an advantage during the first few years of the Gorbachev era when there were many political and ideological barriers to be overcome. Virtually everyone who engaged in political discourse between 1985 and 1988 – whether the doyen of Soviet dissidents, Andrey Sakharov (following his release from exile in December 1986) or the leading conservative figure in the Politburo, Yegor Ligachev – proclaimed support for perestroika. The term, in fact, meant very different things to different people, but it was a convenient shield for a more radical political agenda than could have been explicitly set forth in 1985, a time when even the word 'reform' was still taboo. Little over a year after he became General Secretary Gorbachev went so far as to say that he would equate the word, 'perestroika', with revolution. The scope of the concept expanded over the years, although by 1990–91 a significant section of public opinion had moved beyond perestroika, inasmuch as they envisaged the confederalization or even breakup of the Soviet Union, and not 'simply' transformative change of the political system – including movement to a genuine federalism – and the marketization of the economy. Gorbachev's own view of perestroika changed over time, but even when it developed from reformist into transformative change, he still envisaged it as occurring within the boundaries of the Soviet Union, notwithstanding the fact that the country was to be given a new name (the USS, or Union of Sovereign States).

The concept of glasnost came to occupy a central place in the politics of the Gorbachev era and increasingly it reflected also an important new political reality. A greater openness was advocated by Gorbachev from as early as December 1984, several months before he succeeded Chernenko as Soviet leader. Support for glasnost, following the leadership succession, came both from above (but only from the reformist wing of the new leadership) and from below. In Gorbachev's first year it had reached but a modest level, but after a dismal retreat from even that degree of openness when the disaster at the Chernobyl' nuclear power plant occurred in late April 1986, it developed exponentially. Although a distinction was made by some Russian libertarians between glasnost (a gift from above) and freedom of speech (a right for which no higher authority was required), in fact the former evolved into something virtually indistinguishable from the latter.

An early landmark was the general release of the anti-Stalinist Georgian film, *Repentance*, in November 1986. But by 1990–91 not only Stalin but both Lenin and Gorbachev could be attacked in print and from a variety of very different political standpoints. The concept of glasnost, initially simply an important element in the new thinking, led on to a broadening of the themes and terms of political debate – into areas, indeed, scarcely foreseen by Gorbachev in 1985.

The term, *uskorenie*, was much used in the first two years of the perestroika era but then largely discarded. It was based on the misconception that a radical reform of the economic system could be combined with enhanced economic growth, whereas in reality the dislocation that would be caused by far-reaching reform was always likely to reduce, rather than increase, production in the short term. As this became increasingly clear to Gorbachev and his colleagues, *uskorenie* lost its pride of place in their vocabulary.

The concept of *demokratizatsiya* had a much longer-lasting and more profound impact. As with perestroika, different people meant different things by democratization and Gorbachev's own view of what it entailed was almost certainly broader by 1989–90 than it was in 1985–86. But it was highly significant that the concept of 'democratization' figured in the officially-endorsed 'New Thinking', for this enabled proposals for serious political reform to be advanced. Crucially, under that rubric competitive elections could be advocated, as they were by Gorbachev himself at the 19th Party Conference in 1988 (and actually introduced the following year).

A great many important new concepts found their way into the vocabulary of politics in the Soviet Union between 1985 and 1991. Advocacy of a 'market economy', which for long had been taboo, had become a commonplace by the end of the 1980s. Still more surprising was the endorsement of the concept of pluralism. Gorbachev was the first Soviet leader to use the term other than pejoratively,

although he moved from advocacy of a 'socialist pluralism' or a 'pluralism of opinion' in 1987 to acceptance in principle of 'political pluralism' (along with the legalization of new political parties) in 1990.

Other conceptual innovations that were as alien to the Soviet Communist tradition as political pluralism, but which occurred after 1985, included acceptance of the idea of a 'state based upon the rule of law' (*pravovoe gosudarstvo*), advocacy of the need to develop a 'civil society' (*grazhdanskoe obshchestvo*), and acknowledgement of the desirability of 'separation of powers' and of 'checks and balances' within the political system. In some cases these ideas (which obviously owed a great deal to Western thought and example) were first put forward by independent professionals and later adopted by Gorbachev, in other cases the initiative came from Gorbachev himself or from an important reformist ally in the leadership such as Aleksandr Nikolaevich Yakovlev. AHB

Gorbachev makes an animated intervention at the 19th Conference of the CPSU in 1988 while Andrey Gromyko (right) looks on glumly

NEW THINKING: THE INTERNATIONAL DIMENSION

The revolution in ideology, notably a sharp decline in the role traditional doctrine came to play in policy thinking, was perhaps clearest of all in the international sphere. The heterodox views which powered general ideological revision in international policy first emerged in 1985–86; by the end of 1987 they had taken coherent shape in the form of 'new political thinking'. The origins of this 'new' thinking go back to debates among Soviet international relations specialists in the 1970s which, in turn, drew on Western discussions and literature. Some of these specialists became members of the new foreign policy establishment which emerged under Gorbachev and brought innovative ideas to high office. 'New' thinking prospered in part because Gorbachev, on coming to power, sought fresh analysis to help him break out of the international impasse in which the Soviet Union found itself. A philosophy of 'new political thinking' was elaborated in part to justify and lend an acceptable and enlightened rationale to what many in Moscow considered a policy of concession to the West and withdrawal from global contest. 'New Thinking', however, also had substantive influence on the direction and conduct of foreign policy, shaping as well as reflecting the new leadership's strategy and philosophy.

From the outset, and particularly from 1986–87, the Gorbachev leadership radically reduced the content of traditional ideological elements in both its international analysis and foreign policy practice. While continuing to profess Marxist convictions, leading specialists were extremely eclectic in bringing to bear a wide range of 'bourgeois' perspectives on international affairs. They were encouraged to do so by political leaders concerned with finding effective rather than doctrinally orthodox answers to urgent policy problems. No longer obliged to adhere to traditional ideological dogmas, foreign policy specialists proceeded to assess international developments in a much more realistic fashion, expressing openly at policy level what they had long suggested obliquely in academic analyses.

More realistic perspectives soon emerged on the nature of capitalism and its relationship with socialism. Traditionally capitalist development had been depicted as nurturing the seeds of its own demise. This was supposed to come through class contradictions within capitalist states and conflicts between them. According to 'new thinking', capitalism had adjusted so successfully to internal contradictions that it appeared as a relatively resilient social order. As noted above, many features of capitalism, including pluralism and the market, once viewed as anathema, became implicitly and increasingly explicitly accepted in 'New Thinking' as valid for the Soviet Union under perestroika. Conflicts between imperialist states or 'centres' (the USA, Western Europe and Japan) were no longer seen as necessarily predominating over co-operation between them. Indeed conflict in inter-state relations as such, it was argued, was fast giving way to collaboration.

Central to 'New Thinking' was a revolutionary revision, amounting to a reversal, of the basic relationship between capitalism and socialism. While Khrushchev greatly softened the Stalinist confrontational picture of the relationship by defining it in terms of peaceful co-existence between states, he stressed class and ideological struggle. This 'winner-take-all' notion of the relationship persisted until the perestroika period. New thinking moved towards a positive view of the relationship by radically revising doctrine on the role of socialist and class interests in world affairs. By contrast with

earlier confidence in the strength and international fortunes of socialism, its prospects came to be viewed far more soberly and realistically. There was far less confidence in history determining the ineluctable expansion and world-wide triumph of socialism. The traditional struggle for the world, especially its less developed parts, implicit in the confrontational view of the relationship between imperialism and socialism, gave way to the advocacy of collaboration between the major states to ensure regional stability. And the key to stability was seen in indigenous freedom of choice, a right extended to all states, including communist (or, in Soviet terms, 'socialist') ones.

Underlying these changes was a shift in fundamental assumptions about the dynamics of international affairs. Traditional Marxist-Leninist ideology held that class interest and conflict shaped the development of politics, international as well as domestic. New thinking downgraded class analysis as an explanatory factor and class interests as the determinants of international conflict. Most importantly, Gorbachev was the first Soviet leader formally to subordinate class values to 'all-human' ones. Peace was no longer considered to be associated exclusively with the victory of socialism over capitalism. In the nuclear age peace is considered to be a pre-condition for the survival of mankind and thus not the preserve of any particular class. The new orthodoxy, which was hotly contested by leading conservatives such as Ligachev as early as 1988–89, elevated 'all-human' values and interests above those of class.

The priority of human interests over those of class gave Soviet international thinking, traditionally characterized by its Manicheism, a universalist quality. Global problems, including ecological as well as nuclear threats, made all states and systems interdependent. Concomitant components of this 'globalist' interdependence included mutual security not just in the military but also in the economic sphere. The ascendance of this interdependence philosophy, taken from Western theories of the 1970s, went hand-in-hand with a reinterpretation of peaceful coexistence in terms of collaboration rather than competition. A formal distinction was still drawn between states which must collaborate and systems which might compete as long as they did so peacefully. Yet scope for competition and contestation was greatly circumscribed by official descriptions of the relationship between socialism and capitalism. In his UN speech of December 1988 Gorbachev went as far as to speak of the need for 'co-development', a striking illustration of the remarkable distance 'New Thinking' had taken Soviet ideology on international relations away from established Marxist-Leninist tradition. AP

The Communist Party of the Soviet Union

SOCIAL COMPOSITION

The social composition of the CPSU between 1917 and 1991 is best understood as the outcome of decades of effort to ensure that communist influence should prevail in the public service and in all other posts that could affect social stability, national security or economic production. This was achieved, in part, by creating the expectation that jobs above a certain level of responsibility were conditional on CPSU membership. In consequence the CPSU became increasingly well-educated and 'white-collar' in occupation; the majority of persons on *nomenklatura* lists were party members; and the Party itself soon ceased to be a 'working-class' party, in any except a most abstract and arcane sense.

In absolute numbers in early 1990 there were 19,228,217 members and candidates in the CPSU. This represented nearly 7 per cent of the population,

Soviet propaganda poster of 1973 on how Communism unites different nationalities. The slogan at the top reads: 'Everyone who is honest, join us!'

and about 10 per cent of the eligible (adult) population. These percentages were largely achieved by the rapid expansion of the Party under Khrushchev, and they remained fairly stable after the early 1970s, suggesting that under Brezhnev the optimum party presence in (or party 'saturation' of) the eligible population was thought to have been reached. As General Secretary Gorbachev may have favoured a somewhat lower figure, and he let it be known that party membership would become less of a guarantee of privilege and job advancement than it had been. In March 1990 Gorbachev presided over the amendment of Article 6 of the Constitution and thereby over the Party's withdrawal from its guaranteed monopoly of Soviet politics. This had a major impact on the membership of the CPSU, as on its powers and functions: membership figures began to fall, for the first time since 1953; when the Party was suspended after the August 1991 coup it had already lost about a fifth of its membership.

Of the fifteen union republics only the RSFSR and Georgia had a share of the Party markedly higher than their share of the population. CPSU members had been disproportionately Russian (and these Russians disproportionately from European Russia, old Muscovy) ever since the Civil War, whilst the Georgian figure was a last relic of Stalin's term as General Secretary. In the tables the share of the Central

A Union of Nations

The collapse of the Soviet Union in 1991 revealed the weakness of the system used to govern the largest multinational state in the world.

Among the principal causes of the collapse were the flaws in Soviet federalism; both major and petty, these flaws revealed the deep insensitivity of the Soviet government to the feelings of the ethnic groups that made up their country. A good example of this unthinking chauvinism was the renaming of the Kyrgyz capital, Bishkek, after the Red Army general Frunze. This apparently innocuous move, in line with the renaming of other places in the Soviet Union, entirely ignored the fact that there is no *f* sound in Kyrgyz!

Most such slights were the result of the pro-Russian bias of the Soviet leadership. The worst offender was Stalin (although he himself was a Georgian), who in his Victory Toast in 1945 declared that the Russians were 'the outstanding nation of all the nations of the USSR'. But the same attitude ran through to Gorbachev, who in June 1985 carelessly used 'Russia' when he meant USSR, a revealing mistake for the leader of the country. As late as 1988, when the Russian Orthodox Church was allowed to celebrate its millennium, the equally old Ukrainian and Belorussian Churches remained banned.

The legacy of such insensitivity is a distrust of all things Russian among many non-Russians in the successor states. Though scarcely the responsibility of the Russians as a whole, it is significant that as recently as 1990 the national hymn of the Uzbeks began 'Greetings to the Russian people, our elder brothers'. It will not be easy for the 'younger brothers' patronized for so long to feel they are at last being regarded as equals.

Asian union republics and nationalities in the Party would look greater, and that of the Baltic, smaller if figures for the adult (not total) population had been used. The data for some of the larger union republics also conceal regional variation: around Moscow membership averaged more than 11 per cent of adults in the 1980s, whilst in the Urals and Siberia the figure was about 9 per cent. In the Donets and Dnieper provinces of eastern Ukraine about 10 per cent of adults were in the Party, compared with 7 per cent in the west of Ukraine.

The ethnic distribution of party members is also of interest. The resemblance to their distribution among the union republics is obvious, but some disparities become more vivid once the effects of Russian settlement outside the RSFSR (and of the Armenian diaspora) have been removed. Russians, Ukrainians, Belorussians and Georgians had a larger share of the Party than of the population. Natives of the Baltic union republics had low party membership, as did Germans, Poles and the nationalities of the North Caucasus deported under Stalin. Jews, by contrast, and rather surprisingly, showed very high rates of party membership: the explanation is their overwhelmingly urban residence and high levels of education.

Women were about 30 per cent of the Party in 1989; the proportion had been increasing, because recruitment of females and in female-dominated jobs was encouraged and because older party members were disproportionately male.

In the 1980s about 80 per cent of the Party was in employment. Some occupations, for example administrative grade public servants, editors, factory directors, and army officers, were staffed virtually entirely by party members. There were 1.3 million CPSU members in the armed forces and the police; records on these were kept separately, and their existence and potential as a pressure group within the Party has often been overlooked. About 10 per cent of people employed in agriculture were in the CPSU, somewhat less than 10 per cent of blue-collar

COMMUNIST PARTY MEMBERS, 1952–91

	Party membership	Population (thousands)	Party membership as percentage of population
1952	6,707,539	184,778	3.63
1956	7,173,521	197,902	3.62
1961	9,275,826	216,286	4.29
1966	12,357,308	232,243	5.32
1971	14,372,563	243,891	5.89
1976	15,638,891	255,605	6.12
1981	17,430,413	266,599	6.54
1986	19,004,378	278,784	6.82
1989	19,487,822	286,731	6.80
1990	19,228,217	288,624	6.67
1991 (Jan)	16,516,100	c. 290,500	c. 5.7
(Aug)	c. 15,000,000	c. 290,500	c. 5.1

Source: 'KPSS v tsifrakh' in Partiynaya zhizn', various issues; Naselenie SSSR 1987, p. 8.

COMMUNIST PARTY MEMBERSHIP IN THE REPUBLICS, 1989

Republic	Party membership		Population	
	thousands	%	thousands	%
Russia	c. 10,650	54.65	147,400	51.41
Ukraine	3,302	16.94	52,707	18.03
Belarus	699	3.59	10,200	3.56
Uzbekistan	662	3.40	19,905	6.94
Kazakhstan	841	4.31	16,536	5.77
Georgia	400	2.05	5,443	1.90
Azerbaijan	398	2.04	7,038	2.45
Lithuania	210	1.08	3,690	1.29
Moldova	200	1.03	4,338	1.51
Latvia	184	0.95	2,680	0.93
Kyrgyzstan	153	0.78	4,290	1.50
Tajikistan	127	0.65	5,109	1.78
Armenia	198	1.02	3,288	1.15
Turkmenistan	114	0.59	3,534	1.23
Estonia	112	0.57	1,573	0.55
Armed Forces	c. 1,238	6.35	(c. 5,000?)	—
TOTAL	19,488	100.00	286,731	100.00

Source: Yezhegodnik Bol'shoy Sovetskoy entsiklopedii, 1989; Izvestiya TsK KPSS, no. 2, 1990, p. 61; Pravda 29 April, 9 November, 10 December 1989; Vestnik statistiki 3/90.

COMMUNIST PARTY ETHNIC COMPOSITION, 1989

Republic	Party membership		Population	
	thousands	%	thousands	%
Russians	11,428	58.64	145,155	50.80
Ukrainians	3,132	16.07	44,186	15.46
Belorussians	753	3.86	10,036	3.51
Uzbeks	491	2.52	16,698	5.84
Kazakhs	409	2.10	8,136	2.85
Tatars	405	2.08	6,649	2.33
Azeris	367	1.88	6,770	2.37
Georgians	337	1.73	3,981	1.39
Armenians	293	1.50	4,623	1.62
Jews	215	1.10	1,378	0.48
Lithuanians	156	0.80	3,067	1.07
Moldovans	120	0.62	3,352	1.17
Chuvash	110	0.56	1,842	0.64
Tajiks	92	0.47	4,215	1.48
Mordva	87	0.44	1,154	0.40
Kyrgyz	84	0.43	2,529	0.89
Turkmen	81	0.42	2,729	0.96
Latvians	81	0.41	1,459	0.51
Bashkir	80	0.41	1,449	0.51
Estonians	62	0.32	1,027	0.36
Others	704	3.61	15,308	5.36
TOTAL	19,488	100.00	285,743	100.00

Source: Izvestiya TsK KPSS, no. 2, 1989, p. 140; Vestnik statistiki 3/90. Permanent residents only. Discrepancies in totals due to rounding.

SOCIAL ORIGINS OF COMMUNIST PARTY MEMBERS

	1952	1956	1961	1966	1971	1976	1981	1986	1989
Workers	32.2	32.0	33.9	37.8	40.1	41.6	43.4	45.0	45.4
Peasants	18.0	17.1	17.6	16.2	15.1	13.9	12.8	11.8	11.4
Professional and clerical	49.8	50.9	48.5	46.0	44.8	44.5	43.8	43.2	43.2

Source: 'KPSS v tsifrakh' in *Partiynaya zhizn'*, various issues

industrial workers, whilst the figure was closer to 5 per cent among low-priority, low-paid – and disproportionately female – jobs in the service and retail sectors. During the 1980s an effort began to extend membership more widely among these occupations. Thirty per cent of those with tertiary qualifications (in 1987) were in the Party (making up about a third of it), compared with about 6 per cent of those who had failed to complete secondary school. A similar discrepancy emerges from data on the social origins of party members: about 45 per cent claimed working-class background in 1989, and about 43 per cent 'white-collar' background; the Party worked hard after the death of Stalin to obtain these favourable statistics, but it was nevertheless the case that just under a quarter of white-collar employees entered the CPSU, but no more than about a tenth of workers. Further, because of the enhanced job prospects of party members, these figures did not reflect their current occupation, something on which the Party rarely provided information; but we know that 53 per cent of party members and candidate members in civilian employment in 1990 had white-collar jobs.

Between January 1990 and August 1991 the CPSU lost more than four million members, and many more ceased to pay their party dues. The evidence is that this four million included a disproportionate number of workers and of the poorly educated, and of Russians and Balts. JHM

PARTY STRUCTURE

The Central Control Commission

This body of 165 members was set up at the XXVIII Party Congress in 1990 to supervise party finances and budgeting and to adjudicate disputes over internal party discipline. It was an amalgamation of two bodies which had existed hitherto, a Central Auditing Commission (finance) and a Committee of Party Control (discipline).

Republican and local party organs

Before 1990 district, town, regional and union republican party organizations 'shadowed' the work of the equivalent soviets, and hence their structure was modelled on the territorial administrative structure of the USSR. The combined effects of democratic centralism, *nomenklatura* and the ban on factions created a situation in which their inner bodies – bureaux, secretariats and apparatus – found it easy to assert control over their nominal superiors, the conferences (congresses) and committees that had set them up, and over the membership.

All this was particularly true in the union republics. The party leadership was always conscious of its own strategic vulnerability and of the unpopularity of Soviet government in many republics, and the devices of the leading role of the Party and democratic centralism served to strengthen its control there. The Communist Parties of the union republics had independent-sounding titles and care was taken to appoint persons of the indigenous nationality to most of their high-profile offices; but it was always difficult for republican politicians to defend the interests of their republics, and many were dismissed on charges of nationalist sympathies. This situation began to change in 1988. In a climate of increasingly vigorous self-expression republican party organizations faced the option of losing all authority, or of retaining some by demonstrating their patriotism and independence of the central party organs. The 1990 Congress sought unsuccessfully to counter the Party's collapsing popularity in the union republics by co-opting the First Secretaries of their party organizations into the all-union Politburo; they were permitted to organize their own appointments, programmes and finances, and to appeal against central decisions without at the same time putting them into effect.

The party organizations of some 150 regions were usually more independent than those of the union republics. The typical *oblast'* or *kray* is a region similar in size to a state of the USA, and the First Secretary of the *oblast'* committee (or *obkom*) had powers and status not unlike those of a state governor or a *préfet de département* in France. In his quest for regional support Khrushchev introduced most of these *obkom* First Secretaries into the all-union Central Committee, where they formed a major interest group. In 1988 Gorbachev proposed that soviets be chaired by local First Secretaries; when party authority collapsed in 1990–91 some far-sighted First Secretaries took the opportunity to resign from their party post whilst retaining the chairmanship and a chance of staying in politics.

Primary party organizations

Despite centralization the primary party organizations of the CPSU were always important. It was never practicable to manage entry into the Party or the monitoring of performance except through a locally based unit, and these became the principal functions of primary party organizations. Each party member had to belong to a primary organization, and they had to be set up in all social settings where three or more communists were present on a regular basis; in practice over 80 per cent were formed at the place of work. Those based on administrative workplaces had considerably fewer rights than those in factories and farms to intervene in management's conduct of work (see Party Rule 59). In 1990 there were some 440,000 primary organizations, averaging 43 persons in size. Most managed their affairs on a voluntary, spare-time basis (though there was often an element of hidden subsidy from the workplace); only some 5 per cent, with membership in excess of 150, paid full-time officials – who were then entitled to leave of absence from their normal job. The work of primary organizations was reinforced by that of some 600,000 'party groups'; these were *ad hoc* organizations, without membership functions, formed in such temporary social settings as meetings, soviets or other elected bodies for the purpose of 'carrying out party policy among non-party people' (Rule 67).

After the loss of its political monopoly in 1990 and before its suspension in August 1991 the Party made a brief attempt to adapt the rights of primary organizations to the new conditions in which electoral appeal mattered more than combating infiltration or factionalism. Primary organizations became free to admit members, hire staff and use up to half the membership dues they collected without supervision from above. They were permitted to communicate with each other and jointly form new organizations concerned with common interests and problems; the strict ban on faction was modified so as to permit the establishment of 'platforms', provided these did not set up their own internal discipline. Communist deputies in soviets were no longer obliged to join party groups, and the groups themselves (embryonic parliamentary parties) were granted some tactical autonomy.

The apparat

Before 1991 party committees appointed their own full-time staff, of whom party secretaries were the most important. This *apparat* (apparatus) of full-time party functionaries numbered some 180,000 in 1990. The practice of *nomenklatura* diminished both competitive entry into the apparatus and its accountability, and full-time work allowed many *apparatchiki* to become more experienced and powerful than the part-time members of their 'parent' committees. A common result was that the apparatus came to dominate these committees and came to make policy as well as carry it out. After the amendment of Article 6 of the Constitution the apparatus lost many

of its legal powers (though not its influence) and the 1990 Congress sought to further this process by limiting the term of apparatus appointment to that of the elected committee that set it up.   JHM

THE PARTY *NOMENKLATURA*

The Communist Party's ability to control the appointment and career progress of virtually anyone in a responsible job was one of its key powers. Certain careers – like those of army officers, diplomats, editors or judges – were restricted to those with CPSU membership, and in many others party membership was a precondition for promotion beyond a certain level. But the party's system for the co-ordinated and centralized deployment and monitoring of personnel – the *nomenklatura* system – was more important.

'Nomenklatura' means simply a 'list of names', and in many cases it was, quite literally, a card index. Specifically *nomenklatura* meant a list of the staff one was entitled to appoint; village teachers, for instance, were 'on the *nomenklatura*' of Ministries of Education. But all important posts were also on a party *nomenklatura* and every party committee from the all-union Central Committee down to the humblest *raykom* (district party committee) held a list of posts the occupancy of which it was entitled to confirm, and which were thus 'in its gift'. Such a list would contain the names of the current incumbents of each post, and, as far as possible, of other persons qualified to enter them, at short notice if necessary. It has been estimated that more than two million persons held positions that were on a party *nomenklatura* at some level, positions which might be anywhere in public life (in the state bureaucracy, the economy, the army, the media, teaching, voluntary organizations) and which might in theory be elective or subject to appointment by administrative superiors; the application of *nomenklatura* principles to Soviet elections explains why there was rarely more than one candidate in them. This was not only an elaborate system for the centralized deployment of personnel but also a method of party-political control. The party committee, for instance, that confirmed the rector of a university might contain no one with knowledge of or interest in education; but in ratifying the appointment it might have a lively interest in the capacities of students for political trouble-making!

It seems likely that something of the order of 60,000 posts were on the *nomenklatura* of the all-union Central Committee, that is, controlled in practice by the Politburo, the Central Committee Secretariat, individual members of these two bodies, or other officials in the departments of the Central

Former Communist Party dachas on Kammeny Island, St Petersburg

Right. Young Octobrists and Pioneers in procession on a Moscow street

Communist youth organizations

Committee. It is thought that these posts included: all senior officials at the all-union echelon of the CPSU, the Council of Ministers, the Komsomol, the judiciary, the media, the trade unions and other public organizations; all general officers of the armed forces, KGB and MVD and all commanders down at least to divisional level; all persons officially posted abroad; and, down to the oblast echelon or its equivalent, party secretaries, chairmen of the executive committees of soviets, editors, judges, police and security chiefs and directors of factories 'of all-union significance'.

The *nomenklatura* system enabled the Party to impose its political priorities in most walks of life, but, at the same time, it had two social consequences that may not have been anticipated. Ordinary people came to perceive that the officials with whom they dealt in everyday life were not in any meaningful sense responsible to their administrative superiors, because they had not been appointed by them. The perception set in that politics was the preserve of a remote and hidden élite, and in time the word *nomenklatura* in colloquial language came to denote, not an administrative procedure, but the ruling class that ran and benefited from that procedure. Further, for an official hired under *nomenklatura* procedures, duty to his formal employer was supplemented by loyalty to the committee that had appointed him or to the 'patron' who had got his name placed on the 'reserve for promotion' list. The systematic and co-ordinated character of the *nomenklatura* policy began to be vitiated by 'old-boy networks' that could easily place their own interests above those of the *nomenklatura* system. Both these tendencies were strengthened by Brezhnev's policy of 'stability of cadres', since the latter removed one of the few sanctions the Party had against disobedient or dishonest officials.

From 1988 efforts were made by the Gorbachev leadership to persuade party committees to relinquish their hold on non-party appointments, and this policy was officially accepted by the XXVIII Party Congress – but with less success in practical than in formal terms.   JHM

THE YOUNG OCTOBRISTS

The Young Octobrists (*Oktyabryata*) came into existence in 1923–24. It catered for children aged between six, when formal schooling begins, and nine. The organization essentially prepared them for admission into the Pioneers at the age of ten; based upon groups of five, each under the direction of a Pioneer or younger Komsomol member, it had its own set of rules which enjoined members to study well, be honest and truthful, and to live happily together.

Two national publications, *Veselye kartinki* and *Murzilka*, were produced for this age-group, as were comparable republican journals in the major Soviet languages. The Young Octobrists, like other forms of communist youth organization, were wound up in late 1991.   SLW

THE PIONEERS

Immediately senior to the Young Octobrists, the Pioneers catered for young people aged between ten and fourteen or fifteen. The Pioneer organization was founded in 1922 as an auxiliary to the Komsomol and also to replace the pre-revolutionary scouting bodies; its central council and activities came under the overall direction of the Komsomol. All schoolchildren of the appropriate age were permitted to join if accepted by their local Pioneer organization,

and virtually all who were eligible did so. Entrants were required to take the Pioneer oath, respect the Pioneer Laws in such matters as truth, courtesy and patriotism, and wear the red Pioneer neckerchief, its three corners representing the unity of Pioneers, Komsomol and Communists. According to the Komsomol statute, and jointly with the school, the Pioneers were supposed to bring up their members as 'convinced fighters for the Communist Party cause, inculcate in them a love of labour and of knowledge, [and] assist the formation of the younger generation in the spirit of communist consciousness and morality'. The national Pioneer paper, *Pionerskaya pravda*, had a circulation of 9.8 million in 1990; the Pioneers themselves had 19 million members organized in over 100,000 groups. The Pioneers, like the Komsomol to which they were subordinate, did not survive the end of communist rule in 1991. SLW

KOMSOMOL

Komsomol (All-Union Leninist Communist Union of Youth or VLKSM) was the most important youth organization during the years of communist rule. Immediately senior to the Pioneers, it catered for young people aged between fourteen and twenty-eight and served as an important training ground for party and other officials. The Komsomol was founded in 1918 as an auxiliary to the Communist Party itself, and throughout its history it was closely controlled by the Party and subordinated to its purposes. Komsomol members took part in the Civil War and industrialization and collectivization drives of the late 1920s and 1930s, and many members were prominent in the armed forces and partisan resistance during the Second World War (when the organization won the first of its Orders of Lenin). Total membership grew steadily over the Soviet period – from 21,000 in 1918 to 10.5 million in 1950 and 31.2 million in 1990, although this last figure concealed a substantial fall in membership since the early 1980s. About half of the Soviet population within the relevant age-groups were members of the Komsomol, and more than 150 million adult citizens had at some time been enrolled within its ranks.

The structure of the Komsomol closely paralleled that of the CPSU. Members were admitted by one of the primary Komsomol organizations, of which there were 438,384 at various places of work and study in 1990, and had the right to elect representatives to successive levels in the hierarchy above them, at each of which a committee or bureau was elected to run day-to-day activities. At the apex was the congress of the Komsomol, meeting once every five years, which elected a central committee that was supposed to meet not less often than once every six months. This in turn elected a bureau and a secretariat to guide the work of the organization between its meetings, and also a First Secretary. In 1990, at its XXI Congress, Vladimir Zyukin (born in 1954, and a Russian by nationality) was elected to this position. Like the CPSU, the Komsomol functioned on the basis of democratic centralism, a principle which at least until the late 1980s ensured that there was little effective opposition to firm or even authoritarian central leadership.

According to its revised statute, adopted in 1990, the Komsomol was a 'voluntary, independent sociopolitical organization of Soviet youth, based on federal principles'. Komsomol members were encouraged to further their political education and to take an active part in public life. More than 46 million members were reported to have taken part in the discussion of the 1977 Soviet Constitution, and the Komsomol was allocated seventy-five seats in the Congress of People's Deputies which was first elected in 1989. Komsomol members also assisted in major industrial projects and in harvesting; meetings were held with war and labour veterans; tourist groups were despatched abroad and received into the USSR through the organization's travel agency 'Sputnik'; and regular sporting events were sponsored. Some twenty-seven special brigades from throughout the USSR took part in relief measures after the 1988 Armenian earthquake.

Komsomol members enjoyed some preference in admissions into the CPSU, and in the 1970s and 1980s more than 70 per cent of party recruits came through the Komsomol (although this represented only a small proportion of Komsomol members). Komsomol membership and service were also taken into account in employment and in higher educational admissions and awards. The organization owned three publishing houses, in Moscow (*Molodaya gvardiya*), Kiev and Tashkent; it published the daily newspaper *Komsomol'skaya pravda*, with a circulation of 22 million copies daily in 1990, and 267 other newspapers and journals with a total daily print of 85 million copies. Despite or perhaps because of this substantial institutional superstructure, the Komsomol became increasingly out of touch with Soviet youth during the Gorbachev years and was officially acknowledged to be 'in crisis' by its XXI Extraordinary Congress in 1990. In September 1991, shortly after the attempted coup, the Komsomol formally dissolved itself; it had already suffered the loss of about a quarter of its members since 1990. The daily paper bearing the name of the Komsomol, somewhat incongruously, continued to appear as an independent newspaper after the organization itself had ceased to exist. SLW

New associations and political parties

Not until the Gorbachev era did the Soviet Union see the development of independent pressure groups and only in the last few years of existence of the Soviet state did new political parties make an appearance. Some of the groups were of a nationalist character such as the Popular Fronts which were established in Estonia, Latvia and Lithuania in 1988 and the Karabakh Committee, formed by Armenian intellectuals with the aim of achieving the integration of Nagorno-Karabakh into Armenia. Others embraced a wide variety of causes, representing very different parts of the political spectrum, from *Memorial*, the organization formed to defend the memory of those unjustly persecuted for political 'crimes', and the equally liberal *Aprel'*, an offshoot of the Writers' Union, to the ultra-nationalist and anti-semitic Russian organization, *Pamyat'*.

Not only independent groups but embryonic political parties began to develop between 1989 and 1991. A change to Article 6 of the Soviet Constitution in March 1990 removed the guaranteed 'leading role' of the Communist Party (CPSU) and this meant that parties other than the CPSU, some of which already existed *de facto*, now had a legal right to function. The Communist Party, even at the time of its dissolution in August 1991, was vastly larger than any of the newcomers on the Soviet scene, but it had not been a party in the normal sense of the term. It was, rather, a party-state organization, the leadership of which at every level was not only fully integrated with but actually directing the machinery of state. There was a sharp distinction in terms of power between the full-time professional party apparatus, on the one hand, and the rank-and-file members, on the other. Membership of the Communist Party did, however, help individuals to further their careers and, while only one in ten adults had a CPSU card, such membership was quite simply a precondition of promotion to the most politically sensitive posts. With the rise of an independent public opinion in the Gorbachev era and, especially with the introduction of competitive elections in March 1989, CPSU membership was no longer so obviously an advantage. By 1990–91 Communist Party members were increasingly on the defensive, though in absolute numbers the CPSU was much larger than all the other parties put together.

If the Communist Party, at the time of its suspension in August 1991, still had a membership of

around 15 million, the scores of new parties ranged from those who could be numbered in tens to more serious ones such as the Democratic Party of Russia (DPR), which in 1991 had a membership of around 50,000.

Led by Nikolay Travkin (b. 1946), a prominent public figure who had been a successful manager in the construction industry (and was a member of the CPSU until April 1990), the DPR had its founding congress in Moscow in December 1990. Among prominent figures in the party at the time of its foundation who subsequently broke with Travkin and left the DPR were the chess champion Gary Kasparov (b. 1963) and the economist Academician Stanislav Shatalin (b. 1934). In political orientation, the DPR has been a centrist party and one which came out against the dissolution of the Soviet Union and the creation of a Commonwealth of Independent States in December 1991.

The earliest non-communist party to emerge in Russia, in terms of the date of its official founding congress (4–6 May 1990 in Moscow), was the Social Democratic Party of Russia (SDPR). On 15 March 1991 the party was officially registered by the Ministry of Justice of Russia. In 1990–91 the SDPR was vigorous in its opposition to the CPSU and in its support (in 1991) of the presidential campaign of Boris Yel'tsin as an active participant in the movement, 'Democratic Russia'.

Among the leaders of the SDPR, greatest prominence during its first two years of existence was achieved by Oleg Rumyantsev (b. 1961) who became in 1990 the secretary of the Constitutional Commission of the Russian republic, responsible for drawing up a new Russian Constitution (although that Commission's successive constitutional drafts were eventually discarded by Yel'tsin in 1993). The SDPR, more than most of the new parties, stressed the importance of working through representative organs – the Supreme Soviet of Russia and the local soviets. (The party split in 1993 and Rumyantsev became the leader of a group called the Social Democratic Centre.)

A third new party of consequence to emerge in Russia was the People's Party of Free Russia (PPFR). This party originated in the spring and early summer of 1991 and was based on the group of deputies to the Supreme Soviet of the Russian republic, 'Communists for Democracy', formed in April 1991. Its leader was Aleksandr Rutskoy who was soon to be chosen by Yel'tsin as his running-mate in the Russian presidential elections. Rutskoy duly became Vice-President of Russia. The party he led changed its name from 'Communists for Democracy' to the People's Party of Free Russia (PPFR) in August 1991, a title which was confirmed at its founding congress in October of the same year. The

Nikolay Travkin, pictured in 1990, the year in which his Democratic Party of Russia was founded

support of Rutskoy – and the sixty-six deputies of the Supreme Soviet of Russia who belonged to the PPFR – for a market economy was tempered by concern about the decline in popular living standards and, not least, for the interests of the military-industrial complex.

Of consequence more because of the measure of support attained by its leader than on account of its popularity as a party, the misnamed Liberal Democratic Party (LDP), nevertheless, achieved greater salience than most new political parties during the last two years of the Soviet Union's existence. Its registration as a political party was later, but only temporarily, revoked by the post-Soviet Russian government.

Led by Vladimir Zhirinovsky (b. 1946), this party was actually a breakaway group from a broader political grouping – also called the Liberal Democratic Party – in October 1990. Zhirinovsky was expelled from the parent party for alleged collaboration with the KGB. He espoused an openly imperialist policy, adopting a hard line in defence of maintenance of Soviet power and of Russian domination of the Soviet Union. On an entire range of issues, he adopted positions which were far from liberal and by no means democratic. When Zhirinovsky put the popularity of these views and his party to the test in the Russian presidential election of June 1991, he came third out of six candidates and was beaten only by Yel'tsin – who was, however, overwhelmingly victorious with 57.3 per cent of the popular vote – and Ryzhkov. Zhirinovsky received 7.1 per cent of the votes.

The most important and successful political movement between 1990 and the demise of the Soviet Union at the end of 1991 was the loose coalition known as Democratic Russia. At its first congress in October 1990 it brought together thirty-three different political associations, among them seven parties (including the DPR and the SDPR). Democratic Russia succeeded in establishing local organizations in every region of the country and its support for Yel'tsin played an important part in the first Russian presidential election. At its height, in the summer of 1991, Democratic Russia could claim around 300,000 participants.　　　　AHB/VJG

A new pressure group called the Movement for Democratic Reforms came into existence less than two months before the attempted August coup. Pictured below (from left to right) are three of its major figures, Eduard Shevardnadze, Arkady Volsky and Anatoly Sobchak, at the press conference to launch the movement, 2 July 1991

Aleksandr Rutskoy

Aleksandr Rutskoy was thrust into prominence in Russian political life when Boris Yel'tsin chose him as his vice-presidential running-mate in 1991. The Yel'tsin–Rutskoy team won a convincing victory. While Yel'tsin's popularity at that time was the major factor, Rutskoy played his part by balancing the ticket, reassuring some sections of the military as well as middle-of-the-road voters who feared what they took to be Yel'tsin's radicalism.

Rutskoy was in some ways an unlikely partner. Born in 1947, he joined the military, became a pilot and rose to the rank of air force colonel. He took part in some daring rescues of Russian prisoners during the Soviet intervention in Afghanistan and emerged a much-decorated war hero. Rutskoy was elected from the Kursk region in the 1990 elections for the Congress of People's Deputies of the Russian Republic. Whereas many Afghan veterans were on the conservative wing of Russian politics, Rutskoy for a time gravitated towards reformist circles and by 1991 was one of the leaders of the movement, 'Communists for reform'.

After the failure of the August coup of 1991 – in which Rutskoy played an important part, organizing the defence of the Russian White House – and the banning of the Communist Party, Rutskoy's group was renamed the People's Party of Free Russia. Rutskoy, however, soon became an outspoken opponent of the policies being pursued by Yegor Gaydar and, by extension, those of Yel'tsin. Matters came to a head in September 1993 when Yel'tsin, after suspending Rutskoy from his post of Vice-President, forcibly dissolved the legislature. Rutskoy found himself defending the Russian White House once again, but this time from, rather than with, Yel'tsin. For encouraging armed resistance to the presidential decree, he was arrested on 4 October 1993, but released following an amnesty resolution of the new State Duma in late February 1994.

Rutskoy made it clear he saw a future for himself in Russian politics. In an interview with Russian Independent Television (NTV) on 24 April 1994, he called for a political movement which would unite all the opposition forces and which he was ready to lead.

Soviet 'federalism'

ETHNIC DIVERSITY AND ITS POLITICAL ORGANIZATION

The Soviet Union before 1991 was not a 'nation-state'. In terms of the number, diversity and distribution of its ethnic groups (see 'The Peoples') it was close to unique among states; the best comparisons were with India or South Africa. To organize and maintain a single state among such a population would have been a challenge to any leadership or political philosophy. The Soviet answer was to adopt the formal shape – though not the workings – of federalism, in the Union of Soviet Socialist Republics; its principal features are schematized in the diagram opposite.

Nationality-based territorial administrative divisions of the Soviet Union

Where an American might have thought in terms of three tiers of administration above the immediate community, namely federal, state, and city (or county), his or her Soviet counterpart would have recognized four: all-union, union-republican, provincial, and city or county. Among the territorial units at the union-republican and provincial echelon were four kinds of 'national territorial formation', and these usually bore the name of the largest non-Russian group in their population; this will be called the 'titular' group.

At the two highest echelons, the Soviet Union was a union of fifteen union republics, each of which had some share in the Soviet state frontier. By far the largest of these was the Russian Soviet Federative Socialist Republic or RSFSR; this was itself in formal terms a federation and contained half the Soviet population and three-quarters of its territory. All but the smallest union republics were divided into provinces, some 150 in all. The most common types of province were called *oblast'* or *kray* in

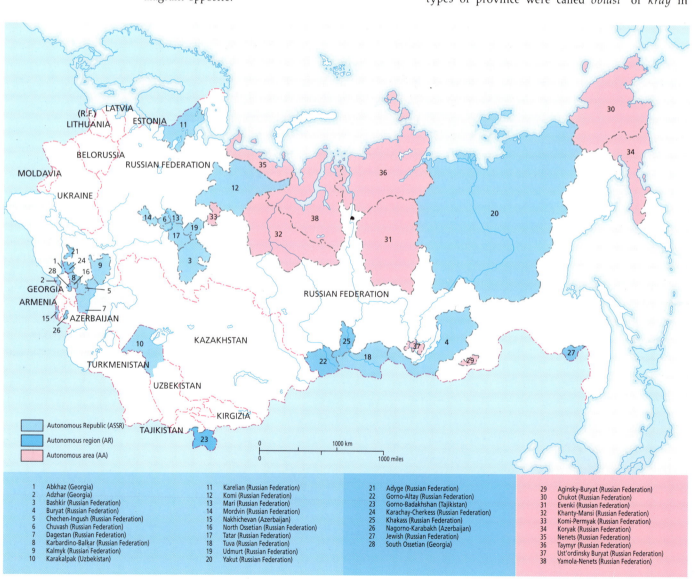

Legend:
- Autonomous Republic (ASSR)
- Autonomous region (AR)
- Autonomous area (AA)

1	Abkhaz (Georgia)	11	Karelian (Russian Federation)
2	Adzhar (Georgia)	12	Komi (Russian Federation)
3	Bashkir (Russian Federation)	13	Mari (Russian Federation)
4	Buryat (Russian Federation)	14	Mordvin (Russian Federation)
5	Chechen-Ingush (Russian Federation)	15	Nakhichevan (Azerbaijan)
6	Chuvash (Russian Federation)	16	North Ossetian (Russian Federation)
7	Dagestan (Russian Federation)	17	Tatar (Russian Federation)
8	Karbardino-Balkar (Russian Federation)	18	Tuva (Russian Federation)
9	Kalmyk (Russian Federation)	19	Udmurt (Russian Federation)
10	Karakalpak (Uzbekistan)	20	Yakut (Russian Federation)

21	Adyge (Russian Federation)	29	Aginsky-Buryat (Russian Federation)
22	Gorno-Altay (Russian Federation)	30	Chukot (Russian Federation)
23	Gorno-Badakhshan (Tajikistan)	31	Evenki (Russian Federation)
24	Karachay-Cherkess (Russian Federation)	32	Khanty-Mansi (Russian Federation)
25	Khakass (Russian Federation)	33	Komi-Permyak (Russian Federation)
26	Nagorno-Karabakh (Azerbaijan)	34	Koryak (Russian Federation)
27	Jewish (Russian Federation)	35	Nenets (Russian Federation)
28	South Ossetian (Georgia)	36	Taymyr (Russian Federation)
		37	Ust'ordinsky Buryat (Russian Federation)
		38	Yamola-Nenets (Russian Federation)

Russian, but equivalent to them in size and powers were the 20 autonomous republics (or ASSRs), all but four of them within the RSFSR; the four largest ASSRs had populations greater than the smallest union republic (Estonia). In addition some provinces or smaller union republics contained autonomous regions (*avtonomnye oblasti*, ARS) or autonomous areas (*avtonomnye okruga*, AAS), usually with a very small titular population. There were eight ARs, and ten AAS, all but three ARS being in the RSFSR.

Some of the political problems of Soviet territorial-administrative structure emerge from the table, especially when its data are compared with those in the tables on Population and on Nationality Composition of the USSR. First, Russians were always more than half of the total Soviet population, and up to a fifth of Russians (in 1989 25 million) lived outside their titular union republic, the RSFSR. In some union republics Russians were close to being the most numerous group, and they formed a clear majority in many ASSRs. Irrespective of policy, there was thus a tendency for Russian interests and personnel to dominate union politics; and present and future governments of Russia must continue to be concerned for the interests of Russians outside Russia proper.

A second group of problems arose from the fact that it was impossible to draw administrative boundaries that circumscribed homogeneous populations. None of the national territorial formations was homogeneous (Armenia came closest to it), and none united all of a titular population (although few Balts or Georgians lived outside their home republics). The titular nationality was sometimes not the largest ethnic group in the population, as in many ASSRs, and in Kazakhstan until the 1980s. Local politics were often dominated by competition for influence and jobs between the titular group and 'immigrants', and, where the latter were Russians, they could readily be thought to have the all-union authorities on their side. Many minorities were enclaves of peoples who had a titular territory somewhere else, and this could give rise to friction between national territorial formations. An example is the Nagorno-Karabakh AR: although its population was more than 70 per cent Armenian and its territory approached to within a few miles of Armenia, it was within and subordinate to Azerbaijan.

Finally there were some nationalities without national territorial formations, who were thus deprived even of the (mainly cultural) opportunities this organization afforded; among these, Germans numbered more than two million and Poles more than a million. Two such groups, the Germans and Crimean Tatars, had had ASSRs which were abolished during the Second World War and never revived. And it should not be forgotten that less than one per cent of Soviet Jews lived in the Jewish AR near Khabarovsk in the Far East.   JHM

The political-administrative structure of the Soviet Union

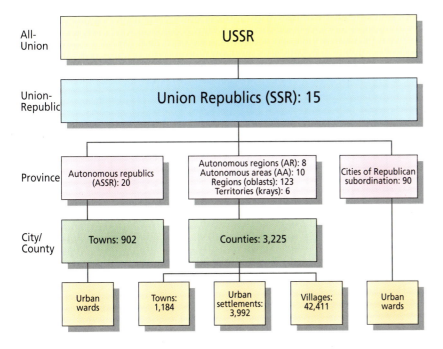

TITULAR AND NON-TITULAR POPULATIONS, 1989

Republic	Population (thousands)	Nationality, of which:		Titular population living outside this territory (%)
		Titular (%)	Russian (%)	
Russia	147,022	81.5	na	17.4
Ukraine	51,452	72.7	22.1	15.3
Belarus	10,152	77.9	13.2	21.2
Uzbekistan	19,810	71.4	8.4	15.3
Kazakhstan	16,464	39.7	37.8	19.7
Georgia	5,401	70.1	6.3	4.9
Azerbaijan	7,021	82.7	5.6	14.3
Lithuania	3,675	79.6	9.4	4.7
Moldova	4,335	64.5	13.0	16.6
Latvia	2,667	52.0	34.0	4.9
Kyrgyzstan	4,258	52.4	21.5	11.8
Tajikistan	5,093	62.3	7.6	24.7
Armenia	3,305	93.3	1.6	33.3
Turkmenistan	3,523	72.0	9.5	7.1
Estonia	1,565	61.5	30.3	6.2

Source: *Vestnik statistiki* 10–12/90; 1, 4, 6/90. Permanent residents only.

PSEUDO-FEDERAL UNION 1922–90

Before and for a short time after the Revolution the Bolsheviks supported national self-determination, but Civil War and the secession of some of the Empire's most prosperous territories led them to overturn independent regimes (such as those in Ukraine and Georgia) and to impose a unitary system of government. Towards the end of his life

Lenin showed a renewed interest in the principle of federalism – but on the assumption that the Communist Party would stay centralized – and it was under his influence that the first Union Treaty was signed in 1922. The union republics that joined were four: the RSFSR (which at that time included Central Asia and Kazakhstan), Ukraine, Belorussia and Transcaucasia (uniting Georgia, Azerbaijan and Armenia). Local élites had a degree of autonomy in the 1920s that was later to be envied.

Stalin's 'Second Revolution' replaced such quasi-federalism with rigid centralization, just as it put an end to other surviving elements of institutional autonomy and pluralism. Non-Russian élites suffered particularly in the purges, programmes of deliberate Russification were pursued (although Stalin was of course not a Russian) and Russians were presented as the 'Elder Brother' nation. It was forecast that the *sblizhenie* (rapprochement) of nations would end in their 'merging' (*sliyanie*). The 'federal' provisions of the 1936 Constitution were among its worst legal fictions. In 1940 the independent Baltic states were pressured into accepting entry into the Union, and in 1941 and after the Great Fatherland War substantial numbers of their élites were deported. During the War seven small nationalities (the Volga Germans and Crimean Tatars, and five from the North Caucasus) were deported *en masse*, and their national territorial formations abolished, for alleged collaboration with the *Wehrmacht*. Under Khrushchev and Brezhnev the brutality and public display of Russian chauvinism were abandoned, some of the deported nationalities were restored to their territories, but the Union remained in practice a unitary and centralized, Russian-dominated state in which attempts to pursue their own interests by the citizens of national territorial formations were punished.   JHM

THE UNION REPUBLICS

Most public office – and especially high-profile or ceremonial office – in the national territorial formations was held by members of indigenous nationalities, and the latter were always over-represented in the feeble Supreme Soviet of the Union before 1989. Yet such officials could do little more than implement policies handed down from above, using budgets which consisted in practice of earmarked grants. The essential characteristics of federalism – the distribution of powers between independent federal and regional governments, clear demarcation of the boundary between them, and mechanisms for the settlement of disputes – were missing from the 1936 and 1977 Constitutions.

This system was maintained above all by the penetration of the Communist Party into all institutions and occupations. It does not appear that there was serious discrimination against non-Russians in regard to entry into the Party; in union republics as elsewhere formal party membership was a prerequisite of most responsible jobs until 1990. But two factors made it difficult for non-Russians to contribute to policy-making on equal terms. Members were bound by the rules of democratic centralism; and the personnel procedures of *nomenklatura* ensured a preponderance of Russians (or of pro-Russian Ukrainians and Belorussians) in the party's (Moscow-based) senior organs and *apparat*. (A similar imbalance was true of the officer corps of the armed forces and KGB, and of the diplomatic corps.) Under *nomenklatura* procedures a small number of key posts in the national territorial formations were reserved for nominees of the central *apparat* – usually Russians, though not, it may be noted, from local Russian minorities. Chief among these posts was that of second Secretary of the local party organization, whose tasks included the selection and deployment of local personnel; this official thus moulded the future élite, both indigenous and Russian, in non-Russian areas.

Yet several things set this system apart from the stereotype of a colonial empire. First, economic development was among the most important of communist priorities and it could not be pursued without introducing literacy, skills and basic welfare pro-

Red Square, Moscow. A typical November 7th demonstration commemorating the Bolshevik revolution of 1917

visions among nationalities that had previously lacked them; and such development, it was held, would moderate if not put an end to perceptions of national identity. The consequence of this policy before the 1960s was a narrowing of the gap between rich and poor regions. (It is another matter that such economic development often lacked diversity – the cotton monoculture in Uzbekistan is an example – and that it prompted widespread perceptions in European Russia, Ukraine and the Baltic republics that these regions or republics had put more into the Union than they got out of it.)

Second, the policy entailed limitations in practice on the imposition from above of Russian language and central plans. In an ethnically diverse society it makes for stability if dealings in the immediate community and workplace are conducted in local languages. In promoting vernacular literacy, therefore, the Communists promoted non-Russian languages and cultures, whilst seeking to depoliticize them and to divorce them from religion and traditional symbols of authority. Economic development led inevitably to an increase in clerical and managerial jobs. The overall consequence was that knowledge of, and publication in, many of the non-Russian languages flourished during the Soviet period – especially in the union republics, whose governments managed education in their own territories. It was central policy that all schoolchildren had to learn Russian, at least as a second language; but it was clear by the 1980s that effective bilingualism was declining in the Baltic region and Central Asia.

The limits of centralization and the scope for local discretion are well illustrated by the division of ministerial responsibilities in the All-Union Council of Ministers. It contained two types of ministry, 'all-union' and 'union-republican'. The former operated directly from Moscow throughout Soviet territory, without formal obligation to take account of local conditions or consult local interests.

Union-republican ministries, by contrast, tended to have tasks whose performance required local knowledge: light industry, agriculture, construction, trade, and such non-economic concerns as health, public order, culture and education. They had branches in the capitals of the union republics and the mere fact that these recruited local staff rendered them open to local influence, at least in the interpretation of central policy as it applied to local conditions.

These factors combined to generate indigenous, bilingual, white-collar élites in the non-Russian nationalities. By the 1980s these were eager to run their own affairs, and had become articulate opponents of Soviet centralization; the old Union had sown the seeds of its own collapse.　JHM

THE FAILURE OF FEDERALISM

Beginning with Estonia in November 1988, but mostly in 1990, all the union republics declared their 'sovereignty'; they were followed by almost all the ASSRS, some ARS and AAS (and even some regions). At the same time most ASSRS claimed the status of union republics (and there was some tendency to merge the status of AAS and ARS). In itself the claim of sovereignty had little legal significance; more serious was the claim by many republics that their legislation could override all-union legislation, a rejection of the division of powers necessary for federation. Although Russian communists had been important beneficiaries of the Soviet system, the new mood extended to Russia also: there the demand was to distinguish firmly between central and Russian interests, and to put the latter first. The Gorbachev administration, free of the constraints of party monopoly, sought to combat these processes and preserve the Union through a renewed interest in federalism. In three important pieces of legislation of April 1990 the political status of Russian and non-Russian languages was codified, a provisional attempt was made at demarcating the all-union from the union-republican spheres of competence, and a procedure for secession from the Union was adopted. Aspects of the demarcation were unclear and the political costs of secession were prohibitive; nevertheless this was pioneering legislation that addressed some of the notorious flaws in the Constitution.

In August 1990 negotiations began between the all-union administration and the Supreme Soviets of the union republics and the ASSRS with a view to drafting a new Union Treaty on a genuinely federal basis. It is clear that these negotiations were difficult to the very end, and doubtful whether a compromise was possible even in principle among the interests of the negotiating parties: most union republics (including the RSFSR) preferred some kind of confederal arrangement; Gorbachev, with the ASSRS, among others, in support, strove for federalism; but substantial elements in the Union and CPSU bureaucracy and in the military-industrial complex were loath to abandon the unitarism that gave them their power, status and livelihood.

Draft texts of the Union Treaty were published in November 1990 and March, June and August 1991. They envisaged a Union of Soviet Sovereign Republics (in place of the Union of Soviet Socialist Republics), to be formed by union republics and ASSRS, many but not all the differences between which would have been eliminated. In a thorough (though somewhat ambiguous) distribution of powers between Union and republics, the Union would have had exclusive powers in the fields of: adoption and amendment of the Constitution; conduct of the Union's foreign, defence and national security policy; management of military industry, atomic energy and the space programme; minting of currency and custody of gold, diamond and hard currency reserves; and administration of a federal police force. The Union's armed forces might not be used for intra-union purposes except in cases of disaster or emergency. Property 'necessary for the exercise of its powers' would have been allocated by member states to the Union, and the union budget was to be financed by union taxes – but 'at rates determined by agreement with the republics'.

Union republics gained exclusive control of such matters as citizenship, the organization of local government, the courts, criminal and civil law, trade and the microeconomy. They might now raise their own taxes and they became the owners of all land, natural resources and property on their territory (except for that assigned to the Union); this would have been their main guarantee against an over-mighty centre. They might conduct their own foreign relations and (by implication) raise their own armed forces for internal purposes, but they undertook not to combine or use force against the Union or other members.

All other powers were to be exercised 'jointly' by union and republican organs. Such 'concurrent' powers exist in many federal systems – but they had existed in the 1922 Treaty, and under Stalin the Union had reduced the republics' share in joint powers to nothing. Republican negotiators suspected that this clause concealed unreconstructed centralism; and the clause which gave the laws of Union and republics supremacy each in their allotted sphere was not unambiguous. The Treaty foresaw a Constitutional Court – an evolution of the existing Committee of Constitutional Supervision – empowered to adjudicate jurisdictional disputes between Union and republics and to determine the constitutionality of legislation and normative acts of government. The major change to central political institutions would have been the creation of an upper house called the Soviet of Republics (in place of the Soviet of Nationalities); its deputies were to be delegated by the legislatures of the republics they represented, and delegates from the same union republic were to vote as one bloc.

The Union Treaty was not without its problems, but it lacked the rhetoric and legal trickery of the 1936 and 1977 Soviet Constitutions and must be treated as a serious attempt to make federalism work in the Soviet Union. Of its clauses, that on taxation

Ethnic distribution of the Soviet population

Slavs
- Russians
- Ukrainians
- Belorussians

Other
- Small nationalities of Christian background
- Nationalities of Muslim background
- Small Asian nationalities
- Sparsely inhabited areas

Cross-hatching indicates a mixture of two or more nationalities with none being dominant

The Mufti of Kazakhstan, Ratbek Nisanbaev (centre) casting his vote in the referendum of March 1991 held in nine of the Soviet Union's fifteen republics on the future of the union. In all, 76 per cent voted in favour of a 'renewed federation of equal sovereign republics'

The development of federalism in the Soviet Union failed for numerous reasons: the extreme diversity of regional and national interests, once they could be freely expressed; the distrust which centuries of Russian hegemony had generated; the failure of Russian politicians to give ethnic politics due attention until it was too late; and widespread inexperience of law and constitutionalism. JHM

The Soviet ministerial system

was the most bitterly contested: all-union and RSFSR representatives fought over this until three weeks before the Treaty was due to be signed on 20 August 1991. RSFSR insistence on, and Gorbachev's ultimate concession of, republican consent to union tax rates were together the main reason why the August coup was launched on 18 August, less than 48 hours before the Union Treaty's signature.

By August 1991 no more than nine union republics were prepared to join the new Union. Six republics (Estonia, Latvia, Lithuania, Moldova, Georgia and Armenia) had already made clear their refusal to sign and had boycotted a referendum on the Treaty held in March 1991. As soon as the coup collapsed most union republics took the opportunity to upgrade their sovereignty to independence, and the three Baltic states gained international and Soviet recognition for their secession from the USSR; these reactions show how important fear of the army had been in prompting support for the Union Treaty. Gorbachev tried for months after the coup – virtually without support – to revive interest in Union (this time a confederal arrangement), but two developments wrecked his hopes: the failure of the Supreme Soviet to pass a budget in late November 1991, followed by Russia's assumption of responsibility for the union budget; and the decision of Ukraine in a referendum on 1 December to sever ties with the Union. A week later the Russian President B.N. Yel'tsin met the leaders of Ukraine and Belarus in Minsk to form the Commonwealth of Independent States, an alliance designed to have no permanent joint institutions other than common command of strategic armed forces. By late December a further eight members (Kazakhstan, the four Central Asian republics, Armenia, Azerbaijan and Moldova) had joined the Commonwealth, and the Soviet Union came to a formal end on 1 January 1992.

The system of ministries and other organs of central administration functioned historically as one of the main institutional elements imposing order across the breadth and diversity of the Soviet state. It comprised the executive and administrative organs of the central Soviet state – the Council of Ministers (renamed the Cabinet of Ministers in 1991) and its permanent apparatus, ministries and the bodies subordinate to them, and the state committees. In practice these bodies were also the source of the bulk of legislative activity, though after 1989 this dominance was to some extent curtailed by the legislative activity of the Congress of People's Deputies and the permanently functioning Supreme Soviet.

As a result of many negative aspects of its activity, particularly in the economy, the ministerial system was frequently the object of criticism by both leading politicians and, after democratization, the general public as well. The reforms of the ministerial system introduced by Gorbachev during the second half of the 1980s were complex and substantial although contested and unfinished. They aimed at reducing the overall power of ministries, at redistributing the remaining power of the system among its constituent elements, and at changing the methods by which ministerial power was exercised. Politically, the ministries became subject to greater scrutiny by the legislative branch, though the overall level of supervision may have been reduced by the abolition of branch departments in the apparatus of the Communist Party's Central Committee.

Economically, the scope of ministerial activity was reduced by enhancing the autonomy of enterprises, and by shifting ministries to more market-based levers of intervention. Legally, the ministries were affected by the move towards a law-governed state (*pravovoe gosudarstvo*) in which individual and corporate property rights could be defended

On parade in Tushino (left to right): Iosif Stalin, Georgy Malenkov and Lavrenty Beria

On parade in Tushino (left to right): Iosif Stalin, Georgy Malenkov and Lavrenty Beria

against state encroachment. However, given the power and influence of the institutions which comprise it, the ministerial system proved far harder to reform in practice than in rhetoric, despite numerous efforts in the course of Soviet history.   SDW

EVOLUTION

When the Bolsheviks came to power in 1917 they created a government which was given a 'revolutionary' name, the Council of People's Commissars, or *Sovnarkom* (renamed the Council of Ministers after the Second World War). Although even in the early days of Soviet power the Politburo and Central Committee were the major bodies of policy-making, *Sovnarkom* under Lenin, whose only formal office was that of its chairman, arguably had a status which it never afterwards regained. Commissariats, some of which were taken over directly from the old tsarist ministries, included foreign affairs, education, labour and the Supreme Council of the National Economy (VSNKh). The last body, especially through its chief administrations (*glavki*) in the period of War Communism, first developed the system of direct central operational control over enterprises which was to become characteristic of the Soviet economy after the end of the New Economic Policy (NEP). In the 1920s commissions of *Sovnarkom* were created, most notably the State Planning Commission (Gosplan), which developed into the complex system of state committees.

Though the power of *Sovnarkom* as a collective body declined after Lenin's death, from 1932 onwards there occurred a vast increase in the number of commissariats created to organize newly emerging branches of industry. The role of Gosplan in managing the economy was also enhanced by the switch from indicative to compulsory planning after 1929. As the 1930s wore on, and especially after 1938, the influence of the People's Commissariat

for Internal Affairs (NKVD) in state administration and the economy became more prevalent. Under Beria it became one of the most powerful institutions in the country, in control of an army of prison labour for work on projects ranging from canal building to advanced scientific research.

The relationship of the ministerial system to Stalinism was a complex one. Some scholars have claimed that the power of the ministries in the Soviet political process represented the triumph of the economic bureaucracy over the Stalinist ideology; others have argued that the ministries were Stalinism's institutional manifestation. In the post-war period, however, it became evident that policies favoured by Stalin were only implemented when they were also in the interests of the ministries.

After Stalin's death and the ousting of Beria, there was a sharp reduction in the power of the NKVD (renamed the MGB in 1946). Security functions were transferred to a new Committee for State Security (KGB), the head of which did not regain a seat in the Politburo until 1973. The power of the ministerial bureaucracy was a factor in the political struggle in 1957 between Khrushchev and the so-called 'anti-party group' which had its power base in the central state apparatus. The subsequent abolition of the ministries and their replacement by regional economic councils (*sovnarkhozy*) was Khrushchev's paradoxical tribute to the power of the ministries in the Soviet system. Characteristic efforts by the Soviet political élite to improve their control over the ministerial system are also evident in this period in Khrushchev's decision to increase the supervisory power of Gosplan and to streamline the Council of Ministers. However, Khrushchev's policy towards the ministerial system was inconsistent, and he developed no alternative to 'administrative-command' methods of instructing enterprises. The *sovnarkhozy* developed negative traits of their own, particularly 'localism', which disrupted overall national economic development and gave ammunition to Khrushchev's political opponents which contributed to his ultimate removal in 1964.

His successors, Brezhnev and Kosygin, restored the system of branch ministries in 1965, though worries about their power and performance were evident from the expectation that ministries would work to implement the concurrent economic reform giving enterprises greater autonomy, and concentrate only on giving general direction to branch development, particularly in the area of science and technology. However, by simultaneously charging ministries with responsibility for plan targets in the branch, the new leaders gave ministries both the motive and the means to oppose successful economic reform, and they quickly came to resemble their pre-1957 predecessors. In many cases, they even had the same personnel.

At the same time, the post-1965 period also saw a number of changes in the ministerial system. The practice under Stalin and Khrushchev whereby the First (or General) Secretary of the Central Committee of the Party also headed the Council of Ministers was prohibited, at least in part because holding both positions put the party leader more directly in the political firing line. While some research suggests that under Khrushchev the Presidium of the Council of Ministers achieved political power on a par with the Presidium of the Central Committee (as the Politburo was known then), under his successor, Brezhnev, the Politburo was clearly pre-eminent. The desire of the leadership to evolve a more technocratic means of management was also evident in the development of the number and responsibilities of state committees.   SDW

THE COUNCIL OF MINISTERS

Though the Constitution of the USSR adopted in 1977 had codified the Council of Ministers as the 'government of the USSR – the highest executive and administrative organ of state power', it did not function as an effective collegial body and despite its long list of formal powers met in full session only quarterly for the largely pre-arranged purpose of approving the quarterly plan figures. The inner Presidium of the Council of Ministers, which comprised the chairman of the Council and the heads of key committees and ministries, met more frequently and was a more powerful executive institution. As part of Gorbachev's efficiency drive, however, the Council of Ministers, and especially its commissions, bureaux and the permanent apparatus of its Presidium, were upgraded in 1987 and described as the 'general headquarters of perestroika'. In part because of a desire of the party leadership at that time to distance itself from direct interference in

the economy, the power of the Council of Ministers was higher in the late 1980s than it had been since Khrushchev. Organizational changes also contributed to its capacity to operate as a collegial body: the size of the Council of Ministers was significantly cut from a figure of well over a hundred members under Brezhnev; the internal apparatus of the Council was also strengthened while the status of the individual ministries was reduced; finally, a new kind of minister began to appear in some non-industrial departments with less of a career bureaucrat background. A new method of ministerial appointment under close scrutiny from the Supreme Soviet showed signs of making the Council of Ministers and its individual members responsible for the conduct of government.

In late 1990 and early 1991, however, further changes occurred in the power, organization, and membership of the Council of Ministers (renamed the Cabinet of Ministers), and in its relationship to other bodies such as the presidency and the legislature, which altered its status yet again, this time in a downward direction. In particular, the dual executive, comprised of either the general secretary or president on the one hand, and the chairman of the Council of Ministers on the other, was abolished by transforming the Cabinet of Ministers as a whole, and its chairman (now called the prime minister), into direct subordinates of the chief executive.

Membership

Membership of the Council of Ministers was sharply reduced in the second half of the 1980s from 115 members in 1984 to 67 in 1989. The Cabinet of Ministers formed in early 1991 consisted of 51 members, a figure which – if the Soviet Union had survived that long – was expected to fall to 36 by the end of 1992 as a result of the conversion of some ministries into corporations and joint-stock companies. Ministers, who had traditionally been approved by the Supreme Soviet in a rubber-stamp procedure, became subject after 1989 to intensive cross-examination by Supreme Soviet committees and parliament as a whole, and in some cases failed to win parliament's approval. Membership of the Council (Cabinet) consisted of its chairman, three first deputy chairmen, nine deputy chairmen who headed bureaux and state commissions, the chairman of the Administrative Department, chairman of the state committees and ministers, and the head of the State Bank.

Structure

The apparatus of the Council (Cabinet) in the last years of the Soviet system was divided as follows:

- A Chairman – from 1985 to 1990 this was Nikolay Ryzhkov until his replacement by

Nikolay Ryzhkov, , Chairman of the Council of Ministers of the USSR from 1985 to 1990, and runner-up to Boris Yel'tsin in the Russian presidential election of 1991

Valentin Pavlov whose participation in the August 1991 coup led to his arrest. Subordinated to the Chairman was a secretariat and an information department which comprised thirty-three full-time aides in 1990.

- A Presidium which included the chairman and his deputy chairmen, the heads of the most important state committees, the Minister of Finance, and the head of the Administrative Department.
- The Administrative Department was the secretariat of the Council and in 1990 consisted of thirteen departments overseeing activity in the economy, industry, metallurgy and geology, territorial development and capital construction, scientific and technological progress, defence industry, personnel and other areas. The department was substantially reorganized after 1989 with cuts in the numbers of subdivisions and a 40 per cent cut in staff levels.
- Standing Committees, which were sub-divided into two types. First, state commissions which guided the Council in general questions concerning: provisions and purchases; economic reform; external economic ties; military-industrial questions; and emergency situations. Some of these state commissions were known to have existed for some time, although the one for economic reform was created only in 1989 when the then serious economic reformer Leonid Abalkin (b.1930) was appointed chairman. Abalkin resigned at the beginning of 1991 and his position was taken by the Prime Minister, Pavlov. The second category consisted of bureaux formed in 1986–87, reviving bodies which had existed in the war period. These were charged with co-ordinating the activities of groups of ministries in the areas of social development, machine building, the fuel and energy complex, and the chemical and forestry complex. Approximately one thousand people were known to work in the various bureaux, though plans for further reform of the Council envisaged cutting the number of bureaux to only three. SDW

THE CABINET OF MINISTERS

Following the constitutional changes of 1990, which created and strengthened the executive presidency, and the 'Law on the USSR Cabinet' passed in March 1991, the Cabinet became an organ of the president's office. Its members, though they continued to be ratified by the Supreme Soviet, were nominated not by the Chairman of the Council of Ministers as had been the case previously, but by the president himself. This consolidated the downgrading in the status of the Cabinet and, especially its chairman, which Nikolay Ryzhkov had publicly opposed before his retirement, and which was already evident in the removal of constitutional references to the Council of Ministers as a legislative and judicial body. In addition, the Cabinet formed in 1991 had an avowedly temporary character, intended to operate while a new Union Treaty was being agreed and while market reforms were being undertaken. Substantially increased participation from republican leaders was also being planned. At the same time, however, the Cabinet maintained considerable formal and informal powers, particularly with regard to the aim of the leadership to secure the continuation of an all-union structure of administration. Within the Cabinet's responsibility, 'in conjunction with the republics', were delegated powers over the budget and currency, all-union economic programmes, fuel and transport policy, administration of defence industry, communications, state security, foreign policy, and social programmes. Less formally, though the president had a nominally supreme status in the executive apparatus, he did not command a developed apparatus of his own, which left him in practical terms even more dependent on the policy inputs of personnel in the Cabinet and the ministries. SDW

MINISTRIES AND STATE COMMITTEES

There were a number of differences between ministries and state committees, though in some cases, as with the Ministry of Finance which was more like a state committee, or the State Committee for Radio and Television (abolished by order of the president in late 1990) which functioned more like a ministry, the distinction was hard to draw. Other differences were eroded as a result of changes made to the ministries in 1991. The most important distinction to be drawn is between the state committee as regulator and the ministry, especially the industrial ministry, as regulated. In practice, of course, the strength of ministerial power often hindered effective regulation. A number of more formal distinctions help explain why. First, the ministry was run on the principles of one-man management (*edinonachalie*) whereby decisions were formally adopted by the order (*prikaz*) of the minister himself. This gave the leading ministerial officials considerable power to direct their own organizations. In state committees, headed by a chairman, decision-making was formally collegial. Changes in the status of the ministry *kollegium*, however, aimed at incorporating republican leaders in the decision-making process, were intended to lead to diminution in the salience of this distinction. Second, ministries had branch jurisdiction and direct power over their subordinates, whereas state committees' jurisdiction cut across ministerial and departmental boundaries, and their decisions were put into effect by the minister's order. Third, ministries had direct responsibility for the performance of their subordinates until 1990, whereas state committees exercised only regulatory functions.

Industrial ministries

The industrial ministries were the institutional backbone of the 'administrative-command system' and were the object of criticism and reform efforts at many times in Soviet history. Some western and Soviet commentators even regard them as the most powerful institutions of the Soviet state which, particularly in the Brezhnev period, were able to function as largely independent fiefdoms. They maintained until the late 1980s very broad powers over resource allocation, scientific and technological development, the development of infrastructure, the environment, and many aspects of social policy. The influence of ministers was supported by their membership in bodies like the Central Committee of the Communist Party.

The efforts of reformers in the political leadership after 1985 to control ministerial power led to a number of changes in their number, structure, functions, personnel, methods of appointment, and relationship with other state bodies. From 1989 ministers were prevented from being members of the Supreme Soviet. However, despite repeated calls after 1987 by politicians for a new law regulating the ministries, the reforms of early 1991 did not fully clarify the ministries' functions.

Number

The number of industrial ministries declined considerably after 1985 as a result of several factors. First, many ministries were merged or had their functions transferred from union to republic subordination. Second, from 1989 ministries sought (and obtained) Council of Ministers and presidential approval to transform themselves into corporations and joint-stock companies. As a result, whereas there were fifty-seven ministries in the economic field in the early 1980s, out of which thirty-four were all-union branch industrial ministries, in the government in 1989 there were only twenty-seven economic ministries in total. In the government formed in 1991, there were only fourteen traditional industrial ministries, many of which were scheduled for liquidation in the following two years. Of the other economic ministries, many were new and designed to support market reform.

Functions

Ministerial functions and powers in the perestroika years were hotly contested. In the traditional command economy, enterprises were subject to direct administrative interference from ministry departments. The efforts of reforming politicians from 1985 were directed at changing ministerial behaviour from operational to regulative management of the sectors under their jurisdiction, while retaining for them a central role in securing state economic policy and in speeding technological development. After the adoption of the resolution on the ministries and the passage of the Law on the Enterprise in 1987, the scope for administrative action over enterprises was legally narrowed, and ministries were expected to manipulate enterprise performance through levers such as state orders, norm-setting, control figures, and deductions from profits. However, when ministries effectively used these powers to undermine the economic reform programme, their powers were cut back further in 1989. There was considerable confusion, not least among ministry officials, about their subsequent role.

Structure

The typical ministry contained the following subunits, although the changes, especially of 1990–91, altered the picture somewhat:

- The Minister was nominated by the Chairman of the Council of Ministers (in 1991 by the president) and approved by the Supreme Soviet. He sat as a member of the Council of Ministers (subsequently the Cabinet). Within the ministry he had a personal secretariat. He signed decisions of the ministry, *prikazy*, which had the force of law, binding on subordinate enterprises and, in some cases, on other ministries as well. He was generally a career member of the department he headed (though from 1985 there was some decline in the frequency of this background in appointments, with a growth in the number of ministers with party or military-industrial backgrounds).
- The branch council, or *kollegium* as it was known until 1988, consisted of members of ministerial departments and administrations and of directors of large enterprises and associations. In an effort to include the republics in central government decision-making, the branch councils in 1991 also contained representatives from economic agencies of republican governments. Decisions of the ministry could be taken in the name of the branch council, and the body had the right of appeal to the Cabinet of Ministers if it disagreed with the decision of the minister.

- There were generally two First Deputy Ministers and six Deputy Ministers who headed various functional departments of general competence within the ministry apparatus. These included planning, technical questions, finance, construction, and environmental protection. A number of Deputy Ministers also supervised 'line administrations' such as the *glavki* (chief administrations) or VPCS (industrial associations) which dealt with operational matters in industry. In 1987, as part of the desire to cut direct ministerial control over enterprises, the industrial associations were formally abolished and efforts were made to strengthen the functional departments. However, production departments were reformed inside the ministerial apparatus which tended to take over old 'line' functions.

The most important structural change in the ministries in the late Soviet period came in 1990 with the combination of self-abolition and transformation into state concerns – as was the case in the gas industry – or the creation within the ministerial structure of associations, corporations, or joint-stock companies. In the huge Ministry of Metallurgy, for example, 25 such sub-structures were created, supposedly as a prelude to privatization.

Personnel

Keeping control over the size of the bureaucracy was among the most salient issues in Soviet politics almost from its inception. If the number of ministerial personnel includes the total number of employees, the figures can be quite staggering. Taking the Ministry of Metallurgy again, it latterly employed a total of 2,753,000 workers, of whom 2,150,000 were in industry. The number of staff in the central apparatus was obviously much smaller, though this did not prevent many critics from accusing the central apparatus of being overblown, incompetent and resistant to reform. Defenders of Soviet state administration, however, attacked the obsession with numbers and suggested that in comparison with other industrial countries, the Soviet bureaucracy, including the ministerial bureaucracy, was actually too small.

A ministry generally contained between 1,000 and 2,000 employees, not including clerical workers, although from 1988 there were cutbacks of up to 30 per cent of total staff. In the central government, for example, staff of ministries and state committees combined fell from 107,000 in 1985 to 85,000 in 1988, although the level stabilized thereafter. The bulk of those released found jobs in other areas of economic administration, often within the newly created associations and corporations. In one notorious case, redundant ministry staff were found doing the same job in a specially created 'research institute'.

State committees

The state committees, especially such a key economic body as Gosplan, were at the core of efforts by the political élite to control the Soviet state. As regulatory bodies, their status was increased after 1965 and in 1978 when they became full members of the Council of Ministers. Although some state committees were abolished during perestroika, new ones were created so their total number remained by 1991 much as it was in the early 1980s. An example of a new state committee was one for environmental protection established in 1988. However, the state committees were also heavily criticized for the weakness of their regulatory activity. Despite repeated calls for improved plan coordination in the 1970s and 1980s, for example, Gosplan was not able to prevent industrial ministries from manipulating plan targets favourably to their interests.

The state committee system was very broad in scope. Committees varied widely in size, importance, and jurisdiction. The most important economic committees were Gosplan, the State Committee for Supply and Material Resources, the State Committee for Prices, and the State Committee for Labour and Social Questions. All of these were substantially reorganized in structure, functions and personnel in the last years of the Soviet era. In Gosplan, for example, personnel was cut from 2,560 in 1987 to 1,095 in 1989. Other important state committees included those for state security (KGB), for press and radio, and for religious affairs.

The central function of the state committee was to exercise general leadership in areas within their jurisdiction, by taking decisions which were obligatory for all relevant ministries – though not directly for sub-ministerial bodies. Gosplan, for example, devised and approved general plan targets and investment budgets which were handed down to individual ministries to be put into operation. The State Committee for Labour and Social Questions, for its part, worked on devising pay scales. Many state committees were structured internally with departments corresponding to the ministries with which they interacted, and there was some evidence of links between the two. As with the ministries, the state committees also found it difficult to define their role in the period of rapid economic reform which undermined many of their functions.

Republican ministerial bodies

It was at the republican level that growth occurred in the ministerial system between 1985 and 1991,

Feliks Dzerzhinsky, a revolutionary from a Polish gentry family and the first head of the Soviet secret police

both in terms of number of personnel employed and in terms of power and influence. Some of this growth was the result of the efforts by the Gorbachev leadership to institutionalize perestroika at the republican level, where it was agreed the central ministries and other authorities had held excessive sway in the past. Numerous enterprises of all-union subordination were transferred to republican authorities. However, in many cases, republican Councils of Ministers were in sharp institutional conflict with the centre over jurisdiction and resources, and republican governments such as that of the RSFSR took a noticeably more anti-ministerial line consolidating all industrial ministries within their territory into a single Ministry for Industry. Disputes between republican bodies and union ministries over enterprises were commonplace in the last years of the Soviet era, and the Russian Federation in particular scored a notable victory as a result of its role in ending the miners' strike of April 1991, when all coal mines were transferred to its control. The expected role of the republics in economic administration was also considerably increased by the draft Union Treaty which was to be signed on 20 August 1991, and this was probably the reason why only one union-level industrial minister made known his opposition to the coup of 18–21 August. The attack on union ministries intensified following the collapse of the coup; almost all were abolished in November 1991, and many of their personnel made unemployed. However, the difficulties of reforming the former Soviet economy are evident from the fact that a large number of former personnel who had operated at the all-union level found positions inside the apparatus of the Russian government. Its Ministry of Industry contains departments which have been compared to the old branch ministries.

SDW

The Committee for State Security (KGB)

The initials KGB are the Russian abbreviation for Committee for State Security, from 1954 to 1991 the main Soviet organization for national security at home and intelligence operations abroad. It was the successor of the Cheka (All-Russian Extraordinary Commission for Combating Counter-Revolution and Sabotage, 1917–22), the GPU (State Political Administration, 1922–23), the OGPU (United State Political Administration, 1923–34), the NKVD (People's Commissariat for Internal Affairs, 1934–43), the NKGB (People's Commissariat for State Security, 1943–46), the MGB (Ministry for State Security, 1946–53) and the MVD (Ministry of Internal Affairs, 1953–54).

In addition to its secret-police functions the Cheka was also in charge of corrective labour camps (later within the GULag system), internal security troops, and press censorship. In 1922 most of these functions passed to the NKVD, to which the GPU was made subordinate. While the OGPU was then separated from the NKVD, this change was reversed in 1934. Although the relevant division of the NKVD was then called the Main Administration for State Security (GUCB), this name was not widely used, and common practice was to refer to the secret police simply as the NKVD. An analogous situation arose in 1953–54, until the KGB was created as a body with ministry status, again separated from the MVD. Although formally part of the USSR Council of Ministers, and thus of the government, in practice the KGB reported primarily to the top communist party organs. In 1989–90, however, this apparently began to change, as accountability to the government and the USSR Supreme Soviet was introduced.

The KGB and its predecessors were headed by F.E. Dzerzhinsky (1917–26), V.R. Menzhinsky (1926–34), G.G. Yagoda (1934–36), N.I. Yezhov (1936–38), L.P. Beria (1938–43 and 1953), V.N. Merkulov (1943–46), V.S. Abakumov (1946–51), S.D. Ignat'ev (1951–53), I.A. Serov (1954–58), A.N. Shelepin (1958–61), V.Ye. Semichastny (1961–67), Yu.V. Andropov (1967–82), V.V. Fedorchuk (1982), V.M. Chebrikov (1982–88), V.A. Kryuchkov (1988–91), and V.V. Bakatin (1991).

For its internal security functions the Cheka, as the Bolsheviks' 'punitive arm', was given very wide powers to detect and suppress 'counter-revolutionary elements' of all sorts. The OGPU concentrated mainly on the Church, 'socially alien' individuals, and former members of opposition parties; then, from 1928, on entrepreneurs and traders, members of the pre-1917 intelligentsia, and – in a series of vast operations – on the peasantry, whom it forcibly collectivized and 'de-kulakized'. The NKVD carried out Stalin's Great Terror of 1934–38, becoming an economic empire on the strength of camp labour, deported numerous Poles, Ukrainians and Balts in 1939–40 and a million Soviet Germans in 1941, and ruthlessly enforced political control in the armed forces and civilian life during the Second World War. The NKGB and MGB, under Beria's protégés, deported to distant territories whole nationalities in 1943–46 for alleged collaboration with the Germans, simultaneously transferring

Stalin's Great Terror

During the Great Terror of 1936–38 Stalin's oppression reached its peak. Leading members of the Communist Party and state officials were prime targets, but no one was safe. Wild denunciations and arbitrary arrests were commonplace:

On 10 August 1937 [member of the Politburo] Kaganovich wrote to the NKVD demanding the arrest of ten responsible officials in the People's Commissariat of Transport. The only grounds were that he thought their behaviour suspicious. They were arrested as spies and shot. He wrote in all thirty-two personal letters to [head of the NKVD] Yezhov, demanding the arrest of eighty-three transport executives.

The North Donets railway was the only line not involved in these sweeping arrests of early 1937. In August, the heads of the line were called to

Moscow and instructed to find saboteurs. An estimate by the Director of Locomotive Service of the line is that about 1,700 out of the 45,000 employees were arrested within months. In mid-November he himself was called to the NKVD and asked how he proposed to end sabotage. As he was unable to think of any cases of sabotage – the line being an exceptionally efficient one – he was bitterly harangued and during the next wave of arrests was pulled in, on 2 December 1937, without a warrant or charge.

His wife and six-year-old son were thrown out of their house two days after his arrest, and he was subjected to severe interrogation, with beatings, together with a number of other prisoners, including several station-masters and the deputy head of the line.

From: Robert Conquest, *The Great Terror* (1968)

suspected collaborators and 'alien elements' from Soviet territories occupied by the Germans, and imprisoning civilians and prisoners of war returning from Germany. They also launched a new general terror in 1949, among the chief targets of which were 'rootless cosmopolitans' (mainly Jews) and former supporters of Zhdanov in Leningrad. On Stalin's death in 1953 Beria used the MVD as his base in his bid for power. His arrest and subsequent execution led to the reduction of KGB powers and its subjection to tight bureaucratic administration to prevent any future escape from party control or deployment in leadership power struggles. Mass terror had been ended in 1953, and torture, previously legalized,

was banned. These setbacks were compounded by Khrushchev's de-Stalinization policy and his claims that the USSR no longer had any political prisoners. Under his successors the KGB's status was restored, and in 1973 its head, Andropov, entered the Politburo. From its grass-roots offices in every workplace of any size the KGB tried to prevent or combat political crime and dissent. The rise since the late 1950s of many types of organized dissent presented it with a serious challenge.

The KGB's role in foreign intelligence (much more central than that of the GRU, the military intelligence organization) became very important after the USSR came fully into international politics in the early 1940s. Agents operated around the world under cover of postings as diplomats, trade officials, journalists, and so on; a Soviet ambassador may not have known who the senior KGB officer (or *resident*) in his embassy was, and had no control over him. From 1945 an average of about fifteen Soviet agents a year, most of them KGB officers, were expelled for espionage or related activities, from a wide range of countries. The organization appeared to have had about half a million employees, of whom some 90,000 were officers, 240,000 were border and internal security troops, and the rest support staff.

From 1988 to 1991 the KGB was subject to increasingly strong public criticism for its record as a ruthless secret police, and claimed no longer to carry out this function. Its main domestic tasks were now said to be counter-intelligence, protecting the Constitution, combating organized crime and terrorism, assisting in the exculpation of innocent victims of past purges, and guarding senior officials, Soviet borders, and high-security sites. Also, cuts in personnel began, especially of some of the border guards

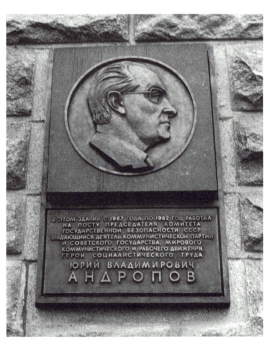

The memorial plaque to Yury Vladimirovich Andropov on the wall of the Lubyanka headquarters of the KGB in Moscow. Andropov, a former secretary of the Central Committee of the CPSU, headed the KGB from 1967 to 1982 before returning to the party Secretariat early in the latter year. He subsequently led the Communist Party from November 1982 until his death in February 1984

Two contrasting heads of the security service. Vladimir Kryuchkov (top), KGB Chairman from 1988 who turned against Gorbachev and his reforms and was a leading figure in the August 1991 coup. He was succeeded by Vadim Bakatin (bottom) who made strenuous efforts to bring the KGB under democratic political control, but whose chairmanship of the organization did not survive the collapse of the Soviet Union at the end of 1991

(who were transferred to the MVD security troops). Sharp political divisions appeared among those KGB officers who entered the political arena.

Towards the end of the Soviet period, hardline elements in the KGB began to manipulate the organization for factional political ends. Vigorous efforts were made to recruit prominent members of oppositional groups; Boris Yel'tsin's telephone conversations were systematically tapped and transcribed; and in summer 1991 the central KGB apparatus was used by the KGB Chairman V.A. Kryuchkov (b. 1924) as a major organizational base for the attempted coup of 18–21 August. In the wake of the coup Kryuchkov was arrested and the KGB was renamed the Interstate Security Service (ISS) under V.V. Bakatin (b. 1937). While a very small Russian KGB subordinate to President Yel'tsin of Russia already existed before the coup, Bakatin radically decentralized the main organization, putting much of it under the jurisdiction of the republics. He also dismembered it by hiving off large sections like foreign intelligence and the border guards, which became independent organizations. In November 1991 the ISS was abolished and all its components on Russian territory were incorporated into an enormously expanded Russian KGB. Very soon the latter was joined to the MVD and renamed the Ministry of Security and Internal Affairs. However, the Russian parliament rejected this merger and in February 1992 it was abandoned and the Russian KGB became the Ministry of Security headed until the summer of 1993 by Viktor Barannikov (b. 1940). It remains a powerful organization, with its personnel and core structures little changed, especially in the provinces. In the fourteen other successor states of the USSR, however, the old KGB structures and, apparently, most of their links with Moscow, have been destroyed, although many former KGB personnel now work for the new security agencies which have been created in each country.   PBR

Elections and representation

ELECTIONS

Open and competitive elections had not been a feature of the tsarist government, and they were not a feature of its Soviet successor until the late 1980s. The elections that took place to the Constituent Assembly in November 1917 were, by general consent, a fair reflection of the wishes of the voters; but although they resulted in a large majority for moderate socialists, the Assembly was dissolved in January 1918 and the Soviet government thereafter permitted no direct challenge to its authority. The outward forms of democracy were generally maintained, at least after 1936, when all citizens were admitted to the franchise on an equal basis and voting became secret. The 1977 Constitution repeated these provisions: all who had reached the age of eighteen had the right to vote (Article 96), each citizen had a single vote and exercised it on an equal basis with other voters (Article 97), and voting was direct and secret (Articles 98 and 99).

In practice, the electoral process was closely controlled by the party authorities, and from the 1930s onwards a single slate of communist and non-party candidates was regularly returned with majorities in excess of 90 per cent. In the 1984 national elections, the last under the old system, turnout had supposedly reached 99.99 per cent and support for the single list of candidates for the two chambers of the Supreme Soviet was recorded as 99.94 and 99.95 per cent respectively. These figures were misleading in several respects. They excluded residents, particularly of the larger cities, who lacked the legal right of abode; and they excluded registered voters who had obtained an absentee certificate allowing them to cast their vote elsewhere, often with no intention of doing so. There were also more straightforward abuses, including parents voting for other family members and officials voting for potential absentees.

Voters who did appear at the polling station were induced to cast a favourable ballot by several other circumstances. One of these was 'passive voting'. The ballot paper invariably contained a single name, with instructions that the voter should 'cross out the names of all the candidates against whom he wished to vote'. A favourable vote was recorded by dropping the ballot paper, unmarked, into the ballot box. A negative vote, however, required the elector to make use of the booth at the side of the polling station in a manner that was likely to attract attention. The single list of candidates was put forward by the Communist Party or another party-controlled organization, which alone enjoyed the right of nomination; and the whole process was managed by electoral commissions on which there was a strong party presence. About three-quarters of the deputies at national level were normally party members, and about half were workers or collective farmers.

Electoral arrangements of this restrictive kind came under increasing criticism from the 1960s onwards, and Gorbachev's speech at the 1986 Party Congress accepted that there would have to be 'correctives'. After a limited experiment in June 1987,

Right. *An elector casting his vote in the Russian republican election of 1990*

in which about 4 per cent of deputies were returned to local soviets from enlarged constituencies with some degree of choice, a more substantial reform was agreed by the 19th Party Conference in July 1988 and legislated the following December. Under the new law, the right of nomination was extended to meetings of voters and an unlimited number of candidates could be put forward. Candidates were required to put forward a 'programme' of their future activity, and could appoint up to ten staff to assist them; they also had 'as a rule' to live or work in the constituency. Voters, for their part, were required to pass through properly appointed booths before casting their vote, and were prohibited from voting on behalf of others.

The first-ever competitive Soviet elections took place on the basis of this law in March 1989. Somewhat controversially, the new supreme legislature, the Congress of People's Deputies, was to be made up of representatives of various public organizations (including the CPSU) as well as deputies elected from ordinary constituencies. In the end, 880 candidates contested the 750 seats that had been reserved for public organizations, but 2,884 candidates were nominated to contest the 1,500 constituencies, with up to twelve candidates competing for a single seat. Public interest was high, and the level of turnout

was 89.8 per cent. In the event, 87.6 per cent of the new deputies were CPSU members, which was a considerable increase on the Party's previous level of representation, but many leading officials were defeated including the prime ministers of Latvia and Lithuania, the mayors of Moscow and Kiev, and the regional party secretary (a Politburo member) in Leningrad. Boris Yel'tsin enjoyed a personal tri-

Votes for Boris Yel'tsin in the presidential election, 12 June 1991

Votes for Boris Yel'tsin (%)

▨	15.2–50.0
▨	50.1–55.0
▨	55.1–60.0
▨	60.1–65.0
▨	65.1–84.8

umph in Moscow, winning nearly 90 per cent of the vote against a party-sponsored opponent.

The republican elections that took place in 1990 showed a similar pattern, with heavy defeats for party officials and sweeping successes for radicals and nationalists. In Lithuania, Latvia and Estonia, which voted in February and March, candidates supported by the Popular Fronts enjoyed a high level of support and formed non-communist administrations. The Slav republics voted in early March, with the radical 'Democratic Russia' coalition taking over 20 per cent of seats in the Russian Congress of People's Deputies and with a corresponding level of success for radicals in Ukraine and Belorussia. The Armenian elections, in May, and the Georgian elections, in October, led to the formation of nationalist administrations. There was much less change in the Central Asian republics, and the level of turnout – over 90 per cent – suggested that traditional practices still exercised some influence. In the first-ever elections for the new post of Russian President in June 1991, Boris Yel'tsin was elected with 57.3 per cent of the vote in a contest with five opponents. Although many procedural issues remained to be resolved, it appeared that political office would increasingly require the freely expressed consent of the electorate.   SLW

'ALL POWER TO THE SOVIETS'

The Soviets of People's Deputies, representative institutions officially referred to as 'organs of state power', originated in the revolutions of 1905 and 1917. At that time they were essentially strike committees of workers' and soldiers' representatives, which sprang up to co-ordinate the revolutionary activity. Their significance was recognized by Lenin, who saw them as genuinely proletarian institutions, and campaigned at the head of the Bolshevik party in 1917 under the slogan 'All power to the soviets'. During the interval between the February and October revolutions, the Petrograd Soviet wielded real influence in competition with the Provisional Government, and the II All-Russian Congress of Soviets endorsed the Revolution on 25 October 1917. The Congress of Soviets became nominally the supreme organ of state power in the new political system, and in the ensuing years soviets (councils) were established throughout the country as the basic institutions in the state to which they gave their name. The soviets thus performed an important symbolic function in the USSR's political rhetoric, linking the evolving present with the country's revolutionary tradition – even though the formal, highly structured and carefully controlled institutions of Soviet rule shared little but the name with the

spontaneous creations of the revolutionary workers.

From December 1988, with the creation of new supreme representative bodies (the Congress of People's Deputies and revamped Supreme Soviets of the USSR and the various republics) and the introduction of genuine contested elections, the slogan of 'All power to the soviets' enjoyed a brief revival and the Soviets of People's Deputies at all levels acquired real power once again, at the expense of both the ministerial system of state administration and the Communist Party. Their actions in passing legislation that challenged the edicts of the emergent presidential government were instrumental in precipitating the crisis that led to the collapse of communist rule.   RJH

SELECTION OF DEPUTIES

The soviets existed from the 1920s until the early 1990s at all levels in the administrative hierarchy, although their political importance fluctuated. The system underwent significant development under the political reforms introduced in the perestroika era by Mikhail Gorbachev, and was further modified in the wake of the collapse of communist rule. From 1 December 1988 until 26 December 1991, the system was headed by the USSR Congress of People's Deputies and its associated USSR Supreme Soviet, with Supreme Soviets in the Union and Autonomous Republics, and over 50,000 local soviets at regional, city, urban and rural district, settlement and village levels. They were elected by the adult population, in an electoral process that traditionally was carefully guided by the Communist Party of the Soviet Union (CPSU). In the process of democratization elections were transformed into genuine contests for position and power, which Boris Yel'tsin exploited with notable effectiveness in the spring of 1989.

The soviets consisted of representatives, the people's deputies, numbering perhaps 30 at village level, and 2,250 in the USSR Congress of People's Deputies, which in turn elected from its own membership 542 deputies to the USSR Supreme Soviet – 271 in each chamber: the Soviet of the Union, and the Soviet of the Nationalities.

There were considerably more than two million deputies at any time, and until the late 1980s a contrived turnover rate of some 50 per cent enabled upwards of five million citizens to serve in a decade. That high rate of managed renewal points to the educational role of the soviets: they were 'schools of communism' (and hence were involved in developing the political culture), rather than organs that debated and influenced policy. That role began to change under the impact of effective elections

The Moscow Kremlin during the Third Congress of People's Deputies, March 1990

and the demise of Communist Party monopoly rule in 1990.

Although intended to serve as representative institutions, the form of 'representation' in the soviets was essentially sociological rather than political: candidates were carefully selected to achieve an appropriate social balance before the electors were invited to endorse the choice at the poll. This thorough vetting and balancing of social categories was done by the political authorities (ultimately the local party committee), and resulted in the broadly representative composition of the soviets; the popularity of the representatives with their electors was always in doubt, however. Local party and state dignitaries formed a core among the deputies, supported by leading workers (in Stalin's day often Stakhanovites) for whom membership was a reward for achievement in production, regardless of their political or administrative aptitudes or even inclinations. Such qualities may have permitted them to perform as a rubber stamp, but they were not conducive to the creation of effective organs of political representation.

The extension of access to the electoral process in the reforms of the late 1980s resulted in electoral success for individuals who enjoyed the confidence of the electors, but whose social composition appeared less 'representative': fewer women, young deputies and workers; in some cases more communists. Even before the abolition of the Communist Party's political monopoly (and its prohibition in the autumn of 1991), certain groups that were previously excluded from the political process – religious and formerly dissident organizations in particular – acquired a new voice within the evolving system. Deputies newly empowered with the legitimacy of a popular mandate attained a chance never before enjoyed to respond to the will of the voters.

FUNCTIONS OF THE SOVIETS

The formal meetings ('sessions') of soviets were held four or six times a year (twice for the USSR Congress of People's Deputies), and in this forum the deputies performed one of their important functions: giving legal force to policy. Throughout almost the whole of the Soviet period, this was an essentially symbolic (although not irrelevant) function, since policy was determined by the Communist Party and simply endorsed by the 'organs of state power'. Soviet commentators emphasized that party committees had no power, and that their decisions were not legally binding on citizens until given the force of law by a decision of the appropriate soviet; political reality, however, meant that the soviets had no option but to comply with the Party's wishes. Legislation, drafted by party bodies, was 'debated' by the deputies, among whom party members were frequently in a majority, passed unanimously by a show of hands, and then implemented by the administrative apparatus in which party members occupied strategic positions.

Under Stalin the soviets had declined into a moribund state. From 1957 onwards the political leadership repeatedly turned its attention to the soviets, with lengthy statements and waves of new legislation, aimed at revitalizing them and finding for them an appropriate role in a society that was becoming more complex and diversified, better educated and less amenable to coercion. From the 1950s Soviet scholars and even politicians came to admit that a vast range of opinions and specific interests existed, apart from the assumed basic goal of building communism, and that the task of the political system was to co-ordinate and aggregate these interests in the policy-making process. Soviets and their deputies had a role to play in this.

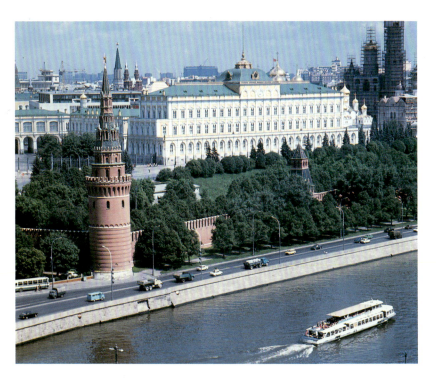

A view from across the River Moskva of the Kremlin building which housed the Supreme Soviet

but inefficient and increasingly corrupt bureaucrats, with whom the deputy would intervene to sort out grievances. This role was enhanced in the Brezhnev era by the selection of better educated, more experienced and more energetic representatives, who were given basic training in the structures and procedures of the Soviet state. Their status was boosted by legislation that conferred a measure of authority formerly lacking, and gave the right to demand fair treatment and an efficient response to petitions on constituents' behalf.

More formally, the majority of deputies took part in the work of the permanent (or standing) commissions, which supervised the administration of health, social welfare, budgeting, industry, transport, agriculture and other specific areas. These bodies, formed by the deputies from among their own number, traditionally possessed certain powers of inspection in checking the efficiency of management. The deputies were thus involved in behind-the-scenes monitoring of policy-making and performance, and acquired some expertise and experience in the functioning of the state administration.

A crucial intention of the reforms from the mid-1980s was to bring the state administration under democratic control, although success was limited. Previously the soviets, although called 'organs of state power', had very little input into the planning process and virtually no authority to challenge the decisions of industrial ministries whose enterprises functioned on their territory; under perestroika the administrators hindered the development of co-operative and private enterprise by simply refusing the supply of raw materials or not allowing premises to be used by such economic undertakings. The legacy of the soviets and their administrative organs was therefore one in which the public could have little confidence. RJH

Such thinking became commonplace in the perestroika era, and the soviets were involved in its implementation. Their ineffectual, passive role was rejected as they increasingly served as forums at which party decisions, including decisions on appointment to ministerial and other positions formerly staffed through the *nomenklatura* system, were challenged and alternatives were discussed and argued over. This development reflected both the positive efforts to shift power from the state and party administrative apparatus to institutions that potentially commanded popular support and the willingness of a new type of representative to use the soviets for the purpose of advancing fresh ideas and policies, often challenging the establishment.

Accordingly, the USSR Supreme Soviet, which met for two sessions annually, each lasting three or four months (rather than a few days, as previously) already exercised genuine policy-making powers, and the party leadership could no longer force through its proposals: in significant areas traditional party policy could even be reversed. Similar developments took place at the republican and regional levels, and clashes between elected soviets and unelected party bodies – and between soviets at different levels – occurred as the new political system emerged.

Apart from their law-making functions, the deputies also represented their constituents informally, a role that had been rather more significant than the legislative function. In the complex bureaucracy, many needs were left unattended to, and a role emerged for the deputy as intermediary between the essentially powerless citizenry and the powerful

PARTY–STATE RELATIONS

Traditionally in Soviet politics, the whole of state administration was 'guided' by the Communist Party: in fact, all organs of state were manipulated by the Party, using a variety of mechanisms. Interlocking membership between party and state institutions ensured that party policy was invariably endorsed by the state bodies, which enjoyed no independent policy-making powers.

A redistribution of political power took place under Gorbachev, which accelerated after the collapse of communist rule that followed the putsch of August 1991. With the election of reformers and representatives of other, non-communist political movements and alternative parties, the Soviet Union began to acquire a system more in conformity with Western traditions. The USSR and republican constitutions were amended in the spring of 1990 to allow for the formation of parties other than the CPSU, and a range of new parties and movements – some splitting from the CPSU, some forming around specific goals (such as independence from the USSR) – competed electorally for control of the law-making agencies of the state.

Spectacular successes by nationalists in the Baltic republics, Georgia, Moldova and parts of Ukraine, in particular, gave control over the state legislative institutions to non-communist and anti-communist forces, who used the democratic process to remove some of the Communist Party's traditional prerogatives and rights. At the all-union level, coalitions of deputies along policy or ideological lines, while offering the hope of the emergence of new, broadly-based parties, in effect served to polarize debate and hindered the establishment of conventional parliamentary politics. The resignation of the Russian Supreme Soviet Chairman, Boris Yel'tsin, from the Communist Party in July 1990, on the grounds that in that position he should stand above parties, was a significant event in the developing debate over the merits of presidential or parliamentary rule. RJH

Constitution

Lenin chairing a meeting of the Council of People's Commissars, 1922

Soviet Constitutions always served as a juridical statement of the current political and social structure. In terms of form they were entrenched, in that their amendment required a two-thirds majority of the members of the legislature. In terms of substance their main functions were: to confer and distribute legislative, executive, judicial and political power; to provide a bill of rights for citizens; and (until 1991) to delimit the scope of the respective authority of the Union and the republics. The USSR Constitution provided the federal framework, while the Union and autonomous republics had their own constitutions which tended to be very similar in structure.

A noteworthy feature of perestroika was the frequent constitutional amendments which it seemed to entail, a process that culminated in the disappearance of the Union in December 1991 and thus of its constitution.

THE 1918 RSFSR CONSTITUTION

The first RSFSR Constitution, adopted by the V All-Russian Congress of Soviets on 10 July 1918, consolidated the tactical victories of the Bolsheviks. Its first part repeated previous decrees stating that all power was in the hands of the soviets (councils) of workers', peasants' and soldiers' deputies, and abolished the private ownership of land and natural resources; the second part listed basic freedoms (conscience, the press, association) and duties (labour and defence) and outlawed privileges which might be used to the detriment of the Revolution; the third part dealt with the organization of the central authority. There was no single elected head of state; supreme power was stated to be vested in the Congress of Soviets composed of representatives of local soviets. This elected the Central Executive Committee (CEC) with up to 200 members, with supreme legislative and administrative power and with authority to appoint the Council of People's Commissars (CPC) composed of eighteen ministries. Local government was to be carried out by a hierarchy of councils (soviets), each with its executive committee for routine administration. Universal suffrage was introduced but was denied to those who employed labour for profit or lived on unearned income, and to 'middlemen' and the clergy. There was no express monopoly of the Bolshevik party. From 1919 to 1922 similar constitutions were adopted in Belorussia, Ukraine, Azerbaijan, Armenia and Georgia and (with variations) in Central Asia.

THE 1924 FEDERAL CONSTITUTION

The various republics united in a formal Federation of 30 December 1922, the Constitution of which was ratified on 13 January 1924. By this, power was

(in theory) merely delegated to the Union and each republic retained the right to secede. The Union was given full capacity in international matters together with control of economic planning, the budget, the armed forces, transport, the judiciary and the basic principles of law in virtually all fields. Supreme authority was still said to be vested in the annual meeting of the indirectly elected Congress of Soviets. Its CEC, however, contained features which were to persist – a two-chamber system consisting of the federal Soviet of the Union (representing the population as a whole) and the Soviet of Nationalities (representing the major ethnic groups in the constituent republics). Its Presidium of (ultimately) 27 members formed a collective head of state with full legislative authority, but accountable to the CEC, and with power to appoint the CPC (that is, the government). No bill of rights was included, those of the republican constitutions remaining in force. During the 1920s, Russia, Belorussia and Ukraine brought their own constitutions into conformity, and there were certain structural changes in the Turkmen and Uzbek republics.

THE 1936 STALIN CONSTITUTION

The Stalin Constitution of 5 December 1936 defined the USSR as 'a socialist state of workers and peasants' and – for the first time – described as their 'vanguard' the Communist Party of the Soviet Union (CPSU). It reaffirmed the socialist ownership of the means of production and enacted a federal bill of rights and duties. Again, in theory, the federal power was delegated and limited, and the right of secession persisted; in practice federal authority was supreme and all-embracing. For the previous Congress of Soviets there was substituted a two-chamber Supreme Soviet with power to amend the Constitution by a two-thirds majority vote. In fact there was no record of any law having failed to secure unanimity. There was no provision for judicial review of the constitutionality of laws. The republican and local organs of power, appropriately adjusted, paralleled the federal structure. In 1940 the Baltic states of Estonia, Latvia and Lithuania were joined to the USSR and Moldavia was created a union republic. So also was the Karelian–Finnish Republic, but in 1956 this was returned to the status of an autonomous republic within the RSFSR. After that and until the collapse of the Soviet Union there were 15 union republics. In addition to the Russian republic they were the: Armenian SSR, Azerbaijan SSR, Belorussian SSR, Estonian SSR, Georgian SSR, Kazakh SSR, Kirgiz SSR, Latvian SSR, Lithuanian SSR, Moldavian SSR, Tadzhik SSR, Turkmen SSR, Ukrainian SSR, Uzbek SSR.

THE USSR CONSTITUTION 1977–88

The de-Stalinization process of the 1950s led, after long delays, to a new draft constitution of May 1977. After widespread public discussion (in which, according to Brezhnev, four-fifths of the adult population took part) and some amendment, it was adopted in October 1977. It was not radically new, stressing in the preamble the 'continuity of ideas and principles' with its three predecessors. It was, however, designed to reflect post-war social and industrial changes, to incorporate the effect of much post-Stalin legislation, and to lay greater emphasis on individual rights.

The first part described the social and political principles of the system. The USSR was defined as 'a socialist state of all the people, expressing the will and interests of the workers, peasants and the intelligentsia and of the working people of all the country's nations and nationalities'. All power was said to belong to the people and was exercised through the Soviet of People's Deputies; the latter could, however, submit matters to nationwide referendum. The state and its agencies were to operate on the basis of socialist legality and to ensure the rights and liberties of citizens. The preamble recited the growth of the CPSU's leading role and, by Article 6, the Party was formally recognized as 'the leading and guiding force of Soviet society, the nucleus of its political system and of state and public organizations'. The economic system was based on socialist ownership of the means of production; all land, minerals, forests, and so on, were owned by the state; private property (called 'personal') was based on earned income and limited to housing, personal effects and the like. The earlier slogan 'he who does not work, neither shall he eat' was replaced by: 'From each according to his ability, to each according to his work'. The provisions on the social system promised the industrialization of agriculture and the development of public services.

The theme of state and individual was developed in the second part, thereby (unlike the Stalin Constitution) preceding the provisions on the state structure. This part laid down the principle of complete equality and lists a bill of rights – work, health care, social security, housing, education, freedom to criticize, and freedom from arrest. Freedom of the press and of assembly was granted for the same aim as before: '. . . in conformity with the people's interests and for the purpose of strengthening and developing the socialist system'. These rights and liberties were declared inseparable from the performance of civic duties: labour, safeguarding the interests of the state, military service, and so on.

The third part (the state structure) reiterated the federal nature of the Union of fifteen republics, confirming the right to secede but (by Article 73) giving wide power to the USSR itself over its constituent parts. Some union republics were subdivided into autonomous republics and regions; thus the RSFSR (the largest) had sixteen of the former and five of the latter organized on ethnic bases. Within federal limits each republic had its own constitution (that of the RSFSR was adopted in April 1978), internal sovereignty and (in theory) the power to enter into international treaties.

The power to enact federal statutes (the highest form of legal act) lay with the two-chamber Supreme Soviet of the USSR, which could also – by a two-thirds majority – adopt amendments to the Constitution. As in previous decades, however, the legislature met for about two weeks a year and until 1988 seemed invariably to act with enthusiastic unanimity.

The role of Head of State was still filled, not by an individual, but by the Supreme Soviet's elected Presidium (a Chairman and thirty-seven members), which acted by edict, amending statutes if necessary (subject to later ratification by the Supreme Soviet); in practice the bulk of legislative activity consisted of parliamentary approval of Presidium edicts. This body also supervised the constitutionality of laws (there was no independent review), and ratified treaties. The government (Council of Ministers) was appointed by, and accountable to, the Supreme Soviet; within its areas of competence it could issue binding regulations.

Appropriate constitutions were then adopted by the Union and autonomous republics: within their competence, their Supreme Soviets exercised similar functions and appointed similar bodies. The local authorities operated, within their territory, through permanent executive committees.

In practice many of the constitutional provisions bore only a tenuous relation to political realities and the whole machinery was controlled by the CPSU.

THE USSR CONSTITUTION 1988–91

Perestroika provoked profound changes in the constitutional structure of the Union and in its relationship with the republics. It also advanced a new juridical theory of its own validity. In place of the 'withering-away of state and law' doctrine of the past, both political and legislative texts announced the creation of a *pravovoe gosudarstvo*; this is a Russian version of the German *Rechtsstaat* and is here translated 'law-governed state'. At first the epithet 'socialist' was added to the noun, but the later Russian legislation chose 'democratic'. This section describes the constitutional changes in the

USSR and the republics from 1988 to 1992, then explains the theory and implementation of the doctrine of the law-governed state, and concludes with the 'war of laws' and the death of the Union.

Constitutional changes

Legislature · Major constitutional amendments were adopted by the Supreme Soviet on 1 December 1988, setting up two legislators in the USSR. Supreme legislative sovereignty was conferred on the Congress of People's Deputies, the 'highest organ of state power'. It was supreme for several reasons: it could legislate on anything; it alone could deal with certain fundamental matters such as the national-state structure and the basic questions of domestic and foreign policy; it alone could call a referendum; it could annul Supreme Soviet statutes; by a two-thirds majority of its members it could override conclusions of the Committee of Constitutional Supervision (below); and (by the same majority) it and it alone could amend the current or enact a new Constitution – it was thus the only body with power to alter its own powers. Nothing expressly allowed Congress to delegate to the Supreme Soviet its own exclusive powers, but since it was the 'highest organ' perhaps it could do so; and in fact it did so delegate the task of electing the first members of the Committee for Constitutional Supervision. Congress consisted of 2,250 deputies, one-third elected by the people on a territorial basis, one-third on a national-territorial basis, and one-third elected by social organizations, including the Party.

From among its members, the Congress elected the 542 members of the bicameral Supreme Soviet – the standing legislature holding two annual sessions of about four months each. Only these two organs could enact statutes strictly so called (*zakony*), although other organs were constitutionally empowered to issue subordinate but general legal norms.

President · The Constitutional amendments of 14 March 1990 created the office of President and greatly curtailed the powers of the Supreme Soviet's Presidium (above all that of legislating by edict). In international relations the president represented the USSR and negotiated and signed treaties. Within the Union he had several important powers in both law-making and executive spheres. It was he who signed legislative bills and could return them unsigned and with objections to the Supreme Soviet, which then needed a two-thirds majority in both chambers to override the presidential veto. He was empowered to issue edicts (*ukazy*) which had binding force throughout the country. He could declare a state of emergency (with the consent of the relevant republic's legislature or, failing that, of the USSR Supreme Soviet) with, if necessary, direct presidential rule. He put forward candidates for the offices of Prime Minister, Procurator General, Supreme Court President and others, and could propose to the Supreme Soviet that the government resign. He was Commander-in-Chief of the Armed Forces and appointed the High Command, could declare a general mobilization and introduce martial law in specific localities. He was assisted by two 'cabinets': the Presidential Council which consisted of his appointees and the Prime Minister; and the Council of the Federation to deal with union/republic issues and comprising the heads of the union republics.

The president was to be directly elected for five years and to serve up to two terms; he could be impeached by a two-thirds vote of Congress. In the event of his death or illness in office, the powers were to pass to the vice-president. The first (and last) Union President, M.S. Gorbachev, was not elected directly but, as a transitional measure, was appointed by the Congress. On 19 August 1991 the Vice-President (G.I. Yanaev, b.1937) announced that, because of the President's inability to perform his duties for health reasons, a state of emergency had been declared and a State Committee was to run the country. Three days later the takeover collapsed and the Vice-President was arrested and detained.

Government · Councils of Ministers were found at union, republic and autonomous republic level and, within their area of competence, had similar powers and duties. The Union Constitution designated the Council as 'the highest executive and administrative agency'. It also possessed law-making powers and could issue decrees and dispositions (but not statutes). The Prime Minister was proposed by the President, approved by the Supreme Soviet and confirmed in office by the Congress; he then collaborated in the appointment by the Supreme Soviet of other ministers. The USSR Council of Ministers was large since it included not only union ministers but the chairs of state committees and of the republic governments. Consequently it was empowered to operate through the permanent agency of its Presidium. In the past it frequently issued decrees in conjunction with the Central Committee of the CPSU.

Status of the Communist Party · The amendments of 14 March 1990 removed the Party's constitutional monopoly. The description of its role as 'the vanguard of all the people' was deleted from the Preamble, and the new version of Article 6 merely listed the Party along with 'other political parties as well as trade union, young people's and other public organizations and mass movements' all of which might participate in public affairs through their elected representatives. Article 7 required all political parties to operate within the law and forbade only those aimed at change by force or the promotion of national or religious discord.

Finally, Article 51 gave citizens the right to form political parties and to participate in mass movements in order to satisfy 'their diverse interests'. Immediately after the failed coup of August 1991, President Gorbachev resigned as General Secretary and very soon both union and RSFSR decrees were issued withdrawing the Party's property and ending its activities.

Republic constitutions · Many of the amendments described above were copied by the republics. With effect from June 1990 the RSFSR introduced a two-tier legislature (a Congress and a bicameral Supreme Soviet) and a year later created the office of President with law-making powers (by decree), power to declare a state of emergency, and the right to put forward candidates for such offices as Prime Minister.

The law-governed state

Until the second half of the 1980s the concept of *der Rechtsstaat*, that is the notion that the state itself is subject to the 'rule of law', was derided; Soviet legal dictionaries described it as an unscientific notion used by the bourgeoisie to mask its own imperialist essence and to inculcate harmful illusions in the masses. In June 1988, however, the resolution on legal reform passed by the CPSU All-Union Conference repeated a phrase used by Gorbachev in his address and described its goal as being the creation of a 'socialist law-governed state'. Subsequently the phrase appeared frequently in legislation and commentary.

Western views on the subject are varied and extensive, but the concept can in essence be reduced to the following propositions. First, it denotes that all authority is subject to the law: legislative power is granted by and subject to the Constitution; executive, governmental, taxing and police powers are bound by Constitution and statute; and all acts of public authorities are constrained by certain general, even if unenacted, principles of law (such as the right to a hearing, and the prohibition against double jeopardy). Secondly, it requires that some trustworthy means exist of keeping both the jurisdiction and the conduct of state organs within these allotted limits; this function is usually assigned to a constitutionally independent judiciary. Thirdly, there is sometimes deduced from the foregoing the proposition that whatever is not forbidden by correctly created law is permitted (a principle adopted by the Party in its very last years of power). Finally, this last statement may be held to mean, not that the state grants permission to the people, but that they confer on the state only such powers to be used by such procedures as they determine.

The Soviet system never attained the aims sketched above. Perhaps the most striking example is the casual frequency with which the union and republic Constitutions were amended. For instance the Supreme Soviet's Land Law Principles Act of 28 February 1990 seemed clearly unconstitutional until, on 14 March, the Congress amended the Constitution's articles on land and property. And the bill on the Committee for Constitutional Supervision would have been similarly vitiated had not the Congress, on enacting it, also amended its constitutional basis.

None the less, the move towards a law-state produced both constitutional changes and institutional innovations. Two institutional amendments must be singled out for special mention: the first aimed at constitutional review of legislative action, the second at judicial review of administrative action.

Committee for Constitutional Supervision (CCS)

The CCS was an independent USSR body whose task was to keep statutory and subordinate law-making within its correct constitutional and legislative limits; counterparts of the USSR CCS emerged at union republic level, and in 1991 the RSFSR created its own Constitutional Court. The union version appeared in the constitutional amendments of 1 December 1988, as amended on 23 December 1989 and 14 March 1990; its basis was in Article 124 and its operation was defined in a Congress statute of 23 December 1989. Its 27 members, including one from each union republic, were to be elected by the Congress from specialists in law and political science, to serve for ten years, and to be independent and subject only to the Constitution. Its meetings were in principle public; its deliberations held in private; its conclusions were reached by simple majority vote and published, with reasons; dissenting opinions might be annexed thereto. The first person to chair the CCS was the jurist S.S. Alekseev (b.1924).

From the point of view of constitutional law, there were several interesting and quite original features of the CCS. First, it could review, for conformity to the Constitution, at either the bill stage or after enactment, Acts of Congress. It reviewed, for conformity to the Constitution and to all legislatively superior norms, Acts of the Supreme Soviet, Edicts of the President, and other subordinate general norms including Government decrees (but not those of individual ministries which could be examined by the Procuracy). It also reviewed union-republic constitutions and laws for compliance with basic constitutional citizens' rights; and was to have supervised the general conformity of republic laws to their USSR counterparts. Secondly – and remarkably – it had the power of self-seisin: that is, it could, of its own motion, select for constitutional review any of the provisions listed above. Thirdly, individuals could not bring suit before it. Fourthly, there was a list of other permitted petitioners, such as one-fifth of the USSR People's Deputies, the President, or a Republic legislature; and the Supreme Court and the Procurator-General could refer a range of subordinate legal norms. Fifthly, the CCS could not itself quash a legal act on the grounds of unconstitutionality. The effects of a CCS conclusion that the provision examined was in breach of the Constitution or other superior norm vary according to the author and nature of the provision, but the general pattern was that the CCS's report was to be forwarded to the author of the provision who would then act to correct it. If, however, the ground of unconstitutionality was a violation of citizens' rights and liberties, the defective provision was void from that moment. Sixthly, the CCS did not, constitutionally speaking, have the upper hand; in the final analysis its conclusions could be rejected by Congress acting by the same majority (two-thirds of members) as that required to amend the Constitution. Finally it may be observed that the USSR's power of self-seisin meant that it could choose to review the whole statute-book back to 1917. Indeed its first self-selected subjects for review included elderly provisions of civil law on the rights of buyers of goods, and the entire internal passport system. In addition it found against certain provisions of Soviet labour law not merely on constitutional grounds, but for failure to comply with international treaties to which the USSR was a party. An important early decision stigmatized as unconstitutional the previous failure to publish many legislative provisions. As a result, in 1991 there was published (and held unconstitutional) a 1967 Decree automatically withdrawing citizenship from those who had left for Israel. Two days after the attempted coup of 18 August 1991 (when Gorbachev was placed under house arrest) became public knowledge on 19 August some members of the Committee, including its chairman S.S. Alekseev, issued in its name a statement calling for strict observance of the Constitution.

Russia's constitutional court

The Russian Federation's counterpart has different functions, reflected in its name. The Court consists of fifteen judges nominated by the Russian President and appointed by the Congress. A quorum is twelve, decisions are by majority vote, and dissents may be published. Its functions fall into four main categories: to decide on conformity to the constitution of international agreements before ratification and of internal statutes after enactment (in this latter respect it is similar to Constitutional Courts elsewhere). Its decision that an enactment is unconstitutional is immediately effective, but suit can be brought only by parliamentary or other official or social organs, and not by ordinary citizens. The Court's second main function, however, allows it to hear complaints by private persons against, not the general norm itself, but its application to the complainant by judicial or administrative organs or officials. In other words the citizen can argue that a particular law is being routinely applied in a way which contravenes his or her constitutional rights. Its third function – and the only one in which it has the power of self-seisin – is to reach conclusions on the constitutionality of international agreements already in force or of the behaviour of the President and other officials. Finally, it could become the forum for disputes between the republics within the Federation but only where this did not imperil its strictly judicial role.

Judicial review

An important tenet of the rule of law is that a person aggrieved by administrative action or inaction should have some adequate and independent means of redress. The complaint will normally be directed, not at some general law envisaged *in toto*, but at an individual decision of a public authority directed towards the specific situation of an individual or legal person – an assessment to tax, the refusal of a residence permit or a trading licence and so on. In addition, complaints against the inaction of bureaucrats are common. In the past, almost the only avenue open to a Soviet citizen was to complain to an administrative superior or to the Procuracy.

Under perestroika, however, the ordinary courts were given power to review unlawful administrative action.

USSR statutes of 1987 and 1989 permitted review of the acts of individual officials and those of administrative organs. The law covered individual, not general, administrative acts (and presumably inaction) by which a citizen was unlawfully deprived of the chance to exercise rights given him or her, by law, or had a duty illegally laid upon him or her. Actions might be brought only by citizens (and not by legal persons, such as companies); complaint was to be first addressed to the administrative superior and, if unsatisfied, brought before the court within one month (though the court might extend this for good reason). The case, and any appeal, were to follow the rules of civil procedure. The law gave the courts no guidance as to what constitutes an unlawful act or other maladministration. If the court found the complaint well-founded it was not itself to annul the act, but was to transmit its decision to the defendant's superior who was required to comply. Another 1989 statute created the crime of intentional failure by an official to carry out the decision of a court. In the Russian Federation the Constitutional Court's power to hear citizens complaints may go some way to providing an alternative remedy.

Union/republic relations: the 'war of laws'

The 1977 USSR Constitution proclaimed itself that of a federal state formed by the voluntary association of the republics (Article 70) and, like that of 1936, confirmed the right of secession (Article 72). Until 1990, however, there was no federal or other legal machinery by which the complexities of secession might be resolved. Furthermore, the Union had jurisdiction over all major political, economic and

Below. Lithuanians asserting their sovereignty in a parliamentary vote, March 1990. In the centre is Algirdas-Mikolas Brazauskas who in 1988 had become First Secretary of the Lithuanian Communist Party. A reformist Communist who had embraced the national cause, Brazauskas in the post-Communist period succeeded Vytautas Landsbergis as President of Lithuania. Below right. In Simferopol', Crimea, November 1991, activists from the Republican Movement of the Crimea gather signatures in support of a demand for a referendum on the status of the peninsula which, under Nikita Khrushchev's influence, was transferred from the Russian republic to Ukraine in 1954

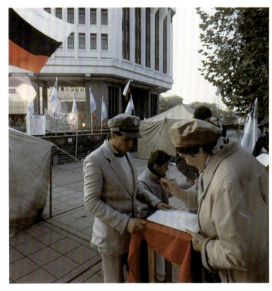

legal issues and had moreover the power to define its own competence by deciding which matters were of all-union importance (Article 72). Article 74 declared that, in case of conflict, union law prevailed over that of a republic; and Article 173 accorded the Union constitution the highest juridical force. Until the late 1980s the constitutions of the republics meshed with these provisions, stating their own right of secession but acknowledging meanwhile the supremacy of union law.

From 1988 onwards, however, the Baltic, and then other republics began to contest the claims of the Union. Power to determine the existence of a conflict between union and republic laws and to declare the latter void was vested by the USSR Constitution in the Presidium of the USSR Supreme Soviet until 14 March 1990. The amendments of that date removed this power. It was not expressly conferred on the President but his Edicts purported to exercise it, basing themselves on Articles 74 and 173 and on the new Article 127.3(1) and (2) which made him guarantor of the Constitution and empowered him to implement the principles of the national-state structure of the USSR. A case in point was the presidential edict on Estonia of 14 May 1990 which held that republic's independence declaration of 30 March to be in breach of both the Constitution and of the USSR Secession Procedure Act – a law not enacted until 3 April, although the Edict fails to mention its date. This Secession statute (which assumed that the competence to lay down the procedure for secession belonged to the Union) provided for referendum, consultations, and a transitional period.

This did not satisfy the republics. An Estonian law of 16 November 1988 proclaimed national sovereignty and provided that union laws would take effect within the republic only if and when registered by the Estonian Supreme Soviet's Presidium. On 30 March 1990 Estonia then struck at the root of the relation by declaring USSR state power 'illegal' and on 16 May provided that the courts and procuracy were freed of subordination to the union structure. In somewhat differing ways, Lithuania declared independence on 11 March 1990 and Latvia on 4 May. Azerbaijan, Moldova, Ukraine, Uzbekistan and, most threateningly, the RSFSR all, in various ways, declared for state sovereignty in the first half of 1990 and began to make treaties with each other. The Ukrainian referendum on 1 December 1991 produced an overwhelming majority for independence and its Supreme Soviet voted not to ratify any new Union Treaty. The immediate juridical response of the USSR President was to issue edicts purporting to annul these acts. The more long-term response was to press for the drafting of a new Union Treaty. The already difficult situation was exacerbated by the claims of the autonomous republics to their own independence – a claim which Karelia asserted against the RSFSR and the Crimea against Ukraine – and by territorial conflict between republics (such as Armenia and Azerbaijan over Nagorno-Karabakh).

Thus, at the end of the Union's life, the law – which as explained above had been seen as a solution – became part of the problem: and statutes, edicts, decrees and decisions became weapons in the war of laws.

BAR

DEATH OF THE UNION

The USSR died in December 1991, but from a strictly legal point of view it is difficult to ascertain either the moment of death or its cause. In formal terms the Union was created by the Treaty between the republics signed on 30 December 1922. On 8 December 1991, three republics – Belarus, Russia, Ukraine, all original parties to the 1922 Treaty – signed an Agreement on the Commonwealth of Independent States (CIS), to which eight other republics (but not Georgia or the Baltic states) soon acceded. The document's preamble declared that the USSR had ceased to exist (although strictly speaking a preamble has itself no legal force). The eleven members of the new CIS undertook to honour the international obligations of the former. The RSFSR accompanied its ratification of the CIS Agreement with a special Law denouncing the 1922 Union Treaty. On 25 December President Gorbachev resigned and on the following day a joint session of the USSR Soviet of the Republics and Soviet of the Union released from their duties the judges of the Supreme Court and the staff of the Procuracy; the Supreme Soviet then declared itself abolished.

Soviet troops arresting an Azeri nationalist in Baku, 1990. Following a pogrom by Azeris against Armenian residents of the capital of Azerbaijan, harsh action was taken by the Soviet army and many Azeris were killed

Under the two-tier legislative system of the USSR Constitution, it is extremely doubtful whether the Supreme Soviet had this power, and many deputies called in vain for a final suicidal session of the Congress of People's Deputies.

At international level the republics have been recognized as the legal successors of the Union but in internal affairs the process leaves several legal gaps. Many matters were regulated only by the union law in force, and the RSFSR has indicated that this will continue to apply unless inconsistent with its own law. But several major pieces of union legislation – especially the new Basic Principles of Civil Law and of Criminal Law – had been enacted during 1991 but were not to come into force until 1992. It seems, then, that as they never became part of union law, they are no part of the republics' systems.   BAR

Legal and penal systems

INTERNAL LAW

The sources of the internal law of the USSR and of the republics may be ranked in the following order, with each lower norm deriving its validity from, and limited by, its superiors. The fundamental law is the Constitution, adopted and amended by a two-thirds majority of the supreme legislative body – formerly the Supreme Soviet and then (in the USSR and the Russian Federation) the Congress of People's Deputies. The Union died in December 1991 and the Commonwealth of Independent States has no independent law-making power or judicial organs; thus the basic norms and courts are those of the republic constitutions. Below them comes legislation, first by the Congress, then by the Supreme Soviet; their bills must be signed by the President. Then come: presidential edicts; government decrees and regulations; and ministerial regulations. Court decisions do not of themselves create general rules of law; but the Supreme Courts have power to issue 'guiding explanations' for lower courts, covering particular areas of law. The fact that these were subject to review by the USSR Committee for Constitutional Supervision suggests that they have legal force.

INTERNATIONAL LAW

It is unclear whether, in the absence of incorporation by one of the methods outlined in the preceding paragraph, any norms of international law were directly effective within the Soviet legal system. Until recently, Soviet authors – while tending to treat the topic as 'bourgeois' – averred that international commitments did not of themselves change Soviet internal law. The Union and Republic Constitutions did not expressly accord Treaty norms primacy over internal laws (unlike, for instance, the constitutions of the USA, Article 6, or of France, Article 55). Furthermore the 1989 Supreme Soviet statute on the court structure stated that the laws to be applied by Soviet judges are those found in the Constitution and in statutes. On the other hand, the 1989 Act of Congress on the Committee for Constitutional Supervision allowed review of Soviet laws for compliance with international treaty obligations. In the last year of the Union several of its statutes provided that any inconsistencies with the rules of international treaties to which the Union was a party were to be resolved in favour of the international norm. But these separate statutory provisions would not be necessary were there any general rule of constitutional law giving priority within the internal legal order to the norms of international treaty law.

LEGAL INSTITUTIONS

Courts

In accordance with the new emphasis on the law-governed state, both constitutional amendment and recent legislation sought to strengthen the position and increase the status of the Soviet court. At first instance, judges sat singly; appellate and review procedure came before a bench of three. There was never a jury for civil cases, nor was there for crime (although some republics began introducing jury trial for major offences). Instead of a jury, lay participation was achieved by the presence, in all first instance hearings, of two people's assessors. The USSR and republic constitutions stated that judges and people's assessors were independent and subject only to law. They were, however, elected (judges for ten, assessors for five years) and subject to recall by their electorate. Supreme Court judges were elected by the Supreme Soviet; those of the tiers below were elected by the corresponding higher soviet: thus the judges of the first tier of district courts were chosen by the soviet of the province or territory of which the district formed part. People's assessors of the lowest tier are directly elected by citizens, and those of the higher courts by the corresponding soviets. Three USSR statutes of 1989 covered the court structure, the status of judges, and the penalties for attempting to influence a court or refusing to conform to its order. The first of these, as regards criminal procedure, gave the right to counsel from the moment of detention, arrest, or indictment, and proclaimed that the accused is deemed not guilty until the contrary is proved by law and declared by court judgment. The second laid down that judges must have a higher legal education and some practical experience.

The court structure was extremely complex. At the summit stood the USSR Supreme Court, dissolved on 26 December 1991. Each republic had its Supreme Court, under which came the courts of the provinces and finally the district people's court. This last is the general court of first instance, although cases of greater importance may begin higher up. After a case has been disposed of at first instance, one appeal (in the sense of a decision on the merits) was normally open to the loser. Proceedings to review the law as stated by the lower court could be instituted by the presidents of higher courts or (and, in practice, usually) the Procuracy. Military tribunals constituted a separate, federal, system under the Military Chamber of the USSR Supreme Court. Disputes between state enterprises fell within the jurisdiction of a distinct, specialized set of arbitration tribunals (*Gosarbitrazh*).

There was no system of binding precedent, but the Supreme Courts at all-union and republican level gave 'guiding explanations' which were (and were meant to be) followed. Monthly law reports were published containing these and a small selection of other decisions. Before the inauguration of the law-state, and the dethronement of the CPSU, the party line was frequently invoked by the Supreme Court, not in its actual decisions but in its instructions to lower courts. Thus its 1986 Plenum Decree No. 15 aimed at improving the observance of the rules of due process and at blocking extra-judicial interference was, paradoxically enough, issued in compliance with the Central Committee's 1986 decree on socialist legality which was itself published in the USSR Supreme Court bulletin. It should also be mentioned that, under secret regulations, areas of the country denominated as falling under a 'special regime' – defence industry sectors and the like – were served by specially selected courts and procuracy which had jurisdiction over all crimes on the territory and all civil cases brought by the population. The most recent decree on this system, signed by Brezhnev in 1979, was not published until 1991.

The Procuracy

In 1722 the Procurator was called 'the eye of the tsar'; in 1990 *Izvestiya* called him 'the eye of the law'. The Soviet Procuracy, introduced by Lenin in 1922, was a distinctively centralist and federal feature of the legal system whose wide function was that of exercising general supervision over all ministries and inferior state and local authorities and departments, officials and citizens (Constitution Article 164). The USSR Procurator-General was proposed by the President, approved by the Supreme Soviet and confirmed by the Congress. He was accountable to these two legislative bodies, and controlled his officials throughout the Union; they were not subject to the authority of their republic or local soviet. The present Russian Procurator-General is likewise the central organ designed to ensure strict observance of the laws by all authorities, including those of the autonomous republics.

To use rather inexact western analogies, the office combines the functions of Federal Attorney, Inspector of Prisons, Attorney-General and Ombudsman. Thus it is the Procurator who supervises investigation in criminal cases, authorizes arrest, prosecutes offenders and supervises prisons; he refers judicial decisions (civil and criminal) to higher courts for review; and he exercises general supervision over the entire administration. This last function makes the Procuracy the channel through which citizens' complaints are considered and, for this, the Procurator may call for documents, explanations and so on. He does not, however, decide the case on its merits but refers the matter by way of 'protest' to the appropriate higher authority. During the attempted coup of August 1991 the USSR Procurator-General was not outspoken in defence of the President; he was removed soon afterwards.

Legal profession

Advocates are under the control of the central Ministry of Justice and, locally, of the justice department of the local executive committee. They must normally be law graduates and have completed a period of practical training. The local Bar admits recruits and administers and supervises the work of the profession. It appoints the head of local law offices where work is distributed and fees, fixed by ministerial tariff, are collected. Advocates are to employ any lawful means to assist their client, whose communication with them is privileged. Representation by advocates in court is not mandatory, though it seems to be usual. In addition to this, advocates give legal advice and draft documents.

Jurisconsults are legal advisers to state enterprises, government agencies, and other institutions and must usually have a law degree. They draft internal rules, contracts and commercial documents and represent their employer in court. In so far as their functions are those of advocates they come under the Ministry of Justice.

Notaries are state officials organized under the Ministry of Justice and usually have either legal education or practical experience. Like their counter-

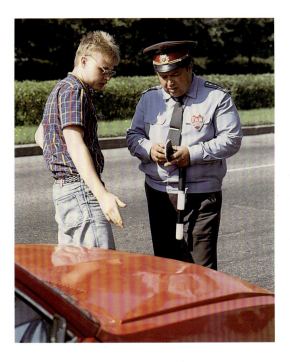

A traffic policeman in action in St Petersburg

tries. A USSR statute of 1991 dealt in general terms with the union and republic police forces, attempting to bring the force into line with glasnost thinking: it was to follow the principles of 'legality, internationalism, [and] humanism'. The 1991 RSFSR statute said much the same. The militia in the USSR was – and in Russia still is – organized under the Ministry of Internal Affairs (MVD) whose structure has been often altered. Not all of the laws governing the militia were published. In general the force is subject both to its own superior agency and to the local soviet. The Russian militia is divided into a criminal investigation branch and a 'local' branch dealing with public order. The police are armed and they have powers to demand identification, to enter buildings and to arrest; to detain vagrants, beggars and drunken persons; to enforce what is left of the internal passport system, with powers of entry into dwellings. They license the possession of firearms, and carry out traffic control including the administration, licensing and inspection of motor vehicles. Militia departments are organized into branches: uniformed police, criminal detection, passport section, state automobile inspection (GAI), prosecuting section (when investigation is not undertaken by the Procuracy or the KGB – Ministry of Security in post-Soviet Russia) and training and administration sections. There is a special transport militia subordinate both to the regular militia and the appropriate transport organization. The Criminal Codes impose stricter penalties (including death) for crimes against the militia, and they may shoot if attacked or to prevent the escape from arrest of an adult male. The force has a civil liability to pay compensation for harm unlawfully caused. In the last years of the USSR and subsequently there appears to have been a serious shortfall in personnel.

The People's Guards

The word here translated 'guards' (*druzhiny*) is an ancient term describing the close advisers and comrades-in-arms (the 'Household Guard') of the medieval Russian princes. In the late 1950s it was revived by RSFSR joint party–government decrees (source of the quotations which follow) as part of a movement to 'enlist working people in the cause of protecting public order and the observance of legality', which also produced 'Comrades' Courts'. They were to be volunteers of 'professional, moral and political qualities' who organized detachments in factories, collective farms, institutions, apartment blocks and so on, directed by party agencies, and with a hierarchical structure up to district or city level; their members were equipped with a guard certificate, badge and arm-band. Their main function was to increase people's 'respect for the law and the rules of socialist community life' – in particular to

parts in western Europe, they attest documents, and draw up conveyances, mortgages, wills and so on.

SUBSTANTIVE LAW

The fundamental principles of the various branches of law were enacted at all-union level and then expanded in the Codes of the republics. Although the system repudiated any formal division into public and private law, one category deals with essentially the public sector: state enterprises, water resources, health, education and the like. A second category directly affects the individual as well as state enterprises and includes criminal law, family law, housing law, labour law and – as the great residual structure – civil law. The RSFSR Civil Code (first enacted in 1922) reads like a simplified version of the German Civil Code. Its General Part defines the legal capacity of both natural and juridical persons, and deals with the major general concepts of private law: the juridical act, representation, and the computation and running of time. It then deals with property, with the major contracts like sale or lease, and with the law of tort or civil wrong. It also includes the law of inheritance and wills (with in principle freedom of testation), and that of copyright. Many of its provisions applied to the legal relations of both individuals and state enterprises.

LAW ENFORCEMENT AGENCIES

The police

Militia is the name given to the police, the latter word being used only of the force in Western coun-

help maintain public order and combat drunkenness, child neglect, road accidents and the like. They also provided support for the agencies of the Ministry of Internal Affairs, the Procuracy and the courts and reported suspected crimes to the police. To carry out these tasks they might demand passports, driving licences and other documents, enter public gatherings (cinemas, sports stadia), detain malefactors for delivery to the police and, in emergencies, commandeer private transport. To assist them they enjoyed free travel on public transport (except taxis) and the free use of office and factory telephones. To protect them, the criminal law equated them with policemen in cases of resistance or violence. Although the activity was unpaid, disability incurred in connection therewith attracted preferential benefits. A good record qualified the guards for extra paid holidays and preference in housing. By 1989, however, some 2.2 million citizens (16 per cent of the force) had left the People's Guards.

As a response to this, and to the shortfall of regular police, slightly different forces were set up in certain towns in 1989, and praised by Gorbachev. Called 'workers' police support detachments' they seem partly to have helped with crime control in general and partly to have mobilized blue-collar sentiment against 'speculators'.   BAR

The Democratic Movement and *samizdat*

THE RISE OF DISSENT

While political opposition of any consequence did not exist in the USSR between the early 1920s and 1988 (except in Ukraine and the Baltic republics, 1944–53), open dissent from various Soviet norms and policies began to emerge soon after Stalin's death ended his system of mass terror in 1953. With important exceptions this dissent did not take on organized forms until 1965–68, years which saw the maturing of the Human Rights Movement. Initially this was primarily a defensive reaction by a few thousand well-educated urban people against the first moves by the post-Khrushchev leadership to reduce the area of conditional freedom opened up for the 'creative intelligentsia' by Khrushchev. By openly resisting political trials and campaigning

for them to be conducted with full observance of the law, these people hoped to reverse what they saw as neo-Stalinist tendencies in policy. As the movement developed, however, it resisted injustices in ever more areas of human rights, and sought reforms and dialogue with the authorities. When these declined to enter into any but occasional and usually indirect discussions, and launched counter measures more readily than reforms, the dissenters increasingly called for support from their fellow-citizens and from organizations abroad.

Many dissenters were concerned not only, or even mainly, with defending the human rights of others, but also with free self-expression – individually or in groups – in such areas as literature, the arts, politics, economics, trade unions, law and religion, determined to exercise a much greater freedom of expression and association than the authorities were usually prepared to grant. This broad community – comprising a wide range of political views – was more informally and loosely structured than the Human Rights Movement, which it incorporated, and was often known as the Democratic Movement. Such a community could develop only because of the ideological vacuum left in much of society by the mass terror, and because the dissenters managed to break down important taboos built up by a related product of the terror, social atomization. Thus dissidents put loyalty to each other above obedience to the secret police (KGB); formed unofficial groups; interceded for persecuted individuals and groups; founded *samizdat* (privately circulated typescript) periodicals to publish independent writing and information on conflict situations involving human rights; spirited *samizdat* material out of the country to be published abroad and, more important, broadcast back into the USSR by foreign radio stations, thus circumventing the censorship which denied them access to Soviet media; and gave press conferences for foreign journalists.

The 10,000-odd *samizdat* items which reached the West between the early 1960s and 1990 vary in length from one-page protest documents to novels and anthologies of 800–900 pages. Among them are dozens of periodicals which came out with some regularity for greater or lesser periods of time. The best known of these was the main organ of the Human Rights Movement, *Khronika tekushchikh sobytiy* (*Chronicle of Current Events*), of which 64 issues (of up to 200 pages each) appeared between 1968 and 1982.

Among the better known groups within the Human Rights Movement were the Initiative Group for the Defence of Human Rights in the USSR (founded in 1969), the Human Rights Committee (formed in 1970 by Andrey Sakharov and others), the Groups to Assist the Implementation of the

Patients, including political prisoners, exercising in partitioned compounds outside the Orel Special Psychiatric Hospital

Right. One of the Meskhetians injured in bloody clashes between Uzbeks and Meskhetians in the Fergana region of Uzbekistan, June 1989

Helsinki Agreements in the USSR (set up in 1976–77 in Moscow, Ukraine, Lithuania, Georgia and Armenia), and the Working Commission to Investigate the Use of Psychiatry for Political Purposes (founded in 1977).

Among the better known *samizdat* authors writing in Russian were Sakharov, Alexander Solzhenitsyn, Andrey Amalrik (1938–80), Vladimir Voynovich (b. 1932), Anatoly Marchenko (1938–86), Petr Grigorenko (1907–87), Alexander Zinov'ev (b. 1922), Roy Medvedev (b. 1925), Zhores Medvedev (b. 1925), Nadezhda Mandel'shtam (1899–1980), Natal'ya Gorbanevskaya (b. 1936), Vladimir Bukovsky (b. 1942) and Valery Chalidze (b. 1938). The best known leader of dissenting artists was Oskar Rabin (b. 1928).

NATIONALIST AND RELIGIOUS PROTEST

The Democratic Movement developed links over time with a wide variety of dissenting national minority groups. Most of these objected to the regime's declared goal that all the peoples of the USSR should eventually merge into a single Soviet people, and saw this as a lightly disguised policy of Russification. One category of groups consisted of those belonging to nations with their own union republics, who sought to assert their constitutional right to considerable autonomy in language, culture, the economy and politics. The most powerful such movement was in Lithuania, where the interlocking of national and religious values (as in Poland) gained for it the support of a majority of the population. The others, in descending order of strength of their open dissent, were in Ukraine, Georgia, Armenia, Estonia and Latvia. Dissent among the Muslims of Central Asia appeared to be quite strong, but largely

covert. Dissenting Russian nationalists, of whom the best known was Solzhenitsyn, opposed the revolutionary internationalism of the regime, its non-Russian ideology, its suppression of important national traditions, its persecution of the Orthodox Church, and its squandering of the national patrimony by foreign sales of raw materials. Most of them, however, enjoyed a certain official tolerance, evidently due to the authorities' hope of gaining more popular support.

A second category consisted of the emigration movements among the USSR's three million Jews and two million Germans, organizations that by their militancy forced the regime in 1971 to allow a significant scale of emigration; between 1968 and the end of 1991 some 740,000 Jews left for Israel and elsewhere, and some 542,000 Germans emigrated, almost all to West Germany.

A final category comprised, first, the Crimean Tatar movement which aimed at return from the exile in Central Asia to which Stalin deported their people (with great loss of life) in 1944; and second, the analogous movement of the Meskhetians, natives of southern Georgia, whose situation differed only in that Stalin did not accuse them of mass collaboration with the German invaders. The Crimean Tatars were absolved of this charge in 1967, after the first stage of a massive lobbying campaign begun in the late 1950s.

The Democratic Movement also developed strong links with dissenting religious groups. Some of

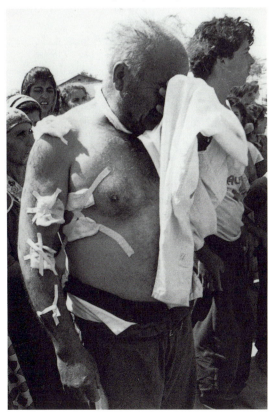

Alexander Solzhenitsyn

The epic sweep of Alexander Solzhenitsyn's life and writings, his emergence in the late 1960s as opposition tribune and 'alternative government', have put many in mind of Lev Tolstoy.

Until the age of twenty-seven Solzhenitsyn was an exemplary Soviet citizen and enthusiast. A contemporary of the Revolution (b. 1918), he was brought up fatherless in southern Russia, and in 1941 graduated in mathematics and physics at the University of Rostov-on-Don while simultaneously completing a correspondence course in creative writing with a Moscow institute. He was decorated as an artillery officer in the Second World War.

Then his life changed. Arrested at his post in 1945 because of politically suspect details in his intercepted correspondence, after two years of interrogation and manual labour he was transferred to one of the scientific research institutes within the prison camp system.

Removed from there in 1950, he did forced labour in Kazakhstan until his release into 'permanent exile' in 1953. In exile he worked as a schoolteacher and survived cancer. Amnestied in 1956, he moved to central Russia.

Solzhenitsyn was admitted to the Writer's Union in 1962, and after an increasingly bitter confrontation with the literary and political authorities was expelled from the Union in 1969 and sent into foreign exile in 1974. From 1976 until his return to Russia on 27 May 1994 he lived in Vermont.

Solzhenitsyn's literary work up to 1970, when he was awarded the Nobel Prize, has a broadly autobiographical basis. The concise masterpiece, *One Day in the Life of Ivan Denisovich* (1962), deals with hard labour in a remote camp; his best novel, *First Circle* (1968), with the captive intellectuals of the prison research team; *Cancer Ward* (1968), with the ideology of disease within the Soviet system. Then, the impassioned three-volume documentary *The GULag Archipelago* (1973–75) speaks for the millions of Solzhenitsyn's fellow-prisoners. The army experience was transmuted into the first part of an epic study of Russian history in the run-up to the October Revolution, *August 1914* (1971); known as *The Red Wheel*, this project occupied Solzhenitsyn in exile and was completed in 1991.

A few of the shorter works had been published in the USSR between 1962 and 1966 (the battles to publish are memorably represented in *The Oak and the Calf*, 1975), but subsequently nothing was permitted until 1988. By 1990 nearly all of Solzhenitsyn's writings had appeared in Russia. The programmatic *How Russia Should be Re-organized* was released in 1990, to a muted response; the tide of political and economic events was running against Solzhenitsyn's pleas for an ethics- and religion-based national revival.

them, like the dissenting sectors of the Baptists, Pentecostals and Adventists, were concerned almost exclusively to resist state control of their activity and achieve greater freedom for religion. Others, like Lithuanian and Ukrainian Catholics, or Russian or Georgian Orthodox, often supported in addition the socio-political aims of their own nationalist movement.

Organized dissent among most denominations began in the early 1960s, in response to Khrushchev's anti-religious campaigns. The Baptists gave a strong lead, quickly developing a high level of *samizdat* activity, which they maintained until the late 1980s. The number of Baptists in prison at any one time decreased from about 250 in the late 1960s

to about 40 in early 1979, but then rose again to over 200 by the mid-1980s, only to decline almost to zero by the end of the 1980s.

FROM REPRESSION TO TOLERANCE

The dissenting groups and movements had considerable achievements to record. Mainly because of the Human Rights Movement's capacity to co-operate with all groups, and act for them as both a sounding-board and a civil liberties organization, the outside world and the Soviet population gained access to extensive and accurate information about their situation. This information and other writings by dissidents contributed substantially to the tarnishing of the official Soviet image of the USSR as a liberalized and contented society ruled by a peace-loving and universally popular regime. The dissenters – with foreign support – also broke down the virtual ban on emigration and made the authorities more hesitant than before about staging political trials or committing well-known figures to psychiatric hospitals; they often preferred to push would-be defendants into exile abroad. On the other hand the dissenters achieved very little liberalization of the law, and may indeed have unwittingly provoked many of the changes in the opposite direction, such as those in the 1977 Constitution which, in effect outlawed dissent. And while the official campaigns to portray dissidents as agents of imperialist powers, or, at best, as swayed by bourgeois propaganda, broadly failed, the Democratic Movement only slowly widened its support base.

The instinctive tendency of the authorities to treat dissent in a defensive, heavy-handed way was partially countered by the dissenting groups' capacity to absorb punishment and still develop, slowly but steadily, in depth and breadth. A second powerful factor – also largely a product of the dissenters' efforts – was the USSR's discovery that access to western technology, goods and credit might be limited unless it curbed somewhat its intolerance of dissent. Underlying this intolerance appeared to be fears about the regime's legitimacy and about the long-term growth potential of dissent. These made the regime's policy toward dissent basically reactionary, and inhibited it from trying to alleviate the root causes. This approach was particularly marked during the crackdowns on dissent of 1972–74 and 1979–85. The latter one was especially severe and eventually supressed most of the dissident groups, although some continued to operate underground. It also put a virtual end to emigration, which only began reviving in 1987.

In 1987–88 the new policies of glasnost and democratization led to the gradual release, although not until 1991 the exculpation, of most political and religious prisoners. Many dissidents were praised in official media for their courage, patriotism, and foresight, and some were published and even elected to various legislatures. A number, such as A.D. Sakharov in Moscow and V.M. Chornovil (b. 1937) in L'vov, assumed positions of political leadership in various groups and parties, or in nationalist movements pressing effectively for the sovereignty or independence of their republics. The root causes of dissent – for example, the persecution of religion and nationalism – were also increasingly addressed. And as access to printing presses, the media, and distribution networks was steadily widened, *samizdat* publications either faded away or became legal. The freedoms of expression, association, and emigration became extensive, and were threatened only by the extreme weakness of the embryonic civil society and the consequent danger of the rise of a new authoritarianism.   PBR

Post-Soviet politics

THE COLLAPSE OF THE SOVIET UNION

The collapse of the Soviet Union had three proximate causes. The August coup revealed how feeble was the hold of the union government on its own institutions, and the defeat of the coup and humiliation of the armed forces removed the major factor that had inhibited union republican élites from pressing their interests. The Baltic states declared independence immediately and this was recognized by the Union on 6 September 1991. The same message of terminal illness was dramatically illustrated on 28 November 1991 when the Union's Supreme Soviet failed to pass a budget for the fourth quarter of the year, thus crippling union finances; Yel'tsin immediately announced that his Russian government would cover union debts, revealing who would be paymaster and the real power in any continued union. Finally on 1 December the Ukrainian electorate, including its Russians, voted overwhelmingly for Ukrainian independence. It was the crushing blow: without Ukraine a union would have been little more than an association of Russia with the financially dependent republics of Central Asia, something Yel'tsin's administration had no intention of promoting. He moved on 7–8 December to replace the Soviet Union with a Commonwealth of

Andrey Sakharov addressing a public meeting, late 1980s

Independent States, membership of which was to be incompatible with union membership. The Commonwealth of Independent States was formed by Russia, Ukraine and Belorussia (now Belarus), and when a further eight members decided to join it on 21 December, it was pointless to continue with the Union. Gorbachev and Yel'tsin agreed that the Soviet Union would cease to exist on 1 January 1992, and Gorbachev resigned as President on 25 December. A handful of Supreme Soviet deputies dissolved that institution the following day.

What almost two years negotiation of the Union Treaty had revealed was that, once diverse national, regional and institutional interests could be freely expressed, there was no common ground for co-operation in the same political system. A democratic Soviet Union could not have worked because a sufficient number of the people on whom this depended did not want it to work. Seventy years of the Soviet experiment had failed to develop sufficient common social or political identity, and in that sense the Soviet Union had been an artificial state.   JHM

THE COMMONWEALTH OF INDEPENDENT STATES

The Commonwealth of Independent States was formed at a meeting in Minsk on 7–8 December 1991 by the leaders of Russia, Ukraine and Belarus. Initially called a 'Slav Union', this title was discarded once eight further union republics – Kazakhstan, Uzbekistan, Armenia, Azerbaijan, Moldova, Tajikistan, Kyrgyzstan and Turkmenistan – decided to join it on 21 December (although the parliaments of Azerbaijan and Moldova did not ratify CIS membership). The three Baltic states and Georgia under Z.K. Gamsakhurdia did not seek to join.

Nationalist demonstration in Estonia, February 1989

Two features are noteworthy in its founding charter. First, 'the application of the norms of third-party states, including those of the former USSR, [was] not permitted on the territory of the states signing this agreement'; this effectively put an end to the Soviet Union. Second, whilst its members agreed to maintain strategic armed forces and nuclear weapons under joint command, to honour the international obligations inherited from the Union, and to co-operate over matters of foreign policy, economics, transport and communications, migration and the environment, they set up no permanent joint institutions for these purposes. In contrast to the various arrangements proposed by the Union Treaty, the Commonwealth was not in legal terms to be a state. Successor states retained the ruble as currency (at least in the interim) and took over such Soviet property as was located on their territory, including, apparently, units of the Soviet armed forces, aircraft and rolling stock.

The Commonwealth was plagued with problems from the outset and within its first six months seemed several times to be on the verge of collapse. Five kinds of problem should be singled out. Four states (Russia, Ukraine, Kazakhstan and Belarus) had inherited nuclear weapons from the Soviet Union and it was difficult to ensure their concentration and/or agreed destruction under international supervision. Some borders between member states – or the allegiance of the residents of border zones – were in dispute (especially in Nagorno-Karabakh, but also the allegiance of the Crimea and of Slavophone parts of Moldova). Some military units, especially the Black Sea Fleet based in the Crimea, challenged their apportionment to new masters. Other member states were caught up in an inflation fuelled in particular by Russia, the largest economy and the possessor of the mints. Animosity between Russia and Ukraine, the Commonwealth's two largest members, was acute over all these issues. Finally many member states were internally unstable and the governments of two (Azerbaijan and Tajikistan) were overthrown by violence before June 1992.   JHM

THE SUCCESSOR STATES

In 1992 the fifteen successor states to the Soviet Union were based precisely on the administrative boundaries of the fifteen Union Republics. (It is possible that in the future more successor states may emerge, if, for instance, the Crimea, Tatarstan or Chechnia succeed in asserting new alignments.) We may classify the fifteen in five groups: (i) Russia, which adopted the title 'Russian Federation' in December 1991; (ii) the Baltic States which left the

Legend:
- Inter-ethnic violence
- Organised armed struggle
- Referendum or ballot on autonomy or independence
- Diplomatic dispute
- Displaced communities

Political flashpoints and ethnic conflict in the late Soviet period and since the dissolution of the USSR

Soviet Union in August 1991 and did not join the Commonwealth of Independent States; (iii) the western states of Ukraine, Belarus and Moldova; (iv) Georgia, Azerbaijan and Armenia in Transcaucasia; (v) the dry steppe or oasis states of Kazakhstan, Uzbekistan, Tajikistan, Kyrgyzstan and Turkmenistan.

Russia resumed its independence with considerable advantages: a population of 147 million, abundant natural resources and manpower, an all-round industrial base, adequate agriculture, a society used to cohesion and obedience, and a developed tradition of statehood. On the debit side it had lost much of the Union's best educated and most productive population, and many of its previous land and sea routes to the West. It is still too early to tell how widely the collapse of the Soviet Union will be interpreted as a defeat for the Russian nation; suffice it to say that, in conditions of economic want and political constraint, such an interpretation would not be surprising. Although more than 80 per cent of the population are Russians, Russia is not without its own internal ethnic tensions: two former autonomous republics of Russia, Tatarstan and Chechnia have striven to maintain a substantial measure of independence.

The three Baltic states of Lithuania, Latvia and Estonia (populations respectively 3.7, 2.7 and 1.6 million) have the advantages of previous experience of statehood and of skilled and disciplined societies. But they possess virtually no sources of fuels or metals, and, combined with their small size, this makes allies, economic and military, indispensable. There are substantial Russian minorities in both Latvia (34 per cent) and Estonia (30 per cent). Belarus (population 10.2 million) resembles the Baltic states in economic terms but has no developed tradition of distinct statehood. Moldova (population 4.3 million) might sooner or later rejoin Romania, with which it shares a common language; but that would only exacerbate the problem of its Russian, Ukrainian and Gagauz (Turkish speaking) minorities who bitterly resented the collapse of the Union. Ukraine, by contrast, with its 51.5 million inhabitants and a reasonable balance among agriculture, resource extraction and manufacturing, appeared to have a better chance than most of evolving into a modern and democratic nation state, but was in deep economic crisis by 1994. It would be politically most vulnerable if disputes with Russia should erode the loyalties of its large (11.4 million) Russian minority.

Transcaucasia began its independence in turmoil. In Georgia (population 5.4 million) two non-

Right. Decapitated statue of Lenin in the Chechen capital of Grozny, 1992. With tension high between Moscow and Chechnia – one of Russia's republics which has maintained a high degree of autonomy from the Russian Federation authorities (refusing, for example, to participate in the December 1993 parliamentary elections) – there has been defacement of what are seen as Russian symbols

Georgian groups, the Ossetes and the Abkhaz, feared Georgian independence and the Georgians themselves were passionately divided over internal politics, expelling their leader Z.K. Gamsakhurdia in January 1992 and replacing him with the former Soviet foreign minister, E.A. Shevardnadze. Armenia (3.3 million) and Azerbaijan (7.0 million) plunged deeper into all-out war over Nagorno-Karabakh. Of the three, Azerbaijan has the most economic resources, but is perhaps politically the most unstable: its government changed hands three times between March and May 1992. By the late summer of 1993 its former Communist Party First Secretary, G. A. Aliev (b. 1923) had returned to power with popular support.

Kazakhstan and Kyrgyzstan (populations 16.5 and 4.3 million) have a number of features in common: a high proportion of Europeans (50 per cent in Kazakhstan and 26 per cent in Kyrgyzstan) and a Muslim population relatively cool towards fundamentalist influences from the south; each began independence under leaders (N.A. Nazarbaev, b.1940; and A. Akaev, b.1944) determined to maintain social consensus and develop market economies. In Tajikistan (5.1 million) Islamic fundamentalists were among the forces that ousted the ex-communist government in May 1992. Of all the successor states Uzbekistan and Turkmenistan (19.8 and 3.5 million) made the smoothest transition to the new order; their formerly communist leaders (I.A. Karimov, b.1938; and S.A. Niyazov, b.1940) turned themselves and their followers to moderate, secular nationalism, and consolidated their powers in 1992–93.   JHM

of many basic commodities on 2 January 1992, thereby attacking the budget deficit and also reducing 'monetary overhang' in the form of people's savings. As the year wore on, prices rose much faster than the government had been prepared for; an initial tight money policy was loosened, and hyperinflation became the latest threat to a Russian economy already suffering from sharp drops in production as well as long-standing technological backwardness.

The essentially free market policies espoused by Gaydar and other young radical reformers in government were criticized from many quarters, including that of Vice-President Aleksandr Rutskoy (b. 1947). In the new political circumstances, the organization which had played an important part in bringing Yel'tsin to power, Democratic Russia, could not maintain either its unity or influence. As it became increasingly divided, other political tendencies and alliances emerged. In June 1992 a new centrist bloc, situated between the radical liberals (personified by Gaydar), on the one hand, and the nationalists and unreconstructed Communists (who themselves formed a loose alliance), on the other, was created. Called the Civic Union, this centrist organization brought together Rutskoy's People's Party of Free Russia, the Democratic Party of Russia led by Nikolay Travkin (b. 1946) and the All-Russian Renewal Union, an association of industrialists and administrators whose principal spokesman

POST-SOVIET RUSSIAN POLITICS

The first year of Russian politics following the collapse of the Soviet Union in December 1991 was dominated by an attempt to introduce radical economic measures and the strains this imposed on relations within the executive and between the executive and legislature. Backed by the authority of President Boris Yel'tsin, who no longer had to share power with Mikhail Gorbachev, the Russian government launched more drastic reform measures than had hitherto been attempted.

The most influential figure in the making of Russian economic policy was Yegor Gaydar (b. 1956), at the beginning of 1992 Minister of Finance and Economics and Deputy Prime Minister and subsequently acting Prime Minister. (Yel'tsin initially kept the prime ministerial as well as presidential powers in his own hands.) Attempting to move more resolutely in the direction of a market economy, Gaydar introduced sharp increases in the prices

Boris Yel'tsin and Ruslan Kasbulatov at a session of the Congress of People's Deputies of Russia in 1990. Yel'tsin, then Chairman of the Supreme Soviet of Russia, and Khasbulatov (left), his First Deputy, were close allies. They remained so throughout 1991 but after the disintegration of the Soviet Union became political enemies

Anti-reformist demonstration by Communist hardliners, Moscow, 1993

was Arkady Vol'sky (b. 1932). The Civic Union, while professing support for a market economy, criticized the 'shock therapy' being proposed by Gaydar and his colleagues. It also took a strong line in defence of the integrity of the Russian state which – as a number of national territories within Russia, including Tatarstan and Chechnia, asserted a high degree of *de facto* independence – showed signs of following the same fissiparous path as that taken by the Soviet Union.

Tensions also grew between government and parliament. Within the Russian Supreme Soviet and its larger outer body, the Congress of People's Deputies, an increasing amount of power fell into the hands of the Chairman, Ruslan Khasbulatov (b. 1942), who made no secret of his dislike of several of the more radical members of Yel'tsin's

team, including Gaydar and the State Secretary, Gennady Burbulis (b. 1945). Khasbulatov, while generally refraining at this stage from attacking Yel'tsin explicitly, did not flinch from challenging his powers. Although he defended this in terms of parliamentary sovereignty, democratic norms and checks and balances, Khasbulatov could not himself escape the accusation of authoritarian tendencies as he tried, for example, to make the newspaper, *Izvestiya*, which had become basically pro-Yel'tsin but relatively independent, a fully-controlled mouthpiece of the leadership of the Supreme Soviet.

Yel'tsin, in his first year as undisputed chief executive and head of state, found himself in many respects facing the same dilemmas and difficulties Gorbachev had encountered. He had to weigh against the demands of marketization the possible social and political consequences of widespread factory closures and large-scale unemployment. He, too, had the problem of creating a genuine federation within a formerly centralized multinational state and, like his predecessor, he issued decrees which were ignored in many parts of the country. Yel'tsin, like Gorbachev, met resistance from the military-industrial complex, unwilling to see the break-up of defence industry, and found his policies under attack from a 'red and brown' alliance of old-style Communists and militant Russian nationalists. Significantly earlier than Gorbachev, Yel'tsin made concessions to his critics and brought into the government a number of more conservative counter-weights to his initial radically reformist team. Yel'tsin and his Foreign Minister, Andrey Kozyrev, were – like Gorbachev and Shevardnadze before them – criticized for pursuing an excessively pro-Western policy and one which did not sufficiently safeguard Russian interests. When, moreover, Yel'tsin prepared to make concessions to the Japanese government in its demand for the return of the Kurile Islands – under Russian jurisdiction since 1945 – he was put under intense pressure from centrist as well as nationalist opinion not to negotiate away any part of the Russian state; bowing to this, he cancelled two days before his planned departure a visit to Japan he was to have made in September 1992.

In economic policy, however, Yel'tsin's government pursued a more radical course than had been attempted under Gorbachev. In October 1992 an ambitious, albeit controversial, privatization scheme was launched, whereby 10,000-ruble vouchers were issued to each citizen in an attempt to shift 70 per cent of Russian industry from state to private ownership. This was partly in response to criticism of 'nomenklatura privatization', whereby sections of the old political and economic élite strove to turn their former control over economic assets into actual ownership. For the population as a whole, the early

Anti-Yel'tsin demonstrator in Moscow. She carries a placard on which the word, 'Liar', is emblazoned on Yel'tsin's picture. The handwritten injunctions on the right read 'Traitor out!' and 'Shame!'

Viktor Chernomyrdin, Prime Minister of Russia since December 1992

Boris Yel'tsin addressing an outdoor meeting in the run-up to the April 1993 referendum, in which a majority of those who voted expressed support for the Russian President

post-Soviet period was one of uncertainty. When the Seventh Congress of People's Deputies of the Russian Federation was held in December 1992, Gaydar and his government encountered fierce criticism. Yel'tsin failed in his attempt to promote Gaydar from acting Prime Minister to the actual Prime Ministership. Gaydar resigned and the Congress elected as Prime Minister one of Yel'tsin's alternative choices, Viktor Chernomyrdin (b. 1938), whose previous experience had been as an energy minister and in the apparatus of the Central Committee of the CPSU. In April 1993 Yel'tsin won a referendum victory in which a majority of those voting expressed confidence in him. That victory did not, however, resolve the increasingly bitter disagreements between executive and legislature. Relations between the President and Vice-President also deteriorated and on 1 September 1993 Yel'tsin took the controversial step of suspending Rutskoy from his duties. On 21 September the Russian President went further, unilaterally dissolving the Congress of People's Deputies and Supreme Soviet. Many deputies refused to be dispersed and passed a resolution transferring presidential power from Yel'tsin to Rutskoy. The standoff came to a bloody end on 3–4 October when, after supporters of Rutskoy had damaged the Moscow mayor's office and unsuccessfully attempted to storm the Ostankino television station, Yel'tsin called up troops to bombard into submission those deputies and their supporters who

had stayed in the parliamentary building, the Moscow White House. There were scores of deaths before Rutskoy and the Supreme Soviet Chairman Khasbulatov surrendered to troops loyal to Yel'tsin and were imprisoned. The Chairman of the Constitutional Court, Valery Zor'kin, who had held Yel'tsin's dissolution of the Congress of People's Deputies and Supreme Soviet to be unconstitutional but had tried to mediate between executive and legislature, was removed from office and the Court itself was suspended by presidential decree.

Elections for a new legislature and a plebiscite on a new Constitution which expanded presidential powers at the expense of parliament were held on 12 December 1993. Voter turnout was low – according even to the official figures less than 55 per cent of the electorate participated – but approximately 60 per cent voted for the Constitution and 40 per cent against. This meant that only 31 per cent of eligible voters had supported the draft Constitution, although an October 1990 Law on the Referendum of the RSFSR had stipulated that on matters affecting the Constitution a majority of all registered voters in the country would be required.

The results of the election for the new parliament were disappointing for Yel'tsin and for the radical economic reformers led by Gaydar. The legislature is composed of two chambers – the Federation Council, with 178 deputies, and the State Duma, with 450 deputies. Not all constituencies participated in the elections and so only 171 of the 178 seats in the Federation Council were filled and 444 in the State Duma. Half the deputies for the Duma were elected in single-member constituencies on a 'first-past-the-post' basis and half from a list of officially-registered movements and political parties. A barrier of 5 per cent of the votes had to be surmounted before a party or bloc could gain representation; eight out of the thirteen contesting the December 1993 election surmounted that barrier.

In the party list component of the election the main victor was Vladimir Zhirinovsky's right-wing and misnamed Liberal Democratic Party with 59 seats, but in the single-member constituencies the reformist grouping, Russia's Choice, did much better and finished overall with a total of 96 seats in the State Duma – more than any other party or movement. However, radical reformers and strongly pro-Yel'tsin groups found themselves in a minority in the lower chamber of the legislature. Not only did Zhirinovsky's party finish second to Russia's Choice in terms of number of seats (and ahead of it in percentage of the vote), but the revived Communists – the Communist Party of the Russian Federation – were a close third.

Although this new legislature had fewer powers than its predecessor, early indications were that it

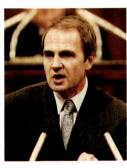

Valery Zor'kin, the Chairman of the Russian Constitutional Court, who tried to mediate between the executive and legislature throughout the first nine months of 1993. Having ruled that President Yel'tsin's forcible dissolution of the Congress of People's Deputies and Supreme Soviet on 21 September was unconstitutional, Zor'kin was forced to resign from his post following the violent denouement at the Moscow White House on 4 October

Vladimir Zhirinovsky, whose strong showing in the December 1993 parliamentary elections made his nationalistic Liberal Democratic Party a force to be reckoned with in the State Duma

would be an uneasy partner for the Russian president. In February 1994 it used the power of amnesty accorded it in the new Constitution to set free Rutskoy and Khasbulatov, and the other rebels of October 1993, and attempted to call a halt to any further trial of the putschists of August 1991. More acceptably for Yel'tsin and Russian reformers, the State Duma simultaneously amnestied prisoners who had been found guilty of economic crimes in the Soviet era (often the kind of entrepreneurial activity now approved).

In both executive and legislature some remnants of the old Soviet system survived (not least in people's consciousness) and neither an effectively-functioning new political system nor a transformed economy had emerged by 1994. It had become increasingly clear that the process of transition to a new order was unlikely to be either smooth or fast.   AHB

POST-SOVIET RUSSIAN LAW

The early post-Soviet period saw the Russian Federation continue the attempt to democratize and to privatize the state. The dual process was encapsulated in the change of adjective from 'socialist' to 'democratic law-governed state'. In whatever way a new Constitution divides political power, early indications were that its legal bases would cover the following: some entrenchment mechanism so that the most fundamental provisions can be amended only by referendum; a recognition that certain international norms operate directly within the national system, and that ratified treaties are superior to Russian statutes; a Bill of Rights; a requirement that all legislation be published; a Constitutional (or Supreme) Court with power to quash all unconstitutional legislation and to hear individual complaints that constitutional rights are being infringed by administrative or judicial practice; an entitlement of all citizens to bring a case whether of private or public law before their 'lawful judge' (German law's concept of *der gesetzliche Richter*). Pressures continue for the criminal law to reflect the liberalization process, with procedure altered to guarantee fair trial and, most importantly, attempts made to improve the practice of the courts and Procuracy. There are also demands for a sharp curtailment of the list of 'administrative violations' under which, although they are technically not crimes, citizens may be fined.

If privatization is to succeed there must be a private law within which it can operate with confidence. There were calls for the new Constitution to permit private ownership of anything, including land, whether as an object of use or as investment. Other pivots of private law are promised. First, there will have to be a coherent system embracing a law of persons, of property, of obligations, and of liability. Secondly, there will be needed a law of commerce dealing with such areas as commercial paper and bankruptcy. As to the first, 'private' co-operatives are now juridical persons and laws on limited liability companies and stock corporations have appeared. The RSFSR 1990 Ownership Act permits citizens to own not merely consumer items but productive assets, shares and securities; the Land Code envisages the privatization of interests in agricultural land; and laws on intellectual property ought to provide protection for patents, trade-marks and the like. On paper, the different contractual patterns of the Civil Code (sale, lease, or loan) are the same as those of the West and, if intelligently used by courts and lawyers, should suffice to facilitate business financing. A consumer protection law will provide for strict product liability. Legislation now states clearly that an owner's property must answer for his debts and a bankruptcy regime is being worked out. The legal regulation of stock transactions, commercial paper, unfair competition and monopoly power is also now under way.

The new Constitution came into being, not under the existing procedures, but under a plebiscite of 12 December 1993, ordered by presidential decree, and contains the features outlined above. It is much more difficult to amend than were its predecessors, requiring a Constitutional Assembly and possible referendum to change the basics and, for the rest, the consent of two-thirds of the component units of the federation. It incorporated international law into the domestic system. In place of the Congress it sets up a bicameral legislature consisting of the Duma (450 seats) and the Federation Council. Federal issues are dealt with in generalities, with the President being given mediating powers. The President's role is strengthened, but his veto on bills can be overridden by special majority, and his power to dissolve Parliament is limited. The Constitutional Court survives on paper. Private property and free enterprise are now enshrined in the Bill of Rights.   BAR

Econo

The Imperial economy

SERFDOM

During the millennium that elapsed between the emergence of Russia as a political entity in the ninth century and the abolition of serfdom in 1861 the country witnessed vast territorial expansion, a rise to imperial status and fundamental changes outside its borders in the economies and societies of Western Europe under the impact of the Industrial Revolution. Throughout, Russia's economy remained backward compared to Western Europe, the bulk of its income and wealth deriving from traditional low-yielding agriculture and artisan industry pursued to an overwhelming extent on a subsistence basis.

One period (roughly ninth to thirteenth century) does not fully conform to this pattern. The basis of wealth creation in Kievan Russia was not agriculture, which was largely primitive, but trade with Byzantium, Western Europe and the Orient. Successive nomadic invasions put an end to this trade, and the devastation following the Mongol invasion of 1240 completed the displacement of the Russian people to the relative safety of the forests of the north-east, the cradle of future Muscovy. The Mongol onslaught and the two and a half centuries of occupation constituted the first major crisis to affect the economy and society of Russia. The low-yielding agricultural economy allowed for little accumulation, while the tribute imposed by the Mongols and their repeated raids and punitive expeditions meant a continuous drain of resources. However, the Mongol fiscal organization based on censuses of households was to be a useful means of resource mobilization in the hands of Moscow rulers, although it is uncertain whether the peasant commune (*mir*), which was to be such a significant feature of Russia's agrarian structure at least until 1906, had its origins here. The *mir* periodically redistributed land among households and regulated agricultural use of common land.

The second major crisis occurred in the sixteenth and early seventeenth century and was associated with the despotic policies of Ivan IV, the Livonian War, civil war and foreign intervention following the extinction of the dynasty. Several consecutive famines depopulated central areas through flight or death, economic activity declined and serfdom began to be imposed. However, this period also saw positive developments: the exploration of the White Sea route, the temporary gain of a foothold on the Baltic, the conquest of Siberia, the freeing of the Volga route from the Tatars – all elements in the growth of trading potential.

The seventeenth century marked the beginnings of a business economy. English and, above all, Dutch merchants activated Russia's internal and foreign trade and turned increasingly to industrial activities with the encouragement of the Russian government. Native businessmen appeared less enterprising: they lacked the resources and experience of their foreign counterparts and were taxed more heavily than the latter. Russian and foreign merchants alike suffered from the ruler's right of pre-emption on the most lucrative goods.

The commercial and industrial advances of the sixteenth and seventeenth centuries were insufficient to meet fully the demands of Peter the Great's military effort in prising open access to the Baltic. While Peter's economic achievements were largely a function of his military ambitions and involved massive state intervention in the provision of capital, markets and labour, in the long run private initiative and autonomous growth were released; the seventeenth century 'manufactory' was the transmitter of technology, skills and entrepreneurship. During the eighteenth century Russia became the single largest exporter of iron and had a virtual monopoly on exports of products such as flax, hemp and tar. The development of ports, canals and roads quickened the pace of internal commerce, as did to some extent the abolition of internal tariffs, the beginning of organized banking, and initially the issue of paper money under Catherine II.

Victory over the Turks gained for Russia access to the Black Sea, opening foreign markets to grain export. However, as price differentials suggest, the isolation of individual regions remained, probably because of transportation difficulties and inadequacies in commercial organization. Private industrial entrepreneurship, no longer foreign only, appeared among serfs, noblemen and merchants,

Previous spread. A Moscow street trader sells off communist labour banners among his display of tourist trinkets. When Soviet constraints on the private sector were lifted most entrepreneurs turned to trading; only later did some begin to turn to production

and operated in areas of consumer rather than state demand. But whereas the Industrial Revolution had had its effect in most of Western Europe and above all in Britain by the end of the Napoleonic wars, relative retardation made Russia assume the role of supplier of foodstuffs and primary products to those industrializing and urbanizing countries. Russia's increased agricultural output (first the fortuitous outcome of Peter the Great's poll tax, and after 1775 consequent upon price rises) was due to area extension rather than to improved yields. The internal market for grain was limited and exports were hampered by the British Corn Laws, distance and inadequate transport. Nevertheless, Russia was far from stagnant: the overall value of manufacturing output grew forty times between 1799 and 1858 – a fivefold increase per head – and made up about 15 per cent of the gross national product. However, though the factory labour force likewise grew about fivefold between 1804 and 1860, it represented only about 1 per cent of the population. Two-thirds of the value of industrial output came from artisan workshops and domestic industry which was scattered over the vast empire. Modern technology began to be employed on a significant scale in two industries working for an internal consumer market, sugar refining and cotton spinning; in the rest of industry handicraft methods prevailed. By the mid-century (1859) only about 7 per cent of the population lived in cities, compared with some 50 per cent in England and Wales and 25.5 per cent in France (1850).

This retardation has been ascribed to various causes. Serfdom, a means for securing not so much supply of labour as of taxes and recruits, was introduced by statute as late as 1649, though it had been evolving since at least the end of the fifteenth century. While it certainly stifled initiative and advance, induced apathy and kept demand low, it

was not the only reason for Russia's long-standing backwardness. Another factor was an excess of government involvement in the economy which crowded out private enterprise and caused commercial decisions to be taken on non-economic grounds, although without state support in the early eighteenth century little economic progress could have been achieved. The physical environment – poor quality soil, climate, distances and location of resources on the periphery – has been a factor both in Russia's poverty before the industrial age and in the high cost and effort involved in economic development since. To this must be added the cost of first attaining and then sustaining Great Power status, which meant a continuous drain of resources away from domestic accumulation through the budget for military and strategic purposes.   OC

INDUSTRIALIZATION

The emancipation of the serfs by an Imperial Manifesto of 19 February 1861 under Alexander II was the dividing line between old and modern Russia. In political terms the Tsar preferred that 'hostility between peasants and their owners' be dealt with 'from above rather than from below', but his government's economic motivation was to foster industry after Russia's defeat – substantially due to inadequate armaments – in the Crimean War: the lifting of the yoke of serfdom would allow manpower to take jobs wherever offered.

The emancipation freed 22 million serfs (40 per cent of the nation) but failed to establish conditions for an independent and prosperous peasantry. Excluding Poland, the land allocated to peasants was on average 13 per cent less than that which they had previously tilled for their own use, and remained subject to redistribution by the *mir*, thereby perpet-

Below. *The Nobel Brothers oilfield, Baku, in the late nineteenth century. Russia was for a time the world's biggest oil exporter. Below right.* Part of the Baku oilfield today. Greatly in need of modernization, the Azerbaijan oil industry has entered into joint ventures with western companies

389

The location of industry in Russia, 1900

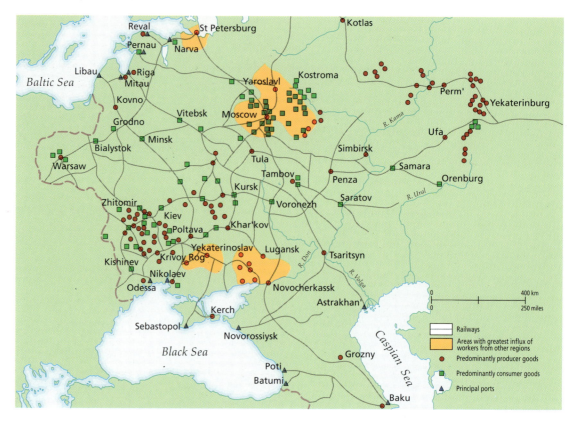

uating the serf's indifference to land improvement. The government financed land allotment to former serfs against redemption dues payable over the ensuing forty-nine years. Reduction of burdens on the peasantry did not begin until 1881, with the abolition of the poll tax on landless peasants, the moderation of redemption dues, and the establishment of a Peasant Land Bank to finance the purchase of land. By the mid-1890s, however, tax arrears had reached equality with tax assessments; peasant and worker unrest increased under the impact of the depression of 1900–02 and continued sporadically, culminating in the uprising of December 1905.

On the eve of emancipation the industrial labour force included 1.2 million serfs but, despite the apparent availability of rural manpower after 1861, employers in mining and manufacturing tended to choose capital-intensive plant. Workshop and individual artisan industry often had a competitive edge over large-scale factory industry, with high fixed costs and overheads, and factories, particularly after the depression, concentrated into larger units or formed cartels. On the eve of the First World War Russia could be described as a 'dual economy' – big modern firms in industry, and small-scale activity in artisan trades and agriculture – a characteristic of many underdeveloped countries, which are unable to rely on direct taxation because of the small share of income arising in money form in the peasant and handicrafts sector. Indirect taxation made the peasant bear much of the cost of the bureaucracy,

state investment and subsidies to guarantee interest on foreign loans. The landowning classes neither saved nor were taxed in proportions that would generate substantial domestic investment and by spending much on travel abroad burdened the balance of payments. West European investment financed the savings and the foreign-exchange gaps.

RUSSIAN ECONOMIC EXPANSION, 1891–1913	
	Increase (%)
Population	37.3
of which urban	68.9
Per capita output of grain	35.3
Per capita industrial output	124.0
Employment in mining, manufacturing and railways	128.5
Length of railway network	132.0

Source: *Cambridge Economic History of Europe*, vol. VII, part 2 (1978)

Railways especially attracted foreign capital for their construction and constituted material security for loans; they stimulated the growth of Russian industries to supply them (for example with rails, rolling stock and coal), provided training for entrepreneurship and management, and greatly widened the Russian market. The Trans-Siberian Railway and other lines distributed peasants deeper into the steppe and the further they settled from towns, the

The Trans-Siberian Railway

A Trans-Siberian railway was first suggested in 1857 by an American named Perry Collins. Nothing came of the idea, however, and it was not until 1891 that the decision to build a railway from the Urals (originally Chelyabinsk) to the Pacific was announced by Imperial decree. Construction started the same year. Building was carried out simultaneously in six sectors, the last of which was not fully completed until 1916.

For many years journeys were delayed by the obstruction of Lake Baykal. During the Russo-Japanese war, a track was laid across the frozen lake in order to speed the delivery of supplies to the Far East. After Russia's defeat in that war, a large new section of track had to be laid because of the shift in borders in Japan's favour.

The main purposes of the railway when it was built were military and economic, the aim being to open up Siberia for settlers. Today largely electrified, the line stretches from Moscow to Vladivostok, a distance of 9,311 km with a journey time of seven days. It is perhaps the best way for the traveller to experience the vastness that is Siberia:

> From now on the Siberian forest, the taiga, thickened, blurring the distant hills with smudges of trees and hiding the settlements that had swallowed so many banished Russians. In places this dense forest disappeared for twenty miles; then there was tundra, a plain of flawless snow on which rows of light-poles trailed into the distance, getting smaller and smaller, like those diagrammatic pictures that illustrate perspective, and the last light-pole a dot. The hugeness of Russia overwhelmed me. I had been travelling for five days over these landscapes and still more than half the country remained to be crossed. I scanned the window for some new detail that would intimate that we were getting closer to Moscow.

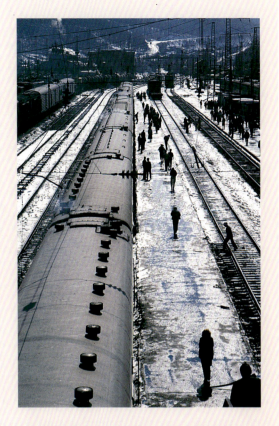

> But the differences from day to day were slight; the snow was endless, the stops were brief, and the sun, which shone so brightly on the taiga, was always eclipsed by the towns we passed through: an impenetrable cloud of smoky fog hung over every town, shutting out the sun. The small villages were different; they lay in sunlight, precariously, between the taiga and the tracks, their silence so great it was nearly visible.

From Paul Theroux, *The Great Railway Bazaar* (1977)

more they committed their grain to the railway for cash disposal (freight tariffs were geared to export sales).

The imposition of a customs tariff in 1885 further fostered industrial investment and, despite relative stagnation in and after the depression of 1900–02, impressive growth was achieved in both industry and agriculture. Farming was stimulated after the 1905 revolution by the Stolypin reform, whereby redemption dues were liquidated from 1907. From October 1906 the peasant could receive an internal passport without the consent of the commune; this gave him the right to settle elsewhere, but most stayed on the land to constitute what Stolypin hoped would be 'a class of small proprietors – this basic cell of the State and in its very nature an adversary of all destructive theories'.   MCK

The Soviet economy

REVOLUTION AND 'WAR COMMUNISM'

It was one of the 'destructive theories' that Stolypin feared – Marxism as interpreted by Lenin – which inspired the Bolshevik victory of 1917, but it is questionable whether the Russian war economy was so grossly inefficient that the tsarist collapse was inevitable once hostilities began. The output of armaments (mainly due to increasing productivity

Compulsory grain delivery to a military collection point under War Communism (Kurgan region, 1918). Introduced to assure supplies to the Red Army during the Civil War, procurement at bayonet point continued after victory over the Whites, for unchecked hyperinflation and rationing that favoured the towns removed incentives for farmers to sell their produce voluntarily

in the munitions industry) expanded substantially in 1915 and 1916 and the civilian standard of living was not reduced before the end of 1916. The economic element in the 1917 revolutions was the withdrawal of labour from farming by conscription to the army and a food supply crisis in 1917. Although there is controversy over the weakness of government wartime industrial organization and whether it was effectively replaced by committees of private manufacturers, the Provisional Government (February–October 1917) introduced a centralized control structure, headed by an Economic Council, with a Supreme Economic Committee as its executive agency. The Soviet authorities transformed that Committee into the Supreme Economic Council ('Vesenkha', from its Russian initials) and Lenin toyed with schemes of a mixed economy and of co-operatives until the emergence of direct worker management – such factory committees constituting a political threat to the local soviets – compelled him to nationalize large-scale industry (28 June 1918). The rest of industry was expropriated on 29 November 1920 and the period to March 1921 is known in retrospect as 'War Communism'.

The exigencies of supply in the Civil War were a major factor in the new Soviet government's choice of complete nationalization, the administration by directive of industry and transport and the compulsory procurement of foodstuffs from farmers. But there was an ideological motive in rejecting use of the market and of the money mechanism – antipathy to the 'spontaneity' of the market and preference for planning in terms of physical targets. The government tolerated, if not encouraged, inflation (in 1920 currency circulation rose from 225 to 1,169 thousand million rubles), characterized by Ye. A. Preobrazhensky (1886–1937), Trotsky's principal economist ally, as 'the machine-gun of the Commis-

sariat of Finance, attacking the bourgeois system in the rear and using the currency laws of that system to destroy it'. All banks were abolished and money itself was on the point of being replaced by 'labour units'. The state budget financed all nationalized production enterprises, which were thereby relieved of having to pay, and to be paid by, one another (the practice became known as 'glavkism', after the name of the administering state agencies). Money wages being almost worthless, payment in kind and rationing predominated. A State Commission for the Electrification of Russia (GOELRO, 1920) drew up a plan on the basis of material balances – that is, of projected availabilities and requirements of energy and industrial material in physical, not money, quantities. To implement it a State Planning Commission (Gosplan) was established in February 1921.
                                                                        MCK

LENIN'S 'NEW ECONOMIC POLICY'

Peasant risings in late 1920 against compulsory procurement of farm produce and the Kronstadt mutiny in early 1921 warned the party leadership against the excesses of a 'command economy'. Lenin secured a Central Committee resolution criticizing Trotsky for 'the degeneration of centralism and militarized forms of work' in December 1920 and presented the X Party Congress in March 1921 with a formula for replacing requisitions in agriculture by a tax related to level of income and numbers of dependants. For that and the following year the tax was levied in kind, but from 1923 it was payable partly (and from 1924 wholly) in cash. The peasant could market the remaining production within a general return to a money economy under the 'New Economic Policy' (NEP).

Inflation was halted by a currency reform (1922–24), introducing a new, partly gold-backed, ruble and a banking system to control money supply (the State Bank in October 1921 and specialized, state-run investment banks during 1922). Decrees of August and December 1921 handed back so much property to private owners that only 8.5 per cent of industrial enterprises remained nationalized. These latter, however, occupied 84 per cent of the labour force, thereby retaining, as Lenin put it, the 'commanding heights' of the economy in the hands of the state. Even at the peak of NEP in 1925–26, private plants produced only 3.5 per cent and foreign concessions (permitted by a decree of March 1923, but withdrawn after September 1928) a mere 0.4 per cent of the output of large-scale industry. State entities were largely restricted to wholesale trade (thereby exercising some control over prices and distribution); 76 per cent of retail turnover was in private hands by 1923.

Bias towards the independent peasantry – politically determined by Lenin's policy of their 'alliance' with the urban working class and economically by the importance of restoring food production – was demonstrated in the 'Scissors Crisis' of 1923–24. On an index 1913 = 100, the price of farm produce was 89 and of industrial goods 276; the symbolism was of a widening of the price 'handles' of the 'scissors' to cut the standard of living of the peasantry. The government ordered state production trusts to reduce prices and until early 1927 continued to keep industrial prices artificially low. The right wing of the Party, as represented by N.I. Bukharin, advocated the maintenance of such preference for farming: sales of foodstuffs at home and for export would generate savings which could be taxed for industrialization. The left – notably Trotsky and Preobrazhensky – urged 'unequal exchange' between country and town, that is a policy of direct exploitation of the agricultural surplus, for rapid industrialization. A temporary curtailment of grain marketed in 1927/28 – deliberately magnified by Stalin into a 'grain crisis' – helped the party Central Committee in July 1928 to adopt a 'high variant' of the draft Five-year Plan and to demand a 'tribute' from the peasantry to furnish the necessary accumulation; in September the fight against the richer farmer (the *kulak*) was equated with that against external class enemies.   MCK

THE PRE-WAR FIVE-YEAR PLANS

The First Five-year Plan was inaugurated on 1 October 1928, and was declared to have been completed in the four and a quarter years to 31 December 1932; it launched a programme of industrial investment on an unprecedented scale (mainly in the capital goods' industries). The Second Five-year Plan (1933–37) consolidated and broadened those projects, while the Third (1938–42) was interrupted by the German invasion of 22 June 1941. In 1928–37 industrial production increased by 12–18 per cent a year, machine-building expanded particularly rapidly, and many new industries were established; tractors, trucks, iron- and steel-making equipment and modern tanks and aircraft, for example, were all produced for the first time on a mass scale. Industrial growth was achieved partly by a massive increase in the labour force: the number of persons employed in industry, including building, increased from 4.3 million in 1928 to 11.6 million in 1937. But capital stock in industry increased much more rapidly than the labour force, so capital per worker rose substantially; consequently, after an initial decline in 1930–32, labour productivity (output per man-year) also increased rapidly. No clear

evidence is available about the efficiency with which resources were utilized, though emphasis was placed throughout these years on growth rather than on care for costs and avoidance of waste. Attention was also devoted to the social services: employment increased at the same rate in education as in industry, and employment in the health services also expanded rapidly.

In contrast, personal consumption per head of population declined in 1928–32, and did not regain the 1928 level until well after the Second World War. The production of industrial consumer goods increased much more slowly than that of capital goods, and, even according to official figures, agricultural production per head of population was about 10 per cent lower in 1937–39 than in 1927–29. The decline in food production per head was even greater, particularly during the First Five-year Plan when there was a catastrophic fall in the number of livestock. In 1932–33 famine was widespread in the countryside and millions died.

While agricultural production did not increase in 1929–41, or increased very slowly, major changes occurred in the structure of agriculture. During enforced collectivization, mainly carried out between the autumn of 1929 and the end of 1931, 20 million individual farms were amalgamated into 250,000 collectives. The boundaries between strips were removed, and arable land was worked in common, using, as they became available, tractors and other agricultural machinery from machine-tractor stations; these gradually replaced the individual's horse and plough. At the same time each collective-farm household also owned some livestock, and retained a personal plot for vegetables and fruit. A large part of collective production, particularly grain, was compulsorily supplied to the state at low prices; but some collective and much personal production were sold on a free market (officially sanctioned in 1932). The collective farm was thus both a repressive instrument for the control of peasant production and a compromise between social and private ownership; planned controls similar to those used in state industry were combined with a market mechanism, which together constituted an effective, if not an efficient, means for increasing the supply of grain to the state. The state in turn sold grain to the rapidly expanding urban population and also (in 1930–32, when machinery imports greatly increased) on the foreign market (annual deliveries were 30 million tonnes in 1938–40 as compared with 10 million tonnes in 1926–28, although the harvest was only 3–4 million tonnes higher). The system also facilitated the release of labour to the towns: the urban population rose from 26 million in 1926 to 56 million in 1939, and most of the increase was due to the flight or migration of peasants from the countryside. But the pressure on the collective farm to supply the state at low prices destroyed incentives, while the slaughter of livestock in 1930–33 greatly reduced capital, including draught power.

The net effect of the introduction of the collective-farm system on the process of industrialization is still disputed: although it provided a crucial, if costly, mechanism for the supply of agricultural products and labour to the state, a large amount of machinery and consumer goods was supplied by industry to agriculture in return for the supply of agricultural products to the towns.

The mechanism of controls over industry was also by directive: materials and capital equipment were allocated to factories and construction sites. The central control of wages, made possible by subordination (by 1929) of the trade unions, restricted urban purchasing power and reduced the standard of living of most of the urban population in favour of expenditure on capital goods.

Neither the industrial nor the collective-farm system consisted simply of physical controls. Rationing of food and consumer goods, introduced in the towns in 1928–29, was abolished in 1935, after which the authorities attempted to balance supply and demand on the retail market: consumer choice, if not consumer sovereignty, to some extent existed. At the same time, most industrial workers and other state employees (those outside the growing forced-labour of the prison camps) remained free to change their jobs; an imperfect market for labour existed. Cost controls and profit-and-loss

accounting, major features of state industry in the 1920s, were resumed and strengthened from 1931 onwards. Thus a money economy, with recognized market elements, existed together with physical planning; and official planning was supplemented and made to work more smoothly by a variety of unplanned black and 'grey' markets.

The achievements were immense: the USSR was transformed into a major industrial power and equipped for defence in the Second World War. Mass unemployment was eliminated, and millions of illiterate or poorly-educated peasants were trained in industrial skills. But the costs and failures were also immense. Many people suffered and died. The planning system was crude; control of quality was difficult; innovation from below was inhibited. Economic and social differentiation were far more extensive than any Soviet Marxist had envisaged before 1930. In 1929–41 a new political, economic and social system was created in the USSR, admired and hated in the West, envied but often misunderstood in countries which were not yet industrialized. The nature of the system is still hotly disputed in Russia today; the prevailing view is that during the Stalin years far more could have been achieved at far less cost.

RWD

PLANNING IN WARTIME AND IN RECONSTRUCTION

In the five months following the German invasion (22 June 1941) 1,500 industrial enterprises were dismantled for shipment east and ten million people were resettled. Mineral extraction and hydro-electricity generation cannot be transferred, and losses of ores and energy at first seriously hindered the war effort. Forced labour, which the Terror of 1937–38 had made available in millions, was extensively used to extract non-ferrous ores in climatically harsh territories – notably at Karaganda in Central Asia, Noril'sk on the Arctic littoral and at Kolyma-Indigirka in the far north-east. Some scientists among those arrested were placed in prison laboratories where their research and development work was especially valuable in the production of military aircraft.

At its nadir in 1942 net material product was two-thirds of the 1940 level (agricultural output, due particularly to the German occupation of Ukraine, was at little more than one-third of pre-war levels), but no less than 55 per cent of it was devoted to military purposes. That the USSR converted to armaments so extensively and so quickly under conditions of extreme shortage (and before lend-lease supplies became available from the USA) was undoubtedly due to central planning on material

INDUSTRIAL OUTPUT IN THE SOVIET PERIOD

Product	1913	1940	1965	1979	1987	1990
Electricity (million MWh)	2	49	507	1,239	1,665	1,726
Oil (million tonnes)	10	31	243	586	624	571
Natural gas (billion cu m)	—	3	128	407	727	815
Coal (million tonnes)	29	166	578	719	760	703
Steel (million tonnes)	4	18	91	149	162	154
Mineral fertilizer (million tonnes)	0.6	0.8	7.4	22	36	32
Sulphuric acid (million tonnes)	0.1	2	9	22	29	27
Synthetic fibres (thousand tonnes)	—	11	407	1,100	1,517	1,477
Metal-cutting machine tools (thousands)	2	58	186	231	156	157
Lorries (thousands)	—	136	380	780	850	774
Motor cars (thousands)	0.1	6	201	1,314	1,332	1,258
Tractors (thousands)	—	32	355	557	567	495
Paper (million tonnes)	0.3	1	3	5	6	6
Cement (million tonnes)	2	6	72	123	137	137
Textiles: cotton (million sq m)	1,817	2,715	5,499	6,974	7,945	7,846
wool (million sq m)	138	155	466	774	690	704
Leather footwear (million pairs)	68	211	486	739	809	843
Domestic refrigerators (thousands)	—	4	1,675	5,954	5,984	6,499
Sugar (million tonnes)	1	2	11	11	14	13

Source: SSSR v tsifrakh 1979 godu. Moscow, 1980; Narodnoe khozyaistvo SSSR v 1990 godu. Moscow, 1991

balances (a technique adopted by other belligerents) and to strict financial controls which inhibited war-time inflation (between 1940 and 1944 industrial wages rose 53 per cent and retail prices increased 120 per cent). The budget ran a significant deficit only in 1941 and 1942, taxation and bond sales matching the enlargement of public expenditure. Supply (chiefly by rail through Persia and by sea to Murmansk) from the western Allies was crucial for opening bottle-necks (as in road transport), but it was the conversion of domestic industry to military needs that was quantitatively decisive for victory.

In conditions of peace the architect of the war economy, N.A. Voznesensky, chairman of Gosplan, attempted to rationalize Stalin's command system: he encouraged economics as a discipline (until 1943 party ideology had rejected any application of 'the law of value' to the public sector) and introduced a far-reaching reform of wholesale prices (January 1949) which would have eliminated subsidies and fostered the profitable operation of state industry. Victim of a struggle within Stalin's entourage in which G.M. Malenkov was victorious), Voznesensky was dismissed in early 1949 and executed a year later. His reforms were annulled and improvements in price relations and in economic administration had to await the death of Stalin (March 1953).

By that time the reconstruction of a severely war-ravaged economy had been completed. The Fourth Five-year Plan (1946–50) had envisaged an increment of net material product, on an index 1940 = 100, from 83 in 1945 to 138 in 1950. The target was abundantly achieved at 173 by overfulfilment for producers' goods which more than offset a serious underfulfilment in farm output (and doubtless also in consumer goods, for which no goal had been published). Shortages of consumer goods would have been worse if most of the cash in personal hands had not been confiscated simultaneously with the lifting of rationing in December 1947, but the real wage of 1928 was only regained in 1952.

Stalin's immediate successors – a 'collective leadership' led by Malenkov – judged a stronger consumer orientation necessary and promulgated in October 1953 ambitious revisions of the Fifth Five-year Plan (1951–55). Though few of these were fulfilled, the output of consumer goods significantly bettered the original goals.

KHRUSHCHEV'S SEVEN-YEAR PLAN

N.S. Khrushchev abandoned the Sixth Five-year Plan (1956–60) and the structure of economic adminstration which had formulated it, but his Seven-year Plan (1959–65) was much more than a revision of targets. It innovated by lengthening the period planned and by introducing rolling targets; broadened the group of priority sectors to include the chemicals industry and private and co-operative housing; accelerated railway electrification and dieselization within a general programme of energy shift from coal to oil and pursued the encouragement of agriculture. Collective farming benefited in September 1953 from price increases for obligatory deliveries and in 1958 from the disbanding of machine-tractor stations, but Khrushchev alienated local party officials in 1962 by dividing the CPSU into agricultural and industrial sections. The objective was to make the Party more directly concerned with economic performance and, in its emphasis on local responsibility, to further the industrial reorganization, which was the issue on which he had defeated the 'anti-party group' in the Politburo. In 1957 all the industrial ministries save that dealing with nuclear engineering and armaments were abolished and their powers divided between the USSR Gosplan, the union-republican Gosplans and newly-established regional economic councils (sovnarkhozy). Since the boundaries of the 105 regional councils coincided with those of oblasts or groups thereof, the first secretary of the oblast party committee had something like the authority of a minister, dealing, however, not with a single branch but with all his region's large-scale industry (smaller enterprises were subordinated to the union republic). The principal aim was to obliterate the ministerial demarcations, which under 'taut planning' induced ministries to produce materials and components for their own plants and often to deliver them across great distances while identical products crossed them within the supply system of another ministry. Unfortunately, the conditions which induced ministries to be self-sufficient obtained also for the regional authorities, and a recentralization began as early as 1962–63, when quasi-ministries returned in the form of state committees, and sovnarkhozy were merged into much bigger units.

THE ECONOMY UNDER BREZHNEV AND KOSYGIN

Khrushchev's reorganizations were castigated as 'harebrained schemes' by the revived 'collective leadership' which replaced him in October 1964. He was also criticized for heavy imports of grain in 1963, because, despite his efforts to foster agriculture, food supplies remained subject to the gross inefficiency of collective and state farming. To pay for North American grain he had also depleted Soviet reserves of gold.

The new administration, within which party General Secretary L. I. Brezhnev, steadily gained precedence over Chairman of the Council of Ministers, A.N. Kosygin, at first conformed in structuring the economy to Stalin's injunction that the rate of growth of producer goods exceed that of consumer goods. The Eighth Five-year Plan (1966–70) laid down a 51 per cent increment for the former and 45 per cent for the latter. In fulfilment, the rates of growth were almost identical (51 and 49 per cent respectively) and the government actually reversed the priorities for the Ninth Plan (1971–75) – a 46 per cent rise for consumer goods and only 43 per cent for producer goods. Two bad harvests reduced supplies for the consumer-goods sector (and required purchases of North American grain) and the achieved growth rates were underfulfilments at 31 and 41 per cent respectively. Under the Tenth Plan (1976–80) investment resources were switched into farming and agriculture-supporting industries, and the overall pace of industrial growth slackened to 24 per cent (against 36 per cent planned).

In March 1965 Brezhnev announced that procurement quotas would be fixed for five-year periods. Such stability would have enabled collective farms to gain a return from investment for themselves without danger of losing some of it to an increased quota. The government failed to adhere to its undertaking and poured investment into collective and state farms. Between 1970 and 1990 each farm worker had an average 7 per cent annual increment in capital, but output declined each year by 1 per cent.

The reform of industrial administration of September 1965 implemented some of the proposals put forward in September 1962 by Ye.G. Liberman (1897–1983), a professor at Khar'kiv, for harnessing the profit motive to enterprise management and liberating contractual relations between enterprises from control by detailed allocations from above. Liberalization was, however, reversed when the leadership convinced itself, for the invasion of Czechoslovakia, that economic devolution was associated with a loss of political control. Modest changes in procedures for managing state industry were made in April 1973 and July 1979, but wholesale and retail prices nevertheless remained both centrally determined and constant for long periods and there was no sense in which the state sector as it entered the 1980s could be seen as a market.

MCK

REFORM ATTEMPTS UNDER PERESTROIKA

At the time of Brezhnev's death (November 1982) the economy already showed signs of rapid deterioration, particularly in respect of living standards. Among other measures this was reflected in the

Yevsey Liberman, whose proposals marked the starting-point of the abortive economic reform of 1965. Liberman suggested that the fulfilment of targets by Soviet state enterprises should be geared to profits earned, not merely to production and technical goals

launching in May 1982 of a comprehensive 'food programme' – another attempt to solve 'finally' the persistent ills of agriculture.

Under Brezhnev's immediate successor, Yu.V. Andropov, the true state of the economy was more openly admitted than before, and a number of measures were taken to strengthen plan discipline as the road to improvement. However, it was not until the election of M.S. Gorbachev as the First Secretary of the Central Committee of the CPSU in March 1985 (following the death of another temporary leader K.U. Chernenko) that a new chapter in the history of the Soviet economy actually began.

At the outset the policy seemed to continue that of Andropov, only with greater vigour and even more explicit criticism of the past (Brezhnev's years in office, especially the later ones, were termed a 'period of stagnation'). The objective was to accelerate growth by stepping up investment outlays and use them for the technological restructuring of industry; combined with emphasis on better utilization of resources (a switch from extensive to intensive methods), this policy was intended to reverse the previous downward trend, as early as during the Twelfth Five-year Plan for 1986–90, and then go on raising the tempo in the 1990s (to 5 per cent annually) in order to double the 1985 national income by the year 2000, with corresponding massive gains for the consumer.

It nevertheless soon became evident that the economic slide would not be stopped, still less reversed, simply by invigorating the command system, and a 'radical reform' of the economic system was launched in June 1987. The main element of the reform was to free industrial enterprises from administrative tutelage and to render the remuneration of personnel and the capacity to expand largely dependent on financial performance (Law on the State Enterprise, 30 June 1987); there was also some encouragement for non-state sectors of the economy, notably co-operatives. These reform measures proved to be not only inadequate in themselves, but also lacking the indispensable economic environment, notably appropriate price relativities and financial mechanism. While reform concepts were radicalized in subsequent years in the direction of full-scale marketization and changes in property rights ('de-statization' and privatization) and an opening up to the outside world, real changes in the system remained far behind concepts and legislation; the economy was in a no man's land wherein an increasingly incapacitated old mechanism had not been replaced by an effective new one. The systemic inconsistency interacted negatively with other factors in its effect on economic performance – a deterioration in the Soviet terms of trade (due to the fall in the world price of oil and gas and of a

National income per capita in Russia, 1989

Thousand rubles per capita	
	3.0-7.9
	2.5-2.9
	2.3-2.4
	1.9-2.2
	1.3-1.8

decline in export availabilities of oil), a number of policy blunders (*inter alia* a severe loss of budget revenue as a result of an ill-conceived anti-alcohol campaign), and failure to deal in time with many political issues including relations between the centre and the republics.

As a result, by 1990 the Soviet economy had plummeted deeply into crisis, reflected in accelerated financial instability, depreciation of the ruble and diminution of its role in the economy, growing shortages and disruption of economic ties between regions and sectors. Even a very good grain harvest in 1990 had little impact on the situation due to the high level of waste in transport, storage and processing. The ambitious programme for the Twelfth Five-year Plan ended with a further and deeper deterioration: according to official statistics the average annual rate of growth of net material product was only slightly above 1 per cent for the five years, while 1990 showed a 4 per cent decline (national income produced). By the beginning of 1991, when the Thirteenth Five-year Period should have started, no draft Plan had been put to the legislature, another sign of the difficulties and uncertainties plaguing the Soviet economy under Gorbachev on the eve of the last decade of the century.

One of the consequences of the defeat of the

August 1991 conservative *coup d'état* was to unlock the economic reform process, the blockage of which in the course of the year 1991 pushed the Soviet economy into an accelerating downward spiral. By the beginning of 1992 the Russian Federation, now firmly led by Yel'tsin, embarked upon a determined drive towards a market economy based – prospectively – on private ownership. Price liberalization, accompanied by a number of measures aimed at tightening monetary and fiscal discipline, as well as by efforts to prompt private enterprise, was to bring a degree of stabilization to the economy – an indispensable condition for arresting the slide and opening the way for structural change. However, the developments which removed the old barriers to economic transformation engendered some formidable new ones arising mainly from the complexities of disintegration of the old Soviet Union but also from the political disarray within the newly-independent states, including Russia. The fall in national output, export, consumption and other economic aggregates (the drop in GDP was estimated at 15 per cent for 1991) deepened in 1992, and this in turn – other causes apart – widened the budget deficit, thus undermining the stabilization programme, as well as threatening the viability of the social 'safety net' so vital for any such process of transformation, but particularly for one conducted under the circumstances of economic collapse. On the other hand, admission of the former Soviet republics to membership of international financial institutions, the International Monetary Fund and the World Bank in the first place, pointed to the possibility of meaningful assistance from outside, which – if coupled with competent, consistent and properly implemented internal policies – could be a major factor in pulling the erstwhile Soviet economy out of the chaos left behind by 70 years of communist rule and the failure of 'perestroika'. But at the end of 1992 the economy remained in disarray.   WB

THE POST-SOVIET ECONOMIES

The difficulties which the successor states would encounter were already evident in 1991 at the end of which the USSR was dissolved. The USSR on average was a poor country permeated by a long-repressed inflation, the release of which by price liberalization could not be long delayed. The fifteen new governments were confronted by a lack of affinity of state-set retail and wholesale prices with the domestic conditions of supply and demand, an unrealistic exchange rate and profound divergences from the relativities of world market prices. But those same characteristics of the Soviet command economy complicate any accurate ranking of the

republics on an external scale of values. The conversion from Soviet rubles to US dollars in the adjoining Table uses the relationship between the domestic and foreign prices of Soviet goods internationally traded at the commercial exchange rate first applied in November 1990. The Soviet average of $1,780 GDP per capita in 1991 was about that of Mexico and the range by republic was from $690 in Tajikistan – comparable to Egypt – to $3,070 in Estonia – similar to Iran. Such GNPs were far below those of the USA, Europe and Japan and demonstrated the emptiness of Stalin's boast for the USSR to 'attain and surpass the levels of the leading capitalist states'.

Since the dismissal of Khrushchev, the last millenarian party leader, few Soviet citizens had believed in such hopes, but the collapse of the regime raised expectations that higher consumption standards could quickly be achieved by the introduction of a market economy, if not necessarily of full-scale capitalism. The dashing of such hopes was reflected in the strong vote for anti-reform parties in the elections of December 1993. By that year Russian GDP had fallen by 38 per cent against the last year of the Soviet regime (1991) and a million were unemployed; so many others were on short time or on minimal pensions that a third of the population – 49 million – were living below the official subsistence level. The International Monetary Fund (which all fifteen states joined in 1992) conforming to its monetary criteria for judging the success of economic reform, advised western governments against fulfilling aid and credit packages offered as bait for change. Of the $28 billion promised for 1993, about $5 billion was delivered. But in comparative terms Russia, for much of the time under a reformist acting or deputy Premier, Yegor Gaydar, backed by Finance Minister Boris Fyodorov, had done quite well. The budget deficit was down from 20 per cent of GDP at the end of 1991 to 9 per cent at the end of 1993; in line with this fall the rate of inflation had declined since price liberalization in January 1992, but still ran at 900 per cent in 1993. Ukraine, without significant reform, fell into hyperinflation, but most other republics were close to the Russian experience, although the degree of their production decline varied. Sound economic policies in Estonia and Latvia kept inflation low, but similarly modest rates in Turkmenistan and Uzbekistan were due to government price control.

The divergence of monetary experience in the states of the CIS (which Georgia joined in 1993, completing the ex-Soviet grouping, save for the three Baltic states), forced all, during 1992–93, to establish their own currencies, but in January 1994 two economic unions were formed – of Russia and Belarus and of Kazakhstan, Kyrgyzstan and Uzbekistan.   MCK

ECONOMIES OF THE REPUBLICS, 1991–92

	Area (million square km)	Population (millions)	Gross domestic product Total (billion rubles)	Per capita rubles	US$	Budget deficit (% GDP)	Retail prices (% increases) 1991	1992[a]
Armenia	30	3.4	15.7	4,605	1,335	−1.0	91	692
Azerbaijan	87	7.2	22.4	3,097	898	−5.2	87	859
Belarus	208	10.3	71.6	6,974	2,022	+2.2	81	777
Estonia	45	1.6	16.7	10,581	3,068	+5.5	212	1053[b]
Georgia	70	5.5	23.5	4,279	1,241	−4.9	81	—
Kazakhstan	2,717	16.9	91.5	5,414	1,570	−8.0	83	690
Kyrgyzstan	199	4.5	15.2	3,392	984	+4.6	88	829
Latvia	65	2.7	22.3	8,317	2,412	+8.0	172	547
Lithuania	65	3.7	32.8	8,781	2,546	+3.2	225	708
Moldova	34	4.3	22.3	5,169	1,499	0.0	97	907
Russia	17,075	148.6	1,130.0	7,603	2,205	−11.3	89	891
Tajikistan	143	5.4	13.0	2,387	692	+3.4	84	667
Turkmenistan	488	3.8	18.6	4,939	1,432	+3.2	85	595
Ukraine	604	51.9	234.0	4,506	1,307	−14.4	83	796
Uzbekistan	447	21.0	56.3	2,681	777	−0.5	83	558
Former USSR	22,403	290.8	1,785.8	6,141	1,781	−18.7[c]	86[d]	840[d]

[a]January–July
[b]January–December
[c]Includes central (all-Union) budget deficit; excludes additions to Savings Bank deposits given as compensation for inflation but frozen until 1994
[d]Excludes Baltic States and Georgia
Source: IMF, *The Economy of the Former USSR in 1991*; *Country Reviews*; *Ecotass*, 12 October 1992

Production

AGRICULTURE

The small-peasant structure of Soviet agriculture was transformed during the 1930s into one of large socialized units – mostly nominally autonomous collectives, but also state farms. The change was brought about with ruthless force and cost millions of lives. Contrary to the intentions of the party leadership, industrialization profited little, if at all, from the process because of the concomitant heavy economic losses; food production per head regained the 1928 level only twenty-five years later. By 1940 a collective farm (*kolkhoz*) worked on average 1,400 ha of agricultural land and was governed under a Model Statute centrally issued in 1935, which allowed for only small variations by regions or individual farms. In 1969, when the average area had by mergers and expansion reached 6,100 ha, a revision of the Statute brought only a little decontrol. The state farm (*sovkhoz*), averaging 17,600 ha in 1979 (12,200 ha in 1940), and others run by public bodies held over half of arable and 77 per cent of total agricultural land. Until 1958 machinery was exclusively owned by the state, either on its own farms or on machine-tractor stations having the dual role of servicing and supervising collective farms in their locality. Under Stalin the rural population lived mainly on the output of collective-farmers' household plots (averaging 0.3 ha) and livestock (state-farm workers were entitled to still smaller plots). This private sector also produced for the free market, as direct sales by producers (but not by intermediaries) were permitted on the 'collective farm market' from 1932; by 1940 such sales accounted for almost 50 per cent of total and 27 per cent of marketed food output. Only with this private production, which by 1989 still accounted for 24 per cent of total output, but only about 10 per cent of the marketed quantities, and – given the

Collectivization under Stalin

The process of collectivizing agriculture in the Soviet Union was arguably the largest and most brutal experiment in social engineering ever attempted. The scale of the undertaking was enormous, as was the human cost.

Collectivization began in 1928 and was largely completed by the mid-1930s. Coupled with it was dekulakization – the liquidation of the wealthier peasants as a class. Estimates for the numbers who died vary widely, but the total was at least six million. The deaths attributable to famine are the least controversial aspect of the figures: Soviet sources admitted that five million people died, while some Western studies claim that the true total was closer to eight million.

The deaths came in two phases; first the Kazakhs, one of the first ethnic groups to be collectivized, were forced to abandon their nomadic pastoral farming and join new crop-growing collectives. At least a million Kazakhs died, and the number of sheep and cattle fell by almost 90 per cent. Stalin noted the effectiveness of famine for forcing peasants into collectives in Kazakhstan, and in 1932 applied what amounted to a deliberate policy of starvation to peasants in Ukraine and the North Caucasus who were not complying with the collectivization process. Up to six million died, mostly in Ukraine.

At the same time, dekulakization was taking its share of victims. Estimates vary considerably as to the number murdered, but the Soviet estimate of one million offered in the 1980s is very conservative; the true figure could have been as high as 6.5 million. In addition, up to 10 million peasants were sent to labour camps where many more would have died.

The true figures may never be known. Most estimates are based on approximate population figures, which were certainly altered to suit Stalin. What is not in doubt is the cold brutality with which famine was used as an instrument of policy in Ukraine; in 1932 and 1933 food held up in transit was allowed to rot rather than be given to the starving peasants who had produced it in the first place.

Propaganda for collectivization in Ukraine, 1929

Right. *Peasant selling bast products. Rural handicrafts were largely destroyed by collectivization, but they are now showing signs of regeneration*

shortages in state shops – was much higher-priced than that originating in the greatly subsidized state deliveries, could the farm population survive.

The changes which took place between Stalin's death in 1953 and the end of the USSR in 1991 did not substantially alter the agrarian system he imposed, but nevertheless modified it in a dozen significant aspects: the prices of agricultural produce were improved, enabling farms to increase investment and labour remuneration; procurement quotas were substituted for the former strict control over production; although with an interlude (1957–63) of efforts to the contrary, restrictions on private-plot production were relaxed; the sown area was enlarged by some 35 million ha of dry-farming land ('virgin lands campaign') during 1954–56; the machine-tractor station system was abolished during 1958–59 and the machines sold off to the collective farms; many collective farms were converted into, or amalgamated with state farms, mainly during 1958–61 but also subsequently up to 1982; a guaranteed minimum wage was introduced into collective farms in 1967–70; industrial supplies for agriculture were increased, mainly after 1961; a new programme for expanding the irrigated areas was inaugurated in 1962 and accelerated in 1966; state farms were put on cost accounting in 1966–70, in replacement of budget funding, and requiring a revision of the prices paid to them (previously lower than those paid to collectives); pursuant to the Party Programme of 1961, some horizontal and vertical integration was undertaken from the late 1960s and more energetically promoted from 1973, but was largely limited to activities immediately connected with farming (machinery repair, local building, and the processing of perishables).

A new period started in the 1980s under Gorbachev, as Central Committee secretary responsible for agriculture from 1978 and as General Secretary from March 1985. The main impulse behind these reforms was the excessive demand for food over supply at the (low) controlled prices, the consequent need for more and more imports, chiefly of grain for livestock feed, and the fast increasing subsidy burden on the state budget. The main characteristics were: renewed encouragement of private plots and other subsidiary production (1978, re-emphasized in 1981); stricter orientation of the wage system towards productive performance in sub-units of the public farms (1983), recognized as applicable also in small, down to family, size units (1986); the permitting of 'peasant' farms on a leasehold (*arenda*) or possession (*vladenie*) basis (1989 and 1990), but not with full private ownership (*sobstvennost'*) of land. Formally, these private farms were accorded equal rights with public farms, but their economic situation has so far remained weak within the overall system.

Management autonomy of the state and collective farms, although formally enacted (Enterprise Law; 1987, New Model Statute for *kolkhozy*, 1988), only during 1991–92, under the impact of crumbling state authority, gained some semi-anarchic reality. There remained an inherent contradiction between macroeconomic directives and microeconomic incentives. The vehicle for reconciling them by 'state orders' of sales, which should be 'advantageous' to the farm, smacked more of imposed plans than of business relations. Russia, however, abolished all compulsory procurement of farm produce from January 1994.

The 'Fundamentals of Legislation' on leasing (November 1989) and on land (February 1990) left it to the former union republics to issue their own specific laws, while the law on property (March 1990) was directly binding for the whole country and did not permit private ownership of land. In this field, too, not only those union republics which declared secession from the USSR, but also the Russian and certain other republics had begun to make their own laws and to permit such ownership of property, although with some limitations. Although all successor states enacted legislation to permit the partition of collective and state farms among households or other applicants (such as workers quitting the non-farm sector), there was rapid change of tenure only in the Baltic states (where former owners could also claim a share). In the CIS by July 1993 only 8.5 per cent of arable land was in private holdings (including the long-standing household plots).

Agricultural investment

Probably the paramount single development since the death of Stalin up to 1990 was the increased supply of capital to agriculture after long neglect.

Below. Comparative area and latitude of the USSR and USA. Bottom. Possibility of drought, May–July. Some of the richest soils lie in drought-prone areas

Below right. Wine jars being prepared for the vintage in Kakhetia, Georgia. The anti-alcohol campaign launched early in the Gorbachev era led to many valuable vineyards being uprooted

Fixed assets in agriculture are officially shown to have increased roughly sixfold during 1979. The next decade saw a slow down. The annual average growth declined to a still respectable rate of 5.3 per cent p.a. during 1980–89. With assets increasing, more reinvestment was needed, and the net effect declined. The inflationary rise of the farm output prices in 1991–92 was exceeded by that of their input prices, which made them reduce their input purchases and resulted in some disinvestment.

Capital supplies in Soviet or Russian agriculture are below those in western industrialized countries.

Compared to Canada, where natural conditions are similar, there were in 1987 2.1 tractors per 100 ha of arable and perennial-crop land against 1.4, eight tractor hp per worker against roughly 60, and one grain combine-harvester for each 145 ha under grain against 130. The supply of fertilizer amounted to 50 kg of effective nutrient equivalent per hectare, somewhat less than in Canada, much below European standards, and has declined since then.

The climate is another factor placing demands on capital investment, for such purposes as the conservation and distribution of water resources or to enable crops to be harvested quickly in adverse weather or to be promptly dried and transported. Only 27 per cent of Soviet territory could be agriculturally utilized, and only 10 per cent was arable; more than one-third is north of 60° latitude. In those agricultural areas where precipitation is sufficient, average temperatures are low and the soils mostly poor (west, north-west and north-east of the European parts), regions with the excellent 'black soil' suffer from barely sufficient precipitation with recurrent years of drought, and the extensive dry-farming stretches of south-eastern Russia, western Siberia and Kazakhstan, while endowed with good soils, are those with the highest risk of drought and wind erosion.

Climatically favoured are the fruit-, wine- and vegetable-growing regions adjacent to the Black Sea and in Transcaucasia, the areas of intensive irrigation farming in Central Asia, and the small monsoon region in the southernmost part of the Far East. In the mountainous and subpolar regions, extensive range farming predominates. Only rarely (in Krasnodar and parts of Ukraine) are the natural conditions comparable to those of the American Midwest. Yet in most areas of the European part yields equal to those

Farm mechanization. 'Dan' harvesters at work in the Kustanay steppe a quarter-century after the region was a focus of Khrushchev's Virgin Lands campaign

Pallets of cheese at a state farm, 1991. As central controls were relaxed by Gorbachev, farms diversified on their own account.

of southern Scandinavia are possible. Thus, the arable land of 0.8 ha per head of the population, although shrinking in recent years, has great potential for output growth and for meeting the likely demand for food.

Food demand and farm production

On a gross basis, the average agricultural production in 1986–90 was three times greater than in 1940 and 1950. In quantitative terms, the nutritional standard has been satisfactory since the late 1950s (3,000 calories per head), but the supply of animal protein and of the finer vegetables and fruit does not yet meet demand. In part such excess demand is due to the inadequate supply, at the retail prices determined by the state, of non-food consumer goods and services; household purchasing power is therefore directed towards the higher-quality foods. With accelerating general inflation, stagnating and even declining output of food and the beginning of the disintegration of the procurement system since 1989, a critical stage had been reached by 1990.

The food crisis had not affected the whole country equally but was exacerbated by the growing regional discrepancies of population and food output growth. Thus, from 1980 to 1990 (end of year figures), the population of Central Asia, excluding Kazakhstan, increased by an annual 3 per cent, but food output by only 1.5 per cent (approximately, as published data included cotton). The sharply contrasting figures for Belorussia were 0.7 and 3.2, for Ukraine 0.4 and 2.1 per cent. These discrepancies either increased inequality or put a growing load on the transport and storage system, or both. The problems were the

worse because of the generally inadequate storage, transport, processing, and distribution capacities, which prevented much food from reaching the consumer. Up to 25 per cent of the grain has been habitually lost on the way to the consumer or to the livestock; the losses have been even greater with fruit and vegetables, and have exceeded 10 per cent with meat and milk.

To stimulate production growth and in part also to compensate for rising input prices, the state has again and again raised the procurement prices actually paid, that is including price supplements, to state and collective farms. From 1980 to 1990 procurement prices rose by roughly 60 per cent, and steep new increases took effect in 1991–92. Partial decollectivization in Russia seems to have been no help to grain production. Against an average for 1976–90 of 101 million tonnes, the crop was 89 million in 1991, 106 million in 1992 and 99 million in 1993.

In order to reduce the demand for food as well as the subsidy, a steep retail price increase was enacted on 2 April 1991. Its effect was very limited, however, as 70 to 80 per cent of the rise effect was compensated for by various income increases. But it was followed by almost full liberalization in early 1992 and an inflationary increase, which reduced demand and consumption.

The output growth was earlier achieved by expanding the cultivated area, and later by increasing yields per hectare and per animal. Productivity per person, on the other hand, has risen only very slowly and in 1979 was barely twice that of 1913, when farm manpower was more than double. Despite an outflow, roughly seven workers are occupied (in full-time equivalent) per 100 ha of arable land. Townsfolk, schoolchildren, students and troops were until the late 1980s brought in in large numbers (16 million was typical) to help with the harvest.

In January 1981 when 30 per cent of cows and 20 per cent of pigs were privately owned, a decree obliged state and collective farms to help assure fodder for private livestock, authorized state farms to give young families livestock free of charge and introduced schemes to encourage state-farm workers and collective farmers to raise the productivity of their plots and livestock. Poor milk yields (2,900 kg per cow in 1990) are an unequivocal indicator of poor breeding and inefficient care of animals, representing low feed-conversion ratios (1.5 of oats-units per unit of milk, 8.0 for pork in public farms). The modest average grain yields (in Russia 1.5 tonnes clean weight in 1986–90) can in part be attributed to climate and to the expansion of grain-growing into·regions of marginal dry-farming. Russian plant breeders have been long renowned for their research, but dissemination of their achievements, including new cropping technology, leaves much to be desired.   K-EW

ENERGY

Sources of energy production

The USSR was one of the world's major energy producers, with a total primary output in 1989 of 2,415.97 million tons of standard fuel (1,689 million

tons of oil equivalent). This was enough to supply domestic needs, to support large exports to energy-deficient Eastern Europe, and to export to the West to earn hard currency. Of the total output about 83 per cent was consumed internally, and the rest was exported, a little less than half to Eastern Europe and the rest elsewhere.

These outputs were supported by large reserves. The USSR's gas reserves were the largest in the world. Its coal reserves, like those of the USA, would suffice to maintain output at current levels for several hundred years. Intensive exploration revealed large oil reserves, but they were not on a scale to match those of the Middle East, and the authorities were depleting them rapidly and recklessly. There were still large untapped hydropower resources, but most were not economical to develop. Not much is known about uranium, but Soviet domestic sources were meagre enough to keep the USSR interested in the breeder reactor from the beginning of its nuclear power programme.

Though abundant, Soviet energy resources were not cheap, and became increasingly expensive to discover, develop, produce, transport and utilize. In the 1960s and early 1970s the energy sector contributed significantly to economic growth on the basis of rich resources, relatively easy production

SOVIET ENERGY PRODUCTION AND CONSUMPTION, 1990[a]

	Output	Import	Export	Net exports	Consumption
Primary electricity[b]					
	138.8	0.3	11.3	11.0	127.8
Natural gas					
	941.1	1.7	125.8	124.1	817.0
Oil					
	816.2	17.3	230.0	212.7	603.5
Coal					
	425.5	5.3	23.5	18.2	407.3
Other (peat, shale, firewood and miscellaneous)					
	39.4	0.0	0.0	0.0	39.4
Total primary energy production					
	2,361.0	24.6	390.6	366.0	1,995.0
Changes in stocks					
MTST					+ 1.7
Total energy consumption					1,996.7

[a]All units in million tons of standard fuel – MTST
[b]Nuclear = 212 BKWH, Hydro = 233 BKWH

Right. Oil drill at the 'super-giant' Samotlor deposits. The severity of winter in the deposits opened up in Siberia and remoteness both from suppliers and energy consumers rendered capital costs high. The Soviet authorities offset this by skimping on further exploration and reliance on short-run extraction methods. Russia paid the price in the 1990s in the form of a sharp decline in oil output. Below. Open-cast mining, a cheap but environmentally damaging method of coal extraction

and transport and a shift in composition towards the cheaper hydrocarbon fuels. Natural gas rapidly increased its share in energy output to become the largest contributor (811 bn.cu.m. in 1991). Since the late 1970s, however, supplying the economy's energy needs has come to be a curb on growth. The energy sources highest in quality, cheapest to produce, and best located with respect to markets have been heavily depleted, and production cost has been rising sharply. Investment requirements have become especially difficult. In the 1960s the energy sector took about 28 per cent of all industrial investment but by the end of the 1980s it was taking almost half. The burden of transporting Siberian energy to the energy-deficient European regions motivated an ambitious programme in capital-intensive nuclear power. Growth of energy output has imposed a heavy cost in the form of environmental damage. The Chernobyl' accident, and a devastating pipeline explosion in the Urals have dramatized these hazards, but others are economically more substantial. Much agricultural land has been lost to the spoil heaps of open-pit mines, and to inundation by hydroelectric projects. Siberian oil and gas development have damaged fragile environments in the north. The burning of high-sulphur coal and the operation of petroleum refineries have polluted air and water basins.

The consumption side of the Soviet energy balance exhibited some peculiarities. Households and automotive transport account for a much smaller share than in industrialized market economies. In future, the successor states will find that increases in these income-elastic uses will spur consumption growth. Energy use per unit of national output is high, and in view of the small use in household and auto transport, energy consumption per unit of output in industry and in agriculture are far above that in the market economies.

Energy consumption has grown about as fast as output – there has been little response to the price revolution in the 1970s that induced sharp cuts in consumption growth in the market economies. Soviet energy planners, in a 'long-range energy programme' that was to take them to the end of the century and beyond foresaw a continuation of this supply-side response, with rapid growth of energy output. But in the era of perestroika it became obvious that this path was not feasible. Oil output peaked at the end of the 1970s, then revived in the early 1980s, but fell again after 1988 (from 624 million tons in 1988 to 570 million tons in 1990, with a further drop to 510 million tons in 1991). None of the economies of the successor states can afford the investment to continue expansion under a supply-side approach, and popular pressure is likely to stall some big energy projects, as it has already some nuclear plants. The energy sector cannot continue to receive the lion's share of a shrinking pie. In 1989 Soviet authorities began cutting total investment, especially in the energy sector.

Energy supply became a constraint on Soviet growth at the end of the 1980s, and in the 1990s this is likely to tighten. How the successor states will deal in future with the conflict between growing energy demand and resource constraints on energy supply expansion is not clear. Intended use of renewable resources can help but little. The USSR cut energy exports to Eastern Europe in the late 1980s, forcing the latter to obtain more of its energy elsewhere. As those economies are marketized, they should curb their inordinate hunger for energy. Given how wastefully the Soviet Union used energy there is large potential for conservation. But how soon economic reform in the successor states can be expected to create cost-conscious, economizing behaviour to conserve energy is uncertain. It does seem that any degree of success in economic reform must be accompanied by strong structural shifts in the energy sector – a rise in the price of energy relative to other goods, and a shrinkage in the sector's total output and claim on investment resources.

The energy sector plays an important role in the drive for regional autonomy: sovereignty over energy resources and control of the hard currency energy outputs can earn is strongly contested between the Russian authorities and those of constituent units (notably Tyumen' oblast and Tatarstan). The hydrocarbon resources of Russia, Kazakhstan, Turkmenistan, Uzbekistan, and Azerbaijan and the coal of Russia and Ukraine put them in a strong bargaining position vis-à-vis the other successor states to be paid in hard currency at world market prices. This will be weakened for Russia if the severe declines in oil and coal output are not reversed. Foreign investment is virtually barred from Russian energy development, but has been welcomed in the other republics.   RWC

METALS

In the second half of the eighteenth century Russia was the world's largest iron producer. This preeminence was lost in the nineteenth century; by 1917 the iron and steel industry was weak in comparison with those of the major powers. The expansion of ferrous metallurgy was a high priority of the pre-war Five-year Plans during which the foundations of modern Soviet industry were laid. The great Ural-Kuznetsk combine was built, leading to a substantial increase in output in the Urals and beyond.

Sources of metal extraction

- ○ Iron
- ◐ Manganese
- ▲ Nickel
- △ Bauxite
- ☐ Copper
- ▨ Tin
- ✛ Gold
- ◑ Polymetallic ores

405

The USSR was the world's largest producer of iron and steel. In 1988 the output of steel was 163 million tonnes, compared with 106 in Japan and 92 in the USA. This lead used to be regarded as a matter of pride, but is now recognized as a product of backwardness. Much of the steel was of low quality in terms of hardness. It was used wastefully in the economy and the production of more modern substitutes was underdeveloped. Production remains heavily concentrated in large combines in Ukraine and Russia (Urals and western Siberia). The industry has a number of technological achievements to its credit, but in recent years has lagged increasingly in the use of such processes as oxygen-converter and electric-arc steel-making, and continuous casting, the latter an original Soviet technology.

The non-ferrous metals industry is largely a product of the Soviet period. By 1941 the industrial production of aluminium, magnesium, nickel, wolfram and other metals had been organized for the first time. In the post-war years expansion was rapid but difficult to measure in the absence of production statistics, an absence reflecting the strategic importance of the industry. The industry is highly concentrated: the thirty largest combines account for approximately half the total output. Major centres of non-ferrous metallurgy are located in Russia (Siberia and the Far East), and Kazakhstan. The ore deposits are frequently located in remote, inhospitable and sparsely populated regions giving rise to high costs, although some activities benefit from the availability of cheap hydroelectric energy. The USSR, unlike other major industrial countries, was highly self-sufficient in all the important non-ferrous metal ores, and had large unexploited mineral reserves; recent priority products have included titanium and zirconium used by the aero-space

industry and semi-conductor and other materials used in electronics technology. Exports of gold (from eastern Russia, Armenia, and Uzbekistan), diamonds (from Yakutia in Russia) and other gem stones play a vital role in the country's foreign economic relations. There was a large favourable balance of trade in non-ferrous metals, but the range of Soviet imports indicated that the quality of domestically produced metals was not always of adequate standard.

During most of the post-war years the ferrous and non-ferrous metals industries were administered by separate ministries, but in 1989 they were merged to create a single, extremely large, Ministry of Metallurgy. The ministry employed 2 million people and accounted for almost 10 per cent of total industrial output. The production of gold and gem stones was administered by a separate body, *Glavalmazoloto*.

The expansion of the metals industry was essential to the growth of Soviet industrial strength, but a heavy price was paid in terms of damage to the environment. New policies are now required of the successor states to restrain the industry's extensive growth and put it on a more efficient and environmentally benign basis. JMC

ENGINEERING

Engineering was by far the largest sector of Soviet industry, accounting for almost 30 per cent of total gross output and employing 16 million people, 43 per cent of the industrial labour force. Before the Revolution the industry was weakly developed; its products were technically backward and the few more advanced branches were dominated by foreign capital. During the 1930s the foundations of a modern machine-building industry were laid with the setting-up of many large new enterprises for the manufacture of machine tools, motor vehicles, tractors, aircraft and heavy machinery. At the same time a strong new production base was created to the east of the Urals, which during the Second World War provided a secure location for military production.

The Soviet engineering industry had civil and military components. Overall management of the former was the responsibility of the Bureau of Machine-building of the USSR Council of Ministers which, following the government reorganization of 1989, oversaw the work of four ministries: those for motor vehicles and agricultural machinery; machine tools and tooling; electrical engineering and instrument making; and heavy, transport and power machine building. Military production was supervised by the Military-Industrial Commission of the

The Novolipetsk steel mill. Far too much investment was directed to metal fabrication

Above. *Female fitter at a locomotive works, Georgia. In the late Soviet period women constituted more than half the labour force.* Above right. *Tractors ready for delivery from the Kirov plant, Leningrad*

Council of Ministers, like the Bureau headed by a deputy prime minister, which handled the work of ministries constituting what in the Soviet Union was known as the 'defence complex'. The principal branches of this complex (official titles in parentheses) were: strategic missiles and space equipment ('general machine building'); armoured vehicles, artillery, small arms and conventional munitions ('defence industry'); aviation, shipbuilding, the radio industry, electronics, and communications equipment. The nuclear weapons industry formerly constituted an additional branch of the defence complex, but in 1989 the ministry concerned ('medium machine building') was merged with the civil nuclear power industry to form a new ministry to be considered part of the fuel and energy industry. Military production represented approximately one-third of total Soviet engineering output.

Areas of particular strength included the production of aircraft, heavy industrial machinery, and equipment for electric-power generation and transmission equipment. In recent years the industry experienced serious problems in matching western achievements in microelectronics and computing: as a result the Soviet standing in information technologies was relatively weak. Under Gorbachev the industry embarked on a major programme of modernization intended to narrow the technological gap, but the results were disappointing. In an attempt to accelerate the process, some backward branches were transferred to the defence industry, which then had a substantial role in the manufacture of equipment for the food and consumer goods industries, medical equipment, and consumer durables. Following the announcement at the end of 1989 of reduced military expenditure, many enterprises of the defence complex have been undergoing partial conversion from military to civilian pro-

duction. It was intended that by 1995 60 per cent of the complex's output would be civilian, compared with 40 per cent in the late 1980s.

An established feature of Soviet foreign trade was the substantial two-way trade in machinery with the European members of Comecon. Soviet engineering products were not competitive, however, in the industrially advanced capitalist countries. Machinery exports represented less than 5 per cent of total Soviet exports to such countries, while machinery imports accounted for 35–40 per cent of total imports from western industrial countries. As the reform of Soviet foreign economic relations gathered pace, joint ventures and other forms of co-operation with western firms were beginning to have an impact on the technological level and quality of Soviet engineering goods, but as they were inherited and augmented by successor states, the industry still faced a formidable task of modernization to bring it fully up to world standards.   JMC

CHEMICALS

The modern Soviet chemical industry was very much the product of its past. The pre-revolutionary industry was markedly backward in respect of the diffusion of chemical technologies, despite Russian scientific advances in chemistry, and the infrastructure of the industry was negligible. Against this background the attempts to develop the chemical industry in the 1930s could be only partially successful. These difficulties were exacerbated further by the dislocation and damage inflicted on chemical plants during the Second World War when many factories were destroyed while others were moved to the East. In the post-war period the industry lagged behind the changes taking place in the major western countries and this fact was recognized by Khrushchev who initiated a major campaign for the development of the industry in the late 1950s and early 1960s. Thus the switch from coal to oil and natural gas as the main sources of organic feedstocks began only in this period – long after a similar movement had occurred in the West.

Khrushchev's policy relied on heavy imports of western chemical plant and these continued under his successors. As a result the industry was more dependent on foreign equipment than any other, while the huge scale of some of these deals and Soviet insistence that suppliers must be compensated by products ('buyback') provoked anxieties among western manufacturers about dumping on the international markets. In practice, however, long construction periods and other problems meant that equipment, even when bought as a complete plant, was rarely used effectively and much remained unused in stores for many years. In addition some Soviet specialists expressed concern that the equipment purchased was not always sufficiently modern and one leading scientist has commented that in the case of the chemical industry the Soviet Union often spent foreign currency not on overcoming its technical backwardness but on reinforcing it.

Administrative responsibility for the manufacture and development of chemicals in the USSR was mainly concentrated in the Chemical and Forestry Complex (*khimiko-lesnoy kompleks*), in the ministries for the chemical industry, the petrochemical industry and for fertilizers, although basic chemicals were also produced by other ministries. The USSR had generous resources of oil, natural gas and minerals (notably apatite and phosphorite) and was for many years the world's leading producer of mineral fertilizers (in 1988 37 million tonnes were produced, calculated in terms of 100 per cent nutrient substances) and was a very substantial producer of relatively simple inorganic and basic organic chemicals. Within each of these general categories, however, quality, variety and technological sophistication tended to be markedly inferior to advanced western countries, particularly in synthetic materials (plastics, fibres and rubber).

Despite its high level of output of chemicals the USSR was a net importer of chemical products. Exports were strongest in unprocessed minerals, fertilizers and inorganic acids, which use relatively simple and established technologies, but these exports were far outweighed by substantial imports of plastics, man-made fibres, agricultural chemicals, pure reagents, additives and catalysts. The USSR obtained around half of its imports from its former Comecon partners but was still very dependent on western countries for the supply of technologically advanced chemical goods in the quantities it required.

In the course of the Eleventh Five-year Plan (1981–85) the Ministry of the Chemical Industry prepared a major programme for the development of the industry (*kompleksnaya programma khimizatsii narodnogo khozyaystva*) which was incorporated in the Twelfth Five-year Plan (1986–90). The programme envisaged an increase in output of 2.4 times and an increase in the share of chemical products in total industrial output from 6.3 per cent to 8.0 per cent. Capital investment would be substantially increased and over half of it would be spent on reconstruction and modernization of existing plants. Despite these measures the following major products remained in short supply: chemical fibres, synthetic detergents, dyes, lacquers and paints, plastics and synthetic resins. The same was true of many small-scale products and their quality was poor. This particularly applied to specially pure substances and a leading scientist pointed out that of 2,000 specially pure substances produced world-wide the USSR produced only 250. An additional problem in recent years has been the increasing concern about the environmental consequences of some chemicals, particularly the excessive use of nitrate fertilizers in agriculture, and the pollution caused by some chemical factories.

There were a number of major institutes under the USSR Academy of Sciences which were concerned with fundamental chemical research. The Ministry of the Chemical Industry had an extensive network of research institutes and other organizations which in 1987 employed over 22,000 scientists. An important contribution was also made by the higher education sector where a number of universities and specialized institutes, as for example the D.I. Mendeleev Chemical Technology Institute, the M.V. Lomonosov Institute of Fine Chemical Technology in Moscow and the Leningrad Technological Insti-

The Razdan mining and chemical combine, Armenia. Environmental pollution was virtually ignored during the Soviet period

Testing television receivers before shipment. Buyers' complaints about quality and product life were legion

tute, carried out research in this field. Despite the large amount of resources devoted to this area the results were unsatisfactory and the industry suffers from many of the problems which beset the Soviet research and development sector as a whole.   MJB

CONSUMER GOODS

The production of consumer goods was always a neglected sector in the Soviet Union. A basic reason was the original emphasis of the First Five-year Plan in 1929–33 on fast industrialization, based on high accumulation and a rapid development of heavy industry. A complementary cause was the extraordinary Soviet priority given to defence. As a result, the consumer was neglected in most regards, and individual consumption was more disregarded than collective consumption. Soviet statistics were so distorted that it was not possible to assess the size of Soviet consumption, though it may be noted that the total wage sum accounted for as little as 42 per cent of the Soviet gross national product in 1988.

The disregard for the production of consumer goods left a strong imprint on all features of this industry, which was one of the most backward parts of the Soviet economy. It received a disproportionately small share of investment, leaving equipment old and frequently obsolete; a lot of work was carried out manually; wages were low; a minimum of research and development was pursued and the quality was miserable.

Since the Soviet Union was not a rich country, the structure of consumer industries was reminiscent of a middle-income country. In 1988 foodstuffs accounted for 41 per cent of the production of consumer industries, heavy industry (consumer durables, chemicals and fuels) for 33 per cent, and light industry (essentially clothes and shoes) for 26 per

cent, according to the official statistics. In reality, the weight of foodstuffs is much greater, since food prices are heavily subsidised, while heavy turnover taxes are levied on clothes, shoes and consumer durables. If some set of western prices were used, foodstuffs would probably make up about two-thirds of the production of consumer goods.

The backwardness of Soviet consumer goods grew more striking in the 1980s, as the USSR was left behind in the proliferation of consumer electronics, particularly video recorders and personal computers. At the end of 1987 the USSR may have possessed 200,000 personal computers, while their number exceeded 25 million in the USA.

Initially, perestroika brought about an even greater preference for heavy industry and engineering, calling for an increase in the already large accumulation. In addition, real Soviet defence expenditures are widely believed to have continued to increase by about 3 per cent a year until 1989.

However, with growing glasnost and democratization, economic priorities were bound to change. The 19th Party Conference of the CPSU in the summer of 1988 marked a breakthrough in this regard. Its final resolution stated: 'The most important task in the socioeconomic sphere is to accelerate the solution of the urgent problems of the people's prosperity.' Similar sentiments had been expressed before, but soon it became apparent that the words had another meaning this time.

After the first partially democratic elections in March 1989, it was no longer politically feasible to call for sacrifices by the consumer. The economic priorities were completely reversed. The consumer was to be favoured, while defence and heavy industry faced sharp cuts. With the collapse of Soviet power in December 1991 the command economy which implemented such priorities fell also: the market economies of the successor states will tend to the same consumer goods share as any other country at a comparable level of economic development.   AÅ

Carpet weaving, Ashgabat, Turkmenistan. The high population with respect to arable land and to industrial capital protected labour-intensive crafts in Central Asia

THE BUILDING INDUSTRY

Despite significant advances during the 1930s, it was not until the mid-1950s that, in order rapidly to expand house building, prefabricated technology began to be introduced on a large scale in the construction industry.

The proportion of all state and co-operative housing in towns erected using large, four-metre wide panels rose from 1.5 per cent in 1959 to over 60 per cent in the 1980s. This expansion has been at the expense of brick-built houses, because of substantial reductions in building time and labour costs associated with panel construction. The use of bricks in the socialized sector declined from 48 per cent in 1970 to 30 per cent in 1980 and was planned to contribute about 10 per cent of all new urban house building by the year 2000.

In 1965 5 per cent of all new 'socialized' (state and co-operative) urban house building (currently 78 per cent of the total urban stock) was of nine or more storeys, by 1980 the figure was 51 per cent. In the case of Moscow, Kiev and St Petersburg construction is almost entirely of blocks of nine, sixteen or more storeys. Almost all blocks of flats in cities of fewer than 100,000 inhabitants are five-storey walk-up blocks. On the whole the latter will remain the norm in all towns with fewer than half a million inhabitants. The 1990s will see a shift from a policy of erecting buildings of nine storeys and higher to one of nine to ten storeys or lower, with greater use being made of one- to four-storey blocks in high density complexes.

Productivity gains notwithstanding, the cost of erecting one square metre of living space almost doubled between 1965 and 1988: the rise in building heights and improved space standards, finishing and equipment has meant higher initial capital investment.

In 1987 the government passed one of its periodic votes of censure on the architectural profession, although recognizing that building production was dictating the activities of architects. The highly centralized nature of standard design work and the predominance of large panel construction have created monotonous and expressionless cities and settlements. The changed emphasis on architecture was reflected in the renaming of the State Committee for Civil Construction and Architecture (*Gosgrazhdanstroy*) the State Committee for Architecture and Town Planning (*Goskomarkhitektura*). This body was subordinate to the State Committee for Construction (*Gosstroy*) which had overall responsibility for co-ordinating research and development in the fields of construction, architecture and the manufacture of building materials. The construction bank (*Stroybank*) had primary responsibility for financial matters within the industry. These committees among others co-ordinated the activities of a number of construction ministries at republican and all-union level; the very largest cities have their own individual construction administrations. During perestroika building contractors and other concerns involved in the building trade were put on full cost accounting and self-financing, and larger enterprises were allowed to combine the functions of design and construction.

The restoration of places of worship and buildings of historical interest has increased considerably and greater stress is being placed on modernization and conservation of older structures. This requires retraining the workforce which, because of the widespread use of students and soldiers and high labour turnover, is poorly skilled – a fact manifested in the very low quality of house building. A new system of wages – payable to groups of workers organized in brigades (*brigadnyy podryad*) who complete a project to a high standard within a contracted period – is now intended to improve standards.

Armies of building workers, known as *shabashniki* (operating as individual tradesmen or in groups), had existed for many years, contracting to work clandestinely for private clients or for public bodies. Working in small gangs their earnings were three to four times greater than the average industrial worker's wage, but their illegal status left them vulnerable to exploitation by their clients who could refuse to pay them for completed work. Under the law on co-operatives of 1988 many formed themselves into legal construction co-operatives (between 1988 and 1991 their number rose from 1,500 to 76,000), but in 1990 they erected only 1.4 per cent of all new housing.

The decision of the Gorbachev administration to expand the private and co-operative housing sectors, required legislation to marketize the 'material-

Restoring an eighteenth-century church on the former Vorontsov estate, south-west of Moscow. Half-forgotten skills were regained in the 1980s and 1990s

One of the numerous office blocks being erected in central Moscow. Many foreign firms were employed to assure western standards in construction during and after perestroika

technical base' of the construction industry with the aim of increasing the supply of building materials. This led to the division of the building labour force into two quite different occupational groups – unskilled building-assembly workers and skilled craftsmen engaged in building rehabilitation, building under contract for individually designed dwellings and carrying out interior decoration for private individuals and organizations.

The construction industry was badly affected by the collapse of the central government in 1991. Absolute falls in the production of building materials and equipment for the industry reached a catastrophic level in the successor states.   GDA

HOUSING

The Soviet state inherited an extremely poorly developed housing stock. By 1924 the four principal forms of present-day housing tenure had been established. Accommodation belonging to factories and tied accommodation attached to various institutions was nationalized (referred to as 'departmental' housing). Other major residential buildings were municipalized and managed by the local soviets, forming another type of state housing tenure. The private sector revived with the introduction of NEP. Cooperatives constituted the fourth form of tenure. Key housing legislation in 1926 and 1928 intended that rents should be tied to money incomes and

should reflect the standard and location of the accommodation. But the rental scale was not indexed and by the 1960s rents had been rendered trivial by inflation and bore no relationship to the accommodation's location or quality.

Destruction caused during the Second World War exacerbated the already extremely acute shortage of accommodation created by investment priorities and rapid urbanization. Little relief was afforded until Khrushchev increased state investment in house building in 1957. Until 1960 greater scope was granted to individuals to build houses in towns. In 1989 21 per cent of urban housing – in terms of space – was privately owned. Their contribution peaked at 14.4 million sq m in 1960 then fell to 5.8 million in consecutive years 1982–85 (a fall from 24.4 per cent to 7.5 per cent of all urban construction).

The accommodation shortage remains acute; according to the 1989 Census, over 15 per cent of the urban population were without their own separate accommodation and had to live in communal flats, hostels or rent space within someone else's property. Some 67 per cent of urban families and single-person households lived in their own flats and 17 per cent in private houses. At the beginning of 1991 14.5 million families were on waiting lists to be rehoused. This, however, underestimated the level of demand and overcrowding. The definition of 'housing need' which allowed a household to join a queue for rehousing normally meant less than 5 sq m per person. If married children living with parents and single adults are taken into account, there was in 1991 a deficit of about 40 million self-contained flats. Waiting times are long and vary considerably: a person living in Minsk who had joined the waiting list in 1976 could expect to receive an offer of accommodation in 1987; the same person in Irkutsk would have been on the list since 1961.

Turmoil and ethnic conflict accompanying and in the wake of the dissolution of the USSR engendered wholly new problems: soldiers without homes, refugees, squatters and homeless people known as *bomzhy*. The number of new flats erected, however, had declined from 2.59 million units in 1960 to 1.99 million in 1985, before rising again to reach 2.3 million in 1987, but declined to 1.8 million in 1990. Investment in housing construction as a proportion of overall capital expenditure followed a similar pattern, falling from 23.5 per cent in 1955–60 to 14.2 per cent in 1976–80, before rising again to 16.3 per cent in 1988. Nevertheless, the amount of per capita living space in urban areas increased from 8.8 sq m in 1960 to 15.1 sq m in 1988. The average room density in towns improved from 2.8 persons per room in 1960 to 1.6 in 1986.

Scarcity gave rise to inequities in distribution and also often to widespread abuse. About 14 per cent

Drab blocks in suburban St Petersburg. Mostly built of large panels, finish was crude and facilities were poor

of families consisting of one or two persons live in self-contained three-roomed flats, while 20 per cent of families with five or more children live in one- or two-roomed flats. Differences among the successor states are also considerable, ranging from 8.7 sq m of overall living space in Tajikistan to 20.3 sq m in Estonia. Moreover, no improvement in per capita provision occurred between 1985 and 1986 in Turkmenistan and Kirghizia while it actually declined in the case of Tajikistan. In comparison with Estonia where each flat on average accommodates 2.8 people, in Central Asia the figure is 4.0–4.3; at the same time the average flat size is 51 sq m in the Baltic states and 47 sq m in Tajikistan.

By the mid-1980s the proportion of the family budget spent on rent amounted to about 1 per cent (and, on average, 3 per cent if charges for communal services were included). This caused pressures for major changes in housing policy culminating in three major decrees in February, March and December 1988. The first, 'On measures to accelerate the development of individual housing construction', aspired to draw upon higher individual incomes and vast personal savings deposits, offering mortgages over twenty-five years in towns and fifty years in the countryside, signalling a reversal of the thirty year decline of the private sector. Enterprises and organizations in towns were given the right to sell houses to their workers. This was followed by a decree 'On measures to accelerate the development of housing co-operatives': in 1990 co-operatives were responsible for 8 per cent of urban building. Unlike earlier legislation governing co-operatives which restricted the latter's activities to building for its members, co-operatives may now also acquire buildings in need of major capital repairs which they renovate and allocate. They may also purchase newly erected or renovated buildings from local soviets and enterprises, whose properties are being offered at huge discounts. Finally, the logic of these developments culminated in the decision to allow local soviets and enterprises to sell their flats to sitting tenants, thereby transferring dwellings controlled by them into private ownership.

The privatization of state housing in Russia has so far been slow. In 1989 it amounted to 0.1 per cent of the total number of state-owned flats, but rose following legislation in July 1991 privatizing state housing. Similar laws already existed in Kazakhstan and Estonia. Each sitting tenant would, on application, be granted 18 sq m of space free of charge, with an extra 9 sq m for the family, but additional space would be heavily taxed. Revenues from the sales must be spent on building new or repairing existing accommodation. The state's role is to be confined to subsidizing new, low-rental housing for low-income groups. The choice facing large sections of the urban population is to become owner occupiers and take responsibility for maintenance, or expect to pay a much higher rent. Not only is the housing problem acute in all successor states, but housing policies could be a potential source of social instability. GDA

Life in the city

Getting home is not easy today. Two really heavy bags in my hands, I've bought everything except the vegetables. I have to stand up in the underground, one bag in my hand, the other by my feet. What a crush. Impossible to read. I stand there and tot up how much I've spent . . . I stop that and start looking at the people sitting down . . . the young men turn their eyes away, close their eyes sleepily, anything so as not to give up their seats. . . . At last we get to Sokol. Everybody leaps up and rushes for the narrow escalators. But I can't, I have my packages of milk and eggs. I drag along in the rear. When I get to the bus stop

there's a queue that'll fill six buses. Should I try and get the one that's filling up? What about my bags? So I try to get on the third bus that comes. But with my hands full I can't hold on to anything, my foot slips off the high step, I get a painful blow on the knee, and just then the bus starts. Everybody yells, I scream. The bus stops, one fellow standing by the door grabs me and pulls me in, and I crash down on to my bags. My knee hurts, in one of my bags there's an omelette now, that's for sure.

From Natal'ya Baranskaya, *One Week Like Any Other* (1969)
Translated by G. S. Smith

CO-OPERATIVES

The first consumer co-operative in Russia was established in Riga in 1865. Because of the strong cultural links between the Baltic states and Germany some regarded Schultze-Delitsch as the spiritual father of the Russian co-operative movement. Others have considered that the idea of consumer co-operatives in Russia originated in the Urals in 1864. The state bureaucracy, suspicious of any coalition of individuals, used a multiplicity of administrative devices to obstruct the development of co-operatives. The chief of police scrutinized the agenda debated by co-operators, supervised their meetings and the governor or mayor was empowered to abolish any society. The movement nevertheless found support amongst representatives drawn from all sections of the population.

At the turn of the century two opposed views on the future of co-operatives prevailed. One regarded co-operation between peasants and among *kustarniki* combined into *artely* to be a viable path out of poverty and torpor. This view sponsored by *narodniki*, the *zemstva* and members of the Socialist Revolutionary Party was regarded by others as doomed to failure. 'Independent workers' co-operatives' formed after 1905 became an arena for the struggle between the Mensheviks, who predominated, and Bolsheviks. Producer co-operatives developed primarily in Siberia. When after a good deal of struggle the Moscow Narodny Bank was granted a charter and opened in 1912, it was in the hands of co-operators. Despite its slow growth, by 1914 Russia had the same number of credit co-operatives as Germany and a greater number of members. On the eve of the October Revolution over 50 per cent of all peasant households in Siberia were members of some form of dairy, credit or consumer co-operative. Although the All-Russian Union of Consumer Co-operatives commanded enormous capital resources, it had few experienced workers.

By 1918 co-operatives emerged as the biggest movement in Russia, possibly as popular as the revolutionary ideas sweeping the country. The Central Union of Co-operative Societies (*Tsentrosoyuz*), founded in 1917, quickly established a world-wide network of offices. The hostility of the Bolsheviks and their interference in co-operative affairs was highly reminiscent of the former tsarist regime, especially prior to 1905. A more favourable attitude began to emerge at the VIII Party Congress in 1919; but the most important turning point came with the publication in 1923 of Lenin's essay, 'On Co-operation' in which he noted that 'socialism is a system of civilized co-operators with socialized ownership of the means of production'. The First Five-year Plan, which had received official approval in May 1929, was originally framed within the principles of NEP and co-operative development. With the decision in autumn 1929 to accelerate collectivization, other forms of agricultural co-operative were phased out, the last closing in 1938; it was to be exactly fifty years before alternatives were again permitted.

The resurrection of co-operatives as a means of providing consumer goods and services may be charted from the Plenary Session of the CPSU in April 1985 to the Law on Co-operatives of July 1988 and the allocation of forty seats to representatives of the co-operative movement in the new Congress of People's Deputies in May 1989.

Under Gorbachev the government sought to create a distinction, through differentiated property forms, between what the state was obliged to do (minimally and maximally) and what corporate bodies and private citizens could both provide and should expect to pay for. Thus state enterprises could be transformed into employee co-operatives either by purchase or by lease. By June 1989 213,700 co-operatives had been registered under the 1988 law, of which 133,000 were already operational, distributed among communal services (31,200); consumer goods production (25,700); catering (6,600); scrap processing (2,600); construction and surveying (14,900); agriculture (4,400); trade and purchasing (6,900); artistic design (3,000); medicine (2,800); entertainment (2,400); research, design and information services (5,800); 26,700 were unclassified. The number of people working in this sector had risen to 2.9 million; the value of output was 12,864 million rubles, and there were on average 22 staff (members and contracted workers) per co-operative. Those with higher education, especially engineers and specialists in information technology, communications and design, were particularly attracted to co-operatives because of their autonomy and greater rewards.

A survey undertaken in April and September 1989 by the then newly-established All-Union Centre for the Study of Public Opinion (VTSIOM) in Moscow, headed by T. I. Zaslavskaya (b. 1927) found 45 per cent of the urban population for and 30 per cent against the further development of co-operatives, with 10 per cent expressing indifference and the remaining 15 per cent offering no answer. Privatization in the successor states offered a more attractive option to small business than co-operatives, but employee shareholding became a significant alternative to the transformation of large state enterprises.   GDA

URBAN DEVELOPMENT

The Soviet Union became a highly urbanized country with more than two-thirds of its population residing in cities or urban-type settlements. The first national census of 1926 showed barely one-sixth of the population so classified and as late as 1960 the majority of Soviet citizens lived in the countryside. Urban development therefore was rapid. In theory at least the evolution of the urban system was to have been guided by precepts and principles intended to ensure rational development of particular places and their harmonious integration into a new settlement system. Agencies of government were early created to oversee the urban development process, notably the State Committee for Civil Construction and Architecture (*Gosgrazhdanstroy*), and the State Committee for Construction (*Gosstroy*). Co-ordination of architectural and urban design activities fell to the Central Urban Planning Institute in Moscow. At the national level *Gosgrazhdanstroy* was responsible to *Gosstroy*, whereas the republican *Gosstroy* agencies were responsible for implementing planning norms established by *Gosgrazhdanstroy*. Strategy was formed around two main concepts: the 'scientific-technical revolution' and agro-industrial integration. Both demanded a perspective on urban development which emphasized networks or systems of interconnected places. But aside from general locational guidelines there was a notable absence of specific policies and programmes to achieve the long-standing objective of a planned development of the settlement system.

From 1933, when a decree was issued stating that cities were not to be created without due regard to their role within the evolving settlement system, close on 1,200 new towns were added to the Soviet scene. Some were former rural settlements reclassified as urban, but hundreds of others were literally new towns. In the latter years of the USSR most new town development took place on the resource or settlement frontier but within the shadow of existing, large cities or urban agglomerations. Because town planning traditionally focused on the city, as distinct from the city and its region, and because the authority of the city soviet and its planning and architectural bureaucracy customarily extended only as far as the city border, little was done to plan the development of the settlement system as opposed to individual cities within it. One consequence was the emergence of urban agglomerations, which came to contain the majority of Soviet city-dwellers. But beyond this, individual cities have frequently grown at rates far in excess of what the planners had intended.

For many years the notion of an optimal size city was widely accepted as an essential feature in the urban development strategy. In the 1920s it was assumed that ideal living conditions for the masses could be achieved in cities of about 50–60,000 population. The Stalin era drive to industrialize produced a spiral of urban growth. By the early 1960s the optimal size city was assumed to be in the order of 200–300,000 people, an increase which reflected changing ideas of scale economies in providing consumer and cultural services as well as the reality of the urban growth process. By the 1970s the basic idea of attempting to control the growth of the larger cities was widely questioned. By the 1980s the concept of an optimal size city had been largely rejected. The reality was that large cities and agglomerations continued to account for a growing proportion of urban dwellers. In 1926 for example, cities of 500,000 or more people comprised less than 3 per cent of the urban population, but when the Union broke up the share of this city size category was close to one quarter of the urban population, which itself had increased dramatically. The number of cities with more than one million inhabitants tells a similar story – in 1959 there were three; by 1987 there were twenty-three – and most fast growing cities are part of agglomerations. Early notions of a rational, planned settlement system proved extremely elusive.

It was not until the 1970s that the Central Urban Planning Institute in Moscow formalized a scheme for planning rural–urban integration throughout the country, a General Scheme for the System of Settlement. Comprising a network of hierarchically organized settlement systems – 60 large, 169 medium and 323 small – when completed it was intended to embrace more than 90 per cent of the total Soviet population. Introduced with considerable fanfare in 1975, the General Scheme was to provide the spatial frame of reference for the development of the economy between the mid-1970s and the turn of the century. While in practical terms it seemed not to have been of great significance, the Scheme was reaffirmed in 1982 and did give tangible expression to the growing preoccupation of many analysts with the long-standing problem of how to eradicate the difference between town and countryside and how to facilitate development in smaller urban centres, especially in the labour surplus region of Central Asia. Moreover, it reflected implicitly the growing attention paid to the role of agglomerations within the Soviet Union. From the 1960s onwards there emerged a concerted effort to turn the attention of all planners away from the individual city to the city region and to the national settlement system. The General Scheme was one manifestation of this tendency; another was interest in the role of the urban agglomeration, typically a network of urban and rural settlements linked to a city of at least 250,000 inhabitants by a transportation system that would permit journeys from dependent settlements to the core-city within two-hours. By this definition, more than three-fifths of the Soviet urban population lived in an agglomeration. But there

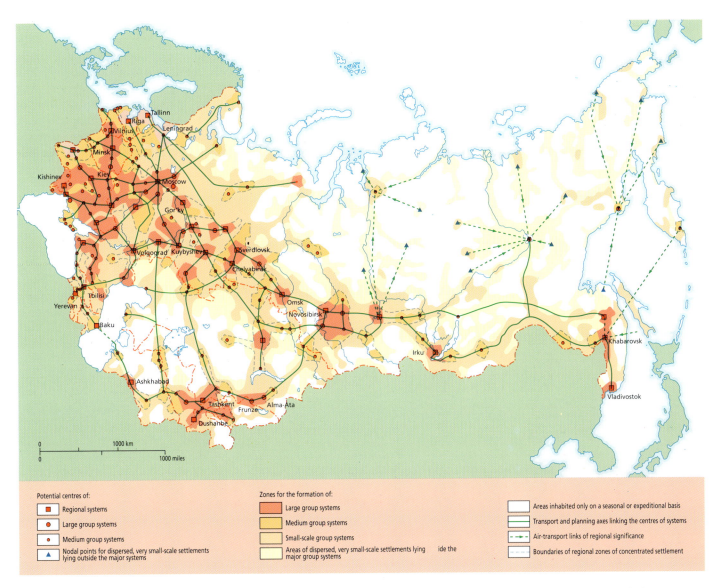

The USSR Gosplan general scheme of settlement, 1975

Potential centres of:

- Regional systems
- Large group systems
- Medium group systems
- Nodal points for dispersed, very small-scale settlements lying outside the major systems

Zones for the formation of:

- Large group systems
- Medium group systems
- Small-scale group systems
- Areas of dispersed, very small-scale settlements lying ide the major group systems

- Areas inhabited only on a seasonal or expeditional basis
- Transport and planning axes linking the centres of systems
- Air-transport links of regional significance
- Boundaries of regional zones of concentrated settlement

were still vast expanses of territory which lay outside such urbanized zones. In the late 1970s it was estimated that about half the area of the Soviet Union was without any permanent settlement.

National and municipal agencies in the successor states did not inherit any juridically based planning regions and must take time before forming their own urban development strategy. Meanwhile, settlement evolves with a momentum of its own and conurbations continue uncontrolled from St Petersburg in the West to Tashkent in the East.

JHB

RURAL SETTLEMENT

Collectivization, the Second World War and industrialization contributed to a decline in the share of the rural population in the USSR (from over two-thirds of the total in 1940 to under one-third in 1989). Out-migration, which was largely responsible for this decline, left agriculture short of labour,

particularly in the Slav regions of the country. In contrast the rural population of the southern republics continued to expand with, by contrast, a problem of agricultural under-employment.

In the 1950s Khrushchev took steps to stem the flow of people from the countryside. His aim was to raise living standards by introducing a new type of 'socialist' settlement into rural regions. Existing village populations were to be consolidated into larger settlements, which would be economic to service and would resemble towns in their design and architecture. Under this policy *rayon* authorities had to classify villages into two groups: those to be expanded and those which were to be phased out (*neperspektivnie*, or non-viable, villages). Khrushchev's successors continued the policy and, under them, some 75 per cent of villages in Russia were classified as non-viable.

In the late 1970s opinion turned against the policy – few districts could afford a radical programme of village liquidation and 'planning blight' in non-viable villages had resulted in a run down of rural services. Under Gorbachev it was officially abandoned. Gorbachev was committed to raising rural living standards and pledged state support for the introduction of basic services to all villages in the Soviet Union. Other measures he proposed included support for private house building and the use of material incentives to encourage urban dwellers to move to farms in the depopulated regions. In post-Soviet Russia the privatization of agriculture is likely to see the continued revival of more remote villages. The process will be further encouraged by the purchase of formerly abandoned rural dwellings as second homes for townspeople. However, the longer term trend is for the rural population to concentrate in large, centrally located villages which can be provided with basic services and amenities. JP

movement, but because there were so many short journeys tonnage loaded on to road vehicles amounted to about 60 per cent of all goods loaded. On the more restricted definition of public service transport the percentages were respectively 2.0 and 52. In passenger traffic the road contribution was higher because of urban movements, the roads carrying about 43 per cent in terms of passenger-kilometres and accounting for 90 per cent of passengers boarding public vehicles. The average length of journey was, however, only about 9 km for passengers and 21 km for freight.

Railways

The first railway in Russia, from the tsar's palace at Tsarskoe Selo to St Petersburg, was opened in 1837 but the main development of the network did not come until the 1850s and 1860s. The Great Siberian (Trans-Siberian) Railway was commenced

The service sector

COMMUNICATIONS

The successor states to the former Soviet Union are faced with immense difficulties in ensuring adequate transport and communications within their vast territories, not only because of the size of the land but because of its varied nature, including great deserts, high mountain ranges, huge swampy tracts and, above all, the climate. In Russia to the length of the winter and the extent of the snow cover is added the effect of the spring thaw, known through history as the *rasputitsa* (the roadless season).

Roads

In both Russia and Ukraine roads have always had a bad reputation; before the railways, travelling great distances on the rutted or muddy tracks was exhausting and frequently hazardous. In spite of sub-zero temperatures, winter was looked upon as the season for travel because temporary 'winter roads' laid on snow and ice provided better conditions, and in spring widespread reconstruction of roads is still necessary. Such conditions have delayed development of extensive motor transport, but recent expansion of vehicle manufacture has resulted in a marked growth in the use of the private car as well as of trucks and buses. The official Soviet view was that road transport should generally be limited to short hauls. In terms of tonne-kilometres of traffic (including farm transport), the roads (on 1990 returns) carried only about 6 per cent of all freight

Potholes

Historically, the roads of Russia were notoriously poor, victims of the extreme climate, and this situation continued throughout the Soviet period. Many Russian and Soviet authors have written about the condition of the roads. The following extract is from a short story by the novelist Vladimir Tendryakov (1923–84) called simply 'Potholes':

What a road! Deep grooves like ravines in the mud, lake-sized puddles with treacherous pitfalls below the dirty water, churned up and furrowed by mile after mile of wheel ruts.

What a road! The everlasting curse of the Gustoy Bor district. Generation after generation of vehicles had grown old before their time on it, ruined by the potholes and the sucking mud.

There is a special organization in Gustoy Bor, the Highways Department. The manager is called Gavril Anufrievich Pypin. He feels a little awkward about his job, and when he meets visitors he hides his embarrassment with a joke. When he introduces himself he stretches out his hand and says, 'Head of the No Highways Department.'

But what can Gavril Anufrievich Pypin do, when last year a paltry five thousand rubles were allocated for road repairs? Five thousand for those forty elemental kilometres!

The only thing that Gavril Pypin could do was to pave the road outside the District Executive Committee with cobblestones and replace the old verst-posts with new kilometre ones. Here they stand, stretching from Gustoy Bor right to the station, a black band on the newly-planed wood marking out the drivers' agony with accuracy, kilometre after kilometre . . .'

From 'Potholes' by Vladimir Tendryakov
Translated by Peter Henry

Moscow–St Petersburg: four hours by rail. The almost straight track on flat terrain between the two cities is ideal for high-speed trains

in 1891, and was at the time the most spectacular railway construction undertaking in the world for sheer length and the crossing of difficult terrain. At first built to rather low engineering standards and for a time running on track across the frozen Lake Baykal in winter and by ferry in summer (until a link was made round the southern shore), it is now one of the finest multi-tracked systems in the world. The USSR was one of the few countries still building new lines on a large scale, a major undertaking being the Baykal–Amur Mainline (BAM), which provides an alternative, more northerly, route across eastern Siberia and should open up vast tracts of territory and valuable deposits.

Railways across the area of the former Soviet Union are among the most intensively used in the world. They are the main freight carriers and also take large numbers of passengers, both on long-distance and suburban services. The mean length of inter-city passenger journeys reported in 1990 was 671 km (including international services) (32 km for suburban services) and the average haul for freight was 962 km, contrasting with the lower averages for road journeys, especially freight. Railways are constructed to a gauge of 1,524 mm (5 feet) so through trains from Eastern Europe need to have bogies changed at the frontiers, but the wider gauge permits more spacious coaches, particularly

noticeable in sleeping cars. The route length in the CIS is over 147,000 km of passenger and freight lines, with 110,000 km of industrial lines adding to the network. Over one-third of the system is electrified with diesel locomotives being used on all other routes.

The railways' share of freight traffic in 1989 was 47 per cent of the total in terms of tonne-kilometres, and about 35 per cent in terms of tonnage loaded (or 31 per cent of public-service transport). They accounted for about 31 per cent of passenger-kilometres covered but only 5 per cent of passenger journeys in terms of bookings. Their share in long distance travel was being eroded by air transport and local journeys by bus, but the railways remain the core of the transport system, especially for freight. The railway system was already regionalized before the country broke up and national takeovers by successor governments were not seriously disruptive.

Air transport

The great distances to be covered in the former Soviet Union encouraged the use of air transport and even winter conditions do not bear as heavily on aircraft as on surface transport, because of the clear skies typically associated with the winter high-pressure climatic conditions of the cold continental areas, and because turbine engines are less difficult to maintain and easier to start under cold conditions than the older piston engines. At the time the country broke up all civil aircraft were under the control of Aeroflot, which was responsible for both internal and overseas air services, agricultural, ambulance, survey, forest fire-fighting and other aerial operations. The scheduled routes covered 146,000 km, of which about one-fifth was accounted for by international links serving more than ninety countries; over 125 million passengers were carried annually, internally and overseas. On domestic routes Aeroflot accounted (on 1989 data) for about

SOVIET PASSENGER TRANSPORT[a]

	1928	1940	1955	1970	1980	1990
Rail	24.5	100.4	141.4	273.6	342.2	417.2
Metro	—	—	—	—	34.3	58.9
Sea	0.3	0.9	1.5	1.6	2.5	1.9
Inland waterways	2.1	3.8	3.6	5.4	6.1	5.6
Road	0.2	3.4	20.9	202.5	407.0	498.9
Air	—	0.2	2.8	78.2	160.6	243.8
TOTAL	27.1	108.7	170.2	561.3	952.7	1,226.3

[a]Units = thousand million passenger-kilometres
Source: *Narodnoye khozyaistvo SSSR v 1990 and earlier years*

SOVIET FREIGHT TRANSPORT[a]

	1928	1940	1955	1970	1980	1990
Rail	93.4	420.7	970.9	2,494.7	3,439.9	3,717.1
Sea	9.3	24.9	68.9	656.1	848.2	944.7
Inland waterways	15.9	36.1	67.7	174.0	244.9	232.5
Pipeline	0.7	3.8	14.7	413.1	1,812.9	2,898.1
Road	0.2	8.9	42.5	64.2	131.5	135.7
Air	—	0.02	0.25	1.9	3.1	3.2
TOTAL	119.5	494.42	1,164.95	3,804.0	6,480.5	7,931.3

[a]General use, excluding agricultural and industrial. Units = thousand million-tonne-kilometres
Source: *Narodnoye khozyaistvo SSSR v 1990 and earlier years*

18 per cent of passenger-kilometres. In terms of numbers boarding, fewer than 0.2 per cent of all travellers departed by air but in some of the more remote regions aircraft provide virtually the sole form of communication, and it was official policy to encourage air travel over long distances by low fares. The average length of a journey was about 1,800 km, while the average freight consignment, including mail, newspaper plates and other items requiring high-speed transit, was carried for 1,900 km. At the other end of the scale, helicopters were extensively used for mainly short journeys but with special roles in lifting heavy items such as oil exploration and development equipment into remote areas. At the Soviet collapse, each successor government took possession of Aeroflot assets, including aircraft which happened to be on its territory on the vesting day.

Water transport

The rivers provided a major means of communication in pre-industrial Russia and valuable routes for the exploration of Siberia. The long period during which they are frozen is a drawback, but great rivers such as the Volga, Dnieper, Don, Ob' and Yenisey are still arteries for the movement of heavy goods and some passenger traffic, in which hydrofoils as well as conventional vessels are employed. Canals provided important links before the railways, and have continued to be developed to provide net-

works such as the Volga–Don Canal, completed in 1952. In the former USSR inland waterways accounted for about 3 per cent of all freight movement (on 1989 statistics), with an average haul of 346 km. They included substantial sea transport on the Caspian Sea and other bodies of water.

In addition the Russian merchant fleet operates many services to other countries; the northern sea route, through Arctic waters, could transport bulky commodities such as timber and minerals for up to eighteen weeks a year with the aid of ice-breakers, including some powered by nuclear reactors. Nearly all ports require the services of ice-breakers for some periods of the winter, the most favourable conditions being at Murmansk, which is ice-bound for about fifty days per year; Vladivostok suffers from ice for over three months and St Petersburg for about six months of each year. In 1966 the Soviet Ministry of Merchant Marine put its international fleet into an autonomous agency to seek external finance for modernization and to operate competitively on world freight markets. Inherited by a consortium of the operators in the successor states, AKP Sovcomflot, with head office in Moscow and subsidiaries throughout the world, became in 1992 the first former Soviet state enterprise outside banking to be fully audited to international standards.

Pipelines

A rapid expansion of pipelines for oil and natural gas was achieved after the Second World War (the first short pipeline was completed in 1879) and by 1989 the combined length was almost 300,000 km. They carried oil, gas, and coal (as slurry), one-tenth of total general-use freight tonnage and one-third in terms of tonne-kilometres. Faulty construction and inadequate maintenance resulted in catastrophic explosions (those near Ufa and Noril'sk being the worst) and to much loss and environmental damage by leakage. The successor states planned more lines, but usually in collaboration with foreign firms.

Urban transit

Urban and suburban movement accounts for most of the road passenger transport and a substantial proportion of the road freight movement. Passenger bus services exist in all large and medium-sized towns, and tramways and trolley-bus lines were never dismantled as they so often were in western larger cities. Suburban railways, mostly electrified, are heavily used; the Moscow Metro is one of the world's most efficient and extensive underground mass-transit systems with about 150 km of routes. Underground railways operate also in St Petersburg, Kiev, Khar'kiv, Tbilisi, Baku, Tashkent, Minsk, Novosibirsk, Nizhny Novgorod, Yerevan and Samara (Kuybyshev) (in order of passengers carried annually). Taxis also provide significant urban and suburban services and decontrol after the break up of the USSR allowed private car owners and drivers of official cars to provide a supplementary service.

Posts and telecommunications

Before the Revolution post and telegraph services were thinly spread even in European Russia and mail was delivered only in towns. They were since developed to give reasonable coverage everywhere. Rail, road, and, especially in recent times, air transport are all involved. Telecommunications, although widely used in preference to the slower postal services (automatic exchanges were installed in most urban areas), were grossly inefficient by modern standards and all successor governments (with Ukraine in the lead) planned sophisticated electronic links and are improving services, with satellites providing long-distance communications.   LJS

CONSUMER SERVICES

Few, if any, areas of the Soviet economy were more neglected than services. The very nature of the Soviet system was alien to the service sector for the ambition was to undertake fast industrialization at the expense of the consumer. Priority was given to heavy industry, notably armaments, and consumption was sacrificed for investment in heavy industry. Another reason for the Soviet neglect of services was that the marxist concept of production was held (many would say erroneously) to exclude them; so-called non-material services were not included in the Soviet concept of national income (net material product). Indeed, many services, notably retail trade, were only considered a cost that should be minimized.

Moreover, many kinds of services are best carried out in small private workshops, which were prohibited for ideological reasons. The Soviet yearning for large scale more often than not led to serious diseconomies of scale in the service sector. The demand for consumer services could hardly be less conducive to central planning. These services need to be spread out to where people live, which means that many entities of a limited scale are necessary. The assortment of demanded services is virtually infinite, rendering aggregate planning futile. Much of the demand for repair services is dependent on the quality of production, over which the authorities have little control. In addition, most service workshops were subordinate to weak republican ministries, which had little or no weight in relation to other administrative bodies.

Slightly over 40 per cent of the Soviet labour force was occupied in the service sector which is approximately the same as in Greece or Portugal, but it must be remembered that the Soviet service sector was amazingly inefficient, and that public administration was classified as service employment. Although no reliable statistics are at hand, it is plain that the Soviet service sector generated a remarkably small share of the national income by international standards.

In short, no field was so neglected as consumer services and no industry was less suitable for a Soviet-type system. Indeed, consumer services are the archetypical activities of small private firms. Whenever private enterprises have been allowed in a Soviet-type economy, they have taken over large segments of consumer services.

The shortcomings of the public service sector have resulted in both extraordinary shortages and a sizeable black economy. A Soviet estimate in the mid-1980s was that the public sector satisfied only one-third of the demand for consumer services, the black sector another third, while one-third of the demand (presumably at given prices) was left unsatisfied. Naturally, this unfortunate situation has forced people to service themselves as far as possible. Estimates of the black service sector vary greatly, but it is clear that tens of millions of people are occupied within it, although most only part-time.

Retail trade

The most characteristic feature of Soviet retail trade was enormous queues. Virtually all commodities worth buying were in very short supply. There were many bottle-necks in the Soviet economy, but retail trade was one of the narrowest. The degree of shortage might be best illustrated by the fact that the words 'buy' and 'sell' largely vanished from the Russian language and were replaced by 'take' and 'give'.

From an international perspective, retail trade was also subject to an unusual degree of centralization. But in retail trade a large co-operative sector persisted beside the state sector, and even a substantial

Above. *Selling outside the store: queuing for sweets, Moscow.* Above right. *Public vegetable market, Irkutsk, Siberia: the produce of household plots could for the most part be freely sold in the Soviet period. After 1991 larger private farms were encouraged to take the place of collective and state farms which had to sell to the state*

Right. *Meat on display at the Central Market, Moscow*

private sector survived in the *kolkhoz* markets, which were in fact private markets. According to the official statistics for 1988, the state sector accounted for 71 per cent of retail sales, the co-operative sector for 26 per cent and the private sector for 2.5 per cent. In reality, private retail sales are much larger. Possibly, the *kolkhoz* markets sell as much as five times the amount the official statistics allege. In addition there are all kinds of illegal sales.

Most of the co-operatives belong to the official consumers' co-operative movement, which hardly differs from the state sector. Co-operative trade dominates in the countryside, while state shops prevail in towns. Since the mid-1980s, a large number of new co-operatives have emerged. Some were controlled from above like the old co-operative shops, but charged prices two to three times higher; they tend to specialize in meat, fruits and vegetables. However, there are also genuine co-operatives which sell at high prices for the profit of a small collective, although their activities were severely circumscribed until 1991.

Even in 1990 the criminal code still prohibited ordinary reselling by private individuals under the heading 'speculation'. As long as the concept of speculation prevailed, private trade was barely feasible. It was limited to peasants' and artisans' own produce.

The efficiency of Soviet trade might have seemed high in terms of sales per shop or per employee, but this was only a reflection of the dismal quality of all sales services. Shops are old-fashioned and dilapidated; packaging is hardly provided; substandard products are not taken away but, on the contrary, dominate the market; there are few places where rudeness developed to the level found in Soviet shops. Technical backwardness is best illustrated by the abacus that still holds it own against even mechanized cash registers in the shops. All these signs of misery were results of the prevalence of the seller's market.

As in other countries with a not very high standard of living, foodstuffs accounted for about half the retail sales. Until 1991 state food prices were very low because of large subsidies, while high prices of other consumer goods were caused by huge turnover taxes. Therefore, if some kind of western price system were used, foodstuffs would probably account for more than 70 per cent of retail sales, suggesting a very low standard of living. Since few shops are equipped with freezers and other chilling equipment, losses of perishable foodstuffs were astounding.

Rationing virtually always existed in the Soviet Union, but most of the time it was organized in a haphazard and regional manner, rendering surveys difficult. In times of growing shortages, as at the end of the 1980s, it proliferated with formal rationing with coupons most common in Russia. Restricted sales, usually at places of work, were so commonplace that they were probably the main source of goods supply. Radical change began as soon as the Soviet state collapsed. On Russian initiative retail prices in all successor countries were liberalized (with a few exceptions) throughout and each government began the privatization of retail shops.

Catering and tourism

Soviet neglect of consumer services left its mark also on catering and tourism. Very little construction of hotels or restaurants took place between the Revolution and the 1960s. In the last two decades, a considerable number of giant hotels were built with up to 5,000 beds each in line with the characteristic Soviet inclination for large scale. In effect, all tourist services are in very short supply, and outside the largest cities no services suitable for foreign tourists exist. Most hotels seem to be full most of the time. For Soviet citizens, prices were very low; foreigners paid many times higher prices which were excessive by international comparison, but the imposition of a realistic exchange rate reversed this situation.

In 1985 Moscow with its nine million inhabitants had only seventy-nine fully licensed restaurants. According to the official statistics, the USSR possessed more than 350,000 catering establishments in 1988, but most were simple canteens that exist at all large enterprises. Towards the end of the 1980s, a significant number of independent co-operative restaurants and bars started appearing. They charged high prices but offered quite decent service. In the post-Soviet period co-operative or private restaurants and bars have proliferated and are gradually improving catering standards.   AÅ

One of Moscow's top restaurants, the Slavyansky Bazar, *formerly a party Central Committee canteen*

Economic institutions

CENTRAL PLANNING

Soviet authorities spoke of their system as 'directive planning', meaning that the plans were obligatory, that they were orders which management must obey. It was distinguished from 'indicative' planning, sometimes practised in the West, whereby governments make forecasts and seek by indirect means to influence the decisions of firms, which themselves are free to act as they think fit in their own interests. In the Soviet system the object was not only to direct but to ensure that compliance with the directives was in the interests of management and labour alike: plan fulfilment had to override all other considerations.

Except for collective farms and the still significant privately owned livestock and household plots, virtually all economic activities were state-owned and state-operated. Thus there was – in a sense – one giant firm divided for administrative convenience into various industries, which were further divided within a planning-and-management hierarchy. The nearest western parallel is the large industrial corporation, where, too, there is a hierarchy, which plans, manages and instructs subordinate units, and where headquarters can dismiss managers who do not obey orders. Not only production but also distribution was in the hands of state organs. Legislation on economic crime forbade individuals to buy and sell for profit (although cabbages grown or dresses made by an individual might be sold by them), or to employ anyone to make goods for sale. Nearly all industrial producers' co-operatives were abolished in 1960–61, but they were revived from 1988.

The complexity of the planning task and the need for a multiplicity of planning organs to carry it out can only be appreciated on examination of the many different aspects of the plan. Since the role of the state in the economy combined planning with management, both the future shape of the economy and the short-term assurance of goals and supplies for each productive enterprise had to be planned and integrated. Thus the current production plan was a multiplicity of interdependent instructions, not only relating supplies and outputs, but also the value of sales, labour productivity and other 'plan indicators'. Because transactions were in money – enterprises sold their output and bought their supplies – there were also financial plans, including profit plans designed to safeguard economic use of resources. Serious problems arose out of the complexity of this plan-and-management system.

Nevertheless, not all activities were centralized; the USSR was a federation of fifteen union republics, each with its own planning structure, and some industries were under republican control. There were also small-scale industries operated by local government bodies. However, the centre exercised a dominant role, because in a modern industrial economy most productive units sent their output all over the country (and sometimes beyond its borders), while drawing supplies from many areas. Therefore regional planning organs, although they played some role in drafting development plans for their regions, had relatively modest powers. From the standpoint of planning, the republics were the wrong size: the Russian republic was much bigger than all the rest put together, and contained half the population, while the smallest, Estonia, had below two million.

The top of the pyramid, in economics and politics alike, was the Politburo. The apparatus of the Central Committee of the Communist Party had economic departments which played an important role, and the Council of Ministers carried out party policy. The State Planning Committee (Gosplan) headed by a deputy premier was the co-ordinating planning agency, responsible to the government. Its task was to ensure the coherence and balance of plans both in the long and in the short term; it was also responsible for allocating key materials and products to the principal users. In this it was assisted by the State Committee on Material-Technical Supply (Gossnab), also headed by a deputy premier. By the method of 'material balances' available supplies of the more important goods were related to estimated requirements (output with the needed inputs), thus identifying the need to increase supplies and/or to cut utilization. These and similar co-ordinating bodies did not themselves administer productive units, which were subordinate to 'industrial' ministries, of which in 1979 there were thirty-one classified as all-union and twenty-two as union-republican. The latter had counterparts at republic level and most administered their enterprises through an industrial association (*obyedineniye*). These latter agencies were categorized as 'industrial' (in which case they may have been all-union, or republican), or 'production' (anything from a merger of small local factories to a giant production complex such as the Noril'sk mines in northern Siberia). These associations grouped enterprises (*predipriyatiya*) all under the supreme auth-

ority of the appropriate ministry, which passed down the plan targets, appointed and dismissed managers (subject to control by party organs) and collaborated with the plan-co-ordinating agencies to ensure that the plans for each ministry were consistent and coherent in relation to the rest of the economy.

On the one hand, the Politburo indicated to the planners the medium-term goals which it desired to pursue, and on the other, there flowed upwards to the planners information, proposals and pressures – the ministries put up schemes for new investments in their branches; republican and local party and state authorities urged the needs of their respective areas; the military planners made their claims, as did those responsible for health, education, housing, and so on. Affecting each flow were issues connected with foreign trade (export needs and opportunities, import requirements), and the co-ordination of investments with those of allies. The political leadership resolved the principal issues of long-term development – the Five-year Plan and 'perspective' plans – and operational priorities in the annual or quarterly plan. Gosplan, together with other co-ordinating agencies, ensured that the plans that finally emerged were internally consistent. If the requirements originally determined by the Politburo added up to more than it was in fact possible to implement, the planners had to so inform their political superiors. For it remained true that one could not build today's factories with tomorrow's bricks.

Enterprise management

Management was not merely the passive recipient of orders which it had to carry out. The proposals it made and the information it provided affected the decisions of its association and ministry and, because the complexity of the task of planning, shared between a number of agencies, could lead to inconsistencies, management may have had to choose between complying with certain instructions at the cost of disobeying others. Moreover, there were so many different products (12 million, according to a 1977 Soviet estimate) that it was quite impossible to tell management exactly what to produce and, with output instructions aggregated, management determined details of the product-mix in negotiation with customers. The material supply system was not wholly reliable, and managers often had to use ingenuity (and sometimes semi-illegal methods) to obtain essential materials and components. These functions were additional to the everyday tasks of actually operating the plant and dealing with labour problems so that although the manager was under the command of the appropriate ministry, he held in fact a key position, and many problems in the Soviet economy arose from the attitudes of management to the instructions of planning and ministerial officials.

Organization chart of the command economy, 1973–91

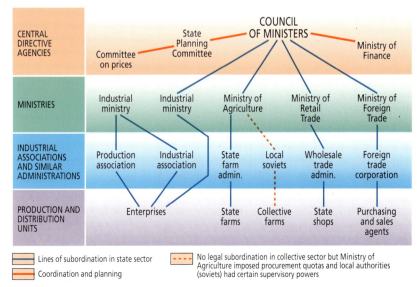

Lines of subordination in state sector

Coordination and planning

No legal subordination in collective sector but Ministry of Agriculture imposed procurement quotas and local authorities (soviets) had certain supervisory powers

Plan indicators

Management was financially rewarded for the fulfilment of plan indicators and penalized for underfulfilment. Even if attention was confined to the plans for output, the central planners faced the problem of ensuring that the product-mix accorded with requirements: to collect information and issue orders about 12 million items was impossible. Plans were in fact made (at some administrative level) in respect of 48,000 items, which meant that on average each plan instruction subsumed 250 sub-items. Plan indicators for output had to be expressed in terms of some total – tonnes, square metres, pairs, rubles – opening management to the temptation to produce whatever best fitted the chosen measure. Examples frequently encountered in the Soviet press were of a plan indicator expressed in weight, inducing management to prefer heavy products, and of garment makers fulfilling plans in money by concentrating on the more expensive clothes. Numerous complaints were printed about construction enterprises, which selected the work which was 'worth' more in terms of plan fulfilment, instead of what was needed to complete the building. Another frequently-criticized effect of plan indicators expressed in money for global output, labour productivity, value of sales or turnover was that the use of costly materials was encouraged, provided that these could be included in the price. A change of plan indicator from global output to 'normed net output' from 1980 was intended to counter such an effect in favour of producing the type or quality required by the user.

Profits might have been a useful criterion in assessing enterprise performance but the price system was such that profitability could be a misleading measure. The reasons were that wholesale prices did not reflect need, demand nor the degree of shortage, and were based on estimated costs which frequently no longer corresponded with actual costs; thus the price schedules established in 1955 were not systematically revised until 1967, and most prices were not revised until 1981. As there were several million prices which had to be fixed by state agencies, many anomalies arose: goods in urgent demand turned out to be unprofitable to produce.

For all these reasons, there were shortages of many goods, even while others turned out to be unsaleable. There was often excess demand both for industrial materials and for consumer goods, accompanied by the phenomena of a sellers' market: queues, hoarding, illegal transactions (the many cases of foreign visitors being asked to sell clothes at inflated prices). These problems were frequently the subject of press comment, and the authorities were aware that quality (of both producer and consumer goods) was often unsatisfactory, reflecting the fact that plans were predominantly quantitative.

The Soviet system was capable of big achievements, and not only in weapons production – for example, the vast and successful investments in extracting oil and gas in north-west Siberia, in the face of formidable natural obstacles. The system seemed to be at its best in large-scale planning of priority projects; the routine of current planning, despite the help of computers, was too overwhelmingly complex.

The end of central planning

By the time that Gorbachev became General Secretary of the Communist Party, the system had lost dynamism, and was suffering increasingly from stagnation and corruption. It was more and more difficult to co-ordinate the activities of economic sectors, ministries, regions, which behaved (in the words of some critics) like 'medieval principalities'. There was a species of 'administrative market', based on the power, influence and bargaining of bureaucratic interest groups. The only way towards a radical reform of the system lay through a substantial extension of the market mechanism.

Already in 1965, under the so-called Kosygin reforms, it had been proposed that administered material allocation be replaced by trade in means of production, which would have logically called for the product-mix to have been determined not by the plan, but by negotiation between customers and suppliers, with freedom to choose suppliers, which in turn would mean competition. However, all this remained on paper. The old system survived, one reason being that prices were fixed without any reference to supply-and-demand, relative scarcities or use-values. This meant that relative profitabilities were no guide either to choice of inputs or to a product-mix in line with user requirements. The same proposal re-surfaced under Gorbachev, and one reason for renewed failure to implement was – again – prices. They were not freed until 1992.

By then the centralized planning system, both in its original and in its partially reformed variants, had disintegrated, along with the Soviet Union itself. The purely political reasons for this disintegration are dealt with elsewhere. It is, however, necessary to stress that the growing economic chaos stimulated separatism, which in turn gave further impetus to the chaos.

Why did the 'marketization' reforms, the endeavour to find some viable combination of plan and market, end in collapse? One reason was inconsistency, arising from unclear aims and conflict between interest groups, especially within the party-state apparatus. Should state ownership predominate, or would there have to be large-scale privatization? Would there still be a state plan, albeit of a new kind? Should prices be set free, even if this meant large increases in the prices of highly subsidized foodstuffs and rents? With so much unclear, the measures taken were half-hearted and contradictory.

Then there were formidable practical problems. There was a lack of market culture, market infrastructure. Management had never learnt about marketing, since customers had been designated by the planners. New commercial banks lacked experienced staff. And among ordinary citizens there was much hostility towards, and lack of understanding of, the logic of marketization: higher prices, reduced job security. Private trade, still illegal until 1991, and the activities of co-operatives, legalized in 1988, were widely regarded as illegitimate speculation. And since, under Gorbachev, there was both *glasnost'* and *demokratizatsiya*, public opinion could not be ignored.

The situation was exacerbated by a loss of control over money and credit. A rapidly increasing budget deficit was financed by money creation, and wages also rose steeply. As prices were prevented from rising, goods disappeared from the shops. Similar imbalances grew also for producer goods. By stages the administrative system of material allocation began to break down, being replaced, especially in and after 1990, by barter deals. A number of commodity exchanges appeared, but they could do little to ensure supplies of materials, while becoming a source of rapid enrichment through the resale of price-controlled goods at much higher free prices. Disruption of supplies led to an accelerated fall in output. The greater powers of national republics and regions were used also for barter deals, obstructing the movement of goods, causing further supply problems. A real market could not function so long as the ruble had so little power to purchase. The freeing of foreign exchanges and limited trade liberalization made it highly profitable to sell anything for hard currency (at an exchange rate which exceeded 150 rubles to the dollar when it was floated in July 1992; at this exchange rate the average Russian earned $4 a month!), while ignoring ruble customers who had nothing 'barterable'.

After the failed coup of August 1991, the USSR disintegrated at the end of that year into fifteen separate states. A year later the so-called Commonwealth which linked a majority of them had not secured a genuine 'common economic space'. The harm that is done by separatism to all the former republics could bring them into a more collaborative relationship, perhaps when and if the ruble regains purchasing power. Meanwhile each successor state proceeded towards a market economy in its own way and at its own pace, Russia with difficulty seeking to implement a radical 'shock-therapy' strategy.   AN

THE FINANCIAL SYSTEM

Central government finance

The Soviet state budget consisted of the revenues of the central and republican governments and local soviets, and summarized the financial flows that reflected the central economic plan. Until the shock revelation in late 1988 that the budget for that year would show a deficit of 90 billion rubles, the state budget had always been manipulated to show a slight surplus, intended to reflect sound financial management. The financial credibility of the Soviet government was thrown immediately into turmoil. The reforms of the perestroika period had been fiscally disastrous, raising expenditure, and cutting revenue, and in addition many republican and local authorities declined to make over to the centre the share of revenue it demanded.

Even two years after the 1988 revelations, the accounts were at best opaque and at worst misleading in that they gave little detail and no clear definition of any item of revenue or expenditure. The main sources of revenue remained (as from the fiscal reform of 1930) turnover tax (the difference between two sets of fixed prices, wholesale and retail) and payments out of the profits of state enterprises. Income tax had been at so low a rate (and so inconsequential that in 1961 the government declared that it would be abolished by 1965), that it provided no more than 9.1 per cent of revenue in 1990. Severe limitations of alcohol sales between 1985 and 1988 reduced revenue from turnover tax; the illicit distilling that the restrictions (to curb alcoholism) engendered reduced government incomes from this source even after they were lifted.

Until 1988, except during the Second World War, the major spending items were termed the 'national economy' and 'sociocultural measures'; defence ran a poor third, but glasnost changed the order sharply. In the budget for 1991 defence ranked as by far the largest item; its 34.9 per cent of expenditure showed both an end to gross (but not all) under-reporting and the shift of particular outlays to separate republican budgets. The redefinition of defence spending put its level at 20.2 billion rubles in 1988 and at 75 billion rubles in 1989, and it is quite possible more defence related spending was included under 'national economy' particularly for defence production and research.

Expenditure on the 'national economy' included until 1991 very large price subsidies, predominantly for agricultural products and subsidies to loss-making enterprises; both forms of non-market-generated income for state enterprises were cut by the price rises then permitted (April 1991 and January 1992). Investment financed from budget funds remained substantial, but declined after the intro-

Large-denomination Soviet ruble notes ceased to be legal tender in 1993. This measure was partly introduced as a way of freezing holdings of rubles in the Soviet successor states other than Russia and was a vain attempt to staunch inflation by physical reduction of the money supply. Prices continued to rise as a result of inter-enterprise debts, government spending and the budget deficit

duction of 'full cost accounting' in 1988 and the emergence of quasi-commercial banking. Compensation to enterprises for price differences between their export receipts and production costs, net of profit on imports, were long an unspecified component of 'national economy' but from 1989 were redesignated 'foreign economic activity', which also incorporated aid to foreign states and interest payments on sovereign debt.

The state budget became more revealing under perestroika, both to offer greater accountability and out of a desire to conform to international standards. Thus the planned budget for 1991 not only identified spending on price subsidies, but also the cost of the KGB and of the Ministry of Internal Affairs and aid to foreign states, and special programmes of aid to Chernobyl' victims, the displaced Crimean Tartars, and the polluted Aral region.

Republican and local finance

Until 1989 the union budget comprehended that of every territorial administration, revenue being allocated to cover authorized expenditure, without surplus or deficit. Even union republics had little autonomy in establishing their planned spending. In 1989, however, the Baltic states secured preferential treatment in the retention of revenues generated on their territory, and opened keen debate on republican and local rights to raise taxes and dispose of revenues. A compromise in early 1991 made the fundamental change that revenues would now be raised by the republics and transferred to the centre according to prior agreement; the initial results of this system indicated that the republics were, in the event, unwilling even to deliver their previously agreed contributions to the union budget, bringing the latter to the verge of bankruptcy as revenue declined, but spending commitments remained the same. From 1992 each successor state formulated an independent budget but the poorer states were in severe straits due to the lack of central subsidies.

The currency

When the USSR collapsed in 1991, the ruble (100 kopeks=1 ruble), the sole permitted means of exchange on the territory of the Soviet Union, was inconvertible, and its rate of exchange varied with the transaction being undertaken and the agents involved; the separation between cash (*nalichny*) and the non-cash money (*beznalichny*) used in inter-enterprise settlements was, however, being dismantled. Soviet monetary policy after 1931 had strictly limited the conversion of the latter into the former in order to maintain control over the amount of liquidity in the consumer sector. Under perestroika this constraint was weakened, first by enterprises using their financial autonomy (from

1 January 1991), and secondly by the non-state sector, particularly the commercial banks being able to increase the velocity of circulation of cash money.

The state has resorted to monetary reforms as an extreme measure to deal with accumulated disequilibrium. The inflation of the early years of the Soviet state was dealt with by an exchange of the depreciated currency (termed *sovznak*) in 1922–24 for a new unit (*chervonets*) at a rate equivalent of one new ruble to 10^{24} old rubles. The inflation of the Second World War was eliminated in 1947 by an exchange of holdings at one new ruble to ten old, prices and payments being unchanged. In 1961 ten old rubles were converted to one new ruble, but all holdings could be exchanged without loss. In a clumsy attempt to reduce the inflationary overhang in January 1991 all 50 and 100 ruble notes were withdrawn and replaced only on proof of having been legally earned. Despite failure then, the Russian Central Bank – without authority from the Finance Minister – demonetized in 1993 all notes issued in previous years. This actually exacerbated inflation because rubles held elsewhere in the CIS were rushed back for exchange. By then all the other successor states had issued their own currencies. The Russian Bank tried again on 1 January 1994 by prohibiting domestic transactions in currency other than the ruble. TA

BANKING

The State Bank of Russia, established in 1860 as the bank of issue, was redesignated the People's Bank in December 1917, abolished in January 1920 and refounded as the State Bank (*Gosbank*) in December 1921. Between 1930 and 1932 all other banks were subordinated to it in the 'mono-bank' system, each designated as Gosbank's agent for designated functions. By the late 1980s there were five – the Bank

Right. *Viktor Gerashchenko who, as Chairman of the Russian Central Bank, was responsive to the demands for credit of Russian industry in the early post-Soviet period and who clashed with such radical reformers as Yegor Gaydar and Boris Fedorov over economic policy*

of Foreign Economic Activity (*Vneshekonombank*), the Industrial-Construction Bank (*Promstroybank*), the Agroindustrial Bank (*Agroprombank*), the Bank for Housing and Communal Economy (*Zhilsotsbank*) and the Savings Bank of the USSR (*Sberegatel'naya Kassa*) – and a number of 'commercial' banks, including co-operative banks, had been authorized.

From 1922 Gosbank had the sole right to issue currency after consultation with Gosplan, the Ministry of Finance, and the Council of Ministers, and was responsible for centralized credit operations, currency operations, and the co-ordination of the 'specialized' banks. Gosbank worked out a national credit plan (approved by the Council of Ministers), participated in the formulation of the state plan, the export–import plan, and the foreign exchange plan, fixed the exchange rate, and set interest rates in consultation with Gosplan and the Ministry of Finance. Vneshekonombank supervised import–export accounts. Promstroybank carried out credit operations for capital investments in industry, construction, transportation, and communication. Agroprombank was responsible for capital investments in agriculture. Zhilsotsbank financed capital investment in so-called non-productive spheres. In fact the two-tier structure of state-owned banks was little different from the previous mono-bank system, since the specialized banks remained effectively under the direction of Gosbank, and at a disadvantage to the few but rapidly increasing number of commercial banks. The latter were free to attract deposits and make loans, and could set their interest rates freely, in contrast to the low fixed 3 per cent rate of the state sector. Commercial banks were set up by individuals, co-operatives and large enterprises.

The banking system played a passive role in the allocation of resources in the Soviet Union. Credit

was automatically granted for activities specified in economic plans. Interest rates played little role in clearing credit markets. Moreover, although Gosbank formally controlled monetary emissions, in reality the money supply was decided by higher authorities. In effect, the Soviet Union lacked an independent monetary authority. During perestroika there were calls for an increase in independence of the banking system, a more active role for credit policy, and the emergence of commercial banks. As of 1989 there were approximately 190 commercial banks in existence. With the breakup of the Soviet Union in late 1991 much of the former Soviet banking structure became part of the Russian financial institution. The former republican branches of the Soviet banking system became part of the central banking structures of the now independent successor states. The early 1990s witnessed an acceleration of monetary growth associated with a decline in enterprise financial discipline and a growing budget deficit problem carried over and exacerbated as the successor states began their separate monetary life. Initially all still used the ruble but during 1992 Estonia issued the kroon, Latvia the Latvian ruble, and Ukraine announced the introduction of its hrivna. Although virtually all the successor states talked of introducing their own currencies, the vast majority remained part of the ruble zone. Issuing authority remained in the hands of Vneshekonombank Russia, which continued under the control of the Russian Supreme Soviet. As of early 1993 the Russian government had yet to create an independent central bank. The bank was still expected to issue currency as directed by political authorities to prop up state enterprises. This monetary policy contributed to the near hyperinflation of the 1990s.

PRG

Mobile branch bank, Moscow 1993. Many commercial banks mushroomed after 1991

INVESTMENT

Historically, investment was financed largely through the medium of non-returnable budgetary grants. Timid reforms of the 1960s increased the importance of retained profits as a source of investment finance, and introduced, for the first time, the principle that major investments could be financed from bank credit. Bank credit, however, remained but a minor source of finance until the end of the USSR. And while the Kosygin reforms greatly increased the importance of profit ploughbacks, they did so in a way that changed the pattern of investment decision taking very little. For the bulk of profit-financed investment continued to be classified as centralized, that is project choice remained the prerogative of higher authorities. Genuinely decentralized investment also increased in importance under the 1965 reform, and by 1972 was accounting for 20 per cent of total state investment. But it suffered under the political and economic reaction which set in during the late Brezhnev years, and by the mid-1970s the scope for enterprises to make independent investment decisions was very limited indeed. It was not until Andropov succeeded Brezhnev that the principle of autonomous enterprise investment decision taking came back into vogue. Under Gorbachev's perestroika programme, decentralized investment was elevated to an unprecedented level of importance, and accounted for over 40 per cent of total state investment.

The stuttering movement towards an investment decision taking system focusing more on the operational production level reflected a desire to move away from the crude mobilizatory investment tactics of the Stalin era. There is a degree of justification in the argument that as long as labour and raw materials were cheap, details of project choice were of secondary importance. But as labour shortage increasingly impinged from the 1960s onwards, and energy extraction costs soared, it became increasingly vital to allocate investment resources on more market-based criteria, to avoid the characteristic problems of sheer gigantomania, 'overstretch' (too many projects), grossly excessive lead-times, and escalating costs, so typical of the centrally planned system.

Although Gorbachev's approach to economic reform was much more radical than that of his predecessors, it bore little fruit in the investment area. During the late 1980s overstretch problems intensified and lead-times lengthened even further, as the rate of completion of new projects faltered. This paradoxical outcome reflects the cruel dilemma which faced Gorbachev. On the one hand, he needed an investment drive to provide the basis for the modernization of the Soviet capital stock without

which perestroika was meaningless. On the other, investment drives still tended, in Soviet conditions, to multiply rather than remove blockages. This in turn reflected a continued failure to provide a market in investment supplies, and to reform the investment finance system with sufficient radicality to break the traditional attitude that 'it is always someone else's money'.

These continued difficulties formed the background to the emergence of the idea that private investment finance might play a significant role in the future. In the successor states legislation permits citizens to own debenture-type shares in enterprises, and the operation of stock exchanges.   DAD

ACCOUNTING AND ENTERPRISE FINANCE

Lenin declared that accounting and control were the main requirements for the proper working of socialist society, but enterprise accounting disintegrated during War Communism and had to be rebuilt slowly on traditional lines during the NEP period. Immediately following the introduction of the First Five-year Plan the 16th Party Conference (1929) resolved that socialist accounting should be a unified system providing the indicators needed for monitoring the implementation of the national plan, and a brief attempt was made in 1931 to create a system for generating both accounting and statistical data. The two data processing systems were distinct but complementary, each containing the stages of recording, reporting and analysis: the statistical flow monitored the realization of the plan and accounting data were for the short-term surveillance of enterprise performance.

The accounting system within central planning

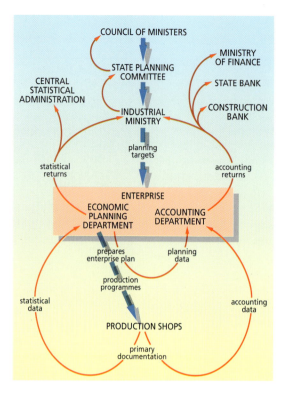

The standard system of accounting, implemented by all enterprises, was the joint responsibility of the Ministry of Finance and the State Committee on Statistics. The former issued the general rules, while more detailed instructions were issued to their subordinate enterprises by ministries. The main features of the system were the national plan of accounts, uniform accounting records and accounting returns, standard procedures for the classification and processing of transactions (such as common rules for asset valuation, treatment of depreciation or profit determination). Historical absorption costing was used for accumulating the cost of commodity output. Financial and cost accounting were integrated into a single system oriented to the requirements of external users. There was a comprehensive disclosure of accounting data to the supervising authorities but the final accounts of enterprises were not made public. A series of *ad hoc* accounting and operating data records serviced the needs of specific enterprise managers. Audits, or inspections, of the accounting records were made by the controlling industrial ministry, the Ministry of Finance and, if criminal activities were suspected, by the Ministry of Internal Affairs.

Soviet accounting evolved as an instrument of control for the centrally administered economy. The managerial uses of accounting data in the appraisal of enterprise performance was neglected.

The disintegration of the USSR, the conversion from Russian to the national languages in the successor states, the desire to create a market mechan-

ism and to develop national policies on accounting and auditing, the emigration of some accounting specialists and the lack of understanding of the role and practices of accounting in a market economy have aggravated the magnitude of the task of accounting reform. Fundamental changes to established accounting practices may well occur slowly although progress is likely to be varied among the successor states.   DTB

PRICES

The nature, functions, and behaviour of prices in the Soviet economy differed in important respects from the characteristics of the price system in a market economy. In the USSR most producer and consumer prices were administratively set, commonly below the levels that would reflect scarcities by balancing supply and demand. Hence, these prices exerted only limited influence on the choices of inputs and outputs in production, or on the purchases of consumer goods and services by households.

Although the allocative function of prices was small, they none the less have played a significant role in economic accounting, namely in the aggregation and comparison in value terms of physically dissimilar goods and services. At the enterprise level, prices were used to aggregate inputs of materials, components, fuels, labour, and machine-time to obtain money costs; to sum in money terms the production and sales of heterogeneous products; and to measure profit as the difference between sales revenue and cost. In turn, government agencies used prices to calculate growth rates of industrial and agricultural production, and to construct 'synthetic' macroeconomic value balances such as national income and product accounts, input–output tables, and the balance of payments. Prices played a necessary part in investment decisions involving capital-output ratios and comparisons of yields (or recoupment periods) of alternative variants. Foreign trade decisions entailed comparisons of foreign and domestic prices (or costs). But the validity of all these calculations was constrained by the extent to which prices failed to reflect relative scarcities.

Prices also are relevant to income distribution, for example through the relationship between retail prices and wages (and transfer payments, like pensions and student stipends). However, the link between money income and real income was weakened throughout almost the entire Soviet period by shortages at shops with below market-clearing prices, formal administrative rationing of some goods and services, and special stores for privileged groups.

Domestic prices

The main components of the Soviet domestic price system were industrial producer prices, agricultural producer prices, and state retail prices.

Industrial producer prices · ('Industrial wholesale prices' in Soviet terminology) were set administratively on the basis of the planned average cost of production of a product by all enterprises in a branch (such as ferrous metallurgy, chemicals or machine building), plus a profit markup. The cost component included direct and indirect labour, materials, fuel and power, amortization allowances, and various overhead expenses. The profit markup was supposed to provide a 'normal' rate of profit, in relation to capital, for the branch as a whole. But the (planned and actual) profitability rate could be above or below 'normal' for an individual enterprise, depending upon its product-mix and the relationship of the actual cost of its output to the planned branch-average cost. From profit, the enterprise paid profits taxes, capital charges, and rents on some natural resources, and used the remainder for reinvestment, bonuses, and facilities for employees.

Quality differentials, and the superiority of new products over earlier models, were intended to be reflected by a set of supplements and discounts to base prices. Supplements increased (or discounts decreased) the prices and profitabilities of products of higher (lower) quality or technological level. Hence, supplements and discounts affected a product's relative contribution to an enterprise's gross and net value of output and sales revenue, as well as to its profits and to bonus funds linked to profits. Consequently, enterprises frequently exaggerated the claimed 'newness' and technological superiority of new products, in an effort to obtain larger price supplements.

The level and structure of Soviet domestic producer prices were divorced from foreign-trade prices charged or paid to foreign trading partners. This separation was accomplished by a system of taxes and subsidies, and multiple exchange rates in settlements for some export and import transactions of Soviet enterprises.

A comprehensive revision of the millions of industrial producer prices was an ambitious task, undertaken infrequently, namely in 1949, 1952, 1955, 1967, and 1982. In consequence the prices in force were usually based on out-of-date planned (branch-average) costs. As a result, not only some individual enterprises but also some entire branches have operated at a loss or with below-normal profits, while others have had above-normal profits.

Because Soviet industrial producer prices did not ordinarily reflect cost or demand accurately, planning agencies often gave enterprises output assign-ments in physical units, in an effort to secure the desired output of products that price–cost relationships rendered 'disadvantageous' for the enterprise. In turn, administrative allocation, rather than price rationing, was commonly used to distribute raw, intermediate and finished goods.

Agricultural producer prices · ('Purchase prices' in Soviet parlance) were supposed to cover the costs of farms operating in 'normal' conditions and provide them profits, part of which could be reinvested to expand their capital stock of buildings, equipment, reproductive livestock, and inventories.

Sales assignments for agricultural products were given to large numbers of farms whose production costs varied widely because of differences in natural conditions, such as soil, topography, rainfall, temperature, and length of growing season. The Soviet practice was to differentiate the prices of many commodities geographically by price zones, in an effort to capture for the state differential rents arising from more favourable natural conditions. These zonal prices were set with reference to the average cost of production in each zone. The aim was to provide, for each product, lower prices but higher profitability in low-cost areas, and higher prices but lower profitability in high-cost areas. In addition, weak farms, with low profitability or losses, have received supplements to the base zonal prices. Nevertheless, many farms delivered livestock, potatoes, eggs, and other products at a loss.

State retail prices · These had three components: the producer price, wholesale and retail trade margins, and, for many goods, a differentiated excise tax (called the 'turnover' tax) or subsidy. Turnover taxes were levied on alcoholic beverages and many non-food consumer goods such as clothing and appliances. Subsidies were provided primarily for food products and services.

Right. Moscow shop selling subsidized dairy products for children. Termed 'milk kitchens', they serve the many Russian families below the poverty line

In principle, for any commodity the turnover tax or subsidy could be set to achieve a market-clearing retail price at which households would buy just the quantity planned for sale in shops, without shortages or surpluses. However, for many years, most consumer goods and services were sold at prices below the market-clearing level, as shown by widespread and persistent shortages. Hence, various forms of non-price rationing distributed the available supply. They included administrative allocation (for instance, of housing), coupons, queuing in actual lines or on waiting lists, influence with sales personnel, access to special stores, and black market transactions.

In contrast, on what used to be called 'collective farm markets', prices of food products sold by farms and farmers to households were and remain determined by supply and demand.

All three kinds of inflationary pressure were experienced during the Soviet period. 'Open' inflation occurs when the overall level of state or free market prices rises, for example as shown by price indexes. 'Hidden' inflation may include price increases for transactions not covered by an official index; reduction in quality of goods sold at unchanged prices; introduction of 'new' goods at higher prices not matched by corresponding increases in quality; and changes in the product-mix that increase the share of higher-priced items and decrease the share of lower-priced items. 'Repressed inflation' refers to excess aggregate demand at fixed prices enforced by price controls, and the resulting involuntary saving reflected in abnormally high accumulation of currency and bank balances.

In 1990–91 industrial wholesale prices were raised sharply to reflect the growth of production costs since the preceding major revision in 1982. The increases in industrial wholesale prices were passed along in higher agricultural purchase prices

and state retail prices. In turn, the rise in state retail prices was partly 'compensated' by increases in wages and transfer payments. As a result, inflationary pressure accelerated.

At the beginning of 1992, as part of economic reform programmes, Russia, and subsequently other republics of the former Soviet Union, began to 'liberalize' the price system by measures intended to make producer and consumer prices more nearly reflect cost and demand. Administratively set prices on many goods and services were initially increased 200–400 per cent, and subsequently raised further. In addition, prices of many goods and services were decontrolled. Wages and transfer payments grew in response, fueling the inflationary process.   MB

Right. *Rises in prices and incomes, 1985–91.*
Far right. *Prices and incomes after the January 1992 price liberalization (index 1990 = 1)*

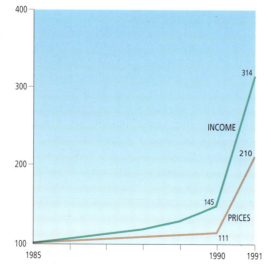

Right. *Women workers were supported in Soviet factories by crèches, kindergartens and health care. Many such on-site facilities were closed after de-subsidization and privatization*

LABOUR AND WAGES

The allocation of labour in the USSR was achieved by a quasi-market where the state has exercised considerable control over wages and conditions of employment but individual workers were free to choose where to work. In the context of perestroika, however, the authorities intended to introduce a system where they would not attempt to set wage rates or determine conditions of work in detail and where some unemployment might occur. But, by the time the USSR disappeared little of the institutional framework for this labour market had been put in place.

Historically, Soviet labour policy was dominated by the rapid growth of non-agricultural employment and by the need to absorb large numbers of peasants and women into industrial employment. This phase has ended for the more industrialized successor states; there will be very little growth in the population of working age for the next ten or twenty years in the Slav or Baltic states. But change in economic structure under the influence of market forces will lead to the need to retrain and redeploy a considerable number of workers. This will influence future labour policy in all the states concerned.

The vast majority of state employees in the former USSR belonged to trade unions. Before 1956 the function of these organizations was largely confined to the administration of social security and the support of management. Subsequently, their role expanded. At local level they were concerned with the resolution of individual grievances; nationally they participated in the formulation of labour policy and the drafting of legislation but had no influence on the determination of wage levels. The development of representative democracy and the emergence of a fully fledged labour market will lead to further changes of role for the unions; but they played only a minor part in the organization of strikes and labour protests during the decline of the Soviet state.

Employment

Population projections show that there will be only modest growth in the population of working age over the next twenty years or so. Only in the Central Asian and parts of the Transcaucasian states will rapid population growth continue. Elsewhere there is unlikely to be much increase in the traditional sources of urban employment growth. In most regions there is no significant difference between male and female participation rates and significant rural–urban migration is unlikely. Finally, in the 1980s, between a sixth and a fifth of the population of pensionable age were economically active; it is doubtful whether this population group contains a sizeable reservoir of labour.

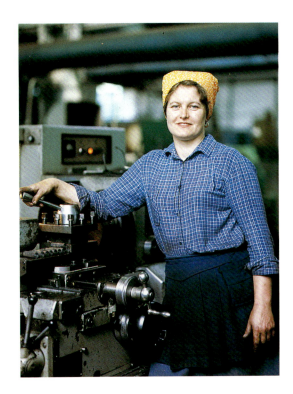

Soviet practice defined the working age as 16–59 years for men and 16–54 years for women. In 1989 the population of working age amounted to 155 million, excluding invalids and certain other categories. This labour force was augmented by 8 million employees of pensionable age, 100,000 foreigners and 300,000 people below working age. Total employment amounted to 139 million. State employment was 120 million and had fallen since about 1986. *Kolkhozy* employed a further 12 million; employment in this sector has been on the decline for twenty years or more. A further 4 to 4.5 million were in individual employment, overwhelmingly on private plots. Finally, some 3 million were employed by non-agricultural co-operatives; this sector had grown very rapidly since 1988. As radical reform continues, the share of individual and co-operative sectors in the total has expanded substantially.

Of the 25 million non-employed persons in 1989, some 12 million were full-time students. Of the remainder, 4 million were reported as women at home with children and an equivalent number were in the armed services. The balance were reported as partially disabled or temporarily unemployed. This estimate makes no allowance for those who choose not to work – perhaps because in the past Soviet labour law imposed an obligation to work on all able-bodied citizens. An alternative estimate, by the State Committee for Labour (*Goskomtrud*), claimed that at the end of 1989 there were 2 million unemployed – those not working but actively seeking a job. Most of these were thought to be in

Central Asia. In late 1993 the Russian Employment Service counted 1 million registered unemployed and 3.7 million only nominally employed. Restructuring and market-induced improvements in efficiency could lead to the shake-out of some 13–19 million workers from the so-called material sphere of production by the end of the century. These will add to existing sources of unemployment and pose new problems for the organizations in the successor states responsible for job placement, industrial training and manpower planning.

Between 1940 and 1956 there were draconian controls on labour mobility and considerable restrictions on freedom of occupational choice. Then the government reverted to a quasi-market to allocate labour; this was associated with an increase in labour turnover. Soviet sociologists considering this problem identified dissatisfaction with career prospects, with conditions of work and with pay as the primary motives for voluntary severance. Among women, the difficulty of reconciling family and career responsibilities also figured largely. Soviet policy was successful in reducing turnover in the ensuing 10 or 15 years. In 1965 turnover amounted to 34 per cent in construction and 21 per cent in industry; in 1975 it was 28 per cent and 19 per cent respectively; and by 1987 it was 17 per cent and 12 per cent.

Turnover is the source of considerable loss of production time. Also, because changes of job are frequently accompanied by changes of occupation, it results in a waste of human capital. In an effort to reduce the costs associated with labour turnover, starting in 1969, labour exchanges and job placement bureaux were established in a number of cities. By 1989 there were more than 800 exchanges and as many as 2,000 bureaux. Too often, however, these organizations are understaffed and poorly financed. It is not clear how much they have contributed to the decline in turnover since, in the middle 1980s, as many as 85 per cent of all new hirings took place at the factory gate.

Industrial training

There was an extensive network of industrial training facilities in the USSR. Formally, there were two separate channels for the acquisition of industrial skills: trade schools and on-the-job training. The first involved attendance for more than six months at a specialized institution where the worker acquired an understanding of the appropriate technical processes as well as practical skills. The number of trade schools was increased considerably in the 1960s and 1970s and there are now about 8,000 of them; but a majority of skilled workers still acquire their training on the shop floor.

On-the-job training is criticized for its restriction to particular skills and its inability to inculcate theoretical understanding; trade schools for limiting training to a few traditional occupations and for a technologically backward and narrow curriculum. Both these criticisms are valid and the system inherited by the successor states is in need of extension and modernization. But any increase in the supply of qualified labour must be drawn from those with adequate general education. And here too there is cause for concern. Steps had been taken to improve the quality of secondary schooling but such improvements take time. Furthermore, some of the apparent shortages in qualified manpower are due to mistakes in industrial location policy, and others can be blamed on inadequacies in the structure of wages.

The wage system

From 1956 to 1991 wage rates for state employees were determined centrally by *Goskomtrud* or its predecessors. As the remuneration of collective farmers was not legally classified as wages before 1966, *Goskomtrud* was never responsible for the earnings of *kolkhozniki*. One consequence of this was that *kolkhozy* were not obliged to pay the minimum wage. There were three general reorganizations of wage and salary scales under the auspices of *Goskomtrud*, in 1957–65, in 1970–77 and a third in 1986–90. It was not clear whether or when radical economic reform would result in the abandonment of attempts to determine the structure of wages administratively.

The methods used to determine the structure of wage rates were the same in all three reorganizations, but under the last wage differentials were to be significantly revised. The 1986–90 reorganization had three objectives: to increase central control by increasing the share of basic wages in take-home pay at the expense of elements under the control of local managements; to widen skill differentials which had become excessively compressed in 1970–77; and to improve incentives by relating differences in earnings more closely to differences in individual performance. It also differed from earlier reorganizations in that the money to pay the higher wages was to come from the enterprises' own resources; on previous occasions, industry could rely upon the state budget for additional funds.

A general picture of the post-1990 structure was as follows. For manual workers, basic wages were to account for 70–75 per cent of take-home pay. The minimum wage was established at 80 rubles a month; in 1970–75 it was set at 70 rubles and in 1957–65 at 40–45 rubles; it was successively raised as steep inflation began in 1991. In the wage-scales proposed for most branches of industry, the top rate was 1.8 times the bottom one; for some workers in machine building and those in ferrous metallurgy there were spreads of 2.0 and 2.3. On most of these scales there

Miners' strike meeting, Prokopievsk, Siberia, in the late Soviet period. The fall in real wages in the coal industry led to strikes which weakened Gorbachev's political position

Right. Beggar woman with icon, central Moscow

are six points. There were the same number of points on most scales after the 1970–77 reorganization, but the spread was only 1.58 in most branches of light industry and 1.86 in much of heavy industry. According to the 1986–90 reorganization, the range of basic wages is 4.06:1 (from a minimum of 81 rubles a month for the least skilled workers in the food industry to 329 rubles for underground workers in coalmining.) This is an increase when compared to the 1970–77 structure, 3.29:1. But is still less than in the 1957–65 structure where it was as high as 5.1:1.

The 1986 reorganization also proposed to increase the basic salaries of office personnel, of managerial and professional staff. These groups were more or less ignored in the previous reorganization and, as a result, they saw differentials between themselves and shop-floor workers eroded. This led to some difficulties in recruitment.

Bureaucratic wage determination in the USSR produced a system that was slow to change. But structural rigidity was accompanied by sustained growth in nominal earnings. Between 1956 and 1986 average earnings in the state sector increased from 74 rubles to 196 rubles a month. At the same time, the standard working week for manual workers fell from 48 to 40 hours. Although there were some increases in the cost of living, until 1986 they were modest by West European standards; as a result there was a steady growth in real wages. In the period since 1987, however, there has been increasing evidence that this system had broken down. The authorities no longer appeared to be in control of wage rates. In the first quarter of 1987, average earnings in the state sector were estimated at 202 rubles a month; in the fourth quarter of 1989 they were reported to be 252 rubles a month. But rapidly rising prices and the increased frequency of stock-outs and redundancies meant that real wages were stagnant or falling.

Income distribution

Information on the distribution of income for years before 1980 is limited. But what is available suggests that as per capita incomes rose after 1958, inequality fell. In 1967 the decile ratio (that is, the ratio of the income of the person whose rank in the distribution is at 90 per cent of income-recipients to that of the person whose rank is at 10 per cent) for state employees was calculated at 3.0; in 1958 it had been 4.1. Although per capita income continued to grow after this date and, indeed, increased by 80 per cent between 1970 and 1988, the trend towards greater equality ceased. It is reported that the decile ratio for the population as a whole (including *kolkhozniki*) in 1988 was 3.45. In 1968 it was estimated to be 3.12–3.14. Such figures suggest that the distribution of income in the USSR was more equal than in Western Europe but less so than in East European socialist countries. Comparisons of this nature should be treated with caution, however, since they take no account of privilege.

More important is the evidence they provide of continuing poverty. The authorities claimed that, in 1965 the poverty line was equal to a per capita income of 50 rubles per month. At that time, it was estimated that approximately 75 million people (43 million state employees and 32 million *kolkhozniki*) had incomes below this level. By 1989 the poverty line had been raised to 78 rubles per month and in the subsequent inflation it was linked to the minimum

wage. There were still 40 million people with incomes below this level before the price liberalization. Poverty is concentrated among pensioners and in Central Asia where families are large. It is not, therefore, only or mainly a consequence of low wages; its alleviation will depend upon appropriate social policies. But the presence of such large numbers on the margin of subsistence acted as a brake on the government's aim of allowing the market to set prices.   AM

The private sector

Since the socialist ownership of the means of production was a Soviet tenet, private ownership, outside the sphere of personal consumption, was perceived by the Soviet authorities as an affront. The word 'private' (*chastny*) was so ideologically repulsive that whenever private activities were allowed they were labelled 'personal' or 'individual'. Even so, the Soviet leadership never eradicated private enterprise, as private enterprise was vital for the subsistence of *kolhozniki*. The policy was rarely stable but vacillated. In agriculture private production from household plots of barely an acre regularly contributed 25–30 per cent of agricultural produce. A substantial share of these products was sold privately by their cultivators at *kolkhoz* markets.

Demonstration in Vilnius, Lithuania, of a balloon produced by a British-Russian joint venture – the Cameron Balloons Company and the Feniks (Phoenix) co-operative, Moscow

The Soviet Constitution of 1977 appeared to offer an opening for small-scale private enterprise. Its Article 13 delimited personal property, but Article 17 explicitly allowed 'individual labour activity'. Yet this clause remained of little significance. Barely 100,000 people were officially registered as privately occupied in the mid-1980s.

A more tolerant attitude towards private enterprise emerged with perestroika. The first major step was the adoption of a 'Law on Individual Labour Activity' in November 1986. It permitted private work in a broad range of handicrafts and services. Hired labour – outside the family – was still not allowed, and the law did not envisage full-time work in the private sector. Furthermore, 'speculation' and the extraction of 'unearned income' remained strictly forbidden; both concepts were legally imprecise but included resales of goods and sales at 'excessive' prices. All individual workers required licences – which local authorities often refused to issue – and taxation was a deterrent. In fact, the new co-operatives that emerged in 1987 were given more liberal conditions and assumed more potent features of private enterprise. Soon they took the lead over 'individual labour activity'.

The successor governments undertook the privatization of state-owned enterprises at varying pace, some confining change to small units. While their combined GNPs dropped by 1992 to 68 per cent of their 1989 levels, private-sector output rose some 35 per cent, doubling its still-modest share of the total.
                                                                     AÅ

Foreign economic relations

Merchandise trade

The foreign trade flows of the USSR were smaller in relation to Soviet gross national product (GNP) than the foreign trade flows of most other countries in relation to their GNP. In 1988 Soviet merchandise exports were equivalent to about 4.3 per cent of Soviet GNP (the latter being estimated in 1988 US dollars). This may be compared with equivalent figures of about 20 per cent for most medium-sized West European countries (such as the UK, Italy or France). There were two main reasons for this modest level of trade activity: the sheer economic size and extensive domestic energy supplies and raw material base of the USSR, and the historically and systematically conditioned tendency towards self-sufficiency in Soviet economic management and policy.

It was also true, however, that if Soviet trade flows and GNP were measured in Soviet established internal (ruble) prices, instead of in dollar prices, the importance of trade to the Soviet economy appeared much larger. This reflected the fact that, even after all the attempts at changing the economic system from 1985 onwards, the domestic and world market price structures remained far apart. Indeed, available evidence on the major revision of internal prices in 1991 suggests that it did not bring the structure of internal prices closer to that of world market prices. Thus some export items appear to be sold at a 'loss' and others at a 'profit' when their dollar or Deutschmark prices are converted back to rubles and there are similar disparities on the import side. In 1989 the 'profits' arising from these disparities were around 7 per cent of GNP.

Despite the continued disjunction between the domestic economy and the world market, there was some increase in the openness of the Soviet economy to the world market under Gorbachev's attempted liberalization. This took two main forms: allowing foreign firms to invest directly in the USSR in the form of joint ventures and, from 1991, wholly owned subsidiaries; and diffusing the right to engage directly in foreign transactions to all Soviet producers, in both the state and the new independent sector. At the same time there was an increase in the illegal and quasi-legal use of foreign currency in the domestic economy, and the beginnings of a legitimate internal currency market.

These developments were severely limited in their practical effect, however, by the failure until the end of the Soviet state to change the domestic economic system into a functioning market economy. Thus

the Soviet ruble was not convertible; the Soviet central authorities retained control over the great bulk of export earnings of convertible currencies; a near-comprehensive system of export and import licensing was in effect, and large flows of taxes and subsidies continued to provide adjustments between internal prices and the foreign-trade prices of export and import items when they were converted to rubles. (The adoption of a much lower official 'commercial' rate for the ruble in late 1990 did not alter this, for the prime disparity was in the structure of relative prices.)

The important practical changes that occurred in Soviet merchandise trade in the Gorbachev era were three in number. First, foreign businesses had easier and more extensive access to Soviet end-users of imports and producers of exports, and could create partnerships with them. Second, the Council of Mutual Economic Assistance, or Comecon, ceased to operate, and the old arrangements for trade on a bilateral clearing basis with Comecon partners were being replaced by payments in hard currency and at world-market prices. Third, Soviet policy makers lost control over trade and payments sufficiently in 1988–90 for the USSR to lose its status in world markets as a top-quality borrower with an outstanding credit rating.

The inheritance of the successor states was the economy of an uncompetitive exporter of manufactures, with arms as the only substantial exception, uncompetitive also in services and farm products. Russia, Ukraine and Kazakhstan could rely on exports of fuel and raw materials, but all needed to import food and technology.   PH

Representatives of Moscow catering services and of McDonald's sign an agreement for the company's first Russian outlet

THE BALANCE OF PAYMENTS

The USSR published merchandise trade statistics but did not publish its balance of payments. Rough orders of magnitude for other components of the balance of payments were, however, estimated.

The Soviet balance of payments was until 1991 made up of two balances of a different nature: those with bilateral trading partners and those with convertible-currency trade partners. The latter were those western and developing countries with whom the USSR conducted trade on a multilateral basis, with settlements in convertible currencies. In bilateral settlements the aim was normally to arrange two-way flows of goods and services so that they balanced over any one year. Imbalances that arose were then cancelled out by increased deliveries from the deficit partner in the following period. A major

Extracting caviar from sturgeon, Astrakhan. Over-fishing and reduction of the water flow on the Volga has greatly reduced production

exception was Soviet aid to bilateral partners (for example, Cuba and India), which involved balancing (in principle) over a period of years. The larger part of Soviet bilateral transactions, however, was with Eastern Europe, merchandise transactions usually showing only small imbalances in any one year. This was probably true also for current-account transactions in total. Soviet current-account transactions with multilateral-settlement partners, however, were a different matter. Both country-by-country and in total, they often exhibited substantial imbalances. The major items in the current account were merchandise trade (including arms), freight transport, tourism and interest on debt. Gold sales, though used as an equilibrating device, could also be viewed as part of the current account, in so far as they came from Soviet production.

Foreign direct investment is permitted by all the successor states but early flows were small; con-

vertible-currency current-account imbalances must hence be offset by reserve changes and by foreign borrowing and lending. In the 1970s and 1980s the USSR, according to Soviet trade returns, generally exhibited a deficit in convertible-currency merchandise trade. It was also making substantial payments of interest on past borrowing. These negative items were usually offset to some extent by hard-currency arms sales (not directly identifiable in the trade returns), net credits on tourism and shipping and gold sales. Net indebtedness fluctuated but was not of the magnitude of the Third World or some of the East European countries.

The central planners' control over payments flows slipped in 1988–90, arrears of payments accumulated, and the Soviet credit rating fell. Net debt rose in 1990 and was approaching maximum sustainable levels in 1991. The switch to hard-currency settlements with Eastern Europe, however, provided some relief and in 1992 international official assistance was perceived as essential by western governments.   PH

FOREIGN BORROWING AND LENDING

The Soviet Union pursued a conservative borrowing policy in the industrialized West until the early 1970s. In the 1950s and 1960s it provided many credits in convertible currencies, rubles and under bilateral clearing to less-developed countries and to its East European allies. During the first period of détente in the 1970s the USSR increased rapidly its borrowings in the West. The (gross) debt grew from $0.2 billion in 1971 to $18 billion in 1980 and reached some $52 billion at the end of 1990. There are estimates that the USSR had more than $10 billion additional debts owned by developing countries (newly industrialized countries in Southeast Asia and Latin America, for example) and Middle Eastern countries (Saudi Arabia). In the second half of the 1980s its net debt position deteriorated with external assets in western banks sharply reduced and reserves fallen to some $5 billion (equivalent to less than two months of convertible currency imports) by the end of 1990.

In the 1970s and 1980s the Soviet Union enjoyed the rating of a first grade borrower on the western financial markets. It borrowed as long as the terms of borrowing were acceptable (and there were no constraints from the creditors side), in order to finance western imports of machinery, equipment, technology, and particularly agricultural products (grain). With its large gold and natural resource base, it was believed in the West that the USSR should have no difficulty in meeting its repayment obligations. It was also believed that the USSR would provide financial assistance to its allies in case of external debt difficulties (the 'umbrella theory'). The events of the early and late 1980s in the East European region proved this not to be true. The political instability and collapsing domestic economy of the late 1980s associated with declining earnings from oil exports (more than 50 per cent of export revenues in recent decades) as a result (amongst other things) of lower quantities of oil available for export, as well as failed efforts to increase exports of manufactured goods, less favourable than expected expansion of natural gas production for export to Western Europe, and shrinking other income (revenues from gold sales and arms sales to developing countries) led to loss of flexibility in Soviet hard-currency trade and debt policies.

In 1989–92 the liabilities towards BIS area banks increased and the current account and the indicators of debt and credit-worthiness deteriorated to alarming levels – a debt service ratio of some 30 per cent and net debt to exports of 140 per cent. The distribution shifted from official and guaranteed debt in the early 1980s in favour of unguaranteed (Euromarket) bank credits, respectively some 21 and 62 per cent of total debt in 1990. As a result of increased demand for foreign funds as well as the lessening of central discipline over total borrowing, the growth of debt accelerated rapidly and reached some $87 billion by the end of 1992. In 1990 the USSR experienced liquidity difficulties with arrears to the West estimated as high as $6 billion. Compared with many developed and developing countries with large external debts, the former USSR still could have been considered as moderately indebted by international standards. However, the fact that the central authorities had to a great extent lost control over international payments and over a significant fraction of reserves has been cause for serious concern in the West. Long-term debt reschedulings will be unavoidable in the future.

Official published Soviet data indicated that the USSR extended credits to many developing and socialist countries and its claims in 1990 totalled over 85 billion rubles (over $125 billion at the then official rate). The greatest number of claims were against Cuba, Vietnam, Mongolia, India, Syria, Poland, Afghanistan, Iraq and Ethiopia, already over-indebted countries scarcely likely to repay debts to Russia and the former Soviet republics, in the short or medium term. The USSR was a net debtor to its former East European allies with the exception of Poland. The financial arrangements for shifting settlements to convertible currencies from 1 January 1991 with these partners did not ease the tension between Russia and the successor states and their former allies.

The successor states had considerable net borrowing requirements in the early 1990s, but encountered severe problems in raising funds in western financial markets and had to rely on public lending. But the infusions of 1992–93 ($2.5 billion by the IMF and $2 billion by the US for grain purchases) were dwarfed by a capital flight estimated during those two years at as much as $25 billion. IZ

FOREIGN DIRECT INVESTMENT

Foreign capital contributed significantly to the industrialization of Russia before the Revolution. Although much of the capital inflow was through bonds issued by the tsarist government, foreign firms played a direct part through their investment in Russian-based operations, especially in the extractive industries. After the Revolution, in the NEP period, Lenin sought with little success to attract foreign firms to reinvest through 'concessions' in many of these same sectors. Thereafter, the extreme centralization of control under Stalin effectively closed the Soviet economy to foreign capital participation. This situation continued after the Second World War. Even in the Brezhnev era, when the USSR sought new avenues for the acquisition of western technology, it eschewed the example of other socialist countries (including several of its Comecon allies) which had taken steps to open the door to foreign equity participation in the form of joint ventures.

Not surprisingly, in view of this history, the 1986 decision of the new Soviet leadership to allow foreign investment in joint enterprises on Soviet territory attracted great interest, at home and abroad. The aim was not only to attract technology and capital to Soviet industry, but to introduce foreign techniques of management and to forge links that would boost manufactured exports to world markets. The follow-up decrees issued in January 1987 proved relatively liberal with regard to form, activities and tax treatment of joint enterprises. The initial limitation on foreign equity to a minority share was relaxed in 1989, as was the stipulation that the managing director be a Soviet citizen, and from 1990 wholly foreign-owned branches and subsidiaries were allowed. The requirement that joint enterprises earn convertible currencies sufficient to cover their convertible expenses and profit repatriation was progressively eased, as measures to expand ruble convertibility were introduced.

The 1987 initiative elicited a positive response. By late 1991 over 5,000 joint enterprises had been officially registered under the new legislation, representing a $6 billion commitment of foreign capital, though well under half were as yet operative. These investments covered a wide range of Soviet industries, services as well as goods.

Demand for foreign consumer goods: a Coca Cola stall. Lack of shops has brought many kiosks to urban pavements as private retailing has expanded

Geologist testing for placer gold in Siberia

Investments abroad by Soviet enterprises also had pre-war roots, but grew most rapidly in the recent post-war period. The first Soviet business operation was the Moscow Narodny Bank, established in London in 1919. By the late 1920s, more than a dozen Soviet business firms and banks had been established abroad. Most disappeared in the 1930s, but a few survived the war and their ranks were swollen by the addition of 178 new companies, most formed after 1965. Altogether, a total of 192 companies with Soviet capital participation were established in 41 countries, with an aggregate capitalization of nearly $1 billion. Most of these investments were concentrated in Western Europe (where the German Federal Republic played a dominant role as host). The remainder were widely scattered in both developed and developing countries. In most cases, Soviet enterprises held all or a majority of the equity. The greatest number of Soviet companies

abroad imported and distributed Soviet products (handling about a third of all Soviet exports to the West) or provided related transport and financial services. Only a few engaged in manufacturing, on a small scale.

Inflows and outflows of foreign direct investment became a feature of the Soviet economy. Their impact on the economic performance of Russia and other successor states, domestically and internationally, are likely to continue to grow in significance.   CHM

GOLD RESERVES

As a gold producer Imperial Russia had a substantial gold reserve (1,566 tonnes in 1913). Soviet gold production was not officially published after 1928 nor did the USSR State Bank reveal its reserves of gold and convertible currency after 1935. Since 1978 its deposits in convertible currency in banks in the industrial West were compiled from returns collected by the Bank for International Settlements ($8,644 million at the end of 1991), although they were more than offset by bank borrowing ($41,216 million at the same date).

The State Bank and its Bank for Foreign Economic Relations used bullion to make up some of the deficit on the balance of payments and in the last years of the USSR such sales and suspected illicit capital flight virtually exhausted the reserves. Statistics published in Moscow in October 1991 showed that the gold reserve had declined from over 2,000 tonnes in 1953 to 260 tonnes in mid-1991.   MCK

THE RATE OF EXCHANGE

The ruble, which dates from the thirteenth century, was originally of silver; Russia did not adhere to the gold standard until 1897. Convertibility into gold was suspended in August 1914 and the value of the paper ruble plummeted in wartime inflation and post-war hyperinflation. A phased currency reform during 1922–24 reintroduced a bullion cover (the 1922 *chervonets* of 10 rubles was issued at 8.6g of gold; the 1924 silver ruble was valued at 18g of silver but was replaced by the 1926 silver *poltinik* of 50 kopeks at 9g). The backing became nominal from 1928 (when the import and export of Soviet currency was prohibited); the *poltinik* was formally withdrawn in 1931 and the *chervonets* in 1936; a gold *chervonets* was sold from 1975 against convertible currency. A devalued paper *chervonets* was introduced in 1936 but withdrawn at the 1947 currency reform. The exchange rate of the ruble then introduced was revalued in 1950 but devalued (to

The first separate currency in the former Soviet Union: the Estonian kroon

pation of Central Asia, opened up land routes to the Orient. Although they were undoubtedly heroic and portentous, the Petrine reforms none the less remained expedient, highly limited to the economic and strategic needs of the hour rather than the construction of a grand modernization strategy.

The modest increase in outward orientation set in motion under Peter received a major impetus from the capitalist enterprises of domestic as well as foreign origin that got under way after the Great Reforms of the second half of the nineteenth century. This movement was particularly effective as a result of the industrialization policies fostered by Vyshnegradsky and later Count Witte. These were aimed at the modernization and industrialization of Russia, in part through the rapid construction of railways, the inputs for which, as well as often their financing, had to be acquired from abroad. On the eve of the First World War, Russia was a major trading nation, exporting one-tenth of its national income and poised for rapid further growth.

Soviet economic isolation

The Soviet government's renunciation of international bond obligations issued by the tsarist regime, which had earmarked foreign savings particularly for railway construction – and the nationalization without compensation in 1918 of foreign assets, which had been mobilized in Western Europe chiefly for the exploitation of oil and other manufacturing endeavours – led to a boycott of trade with the new Soviet state. The signing of the trade agreement with the UK (1921), coinciding as it did with the resumption of a market-oriented economic system under NEP, ushered in a period of moderate reliance on external commerce and some capital inflow. The reversal of that policy by the late 1920s, in the form of forced industrialization and collectivization of agriculture under Stalin, also entailed a relative inward-turning, although the first Soviet industrialization drive of the 1930s depended on buoyant imports financed primarily from exports of grain and primary goods. This search for self-sufficiency through import substitution and the promotion of completely new economic activities was in fact strengthened as a result of the Great Depression and the adverse terms of trade that the USSR experienced.

After the Second World War, the USSR looked upon the external environment as consisting of two 'world economic systems' or camps that would by necessity be antagonistic to each other. It differentiated its external policies accordingly. One focused on the expanding group of socialist countries in Asia and Europe with each of which detailed co-operation, including trade and payments, agreements were signed; in some, especially the countries that had

its 1980 formal gold content of 0.987412g of fine gold) in 1961, when one new ruble was exchanged for ten old rubles. Soviet citizens were permitted to export and reimport up to 30 rubles in banknotes, and to buy for foreign travel $250 worth of currency but the ruble was still a national and inconvertible currency. The exchange rate was set by the State Bank and was for long in the range 0.6–0.7 to the US dollar. It was sharply devalued in November 1990 but a catastrophic decline began only after the demise of the USSR at the end of 1991. The Russian ruble saw its value drop to 1,200 to the dollar in December 1993. The Ukraine *kupon* (standing in for an eventual *hryvnia*), once at par with the ruble, was down to 30,900 at that date, but the Estonian kroon was firmly tied at 8 to the D-mark.　　　MCK

INTERNATIONAL ECONOMIC AGREEMENTS

Before the Revolution

The first recorded Russian economic treaty was that of the year 911 between Prince Oleg of Kiev and the Byzantine emperor. But most medieval commerce was conducted through the privileged trading establishment (*gostiny dvor*), within which the Hanseatic merchants were the principal foreign group, and through great annual fairs such as that of Novgorod. After shaking off the Mongol yoke and the installation of the Romanov dynasty, Peter the Great promoted capitalist commercial relations with Central and Western Europe, while the exploration and colonization of Siberia, and, later, the Russian occu-

sided with the Axis during the war, the Soviet Union mandated the creation of joint-stock companies in key sectors; mutual economic assistance among the members of that group was facilitated through bilateral commissions and group-wide institutions; and the USSR managed to involve itself directly in the steering of economic policy in many of the countries that belonged to the socialist camp. The other revolved around a miscellany of arrangements with developed and developing market economies. On the eve of political détente in the early 1970s, the share of exports in national product was about the same as it was in the second half of the 1920s – perhaps 3 to 4 per cent. Since then, in spite of setbacks with détente, the share of exports in national income has risen to perhaps just under twice that level. But formidable measurement and comparison problems in national accounting and foreign trade data complicate empirical estimates.

The USSR nevertheless kept itself singularly free of formal commitments to international organizations, especially those with an economic mandate. Briefly, as a member of the League of Nations (September 1934 to December 1939), it took part in that agency's economic activities, including the International Labour Office (of which its membership, however, lapsed during 1940–54). It was a founder member (from 1945) of the United Nations (UN) and hence a participant in two Regional Commissions (the Economic Commission for Europe and the present Economic and Social Commission for Asia and the Pacific) and an observer in the other three Regional Commissions, and in all non-regional activities that reside under the auspices of, or are subordinate to, the Economic and Social Council of the UN. Although it participated actively, including the Bretton Woods talks, in the discussions about the post-Second World War global economic framework that had earlier been set in train by the UK and the USA, it refrained in the end from ratifying the Articles of Agreement of the International Monetary Fund and the International Bank for Reconstruction and Development (the World Bank). It did not, however, take part in the discussions in 1946–48 about the post-war International Trade Organization (ITO) and was not invited to participate in the General Agreement on Tariffs and Trade (GATT). Until the 1980s and the advent of perestroika when the 'New Thinking' in foreign relations began to crystallize, the USSR took a negative attitude toward these international economic organizations, which were seen as bulwarks of capitalism ensuring the economic dominance or even hegemony in international trade and finance of key western nations. In the mid-1950s the Soviet Union vigorously sought ratification of the Havana Charter and the creation of the ITO. When this failed to get support, until

1964 the Soviet Union proposed either to resurrect the ITO or to reconceive it under the umbrella of the UN. This attempt in the end was overtaken by events as the developing countries succeeded in the creation of the United Nations Conference on Trade and Development (UNCTAD) as a standing organ of the UN Secretariat, pending the establishment of a more permanent institutionalized specialized agency. Until the mid-1980s the USSR and its allies unambiguously favoured this institution as the centre for enhancing global economic security.

Perestroika and the successor states

Under the influence of the New Thinking the USSR made a first overture to the GATT in August 1986 and gained observer status in May 1990, seeking full contracting party status as soon as possible. It also began to explore some type of association with the IMF and the World Bank. It became an observer of the Asian Development Bank in 1987 and showed interest in other regional development banks. By late 1990 the Group of Seven had reached a compromise on preliminary arrangements for creating a 'special associate' status that would have permitted the institutions to dispense technical advice to the Soviet Union, but not loans.

Until late 1989 the Soviet government put forward proposals on a comprehensive system of global security within the context of the UN, incorporating ideas about strengthening international economic security. This would have involved, but not been limited to, reinforcing the international economic regimes (finance, money, and trade) entrusted to the international economic organizations (World Bank, IMF, and GATT), in terms of both institutional arrangements and agreed-upon rules and regulations. The USSR would not become a full member of the IMF until after fundamental reforms in these organizations, including diluting the veto power, moving toward a stabler exchange rate regime, and emplacing a global monetary anchor through the creation of an 'ideal' world currency or the perfection of the IMF's Special Drawing Rights. IMF membership would essentially be sought in order to gain entry into the World Bank, and hence to have a say over the allocation of the Bank's multilateral development assistance. As part of the New Thinking, Soviet attitudes towards granting official development assistance to developing countries, including the three CMEA developing countries (Cuba, Mongolia, and Vietnam), had by then been shifting favourably toward multilateralizing this assistance institutionally, especially within the context of the UN's specialized agencies and technical co-operation infrastructure, as well as by making commitments in convertible currency rather than domestic rubles, which are difficult to mobilize by non-residents even in the domestic economy. All the successor states except Georgia were admitted to the IMF and Bank in 1992.

The CMEA (Comecon)

After the Second World War Soviet growth efforts revolved around strengthening domestic industrialization and, at least during the Cold War, facilitating economic ties with its political subordinates in Eastern Europe. The Council for Mutual Economic Assistance (CMEA) was founded by the USSR and five East European states (Bulgaria, Czechoslovakia, Hungary, Poland, and Romania) in January 1949. It gradually expanded to encompass ten active full members from June 1978 as well as one associate member (Yugoslavia), nine co-operants (Finland and eight developing countries), and a miscellany of observers; Albania became an inactive, but nominally still full, member in late 1961. From its inception, the USSR was the dominant member. Although it could in principle block any measure that was not to its advantage, owing to its sheer economic and political power, it was not able to carry through some of its schemes for socialist economic integra-

tion. This fundamental weakness was demonstrated once again in the long-drawn-out efforts of the 1980s to infuse the Council with new life and to adopt an integration strategy, supported with an effective mechanism (comprising macroeconomic policies, institutions, and policy instruments), to bring about a Common Market in Eastern Europe too. This Soviet proposal was first tabled by Nikolay Ryzhkov at the 43rd CMEA Session in October 1987. It was formally endorsed by all members but Romania at the 44th Session in July 1988 and remained a theme of active interest, though short on content, until the 45th Session in January 1990, where it was in fact decided to terminate the reform debate of the two preceding years and start afresh. A commission then recommended the dissolution of the CMEA and its replacement by the Organization for International Economic Co-operation. Only the first recommendation was implemented and it was decided to liquidate the CMEA in June 1991.

Relations with the European Community

Although long opposed to West European integration, the USSR decided to recognize realities in 1972 and set in train negotiations, starting in August 1973, between the CMEA and the Commission of the European Community with a view to reaching a bilateral treaty between the two organizations. These negotiations, after much vacillation, concluded on 25 June 1988 with a framework agreement which authorized mutual diplomatic recognition and led in the case of the USSR to a broad trade and co-operation agreement with the Commission, signed in February 1990. The Commission was accorded by the Group of Seven a leading role with the IMF in arrangements for economic assistance to the successor states. By the end of 1993 it had negotiated six agreements with the East European countries, trade and co-operation agreements with the Baltic states and Slovenia, and was in the process of negotiating 'partnership and co-operation' agreements with several CIS countries. JMvanB

Greek-organized course for Russian executives who need to travel abroad: fee $2,500

Society

Social stratification

Social structure and stratification in the USSR developed as a result of three main factors – the historical legacy inherited from pre-revolutionary Russia; the policies of the CPSU and the state it controlled; and the industrialization of Soviet society. Social structure refers to the institutions and the groups, strata, and classes that comprise a society, whereas social stratification denotes the extent to which valued resources and prestige are differentially distributed between groups, strata, and classes. In important ways these factors have been in conflict with each other. The outcome was a system of stratification that was not only different from that found in other industrial societies, but was to prove a barrier to continued economic development. The programme of reconstruction that was initiated during the Gorbachev period involved not only economic and political changes but also qualitative changes in the pattern of social stratification, in the status of social groups, and in the overt expression of competing social interests. In the period following the abolition of the USSR, the pattern of stratification continued to change dramatically.

Russian social structure at the time of the Bolshevik Revolution was still that of a pre-industrial society. Only one in six of the population were workers in industry and services, and a mere one in fifty were specialists or clerical workers, compared to the more than three-quarters of the population who were peasants. The hereditary nobility accounted for only about one per cent of the population, and the merchants, professionals, and clergy taken together amounted to less than one per cent. Approximately 18 per cent of the population were classified as urban. The industrialization programme pursued by Soviet leaders changed this structure and brought it closer to that found in other industrial societies, although the particular circumstances in the USSR created a system of stratification that was in significant ways different. The state's control over wages and employment, and over the distribution of goods and services, gave Soviet stratification a different dynamic from stratification in market economies.

SOVIET VIEWS OF STRATIFICATION

Students of Soviet society have always had to distinguish carefully between official ideology regarding social structure and the actual structure that was developing. Official views of social structure were based on Marxist ideas of the importance of social class. According to this view a social class is defined in terms of its relation to the means of production, the two basic classes being those who own productive property and those who do not. Class relations were by definition always relations of exploitation. Official Soviet theory held that, since the means of production were owned by the population as a whole, there could be no antagonistic classes (and hence no exploitation) in Soviet society. This view defined social stratification as consisting of the working class (defined as all those working for socialized property, such as factories and state-owned farms), and the class of collective farmers (working in *kolkhozy* that were nominally owned by those who worked on them). Since neither of these classes employed the other, there was said to be no antagonism between them, and such conflicts as did exist were said to be vestiges of the past destined to disappear as the society moved closer to communism. Within the

Two Russian paupers, one blind aged 70, the other sighted, aged 58. Albumen print by Iosif Kordysh, 1870s

working class, a distinction was made between manual and non-manual workers, the latter constituting a stratum known as the intelligentsia. This stratum included all those with higher or secondary specialized education or working in occupations that would normally require such education. Officially, Soviet society was said to be moving towards an elimination of these differences as collective farms were transformed into state farms, and as manual labour came more and more to be based on mental work requiring more education. This trend towards greater homogeneity was said to lead also to greater similarity in the material and cultural styles of life.

DEVELOPMENT OF SOCIAL STRATIFICATION

Soviet society changed in a predictable way as it became more industrialized. Thus, that part of the labour force working in industry and construction grew from less than 10 per cent before 1917 to 23 per cent in 1940, and to 39 per cent in 1988. The number of those working in agriculture declined during the same period from 75 per cent to 54 per cent to 19 per cent, and in the sectors dealing with health, education, culture, and science there was a growth from one per cent to 6 per cent to 18 per cent. These changes in the structure of the labour force were accompanied by changes in educational levels. Whereas in 1939 only 10.8 per cent of the population aged ten and above had received more than an elementary education, this had increased to 36.1 per cent by 1959 and to 57 per cent by 1976. By 1984 86.8 per cent of the labour force had at least a secondary education.

Stratification in the USSR should be seen as consisting of two dimensions – the differences due to education, occupation, and income, and those due to special access to privilege. In general, people with more years of education were better off in that they had opportunities to become upwardly mobile, and maybe even move into the ranks of the intelligentsia. On the other hand, more education did not necessarily mean more income, for skilled industrial workers were usually paid more than physicians, scientists, and teachers. Moreover, the policies of the Party and state were often designed to further the move towards greater homogeneity by decreasing wage differentials, especially during the post-Second World War period. While in 1932 the average wages of managerial and technical workers were 163 per cent higher, and those of office workers 50 per cent higher than the wages of skilled workers, by 1985 they were 10 per cent higher and 22 per cent lower than skilled workers respectively. This compression of incomes contributed to declining performance in the economy.

Unlike the situation in other societies, however, income differentials in the USSR were not a good measure of inequality because many goods and services were available only through political connections or through special distribution channels not available to the general public. For example, large apartments, better quality food, better health care, foreign travel, and even access to the best schools, were obtained through special connections and not through purchase on an open market. Since these special privileges provided to the *nomenklatura*, to the party apparat, and to top athletes, scientists, artists, and performers were not publicized, the public's awareness of the true level of stratification was very limited. The policy of glasnost during the Gorbachev era led to public disclosure of the extent of privilege, and to calls for its elimination. As a result, many of the special stores and other facilities were closed and a special commission was appointed to look into the system of privilege.

Social mobility in the USSR was based on different principles at different stages of development. During the first three decades or so, upward mobility depended on meeting certain political requirements; often promotions were based entirely on political criteria, at the expense of technical or other qualifications. During the purges of the 1930s, many people from working-class and peasant backgrounds found themselves rising to higher levels to replace the specialists who were being eliminated. As a result, the upper reaches of the society from the 1950s on were manned by people of modest social origins. As the system matured, however, greater emphasis was put on education as a criterion for advancement, and the society moved more closely to meritocratic principles. Even as late as the 1980s, however, there were many positions in the society

Gravestones at the Novodevichy Cemetery in Moscow, burial-place of many famous Russians and of people from influential Soviet and Russian families

for which there was a political criterion for placement. This was especially true of *nomenklatura* positions. As the emphasis shifted more towards educational qualifications, however, it was the children of the intelligentsia who were most able to compete for higher education, and as a result the intelligentsia became more and more self-recruiting. Thus, the more industrial the society became, the more rigid became the system of stratification.

In reality, the structure of Soviet society was always more complex than the official classification was willing to acknowledge. In fact, it became more heterogeneous rather than less as the process of industrialization developed. The increasing division of labour, the continual creation of new kinds of occupations, increasing educational levels, and the development of new technologies, all led to ever greater differences between people.

An increasing division of labour and occupational differentiation is a normal consequence of industrialization, and results in growing cultural differences, differences in real interests, and more complex competition for available resources. Also, greater skill and technical demands in the workplace usually lead to the desire for more control over life, both at work and in the wider society. These developments in the USSR ran counter to the trends advocated by political leaders, and had they been allowed open expression would have threatened their claim to control over all aspects of social, economic and political life.

CHANGING VIEWS OF STRATIFICATION

The development of empirical sociological research in the USSR from the 1960s on exposed much of the complexity of social structure and stratification. Although compelled to reiterate the official views, researchers found that differences in social status and standard of living were linked to regional and ethnic factors, age differences, urban and rural residence, and to level of occupational skill. During the period of perestroika the scope of enquiry widened, and attention was also drawn to gender differences, and to the special privileges of the party apparat and the *nomenklatura* in general. Investigations into the unequal economic status of women showed that women at mid-career typically earned one-third less than their male counterparts, half of this difference being due to the fact that women were more likely to work in sectors that paid less (40 per cent of women worked in low-skilled, heavy manual and physical labour), and the other half being the result of barriers to the promotion of women. Also, throughout the Soviet period, in every profession

and in the political realm, women became fewer and fewer in number at the higher levels of the occupation.

During the 1980s, and especially during the last part of the decade, sociologists and others began to construct models of Soviet social structure that rejected completely the official views, and also openly challenged the idea that there were no conflicts of interest in Soviet society. Writers such as T.I. Zaslavskaya (b.1927) and others showed that the society had profound conflicts of interest over the distribution of goods, services, and power, and also predicted that perestroika would necessarily involve conflicts as groups struggled to gain new power and influence, or to retain what privileges they already had.

CONSEQUENCES OF PERESTROIKA

Perestroika had important consequences for stratification in several ways. First, incomes came to depend more on effort and efficiency, and this increased the differentials. Second, wages for strategically important occupations, such as teachers and health workers, were increased relative to other occupations. Third, the development of private enterprise created a new stratum of businessmen whose incomes were frequently many times greater than those in the state sector, and whose employees also earned wages two or three times higher than workers in the state sector. By 1990 the number of people working in the legal private sector was at least 5 million, and considerably more if the illegal sector were to be included. Fourth, economic reforms created a significant and growing unemployed population, the conditions of which were made worse by the absence of a developed system of unemployment pay and social services, and the lack of job retraining

Below. *Academician Tat'yana Zaslavskaya, one of the most prominent women in Soviet public life during the Gorbachev era. Zaslavskaya became President of the Soviet Sociological Association in 1986 and from 1988 until after the collapse of the Soviet Union she was Director of the newly-established All-Union Centre for the Study of Public Opinion, based in Moscow.*
Right. *Tat'yana Kol'tsova, one of the new Russian entrepreneurs – the owner of the Red Stars Model Agency in Moscow*

A Russian 'bag lady' – one of a growing number of elderly women and men who live in the streets, in this case in Moscow

and job relocation services. Fifth, those not employed in the economy, such as the elderly, the handicapped, and the homeless found themselves increasingly unable to deal with the shortages of goods and the rapidly increasing prices of those that were available. As a result of these trends the society became increasingly polarized between those who were accumulating wealth (through legal or illegal activities in the developing market economy), and the rest of the population whose standard of living was rapidly declining.

POST-SOVIET STRATIFICATION

By 1992 the official estimate was that 80 per cent of the population was living below the poverty line in Russia alone. This reflected the economic collapse which followed the end of the Soviet period, and the inability of organizations to provide for people's needs. The high level of inflation coupled with considerably slower growth in incomes and entitlements led to increasing poverty. The people who gained during this process were those who were able to take advantage of shortages by engaging in trade, those who were involved in more or less criminal activities, and those members of the former apparat who were able to use their network of connections to acquire property or engage in private business. These developments not only changed the

stratification of the society, they also challenged most people's vision of what constitutes social justice. The long and bitter debate over social justice that took place during the perestroika period occurred precisely because the economic and political changes that were occurring were removing the very foundations on which social stratification had rested for most of the history of the USSR.

Unless the newly-emerging societies in what was formerly the Soviet Union decide to abandon their move to a market economy, and return to central controls of wages, prices, and the distribution of resources, their systems of stratification will continue to change, and will become more like those found in other industrial societies. During the long period of transition, however, poverty will continue to be the fate of large sections of the population.   AJ

Social institutions

MARRIAGE

Soviet citizens could marry at eighteen without their parents' permission and, in certain circumstances, if a baby was expected, marriage could be contracted earlier without permission from parents. In Latvia, Estonia, Moldova, Ukraine, Armenia, Kazakhstan and Kyrgyzstan women may marry at seventeen.

In Soviet society the family was statistically a strong unit with approximately 90 per cent of the population living within a family. According to the 1989 census 65.6 per cent of the population aged sixteen or over were married. Average family size was 3.5 people – 3.3 in urban areas and 3.8 in the countryside. Some 17.5 per cent of marriages were between people of different Soviet nationalities; there were 20.2 per cent such marriages in the towns and 11.8 per cent in rural areas. Such mixed marriages were much more common in some republics than others; they were relatively frequent in Russia, for example, and particularly rare in Armenia. Most couples married between the ages of 21 and 24 (1989). It was common for Soviet citizens to marry twice or more.

When a couple decided to marry they declared their intentions at their local registry office where they were given a date some time in advance to allow them time to reconsider. In some areas the local registry office was called a Wedding Palace and the decor justified the grandeur of the name. Couples were married under chandeliers on a red carpet in

Both in the Soviet Union and in post-Soviet Russia it has been common practice for a newly-wed couple to visit the war memorial or tomb of the unknown soldier and place the bridal bouquet upon it. The picture above was taken in Irkutsk

front of a portrait of Lenin and the national emblem. The bride usually wore white and young couples had in the later Soviet years returned to the tradition of exchanging rings. In any one Wedding Palace it was not uncommon for between thirty and forty weddings to be carried out in one day as each ceremony lasted only six to seven minutes. It was performed by a regally dressed woman-representative of the local soviet who addressed the couple briefly on the obligations of marriage. Some wedding parties remained in the palace for champagne and chocolates there while others proceeded directly to their own celebration, which usually consisted of plenty of food, drink and dancing. This in Russia has traditionally been punctuated by cries of 'Gor'ko, gor'ko' ('Bitter, bitter') to which the couple must respond by kissing until the atmosphere is deemed sweet enough for them to stop. Honeymoons were not a tradition as in the West; it was much more common for parents to move out of the family home for a few days so that the couple could begin married life in unaccustomed privacy.

In larger cities newly-married couples frequently had (and in post-Soviet society still have) no choice but to live with parents, perhaps acquiring a home of their own only if they have children. Most married women work outside the home but the burden of housework still falls chiefly on them rather than their husbands. The relative lack of consumer services and convenience products make the wife's burden particularly heavy.　　　　FO'D

DIVORCE

The tension of overcrowding and overwork must in part explain the high divorce rate although the main reason cited in divorce proceedings is drunkenness.

The number of divorces increased from 0.4 per thousand of the population in 1950 to 3.4 in 1989. The geographical distribution of Soviet divorces was uneven; it was highest in the European and urbanized population of the USSR and lowest in the Caucasus and Central Asia, ranging from 4.2 in Latvia to 1.2 in Armenia. Approximately one-third of all divorces took place in marriages with a duration of four years or fewer.

These divorce figures reflect the fact that in Soviet society divorce was relatively cheap and easy. Payment depended on the couple's income and the authorities decided in each individual case who was responsible for payment. If both husband and wife agreed in wanting a divorce and there were no children, divorce could be carried out in a registry office; otherwise the case had to be heard by a court. In both instances, an attempt was usually made at reconciliation but if this failed a divorce was granted. The court had then to decide about alimony and the custody of any children. It was usually felt that young children need their mother's care although in exceptional cases custody was given to the father. After the divorce it was not uncommon for the couple to have to continue living in one room for some time because of the shortage of living space. There was increasing concern about the number of divorces and their effect on children.　　FO'D

THE FAMILY

Size

The Soviet authorities encouraged parents to have children as, for economic reasons, they wished to ensure a substantial future generation. Nor was the Soviet Union as concerned about spare space and resources as other less well-endowed countries. Parenthood was held in high esteem. Women who produced five or more children were given medals and honorific titles – the Motherhood Medal, second class, for a fifth living child, up to 'Heroine Mother' for a tenth. Material aid was given to pregnant mothers and to parents with young families; a further aspect of the promotion of childbirth was a tax on unmarried men.

Despite these measures the birth-rate was still low. In the 1970s most urban families had only one or two children and, although rural families were larger, the average number of children born to married women was approximately 2.4 (1978). The overall net increase in the population in 1984 was only 8.8 per thousand. Soviet demographers were concerned by the fact that the birth-rate was falling. A 1980 party decision increased family allowances and maternity leave provision. The decline in the birth-rate stopped and birth-rates began to increase during the 1980s. More children were born in the mid-1980s that at any time since before the Second World War.

Data on family size showed large variations from republic to republic and between urban and rural areas. A study of Heroine Mother awards going to women who had brought up at least ten children showed that 87 per cent of them went to Central Asia, an area with ten per cent of the total Soviet population. The highest birth-rate was in the republic of Tajikistan in sharp contrast to the Baltic and the Slav republics where family size was particularly small (1988).

State assistance

In general, conditions for pregnant women were favourable. Employers could not refuse jobs to pregnant or nursing mothers nor could they reduce their pay or dismiss them. Women had the right to be transferred to lighter work in the later months of pregnancy. Gorbachev set about improving conditions for mothers with small children. They were guaranteed one year of paid maternity leave and, if they chose to stay at home with their young babies, they retained the right to return to the same job for up to three years. There was discussion during the perestroika years on how to improve the financial assistance given to young families. One idea proposed by the Moscow City Soviet was to pay the mother a sum of money for her to spend on either the child-care of her choice or to enable her to stay at home with her children.

Child benefits were paid to low-income families; with perestroika the exact nature of these payments varied from region to region.

Illegitimacy

Unmarried mothers in the later Soviet years also received increased benefits. This was not always the case. Stalinist legislation meant that an unmarried mother had no right to benefit and that a child's

illegitimacy was registered on its internal passport – laws abolished only in the 1960s. Illegitimate births increased by about 30 per cent during the 1980s, constituting 8.8 per cent of all births in 1980 and 10.7 per cent in 1989. Increased concern was being voiced about illegitimate children being born to very young mothers. Such babies were more likely to be abandoned or to have low birth weight or be premature, thus affecting the Soviet infant mortality rate which was almost three times higher than that in the USA. An almost complete lack of sex education and of openness about sexual matters (until, at least, the Gorbachev era) was frequently blamed in the press for unwanted pregnancies. However, it seemed probable that many illegitimate births were actually wanted, given the ready availability of abortion in the USSR.

Contraception and abortion

Various kinds of contraception were available in the Soviet Union but on a rather unsophisticated level. Condoms were thick and unlubricated; there were diaphragms but jelly or cream was virtually unobtainable, so they were difficult to use. The loop (IUD) only latterly came into use. Birth-control pills were both produced in the USSR and imported from Hungary but were little used because of shortage of supplies and anxiety about harmful side-effects. Fears about the spread of AIDS led to demands for more and better condoms to be produced. In 1988 it was estimated that condom production was such that each male citizen could have four condoms per year. The black market price was reported to be very high and increasing sharply. In the light of these facts the low birth-rate was surprising. It can be explained by the large-scale use of abortion as a means of birth control.

Abortion had mixed fortunes under Soviet rule. It was legalized in 1920 but then became a criminal offence under Stalin. In 1955, after his death, it was re-legalized and subsequently became available on

Below. Illegitimacy in the USSR, 1989. Below right. Washing condoms for reuse – one manifestation of the shortage of contraceptives in the Soviet Union

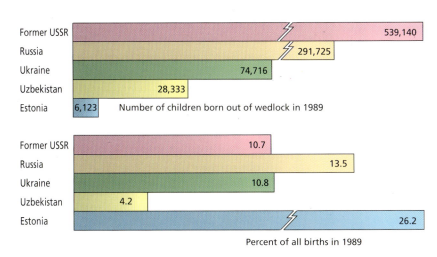

	Number of children born out of wedlock in 1989
Former USSR	539,140
Russia	291,725
Ukraine	74,716
Uzbekistan	28,333
Estonia	6,123

	Percent of all births in 1989
Former USSR	10.7
Russia	13.5
Ukraine	10.8
Uzbekistan	4.2
Estonia	26.2

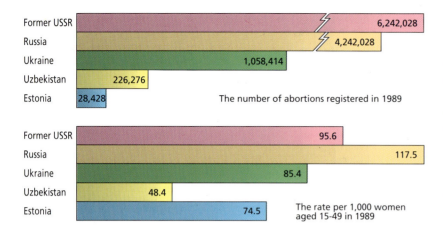

Former USSR	6,242,028
Russia	4,242,028
Ukraine	1,058,414
Uzbekistan	226,276
Estonia	28,428

The number of abortions registered in 1989

Former USSR	95.6
Russia	117.5
Ukraine	85.4
Uzbekistan	48.4
Estonia	74.5

The rate per 1,000 women aged 15-49 in 1989

Abortions in the USSR, 1989. The figures reveal extensive regional variation in the incidence of termination of pregnancy. The percentage rate was much higher in Russia than in the traditionally Muslim Soviet republics

request to any woman who was not more than three months pregnant. It was officially free to any working woman and in 1979 cost only five rubles to any unemployed woman. The medical profession tried to discourage abortion but maintained that if a woman was healthy and allowed at least six months between abortions there was no lasting damage; doctors accepted that it was up to the individual woman to take the decision. In some hospitals the suction method was used but in others the dilatation and curettage process was employed.

In 1989 there were 95.6 legal abortions for every 1,000 women between the ages of fifteen and forty-nine. This compares with 28 per 1,000 in the USA and 12.4 in England and Wales. The figure was particularly high in the Russian republic at 117.5 abortions per 1,000 women and lowest in Azerbaijan at 23.9. In 1989 there were 5.6 million births but 6.9 million abortions. Though abortion was legal, many women sought illegal abortions to avoid official knowledge of their condition or because their pregnancy was already advanced. To reduce that problem, the Ministry of Health in 1989 extended the legal termination date to 28 weeks.   FO'D

WOMEN

From 1917 the Soviet state was officially committed to equality of the sexes. The new Bolshevik government proclaimed equal political rights for men and women and equal pay for equal work. Mothers enjoyed the right to maternity leave with the financial support of full-pay for eight weeks before and after childbirth. Over seventy years later, Russian feminists became concerned that the new 'male democracy', as they dubbed it, might bring an end to earlier legal gains for women.

The 'woman question'

During the Stalin years, propaganda boasted that women had been emancipated and that the 'woman

question' had been 'solved'. But in the 1970s, Soviet social scientists regretted that while 'formal' equality existed, 'factual' equality in everyday life did not. Although socialism of the Soviet type had offered women new opportunities, female labour was still concentrated in low-paid work at the bottom of job hierarchies and very few women held top decision-making posts. Ideologists declared that a 'non-antagonistic contradiction' between work in the home and work in the labour force was to blame. Research into the female 'double burden' or 'double shift' revealed a thirteen to fifteen hour work day, with little help from males in the domestic shift. The shortening of the working week from six to five days increased the amount of time women devoted to housework. On average, women slept one hour fewer than men due to additional chores.

During the Brezhnev era a lively debate raged about the reasons behind the double burden, and its implications for the economy. Under Gorbachev the limits of debate broadened and at an All-Union Conference of Women held in Moscow in January 1987, delegates called for a 'perestroika' of men. As the use of glasnost strengthened, particularly after 1987, 'new' women's issues, previously cloaked in silence, such as the lack of contraceptives, high abortion rates, rape, prostitution, and the self-immolation of women in Central Asia came on to the agenda. After 1988 critical feminists such as Ol'ga Voronina and Ol'ga Lipovskaya condemned the 'male dominated bureaucracy' and 'man's world' and argued that patriarchal stereotypes of gender roles had to be challenged. Concepts such as these, previously ideologically taboo, were now used in women's writings.

Women in the labour-force

Marxist theory holds that women's emancipation results from socialism and from participation in social production. Soviet women, however, were drawn into the labour-force in large numbers after 1928 not because of ideology but due to a demand for workers in an expanding economy and because of a deficit of males. By the mid-1940s, catastrophic wartime losses meant that women of working age outnumbered their male counterparts by 20 million. Women made up 25 per cent of the work-force in 1922, 27 per cent in 1932, 56 per cent in 1945 and stabilized at 51 per cent in 1970. In industry, more than 75 per cent of female labour has been in light industry and under 30 per cent in mining, coal and electrical power. Protective legislation bans women from some forms of arduous physical work.

By 1985 55 per cent of students in higher education and 33 per cent of post-graduates were female. Women made up 71 per cent of specialists employed as teachers, librarians and cultural workers, 36 per

Prostitution

Before glasnost Soviet propaganda maintained that prostitution existed only in capitalist systems where unemployment drove women to it. However, greater openness under Gorbachev revealed that prostitution was a social problem under communism too. Newspaper articles exposed its links to the tourist trade, currency speculation and to the control of women by pimps.

Why did women turn to prostitution? According to one prostitute from Novorossiisk on the Black Sea: 'For most, money is the main thing. Easy money that you don't have to work very hard for, they think. Or fancy clothes.' In one night, prostitutes with foreign clients could earn the equivalent of the average female monthly wage. This was highly attractive in an economy with shortages in which female labour was concentrated at the bottom of job hierarchies in low-paid work. And some women dabbled in occasional prostitution which enabled them to buy basic clothing, such as winter boots.

The percentage of women who turn to prostitution generally increases in periods of growing unemployment and economic hardship. Rationing of selected items in 1989 followed by price increases in April 1991 and an economy increasingly orientated around the US dollar made prostitution more alluring. Massive price rises in January 1992 and the falling value of the ruble made prostitution an even more attractive option, especially since over 70 per cent of the recently unemployed were women.

In this context, schoolgirls view prostitution as a lucrative career choice. A survey at the beginning of the 1990s in Moscow of fifteen- to seventeen-year-olds asked them to rank the top twenty highest-paid jobs. They put prostitution in joint ninth-place alongside director and sales clerk. Prostitution came ahead of diplomat and teacher. In Yel'tsin's Russia 23 per cent of hard-currency prostitutes have enjoyed some higher education.

cent of engineers and 37 per cent of agronomists, livestock specialists and veterinarians. The percentage of women doctors continues to fall, standing in 1990 at 68 per cent, having peaked at 76 per cent in 1960, consistent with the official goals to 'de-feminize' medicine.

Self-financing (*khozraschet*) and a rationalization of the work force were integral to Gorbachev's policy of perestroika. Members of the Soviet Women's Committee and articles in women's magazines expressed the fear that necessary job losses would fall disproportionately on women, as they had during NEP, and that female unemployment would become a serious problem in the 1990s. In fact, some economists explicitly advocated that the impact of unemployment should be cushioned by women rather than men leaving the labour force; they added that this trend might also check falling birth rates among Slavonic peoples. In August 1991 the Soviet television programme *Vremya* informed viewers that most of the workers who had recently lost their jobs were indeed women. This differential pattern of unemployment in industry and in white collar jobs which hits women much harder than men continued in 1992. It became just one of the many problems endured by women in the new Commonwealth of Independent States. Coming at a time of huge price increases and food shortages, women are both angry and frequently in despair.

Women and politics

Another worry for the Soviet Women's Committee after 1989 was the effect of democratization on women's political representation. In the past, fixed quotas of female People's Deputies set 'from above' guaranteed a visible female presence on the soviets. Accordingly, the non-competitive elections in 1985 gave women 50.3 per cent of the seats on local soviets and an average of 36.2 per cent of seats on republic level Supreme Soviets. One year earlier women were chosen for 32.8 per cent of the seats on the all-union Supreme Soviet.

Democratization under Gorbachev ushered in candidate choice. In the 1989 elections to the Congress of People's Deputies, traditional quotas were abolished, although of the 750 seats 'reserved' for social organizations (out of a total of 2,250), the *zhensovety* (or women's councils), were guaranteed 75. The percentage of women elected nevertheless fell substantially to 15.6 per cent. The smaller Supreme Soviet, selected from the Congress, resulted in just 100 of the 542 seats (18.5 per cent) being held by women. Some 44 women sat in the Soviet of the Union and 45 in the Soviet of Nationalities. This contrasted with 233 and 259 respectively in 1984.

The 1990 elections to the Supreme Soviets of the republics and to local soviets resulted in more dramatic falls by almost 30 per cent in female representation. This was because thirteen of the fifteen republics decided to drop 'reserved' seats for social organizations on the ground that they were undemocratic. Just 5.4 per cent of the Russian Supreme Soviet, for example, was female in 1990. Other republics returned slightly higher proportions of women deputies, such as 11.4 per cent in Turkmenistan. Fewer women were also elected to the local soviets, falling to 35 per cent in Latvia, 33 per cent in Russia, 30.2 per cent in Kazakhstan and 23 per cent in Estonia.

Concern about existing and potential reductions in the political representation of women prompted the 1989 Plenary Meeting of the Soviet Women's Committee to discuss the advantages of quotas for women. Even when quotas existed, however, there was a segmentation of representation according to gender. Male deputies enjoyed longer tenure on the soviets and higher status jobs. Turnover among female deputies was significantly higher because they held lower status posts and were less likely to be party members.

Women always had a much lower profile than men in the CPSU. Female membership in the Communist Party increased from 7.4 per cent in 1920, to 13.1 per cent in 1930, 20.7 per cent in 1950, and to 29 per cent in 1988. Women made up just 3.3 per cent of the Central Committee by 1976 (14 out of 426) rising to 4.0 per cent in 1981 (19 out of 470). Only three women ever sat on the Politburo: Yekaterina Furtseva (1957–60); Aleksandra Biryukova (1988–90); and Galina Semenova (1990–91). The female profile after 1988 in developing nationalist movements and in new political parties was similarly weak.

After 1988 a wide range of women's informal groups developed. These included feminist groups,

professional women's associations and religious groups. The Free Association of Feminist Organizations (SAFO), for example, declared that women were discriminated against and that attempts should be made to raise women's consciousness. By contrast, Women for a Socialist Future for our Children supported Leninism, opposed a free market and wished to see Article 6 of the Constitution reinstated. A women's political party was formed in St Petersburg, called the United Party of Women.

The CIS inherited this diversity of women's groups. The future is likely to see lively debates, disagreements and splits. Governments do not wish to be left out of these, but although Boris Yel'tsin in 1992 appointed Yekaterina Lakhova to the government as state secretary for families, mothers and children that post was abolished later in the year with Lakhova becoming a not especially close presidential adviser. MB

CHILDREN

Children were in some ways a privileged group in Soviet society. The state devoted much money and thought to providing good educational and leisure facilities for them. In addition the average adult's love and concern for children could be readily observed; an adult might, for example, even give up a seat on a bus to a child and would almost certainly intervene if a child was noticed either in difficulties or misbehaving. The atmosphere seemed to be primarily one of affectionate discipline.

However, there were also large numbers of disadvantaged children. In 1987 the USSR had a total of 284,000 children in care; 35,000 in 422 infants' homes; 84,000 in 745 children's homes; 71,000 in 237 boarding schools for orphans and 94,000 in regular boarding schools. A further 729,000 children lived not with parents but with other relatives or guardians. The standard of care provided by many of the child care institutions was low – the homes were poorly equipped and the children inadequately fed and clothed.

Upbringing

Most Soviet families – particularly in the urban Russian republic – had only one to two children. It was rare for maternity homes to allow fathers to visit their partners let alone be present at the birth. Babies were usually breast-fed. This was possible even when the mother quickly returned to work as many workplaces provided a crèche. Infants were (and still are) frequently swaddled, at least while in the maternity home, as this was thought to encourage the development of straight bones. By eighteen months toddlers were expected to be toilet-trained.

Below. Newly-born babies in swaddling clothes in a maternity home in Tbilisi, Georgia

Although nappies (diapers) were available, and although mothers gave themselves enormous washing loads, many chose not to use nappies, fearing that their child would become bandy-legged. The crèche and kindergarten served either a particular living area or a workplace. In 1985 51 per cent of all children from two months to school age attended such institutions; in urban areas the proportion rose to three-quarters of all pre-school children. Proportions attending were much lower in the republics of the southern tier of the USSR; this was largely due to a lower demand as more children were cared for within the extended families common in the south. As well as the year-round pre-school facilities there were also seasonal pre-schools (summer camps, for example) serving an estimated one million children in 1983. Despite the extensive network of pre-school facilities there were regular complaints that not enough existed and that those that were available were over-crowded. Many of the young children who did not attend state day-care institutions were looked after by their *babushka* (grandmother). Others were cared for by nannies.

The state and the family shared the responsibility for the upbringing of children. Parents were constantly told that they had to bring up their children to be good Soviet citizens; large numbers of books and pamphlets were published guiding them on how best to do so. If the teachers who were specially responsible for moral education felt parents were not doing a satisfactory job they would not hesitate to contact the parents' workplace so that pressure could be put on them. Prior to the Gorbachev era, particularly recalcitrant parents could have their photograph displayed at their workplace.

Families seemed frequently to indulge their young children. Schools complained, in particular, that many families spoiled their children, always giving them priority in the home, so that disciplinary work carried out in the school was undermined. There was relatively little delinquency among pre-teenagers although there has been concern about rising delinquency rates in the late Soviet and post-Soviet period. Citizens were legally minors up to the age of sixteen; if a minor was accused of a crime, the trial was closed. A particularly difficult child might be referred to a boarding-school for delinquent children. The police devoted some time to crime prevention work, for example by visiting local schools and addressing pupils there.

Recreations

There was a wide range of opportunities provided by the youth organizations and extra-curricular departments of schools. The latter arranged clubs for children with special interests – chess, drama, English, metalwork – in which they could participate

after the school day was over. There were also children's theatres, cinemas, libraries, scientific and sports clubs and so on, often housed in special facilities called Pioneer Palaces. There were Children's Railways run almost entirely by children. Puppet theatres were particularly popular; the Obraztsov Puppet Theatre of Moscow is justly world-renowned. Facilities were better in urban than rural areas. Country children were also less privileged in that they had fewer good specialists to teach them and were frequently expected to work on the land at harvest times.

Soviet children's time was moderately full; they were encouraged to participate in organized leisure activities and also had a substantial amount of homework to do, but children still found time to play informally together, often in the courtyard round which most blocks of flats were built. Most of the games favoured by Russian children were universal – dolls, catapults, skipping, tag, hopscotch, football and blind man's buff were as popular in Russia as elsewhere. More characteristic, particularly in the Russian republic, were carved wooden toys – for instance, the *matryoshka*, which consists of nesting wooden figurines. Large numbers of wooden toys were produced. Children played both their own and organized military games: these aimed to develop a sense of patriotism and to train the young in military and sports skills. Until the mid 1980s at least children were constantly reminded of the Second World War through visits to war memorials and museums and through films and stories about the war.

Children's literature

It has long been part of the Russian tradition for the best adult authors to write for children; Pushkin, Tolstoy and Chekhov did so and their example was followed by many of the best Soviet writers. Samuel Marshak (1887–1964) and Korney Chukovsky (1882–1969) are two of the most delightful of these. Both are particularly well-known for their often humorous poems about animals for small children. Popular Western writers such as Lewis Carroll and A.A. Milne are translated favourites; Mary Poppins, Muffin the Mule and Gerald Durrell's animals are also all familiar to Russian children. Adventure and animal stories are popular but school or pony books are rarely found.

Large editions of magazines for children were also published in the Soviet period; these usually had some degree of educational content – violence and crime, even naughtiness, were not glamorized – but the magazines usually made entertaining reading.

FO'D

Social control and social development

THE MILITARY AND SOCIETY

The Soviet system was characterized by a peculiar degree of integration of the military and society, which has survived in many respects into the post-Soviet era. Many aspects of Soviet society were militarized, but in turn the Communist Party could exert civilian control over the armed forces through bodies down to the local level. One result of this civil-military synthesis was the vulnerability of the Soviet military system to changes and fissures in society at large. Such centrifugal currents in the former USSR in the 1990s have splintered the military forces along national, ethnic and economic lines.

The early Bolshevik leaders developed an ideological commitment to total involvement in the defence effort against external and internal foes, which was reinforced by the experience of the Russian Civil War. In the inter-war years Stalin regarded it as a priority for the Soviet population to become 'war-minded' (psychologically prepared for war) and 'machine-minded' (trained in basic skills for the machinery of war). This effort to mobilize the population was a foundation of Soviet victory in the total war of 1941–45. It was also reflected in post-war efforts to reconstruct the USSR; endless 'campaigns' were launched on 'economic fronts' to fulfil production plans.

The Voluntary Society for Aid to the Army, Air Force and Navy (DOSAAF) acted as a key institution in the military socialization of Soviet youth. It played a large role in running the pre-conscription basic military training programme completed by all youths between the ages of fourteen and seventeen. DOSAAF is under army and, until recently, army-party control. Conscription, which is almost universal, follows at the age of eighteen, and after discharge young men remain liable to reserve training. Until glasnost was introduced the whole population was also subject to relentless, militant state propaganda, which emphasized the threat of 'imperialism' and the ordeals suffered by the Soviet people in the Second World War. Huge military parades used to be held regularly in large cities, and served to reinforce martial values.

The position of the military in society has also been reflected in its organizational role. Before communist rule collapsed commanders of military units or garrisons used to sit on regional and district party committees, which gave them a direct voice in local civilian affairs. These committees have been dissolved but military commanders remain influential figures in their localities. This is reinforced by the pervasiveness of military production in many regions. Until market-oriented reforms commenced military production took precedence in all branches of the Soviet economy and at least five million people remain employed by the defence industry, in addition to those serving in uniform. Whole cities (including what were formerly 'secret cities' serving the nuclear arms establishment) are dependent on military orders. The armed forces are represented in all industrial and academic enterprises concerned with military production and research.

One basic socio-political function of the Soviet armed forces was the 'internationalization' of the many different national groups found in the USSR. Army companies of 80–100 men would often contain up to fifteen different nationalities. Compared to conscripts the officer corps was largely (70 per cent) Russian and even more largely (85 per cent) Slav (Russian, Ukrainian or Belorussian), but it was dispersed over all the republics of the former Union.

Soviet military parade:
Red Square, Moscow, 1984

Successive Soviet leaders aimed to create a focus of loyalty to a *Soviet* Army, transcending national and regional loyalties. But in reality Russian predominance in the forces meant that the army acted more as an instrument for russification of the non-Russian population. Furthermore, growing national divisions in the former USSR were reflected in the army and 'military-patriotic values' have lost much of their former standing in society at large.

The prestige of the military institution and the status of military officers in Soviet society and the successor states have deteriorated steadily since the mid-1980s. A number of developments, which could be debated in the USSR in the climate of glasnost and with the decision in 1990 to end party control over the political organs of the Soviet Army, contributed to this deterioration. First, the steady rise in Soviet military casualties from the occupation of Afghanistan in 1979–89, the poor treatment of Afghan veterans and the ultimate failure of this prolonged military campaign led to disillusionment with military involvement abroad and an increase in social ills, such as drug-taking among recruits. The army's involvement in the massacre of Georgian demonstrators in Tbilisi in 1989 led to growing criticism of its internal role and further tarnished the image of the military. Second, revelations about

the brutality and bullying suffered by recruits (so-called *dedovshchina*), including a claim that as many as 15,000 servicemen had died 'non-combat-related deaths' in 1985–90, shocked the public. Groups such as the Committee of Soldiers' Mothers and the informal military union, 'Shield', developed as lobbies on behalf of servicemen. Third, a shift in policy to reduce military spending and to convert military enterprises to civilian production undercut the priority position of the defence industry and the prestige of working in defence enterprises. Fourth, Gorbachev's decision at the end of 1988 to cut 500,000 men from the army and the eventual decision to withdraw all forces from Eastern Europe resulted in great social hardship, unemployment and disaffection among tens of thousands of officers. The need to set military life on firmer legal grounds and to ensure social provision for demobilized personnel became sensitive political issues. Fifth, the efforts of a number of union republics to set up their own military formations or armies outside central control after 1990 led to a gradual breakdown of the central draft system and loyalty to the Soviet state. This was confirmed by the collapse of the Communist Party and the breakup of the Soviet Union as a single state in 1991.

The Russian armed forces have emerged as the largest single military inheritance of the previous military organization. But a number of republics are set to establish their own armed forces or formations in the 1990s. These different forces are likely to remain multi-national but military officers and personnel have to choose their allegiances. For example, an officer who is a Russian national may become a Ukrainian citizen and serve in Ukraine. In this disorienting situation the supply and housing problems of military personnel have dramatically increased. Central control over former Soviet military forces has weakened, and nationalist sentiments are replacing Communism as the framework for military thinking. The danger exists of these forces being drawn into volatile ethnic disputes in the smaller republics, such as that between Armenia and Azerbaijan. The army in many ways has come to reflect the chaotic social order which has followed the end of Soviet rule.   RA

INTERNAL PASSPORTS

In Soviet Russia and the former Soviet republics all citizens were required from their sixteenth birthday to carry an internal passport. This served as their official means of identification. The passport contained personal data about the holder and his or her family circumstances. In addition to the holder's name, date and place of birth, the passport had

Right. Russian passports being issued in 1992 in Grozny, the capital of semi-independent Chechnia (formerly Chechen-Ingushetia) in southern Russia

entries recording dependent children, marriage and divorce, the names of the holder's parents, military service and place of residence. The passport also included a photograph of the holder taken at age sixteen, to which were added two more at ages twenty-five and forty-five. Passports issued in the non-Russian republics were printed in two languages – Russian and the language of the titular nationality. The nationality entered on a person's passport was determined by the nationality of the holder's parents and, in the case of mixed marriages, a choice had to be made by the holder of which to adopt.

Soviet citizens had to use their internal passports in numerous situations so that carrying them at all times was essential. In any twenty-four hours they might have to show their passports several times as proof of identity. For example, the passport had to be shown when purchasing airline or inter-city rail tickets, when registering at a library or club, when enrolling children in a school or collecting mail or social benefits from the post office or when apprehended, for whatever reasons, by the police. In order to take up a new job, enter higher education, change residence or get married or divorced, the details of a person's passport had to be recorded by the relevant authorities and any necessary amendments made to the details it recorded.

The internal passport system was introduced in 1932 in an attempt to curb the high levels of urban in-migration that accompanied the collectivization of agriculture and forced industrialization during the first five-year plans. This was achieved by restricting passports to urban residents and certain categories of rural wage-earners. Until Khrushchev came to power it was very difficult for collective farm workers to leave their *kolkhoz* and even though restrictions were eased in the 1960s, it was not until the passport reform of 1974 that collective farm workers were entitled automatically to receive an internal passport. Even after that date attempts to leave a *kolkhoz* could be frustrated by collective farm authorities and the local militia illegally witholding passports.

The administration of the passport system was the responsibility of the Ministry of Internal Affairs (MVD). The passport sections of the militia in towns and rural settlements were responsible for ensuring that everybody's passport was correctly endorsed and it was also responsible for issuing residence permits (the *propiska*) and residence discharges (the *vypiska*) to people changing their place of residence. Although on all matters to do with the discharge of passport and living permit regulations the militia was subject to the authority of the executive committee of the local soviet, in reality the decisions it made on individual cases were seldom contested.

Residence permits had to be obtained by all Soviet citizens within three days of arrival at a new place of residence. Although under the regulations introduced in the 1930s a change of residence was defined as the intention to stay in a place for more than one and a half months, changing lifestyles and work patterns in the post-war years meant that this threshold was not strictly enforced. People taking an extended vacation or working on special projects like the Baykal-Amur Mainline railway (BAM) for a few months at a time would generally not apply for residence permits with no adverse consequences. The system of residence permits was, however, increasingly used by the authorities to attempt to contról the growth of large cities. Obtaining a *propiska* for Moscow and the other capitals of the union republics was difficult for anyone not born in the city. Essentially, people who wanted to move to one of the cities to which access was restricted were faced by a vicious circle; a *propiska* could not be issued without proof that the migrant had secured a job and accommodation, yet neither employment nor a place on the housing list was available to anyone unless they were in possession of a *propiska*. Various subterfuges were used by Soviet citizens to get round these regulations, such as contracting fictitious marriages, or obtaining a *propiska* for a suburban location and renting a flat in the city. The most widespread way out of the vicious circle was, however, to apply for a temporary *propiska*. This, in recent decades, became increasingly easy as declining rates of natural population growth in many large cities left them with labour shortages, in particular in the manual and semi-skilled groups.

Enterprises which had a labour shortfall could apply to the city authorities for permission to employ a set number of migrants to whom temporary living permits would be issued. The *limitchiki*, as the people employed under this system came to be called, were discriminated against in various ways; for example they were not permitted to marry whilst in the city and they were obliged to live in dormitories provided by their employer. Other temporary *propiska* holders such as students did not face similar restrictions. In post-Soviet Russia attention has been drawn to the infringement of human rights associated with the limit-worker system but attempts to abolish it have been unsuccessful because of a continuing need to supplement the unskilled and semi-skilled labour force in many large cities. Whether this need will remain in the future will depend upon changes in the labour market associated with economic reform and the decisions made in the various former republics about the system of internal registration for their citizens.

Since the breakup of the USSR, the Moscow and St Petersburg city and regional authorities have resisted legislation intended to abolish the *propiska*. Retention of the system would seem to contradict the principles of a free market economy as well as raising awkward questions about civil liberties. In Moscow the discussions have been particularly heated. Many residents feel threatened by a free-for-all in the housing market and by the prospect of massive immigration if all controls are removed. Yet, it is clear that the intention of the current Russian leadership is to remove the need for a residence permit in the long run. Already there has been a relaxation both in the rules for granting living permits and in their enforcement. People are finding it easier to obtain permission to live in the city, whilst some employers evidently are now prepared to put people on their payroll who do not have a *propiska*. JP

TRADE UNIONS

The trade unions (*professional'nye soyuzy*) were by far the largest public organizations in the USSR and remain so in the CIS. Soviet unions never performed a genuinely independent role. They claimed that under socialism, unions could best serve their members by helping management, the government and the Communist Party to promote production. In the post-communist period organizational fragmentation and economic difficulties have hampered the emergence of strong adversarial unionism. The post-Soviet unions seemed in 1992 to be playing a mixed adversarial and corporatist role.

Historical development

The first Russian trade unions date from 1905. Soon after the October Revolution the Menshevik-dominated union movement was placed under firm Bolshevik control but the Bolsheviks themselves were divided over its role in the new Soviet system. At one end of the spectrum were Trotsky and Bukharin, who pressed for 'statification', the incorporation of the unions into the state machine; at the other, stood A.G. Shlyapnikov (1884–1943) and the Workers' Opposition, who took a syndicalist line. Lenin envisaged unions as non-governmental bodies that would subsume traditional defensive functions within a policy of collaboration with state and management alike. At the X Congress of the CPSU in 1921 Lenin's views prevailed and the unions were defined, in words which remained in currency throughout the Soviet period, as 'a school of administration, a school of economic management and a school of communism'. Any hopes of union autonomy ended in 1929 with the purge of M.P. Tomsky (1880–1937) and other independent-minded union officials; in the next decade the trade unions were reduced to agencies for worker mobilization and welfare administration.

Reappraisal of the unions' role and performance came in the aftermath of Stalin's death. In December 1957 a party Central Committee resolution called for greater union participation in economic planning and more effective union protection of workers' rights, particularly at enterprise level. The economic reforms of the mid-1960s enlarged the scope for union-management negotiation and the 1970 Labour Code enabled unions to strike more of a balance between their production and protection roles, though these remained heavily skewed to party and production interests.

The Brezhnev period

All but a handful of the labour force belonged to a union, more because of the material benefits membership brought than the organizational pressure to join. Members received free legal aid, higher welfare benefits and access to a range of medical, cultural and recreational facilities, all for dues amounting to one per cent of their pay.

Unions were organized on a branch or industrial basis, so that all workers and staff in any one factory institution belonged to the same union. There were thirty or so branch unions, ranging from the aviation industry and rail transport to health and culture. Operating on the principles of democratic centralism, each union had a hierarchy of elected bodies from all-union level, through republican, regional, to local and factory level. At the apex of this organizational pyramid stood the all-union Central Council of Trade Unions. It closely controlled the work of both the central committees of all branch unions and the councils which co-ordinated the various branches at regional and republican level.

At local level the union carried out mobilization, welfare, participation and monitoring tasks. Mobilizing activities included the organization of 'socialist competition', which sought to promote higher productivity. Unions helped management with labour discipline and acted as state agencies in the administration of welfare, collecting contributions and disbursing social insurance and other benefits. Union commissions ran a wide range of cultural and sports facilities, while the union committee supervised catering, housing construction and the allocation of enterprise accommodation.

While the bulk of union work fell into a quasi-state category, some of its activities channelled bureaucratized labour interests into local policy decisions. Local union committees had extensive rights to participate in the drafting of production and social development plans for the enterprise. They also organized standing production conferences to allow workers to scrutinize management performance. In practice, union and labour impact on production plans was small. Somewhat greater influence was exercised by way of the collective agreement drawn up jointly by union and management. This accord specified local working hours, vacations, production quotas, bonus distribution and social benefits. The union committees had co-decision and veto rights on overtime, piece rates, skill grading and, most importantly, dismissals. They also acted as arbiters of unresolved disputes between labour and management, resolving roughly half in workers' favour. Generally, however, local unions were timid in acting against management, seeing their role as helping their employers rather than defending workers' interests.

The same principles guided union policy at national level. On occasion unions used their rights to help draft labour legislation and monitor ministry adherence to the law in order to promote the labour cause. For the most part, though, unions' strict subordination to the Communist Party meant that they played a negligible policy role. Their failure to act for workers prompted occasional attempts to organize unofficial stoppages. In the late 1970s a short-lived effort to establish a Free Trade Union Association was quickly suppressed by police action.

Perestroika and after

The relaxation of policy and party control which accompanied perestroika created unprecedented opportunities for unions to break out of their political and managerial straitjacket. Moves towards independence were slow for organizational and social as well as political and economic reasons. Union

bureaucrats proved somewhat more adept than some of their party counterparts in adapting to changing conditions. More importantly, their retention of control over welfare resources made it easier for them to retain members. Holding on to known security welfare organizations, however conservative they might be, proved attractive for workers facing economic reform which threatened traditional certainties.

In the event, the main impetus to labour and union independence came from strike movements. Sporadic and frequently linked with ethnic protests in 1987–88, direct labour action first made a major impact on the economic and political scene with the large miners' strikes in the summer of 1989. Over a third of a million coalminers in the Siberian Kuzbas and the Ukrainian Donbas regions mounted effective stoppages which forced the government to make major material concessions. Organized by strike committees which transformed themselves into permanent self-governing bodies to monitor the fulfilment of the agreed package, the miners' action completely by-passed the official trade unions. These came under increasing pressure as new independent, albeit small, union groups appeared on the scene and further strikes, including those by the Vorkuta miners in the late autumn of 1989, reflected growing militancy among key labour groups.

The official trade unions, led for a time by G.I. Yanaev – later Vice-President and notional leader of the failed August coup – declared they would free themselves of dependence on Party and management in order to make defence of members' interests their highest priority. In October 1990, responding to centrifugal republican trends as well as to labour militancy, the unions transformed themselves into a new General Confederation of Trade Unions of the USSR, of which the Federation of Independent Trade Unions of Russia was the dominant component. Notwithstanding a self-conscious stand against government plans for price increases and eventual factory closures, the 'new' unions remained dominated by old officials.

In an effort to provide a real alternative to the old union bureaucracy, the miners took a lead in trying to organize regional unions from different sectors. While such attempts proved unsuccessful, coalminers did manage at their Donetsk conference in October 1990 to establish the Independent Union of Miners. Enlisting only a small fraction (4–5 per cent) of the total mine labour force, the new union and the strike committees with which it was closely linked, showed themselves capable of mounting an impressive series of stoppages in the spring of 1991 in defiance of an official ban on direct action in the energy sector. By transferring ownership of the mines to the RSFSR and giving the miners control

From 1989 large-scale miners' strikes became a new social phenomenon in the Soviet Union. In the Kuznetsk Coal Basin, Vorkuta, Karaganda, the Rostov region and the Donetsk Coal Basin miners went on strike, airing both economic and political grievances

over the sales of coal and a share in the proceeds, Boris Yel'tsin bought industrial peace and strengthened the link between the miners and the cause of radical political change.

Such responsiveness to labour militancy probably helped increase worker support for Yel'tsin during the August coup. In an effort to safeguard against labour and especially union opposition to the radical economic programme Yel'tsin sought to introduce after its victory over the putschists, he called on the Federation of Independent Trade Unions of Russia to help the government carry through some of the less popular aspects of marketization for the sake of longer-term improvements in living standards. To harness organized labour aid, Yel'tsin set about institutionalizing their participation in the making of social and economic policy through a 'social partnership' between government, employers and trade unions. All three were represented in the Russian Tripartite Commission on the Regulation of Social and Labour Relations established in January 1992. As each side could veto decisions, agreement had to be reached by negotiation leading to consensus. In the first annual agreement, reached in March 1992, the Russian government pledged to maintain social welfare provisions, including a minimum wage, to cushion the impact of marketization. Employers, for their part, promised to try and minimize the hardships of closures. The unions agreed to price liberalization and privatization plans, and undertook to refrain from organizing strikes as long as the other parties adhered to their side of this corporatist bargain.

If this first agreement marked an encouraging start to a corporatist policy of harnessing union power, its impact on the labour scene in the first half of 1992 was far from clearcut. The fact that strike levels in this period were lower than in early 1991 was due in large part to the readiness of the government to meet the large wage claims of the most militant groups. Miners in the Kuzbas used strike threats to achieve high pay awards as did teachers and medical as well as transport workers. All of these were groups over which the official Russian trade-union federation, and even the Independent Union of Miners or smaller socialist trade unions, exercised little influence. Small independent trade unions proliferated among professional groups as well as among transport and steel workers. Such independent unions remain concentrated on a regional basis and fragmented even within regions and highly militant groups. In the coalmining Donbas region, for instance, there were no fewer than three different miners' unions in mid-1992.

None the less, the right, as from March 1992, of all unions, regardless of size, to negotiate on behalf of their members, augured well for the emergence of a pluralism of unions ready to play an adversarial role in an economic system which promised to give them opponents and partners in the shape of powerful, independent employers.   AP

THE EMERGENCE OF CIVIL SOCIETY

The emergence of substantial elements of a 'civil society' – that is to say, of autonomous associations and organizations neither created nor dominated by the state – was one of the most significant social phenomena in Russia and the former Soviet Union during the second half of the 1980s and the early 1990s. In the first generation following the death of Stalin – from the mid-1950s to the mid-1980s – a freedom of speech in private gradually developed, but this fell far short of anything which could be called civil society. All organizations were subjected to KGB surveillance and party controls and, apart from small and persecuted dissident groups, none could claim to be autonomous social actors. Even religious bodies were penetrated by the political police and the larger and more prominent they were, the higher the price they generally had to pay in political conformism. This was notably true of the Orthodox Church in Russia, although the generalization has to be modified in the case of the Baltic republics where, for example, the Catholic Church in Lithuania came closer to meeting the criterion of an independent social institution.

While even in the early 1990s the successor states to the former Soviet Union were by no means fully-fledged civil societies – as compared, for example, with the countries of Western Europe or North America – the change was remarkable if the comparison is with the Soviet scene in the early 1980s. Serious progress towards the establishment of civil society was first made in the perestroika era and it survived both the attempted coup of August 1991 and the breakup of the USSR in December of the same year (although thereafter with great variations from one of the new states to another).

The years 1986 to 1991 were a period of exceptional growth of autonomous organization. This took the form both of entirely new associations and of the increasing independence of already-existing bodies which had previously been subordinate to the whims of the party-state authorities. The change came about partly as a result of Gorbachev's reforms – conscious effort by a reformist leadership to open up space for societal development – and partly through pressure from below. It was indicative of the genuineness of the embryonic civil society that the new movements and organizations made claims which were mutually contradictory and that many of them were far from congenial to the Communist Party bureaucracy.

An early example of a new and independent organization was the Union of Theatre Workers, established in 1986, while the election of Elem Klimov as First Secretary of the pre-existing Film-Makers' Union earlier in the same year gave that organization an independent voice. Both these arts unions proceeded to use such influence as they possessed to advance the cause of cultural liberalization.

Independent associations founded in the perestroika era were as diverse as the workers' strike committees in the coal-producing areas of Vorkuta, the Kuzbas and the Donbas; the Union of Joint Co-operatives of the USSR (headed by the marketizing reformer, Vladimir Tikhonov, 1927–94); the umbrella organization of newly-founded democratic parties and pressure groups called 'Democratic Russia'; *Memorial*, set up to commemorate the victims of Stalin and to defend those who had suffered political persecution in more recent times; and the mass-based 'Popular Fronts' established in all three Baltic republics in 1988 to pursue nationalist goals.

Other movement in the direction of civil society came with the growing autonomy of organizations which had previously existed but which had been subject to tight controls from above. These included, for example, certain institutes of the Academy of Sciences which in a number of instances showed independence in the perestroika era by electing a new director of their own choosing rather than one foisted upon them by the Academy hierarchy. Scholars in the Academy's constituent institutes also acted autonomously during the elections in 1989 to

the First Congress of People's Deputies of the USSR by rejecting candidates proposed by the Academy leadership and choosing instead radical reformers and democrats. Churches and other religious organizations benefited from a new religious tolerance and acquired a greater autonomy from the state.

An especially important development was the growing freedom of the press and of literary journals. While some publications remained subordinate to party-state authority, a wide diversity of viewpoints began to be represented by existing publications in the second half of the 1980s and through the establishment of new, independent newspapers and periodicals in 1990–91. As early as 1986 the previously conformist weeklies, *Ogonek* and *Moscow News*, acquired new editors and a fresh outlook and began to push wider the boundaries of glasnost. Among the bulkier periodicals, *Nash sovremennik* and *Molodaya gvardiya* became ever more open in their vehement opposition to liberalizing reform, in sharp contrast to the pro-reform stance of their rival monthlies, *Oktyabr'* and *Znamya*.

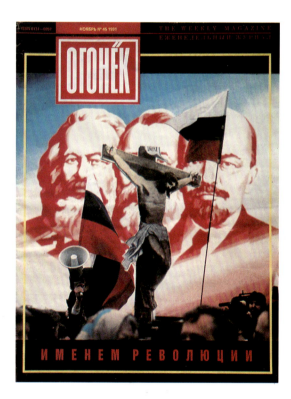

Right. In this cover picture of Ogonek the cross of Christ is superimposed on a poster of Marx, Engels and Lenin. Between 1986 and 1991 Ogonek was one of the liveliest, boldest and most influential of Soviet journals. Before Vitaly Korotich became its editor in 1986 this glossy weekly had been both politically orthodox and boring. In post-Soviet Russia, however, it is no longer on the cutting-edge of political and social commentary

Publishing houses produced the books of long-forbidden writers as different from one another as Orwell, Solzhenitsyn, Berdyaev, Bukharin, Trotsky, Popper, Platonov, Gumilev, Voynovich and Galich. This was not only a manifestation of a developing civil society in that it demonstrated the growing independence of publishing house editors, it was also in itself a stimulus to civic consciousness and independent thinking, bringing hitherto-taboo information and ideas to the reading public.

In post-Soviet Russia financial stringency as well as political pressures from sources both new and old meant that the freedom of the mass media could not be taken for granted and in that important respect the civil society remained a fragile and incomplete creation. Indeed, acknowledgement that the process was still a transitional one came in July 1992 when a new public movement called 'Towards a Civil Society' was founded in Moscow. The very fact, however, that this movement embraced both economic interests and political pressure groups – including, for example, such recently-established associations as the Council of Market Gardeners, the Civil Rights Protection Council and the Council for the Protection of Rights of Leaseholders and Entrepreneurs – showed how great was the social change which had already occurred.   AHB

Deviance

CRIME AND PUNISHMENT

Until the era of glasnost it was impossible to ascertain the extent of criminality in the USSR. Figures were plentiful but were always expressed as a percentage of previous totals; absolute figures were never given. More information is now available: thus, in the first six months of 1990, 126.3 million crimes were reported in the USSR. Of these, some 16 per cent were serious crimes, 58 per cent property offences, 11 per cent street offences, and 12 per cent economic crimes. The figures overall showed a rise of 14.6 per cent over the same period of the previous year. However, the reliability of such data is difficult to evaluate, since there is evidence that some local law enforcement agencies try to keep down the ratio of the number of reported offences to that of arrests and of convictions. In addition a number of relatively minor infractions are not technically classified as crimes and do not figure in the statistics. In any event, the older orthodoxy according to which crime would vanish with the perfection of socialism has long been overtly abandoned.

General crime

In 1991 the USSR Supreme Soviet enacted new Principles of Criminal Legislation, on the basis of which new republic criminal codes were to be introduced. The USSR statute was to come into force on 1 July 1992; but before then the Union had vanished. It covered only the general part of criminal law – general definitions, treatment of minors, accomplices, and so on – and did not contain any definition of specific crimes. At the moment of writing, and under the existing codes, offences against persons and property cover much the same ground as in other countries. Soviet law, however, classified offences into those against the state; against state property; and against citizens. By and large, greater penalties were prescribed for the first two categories. In the first of them, treason included flight abroad or refusal to return until a 1991 Statute provided for free exit and entry to the USSR. In the category of crimes against citizens, refusing treatment for venereal disease is a crime; but blackmail of a private citizen – in the sense of threatening to expose a disreputable truth – is not mentioned. Homosexual acts between consenting adults were a criminal offence until 1993.

It seems that over 80 per cent of convictions concerned standard offences. A number of Soviet sources referred to delinquent counter-cultures, especially among the children of former peasants who had moved to urban surroundings and industrial employment. Their activities were characterized by alcoholism (drink is in the background of one-third of all crimes) and vandalism; in response to this and similar delinquency, intensive campaigns were mounted against 'hooliganism' – the Russian word is taken straight from the English. This is defined as 'intentional actions which grossly violate public order and express an obvious disrespect towards society' and is subject to minimum-sentencing prevention techniques.

Economic crime

Although they have a high latency, some 5 per cent of offences under Soviet rule were classified as economic crimes. The criminal codes had an entire chapter devoted to economic crime covering some twenty infractions. This category tried to deter inefficiency in agriculture and in the state production and distribution network by, for instance, criminalizing the systematic purchase of bread to feed to livestock or the persistent or large-scale issue of poor-quality products by state enterprises; farmers, managers and officials were liable to prosecution. But it covered also a group of offences by ordinary citizens who practised private business involving 'speculation' – the purchase and re-sale of goods for gain; private entrepreneurial activity in the supply of services; and the exercise of a prohibited trade.

Until 1987 most private trades were forbidden. With perestroika a number of ever-more fundamental changes were made. In 1987 the law on 'individual labour activity' granted cautious permission to set up a number of manufacturing and service activities, but without the use of hired labour. More freedom was offered by the 1988 law on co-operatives, although popular hostility led to local restrictions; and the 1991 USSR and RSFSR laws on occupations made it clear that no one was obliged to work for the state, and that there was general freedom in economic activities. In the same year the RSFSR repealed the criminal code provisions on speculation. Alongside this liberalization, appeared a number of general and local legal restrictions. Thus a USSR statute of October 1990 sought to curb 'abuses in trade' during the transition to a market economy and penalized state retail employees who concealed goods from purchasers in order to sell them at higher prices. As well as this problem of conflicting signals, the transition to a market economy has also been accompanied by the rise of organized crime, especially of an economic nature. A 1991 edict of President Gorbachev proposed to devote more manpower to deal with it; the problem, however, persisted in the post-Soviet period.

The converse of criminal economic activity under Soviet law was inactivity, called parasitism – refusal to work and indulgence in an antisocial parasitic existence. The legislation appeared in 1957 and was often amended. The offence was classified with vagrancy and was not explicitly defined in the Code. An unpublished decree of 1975, however, stated that it covered adults who lived for over four months on unearned income while refusing socially useful work, even after official warnings.

Political crime

Apart from the obvious offences of treason, espionage and terrorism, Soviet law prohibited, as an especially dangerous crime, the possession or circulation, with subversive intent, of 'slanderous fabrications' which defamed the Soviet state and social system. In 1966 the conviction for this offence of A.D. Sinyavsky and Yu.M. Daniel' raised certain legal doubts. It was the first public trial for anti-Soviet propaganda of writers of fiction and raised the issues of whether statements put into the mouths of literary characters were to be imputed to the author and whether they were circulated with subversive, or merely artistic, intent. Charged with this offence at his trial in 1972 Vladimir Bukovsky unsuccessfully defended himself by citing the constitutional guarantee of free speech. The problem for the prosecution was that to convict for this offence it had to prove intent to subvert the state; and so, in 1966 new offences were added to the Criminal Code. One was the preparation and circulation of fabrications defamatory of the state and social system; it was not necessary to prove subversive intent, merely that the accused knew the matter to be false. After heated debate in the legislature these

were removed in 1989 to be replaced by a prohibition on calls for the violent overthrow of or change in the system.

Criminal procedure

The Soviet criminal law laid down two prerequisites to criminal liability: the judgment of a court; and the infringement of an express provision of the criminal law. Thus the old rule under which conduct could be punished by 'analogy' with the nearest applicable statute had disappeared. Suspects could be held for up to three days without warrant. Thereafter they could be detained only by court decision or (most commonly) by order of the Procurator until trial; but the maximum period of pre-trial detention was nine months. From 1990 they were entitled to defence counsel from the moment of detention. The trial had to be in public (save where state secrets were involved) and could be held in a factory, on private premises or in the normal courtroom. In addition to professional advocates, the court was allowed to permit representatives of the community (CPSU, trade union, Komsomol) to appear as social accuser or defender. For the most serious offences, some republics began introducing jury trial. The law provided that the accused is deemed not guilty and the court may not transfer the burden of proof; that he or she need not testify and may call evidence; that the verdict must be according to the evidence given; and that a confession alone is not sufficient evidence. The prosecution, both under the former Soviet and the present Russian law, is conducted by the Procurator who may also recommend sentence; he or she is to be guided by the law and 'inner conviction'. In common with European systems, the bench does not merely act as umpire; the judge is expected to question witnesses from the bench and indeed, if the Procurator drops the case during the hearing, the judge must continue it.

Non-criminal sanctions

In a number of cases an offender was subject to sanctioning procedures which did not fall under the Criminal Code or the jurisdiction of the courts. Soviet and Russian law calls these 'administrative offences' which are culpable acts that do not constitute crimes nor lead to a criminal record: they might, for instance, be acts or omissions creating a public nuisance or a breach of particular regulations. Penalties included withdrawal of licences (hunting and driving) and the imposition of corrective labour tasks. Jurisdiction belonged to the local soviets' administrative commissions, the MVD, and a number of other inspectorates. In addition, fines could be imposed by officials for minor traffic violations, public drunkenness, breaches of regulations con-

Andrey Sinyavsky, the Russian prose writer and literary scholar who was arrested in 1965 and sentenced in 1966 for 'anti-Soviet propaganda' in works of fiction which he published abroad under the pseudonym, Abram Terts. After serving seven years in a Soviet labour camp, Sinyavsky was allowed to emigrate to France

cerning passports, rail travel, fire protection and the like. Disciplinary offences at work could be penalized by loss of salary or dismissal. Finally, Comrades' Courts could impose small fines and measures of social pressure.

Punishment

Soviet penal policies frequently changed. The purposes of punishment were stated to be chastisement, re-education and general deterrence. There were twelve types ranging from death, exile (which involved compulsory re-settlement), banishment (which did not), confiscation of property and fines, to social censure. Deprivation of freedom could involve a term in prison or in a labour camp. The latter came in several regimes of varying strictness, depending on the criminality of the person sentenced. The death penalty was never mandatory and did not apply to ordinary murder by a first offender, but until recently could be ordered in a range of cases including large-scale theft of state property, attempts on the life of a policeman or militiaman as well as for some sixteen military offences. A statute of 1991, however, limited the death penalty to treason, aggravated murder or rape, and especially dangerous crimes against peace; it could be applied only to adult males. In general the sentences of imprisonment imposed in the Soviet Union were more severe than in the West. Perestroika brought a questioning of this policy and virtually put an end to banishment and exile.　　　　　　　BAR

Tattooing is as common in Russian as in western jails. Vladimir Penitentiary near Moscow, 1988

Russia's joy is drinking

'Russia's joy is drinking', says the Primary Chronicle . . .

Drunkenness, of course, is evil – for everyone and everywhere. But among us Russians, apart from all the harm it does, in some ways it works for good. Under certain circumstances vodka is the bearer of liberty and even equality and fraternity. I hope no right-thinking person will suspect me of wanting to justify or even glorify drunkenness. But let's not be prigs! 'Someone drunken and skilled has two good things in him', says the proverb.

In Russia people used to drink, and still do, from grief and from joy, because they're tired and to get tired, out of habit and by chance. And more often than not they drink in a group, a company. Even hopeless alcoholics try their best to make sure there's a group of at least three. And when they're under the influence people acquire a freedom that is unknown to non-drinkers – liberty, unprecedented equality and good-hearted fraternity. This is how the Slavophiles and the Westerners used to drink, the reactionaries and the progressives, the learned and the ignorant, poets and painters, actors and barge-haulers; Polezhaev, Ogarev, Apollon Grigor'ev, Musorgsky, Krupin, Blok, Yesenin, Tvardovsky, Ol'ga Berggol'ts . . .

From 'Chem poet zhiv' by Lev Kopelev (1978)
Translated by G. S. Smith

ALCOHOL AND ALCOHOL ABUSE

Russia was historically the land of heavy drinking and various forms of alcohol abuse, and the situation has not changed much since the 1917 Revolution. After some experimentation in the early 1920s with total prohibition of alcohol, the Soviet government reinstituted the tsarist policies – a state monopoly on the production and sales of alcoholic beverages and high prices and taxes.

Excessive drinking and alcoholism are highly complex socio-cultural phenomena, for which no single explanation is possible. In the Soviet case, probably one of the most important factors was the cultural tradition which made drinking a necessary part of socializing and various festivities. This cultural tradition was perpetuated in the USSR by the ready availability of vodka and other beverages in retail trade in all localities and at all hours. Another important factor contributing to heavy drinking was the drabness of the life of the average citizen and the inadequacy of alternative relaxation and entertainment facilities.

Consumption per head rose steadily from the end of the Second World War, doubling during the 1960–80 period. In the early 1980s consumption of state-produced beverages per person aged fifteen years and older was about 11.5 litres of pure alcohol. Of this amount, slightly more than half was consumed in the form of distilled spirits (vodka) and the rest as grape and fruit wine and beer. In addition to this, between 2 and 3 litres of pure alcohol per head were consumed in the form of *samogon* and other illegal home-made beverages. Drinking patterns in the USSR varied greatly by age, sex, and nationality; in the late Soviet period per capita alcohol consumption by Slavs was twice the level of consumption by Muslims.

The overall adverse health and social effects of excessive drinking are also determined by the mode of drinking and the form in which alcohol is consumed. Traditional periodic heavy drinking 'binges', the tendency to consume large quantities of alcohol in a relatively short span of time and without food intake, and the dominance of vodka in the beverage mix make Slav drinking particularly detrimental to health and family.

The social and economic costs of heavy drinking are high. The press and the specialized medical, sociological and legal literature offer impressive evidence of absenteeism, reduced labour productivity, industrial and traffic accidents, and suicide, as well as violent crime associated with alcohol abuse. Social effects are equally significant: alcohol abuse is one of the primary reasons for divorce, and drinking by one of the spouses is often given as the main reason for a family decision not to have children. Heavy drinking leads to cirrhosis of the liver, mental disorders, fatal alcohol poisoning, and cardio-vascular problems. According to official Soviet statistics in the late 1980s, the country had about 4,500,000 alcoholics registered with medical organizations; but the actual number was and is probably three to four times higher. Most Soviet and Western demographers cited alcohol as one of the major reasons for the fact that life expectancy of men (measured at birth) declined from 66.1 years in 1964 to 62.3 in the early 1980s – an alarming and unusual development for a country in peacetime.

Adding the cost of confinement and medical treatment of drinkers and law enforcement to the elements cited above made the total cost of alcohol abuse very high. An accurate ruble figure was difficult to estimate, but in all probability the overall cost was between 5 and 8 per cent of Soviet national income. Many specialists felt that by the early 1980s alcohol abuse had reached crisis level.

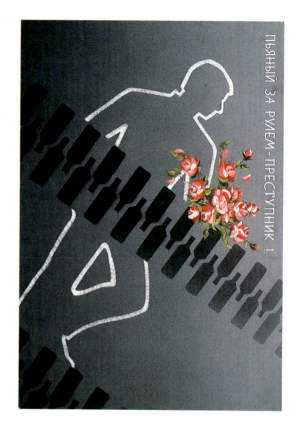

State anti-drinking policies have been haphazard and inconsistent. Excessive drinking was discouraged by penal measures such as stiff fines for public drunkenness and drunken driving including confinement in the so-called 'sobering-up stations', prohibition of selling or serving alcohol to minors, restrictions of hours of sale and locations of vendors of alcoholic beverages, as well as educational campaigns in the press, public lectures, and the like. Alcoholics and chronic heavy drinkers are denied free medical services and were sometimes forcibly placed in treatment centres resembling penal camps. Inebriation during the commission of a crime is treated by courts as compounding the felony. The government also sponsors extensive research programmes on medical effects and treatment of alcoholism. Far less attention, however, has been paid to research on the social causes of alcohol abuse and to the counselling and rehabilitation of heavy drinkers and alcoholics.

Various anti-drinking laws and regulations were, however, not very vigorously enforced while state winery and vodka plants continued to increase their output. During the periodic anti-drinking campaigns, such as in 1958 and 1972, central authorities would order cuts in production of alcoholic beverages and impose other restrictions; after a year or two, the output of the alcohol industry would go up again.

The main reason for slack anti-alcohol policies lies in the singularly important contribution made

A surprisingly frequently-observed Russian winter scene – a drunk asleep on a Moscow pavement, resting on a pile of snow

Health and welfare

The health of the population in the Soviet Union, usually measured by indicators of illness and mortality, was influenced by changing demographic, and environmental conditions, and changing patterns of consumption over time. Given the Soviet Union's authoritarian political system and command economy, health conditions reflected the state's priorities and development strategy to a greater extent than in market-oriented Western countries.

Demographic determinants of health include the age distribution of the population which altered markedly as the share of young people fell and that of the elderly rose from 9 per cent in 1965 to 15 per cent in 1985. Older people in the USSR in the 1980s had experienced considerable deprivation and stress and consequently had a greater tendency to illness than previous generations. In this period the proportion of males rose from 45 to 47 per cent. High rates of birth defects due to poor maternal health and environmental pollution meant that the genetic distribution was less favourable to health than in the past.

There were a number of trends in Soviet consumption that had positive effects on health in the post-Stalin period. Real per capita income rose, as did the population's intake of meat, vegetables and fruit. Educational standards went up, which facilitated more rational decision-making concerning health. However, there were also adverse developments. Adult per capita consumption of alcohol rose from 7 litres of absolute alcohol equivalent in 1965 to a peak of approximately 12 litres by 1985, before it was reduced by Gorbachev's anti-alcohol campaign. Retail sales of tobacco products went up from 1.9 billion rubles in 1965 to 7.3 billion rubles (for 437 billion cigarettes) in 1989. Despite the progress mentioned above, the adult diet continued to have high levels of sugar, salt, fat and carbohydrates but insufficient vitamins. The health of infants was undermined by the inadequate nutritional composition of artificial milk and baby food.

Health conditions were determined as well by developments in the different dimensions of the environment: residential, family, technological, natural and microbiological. In the case of the residential environment, the amount of urban per capita living space rose from 10.3 sq m in 1965 to 15.5 in 1990, but the housing supply remained insufficient to satisfy the population's demand. Most of the new flats were in high-rise buildings located in districts on city outskirts, which were deficient in supporting

by alcohol to state finances. Since the 1950s turnover taxes (sales taxes) on alcoholic beverages have contributed between 10 and 14 per cent of total state budget revenues, accounting for some 40 per cent of all direct and indirect taxes.

The Gorbachev leadership started its quest for improving Soviet economic performance by launching a major anti-drinking campaign in May of 1985. Existing fines and penalties for drunkeness were increased and new ones were introduced. Prices of alcoholic beverages were increased by almost 80 per cent; the price of vodka was boosted from nine to nineteen rubles per litre. The most drastic part of the campaign was the rapid cut in production of alcoholic beverages, the closing of liquor stores and vodka plants, and the destruction of vineyards. Consumption per person of fifteen years and older which stood at 11.2 litres of pure alcohol in 1984 was reduced by 60 per cent to 4.4 litres in 1987. Cuts in state alcohol production and price increases led to the doubling of per capita consumption of *samogon* in the same period. Major losses of tax revenues resulting from output cuts, growth of *samogon* and diversion of sugar to *samogon* production, increases in poisoning by alcohol surrogates, and long queues in front of liquor stores which angered people, forced the government to soften the 1985 anti-drinking measures. Restrictions and penalties were eased and production of alcoholic beverages began to grow. By the early 1990s legal consumption reached 6 litres of pure alcohol per person and the growth continues.   VGT

465

Above. A mother and her five children living in one room of a Moscow communal apartment

Right. Russia finds it difficult to cope with environmental problems. Rubbish dumped in the vicinity of housing estates has become increasingly common with the breakdown of local government

services such as schools, shops, public transportation and crèches. Sanitation in public buildings in the USSR was poor by western standards. Other negative environmental phenomena were the breakup of the family (both extended and nuclear), excessively rapid mechanization and chemicalization of industry, and increases in road traffic without adequate safety programmes. Pollution of air, water, and land was severe across the USSR and catastrophic in some regions. It grew over time due to the industrialization strategy of the Soviet state and its failure to protect the environment. The average annual volume of pollutants entering the water supply rose from 17.6 billion cubic metres in the early 1980s to 33.6 in 1990. The ecological situation was made worse by the April 1986 accident at the Chernobyl′ nuclear reactor that released large amounts of radioactive material into the atmosphere.

In the microbiological environment, antigenic shifts in the influenza virus contributed to epidemics of influenza and the strains of hepatitis became more virulent. A deterioration in public hygiene resulted in a worsening of the bacterial environment and an upsurge in related diseases such as typhoid, salmonellosis, and septicaemia.

In theory, preventive medicine could have ameliorated the influences of negative consumption and environmental factors. But this branch of the health service was poorly funded and ineffectual. As a result, the worsening of health conditions caused greater illness. It proved impossible to eliminate basic nutritional and infectious diseases. In 1989 the rates of six out of eleven reported infectious diseases were higher than the minimum rates achieved in the previous decade (for example, the salmonellosis rate of 55 cases per 100,000 population was twice that of 1986), and virtually all illness rates were

substantially higher than those in the West. Over time there were increases in most forms of degenerative illness. The death rate from heart disease more than doubled from the mid-1960s and the number of first detections of cancer per 100,000 people rose from 177 in 1970 to 236 in 1989. In sum, the poor health conditions meant that the USSR had some of the worst features of the illness patterns found in both underdeveloped countries and industrialized ones with ageing populations.

The transitions from command to market economies in Russia and the other successor states have caused a worsening of health conditions. The policies of price liberalization and wage control have resulted in sharp declines in real per capita income and consumption. This has adversely affected the diet of most members of the population. Unhealthy habits of alcohol and cigarette consumption have been maintained and stress levels have risen. Drastic cuts in social investment have caused a deterioration in housing, the residential environment, safety programmes, and anti-pollution controls. The rapid growth of the private market in food products and the breakdown in state sanitary controls have caused a worsening of the bacterial environment. It is to be hoped that these adverse trends in health conditions will be reversed before they generate markedly higher morbidity and mortality rates.   CD

HEALTH SERVICE

The Soviet Union developed a medical care network that was the world's largest and was original in its organizational model: a national health service in a self-proclaimed socialist society. According to official principles, the health service in the USSR had a socialist character, provided all the population with qualified medical care free-of-charge, was unified and centrally planned, had a preventive orientation, made use of the latest developments in medical science and practice, and involved the population in decision-making. The health service operated in a political and administrative environment determined by the Constitution (Article 42 stated that 'Citizens of the USSR have the right to health protection'), law, Communist Party decrees and resolutions, and ministerial orders. It developed in accordance with five-year and annual plans that were influenced by a health strategy which took into account health conditions (see above), targets, norms and standards of performance of medical establishments, and resource constraints.

The Soviet health service employed 1.3 million doctors (66 per cent of them women) and 3.5 million middle medical personnel (virtually all female) in 1990. Medical staff provided out-patient care through 43,500 polyclinics and dispensaries. In the public, territorial-based system patients were assigned to a local polyclinic and obtained first-contact care from a general doctor called a therapist. If necessary, they were referred to specialists in diagnostic or treatment departments within the same facility. If in-patient care was needed, patients were sent on to the district hospital (in rural areas the polyclinic and hospital were often located in the same building). Further referrals could be made to specialized regional, republican or all-union medical facilities. The Soviet health service possessed 23,900 hospitals of all types, with 3.9 million beds in 1990.

In reality there were considerable deviations from the official principles and descriptions. For example, the health service was fragmented, not unified. The USSR Ministry of Health employed 88 per cent of doctors and controlled about 95 per cent of all medical facilities. These resources were distributed between five subsystems with different organizational forms and performance standards: élite; capital city; industrial; provincial city; and rural. The remaining staff and establishments were attached to closed health services that were financed and managed by a number of ministries with economic or political importance (for example, Ministry of Defence or Ministry of Railways). The theory of popular participation in health service management was quite different from practice as well. The absence of democracy in the traditional Soviet political system prevented citizens from expressing their preferences concerning utilization of national income, which presumably would have been for more spending on consumption (including health) and less on investment and defence. Consumers of medical services had little power to influence the work of either local health departments or medical facilities.

Over recent decades, the demand for medical care increased substantially due to the trends in health conditions, Soviet population growth (from 230 million in 1965 to 290 million in 1991), and the fact that there was no official price barrier to consumption. In the pre-perestroika period the health service was constrained in its supply response by the fact that the government forced it to operate as a low priority branch in a shortage economy. From 1965 to 1985 the health share of the state budget declined from 6.5 to 4.6 per cent. Health expenditure as a percentage of GNP remained under 3 per cent in the USSR and exhibited a downward trend, whereas in the United States it rose from 6.1 to 10.5 per cent.

The Soviet health service responded to the challenge posed by growing demands and limited resources by adopting an extensive development strategy that placed greatest emphasis on expanding output (hospitalizations, outpatient visits, and so on) in quantitative terms and neglected improvements in the quality of services.

Young children being helped back to health at Komarovo Children's Rehabilitation Centre

CIVILIAN HEALTH SERVICE DEVELOPMENT (THOUSANDS), 1950–90

	1950	1960	1970	1979	1990
Doctors	236.9	385.4	577.3	960.5	1,130
Dentists					
with higher education	10.4	16.2	39.6		
with intermediate education	17.7	30.1	51.5		
Middle-grade medical personnel[a]	719	1,388	2,123	2,720	2,886
Pharmacists[b]					
with higher education	12.2	26.5	47.7	68.3[c]	118
with intermediate education	44.9	74.3	120.1	150.2[c]	200
Hospitals	18.3	26.7	26.2	23.2	23
Hospital beds	1,011	1,739	2,663	3,262	3,656
Units providing ambulatory-policlinic care	36.2	39.3	37.4	35.7	41.1

[a]Mainly feldshers, feldsher-midwives, midwives, environmental health officers, nurses, medical laboratory staff, radio-therapists and dental technicians
[b]All pharmacists, not civilian health service alone   [c]1977
Source: *Narodnoe khozyaistvo SSSR*

This expansion was achieved not through improved productivity, but rather by increasing inputs. From 1965 to 1990 the number of doctors more than doubled (from 554,000 to 1.3 million) and the stock of hospital beds rose by 75 per cent from 2.2 to 3.9 million. In 1987 the USSR Minister of Health made the following critique of this policy: 'The pursuit of growing quantities of hospital beds and numbers of outpatient visits has led to a grave situation . . . caring about these numbers, they forgot about quality.'

Despite the substantial growth in the provision of medical care, the population's demand for services and medicines far exceeded their supply. As a consequence, there were chronic shortages and bottlenecks throughout the health service. According to a survey carried out in 1988, only 49 per cent of the population's demand for out-patient services and 52 per cent for hospital care was fully satisfied. In most polyclinics there were queues of patients in crowded waiting rooms, cramped work spaces for staff, insufficient quantities of modern technology, and substandard quarters for diagnostic and treatment units. Hospital beds were often crammed into ward areas in violation of minimum sanitary norms or placed in corridors. There were severe shortages of medical equipment, medicines, and instruments. Virtually no disposable instruments and supplies were available.

One consequence of the pervasive shortages was rationing. This was accomplished in the first instance by dividing the population between the six subsystems of medical care mentioned above. In the 1980s about 6 per cent of the population received relatively high quality care from the medical networks run by the Fourth Main Administration of the Ministry of Health for the party élite and its families, or by the powerful ministries. In contrast, the more than 50 per cent of Soviet citizens who lived in villages or rural district cities were served by backward and deprived medical facilities.

Queuing was another instrument of rationing that was widely used in the health system. In polyclinics patients frequently queued to see the doctor of first contact and again in the specialist department if they were referred onwards. In hospitals, queues involved waiting in bed for diagnostic and treatment facilities to become available.

A third rationing device employed was the waiting list. The practice of rationing was a logical consequence of the chronic excess demand in the medical care market. Its pervasiveness was made possible by the undemocratic nature of the government, which did not have to fear adverse popular feedback through the electoral system. An unusual feature of Soviet practice was the rationing of medical care through closed subsystems within a state-financed national health service.

In any society the health service is the institution with primary responsibility for influencing trends in health indicators, such as illness and mortality rates, through its preventive and curative programmes. Over the past several decades, these rates have been reduced in virtually all industrialized countries, which suggests that their health systems have been successful in fulfilling their tasks. The Soviet Union, however, had a very different experience. From the mid-1960s until the early 1980s the medical system proved incapable of offsetting the effects on the population of the worsening health conditions. In this period all adult age-specific death rates rose. For example, the rate (deaths per 1,000) for the age group 45–49 years went up from 6.0 to 8.0. Reported infant mortality increased from 22.9 deaths per 1,000 live births in 1971 to an estimated 31.1 by 1976 (there is debate over the degree to which this was a statistical as opposed to a real phenomenon). As a consequence, life expectancy declined to 67.7 years (62.3 years for men) in 1980–81 and the crude death rate climbed by 52 per cent, from 7.1 deaths per 1,000 population in 1965 to a peak of 10.8 in 1984.

The Gorbachev regime initiated a reform of the health sector that became more radical over time, especially after 1988. The government introduced an anti-alcohol campaign and provided more funds for consumption and environmental protection programmes. Substantial changes were made in the leadership, organization, and development strategy of health institutions, from the Ministry of Health down to polyclinics. The reorientation of economic plans in favour of welfare during the perestroika period resulted in modest increases in health expenditures and in their budget share (to 5.1 per cent in

Chernobyl'

The aftermath of the explosion of Reactor Four at the Chernobyl' nuclear power station in Ukraine is perhaps the worst of the health problems facing the medical profession in the former Soviet Union. The truth about the disaster only began to emerge years after the event, and the full effects of huge amounts of radioactive material spread over a vast area of Europe can still only be guessed at.

The accident happened in the early hours of 26 April 1986, and it was several days before the Soviet government would even admit that it had taken place. Until 1989 the authorities, both local and national, did all they could to cover up the truth. The extent of the area affected was concealed, and the clean-up workers at the plant had the amount of radiation they were exposed to massively understated on their work records. As late as 1989 Ukrainian health officials were blaming increased levels of cancer on stress caused by 'alarmism' about radiation.

However, as the old officials were replaced by the victors of the democratic elections of 1990, and as campaigns in the press, especially *Komsomol'skaya Pravda*, got under way, the real story began to emerge.

Around 1.5 million Ukrainians alone had been affected, with 10 per cent severely irradiated by Iodine-131. Virtually all of the 600–700,000 clean-up workers reported increased levels of minor illness, and the death rate among this group is already above average. Rates of serious illness such as cancer and childhood leukaemia have increased by 900 per cent in some areas.

The final death-toll is very difficult to guess at. Estimated figures vary from about 5,000 to as many as 250,000 in the former USSR alone. Experience with the effects of fallout from nuclear weapons tests has shown that increased death rates can take up to 40 years to be seen. Whatever

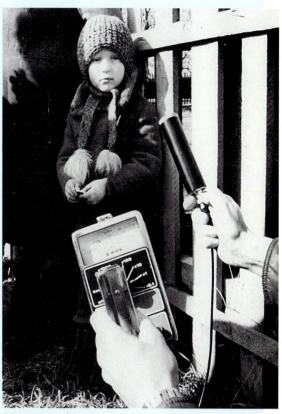

Measuring radiation in the village of Shisheloka, some fifty kilometres from Chernobyl', 1989

the final figure, the medical officials in Ukraine, Belarus and Russia (the worst affected successor states) are facing a huge task in the future, one which may overwhelm already stretched resources. Another problem is getting personnel to work in the affected areas: in 1989, 86 out of 329 medical graduates assigned to one such region refused to go. The poisonous legacy of Chernobyl' will be felt for decades to come.

1989). The reforms affecting both health conditions and the health service had beneficial effects on output indicators. By 1990 the crude death rate was 10.3 deaths per 1,000, infant mortality was 21.8 deaths per 1,000 live births, and life expectancy was 69.5 years.

The breakup of the Soviet Union and the transitions to market systems in its successor states have had profound consequences for the health service. The USSR Ministry of Health was abolished in late 1991 and the existing subsystems were divided between the fifteen independent states. A number of the new governments have announced major health reforms. For example Russia is to transform the health service from a budget-financed national one to a social insurance system. Substantial changes are being made in the organization of polyclinics (more stress is being placed on the family doctor) and hospitals. Private medical care has been legalized, if not encouraged, and some state facilities have been privatized. All medical facilities are now operating in evolving market environments, instead of a command economy, and in more democratic political systems.

Any beneficial impacts of post-Soviet reforms have been more than offset by the effects of economic deterioration, price rises of supplies to the health services, acute shortages of medicines (only about 50 per cent of health service demand was satisfied in 1991), macroeconomic stabilization programmes that are constraining health budgets, and falling real wages of medical staff. The health services in the early stages of transition are undoubtedly less effective than the old Soviet one and health conditions are rapidly deteriorating. This combination is having a negative impact on the health of the population, which is reflected in upward trends in illness and mortality. By late 1991, the death rate in Russia was higher than the birth rate for the first time since the Second World War. The conditions and performance of the health services in the countries of the former Soviet Union are likely to worsen from already low levels in the short term. Significant improvements will only be attained as a result of success in economic transition programmes and massive medical aid from the West.   CD

SOCIAL SECURITY AND WELFARE

Origins

Soviet families had access to an extensive system of welfare benefits designed to provide financial assistance in most of the circumstances in which they suffered temporary or permanent loss of earnings. Formally, most of this system survived the break up of the USSR. But the very rapid rates of inflation experienced in 1992–93, have changed the character of the system and undermined the value of the protection it provides.

The Soviet social security system had its origins in the tsarist workmen's compensation scheme which was extended and made more egalitarian in the 1920s in accordance with Lenin's ideas. After 1928 the system was modified again to reinforce the incentives of the industrialization drive. It was recodified in 1956. State pensions were provided for the collective farm population in 1965 and other programmes were extended to this social group over the next five years. The whole system was recodified again in 1990 and much of that legislation was retained by the successor states.

In addition to income support programmes, there were various free and subsidized services that contributed to the real incomes of Soviet households. These included pre-school child care, free education and medical care. There were also substantial subsidies for housing and a range of basic consumer goods. In the new circumstances of post-Soviet society many of these are under threat – from the new market economics as well as from the lack of resources.

Finance for the welfare system came from a payroll tax supplemented by subventions from general budgetary revenue. In 1991 many programmes were removed from the budget and an attempt was made to reduce or eliminate the subsidy from general taxation. Instead special pension and employment funds were established, financed out of earmarked payroll taxes and employee contributions. In many post-Soviet republics this new system has been preserved; but funds are often insolvent and again in receipt of budgetary subsidies.

Given the nature of the taxes upon which the Soviet budget relied, it is difficult to determine how great was the redistributory impact of the Soviet social security system or how it changed over the years. Nevertheless, the Soviet government made a major investment in the provision of income support. Some of the less developed of the successor states have been unable to maintain it.

Social security

Most social security programmes were related to employment in some way, but there were three benefits that were available to the population more generally: child allowances, family income supplement and student stipends. In the face of accelerating inflation, the first of these has assumed greater and greater prominence. (According to Soviet convention, holiday pay was classified as social security benefit; it was normally included in Soviet statistics of expenditure.)

Old-age and long-service pensions · Civilian state employees are entitled to an old-age pension on reaching the age of sixty (fifty-five for women) provided that they have a record of twenty-five years' employment (twenty for women). The detailed pension entitlement conditions described here refer only to the former Soviet Union and, since 1992, to Russia, as conditions in other post-Soviet states differ and with time will diverge increasingly from the Soviet/Russian model. When the 1990 law came into force, the self-employed and those working for co-operatives and other organizations were also entitled to old-age pensions on the same conditions – provided that contributions had been paid into the state pension fund on their behalf. There are lower retirement ages with correspondingly reduced employment requirements for underground workers and certain other designated categories. Since 1967 collective farmers have been entitled to pensions on the same conditions as state employees. Certain groups (for example, civil aviation pilots) receive long-service pensions rather than old-age pensions.

Under the 1956 law the value of the pension depended upon earnings in the last twelve months before retirement. When the 1990 law came into force, the value depended upon earnings in the last

An aged Caucasian couple. This man and woman photographed in an Azerbaijan village in 1988 were said, somewhat improbably, to have been married for 102 years

five years. Thereby the pension was equal to 55 per cent of terminal average earnings as defined above, with a minimum equal to the minimum wage and a maximum (in 1990) of 266 rubles a month. Supplements were payable to pensioners with dependants. For most pensioners, moreover, no deductions were made in respect of other sources of income and many continued to work after reaching retirement age and receiving a pension. The 1956 law contained no provision for the indexing of pensions, which was a source of some hardship. As a result, the 1990 law contained provision for the periodic review of pensions in response to changes in the cost of living or improvements in economic performance. But these have proved inadequate in conditions of rapid inflation. Pensions, while rising substantially in money terms, failed to keep up with much higher rates of inflation in post-Soviet Russia.

Survivor pensions · When state employees or collective farmers die, their non-working dependants are entitled to a survivor pension. The 1990 law defined non-working dependants as including siblings, children and grandchildren under the age of eighteen years; and parents, grandparents and spouse, provided they are of pensionable age. For certain categories, survivor pensions are paid only if there is no one else obliged by law to support them. The value of the pension depends upon the number of dependants: under the 1956 law, the maximum number in respect of whom benefit was payable was three; under the 1990 law there is no upper limit. Further, benefit is set at one-third of the deceased's earnings for each dependant.

Disability pensions · Disability pensions are paid to those who suffer loss of working capacity as a result of an industrial accident or occupational dis-

ease. They are also payable to those who suffer a general loss of working capacity if they have a sufficient employment record. Benefit levels depend upon prior earnings and the degree of incapacity. After 1970 the regulations covering disability pensions for *kolkhozniki* became broadly similar to those for state employees; before 1965 disability pensions were not paid to collective farmers.

Sickness benefits · Benefits are payable from the first day of incapacity and continue as long as the illness lasts, subject to medical attestation; benefits are payable for up to seven days for workers who remain at home to care for sick children. Sickness benefits were extended to collective farmers in 1970.

Maternity benefits · Since 1968 women state employees have been entitled to 56 days' pre-natal paid leave and a further period of 56 days' leave after the birth of a child. From 1973 women have been entitled to benefits equal to previous average earnings for the full 112 days' leave. Women are further entitled to remain at home until the child's first birthday without loss of job or seniority. Since 1980–85, those who avail themselves of this option have been entitled to a flat-rate benefit. Maternity benefits have been payable to women collective farmers since 1965.

Child allowances · Before 1990 child allowances were payable to all women on the birth of the third and subsequent children at rates that had remained unchanged for more than fifty years. Additional allowances were paid to single mothers and the wives of military personnel. This system was substantially reorganized in 1990 when child allowances were extended to the first and second child. It was modified again in March 1991 by the then prime minister Pavlov to compensate families with children for the significant increase in the cost of living expected to follow from the phasing out of price subsidies on a range of consumer goods. The value of allowances has been raised on several occasions since; these allowances now constitute a major plank in the Russian government's anti-poverty policy.

Family income supplement · Between 1974 and 1990 families with a per capita income below the official poverty line were entitled to payment of 12 rubles per month per child under the age of eight. In 1974 the poverty level was set at 50 rubles a month per capita; in 1988 it was raised to 78 rubles. After 1980 some allowance was made for regional differences in the cost of living in determining entitlement to this benefit. In 1990 the rules governing payment were modified and the value of the benefit was raised to 35 rubles a month. Since 1991 it has been assimilated into the structure of child allowances.

Student grants · In the late 1980s about three quarters of registered full-time students in post-secondary education received stipends or grants. Rates depended upon the subject studied, the year of study and the student's performance. For students in higher education maximum grants were about 80 per cent of the minimum wage and 60 per cent for those receiving secondary specialist training. Increases in student grants have lagged considerably behind the rate of inflation since 1990/91.

Unemployment benefits · Until 1991 there was no system of unemployment compensation in the USSR. It was only in 1988 that redundant workers were guaranteed one month's severance pay. In 1991, however, unemployment benefit schemes were adopted by both the Soviet and the Russian parliaments. Similar schemes were adopted in other successor states. The Russian scheme was amended (and made somewhat less generous) in February 1992. According to the revised scheme, workers laid off from previous employment were entitled to compensation equal to 90 per cent of previous earnings; new entrants and those seeking to return to the labour force after a considerable absence would receive benefits equal to 75 per cent of the minimum wage. Those who quit or were fired for breaches of labour discipline would, it appeared, receive nothing. It was not clear from the regulations for how long these benefits would be paid, but according to the original law, claimants were only entitled to twenty-six weeks' benefit in any twelve month period.

Social assistance · The Soviet social security system did not provide until 1990 a safety net for those without alternative sources of income; it was felt that the guarantee of full employment was sufficient. The 1990 law, however, recognized the inadequacy of existing practice; it proposed the introduction of a so-called social pension for those who did not qualify for old-age, disability or survivor benefits. It proposed that the social pension would be equal to the minimum value of benefits payable under the new regulations. Social pensions are now payable in a number of the successor states, but not all schemes are as generous as that contained in the 1990 all-union law. In some areas social pensions are supplemented by benefits in kind.

Assessment · The various welfare programmes enumerated here made a substantial contribution to the living standards of Soviet families. It is estimated, for instance, that in 1988 income support (including holiday pay) accounted for 13.6 per cent of the personal income of the average family. For those with a per capita income below 75 rubles a month (approximately equal to the official poverty line at

that time) it accounted for as much as 29.1 per cent. Adding the value of such services as medical care and education increased the contribution of government welfare programmes to almost a quarter of the real income of the average Soviet family.

For the same outlay, however, more could have been done to support lower income groups. There are three reasons why the Soviet system failed to achieve this. First, a major part of the system was related to employment. As a result, households where the breadwinner was not in regular employment or whose earnings were low (single parent families, for example) were largely deprived of support. The introduction of family income supplements alleviated the condition of some households, but the narrowness with which entitlement was specified meant that there was still extensive poverty, both rural and urban. Second, regulations governing entitlement were complex and in the past frequently focused upon irrelevant characteristics; inevitably some individuals failed to qualify. Substantial progress, however, towards simplification and universalization was made in the fifteen years before 1990. Finally, the absence of any system of public assistance meant that those who failed to qualify for specific benefits were forced to rely upon the charity of relatives, often reducing the whole extended family to poverty.

Economic collapse, inflation and the attempt to move to a market economy have introduced new threats to family living standards. The social security system has not fully adjusted to these. Poverty remains an ever-present risk in Russia as in the rest of the former Soviet Union. AM

Education

From the late 1980s enormous changes took place in the USSR's education system. Formerly, despite geographical variations, 'Soviet education' was a manageable concept. Latterly, centrifugal tendencies along with fierce resistance to them cast doubt upon its validity. But it makes no sense to survey the fissures in the monolith and post-Soviet departures from it without studying the monolith itself.

PRE-SCHOOL EDUCATION

Pre-school education (*doshkol'noe obrazovanie*) has been differentially available as the day nursery or crèche (*yasli*) for children aged six months to three years, and the nursery school or kindergarten (*det-*

Right. *Children enjoying a game of tug-of-war in Kindergarten no. 6 in the city of Yangiyul in the Tashkent region of Uzbekistan*

sky sad) for those aged three to six or seven. These institutions are increasingly combined (*yasli-sady*). Older and urban children have greater chances of places than younger and rural ones. In 1988 over 17 million or 58 per cent of Soviet children of pre-school age were accommodated on a year-round basis, but this varied greatly by republic, from 71 per cent in Russia and Belorussia to 16 per cent in Tajikistan. There was provision for 69 per cent of urban Soviet children, ranging from 81 per cent in Moldavia to 31 per cent in Azerbaijan, against 40 per cent of rural ones, from 62 per cent in Moldavia to 5 per cent in Tajikistan.

Parents paid a modest income-related sum for meals and also for optional foreign-language teaching, when it was offered. Although the traditional emphasis of Soviet pre-school education was encapsulated in the term for it, *vospitanie* or upbringing, there was pressure on this sector in the last years of the USSR to concern itself more with intellectual development. A major problem was, and remains, the shortage of qualified staff. In 1988, with an average monthly salary of 128 rubles against the national average wage of about 220 rubles, pre-school teaching was one of the lowest-paid occupations in the USSR.

GENERAL EDUCATION

Primary schools

Soviet schooling from the very start was comprehensive ('unified'), coeducational and free of charge, though occasionally inroads were made into these principles. In 1988/89 over 43 million young Soviet citizens were at general schools. Compulsory education used to be for ten years from age seven, with a three-year primary and a five-year middle stage, and with different means of completing it after the eighth year. Under the 1984 school reform, however, the starting age was to be gradually lowered from seven to six.

An extra year was prefixed to the primary stage, making the overall general school course eleven years long. By 1988/89 43 per cent of six-year-olds (38 per cent urban, 51 per cent rural) were following the first-year syllabus. While 72 per cent of these pupils were at general schools, the other 28 per cent were at nursery schools. Some seven-year-olds were in the first year at general school and others in the second.

The lowering of the starting-age was intended to make formal education more efficient, by providing more time and expertise for it. Yet it was resisted by the pre-school lobby as well as by some parents who held sentimental fears about their little ones entering the tough environment of school, with its traditional emphases of hard work, continuous assessment and strict discipline. Implementation of the policy was also delayed by a shortage of accommodation.

The beginner thus entered the primary stage of schooling for three or four years. This might be at either a primary school (*nachal'naya shkola*), or an 'incomplete' secondary school (*nepolnaya srednyaya shkola*) for eight or nine years, or a secondary school proper (*srednyaya shkola*) for ten or eleven years.

In 1975/76 primary schools accounted for nearly one in three general schools but only 2.4 per cent of pupils. By the late 1980s they were no longer significant enough to appear in statistical publications. The model curriculum issued in 1985 covered the native language and literature (plus Russian if this was not Russian), mathematics, environment or nature study, art, music, physical education and labour. The official youth organization for children of primary age was the Octobrists (*oktyabryata*), each class being simultaneously an Octobrist group divided into 'starlets' (*zvezdochki*) of five or six members.

EDUCATIONAL POPULATION (THOUSANDS), 1914–88

Enrolments in	1914/15	1940/41	1965/66	1980/81	1985/86	1988/89
Pre-school	5	1,953	7,673	14,337	16,140	17,354
General schools, full-time	9,656	34,784	43,410	39,546	41,351	43,053
General schools, evening		768	4,845	4,729	3,095	1,083
Vocational–technical schools	106	602	1,701	3,659	3,978	4,048
Secondary specialized schools	54	975	3,659	4,612	4,498	4,372
Higher education	127	812	3,861	5,235	5,147	4,999
TOTAL	9,948	39,894	65,149	72,118	74,209	74,909

Source: *Narodnoe obrazovanie i kul'tura v SSSR* (Moscow, 1989)

An early start to language learning. In this Moscow kindergarten, young children are listening to spoken English

Middle schools

At age ten, according to the 1985 curriculum, children should enter class (form or grade) V. The weekly timetable of twenty-four 45 minute lessons rose to thirty. History and a foreign language – usually English – were now started. Geography and biology (in place of nature study) followed in class VI. Physics, technical drawing and one or two options or electives (*fakul'tativy*) began in the next year, and chemistry in class VIII. Although art and music finished at the end of class VII, all the other subjects continued for all the children. Labour training at this stage was entirely segregated by sex in urban schools – technical studies for the boys, home economics for the girls – but less so in rural areas, where both sexes together did agriculture and basic electronics for 60 per cent of the course. In the summer there was a continuous period of labour practice. At the top of the middle stage, class IX (fourteen-plus) saw the disappearance of technical drawing and the start of new minor courses in principles of Soviet state and law – originally introduced to guard against delinquency – and ethics and psychology of family life.

The uniformed organization for children aged ten to fifteen was the Pioneers (*pionerskaya organizatsiya*). The school class was also a Pioneer detachment (*otryad*). Within this the occupants of a row of desks formed a 'link' (*zveno*) of five to eight members, headed by their chosen 'link-leader' (*zven'evoy*), while the sum total of detachments and Octobrist groups constituted the school's Pioneer brigade (*druzhina*). A detachment was supervised by a leader (*vozhatyy*) who might be a senior pupil or someone from outside the school. The detachment was itself expected to act as the 'collective leader' of an Octobrist group. A senior leader, who sat on the school staff meeting, had oversight of the entire brigade. At both detachment and brigade levels there were elected self-management councils as the official organizers of the Pioneers' activities; elections and organizing alike were under the watchful eye of the older leaders. The Pioneer detachment meeting was the chief traditional context of the school's upbringing effort. In 1990 it was decided to change the name of the organization and to demilitarize and decentralize it. Teachers were routinely urged to concern themselves more with character education, but at least after the primary stage, when subject specialists took over, they tended to be preoccupied with cognitive matters.

Senior schools

After the ninth school year the single path divides into three. Two of these offer vocational or professional training. The third is the two-year senior stage of general schooling (three years in the Baltic states). This has traditionally been the principal route to higher education, taking some 60 per cent of fifteen-year-olds and conferring the certificate (*attestat*) of secondary education, by continuous assessment and examination but without specialization apart from four elective periods per week. Thus the 1985 curriculum continued the study of first language and literature (plus Russian if applicable), mathematics, history, biology, physics, chemistry, the foreign language, physical education and labour training. Geography continued in class X only, but four new subjects were introduced: principles of information science and computer technology, social studies, elementary military training and, in class XI, astronomy.

Only the first of these was fresh to the curriculum, and it had major teething troubles because of a shortage of computers. By 1988, however, the production plan for school computers was 84 per cent fulfilled, though still only 11 per cent of schools had computing laboratories. Social studies constituted the only subject where Marxist-Leninist doctrines were formally taught, since conceptually this would have been extremely difficult at an earlier age; but of course all the other subjects were supposed to be used for political teaching whenever an opportunity occurred. The purpose of the military training course was to prepare boys for call-up and girls for a supportive role in time of war. Only the boys did drill and orienteering, and only the girls had a major component in first aid, but the rest of the syllabus, including weapon-training with small-bore rifles, Kalashnikovs and dummy grenades, was common to both sexes. In 1988, however, the girls' programme was curtailed.

The official youth organization for senior school students, as well as those in vocational, technical and higher education, was the Komsomol (age-range

Handicraft class in a Moscow home for mentally retarded children

fourteen to twenty-eight). Though somewhat selective, it used to be numerically strong in general schools, not least because of its role in supplying a reference for higher education candidates. It had a further significant function in providing leadership for the school Pioneer activities. Glasnost, however, exposed its past sins and greatly diminished its membership. For teachers, Communist Party cells were formed in schools with at least three members; staffs might also be banded together for this purpose.

Special schools

There are a few variants on the general day school with its standardized courses. In the 1980s an estimated 2 to 3 per cent of Soviet children were in special schools or classes for the arts, sport, mathematics and science, languages, and occasionally other subjects. The artistic and academic ones have been in great demand. The special academic 'profiles' now apply to classes VII to XI. Language schools have traditionally specialized from some point in the primary stage, but in 1987 steps were taken to start in-depth language teaching in class VII also. Army (Suvorov) and navy (Nakhimov) schools train cadets for the services. Special schools for the educable handicapped catered for 1.4 per cent of Soviet pupils in 1988/89.

Day care

A child's whole person has been cared for by providing all-day facilities, including hot meals, and also hostels for youngsters from remote rural areas. School dining-halls or at least snack bars exist in three-quarters of schools (96 per cent urban and 67 per cent rural in 1988). The standard of care in the hostels, however, has been a frequent cause for complaint. Extended-day schools (*shkoly prodlennogo dnya*) and groups cater for children up to fifteen whose parents are out at work, by providing supervised homework and leisure activities after lessons (or occasionally beforehand). Younger children predominate, as the older ones seek independence. Although such facilities are convenient, they have never been really popular with parents or children since their supervisory aspect tends to overshadow their caring and upbringing role. Development of the latter, however, is likely to involve additional expenditure on better accommodation and equipment. Thus the extended day has been in decline at a time when the relevant school population has been increasing: whereas in 1985/86 it covered 37 per cent of such children (urban 32 per cent, rural 44 per cent), by 1988/89 the figure was down to 27 per cent (urban 22 per cent, rural 34 per cent). Another 0.15 per cent, mainly children whose parents were unable to give them a proper upbringing because of their domestic or work situation, were at boarding schools.

There is a chronic shortage of school buildings. Perhaps the worst consequence of this is that some schools have to operate on two or even three shifts, in the afternoon and early evening. This involved nearly one in four Soviet children in 1988/89, ranging from 12 per cent in Armenia to 39 per cent in Kyrgyzstan. The situation had improved in the 1970s but was deteriorating again in the 1980s. From an educational point of view, shift working is inefficient because youngsters and teachers tire as the day wears on. Overtime is likely because of the staffing shortage, itself due to poor conditions and pay (averaging 200 rubles in 1990, 40 rubles below the national mean).

Evening schools

The 'evening (shift) general school' (*vechernyaya (smennaya) obshcheobrazovatel'naya shkola*) caters for young adults who for various reasons have been unable to complete their general education. According to 1990 legislation it operates on either a five-year or a three-year basis, respectively offering the major subjects of the middle or senior school course. Thus it omits the foreign language (except as an option), art, music, physical education, labour and military training. Its part-time student body takes the shape of an inverted pyramid, since the more advanced syllabuses are in greater demand. With the spread of compulsory ten-year education, the intake of these schools dwindled over the 1980s – though in 1988/89 they were still providing for over a million students. Adult education of the extra-mural type was furnished more and more by 'people's universities'.

Vocational-technical schools

The vocational-technical education sector trains skilled workers, mainly in the three-year secondary vocational school (*srednee professional'no-tekhnicheskoe uchilishche* or SPTU) which also gives senior-stage general education, or for a shorter period in the ordinary PTU which does not. In the early 1980s these paths were taken respectively by about 20 and 9 per cent of fifteen-year-olds (the latter were also expected to attend evening schools). The 1984 reform envisaged the eventual doubling of the lower-status SPTU at the expense of full-time senior-stage general schooling. This goal proved very elusive and has been abandoned. The dual-provision role of the SPTU involved a workload about 20 per cent heavier than that of general schools, and its quest for appropriate general syllabuses was long and fruitless. Debate continues on the desirability of general education in vocational schools. Entry at seventeen-plus to one-year courses is also possible.

Vocational institutions offer training for over 1,500 skilled occupations. In 1988 they numbered nearly 8,000, with over four million students. Of these, more than 90 per cent were on day courses and 68 per cent at the SPTU, receiving some form of maintenance. Their instructors, earning a monthly average of 200 rubles, had outstripped higher education teachers within three years, an indication of the wage-levels that skill qualifications demand even within the under-resourced educational domain.

Secondary specialized schools

The secondary specialized school (*srednee spetsial'noe uchebnoe zavedenie*) is known for short as the *tekhnikum*, though to be strictly accurate this is industry-related. It offers three- or four-year courses of professional and general education from age fifteen to train 'medium specialists' in such fields as engineering, commerce, nursing, the arts, and pre-school and primary teaching, and shorter courses (about two years) from seventeen-plus without the general-education component. Except for school or PTU leavers with excellent certificates, entrance is by examination, reflecting the *tekhnikum*'s image as second only to higher education.

These schools provide training in over 500 specialisms. In 1988/89 there were more than 4,500 of them, with nearly 4.4 million students. Two in three were on full-time courses, 27 per cent were studying by correspondence, and the rest were evening students. Those training to be teachers numbered 515,400. Full-time students graded 'good' – or sometimes 'satisfactory' – in the twice-yearly examinations received a grant, increased by 25 per cent for excellence but subject to withdrawal for poor performance.

HIGHER EDUCATION

The keynotes of the higher education reform of 1986/87 were quality, intensification and efficient planning. Higher education institutions (*vysshie uchebnye zavedeniya* or *vuzy*) and intakes were to be reduced, specialisms broadened and industrial liaison improved. In 1988/89 the USSR still had 898 of them, mostly organized by branches of the economy and giving higher professional training, but including 69 universities with broader courses. Schoolteachers were trained at the 200 pedagogical institutes and, for middle and senior classes, also at universities. Entrance was, and remains, by competitive examination. In 1988 there were 1.9 candidates per place and in 1989 2.1, but this country-wide

Below. Students in a petrochemistry secondary specialised school (tekhnikum) in Nizhnekamsk, a town in the Tatar republic of the Russian Federation. Below right. The present-day main building of Moscow University, its architectural style betraying its origins in the late Stalin period. Moscow University as an institution was, however, founded in 1755

average conceals wide variables of institutional prestige, disciplines and modes of study. Among the 1989 admissions, over 70 per cent came from general schools, 22 per cent from *tekhnikumy* and 6 per cent from PTU. The five million students comprised 54 per cent full-time (increasing), 35 per cent correspondence and 11 per cent evening (both declining).

Hostel accommodation is cramped but cheap. Grants are modest, often supplemented by part-time jobs, and results-related as with *tekhnikum* students. Most courses have been five-year, with an intensively taught six-day week, continuous assessment, and examinations at the end of each term or semester in January and June. The dropout rate in 1988/89 was 10.6 per cent, mainly because of poor performance. Upon graduation there has traditionally been direction to the first job, except for 'excellent' students, but even before the collapse of the USSR this had begun to be relaxed.

NEW DIRECTIONS IN EDUCATION

The perestroika debate made its mark on education. How should old values and structures be replaced? In October 1986 a group of leading teacher-innovators issued their first manifesto, 'Pedagogy of Co-operation', calling for trust and freedom from fear in schools. Later documents emphasized democratization, individualism and creativity. A debate ensued. The Academy of Pedagogical Sciences (*Akademiya pedagogicheskikh nauk* or APN), spearheading educational research and policy development, was split on the matter but predominantly conservative by inclination. Many teachers also resisted fundamental change.

In February 1988, however, a CPSU plenum criticized the APN and the 1984 reform – as 'evolution, not revolution' – and appeared to back the innovators. In March the USSR's three ministry-level bodies governing education were streamlined into one, the State Committee on Public Education. School and *vuz* syllabuses were modified (with history and social studies courses rewritten and atheism no longer reigning supreme) and a mosaic of educational clubs and experimental schools established. Among school students higher education is said to be losing its appeal.

In July 1989 provisional regulations on secondary general education were published. They mapped out a new structure for the Soviet school. The primary stage of four years was now to begin at age six *or* seven, depending on the child's readiness. Five years of 'main school' (*osnovaya shkola*) were to follow, completing the period of compulsory education. This was a departure from the requirement to achieve eleven years of general schooling by

various means. A two-year third stage continued, but was to be much more diversified. In September 1989 the State Committee issued new model curricula whereby nearly 60 per cent of the content was devolved to republics, regions and schools, and elements of student choice were introduced from the start. The humanities' share was increased by a quarter. Months before the demise of the USSR, the states had begun to introduce their own education policies, but the Russian Federation was keeping quite closely to the 1989 model in 1992. Given the country's problems, plus traditional inertia, it will surely be some time before the model is widely realized.   NJD

Communications and news media

BOOK PUBLISHING

The first dated book known to have been printed in Moscow was the *Apostol* (liturgical acts and epistles) completed by Ivan Fedorov in 1564 – over a century after printing began in Western Europe. Up to the end of the seventeenth century only about 700 books were printed in Russia, nearly all of them religious. Peter the Great encouraged printing for secular purposes, and St Petersburg became the centre of publishing in Russia, which it remained until 1917. Publishing was a monopoly of the state and state-supervised institutions until 1783, and the very limited means of expression thus afforded by the printed word resulted in the widespread clandestine circulation of works in manuscript which persisted into the nineteenth century and surfaced again, as *samizdat*, in the second half of the twentieth. A decree of 1804 codified the practice of censorship for the first time, and institutional censorship of publications was maintained with varying severity throughout the Imperial era and up to the end of Communist Party rule. The first quarter of the nineteenth century saw the beginnings of commercial printing and publishing. The 40 bookshops in the Russia of 1840 had increased to 1,795 by 1893. Measured by copies printed, book output in the later nineteenth century consisted predominantly of textbooks, popular fiction and religious literature.

For 'a time after the Revolution, some private publishing continued to exist beside the newly-established party and government publishers, but

Right. *A typical Russian bookstall. The picture of Lenin, well to the fore in this kiosk, makes it clear that the photograph was taken in the Soviet period – in fact, in November 1987, the seventieth anniversary of the Bolshevik Revolution*

the State Publishing House (*Gosizdat*), set up in 1919, rapidly became the principal book publishing organ. Much printed matter was distributed free, or at very low prices, in the first years after the Revolution, until the New Economic Policy (NEP) in 1921 introduced the principle that publishers should aim to cover their costs from sales. Publishing for the non-Russian peoples of the USSR was greatly increased during the 1920s. In 1930 the Association of State Publishing Houses (OGIZ) was created to co-ordinate the work of the reorganized central publishers. The number of titles and copies published dropped markedly during the years of the purges (1933–38). Strict limitations on treatment and subject-matter were imposed throughout the Stalin era; and from 1953 until the mid-1980s book publishing, like the rest of the media, remained under severe though fluctuating restrictions.

Being subject to lengthy approval and production procedures, books took longer than any other mass medium to reflect Mikhail Gorbachev's policy of glasnost; but by the end of the 1980s the publishing industry was vigorously exploring the new scope which it allowed. The Press Law of 1990 finally legalized genuine pluralism in publishing, but it was not until after the demise of the USSR that the structures of censorship were uprooted in the republics and a real and legal market economy in publishing began to appear.

Control and finance

Centralized control of publishing at ministerial level ended in Russia with the dissolution of the USSR Ministry of the Press in November 1991. The state retains legislation to register publishing-houses, and is still being accused of favouritism and high-handedness in its treatment of the printed media; but publishing is now an activity effectively open to any group or individual able to attract the necessary finance and supplies. Most of the major publishers under party or state control before the USSR's disintegration have remained in business, but operating either as commercial companies, as co-operatives or under sponsorship; and a large number of new, often very small, publishing enterprises are already functioning now that the 'right to publish' is no longer in the gift of party and state authorities.

Publishing, like the rest of post-Soviet industry, has suffered a serious economic downturn in the face of escalating costs for supplies and overheads. State allocation of paper quotas and printing facilities has been replaced by a free market in both these vital commodities. As potential readers find themselves able to afford fewer books, markets are shrinking, and a decline in book production has set in which has badly affected publishers formerly protected by subsidies that allowed the appearance of uneconomic

but approved titles and the maintenance of low prices. Prices for most books and journals are now climbing steeply, but demand for the most popular titles is still sufficient to support a widespread unofficial trade.

Publishers and authors

In 1991 about 1,800 non-state publishing-houses were registered in Russia, in contrast to the 235 publishers functioning in the entire USSR in 1988. An unknown but rapidly-growing number of organizations, government departments, pressure groups, political parties and individuals were also active as publishers.

Publisher–author relations have been radically changed by the greater latitude allowed to contract terms and rights negotiations. Authors are now also free to conduct business abroad without the compulsory intervention of the former All-Union Agency for Authors' Rights, now the Russian Agency for Intellectual Property (RAIS). Authors' rights will be further enhanced by legislation in Russia and the other republics which has paved the way for their adherence to the Berne Convention on copyright protection. In present conditions, however, those rights are difficult to enforce, and pirated editions of popular writers are widely sold.

Book output in the former USSR has fallen sharply, from some 2.5 billion copies in the mid-1980s to fewer than 2 billion in 1991, and the number of titles issued has declined by nearly one-third. Children's books, textbooks and scientific publications have suffered especially in conditions which have reduced their economic attractiveness to publishers. Looking for titles readily saleable in an unstable market, many publishers are giving priority to genres such as detective fiction, the occult, erotica, popular medicine and business manuals. In the successor states other than the Russian Federation, publishing in the national languages is gaining increased prominence at the expense of Russian.   GW

LIBRARIES

The earliest libraries in Russia were the collections of manuscripts, and later of printed books, established in some of the Orthodox monasteries from the eleventh century onwards, and it was only during the eighteenth century that secular libraries began to arise on any scale. The Russian Academy of Sciences received as the nucleus of its library the collection begun by Peter the Great in 1714, and the library of Moscow University was founded in 1755. Although the Imperial Public Library was opened in St Petersburg in 1814, early public library development was slow, underfinanced, and hampered by censorship and widespread illiteracy. After the October Revolution, the Bolshevik government nationalized all libraries, and requisitioned and redistributed many private collections. The growth of libraries was encouraged as an aid to literacy, an educational instrument, and a means of access to approved publications. After extensive destruction during the Second World War, the Soviet library system had expanded by the early 1990s to some 326,000 libraries of all kinds. With the disintegration of the USSR, the administrative control of library systems is now (1992) in a transitional state. Many major libraries have changed their titles, attitudes towards acquisitions, access and services are changing, and economic difficulties in all the republics are seriously restricting library development.

Soviet official policy towards libraries regarded them as a means of educating and ideologically influencing the general public, and as a service essential to research and industry. The formerly strict control over the acquisition of library materials and access to collections was relaxed from 1986 onwards. Thousands of titles consigned by the censor to the *spetskhrany* (special collections) were released to the general reader, and from 1991 such restrictions were in most cases lifted entirely. Despite the importance ascribed now and earlier to library services, widespread neglect over many years of their accommodation and storage needs has been blamed for recent disasters such as the fire at the Academy of Sciences Library in Leningrad in 1988 in which over three million volumes were lost or damaged.

The organization of library services in the former USSR lies largely with ministries and other official organs in the successor republics. Generally speaking, ministries of culture or their equivalents are responsible for the public ('mass') library networks, and education ministries for libraries in schools and other educational institutions. The republics' Academies of Sciences control the libraries of their respective research institutes, and often also some important libraries of national status. A new phenomenon is the libraries, archives and documentation centres attached to the growing number of independently-controlled research, educational and campaigning organizations.

National libraries

The Russian State Library (formerly Lenin Library) in Moscow was founded upon the library of the Rumyantsev Museum, opened in 1862, but is now the principal national library of the Russian Federation, holding by far the largest collections. The former Imperial Public Library, now the State Public Library in St Petersburg, ranks in many respects as a second Russian national library, and holds the largest collection of manuscripts in the country. Another, and probably unique, national institution is the Rudomino Library of Foreign Literature in Moscow, in which is concentrated the country's largest holding of publications issued outside the former Soviet Union. More specialized central libraries of national status in Russia include the State Public Scientific and Technical Library, the State Central Medical Library, and the Central Scientific Agricultural Library. Each of the other successor states to the former Soviet Union has its own 'state library' or 'republic library', serving as the head of the public library network and in particular as a repository of literature relating to that country.

Academy libraries

The Russian Academy of Sciences has within its organization the bulk of the libraries intended for the support of fundamental research in most fields of study. The Library of the Academy of Sciences (BAN) in St Petersburg, the oldest and one of the largest in the country, heads the Academy's library network, complemented by the Library of the Natural Sciences (BEN) and the Institute of Scientific Information for the Social Sciences (INION), both in Moscow. The rapid expansion of the Academy's research facilities in Siberia from the 1950s onwards led to the establishment in Novosibirsk of the State Public Scientific and Technical Library of the Academy's Siberian Division, which is now the leading research library east of the Urals. Many of the Academy's research institutes, such as the Institute for Russian Literature (Pushkin House) have very substantial book and manuscript collections of their own. The Academies of other republics all have their own central and institute libraries.

Public and educational libraries

The number of 'mass' libraries has grown from 13,800 in 1914 to about 130,000 in the early 1990s, and virtually all inhabited areas of the former Soviet Union now have a public library service. Children's library facilities are provided on a similar scale. Nevertheless, library use has been falling markedly in recent years, and there has been mounting concern over public libraries' inability to procure adequate stocks of books in popular demand. In education, school libraries now supply pupils' textbooks, which had previously to be bought for each child.

University libraries, like the institutions they serve, are mostly twentieth-century foundations, but a few, for example Moscow and Kazan', date from the eighteenth century; and outside Russia those of L'vov and Vilnius Universities were established in 1608 and 1570 respectively.

Technical libraries and information services

Industry and construction are served by some 20,000 technical libraries and information centres over the area of the former USSR. Under Soviet rule nearly every branch of industry possessed its own central specialist library at all-union level, but administration is now being recast within each republic. It remains to be seen whether former union services will survive, such as the Centre for Translations of Scientific and Technical Literature and – largest of all – the Institute of Scientific and Technical Information, which in a unique operation prepares and publishes each year Russian summaries of about a million scientific articles from all over the world.   GW

NEWSPAPERS

From the beginning the Soviet leadership attached great importance to the development of the mass media – particularly newspapers, which played an important part in the Bolsheviks' conquest of power and were for some time the only effective means of communication within the country over which they ruled. The number of newspapers, magazines and periodicals accordingly grew rapidly over the years of Soviet rule to stand, in 1990, at 8,434 (of which 172 were dailies, and 43 all-union in character). Newspapers were published, in the same year, in 55 different Soviet languages (5,694 in Russian and

1,253 in Ukrainian) and in 9 foreign languages. The total circulation of all newspapers rose in parallel to a 1990 total of 225 million copies per issue or 47,794 million copies a year. Periodical publications, by 1990, had reached a total of 4,775 titles appearing in 5,694 million copies a year; 62 periodicals appeared weekly, and the average print run was 135,300 copies of each issue.

'A newspaper', Lenin observed, 'is not only a collective propagandist and collective agitator; it is also a collective organizer.' Soviet newspapers and periodicals, accordingly, had different tasks to perform and were different in their coverage and layout from their Western counterparts. The Communist Party daily, *Pravda*, for instance, founded in 1912, normally contained an agitational message with a special emphasis on production achievements upon its front page. Its other five pages were devoted to party affairs, correspondence, foreign news (mostly supplied by TASS, the official news agency), sport, television programmes and the weather (on the back page). *Pravda* had 6.8 million subscribers in 1990. Other important daily papers, which differed from *Pravda* in their coverage and, in the last years of the Soviet era, in their editorial orientation, were: *Izvestiya*, the government daily; *Komsomol'skaya pravda*, the Komsomol daily; *Sel'skaya zhizn'*, a party newspaper intended for a rural readership; *Trud*, the trade-union paper, which enjoyed a spectacular rise in circulation during the 1980s (by 1990 it had over 20 million subscribers); and *Krasnaya zvezda*, the daily organ of the Ministry of Defence.

Influential weekly magazines and periodicals of the perestroika period included: the best-selling *Argumenty i fakty*, which specialized in brief but informative reports on sensitive matters and which in 1990 attained a circulation of over 33 million; the party theoretical journal *Kommunist*; the important literary monthly *Novy mir*; the illustrated weekly *Ogonek*; the weekly *Literaturnaya gazeta*; and the humorous weekly *Krokodil*, founded in 1922. *Ogonek* and the weekly paper *Moscow News* (published in Russian and foreign languages) were the most outspoken supporters of Gorbachev's policy of perestroika after 1985; the Russian newspaper *Sovetskaya Rossiya* and the Komsomol journal *Molodaya gvardiya* were among the publications identified with more conservative positions. A newer independent press, including the aptly named *Nezavisimaya gazeta*, was less obviously partisan.

Sociological studies suggested that the majority of the adult population made considerable use of this substantial diet of newsprint. A survey in Leningrad in the early 1970s found that 75 per cent of those polled read a newspaper every day, and a further 19 per cent did so three or four times a week. Even in relatively remote areas at least half

NEWSPAPER CIRCULATIONS (MILLION COPIES PER ISSUE), 1960–92

	1960	1970	1980	1990	1992
Pravda	6.3	9.2	10.7	6.8	1.4
Izvestiya	2.6	8.4	7.0	9.5	3.8
Komsomol'skaya pravda	3.4	7.7	10.0	21.2	13.4
Trud	1.3	4.1	12.3	20.9	4.3
Literaturnaya gazeta	0.6	1.1	2.8	4.4	0.4
Argumenty i fakty	—	—	—	33.5	25.7

the adult population normally read a newspaper daily, with the younger and better educated particularly likely to do so. More than 670,000 people wrote to *Pravda* in 1988 and the total postbag of the national press was estimated at 60–70 million in the 1980s. No more than a small proportion of the letters could be published, but many of them were followed up and in some cases these investigations could lead to the dismissal of local officials and factory managers. Detailed reports were also presented, on a regular basis, to the party and state leadership.

The role of Soviet newspapers and the electronic media expanded considerably after 1985 as a result of Gorbachev's policy of glasnost in all areas of public life. 'The better people are informed,' the new leader told the Central Committee plenum that elected him, 'the more consciously they act, the more actively they support the Party, its plans and programmatic objectives.' The Gorbachev leadership was accordingly associated with a determined attempt to expand the boundaries of legitimate debate within the columns of the official media.

A whole range of issues that had hitherto been taboo began to receive extended and sometimes sensational treatment. The crimes of the Stalinist years were explored in unprecedented detail, and so too were contemporary issues like prostitution, drug abuse and violent crime. For a small minority, glasnost meant that the achievements of the Soviet past were being improperly neglected; for the great majority, however, glasnost was the single most welcome development of the Gorbachev years.

Glasnost was strengthened considerably by the adoption of a law on the press in 1990, and by corresponding legislation for Russia itself in late 1991. The law on the press nominally abolished censorship, apart from a limited number of cases including the disclosure of state secrets and appeals for the violent overthrow of the state and social system. Any media monopoly was prohibited (again in principle), and individuals and political parties as well as state bodies were given the right to establish their own publications. All means of communication, however, had to be registered with the authorities, and there were criminal penalties for the

Pravda

Although *Pravda* always claimed to be founded on Lenin's initiative, he in fact played little part in the establishment of what was for many decades the authoritative voice of Soviet journalism. Lenin's first article appeared in the paper's thirteenth issue, and his second in its sixty-sixth;

Nikolay Bukharin as editor of Pravda, *accompanied by Lenin's sister, Mariya Ul'yanova. Below. A later (1935) editorial meeting of* Pravda, *with the editor, Mikhail Kol'tsov, left*

several of his articles were modified by more cautious-minded editors, and more than 40 were rejected altogether. *Pravda* none the less reflected Lenin's view that the newspaper should be a 'propagandist, agitator and organizer', and it had the largest circulation of all the Communist papers during the years immediately before the First World War.

Pravda was edited after the Revolution by Nikolay Bukharin, with Lenin's sister Mariya acting as 'responsible secretary'. By the early 1930s, however, effective control had moved to Stalin's personal secretariat, where a department had been established for the direction of all sections of the press. *Pravda* set the tone for press coverage of the repressions of the 1930s, with fabricated letter campaigns in favour of the death penalty as the paper itself demanded a 'dog's death' for all the defendants in the show trials.

Just as it reflected Stalinism, so *Pravda* reflected Khrushchev's reforms, Brezhnev's conservatism and, to a lesser extent, Gorbachev's perestroika. A celebrated digest of letters in 1986, 'Cleansing', spoke openly of party privilege and corruption. The paper none the less lost circulation during the late 1980s as the CPSU itself fell from favour; publication was briefly suspended after the attempted coup in 1991, and in 1992 *Pravda* failed to appear for several weeks. It was rescued, ironically, by a Greek millionaire. But it remains to be seen if there is a mass audience for a paper that so long defended the communist heritage in today's very different society.

'abuse' of freedom of speech or for the dissemination of information that did 'not correspond to reality'. The new law, none the less, did provide a formal basis for a wider range of opinion in the media than had ever existed before, and by the early 1990s the range of publications that could readily be obtained catered for all possible interests – religious, monarchical, ecological, commercial or even pornographic.

Soviet and post-Soviet newspapers and periodicals, despite these developments, experienced new difficulties in the early 1990s. Paper costs increased substantially, delivery became increasingly uncertain, and sometimes the papers themselves failed to appear. There was disillusionment, it seemed, with politics. Nor, by the early 1990s, were there so many sensations to report as had previously been the case. Subscriptions to newspapers and other publications, reflecting these circumstances, fell sharply: *Pravda* was down to 1.4 million subscribers in 1992; *Izvestiya* was down to 3.8 million; and *Trud* to 4.3 million. The measures that were taken

Putting the final touches to Pravda *before printing. The new technology of print production was slow to reach the Soviet Union, and the use of hot metal in typesetting remained common*

by the Russian government to protect the press imposed a further cost, in that papers it regarded as hostile generally received less assistance. Originally the mouthpiece of the Party, the press in the early post-Soviet years was itself discovering some of the unwelcome features of the market system of information it had long condemned in other countries.   SLW

RADIO

The first experimental radio broadcasts in the USSR were made in Nizhny Novgorod in 1919. The construction of a central radio station was undertaken in Moscow the following year, and it began broadcasting in 1922. Further stations were opened in 1924 in Leningrad, Kiev and Nizhny Novgorod, and regular broadcasts throughout the USSR began in the same year. By 1937 some 90 radio transmitters were in operation; by 1990 there were 168 broadcast-

ing centres and over 5,000 local radio stations throughout what was then the USSR, broadcasting in 72 Soviet languages. Broadcasting in union and autonomous republics was in two languages, normally the local language and Russian.

All of these facilities came under the control of the State Committee for Radio and Television of the USSR, whose chairman was a member of the USSR Council of Ministers, and under its counterparts at republican and lower levels of government. After the end of communist rule in 1991 the control of broadcasting shifted almost entirely to republican or local level.

In 1990 the central radio network broadcast fourteen main channels with a total output of 238.7 hours daily. The first channel, as with television, was the main national network for information, socio-political and cultural broadcasts (about 20 hours a day); the second channel, *Mayak*, broadcast news and music on a 24-hour basis. The third channel concentrated upon educational, literary and musical programmes for about sixteen hours daily; and the fourth broadcast music for about nine hours daily. The fifth channel provided information, socio-political and cultural broadcasts for Soviet citizens resident abroad; and the other channels relayed these broadcasts to more remote parts of the country. In 1990 practically the whole country could receive direct radio transmissions; about sixty million citizens, most of them in the main urban areas, could also receive foreign radio broadcasts. From 1991 commercial radio, based on pop music and advertisements, began to make its appearance in the major cities.   SLW

TELEVISION

Television saturated the Soviet Union decades after it had done so in Western Europe and the United States. In 1960 only 5 per cent of the Soviet population could watch television; by 1991 that figure was 97 per cent across the eleven time zones. In every republic at least three-quarters of the households had television sets. Typically, the audience for the nightly news from Moscow was around 150 million people.

The impact of television across this vast audience was considerable. It was increasingly the most important source of information for an overwhelming majority of people in the former Soviet Union. Because of rising costs of newsprint and subscription prices, it is television in Russia and the other successor states that fills the information gap. Even earlier, during the Soviet period, the audience for television was growing so rapidly that its extension eastwards was credited with keeping workers on the

Baykal-Amur Mainline construction project in the harsh climate of the eastern provinces. Its availability was also said to be a principal determinant of job choice among people.

The penetration of television adversely affected the size of film and theatre audiences in the 1970s and 1980s. However, after the August 1991 attempted coup and the effective dissolution of the film-distributing monopoly, foreign films, particularly American ones, brought the audience back to the cinemas. Within a brief time, however, the loose collection of cable television channels had also developed reasonably large local audiences with often pirated versions of American and other countries' films. Until the rules governing cable stations have been codified and enforced, this method of gaining audiences and launching new television studios is likely to continue. Naturally, not all new television systems rely on this method of programming. New studios are engaging in experimental programming and developing alternative news programmes at the local level in individual former republics. Success and penetration depend on capital, access to existing airtime, or acquisition of new satellite capabilities. At present their reach – and its technological underpinning – is limited.

During the Soviet era, there were two national networks, broadcasting in Russian. The First Programme (Channel One), the more widely received, focused on important social and political issues and newsworthy cultural and sports events. In 1982 a Second Programme (Channel Two) was added to feature more experimental and regionally produced programming. St Petersburg television, which, as Leningrad Television produced some of the best television programmes in the country (such as *Fifth Wheel* or, before it became violently sensationalist, *600 Seconds*), could be seen not only in Moscow, but in much of European Russia. (The pro-nationalist and anti-government *600 Seconds* was taken off the air in the autumn of 1993.) In Moscow there are additional channels and each of the former republics has one or more of its own television networks which can receive the two largest networks as well.

Virtually from the beginning of the Gorbachev era, television was enlisted in the battle for glasnost and perestroika. Less radical than newspapers, which have much smaller audiences and depend on more highly educated consumers, television was a powerful giant, termed 'large calibre' by authorities, as opposed to the 'small calibre' of all other media. Because of its enormous reach and large audiences, television underwent during these years a visible tug of war between the powerful right and left wings of the Communist Party. Though the Politburo was in general agreement that television should be made a much more effective instrument of communication, and that this would entail a more sophisticated and differentiated notion of the audience, there were clear divisions as to how far glasnost should be allowed to proceed on the 'blue screen'.

Gosteleradio, the State Committee on Television and Radio Broadcasting, was directed by a Politburo appointee, though the deputy chairman was often the operational power. Television was connected to the Central Committee by 'telephone law' and regular meetings, and the struggle for autonomy of television broadcasting was related to struggles within the Politburo as well as to differences within the various studios in the State Committee. Most pioneering and dedicated to the expansion of glasnost was the division of youth programming, from which such startling new broadcasts as *Twelfth Floor* and *Vzglyad* (Viewpoint) were generated.

Impressive technological upgrading could be seen very early: computer-generated graphics were introduced in 1986; remote pick-ups and live interactive satellite transmissions ('space bridges') became routine. Electronic news gathering (ENG) was expedited by new, mainly foreign-produced, equipment. Editing and sound tracks utilized modern techniques; video clips of rock music grew frequent. News presentation became more personalized, as the impersonal news reader was replaced by an anchor-person.

The news and public affairs programmes regularly featured vigorous discussions of domestic social and economic problems. The provision of several points of view became more widespread, as did appearances by foreign critics of Soviet domestic and foreign policy. The use of opinionated newswriting by broadcasters in referring to foreign governments declined sharply. Live call-in programmes subjected Soviet policy-makers to the grievances of viewers. Uninterrupted live coverage of the contentious sessions of the first Congress of People's Deputies in 1989 was so popular, that its deputy chairman, A.I. Luk'yanov later estimated that a 20 per cent short fall in productivity had occurred during the period.

However, a palpable tension continued to be present as the older system survived and asserted itself as well. One of the earliest and failed tests of the new openness occurred when Chernobyl' exploded. State television did not broadcast adequate or timely information and refrained, or was prevented, from investigative reporting of the crisis. Coverage of the student uprising in Beijing in 1989 was uninformative. *Gosteleradio* essentially took material from the Chinese government and provided no analysis or coverage of its own. It was determined that any other approach would seriously impair the long and difficult restoration of Soviet-Chinese relations – proof that the role of television as political partner of the state had not completely changed. The immensely popular youth programme *Vzglyad* was suspended numerous times and finally cancelled when it attempted to cover the resignation of Foreign Minister Shevardnadze. The growing independence of regional television networks, particularly in the Baltic republics, first drew criticism by Moscow and then violent action as the Lithuanian television tower was stormed and occupied. On this occasion, censorship of the First Programme's news was explicitly acknowledged on air by the rebellious anchor woman Tat'yana Mitkova.

In the early days of glasnost and perestroika, many of these contradictory directions could be traced to the split in the Politburo between Aleksandr Yakovlev and Yegor Ligachev. Their views and values were radically different as were the directions they gave to television programming, in which each displayed a great interest.

In the autumn of 1990, however, in the matter of television, Mikhail Gorbachev decisively sided with the party apparat, the leadership of the military, and the KGB, all of whom sought to rein in political debates on television. He appointed Leonid Kravchenko (b.1938) to head the State Committee, by now officially a state company. Kravchenko saw himself as responsible only to the President and saw the First Programme as the President's channel. This arrangement fell outside the Law on the Press, as Gorbachev in a decree had specifically exempted television from its provisions. Kravchenko reneged on an earlier promise to give the Russian Federation full and immediate authority over the second national channel and so constrained the freedom of television producers and on-air discussants that many left when, the following May, the Russian Federation was given part of the broadcast day on the second channel. From that moment an oppositionist television channel appeared, one that proved a showcase for Boris Yel'tsin and his ideas.

In August 1991 tanks surrounded Ostankino – the television centre of Moscow and the Soviet Union. All counter-programming was suppressed during the four days of the failed coup. None the less, some enterprising and daring newscasters and their immediate superiors managed to broadcast pictures of Yel'tsin defying the coup on a tank at the barricades. Other information was passed on in newscasts, including the negative reaction of foreign countries and many locales within the Soviet Union. In fact, the earliest signs of cracks in the façade of the takeover were visible on television.

Following the putsch and the breakup of the Soviet Union, the *de facto* decentralization of television networks was ratified. The Russian Federation was granted all of Channel Two and part of the assets of Channel One, and each of the other new states claimed their former republican networks. The fate of Channel One – Ostankino – was more complex. Its leadership was replaced and financially it was supported by the Russian government. None the less, by agreement of the Commonwealth, it was to serve as the 'common informational space'. This formula did not clarify in detail how or if financial contributions were to be apportioned and how representation of the many clients and owners (all the states of the Commonwealth) could fairly and justly be determined both in administrative policy-making and on the air, but Russian authority prevailed.

Political constraints have not entirely been displaced by economic ones. For Channels One and Two, 'telephone law' from the central Russian government tends to be diluted by the erosion of governmental power and competition among political actors, all of whom see television as a valuable political resource. The operations of 'their' television networks often come under closer scrutiny by the governments of the newly independent states outside Russia, though the patterns differ from the Baltic west to the Central Asian south. In many cases indigenous policy makers protest against the treatment of their leaders or values on Channels One and Two by cutting off transmissions periodically. This practice, in turn, has a clearly adverse effect on the ability of Russians resident in these states to gain information. It should be recalled that the two Russian-language networks blanketing the area of the former Soviet Union are a key information source for the more than 25 million ethnic Russians and larger number of Russian speakers living outside Russia.

Finally, the introduction of foreign broadcasting is gaining momentum. Such trans-national sources as the BBC and other European broadcasters, Worldnet (programme of the United States Information Agency), CNN, the governments of Turkey and Iran, and others can now reach various parts of the former Soviet Union. In addition, many programmes produced by foreign companies are increasingly seen on television screens.

The clamorous tug-of-war over the control of television by competing élites in the Gorbachev period and the consequent extreme change in the content and packaging of television programming created a reciprocal impact: the identification of television as a crucial political resource for mobilized groups. Expectations about impact have far outstripped even maximalist notions of media effects. It is a measure of the centrality of the television agenda to the opposition that in June 1992 a group of activists led by so-called 'red/brown' politicians (an alliance of extreme nationalists and Communist loyalists), defying the law, laid siege to Ostankino television to demand time for the 'opposition'.

Satellite television is adding to the variety of sources of information and entertainment in post-Soviet Russia, but the satellite dishes add a discordant note to this Moscow building

Indeed, when the field of political competition is filled with dozens of contenders, it is difficult rationally and fairly to allocate time on television. Until the wide array of individuals and movements has jelled into a manageable number of parties, television will be hard pressed to apply rules that the competitors will find equitable and reasonable, while genuinely informing the audience. To further complicate the process, the personalization of politics that television tends to produce may itself militate against the development of the political party as a mediating institution.

In other more subtle ways the struggle for control of the politically powerful medium of television is expressed. For example, in many (not all) independent ventures, there can be found contributions of state property or other resources; investments or partial budgetary contributions from the state; involvement of newly-named incarnations of older institutions; and maintenance of personnel rosters. It is one of the attributes of adaptable political and economic élites that they are able to transform their advantages into new forms. Nevertheless, this method of transition to a market system results in concentrations of holdings and perpetuation of authority that are not wholly visible. Without a firm regulatory system in place, the divisions of property tend to favour previous élites.

In 1993 the storming of Ostankino provided clear proof of the importance of television to mobilize support and claim political legitimacy. Results of the Russian parliamentary elections later that year confirmed earlier conclusions that television significantly helped the candidacy of those who knew how to use it, such as Vladimir Zhirinovsky, with his deliberately 'old-fashioned' campaign for targeted audiences.

The fundamental political dilemma may be characterized as follows: how do democratic reforms proceed in the use of television, the single greatest asset for any political movement, group or party under conditions of crisis? Since the infrastructure (the number of broadcast and cable channels of high penetration) is limited, the rules for fair play not yet in place, and many of the former élites still wielding influence, the solutions are elusive.

Television programmes from foreign broadcasters as well as the developing independent broadcast sector at home provide viewers in the former Soviet Union with a far greater number of choices than had ever been imaginable during the decades of the Soviet system of government. At the same time, certain unresolved issues still complicate news and public affairs coverage. The tensions that mark ethnic relations in some areas are played out on television, and media officials find it difficult to devise a policy of adequate balance that does not exacerbate inflamed relations. Perhaps the most critical political mission for television in the years ahead will be the development of methods for fair and full coverage of divisive ethnic and national issues.   EM

CENSORSHIP

Censorship in the USSR was not a new phenomenon, but it became much more comprehensive and effective in the Soviet period than it had been in Imperial Russia. First introduced officially by Peter the Great, censorship was codified in 1804, substantially liberalized after the 1905 revolution and (with the exception of military censorship) abolished following the February 1917 revolution.

Soviet censorship began on the night of the 24 October 1917 (os) with the confiscation and burning of the latest issue of the liberal newspaper *Russkaya volya*, said to contain 'libellous concoctions'; the paper's printing press was requisitioned on the following day and immediately used to produce copies of the Bolshevik *Rabochy put'*. These actions set the pattern for the next few months, and by the end of July 1918 the Military Revolutionary Committees had succeeded in preventing the regular appearance on communist-held territory of all non-Bolshevik newspapers, although a certain amount of new Menshevik and Socialist Revolutionary political literature circulated in Russia for some time after that. Restrictions on non-Bolshevik publishing were imposed in accordance with the *Decree on the Press* of 27 October 1917 (OS), which stated that 'counter-revolutionary' publications at that juncture were no less dangerous than bombs and machine-guns. This decree (in force until the early 1990s) promised that the 'temporary measures to stop the flood of filth and slander' would be repealed as soon as the new order was consolidated and normal conditions of public life obtained; all administrative interference with the press would then cease and complete freedom within the law would be established. After a decree of 28 January 1918 setting up Revolutionary Press Tribunals, committees of inquiry attached to these bodies were empowered to take swift action against any publications suspected of encroaching on the rights and interests of the revolutionary people (by, for example, printing something critical of Bolshevik policies and practices). In addition, the security police (then the Cheka – Extraordinary Commission for Combating Counter-Revolution and Sabotage) was given the duty of arresting anyone whose publishing activities could be regarded as 'counter-revolutionary'.

The more routine pre-publication censorship at this time was carried out by employees of the Commissariat for People's Enlightenment and in particular, after its establishment in May 1919, of the state publishing house, Gosizdat, which included a Chief Board for Press Affairs. The remaining private book-publishers (who were able to operate until the end of the 1920s and in isolated cases even longer) were also supervised by Gosizdat functionaries at this stage. The military censorship was separate from the civilian branch, but became part of the 'official' Soviet censorship organ, Glavlit, when this body was finally set up on 6 June 1922. Glavlit (initially meaning Chief Board for Literary and Publishing Affairs – after August 1966 the official title became Chief Board for the Preservation of State Secrets in the Press, attached to the USSR Council of Ministers) was designated a Chief Committee of the People's Commissariat of Enlightenment and was headed until 1931 by P.I. Lebedev-Polyansky, the author of the first (1924) book on Lenin's literary and aesthetic views, and then (until 1935) by B.M. Volin. Both had gained valuable experience for the post as chief censor of the Soviet Union by engaging in Bolshevik underground literary activities in Russia before the Revolution. Volin's successors were S.B. Ingulov, N. Sadchikov and K. Omel'chenko, followed in 1957 by P.K. Romanov, a graduate of the Leningrad Institute of Railway Transport Engineering.

The 1922 Statute (*Polozhenie*) states that Glavlit was established to bring together all forms of censorship (*vsekh vidov tsenzury*) of domestic and imported printed works, manuscripts, photographs, drawings and maps that are intended for sale and distribution; it was to compile lists of banned works, and was supplied with broad criteria (such as 'containing agitation against Soviet power') for proscribing harmful items. Publications of certain bodies (the Central Committee, Comintern, the Academy of Sciences, Gosizdat) were 'freed from censorship', apart from being checked for military secrets. The security police (by then known as the GPU – State Political Directorate) was instructed to co-operate with Glavlit to prevent the circulation of banned literature and to 'struggle against' domestic and foreign underground publications. Glavrepertkom (literally, the Main Committee for the Control over Repertoire) was established on 9 February 1923; it was headed by I.P. Trainin, attached to Glavlit, and censored plays, films, circuses, concerts, variety shows, other public performances and, from 1925, gramophone records (both sound track and labels). Slides and photographs had to be submitted to this body for approval before being shown in public, and one or two seats no further back than the fourth row from the stage always had to be kept free for Glavrepertkom's requirements.

By the mid-1920s everything was supposed to be submitted to censorship, including sculptures, drawings, handkerchiefs with pictures on them, book jackets, bus tickets and matchbox labels. In the 1930s items were often reinspected upside-down and back-to-front as an extra precaution against accidental unfortunate juxtapositions. The new censorship statue of 6 June 1931 was more wide-ranging than its predecessor. It now clearly stated that Glavlit (including Glavrepertkom) was concerned also with the pre-publication and post-publication 'control' (this word replaces the term 'censorship' in the 1922 statute) of pictures, radio broadcasts (ballets and television programmes were to be added in due course), lectures and exhibitions, and had its plenipotentiaries not only in publishing houses, printing establishments, editorial offices and radio stations, but also in news agencies, main post offices and customs sheds.

Military (as contrasted to state) secrets are barely mentioned, but Glavlit was instructed to draw up lists of secret information (not merely lists of banned titles). Publications of the main state publishing house (now called OGIZ) were no longer free from Glavlit's preventive 'control'. The final loophole appears to have been closed on 28 August 1939 with the obligatory registration and ringing of carrier pigeons, making evasion of the postal censorship even harder than before. Since then, no substantial changes seem to have taken place in this field, apart from the steadily rising educational level of the censors, until the mid-1980s.

It is very important to stress, however, that Glavlit itself was largely an executive organ and much less important than a range of other factors: current Communist Party policies controlled by the Central Committee; the wishes and whims of the party leader (or one or more of his closest associates); the activities of the security police in suppressing and/or provoking manifestations of dissent; the attitudes of the editor(s) and publisher(s) involved; and the likelihood of self-censorship on the part of the author himself. The Glavlit employee, as a rule, saw not the manuscript but a proof copy, by which stage most of the 'doubtful' passages in the original version had probably been removed, as it was usually fairly clear to all involved what would and would not 'get through' at the Glavlit stage of processing.

No edition of Glavlit's book of rules is available in the West, but it is widely believed that special permission was required (and until the Gorbachev era was rarely given) in every individual case before

Chernobyl' was at first a setback for glasnost as officials both locally and centrally attempted to cover up the scale of the catastrophe. The reaction against the cover-up was, however, such that quite soon the episode led to a loosening of censorship. The environmental consequences of the disaster have far longer-term implications, although the technical effort to restrict the damage was carried out with skill and courage. Here a roof is being erected over the damaged reactor

public mention could be made of such matters as earthquakes, explosions and other disasters in the USSR, the salaries of Soviet government and party officials, and price increases at home or improved living standards anywhere outside the socialist camp. No Soviet publication supplied details about the jamming of foreign radio broadcasts, and the operations of Glavlit itself were also subject to a strict taboo until shortly after Gorbachev came to power when they became an issue of public debate.

Since the 1986 Chernobyl' catastrophe (which seems to have convinced some top Soviet officials of the mortal dangers of concealing and distorting unpleasant information) there has been gradual relaxation of political control over the Soviet and post-Soviet media. Glavlit itself underwent two further changes in its official name and appears to have disintegrated at about the time of the August 1991 attempted coup. According to a chart in the newspaper *Sovershenno sekretno*, No. 1, 1992, shortly before its demise the 'official' censorship agency (headed by its director [*nachal'nik*] V.A. Boldyrev) consisted of four directorates (*upravleniya*) and five departments (*otdely*). Directorate one controlled scientific and technical literature, Directorate two controlled foreign literature, Directorate three co-ordinated the work of the local organs of Glavlit, and Directorate four prepared the 'normative documents' (presumably including the lists of banned topics, facts, titles and authors). Department one dealt with 'secret correspondence', Department two controlled foreign periodicals, Department three controlled the mass media, Department four controlled social, political and artistic literature ('political censorship'), and an unnumbered department handled the transmission of (presumably samizdat, anti-Soviet and 'disinformative') manuscripts abroad.

In 1992 the protection of state and military secrets in Russia was the responsibility of the Ministry of Security (under Colonel General V.P. Barannikov), the Ministry of Internal Affairs (under Lieutenant General V.F. Yerin) and, of course, the Ministry of Defence (this last had representatives on the staff of most of the major newspapers). There was, however, practically no pre-publication censorship, and the problems faced by writers, scholars, scientists, journalists, and cinema directors, were mainly economic, resulting from enormous shortages of, and the virtual monopoly control over and high prices charged for, paper supplies, printing and distribution facilities and film stock. Ironically, this meant that for the general public the availability and range of high-quality Russian literature, journalism and films were no greater than they had been during the Khrushchev and Brezhnev periods, and less than under Gorbachev. MD

Sport and recreation

SPORTS HISTORY

Sport and physical education have their roots deep in Russian history, in the people's traditions, the climate, fears about internal and external foes, the organized sports pioneered largely by Britain, the gymnastics schools of Germany (Jahn), Scandinavia (Ling and Nachtegall) and the Czech lands (Tyrs), and in Prussian military training. The pattern of Soviet sport was shaped as much by these factors as it was by political ideals.

As an industrial society developed in nineteenth-century Russia, liberal noblemen and native industrialists, with foreigners resident in Russia, began to set up private sports clubs in the major cities. These embraced sports such as yachting (the Imperial Yacht Club, dating from 1846), tennis (the Neva Lawn-Tennis Circle, from 1860), ice-skating (the Amateur Skating Society, from 1864), fencing (the Officers' Fencing Gymnasium, from 1857), gymnastics (the Palma Gymnastics Society, from 1863) and cricket (the St Petersburg Tennis and Cricket Club, from 1868). Commercial promoters were also providing, for spectators and gamblers, such professional sports as horse-racing (the St Petersburg Horse-Racing Society, 1826), boxing (Baron Kister's English Boxing Arena, 1895), cycling (the Tsar'skoe Selo Cycling Circle, 1880) and soccer (the Victoria Football Club was the first established soccer club in 1894). Various displays of strength were popular in circuses, featuring such world-famous performers as the Estonian Georgy Hakkenschmidt and the Russian Ivan Poddubny and his wrestling wife Masha Poddubnaya.

At the turn of the century, there were several Russian sports associations and on the eve of the First World War as many as 1,266 Russian sports clubs existed with an average membership of 60 persons. Many of these clubs were located in the main Russian cities, but by no means all. For example, Ukraine had 196 sports clubs with 8,000 members, and Belorussia had 1,000 members in its Sanitas, Sokol, Bogatyr and the Jewish Maccabee sports clubs (Jews being barred from entry to many Russian clubs). In 1912 the government set up its quasi-military Physical Fitness Committee under General Voeykov. The Bolsheviks were therefore to inherit a developing sports movement that was already largely centrally controlled.

Sport in revolution

The first steps to be taken after the Bolsheviks came to power in October 1917 were by no means clear, for there was no pattern to follow. The change-over from criticism of tsarist sport to action in an 80 per cent peasant country in the throes of a world and civil war presented considerable problems.

However, the crucial question being debated was not what form sport should take, but whether competitive sport should exist at all in the new workers' state. After all, some revolutionaries argued, sports such as athletics, soccer, rowing, tennis and gymnastics were invented by the industrial bourgeoisie for their own diversion and character training for future careers as captains of industry and empire. It was thought perfectly natural by some after the Russian Revolution that a new pattern of recreation would emerge, reflecting the dominant values and needs in the new socialist state.

Hygienists and Proletkul'tists

The two major groups that regarded competitive sport as debasing workers' physical culture and inculcating non-socialist habits were known as the Hygienists and the Proletkul'tists (from 'proletarian culture').

To the Hygienists, sport implied competition, games that were potentially injurious to mental and physical health. These included boxing, weight-lifting, wrestling and gymnastics, which were said to encourage individualist rather than collectivist attitudes. They condemned the emphasis on record-breaking and the professionalism of Western sport, and they favoured non-commercialized forms of recreation that dispensed with grandstands and spectators. Sport, they said, diverted attention from providing recreation for all. Their list of 'approved' sports included athletics, swimming and rowing (all against oneself or the clock, rather than an opponent). Since the Hygienists had virtual control over the government body for sport (the Supreme Council of Physical Culture), the sporting press, the Ministry of Health and the physical education colleges, they were extremely powerful. They managed, for

example, to have physical education excluded from the schools, since they believed that it should be integrated into all lessons rather than tacked on to the curriculum artificially. 'The existence of physical education teachers is a sign of pedagogical illiteracy', they claimed.

To the Proletkul'tists, sports that derived from bourgeois society were remnants of the decadent past and part of degenerate bourgeois culture. A fresh start had to be made through labour exercises and mass displays, pageants and folk games. In the decade after the Revolution, many factory yards and farm meadows could be seen full of muscular men and women rhythmically swinging hammers and sickles, simulating work movements in time to music.

The Proletkul'tists went much further than the Hygienists in condemning all manner of games, sports and gymnastics 'tainted' by class society. They invented new games for children, had the manufacture of dolls stopped (because they were thought to foster a maternal disposition among young girls) and organized mass sports activities portraying scenes of world revolution.

Sport for defence, health and integration

Essentially, however, sport during the first few years came to be geared to the needs of the war effort. All the old clubs and their equipment were commandeered for the Universal Military Training Board (*Vsevobuch*) whose main aim was to supply the Red Army with contingents of trained conscripts as quickly as possible. It took over the Physical Fitness Committee and co-ordinated its activities with those of the education and health ministries. A second major consideration then was health. Regular participation in physical exercise was to be a means of improving health standards rapidly and of educating people in hygiene, nutrition and exercise. This campaign could only succeed, in the opinion of N.I. Podvoysky (1880–1948), head of *Vsevobuch*, if the emotional attraction of competitive sport were fully exploited.

Competitive sports began to be organized from the lowest level upwards, culminating in the All-Russia Pre-Olympiads and the First Central-Asian Olympics of 1920. Sports were taken from town to country, from the European metropolis to the Asiatic interior, as an explicit means of involving as many people as possible in organized sport and exercise. A third function of sport was integration. The significance of the First Central-Asian Olympics, held in Tashkent over ten days in early October 1920, may be judged from the fact that this was the first time that Uzbeks, Kyrgyz, Kazakhs and other Turkic peoples, as well as Russians and other Europeans, had competed in any sporting event together.

Sport during the 1920s

Throughout the 1920s the actual amount of sports activity increased substantially. By 1929 sports club membership had risen fifteen-fold since 1913 (from 0.04 to 0.5 per cent of the population). Furthermore, half the officially-recognized sports in the USSR had had their first national championship by 1929, including 14 women's sports.

The big sports contest of the decade was the First Workers' Spartakiad of 1928, with some 4,000 participants, including 600 foreign athletes from 12 countries. In view of the fact that the USSR had few contacts with international sports federations and none with the Olympic movement, this Spartakiad was intended to be a universal workers' Olympics – in opposition to the 'bourgeois' Olympics held that year in Amsterdam with roughly the same programme. Although Soviet sports performance was understandably below top world standards, in some events the USSR did have world-class athletes. Yakov Mel'nikov (1896–1960), for example, had won the 5,000-metre speed-skating event at the Stockholm world championships in 1923.

During the 1920s the Communist Party made clear its own views on physical culture and took it completely under government control. A resolution of 1925 emphasized that physical culture must be an inseparable part of political and cultural education and of public health. This, then, was the definitive statement on the enhanced role of sport in society to which all subsequent policy statements were to refer. Sport had been given the revolutionary role of being an agent of wide-ranging social change. As a means of inculcating standards of hygiene and regular exercise in a predominantly backward peasant country, its therapeutic role was, for example, widely advertised in the three-day anti-tuberculosis campaigns of the late 1920s. Sport was also expected to combat anti-social behaviour: the Ukrainian Party Central Committee issued a resolution in 1926 expressing the hope that 'physical culture would

Right. Old-style Soviet fitness regimentation. Physical exercise in working hours on the shop-floor of a Moscow clock factory

become the vehicle of the new life . . . a means of isolating young people from the evil effects of prostitution, home-made alcohol and the street'. The role given to sport in the countryside was even more ambitious: it was 'to play a big part in the campaign against drunkenness and uncivilized behaviour by attracting village youth to more cultured activities . . . In efforts to transform the village, physical culture is to be a vehicle of the new way of life in all measures undertaken by the authorities – in the fight against religion and natural calamities (drought, floods, frosts and erosion).'

Participation in sport, therefore, might develop healthy minds in healthy bodies. Sport stood for 'clean living', progress, good health and rationality, and was regarded by the Party as one of the most effective instruments in implementing its social policies.

Sport and industrialization

The implications for the sports movement of the economic and political processes of the 1930s were extremely important, for it was then that the organizational pattern of Soviet sport was basically formed – with the sports societies, sports schools, national fitness programme and the uniform rankings system for individual sports. The new society saw the flourishing of all manner of competitive sports with spectator appeal, of leagues, cups, championships, popularity-polls and cults of sporting heroes. All were designed to provide recreation and diversion for the fast-growing urban populace. The big city and security-forces (Dinamo) teams, with their considerable resources, dominated competition in all sports; thus, the Division One soccer league of 1938 included nine Moscow and six Dinamo teams from the cities of Moscow, Leningrad, Kiev, Tbilisi, Odessa and Rostov out of its twenty-six clubs.

Physical culture, Soviet-style, in the Stalin era

The many sports parades and pageants which constituted a background to the sports contests were intended to create 'togetherness' and patriotic feeling. Significantly, sports rallies often began to accompany major political events and festivals (May Day, Anniversary of the Revolution, Constitution Day), thereby linking members of the public, through sport, with politics, the Party and, of course, with their leader.

A relatively close link was re-established in the 1930s between sport and the military, stemming from the conviction that a state surrounded by unfriendly powers must be militarily strong. Sport openly became a means of providing pre-military training and achieving a relatively high standard of national fitness and defence. The two largest and most successful sports clubs in the USSR were those run by the armed forces and the security forces: the Central House of the Red Army (the Central Sports Club of the Army, TSSKA) and Dinamo respectively. After 1931, moreover, the national fitness programme, the GTO, was expressly intended to train people, through sport, for military preparedness and work – the Russian abbreviation GTO (*Gotov k trudu i oborone*) standing for 'Ready for Labour and Defence'.

The Second World War obviously retarded the sports movement, yet had certain far-reaching effects. The war convinced the authorities that they had been correct in 'functionalizing' sport and making nation-wide physical fitness a prime target. It also reinforced a belief in a military bias in physical training and sport. The post-war role of organizations such as the army sports clubs, Dinamo and the civil defence establishment DOSAAF (*Dobrovol'noe obshchestvo sodeystviya Armii, Aviatsii i Flotu* – 'Voluntary Society for Aid to the Army, Air Force and Navy') was to be enhanced and these institutions were to be made the pillars of the entire sports movement. A national physical-fitness programme was to be the main goal, and sports with specific military utility were to become compulsory in all educational institutions and sports societies.

Post-war sport

Competition with the West · With the conclusion of the war and the setting of a new national target – to catch up and overtake the most advanced industrial powers in sport as in all else – the Soviet leaders felt it possible to demonstrate the pre-eminence of sport in Soviet socialist society. Given the limited opportunities elsewhere, sport seemed to offer a suitable medium for pursuing this goal as an area in which the USSR did not have to take second place. This aim presupposed a level of skill in a wide range of sports superior to that existing in the leading Western states. On the eve of the war, that level was already approached or achieved in several sports. Soviet sources assert that by 1939 as many as forty-four unofficial world records had been set, over half (twenty-three) of which were in weight-lifting, the rest being in shooting (nine), athletics (nine), swimming (two) and speed-skating (two).

This trend towards proficiency was strengthened after the war by mobilization of the total, if limited, resources of the entire sports system, by creating full-time, well-remunerated sportsmen and teams, and by giving them considerable backing. Sport was seen as 'one of the best and most comprehensible means of explaining to people throughout the world the advantages of the socialist system over capitalism'.

Urban life and post-war sport · From the late 1950s to the late 1970s there was a steady increase in public and personal prosperity, and in the range and quantity of consumers' goods available, a reduction in working time and a continuing shift in population-balance in favour of the towns. All these factors had a qualitative effect on the pattern of sport.

Increasing prosperity

Soviet sources claimed that both national income and consumption nearly tripled between 1960 and 1977. Part of the resulting increased personal income was undoubtedly being spent on recreation, on the pursuit of a growing variety of activities, particularly outdoor ones, and on personal durables such as skis, skates, tennis and badminton rackets, fishing tackle, tents and, to a lesser extent, on motor-cycles, canoes, dinghies, yachts and cars.

Higher national income also resulted in a more substantial government allocation to sport and the spread of activities that presuppose a certain level of industrial development and economic surplus. For example, motor-racing and rallying, yachting,

Cross-country skiing in Murmansk, northern Russia

karting, various winter sports (bobsleighing, slaloming, ski-jumping), water-skiing, scuba diving, mountaineering, fishing, shooting and the complex of outdoor pursuits that comes under the Russian rubric of 'tourism' all showed appreciable growth in the 1960s and 1970s. Some sports received a new lease of life as industry was able to produce equipment for them – for example, rugby, archery and field hockey. It was in the 1970s that new sports were introduced: squash, hang-gliding, karate and golf. It is significant that the introduction of these new sports came from above. An exception to this was, perhaps, the setting-up of a Soviet pigeon-fanciers' federation in 1975.

State capital investment for the construction of sports facilities grew considerably after the August 1966 government resolutions on sport. For example, some republics increased their expenditure on sport by as much as six to seven times in one year, 1967. The Russian Federation spent twice as much on sport in 1967 as in all the preceding post-war years put together. As a result of this campaign, between 1966 and 1970 the country gained 319 new sports centres, 185 indoor swimming-pools, 31 indoor athletics stadiums and 16 indoor ice-rinks.

Increasing free time

The relationship of work to leisure also altered radically after the war. Not merely was there an increase in the absolute amount of free time, but the reduction in the working day resulted in workers spending less time than previously in such well-defined institutional settings as factory and office. As G.I. Yeliseev, chief of the trade-union sports societies, said, 'whereas recreational activities used to take place in urban sports centres, many have now been transferred to out-of-town sports amenities, recreation camps and parks'. As a consequence, the unions had to 'refit and adapt various buildings, old passenger railway compartments and river steamers, landing-craft, barges and such-like, and to build recreational centres in the countryside'.

The break-through that signalled the greatest revolution in leisure, just as in other industrial countries, was the introduction of the five-day week in March 1967. The boom in camping, fishing, hunting, rock-climbing, pot-holing, water-skiing, motoring and boating (and the relative decline in participation-rates in chess, draughts, gymnastics, table-tennis and boxing) was accounted for partly by longer holidays with pay and partly by the developing cult of the weekend. In 1956 the standard (six-day) week in Soviet industry was 46 hours which by 1978 had decreased to an average working week in industry of 40.6 hours and, in state employment in general, of 39.3 hours in a five-day week with paid annual holidays of 15 days for most employees.

Increasing urbanization

Nearly two-thirds of the Soviet population lived in a relatively modern, urban, industrial society. Whereas only 18 per cent of the population lived in towns in 1926, in 1978 63 per cent (164 million) was urban-based. Town-planning tended to allow for sizeable courtyards for each block of flats and a minimum of sports amenities: one sports centre, one gymnasium and one swimming-pool per 50,000 people. None the less, the problem of providing adequate outdoor amenities for sport became even greater in the most densely-settled urban areas. For example, despite an instruction by the Moscow City Soviet to prevent the commissioning of any new district without the requisite sports amenities, Moscow had only a quarter of the prescribed facilities in 1978 and only one-ninth in the new districts constructed since 1960. In the period 1966–71, some 2,250 sports grounds should have been built, but only 250 (11 per cent) were actually constructed and it was increasingly difficult to accommodate the casual as well as the serious athlete.

Changing recreational pattern

Since the war all these factors affected the Soviet pattern of sport: people tended to form smaller (family) groups for recreation and holidays; there appeared to be an increasing desire to 'get away from it all' rather than to 'get together'. As Soviet writers admitted, the old production-based sports facilities were 'ill-adapted to family forms of free-time activity or to the leisure activities of the small group linked by personal and friendly rather than formal relationships'.

Public and mass sports activities gave place to individual, domestic, family and passive leisure – especially television, now reckoned to be the single most time-consuming leisure activity, taking up a third of all time so spent. It is noteworthy that in 1972 as many as 618 hours of television trans-

Yoga class in Russia during Soviet times

mission-time were devoted to sport (40 per cent of which was coverage of soccer or ice-hockey matches) in contrast with 357 hours in 1966; thus, 11–12 hours a week on television and 14 hours on radio were devoted to sport.

The impact of perestroika

Perestroika had a radical effect on all areas of sport. Efforts were made to provide far more facilities for the public to take up casual sport, to shift the emphasis from élite and functional sport to 'sport for all' and 'for fun'. Official encouragement was given to the establishment of co-operative health, fitness and sports clubs, and for state enterprises to charge fees for use of pool, gym, court and stadium. Independent clubs, including soccer fan clubs, came into being, partly to help curb the serious problem of soccer hooliganism. Previously underprivileged groups brought pressure to bear on the authorities to provide more facilities and attention: to women's sport (especially hitherto discouraged activities like weight-lifting, body-building, soccer, ice-hockey, judo and long-distance running), sport for the disabled (the USSR disabled team took part in its first Paralympics in Seoul in 1988) and rural sport.

Journalists began to talk openly about the darker side of Soviet sport: match-fixing and bribery of referees in the major spectator sports, drug-taking and corruption. What also became clear is that, paradoxically, the sporting success of the Soviet Union increasingly undermined the ideological basis of the sports supremacy policy. To many ordinary people and the new leadership, particularly under Boris Yel'tsin, élite sport, especially as represented in the Olympic Games, reflected all that was bad in the old regime's policies: politics and ideology, hypocrisy, paramilitary coercion, Russian diktat, drug abuse, the exploitation of children, and grossly distorted priorities.

Thus, the striving for world supremacy, largely through Olympic sport, for political purposes – to demonstrate (largely to the Third World) the superiority of Soviet-style communism over US-style capitalism – became utterly discredited. As world chess champion Gary Kasparov put it, 'International victories and titles won by Soviet athletes were supposed to prove yet again the advantages of socialism over capitalism . . . A world chess champion was nothing short of a political post.' What no one previously could say openly, owing to strict censorship, was that Dinamo was the sports society sponsored and financed by the security forces, that athletes devoted themselves full-time to sport and were paid accordingly, that they received bonuses for winning (including dollars), that the National Olympic Committee was a government-run institution and that its Chairman had to be a party member, or that Soviet athletes used drugs.

Soviet champions

Football (International)		Ice-Hockey		Basketball	
World Cup	Semi-final 1966	World Champions	22 times	World Champions (men)	3 times
Olympics	Winners 1956, 1988 (shared)	European Champions	28 times	World Champions (women)	6 times
		Athletics		European Champions (men)	14 times
European Champions	Winners 1960 Runners-up 1964, 1972, 1988	European Cup (men)	6 times	European Champions (women)	20 times
		European Cup (women)	3 times		
Football (Club)		**Volleyball**			
European Cup-Winners Cup	Dinamo Kiev 1975, 1986	World Champions (men)	6 times	**Swimming**	
(Winners)				European Cup (men)	10 times
(Runners-up)	Dinamo Tbilisi 1981 Dinamo Moscow 1972	World Champions (women)	5 times	European Cup (women)	1976
		European Champions (men)	11 times		
European Super-Cup (Winners)	Dinamo Kiev 1975	European Champions (women)	12 times	**Handball** World Champions (women)	1982, 1986
European Footballer of the Year	Lev Yashin, 1963 Oleg Blokhin, 1975 Igor' Belanov, 1986	**Gymnastics**		**Hockey**	
		World Champions (men)	7 times	European Club Champions (men)	Dinamo Alma Ata 1982, 1983
		World Champions (women)	10 times		

Soviet élite sport was always linked to the para-military. In fact, since the end of the Second World War, the East European (and world communist) sports system was dominated by clubs of the security forces (often in Eastern Europe also bearing the Soviet name Dinamo) and the armed forces. Most sports heroes, therefore, have officially been soldiers or police officers, guardians of public order and role models for a disciplined, obedient and patriotic citizenry. So to many people élite sport was identified with paramilitary coercion. Following the breakup of the USSR, the security forces and armed forces sports clubs were largely dismantled.

For non-Russians, who made up about half the 293 million population of the USSR, as well as the old East European communist states, there existed the irritation of having to tolerate a system tailored by Stalin to Russian conditions and imposed from without in contradiction of their own traditions. Youth organizations involved in recreation, like the YMCA and Scouts, were banned in the Baltic states after 1939; the pre-1939 Baltic state Olympic committees were disbanded and their members often persecuted (Estonia's two prewar IOC members, Friedrich Akel and Joakim Puhk, were executed by the NKVD). All this happened in spite of the long traditions and often superior standards existing in the non-Russian states. For example, Lithuania won the European basketball championships in 1937 and 1939; and Estonia competed independently in the

Right. A contestant in full cry during a competition for the loudest voice, Moscow, 1990

Olympics between 1920 and 1936, winning six gold, seven silver and nine bronze medals.

A major reason for the strong anti-élite sport sentiments may be found in the revelations in the media of the long-term state production, testing, monitoring and administering of performance-enhancing drugs for athletes as young as seven or eight. It is this mendacity by members of the old regime – loudly condemning drug abuse in the West as a typical excess of capitalism, while concealing its own involvement in a far more extensive pro-gramme of state manufacture and distribution of drugs – that has brought into question élite and Olympic sport. A television report in late 1989 revealed a document, signed in 1982 by two deputy sports ministers, prescribing anabolic steroids as part of the preparation for Soviet cross-country skiers.

The document set out a programme to test the effects of steroids and for research into ways of avoiding detection. The Soviet coach Sergey Vay-chekovsky, who was in charge of Soviet swimming from 1973 to 1982, admitted that the use of drugs was widespread: 'From 1974 all Soviet swimmers were using banned substances'. A journalist revealed that the world champion super-heavyweight (and 1992 weight-lifting senior coach) Vasily Alexeev 'took anabolic steroids with whose help he beat world records, won two Olympic and European and world championships'. Other sources have uncovered drug-taking and other forms of 'doping' in Soviet cycling, rowing, body-building, gymnastics and athletics.

To many people the worst aspect of the old system was the gap between living standards and ordinary sports and recreation facilities, on the one hand, and the money evidently lavished on élite sport and stars, on the other. Valuable resources were used to buy expensive foreign sports equipment and to pay hard-currency bonuses to athletes who won Olympic and world championship medals.

It should therefore come as no surprise to find that the leaders in the post-perestroika period are radically changing their scale of priorities. They no longer see the need to demonstrate the advantages of socialism, in so far as they are trying to distance themselves from the command economy that has failed so badly and the totalitarian system that accompanied the imposition of communism from above. The old system was none the less generally open to the talents in all sports, probably more so than in the West. It provided opportunities for women to play and succeed, if not on equal terms with men, at least on a higher plane than western women. It gave an opportunity to the many ethnic minorities and relatively small states within the

USSR to do well internationally and helped promote the pride and dignity that sporting success in the glare of world publicity can bring. Nowhere in the world had there been, since the early 1950s, such reverence for Olympism, for Olympic ritual and decorum. One practical embodiment of that was the contribution to Olympic solidarity with developing nations: to the training of Third World athletes, coaches, sports officials, medical officers and scholars at colleges and training camps. Much of this aid was free, though none of it was disinterested. It went to those states whose governments favoured socialism rather than capitalism. Further, no nation outside the Third World did more than the USSR to oppose apartheid in sport and have South Africa banned from world sports forums and arenas.

Today in the former Soviet Union, the international challenge is diluted through lack of state support; the free trade-union sports societies, as well as the ubiquitous Dinamo and armed forces clubs, have given way to private sports, health and recreation clubs; women's wrestling and boxing attract more profit than women's chess and volleyball; the various nationalities prefer their own independent teams to combined effort and success. And right across the country, sports and every other aid is at an end, Third World students having returned home as their support grants have run out. And the successor states are now competitors with other poor nations for development aid from the West. Gone now are the Soviet flag and anthem. Barcelona and Albertville in 1992 were the swan song of the unified team: the 'CCCP' (USSR) logo has been replaced by the colours and emblems of fifteen 'national' teams and Olympic committees, representing Russia, Ukraine, Belarus, Georgia, Armenia, Azerbaijan, Moldova, Kazakhstan, Uzbekistan, Tajikistan, Kyrgyzstan, Turkmenistan, Estonia, Latvia and Lithuania.
                                                    JR

SPORTS ORGANIZATIONS

Overall direction of the sports movement until 1991 was provided by the USSR Committee on Physical Culture and Sport attached to the USSR Council of Ministers. Each of the fifteen union republics had its own Sports Committee. The USSR Sports Committee was the umbrella organization for all other elements of the sports movement: the individual sports federations, the various trade-union sports societies, sports schools, coaching, research, competition, medicine and science.

Sports societies

Actual organization was in the hands of thirty-six sports societies, all but two run by the trade unions;

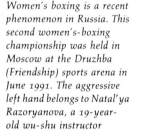

Women's boxing is a recent phenomenon in Russia. This second women's-boxing championship was held in Moscow at the Druzhba (Friendship) sports arena in June 1991. The aggressive left hand belongs to Natal'ya Razoryanova, a 19-year-old wu-shu instructor

they comprised an urban and a rural society for each of the fifteen union republics, four all-union societies (Burevestnik, representing students; Lokomotiv, representing railwaymen; Vodnik, representing river-transport employees; Spartak, representing 'white-collar' workers); and two non-trade-union societies, Dinamo and Labour Reserves, the latter representing students at technical colleges. The one major sports organization outside this framework was the Central Army Sports Club with its garrison sports clubs in many parts of the country.

Each sports society had its own rules, membership cards, badge and colours. It was financed out of trade-union dues (of the one per cent of each employed person's wages that went in union dues, a substantial portion was allocated to sport) and was responsible for building sports centres, acquiring equipment for its members and maintaining a permanent staff of coaches, instructors and medical personnel. All members and their families had the right to use the society's facilities for a nominal fee of 30 kopecks a year (in 1990, representing 0.2 per cent of the average monthly wage), to elect and be elected to its managing committee.

Competitions

Contests were held among sports societies and clubs. Each society had its own local and nation-wide championships for each sport it practised, and its teams played against teams representing other societies. There thus existed nation-wide sports leagues and cup competitions in a whole range of popular sports like soccer, ice-hockey, basket-ball and volley-ball. All the trade-union sports societies had 'teams of masters' in every major town, as did the sports clubs of the armed services and Dinamo.

Payment to athletes

Master sportsmen – who devoted all their time to training and playing a sport during their active careers as sportsmen – were paid by their sports society and the USSR Sports Committee, according to ranking, results and other factors. They were unencumbered by an external job, though not free from studies and 'social duties' and would be coached under the auspices of the society. In the case of Dinamo and the army sports clubs, the sportsmen would hold a commission but would not be expected to undertake normal military service.

As an example of payment (though details were never published for fear of accusation that Olympic rules were being contravened), a footballer in the top national league would have received a basic monthly salary from his sports society of 180 rubles. If he had a Master of Sport ranking or had represented his country, he would have received

another 30 and 40 rubles respectively, paid to him by the USSR Sports Committee. Additionally, he was likely to receive unofficial payments from various organizations associated with his sports society or town team as bonuses for team success and for playing extra matches outside the normal league and cup programme. A player's utility value might also have secured him perquisites such as a good apartment and a car.

Before departing to play in the North American National Hockey League in late 1989, the ice-hockey star Vyacheslav Fetisov declared his monthly earnings to be 450 rubles. Other stars have talked of Olympic winning bonuses: for example, Yelena Vaytsekhovskaya gained 4,000 rubles from the USSR Sports Committee for winning a gold medal at the 1976 Montreal Olympics. The Chairman of the USSR Sports Committee, Marat Gramov, admitted just before the 1988 Seoul Olympics that each Soviet medal-winner would receive 12,000 rubles for a gold medal, 6,000 for a silver and 4,000 for a bronze medal (average monthly income then being 360 rubles). Since the Soviet team won 55 gold medals and 132 medals overall, it must have cost the Sports Committee a million rubles in bonuses alone.

The bulk of foreign earnings of Soviet players abroad has traditionally been taken by the Sports Committee – so much so that the tennis champion Andrey Chesnokov, who won $150,000 for winning the Antwerp Diamond Racket tournament in late 1988, complained that he was not left enough money to eat properly (a mere $25 a day). After a revolt by several top tennis players in 1989, they were permitted to retain up to $1,000 of their winnings.

Spartakiads

The trade unions were directly responsible for organizing competitions within their own sports

Interest in tennis grew in the former Soviet Union during the post-Stalin period and its popularity continues to expand in Russia. Many prominent politicians, including President Yel'tsin, are among the tennis enthusiasts. Few Russian professional players have reached the highest world standards, but one of the most successful has been Natal'ya Zvereva, pictured right

societies and on a nation-wide basis, including the spartakiads. More recently, the word 'spartakiad' was used to denote tournaments for schools, farms, factories, Pioneer camps, and local amateur groups. The main event, however, was the Spartakiad of the Peoples of the USSR, modelled on the Olympic programme and held over the two years preceding each Olympic Games. How important this sports festival was for popularizing sport may be judged from the numbers of people said to participate. Some 23 million took part in the First Summer Spartakiad in 1956, with 9,000 contesting the finals in twenty-one sports. The Sixth Spartakiad, held over 1975 and 1976, had become so massive that for the first time the finals had to be held in all fifteen republican capitals and twelve other major cities; some 55 million people are said to have competed, with 7,094 contesting the finals in twenty-seven sports. Once the period of perestroika began in 1985, the Spartakiads were no longer held.

National fitness programme

The two interlinked elements that underlay the whole sports system were the GTO national fitness programme and the uniform rankings system for individual sports. Both were instituted in the early 1930s and both were intended to serve the twin aims of *massovost'* (mass participation) and *masterstvo* (proficiency). While the GTO set targets for all-round ability in a number of sports and knowledge of the rudiments of hygiene and first aid (for which gold and silver badges were awarded), the rankings system contained a whole set of qualifying standards and titles in individual sports, intended to stimulate the best performers.

It was through the GTO that most Soviet people took part in sport and it was regarded as the foundation of the sports system. The programme (which was revised every ten years on average) had five stages by age which all necessitated a certain minimum performance in running, jumping, throwing, shooting, skiing and gymnastics. Older people could compete only with a doctor's permission. GTO planning quotas were set for every club, society, region and school, and tests were held throughout the year. The main concern of most sports clubs was, in fact, to see that their members obtained their GTO badges. There seems little doubt that most young people were caught up in this fitness campaign: in the decade 1970–80, an estimated average of 18 million people qualified annually for a badge.

The GTO had as its stated aim to make regular participation in sport a permanent feature of the Soviet way of life. The motives behind the programme were fourfold: first, to attract children into sport at an early age, to ensure their later participation and to provide a pool of early talent to develop international success; second, to provide direct military training: a civil-defence test and gas-mask training were to be found at every stage, and rifle-shooting at three stages; the element of military preparation was especially evident for the 16–18 age-group, many of whom would therefore enter the armed forces with some training behind them; third, to cut down absenteeism from work by making workers physically and mentally more alert; and fourth, to channel the zest and energy of young people into healthy recreation.

The ranking system

The sports ranking system was intended to stimulate the best athletes to aim for certain set standards in a particular sport and to help coaches to select promising sportsmen to train with specific targets in mind. A whole complex of qualifying standards existed for the eighty officially-registered sports. These were updated every four years to coincide with the Olympic cycle.

The two top titles (Master of Sport of the USSR, International Class, and Master of Sport of the USSR) were honorary and for life. The only higher award to which an outstanding and internationally-successful athlete might have aspired was Merited Master of Sport of the USSR, but this was a state honorific decoration outside the classification system (like Merited Artist or Merited Teacher of the USSR). In chess and draughts (checkers), the title Grandmaster

The outstanding Soviet pole-vaulter, Sergey Bubka, in action

of the USSR was the equivalent of Master of Sport of the USSR, International Class for other sports. In addition, the title Master of Folk Sport existed for a variety of folk games and sports.

Besides these titles and decorations, the top Soviet sportsmen, coaches and officials were regularly included in the country's 'honours list' up to 1976, when the custom virtually ceased. After the Montreal Olympic Games in 1976, for example, a total of 347 Olympic athletes, coaches and officials received awards, ranging from the supreme honour – the Order of Lenin – to the Order of the Red Banner of Labour. The recipients of the Order of Lenin were four athletes – Ludmilla Turishcheva (b.1952), Nikolay Andriyanov (b.1952), Levan Tediashvili (b.1948) and Ivan Yarygin (b.1950) (two gymnasts and two wrestlers) – three coaches and the Sports Committee chairman Sergey Pavlov (b.1929).

The two top titles were awarded mainly on the basis of international success, but athletes had first to meet all the rankings standards for their sport. Sports rankings one to three were awarded for results achieved in official Soviet competition (all-union championships, spartakiads, cups) and were valid for one or two years only, after which they either lapsed or had to be renewed. Alternatively, athletes could try for a higher ranking. To obtain a second or third ranking, athletes had also to satisfy the requirements of the GTO programme for their particular age category. The qualifying standards for each category were high and were regularly revised to keep pace with changing world standards. Junior rankings were awarded to athletes under eighteen years of age who had also met the qualifying standards of the appropriate GTO programme for their age.

The physical token of having gained one of the titles was a badge and a certificate awarded by the USSR Sports Committee, plus a financial award (30 rubles a month in the case of a Master of Sport). Ranked sportsmen received a badge from the sports society to which they belonged. All such athletes had the right to take part in official competitions and to receive preference in admission to sports schools and colleges of physical education. Along with these rights, however, went certain duties: to conduct oneself in accordance with sporting ethics; to pass on one's expertise and experience to others; to compete on behalf of one's group or club; to improve one's political and cultural standards; to accept constant medical supervision.

Any violation of these obligations might have resulted in losing the ranking or title – a not-infrequent occurrence. In soccer, several players were deprived of their awards for receiving under-cover payments or for behaving badly in public or during matches. Leading athletes were expected to be models of good behaviour at all times.

Finance and facilities

All sports committees throughout the country (each administrative region had its own) received cash from the state budget to finance their work. In 1978 state budgetary allocations to sport and health amounted to 12,600 million rubles. This sum was a very small part (0.03 per cent) of the state budget and represented exactly the same proportion as in 1924. Subsequent state budget allocations were roughly the same. However, the sports committees received finance from the profits of the sports equipment and amenities construction organization, *Glavsportprom*, the state sport publishing agency, *Sovetsky sport*, and the various commercial enterprises and sports events they ran.

All state and public organizations which employed labour contributed to the state social insurance fund in the proportion of 4–9 per cent of their wage funds, depending on the branch of the economy. Part of this social insurance fund was used for sport. It was estimated that over half of all sports amenities built in 1978 were financed out of the funds of state enterprises and government departments.

The trade unions assigned sums of money out of membership dues and other income to their sports societies and clubs. In 1986 they allotted 640 million rubles to sport, about a fifth of their total funds.

An ice sports centre in Medeo, near Alma Ata (now Almaty), Kazakhstan

It has to be noted that, like the country's industrialization in general, facilities for sport were quite recently at an extremely primitive level (many still are), and that much was destroyed in the war. In just one decade (1960–70) the number of stadiums, soccer-pitches, gymnasiums and tennis-courts roughly trebled; indoor swimming-pools, ski-jumps and indoor athletics stadiums grew from virtually nothing to over 1,000, nearly 100 and 50 respectively. By 1986 the country had a total of 3,750 sports centres, 71,000 gymnasiums, 2,500 swimming-pools, 145,000 soccer-pitches and 850,000 playing-fields.

The 1980 Moscow Olympics generated a wave of construction of world-class facilities for the full range of sports, and it was only thereafter that the USSR had even a few amenities comparable to those in the rest of the developed world. Even today, not only for mass participation but also for teams in the top leagues, only a relatively small number of soccer pitches are available; and the quality of playing surfaces in most stadiums is well below world standards. There were in 1989 only seven stadiums with a crowd capacity of over 50,000 in the entire Soviet Union. By comparison, California alone had nine such stadiums. In the same year there were only four indoor arenas in the USSR that could seat more than 10,000 people. Two of these were constructed in the 1980s and are vast – the indoor Olympic Stadium in Moscow (35,000–40,000) and the Lenin Concert and Sport Complex in Leningrad (21,000–25,000). Until these two ultra-modern facilities were built, the largest arenas in the former Soviet Union were the Palaces of Sport in Moscow (12,000–14,000) and in Tbilisi (10,000). Again, by contrast, California had nine such facilities. Most arenas in the successor states other than Russia are quite small. The largest building outside Russia for ice hockey is in Kiev (6,700 capacity). The arena of the

Sports committees, societies and clubs also received income from renting out and using sports facilities and from making, lending and selling equipment. Dinamo was in the fortunate position of being the biggest manufacturer of sports equipment in the country, operating over fifty plants and many retail sports shops; most of the 22 million rubles it spent on sport in 1986 came from its own business enterprises.

One means by which the government was able to raise money for sport was by sponsoring sports lotteries. This began in 1964 as one method of helping to finance the Soviet Olympic team's attendance at the Tokyo Games. From 1970 monthly lotteries were run to obtain money for sports amenities. Three different monthly lotteries were operating simultaneously in the four years up to the 1980 Olympics, called 'Sportloto', 'Sportloto-2' and 'Sprint'. In each lottery half the revenue from ticket sales went to sport, and half to prizes ranging from saloon cars to sports equipment.

Children exercising at the unusual Sambo-70 sports school attended by males aged ten to fifty

One of the most famous of all Soviet gymnasts, Ol'ga Korbut (b. 1955). Her daring innovations had a great impact on women's gymnastics throughout the world, and she won two gold and two silver medals at the 1972 Olympics

top Zhalgiris basketball team of Kaunas in Lithuania holds only 4,500. Similarly, by contrast with the USSR's 102 artificial skating rinks in 1989, Canada had 10,000, the USA 1,500 and Sweden 343; by contrast with the USSR's 2,500 swimming pools, the USA had over a million.

Much depended on local initiative and the inclination (and ability) of factories, farms, city councils or republics to allocate money for sports purposes; some are much better equipped than others. On the whole, however, the European, more industrialized republics were better off in sports facilities than were Turkmenia, Kyrgyzstan and Tajikistan – a gap which the independent states will find difficult to close.

Sports schools

All schoolchildren and students in the Soviet Union were expected to reach certain standards in physical education and sport, and the institutions themselves had to meet official targets. Young people who wished to pursue a sport seriously after school hours could do so in one of several specialized sports establishments. At the base of the pyramid was the children's and young people's sports school which young people could attend outside their normal

school hours (they were, in fact, 'clubs' in the western sense). There were over 5,525 such schools with a membership of two million children in 1990. Attempts were made to spread the net as wide as possible both to catch potential talent and to distribute facilities fairly evenly between the republics. Children were normally considered for these schools on the recommendation of their school physical education teacher or at the request of their parents. Attendance and coaching were free, entry age depended upon the sport – for swimming and gymnastics, seven or eight years (or earlier), for cycling and speed-skating, thirteen to fourteen years. Moscow Dinamo had a gymnastics section for four- to six-year-olds, and the Minsk Dinamo 'soccer nursery' took young boys aged six or seven years. Coaching was usually intensive and classes were often long and frequent; for example, eleven- to thirteen-year-olds might attend three evenings a week for two-hour sessions; those working for their Master of Sport ranking might attend four or five.

Originally it was intended for the sports schools to cultivate up to ten sports, but most concentrated on no more than three, some only on a single sport; these were known as specialist children's and young people's sports schools, and all leading football (soccer) and ice-hockey clubs ran their own. They were a vital key to Soviet sporting success, especially in the Olympics; in fact, of the thirty-seven sports pursued in the schools in 1990, only four were outside the Olympic programme: acrobatics, chess, handball and table-tennis. The most popular were athletics, basketball, gymnastics, volleyball, swimming and skiing.

Finance and administration were provided through the local education authorities (over 50 per cent of schools), the trade-union sports societies, and the big sports clubs run by Dinamo and the armed forces.

Full-time 'sport-oriented' day-schools combined a normal school curriculum with sports training, on the model of 'foreign-language-oriented' schools; they took children aged seven upwards from the neighbouring catchment area and offered superior facilities.

The sports proficiency schools (sixteen- to eighteen-year-olds) and higher sports proficiency schools (eighteen years and over) provided both extra-curricular training for schoolchildren and students and short-term vacation courses.

In 1967 a new sports society for young people, *Yunost'* was set up to co-ordinate the activities of all these schools and to ensure that minimum standards were established for facilities, coaches, age and other entrance qualifications. At the apex of the pyramid were the sports boarding-schools of which there were twenty-six in 1979. The USSR opened its first boarding-school on an experimental basis in Tashkent in 1962, modelled on similar schools found in the GDR since 1949. Others followed in each of the fifteen union republics, then in some provincial centres, and in 1970 a special government resolution set an official seal of approval on their existence. Only sports in the Olympic programme were pursued; like the mathematical, musical and other special schools they adhered to the standard Soviet curriculum but they had an additional study load in sports theory and practice. Pupils were accepted from between seven and twelve years, and stayed on until eighteen – a year longer than at normal day-schools; they were served by the best coaches and amenities, nurtured on a special diet, kept constantly under the supervision of doctors and sports instructors, and stimulated by mutual interest and keen enthusiasm. By the time of the USSR's dissolution in late 1991, there were a total of forty sports boarding schools – far more than in any other country.   JR

INTERNATIONAL SPORT

Soviet participation in international sport before the war falls roughly into three periods: 1917–28, when the Soviet authorities pursued a policy of promoting world revolution and proletarian internationalism; 1929–39, when the policy changed towards strengthening the USSR as a major state; 1939–41, when the Soviet leaders developed relations with the Axis powers.

On the assumption that world revolution was not far distant and that, until then, the world would be split irreconcilably into two hostile camps, the Soviet authorities after 1917 at first ignored 'bourgeois' sports organizations, refused to affiliate to their international federations and boycotted most of their competitions. The Olympic Games in particular were characterized as designed 'to deflect the workers from the class struggle while training them for new imperialist wars'.

Initially then, excursions beyond Soviet borders were almost entirely confined to competing against foreign workers' teams, such as the Finnish Labour Team (TUL), and the French communist trade-union (CFGT) team. As the 1920s wore on, the need to coexist (especially with the USSR's neighbours), a desire to compete against the world's best teams and the consideration that the 'bourgeoisie' in certain backward states were playing a progressive role brought some limited contacts.

For the most part, however, as long as the USSR remained isolated and weak internationally, foreign sports relations were restricted to workers' sports organizations and reflected the policy of the Com-

munist International (Comintern). Soviet foreign sports policy was, in fact, largely identical with and conducted through the International Association of Red Sports and Gymnastics Organizations, better known as Red Sport International (RSI). The RSI was formed at the First International Congress of representatives of revolutionary workers' sports organizations in July 1921. The founders were workers' sports organizations from eight countries: Czechoslovakia, Finland, France, Germany, Hungary, Italy, the USSR and Sweden (by 1924, it included Norway, Uruguay and the USA). After 1928 the former policy changed both in relation to 'bourgeois' states and towards the social democratic countries. As a result, sports ties developed with the first, but were curtailed with the second. Although the USSR did not try to affiliate to international sports federations, it did send its best sportsmen abroad to compete against the world's best.

When war broke out in Europe and the German-Soviet Non-Aggression Pact was signed, Soviet sports contacts were confined to the Axis powers. In fact, more sports contests took place between Soviet and German sportsmen during 1940 than between the sportsmen of the USSR and all 'bourgeois' states put together in all the years since 1917: some 250 German athletes competed in the USSR and 175 Soviet athletes in Germany between September 1939 and the end of 1940.

Immediately after the war, Soviet sports associations affiliated to nearly all the major international

Right. Sambo wrestling in Russia. The picture was taken at the fourteenth world championships held in the Lenin stadium in Moscow in December 1990. The photograph is from the final in the juniors over 100 kilograms class. Orgibold (left) from Mongolia defeated Fujita of Japan

federations and Soviet athletes were competing regularly at home and abroad against foreign 'bourgeois' opposition. Soviet sport became an instrument of foreign policy, both to advertise the advantages of Soviet-style socialism among communist states and to influence Third World countries through the provision of instructors and assistance in building sports amenities.

Between 1946 and 1958 the USSR joined thirty international federations and by 1975, forty-eight, thereby embracing nearly all the major world sports. Furthermore, 236 Soviet officials held posts in international sports organizations in 1978.

Not only did affiliations take place, but Soviet athletes quickly established a world dominance, often on their début in world sport. In 1948 Mikhail Botvinnik (b.1911) won the world chess title and, in 1949, Lyudmilla Rudenko (b.1904) won the women's world chess title; both titles were to be long held by the USSR with the exception of 1972–74 when the men's title was held by Bobby Fischer of the USA. In 1945 Moscow Dinamo football team came to Britain and played four matches without defeat against leading British clubs. In weight-lifting, wrestling, volley-ball and ice-hockey, Soviet teams established a supremacy they subsequently maintained.   JR

THE OLYMPIC GAMES

Russia was a founding member of the modern Olympic movement and Russian athletes first participated in the Olympic Games in 1908 – the Fourth Olympics, held in London. A team of five contestants, sponsored by voluntary contributions, did surprisingly well, winning a gold medal in figure-skating and two silvers in wrestling, taking fourteenth place overall out of twenty-two nations. For the next Olympics, held in Stockholm in 1912, the Russian sports societies were prepared to sponsor a much larger contingent. The government, appreciating the prestige value at home of sports success, set up a Russian Olympic Committee (ROC) headed by Baron F. Meyendorf. With generous government backing and organization, a team of 169 athletes (half of them army officers) gathered to take part in fifteen sports in the Olympic programme. In fact, half the group failed to reach Stockholm because they missed the boat and Russia ultimately shared a disappointing fifteenth place with Austria, out of twenty-eight countries, and won few medals (in wrestling, gymnastics, shooting and yachting).

Although it was to be another forty years before Russia was to compete again in the Olympics, the International Olympic Committee (IOC) continued to recognize the old Russian Olympic Committee

for several years after 1917, and such ROC notables as Prince Urusov, Count Ribopierre, Baron Villebrand and General Butovsky all served on the IOC in the period before the Second World War.

Despite initial post-Second World War successes, the USSR moved cautiously into Olympic competition. Only in April 1951 was a Soviet Olympic Committee formed and, in May, accepted by the IOC. The USSR made its Olympic début at the fifteenth Summer Olympic Games, held in Helsinki in 1952. Soviet athletes contested all events in the programme with the exception of field hockey and, although they gained fewer gold medals than the USA (22:40), they gained more silver (30:19) and bronze (19:17) and tied with the USA in points allotted for the first six places (according to the system used in the *Olympic Bulletin*).

The USSR took no part in the 1952 Winter Olympics and made its winter début only in 1956 at Cortina d'Ampezzo in Italy. There it amassed most medals and points, winning gold medals in speed-skating, skiing and ice-hockey.

From the débuts in 1952 and 1956 up to 1988, the USSR 'won' every Olympic Games with the sole exception of 1968, when it came second to Norway in winter and second to the USA in summer, and the winter Games of 1980 and 1984, when it was placed second to East Germany. It also provided the most versatile as well as the most successful performance in the Olympics: at the 1988 Seoul Olympics, Soviet athletes won medals in all sports,

OLYMPIC GAMES PERFORMANCE, 1952–92

Year	Summer Games				Nearest rival		Winter Games				Nearest rival	
	gold medals	medal total	points[a]	position	medals	points[a]	gold medals	medal total	points[a]	position	medals	points[a]
1952[b]	22	71	494	1	76	494[c]	—	—	—	—	—	—
1956	37	98	624.5	1	74	498[c]	7	16	103	1	11	66.5[d]
1960	43	103	683	1	71	463.5[c]	7	21	146.5	1	7	62.5[e]
1964	30	96	608.3	1	90	581.8[c]	11	25	183	1	15	89.3[f]
1968	29	91	591.5	1	106	709[c]	5	13	92	2	14	103[f]
1972	50	99	665.5	1	93	636.5[c]	8	16	120	1	14	83[g]
1976	47	125	788.5	1	90	636.5[g]	13	27	201	1	19	138[g]
1980	80	195	1476	1	121	779[g]	10	22	148	2	23	155[g]
1984[h]	—	—	—	—	—	—	6	25	152	2	24	171[g]
1988	55	132	811	1	102	703[g]	12	32	196	1	23	155[g]
1992[i]	45	152	768	1	108	717[c]	7	22	135	2	28	179[j]

[a]*Olympic Bulletin* points allocation: seven points for first place, five for second and so on down to one point for sixth place
[b]No USSR participation in Winter Games   [c]USA   [d]Austria   [e]Sweden   [f]Norway
[g]East Germany   [h]No USSR participation in Summer Games   [i]'Unified Team' (USSR minus Latvia, Lithuania, Estonia and Georgia)   [j]Germany

coming first in ten sports, second in seven, and third in six; of the 464 Soviet athletes competing, as many as 288 won medals, with 130 taking gold. At the last Olympics (Barcelona, 1992) a joint team from the former Soviet Union won 112 medals, including 45 gold – fewer than at Seoul, but well ahead of its closest rival, the USA. The three Baltic states competed independently; Estonia and Lithuania both won one gold and one bronze medal, Latvia two silver and one bronze. All these results suggested that the USSR had gone a considerable way

towards achieving its aim of world supremacy in Olympic sports. Discussing earlier successes, pre-perestroika, Soviet writers left no doubt that they saw it as a victory for the communist system generally.

The Moscow Olympics, 1980
The twenty-second Olympic Games were held in Moscow from 19 July to 3 August 1980. Yachting events were held in Tallinn, and soccer preliminaries in Kiev, Minsk and Leningrad. This was the only

The 1992 Winter Olympics. The 'Unified Team' of the former USSR (minus the three Baltic states and Georgia) are here playing one of their major ice hockey rivals, Czechoslovakia

time in modern Olympic history that a communist country had staged the summer Olympics. Despite a partial boycott led by the USA over the USSR's invasion of Afghanistan, a total of sixty-eight nations attended the Games (seventy-two attended in Montreal, 1976). In retaliation for the US-led boycott of Moscow, the USSR and most other Warsaw Pact states boycotted the 1984 Summer Olympics held in Los Angeles.   JR

CHESS

The special affinity between the game of chess and the peoples of Russia and the Soviet Union is a complex phenomenon. In part it can be regarded as a social reality. The sheer popularity of the game, stimulated by systematic use of state patronage from the 1920s onwards, and the competitive success of leading Russian players, especially since 1945, come into this category. But Soviet chess was also an ideological construct, an evolving set of ideas linking the qualities of the game with the forces supposedly most characteristic and beneficial in Soviet culture. Nourished on practical success, this ideology in turn provided the rationale for continued state sponsorship from the 1920s to the 1980s, constraining Soviet chess writers to describe both the game and their own approach to it in politically correct terms. The resultant theory of the 'Soviet school of chess', already riven by internal contradictions in the 1970s and 1980s, could hardly be expected to survive the fragmentation of the Soviet Union, whatever the practical fortunes of the game.

Despite this, the legacy of chess remains significant. Because the chess movement was able to claim relatively early successes, it frequently served as a model, in both organization and ideology, for other sports and cultural activities. Chess was chosen as a means of advancing some of the most characteristic preoccupations of modern (and earlier) Russian rulers: the promotion of mass education, incentives for individual self-improvement, the demonstration of ability to compete successfully with the West. Many other states have pursued a similar agenda of modernization in the twentieth century, but in Russia uniquely chess was assigned a role of some importance as a catalyst in the process of change.

Early history
Most historians are agreed that chess was invented in northern India and cannot be documented before about 600 AD, but this did not prevent Soviet archaeologists from claiming that animal figurines of the second century AD excavated in Uzbekistan in 1972, were chess pieces. Doubt attaches even to other finds attributed to the eleventh and twelfth centuries,

though it is perfectly possible that chess had reached Russia by then, spreading directly from India through Central Asia or, as the later Russian terminology would suggest, through Persia. The earliest certain references to chess in Russian texts date from the thirteenth century, the first of a long series of ecclesiastical bans on it. Despite these, anecdotal references by western travellers in the sixteenth and seventeenth centuries suggest that chess was then quite popular, in noble circles at least.

That popularity continued into the eighteenth and nineteenth centuries, but with one significant change. The rules of chess had undergone substantial alteration in Western Europe around the year 1500 and it was the modern form which now began to establish itself in Russia. The first printed books on chess in Russian, those of I. Butrimov (1821) and A.D. Petrov (1824), perfectly reflect this development, being heavily based on the contemporary western literature. Such issues were even more apparent in the Asiatic territories attached to the Russian Empire, all of which possessed their own native forms of the game dating back at least to the Mongol period. The final displacement of these native variants by standardized modern chess was in fact one of the achievements of the Soviet regime after 1920. A nationalist emphasis on the antiquity and continuous presence of chess in Russia is therefore one-sided. The development of chess also exemplifies another abiding feature of Russian history, both before and after 1917: tension between native cultural forms and those imposed by western-influenced ruling élites.

The first international chess tournament took place in London in 1851, but such events were held in Russia, at St Petersburg, only in 1895–96, 1909 and 1914. M.I. Chigorin (1850–1908), the leading Russian player of the period, contested two matches for the World Championship in 1889 and 1892 but competitive chess at this level was sustained by a relatively small number of wealthy patrons, despite the later Soviet emphasis on the popularity of the game among intellectuals and political radicals in the tsarist period. Many Russian players who aspired to develop their careers spent much of their time abroad, where tournaments and patronage were more widely diffused. Leading figures, notably the future world champion A.A. Alekhin (1892–1946), then naturally emigrated, after 1917 if not before. Though it is sometimes said that there were twenty-two 'Russian' chess masters by 1914, this figure conveys an inflated impression of the progress made in Russia itself.

1920–1945
The initial decision of Soviet leaders after 1920 to promote chess and treat it as more than a bourgeois

diversion is not easy to explain. However, the role of A.F. Il'in-Zhenevsky (1894–1941), an influential Bolshevik and keen chess player, was crucial. Il'in used the military training organization (*Vsevobuch*) of which he was head to recruit leading players for a Russian chess championship in 1920. He then initiated a campaign to persuade the authorities of the value of chess in promoting first military training, and then literacy and social discipline generally. Success was achieved by 1924 with the creation of the All-Soviet Chess Section; chess organization was henceforth to be controlled by this state body, headed by the leading political figure N.V. Krylenko (1885–1938), who also edited its magazine *64*. Throughout the 1920s and the early 1930s the key arguments for the promotion of chess were those of internal policy. The Chess Section claimed increases in the number of registered players, from 24,000 in 1924 to 150,000 in 1929, and to 500,000 in 1934. It continually reported on its successes in mass education, and on the role of chess in politicizing factories and trade unions during the period of the First Five-year Plan (1928–1932). More elaborate theories were put forward to justify all this, by writers such as the historian M.S. Kogan and the three Soviet psychologists who reported on the qualities of chess in 1926, laying stress on its dialectical nature and close correspondences with Marxist-Leninist thought.

Although the number of recognized masters grew to almost fifty by 1939, few of them had a chance to experience international competition. The world's leading players did attend a tournament in Moscow in 1925, but the Russian winner Ye.D. Bogolyubov (1889–1952) continued to live in exile, like Alekhin, while Soviet players had only limited success. The result was that future experiments of this kind were postponed into the mid-1930s. Nor would the Soviet authorities have anything to do with the Inter-

national Chess Federation (FIDE) founded in Paris in 1924. This approach only began to change with the successes of the leading Soviet master M.M. Botvinnik who established himself in several tournaments held in 1935–36, two of them in Moscow, as one of the strongest players in the world. His status as a potential world championship contender encouraged Soviet leaders to maintain chess events even during the subsequent war years, though in his later memoirs *Achieving the Aim* (1978), Botvinnik made much of the struggles he had to conduct within the system to bring this about.

1945–1985

The accumulated success of Soviet chess training burst upon the rest of the world after the war, with crushing victories over the USA, by 15 : 4 in a 1945 radio match, and by 12 : 7 in a return match played in Moscow. Not just Botvinnik and the Estonian Paul Keres (1916–75), but younger players such as V.V. Smyslov (b.1921), Ye.I. Boleslavsky (1919–77) and D.I. Bronstein (b.1924) were now also of world class. Stimulated by these results, and by the opportunity arising from the death of the reigning world champion Alekhin in 1946, the Soviet chess authorities opted to join FIDE in 1947 and to participate in the 1948 World Championship Tournament, which was duly won by Botvinnik. Botvinnik then retained the title until 1963, ceding it only briefly to Smyslov in 1957–58 and the Latvian M.N. Tal' (1936–92) in 1960–61. His successors T.V. Petrosyan (1929–84), from 1963 to 1969, and B.V. Spassky (b.1937), from 1969 to 1972, were also Soviet players. USSR teams also won every biennial 'Olympiad' team tournament from 1952 until 1976.

Such a degree of dominance over a widely pursued competitive activity is striking. Limited western investment in chess, as compared with other sports, can only be part of the explanation. The severest competition in these years came from Eastern European countries who had imitated Soviet techniques of training and sponsorship. It cannot be doubted that chess had now acquired an unprecedented role in Russian social and cultural life. The number of officially registered players neared 2 million by 1960 and passed 4 million by 1977. The popular book by A.A. Kotov and M.M. Yudovich, *The Soviet School of Chess* (1951 and subsequent editions) became the orthodox account, tracing success from the initial inspiration of Chigorin, through the achievements of Botvinnik, and others, but ultimately relating it to the dawning cultural superiority of the Soviet Union in all fields.

Yet there were problems. Complaints were voiced from the 1950s onwards that leading players neglected educational work in favour of pursuing their careers. The Soviet Chess Federation had become a

Gary Kasparov displaying his virtuoso talents in a simultaneous chess contest against a large number of young opponents

Anatoly Karpov (left), who became a chess master at fourteen and international grandmaster at nineteen, held the world chess championship for ten years until Gary Kasparov (right) wrested the title from him in 1985. Kasparov, twelve years Karpov's junior, was only twenty-two when he became world champion. In the early 1990s he continued to maintain his pre-eminence. The rivals are seen here in the United States in October 1990 before their world tournament. Mayor Dinkins of New York is in the centre

large patronage organization dispensing privileges including foreign travel to its favoured members, and controlled by influential cliques of party figures. In contrast to the 1920s, the justification was now provided largely by the prestige of international victories, which left the whole system highly vulnerable when the world championship was lost to the American Robert (Bobby) Fischer in 1972, with a consequent upsurge of interest in chess in the West. Internal tensions in Soviet chess were also signalled by a growing trickle of emigration, notably the defection in 1976 of V.L. Korchnoy (b.1931), who contested matches for the world championship in 1978 and 1981. The mainstay of the system in these years, as many leading players of the post-war generation neared retirement, was A.Ye. Karpov (b.1951) who retained the world title from 1975 to 1985, holding off Korchnoy's challenge and being rewarded (like Botvinnik and Smyslov before him) with the Order of Lenin.

Since 1985

The shifts in chess brought about by reform and fragmentation since 1985 constitute an interesting case study of political change in an area of social life long held up as characteristically Soviet. As in other spheres, the new forces worked in tandem with existing internal tensions. The world championship passed in 1985 to a younger player, G.K. Kasparov (b.1963), who has since retained the title in three further matches (1986, 1987, 1990). But Kasparov soon made accusations, which he repeated in *Child of Change* (1987) that he had only escaped a plot to disqualify him in 1985 through a personal approach to the future Politburo member A.N. Yakovlev. Without Gorbachev's accession to power and the reform Plenum of April 1985, a political outsider like himself would never have been given a fair chance. Like Botvinnik and Korchnoy before him, Kasparov in his autobiographical writing adopted the characteristic stance of the individual battling against injustice in the system. The difference is that whereas Botvinnik implied that Soviet society was ultimately benevolent, and true merit would be acknowledged, Korchnoy's book took the opposite view. Kasparov himself moved on from his praise for Gorbachev and hopes for the future in 1987 to overt criticism as disorder grew in his native republic of Azerbaijan; in 1989 he was briefly associated with N.I. Travkin's Democratic Party. In 1989 Karpov became a member of the Congress of People's Deputies of the USSR.

Chess players continue to have a role as public figures, if only because they continue to be successful, leading the way in the sporting representation of the newly independent states. Thirteen former Soviet republics participated in the international Chess Olympiad of June 1992 and six of them (Russia, Uzbekistan, Armenia, Latvia, Georgia, Ukraine) finished in the top ten (out of 112), Kasparov's Russian team taking the gold medal. Chess continues to be popular in most parts of the former Soviet Union, though exaggerated claims for its standing are currently being put to the test, as organizations are disrupted, subsidies cease to be paid, and books and magazines cannot be printed for lack of paper. If the promotion of chess in the Soviet Union since the 1920s has been a fascinating experiment, it remains an incomplete one.　RE

The armed forces

THE IMPERIAL ARMED FORCES

The army

Such military successes as Russia scored in the seventeenth century must be put down to the enfeeblement and disarray of its main adversary, Poland, rather than to the effectiveness of its own motley armies. At the end of the century, out of 200,000 men who could be put into the field perhaps 20,000 were useful soldiers. The creation of an efficient regular army was made necessary by the territorial ambitions of Peter the Great. He gave an indication of his intentions in 1687, when he was fifteen, by forming from among his 'play troops' the two élite units which later became the Preobrazhensky and the Semenovsky Guards Regiments. But the establishment of a large standing army organized, uniformed, armed, equipped, trained and provisioned in imitation of the best 'German' (West European) models began in 1699, and was accelerated by Peter's discomfiture at the hands of the boy-king Charles XII of Sweden at Narva in 1700.

Two enactments (1699 and 1705) made all males of the tax-paying classes (that is, all except the gentry) liable to conscription for life. (The obligation of the gentry to serve the state either in the armed forces or in administration, which Peter generalized and tried ruthlessly to enforce, was gradually relaxed by his successors and abolished in 1762.) The duration of conscript service was reduced to twenty-five years in 1793, twenty in 1834 and twelve in 1855. Selection of recruits was left to their communities, but on private estates landowners rather than peasant communes made the choice, and often abused this power for punitive or mercenary purposes. The custom of avoiding service by purchasing a voluntary substitute was established early, and legalized from the 1840s.

The general overhaul of Russia's antiquated institutions after the Crimean War produced, as part of the programme of 'Great Reforms', the Military Reform of 1874. Its author, General D.A. Milyutin (1816–1912), among other things introduced universal conscription. Males of all classes became liable to serve at twenty-one, and about a quarter of each

annual contingent was picked by lot to serve for six or seven years with the colours followed by nine or eight in the reserve. The privileged now were not the gentry as a class, but the educated: a university student was required to serve no more than six months.

From Peter's time onwards Russia maintained a larger army in peacetime than any other European country. Its size in the eighteenth and for much of the nineteenth century must be explained in part by its role in internal security, and particularly in suppressing peasant disorders. In the later years of the empire Russia (and at times its allies) hoped that sheer numbers would compensate for chronic failure, in spite of strenuous efforts, to keep abreast of the other great powers in military technology. At the end of the nineteenth century Russia had 850,000 men under arms, and in 1914 was able to mobilize 6,600,000 in a matter of months.

The great successes of the Imperial Army were won in the eighteenth and early nineteenth century – Peter's Great Northern War, the humiliation of Prussia in the Seven Years War, Catherine the Great's Turkish wars, the Russian contribution to the demolition of Napoleon. Thereafter, Russia's military history was a tale of disasters (the Crimea, the war with Japan of 1904–05, the First World War), interspersed by minor successes too hard won (the war with Turkey, 1877–78). Russia owed its great victories not only to the legendary endurance and courage of its common soldiers, and to an occasional genius such as A.V. Suvorov (1729–1800) among its generals, but to its success in the first period in keeping up with and adapting western organizational and training methods and western weaponry. Explanations for the disasters of 1854–55, 1904–05 and 1914–17 must include economic and technical backwardness, the inadequacies of the internal transport system, and administrative failures which greatly aggravated difficulties of supply.

The navy

Russia had no navy before Peter the Great: even attempts to police the lower waters of the Volga with foreign-built vessels had failed ingloriously. The first (and archetypal) Russian naval success was the capture of Azov in 1696: Peter's new fleet, operating in support of land forces, closed the ring around the fortress from the sea. Vessels built in

Previous spread.
Dismantling a tank at a military hardware factory, 1993. The aim is to adapt vehicles for civilian use under the military conversion programme

Nicholas II (centre), pictured with his retinue at the Tsar's headquarters in Mogilev in 1916

newly conquered Baltic ports played a major part in Russia's triumph in the Great Northern War, and it was the seaborne invasion of the Swedish mainland in 1719 which convinced western Europe that Russia had firmly established itself as a formidable military power. Although naval ships took a notable part in geographical explorations, the navy's role throughout the imperial period was largely confined to defence of Russia's shores and support of land-based operations in the Baltic and the Black Sea. As a rule, Russia took naval action further from base – in the Mediterranean in 1770 (Battle of Chesme and blockade of the Dardanelles) and in 1827 (Navarino) – only when other great powers were sympathetic and helpful. Famous admirals included F.F. Ushakov (1743–1818), P.S. Nakhimov (1803–55) and S.O. Makarov (1848–1904). Imperial Russia's most grandiose naval enterprise was also its most disastrous: the fleet under Admiral Z.P. Rozhdestvensky (1848–1909), after a voyage from the Baltic of over seven months, was smashed by the Japanese off Tsushima in May 1905, and only three out of thirty-eight vessels limped home to Vladivostok.   HTW

THE SOVIET NAVY

Care for the tsarist fleet had long been sporadic, and the Imperial Russian navy was relatively ineffective in the First World War. Sailors of the Baltic fleet played a prominent part part in the Revolution of 1917, but mutinied against the Bolsheviks in 1921. Despite ambitious pre-war plans of construction, and though entering the Second World War with the world's largest submarine fleet, the Soviet high-seas navy in this war achieved negligible results: river flotillas made a useful contribution, however, and many Soviet sailors fought on land. In 1945 the much-reduced navy amounted barely even to a coastal defence force.

Development, set back by the war, was resumed at first purely on conventional lines. However, while there were many shifts of priority a huge and modern fleet, able to undertake both defensive and offensive missions, and thus fundamentally altering the balance of power at sea, was built up. The USSR at first concentrated on seaward defence, as if to repulse a D-Day style invasion: many small short-range submarines were built. By 1950 western aircraft-carriers flying nuclear-armed aircraft of longer range began to be seen as the greater danger, and accordingly the accent shifted to the production of longer-range aircraft and submarines and of missile-armed surface combatants. By 1960 the primary threat was perceived to have shifted from carriers to Polaris nuclear-powered ballistic-missile-launching submarines, to counter which required more attention to anti-submarine warfare (ASW). The USSR also began to build its own naval deterrent force, comprising submarines (both nuclear- and conventionally-powered) equipped with cruise and ballistic missiles and stationed mainly with the Northern fleet (see below). The aim was a balanced force

The Russian fleet in port at Vladivostok

for exercising sea-denial (the capability for which increased) and to a smaller extent sea control. Although very strong in a number of dimensions the Soviet navy had much less embarked aviation than the US navy, and aside from nuclear strategic deterrence was far less able to project power ashore.

The Soviet navy held exercises on an increasing scale, especially in the final years of five-year plans (1965, 1970, 1975), which also extended into more distant waters. The exercise *Okean* in 1975 involved more than 200 ships (as well as aircraft) around Eurasia. The navy's role in 'protecting state interests' came to be mentioned increasingly often and to a certain degree amounted to gunboat diplomacy. A patrol was maintained off Guinea, and the navy escorted Cuban and East German troops to Africa. Potential naval, or naval with air, facilities attracted the USSR towards several African states. The USSR needed to safeguard its sea lanes to clients and allies (Angola, Cuba, Vietnam) and to protect its fishing and merchant fleets, then among the largest in the world; on the other hand, it was less dependent on sea links than NATO, whose communications could have been attacked by a Soviet force of conventional submarines several times bigger than NATO's.

It was a handicap that the USSR had to divide its navy among four widely separated fleet areas: the Arctic Ocean, Baltic Sea, Black Sea and Pacific Ocean. Internal waterways link the three European fleet areas but only for small vessels. Movement between the fleet areas otherwise involved passage through NATO-dominated straits or was feasible (via the northern sea route) only in summer. The Northern fleet (stationed in the Arctic) was the largest and most important of the four, the Pacific fleet the next largest. Shallow waters restrict the draught of ships leaving the Baltic and preclude there the passage of submerged submarines, while the Black Sea exit is theoretically regulated by the Montreux Convention of 1936, although in practice the passage of Soviet carriers was not hindered. Generally, the USSR was poorly placed in comparison with NATO for oceanic access, due to a combination of distance and narrow angles of exit. The principal Soviet naval bases were along the Murmansk fjord, Kronstadt and other Baltic ports, Sevastopol' in the Black Sea and Vladivostok, Petropavlovsk and Cam Ranh (Vietnam) in the Far East. From 1964 a naval presence was maintained in the Mediterranean. A small force was kept in the Indian Ocean. In the later Soviet period the relative strength of the combined Pacific and Indian Ocean fleets was increased.

Fleet balance

The Soviet navy had approximately the same number of cruisers, destroyers and frigates, and nuclear-powered submarines as the US navy; on the other hand, it had many more conventionally powered submarines, patrol boats and mine-warfare ships. Historically it had had fewer and smaller aircraft carriers, but the first larger carrier, of 65,000 tonnes, *Tbilisi*, was completed in 1989 with still larger vessels on the slipways. Soviet submarines included the largest in the world, *Typhoon* (30,000 tonnes). While the overall emphasis on submarines continued, *Kirov*, a very heavily armed 23,000 tonne rocket cruiser, has no parallel in western navies and is the largest surface warship apart from aircraft carriers to be built anywhere since 1945 (though of lesser tonnage than the recommissioned US *Missouri* class). However, the Soviet navy's ability to operate over long periods in distant waters was constrained by its refuelling limitations.

Soviet ships with sophisticated detection equipment invariably accompanied NATO exercises; a specialized class of spy-ships, *Balzam*, was introduced recently. The USSR also had the world's largest oceanographic fleet.

Naval design

The Imperial Russian navy had been technically innovative: Russians were the first to employ the torpedo in war, and pioneered detonation of mines by remote control; circular ironclads were built to the design of Admiral A.A. Popov (1821–98). Yet in the present century, until the mid-1950s, Soviet warships showed little evidence of originality. In the 1930s Italian design influence was strong and, immediately after the Second World War, so was German influence. By contrast, later designs showed striking originality: the Soviet navy installed the first surface-to-surface guided missiles (1959–61), the first all-gas-turbine power (1963), the first submarine-mounted cruise missiles (1958), the first Gatling-type guns to shoot down incoming missiles, and the first sizeable embarkation of vertical take-off and landing aircraft (1976). It had large numbers of hovercraft for amphibious work. In contrast to their predecessors, the newer generation of Soviet warships tended to be relatively small and fast, while crammed with diversified and partly new weapon systems. This applied to guided-missile destroyers, helicopter-carriers, missile corvettes and smaller missile-armed craft. Both nuclear and conventionally-powered submarines could launch ballistic

Inside a Soviet submarine

missiles, whereas western navies employ only nuclear platforms for this purpose. Soviet submarines mounted cruise missiles much earlier than in the West; this indicated an unusual design effort. Such efforts were sometimes initiated in haste in order to get to sea some counter to an envisaged threat.

Soviet vessels maximized simultaneous firepower, especially for defending the ship herself (whereas in western task forces protection is partly delegated to escorts), but probably carried fewer reloads than western warships (or in the case of aircraft-carriers, fewer aircraft). Recent Soviet design priorities may have parallelled those of Allied warships in the Second World War while Western designs emphasized electronics and habitability. The conspicuous weapon clusters and uncovered radars of Soviet surface combatants generated – perhaps intentionally – a menacing look.

The visible hardware partly compensated for the paucity of published information, but many uncertainties remained. The navy was thought to lag behind NATO in most aspects of anti-submarine warfare (ASW), including sonar, but to lead in electronic counter-measures. Soviet mine warfare was highly advanced. Shipborne weapons were chiefly missiles, but ASW relied less on torpedoes and more on multiple rocket-launchers than western ships did. Nuclear warheads were carried in large numbers and nuclear-ballistic capability readiness was high. A recent improvement was made in torpedo design. Most gun calibres were 76mm or less, but the latest have larger calibres – up to 180mm being mounted in the *Sovremennyy* class. Soviet ships built in recent decades were unarmoured; while this was true of navies generally, the more exposed weapons on Soviet vessels increased vulnerability. Soviet warships had good sea-keeping qualities and were relatively stable. Once notoriously noisy, more recent Soviet submarines were almost as quiet as US boats and could dive deeper.

The Soviet navy latterly built larger ships, with some Western features, such as a ski-jump take-off on the aircraft-carrier *Tbilisi*. It also commissioned specialized ships based on Western models, such as the *Udaloy* and *Sovremennyy* classes (for ASW and anti-surface warfare respectively).

Construction and maintenance

Apart from certain landing ships all Soviet warships were constructed in the USSR. Gor'ky (Nizhny Novgorod, on the Volga) has one of the main submarine-building yards. Large vessels were built in the Leningrad area, at Nikolaev and more recently at Severodvinsk (near Arkhangel'sk); the latter, together with Komsomol'sk-na-Amure, specialized in nuclear submarines.

The navy kept more of its ships in port (or if on station, at anchor) than NATO navies did; this lowered fuel costs and wear and tear, but must have impaired training and suggested fairly low operational readiness. Similarly, the multiplicity of shipborne weapons and sensors indicated uncertain reliability, resulting perhaps from the high conscript content among crews (see below). Probably for this same reason Soviet warships were basically factory-maintained, rather than user-maintained as in the West; the Soviet practice reduced spatial and professional demands on board, but also reliability, especially on longer cruises. The ships were able, however, to make use of repair facilities in many countries, including Yugoslavia, Thailand and former British facilities at Singapore.

The navy imposed a considerable economic burden, representing (according to US estimates based on direct costing) almost 20 per cent of defence spending; that is, not far below that of the ground forces with their far greater manpower. Investment (primarily procurement of material) comprised about four-fifths of this, calling chiefly on engineering and electronics, design and scientific research.

Naval aviation

Naval aviation was fairly equally divided among the four fleet areas attached to the respective fleets. Bear (reconnaisance) and Badger (missile-armed) aircraft were reinforced from 1974 by several hundred Backfire (Tu-22M/26) strike planes. Substantial numbers of these were based in the Pacific area, a fact which caused concern in Japan. Aviation was primarily shore-based, with less use of helicopters than in the US navy. However, shipborne planes included the Hormone helicopter, the Fitter and the Forger.

Naval infantry

Numbering some 14,000 highly trained men, naval infantry would in wartime probably have been entrusted with offensive missions, such as the seizure of NATO-held straits.

Personnel

From January 1956 to December 1985 the navy was commanded by Admiral of the Fleet S.G. Gorshkov (1910–88), who published in 1962 a series of studies on Russian and Soviet seapower. His successor was Admiral V.N. Chernavin (b. 1928). Compared with western navies, Soviet naval officers provided a larger proportion of narrowly specialized skills and remained longer on the same ship. Their training placed less emphasis on meeting unexpected contingencies. Living quarters, though improved, remained cramped and spartan by comparison with NATO navies. In the Brezhnev era one ship (*Storozhevoy*, 1975) mutinied. A number of accidents at sea have been reported (especially in 1989), as well as a huge explosion at Severomorsk (Northern fleet area) in May 1984. Over four-fifths of Soviet sailors were conscripts (for three years if afloat) and the re-enlistment rate was low.

Post-Soviet developments

In August 1992 the Russian President Boris Yel'tsin and the Ukrainian President Leonid Kravchuk took over joint personal command of the Black Sea fleet until 1995. In September 1993, with Ukraine's economy in extreme difficulties, Kravchuk apparently agreed to hand over the Ukrainian share of the fleet to Russia as a way of paying its economic debts. But divisions within the Ukrainian leadership left the position uncertain.   RH

Below. Helicopters on a training mission on board the cruiser, Novorossiysk. *Below right. A hovercraft belonging to the Black Sea fleet*

THE RED ARMY

Military power played an instrumental role in the evolution of the Soviet state and system. The revolutionary Bolshevik regime, determined to exercise power alone, was swiftly confronted with internal and external opposition. These exigencies not only called for powerful armed forces, but for measures which would ensure their loyalty and reliability. The complex challenges of revolution, civil war and international isolation instilled a highly disciplined approach to the use of force, as well as a fusion of political and military considerations which was a notable feature of the USSR throughout its history.

Early years

The Workers' and Peasants' Red Army (RKKA) was formed on 18 January 1918. Initially, it was an all volunteer force composed of workers and poor peasants, who were screened for reliability by special military committees staffed by party workers. Motivated as these soldiers were, their strength (300,000 by May 1918) was clearly inferior to that of the anti-Bolshevik troops facing them. Under the impetus of Trotsky, People's Commissar for War between 1918 and 1925, the Central Committee on

Lenin, accompanied by a group of officers, reviews the ranks of militia volunteers gathered in Red Square in 1919

29 May 1918 enacted a decree making military service compulsory for members of the working class and poor peasantry. 'Military specialists', including 50,000 ex-tsarist officers, were also inducted. The performance of all commandos was strictly monitored by cadres of political commissars, who were empowered to countersign their orders and countermand them when necessary. In addition, 'special departments' (*Osobye Otdely – OO*) of the Cheka were attached to military units with the task of providing counter-intelligence and curbing anti-Bolshevik penetration in a force which, by 1920, was overwhelmingly (83 per cent) composed of conscripts. As the staff of the Red Army expanded, numbers rose to 550,000 by September 1918 and to 5.5 million by the end of 1920.

The Civil War (and the Russo-Polish War of 1920) left a strong imprint on Soviet military commanders and did much to shape their future operational style. First, the war was seen as a clash of coalitions in which victory depended on the ability to harness different classes, nations and (thanks to foreign intervention) states to common ends. In this respect it merely confirmed the primacy assigned to the 'political factor' by pre-revolutionary Russian military theorists, by the military theorist Karl von

Clausewitz (1780–1831), and especially by Lenin himself.

Secondly, the Civil War was a war of manoeuvre and vast spatial scope, conducted without fixed front and rear lines. It taught staff officers and commanders to plan operations on a large scale, to co-ordinate activity on different fronts and between different arms of service.

Finally, the war underscored the importance of possessing a large conscript base and an efficient mobilization system. After 1920 this became a critical concern, as the dire economic condition of the country forced a severe contraction of the standing army from 5.5 million to a mere 500,000 by the end of 1924. The military service law of 1925 established short-term, rudimentary but universal military training for the population, whilst the army was transformed into a mixed cadre-territorial force, built around a small nucleus of professionals.

The architect of the new system, M.V. Frunze (1885–1925), who became Chief of the General Staff in May 1924 and replaced Trotsky as Chairman of the Revolutionary Military Council in January 1925, curtailed the authority of political commissars and restored 'single command' (*edinonachalie*) in military units. He also played an instrumental role

Red Army soldiers, c. 1937

in establishing a unified 'military doctrine' which standardized training, procurement and operational concepts within the framework of an overarching and official view of future war. Building upon this foundation, M.N. Tukhachevsky (1893–1937), B.M. Shaposhnikov (1882–1945), A.I. Svechin (1878–1938), V.K. Triandafillov (1894–1931) and other senior military figures strengthened the General Staff system, expanded operational research and schooled a new generation of commanders in the 'combined arms' challenges posed by tanks, artillery and aircraft.

The 1930s: growth and regression

By the early 1930s, internal consolidation and a worsening international environment made expansion feasible as well as necessary. Before 1935, 74 per cent of Red Army formations were organized on territorial lines, with conscripts training near their places of work and serving in their localities. Although this structure minimized economic disruption and social disaffection with military service, it greatly reduced military effectiveness. It also raised worrying concerns about the concentration of ethnic groups in particular units. In 1935 the Politburo decided to phase out territorial formations and, at the same time, expand the size of the regular army. By the end of 1936 the proportion of territorial formations had fallen to 23 per cent. Concurrently, the size of the army rose from 900,000 (in 1933) to 1.5 million by 1938.

The First and Second Five-year Plans complemented these measures, but they were not rearmament programmes as such. Stalin aimed to create an advanced scientific, technological and manufacturing base that could produce both capital goods and military goods and thereby support successive generations of armament when the need arose.

Even before the plans bore fruit, Deep Operations became official military doctrine (1933). It placed the emphasis firmly on surprise, manoeuvre, and deep offensive thrusts of armour into the heart of the enemy's territory with a view to bringing about his collapse in the shortest possible time. Mechanized (and later tank) corps were formed, experiments with airborne landings (*desants*) conducted, and tank, artillery and aircraft production was vastly increased.

To the mystification of contemporary (and current) observers, these advances were cut to the quick by the military purges (May 1937 to September 1938) which led to the imprisonment or execution of over 70 per cent (35,000) of senior officers and, after a thirteen-year hiatus, saw the political commissar system reimposed with its original rigour. The operational consequences of this upheaval were profound. Misreading the lessons of the Spanish

Marshal Zhukov

Georgy Konstantinovich Zhukov (1896–1974) was the outstanding military leader of the Red Army during the Second World War, and was also a powerful player in the political arena for the four years after Stalin's death in 1953. He was rightly considered the successor to the great Russian generals of the past, such as Suvorov, Kutuzov and Brusilov.

After fighting in the First World War Zhukov joined the Red Army in 1918, and rose rapidly through the ranks, becoming a senior commander by the late 1930s. During this period he worked with Tukhachevsky, and he took on board the latter's modernizing ideas.

Zhukov managed to avoid the fate of many senior officers (including Tukhachevsky himself) during the purges, and distinguished himself in 1939 by inflicting a crushing defeat on Japanese forces in Outer Mongolia, using the tactics he was to utilize soon afterwards against the Germans.

Zhukov was Chief of the General Staff at the time of the Nazi invasion in 1941, but it was the incompetence of his colleagues that was blamed for the disasters of that year. Zhukov organized the heroic defence of Leningrad in the first months of the war, and then worked with Stalin in the defence of Moscow. As the tide of the war turned, Zhukov was responsible for many of the Red Army's successes, among them the victory at Stalingrad, the relief of Leningrad and the huge tank battle at Kursk (all in 1943). He also organized and led the Soviet advance on Berlin in 1944.

In peacetime however, Zhukov found himself demoted by Stalin, who was jealous of his popularity, and he narrowly escaped arrest by Beria's secret police. After Stalin's death in 1953 he became Defence Minister, where he began the modernization of the Soviet armed forces. In 1957 he gave vital support to Khrushchev in his struggle with the 'anti-party group'. Nevertheless Khrushchev, fearing Zhukov's power, influence and popularity, dismissed him later in the same year. Zhukov concentrated the last years of his life on writing his memoirs. He died in 1974.

Civil War, a now deficient High Command dismantled independent tank corps and redistributed tanks amongst infantry units. The disastrously ill-planned operation against Finland (December 1939 to March 1940) produced 200,000 Soviet casualties in the month of December alone and exposed the Red Army's deficiencies to the world. Yet, the sole force to have escaped the purge, the Far Eastern army under command of General (later Marshal) Zhukov (1896–1974), inflicted a stunning defeat on the Japanese Kwantung army at Nomonhan/Khalkhin Gol in the summer of 1939: a defeat which induced the Japanese to conclude, and subsequently honour, a neutrality agreement with Stalin on the eve of Germany's invasion of the USSR.

The Great Fatherland War

Operation Barbarossa, launched by Hitler on 22 June 1941, achieved complete strategic surprise, and by October over two million Soviet soldiers had surrendered. A vast war potential remained, but it

would prove irrelevant unless the Soviet government traded space for time and transformed blitzkrieg into a prolonged contest.

Soviet military historians divided the war into three periods. In the first (22 June 1941 to 18 November 1942), the Soviet Union transformed an unprecedented military débâcle into an orderly 'strategic defensive operation'. The Red Army, savaged by the German offensive and still handicapped by the purges, none the less showed a remarkable ability to learn from mistakes and restructure its tactical order of battle. This ability to amend and adapt, along with an excellent mobilization system established in the 1920s and 1930s, proved vital to the country's survival during these first few months.

During the second period (19 November 1942 to 31 December 1943), Soviet forces fought for, and finally gained, the strategic initiative. It was during this period that the concepts underpinning 'Deep Operations' were first put to effective use. Like the German concept of blitzkrieg which developed alongside it, Deep Operations employed tanks, artillery and artillery and aircraft to disorientate the opponent and penetrate to the depths of his deployment. But unlike blitzkrieg, which allowed tactical success to determine the larger operational plan, Deep Operations firmly subordinated tactical commanders (division level and below) to operational commanders (army and front). These, in turn, were given enormous scope to select and alter axes of advance and exploit opportunities as they arose. Thanks to its mastery of this distinct 'operational' level of warfare, the Red Army eventually proved able to defeat German forces equal in strength and tactically superior to their own.

The final period (usually dated from July 1944) took the war outside Soviet territory. Even before this date, Polish and Czech units, raised, trained and equipped in the USSR, had been incorporated into the Soviet command structure and order of battle. To these were added Romanian and Bulgarian forces in late 1944. The experience gained in the command and control of foreign forces (550,000 by the war's end), as well as non-Russian units in the Red Army, had a strong influence on the future command-and-control system of the Warsaw Pact.

The scale of disaster and achievement during the Second World War is more easily measured than comprehended. The Red Army destroyed or disabled 607 German divisions in 51 strategic operations. Despite the loss of 70 per cent of housing and industry in the European USSR, Soviet military historians claim that they produced over twenty times the quantity of munitions supplied by Allied lend-lease.   JGS

THE SOVIET AIR FORCES

From the 1930s onwards, the Soviet Union coupled heavy investment in airpower with a combined arms approach towards its employment. This and the Soviet practice of dividing services by function rather than environment, gave air forces a distinctly subordinate role in the Soviet military structure.

In peacetime, Soviet air forces were divided into two arms of service, the Air Defence Forces (PVO) and Air Forces (VVS). Additionally, a substantial land-based (and smaller sea-based) inventory of bombers and strike aircraft was maintained by Soviet Naval Aviation (a branch of the navy) and a large combat and transport helicopter component by Army Aviation (a branch of the Ground Forces). In wartime front commanders had direct control of 'air forces' within their zones of responsibility. Control over strategic 'aviation armies' was exercised by the Supreme High Command (VGK) through the General Staff's Main Operations Directorate, or

through their regional extensions, the High Commands (GK) of Theatres of Military Activity (TVD).

In the late 1920s, Soviet military scientists concluded that airpower (along with armour) would revolutionize warfare, but they rejected the view held by western airpower enthusiasts that air forces could achieve strategic results on their own. The country's long, exposed frontiers persuaded a General Staff dominated by Ground Forces commanders that air power would be the third dimension of a land battle: a view borne out by the Great Fatherland War, which saw the ground attack aircraft successfully deployed as a form of long-range artillery. The advent of nuclear weapons enlarged the (hitherto negligible) strategic role of the air force. But the priority accorded to inter-continental ballistic missiles (ICBM) (under custody of the Strategic Rocket Forces) and the growing importance of submarine-launched ballistic missiles (SLBM) still limited this role, as did the General Staff, who would have co-ordinated nuclear strikes and taken command of the forces executing them.

The organization adopted for the air forces in March 1942 survived in its essentials until 1978. These forces were divided into Long-range Aviation (DA), with exclusive responsibility for strategic targets and Tactical Air Armies (later termed Frontal Aviation), with a primarily defensive battlefield mission. To these components Military Transport Aviation (VTA) was added in the 1950s, and the Air Defence Forces of the Homeland (PVO Strany) was established as a separate arm of service with its own Commander-in-Chief in 1954.

The 1978–81 reorganization arose out of the establishment of high commands of forces in the USSR's four contiguous TVD's and a more favourable assessment of the possibility of defeating NATO by non-nuclear means. Whereas previously, nuclear forces would have dealt a disarming initial blow to NATO's' defences, from this point (1981) onwards war would have been initiated by a non-nuclear 'strategic air operation', targeted against air bases, nuclear delivery means, command-and-control and other vital assets to the depth of NATO's deployment. To this end Long-range Aviation and some Frontal Aviation assets were combined into five strategic Aviation Armies, four of them structured primarily for a theatre strategic role. Remaining Frontal Aviation assets, greatly strengthened in size and capability, were reorganized into Air Forces of Military Districts and Groups of Forces (AFMD/GOF).

Hardly was this reorganization complete than the 1982 Israel–Syrian air war disrupted these calculations. By 1984 the General Staff warned that a third 'revolution in military affairs' would eliminate many of the advantages upon which the USSR's offensive military potential had been based. This revolution, coupled with Gorbachev's 'New Thinking', produced a more defensive configuration after 1988 for AFMD/GOF, which none the less retained a strong counter-offensive capability. However, with the dissolution of the Warsaw Pact and the redeployment of forces to the Soviet homeland, the General Staff warned that 'defensive sufficiency' could turn into defencelessness unless offensive capabilities were recovered. More recently, the Gulf War persuaded them that air forces would require pre-emptive as well as offensive capabilities if they were to foil attack.

Like the air forces, the air defence forces (renamed *Voyska* PVO in 1981) were substantially reorganized after 1978. Whereas PVO *Strany* overlapped organizationally with the Ground Forces air defence troops, the new organization freed PVO to concentrate exclusively on strategic tasks. In peacetime air defence troops were geographically divided into five air defence districts, each containing five air defence

Below. The 'Russian Vityazi' squadron. Bottom. Combat vehicles taking part in the military parade on the fortieth anniversary of victory in the Great Patriotic War: 9 May 1985

zones. In wartime PVO, like all strategic forces, came under the direct command of the VGK and General Staff.

Organizationally the PVO was divided into three branches: Fighter Aviation (IA) with upwards of 2,000 interceptors dedicated to strategic air defence; Zenith Rocket Troops (ZRV) operating more than 9,000 surface-to-air missile (SAM) launchers at over 900 sites; and Radio-Technical Troops (RTV), employing three layers of satellite warning, ground-based early warning out to 6,000 km, and over 7,000 surveillance, target acquisition and missile control radars. RTV also operated the Moscow ABM system, the ground-based anti-satellite (ASAT) system and a variety of damage assessment systems. JGS

THE SOVIET ARMED FORCES 1945–91

The Red Army was renamed the Soviet Army in March 1946. Although it was a much transformed and vastly more capable force than its predecessor, it attached enormous weight to its history and operational experience. The Soviet armed forces differed from their NATO counterparts in four key respects.

First, substantial military forces were maintained outside the jurisdiction of the Ministry of Defence. The internal troops (*Vnutrennye Voyska* – VV) of the Ministry of Interior (MVD) possessed a substantial (though far from limitless) capability to combat armed internal insurgency. More significant were the armed forces of the Committee for State Security (KGB). These included the heavily armed border troops, as well as rather smaller numbers of state security troops (whose functions included guarding nuclear warheads). Additionally, military counter-intelligence lay within the exclusive domain of the KGB Third Chief Directorate (as opposed to military intelligence activity, which was subordinate to the Chief Intelligence Directorate (GRU) of the general staff).

Second, the USSR differed from NATO countries in the mechanisms it evolved for maintaining political control over its forces. At higher levels, control was exercised by military councils, and senior appointments had to have the endorsement of the KGB and the Administrative Organs Department of the CPSU Central Committee. In deployed formations, political authority was imposed directly through a corps of 'political deputies' (*zampoliti*), subordinate to the Main Political Directorate of the Soviet Army and Navy (GLAVPU), which operated as the Central Committee's military branch. Unlike their predecessors, the political commissars (*zampoliti*) had no voice in operational matters, but they remained the senior political authorities in their units, with important prerogatives in personnel policy, promotions and political education.

The third contrast was the maintenance in the Soviet armed forces of a powerful General Staff along Prussian lines. In peacetime the General Staff acted as the working organ of the Defence Council and Ministry of Defence; in wartime as the planning organ and transmission belt for the headquarters (*Stavka*) of the Supreme High Command (VGK). Long considered the 'brain of the army', the General Staff possessed impressive prerogatives over the five armed services and, for much of its existence, maintained an unchallenged dominance over military-technical policy.

The fourth difference was the immense importance attached to 'military doctrine' and 'military science': the former was an official and binding 'system of views' about future war, divided into 'socio-political' and 'military-technical' components; the latter was a coherent but evolving 'system of knowledge' embracing all those disciplines relevant to the waging of war and the preparation for it. Together military doctrine and science lent coherence to the diverse aspects of defence policy-making, facilitated the allocation of resources to defence production and enabled civil and military participants in the defence structure to operate within a common analytical framework.

Soviet military doctrine 1945–85

The immediate post-war period (1945–53) was characterized by an incongruous mixture of activism and inertia. Whilst substantially reduced in size (from 11 million men to 3 million between 1945–48, rising again to about 5 million in 1953), the Ground Forces were extensively modernized, the Air Defence Forces (PVO *Strany*) established as an independent service, and substantial nuclear and missile programmes set in motion. In contrast theoretical debate was rigidly constrained by Stalin's five 'permanently operating factors' of war, which made it impossible to give serious consideration to the effects of strategic surprise or to the implications of nuclear weapons, even as they were being designed, built and deployed.

At the instigation of the post-Stalin political leadership, the military establishment conducted two major debates in the 1950s. The first (1953–55) elevated surprise to a fundamental principle of 'military art' (armed combat) and concluded that nuclear weapons would alter future war, but not decisively. In the interests of modernization and economy, the armed forces were again reduced in size (from 5.8 to 3.6 million between 1955 and 1958) and partially restructured for nuclear operations. The second debate (1957–59) went further, concluding that nuclear weapons and guided missiles had produced a 'revolution in military affairs'. This conclusion formed the basis of a new military doctrine, unveiled by Khrushchev in January 1960.

The 1960 doctrine postulated that a future war would be nuclear from the outset and waged without limitation in a 'decisive clash' between 'two opposed world systems'. Although the USSR would never initiate such a war, it would need to acquire forces capable of 'foiling' (pre-empting) attack, delivering disarming blows upon the opponent and limiting damage to the Soviet homeland. Accordingly Khrushchev established the Strategic Rocket Forces as the senior armed service, but his neglect of traditional services and demands for further manpower reductions (1.2 million) alarmed his senior military commanders.

Following his removal in October 1964, Khrushchev was denounced for overestimating the potential of nuclear weapons and neglecting the country's defences. Between 1965 and 1985 the armed forces grew from 3.2 to 5.5 million men, nuclear weapons were modernized and deployed in quantity, and conventional forces were restructured for both nuclear and non-nuclear contingencies. With the encouragement of Marshal A.A. Grechko (1903–76; Minister of Defence 1967–76), a more balanced force structure evolved in response to changes in NATO's strategy, nuclear parity and a revised (and unfavourable) assessment of nuclear effects on the battlefield. Until the mid-1970s, nuclear escalation in a NATO–Warsaw Pact conflict was considered probable, if no longer inevitable, but as capabilities improved, so did hope of deterring escalation and confining operations below the nuclear threshold.

Under the stewardship of Marshal N.V. Ogarkov (1917–94; Chief of the General Staff, 1977–84), the Soviet armed forces acquired the capability to conduct high-speed, all conventional strategic offensive operations. NATO's economic strengths and the risk of nuclear use made it imperative to revive pre-war 'Deep Operations' concepts, emphasising surprise, mobility, the rapid penetration of the enemy's depths and the achievement of decisive results in an 'initial period' of hostilities. Despite sustained progress on these fronts, Ogarkov's efforts were considerably set back by NATO's deployment of ground-launched cruise missiles (GLCM) and Pershing II and its development of advanced warning, reconnaissance and strike capabilities in the early 1980s.

On the political–military front the deterioration in Sino-Soviet relations both widened and complicated the planning framework during this period. Nevertheless, in 1974, 'external' functions were added to the armed forces in support of the 'social and national liberation struggle' in the Third World. Logistics, intelligence and limited combat support

Dmitry Yazov, Soviet Minister of Defence, 1987–91, and one of the leaders of the attempted coup against Mikhail Gorbachev in August 1991. Born of peasant parents in a small village in the Omsk region in Siberia in 1923, Yazov fought in the Second World War and in the post-war era rose to the rank of General by 1984. He was appointed Minister of Defence in May 1987 over the heads of a number of more senior colleagues. He shared the suspicion of growing political pluralism of many in the higher ranks of the army and their anxiety that the loss of Soviet military positions in Eastern Europe might be followed by the disintegration of the USSR itself. By participating in the August 1991 coup, he unwittingly helped to accelerate that process

in Angola and Ethiopia proved decisive in both conflicts. Despite these successes, it appears that Ogarkov and his First Deputy, S.F. Akhromeev (1923–91; Chief of the General Staff, 1984–88), advised against invading Afghanistan in 1979.

Developments since 1985

Mikhail Gorbachev had as dramatic an impact on the Soviet armed forces as on any other Soviet institution. By turning military policy into a subject of public debate, he challenged deep-seated traditions. But he also restored traditions – and Leninist disciplines – by subordinating military policy to the political goals of the state and the economic means available.

Gorbachev's initial forays into the military sphere were limited and cautious. But he readily grasped that 'new thinking' in foreign policy would prove stillborn without corresponding changes to military doctrine. Although the socio-political side of this doctrine – the justification for war – had long been 'defensive', its military-technical content – the methods of waging war – had always been 'offensive'. The shift towards 'reasonable sufficiency' and a 'strictly defensive' doctrine was initiated by Gorbachev at the XXVII Party Congress (January 1986) and then codified in the Warsaw Pact's communiqué of 29 May 1987. From the latter date onwards, official pronouncements and arms control proposals emphasized the subordination of military doctrine to 'war prevention', the removal of capabilities for surprise attack and the principle of asymmetrical reductions to equal and lower force levels.

Marshal S.F. Akhromeev argued that these changes were, in their essentials, dictated by military as well as by political need. As in the 1920s and 1950s, the military establishment was reminded of the 'laws' relating military potential to scientific–economic potential. Moreover, a 'revolutionary turn in military affairs' now made economic reconstruction urgent. In the early 1980s Marshal Ogarkov had warned that conventional weapons based on new physical principles would transform war as profoundly as nuclear weapons had done. By 1985 the warnings were being heeded. Yet unlike Ogarkov, Akhromeev believed that the danger of war was low and that modernization could be accompanied, indeed facilitated, by retrenchment. Both he and his successor, Colonel General M.A. Moiseev (b.1939), saw merit in a foreign policy which, through détente, arms control and well-judged concessions, could provide a 'breathing space' for modernization and discourage NATO from exploiting its technological advantages.

If the high command accepted Gorbachev's overall priorities, it still found much to dispute in their practical implementation. Army General (then Marshal) D.T. Yazov (Minister of Defence, 1987–91) and other senior officers insisted on distinguishing 'defensive sufficiency' from the 'defensive defence' advocated by a number of Soviet civilian specialists. Whilst forswearing capabilities for launching a pre-emptive offensive war, they were adamant that effective defence was impossible without strong (operational and strategic) counter-offensive capabilities.

Arms proposals and unilateral reductions also aroused controversy, despite the substantial role which the General Staff had had in crafting them. The Treaty on Intermediate-range Nuclear Forces (INF), concluded in December 1987, eliminated the weapons of greatest concern to Western Theatre (TVD) commanders (the United States' GLCM and Pershing II), though at the cost of highly asymmetrical reductions (of SS-20) and the loss of a major component of a Soviet strategic offensive (SS-23). The unilateral reductions announced by Gorbachev on 7 December 1988 (including six tank divisions from central Europe) failed to soften NATO's negotiating stance in the Conventional Forces in Europe (CFE) negotiations (begun in March 1989). The CFE treaty itself maintained, to Soviet advantage, the discrepancy in mobilization and reinforcement potentials between NATO and the USSR, yet it also eliminated the capacity of the Soviet armed forces to attack NATO's central region unexpectedly by conventional means.

These controversies were exacerbated, but also overshadowed, by the disintegration of the Warsaw Pact, the deterioration of the Soviet economy and finally the breakup of the Soviet Union itself. A substantial but selective withdrawal of Soviet forces from central Europe, preserving essential infrastructure, logistics and command assets, would not have harmed Soviet military interests. But the wholesale loss of these assets, the defection of allies and the Gulf War in early 1991 roused the General Staff to restate their view that security could not be achieved by political means alone.

Organization

The transformation of Soviet society after 1985 affected, first, the accountability of the armed forces and the control of military policy; second, the organization of the defence–industrial complex; and third, the conditions of military service. None the less, the military system had deep roots, and its defenders have waged a determined struggle to preserve its essential features.

Before 1989 effective authority over the five armed services (strategic rocket forces, ground forces, air defence forces, air forces, and navy) was vested in the CPSU Politburo, which exercised dominance over all aspects of defence policy through the

USSR Defence Council. Membership of the latter body was formally confined to top civilian leaders with defence and security responsibilities. But in practice the Defence Council provided close civil–military interaction through participation of the General Staff (which provided administrative support) and its standing bodies of permanent advisers and consultants. This CPSU dominance was substantially reinforced by personnel appointment and oversight prerogatives of the CPSU Central Committee, by military councils operating in military districts, fleets and groups of forces, by the chief political directorate of the armed forces (GLAVPU) and by party organizations in individual military

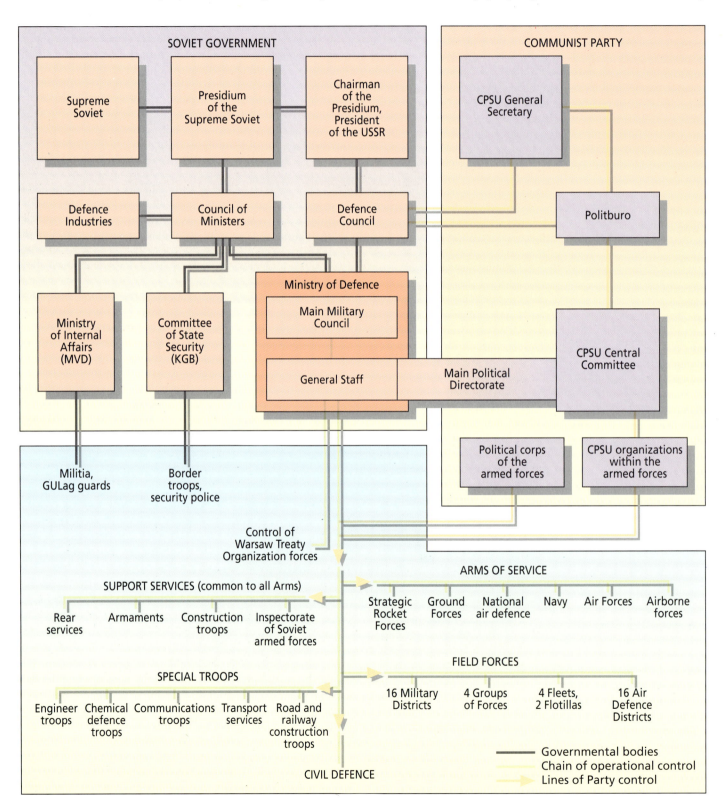

units. Not only did these mechanisms ensure party and state control, they confined debate (and knowledge) about defence matters to a small and closed circle.

An equally cohesive arrangement applied to the nine (later eight) ministries, 5,000 or so enterprises and 600–800 research and development establishments belonging to the defence industrial complex. The Military–Industrial Commission (VPK) of the Council of Ministers, with close ties to Gosplan and the Central Committee's Defence Industry Department (later abolished), possessed the legal and administrative means to co-ordinate defence production and ensure that enterprises received the resources they required. Production of end product weapons was supervised by the 'military representatives' (*voenpredy*) of the individual armed services, empowered to reject substandard output at enterprise expense. Moreover, substantial civil production (40 per cent of defence industry's output) was located in the defence complex, providing a large reserve capacity in event of war. This integrated and almost autarchic system – which produced weapons in one-half the time and one-half the cost of its NATO counterparts – was seen as a vital component of Soviet military power.

A third and no less vital feature of the traditional system was a conscript army with extensive reserves and a rapid mobilization capability. In principle, the Soviet army was a reserve force, composed for the most part of semi-deployed formations (50–75 per cent strength) and 'cadre' formations (15–30 per cent), the former of which could be made combat effective within one to three days and the latter within three weeks. Key to the effective running of this system were military commissariats (*voenkomaty*) which administered the twice-yearly call-up of conscripts, mobilized reservists and maintained records of 'human and economic resources' within the USSR's sixteen (later fourteen) military districts and four fleets. These districts and fleets were territorial–administrative entities designed to ensure civil–military co-ordination in peacetime and rapid transition from peace to war.

Four developments undermined, and finally destroyed, this tried and proven system: (1) the dissolution of the CPSU, which dislocated the traditional system of accountability and supervision;

Gruppovshchina

As the Soviet Union crumbled in the late 1980s, the military began to follow suit. In addition to divisions between reformers and conservatives, the ethnic tension that was so marked a feature of Soviet society in general made its presence felt in the armed forces.

One of the greatest difficulties faced by the army in particular was fulfilling the quotas for new soldiers to be drafted from certain republics. The reasons were of course political, with independence-minded republican leaders trying openly to score points against the central Soviet government. Public support for the local leaderships was guaranteed because of one phenomenon in particular: the upsurge in inter-ethnic bullying (*gruppovshchina*) that occurred in the armed forces in the late 1980s.

Racial and ethnic tension had always existed in the Soviet military, despite official propaganda, but in the increasingly politicized atmosphere of the Gorbachev era two new factors came into play. First, the problem itself became worse. Secondly, glasnost meant that for the first time the general public was made aware of what was going on. In 1988–89 the bullying of non-Russian recruits by Russians, both officers and fellow conscripts, became a major issue in the media in the Baltic states and Transcaucasia. In one case a young Lithuanian shot and killed eight Russian soldiers after they had beaten him up. Human rights activists pointed revealingly to the large number of recruits who died every year in suspicious circumstances.

The military denied that the problem of ethnic abuse was endemic, but senior officers admitted that some Russians were angered by the separatist movements in certain republics, and that tension had increased as a result. The reaction in republics such as Lithuania was to try to insist that recruits served only in or near their native republics. When this was rejected by the central authorities, the republics countered by refusing to provide the recruits demanded by the army. Inter-ethnic bullying in the military thus became yet one more issue that drove the republics, in particular the Baltic states, towards independence from the USSR.

(2) challenges by legislators and civilian specialists to the General Staff's *de facto* monopoly over military-technical policy; (3) the dismantling of the command-administrative system in the national economy; and (4) the decisions of several successor states to form their own national armies.

The election of a Congress of People's Deputies and Supreme Soviet in 1989 had earlier launched a new stage in a three-year-long battle to define and control the future course of military policy. Before this point advocates of radical military reform were concentrated in the research institutes of the USSR Academy of Sciences, an institutional base which made it possible to contest but not control the activities of the General Staff. The new Supreme Soviet set up a forty-three-member Committee on Questions of Defence and State Security, with three sub-committees (Armed Forces, Defence Industry, and State Security). Although the Committee was overwhelmingly conservative – 90 per cent of its members being connected with the defence complex – its small radical wing was intent on seeing the Supreme Soviet displace the Party and Defence Council as the directing organ of the armed forces. In December 1989 a commission under the chairmanship of a naval aviation political officer, Major Vladimir Lopatin (b. 1960), tabled a draft reform programme calling for the de-politicization of the armed forces and dissolution of GLAVPU, the phasing out of conscription and the restoration of national-territorial formations.

In February and March 1990 the Party and armed forces counter-attacked. A 'counter-commission', set up by the Central Committee and chaired by the Chief of the General Staff, Army General M.A.

Building a Mig-29 in a Moscow factory

Moiseev, secured Gorbachev's approval to draw up the state's official reform package. In August Gorbachev reversed a decision, made six months earlier, to transfer the Defence Council's prerogatives to the newly formed Presidential Council. This 'reconstructed' Defence Council, under Gorbachev's chairmanship, operated with a narrow membership under the stewardship of its First Deputy Chairman, O.D. Baklanov (b. 1932), a senior party official with long-standing ties to the armed forces, who also chaired the Central Committee's Commission on Military Policy. By the summer of 1990 dominance of military-technical policy had reverted to the General Staff, for whom the paramount task of 'military reform' was the technological modernization of the armed forces.

That task proved exceedingly difficult to achieve under the existing economic conditions. A sharp drop in military equipment orders in 1989, coupled with efforts under way since 1988 to convert additional military capacity to civil production, weakened the integrity of the defence complex, reduced earnings and put skilled workers and technical specialists out of work. Demands for coherence and 'economic order' from an increasingly politicized defence-complex leadership eventually produced a State Programme for Conversion, submitted to the Supreme Soviet in the summer of 1990. The plan called for modest to substantial measures of conversion in approximately 400 defence-complex enterprises and the resubordination of some 100 (additional) civilian enterprises to defence production ministries. By 1995 it was envisaged that the present share of non-military output in the complex (40 per cent) should rise to 60 per cent.

Radicals (who put forward an alternative plan) found much to criticize in the State Programme: it was drawn up by those who had the most to lose from radical change: the military-industrial complex, the defence departments of Gosplan and the Ministry of Defence; it was based upon command-administrative methods that were incompatible with comprehensive market reform; participating enterprises would remain in the defence complex, subordinated to the established ministerial structure; the form of conversion prescribed was partial and reversible. None the less, until this or an alternative programme was adopted and implemented, the economic interests of the armed forces would continue to suffer.

Personnel

'Human resources' posed three of the most vexing challenges for the military leadership between 1985 and August 1991: integrating sophisticated technology into a conscript army of deteriorating standard; maintaining the legitimacy of a multi-national army which had lost its ideological foundation; preserving an integrated army in a union dissolving into its component parts.

From a conscript's perspective, the Soviet military system, orientated around two semi-annual call-ups, was essentially a training system, instilling basic combat skills through drill. From 1968 the two-year conscription period (three years for the navy and air force) was supplemented by 140 hours of pre-induction training and reserve obligations to age fifty. Soviet NCOs, two-thirds of them conscripts themselves, were tough disciplinarians and competent drillmasters, but they lacked the versatility and technical skills of the long-service NCOs who form the backbone of most NATO armies. The junior

Below. Training in unarmed self-defence in the Soviet army, 1990. Bottom. Instruction in the Nakhimov Military Naval Academy, Leningrad, 1989

officer therefore bore a great burden in this system: at one and the same time commander, clerk and mechanic, performing routine tasks which in the British army are carried out by corporals and sergeants.

Within these confines, the centralized system of conscription and manpower allocation had been quite effective at meeting the specific requirements of individual arms of service, despite a wide variation in the national composition, educational level and political reliability of the conscript pool. But even before the dissolution of the Soviet Union demographic changes were taxing this system to its limits. Whereas conscripts from the Transcaucasus and Central Asia made up 14 per cent of the two 1970 call-ups, this proportion had risen to 37 per cent by 1989. In the same period the number of recruits per call-up who lacked a functional command of the Russian language rose from 9,500 to 114,000 (one-eighth of the cohort). Even élite services like the Strategic Rocket Forces began to suffer in an army which, on average, was forced to assign from nine to eighteen nationalities per company and twenty-five to thirty-seven per regiment. Consequently, *gruppovshchina* (inter-ethnic bullying) displaced the notorious *dedovshchina* (cross-generational bullying) as the principal hazard of barracks life, accounting for 80 per cent of 'non-regulation relations' in the armed forces.

Demographic pressures upon quality were compounded by three others: the reinstatement of student deferments in 1989 (which deprived the forces of 200,000 of their most educated conscripts), the declining prestige of the military profession and the dramatic alterations to the size and shape of the army imposed by troop withdrawals from central Europe.

Diminished career prospects sharply reduced applications to the 150 officer-commissioning higher military colleges which, before a 30 per cent shrinkage was announced in 1990, constituted 15 per cent of Soviet institutions conferring higher education degrees. The 23 military academies and institutes awarding advanced degrees also began to suffer owing to the drop in retention rates. Of those officers applying for discharge in 1989, 70 per cent were under twenty-five, and over 75 per cent had ratings of 'efficient and conscientious' or higher.

Ironically, the planned contractions of the military establishment, (including the December 1988 reductions) were expected to have the opposite effect, weeding out the lacklustre and incompetent and, on the principle of 'better fewer, but better', building a flexible, high-technology force. But the dismantling of the four groups of forces in central Europe in 1990–91 plunged a system already under stress into turmoil. In short order, 500 senior com-

manders had to be reassigned or discharged. By October 1990 the number of marshals, generals and admirals alone had fallen from the January 1989 figure of 2,500 to roughly 2,000. By June 1991 270,000 young officers and senior NCOs lacked accommodation for their families, and 50 per cent of young officer families were earning an income below the official poverty level of 100 rubles per month.

It is therefore not surprising that 4 million rubles of the 1991 defence budget was earmarked for social programmes, or that officer's salaries were to rise, sharply. Moreover, contract service for senior NCOs,

A protest against the deaths in non-combat situations of thousands of Soviet servicemen. Such protests only became possible during the Gorbachev era, but the Ministry of Defence maintained its silence

already underway in the navy, was to be extended to the SRF and airborne troops between 1991 and 1994.

A crisis of authority

Of the two crises of authority in the USSR, Party and state, the former did not transform radically the character of Soviet military life until the Party itself was dissolved in 1991. Party activity remained an important factor in promotion and preferment after 1985. According to military spokesmen, 37,000 party cells held their assemblies in 1990, and membership remained fairly constant at over 1 million (70 per cent of them officers). None the less, the Komsomol's striking decline (from 40 to 23.6 million members between 1987 and 1991), had obvious implications for the armed forces, as did the demands for dissolution of GLAVPU by a growing body of younger officers. The XXVIII Party Congress stopped well short of this, transforming GLAVPU into a 'neutral arm of the state', ending its subordination to the Central Committee and its supervision of party cells, but otherwise leaving the apparatus intact.

It was the decline of the centre's authority which posed an earlier and more immediate threat to the military system. By August 1991 six republics (Armenia, Georgia, Latvia, Lithuania, Moldova and Ukraine) had announced their intention to create their own armed forces and defence ministries, while a further four (Azerbaijan, Belarus, Estonia, and Uzbekistan) had passed resolutions forbidding their conscripts to serve outside their borders. The centre responded to these developments, *inter alia*, by shifting responsibility for draft fulfilment from the military commissariats (*voenkomaty*), which did not possess powers of enforcement, to local authorities. Many of the latter, however, simply defied instructions. According to official figures, draft evaders from the five republics worst affected represented only 7 per cent of the conscript pool. But given the low call-up figures announced for Moscow and Leningrad in 1990 (25 per cent), the figures released for the Russian Republic were, not altogether surprisingly, treated with scepticism.

With the dissolution of the Soviet state, the military establishment may have had little choice but to carry on as they did during Gorbachev's final months in power: compromising with those who would compromise with them and fighting rearguard actions against those who would not. Such actions have met with some success. None the less, it would be unwise to underestimate the level of discontent in the armed forces or discount the dangers it might pose in post-Soviet Russia. JGS

DRAFT FULFILMENT BY REPUBLIC, 1989–91[a]

Republic	Spring 1989[b] (%)	Spring 1990[b] (%)	Autumn 1990[c] (%)	Overall 1990[d] (%)	Spring 1991[e] (%)
Armenia	100.0	7.5	37.5	22.5	16.5
Azerbaijan	97.8	100.0	58.0	84.0	100.0
Belarus	100.0	98.9	82.0	90.4	100.0
Estonia	79.5	40.2	31.6	35.9	30.3
Georgia	94.0	27.5	10.0	18.5	8.2
Kazakhstan	100.0	99.2	100.0	100.0	90.0+
Kyrgyzstan	100.0	89.5	100.0	100.0	90.0+
Latvia	90.7	54.2	25.3	39.5	30.8
Lithuania	91.6	33.6	16.5	25.1	12.3
Moldova	100.0	100.0	92.0	96.0	81.5
Russia	100.0	98.6	92.2	95.4	100.0
Tajikistan	100.0	92.7	94.1	93.4	90.0+
Turkmenistan	100.0	90.2	100.0	96.1	90.0+
Ukraine	97.6	99.4	91.0	95.1	100.0
Uzbekistan	100.0	87.4	83.6	85.6	84.6

[a]Percentage of youths answering the draft only. Owing to exemptions, only 49% of those eligible were called up in 1989
[b]*Krasnaya Zvezda*, 7 December 1990
[c]Estimates only. (Source: Craig Oliphant, SSRC, Sandhurst)
[d]Soviet Central TV, 14 April 1991
[e]*Izvestiya*, 22 July 1991, reporting a shortfall of 'more than 500,000' conscripts

The Black Sea fleet crisis

When the Soviet state collapsed, a bitter dispute erupted between Russia and Ukraine over the future of the Black Sea fleet. The third largest of the former Soviet fleets, it has its main base at Sevastopol' in the Crimea. Russian politicians and military leaders, however, tend to view the fleet as part of the historic defences of the Imperial Russian and Soviet states. Once the USSR was dissolved they claimed that the fleet should fall under CIS or even Russian control.

The leadership in Kiev, in contrast, insisted on the ships coming under Ukrainian national control. Ukraine hardly needed a fleet of this size to defend its coast, and did not have the means to maintain so large a naval force. But Ukrainian nationalists viewed the struggle over ownership as a test of the fledgling independence of their state. Passions surrounding the dispute were inflamed on both sides by political sniping over the status of the Crimean peninsula, which was transferred from Russia to Ukraine by the Soviet government in 1954.

Efforts to agree on a division of the fleet reached deadlock in the spring of 1992 and military friction increased as Kiev and Moscow competed for its loyalty. The crisis was only defused at a summit in June 1992 when Presidents Yel'tsin and Kravchuk agreed to take over joint personal operational and strategic command of the fleet for a transitional period to 1995. This agreement temporarily turned the Black Sea fleet into a joint Ukrainian-Russian force. Subsequently a 1993 agreement by Kravchuk to meet Ukrainian economic debts to Russia by ceding Russia control of the entire fleet was hotly disputed in Kiev. The future of the fleet in 1994 remained uncertain; in practice many of the vessels may be sold off or scrapped.

Part of the Black Sea fleet in the port of Sevastopol'

THE WARSAW PACT

The Warsaw Treaty Organization (WTO), comprising Bulgaria, Czechoslovakia, the GDR, Hungary, Poland, Romania, the USSR and (until 1968) Albania, was established on 14 May 1955, ostensibly but only partially in response to the admission of the Federal Republic of Germany into NATO.

Before its establishment the USSR's central and East European clients, tied to the USSR by bilateral defence treaties, maintained 1.5 million men under arms, supervised by thousands of Soviet advisers posted down to regimental level. After Stalin's death a less direct but more institutionalized form of supervision was deemed appropriate. Additionally, by this time, the impact of nuclear weapons made it desirable to standardize training, force structures and equipment within a multilateral framework.

Despite the Pact's formal symmetry with NATO, its role, from its founding up to its dissolution in 1991, was limited to administration, training and (after 1969) consultation. Its supreme political organ, the Political Consultative Committee, whilst required to meet twice a year, functioned at Soviet convenience, failing to meet at all between 1956 and 1958 or during the 1968–69 Czechoslovak crisis. Its principal military organ, the Joint High Command, was given no operational authority over military forces, and subordinate multinational commands analogous to NATO's AFNORTH, AFCENT and AFSOUTH were never established. In crisis and war, command and control of each member's forces would have passed directly from its national defence ministry to the Soviet General Staff and its designated Theatre commanders. It is precisely by such means that Bulgarian, GDR, Hungarian and Polish units were incorporated into the twenty-six-division force that invaded Czechoslovakia in 1968.

In practice the Warsaw Pact performed both an external and an internal function. Externally it was designed to support a 'theatre strategic operation' against NATO, waged according to a military doctrine of 'coalition warfare' which was binding upon Warsaw Pact members. This doctrine deprived non-Soviet Warsaw Pact (NSWP) forces of the capacity to conduct independent operations above the tactical (divisional) level. Divisions were designed to be interchangeable, inserted where required into 'higher formations' (armies of four to five divisions and fronts of two to five armies) under Soviet commanders who controlled most significant intelligence, communications and logistics assets. Through this system, formations of the same nationality could be separated, maximizing Soviet control over each, and minimizing opportunities for insubordination.

The internal function of the Pact was to render local armies incapable of interfering with the activities of the Soviet armed forces on their national territories. Thanks to the organization which 'coalition warfare' doctrine imposed upon them, these armies were neither integrated nor cohesive entities, and neither the training system nor the elaborate schedule of joint exercises enabled their commanders to familiarize themselves with local conditions. After the Soviet troop withdrawal in 1958, Romania waged a long and ultimately successful struggle to extricate itself from Warsaw Pact doctrine. The attempt by the Czechoslovak General Staff to do the same was halted when the Prague Spring was crushed in August 1968.

Reliability, always seen as problematic, was addressed by institutional mechanisms replicating those found in the Soviet armed forces: party cells in each sub-unit and party membership as a requirement for advancement; political officers, accountable to political directorates under Central Committee control; military counter-intelligence networks of security services; élite armed detachments and workers' militias responsible to interior ministries and state security organs.

Soviet supervision of these mechanisms was conducted through three channels: the headquarters and staff of the Soviet military representative in each country; Warsaw Pact advisory organs (for example, the WTO chief political directorate); and the KGB. Additionally, the educational system – which placed a large number of mid-ranking and all senior NSWP officers in Soviet academies – enabled the Soviets to identify and, in turn, advance the career prospects of reliable and capable officers.

Despite the USSR's dominance and its undoubted control over the WTO, its non-Soviet members found it possible on occasion to use the Political Consultative Committee to assert joint or particular interests: for example, to deny the USSR military assistance in its border confrontation with China (1969); to register concern about nuclear missile deployments (1984); and throughout the 1970s and 1980s, to resist Soviet demands for greater integration and higher defence spending. Although these demands escalated during the first two years of Gorbachev's tenure, the adoption of a 'purely defensive' military doctrine on 29 May 1987 led, by stages, to significant Soviet-sanctioned force reductions in Poland and Czechoslovakia, whilst in no respect changing the doctrine's 'coalition' aspects.

Only after the democratic revolutions of 1989 did central European governments take the first difficult steps to establish national military doctrines. Despite anxieties over German unification, by the summer of 1990 Czechoslovakia, Hungary and Poland had concluded that continued WTO membership was incompatible with this aim. In response to the changed situation in Europe, the military structures of the Pact were formally dissolved in April 1991 and the political structures dissolved on 1 July 1991. JGS

Soviet tanks in Wenceslas Square, Prague, as the military intervention of Soviet and other Warsaw Pact troops brought the Prague Spring to an end in August 1968

Strategic arms

THE MILITARY USE OF SPACE

Both the USSR and the USA were dependent on space systems for the support of military operations. However, while many American military support functions are primarily provided by space systems, the USSR maintained terrestrial systems in parallel with the development of space systems. To that extent they were less vulnerable to anti-satellite attack (ASAT). From 1957 the USA and USSR, while increasing the numbers of operational satellites in orbit, maintained parity. Until 1989, however, the number of Soviet space launches was some three or four times that of the USA. American satellites and their ground control stations can achieve 'assured mission capabilities' for long periods. The Soviet approach was for short-lived and less sophisticated satellites, but extensive launch facilities provided the Soviet Union with an advantage in space support responsiveness, including a surge launch capability which would have been useful in wartime.

The USSR employed satellites for numerous purposes including: reconnaissance by means of imagery, electronic and radar collection techniques; missile launch detection and warning of attack; ocean surveillance and targeting; command and control communications; navigational aids; and meteorological forecasting. The Soviet Union possessed an ASAT capability based on a co-orbital interceptor situated at the Tyuratum cosmodrome in Kazakhstan. The system probably became operational in 1971 and routine tests were carried out until 1983 when the USSR unilaterally announced a moratorium on launching ASAT weapons. Since then ground-based tests and practices have been routinely

conducted. Other potential ASAT capabilities include the exo-atmospheric Galosh ABM system defending Moscow and, at the Sary Shagan range in Kazakhstan, test equipment and a ground-based laser, which may be powerful enough to damage unprotected satellites in near-earth orbit.

Until 1988 the USSR conducted over 90 space launches a year but this dropped to about 75 a year by 1991. At least 160 satellites are maintained in orbit. In 1982 during the period of the Anglo-Argentinian war in the South Atlantic the USSR launched twenty-eight satellites in sixty-nine days. The normal launch rate was roughly one every five days. The USSR also developed a space shuttle system, the Buran, but this was launched only once, in 1988, in an unmanned mode and under fully automatic control. The USSR established the Mir space station which has been continuously manned since mid-1989 and is undoubtedly conducting military as well as civil research. Mir has six docking ports and so can be quickly and extensively reinforced in times of crisis.   AD

STRATEGIC NUCLEAR FORCES

The USSR's strategic nuclear forces were split between the navy and the air, and strategic rocket forces. All these nuclear elements have now been concentrated in the Strategic Deterrent forces and are under the command of the Commonwealth of Independent States.

The Strategic Rocket Forces (SRF) were the strongest arm of the USSR's offensive nuclear capability but represent a smaller proportion of the strategic nuclear forces of the CIS. In June 1992 SRF deployed 1,400 intercontinental ballistic missiles (ICBM) mounting 6,600 warheads compared to 1,398 ICBMS with under 5,000 warheads in 1979. There are 832 submarine-launched ballistic missiles (SLBM) mounting about 2,700 warheads compared with 1,028 SLBMS with around only 1,500 warheads in 1979. In the same year there were 156 strategic bombers armed with bombs only, while today there are 170 strategic bombers of which nearly half can carry a number of stand-off or cruise missiles. Of these strategic weapons, 104 ICBMS and 40 strategic bombers were located in Kazakhstan, 80 mobile ICBMS in Belarus and 176 ICBMS and 20 bombers in Ukraine; the remainder, including all ballistic missile submarines, are held by Russia.

The last five years of the Soviet era saw significant changes in the USSR's nuclear weapons deployment. For the first time mobile ICBMS were brought into service. All ground-launched missiles, including cruise missiles (GLCM) with ranges between 500 and 5,500 km were eliminated by 1 June 1991 in

Russian mobile missile launcher, 1992

accordance with the terms of the Intermediate Nuclear Forces Treaty which came into force in June 1988. The Soviet Union destroyed close to 900 missiles.

The Strategic Arms Reduction Treaty (START) was signed in Moscow on 31 July 1991. The treaty required both the Soviet Union and the USA to reduce their strategic nuclear forces to 1,600 delivery weapons and 6,000 nuclear warheads (according to counting rules which in effect allowed the limits for warheads to be exceeded). The importance of START does not lie in the reductions of strategic weapons. While these will be considerable, they will fall short of original expectations. Some 800 delivery vehicles and over 5,000 warheads for the Soviet Union and 250 delivery vehicles and over 3,500 warheads for the USA were to be eliminated but both sides could keep more than sufficient weapons to maintain deterrence. The most significant clauses of the treaty concern the development of future weapons and verification of weapons' holdings which will be both extensive and intrusive.

Since then, on 23 May 1992, Belarus, Kazakhstan, Russia, Ukraine and the USA signed a protocol to START. It was agreed that these four republics of the former Soviet Union, as successor states, would assume the treaty obligations of the former USSR. Belarus, Kazakhstan, and Ukraine further committed themselves to adhere to the Non-proliferation Treaty as non-nuclear weapon states in the shortest possible time. The treaty was subsequently ratified, but with especially strong reservations on Ukraine's part. On 16 June 1992 Presidents Bush and Yel'tsin met in Washington and signed a joint understanding on further substantial reductions in strategic offensive weapons; these would be effected in two stages. In the first, to be completed within seven years of START coming into force, strategic weapons would be reduced to no more than an overall total of between 3,800 and 4,250 warheads to be held by

each country. The second stage, to be completed by the year 2003, would reduce each side's overall warhead total to between 3,000 and 3,500. All multiple, independently-targetable re-entry vehicles (MIRV) ICBMs would be eliminated, and no more than 1,700 SLBM warheads would be deployed by each side. A significant change to START counting rules for bombers was agreed. Instead of attributing a number of weapons to aircraft which can be equipped to carry more, the new rule is that bombers will be counted as carrying the number of weapons that they are capable of carrying. On 3 January 1993 President Yel'tsin and President Bush signed a START 2 agreement which extended the cuts, provided both Belarus and Ukraine complied fully with START 1 and subject to the ratification by the Russian parliament of the START 2 document.

Strategic rocket forces

The SRF are a separate service with equal status to the army, navy, air force and air defence force. Its manpower numbers some 144,000 and it is organized in five rocket armies which are sub-divided into divisions and brigades. In common with other areas of defence design and production, a number of design bureaux develop ballistic missiles for the SRF. There are, therefore, normally two or more different systems of the same generation of missile in service at any time.

The ICBM force has been constantly up-graded with both the introduction of new missile systems and the modification of older models. The backbone of the SRF is its force of fourth generation ICBMs comprising some 700 SS-17, SS-18 and SS-19 ICBMs; all have a maximum range of 10,000 km (11,000 for SS-18) and all are equipped with MIRV; four, ten and six respectively. All will have to be eliminated under the June 1992 agreement. The two older systems are already being retired: the SS-11, first introduced in 1965, has three warheads (not independently targetable) and the SS-13 is a single warhead missile first operational in 1966. The latest additions, SS-24 and SS-25 are both mobile ICBMs and came into service in 1987 and 1985 respectively. The SS-24 is a rail-mobile system, though some have been deployed in silos. It can carry up to ten MIRV 550 kiloton warheads, its maximum range is 10,000 km and with an estimated 'circular error probability' (CEP) of 200 metres it is more accurate than the fourth generation systems. Production of the SS-24 ceased on 1 January 1991 with 36 rail-mobile and 56 silo-based missiles deployed. All will be eliminated under the June 1992 agreement. The second mobile ICBM is the SS-25 which is road-mobile and of which over 340 have so far been deployed, 80 of which are located in Belarus. The SS-25 is a single warhead missile with a yield of

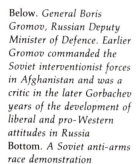

Below. *General Boris Gromov, Russian Deputy Minister of Defence. Earlier Gromov commanded the Soviet interventionist forces in Afghanistan and was a critic in the later Gorbachev years of the development of liberal and pro-Western attitudes in Russia*
Bottom. *A Soviet anti-arms race demonstration*

and IV; and six of the latest class of Typhoon first deployed in 1982. There are no reports of any new class of missile submarine under construction. With one exception each new sub-class was fitted with a new type of SLBM. Each generation of SLBM showed improvements in range and accuracy. Early models were single warhead missiles and developments progressed through MRV to MIRV, the latest version being the ten MIRV warhead SS-N-23 with a range of 8,300 km. MIRV warheads for SLBMs were not restricted by the June 1992 agreement. All told: Russia could deploy a maximum of 832 SLBMs, if all submarines were operational and at sea, whereas in practice probably only about 20 per cent are kept on station at any one time.

Strategic bombers

Soviet strategic aviation contained both long- and medium-range bombers but only the former could be classified as strategic in the treaty sense of the word. For arms control purposes bombers would be divided into air-launched cruise missiles (ALCM) capable and non-ALCM capable; for treaty purposes countable ALCMs are those with a range in excess of 600 km and the USSR had only one such ALCM in service, the 1,600 km range AS-15 which carries a 250 kiloton warhead. The long-range bomber force comprises 150 Tu-95 Bear (89 classed as non-ALCM capable, with the ALCM capable bombers located in Ukraine and Kazakhstan) and 20 ALCM capable Tu-160 Blackjack in Ukraine.

Nuclear war policy

The Soviet Union repeatedly declared that it would not be the first nation to use nuclear weapons and, while openly admitting that no side could win a nuclear war, still seemed more concerned with waging war and did not recognize deterrence as a concept, but only as a by-product of capability. Soviet policy in the event of a possible nuclear exchange was to pre-empt an enemy attack by a massive nuclear strike. If they failed to launch a pre-emptive strike, the possibility of a launch under attack still existed, as the USSR's warning system would have provided the High Command with up to thirty minutes warning of an ICBM attack. The Soviet Union, therefore, put more effort into developing its first strike capability, as witnessed by the allocation of 54 per cent of its strategic warheads to silo-based ICBMs. Other measures showed a determination to emerge from a nuclear war, which military theorists considered might be of a protracted nature, in a more favourable position than their enemy. These measures included: a command, control and communications system designed to ensure maximum surviveability; massive investment in an anti-ballistic missile (ABM) system and in air defences.   AD

Top. United States inspectors checking on the destruction of Russian missiles. Above. Military musicians in Moscow's Gor'ky park

550 kilotons, its range is 10,500 km and it also has a CEP of 200 metres; production of the SS-25 continues. The USA has no operational mobile ICBMs and development of a rail-mobile version of the MX Peacekeeper has been cancelled.

Submarine-launched ballistic missiles (SLBM)

The Soviet Union first brought submarines especially designed to carry SLBMs into service in the 1950s, in the form of the Golf and Hotel classes (NATO designations) whose later versions each carried six missiles. The last of these two classes was de-commissioned in late 1990. The Soviet custom was to design the submarine and its missiles as a package and so few classes mounted the same missile as another class. The navy now fields fifty-five nuclear submarines in three basic classes: six Yankee I, first deployed in 1968 and now being withdrawn from service; forty-three Delta I, II, III

International relations

Muscovy and Imperial Russia

THE EXPANSION OF TSARIST RUSSIA

Muscovy became an independent state in 1480 when the Tatar yoke was thrown off by Ivan III who, after his marriage in 1472 to Sofia, the only niece of the last Byzantine emperor, also initiated Muscovy's claim to be Byzantium's successor as leader of the Orthodox world ('Moscow is the Third Rome'). Ivan III also asserted Moscow's claim to the former lands of Kievan Russia, acquired by Lithuania, and gained access to the Baltic. Modest diplomatic contacts with many western states were started. Muscovite control of northern Russia was completed by Vasily III. Under Ivan IV (the Terrible), first to be crowned 'Tsar of All the Russias' (the Russian principates now assembled under Muscovite rule), Muscovy conquered the Tatar khanates of Kazan' (1552) and Astrakhan' (1556), and expanded into western Siberia (1583). The Crimean Tatars, however, remained a great menace, and in the Livonian War (1558–83) against Poland–Lithuania (fully united in 1569) and Sweden, Ivan failed to acquire the lands of the Teutonic Order and lost Muscovy's narrow Baltic coastline. A difficult sea route to the west via Arkhangel'sk was, however, opened by the English in 1553. Under Fedor I, an independent Russian Orthodox patriarchate was established (1588). Following the death of Boris Godunov, violent dynastic and social conflicts erupted, and during the Time of Troubles Muscovite power was eclipsed. Polish intervention in 1609–12 and the Polish king's ambition to promote Catholicism provoked a successful national rising, and Mikhail Romanov was elected tsar in 1613. Under him Muscovy still remained on the defensive. Novgorod was recovered from Sweden (1617), but relations with Poland proved complex; in 1634 Władysław IV of Poland renounced his claim to the Muscovite throne but retained Smolensk. In 1648, however, a Ukrainian Cossack rising against Polish rule, and Ukraine's incorporation in 1654 by Tsar Alexis, precipitated a major Russo-Polish war which resulted in the partition of the Ukraine along the Dnieper (1667). A war with Sweden (1656–58) was inconclusive. An 'eternal peace' with Poland (1686) brought the permanent acquisition of Kiev and membership, with Poland, Austria and Venice, of the Holy League against Turkey, but with little success for Russia. A treaty with China excluded Russia from the Amur basin (1689).

The birth of the Russian Empire

By 1696, when Peter I acquired sole power, Muscovy was no longer isolated and was open to western cultural and technological ideas. Peter accelerated this process and during the Great Northern War (1700–21) against Sweden altered the balance of power in northern and eastern Europe. Humiliatingly defeated at Narva (November 1700), Peter consolidated his forces while Charles XII of Sweden pursued Peter's ally, Augustus II of Poland and Saxony. Peter conquered Ingria and founded St Petersburg (May 1703) but failed to secure peace in 1707 and had to face a Swedish invasion from Poland in 1709. Peter's decisive victory at Poltava (July 1709) did not immediately end the war, but Russia's access to the Baltic was now assured. However, Peter fared badly against Turkey, where Charles XII took refuge. An invasion of Turkey (1711) during which Russia, for the first time, sought Balkan Christian support, ended disastrously, and Peter had to relinquish Azov (captured in 1696) and to promise not to interfere in Poland. Despite this promise, Peter restored Augustus II, and in 1716–17 re-established Russian influence in Poland.

The Swedish war was vigorously pursued in Germany, Denmark and Finland; the new Russian fleet defeated the Swedes at Hangö (July 1714), and in July 1719 Russian forces landed in Sweden proper. By the peace treaty of Nystad (August 1721) Russia acquired Ingria, Estonia and Swedish Livonia with Riga. The victorious Peter assumed the title of emperor. Dynastic links with Courland, Mecklenburg and Holstein–Gottorp were also established.

However, there was growing concern in England, Germany and elsewhere at the rise of the new northern colossus. In 1722–23 Russia won the south shore of the Caspian from Persia and, although it failed to establish diplomatic and trading relations

Previous spread. *Boris Yel'tsin and Bill Clinton at their Vancouver summit meeting, 1993*

Peter the Great in France, meeting Louis XV. Painting by Louise Marie Jeanne Hersent (1784–1862)

with China, the subjugation of Kamchatka continued.

Although none of Peter I's immediate successors possessed his formidable qualities, Russia's growing international importance was maintained. During the period 1725–40 Russian foreign policy was largely guided by A.I. Ostermann (1687–1747), who opposed French influence and supported Austria. During the War of the Polish Succession (1733–35) Empress Anne fought the French-sponsored candidate Leszczyński and helped to install the Saxon Augustus III. In 1732 Peter I's Persian conquests were surrendered, but another Turkish war (1735–39) brought Russia Azov, though not the right to enter the Black Sea. Sweden declared war in 1741 only to lose south-eastern Finland in 1743.

In the Seven Years War (1756–62) Russia adhered to the Franco-Austrian alliance (January 1757), fought successfully against Prussia, and in 1760 occupied Berlin. However, the accession of Peter III brought about an instantaneous reconciliation and an alliance with Prussia which continued under Catherine II until 1788.

Conquests of Catherine the Great

Under Catherine II Russia's international influence and prestige received a new impetus. Catherine secured the election of Stanisław Poniatowski as king of Poland (1764) but opposed constitutional reform there, and in 1768 imposed a formal Russian protectorate over Poland. An uprising in Poland won Franco-Austrian assistance, and brought Turkey into open war against Russia (1769). The ensuing serious international complications were resolved by the first partition of Poland (1772), which gave Russia Vitebsk and Mogilev. The Russo-Turkish treaty of Kutchuk–Kainardzhi (July 1774) established the independence of the Crimean khanate; Russia annexed Kerch and the territory between the Bug and Dnieper, secured a free passage for its merchant ships through the Turkish Straits, and acquired ill-defined rights to protect Turkey's Christians. Russia's international prestige was greatly enhanced by the victory over Turkey. The Russian protectorate over Poland was confirmed in 1775, Russia became a guarantor of the constitution of the Holy Roman Empire in 1779, and during the American War of Independence lent its weight to the League of Armed Neutrality (1780) against British claims to search neutral vessels in wartime.

Turkey, however, loomed large again. In association with G.A. Potemkin (1739–91), Catherine devised the 'Greek project' to restore Byzantium under her grandson Constantine, and to liberate Orthodox Christians from Turkish rule. This ambitious scheme made necessary a rapprochement with Austria (1781). The Crimea was annexed and a protectorate imposed over Georgia (1783), but the war against Turkey (1787–92) brought limited success; the situation was further complicated in 1788 by a Swedish attack and by the overthrow of the Russian protectorate in Poland. Although peace was signed with Sweden at Verelä (August 1790), Prussian alliances with Poland and Turkey, and the threat of combined action by the European powers against Russia with British participation in spring 1791 tested Catherine's resilience to the utmost. She refused to budge, the potential anti-Russian coalition disintegrated, and after the Treaty of Jassy with Turkey (January 1792), whereby she postponed implementing the 'Greek project', Catherine turned to deal with Poland whose reformed constitution of 1791 she overthrew in summer 1792. She then proceeded, in collusion with Prussia, with the second partition of Poland (1793). The defeat of Kościuszko's uprising brought about the third and final partition of Poland in 1795; 62 per cent of pre-partition Poland was now in the Russian Empire. Catherine died in November 1796 before another extravagant campaign to destroy the Ottoman Empire could be implemented.

Paul I was hostile to the French Revolution and after Bonaparté's seizure of Malta (June 1798) joined the Second Coalition against France. Despite Russian successes in the Ionian Islands and Italy, relations with Austria turned sour, as well as with Britain over an expedition to Holland and Russian designs on Malta. Paul abandoned the coalition, organized the second League of Armed Neutrality against Britain (December 1800) and started negotiations for a French alliance. He turned to planning Turkey's downfall and annexed Georgia, but a Cossack force sent to conquer India was recalled after his murder in March 1801.

The zenith of tsarist power

Under Alexander I Russian influence was to reach its highest point in the imperial period. He restored good relations with Britain and France in 1801. However, the new Anglo-French war (1803), the Duc d'Enghien's execution, and the proclamation of Napoleon as emperor in 1804 moved him to support the Third Coalition of which the Anglo-Russian alliance (April 1805) was the core. But disaster struck; despite Alexander's warm friendship with the Prussian king and queen, Prussia did not participate militarily and the defeat of the Russian and Austrian armies at Austerlitz (December 1805) compelled Austria to sue for peace. Russian military operations resumed when Prussia finally challenged France in September 1806. Prussia's collapse and Russia's defeat at Friedland (June 1807) led to the Treaty of Alliance signed by Napoleon and Alexander at Tilsit in July 1807. Russia severed relations with Britain, helped to enforce Napoleon's Continental System by attacking Sweden and annexing Finland (September 1809), and discussed with France a partition of Turkey, yet again at war with Russia

since October 1806. Despite the two emperors' second meeting at Erfurt (September–October 1808), Russia's support of France during the Franco-Austrian war of 1809 was half-hearted, while the enlargement of the Napoleonic Duchy of Warsaw (created at Tilsit) increased Russia's fears for her ex-Polish provinces. In fact the Franco-Russian alliance was under a growing strain. Experiencing economic difficulties, Russia modified the stiff anti-British tariffs demanded by Napoleon. In January 1811 Napoleon annexed Oldenburg, the heir to which was Alexander's brother-in-law. Alexander secured an alliance with Sweden (April 1812) and signed a well-timed peace treaty with Turkey (May 1812), which ceded Bessarabia. A nine-year war with Persia was terminated when that country renounced its claims to a large area in the Caucasus in October 1813.

Napoleon attacked Russia on 24 June 1812 and entered Moscow on 14 September. Alexander's refusal to negotiate, the burning of Moscow, and an early winter compelled the French to withdraw. Disregarding contrary advice and determined to liberate Europe, Alexander pursued them across the Russian border. He was joined by Prussia (February 1813), Sweden and Austria (August), and received the necessary subsidies from Britain. On 31 March 1814 Alexander entered Paris in triumph; he insisted that Louis XVIII could be restored only as a constitutional monarch. At the Congress of Vienna (September 1814–June 1815) Alexander acquired most of the Duchy of Warsaw as a constitutional kingdom of Poland in union with Russia.

The vague Holy Alliance initiated by Alexander in September 1815, which was to commit all rulers to govern according to the precepts of Christianity, had less effect in preserving peace than the periodic international congresses provided for by the renewed Quadruple Alliance of November 1815. At the Congresses of Troppau (1820), Laibach (Ljubljana) (1821) and Verona (1822) Alexander supported the policy of intervention advocated by Metternich, against revolutions in Italy, Spain and South America, but his offers of Russian troops were politely refused. Diplomatic relations with the USA, which date from 1808, were not strained by the Monroe Doctrine; Alexander admired the American republic and Russia agreed to restrict its territory in America to Alaska (April 1824).

Alexander's new policy of 'legitimacy' proved difficult to uphold when the Greeks rose against Turkey in 1821, and Nicholas I finally agreed, in conjunction with Britain, to mediate for Greek autonomy (1826). Turkish indignation after the destruction of the Turkish fleet at Navarino (October 1827) drove Russia into another successful war in April 1828. The Treaty of Adrianople (September

Napoleon's retreat from Moscow portrayed by Ernest Meissonier (1815–91)

Napoleon's retreat from Moscow

When the French Emperor Napoleon attacked Russia in June 1812, his invasion force numbered some 370,000 men, later reaching a total of about 600,000. In December of the same year, the remnants of this force retreated across the Niemen river into Prussia. Fewer than 5,000 remained as organized military units, and the total number of men who left Russia that winter was no more than 100,000. Yet this crushing defeat was achieved by the Russians without winning a single major battle.

The initial French attacks were successful, but on at least two occasions in the summer of 1812 hesitation on the part of Napoleon's generals allowed large Russian forces to escape from very difficult situations. These failures combined with Napoleon's desire to inflict a rapid defeat on Russia to sow the seeds of disaster. Rather than pausing for the winter at Minsk or Smolensk, the Emperor pushed on to Moscow.

The battle of Borodino, fought before Moscow in September 1812, was bloody but indecisive. Both armies suffered huge casualties, and the Russians under Kutuzov retreated beyond Moscow.

The burning of the city that followed its occupation by the French is a much-disputed event. Both sides have been blamed for deliberately setting it alight. However it seems most likely that a wooden city, unusually hot summer weather, and the fact that the Russians had removed all the fire-fighting equipment, in combination with victorious soldiers and alcohol meant that a destructive fire was almost inevitable.

As the French were forced to retreat from a city in flames, the hugely skilful campaign fought by Kutuzov came to fruition. Avoiding a large battle, the Russian commander carefully shepherded the French away from the south, where Napoleon wanted to go, and forced them to retreat back through areas already devastated by war. Starvation, illness and highly effective guerrilla campaigns demoralized the weakened French armies. Napoleon managed to extricate himself and some of his remaining forces from a last battle near the Prussian frontier, but after this the Russian winter set in and cold and starvation finished off the rest of his troops. By 1813 only a pitiful skeleton of the Grand Army remained.

1829) gave Russia the mouth of the Danube, territories along the eastern Black Sea coast and in the Caucasus, guaranteed Russian trade in the Black Sea, and established Russian influence in Moldavia and Wallachia. With Britain and France, Russia established an independent Greek kingdom in 1830, and its domination of Turkey was obvious.

The Caucasus

Russia's strategic position on the Black Sea had been reinforced under Alexander I. The eastern Georgian kingdom – a Russian protectorate since the reign of Catherine the Great – was annexed in 1801. The subjugation of the remaining Georgian principalities, such as Mingrelia and Imeretiya, led to war with Persia (1804–13), which had to cede most of

eastern Transcaucasia along the Kura and Araxes rivers (including Baku, and the Azerbaijan lowlands), and to recognize Russia's right to maintain a fleet on the Caspian. Persia denounced the 1813 Gulistan treaty in June 1826 but was beaten by Field-Marshal I. F. Paskevich (1782–1856); with the Treaty of Turkmanchay (February 1828) it surrendered the khanates of Nakhichevan and Yerevan (Persian Armenia and the Azerbaijan highlands).

The struggle with Turkey for the western Caucasus started in 1828, but although the acquisition of the eastern Black Sea littoral (including Anapa and Poti) in 1829 completed the formal annexation of the Caucasus, Russia had to face a protracted war from 1834 to 1859 against Muslim mountain peoples in the Chechen area and Dagestan under the *imam* Shamil. Russia completed its conquest in Transcaucasia in 1878 when it received Kars, Ardahan and Batumi from Turkey under the Treaty of Berlin.

Russia and the Eastern Question

Revolutions in France, Belgium and Russian Poland in 1830 augmented Nicholas I's fear of subversion and prompted a renewal of the hitherto strained Holy Alliance with Austria and Prussia (1833). But the Eastern Question re-emerged as the dominant problem when the Sultan was obliged to accept Russian help against Mehemet Ali, the Egyptian pasha and France's protégé (1831–33). Although the Russo-Turkish alliance treaty of Unkiar Skelessi (July 1833) did not give Russia new advantages in the Straits, it provided legalistic justification to intervene in Ottoman affairs, to which Britain in particular objected. Nicholas, however, was aware of the dangers of unilateral action and hoped to disrupt the Anglo-French entente. He therefore co-operated with Britain, Austria and Prussia (London Convention, July 1840) in compelling the Egyptians to retreat after the second Egyptian–Turkish war (1839–40), and in replacing the Unkiar Skelessi treaty with the Straits Convention (July 1841), to which a humiliated France also acceded. Palmerston considered the convention a British success since it confirmed that the Straits was an international and not just a Russo-Turkish problem. While Russo-French relations cooled, Nicholas courted Britain with offers of a common policy to preserve Turkey in the short run but to prepare in advance for what Nicholas considered the inevitability of Turkey's disintegration. He obtained an erroneous impression that Lord Aberdeen had committed Britain in 1844 to co-operation with Russia.

The 1848 revolutions in Europe horrified Nicholas, whose subsequent actions were to earn him the nickname of 'gendarme of Europe'. Russian forces overwhelmed the Romanian patriots and restored Russo-Turkish control in Moldavia and Wallachia (May 1849), and in March 1849, fearing Austria's collapse, Nicholas speedily accepted Vienna's request to help crush the Hungarian struggle for independence. He opposed the movement for German unity, successfully supporting Denmark over Schleswig and Holstein (mid-1848), and then Austria in restoring the German Confederation (1850).

The Crimean War

Russia's influence in Europe, now at its peak, was to be drastically reduced by the Crimean War (1854–56). A dispute with France and Turkey over rival Catholic and Orthodox claims to control the Holy Places in Palestine provoked Nicholas to demand of the Turkish government guarantees not only for the Orthodox Church but also for the entire Orthodox population of Turkey, the object of A.S. Menshikov's (1787–1869) mission of February 1853. Nicholas strove for a peaceful settlement of the crisis, but his diplomatic efforts were defeated by widespread Russophobia in France and Britain and by Turkish truculence. Turkey declared war on Russia (November 1853) as did Britain and France (March 1854). Nicholas I died in February 1855 amidst the ruins of his foreign policy; the Crimean War exposed Russia's fundamental weakness and the Austrian ultimatum of December 1855 finally compelled Alexander II to sue for peace.

By the Treaty of Paris (March 1856) Russia ceded Bessarabia to Moldavia and, most humiliating of all, accepted the neutralization of the Black Sea region; Ottoman territorial integrity was guaranteed. Though Napoleon III proved less hostile to Russia than Palmerston, Alexander II disapproved of Italian unification (1859–60) and moved closer to Prussia, a process much accelerated by Bismarck's offers of assistance, in contrast to Anglo-French hostility, during the Polish insurrection of 1863–64. The Russo-Prussian rapprochement benefited both states; it permitted Bismarck to defeat Austria (1866) and France (1870–71), and enabled Russia to repudiate unilaterally in October 1870 the clauses of the 1856 treaty neutralizing the Black Sea. Although resented in Britain, Russia's action was recognized by the London Conference (March 1871). Russia and Germany were soon reconciled with Austria–Hungary, and the Three Emperors' League, reminiscent of the former conservative Holy Alliance, was formed in 1873.

Central Asia and the Far East

Expansion into the nomad-populated steppes between the Caspian and the Aral seas dates from the 1820s, and the Aral Sea was reached by 1846. In 1853 General V.A. Perovsky (1795–1857) took the fortress of Ak-Mechet (Perovsk) on the river Syr Darya along which a line of forts was established. In the east, working from Semipalatinsk, the Russians crossed the River Ili and founded Verny (Alma-Ata) in 1854. The advance on the established khanates of Kokand and Khiva and the emirate of Bukhara, with which Russia already had trading links, began in 1864–65 when General M.G. Chernyaev, acting largely on his own initiative, attacked Tashkent, the Kokand capital, and provoked the emir of Bukhara to declare a 'holy war'. The resulting Russian invasion was accompanied by the creation of a new province of Turkestan (1866) under K.P. Kaufman (1818–82), and led to the establishment of Russian protectorates in Kokand and Bukhara (January and June 1868) and subsequently in Khiva (1873). The

Russian expansion in Europe and the Caucasus, 1689–1914

North Sea

Barents Sea

KOLA PENINSULA

NORWAY

SWEDEN

Gulf of Bothnia

FINLAND

1809

• Archangel'sk

1809

Nystad

KARELIA

Stockholm •

Helsingfors •

1743

1721

Vyborg

Reval •

St Petersburg
(founded 1703)

Baltic Sea

ESTONIA

INGRIA

1721

LIVONIA

• Pskov

• Novgorod

Riga

Königsberg

COURLAND

1795

1772

• Tver'

Danzig

Tilsit •

Vilnius •

1807

LITHUANIA

• Vitebsk

• Smolensk

Nizhny
Novgorod

• Moscow

GERMANY

Warsaw •

• Minsk

• Kazan'

Brest •

1793

Pinsk

1772

RUSSIA

1815

Cracow •

1795

POLAND

L'vov •

Tarnopol
1809-15

1793

• Kiev

• Samara

AUSTRIA-

HUNGARY

UKRAINE

• Khar'kov

• Saratov

Jassy •

BESSARABIA
1812

ZAPOROZHE
COSSACKS

• Poltava

JEDISAN
1792

1774

1783

Taganrog

• Tsaritsyn

ROMANIA

Odessa •

• Kherson

Azov
(Russia 1699-1711
and from 1739)

Bucharest •

Lost
1856-78

CRIMEAN
KHANATE

Sea of
Azov

1783

1783

• Astrakhan

Danube Delta
Russian 1829-56

Sebastopol

Kerch •

KUBAN
(CIRCASSIAN TRIBES)

1864

BULGARIA

*Black
Sea*

1829

1801

1784

1858

*Caspian
Sea*

Constantinople •

Sinope •

Poti 1829

1803-04

DAGHESTAN

1859

Batumi •

1878

• Tiflis

1806

TURKEY

GEORGIA

Kars •

ARMENIA

1805

Baku •

Yerevan •

1828

AZERBAIJAN

1813

PERSIA

• Tehran

Poland-Lithuania in 1689, showing lines of partition 1772 and 1793; totally dismembered 1795

Swedish territory 1689

Ottoman Empire (with vassal and allied states) 1689

Persia at the end of the 18th century (the Persian frontier with the Ottoman Empire fluctuated considerably during the 18th century)

Eastern frontier of Poland-Lithuania in 1654-67

Partitions of Poland

Other international frontiers 1914

PERSIA Russia's neighbours and other states 1914

1689

1725

1796

1815

1914

Territory held temporarily by Russia with dates of accession (Tarnopol; Danube Delta)

Territory lost by Russia but subsequently recovered (South Bessarabia, Azov)

Territory acquired from Persia in 1723 but lost in 1732

latter two states retained this status until 1917, but a rising in Kokand in 1875 brought about its total annexation under the name of the Fergana region (February 1876). Advances in eastern Turkestan also involved friction with China over the Kuldja (I-ning) province in Sinkiang, only a small part of which Russia was permitted to retain under the Treaty of St Petersburg, 1881.

Next was the turn of the Turkmen tribes east of the Caspian Sea. Although Krasnovodsk was founded in 1869, it was only in 1881 that General M.D. Skobelev took Geok-Tepe. The war scare with Britain, caused by Russia's seizure of Merv (February 1884) and of the Afghan fort of Kushka (February 1885), ended with a joint delimitation of the Russo-Afghan frontier in 1885–87 which left the Zulfikar pass in Afghanistan. The acquisition of a slice of the Pamir region in 1895 concluded Russia's southward growth which had frequently excited British concern for India.

In the Far East – following the expeditions of Captain G.I. Nevel'skoy (c.1814–76) – the enterprising governor-general of East Siberia, N.N. Murav'ev-Amursky (1809–81), founded Nikolaevsk near the Amur estuary (1850), and led a force up the river and founded Khabarovsk (1854). In May 1858 Russia annexed the north bank of the Amur, acquiring also a share in the administration of the Ussuri region (Treaty of Aygun). Both terri-

tories were finally yielded by China in November 1860 (Treaty of Peking). The foundation of Vladivostok in the same year symbolized Russia's power on the Pacific. Murav'ev also occupied northern Sakhalin in 1852–53 and the island was administered jointly with Japan until 1875 when, in return for recognizing Japanese sovereignty over the Kurile Islands, the whole of Sakhalin passed to Russia.

The end of the nineteenth century saw a revived interest in the Far East associated with the Trans-Siberian Railway (begun 1891), the colonization of Siberia, and the finance minister S. Yu. Witte's (1849–1915) schemes for the economic penetration of China. Growing financial and diplomatic influence led to a secret Russo-Chinese defensive treaty (June 1896) and to indirect Russian control of the broad-gauge trans-Manchurian railway which considerably shortened the journey to Vladivostok. Paramount Russian influence in Korea was accepted by Japan (June 1986) while in March 1898, as a result of the Kiaochow crisis, Russia extracted a twenty-five-year lease on the Liaotung peninsula, including Port Arthur (Lü-shun) – Russia's first ice-free port in the Far East – with a rail link to Harbin. During the Boxer Rising in China (1900) Russian troops occupied the whole of Manchuria where they remained until their defeat at Japanese hands in 1905 when south Sakhalin and Port Arthur were lost.

Russian expansion in Asia, 1689–1914

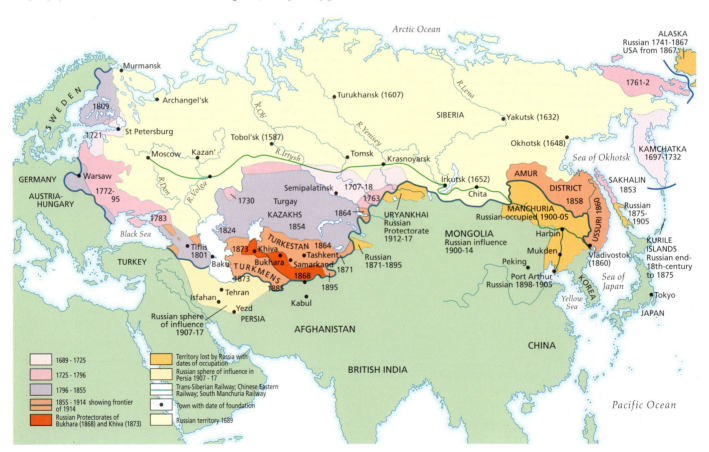

The defence of Sevastopol' during the Crimean War

The South Slavs

Anti-Turkish revolts in Herzegovina and Bulgaria in 1875–76, Serbia's defeat at Turkish hands in 1876–77, and growing nationalist and Panslav sentiments in Russia moved Alexander II, after several efforts to secure international intervention, to declare war on Turkey to liberate the Balkan Slavs (April 1877). The San Stefano treaty (March 1878), which created a large Bulgaria dependent on Russia, met with considerable opposition, especially British; Russia had to back down over Bulgaria, which was reduced in size and divided at the Congress of Berlin (June–July 1878), although regaining south Bessarabia (lost in 1856). Alexander II returned to the Three Emperors' League, formally joined by Alexander III in June 1881, which sanctioned Austrian control of Bosnia–Herzegovina and checked Panslav tendencies in Russian policy.   WHZ

TSARIST RUSSIA IN DECLINE

The German and Austrian alliances within the Three Emperors' League proved valuable during a war scare with Britain over Afghanistan (1885), but less so during the crisis, caused by the union of Bulgaria and East Rumelia (1885–86), which ended Russian influence in Sofia. The trilateral agreement was succeeded by a direct 'reinsurance' treaty with Germany only (June 1887). Tariff and financial problems, the end of Bismarck's moderating influence (March 1890), and recognition that the Triple Alliance of Germany, Austria–Hungary and Italy (1882, 1887) was incompatible with obligations to Russia, moved Kaiser Wilhelm II not to renew the Reinsurance Treaty in 1890. This encouraged Russian rapprochement with France which now provided Russia with loans. After seemingly ominous German behaviour and the renewal of the Triple Alliance in May 1891, and fearing isolation, Alexander III, although originally hostile to French republicanism, concluded a fateful political and military alliance with France (ratified August 1894).

War with Japan

Divided opinions and pressures in St Petersburg initially led to confusion and some inconsistency in Russian policy under Nicholas II. Although Russia unsuccessfully proposed the international reduction of armaments at the Hague peace conferences in 1899 and 1907, the construction of the Trans-Siberian Railway and concepts of Russia's 'Asiatic mission' resulted in an aggressive Far Eastern policy. The peaceful penetration of China was facilitated by Russian mediation during the Sino-Japanese war of 1894–95, Russian loans and the subsequent Russo-Chinese treaty (June 1896) granting Russia a railway concession across Manchuria, shortening thereby the route to Vladivostok (founded in 1860). However, the lease of Port Arthur imposed by

539

Russia (March 1898) and the occupation of Manchuria (July 1900) not only violated the treaty with China but brought Russia into conflict with Japanese ambitions in Korea. Russia's defeat in the war against Japan (February 1904–May 1905), which contributed to the outbreak of revolution at home, forced Russia to recognize Japanese influence in Korea, to evacuate Manchuria and to surrender Port Arthur, south Sakhalin and the South Manchurian Railway (Treaty of Portsmouth, USA, September 1905). To contain Japan's power and American economic involvement in Manchuria, Russia moved closer to Japan, winning its consent to a Russian sphere of influence in north Manchuria and Outer Mongolia (1907, 1910, 1912).

Consolidation of the Triple Entente

Moves to revive a Russo-German alliance and Nicholas II's inept 'private' treaty with Wilhelm II at Björkö (July 1905) were abandoned as incompatible with the 1894 Russo-French treaty, while improved relations with Japan encouraged Russia to seek an arrangement with Britain (Japan's ally since 1902) on Asian matters, including the division of Persia into zones of influence (August 1907). A Triple Entente of Britain, France and Russia was by no means a certainty but growing suspicions of Germany, and above all Russia's retreat, due to military unreadiness, in the face of Austro–German solidarity during the 1908 Bosnian crisis (Austria–Hungary formally annexed Bosnia and Herzegovina), widened the gap between Russia and the two Germanic powers. In 1908–09 the foreign minister A. P. Izvolsky (1856–1919) also failed to revise the Straits Convention to permit the free passage of Russian warships in and out of the Black Sea.

International relations were further complicated by the two Balkan Wars of 1912–13, which deprived

Emperor Nicholas II with the French President, Raymond Poincaré, on board the yacht, Shtandart, *during Poincaré's visit to Russia, July 1914*

Turkey of most of its remaining European territory. Without abandoning Russia's long-term ambitions for the Straits, and despite considerable Panslav agitation at home, Izvolsky's successor S.D. Sazonov (1861–1927) tried to prevent, and then to localize the Balkan conflict (as at the London Conference, December 1912) and insisted on reducing Serbia's and Montenegro's gains, and on creating an Albanian state. Sazonov's concern to avoid a wider conflict for which Russia was not prepared was probably sincere, but the Balkan Wars and the appointment of a German general to command a Turkish army corps in November 1913 increased anti-German feeling and revived Russia's concern for the Straits; ideas for conquering Constantinople were mooted in December 1913–February 1914.

Notwithstanding occasional Russian disagreements with Britain (such as over Persia), the secret Russo-French naval convention (July 1912), President Poincaré's visits to Russia (August 1912 and July 1914) and Russo-British naval talks (May 1914) illustrated how the states of the Triple Entente had come closer together by the time of Archduke Franz Ferdinand's assassination at Sarajevo (28 June 1914). Russia was not prepared to see Austria–Hungary defeat Serbia, and the Great Powers' mobilization systems and interlocking alliances undermined all international attempts to avert a general war. Russian mobilization after the Austrian declaration of war on Serbia (28 July) led to Austrian, and then German and French mobilization. Germany declared war on Russia on 1 August, and on France on 3 August; Britain declared war on Germany on 4 August; Austria declared war on Russia on 6 August.

Russia in the First World War

Although the military fortunes of Imperial Russia fluctuated in 1914–17, it remained loyal to the anti-German coalition, formalized by treaty on 5 September 1914, and provided valuable assistance to relieve German pressure on the western front. Badly mauled in East Prussia (August–September), the Russians fared better against Austria in Galicia (September) and checked a German attack in Poland (October–December). A big German–Austrian offensive in 1915, however, pushed the front east of Lithuania and Poland where it roughly remained, except for General A.A. Brusilov's (1853–1926) offensive in June–September 1916, until the Russian collapse in mid-1917.

Russia's war aims, outlined by Sazonov in September 1914, favoured French and South Slav aspirations at Germany's and Austria–Hungary's expense, and included the Russian annexation of East Galicia and the re-unification of ethnic Poland as an autonomous region under the tsar. Turkey's entry into the war against Russia (October 1914) provided Russia with the opportunity to demand, as a major war aim, the annexation of Constantinople and the Straits, to which Britain and France, despite their traditional policies, consented in March and April 1915. The general disruption caused by the First World War in Russia contributed to the February 1917 revolution. After Nicholas II's abdication, the Provisional Government tried to honour all tsarist commitments to the Entente, and the foreign minister P. N. Milyukov (1859–1943) reiterated Russia's claim to Constantinople (March 1917). Although the principle of a defensive war without indemnities or annexations was next adopted, intense war weariness grew, and the attempt by A.F. Kerensky (1881–1970), then prime minister, to continue fighting was a major cause of the government's downfall in October 1917. WHZ

The Baltic states, 1918–45

Map legend:
- International boundaries in 1937
- Memel (Klaipeda) Territory occupied by Lithuania, 1923-39
- Vilnius Province occupied by Poland, 1920-39
- Land ceded to the RSFSR IN 1945

Non-Soviet territories between the wars

THE BALTIC STATES, 1918–40

Estonia, Latvia and Lithuania were declared independent in 1918, after the Russian empire had disintegrated. Initially, their independence was endangered by the expansion of socialist revolution from Russia and by repeated German efforts to secure hegemony over them. By 1920, with military and diplomatic support from the Western Allies, these small states had overcome such threats. The new republics adopted broadly similar democratic constitutions, though communist parties were proscribed. Power lay with one-chamber legislatures, while executive authority remained weak throughout. Proportional representation produced numerous, usually small political parties, especially in Latvia, where regional parties that flourished in largely Catholic Latgalia raised the total to forty-four. Frequently changing coalition governments and political instability were the consequence, since no one party could consistently command a majority.

Parliamentary democracy did not survive long. In 1926 the Populist Socialist government in Lithuania, unpopular for its conciliatory policies toward the Soviet Union, communists and minorities and for its failure to solve the current economic crisis, was overthrown by an alliance of Nationalists (*Tautininkai*) and army officers, tacitly supported by some leading Christian Democrats. An aggressively authoritarian regime was established. The pretensions to power of more extremist right-wing movements, led by Prime Minister A. Voldemaras, were crushed by President A. Smetona in 1929, and again in 1934, after which Smetona's government itself became increasingly authoritarian, chauvinist and corporate. Partial liberalization occurred in 1939 after Lithuania humiliatingly was forced to concede opening diplomatic relations with Poland in 1938 despite the latter's occupation of Vilnius (Wilno) since 1920, and to Germany's claim to Klaipeda in March 1939. The outbreak of the Second World War curtailed further developments.

In Estonia and Latvia the governing centrist and right Agrarian and Populist Parties steadily gained popular electoral support at the expense of the Socialists. In 1934, amidst economic depression, K. Päts in Estonia and K. Ulmanis in Latvia – nationalists as was Smetona – supported by the army and the conservatives, staged peaceful, right-wing coups. Authoritarian, self-avowedly nationalist, semi-corporatist regimes were established, more repressive in Latvia, although at the same time more extreme fascist movements were suppressed.

These republics remained ethnically and confessionally heterogeneous. Estonia (1.13 million population, 1934) was the most homogeneous, being 88 per cent Estonian, with, in decreasing importance, Russian, German, Swedish, Jewish and other minorities, and 78 per cent Lutheran. Lithuania (2.03 million population, 1923) was 84 per cent Lithuanian, with Jewish, Polish, Russian, German, Lettish and other minorities, and 81 per cent Catholic. Latvia (1.95 million population, 1935) was the most diverse, being 75 per cent Lettish, with Russian, Jewish, German, Polish and other minorities, and 57 per cent Lutheran, with most of the 24 per cent Catholics in Latgalia. While the German, Polish and Russian minorities lost their former power, as with all minorities they were at first guaranteed linguistic, educational and cultural freedom. In the 1930s their rights were increasingly restricted by the dominant indigenous nationalities.

The agrarian reforms after 1918, which divided up the large estates, strengthened the rural character of these states. The reforms were designed to destroy the economic power of the foreign (German, Polish and Russian) landlords, to avert potential peasant unrest produced by land hunger, and to strengthen the rural communities, regarded as the basis and symbol of nationhood. While many new smallholdings were scarcely profitable, agrarian productivity did rise, in part as the result of state aid. The majority, especially of the native peoples, remained employed in agriculture in the 1930s – 60 per cent of the working population in Estonia, 66 per cent in Latvia and 77 per cent in Lithuania.

Industry, previously insignificant in Lithuania and devastated by war in Estonia and Latvia, was also built up. Separation from the old Russian empire compelled the republics, lacking internal resources and markets, to develop small-scale industries, often offshoots of agriculture and designed to satisfy their own needs – although Estonia and Latvia chose not to rebuild their large-scale industries for fear of nurturing a revolutionary proletariat. Trade, too, had to be reoriented towards Western Europe, where the bulk of their primarily agricultural exports went. In the 1930s state intervention in trade and industry increased, to keep these sectors under national control and to protect the economy from the vicissitudes of world trade.

Unable to unite, partly since Estonia and Latvia aimed to avoid involvement in Lithuania's territorial disputes with Poland over Vilnius and with Ger-many over Klaipeda, and lacking effective support from the West, they were forcibly incorporated into the Soviet Union in 1940. In the summer of 1989 the Soviet authorities acknowledged publicly that contrary to existing agreements respecting the sovereignty of the Baltic states, the secret protocols attached to the Molotov–Ribbentrop Pact of 23 August 1939, effectively consigned them to the Soviet sphere of influence.   RIK

BESSARABIA, 1918–44

The territory between the rivers Prut and Dniester was an integral part of the Danubian Principality of Moldova, annexed by the Russian empire in 1812. Although its borders were redrawn in 1856 and 1878, Bessarabia remained a province of Russia until 1917, with a population which was almost entirely illiterate and a russified local nobility.

After the overthrow of the tsar, a 'Moldovan National Democratic Party' was established in March 1917, its main policy being the distribution of land to peasants, the establishment of a sovereign Bessarabian republic and the ultimate aim of union within a federated Russian state. Very quickly, however, it became clear that the disintegration of the empire presented the province with a completely different set of problems. In the north, Ukraine advanced territorial demands on Bessarabia; in the south, the Romanian government (then defeated by German forces and residing in exile only 50 km from Bessarabia's borders) had its own plans for the province. Rejecting the demands of both neighbours, the Bessarabians established their own parliament, the Sfatul Ţării, on 20 October 1917. Composed mainly of ethnic Romanians, but also representing some members of other ethnic groups in the province, the Sfat proclaimed the creation of a Moldovan People's Republic in December. Yet by January 1918, Bolshevik soldiers were seizing control of parts of Chişinău and the Sfatul Ţării asked for Romanian military help. Eleven Romanian divisions crossed the Prut frontiers almost immediately in an operation initially aimed to safeguard Romania's rear in its fight against Germany and Austria–Hungary. However, the Romanian authorities swiftly took control over most of the administration and on 27 March 1918, the Sfatul Ţării decreed the conditional union of the Moldovan republic with the Kingdom of Romania, an act whose significance is contested to this day. The USSR always regarded the union as null and void, on the grounds that it was imposed by the Romanian authorities and implemented by an assembly which represented no one; for the Romanians, the union represents the triumph of nationalism against diversity.

Regardless of the fact that the methods by which the union was achieved were hardly democratic, it is nevertheless obvious that throughout the subsequent twenty years, Bessarabians regarded themselves as nothing but equal to all other Romanians, although they often complained about the treatment which they received from the authorities in Bucharest. In essence, Bessarabians always doubted whether they could join a Romanian state still ruled by a cabal of king and wealthy landowners and when they united with Romania in 1918, they did so on two conditions. The first was for the immediate distribution of land to all peasants and the second related to the complete 'democratization' of Romania's political life. Although these conditions were subsequently rescinded under Romanian pressure, Bessarabians persisted in their belief that they were deceived by their brethren for, while land was redistributed according to their requirements, Romania never became a democratic state in which the Bessarabian peasants could have their say. Other Romanians would readily acknowledge today that Bessarabia was badly governed throughout the inter-war period. Its representatives in the Romanian parliament in Bucharest were always seen as dangerous radicals, espousing populist peasant ideas and eschewing complete integration into the country's corrupt political life. As a result, Bessarabian deputies were marginalized and often proved unable to voice their particular concerns. Furthermore, Romania's territorial conflicts with its neighbours only increased their plight.

The Soviet government persistently refused to recognize Bessarabia's union with Romania, partly because of a wish to see the borders of imperial Russia restored and partly because the province bordered on the Danube river and its possession was of great strategic interest. In 1920 Britain and France agreed to recognize Romania's possession of Bessarabia but, since this agreement was ultimately connected to all the other peace treaties at the end of the First World War, it was dependent on the ratification by all major victorious powers. Since this never happened, Romania was left in a state of perpetual insecurity, facing a mighty northern neighbour clearly determined to recover its lost lands. Throughout the 1920s, armed incursions were encouraged by the USSR across the entire frontier with Romania and in 1924, a peasant *jacquerie* at Tatar Bunar was put down with great bloodshed. As a result, Bessarabia remained for almost the entire period between the wars under martial law, while Romania's diplomats attempted to negotiate a settlement with the Soviet Union. Diplomatic relations between the two states were only established in 1934 and ambassadors were exchanged a year later. However, this trend – encouraged by

Romania's astute Foreign Minister, Titulescu – ended in 1936 when King Carol II abruptly dismissed his minister and changed political course.

Despite the general neglect of the province, Bessarabia experienced some progress during the period of its union with Romania. The vast estates, held by absentee and often foreign landowners, were broken up and divided between local inhabitants. The University of Iaşi (Jassy) established a branch at Chişinău, first for the study of theology but subsequently also for the higher education of agricultural experts. Additionally, illiteracy was greatly reduced through the imposition of compulsory elementary education and the extension of grants for pursuing studies at other Romanian higher education establishments. A great deal of local literature was published by both the Romanian majority and the ethnic minorities, and the central authorities invested heavily in the development of the province's infrastructure, particularly in roads and railways. The majority of Romania's capital investors, however, preferred to avoid this troublesome province and Bessarabia remained an overwhelmingly agricultural region.

A secret protocol to the Molotov–Ribbentrop Pact signed on 23 August 1939 allotted Bessarabia to the Soviet 'sphere of interest' and on 26 June 1940, Romania's ambassador in Moscow was handed an ultimatum demanding the immediate cession of the territory. Interestingly, however, Stalin was initially not contemplating establishing a separate

Right. The Soviet–Nazi Pact of 1939: Stalin shakes the hand of Hitler's Foreign Minister, Joachim von Ribbentrop

republic on Bessarabia's lands, for the Soviet Union demanded the return of the territory on the grounds that it was inhabited 'mainly by Ukrainians'. A month after Soviet troops marched into Chişinău, the Moldavian Soviet Socialist Republic was, however, established and this lasted until Romania joined Nazi Germany in its attack on the Soviet Union in 1941. Swiftly repossessed, Bessarabia reverted to Romanian control; where it remained until the Soviet forces returned in 1944. Romania's politicians made every effort in the closing stages of the Second World War to obtain western support for their claim to the province but the Allies, who negotiated with Romanian emissaries in Egypt and Turkey, were unwilling to support such claims. Realizing that it could no longer withstand the might of the advancing Soviet forces, Romania repudiated its alliance with Nazi Germany on 23 August 1944 and signed an armistice with the Soviet Union. The much neglected province of Bessarabia (already under Soviet military control by that time) reverted to its 1940 status as the Moldavian Soviet Socialist Republic. JE

EASTERN POLAND, 1921–39

At the Yalta Conference in February 1945, Churchill, Roosevelt and Stalin agreed 'that the eastern frontier of Poland should follow the Curzon Line with digressions from it in some regions of five to eight kilometres in favour of Poland'. As a result, a substantial area which had been part of the Polish state between 1921 and 1939 was incorporated into the Soviet Union. This included the provinces of Wilno (Vilnius), Nowogródek, Polesye, Volynia, Stanisławów and Tarnopol and the eastern parts of the provinces of Lwów (L'vov) and Białystok which made up nearly 48 per cent of the surface area of the pre-war Polish state. It was largely agricultural and dominated by great estates – nearly half of all holdings in 1921 were larger than 50 ha. Compared to the rest of Poland, these lands were also rather poor and the state of agriculture was, by and large, primitive. In the northern provinces its progress was hampered by inadequate communications and the rather swampy nature of much of the land, while in the south the abolition of serfdom under Austrian rule had created a plethora of small and unviable holdings. Some industrial development had taken place, particularly the oil and gas wells around Drohobycz and sawmills and wood processing plants in the northern areas which were rich in forests.

Eastern Poland, referred to in Polish as the 'Kresy' or borderlands, was multinational: according to the census of 1931, of the 11.1 million people in the

seven eastern provinces, 43 per cent were Polish-speaking, 38 per cent gave Ukrainian as their mother tongue, 13.5 per cent stated that they spoke Belorussian or the local language, and 8.3 per cent gave Yiddish or Hebrew as their mother tongue. In addition, there were about 70,000 Lithuanians near that border and some 56,000 Russians scattered across the whole area. These figures were the product of considerable administrative pressure and almost certainly understate the number of Ukrainians and Belorussians while overstating that of Poles, who were found everywhere in the Kresy as landowners and officials and formed the majority of the population in the larger towns, above all Wilno and Lwów. There was also a large Polish peasant population in the two north-eastern provinces of Wilno and Nowogródek and in East Galicia. The Ukrainians were the largest group in East Galicia and Volynia and were also found in the provinces of Lublin and Polesie. Those who lived in the former Austrian territories were largely Uniate in religion – Catholics of the Eastern Rite – while in the former Russian areas, Orthodoxy had struck successful roots after the forced reconversion of 1839. The Belorussians, concentrated in the provinces of Polesie, Nowogródek and Wilno, were also largely Orthodox, though there was a substantial Catholic minority, made up largely of those who had left the Orthodox Church after the Toleration Edict of 1905. The Jews were almost entirely urban, forming the bulk of the population of the smaller towns and also constituting a significant minority in Wilno and Lwów.

Control of the Kresy had long been a source of dispute between Russian and Poland. Class and national antagonisms also overlapped there, since the peasantry was largely Belorussian or Ukrainian while the landowners were Polish. Religious differ-

Right. Frontier changes in Poland between 1939 and 1945

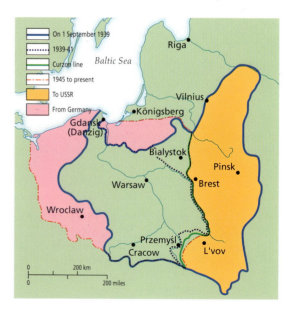

	On 1 September 1939
	1939-41
	Curzon line
	1945 to present
	To USSR
	From Germany

ences further intensified the bitterness of the land-hungry peasantry, whose national and social aspirations had been greatly stimulated by events during and after the First World War. In the period between 1916 and 1923 when the whole area was definitively recognized as part of the Polish state, it was ruled at times by the Bolsheviks, by Ukrainian, by Belorussian and by Lithuanian nationalists. Thus it is hardly surprising that the politics of the region throughout the inter-war period were dominated by national questions, and that the Polish authorities were never able to establish a firm basis of popular support for their rule. Among the Ukrainians, the strongest political orientation was nationalist in character, particularly in East Galicia, with its long tradition of semi-parliamentary government. Here the major political party was the Ukrainian National Democratic Organization (UNDO) while more violent para-military groups also had some support. Communist and leftist groups were much weaker, though they had some backing in Volynia. In the Belorussian areas, there was a greater willingness to co-operate with the Poles and the nationalist groupings were generally rather weaker. Pro-Soviet and pro-communist sentiments were strong, however, and from 1921, the Belorussian Revolutionary Organization, which demanded the union of the whole of Belorussia under Soviet rule, began to engage in guerrilla activities.

Until the coup of May 1926, which brought Marshal Piłsudski back to power, Polish policy in the Kresy was marked both by a lack of consistent planning and by the use of officials whose chauvinism was strongly resented by the majority of the population. Piłsudski hoped to initiate a new policy towards the minorities. The goal of national assimilation was to be renounced and instead conditions were to be created to make possible assimilation to the state structure. The inadequacy of many Polish officials, coupled with the strength of local Polish sentiment, made real changes hard to introduce. In addition, the repression which followed an upsurge of communist agitation in Belorussia in 1927 and large-scale nationalist sabotage in East Galicia in the summer of 1930 exacerbated relations. So, too, did the impact of the Great Depression which was felt most acutely by the rural population and which brought to an effective end any attempt to give land on a large scale to Belorussian and Ukrainian peasants.

The 1930s saw some improvement in the situation in the Kresy. Communist strength in both the Ukrainian and Belorussian areas was undermined by the shock caused by collectivization in the USSR and by splits in the Communist Parties of western Ukraine and western Belorussia. Among the Ukrainians, a feeling also developed that the strategy of

a frontal assault on the Polish state had proved unsuccessful and that some accommodation should be sought. This lay at the basis of the policy of 'normalization' adopted by the UNDO in 1935. Some improvement in relations with the Polish government was achieved, but the policy collapsed in the face of the foreign policy successes of Hitler, whom the Ukrainian nationalists expected to satisfy their aspirations, and it was formally dropped in February 1938. Hitler's abandonment of the Ukrainians in sub-Carpathian Ruthenia to Hungarian rule caused a revival of the pro-Polish orientation, but its exponents did not feel any great conviction in its success. In Volynia too, attempts by the local military commanders to reconvert the Orthodox population to the Uniate Church were also bitterly resented.

Pressures for Polonization were stepped up in the Belorussian areas in these years and the government also tried to foster economic development there. This was not very successful, but at the same time the area remained politically quiescent and there was no revival of the terrorism of the mid-1920s. By 1939, although the majority of the population was considerably discontented with its position, support for the incorporation of the Kresy in the USSR was far weaker than it had been a decade earlier. In the early 1990s the area has become an important base for both the Belorussian and Ukrainian national revival.　　　　　　　　　　　　　ABP

The rise and fall of Soviet power

SOVIET FOREIGN POLICY, 1917–45

Trotsky, Soviet Russia's first Commissar for Foreign Affairs, announced that his duties would be to issue a few proclamations and shut up shop. Intended as revolutionary bravado, his words were none the less prophetic. For nearly four years the new Soviet state had little opportunity to pursue an active foreign policy. Once the belligerent peoples had been urged to conclude a 'peace without annexations and indemnities', once the secret arrangements between Russia and its former allies had been published, Trotsky had only one, far less enjoyable, task to perform before moving on to the Commissariat for War, handing over foreign affairs to G. V. Chicherin (1872–1936). This was to make peace with Germany.

The exorbitant demands tabled by the German negotiators in the Brest–Litovsk peace talks (22 December 1917(NS)–3 March 1918) were the occasion of the first major split within the new Soviet leadership. Left Communists, N.I. Bukharin prominent amongst them, were for defying the Germans and risking a 'revolutionary war' in the hope of raising the proletariat of western Europe in support of the 'first workers' state'. Trotsky and his supporters, less rash though scarcely less unrealistic, were for breaking off negotiations and adopting a stance of 'neither peace nor war'. A show of force by the Germans in February, and a threat of resignation from Lenin, brought the Bolshevik Central Committee to its senses. Under the Treaty of Brest–Litovsk, Russia gave up all claim to Finland, the Baltic states, Poland, Ukraine and parts of Belorussia (areas already outside its control). The government of the drastically reduced Soviet state withdrew to a safe distance, and henceforward Moscow was its capital.

Civil War and intervention

Brest–Litovsk saved the Soviet regime from demolition at the hands of the Germans, and inevitably drew upon itself the wrath of the Western Allies. France, Britain and Japan landed troops on Russia's coasts in the spring of 1918, originally to prevent the Germans from seizing bases and arms depots, and if possible to reconstitute an eastern front. Some statesmen and soldiers in the Allied countries would have attempted something more ambitious: a punitive and prophylactic crusade against Bolshevism after the collapse of the Central Powers. Such plans were made unrealistic by divisions within and between Allied governments, and by the war weariness of their peoples. In the event, the interventionists could give only logistic and moral support to the White armies and their political appendages, and to anti-Bolshevik regimes on the periphery of the old Russian empire. By doing so they helped to prolong the Civil War until late 1920. In the last stages of the Civil War the armies of the newly restored Polish republic thrust deep into Ukraine. Driven back, the Poles held and defeated the Russians on the approaches to Warsaw ('the miracle on the Vistula', August 1920), and under the Treaty of Riga (March 1921) which concluded the war they were able to extend their frontier eastwards at the expense of Ukraine and Belorussia. For the Soviet state, this was the last aggressive military action it would undertake (outside its own frontiers) until 1939. The last of the White armies (that of General P.N. Wrangel, 1878–1928) was defeated and evacuated in the autumn of 1920. With the end of organized White resistance, intervention also ceased, though the Japanese abandoned the Soviet Far Eastern provinces only in 1922, under US pressure.

Diplomacy and disruption

To the Bolshevik leaders the Soviet state's security, its hopes of 'building socialism' fairly quickly, and (to some of them) even its ideological legitimacy depended upon the establishment of kindred, and helpful, regimes in other, more advanced countries. The fires of revolution which sprang up in defeated Germany and Austria–Hungary were, however, quickly extinguished. The attempt to make a prostrate Poland the bridge between the Russian 'proletariat' and its German 'brothers' was frustrated in 1920. Well into the decade, the Soviet leaders fitfully hoped and worked for the revolution which would bring at least one major European or Asian country into the camp of socialism.

Soviet Russia, however, was forced to play a dual role: it was the (self-proclaimed) centre of the world revolutionary cause, but it was also a state amongst other states, most of them hostile and suspicious. Backward, impoverished and enfeebled by war and civil war, terribly vulnerable, Soviet Russia for the immediate future urgently needed 'normal' relations with states which, ultimately, it hoped to subvert.

This duality came out clearly in the behaviour and publications of the Third (Communist) International (Comintern), set up in Moscow in March 1919. This body was, in intention, a single political party of which the new Communist Parties in particular countries (formed largely by fission from existing socialist parties) were to be only 'sections', adjusting their policies to a world revolutionary strategy determined in Moscow. At times, this strategy might require a member party to abate its revolutionary

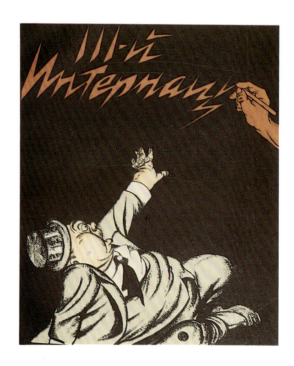

ardour, or even to go out of existence (as happened with the Turkish Communist Party in the early 1920s). In general, communists in other countries were required to prepare themselves for the ultimate overthrow of their governments and simultaneously to persuade those governments to maintain good relations and to trade with the Soviet state.

Soviet Russia began its struggle to normalize relations with the world outside by signing a series of treaties with neighbouring states (with Estonia, 2 February 1920; Lithuania, 12 July 1920; Latvia, 11 August 1920; Finland, 14 October 1920; Poland, 18 March 1921; Iran, 26 February 1921; Afghanistan, 28 February 1921; Turkey, 16 March 1921; and Mongolia, 5 November 1921) which might render them less likely to serve as bases for a renewed imperialist crusade or as a barrier to Soviet trade. Commercial relations with major European trading countries were established almost as the Civil War ended, but full diplomatic recognition was accorded by the victors of the First World War later, and grudgingly: by Britain, France and Italy in 1924, by the USA not until 1933. The Soviet government's repudiation of pre-revolutionary debts, its failure to compensate foreign owners of nationalized property, its insistence whenever these subjects were raised that Russia too was entitled to compensation for damage done by the Civil War and the 'intervention', greatly complicated dealings with the West. Soviet subversive activities, real enough (though western ill-wishers sometimes saved themselves trouble by trumping up evidence), exacerbated relations with capitalist countries, twice, for instance, resulting in a breach between Russia and Britain (1924 and 1927). To Britain, Soviet support of national liberation movements in the empire, and of anti-British sentiments and actions in the Middle East, was a special source of annoyance. France was preoccupied rather by the Soviet threat to arrangements made at and after Versailles for the containment of a disarmed Germany and the extraction of reparations from that country. No love was lost between Soviet Russia and some of the East European states (Poland and Romania in particular) which France saw as a partial replacement for tsarist Russia as allies to the east of Germany, and also as a *cordon sanitaire* between Bolshevism and the West.

Soviet Russia's first big success in breaking out of isolation came in April 1922. Soviet and German representatives, dissatisfied with their treatment at the Genoa Conference, met privately at Rapallo and concluded a Treaty (16 April 1922) which was the foundation of lively commercial relations throughout the 1920s and also provided opportunities for Germany to begin surreptitiously rebuilding its military strength in defiance of restrictions imposed

at Versailles. The weak Germany of the 1920s clung to its special arrangement with Russia in spite of another communist attempt, openly encouraged not only by Comintern but by senior Soviet leaders, to launch a revolution in 1923, and in spite of the development of the German Communist Party in the late 1920s into a threat to democratic government rivalled only by the Nazi Party.

The constant fear of the USSR (as Soviet Russia became in 1922) was that it might be attacked before it had time to construct the economic basis for a war against one or – more likely – several capitalist countries. (The inevitability of such wars was, until 1956, axiomatic.) It viewed apprehensively not merely international agreements with a frankly anti-Soviet slant (until the mid-1930s there were none of importance), but also such attempts to regulate Europe's security problems as the Locarno Treaty of October 1925, which made Germany an equal partner for diplomatic purposes with the western powers, confirmed that country's western frontiers while not expressly mentioning those to the east, and prepared the way for Germany's admission to the League of Nations. (The official Soviet view was that the League existed primarily to co-ordinate imperialist machinations against the 'first workers' state'.) To safeguard itself against the implications it read into Locarno, the USSR made a Treaty of Friendship and Neutrality with Germany (24 April 1926), re-embodying and greatly reinforcing the agreements made at Rapallo. It also took an active part in international discussions on arms limitation, to which, however, its main contribution, the proposal for immediate universal and total disarmament put to the Preparatory Commission of the League of Nations in November 1927, was demagogic rather than strictly practical in intent. The USSR showed its eagerness to delay what it regarded as the ultimately inevitable breakdown of peaceful co-existence by associating itself with other international enterprises in whose efficacy it had little faith: thus, it adhered in September 1928 to the Kellog–Briand Pact, and in accordance with this joined a number of neighbouring countries in renouncing aggression as an instrument of policy.

The foreign policy of the USSR in the years 1921–39 was essentially defensive. But self-defence as Soviet leaders understood it was always compatible with, indeed always demanded, active encouragement of foreign Communist Parties with some prospect of seizing power. The tactics urged on such parties by Comintern (which meant in effect by the Soviet faction currently in control of that body) were often misconceived and sometimes disastrous. Perhaps the most serious setback to the cause of 'world revolution' between the wars was the massacre of Chinese communists in 1927, and the subsequent withdrawal of the Chinese Communist Party's enfeebled remnant into remote rural areas. Chinese communists never forgot that they had put themselves at Chiang Kai-shek's mercy by following Soviet advice.

The USSR and the rise of Hitler

Trotsky and his followers in the USSR and elsewhere found the explanation for the Chinese débâcle in Stalin's stubborn attachment to policies which they had declared obsolete. The exigencies of Stalin's drive for supremacy clearly distorted the official Soviet interpretation of international developments and Soviet policy in the late 1920s. Thus, a totally artificial war scare, which identified Britain and more particularly France as potential aggressors against the USSR, served to dramatize the urgency of rapid industrialization and of forced collectivization which, according to Stalin, was the essential preliminary. Comintern urged on its clients everywhere a policy of 'class against class' – of communist struggle against all other political forces – on the grounds that ever acuter contradictions between and within capitalist countries, exacerbated by economic stagnation and collapse, would lead to a new upsurge of working-class militancy. Non-revolutionary social democratic and labour parties were condemned as 'social fascists', and as more dangerous enemies of the workers' cause than the fascists themselves. There can be no certainty that, but for Comintern, German socialists and communists would have joined in resisting the Nazi threat, or that their combined strength would in any case have sufficed. What is certain is that the 'class against class' doctrine ruled out joint resistance in advance, and indeed directed communist militancy primarily against socialists rather than against Nazis.

The USSR was slow to recognize that Hitler was a much more serious threat to peace, and to itself, than Britain or France had ever been. Indeed, it saw the Nazi regime to begin with as merely an 'alternative instrument' to which capitalism resorted when parliamentary democracy with 'social fascist' (social democratic) participation ceased to serve its purposes. The advent of Hitler, in fact, showed that capitalism was desperate, and the triumph of communism imminent! The USSR, in the meantime, saw no reason why relations with Nazi Germany should be more difficult than with any other 'bourgeois' regime, and for two or three years commercial exchanges between the two countries continued, unaffected by Hitler's persecution of German communists.

Collective security

The increasingly truculent and reckless behaviour of Japan and Germany in the course of the 1930s compelled the USSR to move, tentatively, closer to the Western democracies which it had previously regarded as its main enemies. This modification of Soviet policy should be seen as reinsurance rather than as recognition of a real community of interest. As Stalin put it (at the XVII Congress of the CPSU in 1934) 'we were not in the past oriented towards Germany, and are not now oriented towards Poland and France. Our orientation, past and present, is exclusively towards the USSR'. Though he went on to speak of rapprochement with 'countries not interested in a breach of the peace' he was clearly serving notice that the USSR would accept whatever alliances its own security seemed to demand.

The Japanese occupation of Manchuria (1931), the departure of Japan (in March 1933) and Germany (October 1933) from the League of Nations, the conclusion of the anti-Comintern pact between Germany and Japan in November 1936 and Italy's adherence to it in November 1937 made the quest for precautionary alliances a matter of increasing urgency. The USSR established relations with the USA (December 1933), joined the despised League of Nations (September 1934) and concluded 'mutual aid' pacts with France and with Czechoslovakia (May 1935), and a Non-Aggression Treaty with China (August 1937). The Soviet–Czechoslovak treaty stipulated that French assistance to the country attacked was a necessary condition of assistance from the other party to the agreement, and Germany had no difficulty in ignoring it.

In support of the Soviet drive for 'collective security', Comintern at its Seventh Congress in July–August 1935 abandoned the 'class against class' policy and called on member parties to establish 'Popular Fronts' with all political forces, of whatever complexion, which favoured resistance to Nazism and to Japanese militarism. 'Popular Front' governments came into being in France, Spain and Chile. It was Spain during its Civil War which most vividly illuminated the realities of Soviet policy. Support – in arms, communist volunteers and Soviet military advisers – for the Republican cause went with ruthless (and even murderous) measures to centralize political and military control of the 'Popular Front' in communist hands. Neither the anti-Comintern pact, nor the fact that in 1937 they were intervening on opposite sides in Spain, provoked a final breach between Germany and the USSR: on the contrary, the two countries in 1937 began discussing in Berlin a possible *modus vivendi*.

The Molotov–Ribbentrop Pact

If the Soviet campaign for 'collective security' was never more than a manoeuvre it cannot be said that the Western democracies did much to encourage or deserve a firm Soviet commitment to an anti-Nazi

Delegation of Spanish Republicans – including some wounded in the Spanish Civil War – at the May Day Parade in Moscow, 1937

alliance. Even when they abandoned all hope of checking Hitler by appeasement the British and French governments made only cautious and grudging attempts to involve the USSR in joint resistance to further German aggrandizement. Their half-heartedness is understandable: previous Soviet behaviour gave no reason to believe that the USSR would ever take military action unless it was attacked; the Red Army had, it was thought, been seriously weakened by the massacre of its high command, and a large proportion of its officer corps, in the Great Terror; and the USSR could put itself in a strong strategic position against Germany only on the territory of Poland and the Baltic republics. Stalin believed that even if he allied himself with them the democracies would leave the USSR to 'pull the chestnuts out of the fire' if war came. He preferred a prophylactic Non-Aggression Pact with Germany (23 August 1939) which gave Hitler a free hand in the West, followed by the Agreement on Friendship and Frontiers (28 September 1939). Germany and the USSR partitioned and occupied Poland, described by V.M. Molotov on this occasion as 'the freakish creation of Versailles'. The USSR also took advantage of the war in Western Europe to attack Finland and annex Estonia, Latvia and Lithuania. In preparation for this rapprochement with Germany, Stalin had executed or consigned to prison camps many of the European communist leaders in exile in the USSR. Communists abroad were ordered (not all of them obeyed) to treat the war as a clash between rival imperialisms, to deny their governments support against Germany, and to work for a negotiated peace. Stalin would subsequently claim that the Non-Aggression Pact was intended only to give the USSR a breathing space before the inevitable conflict with Germany. More probably, he hoped for a stalemate which would leave a relatively stronger USSR with its territorial gains. In the two years before the German attack Stalin dismissed as mischievous Western warnings about German intentions, avoided reinforcing forward defences for fear

of provoking Hitler, and gave substantial material assistance to Germany. Stalin's description of the German invasion as 'perfidious' makes sense only if we suppose that he expected Hitler to respect his benevolent neutrality.

The German invasion of the USSR on 22 June 1941 instantly converted the 'imperialist war' into a 'people's war against fascism'. Churchill hastened to assure Stalin of British support, and the USA (still neutral) extended lend-lease arrangements to the USSR.

The Grand Alliance

Relations within the Grand Alliance were frequently uneasy. Stalin as a rule found Roosevelt much easier to work with (and upon) than Churchill. The President of the USA believed that the USSR was interested only in guarantees of its own security, that it would work for a world of 'peace and democracy' after the war, and (surely his most memorable statement) that 'Stalin is not an imperialist'. American *naïveté*, Britain's relatively weak position within the Alliance, and the need to encourage and at times placate the country which did in fact bear the brunt of the war in Europe, resulted in a series of diplomatic agreements which greatly extended the area of direct and indirect Soviet rule, and which after 1945 in large measure determined Soviet foreign policy. Churchill, in Moscow in October 1944, suggested a division of post-war Europe into spheres of influence which guaranteed Soviet preponderance in Romania and Bulgaria, and equal British and Soviet shares in Greece. At the Yalta Conference in February 1945 the Western leaders accepted as the provisional government of Poland the communist administration installed in Lublin by the USSR: it was to be enlarged to include politicians of other parties, and 'free and unfettered' elections would eventually be held, but the Polish communists and the USSR were only briefly embarrassed by these commitments. At the Potsdam Conference in July–August 1945 decisions were taken which would later result in the division of Germany into two sovereign states, one of which became for long the most useful and loyal of Soviet satellites. Also at Yalta, a bilateral agreement between the USA and the USSR, subsequently accepted by Churchill, awarded the USSR considerable territorial gains at the expense of Japan (and Japanese-occupied China) in return for its belated, brief and probably unnecessary participation in the war in the Far East.   HTW

THE COLD WAR

Between 1945 and 1948 the Soviet Union extended its control over most of the European neighbours

Yalta, February 1945.
Seated (left to right) are
Stalin, Roosevelt and
Churchill

bordering on its frontier and briefly also over North Korea, Manchuria and northern Iran, giving rise to fears in the West of an ideological conspiracy. It would seem preferable to see such Soviet domination as the consequence of victory in the Second World War. Whatever Soviet intentions may have been, equally important were the interpretations of these events by Western decision-makers. To the American scholar and diplomat George Kennan, Soviet action was a 'fluid stream which moves constantly, wherever it is permitted to move', until 'it has filled every nook and cranny available to it in the basin of world power', and the appropriate response was the vigilant application of counterforce. This was the policy of containment.

The Soviet government, for its part, saw itself as peace-loving. The Red Army, which at its peak in 1945 numbered some 11.3 million men, was reduced to about 2.8 million men by 1947. Until 1949 the USA enjoyed a monopoly of nuclear weapons. One Soviet economist expressed views which appeared to contradict the two-camp image of the world endorsed by orthodox Soviet spokesmen such as Zhdanov or by foreign communists such as Marshal Tito of Yugoslavia. The economist Ye.S. Varga (1879–1965) wrote that the economy of the United States was not inevitably heading towards a slump and that it possessed the means of reconstruction; he did not believe that the West would pursue an aggressive policy towards the USSR and he discerned the importance of decolonization exemplified in the British withdrawal from India.

The iron curtain

On 9 February 1946, on the eve of the elections to the Supreme Soviet, Stalin made his election address. It was a moderate statement of the Soviet view. Although he admitted that the Second World War

had been from the outset 'a war of liberation', he also said that it had been the inevitable result of the development of monopoly capitalism and that capitalism might cause a future war. He envisaged an ambitious programme of heavy industrial development to guarantee the USSR 'against all eventualities' – that is, against an 'imperialist assault'. In an obvious reference to a nuclear bomb he promised Soviet scientists such support as would enable them to 'surpass the achievements of science beyond the boundaries of our country'.

The speech caused consternation in the West. Churchill's speech on 5 March 1946 at Fulton, Missouri in its turn caused consternation in the USSR. Although Churchill at the time was in opposition to a Labour government, his international reputation, combined with the presence of President Truman in the audience, gave his words the character of an official statement of British policy. He spoke of an iron curtain dividing Europe – and so indeed it was. By 1948 the whole of Eastern Europe with the exception of Finland in the north and Greece in the south was under Soviet and communist control. In Poland in January 1947 the communist-dominated bloc received 80 per cent of the votes. In Romania in November 1946 the communist-led bloc won 372 out of 414 parliamentary seats. In Bulgaria the elections of October 1946 placed parliament into the hands of the communists. Only in Hungary and Czechoslovakia was there some delay. In the elections of November 1945 in Hungary the communists polled 17 per cent of the votes, but in the equally free Czechoslovak elections of May 1946 the communists polled 38 per cent of votes. The Hungarian democratic triumph was not to last long: using what the Hungarian communist leader M. Rákosi later described as 'salami tactics', the Hungarian communists, with the active support of the Soviet occupation authorities, destroyed the opposition in one year. Czechoslovakia was to enjoy immunity until February 1948.

Soviet involvement in these events is sometimes, but not always, clearly documented. Thus in Hungary, the secretary-general of the Smallholders Party, I. Kovacs, was arrested, not by the Hungarian police but by the Soviet authorities. Earlier in Romania a government had been forced on King Michael by the Soviet deputy foreign minister himself. More examples of direct Soviet intervention were provided by the correspondence between the Soviet and Yugoslav communists published in the aftermath of the Tito–Stalin split showing that the USSR expected to be consulted on all senior state and party appointments. The economies of satellite countries were modelled on the Soviet example and exploited by Soviet-controlled joint-stock companies. Control was strengthened and opposition cowed by the judicial murder in 1949 of L. Rajk in Hungary and of T. Kostov in Bulgaria and by the major purge trial in Prague in 1952, prepared and conducted with the collaboration of the Soviet security apparatus.

Outside Europe Soviet control was even more evident. In November 1945 a 'democratic government' of Azerbaijan was set up under the aegis of the Red Army in northern Iran, followed in March 1946 by a Kurdish republic. Reaction from the Western powers, from the Security Council of the United Nations and even from the Iranian government was firm and by the end of 1946 the Soviet forces withdrew. This incident convinced President Truman that Soviet and communist (to many these terms were interchangeable) imperialists would back down if firmly resisted. There were to be no more Munichs.

Conflict over Germany and Berlin

Germany became a primary area of conflict. At the end of 1945 the US Secretary of State J. Byrnes had suggested both to the USSR's foreign minister V.M. Molotov and to Stalin a four-power pact to keep Germany demilitarized, but they showed little interest, being more concerned with the question of reparations. At the Potsdam Conference it had been agreed that each of the four occupying powers should take reparations from its own zone; in addition the USSR was to receive 15 per cent of all industrial capacity removed from the Ruhr (in the British zone) in return for Soviet deliveries of raw materials and food. To the USSR reparations were vital: in February 1946 the leading economist N.A. Voznesensky (1903–50) even formulated the slogan 'Reparations for the fulfilment of the Five-year Plan'. The Soviet refusal to account for the raw materials exported from their zone or the capital goods and

equipment dismantled hampered any attempt to treat Germany as an economic unit, and proved costly to Britain and the USA. Thus in April 1946 all reparation payments from the West to the Soviet zone ceased.

The USSR and the Western powers accepted and consolidated the division of Germany. In the Soviet zone the ruling Socialist Unity Party had been formed by the enforced amalgamation of the Socialist and Communist Parties. Since in the October 1946 municipal elections in Berlin this party had polled only 19.8 per cent of votes, the Soviet authorities were unlikely to hazard the fate of their regime in Eastern Germany to the chance of a free election. In March 1948 Marshal V.D. Sokolovsky (1897– 1968) left the Allied Control Council on the grounds that a quadripartite basis for governing Germany no longer existed. The Western occupying powers had meanwhile decided on the introduction of a new currency – the Deutschmark – to be the foundation of economic rebirth. It was not intended to apply to West Berlin. When the USSR in its turn introduced a new mark and applied it to the whole of Berlin the West retaliated by extending the Deutschmark to West Berlin. As early as March 1948 the Soviet authorities had begun to impede road traffic to Berlin and in June they imposed a total blockade, which was not lifted until May 1949. Much to their surprise the British, the Americans and the French possessed in the airlift the will and the technical capacity to keep Berliners fed, clothed and warm. For the Soviet Union the failure to force the West out of Berlin was a serious setback. It was not the nuclear bomb, whose destructiveness had been demonstrated on two Japanese cities, which made the Soviet government amenable to American pressure. In war it might prove the ultimately decisive weapon but its use in negotiation was limited. The expansion of Soviet power was greatest during the years when the USSR had no nuclear weapon.

The Truman Doctrine and Marshall Aid

The year 1947 began the long-term involvement of the USA in Europe to fill the vacuum created by the eclipse of Germany and the decline of British and French power. The British government announced that it could no longer support Greece financially and would withdraw its forces – the Greeks were fighting a communist partisan army supported from Albania, Yugoslavia and Bulgaria. On 12 March Truman proposed economic aid to the Greeks and the Turks. The Truman Doctrine was swiftly followed by the Marshall Plan to reverse the economic decline of Europe by extending aid to all European countries. In June 1947 the foreign ministers of France, Britain and the USSR met in Paris to discuss how best to make use of the Marshall offer. The

During the tense period of the Berlin blockade in 1948–49 cargo planes, flying day and night, brought food and supplies – even loads of coal – to the people of Berlin. Here Berlin children watch from a hillside as a United States airlift plane approaches Berlin's Tempelhof airport

differences between them were fundamental. Molotov was unwilling to allow the Soviet economic position to be discussed or scrutinized and to the undisguised relief of the Americans he withdrew. The British and French governments then summoned the other European nations to a conference. Czechoslovakia wanted to send delegates but Stalin summoned its ministers to Moscow, and after a reprimand they rejected Marshall Aid.

The West was taking both political and military countermeasures. In 1947 the Communist Parties which had participated in the governments of France, Italy, Belgium and Austria were all forced into opposition. Militarily the West was also coming together and the North Atlantic Treaty Organization (NATO) was set up in April 1949.

The Cominform and Czechoslovakia

In turn the USSR took defensive measures. The Communist Parties of the Soviet Union, of the East European satellites and of Czechoslovakia, France and Italy met in Poland in September 1947 to establish the Communist Information Bureau (Cominform). Zhdanov, who was in frequent telephone contact with Stalin, stressed that the isolation of the Communist Parties from each other was harmful: unity and co-operation under Soviet surveillance was the new slogan. The popular front politics which had been revived at the time of the German invasion of the Soviet Union were abandoned. The world was now divided into the camp of imperialism and the camp of the 'new democracies', which could also depend on the support of the peoples of Indonesia, Vietnam, India, Egypt and Syria. The new Cominform policy was soon put into effect. The Czechoslovak Communist Party took advantage of a government crisis which it had not itself created to assume power. A Soviet deputy foreign minister supervised the take-over, and in February 1948 President E. Beneš accepted the new communist government of K. Gottwald. The Prague coup d'état, coming ten years after Czechoslovakia had been abandoned at Munich, profoundly shocked western public opinion.

Stalin against Tito

At the founding of the Cominform the Yugoslav delegation had been instructed to denounce the policy of the French and Italian communists. Now, it was the turn of the Yugoslavs – Tito and his communists were condemned by the Cominform for pursuing an independent policy – over claims to Trieste, over plans for a Balkan federation, and over the Greek Civil War (1946–49). In a world which believed in a communist conspiracy, Tito's actions were seen as the responsibility of Stalin and the Soviet government feared involvement in conflict

with the Western powers over matters which were not of their choosing. While no great power would for long tolerate a situation where its policy could be influenced by a satellite, Stalin's mistake was to believe that 'if he shook his little finger there would be no Tito'. The vigilance of the Yugoslav secret police, modelled on the Soviet security apparatus, saw to it that no internal threat to Tito's rule ever materialized. Yugoslav defiance was a serious blow to the USSR in south-eastern Europe. It brought the Greek Civil War to an end, it led to Yugoslav non-alignment, and in the fullness of time it was to create an alternative centre of communist power.

Alliance with China

The year 1946 began inauspiciously for the Chinese communists. In November 1945 the Kuomintang (the Nationalist Party) had forced its way into Manchuria and Soviet forces withdrew in the spring of 1946. Stalin regarded the Chinese communists with suspicion: he did not believe that they could defeat Chiang Kai-shek and he overestimated the extent to which the USA was prepared to support the Nationalists. He advised the communists to dissolve their army and join Chiang's government – a policy similar to that which Communist Parties were pursuing in Europe. In any case gestures of reconciliation were essential. In December 1945 the American General Marshall arrived in China on a mission of mediation and in January 1946 Zhou En-lai as representative of the Chinese Communist Party agreed to a truce proposed by Marshall. In fact fighting between the Kuomintang and the communists never ceased but it only became all-out war in January 1947 after Marshall had left China.

The Soviet authorities were reluctant to accept a communist victory. For Stalin a truncated nationalist China was preferable to a Chinese super power, but it was not to be. In January 1949 Chiang retired from the presidency. His successor Li Tsung-jen approached the Soviet ambassador, with whom he reached a tentative agreement, providing for Chinese neutrality in any future conflict and the elimination of American influence, combined with Sino-Soviet co-operation. But Li was driven from the capital and the People's Republic was proclaimed on 1 October 1949. Soviet political and military advisers had been attached to the Chinese communist forces, and Stalin's attempts to keep China divided and weak did not cease. In July 1949 a Manchurian communist delegation headed by Kao Kang visited Moscow to sign a barter agreement and in August a North-Eastern People's Government headed by Kao was established in Mukden. At the end of the year Stalin had to deal with the real master of China. Mao Zedong stayed in Moscow from December 1949 to February 1950, absenting himself during a vital period of consolidation of the Chinese regime to negotiate at length with the reluctant Stalin. It is believed that Mao reckoned China's needs as being between 2 and 3 billion dollars: he obtained 300 million dollars in loans, and signed a friendship and mutual assistance treaty agreeing to collaborate against future Japanese aggression or against 'any other state that may collaborate with Japan.' Mao could not persuade the USSR to release its hold over Outer Mongolia, but he was promised the return of Port Arthur and the Chinese Changchun railway by 1952. This surrender, however, was to become inoperative if either of the signatories became involved in war in the Far East.

Very soon after the signature of the treaty the Chinese were to be involved in war. Communism was very much on the move in Asia. Ho Chi Minh in Indochina had already raised the standard of revolt as early as December 1946. Communist-led insurrections broke out in Malaya, Burma, the Philippines and Indonesia in the spring of 1948, possibly on a signal given by Zhdanov at the Calcutta youth conference in February.

The Korean War

The attention of the world was soon to turn to Korea. On 25 June 1950 the North Korean army crossed the 38th parallel dividing the north from the south. In the temporary absence of the Soviet representative from the Security Council (in protest at the refusal to recognize Communist China) further resistance to the North Korean invasion was organized under the auspices of the United Nations. In spite of initial success the North Koreans were soon pushed back by the Americans. When United Nations forces approached the Yalu river dividing Korea from China, the Chinese intervened (in October). It was not until June 1951 that the front was stabilized, roughly on the 38th parallel, and formal negotiations for a truce continued until 1954.

The war had been another Soviet miscalculation. Not only did its government face the prospect that the North Korean outpost might be lost but there was world-wide condemnation of North Korea, of the Chinese, and of the Soviet Union. In the United Nations Security Council and General Assembly (to which the USSR hurriedly returned after its earlier boycott) the Soviet foreign minister A. Ya. Vyshinsky (who had succeeded Molotov in 1949) and the chief Soviet delegate Ya. A. Malik (b.1906) made attempts to bring the war to an end. The Uniting for Peace resolution and the General Assembly condemnation of Chinese intervention showed the extent to which the USSR was isolated.

The war also accelerated the rearmament of the West, bringing a military contribution from the Federal Republic of Germany (FRG) to the anti-Soviet alliance. The USSR reacted vehemently. It believed that in opposing German rearmament it would gain the support of many non-communists just as its peace appeal found an echo in the hearts of those who had little sympathy for communism. From 1950 onwards Soviet and East European protests multiplied. A foreign ministers' conference in Prague condemned such rearmament; the GDR appealed directly to the FRG and its parliament; and finally the Soviet Union protested in a note to the other occupying powers in May 1952. The Soviet plan for German unification, which went very far to meet previous Western objections, was rejected both by the Western powers and by the FRG under Chancellor K. Adenauer.

The failures in Soviet policy after 1949 compared to the successes of the immediate post-war years imposed changes which were indicated in a complex way in 1952. Stalin's last work *The Economic Problems of Socialism in the USSR* appeared, and was followed by the XIX Party Congress in November at which G.M. Malenkov presented the Central Committee's report and Stalin gave only a short address, to foreign communists. The book and speeches represent some reappraisal of policy, Stalin maintaining that although the contradictions between capitalism and socialism were the major factor of politics, it was the contradictions within capitalism itself that would cause war: 'in order to eliminate the inevitability of wars it is necessary to destroy imperialism'. More than this – both Stalin and Malenkov stated that the resentment of world capitalism to domination by American capitalism would grow, that in any case capitalism was approaching economic ruin, and that this would inevitably strengthen the camp of socialism. It is, however, more than likely that Stalin's evaluation was based on the increasing military strength of the USSR rather than on the economic weakness of capitalism. By 1951 the Soviet army numbered some five million men, the USSR had a modest stockpile of atomic weapons, estimated at about sixty – the American arsenal was perhaps ten times larger – and Soviet nuclear physics and space research was moving forward rapidly.

Finally, the two Soviet leaders stressed that the peace movement could help to divert or nullify the aggressive tendencies of capitalism. Few concrete results emerged from this new policy in the five months before Stalin's death. To an American journalist he expressed the wish that the war in Korea should be brought to an end, and to two Indian diplomats he voiced his fear of the consequence of war for the USSR. Shortly after his death (5 March 1953) his successors began to implement the policies which had been merely hinted at in the previous two years and one of the first initiatives resulted in the signing of an armistice by the United Nations and North Korean military representatives at Panmunjon on 27 July 1953.   HH

THE 'NEW COURSE'

Although Stalin left to his successors a strong and united camp with a single centre, it was surrounded by Western bases. The necessary defence expenditure retarded economic recovery from the terrible devastation of the Second World War. Equally, the fissiparous influences within the camp, already visible in Yugoslavia under Tito, could not be contained indefinitely. First Malenkov, with his 'New Course', and then Khrushchev, under the banners of 'peaceful coexistence' and 'separate paths to socialism', tried to break out of the foreign policy constraints imposed both by the Stalinist inheritance and by Western containment.

Although the June 1953 uprising in East Berlin was suppressed by Soviet tanks, the USSR's treatment of its allies did soften: leaders such as Poland's W. Gomułka and Hungary's E. Gerö were released from prison, and the first steps toward rapprochement with Yugoslavia were taken with Khrushchev's visit to Belgrade in May 1955. The signing of the Austrian State Treaty that month produced the withdrawal of Soviet and Western forces from Austria as a prelude to Austria's declaration of neutrality. In the autumn the establishment of Soviet diplomatic relations with the FRG removed the issue of the future unity of Germany from the Soviet Union's immediate foreign policy agenda and seemed to augur well for a period of peaceful coexistence which would allow of more attention to domestic issues.

In the West, however, the memory of the Korean War, the announcement by Malenkov in August 1953 that the USSR possessed the hydrogen bomb, and the French withdrawal from Indochina in 1954, combined with the anti-communist spirit of the McCarthy era to produce an American commitment to large-scale retaliation against any further communist advances which it was feared might produce a chain reaction: the image evoked was of 'falling dominoes'. To this end two alliances comprising the USA and the UK and states in south-eastern Asia and in the Middle East were established – the South-East Asia Treaty Organization (SEATO) at Manila in 1954, and the Central Treaty Organization (CENTO) after agreement in Baghdad in 1955. In Europe, the decision was taken in May 1955 to admit the FRG to the North Atlantic Treaty Organization (NATO).

The Soviet government reacted by setting up the Warsaw Treaty Organization which bound the East European states into a close military alliance with Moscow, and by encouraging the nascent non-aligned movement which held its first conference in Bandung (Indonesia) in April 1955. There Tito, China's Premier Zhou En-lai, India's Prime Minister Nehru and Egypt's President Nasser emerged as opponents of the rigid division of the world into two camps. Rejected by the US Secretary of State J.F. Dulles as an 'immoral and short-sighted conception', non-alignment was nurtured by the USSR throughout the 1950s and 1960s as beneficial to the achievement of Soviet objectives.   KD

CRISES OF THE 1950S AND 1960S

Beginning with the large supply of arms to Egypt in 1955, the Soviet leaders made clear their willingness to provide military and economic aid to those

On 24 October 1956 a massive revolt of Hungarians took place against their Communist rulers. It lasted until 12 November, by which time Soviet troops had quelled the armed resistance. Hungarian revolutionaries are here seen on the streets of Budapest before their uprising was finally crushed

states not allied with the West. This policy reaped particular benefits after the October 1956 intervention in Egypt by Britain, France and Israel, aimed at the overthrow of Nasser following nationalization of the Suez Canal Company in the previous July. The failure of the invasion, with the Soviet threat of force to bring about a cease-fire, enhanced Soviet prestige in the Third World.

Poland and Hungary

If the Middle East crisis had the effect of improving Soviet standing in the Arab world, it also distracted world public opinion from Soviet behaviour in Eastern Europe. Khrushchev's speech denouncing Stalin to the XX Party Congress in February 1956 sent shock-waves through the world communist movement. Riots which broke out in Poland during the summer led to popular demands for leadership changes. When it became clear both that the Poles would resist any Soviet invasion and that the reforms proposed would not undermine Soviet–Polish relations, the USSR permitted W. Gomułka to become First Secretary of the Polish Party and withdrew a Soviet citizen of Polish origin (Marshal K.K. Rokossovsky, 1896–1968) from his post as Polish Minister of Defence. Developments in Hungary, in particular the far-reaching economic reforms planned and the proposed withdrawal from the Warsaw Treaty Organization, alarmed the Soviet government. Soviet troops entered Budapest to substitute a government under Kádár for that of Nagy.

Berlin

Although that invasion halted for twelve years any radical divergence of East European policies from those embraced by the USSR, Soviet attention remained firmly focused on central Europe, where the series of crises over Berlin between 1958 and 1961 threatened to erupt into another world war. The Soviet note on the status of Berlin, sent to the USA, France and the United Kingdom in November 1958, proposed making Berlin a free city with access to it governed by the GDR. The note declared that if after six months no consensus had been reached, the USSR unilaterally would 'carry out the planned measures through an agreement with the GDR,' a move designed to force the West to extend *de facto* diplomatic recognition to that government.

In the face of a categorical Western refusal to renegotiate the status of Berlin, the situation was defused only when Khrushchev agreed to send A.A. Gromyko to a foreign ministers' conference in 1959. Although that meeting was inconclusive, prospects for a settlement improved after Khrushchev's visit to the USA immediately afterwards, during which President Eisenhower accepted that a solution to the Berlin question had to be found. The following year agreement was reached to hold four-power talks in Paris, with the German question on the agenda. On 4 May 1960, however, only days before the summit meeting was to convene, Khrushchev announced that a U-2 high-altitude reconnaissance aircraft piloted by an American, Gary Powers, had been

Crises in the balance of power, 1945–80

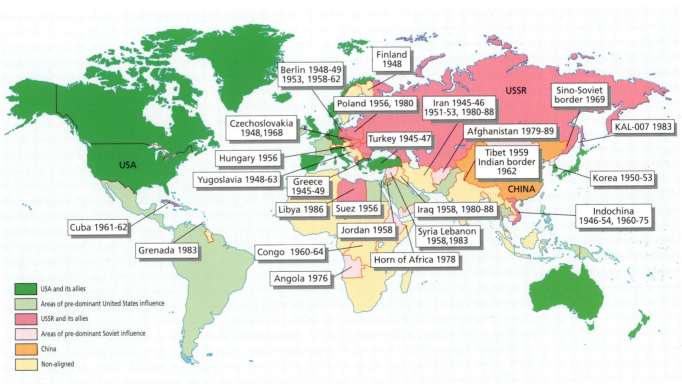

Legend:
- USA and its allies
- Areas of pre-dominant United States influence
- USSR and its allies
- Areas of pre-dominant Soviet influence
- China
- Non-aligned

Nikita Khrushchev and Richard Nixon conduct a public political argument in Moscow, 1959

shot down over Soviet territory, and abruptly curtailed the conference.

The inauguration of J.F. Kennedy as President of the USA in January 1961 brought hopes that a new era in East–West relations might ensue. Yet at their first meeting in Vienna during June, Khrushchev gained the impression that Kennedy was both inexperienced and reckless, judging from his handling of the unsuccessful Bay of Pigs attempt to overthrow Castro's new regime in Cuba in April 1960. As a result, Khrushchev renewed the Soviet threat that if no agreement were reached on Berlin by the end of the year, the USSR would sign a separate treaty with the GDR.

When no positive response was forthcoming, the Soviet government allowed the GDR to build a wall around West Berlin, thus achieving the minimum objective of stopping the flow of East Germans to the West via Berlin, but failing either to renegotiate the status of that city or to obtain recognition of the post-war division of Europe.

The Cuban missile crisis

The crisis over Berlin had both exacerbated, and been exacerbated by, the arms race between the USSR and the USA, initiated by the 1957 Soviet launchings of an intercontinental ballistic missile and an unmanned space satellite (Sputnik 1). By 1962, however, the USA had regained strategic superiority which the Soviet Union thereupon attempted to undermine by placing ballistic missiles in Cuba within range of American cities. The Soviet assessment of Kennedy proved to be incorrect, for on 22 October he ordered a full alert and a naval blockade of Cuba. Six days later a crisis was averted when the Soviet leadership acquiesced in the removal of the missiles. In the two years which remained of Khrushchev's tenure in office, a number of important steps were taken to improve East–West relations, including the 1963 agreement to install a 'hot line' telephone between the Kremlin and the White House and the conclusion in the same year of a partial nuclear test-ban treaty.

China: the split

Khrushchev's management of the crises in Berlin and Cuba had done little to appease opposition within the Soviet Politburo, and was viewed with equal alarm by the Chinese government. Mao Zedong, in response to advances in Soviet power, had optimistically declared as early as 1957 that 'The East Wind is prevailing over the West Wind' and must have hoped that with the acquisition of its own nuclear weapons and with other forms of Soviet military aid, China would soon emerge as an equal partner in a strong revolutionary alliance with Moscow. Soviet refusal to aid China in retaking

Looking east into the no-go area beyond the Berlin Wall, 1975

Top. *Left to right: Yury Gagarin (the world's first cosmonaut), Nikita Khrushchev, President Sukarno of Indonesia and Leonid Brezhnev in the Kremlin, 1962. Above. The Soviet ship, Svirsk, on its return to Russia, 18 August 1967, after it had been attacked by Red Guards when it docked in China*

the off-shore islands of Quemoy and Matsu from Taiwan in 1958 and the cancellation by Moscow of its nuclear co-operation agreement with Beijing the following year resulted, by 1960, in the withdrawal of all Soviet technicians from China. At first Albania, which supported Chinese claims against Moscow, was singled out as a proxy for Soviet condemnation of China, but during 1963 the two sides engaged in open polemics. By 14 October 1964, when Khrushchev was replaced as party leader by Brezhnev, therefore, there were very few areas of the world which did not demand the immediate attention of his successors.

The day after L.I. Brezhnev and A.N. Kosygin took office, the Chinese tested their first nuclear bomb, thus gaining a place among the nuclear powers. Despite an initial lull in the polemics, it soon became apparent that no long-term rapprochement between Moscow and Peking was possible. The failure of Kosygin's visit to China in February 1965, aimed at agreeing on a common approach to combat the American bombing of North Vietnam, under-

lined the continuing mistrust by China of Soviet intentions in south-east Asia. Mao also was convinced by this time that the new Soviet leadership would do nothing to prevent the corruption and bureaucratization which he believed characterized Soviet-style regimes. To demonstrate that China would take a different path, he initiated in 1965 the Great Proletarian Cultural Revolution, which had the effect of isolating China from the world arena while at the same time reducing Sino-Soviet relations to their lowest point.

East–West tensions

This was also a time of changes and uncertainty in East–West relations. The escalation of the United States involvement in the Indochina war strained Soviet–American relations, and also exposed the Soviet leaders to criticism within their own camp from those who favoured the concomitant increase in the Soviet backing of North Vietnam. The USSR showed itself to be equally cautious in its response to the June 1967 Middle East war: while providing the Arab states with arms and diplomatic support, it proved unwilling, or unable, to intervene decisively to prevent the overwhelming Arab defeat which followed Israel's pre-emptive strike.

In Europe, de Gaulle's withdrawal of France from participation in NATO in March 1966 produced a positive reaction from the USSR, which welcomed any sign of weakness within the Atlantic alliance. The Soviet leaders did not respond favourably, however, to changes in the foreign policy of the FRG which, beginning with the 'Grand Coalition' government of W. Brandt and K. Kiesinger of 1966, attempted to 'build bridges' between the FRG and Eastern Europe. Romania's decision in January 1967 unilaterally to establish diplomatic relations with the FRG marked the most dramatic gesture thus far of its independence from Soviet policy. It also created a crisis in the East European alliance, only temporarily resolved by a resolution of the Karlovy Vary (Czechoslovakia) Conference of April 1967, which demanded the FRG's recognition of GDR sovereignty as a precondition for the establishment of relations between the FRG and any East European state.

The invasion of Czechoslovakia

The 1968 crisis in Czechoslovakia threatened to weaken bloc unity and undermine Soviet control over East European domestic and foreign policies. Although the USSR did not intervene to prevent the downfall of A. Novotný, the Stalinist First Secretary of the Czechoslovak Communist Party, it soon became apparent that the new leadership, headed by A. Dubček, was planning to introduce reforms far beyond limits thought to be acceptable to Moscow. Cadre changes and reforms in Party and state, freedom of the press, and a more European-oriented foreign policy were some of the issues at the centre of the many bilateral and multilateral negotiations held between the Czechoslovak and the other ruling Communist Parties throughout the spring and summer. Recognition that Czechoslovakia would not willingly abandon its new course, and fear that such reforms would spread into Eastern Europe while at the same time affecting the future reliability of Czechoslovakia as a member of the Warsaw Treaty Organization, were the major factors which produced the 21 August invasion of Czechoslovakia by the forces of the USSR, the GDR, Poland, Hungary, and Bulgaria. Although the Soviet Union initially failed to install an alternative government in Czechoslovakia it eventually succeeded in suppressing the reform movement, stationing Soviet troops on Czechoslovak territory and – in April 1969 – replacing Dubček with the more conservative G. Husák.

The invasion of Czechoslovakia may have reasserted Soviet dominance in Eastern Europe, but its repercussions on Soviet foreign policy were wide-reaching. Any hope that either Yugoslavia or Romania could soon be brought back under Soviet control was shattered when each denounced the 'Brezhnev doctrine' of limited sovereignty which had been used to justify the invasion. Most of the non-ruling Communist Parties also distanced themselves from the Soviet line after the invasion, and it was from this time that Moscow found it difficult to assert authority over the Eurocommunist movement. The invasion also provoked a sharp reaction in Beijing, with the war of words escalating to armed border clashes on the Ussuri River in March 1969.   KD

DÉTENTE

The Czechoslovak crisis scarcely disturbed the process of improvement in East–West relations which came to be known as détente. For Moscow, détente with Washington through arms control appeared a desirable way of codifying the military parity the Soviet Union had achieved by 1970 as well as improving political relations with the USA. This was particularly important because of continuing Soviet tensions with China. The importance Brezhnev attached to better relations with Washington was underscored by his insistence, despite much domestic opposition, on holding a summit in Moscow,

Unarmed resistance by Czechs on the streets of Prague following the Soviet invasion of August 1968 which put an end (for more than twenty years) to radical reforms in Czechoslovakia

not long after the Americans had mined Haiphong harbour. The resulting agreements, notably those on Strategic Arms Limitations (SALT 1), provided the cornerstone of superpower détente. They were supplemented by the agreement on the prevention of nuclear war signed at the Washington summit of June 1973. By 1974, however, superpower détente had run into difficulties, with Nixon's resignation over Watergate and the linkage, in the Jackson–Vanik amendment, of US–Soviet trade with the lifting of restrictions on Jewish emigration from the USSR. While emigration was eased, Moscow in 1975 repudiated the trade agreement it had signed with Washington in 1972.

Strains over economic and human rights issues were paralleled by problems détente encountered when applied to the Third World. It was here that the differences between the Soviet and American understanding of the détente 'rules of the game' most clearly emerged. As stipulated in the 1972 Basic Principles agreement, these rules were ambiguous. They encompassed both the Soviet formula of peaceful coexistence, which Moscow saw as permitting continuing global competition, and the American emphasis on mutual restraint, which Washington saw as constraining Soviet activity in the Third World. The Middle East crisis of October 1973 demonstrated the continuity of Soviet – and indeed US – policy, détente notwithstanding. Moscow made some efforts to warn Washington of the impending conflict, but continued to send large military supplies to its allies and intervened to save Egypt from complete humiliation.

Détente was also strained by Soviet moves to exploit new opportunities to expand influence in Africa by intervening, together with its Cuban allies, in Angola in 1975–76 and the Horn in 1977–78. The final blow to superpower détente came with the Soviet invasion of Afghanistan in December 1979, the first instance of a large-scale incursion by Moscow beyond the sphere of influence it established in the wake of the Second World War. Undertaken to secure Soviet control in an area seen as vulnerable to both Islamic and Western influence, the invasion triggered a far sharper reaction (including the non-ratification of the SALT 2 accords of 1979) than the ageing Brezhnev leadership had anticipated. Criticism of the Soviet Union strengthened with the

Andrey Gromyko

Andrey Gromyko was for many years the personification of Soviet foreign policy. He served as Foreign Minister from 1957 until his 'promotion' to the honorific post of Chairman of the Presidium of the Supreme Soviet (the official head of the Soviet state) in 1985. An extraordinary survivor, he had during his career official meetings with every American President from Roosevelt to Reagan.

Gromyko was born in Belorussia in 1909, the son of a peasant family that took its name from that of their village, Starye Gromyki. He joined the diplomatic service in 1939 as part of a new intake replacing those purged by Stalin. There he quickly came to the attention of the Foreign Minister, Molotov. In 1943 Gromyko became the Ambassador to the United States. He also led the Soviet delegation at the Dumbarton Oaks conference that resulted in the creation of the United Nations.

After the death of Stalin in 1953, Gromyko served as Molotov's deputy in the Ministry of Foreign Affairs. When Molotov was removed from the Politburo by Khrushchev in 1957, it might have been expected that Gromyko would follow his patron into obscurity. Gromyko's political adroitness resulted, however, in his being

promoted to Foreign Minister to replace Shepilov, another member of the 'anti-party group'. Until 1964 Khrushchev took the lead in foreign affairs, and the Minister occupied a back seat. Under Brezhnev, though, Gromyko became increasingly powerful, particularly after he was made a full Politburo member in 1973.

In the early 1980s Gromyko was at the height of his influence as the USSR endured a succession of sick and dying General Secretaries, and it was Gromyko who gave decisive support to Mikhail Gorbachev after Chernenko's death in 1985. Despite

Above left. *Nikita Khrushchev pounds the desk at the United Nations in October 1960 while Andrey Gromyko hides his embarrassment with an apparently approving smile.* Above right. *Gromyko in May 1985*

this, Gromyko did not fit in with Gorbachev's new thinking and he was replaced as Foreign Minister in June of the same year. In recognition of his support, the new Soviet leader gave Gromyko the ceremonial position of head of state, in which he served until his retirement in 1988. He died the following year.

imposition of martial law in Poland in December 1981, though on this issue as on Third World tensions, West Europeans reacted less sharply than the Americans.

In Europe détente proved more resilient because it was based on a more realistic set of expectations and understandings, notably between the Soviet Union and the FRG. Negotiations for the normalization of relations with the FRG accelerated after the coming to power in 1969 of the Social Democrat-led coalition headed by Willy Brandt. The Treaty of Non-Aggression signed in Moscow in August 1970, together with the 1971 Four-power Agreement on Berlin, laid the foundations for the all-European collective security agreement the Soviet Union had long promoted. Negotiations on economic and political issues resulted in the 1975 Helsinki Final Act on Security and Co-operation in Europe. By recognizing existing frontiers as 'inviolable', the Final Act

provided the legitimation of the post-war European order which Mosow had long sought.

In return, the Soviet Union participated in negotiations on 'mutual and balanced force reductions' (which dragged on fruitlessly for nearly two decades) and signed general human rights conventions. Human rights figured centrally in the Helsinki review conferences at Belgrade (1977–78) and Madrid (1980–83) whose acrimonious proceedings took place against the backdrop of developments – Afghanistan, Poland, and the deployment of SS-20 Soviet missiles – which reflected and fuelled rising tension between Moscow and the West. The year 1983 saw the height of what some dubbed the Second Cold War: a Korean airliner (KAL 007) was shot down in the Soviet Far East, President Reagan launched his Strategic Defence Initiative (SDI), and the Soviet delegation walked out of the Geneva arms control talks. During his brief term of office Andropov tried to defuse the tension; not until Chernenko's last days (January 1985), however, was a decision taken to return to the Geneva negotiating table. AP

Below. *Soviet troops in Afghanistan.* Bottom. *Inside a Soviet spacecraft – a Soviet-French joint flight, June 1982*

CO-OPERATION UNDER GORBACHEV

Only after Gorbachev became General Secretary in March 1985 and Shevardnadze replaced Gromyko as Foreign Minister in July, did Moscow show willingness actively to renew détente through arms control agreements. In making arms control his initial top foreign policy priority, Gorbachev sought generally to create a safer international climate for domestic reform and, more specifically, to ease the Soviet military burden by constraining the arms race, especially the technological challenge symbolized by SDI. To these ends Gorbachev announced a unilateral moratorium on nuclear testing (launched in August 1985 and subsequently extended to the end of 1986) and held a summit meeting with Reagan at Geneva in November 1985.

The January 1986 Soviet plan to eliminate nuclear weapons by the year 2000 smacked of traditional propaganda, but its anti-nuclear thrust gained force with the accident at Chernobyl' (April 1986) and Gorbachev's determination to bring about deep cuts in nuclear arsenals. The strength of that determination was indicated by his decision to reverse previous Soviet positions on Western inspection of compliance with arms control accords. Under the Stockholm agreement of September 1986 Moscow accepted on-site verification of limits on troop exercises.

In an attempt to force the pace of negotiations with the United States at the Reykjavik summit in October 1986, Gorbachev proposed halving strategic arsenals and eliminating intermediate ones. While Reykjavik foundered on the issue of the Strategic Defence Initiative, Soviet willingness in March 1987 to decouple the question of intermediate missiles from that of banning space weapons, such as those involved in SDI, made possible the successful negotiation of a treaty signed at the Washington summit of December 1987 which eliminated intermediate (INF) and shorter-range missiles from Europe.

Despite the remarkable overall improvement in relations with the USA, affirmed by the summits in Moscow (May 1988) and Malta (December 1989) agreement proved elusive on space weapons, the Anti-Ballistic Missile Treaty and strategic arms. Not until the Washington summit of May–June 1990 was an outline strategic arms accord struck, by which time these issues had become somewhat overshadowed by conventional disarmament and the speed of political change.

The radical moves on arms control made under Gorbachev reflected major shifts in Soviet thinking on security. Rather than viewing security primarily in terms of matching the military capabilities of all possible adversaries, the new policy emphasized a 'reasonable sufficiency' of armed force. Soviet military doctrine was revised to give precedence to defence so as to help reduce chances of conflict and dispel the Western image of the Soviet threat as well as to help change the enemy image of Western imperialism within the USSR. Soviet 'new thinking' saw security in a nuclear world as mutual and incompatible with physical or psychological confrontation. The thrust of the argument was that security and indeed influence in an interdependent world rests on technological and economic capability rather than military might, as the success of West Germany and Japan testified. Past Soviet preoccupation with the military dimension was seen to have brought

expensive insecurity which helped cement the Western alliance and overburden the Soviet economy. Gorbachev therefore sought to de-militarize security policy and reduce the weight of defence expenditure. At the end of 1988 he announced a 14.2 per cent cut in total military spending (given as 77.3 billion rubles in 1989) and a 19.5 per cent reduction in arms production over the following two years. A programme of industrial conversion was launched to increase the proportion of civilian production of the defence sector from 40 per cent to 60 per cent by 1995. If the speed and scale of de-militarization aroused concern among the Soviet military, most acknowledged that disarmament and new security thinking were the only realistic way forward for the country given its domestic economic problems.

The Third World

This realistic approach, central to 'new thinking', was also applied to transform Soviet policy in the Third World. In the light of Gorbachev's cost–benefit approach, Soviet economic and military investments in developing countries, made to increase global influence, appeared an expensive luxury for a state in deep economic crisis. The Soviet Union could simply not afford the costs of such global confrontation which, leaving military expenditure aside, had amounted to 700 billion rubles for the 1970s and 1980s.

Political liability compounded economic burden, as Gorbachev recognized far more readily than his predecessors that Soviet investment in the Third World had rarely brought effective influence, let alone 'socialist' development. Moscow's efforts to extend influence had actually damaged relations with many Third World states as well as having exacerbated tensions with the West.

Afghanistan stood out as the the most obvious instance of such costs and became the most striking example of the radical change in Soviet global policy under Gorbachev. At the XXVII Party Congress in February 1986 he described Afghanistan as a 'bleeding wound' and in the months that followed tried to staunch the material losses (60 billion rubles over the course of the war) and human casualties (over 13,000 Soviet dead) by political rather than military means. When a strategy of ceasefire and political 'reconciliation' failed to stabilize the Najibullah regime, Moscow pressed forward with negotiations with the USA, Afghanistan and Pakistan, all of whom were signatories to the Geneva accords of April 1988 which brought the complete withdrawal of Soviet troops by February 1989. Ending the occupation of Afghanistan lent further credibility to Gorbachev's new foreign policy not only in the West but also in Asia.

Soviet chemical weapons in the process of being destroyed

Afghanistan

The invasion of Afghanistan in December 1979 marked the high tide of Soviet use of military force for expansion in the Third World. The withdrawal of troops in 1988–89 provided the most dramatic evidence of the revolutionary change in Moscow's foreign policy and ushered in its general withdrawal from global competition with the West.

Afghanistan had been a sphere of traditional Russian interest in the nineteenth century and continued to be an area of Soviet involvement. The post-war period saw growing economic links and after 1973 increasing Soviet political and military influence. A coup in 1978, which brought the Marxist-oriented People's Democratic Party of Afghanistan to power, took Moscow by surprise. The new leader, Noor Mohammed Taraki, signed a Treaty of Friendship with the USSR but proved unable to control his party's warring Khalq and Parcham factions. Growing instability posed a threat to the 7,000 or so Soviet advisers in the country, 100 of whom were killed in spring 1979 in the Herat uprising.

Haffizulah Amin, who came to power in September the same year, was distrusted by Moscow for his extreme views and lack of success against Mujahideen opposition. A core Soviet leadership group (Brezhnev, Gromyko and, critically, Ustinov and Andropov) took a final decision on 12 December 1979 to replace Amin with the more moderate Babrak Karmal and provide military support to stabilize the situation. While the political objective was achieved on 27–28 December, the 75–80,000-strong military contingent, soon strengthened to a maximum of 108,000, rapidly found itself entangled in guerrilla warfare against 40,000 Mujahideen supplied militarily by the West, which saw Soviet intervention as marking the end of détente.

UN-sponsored negotiations on Afghanistan started in 1981 but were blocked by a rigid Soviet stance which softened only after Gorbachev's accession to power. In December 1985 a decision was taken to move rapidly towards a military withdrawal, a shift signalled by Gorbachev's description of Afghanistan at the XXVII Party Congress as a 'bleeding wound'. The new Soviet leader was concerned at the three-fold haemorrhage occasioned by the war: the economic cost of five billion rubles a year; the mounting domestic unpopularity of a conflict that left over 13,000 Soviet soldiers dead and more than 35,000 wounded; and, perhaps most decisively, the international diplomatic cost of a seemingly unwinnable war.

In July 1986 Moscow announced the withdrawal of 8,000 troops as a token of a novel emphasis on political means to resolve the conflict, underscored from January 1987 by the policy of 'national reconciliation' espoused in Kabul by President Najibullah (who had replaced Karmal in May 1986). In February 1988 Gorbachev held out the prospect of total military withdrawal to help move the UN-sponsored negotiations to a successful conclusion. The Geneva accords of April 1988 included agreements between Afghanistan and Pakistan as well as a Soviet–US Declaration on International Guarantees which underwrote the settlement and pledged mutual restraint on external aid to either side.

The withdrawal of Soviet troops began on 15 May 1988 and was completed on schedule by 15 February 1989. Military disengagement from Afghanistan eased rapprochement with Beijing, helped improve regional collaboration with Washington and presaged the general Soviet withdrawal from global competition that followed.

Top. *Soviet troops withdrawing from Afghanistan*. Above. *Mujahideen troops, October 1984*

Resolution of the immediate Afghan problem removed one of the three 'obstacles' which had impeded the improvement of relations with China ever since Moscow had tried to promote rapprochement in the early 1980s. Identifying Sino-Soviet relations as one of his top priorities, Gorbachev removed the remaining obstacles by conceding key Chinese border claims and successfully helping to get a Vietnamese pledge to withdraw forces from Kampuchea. Gorbachev's May 1989 visit to Beijing, though overshadowed by the events in Tiananmen Square, sealed the normalization of relations and opened the way to a strengthening of political and economic ties. Rapprochement with Beijing made possible reductions of Soviet forces along the Chinese border and eased the task of building a new security order in the Asia–Pacific region as set out in Gorbachev's Vladivostok speech of July 1986.

The rather ambitious Vladivostok vision of building Helsinki-like structures gave way to a more realistic policy, detailed at Krasnoyarsk (September 1988) of constructing new networks of diplomatic and economic ties, such as those promoted by Shevardnadze on his grand tour of Asia and the Pacific in 1987. While Soviet standing in the area undoubtedly improved, the combination of demilitarization and economic weakness limited Moscow's prospects for major regional influence. Continuing differences over the Kurile islands kept relations with Japan cool throughout the Gorbachev years and into the Yel'tsin era. As far as other states in the region were concerned, notably South Korea, the new, non-ideological Soviet approach made possible a successful diversification of economic and political relations throughout the region.

More broadly, the removal of ideological confrontation from Soviet global policy brought a shift towards the acceptance of a predominantly Western international order. This was evident in the new co-operative stance taken towards economic and political international organizations, particularly the United Nations. In a seminal article in September 1987, Gorbachev strongly advocated co-operation with the UN and an enhanced role for the Security Council in the resolution of regional conflicts. Such declaratory policy was translated into practice by Shevardnadze's willingness actively to make use of the UN in collaborating with the United States and other interested parties in resolving conflicts in southern Africa and Cambodia. The new Soviet determination to foster international co-operation rather than rivalry was evident in Moscow's accommodating stance on the Gulf crisis of 1990–91 and the whole complex of issues involved with the Middle East peace process. Even if actual withdrawal from Third World involvement was gradual – considerable presence was maintained in Cuba until 1992 – there was no doubt that Moscow was serious about abandoning its extensive economic, military and, to a great extent, even its political presence in the Third World.

Europe

While withdrawal from the traditional Soviet global role in itself gave Gorbachev's foreign policy changes a revolutionary significance, it was in Europe that

Demolishing the Berlin Wall, 1989

his policies brought about the most spectacular transformation of the established international order.

If under Khrushchev and Brezhnev European policy was often regarded as a subset of relations with the United States, under Gorbachev it assumed far greater importance in its own right. Early efforts to mend diplomatic fences with Britain, France and West Germany (FRG) made disappointing progress towards construction of the Common European House which Gorbachev set as his neo-Helsinki goal in October 1985. Gradually evidence of new Soviet flexibility on human rights and arms control created greater trust which facilitated warmer relations with the key West European states, notably the FRG. Rapprochement came through frequent meetings with the FRG foreign minister Genscher and was marked by Chancellor Kohl's visit to Moscow in October 1988 and Gorbachev's return stay in Bonn the following June. For Moscow, closer relations with the FRG promised much needed economic assistance as well as providing a key element of the foundations of the Common European House. For Bonn, better relations were important for security and more positively for the further improvement of ties with East Germany (GDR). General rapprochement between Eastern and Western Europe was given a fillip by the establishment of official relations in June 1988 between the European Community and the Council for Mutual Economic Assistance (CMEA).

Glasnost and perestroika in the Soviet Union and Gorbachev's promotion of closer ties and stress on European interdependence, as in his July 1989 speech to the Council of Europe, encouraged more radical change in East European domestic and foreign policy than Moscow intended. Initially, Gorbachev attempted to invigorate established economic (CMEA) and security (Warsaw Pact) mechanisms to improve co-ordination among the communist states. In late 1986 he informed East European leaders that Moscow would no longer bale them out of domestic crises. Declarations in spring 1987, rejecting the existence of any one correct model of socialism, and statements in 1988, proclaiming that all states had the right to freedom of choice, signalled the public disavowal of the Brezhnev doctrine of limited sovereignty which had been used to justify the 1968 invasion of Czechoslovakia. Throughout 1987 and 1988 Gorbachev applauded Polish and Hungarian leaders for undertaking reforms and cautiously urged their conservative counterparts in Czechoslovakia, the GDR, Bulgaria and Romania to follow suit. Rejecting old-style Soviet intervention as counter-productive in both regional and all-European contexts, Moscow accepted the emergence of a non-communist government in Poland in the summer of 1989. Gorbachev's permissive policy was most strikingly shown in his encouragement of leadership change in East Germany and approval of the decision to breach the Berlin Wall in November 1989. The radically new Soviet *laissez faire* attitude catalysed a snowballing of revolutionary developments which brought an end to the division of Germany and Europe far more rapidly than anyone in Moscow, and indeed elsewhere, had anticipated.

Moscow acceded to Hungarian and Czechoslovak demands in early 1990 for the withdrawal of Soviet troops. The Kremlin sought to make a virtue of necessity by linking withdrawal from Eastern Europe with an accelerated reduction of all forces on the central front, a process set in motion by the Soviet announcement in December 1988 of a unilateral cut of 500,000 troops in Europe. Deeper reciprocal cuts were agreed at the conventional forces in Europe (CFE) negotiations in 1989–90. Faced with growing pressure for German unification, Moscow first attempted to slow the process and devise ways in which to avoid a united Germany from becoming a full member of the Western military alliance. However, by the spring of 1990 Gorbachev seemed to accept there was nothing he could do to prevent

the eastern part of Germany from joining NATO. In June 1990, at Zheleznovodsk, Gorbachev and Kohl signed an accord in which Moscow agreed to German membership in NATO in return for assurances on the size of the German army and considerable financial assistance to help withdraw and re-house Soviet troops.

The final phase of Gorbachev's policy on Germany was in many ways a rational response to overwhelmingly difficult circumstances. His erstwhile Warsaw Pact allies themselves favoured German membership of NATO and the West refused to help slow the pace either of change or military realignment. Washington and especially Bonn overcame any misgivings about too rapid a rate of change, given the imminent prospect of the complete collapse of East Germany flooding the Federal Republic with refugees. Effective Soviet opposition would have required willingness to use force. This Gorbachev and Shevardnadze realized would have lost many of the gains they had made in foreign policy and jeopardized the whole process of reform at home, giving conservative arguments the upper hand.

Conservatives in Moscow quickly latched on to foreign policy concessions in Europe to berate the

Below. American Secretary of State George Shultz and Shevardnadze exchange signed agreements as Ronald Reagan and Mikhail Gorbachev look on

Eduard Shevardnadze

At different times during Eduard Shevardnadze's remarkable career, this unusual and skilful politician has been Communist Party leader in his native Georgia, USSR Foreign Minister, and elected head of state in independent, post-Soviet Georgia. It is, however, as the Soviet Foreign Minister who helped Mikhail Gorbachev transform Soviet relations with the West and with Eastern Europe that he

has achieved greatest international renown.

Shevardnadze, the son of a schoolteacher, was born in the Georgian village of Mamati on 25 January 1928. His parents wanted him to become a doctor and he entered Tbilisi Medical College upon completion of his schooling. After joining the Communist Party, however, he was offered a post in the Komsomol which he accepted. Following further studies in the Party School in Tbilisi and at the Kutaisi Pedagogical Institute, he embarked on a political career. He rose through the Komsomol and party hierarchy in Georgia until in 1964 he became First Deputy Minister (and from 1965 Minister) for the Maintenance of Public Order (renamed MVD in 1968). Shevardnadze was thus in charge of the ordinary police in Georgia, not – as is commonly but wrongly asserted – the KGB.

Having taken the risk of exposing the corruption that extended to the top of the party structure in Georgia, Shevardnadze, at the age of 44, was himself appointed First Secretary of the Georgian Communist Party. This post he held from 1972 until 1985 when Gorbachev, a long-standing

friend and like-minded reformer, surprised the world by bringing him to Moscow as Soviet Foreign Minister, making him a full member of the Politburo.

Although Shevardnadze made enemies among Russian nationalists and unreconstructed communists, he became popular both with Russian liberals and with democrats in the West. When he felt too many concessions were being made to conservative forces at home, he resigned as a minister in a dramatic speech in December 1990, warning of impending dictatorship – just eight months before the attempted coup.

In March 1992 Shevardnadze took another political – and physical – risk by returning to his native Georgia, by then racked by civil war. He was seen by a majority of Georgians as the one person who might bring stability to their country and became head of the ruling State Council. In free elections in October of the same year Shevardnadze was strongly supported and was elected chairman of the parliament. In a final break with his communist past, he was baptized into membership of the Georgian Orthodox Church in late 1992.

Gorbachev leadership for losing all that the Soviet Union had fought for in the Second World War. New thinking had left the USSR with no allies, exposed economically, and now increasingly strategically, to a capitalist world which still posed a threat to Soviet security. Bitter attacks were launched in particular against Shevardnadze for losing Eastern Europe and kow-towing to the United States. Soviet support for the thrust of American policy in the Gulf in late 1990 was seen as exemplifying this new dependence on Washington.

It was in part the growing vehemence of such assaults, and the failure of Gorbachev to help deflect them, which prompted Shevardnadze to resign as foreign minister in December 1990. Meant as a warning against the growing power of the conservatives, the resignation was followed by a marked 'rightward' turn in foreign, as in domestic, policy. There was an effort, led by conservatives in the Central Committee and permitted by the new foreign minister Aleksandr Bessmertnykh, to circumscribe the security alignment of the Eastern European states through new treaties along the lines of that signed by Romania in April 1991. Unsuccessful attempts were made, through Primakov's shuttle missions, to play a more active role in the Gulf crisis and take a more independent stance towards the West. Kryuchkov and Pavlov attacked Western financial and business and intelligence circles for seeking to exploit Soviet economic difficulties. In the event, it was the failure of the coup they played a part in mounting in August 1991 which accelerated the further westernization of Moscow's foreign policy and catalysed the republican disintegration which brought an end to Soviet foreign policy as such by hastening the demise of the USSR.

Republicanization

New thinking and the revolution in foreign policy in a sense helped to catalyse the centrifugal forces of nationalism which undermined the Soviet Union. By rejecting the 'fortress mentality' and external threat, Gorbachev and Shevardnadze weakened the national myths which had helped legitimize central rule. By weakening the fabric and morale of the security and armed forces they reduced the power of the centre to enforce its rule.

Integral to republics' efforts to achieve sovereignty was a desire to create their own foreign policies. These were a basic attribute of sovereignty as well as a practical instrument for achieving recognition as independent states. The Baltic republics led the way in carving out foreign policy independence from 1989. By late 1990 the Caucasian and Central Asian republics, notably Kazakhstan, were establishing their own external ties. More damaging to Moscow's ability to conduct a Soviet foreign policy were the steps taken by Ukraine and, especially, the RSFSR, to forge their own links with the outside world. An independent foreign policy and non-aligned status formed part of the July 1990 Ukrainian declaration of sovereignty. Kiev started to vote independently of Moscow at the United Nations and build its own economic and diplomatic links with Eastern and Western Europe, notably with Germany. There was also an exchange of presidential visits in 1991 with America, even if Washington remained wary of undermining Gorbachev's foreign policy authority. Given this concern, the Americans and the West in general remained somewhat hesitant before August 1991 in responding to Yel'tsin's efforts to challenge Gorbachev's right to negotiate about Russian assets (including gold) and to win international recognition for an independent RSFSR.

Gorbachev's and Shevardnadze's moves to coordinate the embryonic foreign policies of the republics with that of the centre proved ineffective. The enormous fillip the failed August coup lent centrifugal forces undermined the attempts of the new Union foreign minister, Boris Pankin, to salvage central foreign policy authority through a new Union Ministry of External Relations, established in November 1991. Hopes that Shevardnadze, who was brought back as minister, would increase the new body's chances of survival proved forlorn. Union foreign policy disappeared along with the USSR in December 1991 and the ministry building was taken over by the Russian foreign ministry, headed by Andrey Kozyrev. AP

Right. *German Chancellor Helmut Kohl and Soviet President Mikhail Gorbachev in Kiev, July 1991.* Below. *Eduard Shevardnadze, as Soviet Foreign Minister, meets British Prime Minister Margaret Thatcher in London*

RUSSIAN FOREIGN POLICY

The Russian Federation quickly established itself as the 'continuer' (rather than strictly the successor) state of the USSR, assuming the Soviet permanent seat on the UN Security Council as well as the effective command of all but a fraction of the armed forces of the new Commonwealth of Independent States (CIS). The early months of the CIS saw intense tussles over the precise division of armed forces between the new states. By mid-1992 it seemed clear that members of the CIS were determined to establish their own armed forces and deploy them in support of their own foreign policy objectives.

Running their own foreign policies posed considerable resource problems for the non-Russian states; most, for instance, had initially to share Russian embassy facilities. Superior material resources did not, however, help Russia to resolve the difficulties of defining a new foreign policy based on Russian national interests rather than on the traditional imperial ones of the Soviet period. The nature of Russian national interests and strategies within the CIS and beyond became the subject of a vigorous debate. Many participants in the debate, including the Russian foreign minister, Kozyrev, criticized new thinking for attempting to construct a new ideology and a new mission based on the Soviet Union as the embodiment of international morality. Instead, they contended, Russia needed a highly pragmatic policy founded on a calculus of political and economic advantage to secure the democratic economic and political reform which would ensure its great, rather than super, power status in the post-Cold War international order. Other participants in these discussions, of a more strongly nationalist persuasion, depicted national interest in more expansive patriotic colours, stressing the need for policy to advance Great Russian culture and values. The pragmatists and the patriots, to simplify a more variegated picture, argued for somewhat different priorities for Russian foreign policy.

All agreed that the most important and urgent priority was to build new and stable relations with 'near abroad', with neighbouring former republics of the old Soviet Union. Indeed in early 1992 most of Yel'tsin's and Kozyrev's time was spent in trying to give the embryonic CIS some substance. Even on economic issues, little headway was made towards co-operation as the new states concentrated their efforts on establishing ties with hard-currency partners rather than trying to re-shape those with Russia of whose imperialist proclivities they remained highly suspicious.

Dramatic disputes surrounded the disentanglement of military ties. The establishment of a Russian army in May 1992 marked the effective end of attempts to set up CIS ground forces. By summer 1992 it appeared that only strategic nuclear forces would come under notional CIS, effectively Russian, command. And even here Kazakhstan, and more particularly Ukraine, harboured ambitions to retain some independent nuclear capacity so as to safeguard security against a potential threat from Russia. Similar apprehensions plus national pride on both sides underlay the prolonged tug-of-war over the Black Sea fleet. In summer 1992 pragmatic arguments for settling the issue through negotiation seemed to prevail, though patriotic voices urging greater assertiveness remained forceful. The same kind of division on Russian CIS policy emerged over the best ways in which to safeguard the rights of the 25 million or so Russians living in other Commonwealth states. Those in the Crimea (Ukraine) and the Dniester region of Moldova presented the greatest policy problems. In early 1992 the Russian government, notwithstanding nationalist calls for a tough line, seemed satisfied with the granting of Crimean regional autonomy and sought a co-operative, peacekeeping solution to the Dniester conflict.

Differences within Russia over policy towards other CIS states extended further afield. The pragmatists, including Kozyrev, were associated with advocating a Western foreign policy orientation while the patriots, including the then Vice-President Aleksandr Rutskoy, favoured a more Eurasian focus.

Much of Yel'tsin's early foreign policy energy concentrated on building on the military, political and especially economically profitable relations with the West pioneered under Gorbachev. Western Europe, particularly Germany, remained an important concern. However, Moscow was now further separated from Western Europe by an independent Ukraine which was viewed as a direct competitor, particularly as far as Eastern Europe and Germany were concerned. This heightened the importance of consolidating ties with America where Russia's huge military arsenal gave it a comparative advantage. In January 1992 Yel'tsin proposed cuts in strategic weapons going far deeper than those envisaged in previous talks. He welcomed membership of the new North Atlantic Consultative Council and talked of the long-term Russian aim to join NATO. The Camp David joint declaration of February 1992 described relations between Moscow and Washington as based on 'friendship and partnership' and 'a common commitment to democracy and economic freedom'.

It was the search for material aid to further plans for achieving such economic freedom through marketization that dominated Russia's western foreign policy orientation in the first half of 1992. Russia joined the IMF in April 1992 and Yel'tsin did

Top left. *Russian troops minesweeping in Moldova.* Top right. *Russian paratroopers about to join the UN multi-national peacekeeping forces in former Yugoslavia, 1992.* Above. *President Boris Yel'tsin and Mrs Naina Yel'tsin on a visit to Britain, with Prime Minister John Major and Mrs Norma Major*

his utmost, as at the Munich G7 summit in July, to display a determination to keep radical reforms on course so as to benefit from the $18 billion aid package (out of a total $24 billion for the CIS) funded by the leading industrialized countries. Yel'tsin's apparent willingness to adjust domestic economic policy to IMF specifications provoked growing criticism from a wide spectrum of opinion.

Closely connected with such criticism of the overly western direction of Russian foreign policy were more fundamental and more positive arguments advocating greater attention to relations with states to the south and east. The rationale for such a southward or Eurasian policy orientation was three-fold. The first, CIS-focused, highlighted the importance of the Central Asian states, especially Kazakhstan, to the viability of any kind of Commonwealth. With or without a Commonwealth it was important to build good relations so as to prevent any Central Asian states linking up with Islamic regions within Russia. The second line of argument was that Russia had to focus on its southern neighbours, as well as on the states of South Asia and

the Middle East, both to pre-empt threats from those directions and to carve out new markets. Practical steps to follow such recommendations were evident in the close relationship fostered between Moscow and Alma Ata as well as attempts to build ties with Turkey and Iran, the two most important external actors actively interested in Central Asia.

The final strand of the case for a Eurasian rather than overwhelmingly western policy orientation rested on minimizing threats and maximizing economic and political benefits. If, as many participants in the debate agreed, the post-Cold War international order was likely to see conflicts shift increasingly to a north–south axis, it was vital for Russia, geographically straddling the divide, not to align only with the West. Apart from the security considerations, a more balanced alignment would widen the range of possible sources of aid and accessible markets for goods which could not be sold in the West. At the level of global political influence, many saw Russia as capable of exercising the influence worthy of a Great Power through a Eurasian policy that built on her geostrategic position. As of late 1993 the most significant trend was the strengthening of Russian security within the southern part of the former Soviet Union, enforcing a kind of 'Monroe Doctrine' over the whole region. It was still too early to draw any firm conclusions about the results of the debate on Russia's external orientation or the direction its foreign policy might take. There were signs, however, that having overcome the old Soviet duality of international ideological mission and national state interest, Russian foreign policy would have to cope with the older duality inherent in straddling Europe and Asia. AP

AA Autonomous area

ABM Anti-ballistic missile

ALCM Air-launched cruise missiles

apparat Administrative personnel of the Communist Party (especially) or the government

AR Autonomous region (oblast); nationality-based administrative division; part of a kray or union republic

ASAT Anti-satellite attack

ASSR Autonomous Soviet Socialist Republic; nationality-based division of a union republic; administratively comparable to an oblast

ASW Anti-submarine warfare

BAM Baykal-Amur Mainline – a Siberian railway project

bomzhy Homeless people – literally those 'without a registered place to live'

CFE Conventional Forces in Europe; talks concluded in December 1987

Cheka (*Vecheka*) All-Russian Extraordinary Commission (of the Council of People's Commissars) for combating Counter-Revolution, Sabotage and Speculation; the state security and intelligence organ, 1917–22

CIS Commonwealth of Independent States

Comecon (CMEA) Council for Mutual Economic Assistance; economic grouping of the USSR, six East European states, Cuba, Mongolia and Vietnam

Cominform Communist Information Bureau, 1947–56

Comintern The Third (Communist) International, 1919–43

CPSU Communist Party of the Soviet Union

dedovshchina Cross-generational bullying in the armed forces

demokratizatsiya Democratization

DOSAAF Voluntary Society for Aid to the Army, Air Force and Navy

FRG Federal Republic of Germany

GDR German Democratic Republic

glasnost' Glasnost; openness

glavk Chief administration within a ministry or under the Council of Ministers

Glavlit Main Directorate for Literary and Publishing Affairs; official censorship organ

GlavPU Main Political Directorate of the Armed Forces

GLCM Ground-launched cruise missile

GOELRO State Commission for the Electrification of Russia

Gosarbitrazh Arbitration tribunals to settle disputes between enterprises

Gosbank State Bank

Gosplan State Planning Committee (Commission)

Gossnab State Committee on Material-Technical Supply

GPU State Political Administration; the state security and intelligence organ, 1922–23 (see OGPU)

gruppovshchina Inter-ethnic bullying in the armed forces

GTO *Gotov k trudu i oborone* (Ready for labour and defence) – the national fitness programme

guberniya Pre-revolutionary administrative division of the Russian Empire (translatable as 'province')

GULag Main Administration for Camps under the state security organs

ha Hectares

ICBM Inter-continental ballistic missile

INF Intermediate Nuclear Forces; treaty concluded in December 1987

KGB Committee for State Security (name of state security police, 1954–1991)

kolkhoz Collective farm

kray Territory; division of a union republic, administratively comparable to an oblast; generally containing one or more nationality-based territorial divisions

LSR Left Socialist Revolutionaries

Memorial Organization set up in the mid-1980s to commemorate and campaign on behalf of the victims of the purges

MGB   Ministry for State Security, 1946–53

mir   Village commune in pre-revolutionary Russia

Mir Isskustva *The World of Art* – journal of the World of Art Association, founded by Diaghilev and others

MIRV   Multiple, independently-targetable re-entry vehicles

MKhAT Moscow Arts Theatre

MVD   Ministry of Internal Affairs; state security and intelligence organ, 1953–54

NBC   Nuclear ballistic capability

NEP   New Economic Policy, 1921–28; initiated by Lenin

NKGB   People's Commissariat for State Security, 1943–46

NKVD   People's Commissariat for Internal Affairs; state security and intelligence organ, 1934–43

nomenklatura   List of responsible posts and of suitable holders of them; refers especially to appointments which required approval of Communist Party organs

NS   New Style or Gregorian calendar. Imperial Russia continued to use the Julian (Old Style) calendar which had been superseded in all other European states in the seventeenth or eighteenth centuries. A Soviet decree (26 January 1918) fixed 1 February 1918 (OS) as 14 February 1918, for the New Style to come into force

NSWP   Non-Soviet Warsaw Pact forces

oblast'   Region; administrative division in contemporary Russia and former Soviet republics

OGPU   Unified State Political Administration; the state security and intelligence organ, 1923–24

okrug   Autonomous area (AA)

OS   Old Style or Julian calendar; see NS

perestroyka   Perestroika; reconstruction

Politburo   Political Bureau of the Central Committee of the CPSU

pravovoe gosudarstvo   Law-governed state

profsoyuzy   Trade Unions

propiska   Residence permit

PVO strany   Air-defence forces of the homeland

rayon   Administrative district within a republic, kray, oblast, okrug or city

RKKA   *Raboche-Krest'yanskaya Krasnaya Armiya* (Workers' and Peasants' Red Army)

RTV   Radio-Technical Troops

RSFSR   Russian Soviet Federative Socialist Republic

SALT   Strategic Arms Limitation Treaty and talks (between the USSR and the USA)

samizdat   'Self-publishing'– the clandestine production and circulation of writings

sblizhenie   rapprochement or coming-together (of nationalities)

SLBM   Submarine-launched ballistic missile

sliyanie   merging (of nationalities)

sovkhoz   State farm

Sovnarkom   Council of People's Commissars (CPC)

Sovnarkhozy   Regional economic councils

SR   Socialist Revolutionary Party

SRF   Strategic Rocket Forces

SSR   Soviet Socialist Republic, one of the fifteen which comprised the Soviet Union

START   Strategic Arms Reduction Treaty, signed in Moscow, 31 July 1991

Stavka   Military Headquarters

TVD   Theatres of Military Action

uezd   Pre-revolutionary administrative division of a province (*guberniya*), translatable as 'county'

uskorenie   acceleration

VASKhNIL All-Union Lenin Academy of Agricultural Science

verst   1.07 km/0.55 miles

Vesenkha   Supreme Economic Council

VPK   Military-Industrial Commission

VTA   Military Transport Aviation

VUZ   Higher education institution

VV   Internal troops of Ministry of Interior

VVS   Air Forces

WTO   Warsaw Treaty Organization

zemstvo   Pre-revolutionary elected organ of local government

ZRV   Zenitnye Raketnye Voyska – anti-aircraft troops

General reference works

Archie Brown, ed., *The Soviet Union: A Biographical Dictionary*, London, 1990; New York, 1991

Leonard Geron and Alex Pravda, eds., *Who's Who in Russia and the New States*, London and New York, 1993

Wolfgang Kasack, *A Dictionary of Russian Literature since 1917*, New York, 1988

Tania Konn, ed., *Soviet Studies Guide*, London, 1992

Robin Milner-Gulland, *A Cultural Atlas of Russia*, Oxford and New York, 1989

Harold Shukman, ed., *The Blackwell Encyclopedia of the Russian Revolution*, Oxford, 1988

Victor Terras, *A Handbook of Russian Literature*, New Haven and London, 1985

S.V. Utechin, *Everyman's Concise Encyclopedia of Russia*, London and New York, 1961

The physical environment

V.D. Aleksandrova, *Vegetation of the Soviet Polar Deserts*, Cambridge, 1988

L.S. Berg, *The Natural Regions of the USSR*, New York, 1950

A.A. Borisov, *Climates of the USSR*, Edinburgh, 1965

Yu. I. Chernov, *The Living Tundra*, Cambridge, 1985

J.C. Dewdney, *The USSR* (Studies in Industrial Geography), London, 1978

G. and L. Durrell, *Durrell in Russia*, London, 1986

Murray Feshbach and Alfred Friendly, Jr, *Ecocide in the USSR: Health and Nature under Siege*, New York, 1992

I.P. Gerasimov, D.L. Armand and K.M. Yefron, eds., *Natural Resources of the Soviet Union: Their Use and Renewal*, San Francisco, 1971

I.P. Gerasimov and M.A. Glazovskaya, *Fundamentals of Soil Science and Soil Geography*, Israel Program for Scientific Translation, 1965

J.R. Gibson, *Feeding the Russian Fur Trade: Provisionment of the Okhotsk Seaboard and the Kamchatka Peninsula, 1639–1856*, Madison, 1969

G.M. Howe, *The Soviet Union*, Harlow, 2nd edn, 1986

Barbara Jancar, *Environmental Management in the Soviet Union and Yugoslavia*, Durham, North Carolina, 1987

R.G. Jensen, T. Shabad and A.W. Wright, eds., *Soviet Natural Resources in the World Economy*, Chicago, 1983

Michael Kaser and Santosh Mehrotra, *The Central Asian Economies after Independence*, London, 1992

A. Knystautas, *The Natural History of the USSR*, London, 1987

B. Komarov, *The Destruction of Nature in the Soviet Union*, New York, 1978

Paul E. Lydolph, *Climates of the Soviet Union*, Amsterdam, 1978

Paul E. Lydolph, *Geography of the USSR*, 5th edn, Elkhart Lake, Wisconsin, 1990

R. St J. Macdonald, ed., *The Arctic Frontier*, Toronto, 1966

N.T. Mirov, *Geography of Russia*, New York and London, 1951

R. Mnatsakanian, *The Environmental Legacy of the Former Soviet Republics*, Edinburgh, 1992

D.V. Nalivkin, *The Geology of the USSR*, Oxford, 1960

Philip R. Pryde, *Conservation in the Soviet Union*, Cambridge, 1972

Philip R. Pryde, *Environmental Management in the Soviet Union*, Cambridge, 1991

G. St George, *Soviet Deserts and Mountains*, Amsterdam, 1974

Fred Singleton, ed., *Environmental Problems in the Soviet Union and Eastern Europe*, London, 1987

V.I. Smirnov, ed., *Ore Deposits of the USSR*, 3 vols, London, 1977

J. Sparks, *Realms of the Russian Bear: A Natural History of Russia and the Central Asian Republics*, London, 1992

D. Sulimirski, *Prehistoric Russia*, London, 1970

S.P. Suslov, *Physical Geography of Asiatic Russia*, London, 1961

Leslie Symons, ed., *The Soviet Union: A Systematic Geography*, London, 1983

Charles E. Zeigler, *Environmental Policy in the USSR*, London, 1987

The peoples

W.E.D. Allen, *A History of the Georgian People: From the Beginning down to the Russian Conquest in the Nineteenth Century*, London, 1971

M. Altshuler, *Soviet Jewry since the Second World War: Population and Social Structure*, New York, 1987

T.E. Armstrong, *Russian Settlement in the North*, Cambridge, 1965

R.P. Bartlett, *Human Capital: The Settlement of Foreigners in Russia, 1762–1804*, Cambridge, 1979

J.H. Bater, *The Soviet City*, London, 1980

Ralph S. Clem, ed., *Research Guide to the Russian and Soviet Censuses*, Ithaca and London, 1986

Robert Conquest, *The Nation Killers*, London, 1970

N. Dima, *Bessarabia and Bukovina: The Soviet-Romanian Territorial Dispute*, New York, 1982

I. Fleischhauer and B. Pinkus, *The Soviet Germans: Past and Present*, London, 1986

J. Forsyth, *A History of the Peoples of Siberia: Russia's North Asian Colony, 1581–1990*, Cambridge, 1992

R.A. French and F.E.I. Hamilton, eds., *The Socialist City*, London, 1979

A. Giesinger, *From Catherine to Khrushchev: The Story of Russia's Germans*, Battleford, 1974

Zvi Gitelman, *A Century of Ambivalence. The Jews of Russia and the Soviet Union: 1881 to the Present*, London, 1988

M.F. Hamm, *The City in Russian History*, Lexington, Kentucky, 1976

David Hooson, *The Soviet Union: People and Regions*, Belmont, California and London, 1966

Richard Hovannisian, *Armenia on the Road to Independence, 1918*, Berkeley and Los Angeles, 1967

Richard Hovannisian, *The Armenian Republic*, 2 vols., 2nd edn, Berkeley and Los Angeles, 1982

Caroline H. Humphrey, ed., *Peoples of the Earth, XIV: USSR East of the Urals*, Verona, 1973

Zev Katz *et al*, eds., *Handbook of Major Soviet Nationalities*, New York, 1975

D. Kendrick and G. Puxon, *The Destiny of Europe's Gypsies*, London, 1972

Lionel Kochan, ed., *The Jews in Soviet Russia since 1917*, Oxford, 1978

Lawrence Krader, *Social Organisation of the Mongol-Turkic Pastoral Nomads*, The Hague, 1964

David M. Lang, *A Modern History of Soviet Georgia*, London, 1962

David M. Lang and C. Walker, *Armenians*, London, 1977

M.G. Levin and L.P. Potapov, *The Peoples of Siberia*, Chicago, 1964

Robert A. Lewis and Richard H. Rowland, *Population Redistribution in the USSR: Its Impact on Society 1897–1977*, New York, 1979

Robert A Lewis, Richard H. Rowland and R.S. Clem, *Nationality and Population Change in Russia and the USSR: An Evaluation of Census Data, 1897–1970*, New York and London, 1976

James W. Long, *From Privileged to Dispossessed: The Volga Germans 1861–1917*, Lincoln, Nebraska, 1988

James W. Long, *The Volga Germans*, Winnipeg, 1989

Mary Kilbourne Matossian, *The Impact of Soviet Policies in Armenia*, Leiden, 1962

Alexander J. Motyl, *Dilemmas of Independence: Ukraine after Totalitarianism*, New York, 1993

Judith Pallot and Denis J.B. Shaw, *Landscape and Settlement in Romanov Russia 1613–1917*, Oxford, 1990

Judith Pallot and Denis J.B. Shaw, *Planning in the Soviet Union*, London, 1981

Paula G. Rubel, *The Kalmyk Mongols: A Study in Continuity and Change*, The Hague, 1967

Graham Smith, ed., *The Baltic Republics in Revolt: National Separatism in Estonia, Latvia and Lithuania*, London, 1992

Graham Smith, ed., *The Nationalities Question in the Soviet Union*, London and New York, 1990

Ronald G. Suny, *Looking Toward Ararat: Armenia in Modern History*, Bloomington, Indiana, 1993

Ronald G. Suny, *The Making of the Georgian Nation*, London, 1989

Donald W. Treadgold, *The Great Siberian Migration*, Princeton, 1957

V. Stanley Vardys, *The Catholic Church, Dissent and Nationality in Soviet Lithuania*, Boulder, 1978

Christopher Walker, *Armenia, the Survival of a Nation*, Beckenham and New York, 1980

Geoffrey E. Wheeler, *Racial Problems in Soviet Muslim Asia*, Oxford, 1962

Geoffrey E. Wheeler, *The Peoples of Soviet Central Asia*, London, 1966

Religion

C. Bawden, *Shamans, Lamas and Evangelicals*, London, 1985

Trevor Beeson, ed., *Discretion and Valour*, London, 1982

G. Bennigsen and C. Lemercier-Quelquejay, *Islam in the Soviet Union*, New York, 1967

Michael Bourdeaux, *Gorbachev, Glasnost and the Gospel*, London, 1990

Michael Bourdeaux, *Religious Ferment in Russia*, London, 1968

James Cracraft, *The Church Reform of Peter the Great*, London, 1971

J.S. Curtiss, *Church and State in Russia: The Last Years of the Empire 1900–1917*, New York, 1940

J.S. Curtiss, *The Russian Church and the Soviet State 1917–1950*, Boston, Mass., 1953

Jane Ellis, *The Russian Orthodox Church: A Contemporary History*, London, 1988

G.P. Fedotov, *The Russian Religious Mind*, 2 vols., Cambridge, Mass., 1946–1966

W.C. Fletcher, *Religion and Soviet Foreign Policy 1954–1970*, London, 1973

W.C. Fletcher, *The Russian Church Underground*, Oxford, 1973

G. Florovsky, *The Ways of Russian Theology*, 2 vols., Belmont, Mass., 1977

Sergei A. Hackel, *The Orthodox Church*, London, 1971

H.M. Hayward and W.C. Fletcher, eds., *Religion and the Soviet State*, London, 1969

W. Kolarz, *Religion in the Soviet Union*, London, 1961

Christel Lane, *Christian Religion in the Soviet Union: A Sociological Study*, London, 1978

R.H. Marshall, ed., *Aspects of Religion in the Soviet Union 1917–1967*, Chicago and London, 1971

Dimitri Obolensky, *The Byzantine Commonwealth: Eastern Europe 500–1453*, London, 1971

Walter Sawatsky, *Soviet Evangelicals since World War II*, Kitchener, Ontario, 1981

V. Stanley Vardys, *The Catholic Church, Dissent and Nationality in Soviet Lithuania*, Boulder, 1978

Philip Walters, ed., *World Christianity: Eastern Europe*, Eastbourne, 1989

History

Edward Acton, *Russia*, London and New York, 1986

J.T. Alexander, *Catherine the Great: Life and Legend*, Oxford, 1989

Edward Allworth, ed., *Central Asia: 120 Years of Russian Rule*, Durham, NC and London, 1989

M.S. Anderson, *Peter the Great*, London, 1978

Robert Auty and Dimitri Obolensky, eds., *An Introduction to Russian History*, Companion to Russian Studies, I, Cambridge, 1976

P.L. Barbour, *Dimitri, Tsar and Great Prince of All Russia, 1605–1606*, London, 1967

Isaiah Berlin, *Russian Thinkers*, London, 1978

Jerome Blum, *Lord and Peasant in Russia from the Ninth to the Nineteenth Centuries*, Princeton, 1961

Archie Brown, ed., *Political Leadership in the Soviet Union*, London and Bloomington, 1989

E.H. Carr, *History of Soviet Russia*, 14 vols., London, 1952-78

B.E. Clements, B.A. Engel, C.D. Worobec, eds., *Russia's Women: Accommodation, Resistance, Transformation*, Berkeley, 1991

E. Clowes, S.D. Kassow, J.L. West, eds., *Between Tsar and People: Educated Society and the Quest for Public Identity in Late Imperial Russia*, Princeton, 1991

Stephen Cohen, *Bukharin and the Bolshevik Revolution: A Political Biography 1888-1938*, London, 1974

Robert Conquest, *Kolyma: The Arctic Death Camps*, London, 1978

Robert Conquest, *The Great Terror: A Reassessment*, London, 1990

Robert O. Crummey, *The Formation of Muscovy, 1304–1613*, London and New York, 1987

R.W. Davies, *Soviet History in the Gorbachev Revolution*, London, 1989

Paul Dukes, *The Making of Russian Absolutism 1613–1801*, 2nd edn, London, 1990

D.M. Dunlop, *The History of the Jewish Khazars*, Princeton, 1954

Timothy Dunmore, *The Stalinist Command Economy*, London, 1980

Ben Eklof and S.P. Frank, eds., *The World of the Russian Peasant: Post-Emancipation Culture and Society*, Boston and London, 1990

T. Emmons and W. Vucinich, eds., *The Zemstvo in Russia: An Experiment in Local Self-Government*, Cambridge, Mass., 1982

Laura Engelstein, *The Keys to Happiness. Sex and the Search for Modernity in Fin-de-siècle Russia*, Ithaca and London, 1992

J.L.I. Fennell, *Ivan the Great of Moscow*, London, 1963

J.L.I. Fennell, *The Emergence of Moscow, 1304–1359*, London, 1968

Sheila Fitzpatrick, *The Commissariat of Enlightenment: Soviet Organization of Education and the Arts under Lunacharsky*, Cambridge, 1970

J. Arch Getty, *Origins of the Great Purges: The Soviet Communist Party Reconsidered, 1933–1938*, Cambridge, 1985

Geoffrey A. Hosking, *A History of the Soviet Union*, London, 1985; revised edn, London, 1992

Geoffrey A. Hosking, *The Russian Constitutional Experiment: Government and Duma 1907–1914*, Cambridge, 1973

R.C. Howes, *The Testaments of the Grand Princes of Moscow*, Ithaca, 1967

L.A.J. Hughes, *Sophia, Regent of Russia 1654–1704*, New Haven and London, 1990

D.M. Kaiser, *The Growth of Law in Medieval Russia*, Princeton, 1981

George Katkov, *Russia: February 1917*, London and New York, 1967

George Katkov, ed., *Russia Enters the Twentieth Century, 1894–1917*, London, 1971

J.P. Le Donne, *Absolutism and Ruling Class. The Formation of the Russian Political Order 1700–1825*, New York and Oxford, 1991

Moshe Lewin, *The Making of the Soviet System*, London, 1985

Moshe Lewin, *Russian Peasant and Soviet Power: A Study of Collectivization*, London, 1968

Dominic Lieven, *Nicholas II: Emperor of All the Russias*, London, 1993

P. Longworth, *Alexis, Tsar of All the Russias*, London, 1984

P. Longworth, *The Cossacks*, London, 1969

P. Longworth, *Three Empresses: Catherine I, Anne and Elizabeth of Russia*, London, 1972

Isabel de Madariaga, *Catherine the Great: A Short History*, London, 1990

Isabel de Madariaga, *Russia in the Age of Catherine the Great*, New Haven and London, 1981; reissued 1991

J.P. Mallory, *In Search of the Indo-Europeans: Language, Archeology and Myth*, London, 1989

R. Manning, *The Crisis of the Old Order in Russia: Gentry and Government*, Princeton, 1982

Mary McAuley, *Bread and Justice: State and Society in Petrograd 1917–1922*, Oxford, 1991

Roderick E. McGrew, *Paul I of Russia 1754–1801*, Oxford, 1992

Robert H. McNeal, ed., *Russia in Transition: 1905–1914: Evolution or Revolution?*, Huntington, 1976

Robert H. McNeal, *Stalin: Man and Ruler*, London, 1988

Roy Medvedev, *Let History Judge: The Origins and Consequences of Stalinism*, revised edn, Oxford, 1989

W.E. Mosse, *Alexander II and the Modernization of Russia*, London, 1958

B. Nørretranders, *The Shaping of the Tsardom of Muscovy*, London, 1964

Alec Nove, ed., *The Stalin Phenomenon*, London, 1993

Dimitri Obolensky, *The Byzantine Commonwealth: Eastern Europe, 500–1453*, London, 1971

S. Piggott, *The Earliest Wheeled Transport, from the Atlantic to the Caspian Sea*, London, 1983

Richard Pipes, *The Russian Revolution 1899–1919*, London, 1990

Marc Raeff, *Imperial Russia, 1682–1825: The Coming of Age of Modern Russia*, New York, 1971

Georg von Rauch, *A History of Soviet Russia*, New York, 1957

N.V. Riasanovsky, *A History of Russia*, 5th edn, Oxford and New York, 1993

T.H. Rigby, *Lenin's Government: Sovnarkom 1917–1922*, Cambridge and New York, 1979

T.H. Rigby, Archie Brown and Peter Reddaway, eds, *Authority, Power and Policy in the USSR*, London and New York, 1980

Hans Rogger, *Russia in the Age of Modernization and Revolution, 1881–1917*, London, 1983

Tamara Talbot Rice, *The Scythians*, London, 1957

M. Rostovtzeff, *Iranians and Greeks in Southern Russia*, Oxford, 1922; New York, 1969

S.I. Rudenko, *Frozen Tombs of Siberia* (trans. M.W. Thompson), London, 1970

Leonard Schapiro, *Russian Studies*, London, 1986

Leonard Schapiro, *The Communist Party of the Soviet Union*, 2nd edn, London, 1970

Leonard Schapiro, *The Origin of the Communist Autocracy: Political Opposition in the Soviet State 1917–1922*, London, 1955

Albert Seaton *The Russo-German War, 1941–1945*, London, 1971

Robert Service, *Lenin: A Political Life*, 3 vols., London, 1985, 1991 and 1994

Robert Service, *The Russian Revolution 1900–1927*, 2nd ed., London, 1991

Hugh Seton-Watson, *The Russian Empire 1801–1917*, Oxford, 1967

Harold Shukman, *Lenin and the Russian Revolution*, London, 1966

R.E.F. Smith and David Christian, *Bread and Salt: A Social and Economic History of Food and Drink in Russia*, Cambridge, 1984

T. Sulimirski, *The Sarmatians*, London, 1970

Michel Tatu, *Power in the Kremlin*, London, 1969

Donald W. Treadgold, *Twentieth-Century Russia*, 7th ed., Boulder, 1990

Robert C. Tucker, *Stalin as Revolutionary 1879–1929*, London, 1974

Robert C. Tucker, *Stalin in Power: Revolution from Above, 1928–1949*, New York and London, 1990

Adam Ulam, *Lenin and the Bolsheviks*, London, 1966

Adam Ulam, *Stalin: The Man and his Era*, New York, 1973

J. Urry, *None but Saints. The Transformation of Mennonite Life in Russia 1789–1889*, Winnipeg, 1989

A.A. Vasiliev, *The Goths in the Crimea*, Cambridge, Mass., 1936

G.V. Vernadsky, *Kievan Russia*, New Haven, 1948

G.V. Vernadsky, *The Mongols and Russia*, New Haven, 1953

G.V. Vernadsky, *Russia at the Dawn of the Modern Age*, New Haven, 1959

G.V. Vernadsky, *The Tsardom of Muscovy*, New Haven, 1969

G.V. Vernadsky *et al*, eds., *A Source Book for Russian History from Early Times to 1917*, New Haven and London, 1972

Andrzej Walicki, *A History of Russian Thought from the Enlightenment to Marxism*, Oxford, 1980

B.D. Wolfe, *Three Who Made a Revolution*, New York, 1948

R.E. Zelnik (ed. and trans.), *A Radical Worker in Tsarist Russia: The Autobiography of Semen Ivanovich Kantachikov*, Stanford, 1986

Art and architecture

M.I. Artamonov, *Treasures from Scythian Tombs*, London, 1969

Robert Auty and Dimitri Obolensky, eds., *An Introduction to Russian Art and Architecture*, Companion to Russian Studies, III, Cambridge, 1980

G. Azargay, *Sogdiab Painting*, Berkeley, 1981

Alan Bird, *A History of Russian Painting*, Oxford, 1987

John E. Bowlt, ed., *Russian Art of the Avant-Garde: Theory and Criticism 1902–1934*, New York, 1976; 2nd edn, London, 1988
Martin Brown, *Art under Stalin*, Oxford, 1991
William C. Brumfield, *A History of Russian Architecture*, Cambridge, 1993
William C. Brumfield, *The Origins of Modernism in Russian Architecture*, Berkeley, 1991
William C. Brumfield, ed., *Reshaping Russian Architecture: Western Technology, Utopian Dreams*, Cambridge, 1990
William C. Brumfield and Milos M. Brumfield, eds., *Christianity and the Arts in Russia*, Cambridge, 1992
M. Bussagli, *Paintings of Central Asia*, Geneva, 1963
James Cracraft, *The Petrine Revolution in Russian Architecture*, Chicago, 1988
Lydia Dournovo, *Armenian Miniatures*, London, 1961
Sheila Fitzpatrick, ed., *Cultural Revolution in Russia, 1928–1931*, Bloomington, 1978
Igor Golomstock, *Totalitarian Art*, London, 1990
I. Golomstock and A. Glezer, *Unofficial Art from the Soviet Union*, London, 1977
Camilla Gray, *The Great Experiment: Russian Art 1863–1922*, London and New York, 1962; revised and enlarged edn by Marian Burleigh-Motley, London, 1986
Mikhail Guerman, *Soviet Art, 1920s–1930s*, New York, 1988
G.H. Hamilton, *The Art and Architecture of Russia*, Harmondsworth, 2nd edn, 1975
C. Holme, ed., *Peasant Art in Russia* (Studio Special), London and New York, 1912
K. Jettmar, *Art of the Steppes*, New York, 1967
D. Marshall Lang, *The Georgians*, London, 1966
Yu. Ovsyannikov, *The Lubok*, Moscow, 1968
Tamara Talbot Rice, *The Ancient Arts of Central Asia*, London, 1965
Tamara Talbot Rice, *A Concise History of Russian Art*, London, 1963
Dmitry V. Sarabianov, *Russian Art: From Neoclassicism to the Avant Garde, 1800–1917*, New York and London, 1990
Albert J. Schmidt, *The Architecture and Planning of Classical Moscow*, Philadelphia, 1989
Leonid Uspensky, *Theology of the Icon*, 2 vols., Crestwood, NY, 1992
Leonid Uspensky and Vladimir Lossky, *The Meaning of Icons*, Crestwood, NY, 1982
Elizabeth Valkenier, *Ilya Repin and the World of Russian Art*, New York, 1990
Elizabeth Valkenier, *Russian Realist Art, the State and Society*, New York, 1989
Elizabeth Kridl Valkenier, ed., *The Wanderers. Masters of 19th-Century Russian Painting*, Austin, Texas, 1990
Miuda Yablonskaia, *Women Artists of Russia's New Age*, London, 1990

Language and literature

Robert Auty and Dimitri Obolensky, eds., *An Introduction to Russian Language and Literature*, Companion to Russian Studies, II, Cambridge, 1977
Christopher Barnes, *Boris Pasternak: A Literary Biography*, I, Cambridge, 1989
Brian Boyd, *Nabokov: The Russian Years*, London, 1990
Jeffrey Brooks, *When Russia Learned to Read. Literacy and Popular Literature, 1861–1917*, Princeton, 1985
Deming Brown, *Soviet Russian Literature since Stalin*, Cambridge, 1978
Deming Brown, *The Last Years of Soviet Russian Literature: Prose Fiction 1975–1991*, Cambridge 1994
Edward J. Brown, *Russian Literature since the Revolution*,

Cambridge, Mass. and London, 1982
William E. Brown, *A History of Eighteenth-Century Russian Literature*, Ann Arbor, 1980
William E. Brown, *A History of Seventeenth-Century Russian Literature*, Ann Arbor, 1980
William E. Brown, *A History of Russian Literature in the Romantic Period*, 4 vols., Ann Arbor, 1986
Katerina Clark, *The Soviet Novel: History as Ritual*, Chicago, 1980
Katerina Clark and Michael Holquist, *Mikhail Bakhtin*, Cambridge, Mass. and London, 1984
D.P. Costello and I.P. Foote, eds., *Russian Folk Literature*, London, 1967
D. Cizevskij, *History of Russian Literature from the Eleventh Century to the End of the Baroque*, The Hague, 1962
Efim Etkind, Georges Nivat, Ilia Serman, Vittorio Strada, eds., *Histoire de la littérature russe*, 7 vols., Paris, 1987–92
John Fennell and A.D. Stokes, *Early Russian Literature*, London, 1974
Richard Freeborn, *The Rise of the Russian Novel*, Cambridge, 1973
Julian Graffy and Geoffrey A. Hosking, eds., *Culture and the Media in the USSR Today*, London, 1989
N.K. Gudzy, *A History of Early Russian Literature* (trans. S. Wilbur Jones), New York, 1970
Max Hayward, *Writers in Russia 1917–1978*, London, 1983
Barbara Heldt, *Terrible Perfection: Women and Russian Literature*, Bloomington, 1992
Ronald Hingley, *A New Life of Anton Chekhov*, London, 1976
Ronald Hingley, *Russian Writers and Society, 1917–1978*, London, 1979
Geoffrey Hosking, *Beyond Socialist Realism: Soviet Fiction since Ivan Denisovich*, London, 1980
Linda J. Ivanits, *Russian Folk Belief*, Armonk, NY and London, 1989
Malcolm V. Jones, *Dostoevsky after Bakhtin*, Cambridge, 1990
Malcolm V. Jones, ed., *New Essays on Tolstoy*, Cambridge, 1978
Simon Karlinsky, *Marina Tsvetaeva: The Woman, her World, and her Poetry*, Cambridge, 1985
Simon Karlinsky, *Russian Drama from its Beginnings to the Age of Pushkin*, Berkeley, Los Angeles, and London, 1985
Simon Karlinsky and Alfred Appell, Jr., eds., *The Bitter Air of Exile: Russian Writers in the West, 1922–72*, rev. edn, Berkeley and London, 1977
Catriona Kelly, *A History of Russian Women's Writing 1820–1992*, Oxford, 1994
D.S. Likhachev, *The Great Heritage: The Classical Literature of Old Rus* (trans. Doris Bradbury) Moscow, 1981
John E. Malmstad, ed., *Andrei Bely: Spirit of Symbolism*, Ithaca and London, 1987
Nadezhda Mandelstam, *Hope against Hope* (trans. Max Hayward), London, 1971
Nadezhda Mandelstam, *Hope Abandoned* (trans. Max Hayward), London, 1974
Vladimir Markov, *Russian Futurism*, Berkeley and Los Angeles, 1968
W.K. Matthews, *Russian Historical Grammar*, London, 1960
Lesley Milne, *Mikhail Bulgakov: A Critical Biography*, Cambridge, 1991
D.S. Mirsky, *A History of Russian Literature*, London, 1949 and subsequent editions
Charles Moser, ed., *The Cambridge History of Russian Literature*, 2nd enlarged edn, Cambridge, 1992
Richard Peace, *Dostoevsky: An Examination of the Major Novels*, Cambridge, 1971
Valentina Polukhina, *Joseph Brodsky: A Poet for our Time*, Cambridge, 1989

Avril Pyman, *The Life of Alexander Blok*, 2 vols., Oxford, 1979-80

Michael Scammell, *Solzhenitsyn: A Biography*, New York and London, 1984

Barry P. Scherr, *Russian Poetry: Meter, Rhythm, and Rhyme*, Berkeley and London, 1986

Frank Friedeberg Seeley, *Turgenev: A Reading of his Fiction*, Cambridge, 1991

David Shepherd, *Beyond Metafiction. Self-Consciousness in Soviet Literature*, Oxford, 1992

Gerald S. Smith, *Contemporary Russian Poetry: A Bilingual Anthology*, Bloomington, 1993

Gerald S. Smith, *Songs to Seven Strings: Russian Guitar Poetry and Soviet 'Mass Song'*, Bloomington, Indiana, 1984

Yu.M. Sokolov, *Russian Folklore* (trans. Catherine Ruth Smith), Folklore Associates, Hartboro, Penn., 1966

Gerald Stone and Bernard Comrie, *The Russian Language since the Revolution*, Oxford, 1978

Gleb Struve, *Russian Literature under Lenin and Stalin*, London, 1972

Victor Terras, *A History of Russian Literature*, New Haven and London, 1992

A.P. Vlasto, *A Linguistic History of Russia to the End of the Eighteenth Century*, Oxford, 1986

Cultural life

A. Benois, *Reminiscences of the Russian Ballet*, London, 1941

David Brown, 'Russia', in F.W. Sternfeld, ed., *A History of Western Music*, V, London, 1973

John Bushnell, *Moscow Graffiti: Language and Subculture*, Boston, 1990

Leo Fagin, ed., *Russian Jazz: New Identity*, London, 1985

M.I. Glinka, *Memoirs* (trans. R.B. Mudge), Oklahoma, 1963

Julian Graffy and Geoffrey A. Hosking, eds., *Culture and the Media in the USSR Today*, London, 1989

Tamara Karsavina, *Theatre Street*, London, 1930 (reprinted 1961)

Catriona Kelly, *Petrushka: The Russian Carnival Puppet Theatre*, Cambridge, 1990

Vera Krasovskaya, *Nijinsky*, New York, 1979

Anna Lawton, *Kinoglasnost: Soviet Cinema in our Time*, Cambridge 1992

Anna Lawton, ed., *The Red Screen: Politics, Society, and Art in Soviet Cinema*, London, 1992

J. Leyda, *Kino: A History of Russian and Soviet Film*, London, 1960

V.N. Nemirovich-Danchenko, *My Life in the Russian Theatre*, New York, 1936

R.S. Ralston, *The Songs of the Russian People as Illustrative of Slavonic Mythology and Russian Social Life*, London, 1872 (reprinted 1970)

N.A. Rimsky-Korsakov, *My Musical Life*, New York, 1942

Princess Romanovsky-Krassinsky, *Dancing in Petersburg: The Memoirs of Kschessinskaya*, London, 1960

Natalia Roslavleva, *Era of the Russian Ballet, 1770–1965*, London, 1966

Konstantin Rudnitskii, *Russian and Soviet Theatre: Tradition and the Avant-Garde*, London, 1988

Robert Russell and Andrew Barratt, eds., *Russian Theatre in the Age of Modernism*, Basingstoke, 1990

Timothy W. Ryback, *Rock Around the Bloc: A History of Rock Music in Eastern Europe and the Soviet Union*, Oxford and New York, 1990

B. Schwarz, *Music and Musical Life in Soviet Russia 1917–1970*, London, 1972; enlarged edn, Bloomington, 1983

Gerald Seaman, *History of Russian Music: From its Origins to Dargomyzhsky*, I, Oxford, 1967

Harold B. Segel, *Twentieth-Century Russian Drama from Gorky to the Present*, New York, 1979

Yu. Slonimsky, *The Soviet Ballet*, New York, 1947 and 1973

K.S. Stanislavsky, *An Actor Prepares*, New York, 1989

S. Frederick Starr, *Red and Hot: The Fate of Jazz in the Soviet Union*, New York, 1983

Richard Stites, *Russian Popular Culture: Entertainment and Society since 1900*, Cambridge, 1992

Richard Taylor, *The Politics of the Soviet Cinema, 1917–1929*, Cambridge, 1979

Richard Taylor and Ian Christie, eds., *The Film Factory. Russian and Soviet Cinema in Documents, 1896–1939*, London and Cambridge, Mass., 1988

Richard Taylor and Derek Spring, eds., *Stalinism and Soviet Cinema*, London and New York, 1993

Artemy Troitsky, *Back in the USSR: The True Story of Rock in Russia*, London, 1987

Artemy Troitsky, *Tusovka*, London, 1990

R.J. Wiley, *Tchaikovsky's Ballets*, Oxford, 1985

R.J. Wiley, ed., *A Century of Russian Ballet: Documents and Eyewitness Accounts, 1810–1910*, Oxford, 1990

Nick Worrall, *Modernism to Realism on the Soviet Stage: Tairov, Vakhtangov, Okhlopov*, Cambridge, 1989

Denise J. Youngblood, *Soviet Cinema in the Silent Era, 1918–1935*, Austin, Texas, reprinted 1991

The sciences

Ronald Amann and Julian Cooper, eds., *Industrial Innovation in the Soviet Union*, New Haven and London, 1982

Ronald Amann, Julian Cooper and R.W. Davies, eds., *The Technological Level of Soviet Industry*, New Haven and London, 1977

V.A. Anuchin, *Theoretical Problems of Geography*, Columbus, 1977

T. Armstrong, *The Russians in the Arctic: Aspects of Soviet Exploration and Expoitation of the Far North, 1937–1941*, London, 1960

Kendall E. Bailes, *Technology and Society under Lenin and Stalin: Origins of the Soviet Technical Intelligentsia, 1917–1941*, Princeton, 1978

Harley D. Balzer, *Soviet Science on the Edge of Reform*, Boulder, 1989

J.S. Berliner, *The Innovation Decision in Soviet Industry*, Cambridge, Mass., 1976

Michael J. Berry, ed., *Science and Technology in the USSR*, London, 1988

Sidney Bloch and Peter Reddaway, *Russia's Political Hospitals: The Abuse of Psychiatry in the Soviet Union*, London, 1977

Robert W. Campbell, *Soviet Energy Technologies: Planning, Policy, Research and Development*, Bloomington, 1980

Martin Cave, *Computers and Economic Planning: The Soviet Experience*, Cambridge, 1980

A.C. Crombie, ed., *Scientific Change*, London, 1961

Frederic J. Fleron, Jr, ed., *Technology and Communist Culture*, Eastbourne and New York, 1977

Stephen Fortescue, *Science Policy in the Soviet Union*, London, 1990

Stephen Fortescue, *The Communist Party and Soviet Science*, London, 1986

D.W. Freshfield, *The Exploration of the Caucasus*, London, 1902

Nancy Frieden, *Russian Physicians in an Era of Reform and Revolution, 1856–1905*, Princeton, 1981

K.W. Gatland, *Robot Explorers*, London, 1972

I.P. Gerasimov, ed., *A Short History of Geographical Science in the Soviet Union*, Moscow, 1976

Loren R. Graham, *Science, Philosophy and Human Behavior in the Soviet Union*, New York, 1987

Loren R. Graham, ed., *Science and the Soviet Social Order*, Cambridge, Mass., 1990

Loren R. Graham, *Science in the Soviet Union: A Short History*, Cambridge and New York, 1993

G. Heiken, D. Vaniman and B. French, eds., *Lunar Sourcebook*, Cambridge, 1991

Raymond Hutchings, *Soviet Science, Technology, Design: Interaction and Convergence*, Oxford, 1976

Gordon Hyde, *The Soviet Health Service: A Historical and Comparative Study*, London, 1974

David Joravsky, *Russian Psychology: A Critical History*, Oxford, 1989

David Joravsky, *Soviet Marxism and Natural Science, 1917–32*, New York, 1961

David Joravsky, *The Lysenko Affair*, Cambridge, Mass., 1970

Paul R. Josephson, *Physics and Politics in Revolutionary Russia*, Los Angeles, 1991

Michael Kaser, *Health Care in the Soviet Union and Eastern Europe*, London and Boulder, 1976

Edward J. Kormondy and J. Frank McCormick, eds., *Handbook of Contemporary Developments in World Ecology*, Westport, Conn., 1981

Alex Kozulin, *Psychology in Utopia*, Cambridge, Mass., 1984

Malcolm Lader, *Psychiatry on Trial*, Harmondsworth, 1977

D.V. Lebedev *et al*, *An Outline of the History of the V.L. Komarov Botanical Institute of the USSR Academy of Sciences (1714–1961)* (trans. D.M. Kershner and G.E. Ben, ed. P.A. Baranov), Moscow-Leningrad, 1962

R. Lewis, *Science and Industrialisation in the USSR*, London, 1979

Linda L. Lubrano and Susan Gross Solomon, eds., *The Social Context of Soviet Science*, Boulder and Folkestone, 1980

R.E. McGrew, *Russia and the Cholera 1823–1832*, Madison, 1965

Zhores A. Medvedev, *Soviet Science*, New York, 1978; Oxford, 1979

Zhores A. Medvedev, *The Medvedev Papers: The Plight of Soviet Science Today*, London and New York, 1971

B.N. Menshutkin, *Russia's Lomonosov: Chemist, Courtier, Physicist, Poet* (trans. J.E. Thal and E.J. Webster), Princeton, 1952

D.V. Nalivkin, *Geology of the USSR* (trans. N. Rast), Edinburgh, 1973

L.E. Neatby, *Discovery in Russian and Siberian Waters*, Columbus, 1973

E. Riabchikov, *Russians in Space*, London, 1972

P. Sager, *The Technological Gap between the Superpowers* (trans. C. Rieser), Berne, 1972

A.D. Sakharov, *Progress, Co-Existence and Intellectual Freedom*, London, 1969

P.H. Schultz, *Moon Morphology*, Austin, Texas, 1976

S.G. Shetler, *The Komarov Botanical Institute: 250 Years of Russian Research*, Washington, 1967

A.C. Sutton, *Western Technology and Soviet Economic Development*, 3 vols., *1917–1930, 1930–1945, 1945–1965*, Stanford, 1968, 1971, 1973

J.R. Thomas and U.M. Kruse-Vaucienne, eds., *Soviet Science and Technology: Domestic and Foreign Perspectives*, Washington DC, 1977

J.L. Turkevich, *Chemistry in the Soviet Union*, Princeton, 1965

Alexander Vucinich, *Science in Russian Culture: A History to 1860*, London, 1963

Alexander Vucinich, *Science in Russian Culture: 1861–1917*, Stanford, 1970

Alexander Vucinich, *Empire of Knowledge: The Academy of Sciences of the USSR (1917–1970)*, Berkeley, 1984

D.R. Weiner, *Models of Nature: Ecology, Conservation and Cultural Revolution in Soviet Russia*, Bloomington, 1988

J. Wilczynski, *Technology in Comecon*, New York, 1974

E. Zaleski, J.P. Kozlowski, H. Weinert, R.W. Davies, M.J. Berry and R. Amann, *Science Policy in the USSR*, Paris (OECD), 1969

A. Zauberman, *The Mathematical Revolution in Soviet Economics*, Oxford, 1975

A. Zauberman, *Mathematical Theory in Soviet Planning*, Oxford, 1976

Politics

Christopher Andrew and Oleg Gordievsky, *KGB: The Inside Story of its Foreign Operations from Lenin to Gorbachev*, London, 1990

Isaiah Berlin, *Russian Thinkers*, London, 1978

Seweryn Bialer, *Stalin's Successors: Leadership, Stability and Change in the Soviet Union*, Cambridge, 1980

Seweryn Bialer, ed., *Politics, Society and Nationality Inside Gorbachev's Russia*, Boulder and London, 1989

Ian Bremner and Ray Taras, eds, *Nations and Politics in the Soviet Successor States*, Cambridge and New York, 1993

Archie Brown, ed., *New Thinking in Soviet Politics*, London and New York, 1992

Archie Brown, *The Gorbachev Factor*, Oxford and New York, 1995

Abraham Brumberg, ed., *Chronicle of a Revolution: A Western-Soviet Inquiry into Perestroika*, New York, 1990

Mary Buckley, *Redefining Russian Politics and Society*, Boulder 1993

William E. Butler, *Soviet Law*, London, 1983

Stephen F. Cohen and Katrina vanden Heuvel, *Voices of Glasnost: Interviews with Gorbachev's Reformers*, New York, 1989

Timothy J. Colton and Robert Legvold, eds., *After the Soviet Union: From Empire to Nations*, New York and London, 1993

Alexander Dallin and Gail W. Lapidus, eds., *The Soviet System in Crisis*, Boulder and London, 1991

Karen Dawisha and Bruce Parrott, *Russia and the New States of Eurasia. The Politics of Upheaval*, Cambridge, 1994

John B. Dunlop, *The Rise of Russia and the Fall of the Soviet Empire*, Princeton, 1993

Merle Fainsod, *Smolensk under Soviet Rule*, London, 1958

Theodore H. Friedgut, *Political Participation in the USSR*, Princeton, 1979

Jeffrey W. Hahn, *Soviet Grassroots*, Princeton, 1988

Neil Harding, *Lenin's Political Thought*, 2 vols., London, 1977, 1981

Ed A. Hewett and Victor H. Winston, eds., *Milestones in Glasnost and Perestroika: Politics and People*, Washington, 1991

Ronald J. Hill, *Soviet Politics, Political Science and Reform*, Oxford, 1980

Ronald J. Hill and Peter Frank, *The Soviet Communist Party*, 3rd edn, London, 1986

Geoffrey A. Hosking, Jonathan Aves and Peter J.S. Duncan, *The Road to Post-Communism: Independent Movements in the Soviet Union 1985–1991*, London and New York, 1992

Jerry F. Hough, *The Soviet Prefects*, Cambridge, Mass., 1969

Jerry F. Hough and Merle Fainsod, *How the Soviet Union is Governed*, Cambridge, Mass. and London, 1979

Gayle D. Hollander, *Soviet Political Indoctrination*, London and New York, 1972

Eugene Huskey, ed., *Executive Power and Soviet Politics: The Rise and Decline of the Soviet State*, Armonk and London, 1992

Peter Juviler, *Revolutionary Law and Order: Politics and Social Change in the USSR*, New York, 1976

Robert Kaiser, *Why Gorbachev Happened: His Triumphs and His Failures*, New York, 1991

Rasma Karklins, *Ethnic Relations in the USSR: The Perspective from Below*, Boston, 1985

Amy Knight, *The KGB: Police and Politics in the Soviet Union*, London, 1988

Vladimir Kuzichkin, *Inside the KGB: Myth and Reality*, London, 1990

George Leggett, *The Cheka: Lenin's Political Police*, Oxford, 1981

Wolfgang Leonhard, *Three Faces of Marxism*, New York, 1974

Mary McAuley, *Soviet Politics 1917–1991*, Oxford, 1992

Roy A. Medvedev, *On Socialist Democracy*, New York and London, 1975

John Miller, *Mikhail Gorbachev and the End of Soviet Power*, London, 1993

John Morrison, *Boris Yeltsin*, Harmondsworth, 1991

Bohdan Nahaylo and Victor Swoboda, *Soviet Disunion: A History of the Nationalities Problem in the USSR*, London and New York, 1990

Peter Reddaway, ed., *Uncensored Russia: The Human Rights Movement in the Soviet Union*, London, 1972

T. H. Rigby, *Communist Party Membership in the USSR 1917–1967*, Princeton, 1968

T. H. Rigby, *Political Elites in the USSR: Central Leaders and Local Cadres from Lenin to Gorbachev*, Aldershot and Brookfield, Vermont, 1990

T. H. Rigby, *The Changing Soviet System*, Aldershot and Brookfield, Vermont, 1990

Angus Roxburgh, *The Second Russian Revolution*, London, 1991

Amin Saikal and William Maley, eds., *Russia in Search of its Future*, Cambridge, 1994

Andrei Sakharov, *Sakharov Speaks*, London, 1974

Andrei Sakharov, *Memoirs* (trans. Richard Lourie), New York, 1990

Andrei Sakharov, *Moscow and Beyond: 1986 to 1989* (trans. Antonina Bouis), New York, 1991

Richard Sakwa, *Russian Politics and Society*, London, 1993

Leonard Schapiro, *The Communist Party of the Soviet Union*, 2nd edn, London, 1970

Robert Sharlet, *Soviet Constitutional Crisis from De-Stalinization to Disintegration*, Armonk, 1992

H. Gordon Skilling and Franklyn Griffiths, eds., *Interest Groups in Soviet Politics*, Princeton, 1971

Graham Smith, ed., *The Nationalities Question in the Soviet Union*, London and New York, 1990

Anatoly Sobchak, *For a New Russia*, London, 1992

William Taubman, *Governing Soviet Cities: Bureaucratic Politics and Urban Development in the USSR*, New York, 1973

Rudolf L. Tökés, ed., *Dissent in the USSR*, Baltimore and London, 1975

Robert C. Tucker, *The Soviet Political Mind*, London, 1963

Robert C. Tucker, ed., *Stalinism: Essays in Historical Interpretation*, London, 1963

Michael Urban, *More Power to the Soviets: The Democratic Revolution in the USSR*, Aldershot, 1990

S. V. Utechin, *Russian Political Thought*, London, 1963

Stephen White, *After Gorbachev*, Cambridge, 1993

Stephen White, Alex Pravda and Zvi Gitelman, eds., *Developments in Russian and Post-Soviet Politics*, London, 1994

Stephen Whitefield, *Industrial Power and the Soviet State*, Oxford and New York, 1993

Boris Yeltsin, *Against the Grain*, London, 1990

Economy

Ronald Amann and Julian Cooper, eds., *Technical Progress and Soviet Economic Development*, Oxford, 1986

Gregory D. Andrusz, *Housing and Urban Development in the USSR*, London, 1984

Anders Åslund, *Gorbachev's Struggle for Economic Reform*, 2nd edn, London, 1991

D. T. Bailey, ed., *Accounting in Socialist Countries*, London, 1988

Harley D. Balzer, *Soviet Science on the Edge of Reform*, Boulder, 1989

John Barber and Mark Harrison, *The Soviet Home Front 1941–45. A Social and Economic History of the USSR in World War II*, London, 1991

J. Berliner, *The Innovation Decision in Soviet Industry*, Cambridge, Mass., 1976

Michael J. Berry, ed., *Science and Technology in the USSR*, London, 1988

W. L. Blackwell, *The Beginnings of Russian Industrialization, 1800–1860*, Princeton, 1968

Jozef M. van Brabant, *Centrally Planned Economies and International Economic Organizations*, Cambridge, 1990

Robert Campbell, *Soviet Energy Technologies*, Bloomington, 1983

Robert Campbell, *The Economics of Soviet Oil and Gas*, Baltimore, 1968

E. H. Carr and R. W. Davies, *Foundations of a Planned Economy*, I, London, 1969

Olga Crisp, *Studies in the Russian Economy before 1914*, London, 1976

R. W. Davies, *The Socialist Offensive: The Collectivisation of Soviet Agriculture, 1929–1930*, London, 1980

R. W. Davies, *The Industrialization of Soviet Russia*, 3 vols., London and Cambridge, Mass., 1980–89

Leslie Dienes and Theodore Shabad, *The Soviet Energy System*, New York, 1979

Maurice H. Dobb, *Soviet Economic Development since 1917*, 6th edn, London and New York, 1966

David A. Dyker, *The Process of Investment in the Soviet Union*, Cambridge, 1983

J. Eatwell, M. Milgate and P. Newman, eds., *Problems of the Planned Economy*, London, 1990

M. Ellman and V. Kontorovich, eds, *The Disintegration of the Soviet Economic System*, London, 1992

M. E. Falkus, *The Industrialization of Russia 1700–1914*, London, 1972

Perdita Fraser, *The Post-Soviet States and the European Community*, London, 1992

J. T. Fuhrmann, *The Origins of Capitalism in Russia: Industry and Progress in the Sixteenth and Seventeenth Centuries*, Chicago, 1972

G. Garvy, *Money, Financial Flows, and Credit in the Soviet Union*, Cambridge, Mass., 1977

Peter Gatrell, *The Tsarist Economy 1850–1917*, London, 1986

Kenneth R. Gray, ed., *Soviet Agriculture: Comparative Perspectives*, Ames, Iowa, 1990

P. R. Gregory and R. C. Stuart, *Soviet Economic Structure and Performance*, 4th edn, New York, 1990

Thane Gustafson, *Crisis amid Plenty: The Politics of Soviet Energy under Brezhnev and Gorbachev*, Princeton, 1989

C. D. Harris, *Cities of the Soviet Union: Studies of their Functions, Size, Density and Growth*, Chicago, 1970

Stefan Hedlund, *Private Agriculture in the Soviet Union*, London and New York, 1989

Ed A. Hewett, *Energy, Economics, and Foreign Policy in the Soviet Union*, Washington, 1984

Ed A. Hewett, *Reforming the Soviet Economy: Equality versus Efficiency*, Washington, 1988

Ed A. Hewett and Victor H. Winston, eds., *Milestones in Glasnost and Perestroika: The Economy*, Washington, 1991

Malcolm R. Hill and Richard McKay, *Soviet Product Quality*, London, 1988

F.D. Holzman, *International Trade under Communism: Politics and Economics*, London, 1976

Michael Kaser, *Soviet Economics*, London and New York, 1970

Michael Kaser and Santosh Mehrotra, *The Central Asian Economies after Independence*, London, 1992

E.S. Kern, ed., *Land Reform and the Problems of Land Legislation* (FAO), Rome, 1992

L. Kirsch, *Soviet Wages*, Cambridge, Mass., 1972

David Lane, ed., *Russia In Flux*, Aldershot, 1992

Margot Light, *The Soviet Theory of International Relations*, Hemel Hempstead, 1988

Alastair McAuley, *Economic Welfare in the Soviet Union*, London, 1979

Carl McMillan, *Multinationals from the Second World*, London, 1987

B. Nahaylo, *The New Ukraine*, London, 1992

Alec Nove, *An Economic History of the USSR*, 3rd edn, London, 1992

Alec Nove, *The Soviet Economic System*, 3rd edn, London, 1987

Judith Pallot and Denis J.B. Shaw, *Planning in the Soviet Union*, London, 1981

G.T. Robinson, *Rural Russia under the Old Regime*, 2nd edn, London, 1967

Peter Rutland, *The Politics of Economic Stagnation in the Soviet Union*, London, 1993

N.Shmelov and V. Popov, *The Turning Point. Revitalizing the Soviet Economy*, London, 1990

R.E.F. Smith, *Peasant Farming in Muscovy*, Cambridge, 1977

Jonathan Stern, *The Russian Energy Industry*, London, 1993

Pekka Sutela, *Economic Thought and Economic Reform in the Soviet Union*, Cambridge, 1991

L. Symons, *Russian Agriculture: A Geographic Survey*, London, 1972

L. Symons and C. White, eds., *Russian Transport: An Historical and Geographical Survey*, London, 1975

The Cambridge Economic History of Europe, Cambridge, vols. I, 1966; VI, 1966; VII, 1978; and VIII, 1981

The East-West Business Directory 1991/92, New York, 1992

J.A. Underhill, *Soviet New Towns: Housing and National Urban Growth Policy*, Washington, 1976

K.-E. Wädekin, ed., *Communist Agriculture: Farming in the Soviet Union and Eastern Europe*, London and New York, 1990

World Investment Directory, II, *Central and Eastern Europe*, New York, 1992

Iliana Zloch-Christy, *East-West Financial Relations: Current Problems and Future Prospects*, Cambridge, 1991

A. Zwass, *Money, Credit, and Banking in the Soviet Union and Eastern Europe*, New York, 1979

Society

Dorothy Atkinson, Alexander Dallin and Gail Lapidus, eds., *Women in Russia*, Berkeley and London, 1978

David Wedgwood Benn, *Persuasion and Soviet Politics*, Oxford, 1989

Harold J. Berman, *Justice in the USSR*, Cambridge, Mass., 1963

Sidney Bloch and Peter Reddaway, *Russia's Political Hospitals: The Abuse of Psychiatry in the Soviet Union*, London, 1977

J. Brine, M. Perrie and A. Sutton, eds., *Home, School and Leisure in the Soviet Union*, London, 1980

Emily Clark Brown, *Soviet Trade Unions and Labor Relations*, Cambridge, Mass., 1965

Mary Buckley, ed., *Perestroika and Soviet Women*, Cambridge, 1992

David Christian, *Living Water: Vodka in Russian Society on the Eve of the Emancipation*, Oxford, 1990

Walter D. Connor, *Deviance in Soviet Society: Crime, Delinquency and Alcoholism*, New York, 1972

Walter D. Connor, *The Accidental Proletariat*, Princeton, 1991

Robert Conquest, *Kolyma: The Arctic Death Camps*, London, 1978

Martin Dewhirst and Robert Farrell, eds, *The Soviet Censorship*, Metuchen, NJ, 1973

John Dunstan, ed., *Soviet Education under Perestroika*, London and New York, 1992

R. Eales, *Chess: The History of a Game*, London, 1985

Linda Edmondson, ed., *Women and Society in Russia and the Soviet Union*, Cambridge, 1992

Beatrice Farnsworth and Lynne Viola, eds., *Russian Peasant Women*, Princeton, 1992

Murray Feshbach and Alfred Friendly, Jr., *Ecocide in the USSR: Health and Nature under Siege*, New York, 1992

Sheila Fitzpatrick, *Education and Social Mobility in the Soviet Union, 1921–1934*, Cambridge and New York, 1979

S. Francis, ed., *Libraries in the USSR*, London, 1971

Nigel Grant, *Soviet Education*, 4th edn, Harmondsworth, 1979

Horst Herlemann, ed., *Quality of Life in the Soviet Union*, Boulder, 1987

Leslie Holmes, *The End of Communist Power: Anti-Corruption Campaigns and Legitimation Crisis*, Oxford, 1993

M.W. Hopkins, *Mass Media in the Soviet Union*, New York, 1970

Geoffrey A. Hosking, *The Awakening of the Soviet Union*, London, 1990

Anthony Jones, Walter Connor, and David Powell, eds., *Soviet Social Problems*, Boulder, 1991

Anthony Jones and William Moskoff, *KO-OPS: The Rebirth of Entrepreneurship in the Soviet Union*, Bloomington, 1991

Ellen Jones, *Red Army and Society: A Sociology of the Soviet Military*, London, 1985

Ellen Jones and Fred W. Grupp, *Modernization, Value Change and Fertility in the Soviet Union*, Cambridge, 1987

Michael Kaser, *Health Care in the Soviet Union and Eastern Europe*, London and Boulder, 1976

A. Kassof, *The Soviet Youth Program: Regimentation and Rebellion*, Cambridge, Mass. and London, 1965

Basile Kerblay, *Modern Soviet Society*, London and New York, 1983

Jeffrey Klugman, *The New Soviet Elite: How They Think and What They Want*, New York, 1989

Vitaly Korotich and Cathy Porter, eds., *The New Soviet Journalism*, Boston, 1990

A. Kotov and M. Yudovich, *The Soviet School of Chess*, Moscow, 1958; New York, 1961

David Lane, *Soviet Society under Perestroika*, London, 1992

Gail Lapidus, *Women in Soviet Society: Equality, Development and Social Change*, Berkeley, 1978

Alastair McAuley, *Economic Welfare in the Soviet Union*, London, 1979

Brian McNair, *Glasnost, Perestroika and the Soviet Media*, London, 1991

Bernice Madison, *Social Welfare in the Soviet Union*, Stanford, 1968

Mervyn Matthews, *Class and Society in Soviet Russia*, London, 1972

Mervyn Matthews, *Patterns of Deprivation in the Soviet Union under Brezhnev and Gorbachev*, Stanford, 1989

Zhores and Roy Medvedev, *A Question of Madness*, London, 1971

Ellen Mickiewicz, *Split Signals: Television and Politics in the Soviet Union*, Oxford, 1988

Elena Molokhovets, *Classic Russian Cooking: A Gift to Young Housewives*, trans. and introduced by Joyce Toomre, Bloomington and Indianapolis, 1992

James Muckle, *Portrait of a Soviet School under Glasnost*, London, 1990

Alec Nove, *Glasnost in Action: Cultural Renaissance in Russia*, London, 1989

Felicity O'Dell, *Socialization through Children's Literature: The Soviet Example*, Cambridge, 1978

L. Pearson, *Children of Glasnost*, Toronto, 1990

Miranda B. Remnek, ed., *Books in Russia and the Soviet Union: Past and Present*, Wiesbaden, 1991

D.J. Richards, *Soviet Chess: Chess and Communism in the USSR*, Oxford, 1965

James W. Riordan, *Sport in Soviet Society: Development of Sport and Physical Education in Russia and the USSR*, Cambridge, 1977

Blair A. Ruble, *Soviet Trade Unions: Their Development in the 1970s*, Cambridge, 1981

Michael Ryan, *The Organization of Soviet Medical Care*, Oxford, 1978

Michael Ryan and Richard Prentice, *Social Trends in the Soviet Union from 1950*, London, 1987

Michael Sacks and Jerry Pankhurst, eds., *Understanding Soviet Society*, London, 1988

Vladimir Shlapentokh, *Public and Private Life of the Soviet People: Changing Values in Post-Soviet Russia*, New York and Oxford, 1989

Hedrick Smith, *The New Russians*, New York, 1990

Alexander Solzhenitsyn, *The Gulag Archipelago*, 3 vols., London, 1974-78

Richard Stites, *The Women's Liberation Movement in Russia*, Princeton, 1978

J.J. Tomiak, *The USSR* (World Education Series), Newton Abbot and North Pomfret, 1962

Vladimir G. Treml, *Alcohol in the USSR: A Statistical Study*, Durham, NC, 1982

Vladimir G. Treml, *Gorbachev's Antidrinking Campaign: A Noble Experiment or a Costly Exercise in Futility?*, New York, 1987

Arkady Vaksberg, *The Soviet Mafia*, London, 1991

Michael Voslensky, *Nomenklatura*, New York, 1984

R.G. Wade, *Soviet Chess*, London, 1968

Gregory Walker, *Soviet Book Publishing Policy*, Cambridge, 1978

Gregory Walker, *Book Publishing in the USSR: Reports of the Delegations of US Book Publishers Visiting the USSR*, 2nd edn, Cambridge, Mass and Oxford, 1972

Valentina Wasson and R. Gordon Wasson, *Mushrooms, Russia and History*, 2 vols., New York, 1957

M. Yanowitch, *Controversies in Soviet Social Thought*, Armonk, NY, 1991

M. Yanowitch, *New Directions in Soviet Social Thought*, New York, 1989

M. Yanowitch, *Social and Economic Inequality in the Soviet Union*, London, 1977

M. Yanowitch and W.A. Fischer, *Social Stratification and Mobility in the USSR*, New York, 1973

Tatiana Zaslavskaia, *The Second Socialist Revolution*, Bloomington, 1990

Military power

Roy Allison, ed., *Radical Reform in Soviet Defence Policy*, London, 1992

John Baylis and Gerald Segal, eds., *Soviet Strategy*, London, 1981

R. Bond, ed., *The Soviet War Machine*, 2nd edn, London and New York, 1977

Alexander Boyd, *The Soviet Air Force since 1918*, London, 1977

S. Breyer and N. Polmar, *Guide to the Soviet Navy*, Washington and London, 1978

Timothy J. Colton, *Commissars, Commanders and Civilian Authority: The Structure of Soviet Military Politics*, Cambridge, Mass. and London, 1979

Timothy J. Colton and Thane Gustafson, eds., *Soldiers and the Soviet State: Civil-Military Relations from Brezhnev to Gorbachev*, Princeton, 1990

Christopher Donnelly, *Red Banner: The Soviet Military System in Peace and War*, Coulsdon, 1988

John Erickson, *The Soviet High Command*, London, 1962

John Erickson, ed., *Soviet Military Power and Performance*, London, 1979

David Footman, *Civil War in Russia*, London, 1961

Raymond Garthoff, *Soviet Military Policy*, London, 1966

K.W. Gatland, *Missiles and Rockets*, London and New York, 1975

Richard Hellie, *Enserfment and Military Change in Muscovy*, Chicago, 1971

A.L. Horelick and M. Rush, *Strategic Power and Soviet Foreign Policy*, Chicago, 1966

Michael McGwire, *Military Objectives in Soviet Foreign Policy*, Washington, 1987

Michael McGwire and J. McDonnell, eds., *Soviet Naval Influence: Domestic and Foreign Dimensions*, New York and London, 1975

M. Mitchell, *The Maritime History of Russia: 848–1948*, London, 1949

W.E. Odom, *The Soviet Volunteers*, Princeton, 1973

Bryan Ranft and Geoffrey Till, *The Sea in Soviet Strategy: Strengths and Liabilities*, Boulder, 1986

Harriet Fast Scott and William F. Scott, *Soviet Military Doctrine: Continuity, Formulation and Dissemination*, Boulder, 1988

James Sherr, *Soviet Power: The Continuing Challenge*, 2nd edn, London and New York, 1991

G. Stewart, *The White Armies of Russia*, New York, 1933

Norman Stone, *The Eastern Front, 1914–1917*, London, 1975

V.D. Sokolovsky, *Soviet Military Strategy*, Moscow 1968

P.H. Vigor, *The Soviet View of War, Peace and Neutrality*, London and Boston, 1976

A.K. Wildman, *The End of the Russian Imperial Army: The Old Army and the Soldiers Revolt (March-April 1917)*, Princeton, 1980

Thomas Wolfe, *Soviet Power and Europe, 1945–1970*, Baltimore, 1970

P.T. Yegorov, *Civil Defence: Soviet Handbook* (trans. USAF), Washington, 1976

International relations

M.S. Anderson, *The Eastern Question 1774–1923: A Study in International Relations*, London, 1966

J.F. Baddeley, *The Russian Conquest of the Caucasus*, London, 1908

Max Beloff, *The Foreign Policy of Soviet Russia, 1929–1941*, Oxford, 1947–49

Seweryn Bialer, ed., *The Domestic Context of Soviet Foreign Policy*, London, 1981

Zbigniew Brzezinski, *The Soviet Bloc: Unity and Conflict*, Cambridge, Mass., 1967

A. Dallin, *The Rise of Russia in Asia*, London, 1950

A. Dallin, *The Soviet Union at the United Nations*, New York, 1963

Karen Dawisha and Philip Hanson, eds., *Soviet-East European Dilemmas: Coercion, Competition and Consent*, London, 1981

Jane Degras, ed., *Calendar of Documents on Soviet Foreign Policy*, I–III, London, 1951–53

Jane Degras, ed., *The Communist International 1919–1943: Documents*, I–III, Oxford, 1956–65

H. Feis, *From Trust to Terror: The Onset of the Cold War, 1945–1950*, London, 1970

L. Fischer, *The Soviets in World Affairs*, 2 vols, London, 1930; 2nd edn, Princeton, 1951

Frederic Fleron, Erik Hoffman and Robbin Laird, eds., *Contemporary Issues in Soviet Foreign Policy: From Brezhnev to Gorbachev*, New York, 1991

Raymond Garthoff, *Detente and Confrontation: Soviet-American Relations from Nixon to Reagan*, Washington, 1985

Raymond Garthoff, *Reflections on the Cuban Missile Crisis*, Washington, 1989

Charles Gati, *The Bloc that Failed*, London, 1991

Galia Golan, *Soviet Policies in the Middle East*, Cambridge, 1990

W.E. Griffith, *Sino-Soviet Relations*, Cambridge, Mass., 1964

Patricia Kennedy Grimsted, *The Foreign Ministers of Alexander I: Political Attitudes and the Conduct of Russian Diplomacy 1801–1825*, Berkeley and Los Angeles, 1969

Harry Hanak, *Soviet Foreign Policy since the Death of Stalin*, London, 1972

Jonathan Haslam, *Soviet Foreign Policy 1930–33: The Impact of the Depression*, London, 1983

Jonathan Haslam, *The Soviet Union and the Struggle for Collective Security in Europe, 1933–39*, London, 1984

J. Hiden and P. Salmon, *The Baltic Nations and Europe. Estonia, Latvia and Lithuania in the 20th Century*, London, 1991

David Holloway, *The Soviet Union and the Arms Race*, New Haven and London, 1983

Jerry F. Hough, *The Struggle for the Third World: Soviet Debates and American Options*, Washington, 1986

B. Jelavich, *St Petersburg and Moscow: Tsarist and Soviet Foreign Policy, 1814–1974*, Bloomington, 1974

N.A. Khalfin, *Russia's Policy in Central Asia, 1857–1868*, London, 1964

Andrzej Korbonski and Francis Fukuyama, eds., *The Soviet Union and the Third World: The Last Three Decades*, Ithaca and London, 1987

Robbin Laird and Erik Hoffman, eds., *Soviet Foreign Policy in a Changing World*, New York, 1986

Walter LaFeber, *America, Russia and the Cold War, 1945–1975*, 3rd edn, New York, 1976

I.J. Lederer, ed., *Russian Foreign Policy: Essays in Historical Perspective*, London, 1962

D.C.B. Lieven, *Russia and the Origins of the First World War*, London, 1987

Margot Light, *The Soviet Theory of International Relations*, Brighton, 1988

A. Lobanov-Rostovsky, *Russia and Asia*, New York, 1933; Ann Arbor, 1951

Robert H. Lord, *The Second Partition of Poland: A Study in Diplomatic History*, Cambridge, Mass., 1915

Vojtech Mastny, *Russia's Road to the Cold War: Diplomacy, Warfare and the Politics of Communism, 1941–1945*, New York, 1979

Michael MccGwire, *Perestroika and Soviet National Security*, Washington, 1991

Joseph L. Nogee and Robert H. Donaldson, *Soviet Foreign Policy since World War II*, 3rd edn, New York, 1988

Alex Pravda, ed., *The End of the Outer Empire. Soviet-East European Relations in Transition, 1985–90*, London, 1992

Hugh Ragsdale, ed., *Imperial Russian Foreign Policy*, Cambridge and New York, 1993

George von Rauch, *The Baltic States: The Years of Independence. Estonia, Latvia, Lithuania, 1917–1940*, London, 1974

L. Sabaliunas, *Lithuania in Crisis, 1939–1940*, Bloomington, 1972

Amin Saikal and William Maley, eds., *Soviet Withdrawal from Afghanistan*, Cambridge, 1989

Morton Schwartz, *The Foreign Policy of the USSR: Domestic Factors*, Encino, California, 1975

Hugh Seton-Watson, *Neither War nor Peace*, London, 1961

Eduard Shevardnadze, *The Future Belongs to Freedom*, London, 1991

Marshall D. Shulman, *Stalin's Foreign Policy Reappraised*, Cambridge, Mass., 1963

Michael Sodaro, *Moscow, Germany and the West from Khrushchev to Gorbachev*, London, 1991

B.H. Sumner, *Peter the Great and the Emergence of Russia*, London, 1950

Adam B. Ulam, *Expansion and Coexistence: Soviet Foreign Policy 1917–73*, New York, 1974

Jiri Valenta and William C. Potter, eds., *Soviet Decision Making for National Security*, London, 1984

G. Wheeler, *The Modern History of Soviet Central Asia*, London, 1964

Daniel Yergin, *Shattered Peace: The Origins of the Cold War and the National Security State*, Boston, 1978

Daniel Yergin and Thane Gustafson, *Russia 2010 and What it Means for the World*, London and New York, 1994

W.H. Zawadzki, *A Man of Honour: Adam Czartoryski as a Statesman of Russia and Poland, 1795–1831*, Oxford, 1993

A. Zóltowski, *Border of Europe: A Study of the Polish Eastern Provinces*, London, 1950

Hutchison = Hutchison Library
SCRSS = Society for Co-operation in Russian & Soviet Studies

Title page, opposite page 1, 5b, 7, 8t, 10t, 15b, 16br, 17l, 17r, 21tr, 28, 31r, 39, 41tl, 41tc, 42t, 42bl, 42r, 44t, 49, 52, 54l, 54r, 55, 56, 61t, 65tl, 66, 72t, 74, 75, 76b, 78t, 79t, 79b, 80bl, 80br, 82t, 83b, 85l, 86, 87, 88b, 89b, 89tr, 90t, 93t, 96t, 98t, 100l, 104l,b, 107r, 108, 114bl,br, 113tr,b, 114t, 116b, 117t, 117br, 121t,b, 122, 123l, 124, 126, 127t,b, 129l, 133, 137 , 138r, 139r,l, 142t, 142b, 146, 150, 153t, 156, 162, 163tr,b, 164t, 166tl, 167t, 171t, 173, 174, 176t, 177, 178, 179, 180, 181b, 182, 183b, 184, 188, 189, 190t, 191tr, 192, 193, 194, 197br, 198, 201, 203, 210t, 211t, 212, 214, 216b, 217, 220, 221, 223, 224, 226, 228, 229b, 230, 233t,br, 240, 247t, 249, 259, 260, 262, 264, 265b, 266b, 271b, 272t, 278l, 284, 287, 288t, 292, 293, 312t, 304, 305, 306t, 308, 310, 312b, 313b, 314, 320, 321, 322tr,b, 323, 324, 325t, 331b, 336b, 331, 332t, 338t, 346, 347, 353, 354, 356, 359, 361, 365, 371r, 372, 377b, 383t, 384, 385, 389l, 392, 396, 399, 401, 402b, 404b, 408, 418bl,br, 426t, 434, 439, 442, 455, 462, 464, 473, 476l, 487, 492, 493, 494, 496, 498, 501, 504, 506, 509, 515, 517, 519, 523t, 527, 528t, 540, 549, 556t, 557, 560t, 567tr, Novosti Photo Library (London); 5t, 6b, 10bl, 45b, 57, 65bl, 80t, 91, 93b, 103t, 168tr, 169bl, 169tr, 386, 425, 448, 510, John Massey Stewart; 6t, 9b, 21b, 33r, 35t, 38, 43, 50, 65tr, 137r, 364, Eastlight/Still Pictures; 8b, 9t, 36, 47b, 62b, 64, 197bl, 252b, Victoria Jvleva/Hutchison; 10br, 171br, 411, 488, Oleg Svyatoslavsky/Life File; 11b, Bobby Meyer/Hutchison; 14t, 15t, 20t, 319b, 407l, 412t, 420tl,tr, Hjalte Tin/Still Pictures; 14b, 69, 158, Hutchison; 16tr, R Van Nostrand/Frank Lane Picture Library; 16tl, Francois Gohier/Ardea, London; 16bl, Silvestris/Frank Lane Picture Library; 22, 175b, 209, 288b, 317b, 338b, 340, 402t, 409t, 433t, 459, 489, 490, 512l, 513, 539, 546, 564, SCRSS; 31l, 478, Liba Taylor/Hutchison; 33l, 153c, 491, 528b, Sergei Verein/Life File; 35b, 40b, 41bl, 45t, 129r, 136b, 138l, 144, 152br, 241, 263, 265t, 267, 268t, 269t, 294, 295, 296, 298, 306b, 317t, 325b, 326, 362, 371l, 380, 406, 407r, 417, 430, 438b, 441, 449, 463l, 467t, 471, 482, 511, 512r, 522, 523b, 526, 529t, 530, 557t, 558, 560b, 561, 562t, 565t, 567b, Frank Spooner Pictures; 37, 62t, Dave Brinicombe/Hutchison; 40t, T E Clark/Hutchison; 41tr, Sarah Errington/Hutchison; 41br, 487, Tordai/Hutchison; 44b, 154, 248t, 319t, 412b, Robert Harding Picture Library; 46, Sergei Buzasovski/Hutchison; 47t, Melanie Friend/Format; 51, Yuri Shpagin/Hutchison; 58, Anatoly Therei/Hutchison; 59, 94, 96b, 97, 98b, 100r, 101, 102, 103b, 104t,r, 105l,r, 106, 107l, 109, 110, 111, 112, 113tl (photo: Boris Kudoyarov), 115, 116t, 117bl, 123r, 128c, 147, 190b, 191tl, 218, 222, 225, 229tl, 232, 233bl, 234, 235, 237, 270, 274l, 334, 360, 366, 481t, 543, 556b, David King Collection; 60, ©Keston College/Keston College Photo Archive; 61b, 436, A Grachtchenkov/Hutchison; 63, Vladimir Birgus/Hutchison; 71, Comstock/Ted Spiegel/SGC; 72b, Erich Lessing/Archiv für Kunst und Geschichte, Berlin; 76b, 78b, Archiv für Kunst und Geschichte, Berlin; 80t, 160t, 164bl, Michael Holford; 81b, 83t, 85r, 88t, Michael Holford (Collection of Countess Bobrinskoy); 82b, Mary Evans Picture Library; 84, 89tl, The Royal Collection©1994 Her Majesty the Queen; 128, Archie Brown/print by Chris Honeywell, Oxford; 131, 132, 268br, 272b, 276, 277, 282t, 378, 379, 495, 499, 500, 525, 529b, 559r, 562b, 564, 565b, Rex Features; 136t, Heidi Bradner/Panos Pictures; 148, Emile S./Hutchison; 155, Tamara Talbot Rice; 152bl, Christopher Rennie/Robert Harding Picture Library; 152tl,tr, 153br, 191b, 498t, David Williamson, London; 157, 460, Douglas Brown; 160b, 161c,r, 163tl, 164br, Private Collection; 166tr, 170b, 176b, 375, 400, 476r,

Allan Gordon/Life File; 165, Steven Burr Williams/The Image Bank; 167c, Audrey Baskakov/Hutchison; 168b, 167b, 168tl, 269b, 335, Terence Waeland/Life File; 170t, Terry O'Brien/Life File; 171bl, 172, 175t, 166b, 253, 303, 313t, 344b, 391, 420b, 421, 433b, 435t, 438t, 445, 447, 453, 466b, Jim Holmes; 181t, Tretyakov Gallery, Moscow/Bridgeman Art Library, London; 183t, Astrakhan Picture Gallery, Russia/Bridgeman Art Library, London; 185, 197t, State Russian Museum, St Petersburg/Bridgeman Art Library, London; 186b, 187, Stephen White; 208, 211b, 255, 275t, Mary Evans Picture Library; 210b, 248b, 251, 274r, 275th, Hulton Deutsch Collection; 213, 216t, 272t, 280, 281b, 282bl,br, 283t, British Film Institute; 219, Mary Evans Picture Library/Sigmund Freud Copyright; 236, Karsh/Camera Press; 238, Oleg Parskin/Hutchison; 244, Ashmolean Museum, Oxford; 250, Mary Evans Picture Library/Ida Kar; 252t, Clive Barda/Performing Arts Library; 257t, Yuri Shpagin/Hutchison; 257b, G. Seaman; 258, Performing Arts Library; 266t, 344t, 382, 383b, 426b, 427, 451, 456, 485, David Kampfner/Life File; 268bl, 279, 281t,c, 283b, Kobal Collection; 271t, 350, M. Shishanov/Life File; 278r, Linda Rich; 297, Bodleian Library, Oxford; 301, Rodger Jackman/Oxford Scientific Films; 327, Piet Smolders; 328, Ferdinando Scianna/Magnum; 336t, David Joravsky; 377t, ©A.R.C./photo courtesy of Keston College Photo Archive; 389r, Trevor Page/Panos Pictures; 404t, Howard Sochurek/John Hillelson Agency; 409b, 429, 466t, 474, 475, Jeremy Hartley/Panos Pictures; 410, Bobby Meyer/Hutchison; 418t, Mike Potter/Life File; 431, Igor Gavrilov/Hutchison; 435b, courtesy of McDonald's; 446l, 559l, Popperfoto; 446r, 465, Jim Holmes/Panos Pictures; 452, Jorgen Schytte/Still Pictures; 453b, Eddy Tan/Life File; 463r, Eric Bach/BritStock–IFA; 469, Associated Press; 497, Steve Powell/Allsport; 502, Bob Thomas Sports Photography; 505, Les Stone/Sygma; 521, Andrew Watson/Life File; 524, 567tl, Chris Stowers/Panos Pictures; 533, Lauros-Giraudon; 535, Musée d'Orsay, Paris/Bridgeman Art Library; 550, Imperial War Museum, London; 551, Sygma; 554, Raymond Darolle/Sygma; 563, D. Aubert/Sygma

Maps on pages 28, 362 and 379 by AVB and LVS (see list of contributors, pages vii and ix)

INDEX